P9-DGL-425

Thailand

Chiang Mai
Province
p230

Northern
Thailand
p291

Northeastern
Thailand
p407

Central
Thailand
p151

Bangkok &
Around
p54

Ko Chang &
Eastern Seaboard
p188

Hua Hin &
the Upper
Gulf
p493

Phuket &
the Andaman
Coast
p597

Ko Samui
& the
Lower Gulf
p526

THIS EDITION WRITTEN AND RESEARCHED BY

China Williams,

Mark Beales, Tim Bewer, Celeste Brash, Austin Bush, David Eimer,

Adam Skolnick

Contents

PÀT TAI: FOOD SPOTTER'S GUIDE P726

PEOPLE & CULTURE P705

Contents

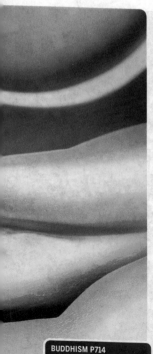

BUDDHISM P714

Contents

ON THE ROAD

AYUTHAYA P154

KAREN HILL TRIBE P708

Contents

LOI KRATHONG P31

Welcome to Thailand

Friendly and fun-loving, exotic and tropical, cultured and historic, Thailand radiates a golden hue from its glittering temples and tropical beaches to the ever-comforting Thai smile.

Sand Between Your Toes

With a long coastline (actually, two coastlines) and jungle-topped islands anchored in azure waters, Thailand is a tropical getaway for the hedonist and the hermit, the prince and the pauper. This paradise offers a varied menu: playing in the gentle surf of Ko Lipe, diving with whale sharks in Ko Tao, scaling the sea cliffs of Krabi, kiteboarding in Hua Hin, partying on Ko Phi-Phi, recuperating at a health resort in Ko Samui and feasting on the beach wherever sand meets sea.

Sacred Spaces

The celestial world is a close confidant in this Buddhist nation and religious devotion is colourful and ubiquitous. Gleaming temples and golden Buddhas frame both the rural and modern landscape. Ancient banyan trees are ceremoniously wrapped in sacred cloth to honour the resident spirits, and fortune-bringing shrines decorate humble homes as well as monumental malls, while garland-festooned dashboards ward off traffic accidents. Visitors can join in on the conversation through meditation retreats in Chiang Mai, religious festivals in northeastern Thailand, underground cave shrines in Kanchanaburi and Phetchaburi, and hilltop temples in northern Thailand.

Fields & Forests

In between the cluttered cities and towns is the rural heartland, a mix of rice paddies, tropical forests and squat villages tied to the agricultural clock. In the north, the forests and fields bump up against toothy blue mountains decorated with silvery waterfalls. In the south, scraggly limestone cliffs poke out of the cultivated landscape like prehistoric skyscrapers. The usually arid northeast beams an emerald hue during the rainy season when tender green rice shoots carpet the landscape.

A Bountiful Table

Adored around the world, Thai cuisine expresses fundamental aspects of Thai culture: it is generous, warm, refreshing and relaxed. Each Thai dish relies on fresh, local ingredients – pungent lemongrass, searing chillies and plump seafood. A varied national menu is built around the four fundamental flavours: spicy, sweet, salty and sour. Roving appetites go on eating tours of Bangkok noodle shacks, seafood pavilions in Phuket and Burmese market stalls in Mae Hong Son. Cooking classes reveal the simplicity behind the seemingly complicated dishes, and mastering the market is an important survival skill.

Why I Love Thailand

By China Williams, Author

When I step off the plane after a gruelling trip across a continent and an ocean, I slip into my Thai 'skin' and the rhythms of the country: chit-chatting with locals, eating at roadside noodle joints, climbing aboard shared taxi pick-up trucks, *wâi*-ing at sacred temples, slipping off my shoes with ease and craving rice for breakfast. The beaches and the jungles are all fine, but I prefer the cities, where life spills out on to the street and the markets are packed with people and produce. Life is pleasant here and best of all, Thais shower my children with attention and affection.

For more about our authors, see page 800

Above: Monk praying in front of Buddha statues

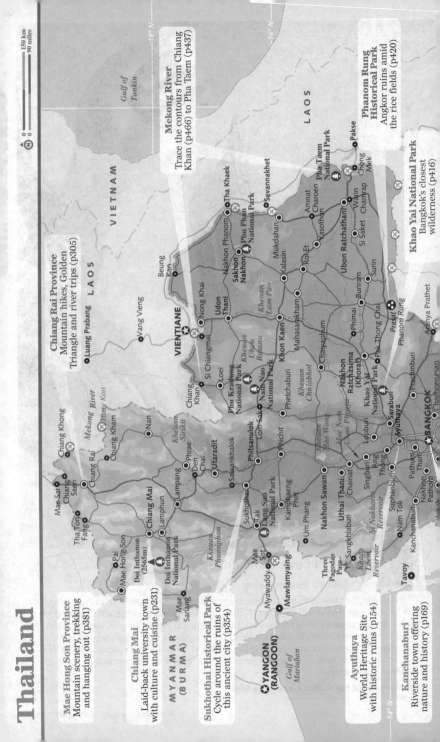

Thailand

Mae Hong Son Province
Mountain scenery, trekking and hanging out (p381)

Chiang Mai
Laid-back university town with culture and cuisine (p231)

Sukhothai Historical Park
Cycle around the ruins of this ancient city (p354)

Ayuthaya
World Heritage Site with historic ruins (p154)

Kanchanaburi
Riverside town offering nature and history (p169)

Chiang Rai Province
Mountain hikes, Golden Triangle and river trips (p305)

Mekong River
Trace the contours from Chiang Khan (p466) to Pha Taem (p437)

Phanom Rung Historical Park
Angkor ruins amid the rice fields (p420)

Khao Yai National Park
Bangkok's closest wilderness (p416)

150 km
90 miles

Gulf of Tonkin

VIETNAM

LAOS

MYANMAR (BURMA)

Gulf of Martaban

Luang Prabang

Vang Vieng

VIENTIANE

Beung Kan

Nong Khai

Nakhon Phanom

Tha Khaek

Savannakhet

Pakse

Chong Mek

Pha Taem National Park

Amnat Charoen

Yasothon

Mukdahan

Kalasin

Ubon Ratchathani

Si Saket

Warin Chamrap

Roi Et

Sakhon Nakhon

Phu Phan National Park

Udon Thani

Si Chiangmai

Loei

Phu Kradung National Park

Khon Kaen

Mahasarakham

Buriram

Surin

Phimai

Prasat Phanom Rung

Chaiyaphum

Nakhon Ratchasima (Khorat)

Khao Yai National Park

Pak Thong Chai

Aranya Prathet

Chachoengsao

Mae Sai

Chiang Saen

Chiang Khong

Mae Hong Son

Pai

Tha Ton

Fang

Chiang Rai

Chiang Kham

Nan

Pray Kon

Mekong River

Chiang Khan

Lampang

Lamphun

Chiang Mai

Doi Inthanon (2565m)

Doi Inthanon National Park

Mae Sot

Mae Sariang

Myawaddy

Mawlamyaing

YANGON (RANGOON)

Tavoy

Three Pagodas Pass

Sangkhlaburi

Kanchanaburi

Nam Tok

Khao Laem Reservoir

Si Nakharin Reservoir

Suphanburi

Um Phang

Kamphaeng Phet

Mae Sot

Tak

Lan Sang National Park

Sukhothai

Sawankhalok

Phitsanulok

Lom Sak

Phetchabun

Phichit

Uttaradit

Den Chai

Phrae

Nakhon Sawan

Uthai Thani

Chainat

Singburi

Ang Thong

Lopburi

Saraburi

Ayuthaya

Pathum Thani

Nakhon Pathom

BANGKOK

Prachinburi

Kheuan Sirikit

Kheuan Phumiphon

Kheuan Ubon Ratana

Kheuan Lam Pao

Kheuan Chulabhon

Kheuan Mae Wong

Mae Nam Chao Phraya

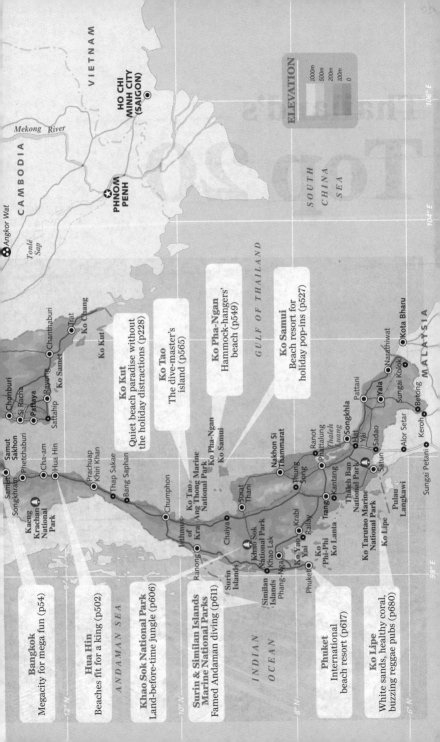

ELEVATION

1000m
500m
200m
100m
0

Bangkok
Megacity for mega fun (p54)

Hua Hin
Beaches fit for a king (p502)

Khao Sok National Park
Land-before-time jungle (p606)

Surin & Similan Islands Marine National Parks
Famed Andaman diving (p611)

Phuket
International beach resort (p617)

Ko Lipe
White sands, healthy coral, buzzing reggae pubs (p680)

Ko Kut
Quiet beach paradise without the holiday distractions (p228)

Ko Tao
The dive-master's island (p565)

Ko Pha-Ngan
Hammock-hangers' beach (p549)

Ko Samui
Beach resort for holiday pop-ins (p527)

CAMBODIA

VIETNAM

Mekong River

Angkor Wat

Tonlé Sap

PHNOM PENH

HO CHI MINH CITY (SAIGON)

SOUTH CHINA SEA

GULF OF THAILAND

ANDAMAN SEA

INDIAN OCEAN

MALAYSIA

Chonburi
Si Racha
Pattaya
Sattahip
Rayong
Ko Samet
Chanthaburi
Trat
Ko Chang
Ko Kut

Samut Sakhon
Samut Songkhram
Phetchaburi
Cha-am
Hua Hin
Kaeng Krachan National Park
Prachuap Khiri Khan
Thap Sakae
Bang Saphan
Chumphon

Isthmus of Kra
Ranong
Surin Islands
Similan Islands
Phang-Nga
Khao Lak
Khao Sok National Park
Phuket
Ko Yao Yai
Ko Phi-Phi
Krabi
Railay
Ko Lanta

Chaiya
Surat Thani
Ko Tao
Ang Thong Marine National Park
Ko Pha-Ngan
Ko Samui

Nakhon Si Thammarat
Thung Song
Trang
Kantang
Thaleh Ban National Park
Ko Tarutao Marine National Park
Ko Lipe
Pulau Langkawi

Ranot
Phatthalung
Thaleh Luang
Songkhla
Hat Yai
Satun
Sadao
Alor Setar

Pattani
Yala
Narathiwat
Sungai Kolok
Betong
Keroh
Sungai Petani

Kota Bharu

106° E
104° E
98° E
96° E
12° N
10° N
8° N
6° N

Thailand's
Top 20

Bangkok Nightlife

1 Despite what your dodgy uncle may have told you, having a fun night out in Bangkok (p121) no longer needs to involve ping-pong balls or the word 'go-go'. The nightlife scene in today's Bangkok touches on all points from trashy to classy, with a distinct emphasis on unpretentious Thai-style fun. Start your night in a bar perched on a skyscraper, throw in a few roadside beers, and finish up at a basement-level music pub; in Bangkok, a night out is whatever you want it to be.

Chatuchak Weekend Market

2 In a city obsessed with commerce, Chatuchak (p134) takes the prize as Bangkok's biggest, baddest market, and is yet another reason to plan your visit to the city around a weekend. Silks and sneakers, fighting fish and fluffy puppies, not to mention some pretty good food – if it can be sold in Bangkok, you'll find it here. Come early and be prepared for some serious collective bargaining as half of Bangkok squeezes into the market's narrow lanes.

NIKADA / GETTY IMAGES ©

JULIET COOMBE / GETTY IMAGES ©

Chiang Rai Province

3 The days of the Golden Triangle opium trade are over, but Chiang Rai (p305) still packs intrigue in the form of fresh-air fun, such as trekking and self-guided exploration. It's also a great destination for unique cultural experiences, ranging from a visit to an Akha village to a stay at the Yunnanese hamlet of Mae Salong (Santikhiri; p315). From the Mekong River to the mountains, Chiang Rai is arguably Thailand's most beautiful province, and if you've set your sights further, it's also a convenient gateway to Myanmar and Laos. Above: Wat Rong Khun ('White Temple'; p309)

Sukhothai Historical Park

4 Step back 800 years in time at Thailand's most impressive historical park (p354). For a classic Thailand experience, explore the ruins of this former capital by bicycle; wind leisurely through the crumbling temples, graceful Buddha statues and fish-filled ponds. Worthwhile museums and good-value accommodation round out the package. Despite its popularity, Sukhothai rarely feels crowded, but for something off the beaten track, head to nearby Si Satchanalai-Chaliang Historical Park (p364), where you might be the only one scaling an ancient stairway. Top right: Dancers at Sukhothai Historical Park

Chiang Mai

5 The cultural capital of the north, Chiang Mai (p230) is beloved by culture geeks, temple-spotters and families. The old city is jam-packed with temples born during the once independent Lanna kingdom. Cooking schools teach visitors the art of Thai food. The scenic countryside boasts jungle treks, elephant encounters and minority villages. And the city enjoys fantastic dining thanks to imports such as Japanese sushi and Burmese curries, as well as home-grown northern specialities and vegetarian fare. Bottom right: Wat Chiang Man (p237)

Phetchaburi

6 A delightful mix of culture and nature combine in this provincial capital (p495), a close and quiet alternative to the hectic streets of Bangkok. Explore an antique hilltop palace, sacred cave shrines and bustling temples. Wander the old shophouse neighbourhood filled with do-it-yourself businesses run by Thai aunties and grannies. Then head off to the wilds of Kaeng Krachan National Park (p499) to spot wild gibbons and exotic birds. Phetchaburi is also a smart layover for travellers returning from the south. Below: Phra Nakhon Khiri Historical Park, Phetchaburi

Ayuthaya

7 A once vibrant, glittering capital packed with hundreds of temples, Ayuthaya (p154) today only hints at its erstwhile glory. Cycle around the brick-and-stucco ruins, which form part of a Unesco World Heritage Site, and try to imagine how the city must have looked in its prime, when it greeted merchants from around the globe. On the outskirts of the city sit several more attractions, including an enormous handicraft centre, the most eclectic royal palace you'll ever see and a water theatre. Right: Wat Chai Wattanaram (p157)

6

VAYU PERLEY / GETTY IMAGES ©

Pai

8 Combine a beautiful mountain valley, a party scene reminiscent of a Thai island, an old-school hippie vibe and laid-back northern Thai roots and you have Pai (p381), still reigning as northern Thailand's coolest destination. Its popularity means it can get crowded, especially at the peak of Thailand's 'winter' in December and January. But a huge spread of accommodation houses every budget and style and a host of outdoor and laid-back activities means your visit won't be quite like anybody else's.

INGOLF POMPE / GETTY IMAGES ©

Railay & Krabi

9 At the tip of the Krabi peninsula are some of Thailand's most famous natural features: the soaring limestone karsts of Railay (p649), anchored in the ocean. The beaches have sugar-white sand and the forested interior is traversed by foot traffic, not cars. No traffic jams, no transport hassles. Visitors come and go by long-tail boats. Come to lounge, swim, dive or rock climb. Beginners can learn basic skills, and some stay long enough to get good enough to do a free solo on a pinnacle then tumble harmlessly into a cobalt sea. Above left: Ko Poda, Railay

Kanchanaburi

10 Walks on the wild side are the main reason to visit Kanchanaburi (p169), where dragon-scaled limestone mountains gaze down upon dense jungle. Trek past silvery waterfalls and rushing rivers in search of elusive tigers and gibbons, then spend the night at a homestay organised through an ethnic group. Once you've explored this western province's wartime past – the infamous Bridge Over the River Kwai is here – hold on tight to experience the growing number of adventure activities. Above right: Death Railway Bridge (Bridge Over the River Kwai)

Mekong River

11 From the historic timber shophouses of Chiang Khan (p469) to the waterfalls of Pha Taem National Park (p440), northeast Thailand's glorious arc of the Mekong River offers an incomparable smorgasbord of culture and beauty. Chase the meandering river aboard a rickety bus, long-tail boat or even a bicycle. View the cross-pollination of Thai-Lao culture in local fishing villages, Nong Khai's bizarre sculpture park, prehistoric rock paintings in Ubon Ratchathani, holy temples and elephant villages. Those who follow this little-visited trail will be rewarded with true traveller's tales.

11

Ko Pha-Ngan

12 Famous for its sloppy, techno-fuelled Full Moon parties, Ko Pha-Ngan (p549) has graduated from a sleepy bohemian island to an Asian Ibiza. Comfort seekers have an alternative to Ko Samui thanks to a bevy of boutique bungalows. And on the northern and eastern coasts, the ascetic hammock hangers can still escape enough of the modern life to feel like castaways (well-fed ones, of course). Just offshore is Sail Rock, one of the gulf's best dive sites. Right: Poolside yoga in Ko Pha-Ngan

HENRIK SORENSEN / GETTY IMAGES ©

12

Phuket

13 An international beach resort, Phuket (p617) is an easy-peasy destination for all ages. You can fly in from Bangkok (or directly from China), and then retreat into a five-star resort or arty boutique hotel for a trouble-free tropical vacation. There are slinky stretches of sand, hedonistic party pits and all the mod-cons needed for 21st-century rest and recreation. Plus there are day trips to mangrove forests, monkey-rescue centres and a ton of water sports, from diving to surfing (when the weather is right). Below left: Patong beach

Ko Lipe

14 Where creature comforts meet laid-back island escape, Ko Lipe (p680) takes work to reach but the ever-growing devotees agree that it's worth it. The days of desertion are over, especially in the high season when the island is overrun, but it is still a wonderful blend of white-sand beaches, authentic Thai kitchens, groovy guesthouses, boutique resorts and nature adventures in the national park. The diving and living are best here during the early wet season (May and June). But keep that hush-hush. Below right: Pattaya beach

CHRISTER FREDRIKSSON / GETTY IMAGES ©

Surin & Similan Islands Marine National Parks

15 The world-renowned dive sites off the Surin (p611) and Similan Islands (p612) have anchored Thailand as a global diving destination. Live-aboard trips set out from Khao Lak, allowing for more time at the famous sites where you can meet the local manta rays and whale sharks. The islands are an attraction in their own right, with jungle-filled interiors and smooth white beaches surrounded by decent coral reefs.

Top: School of fish, Similan Islands Marine National Park

Hua Hin

16 Long a royal retreat, anyone can play in Hua Hin (p502) now. This city by the sea offers a unique mix of beaches, history and culture. You can explore the secluded coastline to the south, wander through the impeccably manicured gardens of a Thai royal palace or just laze on the beach watching the kite-boarders twisting and turning above the waves. And you can feast like a king at any time, whether at the amazing night market or in one of the many celebrated seafood restaurants.

Khao Sok National Park

17 A deep, dark jungle hugs the midsection of southern Thailand. This ancient rainforest (p607) is filled with long sweaty hiking routes up dramatic limestone formations that reward with postcard-perfect views. Birds and bats call this forest home, as does the rare *Rafflesia kerrii*, one of the stinkiest flowers on the planet. Reward all your outdoor work with riverside camping and listen to the symphony of the jungle. Just remember to wear leech-proof gear to prevent an involuntary blood donation.

Ko Kut

18 Still looking for that paradise island where the crowds are thin, the water aquamarine and clear, and the beaches wide and long? Try Ko Kut (p228). There's Hat Khlong Chao, one of the most beautiful stretches of sand anywhere in Thailand, fine snorkelling and hidden waterfalls to trek to. Best of all, Ko Kut retains a supremely unhurried pace of life that visitors soon find themselves imitating. There's nothing in the way of nightlife, apart from listening to the ocean. But that's why you're here.

ANDERS BLOMQVIST / GETTY IMAGES ©

TOM COCKREM / GETTY IMAGES ©

Khao Yai National Park

19 Here you'll find elephants, monkeys, gibbons, hornbills, pythons, bears, a million bats and a few wily tigers. Wildlife sightings are almost at the mercy of chance, but your odds are excellent at this vast Unesco World Heritage–listed reserve (p419), just a few hours out of Bangkok. And even if you don't meet many big animals, the orchids, birds, waterfalls and sense of adventure that inevitably arises when trekking in the jungle guarantee a good day. Khao Yai's mix of scenery, accessibility and beauty is hard to beat.

Phanom Rung Historical Park

20 Perched high atop an extinct volcano, the biggest and best Khmer ruin (p423) in Thailand is special. As you amble along the promenade, up the stairs and over the *naga*-flanked bridges, the sense of anticipation builds. And when you enter the temple, completely restored and still rich with Hindu sculpture, you will experience a moment of timelessness. While Phanom Rung is not as awe-inspiring as Cambodia's Angkor Wat, the experience here is impressive and different enough that you should visit both.

Need to Know

For more information, see Survival Guide (p747)

Currency
Thai baht (B)

Language
Thai

Visas
International air arrivals receive 30-day visa; 15-day visa at land borders; 60-day tourist visa through application at a Thai consulate.

Money
ATMs widespread and charge a 150B foreign-account fee. Visa and MasterCard accepted at upmarket places.

Mobile Phones
Get inexpensive pre-paid SIM cards for GSM phones. 3G is available.

Time
GMT plus seven hours

When to Go

Mae Hong Son
GO Nov–Mar

Chiang Mai
GO Nov–Feb

BANGKOK
GO Nov–Feb

Ko Samui
GO Dec–Aug

Phuket
GO Oct–Apr

Tropical climate, rain year-round

Tropical climate, wet & dry seasons

High Season
(Nov–Mar)

➡ A cool and dry season follows the monsoons, meaning the landscape is lush and temperatures are comfortable.

➡ Western Christmas and New Year's holidays bring crowds and rates increase 50% at the beaches.

Shoulder Season
(Apr–Jun, Sep & Oct)

➡ Hot and dry (April to June) but less so in higher elevations.

➡ Beaches aren't crowded and the ocean provides the air-con.

➡ September and October are ideal for the north and the gulf coast.

Low Season
(Jul–Oct)

➡ Monsoon season can range from afternoon showers to major flooding.

➡ Some islands shut down and boat service is limited during stormy weather.

➡ Be flexible with travel plans.

Websites

Tourism Authority of Thailand (TAT; www.tourismthailand.org) National tourism department covering info and special events.

Thaivisa (www.thaivisa.com) Expat site for news and discussions.

Lonely Planet (www.lonely planet.com/thailand) Country profile and what to do and see.

Bangkok Post (www.bangkok post.com) English-language daily.

The Nation (www.nationmulti media.com) English-language daily.

Thai Language (www.thai -language.com) Online dictionary, Thai tutorials.

Important Numbers

Thailand's country code	☎66
Emergency	☎191
International access codes	☎001
	☎007
	☎008
	☎009
Operator-assisted international calls	☎100
Tourist police	☎1155

Exchange Rates

Australia	A$1	32B
Canada	C$1	30B
Euro zone	€1	42B
Japan	¥100	32B
New Zealand	NZ$1	26B
UK	£1	50B
USA	US$1	31B

For current exchange rates see www.xe.com.

Daily Costs

Budget: Less than 1000B

➡ Basic guesthouse room: 300–800B

➡ Market or street stall meal: 40–60B

➡ One beer: 100B

➡ Getting around town with public transport: 20–50B

Midrange: 1000–3000B

➡ Flashpacker guesthouse or midrange hotel room: 800–1500B

➡ Western lunches and seafood dinner: 150–350B

➡ Organised tour or activity: 1000–1500B

➡ Motorbike hire: 300–500B

Top End: More than 3000B

➡ Boutique hotel room: 3000B

➡ Fine dining: 350–500B

➡ Private tours: 1500B

➡ Car hire: 1500B

Opening Hours

Banks and government offices close for national holidays. Some bars and clubs close during elections and on certain religious public holidays when alcohol sales are banned.

Banks 9.30am–3.30pm Monday to Friday; 24hr ATMs

Bars 6pm–midnight

Clubs 8pm–2am

Government Offices 8.30am–4.30pm Monday to Friday; some close for lunch (noon–1pm)

Restaurants 8am–10pm; some local restaurants are open only to 3pm or 4pm

Shops 10am or 11am to 9pm

Arriving in Thailand

Suvarnabhumi International Airport (Bangkok; p765) The Airport Rail Link provides local service (45B, 30 minutes, every 15 minutes from 6am to midnight) to Phaya Thai station and express service (90B, 15 minutes, hourly from 6am to midnight) to Makkasan station (Bangkok City Air Terminal). Taxis cost 200B to 300B plus 50B airport surcharge and tolls; about an hour to the city.

Don Muang International Airport (Bangkok; p765) Airport bus A1 runs to BTS Mo Chit; bus A2 runs to BTS Mo Chit and BTS Victory Monument. Both cost 30B and run hourly (9am to midnight). Ordinary trains run to Hualamphong station (5B to 10B, one hour, hourly from 4am to 11.30am and 2pm to 9.30pm). Taxis cost 300B to 400B, plus 50B charges/fees.

Chiang Mai International Airport (p765) Taxis from the airport are a flat 120B.

Phuket International Airport (p765) Hourly buses run to Phuket Town (90B, 6am to 7pm). Minivans run to Phuket Town (150B) and the beaches (180B). Metered taxis (550B) run to the beaches and Phuket Town.

Getting Around

Buses Extensive and affordable for travel between towns.

Air Cheap domestic connections on budget airlines.

Trains Slow but scenic between Bangkok and Chiang Mai or Bangkok and Surat Thani.

Car & Motorcycle Easy to rent for local touring.

For much more on **getting around**, see p765

First Time Thailand

For more information, see Survival Guide (p747)

Checklist

➡ Make sure your passport is valid for at least six months

➡ Purchase your international and domestic flight tickets

➡ Apply for a tourist visa for visits longer than 30 days from a Thai consulate

➡ Organise travel insurance, diver's insurance and international driving permit

➡ Visit the doctor for a check-up and medical clearance if you intend to scuba dive

➡ Inform your bank and credit-card company of your travel plans

What to Pack

➡ Driving licence and international driving permit

➡ Phrasebook

➡ Power converter

➡ GSM mobile phone and charger

➡ A week's worth of lightweight clothes

➡ Hat and sunglasses

➡ Comfortable sandals

➡ Earplugs

➡ Rain gear and dry pack if travelling in the rainy season

Top Tips for Your Trip

➡ Eat at the market or the street stalls for real Thai grub.

➡ Hop aboard local transport. It is cheap and a great way to hang out with the locals.

➡ Rent a bicycle to tour towns and neighbourhoods.

➡ Learn a few Thai phrases and always smile.

➡ Avoid the first-timer scams: one-day gem sales in Bangkok, insane transport prices, dodgy tailors.

➡ Figure out how to bargain without being a jerk.

What to Wear

In general, light, loose-fitting clothes will prove the most comfortable in the tropical heat. It's worth bringing one jacket that can double as rain gear and keep you warm in higher elevations and on air-conditioned buses. When you visit temples, wear clothes that cover to your elbows and knees. Bring a dress-up outfit if you plan on clubbing in Bangkok or fine-dining in Phuket.

Sleeping

Finding a place to stay in Thailand is easy. For piece of mind, book a room for your arrival night; after that, you can wing it. Vacancies become scarce during certain holidays and peak travel periods. Each destination gives advice on when bookings are recommended. See p754 for more accommodation information.

➡ **Guesthouses** Our favourite are these family-run options, usually in a converted house or apartment building. Rooms range from basic (bed and fan) to plush (private bathroom and air-con).

➡ **Hotels** From boutique to stodgy, hotels offer comfortable, mainly modern rooms, with extra services like breakfast included in the rate and sometimes a swimming pool.

➡ **Hostels** As prices and standards within Thailand's guesthouses have increased, dorms have become better value. Good for solo travellers.

Money

Most places deal only with cash. Some credit cards are accepted in high-end establishments.

ATMs are widespread but there is a 150B foreign-transaction fee in addition to whatever fees your home bank charges. To keep ATM withdrawals to a minimum, take out as much cash as you feel comfortable carrying. Most ATMs allow 20,000B, which should last about a week.

For more information, see p758.

Bargaining

If there is no posted price, then bargaining is acceptable. Ask the price, follow up by asking for a discount, offer a counter and accept what is offered in return. Always smile and don't start bargaining if you're not interested in buying.

Tipping

Tipping is not standard but it is appreciated. If there is a small bit of change from a restaurant bill or metered taxi fare, it is common to offer it as a tip.

Tips for Sticking to a Budget

➡ Track your expenses.

➡ Use local transport.

➡ Travel with a companion to share lodging costs.

➡ Eat at the market.

➡ Save souvenir shopping until the end of your trip.

➡ Take buses or trains instead of planes for long-distance travel.

RICHARD ASHWORTH / ROBERT HARDING / GETTY IMAGES ©

Wat Phra That Lampang Luang (p303)

Etiquette

Thais are generally very understanding and hospitable, but there are some important taboos and social conventions.

➡ **Monarchy** Never disrespect the royal family with disparaging remarks. Treat objects depicting the king (like money) with respect.

➡ **Temples** Wear clothing that covers to your knees and elbows. Remove your shoes when you enter a temple building. Sit with your feet tucked behind you to avoid pointing the bottom of your feet at Buddha images. Women should never touch a monk or a monk's belongings; step out of their way on footpaths and don't sit next to them on public transport.

➡ **Modesty** At the beach, avoid public nudity or topless sunbathing. Wear a cover-up to and from the beach.

➡ **Save Face** Never get into an argument with a Thai. It is better to smile through any social friction.

Language

Tourist towns are well stocked with English speakers, though bus drivers, market vendors and taxi drivers are less competent so it helps to know some basics.

Thailand has its own script. Street signs are always transliterated into English, but there is no standard system so spellings vary widely. Not all letters are pronounced as they appear ('Ph' is an aspirated 'p' not an 'f').

See Language (p779) for more information.

What's New

Fly Everywhere

Air routes now link every provincial capital to Bangkok, so you can skip those frigid overnight bus journeys. You can also fly from Phuket and Chiang Mai to major Chinese cities. And Ko Pha-Ngan's drunken Full Moon raves just got easier to get to; a privately owned airport served by Kan Air's turboprop planes is scheduled to open in 2014.

Asia Discovers Itself

Chinese, Indians, Koreans, Singaporeans and more – Asia's emerging middle class is backpacking, package touring and week-ending in Thailand. Russians are on board too, especially for the Gulf of Thailand beaches.

Overlanding to/from Myanmar

The cloistered country of Myanmar is now 'open' and foreigners can enter and exit from one of four land borders with Thailand. Well, sort of. The most open crossing is Mae Sot to Myawaddy.

Take Me to Angkor

There is a new government bus from Bangkok direct to Siem Reap that cuts out some of the hassles of the infamous Aranya Prathet–Poipet border. Though the scams are tenacious and there's still the line at Cambodian immigration.

Hip Hostels

Bangkok and Chiang Mai have sprouted hip hostels, where sleeping with the pack means saving baht and scoring style points. Now solo travellers have an alternative to single occupancy.

Coral Bleach Job

In recent years, rising sea temperatures have caused coral bleaching and even coral death. Snorkelling sites in shallow waters have been hit the worst. Thanks a lot, global warming.

What a Wreck

Ko Chang and Ko Tao both have new wreck dives created by decommissioned Thai navy ships. In Tao the wreck dive is accessible to novice divers with regular scuba gear. Meanwhile, Ko Pha-Ngan has cheap scuba schools and Ranong now has live-aboards.

Bridging Borders

The fourth Mekong River bridge now links Laos to Thailand via Huay Xai–Chiang Khong, making the crossing faster and easier for shipping and passenger travel to Laos and Yunnan, China.

Caffeinated & Cultured Chiang Mai

New and professional culture museums have replaced the government offices that once occupied Chiang Mai's old city, and cafes and fruit-shake stands outnumber 7-Elevens.

Local Press Knows Best

Protests have been in full swing in Bangkok of late and there is seemingly no good solution ahead. Stay informed about rally sites (and avoid them) through the local press. Follow Richard Barrow on Twitter for breaking news.

For more recommendations and reviews, see **lonelyplanet.com/thailand**

If You Like...

Wildlife Encounters

Khao Yai National Park Spot elephants, monkeys, snakes and creepy-crawlies in Thailand's oldest national park. (p419)

Ao Khanom A lovely and un-touristed bay south of Surat Thani that hosts pink dolphins, a rare albino breed. (p584)

Um Phang An isolated and untamed corner of Thailand where forest creatures still roam. (p376)

Chiang Mai Meet domesticated elephants in sanctuaries, forested camps and mahout-training programs. (p253)

World-Class Pampering

Ko Samui Get thin, aligned and beautified on this wellness retreat island. (p532)

Bangkok A massage in the City of Angels is an ordinary errand, like picking up dry cleaning or going to the post office. (p88)

Phuket Five-star spas make pampering an all-day affair on this resort island. (p617)

Chiang Mai This low-key city does massages for the masses without the painful 'spa' price tag. (p254)

Diving & Snorkelling

Thailand is among the world's top dive sites with warm and clear seas.

Surin Islands & Similan Islands Marine National Parks These Andaman islands have dramatic rocky gorges, hard and soft coral reefs and a laundry list of marine life. (p611)

Ko Lanta The ocean's version of a grocery store attracts manta rays, whale sharks and other large pelagic fish to this Andaman island. (p662)

Ko Tao With cheap dive schools and shallow waters, Ko Tao remains the scuba-training headquarters. (p565)

Ko Lipe Dive sites with healthy coral, a deep pinnacle and good visibility in the early rainy season. (p680)

Fabulous Food

Thai food is super delicious, remarkably convenient and ridiculously cheap.

Curries

Curries The soup that eats like a meal, Thai curry is pungent, fiery and colourful. Bangkok, southern Thailand and northern Thailand all whip up their own variations.

Isan cuisine The northeast's triumvirate dishes – *gài yâhng* (grilled chicken), *sôm·đam* (spicy green papaya salad) and *kôw nĕe·o* (sticky rice) – have converts across the country.

Seafood Grilled prawns, spicy squid stir-fries, crab curries, fried mussels – get thee to the coast and dine on the fruits of the sea.

Fruits Luscious, dessert-like tropical fruits are piled into pyramid displays at day markets or arranged like precious jewels in vendors' glass cases.

Cooking Courses Learn how to replicate the tricks of the trade at cooking schools in Bangkok (p93) or Chiang Mai (p252).

Temples & Ruins

From glittering Buddhist temples to ancient Khmer sanctuaries.

IF YOU LIKE... SMALL TOWNS

Head to Nong Khai (p457), Tha Ton (p284), Chiang Khong (p327), Lampang (p297) and Prachuap Khiri Khan (p516) – small towns worth hanging around.

Bangkok The city's most exalted Buddha figure resides comfortably in Wat Phra Kaew, the seat of Thai Buddhism. (p55)

Ayuthaya The ruins of this fabled city stand testament to Thailand's formative years. (p154)

Sukhothai This ancient city is the capital of one of Thailand's first home-grown kingdoms. (p354)

Chiang Mai Chiang Mai's old walled city is filled with antique teak temples. (p231)

Phanom Rung This Khmer outpost built in the Angkor style has surveyed the rural landscape for centuries. (p423)

Outdoor Adventures

Trek, paddle and be carried through deep forests.

Kanchanaburi Waterfall-spotting, rafting and elephant riding just a short journey from Bangkok. (p169)

Mae Hong Son Trekking groups head off into the mountainous frontier between Thailand and Myanmar to visit ethnic hill-tribe villages. (p393)

Ko Chang When you tire of the sea, plunge into the jungle-covered hills where local guides have played since childhood. (p214)

Khao Sok National Park Canoe and hike through Thailand's ancient rainforest studded with limestone mountains. (p607)

Krabi Claw your way up the limestone cliffs at Railay for a breathtaking and breathless ocean view. (p643)

Chiang Mai Every activity known to athletes – mountain biking, kayaking, abseiling, trekking, ziplining – has a following in this nature-loving town. (p231)

(Top) Climbing at Hat Ton Sai (p653)
(Bottom) Marine life, Ko Tao (p565)

Month by Month

January

The weather is cool and dry, ushering in the peak tourist season.

✦ Chinese New Year

Thais with Chinese ancestry celebrate the Chinese lunar new year *(drùd jeen)* with a week of house-cleaning and fireworks.

February

Still in the high season; snowbirds flock to Thailand for sun and fun.

✦ Makha Bucha

One of three holy days marking important moments of Buddha's life, Makha Bucha *(mah·ká boo·chah)* falls on the full moon of the third lunar month. It is a public holiday.

✦ Flower Festival

Chiang Mai displays its floral beauty during a three-day period. The festival highlight is the flower-decorated floats that parade through town.

March

Hot and dry season approaches and the beaches start to empty out. This is also Thailand's semester break ('mid term'), and students head out on sightseeing trips.

☆ Pattaya International Music Festival

Pattaya showcases pop and rock bands from across Asia at this free music event, attracting busloads of Bangkok university students.

✦ Kite-Flying Festivals

During the windy season, colourful kites battle it out over the skies of Sanam Luang in Bangkok and elsewhere in the country.

✦ Golden Mango Season

Luscious ripe mangoes come into season from March to June and are sliced before your eyes, packed in a container with sticky rice and accompanied with a sweet sauce.

April

Hot, dry weather sweeps across the land. Though the tourist season is winding down, make reservations well in advance – the whole country is on the move for Songkran.

✦ Songkran

Thailand's traditional new year (12–14 April) starts out as a respectful affair then degenerates into a water war. Morning visits to the temple involve colourful processions and water-sprinkling ceremonies of sacred Buddha images. Afterwards, Thais load up their water guns and head out to the streets for battle. Chiang Mai and Bangkok are the epicentres.

May

Leading up to the rainy season, festivals encourage plentiful rains and bountiful harvests. Prices are low and tourists are few but it is still incredibly hot.

✿✿ Royal Ploughing Ceremony

This royal ceremony employs astrology and ancient Brahman rituals to kick off the rice-planting season. Sacred oxen are hitched to a wooden plough and part the ground of Sanam Luang in Bangkok.

✿✿ Rocket Festival

In the northeast, where rain can be scarce, villagers craft bamboo rockets *(bâng fai)* that are fired into the sky to encourage precipitation. This festival is celebrated in Yasothon, Ubon Ratchathani and Nong Khai.

✿✿ Visakha Bucha

The holy day of Visakha Bucha *(wí·săh·kà boo·chah)* falls on the 15th day of the waxing moon in the sixth lunar month and commemorates the date of the Buddha's birth, enlightenment and *parinibbana* (passing away).

June

In some parts of the country, the rainy season is merely an afternoon shower, leaving the rest of the day for music and merriment. This month is a shoulder season.

☆ Hua Hin Jazz Festival

Jazz groups descend on this royal retreat for a musical homage to the king, an accomplished jazz saxophonist and composer.

✿✿ Phi Ta Khon

The Buddhist holy day of Bun Phra Wet is given a

(Top) Lanterns float in the night sky for the Loi Krathong holiday

(Bottom) Water fights in Chiang Mai mark Songkran, Thailand's traditional New Year celebration

Carnival makeover in Dan Sai village in northeast Thailand. Revellers disguise themselves in garish 'spirit' costumes and parade through the streets wielding wooden phalluses and downing rice whisky. Dates vary between June and July.

July

The start of the rainy season ushers in Buddhist Lent, a period of reflection and meditation. Summer holidays bring an upsurge in tourists.

☆ Asanha Bucha

The full moon of the eighth lunar month commemorates Buddha's first sermon, in which he described the religion's four noble truths. It is considered one of Buddhism's holiest days.

☆ Khao Phansaa

The day after Asanha Bucha marks the beginning of Buddhist Lent (the first day of the waning moon in the eighth lunar month), the traditional time for men to enter the monastery. In Ubon Ratchathani, traditional candle offerings have grown into a festival of elaborately carved wax sculptures.

August

Overcast skies and daily showers mark the middle of the rainy season.

☆ HM the Queen's Birthday

Celebrated on 12 August, the Queen's Birthday is a public holiday; it's also rec-

ognised as Mother's Day throughout the country.

October

Religious preparations for the end of the rainy season and the end of Buddhist Lent begin. The monsoons are reaching the finish line (in most of the country).

☆ Vegetarian Festival

A holiday from meat is taken for nine days in adherence with Chinese beliefs of mind and body purification. In Phuket the festival gets extreme, with entranced marchers turning themselves into human shish kebabs.

☆ Ork Phansaa

The end of Buddhist Lent (three lunar months after Khao Phansaa) is marked by the *gà·tǐn* ceremony, in which new robes are given to the monks by meritmakers.

☆ King Chulalongkorn Day

Rama V is honoured on the anniversary of his death at the Royal Plaza in Dusit. Held on 23 October.

November

The cool, dry season has arrived and if you get here early enough, you'll beat the tourist crowds. The beaches are inviting and the landscape is lush.

☆ Surin Elephant Round-Up

Held on the third weekend of November, Thailand's

biggest elephant show celebrates this province's most famous residents.

☆ Loi Krathong

One of Thailand's most beloved festivals, Loi Krathong is celebrated on the first full moon of the 12th lunar month. Small origami-like boats (called *kràthong* or *grà·tong*) festooned with flowers and candles are sent adrift in the waterways.

☆ Lopburi Monkey Festival

During the last week of November, the town's troublesome macaques get pampered with their very own banquet, while meritmakers watch merrily.

December

The peak of the tourist season has returned with fair skies, busy beach resorts and a holiday mood.

☆ HM the King's Birthday

Honouring the king's birthday on 5 December, this public holiday hosts parades and merit-making events. Everyone wears pink shirts, pink being the colour associated with the monarchy.

Plan Your Trip
Itineraries

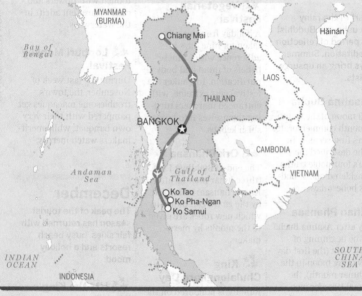

FELIX HUG / GETTY IMAGES ©

(2 WEEKS) Thailand's Highlights

Thanks to expanded domestic air travel, you can do a highlights tour of Thailand, sampling the beaches, mountains and cities. And remember that there are plenty of 'hidden' spots in the midst of crowded tourist centres.

Start off in **Bangkok**, where you can master the public transit system, visit the gleaming temples of Wat Phra Kaew and Wat Pho, explore the shopping malls and party like a rock star. Getting lost in Bangkok is an under-appreciated attraction and neighbourhoods like Chinatown have

people-packed streets where you'll see the weird and the wonderful.

Fly up to **Chiang Mai**, which can keep you busy for several days with Thai cooking classes, temple-spotting, monk chats and fabulous food. Then there is the surrounding countryside explored on road trips through the mountains, trekking to hill-tribe villages, elephant encounters and ziplining through the forest. Don't forget to visit the cool highlands of Doi Suthep or Doi Inthanon, two famous northern mountains.

Elephant ride, Chiang Mai (p230)

Reward all of your hard work getting to know Thai culture with a getaway to the tropical island of **Ko Samui**, an international resort jam-packed with package tourists, hotels and even traffic. But there are quiet corners and a buffet of beaches to suit every sand hunter. Bangkok Airways runs at least one direct flight between Chiang Mai and Samui per day, but book way in advance for a cheaper fare. While there, spend a day exploring the uninhabited Ang Thong National Marine Park.

Dial down your vacation with a stop in **Ko Pha-Ngan**, an easy boat trip from Ko Samui. Head to one of its overblown rave parties or time your visit to miss the crowded and sloppy event for some laid-back hammock hanging or diving instead. Next door is little **Ko Tao**, the Gulf of Thailand's dive certification centre; there are also near-shore reefs if you need to greet the fishes after breakfast.

Return to Bangkok with a tan, a Thai recipe book and lots of travel tales for the water cooler.

IAN TROWER / GETTY IMAGES ©

4 WEEKS Essential Thailand

The classic Thailand trip meanders through almost every corner of the kingdom. If you need to save time, hop on a flight – planes go everywhere.

Start off in **Bangkok**, and then take a train north to the ancient capital of **Ayuthaya**. Make a brief detour to the monkey town of **Lopburi**. From here, follow the culture trail north to **Sukhothai**, where you can cycle through the historic and crumbling ruins of another ancient capital. Hightail it to **Chiang Mai**, the laid-back 'lady' of the north. Then switchback into the mountains to the party scene of **Pai**. Climb deeper into the hills to the Myanmar-influenced town of **Mae Hong Son**. Loop back to Chiang Mai.

By now the beach is calling, so fly to the Gulf of Thailand and thread through **Ko Samui** for air connections, **Ko Pha-Ngan** for beach bumming and partying, and **Ko Tao** for diving and snorkelling.

Bus over to the Andaman Coast and its limestone mountains jutting out of the sea. **Ko Phi-Phi** is the prettiest, priciest and partiest of them all. Little **Ko Jum** holds tight to a fast-disappearing beach-shack, hippie vibe. **Ko Lanta** has gentrified into a package-tour destination, but the dive scene is the real attraction. Rock climbers opt for nearby **Krabi**.

If you've got the itch for more sand then continue down the peninsula to the **Trang Islands**, another collection of limestone sea mountains and gin-clear water. Or opt for the islands offshore from Satun. There's emerging and mid-range **Ko Bulon Leh**, rustic **Ko Tarutao** or overblown but still well-loved **Ko Lipe**.

Or you could skip the beaches south of Krabi and instead take a cultural antidote to the northeast, the agricultural heartland. Transit through Bangkok and then crawl through the jungles of **Khao Yai National Park**. From here, head to **Nakhon Ratchasima (Khorat)**, a transit point for trips to the Angkor ruins at **Phimai**. Follow the Khmer trail east to **Phanom Rung**, the most important and visually impressive of the Angkor temples in Thailand. Surrounding Phanom Rung are a handful of smaller, more remote temples known for their regal but forgotten ambience.

BLAKE KENT / DESIGN PICS / GETTY IMAGES ©

Top: View from Ko Phi-Phi Don (p654)
Bottom: Diving in Ko Tao (p565)

Off the Beaten Track: Thailand

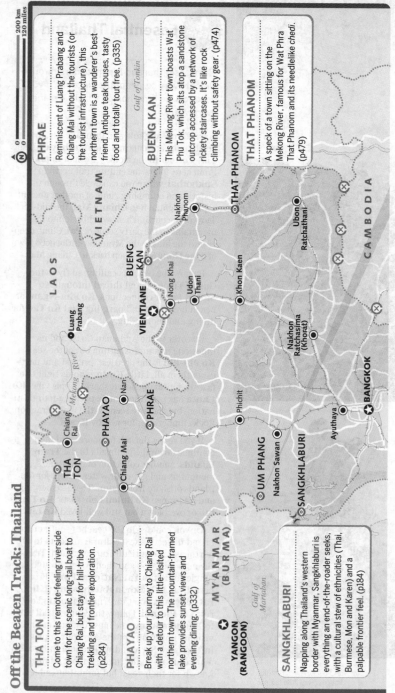

PHRAE

Reminiscent of Luang Prabang and Chiang Mai without the tourists (or the tourist infrastructure), this northern town is a wanderer's best friend. Antique teak houses, tasty food and totally tout free. (p335)

BUENG KAN

This Mekong River town boasts Wat Phu Tok, which sits atop a sandstone outcrop accessed by a network of rickety staircases. It's like rock climbing without safety gear. (p474)

THAT PHANOM

A speck of a town sitting on the Mekong River, famous for Wat Phra That Phanom and its needlelike chedi. (p479)

THA TON

Come to this remote-feeling riverside town for the scenic long-tail boat to Chiang Rai, but stay for hill-tribe trekking and frontier exploration. (p284)

PHAYAO

Break up your journey to Chiang Rai with a detour to this little-visited northern town. The mountain-framed lake provides sunset views and evening dining. (p332)

SANGKHLABURI

Napping along Thailand's western border with Myanmar, Sangkhlaburi is everything an end-of-the-roader seeks, with a cultural stew of ethnicities (Thai, Burmese, Mon and Karen) and a palpable frontier feel. (p184)

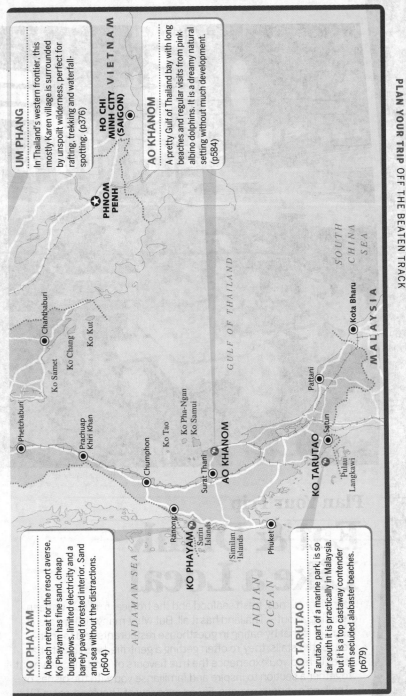

UM PHANG

In Thailand's western frontier, this mostly Karen village is surrounded by unspoilt wilderness, perfect for rafting, trekking and waterfall-spotting. (p376)

AO KHANOM

A pretty Gulf of Thailand bay with long beaches and regular visits from pink albino dolphins. It is a dreamy natural setting without much development. (p584)

KO PHAYAM

A beach retreat for the resort averse, Ko Phayam has fine sand, cheap bungalows, limited electricity and a barely paved forested interior. Sand and sea without the distractions. (p604)

KO TARUTAO

Tarutao, part of a marine park, is so far south it is practically in Malaysia. But it is a top castaway contender with secluded alabaster beaches. (p679)

Vendors line Th Yaowarat, Bangkok's Chinatow

Plan Your Trip

Eat & Drink Like a Local

Incendiary curries, fresh seafood and the tropical fruit you've been dreaming about – Thailand has it all. But what many visitors aren't aware of is that by eating in guesthouse restaurants and tourist-frequented stalls, they're often getting a gentrified version of Thai food. To help you experience the true flavours of Thailand, we've put together a section to inspire and familiarise you with the dishes of Thailand's various regions. For an overview of Thai food, see p721.

The Year in Food

Summer (Mar–Jun)

Thailand's hot season is the best time of year for fruit. Durian, mangoes, mangosteen and lychees are all at their juicy peak during these months.

Rainy Season (Jul–Oct)

One holiday to look out for during the rainy season is Thailand's annual Vegetarian Festival (typically held in late September or early October). The festival is celebrated particularly in towns with large Chinese populations, such as Bangkok, Phuket Town and Trang.

Winter (Nov–Jan)

During Thailand's brief cool season, open-air beer halls, many serving spicy Thai drinking snacks, spring up in the country's larger cities.

Food Experiences

Top Local Restaurants

➡ **Krua Apsorn, Bangkok** This award-winning restaurant has a thick menu of decadent Bangkok- and central Thailand–style fare. (p113)

➡ **Jay Fai, Bangkok** Lauded shophouse that specialises in seafood-heavy stir-fries that blur the line between Thai and Chinese cuisines. (p114)

➡ **Kow Soy Siri Soy, Chiang Mai** At lunchtime, locals swoop in on motorbikes to slurp down a bowl of rich and spicy *kôw soy* – northern Thai curry noodle soup. (p263)

➡ **Lung Eed, Chiang Rai** Simple but profoundly delicious northern-style chicken *lâhp* (a type of minced meat 'salad'). (p311)

➡ **Hua Hin Koti, Hua Hin** You know a restaurant is good in Thailand when the queue for a table stretches around the corner. (p510)

➡ **Gai Yang Rabeab, Khon Kaen** *Gài yâhng* (grilled chicken) and *sôm·dam* (spicy green-papaya salad) done right, with never a thought of compromising for *fa·ràng* (Western) tastes. (p445)

➡ **Ging Pagarang, Ko Samui** Locals know this is one of the island's best beachside places to sample authentic Samui-style seafood. (p544)

➡ **Bao Pradit, Mukdahan** An English menu lets you order dishes made of ant eggs, rattan, wild boar and other local ingredients. (p487)

➡ **Kruthara, Krabi** One of Thailand's very best seafood kitchens attracts domestic tourists from around the country. (p649)

➡ **Moom Aroy, Si Racha** Choose from a vast seafood menu at this long-standing open-air place perched over the sea. (p189)

Cooking Courses

A standard one-day course usually features a shopping trip to a local market to choose ingredients, followed by preparation of curry pastes, soups, curries, salads and desserts.

➡ **Helping Hands, Bangkok** (p93)

➡ **Chiang Mai Thai Cookery School, Chiang Mai** (p252)

➡ **Koh Chang Thai Cookery School, Ko Chang** (p218)

➡ **Pai Cookery School, Pai** (p385)

➡ **Suay Cooking School, Phuket Town** (p622)

Regional Specialities

Unlike the way it is often touted abroad, Thai food is anything but a single entity and is made up of a vast repertoire of ingredients, cooking techniques and dishes that can often pinpoint a particular province, or even a town.

Bangkok & Central Thai Cuisine

When foreigners think of Thai food, they're often thinking of the dishes of Bangkok and the central plains. A wealth of agriculture, access to the sea and the influence of foreign cuisines have come together in a cuisine that is both sophisticated and diverse. For a list of must-eat Bangkok- and central Thai–style dishes, see p111.

Northern Thai Cuisine

You may have heard of *kôw soy* (curry noodle soup), but most people, including many Thais, would be hard-pressed to name more than a few northern Thai dishes. In addition to being the country's least-known regional cuisine, northern Thai food is probably also the most seasonal, largely due to the north's elevation and climate. For more on northern Thai food, see p359.

Northeastern Thai Cuisine

Northeastern Thai food is undoubtedly Thailand's most rustic regional cooking style, and is most likely indicative of what the ethnic Tai people have been eating for hundreds, if not thousands, of years. Spicy, tart flavours and simple cooking methods such as grilling and soups dominate the northeastern kitchen, in which the predominant carb is sticky rice. For the must-eat northeastern Thai dishes, see p414.

Southern Thai Cuisine

You probably didn't notice it in the guesthouse food you've been served, but the dishes of Thailand's southern provinces are arguably the country's spiciest. Eat outside the tourist track and you'll find an entire repertoire of incendiary soups, piquant curries and full-flavoured stir-fries. For more on the food of Thailand's southern provinces, see p541.

Ethnic Specialities

In addition to geography, the country's predominant minorities – Muslims and Chinese – have had different but profound influences on the local cuisine.

Salak – one of Thailand's indigenous fruits (p723)

Thai-Muslim Cuisine

Muslims are thought to have first visited Thailand during the late 14th century. Along with the Quran, they brought with them a cuisine based on meat and dried spice from their homelands in India and the Middle East. Nearly 700 years later, the impact of this culinary commerce can still be felt.

While some Muslim dishes such as *ro·ti,* a fried bread similar to the Indian *paratha,* have changed little, if at all, others such as *gaang mát·sà·màn* are a unique blend of Thai, Indian and Middle Eastern cooking styles and ingredients. In more recent years, additional Muslim dishes have arrived via contact with Thailand's neighbour to the south, Malaysia.

Common Thai-Muslim dishes include the following:

➡ *Gaang mát·sà·màn* – 'Muslim curry' is a rich coconut milk–based dish, which, unlike most Thai curries, gets much of its flavour from dried spices. As with many Thai-Muslim dishes, there is an emphasis on the sweet.

➡ *Kôw mòk* – biryani, a dish found across the Muslim world, also has a foothold in Thailand.

Fresh-fruit drink stand, Bangkok

Here the dish is typically made with chicken and is served with a sweet and sour dipping sauce and a bowl of chicken broth.

➡ *Má·đà·bà* – known as *murtabak* in Malaysia and Indonesia, these are *ro·ti* that have been stuffed with a savoury or sometimes sweet filling and fried until crispy.

➡ *Sà·đé* (satay) – the savoury peanut-based dipping sauce served with these grilled skewers of meat is often mistakenly associated with Thai cooking.

➡ *Sà·làt kàak* – literally 'Muslim salad' (*kàak* is a somewhat derogatory word used to describe people or things of South Asian and/or Muslim origin), this dish combines iceberg lettuce, chunks of firm tofu, cucumber, hard-boiled egg and tomato, all topped with a sweet peanut sauce.

➡ *Súp hǎhng woo·a* – oxtail soup, possibly a Malay contribution, is even richer and often more sour than the 'Buddhist' Thai *đôm yam*.

Thai-Chinese Cuisine

Immigrants from southern China have been influencing Thai cuisine for centuries,

and it was Chinese labourers and vendors who most likely introduced the wok and several varieties of noodle dishes to Thailand.

Thai-Chinese dishes you're likely to run across include the folllowing:

➡ *Bà·mèe* – Chinese-style wheat and egg noodles are typically served with slices of barbecued pork, a handful of greens and/or wontons.

➡ *Gǒo·ay đěe·o kôo·a gài* – wide rice noodles fried with little more than egg, chicken, squid and garlic oil; a popular dish in Bangkok's Chinatown.

➡ *Kôw kǎh mǒo* – braised pork leg served over rice, often with sides of greens and a hard-boiled egg, is the epitome of the Chinese-style one-dish meal.

➡ *Kôw man gài* – chicken rice, originally from the Chinese island of Hainan, is now found in just about every corner of Thailand.

➡ *Sah·lah·bow* – Chinese-style steamed buns are a favourite at old-school Chinese-style coffee shops across Thailand.

Ko Pha-Ngan (p549)

Plan Your Trip

Choose Your Beach

It's a terrible dilemma: Thailand has too many beaches. Choices can be daunting even for those visiting a second time and development is so rapid that where you went five years ago may now be completely different. Here, we break it down for you so you can find your dream beach.

Best Beaches for...

Peace–Action Balance

Ko Mak Beach bar scene, explore-ably flat and tonnes of beach.

Ko Phayam Bike back roads to empty beaches or to parties.

Hat Mae Nam Quiet Ko Samui beach close to lots of action.

Ko Bulon Leh Chilled-out vibe but lots to do.

Kids

Dolphin Bay Low-key scenic bay close to Bangkok.

Hua Hin Mainland resort with a long gulf-side coastline.

Ko Ngai (Trang Islands) Shallow Andaman bay with coral reefs.

Ko Lanta Build sandcastles all day on this Andaman package-tour island.

Local Culture

Ko Yao Noi Thai-Muslim fishing island with beautiful karst scenery.

Ko Sukorn Agricultural and fishing gem filled with mangroves and water buffalo.

Ko Phra Thong Look for rare orchids with *chow lair*.

Hua Hin Recreate with middle-class Thais in this urban beach getaway.

Quick & Easy Access from Bangkok

Nowadays the closest beaches to Bangkok aren't necessarily the quickest and easiest to get to. There are international flights direct to Phuket and Ko Samui that allow you to skip the big city altogether, and flights from Bangkok (and some Southeast Asian countries) can shuttle you to several southern towns with ease.

If you don't want or can't afford to fly, but are still short on time, the closest beach island to Bangkok is Ko Samet (count on around four hours total travel time) while the closest beach resort is Pattaya (1½ hours). The next-closest stops by land are the beach towns of Cha-am (2½ hours) and Hua Hin (three hours). It takes around six hours to get to Ko Chang which beats the minimum of 10 hours to reach the lower gulf islands. If you're in a hurry and want to take the bus, anywhere on the Andaman Coast is not your best choice.

To Party Or Not To Party

Where

A big percentage of travellers to southern Thailand want to party. If there are buckets of sugary cocktails and cheap beer, hordes or revellers will turn up and give the night their all. For other visitors, this sounds like a complete nightmare.

Luckily it's as easy to escape the madness as it is to join in. The main party zones are well known to be just that. Anywhere you go that's not a major tourist enclave will have peace and quiet on offer. Small towns will have zero nightlife and a few beaches sit somewhere in between where you can have a nice sunset drink or maybe stay out till midnight at small, fun bars.

The Girly Bar Issue

Bangkok, Pattaya and Phuket are the capitals of push-up bras and 'hello meesta', while Hat Lamai on Ko Samui is the centre of this small universe in the lower gulf islands. Islands like Ko Samet and Ko Chang and mid-sized towns such as Hat Yai and Ao Nang have small enclaves of questionable massage parlors and bars with the telltale pole dancer silhouette on the sign, but it won't be in your face. Smaller islands and towns will be clear of this sort of thing, at least on the surface.

Your Party Level

Level One: Dead Calm Surin & Similan Islands, Laem Son National Park, Hat Pak Meng & Hat Chang Lang

Level Two: A Flicker of Light Ko Tarutao, Ko Libong, Prachuap Khiri Khan

Level Three: There's a Bar Ko Yao Islands, Ao Khanom, Ko Kut

Level Four: Maybe a Few Bars Hat Khao Lak, Ko Muk, Ao Thong Nai Pan (Pha-Ngan)

Level Five: Easy to Find a Drink Hua Hin, Bo Phut (Samui), Ao Nang

Level Six: There's A Beach Bar Scene Ko Mak, Ko Phayam, Railay

Level Seven: Magic Milkshake Anyone? Ko Lanta, Ko Chang, Ban Tai (Pha-Ngan)

Level Eight: I Forget What Eight Was For Hat Lamai (Samui), Ko Lipe, Ko Samet

Level Nine: What Happened Last Night? Hat Chaweng (Samui), Pattaya, Ko Tao

Level Ten: Don't Tell Me What Happened Last Night Patong (Phuket), Ko Phi-Phi, Hat Rin (Ko Pha-Ngan)

Resort Town Personalities

The personality of a Thai resort town depends a lot on the prices. In places where midrange options dominate, you'll usually find package tourists, rows of beach loungers and umbrellas along the beach, and plenty of big boats full of snorkelling tours.

At upscale places things settle down. The ritzier beaches of Phuket like Surin and Ao Ban Tao are among the quieter on the island yet still have plenty of dining and cocktail options. Ko Kut off the eastern seaboard has lovely resorts on some of the country's most unspoiled beaches, while the more secluded beaches of northeastern Ko Samui have some of the most luxurious resorts in Thailand. Once you go very high end, privacy and seclusion become a bigger part of the picture.

There are a few remaining beach huts that are often found on some of the country's most secluded beaches. See our Off The Beaten Track feature for details.

Activities

Diving & Snorkelling

The Andaman Coast and Ko Tao in the lower gulf have the best undersea views in the country. Islands like Ko Samui and Ko Lanta that don't have great snorkelling from the beach will have snorkelling tours to nearby sites.

Climbing

Railay is the best-known place to climb in southern Thailand; it has the best set up for beginners and a fun scene. Ko Phi-Phi has some great climbing options, and there are more off-the-beaten-path climbing options around Krabi. The Ko Yao islands are slowly getting bolted and offer horizons to more seasoned climbers.

Hiking

The mainland national parks like Khao Sok have the most jungle walking opportunities, but more forested islands such as Ko Chang, Ko Pha-Ngan and Phuket have great hiking.

Culture

For a taste of authentic Thai culture, head to Trang, Surat Thani or Songkhla, to lesser known islands like Ko Si Chang or Ko Sukorn, or to the south coast of Ko Samui or the east coast of Ko Lanta. But even tourist central Patong or Ko Phi-Phi can give you a taste of what's beyond resort land, just by eating at food stalls and talking to the owners, smiling a lot and being open to interactions with locals.

WHEN TO GO

REGION	JAN–MAR	APR–JUN	JUL–SEP	OCT–DEC
Bangkok	Hotter towards March	Hot and humid rainy season	Cooler towards December	
Eastern Seaboard	Peak season; thins towards March	Rainy season begins in May	Some islands close for the monsoon	Cooler weather; low hotel rates
Southern Gulf	Hot and dry	Hot and dry	Occasional rains and strong winds	Occasional rains and strong winds
Lower Gulf	Clear and sunny	Hot and dry	Clear and sunny	Monsoon and rough waters
Northern Andaman	High season; high prices	Fringe season with iffy weather	Rainy season and surf season	High season picks up again
Southern Andaman	High season	Monsoons usually begin in May	Some resorts close for rainy season	Crowds return with the sun

OVERVIEW OF THAILAND'S ISLANDS & BEACHES

BEACHES	PACKAGE, HIGH-END TOURISTS	BACK-PACKERS	FAMILIES	PARTIES	DIVING & SNORKELLING	PERSONALITY
Ko Chang & Eastern Seaboard						
Ko Samet	✓	✓	✓	✓		Pretty beach, easy getaway from Bangkok
Ko Chang	✓	✓	✓	✓	✓	International resort, mediocre beaches, jungle interior
Ko Wai		✓	✓		✓	Primitive day-tripper, deserted in the evening
Ko Mak	✓	✓	✓			Mediocre beaches, great island vibe
Ko Kut	✓	✓	✓			Pretty semi-developed island, great for solitude
Hua Hin & the Upper Gulf						
Hua Hin	✓	✓	✓			International resort, easy access to Bangkok
Pranburi & Around	✓		✓			Quiet and close to Bangkok
Ban Krut			✓			Low-key and popular with Thais
Bang Saphan Yai	✓	✓				Cheap mainland beach
Ko Samui & the Lower Gulf						
Ko Samui	✓	✓	✓	✓		International resort for social beach-goers
Ko Pha-Ngan	✓	✓	✓	✓	✓	Popular beach, with boozy Hat Rin
Ko Tao	✓	✓	✓	✓	✓	Dive schools galore
Ang Thong		✓	✓			Gorgeous karst scenery, rustic
Ao Khanom		✓	✓			Quiet, little known
Phuket & the Andaman Coast						
Ko Chang (Ranong)		✓	✓		✓	Rustic
Ko Phayam		✓	✓			Quiet, little known
Surin & Similan Islands		✓			✓	Dive sites accessed by live-aboards
Ko Yao	✓	✓	✓			Poor beaches but nice vibe, great scenery
Phuket	✓	✓	✓	✓	✓	International resort for social beach-goers
Ao Nang	✓	✓	✓		✓	Touristy, close to Railay
Railay	✓	✓	✓			Rock-climbing centre
Ko Phi-Phi	✓	✓		✓	✓	Pretty party island
Ko Jum	✓	✓	✓			Mediocre beach, nice island vibe
Ko Lanta	✓	✓	✓		✓	Emerging package tourist scene
Trang Islands	✓	✓	✓		✓	Ko Ngai good for kids
Ko Bulon Leh		✓	✓		✓	Pretty beaches, little known
Ko Tarutao		✓	✓			Semi-developed national park
Ko Lipe	✓	✓	✓	✓	✓	Hot spot, handy for visa runs
Ko Adang		✓			✓	Popular with day-trippers

Top: Ko Lipe (p680)

Bottom: Rock-climbing in Krabi (p643)

Plan Your Trip
Travel with Children

Looking for an exotic destination that the kids can handle? Thailand has it: beaches, mountains, elephants, sparkling temples and bustling markets; there's something for each age range. Plus Thais are serious 'cute' connoisseurs and exotic-looking foreign children trump stuffed animals and fluffy dogs.

Thailand for Children

Small children are instant celebrities in Thailand and attract paparazzi-like attention. Babies do surprisingly well with their new-found stardom, soaking up adoration from gruff taxi drivers who transform into loving uncles wanting to play a game of peekaboo (called *'já ăir'*). If you've got a babe in arms, food vendors will often hold the child while you eat, taking the child for a brief stroll to visit all the neighbours.

At a certain age, kids can develop stranger anxiety, which doesn't mix well with the Thai passion for children. For the preschool set, who are becoming self-conscious but still have major cute quotient, stick to tourist centres instead of trotting off to far-flung places where foreigners, especially children, will attract too much attention. A polite way to deflect spectators is to say the child is 'shy' *('ki aye')*. Thais understand this emotion.

Older children should be safe from Thai attention, though they might get nervous about the cities' natural chaos and the confusion that arises from being in a new place and having to negotiate transport. Consider giving your children a role in travel planning: reading the map, setting up an itinerary or carrying the water bottles. You're moulding future travellers.

Best Regions for Kids

Eastern Seaboard & Ko Chang
Shallow seas are kind to young swimmers and the low evening tides make for good beach-combing. Older children will like the interior jungle, elephant camp and mangrove kayaking.

Southern Gulf
Hua Hin has a long sandy coastline for pint-sized marathons and hillside temples for monkey spotting. Phetchaburi's cave temples have bats.

Ko Samui & Lower Gulf
Older children can snorkel at Ko Tao without worry. Ko Samui, especially its northern beaches, is a hit with pram-pushers and toddlers, while Hat Chaweng is social and commercial; ideal for teens.

Phuket & Andaman Coast
Phuket has amusements galore (from theme parks to surf schools), though steer clear of the Patong party scene. There are at least a dozen islands along this coast where families can frolic in the sea.

Chiang Mai
Families come in droves during European summer holidays to expose their kids to culture, ride elephants and cycle about town.

Thai cities can be claustrophobic and the heat can make it difficult to wear out energetic children. Staying at a hotel with a pool will give the kids enough exercise not to bounce off the proverbial walls.

To smooth out the usual road bumps of dragging children from place to place, check out Lonely Planet's *Travel with Children,* which contains useful advice on how to cope with kids on the road, with a focus on travel in developing countries.

Children's Highlights

Children will especially enjoy the beaches, as most are shallow, gentle bays good for beginner swimmers. The further south you go, the clearer the water. The bays are often fringed with near-shore reefs and curious fish swim by for a visit.

Animal amusements abound in Thailand, though standards are often below those in the West. Chiang Mai is the centre of elephant tourism; here tourists can bathe, ride and learn about elephant welfare. Many beach resorts, such as Phuket and Ko Chang, also have wildlife encounters. Lopburi is overrun with monkeys who cause all sorts of mayhem.

Outdoor activities – trekking, ziplining, bamboo rafting – will appeal to older children. Chiang Mai, Kanchanaburi, southern beach resorts and tourist centres in Northern Thailand all have a variety of nature sports that are family friendly.

Bangkok is great fun for those in awe of construction sites: the city is filled with cranes, jackhammers and concrete-pouring trucks. Then there's the aboveground BTS (Skytrain), and shopping malls complete with escalators (a preschool favourite). The city's immense shopping options will appeal to tweens and teens.

Getting around can also be amusing. Kids on a train kick might like an overnight journey. On the train they can walk around and they're assigned the lower sleeping berths with views of the stations. The author's preschooler loved the speedboats they took to get around the Ko Chang archipelago.

Even temples can be engaging places for children. The climb to hilltop temples, marvelling at the resident monkeys and cave shrines, is a great way to expend energy. Merit-making at a Buddhist temple is surprisingly child-friendly – there are the burning joss sticks, the bowing in front of the Buddha and the rubbing of gold leaf on the central image. It is a very active process that can involve the kids. Most temples have a fortune-telling area, where you shake a bamboo container until a numbered stick falls out. The number corresponds to a printed fortune. A variation on this is to make a donation into a pot (or in some cases an automated machine) corresponding to the day of the week you were born and retrieve the attached fortune.

STORIES FOR THE SCRAPBOOK

After two children and four trips to Thailand with them as my research assistants, these are some of the tales that we share at the dinner table when they feel like going on a memory walkabout.

'My son's last visit to Thailand was when he was four and we researched the eastern seaboard together. At the time his highlights were the hotels that had two complimentary soaps (four-year-olds are easily impressed); 7-Elevens, where his babysitter would buy him cookies; and pineapple ('Dad, have you ever heard of pineapple before?' he asked during a phone call home). The mosquito net we slept under in Ko Kut became our very own bat cave. And his great triumph was when he outran the Thai ladies on the beach who wanted to shower him with love pinches.

On my most recent trip, I brought my one-year-old daughter along to break in her passport. We were based in Chiang Mai and she loved all of Thailand's cats and dogs, waved at passersby and was well photographed by Thais and Chinese tourists. She screeched wildly for noodles and protested violently when I didn't get off at every stop on Bangkok's BTS. She was surprised when we returned home that strangers didn't want to hold her.'

By Lonely Planet Thailand guidebook author, China Williams

Planning & Practicalities

Amenities specially geared towards young children – such as child-safety seats for cars, high chairs in restaurants or nappy-changing facilities in public restrooms – are virtually nonexistent in Thailand. Therefore parents will have to be resourceful in seeking out substitutes or just do without.

Baby formula and nappies (diapers) are available at minimarkets and 7-Elevens in the larger towns and cities, but sizes are usually small, smaller and smallish. If your kid wears size 3 or larger, head to Tesco Lotus, Big C or Tops Market stores. Nappy rash cream is sold at pharmacies.

Hauling around little ones can be a challenge. Thailand's footpaths are often too crowded to push a pram, especially full-size SUV versions. Instead opt for a compact umbrella stroller that can squeeze past the fire hydrants and mango carts and can be folded up and thrown in a túk-túk (pronounced *đúk đúk;* three-wheeled motorised vehicle). A baby pack is also useful, but make sure the child's head doesn't sit higher than yours: there are lots of hanging obstacles poised at forehead level.

Eating with Kids

Worrying about food occupies a lot of parental bandwidth and the vagaries of children's food preferences are further complicated by a cuisine known for its spiciness. Luckily, even Thai children are shielded from chillies and there are a handful of child-friendly dishes that every server can recommend. Because of the heat, remember to keep your little ones well hydrated, either with water or a variety of fruit juices, including fresh young coconuts or lime juice (a surprising hit with kids).

➡ *kài jee·o* (omelette) – more oily than the French style but a safe, non-spicy restaurant or street-stall option.

➡ *gài yâhng/tôrt* (grilled/fried chicken) – common market and street stall meal.

➡ *kôw nĕe·o* (sticky rice) – straight-up carbs but picky eaters won't resist; sold in markets alongside grilled or fried chicken.

➡ *gài pàt mét má·môo·ang* (chicken stir-fried with cashew nuts) – mild stir-fry, popular at restaurants.

➡ *kôw man gài* (Hainanese chicken rice) – a popular morning and afternoon meal sold at speciality shops.

Health & Safety

For the most part parents needn't worry too much about health concerns. Regular hand washing should be enforced. Thai children are bathed at least twice a day and powered afterwards to reduce skin irritation from the humid climate; foreigners should aim for at least daily showers. Children should be warned not to play with animals as rabies is relatively common and some pets have bad manners.

Dengue is an increasing concern in Thailand and reached a 20-year-high rate of infection during the rainy season of 2013. Parents should take care to prevent mosquito bites (a difficult task) in children. Repellent creams containing 12% DEET are widely available. If your child is bitten, there are a variety of locally produced balms that can reduce swelling and itching. All the usual health precautions apply.

Children familiar with urban environments will do well in Thailand's cities, where traffic is chaotic and pedestrian paths are congested. Thai cities are very loud and can be a sensory overload for young children. Be sure that your child understands street safety guidelines as it will be difficult to focus on your instructions amid all the street noise outside.

Regions at a Glance

Bangkok & Around

Culture
Food
Nightlife

Classic Siam

The great temples along Mae Nam Chao Phraya (Chao Phraya River) are national pilgrimage sites cradling revered religious symbols and the country's test displays of classical art and architecture.

More is Better

The residents of this multi-wát city love to eat. Food can be found in every nook and cranny, from noodle pushcarts and grease-stained wok shops to fine dining and fashion-minded cafes. All of Bangkok's expat communities have their culinary outposts, providing comfort to the home-sick and exotic flavours to everybody.

Toast the Stars

The quintessential night out in Bangkok is still a plastic table filled with sweating Beer Changs but rooftop bars, with cool breezes and fizzy cocktails, make better Instagram pictures.

p54

Central Thailand

Culture/History
Mountains
Festivals

Rest & Ruins

The ruins of Ay-uthaya, Thailand's greatest empire, is an Unesco World Heritage Site. Ami-able Lopburi and its ancient ruins are informally ruled by a troop of monkeys. Kanchanaburi is the final resting place for WWII POWs.

Mountain Journeys

Kanchanaburi is the gateway to the misty Myanmar-bordering moun-tains of western Thailand. Rivers and waterfalls carve the contours and a collection of parks makes this one of Thailand's wildest corners.

Mother Waters

This fertile river plain is often cel-ebrated during religious festivals, such as Loi Kratong in Bang Pa In Pal-ace, and Ayuthaya's International Swan Boat Races.

p151

Ko Chang & Eastern Seaboard

Beaches
Diving/Snorkelling
Small Towns

A Chain of Islands

Jungle-covered Ko Chang is loved for its tropical ambience and party scene. Quiet Ko Kut excels in seaside seclusion, Ko Mak boasts a laid-back island vibe and little Ko Wai has the prettiest views you've ever seen.

Scuba Hero

Surrounding Ko Chang is a national marine park filled with beginner-friendly dives. Seamounts and rock pinnacles serve as shelter for schooling fish and turtles.

Provincial Prominence

Tourists often over-look Chanthaburi, famous for a week-end gem market, and Trat, a transit link to Ko Chang, that are both charming for their ordinariness and middle-class prosperity.

p188

Chiang Mai Province

Culture/History
Food
Outdoor Adventures

Lanna Latitudes

A refreshing counterpoint to Bangkok's mayhem, Chiang Mai proudly displays northern Thailand's unique history and culture in its antique-fortified city. Culture geeks come for sightseeing or courses.

Curries & Noodles

Northern Thailand has its own versions of standard Thai dishes, reflecting its cooler climate and proximity to Yunnan and Myanmar. Chiang Mai converts the carnivores with its vegetarian, health food.

Commute into the Hills

Just beyond the city limits is a lush and mountainous landscape that can be explored on muddy hikes, river paddle tours, zipline courses or aboard an elephant.

p230

Northern Thailand

Culture/History
Mountains
Food

Ancient Kingdoms

Ancient city-states with fortressed walls and sandstone Buddhist monuments sprang up throughout northern Thailand. Sukhothai is the most atmospheric.

Misty Mornings

The terrain climbs into the highlands shared with Laos and Myanmar. Winding roads and scenic vistas are highlights of Chiang Rai and Mae Hong Son Provinces. Tucked into high-altitude valleys are villages of ethnic minorities.

Comfort Food, Northern Style

The north's cooler climate features a menu of hearty pork stews, influenced by Thai, Shan and Yunnan cuisine. The signature dish is *kôw soy,* a mild curry served over noodles.

p291

Northeastern Thailand

Culture/History
Food
Festivals

Ancient Angkor

The northeast was once a remote frontier of the great Angkor empire, based in present-day Cambodia, which built miniature versions of Angkor Wat throughout the countryside.

Powered by Sticky Rice

During the rainy season, the landscape transforms into an emerald hue of tender rice shoots. To appreciate the agricultural rhythms, homestays place visitors smack in the middle of the paddies complete with water buffaloes.

Fireworks & Fireballs

There isn't much to see in the northeast until a festival fires up. Mysterious fireballs erupt from Mekong River near Nong Khai and huge candle sculptures are paraded through Ubon Ratchathani.

p407

Hua Hin & the Upper Gulf

Culture/History
Beaches
Food

Royal Coast

Successive Bangkok kings escaped to this coastal getaway, which includes Phetchaburi and its historic hilltop palace and cave shrines, and Hua Hin, still serving as the king's seaside retreat.

Surf & Turf

Beach lovers looking for a sense of place will find it in Prachuap Khiri Khan, a mellow small town with karst-studded bays, and Hua Hin, a mod-con seaside resort ideal for families and honeymooners.

Beach Grub

With its proximity to Bangkok and popularity with domestic tourists, this region excels in local-style seafood, served in the raucous Hua Hin night market, by roaming vendors in Cha-am or at oceanfront restaurants.

p493

Ko Samui & the Lower Gulf

Beaches
Diving/
Snorkelling
Nightlife

Bronzing Bodies

The three sister islands of the lower gulf have been pursued by smitten island-hoppers for decades. Samui caters to resort-style vacations with stunning sugar-white beaches, while Ko Pha-Ngan goes bohemian with cosy coves.

Diver Down

The warm gentle seas and wallet-friendly prices keep Ko Tao beloved for dive training, but Ko Pha-Ngan is close behind.

Rave at the Moon

Ko Pha-Ngan becomes a huge uni campus during its Full Moon Parties when tonnes of people storm the beach to rave at the moon. Booze buckets, day-glo paint and drunken foolishness abound.

p526

Phuket & the Andaman Coast

Scenery
Beaches
Diving/
Snorkelling

Karst Cathedrals

Limestone mountains jut out of jewel-coloured waters with monumental stature. A variety of sports, based in Krabi and Ko Yao, turn the pinnacles into an outdoor playground.

Goldilocks Beaches

Andaman beaches come in every shape and flavour. Phuket excels in comfort for the holidaying masses. But there are backwater islands without 24-hour electricity, pretty Ko Phi-Phi and well-loved Ko Lipe.

Cousteau Territory

Big fish, coral gardens, clear waters – diving and snorkelling sites include the world-renowned Similan Islands and Surin Islands Marine National Parks.

p597

On the Road

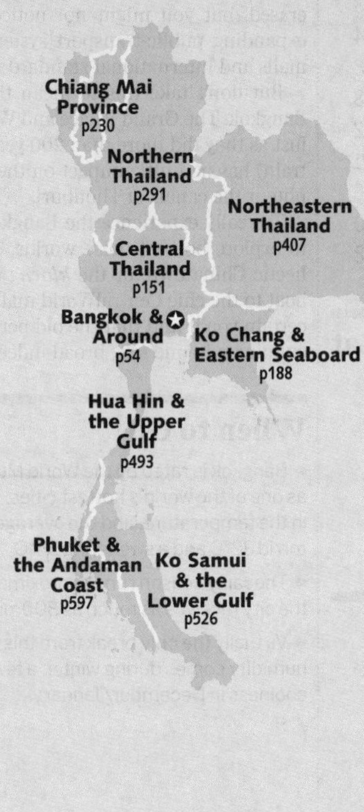

Chiang Mai
Province
p230

Northern
Thailand
p291

Northeastern
Thailand
p407

Central
Thailand
p151

Bangkok &
Around
p54

Ko Chang &
Eastern Seaboard
p188

Hua Hin &
the Upper
Gulf
p493

Phuket &
the Andaman
Coast
p597

Ko Samui
& the
Lower Gulf
p526

Bangkok & Around

Includes ➡

Best Places to Eat

➡ nahm (p116)

➡ Krua Apsorn (p113)

➡ Street food in Chinatown (p117)

➡ Eat Me (p115)

➡ Jay Fai (p114)

Best Places to Stay

➡ Siam Heritage (p105)

➡ AriyasomVilla (p109)

➡ Metropolitan by COMO (p106)

➡ Bangkok Tree House (p111)

➡ Lamphu Treehouse (p100)

Why Go?

Formerly the epitome of the elderly Asian metropolis, in recent years Bangkok has gone under the knife and emerged as a rejuvenated starlet. Her wrinkles haven't totally been erased, but you might not notice them behind the ever-expanding public-transport system, air-conditioned mega-malls and international-standard restaurants.

But don't take this to mean that there's no more 'real' Bangkok. The Grand Palace and Wat Phra Kaew still sparkle just as they did more than 200 years ago, and the BTS (Skytrain) has had little impact on the shophouses of Banglamphu or the canals of Thonburi.

To really experience the Bangkok of today, it's necessary to explore both of these worlds. Take the MRT (metro) to hectic Chinatown, or the *klorng* (canal, also spelt *khlong*) boat to the chic CentralWorld mall, and along the way we're certain you'll find that the old personality and the new face culminate in one sexy broad indeed.

When to Go

➡ Bangkok is rated by the World Meteorological Organisation as one of the world's hottest cities. There's little fluctuation in the temperature, and the average high sways between a torrid 32°C and a sweltering 34°C.

➡ The rainy season runs approximately May to October, when the city receives as much as 300mm of rain monthly.

➡ Virtually the only break from this relentless heat and humidity comes during winter, a few weeks of relative coolness in December/January.

History

Now the centre of government and culture in Thailand, Bangkok was a historical miracle during a time of turmoil. Following the fall of Ayuthaya in 1767, the kingdom fractured into competing forces, from which General Taksin emerged as a decisive unifier. He established his base in Thonburi, on the western bank of Mae Nam Chao Phraya (Chao Phraya River), a convenient location for sea trade from the Gulf of Thailand. Taksin proved more of a military strategist than a popular ruler. He was later deposed by another important military general, Chao Phraya Chakri, who in 1782 moved the capital across the river to a more defensible location in anticipation of a Burmese attack. The succession of his son in 1809 established the present-day royal dynasty, and Chao Phraya Chakri is referred to as Rama I.

Court officials envisioned the new capital as a resurrected Ayuthaya, complete with an island district (Ko Ratanakosin) carved out of the swampland and cradling the royal court (the Grand Palace) and a temple to the auspicious Emerald Buddha (Wat Phra Kaew). The emerging city, which was encircled by a thick wall, was filled with stilt and floating houses ideally adapted to seasonal flooding.

Modernity came to the capital in the late 19th century as European aesthetics and technologies filtered east. During the reigns of Rama IV (King Mongkut; r 1851–68) and Rama V (King Chulalongkorn; r 1868–1910), Bangkok received its first paved road (Th Charoen Krung, formerly known as New Road) and a new royal district (Dusit) styled after European palaces.

Bangkok was still a gangly town when soldiers from the American war in Vietnam came to rest and relax in the city's go-go bars and brothels. It wasn't until the boom years of the 1980s and 1990s that Bangkok exploded into a fully fledged metropolis crowded with hulking skyscrapers and an endless spill of concrete that gobbled up rice paddies and green space. The city's extravagant tastes were soon tamed by the 1997 economic meltdown, the effects of which can still be seen in the numerous half-built skyscrapers. Nearly two decades later, many of these still exist, but are becoming increasingly obscured behind a modern public transport system and the seemingly endless high-rise condos and vast glass-fronted mega-malls that have come to define the Bangkok of today.

◎ Sights

◎ Ko Ratanakosin เกาะรัตนโกสินทร์

Welcome to Bangkok's birthplace. The vast city we know today emerged from Ko Ratanakosin, a tiny virtual island ('Ko') made by dredging a canal around Mae Nam Chao Phraya during the late 18th century. Within this area you'll find the glittering temples and palaces that most visitors associate with the city. Ko Ratanakosin's riverfront setting is also home to several museums, markets and universities. All these sights are within walking distance of each other and are best visited early in the morning before the day comes to a boil.

The river ferry pier at Tha Chang is the most convenient access point.

★ Wat Phra Kaew & Grand Palace   BUDDHIST TEMPLE, HISTORICAL SITE

(วัดพระแก้ว, พระบรมมหาราชวัง; Map p62; Th Na Phra Lan; admission 500B; ⊘8.30am-4pm; 🚤 Tha Chang) Also known as the Temple of the Emerald Buddha, Wat Phra Kaew is the colloquial name of the vast, fairy-tale compound that also includes the former residence of the Thai monarch, the Grand Palace.

This ground was consecrated in 1782, the first year of Bangkok rule, and is today Bangkok's biggest tourist attraction and a pilgrimage destination for devout Buddhists and nationalists. The 94.5-hectare grounds encompass more than 100 buildings that represent 200 years of royal history and architectural experimentation.

Housed in a fantastically decorated bòht (chapel), the Emerald Buddha is the temple's primary attraction. For more on this and other highlights of the temple compound, see p60.

Except for an anteroom here and there, the buildings of the Grand Palace are now put to use by the king only for certain ceremonial occasions, such as Coronation Day.

Borombhiman Hall, a French-inspired structure that served as a residence for Rama VI, is occasionally used to house visiting foreign dignitaries. The building to the west is Amarindra Hall (open from Monday to Friday), originally a hall of justice but used today for coronation ceremonies.

The largest of the palace buildings is the Chakri Mahaprasat, the Grand Palace Hall. Thai kings housed their huge harems in the inner palace area, which was guarded by combat-trained female sentries.

Bangkok & Around Highlights

1 Basking in the glow of all the gold at **Wat Phra Kaew & Grand Palace** (p55)

2 Taking in the immense Buddha statue at **Wat Pho** (p58)

3 Skipping between sightseeing spots on **a cruise of Bangkok's canals** (p97)

4 Encountering the best of Thai architecture and artwork at **Jim Thompson House** (p79)

5 Burning baht at **Chatuchak Weekend Market** (p134)

6 Learning to make authentic Thai dishes at one of Bangkok's **cooking schools** (p93)

7 Toasting the stars and the twinkling

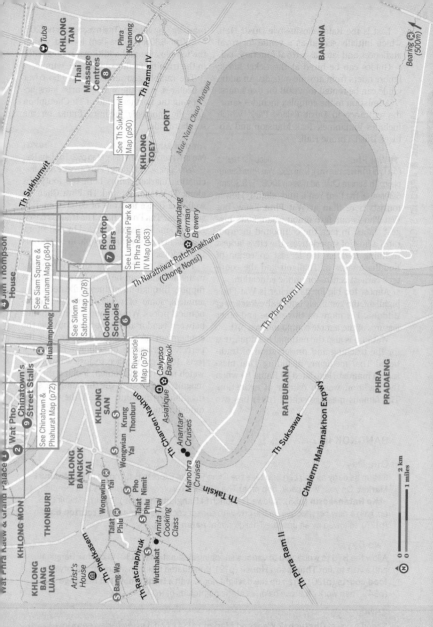

skyscraper lights
atop one of the city's
rooftop bars (p125)

8 Being blissfully
pounded into
submission at one of
Bangkok's terrific-
value **Thai massage
centres** (p94)

9 Eating yourself
into a stupor at
**Chinatown's street
stalls** (p117)

10 Getting out of
Bangkok and visiting
the nearby canalside
town of **Amphawa**
(p148)

Last is the Ratanakosin-style Dusit Hall, which initially served as a venue for royal audiences and later as a royal funerary hall.

Guides can be hired at the ticket kiosk; ignore offers from anyone outside. An audio guide can be rented for 200B for two hours.

Admission to the complex includes same-day entrance to Dusit Palace Park, which includes Vimanmek Teak Mansion and Abhisek Dusit Throne Hall.

★ Wat Pho   BUDDHIST TEMPLE
(วัดโพธิ์ (วัดพระเชตุพน); Map p62; Wat Phra Chetuphon; Th Sanam Chai; admission 100B; ⊙ 8.30am-6.30pm; ☒ Tha Tien) You'll find (slightly) fewer tourists here than at Wat Phra Kaew, but Wat Pho is our fave among Bangkok's biggest sights. In fact, the compound incorporates a host of superlatives: the city's largest reclining Buddha, the largest collection of Buddha images in Thailand and the country's earliest centre for public education.

Almost too big for its shelter is Wat Pho's highlight, the genuinely impressive Reclining Buddha. For more on this statue and other features of the temple compound, see p70.

Wat Pho is also the national headquarters for the teaching and preservation of traditional Thai medicine, including Thai massage, a mandate legislated by Rama III when the tradition was in danger of extinction. The famous massage school (p94) has two massage pavilions (Thai massage per hr 420B; ⊙ 8.30am-6.30pm; ☒ Tha Tien) located within the temple area and additional rooms within the training facility outside the temple.

The rambling grounds of Wat Pho cover 8 hectares, with the major tourist sites occupying the northern side of Th Chetuphon and the monastic facilities found on the southern side.

Amulet Market   MARKET
(ตลาดพระเครื่องวัดมหาธาตุ; Map p62; Th Maha Rat; ⊙ 7am-5pm; ☒ Tha Chang) This arcane and fascinating market claims both the footpaths along Th Maha Rat and Th Phra Chan, as well as a dense network of covered market stalls near Tha Phra Chan. The trade is based around small talismans prized by collectors, monks, taxi drivers and people in dangerous professions.

Potential buyers, often already sporting many amulets, can be seen bargaining and flipping through magazines dedicated to the amulets, some of which command astronomical prices. While money changes hands between vendor and customer, both use the euphemism of 'renting' to get around the perceived crassness of selling religious objects. It's a great place to just wander and watch men (rarely women) looking through magnifying glasses at the tiny amulets, seeking hidden meaning and, if they're lucky, hidden value.

BANGKOK IN...

One Day
Get up as early as you can and take the Chao Phraya Express Boat north to **Nonthaburi Market**. On your way back, hop off at Tha Chang to explore the museums and temples of **Ko Ratanakosin** (p55), followed by lunch in **Banglamphu** (p65). After freshening up, gain a new perspective on the city with sunset cocktails at one of the **rooftop bars** (p125), followed by an upscale Thai dinner at **nahm** (p116).

Two Days
Allow the BTS to whisk you to various shopping destinations (p130) in central Bangkok and a visit to **Jim Thompson House** (p79), punctuated by lunch at one of the city's **food courts** (p120). Wrap up the daylight hours with a **traditional Thai massage** (p94). Then work off those calories at the nightclubs of **RCA**.

Three Days
Spend a day at **Chatuchak Weekend Market** (p134), or if it's a weekday, enrol in a **cooking school** (p93). Now that you're accustomed to Bangkok's noise, pollution and traffic, you're ready for a street-food dinner in **Chinatown** (p117).

Four Days
At this point you may be itching to get out of the city. Convenient escapes include **Ko Kret** (p148), a car-less island north of Bangkok, or a long-tail boat ride through **Thonburi's canals** (p94).

LOCAL KNOWLEDGE

HOW TO BLEND IN WITH THE BANGKOKIANS

➡ **Eat your way through Bangkok** Thais love to eat. We eat all day – there is no such thing as mealtime. Throughout the day fill your stomach with fruit or deep-fried wonders such as quail eggs, fish balls and dim sum. If you're too scared of the skewered meats in the streets, try a mall food court. Also, don't forget to Instagram every dish.

➡ **Everyone is your family** In the old days, villagers considered each other a part of their family, a tradition that extends to the Bangkok of today. Your food vendor, your 7-Eleven clerk or your taxi driver can become your family in an instant. You don't need to know their names, simply guesstimate their age and refer to them as *pêe* (older brother/sister), *nórng* (younger brother/sister), *lung* (uncle) or *bǎh* (auntie).

➡ **Approach the BTS like a war zone** Battle your way onto the BTS (Skytrain) and push your way out as no one will move for you. Fight for your spot as no one will share the hand straps with you. And run for your life, otherwise the turnstile gates will crush you.

➡ **Relax, you're in Bangkok** Bangkok may look like a busy city, but it only appears that way. You'll find food vendors, shopkeepers, cafe waitresses and taxis drivers napping on the job (yes, even taxi drivers who are driving). Incorporate this routine into your sightseeing: find yourself a nice secluded spot at Wat Pra Kaew and pretend to be 'meditating', or book a massage at Wat Pho.

By Kitty Chirapongse

Also along this strip are handsome shop-houses overflowing with family-run herbal-medicine shops.

Museum of Siam MUSEUM
(สถาบันพิพิธภัณฑ์การเรียนรู้แห่งชาติ; Map p62; www.museumsiam.com; Th Maha Rat; admission 300B; ⊙10am-6pm Tue-Sun; ⏏Tha Tien) This fun museum employs a variety of media to explore the origins of the Thai people and their culture. Housed in a European-style 19th-century building that was once the Ministry of Commerce, the exhibits are presented in an engaging, interactive fashion not often found in Thailand. They are also refreshingly balanced and entertaining, with galleries dealing with a range of questions about the origins of the nation and its people.

Each room has an informative narrated video started by a sensory detector, keeping waiting to a minimum. An Ayuthaya-era battle game, a room full of traditional Thai toys and a street vending cart where you can be photographed pretending to whip up a pan of *pàt tai* (fried noodles) will keep kids interested for at least an hour, adults for longer. Check out the attached shop for some innovative gift ideas.

National Museum MUSEUM
(พิพิธภัณฑสถานแห่งชาติ; Map 62; 4 Th Na Phra That; admission 200B; ⊙9am-4pm Wed-Sun; ⏏Tha Chang) Often touted as Southeast Asia's big-gest museum, Thailand's National Museum is home to an impressive collection of religious sculpture, best appreciated on one of the museum's twice-weekly guided **tours** (free with museum admission; ⊙9.30am Wed & Thu).

Most of the museum's structures were built in 1782 as the palace of Rama I's (King Praphutthayotfa; r 1782–1809) viceroy, Prince Wang Na. Rama V turned it into a museum in 1874, and today the institute consists of three permanent exhibitions spread out over several buildings.

The **history wing** has made impressive bounds towards mainstream curatorial aesthetics with a succinct chronology of prehistoric, Sukhothai-, Ayuthaya- and Bangkok-era events and figures. Gems include King Ramkamhaeng's inscribed stone pillar, said to be the oldest record of Thai writing; King Taksin's throne; the Rama V section; and the screening of a movie about Rama VII, *The Magic Ring*.

The **decorative arts and ethnology exhibit** covers every possible handicraft: traditional musical instruments, ceramics, clothing and textiles, woodcarving, regalia and weaponry. The **archaeology and art history wing** has exhibits ranging from prehistoric to the Bangkok period.

In addition to the main exhibition halls, the **Buddhaisawan (Phutthaisawan) Chapel** includes some well-preserved original murals

Wat Phra Kaew & Grand Palace

EXPLORE BANGKOK'S PREMIER MONUMENTS TO RELIGION AND REGENCY

This tour can be covered in a couple of hours. The first area tourists enter is the Buddhist temple compound generally referred to as Wat Phra Kaew. A covered walkway surrounds the area, the inner walls of which are decorated with the **murals of the *Ramakian* ❶** and **❷**. Originally painted during the reign of Rama I (r 1782–1809), the murals, which depict the Hindu epic the *Ramayana*, span 178 panels that describe the struggles of Rama to rescue his kidnapped wife, Sita.

After taking in the story, pass through one of the gateways guarded by **yaksha ❸** to the inner compound. The most important structure here is the **bòht, or ordination hall ❹**, which houses the eponymous **Emerald Buddha ❺**.

Kinaree
These graceful half-swan, half-women creatures from Hindu-Buddhist mythology stand outside Prasat Phra Thep Bidon.

Borombhiman Hall

Prasat Phra Thep Bidon

Phra Si Ratana

The Murals of the *Ramakian*
These wall paintings, which begin at the eastern side of the Wat Phra Kaew, often depict scenes more reminiscent of 19th-century Thailand than of ancient India.

Hanuman
Rows of these mischievous monkey deities from Hindu mythology appear to support the lower levels of two small *chedi* near Prasat Phra Thep Bidon.

Head east to the so-called Upper Terrace, an elevated area home to the **spires of the three primary** *chedi* **6**. The middle structure, Phra Mondop, is used to house Buddhist manuscripts. This area is also home to several of Wat Phra Kaew's noteworthy mythical beings, including beckoning *kinaree* **7** and several grimacing **Hanuman** **8**.

Proceed through the western gate to the compound known as the Grand Palace. Few of the buildings here are open to the public. The most noteworthy structure is **Chakri Mahaprasat** **9**. Built in 1882, the exterior of the hall is a unique blend of western and traditional Thai architecture.

The Three Spires
The elaborate seven-tiered roof of Phra Mondop, the Khmer-style peak of the Prasat Phra Thep Bidon, and the gilded Phra Si Ratana *chedi* are the tallest structures in the compound.

Emerald Buddha
Despite the name, this diminutive statue (it's only 66cm tall) is actually carved from nephrite, a type of jade.

Amarindra Hall

The Death of Thotsakan
The panels progress clockwise, culminating at the western edge of the compound with the death of Thotsakan, Sita's kidnapper, and his elaborate funeral procession.

Chakri Mahaprasat
This structure is sometimes referred to as *fa·ràng sài chá·dah* (Westerner in a Thai crown) because each wing is topped by a *mon·dòp*: a spire representing a Thai adaptation of a Hindu shrine.

Dusit Hall

Yaksha
Each entrance to the Wat Phra Kaew compound is watched over by a pair of vigilant and enormous *yaksha*, ogres or giants from Hindu mythology.

Bòht (Ordination Hall)
This structure is an early example of the Ratanakosin school of architecture, which combines traditional stylistic holdovers from Ayuthaya along with more modern touches from China and the West.

Ko Ratanakosin, Banglamphu & Thonburi

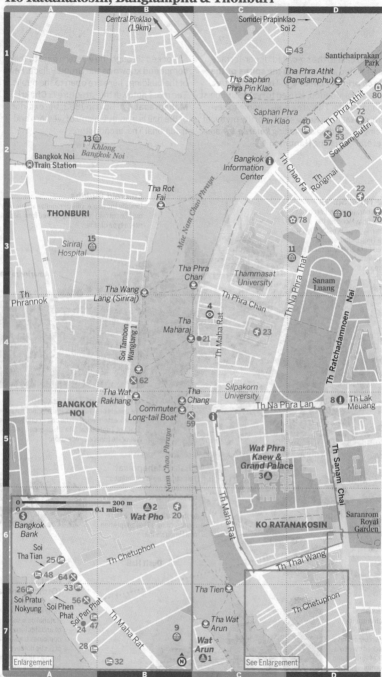

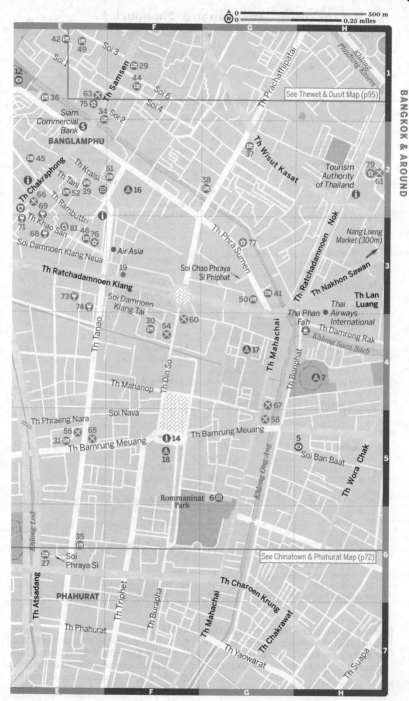

Ko Ratanakosin, Banglamphu & Thonburi

and one of the country's most revered Buddha images, Phra Phut Sihing. Legend says that the image came from Sri Lanka, but art historians attribute it to 13th-century Sukhothai.

Lak Meuang
MONUMENT

(ศาลหลักเมือง; Map p62; cnr Th Sanam Chai & Th Lak Meuang; ◎ 6.30am-6.30pm; 🛥 Tha Chang) **FREE**
Serving as the spiritual keystone of Bangkok, Lak Meuang is a phallus-shaped wooden pillar erected by Rama I during the found-

ing of the new capital city in 1782. Part of an animistic tradition, the pillar embodies the city's guardian spirit (Phra Sayam Thewathirat) and also lends a practical purpose as a marker of the town's crossroads and measuring point for distances between towns.

If you're lucky, a *lá·kon gâa bon* (commissioned dance) may be in progress. Brilliantly costumed dancers measure out subtle movements as gratitude to the guardian spirit for granting a worshipper's wish.

National Gallery
ART GALLERY
(พิพิธภัณฑ์สถานแห่งชาติหอศิลป์ (หอศิลป์เจ้าฟ้า); Map p62; ngbangkok.wordpress.com; 4 Th Chao Fa; admission 200B; ☺9am-4pm Wed-Sun; ⚑Tha Phra Athit (Banglamphu)) Housed in a building that was the Royal Mint during the reign of Rama V, the National Gallery's permanent exhibition is admittedly a rather dusty and dated affair. Secular art is a relatively new concept in Thailand and most of the country's best examples of fine art reside in the temples for which they were created – much as historic Western art is often found in European cathedrals. As such, most of the permanent collection here documents Thailand's homage to modern styles.

More interesting are the rotating exhibits held in the spacious rear galleries; take a look at the posters out front to see what's on.

◉ Banglamphu บางลำพู

Adjacent to Ko Ratanakosin, Banglamphu suffers from an extreme case of bipolar disorder, encompassing both the most characteristically old-school-Bangkok part of town as well as Th Khao San, a brash, neon-lit decompression zone for international backpackers. Depending on which one you fancy, it's not difficult to escape the other – another of Banglamphu's charms. The bulk of Bangkok's classic buildings are found in this area, as well as lots of authentic Bangkok-style cuisine and culture.

Although admittedly less grand than those of its neighbour, Banglamphu's sights are a worthwhile window into the Bangkok of yesteryear – a city that's quickly disappearing.

Golden Mount
BUDDHIST TEMPLE
(ภูเขาทอง; Map p62; off Th Boriphat; admission to summit of Golden Mount 10B; ☺7.30am-5.30pm; ⚑Tha Phan Fah) Even if you're wát-ed out, you should take a brisk walk to the Golden Mount. Serpentine steps wind through an artificial hill shaded by gnarled trees, some

of which are signed in English, and past graves and pictures of wealthy benefactors. At the peak, you'll find a breezy 360-degree view of Bangkok's most photogenic side.

This artificial hill was created when a large stupa, under construction by Rama III (King Phranangklao; r 1824–51), collapsed because the soft soil beneath would not support it. The resulting mud-and-brick hill was left to sprout weeds until Rama IV (King Mongkut; r 1851–68) built a small stupa on its crest. Rama V later added to the structure and housed a Buddha relic from India (given to him by the British government) in the stupa. The concrete walls were added during WWII to prevent the hill from eroding.

Every year in November there is a big festival on the grounds of Wat Saket, which includes a candlelit procession up the Golden Mount.

Wat Suthat
BUDDHIST TEMPLE
(วัดสุทัศน์; Map p62; Th Bamrung Meuang; admission 20B; ☺8.30am-8.30pm; ⚑klorn boat to Tha Phan Fah) Begun by Rama I and completed in later reigns, Wat Suthat boasts an immense *wí·hǎhn* (sanctuary) with gilded bronze

> ### ⓘ DRESS FOR THE OCCASION
>
> Many of Bangkok's biggest tourist attractions are sacred places, and visitors should dress and behave appropriately. In particular at Wat Phra Kaew & Grand Palace and in Dusit Park, you won't be allowed to enter unless you're well covered. Shorts, sleeveless shirts or spaghetti-strap tops, short skirts, capri pants – basically anything that reveals more than your arms (certainly don't show your shoulders), knees and head – are not allowed. This applies to men and women. Violators can expect to be shown into a dressing room and loaned a sarong before being allowed to go in.
>
> For walking in the courtyard areas you are supposed to wear shoes with closed heels and toes, although these rules aren't as zealously enforced. Regardless, footwear should always be removed before entering any main *bòht* (chapel) or *wí·hǎhn* (sanctuary). When sitting in front of a Buddha image, tuck your feet behind you to avoid the highly offensive pose of pointing your feet towards a revered figure.

ℹ️ TRANSPORT TIPS

Despite the abundance of attractions, Ko Ratanakosin and Banglamphu are still isolated from the more modern forms of public transport. The Chao Phraya Express Boat is probably the most efficient way of reaching the area, and the *klorng* (canal; also spelt *khlong*) taxi along Khlong Saen Saeb to eastern Banglamphu is another convenient option if you're coming from the Siam Sq or Sukhumvit areas. The closest BTS station is Ratchathewi.

Buddha images (including Phra Si Sakayamuni, one of the largest surviving Sukhothai bronzes) and incredibly expansive *jataka* (stories of the Buddha's previous lives) murals, making it one of Bangkok's more impressive Buddhist temples.

The *wát* also holds the rank of Rachavoramahavihan, the highest royal-temple grade; the ashes of Rama VIII (King Ananda Mahidol; r 1935–46), the current king's deceased older brother, are contained in the base of the main Buddha image in the *wí·hǎhn*.

Ban Baat   NEIGHBOURHOOD

(บ้านบาตร, Monk's Bowl Village; Map p62; Soi Ban Baat; ⏰8am-5pm; 🚤klorng boat to Tha Phan Fah) **FREE** This is the only surviving village established by Rama I to make the *bàht* (rounded bowls) that the monks carry to receive food alms from faithful Buddhists every morning. Today the average monk relies on a bowl mass-produced in China, but the traditional technique survives in Ban Baat thanks to patronage by tourists.

About half a dozen families still hammer the bowls together from eight separate pieces of steel representing, they say, the eight spokes of the Wheel of Dharma (which symbolise Buddhism's Eightfold Path). The joints are fused in a wood fire with bits of copper, and the bowl is polished and coated with several layers of black lacquer. A typical output is one bowl per day. If you purchase a bowl, the craftsperson will show you the equipment and process used.

Wat Ratchanatdaram   BUDDHIST TEMPLE

(วัดราชนัดดาราม; Map p62; Th Mahachai; ⏰8am-5pm; 🚤klorng boat to Tha Phan Fah) **FREE** Wat Ratchanatdaram dates from the mid-19th century and in addition to Loha Prasat, the

metallic, castlelike monastery, is home to a well-known market selling Buddhist *prá pim* (magical charm amulets) in all sizes, shapes and styles.

Sao Ching-Cha   MONUMENT

(เสาชิงช้า, Giant Swing; Map p62; Th Bamrung Meuang; ⏰24hr; 🚤klorng boat to Tha Phan Fah) **FREE** This spindly red arch formerly hosted a Brahman festival in honour of Shiva, in which participants would swing in ever-higher arcs in an effort to reach a bag of gold suspended from a 15m bamboo pole. Many died trying and the ritual was discontinued during the reign of Rama VII (King Prajadhipok; r 1925–35).

In 2007 the decaying swing was ceremoniously replaced with the current model, made from six specially chosen teak logs from Phrae Province in northern Thailand.

Phra Sumen Fort &

Santichaiprakan Park   NOTABLE BUILDING, PARK

(ป้อมพระสุเมรุ, สวนสันติชัยปราการ; Map p62; Th Phra Athit; ⏰5am-10pm; 🚤Tha Phra Athit) **FREE** Beside Mae Nam Chao Phraya in Banglamphu stands one of Bangkok's original 18th-century forts. Built in 1783 to defend against potential naval invasions and named for the mythical Phra Sumen (Mt Meru) of Hindu-Buddhist cosmology, the octagonal brick-and-stucco bunker was one of 14 city watchtowers that punctuated the old city wall alongside Khlong Rop Krung (now Khlong Banglamphu but still called Khlong Rop Krung on most signs). Apart from Mahakan Fort, this is the only one still standing.

Alongside the fort and fronting the river is the small, grassy Santichaiprakan Park with an open-air pavilion, river views, cool breezes and a bohemian mix of alternative young Thais and fisherman-pants-wearing, fire-stick-twirling backpackers. It's an interesting place to sit, people-watch and see what are said to be the last two *lam·poo* trees in Banglamphu.

Wat Bowonniwet   BUDDHIST TEMPLE

(วัดบวรนิเวศวิหาร; Map p62; www.watbowon. org; Th Phra Sumen; ⏰8.30am-5pm; 🚤Tha Phra Athit) **FREE** Founded in 1826, Wat Bowonniwet (Wat Bowon) is the national headquarters for the Thammayut monastic sect, a reformed version of Thai Buddhism. Rama IV, who set out to be a scholar, not a king, founded the Thammayuts and began the royal tradition of ordination at this temple. In fact, Mongkut was the abbot of Wat Bowon for several years. Rama IX (King Bhumibol Adulyadej; r 1946–present) and Crown Prince Vajiralongkorn, as well as several other males in the royal family, have been ordained as monks here.

The murals in the panels of the *bòht* of this temple are noteworthy, and include Thai depictions of Western life (possibly copied from magazine illustrations) during the early 19th century.

THANON KHAO SAN

Th Khao San, better known as Khao San Rd, is genuinely unlike anywhere else on earth. It's an international clearing house of people either entering the liberated state of travelling in Southeast Asia or returning to the coddling bonds of first-world life, all coming together in a neon-lit melting pot in Banglamphu. Its uniqueness is probably best illustrated by a question: apart from airports, where else could you share space with the citizens of dozens of countries at the same time, people ranging from first-time backpackers scoffing banana pancakes to 75-year-old grandparents ordering G&Ts, and everyone in between, including hippies, trendies, squares, style queens, package tourists, global nomads, people on a week's holiday and those taking a gap year, of every colour and creed looking at you looking at them looking at everyone else?

Th Khao San (pronounced *cow-sarn*), meaning 'uncooked rice', is perhaps the most high-profile bastard child of the age of independent travel. Of course, it hasn't always been this way. For its first two centuries or so it was just another unremarkable road in old Bangkok. The first guesthouses appeared in 1982, and as more backpackers arrived through the '80s the old wooden homes were converted one by one into low-rent dosshouses. By the time Alex Garland's novel *The Beach* was published in 1997, with its opening scenes set in the seedier side of Khao San, staying here had become a rite of passage for backpackers coming to Southeast Asia.

The publicity from Garland's book and the movie that followed pushed Khao San into the mainstream, romanticising the seedy, and stereotyping the backpackers it attracted as unwashed and counterculturalist. It also brought the long-simmering debate about the relative merits of Th Khao San to the top of backpacker conversations across the region. Was it cool to stay on KSR? Was it uncool? Was this 'real travel' or just an international 'anywhere' surviving on the few baht Western backpackers spent before they headed home to start their high-earning careers? Was it really Thailand at all?

Perhaps one of Garland's characters summed it up most memorably when he said: 'You know, Richard, one of these days I'm going to find one of those Lonely Planet writers and I'm going to ask him, what's so fucking lonely about the Khao San Road?'

Today more than ever the answer would have to be: not that much. With the help of all that publicity, Khao San continued to evolve, with bedbug-infested guesthouses replaced by boutique hotels, and downmarket TV bars showing pirated movies transformed into hip design bars peopled by flashpackers in designer threads. Th Khao San even briefly hosted an Apple store. But the most interesting change has been in the way Thais see Khao San.

Once written off as home to cheap, dirty *fa-ràng kêe nók* (stingy foreigners), the Banglamphu of today is arguably one of the city's edgiest districts. Attracted in part by the long-derided independent traveller and their modern ideas, the city's own counterculture kids have moved in and brought with them a tasty selection of small bars, organic cafes and shops. Indeed, Bangkok's indie crowd has proved to be the Thai spice this melting pot always lacked.

Not that Khao San has moved completely away from its backpacker roots. The strip still anticipates every traveller need: meals to soothe homesickness, cafes and bars for swapping travel tales about getting to the Cambodian border, tailors, travel agents, teeth whitening, secondhand books, hair braiding and, of course, the perennial Akha women trying to harass everyone they see into buying wooden frogs. No, it's not very lonely at all....

By Andrew Burke

◎ Thonburi ธนบุรี

Directly across the river from Banglamphu is Thonburi, which served a brief tenure as the Thai capital after the fall of Ayuthaya. Today the area along both sides of the river is easily accessed from Bangkok's cross-river ferries, and there are museums and temples in Thonburi that are historical complements to those in Ko Ratanakosin.

It's calm enough on the right bank of the Mae Nam Chao Phraya to seem like another province. The attractions here are relatively few, but *fàng ton* (the colloquial name for the district) is a great area for aimless wandering among leafy streets.

★ Wat Arun   BUDDHIST TEMPLE

(วัดอรุณฯ; Map p62; www.watarun.net; off Th Arun Amarin; admission 50B; ⊗ 8am-6pm; 🚢 cross-river ferry from Tha Tien) Striking Wat Arun commands a martial pose as the third point in the holy trinity (along with Wat Phra Kaew and Wat Pho) of Bangkok's early history. After the fall of Ayuthaya, King Taksin ceremoniously clinched control here on the site of a local shrine (formerly known as Wat Jaeng) and established a royal palace and a temple to house the Emerald Buddha. The temple was renamed after the Indian god of dawn (Aruna) and in honour of the literal and symbolic founding of a new Ayuthaya.

It wasn't until the capital and the Emerald Buddha were moved to Bangkok that Wat Arun received its most prominent characteristic: the 82m-high *prang* (Khmer-style tower). The tower's construction was started during the first half of the 19th century by Rama II (King Phraphutthaloetla Naphalai; r 1809–24) and was later completed by Rama III. Not apparent from a distance are the ornate floral mosaics made from broken, multihued Chinese porcelain, a common temple ornamentation in the early

Ratanakosin period, when Chinese ships calling at the port of Bangkok discarded tonnes of old porcelain as ballast. At press time, it had been announced that the *prang* would be closed for as long as three years due to renovation. Visitors can enter the compound, but cannot, as in previous years, climb the tower.

Also worth an inspection is the interior of the *bòht*. The main Buddha image is said to have been designed by Rama II himself. The murals date from the reign of Rama V; particularly impressive is one that depicts Prince Siddhartha encountering examples of birth, old age, sickness and death outside his palace walls, an experience that led him to abandon the worldly life. The ashes of Rama II are interred in the base of the presiding Buddha image.

Cross-river ferries from Tha Tien run over to Wat Arun every few minutes from 6am to 8pm (3B).

Royal Barges National Museum   MUSEUM

(พิพิธภัณฑสถานแห่งชาติ เรือพระราชพิธี (เรือ พระที่นั่ง); Map p62; Khlong Bangkok Noi or 80/1 Th Arun Amarin; admission 100B, camera/video 100/200B; ⊗ 9am-5pm; 🚢 Tha Saphan Phra Pin Klao) The royal barges are slender, fantastically ornamented vessels used in ceremonial processions along the river. The tradition dates back to the Ayuthaya era, when most travel (for commoners and royalty) was by boat. Today the royal barge procession is an infrequent occurrence, most recently performed in 2012 in honour of the king's 85th birthday. When not in use, the barges are on display at this Thonburi museum.

Suphannahong, the king's personal barge, is the most important of the boats. Made from a single piece of timber, it's the largest dugout in the world. The name means 'Golden Swan', and a huge swan head has been carved into the bow. Lesser barges feature bows that are carved into other Hindu-Buddhist mythological shapes such as *naga* (mythical sea serpent) and *garuda* (Vishnu's bird mount). Historic photos help envision the grand processions in which the largest of the barges would require a rowing crew of 50 men, plus seven umbrella bearers, two helmsmen and two navigators, as well as a flagman, rhythm-keeper and chanter.

The most convenient way to get to the museum is by taking a motorcycle taxi (ask the driver to go to *reu·a prá têe nâng*) from Tha Saphan Phra Pin Klao. The museum is

---

ℹ️ SNAPPING WAT ARUN

Sublime sunset views of Wat Arun can be caught from across the river at the riverfront warehouses and docks off Th Maha Rat, although some enterprising locals have taken to charging a 20B 'fee'. Another great – and free, with the purchase of a drink, that is – viewpoint is from Amorosa (p125), the rooftop bar at Arun Residence.

also an optional stop on long-tail boat trips through Thonburi's canals.

Artist's House ART GALLERY

(บ้านศิลปิน; www.klongbangluang.com; Khlong Bang Luang; ⏰10am-6pm) **FREE** Sort of a gallery, kind of a coffee shop, more a cultural centre... It's hard to pin down this old wooden house at the edge of Khlong Bang Luang. Food is available on weekends as well a free traditional Thai puppet show scheduled for 2pm, but the best excuse to come is simply to soak up the old-world Thai vibe.

Artist's House is most easily accessible via Soi 3, Th Charansanitwong; cross the canal at the bridge by the 7-Eleven, turn left and it's about 100m down.

⊙ Chinatown & Phahurat เยาวราช/ พาหุรัด

Bangkok's Chinatown (called Yaowarat after its main thoroughfare, Th Yaowarat) is the urban explorer's equivalent of the Amazon Basin. The highlights here aren't necessarily tidy temples or museums, but rather a complicated web of tiny alleyways, crowded markets and delicious street stalls. Unlike other Chinatowns around the world, Bangkok's is defiantly ungentrified, and getting lost in it is probably the best thing that you could do.

The neighbourhood dates back to 1782 when Bangkok's Chinese population, many of whom were labourers hired to build the new capital, were moved here from today's Ko Ratanakosin area by the royal rulers. Relatively little has changed since then, and you can still catch conversations in various Chinese dialects, buy Chinese herbal cures, and taste Chinese dishes not available elsewhere in Thailand.

Getting in and out of Chinatown is hindered by horrendous traffic. The river ferry stop at Tha Ratchawong was previously the easiest way to reach the district; however, the advent of the MRT has put the area a brief walk from Hualamphong Train Station.

At the western edge of Chinatown is a small but thriving Indian district, generally called Phahurat. It's a seemingly endless bazaar uniting flamboyant Bollywood fabric, photogenic vendors selling *paan* (betel nut for chewing), several shops stocked with delicious northern Indian-style sweets and dozens of Indian-owned stores selling all kinds of fabric and clothes.

BANGKOK & AROUND SIGHTS

THE CHINESE INFLUENCE

In many ways Bangkok is as much a Chinese city as it is Thai. The presence of the Chinese in Bangkok dates back to before the founding of the city, when Thonburi Si Mahasamut was little more than a Chinese trading outpost on Mae Nam Chao Phraya. In the 1780s, during the construction of the new capital under Rama I, Hokkien, Teochiew and Hakka Chinese were hired as coolies and labourers. After the job was done, the Chinese were relocated to the districts of Yaowarat and Sampeng, today known as Bangkok's Chinatown.

During the reign of King Rama I, many Chinese began to move up in status and wealth. They controlled many of Bangkok's shops and businesses, and because of increased trading ties with China, were responsible for an immense expansion in Thailand's market economy. Visiting Europeans during the 1820s were astonished by the number of Chinese trading ships in the Chao Phraya River, and some assumed that the Chinese formed the majority of Bangkok's population.

The new-found wealth of certain Chinese trading families created one of Thailand's first elite classes that was not directly related to royalty. Known as *jôw sŏo·a*, these 'merchant lords' eventually obtained additional status by accepting official posts and royal titles, as well as offering their daughters to the royal family. Today it is thought that more than half of the people in Bangkok can claim some Chinese ancestry.

During the reign of Rama III, the Thai capital began to absorb many elements of Chinese food, design, fashion and literature. The growing ubiquity of Chinese culture, coupled with the tendency of the Chinese men to marry Thai women and assimilate into Thai culture, meant that by the beginning of the 20th century there was relatively little that distinguished many Chinese from their Siamese counterparts.

Wat Pho

A WALK THROUGH THE BIG BUDDHAS OF WAT PHO

The logical starting place is the main *wí•hǎhn* (sanctuary), home to Wat Pho's centrepiece, the immense **Reclining Buddha ❶**. Apart from its huge size, note the **mother-of-pearl inlays ❷** on the soles of the statue's feet. The interior walls of the *wí•hǎhn* are covered with murals depicting previous lives of the

Buddha, and along the south side of the structure are 108 bronze monk bowls; for 20B you can buy 108 coins, each of which is dropped in a bowl for good luck.

Exit the *wí•hǎhn* and head east via the two **stone giants ❸** who guard the gateway to the rest of the compound. Directly south of these are the four towering **royal chedi ❹**.

Continue east, passing through two consecutive **galleries of Buddha**

Phra Ubosot
Built during the reign of Rama I, the imposing *bòht* (ordination hall) as it stands today is the result of renovations dating back to the reign of Rama III (r 1824–51).

Southern
Wí•hǎhn

Buddha Galleries
The two series of covered hallways that surround the Phra Ubosot feature no fewer than 394 gilded Buddha images, many of which display classic Ayuthaya or Sukhothai features.

Eastern
Wí•hǎhn

Massage Pavilions
If you're hot and footsore, the two air-conditioned massage pavilions are a welcome way to cool down while experiencing high-quality and relatively inexpensive Thai massage.

Phra Buddha Deva Patimakorn
On an impressive three-tiered pedestal that also holds the ashes of Rama I is this Ayuthaya-era Buddha statue originally brought to the temple by the monarch.

Northern
Wí•hǎhn

Western *Wí•hǎhn*

statues **5** linking four *wí•hǎhn*, two of which contain notable Sukhothai-era Buddha statues; these comprise the exterior of **Phra Ubosot** **6**, the immense ordination hall that is Wat Pho's second-most noteworthy structure. The base of the building is surrounded by bas-relief inscriptions, and inside is the notable Buddha statue, **Phra Buddha Deva Patimakorn** **7**.

Wat Pho is often referred to as Thailand's first university, a tradition that continues today in an associated traditional Thai medicine school and, at the compound's eastern extent, two **massage pavilions** **8**.

Interspersed throughout the eastern half of the compound are several additional minor *chedi* and rock gardens.

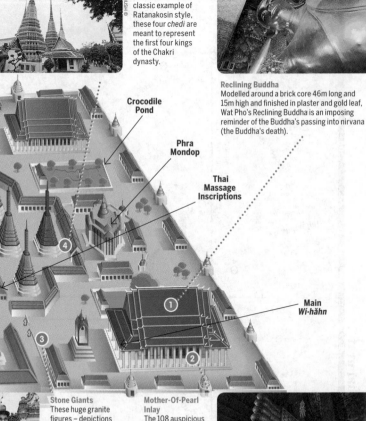

Royal Chedi
Decorated in coloured tiles in a classic example of Ratanakosin style, these four *chedi* are meant to represent the first four kings of the Chakri dynasty.

AUSTIN BUSH ©

Reclining Buddha
Modelled around a brick core 46m long and 15m high and finished in plaster and gold leaf, Wat Pho's Reclining Buddha is an imposing reminder of the Buddha's passing into nirvana (the Buddha's death).

AUSTIN BUSH ©

Crocodile Pond

Phra Mondop

Thai Massage Inscriptions

Main *Wí•hǎhn*

Stone Giants
These huge granite figures – depictions range from Chinese opera characters to Marco Polo – originally arrived in Thailand in the 19th century as ballast aboard Chinese junks.

AUSTIN BUSH ©

Mother-Of-Pearl Inlay
The 108 auspicious *lák•sà•nà*, physical characteristics of the Buddha, are depicted on the soles of the feet of the Reclining Buddha.

AUSTIN BUSH ©

Chinatown & Phahurat

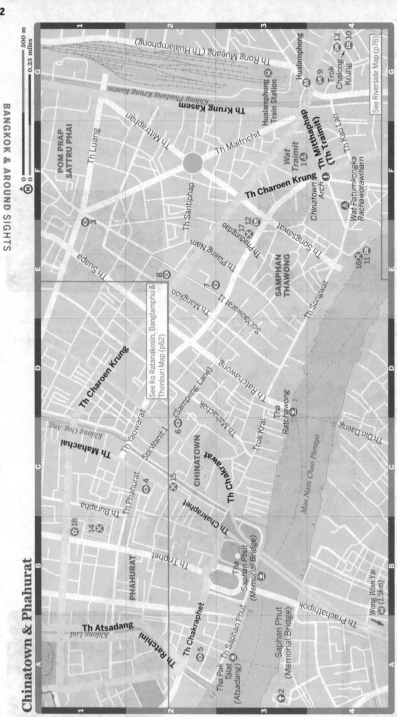

0 500 m
0 0.25 miles

★ **Wat Traimit** BUDDHIST TEMPLE

(วัด ไตรมิตร, Temple of the Golden Buddha; Map p72; Th Mitthaphap (Th Traimit); admission 40B; ⊘ 8am-5pm; ☷ Tha Ratchawong, Ⓜ Hua Lamphong exit 1) The attraction at Wat Traimit is undoubtedly the impressive 3m-tall, 5.5-tonne, solid-gold Buddha image, which gleams like, well, gold. Sculpted in the graceful Sukhothai style, the image was 'discovered' some 40 years ago beneath a stucco or plaster exterior when it fell from a crane while being moved to a new building within the temple compound. It has been theorised that the covering was added to protect it from marauding hordes, either during the late Sukhothai period or later in the Ayuthaya period when the city was under siege by the Burmese. The temple itself is said to date from the early 13th century.

Donations and a constant flow of tourists have proved profitable, and the statue is now housed in a new four-storey marble structure. The 2nd floor of the building is home to the **Phra Buddha Maha Suwanna Patimakorn Exhibition** (Map p72; admission 100B; ⊘ 8am-5pm Tue-Sun), which has exhibits on how the statue was made, discovered and came to arrive at its current home, while the 3rd floor houses the **Yaowarat Chinatown Heritage Center** (Map p72; admission 100B; ⊘ 8am-5pm Tue-Sun), a small but engaging museum with multimedia exhibits on the history of Bangkok's Chinatown and its residents.

Talat Mai MARKET

(ตลาดใหม่; Map p72; Soi 6 (Trok Itsaranuphap), Th Yaowarat; ⊘ 6am-6pm; ☷ Tha Ratchawong, Ⓜ Hua Lamphong exit 1 & taxi) With nearly two centuries of history under its belt, 'New Market' is no longer an entirely accurate name for this strip of commerce. Essentially it's a narrow covered alleyway between tall buildings, but even if you're not interested in food the hectic atmosphere and exotic sights and smells culminate in something of a surreal sensory experience.

While much of the market centres on Chinese cooking ingredients, the section north of Th Charoen Krung (equivalent to Soi 21, Th Charoen Krung) is known for selling incense, paper effigies and ceremonial sweets – essential elements of a traditional Chinese funeral.

Wat Mangkon Kamalawat BUDDHIST TEMPLE

(วัดมังกรกมลาวาส; Map p72; cnr Th Charoen Krung & Th Mangkon; ⊘ 6am-6pm; ☷ Tha Ratchawong, Ⓜ Hua Lamphong exit 1 & taxi) **FREE** Clouds of incense and the sounds of chanting form

the backdrop at this Chinese-style Mahayana Buddhist temple. Dating back to 1871, it's the largest and most important religious structure in the area, and during the annual Vegetarian Festival, religious and culinary activities are particularly active here.

Flashlight Market MARKET

(ตลาดไฟฉาย; Map p72; cnr Th Phlap Phla Chai & Th Luang; ⊘ 5am Sat-5pm Sun; ☷ Tha Ratchawong, Ⓜ Hua Lamphong exit 1 & taxi) This street market extends west from the Phlap Phla Chai intersection, forging a trail of antiques, secondhand items and, well, sometimes just plain junk, along the area's footpaths. It's open 36 hours, but is at its busiest on Saturday night, when a flashlight is needed to see many of the goods for sale.

Gurdwara Siri Guru Singh Sabha SIKH TEMPLE

(พระศาสนสถานคุรุดวารา; Map p72; off Th Chakraphet; ⊘ 9am-5pm; ☷ Tha Saphan Phut (Memorial Bridge)) **FREE** Reportedly this is the second-largest Sikh temple outside India. Devoted to the worship of the *Guru*

OFF THE BEATEN TRACK

BIZARRE BANGKOK MUSEUMS

If looking at stuffed tigers and Buddha statues just isn't doing it for you, then consider a visit to one of these quirky institutions.

➡ **Songkran Niyomsane Forensic Medicine Museum & Parasite Museum** (พิพิธภัณฑ์นิติเวชศาสตร์สงกรานต์นิยมเสน; Map p62; 2nd fl, Adulyadejvikrom Bldg, Siriraj Hospital; admission 40B; ⊗9am-4pm Mon-Sat; 🚤Tha Wang Lang (Siriraj)) This gory institution contains the various appendages and remnants of famous murders, including the bloodied T-shirt from a victim who was stabbed to death with a dildo. If you're still with us at this point, you'll probably also enjoy the adjacent **Parasite Museum**. The easiest way to reach the museum is by taking the river-crossing ferry to Tha Wang Lang (on the Thonburi side) from Tha Chang. At the exit of the pier, turn right to enter Siriraj Hospital, and follow the green signs.

➡ **Ancient City** (เมืองโบราณ, Muang Boran; www.ancientcity.com; 296/1 Th Sukhumvit, Samut Prakan; adult/child 500/250B; ⊗8am-5pm) Claiming to be the largest open-air museum in the world, the site covers more than 80 hectares of peaceful countryside littered with 109 scaled-down facsimiles of many of the kingdom's most famous monuments. It's an excellent place to explore by bicycle (per day 50B), as it is usually quiet and never crowded. Ancient City lies outside Samut Prakan, which is accessible via air-conditioned bus 511 from Bearing BTS station at the east end of Th Sukhumvit. Upon reaching the bus terminal at Pak Nam, board minibus 36, which passes the entrance to Ancient City.

➡ **Bangkokian Museum** (พิพิธภัณฑ์บางกอก; Map p76; 273 Soi 43 (Soi Saphan Yao), Th Charoen Krung; admission free; ⊗10am-4pm Wed-Sun; 🚤Tha Si Phraya) Consisting of three wooden houses, this family-run museum is a window into Bangkok life during the 1950s and 1960s. Particularly interesting is the traditional Thai kitchen.

➡ **Corrections Museum** (พิพิธภัณฑ์ราชทัณฑ์; Map p62; 436 Th Mahachai; admission free; ⊗9am-4pm Mon-Fri; 🚌508, klorng taxi to Tha Phan Fah) Learn about the painful world of Thai-style punishment at what's left of this former jail. Life-sized models re-enact a variety of horrendous executions and punishments, encouraging most visitors to remain law-abiding citizens for the remainder of their visit.

Granth Sahib, the 16th-century Sikh holy book, which is itself considered to be a 'living' guru and the last of the religion's 10 great teachers. Visitors are welcome, but you must remove their shoes.

Church of Santa Cruz　　　　CHURCH
(โบสถ์ซางตาครูส; Map p72; Soi Kuti Jiin; ⊗7am-noon Sat & Sun; 🚤river-crossing ferry from Tha Pak Talat (Atsadang)) FREE Dating back to 1913, this Catholic church holds relatively little interest unless you visit on a Sunday. But the surrounding neighbourhood, a former Portuguese concession dating back to the Ayuthaya period, is worth a wander for its old-school riverside atmosphere and Portuguese-inspired cakes, *kà·nŏm fa·ràng.*

◉ Riverside ข้างแม่น้ำ

Talat Noi　　　　NEIGHBOURHOOD
(ตลาดน้อย; Map p76; ⊗7am-7pm; 🚤Tha Marine Department) Bordered by the river, Th Songwat, Th Charoen Krung and Th Yotha, this ancient neighbourhood is a fascinating jumble of tiny alleys, greasy machine shops and traditional architecture. Located opposite the River View Guest House, **San Jao Sien Khong** (ศาลเจ้าเซียนโค้ง; Map p76; admission free; ⊗6am-6pm) is one of the city's oldest Chinese shrines and is also one of the most atmospheric areas to be during the annual Vegetarian Festival.

◉ Silom & Sathon สีลม/สาธร

The business district of Th Silom has only a handful of tourist attractions scattered among the corporate hotels, office towers

BANGKOK FOR CHILDREN

There aren't a whole lot of attractions in Bangkok meant directly to appeal to the little ones, but there's no lack of locals willing to provide attention. The website www.bangkok.com/kids has an excellent spread of things to do for kids, and www.bambiweb.org is a useful resource for parents of young children in Bangkok.

If visiting with young kids, keep in mind that car seats are almost nonexistent, and even if you bring your own, most taxis have no seatbelt in the back. For moving by foot, slings are often more useful than prams as Bangkok's sidewalks are famously uneven.

Kid-Friendly Museums

Although not specifically child-targeted, the Museum of Siam (p59) has lots of interactive exhibits that will appeal to children.

Outside of town, Ancient City (p74) recreates Thailand's most famous monuments. They're linked by bicycle paths and were practically built for being climbed on.

Parks & Amusement Parks

Lumphini Park (p78) is a trusty ally in the cool hours of the morning and evening for kite-flying (during February and March) as well as for stretching the legs and lungs. Nearby, kids can view lethal snakes become reluctant altruists at the adjacent antivenin-producing Queen Saovabha Memorial Institute snake farm (p77).

Siam Park City (☑0 2919 7200; www.siamparkcity.com; 203 Th Suansiam; admission 120-900B; ☺10am-6pm; Ⓢ Mo Chit exit 1 & taxi) features more than 30 rides and a water park with the largest wave pool in the world, while **Dream World** (☑0 2577 8666; www.dreamworld.co.th/2011; 62 Moo 1, Th Rangsit-Nakornnayok, Pathum Thani; adult/child 150/120B; ☺10am-5pm Mon-Fri, to 7pm Sat & Sun; Ⓢ Mo Chit exit 1 & taxi) boasts a snow room. Both lie north of Bangkok and are accessible by taxi from Mo Chit BTS station.

Rainy-Day Fun

MBK Center (p131) and Siam Paragon (p132) both have bowling alleys to keep the older ones occupied. Siam Discovery Center has a branch of **Madame Tussaud's** (Map p84; www.madametussauds.com/Bangkok/en/; 6th fl, Siam Discovery Center; adult/child 800/600B; ☺10am-8pm; Ⓢ Siam exit 1).

Krung Sri IMAX (Map p84; ☑0 2129 4631; www.majorcineplex.com/en/cinema/paragon-cineplex/; 5th fl, Siam Paragon, 991/1 Th Phra Ram I; tickets 250-1200B; Ⓢ Siam exits 3 & 5) screens special-effects versions of Hollywood action flicks and nature features.

Bangkok's biggest indoor playground is **Fun-arium** (Map p90; ☑0 2665 6555; www.funarium.co.th; 111/1 Soi 26, Th Sukhumvit; admission 110-320B; ☺9am-7pm; Ⓢ Phrom Phong exit 1 & taxi), which has coffee and wi-fi for parents. Slightly older kids can land a plane, record an album, make sushi, or, er, perform a root canal at **KidZania** (Map p84; ☑0 2683 1888; bangkok.kidzania.com/en/; 5th fl, Siam Paragon, 991/1 Th Phra Ram I; adult/child 650/400B; ☺10am-5pm Mon-Fri, 10am-3pm & 4-9pm Sat & Sun; Ⓢ Siam exits 3 & 5), a new and impressive learn-and-play centre.

Zoos & Animals

Dusit Zoo (สวนสัตว์ดุสิต (เขาดิน); Map p95; Th Ratchawithi; adult/child 100/50B; ☺8am-6pm; Ⓢ Phaya Thai exit 3 & taxi) covers 19 hectares with caged exhibits of more than 300 mammals, 200 reptiles and 800 birds, including relatively rare indigenous species such as banteng, gaur, serow and some rhinoceros. There are shady grounds plus a lake in the centre with paddleboats for hire and a small children's playground.

A massive underwater world has been recreated at the **Siam Ocean World** (สยาม โอเชี่ยนเวิร์ล; Map p84; www.siamoceanworld.com; basement, Siam Paragon, 991/1 Th Phra Ram I; adult/child 900/700B; ☺10am-9pm; Ⓢ Siam exits 3 & 5) shopping-centre aquarium. Gaze into the glass-enclosed deep-reef zone or view the daily feeding of penguins and sharks. For a budget version, join the novice monks and other children as they sprinkle fish food (sold on the pier) into the river at Tha Thewet, transforming the muddy river into a brisk boil of flapping bodies.

Riverside

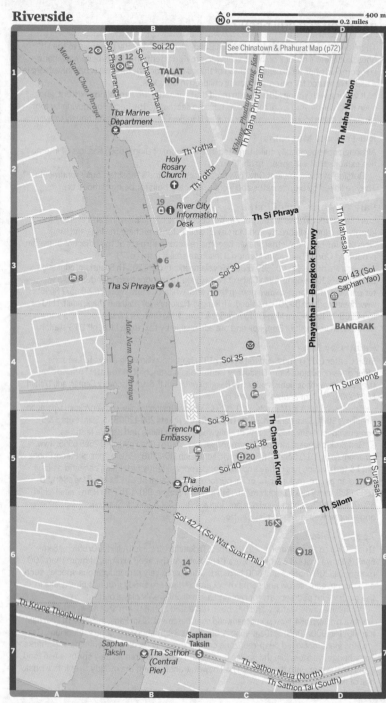

0 400 m
0 0.2 miles

See Chinatown & Phahurat Map (p72)

TALAT NOI

Tha Marine Department

Holy Rosary Church

River City Information Desk

Th Yotha

Th Si Phraya

Tha Si Phraya

Soi 30

BANGRAK

Soi 43 (Soi Saphan Yao)

Soi 35

Th Surawong

Soi 36

French Embassy

Soi 38

Th Charoen Krung

Soi 40

Tha Oriental

Th Silom

Soi 42/1 (Soi Wat Suan Phlu)

Th Krung Thonburi

Saphan Taksin

Saphan Taksin

Tha Sathon (Central Pier)

Th Sathon Neua (North)

Th Sathon Tai (South)

Mae Nam Chao Phraya

Phayathai – Bangkok Expwy

Th Maha Nakhon

Th Mahesak

Th Surasak

Soi Phanurangsi

Soi Charoen Phanit

Klong Phadung Krung Kasem

Th Maha Phrutharam

Riverside

and wining-and-dining restaurants. As you get closer to the river, the area becomes spiced with the sights and smells of its Indian and Muslim residents. Moving north along Th Charoen Krung, the area adjacent to the river was the international mercantile district during Bangkok's shipping heyday.

Traffic is notoriously sticky in this part of town, but the BTS, the MRT stops at Si Lom and Lumphini, and Chao Phraya Express Boat pier at Tha Sathon (Central Pier) provide some transport relief.

MR Kukrit Pramoj House   MUSEUM
(บ้านหม่อมราชวงศ์คึกฤทธิ์ปราโมช; Map p78; Soi 7 (Soi Phra Phinit), Th Narathiwat Ratchanakharin; adult/child 50/20B; ⊙10am-4pm; ⑤Chong Nonsi exit 2) Author and statesman Mom Ratchawong (MR, an honourary royal title) Kukrit Pramoj (1911–95) once resided in this charming complex now open to the public for tours. Surrounded by a garden famed for its Thai bonsai trees, five teak buildings introduce visitors to traditional Thai architecture, arts and to the former resident, who wrote more than 150 books (including the highly respected *Four Reigns*), served as prime minister of Thailand in 1974 and 1975, and spent 20 years decorating this house.

Queen Saovabha Memorial Institute   ZOO
(สถานเสาวภา, Snake Farm; Map p78; cnr Th Phra Ram IV & Th Henri Dunant; adult/child 200/50B; ⊙9.30am-3.30pm Mon-Fri, to 1pm Sat & Sun; Ⓜ Si Lom exit 1, ⑤Sala Daeng exit 3) Snake farms tend to gravitate towards carnivalesque rather than humanitarian, except at the Queen Saovabha Memorial Institute. Founded in 1923, the snake farm gathers antivenin from venomous snakes. This is done by milking the snakes' venom, injecting it into horses, and harvesting and purifying the antivenin they produce. The antivenins are then used to treat human victims of snake bites.

The leafy grounds are home to a few caged snakes (and a constant soundtrack of Western rock music), but the bulk of the attractions are found in the Simaseng Building, at the rear of the compound. The ground floor houses several varieties of snakes in glass cages. Regular milkings (⊙11am Mon-Fri) and snake-handling performances (⊙2.30pm Mon-Fri, 11am & 2.30pm Sat & Sun) are held at the outdoor amphitheatre.

Sri Mariamman Temple   HINDU TEMPLE
(วัดพระศรีมหาอุมาเทวี (วัดแขก), Wat Phra Si Maha Umathewi; Map p78; cnr Th Silom & Th Pan; ⊙6am-8pm; ⑤Surasak exit 3) FREE Standing out, even among Bangkok's golden wát, this Hindu temple virtually leaps off the block. Built in the 1860s by Tamil immigrants in the centre of a still thriving ethnic enclave, the structure is a stacked facade of intertwined, full-colour Hindu deities.

In the centre of the main shrine is Jao Mae Maha Umathewi (Uma Devi, also known as Shakti, Shiva's consort), and along the left interior wall sit rows of Shiva, Vishnu and other Hindu deities, as well as

Silom & Sathon

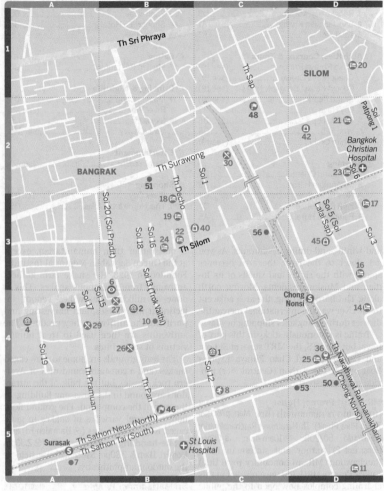

a few Buddhas, so that just about any non-Muslim, non-Judaeo-Christian Asian can worship here.

Thais call this temple Wat Khaek – *kàak* is a colloquial expression for people of South Asian descent. The literal translation is 'guest', a euphemism for a group of people that locals don't particularly want as permanent residents; hence most Indians living permanently in Thailand don't appreciate the term.

◉ Lumphini Park & Th Phra Ram IV สวนลุมพินี/ถนนพระราม ๔

The main attraction in this hyper-urban part of town is, rather paradoxically, the city's single largest green zone.

The MRT, with stops at Lumphini and Silom, is the best way to reach this area.

★**Lumphini Park**　　　　　　　PARK
(สวนลุมพินี; Map p83; bounded by Th Sarasin, Th Phra Ram IV, Th Witthayu (Wireless Rd) & Th Ratchadamri; FREE; ⊘ 4.30am-9pm; M Lumphini exit

Thai-Chinese are practising *taijiquan* (t'ai chi). The park reawakens with the evening's cooler temperatures – aerobics classes collectively sweat to a techno soundtrack. Giant monitor lizards can be seen at just about any time, and late at night the borders of the park are frequented by streetwalking prostitutes, both male and female.

◉ Siam Square & Pratunam
สยามสแควร์/ประตูน้ำ

Commerce, mainly in the form of multi-storey mega-malls, forms the main attraction in this part of town, but there are a couple of sights that don't involve credit cards. The BTS stop at Siam and *klorng* taxis provide easy access to most sights here.

★ **Jim Thompson House**   HISTORICAL BUILDING
(Map p84; www.jimthompsonhouse.com; 6 Soi Kasem San 2; adult/child 100/50B; ⊙9am-5pm, compulsory tours in English & French every 20min; ⓢklorng boat to Tha Saphan Hua Chang, ⓢNational Stadium exit 1) This jungly compound is the former home of the eponymous American silk entrepreneur and art collector. Born in Delaware in 1906, Thompson briefly served in the Office of Strategic Services (the forerunner of the CIA) in Thailand during WWII. Settling in Bangkok after the war, his neighbours' handmade silk caught his eye and piqued his business sense; he sent samples to fashion houses in Milan, London and Paris, gradually building a steady worldwide clientele.

In addition to textiles, Thompson also collected parts of various derelict Thai homes and had them reassembled in their current location in 1959. Some of the homes were brought from the old royal capital of Ayuthaya; others were pulled down and floated across the *klorng* from Baan Krua, including the first building you enter on the tour. One striking departure from tradition is the way each wall has its exterior side facing the house's interior, thus exposing the wall's bracing system. His small but splendid Asian art collection and his personal belongings are also on display in the main house.

Thompson's story doesn't end with his informal reign as Bangkok's best-adapted foreigner. While out for an afternoon walk in the Cameron Highlands of western Malaysia in 1967, Thompson mysteriously disappeared. That same year his sister was murdered in the USA, fuelling various conspiracy

3, Si Lom exit 1, ⓢ Sala Daeng exit 3, Ratchadamri exit 2) Named after the Buddha's place of birth in Nepal, Lumphini Park is the best way to escape Bangkok without leaving town. Shady paths, a large artificial lake and swept lawns temporarily blot out the roaring traffic and hulking concrete towers. There are **paddleboats** (Map p83; per 30min 40B) for lovers, a **playground** (Map p83) for the kids, and open-air concerts on Sunday afternoon.

One of the best times to visit the park is before 7am, when the air is fresh (well, relatively so for Bangkok) and legions of

Silom & Sathon

theories. Was it communist spies? Business rivals? Or a man-eating tiger? Although the mystery has never been solved, evidence revealed by American journalist Joshua Kurlantzick in his profile of Thompson, *The Ideal Man,* suggests that the vocal anti-American stance Thompson took later in his life may have made him a potential target of suppression by the CIA.

Beware well-dressed touts in soi near the Thompson house who will tell you it is closed and try to haul you off on a dodgy buying spree.

Erawan Shrine   MONUMENT
(ศาลพระพรหม; Map p84; cnr Th Ratchadamri & Th Ploenchit; ⊙6am-11pm; ⑤Chit Lom exit 8) **FREE**
The Erawan Shrine was originally built in

1956 as something of a last-ditch effort to end a string of misfortunes that occurred during the construction of the hotel, at that time known as the Erawan Hotel. After several incidents ranging from injured construction workers to the sinking of a ship carrying marble for the hotel, a Brahmin priest was consulted. Since the hotel was to be named after the elephant escort of Indra in Hindu mythology, the priest determined that Erawan required a passenger, and suggested it be that of Lord Brahma. A statue was built, and lo and behold, the misfortunes miraculously ended.

Lingam Shrine   MONUMENT
(ศาลเจ้าแม่ทับทิม; Map p84; Swissôtel Nai Lert Park, Th Witthayu (Wireless Rd); ⊙24hr; ☷klorng boat to

Tha Witthayu, Ⓢ Phloen Chit exit 1) FREE Clusters of carved stone and wooden phalli surround a spirit house and shrine built by millionaire businessman Nai Lert to honour Jao Mae Thap Thim, a female deity thought to reside in the old banyan tree on the site. Someone who made an offering shortly thereafter had a baby, and the shrine has received a steady stream of worshippers – mostly young women seeking fertility – ever since.

To get here if facing the entrance of the Swissôtel, follow the small concrete pathway to the right that winds down into the bowels of the building beside the car park. The shrine is at the end of the building next to the canal.

◉ Sukhumvit สุขุมวิท

The BTS is the primary public-transport option, although the MRT intersects at Sukhumvit station.

Ban Kamthieng   MUSEUM
(บ้านคำเทียง; Map p90; Siam Society, 131 Soi 21 (Asoke), Th Sukhumvit; adult/child 100B/free; ⊘9am-5pm Tue-Sat; Ⓜ Sukhumvit exit 1, Ⓢ Asok exit 3 or 6) Ban Kamthieng transports visitors to a northern Thai village complete with informative displays of daily rituals, folk beliefs and everyday household chores, all within the setting of a traditional wooden house. This museum is operated by and shares space with the Siam Society, publisher of the renowned *Journal of the Siam Society* and a valiant preserver of traditional Thai culture.

BANGKOK & AROUND SIGHTS

BANGKOK'S ART GALLERIES

Although its hyper-urban environment seems to cater to the inner philistine in all of us, Bangkok has a low-key but burgeoning art scene. In recent years, galleries seem to have been opening on a weekly basis, and Bangkok also acts as something of a regional art hub with works by emerging artists from places such as Myanmar and Cambodia. To find out what's happening while you're in town, pick up a free copy of the excellent **BAM!** (Bangkok Art Map; www.facebook.com/bangkokartmap).

Our picks of the city's better galleries:

➡ **Kathmandu Photo Gallery** (Map p78; www.kathmandu-bkk.com; 87 Th Pan; ⊘11am-7pm Tue-Sun; Ⓢ Surasak exit 3) FREE Bangkok's only truly dedicated photography gallery is located in a restored Sino-Portuguese shophouse. The small upstairs gallery plays host to changing exhibitions by local and international artists and photographers.

➡ **Silom Galleria** (Map p78; 919/1 Th Silom; ⊘6am-10pm; Ⓢ Surasak exit 3) Not a gallery per se, but the top floors of this abandoned-feeling mall are home to some of Bangkok's best commercial galleries: **Number 1 Gallery** (www.number1gallery.com; 4th fl, Silom Galleria, 919/1 Th Silom; ⊘10am-7pm Mon-Sat; Ⓢ Surasak exit 3) features edgy contemporary Thai art, **Tang Gallery** (5th fl, Silom Galleria, 919/1 Th Silom; ⊘11am-7pm Mon-Sat; Ⓢ Surasak exit 3) showcases the work of contemporary Chinese artists, and **Thavibu** (www.thavibu.com; 4th fl, Silom Galleria, 919/1 Th Silom; ⊘11am-7pm Tue-Sat; Ⓢ Surasak exit 3) focuses on the work of Vietnamese and Burmese artists.

➡ **Bangkok Art & Culture Centre** (BACC; Map p84; www.bacc.or.th; cnr Th Phayathai & Th Phra Ram I; ⊘10am-9pm Tue-Sat; Ⓢ National Stadium exit 3) FREE This multistorey building, located smack-dab in the centre of Bangkok, combines revolving exhibitions and art-themed commerce.

➡ **100 Tonson Gallery** (Map p84; www.100tonsongallery.com; 100 Soi Tonson; ⊘11am-7pm Thu-Sun; Ⓢ Chit Lom exit 4) FREE A private gallery showcasing the work of domestic and international emerging and high-profile painters, sculptors and conceptual artists.

➡ **H Gallery** (Map p78; www.hgallerybkk.com; 201 Soi 12, Th Sathon Neua (North); ⊘10am-6pm Wed-Sat, by appointment Tue; Ⓢ Chong Nonsi exit 1) FREE Leading commercial gallery for emerging Thai abstract painters.

➡ **Museum of Contemporary Art** (MOCA; www.mocabangkok.com; 3 Th Viphavadee Rangsit; admission 180B; ⊘10am-6pm Tue-Sun; Ⓢ Mo Chit exit 1 and taxi) A huge new complex north of town, MOCA spans five floors of pieces by the cream of the crop of Thailand's contemporary artists. It's *the* place to go to take in the spectrum of modern Thai art from breathtaking to not-so-good.

⊙ Thewet & Dusit เทเวศน์/ดุสิต

Bangkok's royal district is one of wide streets, monuments and greenery.

A brief walk from Chao Phraya Express Boat pier at Thewet, or a taxi hop from Phaya Thai BTS station will get you to the sights listed below.

Wat Benchamabophit   BUDDHIST TEMPLE

(วัดเบญจมบพิตร (วัดเบญจะฯ); Map p95; cnr Th Si Ayuthaya & Th Phra Ram V; admission 20B; ⊙ 8am-6pm; S Phaya Thai exit 3 & taxi) You might recognise this temple from the back of the 5B coin. Made of white marble imported from Italy, Wat Ben, as it's colloquially known, was built in the late 19th century under Rama V. The base of the central Buddha image, a copy of Phitsanulok's Phra Phuttha Chinnarat, contains his ashes.

The courtyard behind the *bòht* has 53 Buddha images (33 originals and 20 copies) representing every *mudra* (gesture) and style from Thai history, making this the ideal place to compare Buddhist iconography. If religious imagery isn't your thing, the temple still offers a pleasant stroll beside landscaped canals filled with blooming lotus and Chinese-style footbridges.

Dusit Palace Park   MUSEUM, HISTORICAL SITE

(วังสวนดุสิต; Map p95; bounded by Th Ratchawithi, Th U Thong Nai & Th Ratchasima; adult/child 100/20B or free with Grand Palace ticket; ⊙ 9.30am-3.15pm Tue-Sun; ☱ Tha Thewet, S Phaya Thai exit 2 & taxi) Following Rama V's first European tour in 1897, he returned home with visions of European castles swimming in his head and set about transforming these styles into a uniquely Thai expression – today's Dusit Palace Park. The royal palace, throne hall and minor palaces for extended family were all moved here from Ko Ratanakosin, and today this complex holds a house museum and other cultural collections.

Originally constructed on Ko Si Chang in 1868 and moved to the present site in 1910, **Vimanmek Teak Mansion** (Map p95; 16 Th Ratchawithi, within the Dusit Palace compound; ⊙ 9.30am-4pm, last entry 3.15pm) contains 81 rooms, halls and anterooms, and is said to be the world's largest golden-teak building, allegedly built without the use of a single nail. The mansion was the first permanent building on the Dusit Palace grounds, and served as Rama V's residence in the early 1900s. The interior of the mansion contains various personal effects of the king

and a treasure trove of early Ratanakosin art objects and antiques. Compulsory tours (in English) leave every half-hour between 9.45am and 3.15pm, and last about an hour.

The nearby **Ancient Cloth Museum** (Map p95; ☑ 0 2628 6300; Th Ratchawithi, Dusit Palace Park; ticket for all Dusit Palace Park sights 250B or free with Grand Palace ticket; ⊙ 9.30am-4pm; ☐ 510, 72, ☱ Tha Thewet) presents a beautiful collection of traditional silks and cottons that make up the royal cloth collection.

Originally built as a throne hall for Rama V in 1904, the smaller **Abhisek Dusit Throne Hall** (Map p95; ☑ 0 2628 6300; Th Ratchawithi, Dusit Palace Park; admission full 250B, or free with Wat Phra Kaew & Grand Palace ticket; ⊙ 9.30am-4pm; ☐ 510, 72, air-con 10, 16, 18, ☱ Tha Thewet) is typical of the finer architecture of the era. Victorian-influenced gingerbread architecture and Moorish porticoes blend to create a striking and distinctly Thai exterior. The structure itself is more interesting than the display of regional handiwork crafted by members of the Promotion of Supplementary Occupations & Related Techniques (Support) foundation, an organisation sponsored by Queen Sirikit.

Near the Th U Thong Nai entrance, two large stables that once housed three white elephants – animals whose auspicious albinism automatically make them crown property – are now the **Royal Thai Elephant Museum** (Map p95; ☑ 2628 6300; Th Ratchawithi, Dusit Palace Park; admission full 250B, ticket for all Dusit Palace Park sights free with Grand Palace ticket; ⊙ 9.30am-4pm; ☐ 510, 72). One of the structures contains artefacts and photos outlining the importance of elephants in Thai history and explaining their various rankings according to physical characteristics. The second stable holds a sculptural representation of a living royal white elephant. Draped in royal vestments, the statue is more or less treated as a shrine by the visiting Thai public.

Because this is royal property, visitors should wear long pants (no capri pants) or long skirts and shirts with sleeves.

Rama V Memorial   MONUMENT

(พระบรมรูปทรงม้า; Map p95; Th U Thong Nai; ⊙ 24hr; S Phaya Thai exit 3 & taxi) FREE The bronze figure on horseback is Rama V, the Thai king widely credited with steering the country into the modern age and for preserving Thailand's independence from European colonialism. He is also considered a champion of the common person for his

Lumphini Park & Th Phra Ram IV

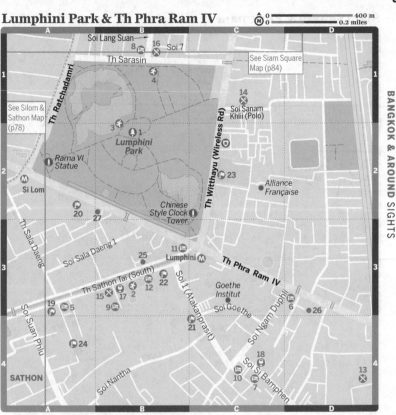

Lumphini Park & Th Phra Ram IV

Siam Square & Pratunam

PRATUNAM

PLOENCHIT

See Lumphini Park &
Th Phra Ram IV Map (p83)

Siam Square & Pratunam

abolition of slavery and corvée (the requirement that every citizen be available for state labour when called on).

Rama V's accomplishments are so revered, especially by the middle class, that his statue attracts worshippers (particularly on Tuesdays, the day of his birth), who make offerings of candles, flowers (predominantly pink roses), incense and bottles of whisky. The statue is also the site of a huge celebra-

tion on 23 October, the anniversary of the monarch's death.

The domed neoclassical building behind the statue is **Ananta Samakhom Throne Hall** (พระที่นั่งอนันตสมาคม; www.artsofthe kingdom.com; Th U Thong Nai; admission 150B; ⏰10am-6pm Tue-Sun; ⓢPhaya Thai exit 3 & taxi), originally built as a royal reception hall during the reign of Rama V, but not completed until 1915, five years after his death. Today the building houses an exhibit called Arts of the Kingdom, which, like the nearby Abhisek Dusit Throne Hall, displays the products of Queen Sirikit's Support foundation.

◉ Ratchathewi ราชเทวี

Suan Pakkad Palace Museum   MUSEUM
(วังสวนผักกาด; Map p96; Th Si Ayuthaya; admission 100B; ⊗9am-4pm; ⑤Phaya Thai exit 4) The overlooked treasure of Suan Pakkad is a collection of eight traditional wooden Thai houses that was once the residence of Princess Chumbon of Nakhon Sawan and before that a lettuce farm – hence the name. Within the stilt buildings are displays of art, antiques and furnishings, and the landscaped grounds are a peaceful oasis complete with ducks, swans and a semi-enclosed garden.

The diminutive Lacquer Pavilion, at the back of the complex, dates from the Ayuthaya period and features gold-leaf *jataka* and Ramayana murals, as well as scenes from daily Ayuthaya life. The building originally sat in a monastery compound on Mae Nam Chao Phraya, just south of Ayuthaya.

Larger residential structures at the front of the complex contain displays of Khmer-style Hindu and Buddhist art, Ban Chiang ceramics and a very interesting collection of historic Buddhas, including a beautiful late U Thong-style image.

🏃 Activities

Meditation

Although at times Bangkok may seem like the most un-Buddhist place on earth, there are several places where instruction in Theravada Buddhist meditation is done in English. Additional sources of information include **Dharma Thai** (www.dhammathai.org), which has a rundown on several prominent *wát* and meditation centres. For background information on Buddhism, see p714.

House of Dhamma   MEDITATION
(Map p112; ☑0 2512 6083; www.houseofdhamma.com; 26/9 Soi 15, Th Lat Prao; fee by donation; ⊗lessons 10am-5pm Wed-Sun; Ⓜ Phahon Yothin exit 5) Helen Jandamit has opened her suburban Bangkok home to meditation retreats and classes in *vipassana* (insight meditation). Check the website to see what workshops are on offer and be sure to reserve a spot at least 10 days in advance.

Wat Mahathat   MEDITATION
(Map p62; 3 Th Maha Rat; 🚤Tha Chang) This temple is home to two independently operating meditation centres. The **Meditation Study and Retreat Center** (Map p62; ☑0 2222 6011; Section 5, Wat Mahathat, Th Maha Rat; donations accepted; ⊗lessons 7am, 1pm & 6pm; 🚤Tha Chang) offers daily meditation classes. Taught by English-speaking Phra Suputh Chainikom (Kosalo), classes last three hours. The **International Buddhist Meditation Center** (Map p62; ☑0 2623 6326; www.mcu.ac.th/IBMC/; Wat Mahathat, Th Maha Rat; donations accepted; 🚤Tha Chang) offers a regimented daily program of meditation. With both programs, longer stays, including accommodation and food, can be arranged, but students are expected to follow a strict regimen of conduct.

Thai Boxing

Training in *moo·ay tai* (also spelt *muay thai*) for foreigners has increased in popularity in the last decade or so and many camps all over the country are tailoring their programs for foreign fighters. The following camps provide instruction in English and accept men and women. The website **Muay Thai Camps** (www.muaythaicampsthailand.com) contains additional information on Thailand's various training centres.

MuayThai Institute   THAI BOXING
(☑0 2992 0096; www.muaythai-institute.net; Rangsit Stadium, 336/932 Th Prachatipat, Pathum Thani; 10-day course from 8000B; ⑤Mo Chit exit 3 & taxi) Associated with the respected World Muay Thai Council, the institute offers a fundamental course (consisting of four levels of expertise), as well as courses for instructors, referees and judges.

Sor Vorapin Gym   THAI BOXING
(Map p62; ☑0 2282 3551; www.thaiboxings.com; 13 Th Kasab; per session/month 500/9000B; ⊗lessons 7.30-9.30am & 3-5pm; 🚤Tha Phra Athit (Banglamphu)) Specialising in training foreign students of both genders, this gym is sweating distance from Th Khao San. More serious training is held at a gym outside the city.

Fairtex Muay Thai   THAI BOXING
(☑0 2386 6117; www.fairtexbangplee.com; 99/5 Mu 3, Soi Buthamanuson, Th Thaeparak, Samut Prakan; tuition & accommodation per day 1450-1850B; ⑤Chong Nonsi exit 2 & taxi) A popular, long-running camp south of Bangkok.

Krudam Gym   THAI BOXING
(Map p90; ☑08 7111 7115, 08 4108 6652; www.krudamgym.com; Soi 24, Th Sukhumvit; per lesson 500B; ⊗10am-9pm Mon-Fri, 10am-7.30pm Sat-

Sun; **S** Phrom Phong exit 2) Headed by Dam Srichan, a former professional boxer, this small gym in central Bangkok offers 1½-hour open lessons for all skill levels, including for children. See website for times.

Thai Massage

A good massage is the birthright of every Bangkokian, and the joy of every visitor. Correspondingly, places offering massage are everywhere in Bangkok, and they range dramatically in quality, depending on if they offer massage or 'massage'. To avoid the latter, stay clear of the places that advertise via hard-selling, scantily dressed women.

If it's your first time in the hands of a Thai masseur/masseuse, it's probably a good idea to discard any previous massage experience, as many visitors find the experience equal parts painful and relaxing. Traditional Thai massage is based on yogic techniques for general health that involve pulling, stretching, bending and manipulating pressure points. If done well, a traditional massage will leave you sore but revitalised. A full-body Thai massage often also involves herbal heat compresses (oil treatments are generally associated with 'sexy' massage).

Depending on the neighbourhood, prices for an hour-long, full-body massage in a no-frills, small parlour will run from approximately 200B to 400B.

Some recommended places are:

Health Land THAI MASSAGE
(www.healthlandspa.com; Thai massage 2hr 500B; ⊙ 9am-midnight) A winning formula of affordable prices, expert treatments and pleasant facilities has created a small empire of Health Land centres with branches at **Ekamai** (Map p90; ☑ 0 2392 2233; 96/1 Soi Ekamai 10; Thai massage 2hr 500B; ⊙ 9am-midnight; **S** Ekkamai exit 2 & taxi), **Sathon** (Map p78; ☑ 0 2637 8883; 120 Th Sathon Neua (North); Thai massage 2hr 500B; ⊙ 9am-midnight; **S** Surasak exit 3) and **Sukhumvit** (Map p90; ☑ 0 2261 1110; 55/5 Soi 21 (Asoke), Th Sukhumvit; Thai massage 2hr 500B; ⊙ 9am-midnight; **M** Sukhumvit exit 1, **S** Asok exit 5).

Asia Herb Association THAI MASSAGE
(www.asiaherbassociation.com; Thai massage per hr 400B, Thai massage with herbal compress 1½hr 900B; ⊙ 9am-midnight) With outposts at **Phrom Phong** (Map p90; ☑ 0 2261 7401; 33/1 Soi 24, Th Sukhumvit; Thai massage per hr 400B, Thai massage with herbal compress 1½hr 900B; ⊙ 9am-midnight; **S** Phrom Phong exit 4), **Sawadee** (Map p90; ☑ 0 2261 2201; 20/1 Soi 31, Th Sukhumvit;

Thai massage per hr 400B, Thai massage with herbal compress 1½hr 900B; ⊙ 9am-midnight; **S** Phrom Phong exit 5) and **Thong Lor** (Map p90; ☑ 0 2392 3631; 58/19-25 Soi 55 (Thong Lor), Th Sukhumvit; Thai massage per hr 400B, Thai massage with herbal compress 1½hr 900B; ⊙ 9am-midnight; **S** Thong Lo exit 3), this Japanese-owned chain specialises in massage using *prà·kóp*, traditional Thai herbal compresses stuffed with 18 different herbs.

Ruen-Nuad Massage Studio THAI MASSAGE
(Map p78; ☑ 0 2632 2662; 42 Th Convent; Thai massage per hr 350B; ⊙ 10am-9pm; **M** Si Lom exit 2, **S** Sala Daeng exit 2) Set in a refurbished wooden house, this charming place successfully avoids both the tackiness and New Agedness that characterise most Bangkok massage joints. Prices are approachable, too.

Coran THAI MASSAGE
(Map p90; ☑ 0 2726 9978; www.coranbangkok.com; 94-96/1 Soi Ekamai 10, Soi 63 (Ekamai), Th Sukhumvit; Thai massage per hr 600B; ⊙ 11am-10pm; **S** Ekkamai exit 4 & taxi) A minimalist-feeling spa housed in a Thai villa. Stone, aroma and Thai herbal compress massage are also available.

Baan Dalah THAI MASSAGE
(Map p90; ☑ 0 2653 3358; www.baandalahmindbodyspa.com; 2 Soi 8, Th Sukhumvit; Thai massage per hr 350B; ⊙ 10am-midnight; **S** Nana exit 4) Calling itself the 'Family Friendly Spa of Thailand', this place does correspondingly G-rated massage in a simple setting.

Spas

Unless you've spent your entire visit in an air-conditioned bubble (entirely possible in today's Bangkok), at some point you may want to rid yourself of the negative effects of the city's urban environment. This can take the form of a simple scrub or multistage treatments with a customised choice of aromas and oils and a team of staff. There are countless spas in Bangkok, many of them in the city's high-end hotels with high-end price tags to match. To round down your choices, visit www.spasinbangkok.com or consider one of the following:

Banyan Tree Spa SPA
(Map p83; ☑ 0 2679 1052; www.banyantreespa.com; 21st fl, Banyan Tree Hotel, 21/100 Th Sathon Tai (South); massage packages from 3200B, spa packages from 6000B; ⊙ 10am-10pm; **M** Lumphini exit 2) A combination of highly trained staff and

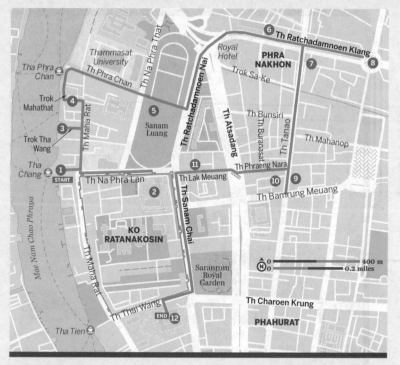

City Walk
Old Bangkok

START THA CHANG
FINISH WAT PHO
DISTANCE ABOUT 4KM
DURATION FOUR TO SIX HOURS

The bulk of Bangkok's 'must-see' destinations are in and around the former royal district, Ko Ratanakosin. It's best to start early to beat both the heat and the hordes. Remember to dress modestly to gain entry to the temples. Also ignore any strangers offering advice on sightseeing or shopping.

Start at ❶ **Tha Chang**. Proceed east to the main gate of ❷ **Wat Phra Kaew & Grand Palace**, two of Bangkok's most famous attractions. Otherwise, head north along Th Maha Rat, and immediately after passing the cat-laden newsstand (you'll know it when you smell it), turn left into ❸ **Trok Tha Wang**, a narrow alleyway holding a hidden classic Bangkok neighbourhood.

Turn left into crowded Trok Mahathat to discover the cramped ❹ **amulet market**. Exiting the market at Tha Phra Chan, cross Th Maha Rat and continue east until you reach ❺ **Sanam Luang**, the 'Royal Field'.

Cross Th Ratchadamnoen Nai and go north, turning right at the Royal Hotel onto ❻ **Th Ratchadamnoen Klang**, Bangkok's own Champs Élysées. Continuing east, at the intersection with Th Tanao, you'll see the ❼ **October 14 Memorial**, commemorating the civilian demonstrators who were killed on 14 October 1973 by the military during a pro-democracy rally. In the distance you'll see the ❽ **Democracy Monument**, erected in 1932.

After a lunch stop at ❾ **Poj Spa Kar** or ❿ **Chote Chitr**, enter Th Phraeng Nara, crossing Khlong Lod, and continue west along Th Lak Meuang to the home of Bangkok's city spirit, ⓫ **Lak Meuang**.

Head south along Th Sanam Chai and turn right onto Th Thai Wang, which will escort you to the entrance of ⓬ **Wat Pho**, home of the giant Reclining Buddha.

BANGKOK & AROUND

Th Sukhumvit

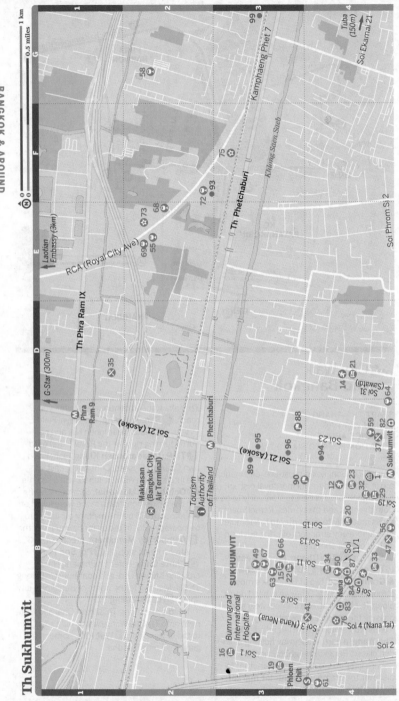

Th Phra Ram IX

Soi 21 (Asoke)

RCA (Royal City Ave)

Th Phetchaburi

Kamphaeng Phet 7

Khlong Saen Saeb

Laotian
Embassy (3km)

G-Star (300m)

Phra
Ram 9

Makkasan
(Bangkok City
Air Terminal)

Tourism
Authority
of Thailand

Phetchaburi

Soi 21 (Asoke)

Soi 23

Soi 31
(Sawatdi)

Soi Ekamai 21

Tuba
(150m)

Soi Phrom Si 2

Th Sukhumvit

SUKHUMVIT

Bumrungrad
International
Hospital

Soi 15

Soi 13

Soi 11

Soi 11/1

Soi
11/1

Soi 5

Soi 3 (Nana Neua)

Nana

Soi 4 (Nana Tai)

Soi 2

Soi 1

Phloen
Chit

Soi 19

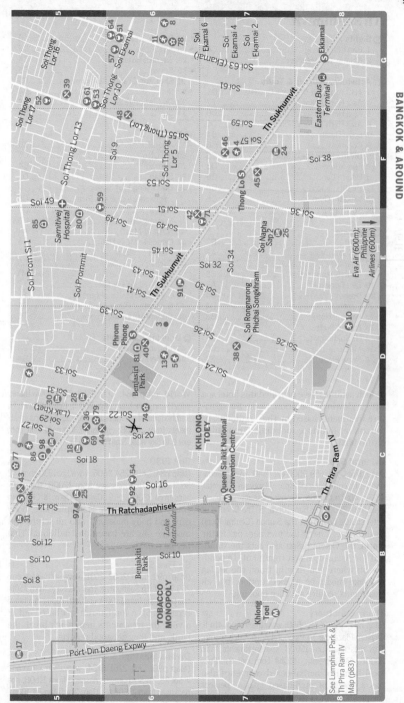

Soi Thong Lor 16
64
51
57 Soi Ekamai
Soi Thong Lor 10
5
8
11
78
Soi Ekamai 6
Soi Ekamai 4
Soi Ekamai 2
Soi 63 (Ekamai)
Ekamai
39
61
53
Soi Thong Lor 17
52
Soi Thong Lor 13
48
Soi 55 (Thong Lor)
Soi 61
Eastern Bus Terminal
Th Sukhumvit
Soi 9
Soi Thong Lor 5
46
4
Soi 57
24
Soi 59
Soi 49
59
Soi 53
Thong Lo
45
Soi 38
Th Sukhumvit
85
80
Samitivej Hospital
Soi 51
42
1
Soi 36
Soi Prom S1
Soi 49
Soi 45
Soi 49
Soi Napha Sap 2
26
Eva Air (600m);
Philippine Airlines (600m)
Soi Prommit
Soi 43
Soi 32
Soi 34
91
Soi 41
Th Sukhumvit
Soi 30
Soi 39
3
Phrom Phong
Soi 26
Soi Rongnarong Phichai Songkhram
Soi 33
6
Benjasiri Park
81
40
13
5
Soi 24
38
10
Soi 31
28
Soi 30 (Lak Khet)
Soi 29
79
36
Soi 22
74
KHLONG TOEY
Soi 27
27
86
98
18
69
44
Soi 20
9
77
43
18
Soi 18
Asok
31
92
54
Soi 16
25
Soi 14
Queen Sirikit National Convention Centre
Th Ratchadaphisek
97
17
Soi 12
Lake Ratchada
Th Ratchadaphisek
Soi 10
Benjakiti Park
Soi 8
Soi 10
TOBACCO MONOPOLY
Khlong Toei
Th Phra Ram IV
2
Port-Din Daeng Expwy

See Lumphini Park & Th Phra Ram IV Map (p83)

Th Sukhumvit

hi-tech facilities have provided this hotel spa with a glowing reputation. Come for signature treatments based in Thai traditions, or the more futuristic-sounding 'Tranquility Hydro Mist'.

Oriental Spa SPA
(Map p76; ☑ 0 2659 9000 ext 7440; www.mandarinoriental.com/bangkok/spa; Mandarin Oriental, 48 Soi 40, Th Charoen Krung; massage/spa packages from 2900B; ⊙ 6am-10pm; ☑ Tha Oriental or hotel shuttle boat from Tha Sathon (Central Pier)) Regarded as among the premier spas in the world, the Oriental Spa also sets the standard for Asian-style spa treatment. Depending on where you flew in from, the jet lag massage might be a good option, but all treatments require advance booking.

Thann Sanctuary SPA
(Map p84; ☑ 0 2658 0550; www.thann.info; 4th fl, Gaysorn Plaza, cnr Th Ploenchit & Th Ratchadamri; Thai massage from 1500B, spa treatments from 2800B; ⊙ 10am-9pm; ☑ Chit Lom exit 9) This local brand of herbal-based cosmetics also has a series of mall-based spas – perfect for post-shopping therapy. Also at Central-

World (Map p84; ☑ 0 2658 6557; www.thann. info/thann_sanctuary.php; 2nd fl, CentralWorld, Th Ratchadamri; Thai massage from 1500B, spa treatments from 2800B; ⊙ 10am-7.30pm; ☑ Chit Lom exit 9 to Sky Walk, Siam exit 6 to Sky Walk).

Spa 1930 SPA
(Map p84; ☑ 0 2254 8606; www.spa1930.com; 42 Soi Tonson; Thai massage from 1200B, spa packages from 3800B; ⊙ 9.30am-9.30pm; ☑ Chit Lom exit 4) The menu here is simple (face, body care and body massage), and all scrubs and massage oils are based on traditional Thai herbal remedies.

So Thai Spa SPA
(Map p90; ☑ 0 2662 2691; www.sothaispa.com; 269 Soi 31, Th Sukhumvit; Thai massage from 750B, spa packages from 1300B; ⊙ 10am-10pm; ☑ Phrom Phong exit 5) A foreign-run spa based out of a villa, the treatments here won't break the bank, and they get good reports.

Divana Massage & Spa SPA
(Map p90; ☑ 0 2261 6784; www.divanaspa.com; 7 Soi 25, Th Sukhumvit; massage from 1150B, spa packages from 2350B; ⊙ 11am-9pm Mon-Fri, 10am-

9pm Sat & Sun; Ⓜ Sukhumvit exit 2, Ⓢ Asok exit 6) This place retains a Thai touch with a private and soothing setting in a garden house.

🍴 Courses

Cooking

Imagine the points you'll rack up if you can make authentic Thai dishes for your friends back at home. A visit to a Thai cooking school has become a must-do for many Bangkok itineraries, and for some visitors it's a highlight of their trip.

Courses range in price and value, but a typical half-day course should include at least a basic introduction to Thai ingredients and flavours, and a hands-on chance to both prepare and cook at least four dishes. Most schools offer a revolving cast of dishes that change on a daily basis, making it possible to study for a week without repeating a dish. Many courses include a visit to a market, and nearly all lessons include a set of printed recipes and end with a communal lunch consisting of your handiwork.

Helping Hands COOKING
(📞 08 4901 8717; www.cookingwithpoo.com; 1200B; ⏱ lessons 8.30am-1pm) This popular cookery course was started by a native of Khlong Toey's slums and is held in her neighbourhood. Courses, which must be booked in advance, span four dishes and include a visit to Khlong Toey Market and transport to and from **Emporium** (Map p90; www.emporiumthailand.com; cnr Soi 24 & Th Sukhumvit; ⏱ 10am-10pm; Ⓢ Phrom Phong exit 2).

Baipai Thai Cooking School COOKING
(📞 0 2561 1404; www.baipai.com; 8/91 Soi 54, Th Ngam Wong Wan; 2200B; ⏱ lessons 9.30am-1.30pm & 1.30-5.30pm Mon-Sat) Housed in an attractive suburban villa, and taught by a small army of staff, Baipai offers two daily lessons of four dishes each. Transport is available.

Silom Thai Cooking School COOKING
(Map p78; 📞 08 4726 5669; www.bangkokthaicooking.com; 68 Soi 13, Th Silom; 1000B; ⏱ lessons 9am-12.30pm, 1.40-5.30pm & 6-9pm; Ⓢ Chong Nonsi exit 3) The facilities are basic, but Silom crams a visit to a market and instruction of five to

six dishes into 3½ hours, making it the best bang for your baht. Located at the very end of Soi 13, Th Silom – follow the signs.

Blue Elephant Thai Cooking School
COOKING

(Map p78; ☑0 2673 9353; www.blueelephant. com; 233 Th Sathon Tai; course 2800B; ⊘lessons 8.45am-1.30pm & 1.30-4.30pm Mon-Sat; ⑤Surasak exit 2) Bangkok's most chichi Thai cooking school offers two lessons daily. The morning class squeezes in a visit to a local market, while the afternoon session includes a detailed introduction to Thai ingredients.

Amita Thai Cooking Class
COOKING

(☑0 2466 8966; www.amitathaicooking.com; 162/17 Soi 14, Th Wutthakat, Thonburi; 3000B; ⊘lessons 9.30am-1pm Thu-Tue) In a canalside house in Thonburi, a course here includes a romp in a herb garden and instruction in four dishes. The fee covers transportation, including boat transfer from Tha Maharaj.

Thai Massage

Wat Pho Thai Traditional Medical and Massage School
THAI MASSAGE

(Map p62; ☑0 2622 3551; www.watpomassage. com; 392/25-28 Soi Phen Phat; lessons from 2500B; ⊘lessons 9am-4pm; ⓩTha Tien) Offers basic and advanced courses in traditional Thai massage; basic courses span 30 hours spread over five days and cover either general massage or foot massage. The advanced level spans 60 hours, requires the basic course as a prerequisite, and covers therapeutic and healing massage. Other advanced courses include oil massage and aromatherapy, and infant and child massage. Also offers massages to the public.

The school is outside the temple compound in a restored Bangkok shophouse on unmarked Soi Phen Phat – look for Coconut Palm restaurant.

☞ Tours

If you would like someone to guide you through Bangkok, recommended outfits include **Tour with Tong** (☑08 1835 0240; www.tourwithtong.com; day tour from 1500B), whose team conducts tours in and around Bangkok, and **Thai Private Tour Guide** (☑08 9661 6706, 08 9822 1798; www.thaitourguide.com; day tour from 2000B), where Ms Pu and TJ get good reviews.

Walking & Speciality Tours

Although the pollution and heat are significant obstacles, Bangkok is a fascinating city to explore on foot. If you'd rather do it with an expert guide, **Bangkok Private Tours** (www.bangkokprivatetours.com; half-/full-day walking tour 4700/6000B) conducts customised walking tours of the city. And foodies may appreciate the offerings at **Bangkok Food Tours** (☑08 9126 3657; www.bangkokfoodtours.com; tours from 850B), which offers daytime culinary tours of Bangkok's Bang Rak neighbourhood and night-time tours of Chinatown.

DON'T MISS

BANGKOK'S CANALS

For an up-close view of the city's famed canals, long-tail boats are available for hire at Tha Chang, Tha Tien, Tha Oriental and Tha Phra Athit. Prices at Tha Chang are the highest and allow little room for negotiation, but you stand the least chance of being taken for a ride or hit with tips and other unexpected fees.

Trips explore the Thonburi canals **Khlong Bangkok Noi** and, further south, **Khlong Mon**, taking in the Royal Barges National Museum, Wat Arun and a riverside temple with fish feeding. Longer trips diverge into **Khlong Bangkok Yai**, further south, which offers more typical canal scenery, including orchid farms. On weekends, you have the option of visiting the Taling Chan floating market (p136). However, to actually disembark and explore any of these sights, the most common tour of one hour (1000B, up to eight people) is simply not enough time and you'll most likely need 1½ (1300B) or two hours (1500B). Most operators have set tour routes, but if you have a specific destination in mind, you can request it.

If you'd prefer something longer or more personal, **Pandan Tour** (☑0 2689 1232, 08 7109 8873; www.thaicanaltour.com; tours from 1995B) conducts a variety of mostly full-day tours.

A cheaper alternative is to take the **commuter long-tail boat** (25B; ⊘4.30am-7.30pm) from Tha Chang to Bang Yai, at the distant northern end of Khlong Bangkok Noi.

Thewet & Dusit

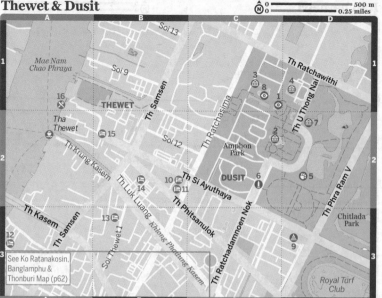

BANGKOK & AROUND TOURS

Thewet & Dusit

◎ Sights
1 Abhisek Dusit Throne Hall C1
2 Ananta Samakhom Throne Hall C2
3 Ancient Cloth Museum C1
4 Dusit Palace Park D1
5 Dusit Zoo.. D2
6 Rama V Memorial C2
7 Royal Thai Elephant Museum D2
8 Vimanmek Teak Mansion C1
9 Wat Benchamabophit D3

⊜ Sleeping
10 Baan Tepa Boutique House B2
11 Hi Baan Thewet B2
12 Khaosan Baan Thai............................. A3
13 Phra-Nakorn Norn-Len B3
14 SSIP Boutique B2
15 Taewez Guesthouse B2

⊗ Eating
16 Kaloang Home Kitchen A1

Bicycle & Segway Tours
Although some cycling tours tackle Bangkok's urban neighbourhoods, most take advantage of the nearby lush, undeveloped district to the south known as Phra Pradaeng, where narrow walkways crisscross irrigation canals that feed small-scale fruit plantations and simple villages.

Grasshopper Adventures   BICYCLE TOUR
(Map p62; ☏0 2280 0832; www.grasshopperadventures.com; 57 Th Ratchadamnoen Klang; tours from US$32; ⊙8.30am-6.30pm Mon-Fri; ⊛klorng boat to Tha Phan Fah) This lauded outfit runs a variety of bicycle tours in and around Bangkok, including a night tour and a tour of the city's green zones.

ABC Amazing Bangkok Cyclists   BICYCLE TOUR
(Map p90; ☏0 2665 6364; www.realasia.net; 10/5-7 Soi Aree, Soi 26, Th Sukhumvit; tours from 1300B; ⊙daily tours at 8am, 10am, 1pm & 6pm; Ⓢ Phrom Phong exit 4) Operating for more than a decade, the bike-based tours here purport to reveal the 'real' Asia by following the elevated walkways of the city's rural canals. A variety of city tours are available as well.

Co van Kessel Bangkok Tours   BICYCLE TOUR
(Map p76; ☏0 2639 7351; www.covankessel.com; ground fl, River City, 23 Th Yotha; tours from 950B; ⊙6am-7pm; ⊛Tha Si Phraya/River City) This Dutch-run outfit offers a variety of tours in Chinatown, Thonburi and Bangkok's green zones, many of which also involve boat rides. Tours depart from the company's office in the River City shopping centre.

Ratchathewi

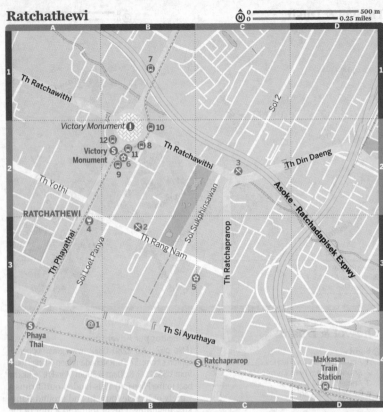

Ratchathewi

Bangkok Bike Rides BICYCLE TOUR
(☎ 0 2381 7490; www.bangkokbikerides.com; tours from 1000B) A division of the tour company Spice Roads, it offers a variety of tours, both urban and rural. Hotel pick-up is provided; otherwise tours commence from a spot near Soi 26, Th Sukhumvit.

Segway Tour Thailand SEGWAY TOUR
(Map p62; ☎ 0 2221 4525; www.segwaytourthailand.com; Maharaj Pier Bldg, Tha Maharaj, off Th

Maha Rat; half-day tour 3500B; ⊙ 8.30am-6.30pm Tue-Sun; ⚲ Tha Maharaj) This outfit runs half-day Segway tours of Bangkok and longer tours elsewhere, including Ayuthaya.

River & Canal Trips

Glimpses of Bangkok's past as the 'Venice of the East' are still possible today, even though the motor vehicle has long since become the city's conveyance of choice. Along the river and the canals is a motley fleet of watercraft, from paddled canoes to rice barges. In these areas many homes, trading houses and temples remain oriented towards life on the water, providing a fascinating glimpse into the past when Thais still considered themselves *jôw nám* (water lords).

The most obvious way to commute between riverside attractions is on the public ferries run by Chao Phraya Express Boat (p146). The terminus for most northbound boats is Tha Nonthaburi and for most southbound boats it's Tha Sathon (also called Central Pier), near Saphan Taksin BTS station, although some boats run as far north as Pak Kret, in Nonthaburi, and as far south as Wat Ratchasingkhon.

For a more customised view, you might consider chartering a long-tail boat along the city's canals; for details see the boxed text on p94.

A little faster than the days of sailing ships, river cruises from Bangkok north to the ruins of the former royal capital of Ayuthaya take in all the romance of the river. Most trips include a guided tour of Ayuthaya's ruins with a stop at the summer palace of Bang Pa-In.

Asian Oasis   RIVER CRUISE
(Map p84; ☑ 08 1496 4516, 08 8809 7047; www.asian-oasis.com; 7th fl, Nai Lert Tower, 2/4 Th Witthayu (Wireless Rd); ⊙ 9am-5pm Mon-Fri; Ⓢ Phloen Chit exit 1) Cruise the Chao Phraya River aboard a fleet of restored rice barges with old-world charm and modern conveniences. Trips include either an upstream or downstream journey to/from Ayuthaya, including a night on the boat, with bus transfer in the opposite direction.

Anantara Cruises   RIVER CRUISE
(☑ 0 2477 0770; www.bangkok-cruises.anantara.com; 25,000-72,000B) Operated by the Anantara Bangkok Riverside Resort & Spa are two restored teak rice barges decorated with antiques, Persian carpets and luxury sleeping berths. The trip is a three-day, two-night excursion to Ayuthaya, and rates are all-inclusive.

Dinner Cruises

A dinner cruise along Mae Nam Chao Phraya is touted as an iconic Bangkok experience, and several companies cater to this. Yet it's worth mentioning that, in general, the vibe is pretty cheesy, with loud live entertainment and mammoth boats so brightly lit inside you'd never know you were on the water. The food, typically served as a buffet, usually ranges from mediocre to forgettable. But the atmosphere of the river at night, bordered by illuminated temples and skyscrapers, and the cool breeze chasing the heat away, is usually enough to trump all of this.

The vast majority of cruises depart from, or very near, the pier at River City; the **information desk** (☑ 0 2639 4532, 0 2237 0077; www.rivercity.co.th; ground fl, River City, 23 Th Yotha; ⊙ 10am-10pm; ⚲ Tha Si Phraya/River City, or shuttle boat from Tha Sathon) there is your one-stop-shop for all things dinner-cruise related, and tickets can be purchased in advance for White Orchid and Wan Fah, in addition to **Chaophraya Cruise** (Map p76; ☑ 0 2541 5599; www.chaophrayacruise.com; 1700B; ⊙ cruise 7-9pm), **Chao Phraya Princess** (Map p76; ☑ 0 2860 3700; www.thaicruise.com; 1400B; ⊙ cruise 7.45-9.45pm) and **Grand Pearl** (Map p76; ☑ 0 2861 0255; www.grandpearlcruise.com; 1700B; ⊙ cruise 7.30-9.30pm). Hotel transfer is generally included in the ticket price.

Manohra Cruises   DINNER CRUISE
(☑ 0 2476 0022; www.manohracruises.com; 1400-1990B; ⊙ cruise 7.30-9.30pm) This cruise takes place aboard a restored teak rice barge, and probably has the best food of the lot; departs from Anantara Bangkok Riverside Resort & Spa, acessible via hotel shuttle boat from Saphan Taksin.

Wan Fah   DINNER CRUISE
(Map p76; ☑ 0 2622 7657; www.wanfah.in.th/eng/dinner; 1300B; ⊙ cruise 7-9pm) The buxom wooden boats here are more intimate than most. Dinner options include a standard or seafood set menu.

Loy Nava   DINNER CRUISE
(Map p76; ☑ 0 2437 4932; www.loynava.com; from 1648B; ⊙ cruises 6-8pm & 8.10-10.10pm) Operating since 1970, and quite possibly the original Bangkok dinner cruise. A vegetarian menu is available.

White Orchid   DINNER CRUISE
(Map p76; ☑ 0 2476 5207; www.thairivercruise.com; 1400B; ☺ cruise 7.45-9.45pm) One of the larger boats; entertainment here is provided by *gà·teu·i* (transsexual) performers.

✵ Festivals & Events

In addition to the national holidays, there's always something going on in Bangkok. Many Thai holidays are based on the lunar calendar, which varies year to year, so check the website of the Tourism Authority of Thailand (p140) or the Bangkok Information Center (p140) for exact dates.

February & March

Chinese New Year   NEW YEAR
(☺ Jan or Feb) Thai-Chinese celebrate the lunar New Year with a week of housecleaning, lion dances and fireworks. Most festivities centre on Chinatown. Dates vary.

Kite-Flying Season   KITE-FLYING
During the windy season, colourful kites battle it out over the skies of Sanam Luang and Lumphini Park.

April & May

Songkran   NEW YEAR
(☺ mid-Apr) The celebration of the Thai New Year has morphed into a water war with high-powered water guns and water balloons being launched at suspecting and unsuspecting participants. The most intense water battles take place on Th Khao San.

**Royal Ploughing
Ceremony**   PLANTING CEREMONY
(☺ May) His Majesty the King (or lately the Crown Prince) commences rice-planting season with a ceremony at Sanam Luang. Exact dates vary.

August

Queen's Birthday   MOTHER'S DAY
(☺ 12 Aug) The queen's birthday is recognised as Mother's Day throughout the country. In Bangkok, festivities centre on Th Ratchadamnoen and the Grand Palace.

September & October

Vegetarian Festival   FOOD
(☺ Sep or Oct) A 10-day Chinese-Buddhist festival wheels out yellow-bannered streetside vendors serving meatless meals. The greatest concentration of vendors is found in Chinatown. Dates vary.

**International Festival of Dance &
Music**   MUSIC, DANCE
(www.bangkokfestivals.com; ☺ Sep or Oct) An extravaganza of arts and culture sponsored by the Thailand Cultural Centre.

King Chulalongkorn Day   ROYAL EVENT
(☺ 23 Oct) Rama V is honoured on the anniversary of his death at the Royal Plaza in Dusit. Crowds of devotees come to make merit with incense and flower garlands.

November

Loi Krathong   FULL MOON
(www.loikrathong.net/en; ☺ early Nov) A beautiful full-moon festival where, on the night of the full moon, small lotus-shaped boats made of banana leaf and containing a lit candle are set adrift on Mae Nam Chao Phraya.

Krating Daeng Fat Fest   MUSIC
(www.facebook.com/fatradio; ☺ early Nov) Sponsored by FAT 104.5FM radio, Bangkok's indie-est indie bands gather for an annual fest.

Bangkok World Film Festival   FILM
(www.worldfilmbkk.com; ☺ mid-Nov) Homegrown talent and overseas indies arrive on the silver screens.

December

King's Birthday   ROYAL EVENT
(☺ 5 Dec) Locals celebrate their monarch's birthday with lots of parades and fireworks.

🛏 Sleeping

At first glance, deciding where to lay your head in Bangkok appears an insurmountable task – there are countless hotels in virtually every corner of this sprawling city.

Making the job slightly easier is the fact that where you stay is largely determined by your budget. Hotel rooms in Bangkok are generally more expensive than elsewhere in Thailand, but don't fret as there's a huge variety and significant discounts can be had, making accommodation excellent value overall. Banglamphu and the tourist ghetto of Th Khao San still hold the bulk of Bangkok's budget accommodation, although the downside is that it can be difficult to get to other parts of town. Cheap rooms are also available around lower Th Sukhumvit, although you'll have to put up with sex tourists and touts. Chinatown also has its share of hotels in this category, with the added bonus of anonymity. And there's an OK selection of budget digs on Soi Ngam Duphli, near Th Sathon.

Those willing to spend a bit more can consider staying in 'downtown' Bangkok. Both Th Sukhumvit and Th Silom have solid midrange options, typically within walking distance of the BTS or MRT. The sois (streets) opposite the National Stadium, near Siam Sq, have some good budget/midrange options, and have the benefit of being close to the BTS.

Upper Sukhumvit is home to many of Bangkok's boutique and upscale designer hotels. The city's most legendary luxury hotels are largely found along the riverside near Th Silom.

Ko Ratanakosin

Ko Ratanakosin, the most touristed area of Bangkok, was until relatively recently utterly devoid of lodging options. But with the advent of the boutique-hotel craze, riverside shophouses are being transformed into charming tourists' nests; in the last year or so, a handful of attractive midrange hotels have sprung up in converted shophouses just off Th Maha Rat.

Royal Tha Tien Village　　　HOTEL **$$**
(Map p62; ☑08 9555 1683; www.facebook.com/theroyalthatienvillage; 392/29 Soi Phen Phat; r 1000-1200B; ❋ @ ⚛; ☻ Tha Tien) The five rooms here are relatively plain, but TV, fridge, air-con, lots of space and shiny wood floors, plus a cosy homestay vibe, edge this new place into the recommendable column.

Chetuphon Gate　　　HOTEL **$$**
(Map p62; ☑0 2622 2060; www.chetuphon-gate. com; Soi Pratu Nokyung; r 1800-2200B; ❋ @ ⚛; ☻ Tha Tien) Nine new and attractive rooms located above a coffee shop; the cheapest can feel rather tight, so opt for the 'deluxe' rooms, which feature beds on an elevated platform and a bit more space.

Arom D Hostel　　　HOTEL **$$**
(Map p62; ☑0 2622 1055; www.aromdhostel.com; 336 Th Maha Rat; incl breakfast dm 800B, r 2250B; ❋ @ ⚛; ☻ Tha Tien) The rooms and dorm beds here are united by a cutesy design theme and a host of inviting communal areas including a rooftop deck, computers, a ground-floor cafe and TV room.

Chakrabongse Villas　　　HOTEL **$$$**
(Map p62; ☑0 2622 1900; www.chakrabongsevillas. com; 396/1 Th Maha Rat; incl breakfast r 5000B, ste 10,000-25,000B; ❋ @ ⚛; ☻ Tha Tien) This compound incorporates three sumptuous but cramped rooms and four larger suites and villas, some with great river views, all surrounding a still-functioning royal palace dating back to 1908. There's a pool, jungle-like gardens and an elevated deck for romantic riverside dining. No walk-ins.

Sala　　　HOTEL **$$$**
(Map p62; ☑0 2622 1388; www.salaresorts.com; Soi Tha Tian; incl breakfast r 3500-5500B, ste 10,500B; ❋ @ ⚛; ☻ Tha Tien) This new riverside place boasts a sleek, modernist feel – an intriguing contrast with the former warehouse it's located in. The 17 rooms, decked out in black and white and boasting open-plan bathrooms and big windows looking out on the river and Wat Arun, aren't particularly huge, but will satisfy the fashion-conscious.

Aurum: The River Place　　　HOTEL **$$$**
(Map p62; ☑0 2622 2248; www.aurum-bangkok. com; 394/27-29 Soi Pansuk; r incl breakfast 3700-4600B; ❋ @ ⚛; ☻ Tha Tien) The 12 modern rooms here don't necessarily reflect the grand European exterior of this refurbished shophouse. Nonetheless, they're comfortable and well-appointed, and most offer fleeting views of Mae Nam Chao Phraya.

ⓘ THINKING AHEAD

The rates listed in this chapter are high-season rack rates; ie the highest price a hotel will generally charge for a room. However, there's no reason you should be paying this much, especially if you know ahead of time when you'll be in town. Booking rooms online can lead to savings of at least 20%, and often more, at many of Bangkok's leading hotels. This can be done directly through the hotel websites or by sites such as **Lonely Planet's Hotels & Hostels** (www.hotels.lonelyplanet.com), which features thorough reviews from authors and traveller feedback, and a booking facility.

It can also work to your advantage to simply call the hotel and book ahead; sometimes desk staff collect a commission on walk-ins and are reluctant to discount, something that can be remedied by a pre-emptive phone call and an inquiry about the lowest possible rate.

Banglamphu & Around

Although Banglamphu is ground zero for budget accommodation in Bangkok, this doesn't necessarily mean it's the only or even the best place in Bangkok for a cheap room. But prices are generally low, and services such as internet cafes, travel agents and beer stalls are available in abundance, making it a convenient base.

It would be impossible to list all of Banglamphu's accommodation options here. Instead, we've chosen a select few that stand out, generally those away from Th Khao San, which can get pretty hectic. If you've got the time, explore a bit and check out a few places before making a decision – there are increasingly attractive options spanning all price levels on outlying streets such as riverside Th Phra Athit, leafy Soi Ram Buttri and the residential side streets off Th Samsen. During the high season (December to February), however, it's probably a wise idea to take the first vacant bed you come across. The best time of day to find a vacancy is around check-out time, at 10am or 11am.

Fortville Guesthouse HOTEL $
(Map p62; ☎ 0 2282 3932; www.fortvilleguesthouse.com; 9 Th Phra Sumen; r 790-1120B; ❋ @ ☎; ☻ Tha Phra Athit (Banglamphu)) The rooms here are stylishly minimal, and the more expensive ones include perks such as fridge, balcony and five hours of free wi-fi.

Rambuttri Village Inn HOSTEL $
(Map p62; ☎ 0 2282 9162; www.rambuttrivillage.com; 95 Soi Ram Buttri; r 650-1150B; ❋ ☎ ☀; ☻ Tha Phra Athit (Banglamphu)) If you're willing to subject yourself to the relentless gauntlet of tailors along the path approaching it ('Excuse me, suit?'), this plain and busy place has an abundance of good-value rooms and a rooftop pool.

Rajata Hotel HOTEL $
(Map p62; ☎ 0 2628 8084; www.rajatahotel.com; 46 Soi 6, Th Samsen; r 850-900B; ❋ @ ☎; ☻ Tha Phra Athit (Banglamphu)) This defiantly old-school hotel is a comfortable choice for those who don't want to stay on Th Khao San, but who don't want to be too far away.

Wild Orchid Villa HOTEL $
(Map p62; ☎ 0 2629 4378; www.wildorchidvilla.com; 8 Soi Chana Songkhram; r 300-1800B; ❋ ☎; ☻ Tha Phra Athit (Banglamphu)) The cheapies here are some of the tiniest we've seen anywhere, but all rooms are clean and neat, and come in a bright, friendly package. Wild Orchid is popular, so it's best to book ahead.

★**Lamphu Treehouse** HOTEL $$
(Map p62; ☎ 0 2282 0991; www.lamphutreehotel.com; 155 Wanchat Bridge, off Th Prachathipatai; incl breakfast r 1450-2500B; ste 3600-4900B; ❋ @ ☎ ☀; ☻ Tha Phan Fah) Despite the name, this attractive midranger has its feet firmly on land and, as such, represents a great value. The rooms, panelled in wood and decorated with subtle Thai accents, are attractive and inviting, and the rooftop bar, pool, internet, restaurant and quiet canal-side location ensure you may never feel the need to leave.

A new annexe a couple of blocks away increases your odds of snagging a reservation.

Feung Nakorn Balcony HOTEL $$
(Map p62; ☎ 0 2622 1100; www.feungnakorn.com; 125 Th Fuang Nakhon; incl breakfast dm 600B, r 1650B, ste 2000-3000B; ❋ @ ☎; ☻ Tha Phan Fah) Set in a former school, the 42 rooms here surround an inviting garden courtyard and are generally large, bright and cheery. Amenities such as a free minibar, safe and flat-screen TV are standard, and the hotel has a quiet, secluded location away from the strip, with capable staff. A charming and inviting, if not extremely great-value, place to stay.

Hotel Dé Moc HOTEL $$
(Map p62; ☎ 0 2282 2831; www.hoteldemoc.com; 78 Th Prachathipatai; r incl breakfast 2549-2804B; ❋ @ ☎ ☀; ☻ Tha Phan Fah) The rooms at this 1960s-era hotel feel spacious, with high ceilings and generous windows, although the furnishings, like the exterior, are still stuck in the previous century. The grounds include an inviting and retro-feeling pool and cafe, and complimentary transport to Th Khao San and free bike rental are thoughtful perks. Hefty online discounts are available.

Sam Sen Sam Place GUESTHOUSE $$
(Map p62; ☎ 0 2628 7067; www.samsensam.com; 48 Soi 3, Th Samsen; r incl breakfast 590-2500B; ❋ @ ☎; ☻ Tha Phra Athit (Banglamphu)) One of the homiest places around, this colourful, refurbished antique villa gets glowing reports about its friendly service and quiet location. Note that the cheapest rooms are fan-cooled and share a bathroom.

Sourire HOTEL $$
(Map p62; ☎ 0 2280 2180; www.sourirebangkok.com; Soi Chao Phraya Si Phiphat; r incl breakfast 1500-3500B; ❋ @ ☎; ☻ Tha Phan Fah) More home than hotel, the 38 rooms here

SMALLER IS BETTER

The research trip for this edition revealed several attractive hotels and guesthouses with fewer than 10 rooms. Some of our faves:

➔ ★ **Arun Residence** (Map p62; ☎ 0 2221 9158; www.arunresidence.com; 36-38 Soi Pratu Nokyung; r incl breakfast 4000-4200B, ste incl breakfast 5800B; ❄ @ ☎; ⛴ Tha Tien) Although strategically located on the river directly across from Wat Arun, this multilevel wooden house boasts much more than just brilliant views. The six rooms here manage to feel both homey and stylish, some being tall and loftlike, while others cojoin two rooms (the best is the top-floor suite with its own balcony).

➔ ★ **Loy La Long** (Map p72; ☎ 0 2639 1390; www.loylalong.com; 1620/2 Th Songwat; incl breakfast dm 1100B, r 2100-4000B; ❄ @ ☎; ⛴ Tha Ratchawong, Ⓜ Hua Lamphong exit 1 & taxi) Rustic, retro, charming – the six rooms in this 100-year-old wooden house can lay claim to more than their fair share of personality. And united by breezy, inviting nooks and crannies, and a wonderful location elevated over Mae Nam Chao Phraya, the whole place is also privy to a hidden, almost secret, feel.

➔ **Bhuthorn** (Map p62; ☎ 0 2622 2270; www.thebhuthorn.com; 96-98 Th Phraeng Phuthon; r incl breakfast 4200-5200B; ❄ @ ☎; ⛴ Tha Phan Fah) Travel a century back in time by booking one of the three rooms in this beautiful antique shophouse located in a classic Bangkok neighbourhood. They're not particularly huge, but are big on atmosphere and come equipped with both antique furnishings and modern amenities. The sister hotel, **Asadang** (Map p62; ☎ 08 5180 7100; www.theasadang.com; 94-94/1 Th Atsadang; r incl breakfast 3300-6600B; ❄ @ ☎), a couple of blocks away, offers a similar package.

➔ **Littlest Guesthouse** (☎ 0 2675 6763; 77 Th Sathon Tai (South); r incl breakfast 2500B; ❄ ☎; Ⓢ Surasak exit 2) Located in a secluded alleyway steps from the BTS is this tiny, home-bound boutique. Inside, you'll find three rooms that are spacious and spotless, attractively decked out in contemporary/artsy furnishings, and boasting lots of natural light.

➔ **Café Ice Residence** (Map p78; ☎ 0 2636 7831; cafeiceresidences@gmail.com; 44/4 Soi Phiphat 2; r incl breakfast 1900-3300B; ❄ @ ☎; Ⓢ Chong Nonsi exit 2) More home than hotel, the nine rooms in this spotless, classy villa are inviting, spacious and comfortable. Filled with subtle yet attractive furnishings, they also share a location with a Thai restaurant and a quiet street.

➔ **Baan Dinso** (Map p62; ☎ 08 6815 2200; www.baandinso.com; 113 Trok Sin; r incl breakfast 1400-3500B; ❄ ☎; ⛴ Tha Phan Fah) This antique wooden villa may not represent the best deal in Bangkok, but for accommodation with a nostalgic feel and a palpable sense of place, it's almost impossible to beat. Of the nine small-yet-spotless rooms, five have en suite bathrooms, while all have access to functional and inviting communal areas.

➔ **Baan Tepa Boutique House** (Map p95; ☎ 0 2281 4332; www.baantepa.com; 245/1 Soi 9, Th Si Ayutthaya; r incl breakfast 1100-1800B; ❄ @ ☎; ⛴ Tha Thewet) The eight rooms in this 80-year-old wooden house are small, and the decor edges towards the chintzy, but the charm and hospitality are abundant and authentic.

exude a calming, matronly feel. Soft lighting, comfortable, sturdy wood furniture and the friendly, aged owners round out the package. To reach the hotel, follow Soi Chao Phraya Si Phiphat to the end and knock on the tall brown wooden door immediately on your left.

Diamond House　　　　　　　HOTEL $$
(Map p62; ☎ 0 2629 4008; www.thaidiamond-house.com; 4 Th Samsen; r 1100-1700B, ste 3600B;

❄ @ ☎; ⛴ Tha Phra Athit (Banglamphu)) Despite sharing real estate with a Chinese temple, there's no conflict of design at this eccentric hotel. Most rooms have beds on raised platforms, and are outfitted with stained glass, dark, lush colours and chic furnishings. There's a lack of windows, and some of the suites aren't much larger than the cheaper rooms, but a rooftop deck and an outdoor Jacuzzi make up for this.

BATHROOMLESS IN BANGKOK

If you don't require your own en suite bathroom, Bangkok has heaps of options, ranging from hi-tech dorm beds in a brand-new hostel to private bedrooms in an antique wooden house. Some of our picks:

➡ ★ **Lub*d** (Map p84; 0 2634 7999; www.lubd.com; Th Pha Ram I; dm 600-650B, r 1500-2000B; ❄ @ 🛜; S National Stadium exit 1) The title is a play on the Thai *làp dee*, meaning 'sleep well', but the fun atmosphere here might make you want to stay up all night. There's an inviting communal area stocked with games and a bar, and thoughtful facilities ranging from washing machines to a theatre room. If this one's full, there's another branch just off **Thalon Silom** (Map p78; 0 2634 7999; www.lubd.com; 4 Th Decho; dm 450-475B, r 550-850B; ❄ @ 🛜; S Chong Nonsi exit 2).

➡ **NapPark Hostel** (Map p62; 0 2282 2324; www.nappark.com; 5 Th Tani; dm 440-550B; ❄ @ 🛜; 🚤 Tha Phra Athit (Banglamphu)) This well-run hostel features dorm rooms of various sizes, all of which boast podlike beds outfitted with power points, mini-TV, reading lamp and wi-fi. Free bicycles and hypersocial communal areas ensure you may not actually get the chance to plug in.

➡ **Khaosan Baan Thai** (Map p95; 0 2628 5559; www.khaosanbaanthai.com; 11/1 Soi 3, Th Samsen; r incl breakfast 390-730B; ❄ @ 🛜; 🚤 Tha Phra Athit (Banglamphu)) This tiny wooden house holds 10 rooms decked out in cheery pastels and hand-painted bunny pictures. Half of the rooms are fan-cooled, and most are little more than a mattress on the floor, but warm service and an authentic homestay vibe compensate for this.

➡ **Silom Art Hostel** (Map p78; 0 2635 8070; www.silomarthostel.com; 198/19-22 Soi 14, Th Silom; dm 380-550B, r 1200-1500B; ❄ @ 🛜; S Chong Nonsi exit 3) Quirky, artsy, bright and fun, Silom Art Hostel combines recycled materials, bizarre furnishings and colourful art to arrive at a hostel that's quite unlike anywhere else in town. It's not all about style though: beds and rooms are functional and comfortable, and share clean bathrooms and appealing communal areas.

➡ **HQ Hostel** (Map p78; 0 2233 1598; www.hqhostel.com; 5/3-4 Soi 3, Th Silom; dm 380-599, r 1300-1700B; ❄ @ 🛜; M Si Lom exit 2, S Sala Daeng exit 2) A flashpacker hostel in the polished-concrete-and-industrial-style mould, HQ includes four- to 10-bed dorms, a few private rooms and inviting communal areas in a narrow multistorey building in the middle of Bangkok's financial district.

➡ **Saphaipae** (Map p76; 0 2238 2322; www.saphaipae.com; 35 Th Surasak; dm 330-460B, r 1700-2000B; ❄ @ 🛜; S Surasak exit 1) The bright colours, chunky furnishings and bold murals in the lobby of this new hostel give it the vibe of a day-care centre for travellers – a feel that continues through to the playful communal areas and rooms. Dorms and rooms are well-equipped, and there's heaps of useful travel resources and facilities.

➡ **Suneta Hostel Khaosan** (Map p62; 0 2629 0150; www.sunetahostel.com; 209-211 Th Kraisi; incl breakfast dm 440-590B, r 900-1090B; ❄ @ 🛜; 🚤 Tha Phra Athit (Banglamphu)) This young hostel gets rave reviews for its retro-themed design, comfy dorms and friendly service.

➡ **S1 Hostel** (Map p83; 0 2679 7777; 35/1-4 Soi Ngam Duphli; dm 350B, r 600-1200B; ❄ @ 🛜; M Lumphini exit 1) A huge new hostel with dorm beds and private rooms decked out in a simple yet attractive primary colour scheme. A host of facilities (laundry, kitchen, rooftop garden) and a convenient location near the MRT make it great value.

➡ **HI-Sukhumvit** (Map p90; 0 2391 9338; www.hisukhumvit.com; 23 Soi 38, Th Sukhumvit; incl breakfast dm 350B, r 650-1500B; ❄ @ 🛜; S Thong Lo exit 4) The dorms here are admittedly rather plain, but clean bathrooms and a location in a quiet residential area with easy access to street food make it comfortable and convenient.

➡ **New Road Guesthouse** (Map p76; 0 2630 9371; www.newroadguesthouse.com; 1216/1 Th Charoen Krung; dm 160-250B, r 280-2500B; ❄ @ 🛜; 🚤 Tha Oriental) The fan-cooled dorms here, among the cheapest accommodation in all of Bangkok, are surprisingly clean and welcoming.

Villa Cha-Cha
HOTEL $$

(Map p62; 0 2280 1025; www.villachacha.com; 36 Th Tani; r 1000-3200B; ✳❄✈; Tha Phra Athit (Banglamphu)) Wind between statues, lounging residents, an expansive restaurant and a tiny pool to emerge at this seemingly hidden but popular hotel. A few clumsy stabs have been made at interior design, but the real draw is the social, resort-like atmosphere.

Rikka Inn
HOTEL $$

(Map p62; 0 2282 7511; www.rikkainn.com; 259 Th Khao San; r 1150-1450B; ✳@❄✈; Tha Phra Athit (Banglamphu)) Boasting tight but attractive rooms, a rooftop pool and a location right in the middle of all the action on Th Khao San, the Rikka is one of the area's most convenient and better-value midrangers.

Penpark Place
HOTEL $$

(Map p62; 0 2628 8896; www.penparkplace. com; 22 Soi 3, Th Samsen; r 330-1650B; ste 2100B; ✳@❄; Tha Phra Athit (Banglamphu)) This former factory has been turned into a good-value budget/midrange hotel. Rooms in the original building are little more than a bed and a fan, but a newer add-on sees a handful of well-equipped apartment-like rooms and suites.

New Siam Riverside
HOTEL $$

(Map p62; 0 2629 3535; www.newsiam.net; 21 Th Phra Athit; r incl breakfast 1490-3990B; ✳@❄; Tha Phra Athit (Banglamphu)) Of the few places along Th Phra Athit taking full advantage of the riverside setting, this is the cheapest of the lot, and has comfortable rooms with tiny bathrooms. But the real value is in the amenities (internet, travel agent, restaurant) and the location on one of the city's more pleasant streets.

Old Bangkok Inn
HOTEL $$$

(Map p62; 0 2629 1787; www.oldbangkokinn.com; 609 Th Phra Sumen; incl breakfast r 3690-7790B; ✳@❄; Tha Phan Fah) Providing the dictionary definition of a honeymoon hotel, the 10 rooms in this refurbished antique shophouse are decadent and sumptuous, blending rich colours and heavy wood furnishings. All have computers for personal use, and some have two levels and semi-outdoor bathrooms.

Praya Palazzo
HOTEL $$$

(Map p62; 0 2883 2998; www.prayapalazzo.com; 757/1 Somdej Prapinklao Soi 2, Thonburi; incl breakfast r 7000-9000B; ste 12,000-19,000B; ✳❄✈; Tha Phra Athit (Banglamphu)) After lying dormant for nearly 30 years, this elegant 19th-century mansion has been reborn as an attractive riverside boutique hotel. The 17 rooms can feel rather tight, and river views can be elusive, but the meticulous renovation, handsome antique furnishings and a bucolic atmosphere convene in a boutique hotel with legitimate old-world charm.

Baan Chantra
HOTEL $$$

(Map p62; 0 2628 6988; www.baanchantra. com; 120 Th Samsen; r incl breakfast 2400-3500B; ✳@❄; Tha Phra Athit (Banglamphu)) This beautiful converted house dating back to 1936 is without pretensions, preferring to be comfortable and roomy rather than fashionable and pinched. Many of the house's original teak details remain, and the 'deluxe' room boasts a sunny patio and an in-room computer.

Chinatown & Phahurat

Bangkok's Chinatown isn't the most hospitable part of town, but for those who wish to stay off the beaten track it's an area where travellers can remain largely anonymous. There's a decent selection of accommodation, much of it just off busy streets, so be sure to assess the noise situation before choosing your room. The area used to be a nightmare to get to, but the MRT stop at Hua Lamphong has improved things immensely.

If you're arriving in Bangkok by train and can't be bothered to search elsewhere for accommodation, there are a few great budget choices near Hua Lamphong train station, including the budget places listed here.

Siam Classic
GUESTHOUSE $

(Map p72; 0 2639 6363; www.siamclassic-hostel.com; 336/10 Trok Chalong Krung; r incl breakfast 500-1200B; ✳@❄; Hua Lamphong exit 1) The rooms here don't include much furniture, but a genuine effort has been made at making them feel comfortable, tidy and even a bit stylish. An inviting ground-floor communal area encourages meeting and chatting, and the whole place exudes a welcoming homestay vibe.

Baan Hua Lampong
GUESTHOUSE $

(Map p72; 08 3323 6806; www.baanhualampong.com; 336/20-21 Trok Chalong Krung; incl breakfast dm 220B; r 290-700B; ✳@❄; Tha Ratchawong, Hua Lamphong exit 1) Repeat visitors rave about the homey setting and warm, personal service at this guesthouse.

@Hua Lamphong
HOSTEL $

(Map p72; ✆0 2639 1925; www.at-hualamphong. com; 326/1 Th Phra Ram IV; dm 350-400B, r 690-950B; ✾@�; 🚤Tha Ratchawong, Ⓜ Hua Lamphong) Plain-yet-clean dorm beds and rooms can be found at this new-feeling hostel across the street from the train station.

Shanghai Mansion
HOTEL $$$

(Map p72; ✆0 2221 2121; www.shanghaimansion. com; 479-481 Th Yaowarat; incl breakfast r 3200B, ste 4500B; ✾@�; 🚤Tha Ratchawong, Ⓜ Hua Lamphong exit 1 & taxi) Easily the most consciously stylish place to stay in Chinatown, if not in all of Bangkok. This award-winning boutique hotel screams Shanghai circa 1935 with stained glass, an abundance of lamps, bold colours and cheeky Chinatown kitsch. If you're willing to splurge, ask for one of the bigger streetside rooms with tall windows that allow more natural light.

Riverside

Accommodation on either bank of Mae Nam Chao Phraya tends to diverge between upscale and hostel, with little in between.

River View Guest House
HOTEL $

(Map p76; ✆0 2234 5429; www.riverviewbkk.com; 768 Soi Phanurangsi, Th Songwat; dm 250B, r 400-1500B; ✾�; 🚤Tha Marine Department) After 20 years, this towering budget staple is finally receiving a much-needed renovation. The rooms that have been renovated are spacious and relatively modern, although the halls and exterior remain in a rather gritty time warp. To get there, heading north on Th Charoen Krung from Th Si Phraya, take a left onto Th Songwat, then the second left onto Soi Phanurangsi. You'll start to see signs at this point. Has a rooftop bar, River Vibe (p125).

Swan Hotel
HOTEL $$

(Map p76; ✆0 2235 9271; www.swanhotelbkk.com; 31 Soi 36, Th Charoen Krung; r incl breakfast 1200-2000B; ✾@�; 🚤Tha Oriental) The 1960s-era furnishings date this classic Bangkok hotel despite recent renovations. But the rooms are airy and virtually spotless, and the antiquated vibe provides the Swan, in particular its pool, with a funky, retro feel.

P&R Residence
HOTEL $$

(Map p76; ✆0 2639 6091; www.pandr-residence. com; 34 Soi 30, Th Charoen Krung; r 900-1800B; ✾�; 🚤Tha Si Phraya/River City) There's nothing fancy about the P&R, but its 20 rooms are comfortable and clean, if a bit frumpy, and it's very fairly priced for this atmospheric corner of town.

Mandarin Oriental
HOTEL $$$

(Map p76; ✆0 2659 9000; www.mandarinoriental. com; 48 Soi 40, Th Charoen Krung; incl breakfast r 15,150-30,000B; ste 27,500-160,000B; ✾@�; 🚤Tha Oriental, or hotel shuttle boat from Tha Sathon (Central Pier)) For the true Bangkok experience, a stay at this grand old riverside hotel is a must. The majority of rooms are in the modern and recently refurbished New Wing, but we prefer the old-world ambience of the Garden and Authors' Wings. The hotel is also home to one of the region's most acclaimed spas, a legendary fine dining restaurant, a cooking school and the Bamboo Bar (p129).

Peninsula Hotel
HOTEL $$$

(Map p76; ✆0 2861 2888; www.peninsula.com; 333 Th Charoen Nakhon, Thonburi; r incl breakfast 14,000-25,000B, ste 70,000-130,000B; ✾@�; 🚤hotel shuttle boat from Tha Sathon (Central Pier)) After nearly 15 years in Bangkok, the Pen still seems to have it all: the location (towering over the river in Thonburi), the rep (it's consistently one of the highest-ranking luxury hotels in the world) and one of the highest levels of service in town. If money is no obstacle, stay on one of the upper floors where you literally have all of Bangkok at your feet.

Shangri-La Hotel
HOTEL $$$

(Map p76; ✆0 2236 7777; www.shangri-la.com; 89 Soi 42/1 (Soi Wat Suan Phlu); incl breakfast r 7600-11,300B, ste 12,800-120,000B; ✾@�; Ⓢ Saphan Taksin exit 1) A recent facelift has the long-standing Shangri-La looking better than ever. And a convenient location near the BTS, generous rates, a resortlike riverside atmosphere and ample activities and amenities make it a clever choice for families.

Millennium Hilton
HOTEL $$$

(Map p76; ✆0 2442 2000; www.bangkok.hilton. com; 123 Th Charoen Nakorn, Thonburi; incl breakfast r 10,000-12,000B, ste 13,000-13,800B; ✾@�; 🚤hotel shuttle boat from Tha Sathon (Central Pier)) As soon as you enter the dramatic lobby, it's obvious that this is Bangkok's youngest, most modern riverside hotel. Rooms, all of which boast wide-screen river views, follow this theme and are decked out with funky furniture and Thai-themed photos. A glass elevator and an artificial beach are just some of the fun touches.

Silom & Sathon

The city's financial district along Th Silom is not the most charming area of town, but it allows convenient access to nightspots and to the BTS and MRT. There's a decent mix of budget and midrange, while some of Bangkok's most famous top-enders are also along this stretch of the river, and can be reached via the complimentary hotel ferries from Tha Sathon (Central Pier).

Th Sathon is home to several top-end hotels, but the area as a whole lacks atmosphere, the primary feature being the vast eponymous road.

Glow Trinity Silom
HOTEL $$

(Map p78; ☑ 0 2231 5050; www.zinchospitality.com/glowbyzinc/silom; 150 Soi Phiphat 2; incl breakfast r 1900-2600B, ste 3600B; ❋ @ ⚛ ☎; ⑤ Chong Nonsi exit 2) A sophisticated-feeling hotel at a midrange price, Glow has contemporary-feeling, tech-equipped rooms and great service, and pool and fitness can be accessed next door. The suites aren't worth the extra baht unless you really need a bit more space and a bigger TV.

Smile Society
HOTEL $$

(Map p78; ☑ 08 1343 1754, 08 1442 5800; www.smilesocietyhostel.com; 30/3-4 Soi 6, Th Silom; incl breakfast dm 450B, r 1400-1700B; ❋ @ ⚛; Ⓜ Si Lom exit 2, ⑤ Sala Daeng exit 1) Part boutique, part hostel, this four-storey shophouse combines small but comfortable, well-equipped rooms and dorms with spotless shared bathrooms. A central location, a communal area with TV and free computers, and helpful, English-speaking staff are additional perks.

Baan Saladaeng
HOTEL $$

(Map p78; ☑ 0 2636 3038; www.baansaladaeng.com; 69/2 Soi Sala Daeng 3; r incl breakfast 999-1799B; ❋ ⚛; Ⓜ Si Lom exit 2, ⑤ Sala Daeng exit 4) Of the handful of pint-sized boutique hotels along Th Sala Daeng, Baan Saladaeng is the most welcoming. The lobby's cheery primary colour theme carries on into the 11 rooms, with those on the upper floors being the largest and airiest.

Rose Hotel
HOTEL $$

(Map p78; ☑ 0 2266 8268; www.rosehotelbkk.com; 118 Th Surawong; incl breakfast r 1950-2250B, ste 3300-3800B; ❋ @ ⚛ ☎; Ⓜ Si Lom exit 2, ⑤ Sala Daeng exit 1) Don't let the unremarkable exterior fool you – the convenient location, modern rooms, pool, gym and sauna make this Vietnam War–era vet a pretty solid deal.

The only downside is the overpriced wi-fi (per day 300B).

Bangkok Christian Guest House
HOTEL $$

(Map p78; ☑ 0 2233 2206; www.bcgh.org; 123 Soi Sala Daeng 2; r incl breakfast 1100-2860B; ❋ ⚛; Ⓜ Si Lom exit 2, ⑤ Sala Daeng exit 2) This somewhat institutional-feeling guesthouse is a wise choice for families on a budget, as some rooms have as many as five beds and there's a 2nd-floor children's play area.

★ Siam Heritage
HOTEL $$$

(Map p78; ☑ 0 2353 6101; www.thesiamheritage.com; 115/1 Th Surawong; incl breakfast r 2900B, 4000-9300B; ❋ @ ⚛ ☎; Ⓜ Si Lom exit 2, ⑤ Sala Daeng exit 1) Tucked off busy Th Surawong, this classy boutique hotel oozes with homey Thai charm – probably because the owners also live in the same building. The 73 rooms are decked out in silk and dark woods with classy design touches and thoughtful amenities. There's an inviting rooftop garden/pool/spa, and it's all cared for by a team of charming and professional staff. Highly recommended.

W Bangkok
HOTEL $$$

(Map p78; ☑ 0 2344 4314; www.whotels.com/bangkok; 106 Th Sathon Neua (North); incl breakfast r 9000-10,350B, ste 11,250-154,350B; ❋ @ ⚛ ☎; ⑤ Chong Nonsi exit 1) A massive, stylish, big-chain newbie, the W has correspondingly young-feeling rooms with cheeky touches (think Thai boxing–themed decor) and hi-tech amenities. Ample glitter and glass, a lobby bar and a pool that literally glows are just some of the elements that make this a contender for Bangkok's clubbiest hotel.

Triple Two Silom
HOTEL $$$

(Map p78; ☑ 0 2627 2222; www.tripletwosilom.com; 222 Th Silom; incl breakfast r 3400-3800B, ste 7900B; ❋ @ ⚛; ⑤ Chong Nonsi exit 3) Rooms here resemble sleek modern offices – in a good way. But don't worry, with huge bathrooms and inviting-looking beds, you'll be inspired to relax, not work. Guests can use the rooftop garden, but have to go next door to the sister Narai Hotel for the swimming pool and fitness centre.

Dusit Thani
HOTEL $$$

(Map p78; ☑ 0 2200 9000; www.dusit.com; 946 Th Phra Ram IV; incl breakfast r 5580B, ste 12,330-14,830B; ❋ @ ⚛ ☎; Ⓜ Si Lom exit 2, ⑤ Sala Daeng exit 4) At one point the tallest building in the country, this venerable luxury hotel is a testament to how much things have changed in Bangkok. Renovations have most of the rooms looking more contemporary than the flagrantly 1970s exterior would suggest, but the hotel remains notable more for its convenient location and great views than for its hip factor.

Anantara Sathorn
HOTEL $$$

(Map p78; ☑ 0 2210 9000; www.bangkok-sathorn. anantara.com; 36 Th Narathiwat Ratchanakharin (Chong Nonsi); incl breakfast r 4800-5300B, ste 6800B; ✳ @ 🛜 🌊; 🚇 Chong Nonsi exit 1) If you're the type who prefers an apartment over a hotel room, consider this branch of the Anantara chain. The 'Deluxe' rooms are spacious, come equipped with a (relatively) functional kitchenette and dining room, and share inviting facilities, ranging from pool to tennis court.

🏞 Lumphini Park & Th Phra Ram IV

If you were hitting the Asian hippie trail back in the 1970s, you would have laid your love beads at a guesthouse in Soi Ngam Duphli, off Th Phra Ram IV, not too far from Lumphini Park. Despite the decades that have passed, it's still an OK area for budget accommodation, particularly along Soi Si Bamphen. There are also more upmarket options, and getting there has been made even easier by the MRT stop at Lumphini.

ETZzz Hostel
HOSTEL $

(Map p83; ☑ 0 2286 9424; www.etzhostel.com; 5/3 Soi Ngam Duphli; dm 250-350B, r 900B; ✳ @ 🛜; 🚇 Lumphini exit 1) The private rooms at this brand-new shophouse-based hostel are rather overpriced, but the tidy dorm, shiny facilities and convenient location feel just right.

Chaydon Sathorn
HOTEL $$

(Map p83; ☑ 0 2343 6333; www.chaydonsathorn. com; 31 Th Sathon Tai (South); r incl breakfast 2000-2600B; ✳ @ 🛜; 🚇 Lumphini exit 2) The former King's Hotel has been reborn as a no-frills midranger, right in the middle of the embassy district. The primary colours and bold lines of the design scheme make up for the lack of natural light in some rooms.

Hansaah Guesthouse
GUESTHOUSE $$

(Map p83; ☑ 08 5159 2811; www.hansaah.com; 44/7 Soi Si Bamphen; r incl breakfast 1300-1700B; ✳ 🛜; 🚇 Lumphini exit 1) The seven rooms here, located above a restaurant in a converted shophouse, feel homey and come equipped with convenient and functional amenities. A

good choice for those wishing for an anonymous, unhotel-like stay.

★ Metropolitan by COMO
HOTEL $$$

(Map p83; ☑ 0 2625 3333; www.comohotels.com/ metropolitanbangkok; 27 Th Sathon Tai (South); incl breakfast r 9220-11,220B, ste 12,200-78,720B; ✳ @ 🛜 🌊; 🚇 Lumphini exit 2) The exterior of Bangkok's former YMCA has changed relatively little, but a peek inside reveals one of the city's sleekest, sexiest hotels. A recent renovation has all 171 rooms looking better than ever in striking tones of black, white and yellow. It's worth noting that the 'City' rooms tend to feel a bit tight, while the two-storey penthouse suites feel like small homes.

Sukhothai Hotel
HOTEL $$$

(Map p83; ☑ 0 2344 8888; www.sukhothai. com; 13/3 Th Sathon Tai (South); incl breakfast r 11,000-12,000B, ste 14,000-79,500B; ✳ @ 🛜 🌊; 🚇 Lumphini exit 2) As the name suggests, the Sukhothai employs brick stupas, courtyards and antique sculptures to create a peaceful, almost templelike atmosphere. The recently remodelled rooms contrast this with hi-tech TVs, phones and yes, toilets. If you can afford the outlay, this is one of Bangkok's classiest luxury options.

Sofitel So
HOTEL $$$

(Map p83; ☑ 0 2624 0000; www.sofitel.com; 2 Th Sathon Neua (North); incl breakfast r 7415-11,417B, ste 15,654-31,450B; ✳ @ 🛜 🌊; 🚇 Lumphini exit 2) Taking inspiration from (and featuring amazing views of) adjacent Lumphini Park, this is one of a handful of large-yet-hip name-brand hotels to open in Bangkok in the last couple years. A four elements-inspired design theme sees no two rooms looking quite the same, but all feeling spacious and stylish, modern and young.

LUXX XL
HOTEL $$$

(Map p83; ☑ 0 2684 1111; www.staywithluxx.com; 82/8 Soi Lang Suan; incl breakfast r 2500-7000B, ste 13,000-22,000B; ✳ @ 🛜 🌊; 🚇 Ratchadamri exit 2) LUXX oozes with a minimalist hipness that wouldn't be out of place in London or New York. Floor-to-ceiling windows allow heaps of natural light, suites have an added kitchenette, and all rooms are decked out with appropriately stylish furnishings. There's another slightly cheaper (and smaller) branch (Map p78; ☑ 0 2635 8800; www. staywithluxx.com; 6/11 Th Decho; r incl breakfast 1799-2999B; ✳ @ 🛜; 🚇 Chong Nongsi exit 3) on Th Decho, off Th Silom.

Siam Square & Pratunam

For centrally located accommodation, there's really no better destination than the area surrounding Siam Sq. Home to the intersection of the two BTS lines, and only a brief-ish (depending on traffic) taxi ride to older parts of town, this is about as convenient as it gets in ever-expanding Bangkok.

For those on a budget who also need a central location, a low-key backpacker community exists along Soi Kasem San 1, across from the National Stadium.

Reno Hotel
HOTEL **$$**

(Map p84; 0 2215 0026; www.renohotel.co.th; 40 Soi Kasem San 1; r incl breakfast 1590-2390B; ❄@🛜☂; Ⓢ National Stadium exit 1) The rooms here are relatively large, if somewhat dark, and reflect the renovations evident in the lobby and exterior. But the cafe and pool of this Vietnam War–era hotel still cling to the past.

Wendy House
HOSTEL **$$**

(Map p84; 0 2214 1149; www.wendyguesthouse. com; 36/2 Soi Kasem San 1; r incl breakfast 1100-1450B; ❄@🛜; Ⓢ National Stadium exit 1) The rooms here are small and basic, but exceedingly clean and relatively well stocked (TV, fridge) for this price range.

Golden House
HOTEL **$$**

(Map p84; 0 2252 9535; www.goldenhouses.net; 1025/5-9 Th Ploenchit; r incl breakfast 1800-2000B; ❄🛜; Ⓢ Chit Lom exit 1) With parquet flooring and built-in wooden furniture, the 27 rooms here are more like modern Thai condos than hotel rooms. The beds are huge, but just like those of Thai condos, they have the potential to sag.

Siam@Siam
HOTEL **$$$**

(Map p84; 0 2217 3000; www.siamatsiam.com; 865 Th Phra Ram I; r incl breakfast 5000-8000B; ❄@🛜☂; Ⓢ National Stadium exit 1) A seemingly random mishmash of colours and industrial/recycled materials result in a style one could only describe as 'junkyard chic' – but in a good way, of course. The rooms, which largely continue the theme, are between the 14th and 24th floors, and offer terrific city views. There's a spa, a rooftop restaurant and a pool on the 11th floor.

Hansar
BOUTIQUE HOTEL **$$$**

(Map p84; 0 2209 1234; www.hansarbangkok. com; 3 Soi Mahadlekluang 2; incl breakfast r 5225B, ste 5700-24,000B; ❄@🛜☂; Ⓢ Ratchadamri exit 4) The new Hansar can claim that elusive intersection of style and value. All 94 rooms here are handsome and feature huge bathrooms and giant desks, but the smallest (and cheapest) studios are probably the best deal, as they have a kitchenette, washing machine, stand-alone tub, free wi-fi and balcony.

Okura Prestige
HOTEL **$$$**

(Map p84; 0 2687 9000; www.okurabangkok.com; 57 Th Witthayu (Wireless Rd); incl breakfast r 14,000-25,000B, ste 29,000-150,000B; Ⓟ❄@🛜☂; Ⓢ Phloen Chit exit 5) The Bangkok venture of this Japanese chain – to date the first branch outside of its homeland – is, unlike other recent, big-name openings in Bangkok, distinctly un-flashy. But we liked the minimalist, almost contemplative feel of the lobby and the 240 rooms, and the subtle but thoughtful, often distinctly Japanese touches.

Vie
HOTEL **$$$**

(Map p84; 0 2309 3939; www.viehotelbangkok.com; 117/39-40 Th Phayathai; incl breakfast r 3400B, ste 5400B; ❄@🛜☂; Ⓢ Ratchathewi exit 2) Vie combines a convenient location and a casual atmosphere in one attractive package. The service gets good reports, there's an emphasis on wining and dining, and if you're considering upgrading, the duplex suites are spacious and offer great city views.

Lit
HOTEL **$$$**

(Map p84; 0 2612 3456; www.litbangkok.com; 36/1 Soi Kasem San 1; incl breakfast r 7000-8000B, ste 9000-10,000B; ❄@🛜☂; Ⓢ National Stadium exit 1) This architecturally striking new hotel has a variety of modern-feeling rooms united by a light theme. Check out a few, as they differ significantly, and some features, such as a shower that can be seen from the living room, aren't necessarily for everybody.

Asia Hotel
HOTEL **$$$**

(Map p84; 0 2217 0808; www.asiahotel.co.th; 296 Th Phayathai; incl breakfast r 3700-4800B, ste 8000-10,000B; ❄@🛜☂; 🚇Tha Ratchathewi, Ⓢ Ratchathewi exit 1) A renovation has left this tour-group staple looking slightly more modern than the 1970s-era lobby would suggest. Connected to the BTS, it's a convenient place to stay, although the 700B per day wi-fi fee takes the value factor down a couple of notches.

Sukhumvit

This seemingly endless urban thoroughfare is Bangkok's unofficial International Zone and also boasts much of the city's accommodation.

There's a bit of everything here, from the odd backpacker hostel to sex tourist hovels and five-star luxury. The former two are largely located between Soi 1 and Soi 4, while the latter doesn't begin to appear until you reach Soi 12 or so.

In general, because visitors with larger budgets stay in Sukhumvit, tourist services are more expensive here than in Banglamphu. The trade-off is access to food from virtually every corner of the globe, heaps of nightlife options and easy access to both the BTS and MRT.

Suk 11 HOTEL $
(Map p90; ✆ 0 2253 5927; www.suk11.com; 1/33 Soi 11, Th Sukhumvit; r incl breakfast 535-1712B; ✳ @ 🖱; ⑤ Nana exit 3) Extremely well run and equally popular, this rustic guesthouse is an oasis of woods and greenery in the urban jungle that is Th Sukhumvit. The basic rooms are clean and comfy, if a bit dark, and the cheapest ones share bathrooms. Although the building holds nearly 70 rooms, you'll still need to book at least two weeks ahead.

Bed Bangkok HOSTEL $
(Map p90; ✆ 0 2655 7604; www.bedbangkok.com; 11/20 Soi 1, Th Sukhumvit; dm 390B, r 800-1200B;

✳ @ 🖱; ⑤ Phloen Chit exit 3) This hostel manages to maintain a cosy feel despite the industrial-design theme. The friendly service and convenient location just about make up for the rather hard dorm beds.

Atlanta HOTEL $
(Map p90; ✆ 0 2252 1650; www.theatlantahotel-bangkok.com; 78 Soi 2, Th Sukhumvit; incl breakfast r 650-1000B; ste 950-1850B; ✳ @ 🖱 ✳; ⑤ Nana exit 2) Defiantly antiquated and equal parts frumpy and grumpy, this crumbling gem has changed very little since its construction in 1952. The opulent lobby stands in stark contrast to the simple rooms, and the frantic anti-sex tourist tone can be rather disturbing, but the inviting pool (allegedly the country's first hotel pool) and delightful restaurant (for guests only) are enough incentive to get past these.

Napa Place HOTEL $$
(Map p90; ✆ 0 2661 5525; www.napaplace.com; 11/3 Soi Napha Sap 2; r incl breakfast 2589-4826B; ✳ @ 🖱; ⑤ Thong Lo exit 2) Hidden in the confines of a typical Bangkok urban compound is what must be the city's homiest accommodation. The 12 expansive rooms have been decorated with dark woods from the fam-

---

LATE-NIGHT TOUCHDOWN

A lot of nail-biting anxiety is expended on international flights arriving in Bangkok around midnight. Will there be taxis into town? Will there be available rooms? Will my family ever hear from me again? Soothe those nagging voices with the knowledge that most international flights arrive late and that Bangkok is an accommodating place. Yes, there are taxis and even an express train service that runs until midnight.

If you haven't already made hotel reservations, a good area to look for a bed is lower Sukhumvit – it's right off the expressway and hotels around Soi Nana such as Federal Hotel (p109) are used to lots of late-night traffic and won't break your bank. Alternatively, you could always go to Th Khao San, which stays up late, is full of hotels and guesthouses, and sees a near-continuous supply of 'fresh-off-the-birds' just like you.

If, for some reason, you can't stray too far from the airport, these places provide a more than adequate roof.

Suvarnabhumi International Airport

➡ **Grand Inn Come Hotel** (✆ 0 2738 8189; www.grandinncome-hotel.com; 99 Moo 6, Th Kingkaew; incl breakfast r 1250-2200B; ste 3600-3800B; ✳ @ 🖱) Solid midranger 10km west of the airport, with airport shuttle and self-professed 'lively' karaoke bar.

➡ **Novotel Suvarnabhumi Airport Hotel** (✆ 0 2131 1111; www.novotelairportbkk.com; incl breakfast r 4000-6000B; ste 7000B; ✳ @ 🖱) With 600-plus luxurious rooms in the airport compound.

Don Muang Airport

➡ **Amari Airport Hotel** (✆ 0 2566 1020; www.amari.com/donmuang; 333 Th Choet Wutthakat; incl breakfast r 1450-1850B; ste 2850B; ✳ @ 🖱 ✳) Directly opposite Don Muang Airport.

ily's former business and light brown cloths made by Thai weavers, and the cosy communal areas couldn't be much different from the suburban living room you grew up in.

Sacha's Hotel Uno
HOTEL $$

(Map p90; ✆0 2651 2180; www.sachas.hotel-uno.com; 28/19 Soi 19, Th Sukhumvit; r incl breakfast 2472-3531B; ❄@🌐; Ⓜ Sukhumvit exit 1, Ⓢ Asok exit 1) Soi 19 and around are home to a handful of good-value, stylish hotels that barely edge into the midrange category, including Uno, surprisingly sophisticated for this price range. Its 56 rooms are comfortable and equally well equipped for work or play.

Silq
HOTEL $$

(Map p90; ✆0 2252 6800; www.silqbkk.com; 54 Soi 19, Th Sukhumvit; r incl breakfast 2800-3700B; ❄@🌐; Ⓜ Sukhumvit exit 1, Ⓢ Asok exit 1) Many of the 46 rooms at Silq feel larger than they are thanks to expansive windows.

Fusion Suites
HOTEL $$

(Map p90; ✆0 2665 2644; www.fusionbangkok.com; 143/61-62 Soi 21 (Asoke), Th Sukhumvit; r incl breakfast 2600-5200B; ❄@🌐; Ⓜ Sukhumvit exit 1, Ⓢ Asok exit 1) A disproportionately funky hotel for this price range; unconventional furnishings provide the rooms with heaps of style, although the cheapest can feel a bit dark.

Baan Sukhumvit
HOTEL $$

(Map p90; ✆0 2258 5622; www.baansukhumvit.com; 392/38-39 Soi 20, Th Sukhumvit; r incl breakfast 1440-1540B; ❄@🌐; Ⓢ Nana exit 3) One of a handful of midrangers located on this small side street off Soi 20, Baan Sukhumvit's 12 rooms exude a homey, cosy atmosphere. A newer branch is around the corner on Soi 18.

Federal Hotel
HOTEL $$

(Map p90; ✆0 2253 0175; www.federalbangkok.com; 27 Soi 11, Th Sukhumvit; r incl breakfast 1300-1600B; ❄@🌐🏊; Ⓢ Nana exit 4) You wouldn't know it from the exterior, but after more than 50 years 'Club Fed' finally decided to get a makeover. The upstairs rooms are comfortable and almost contemporary, but elements of the ground-floor rooms still scream 1967. The real draws are the convenient location, the frangipani-lined pool and the time-warped US-style coffeeshop.

Stable Lodge
HOTEL $$

(Map p90; ✆0 2653 0017; www.stablelodge.com; 39 Soi 8, Th Sukhumvit; r 1600-1800B; ❄@🌐🏊; Ⓢ Nana exit 4) A renovation has given a bit of life to the somewhat aged rooms here, and the spacious balconies offer great city views (though we were slightly disappointed the faux-Tudor theme of the downstairs restaurant doesn't carry on into the rooms).

Preme
HOSTEL $$

(Map p90; ✆0 2259 6908; www.premehostel.com; 2 Soi 25, Th Sukhumvit; incl breakfast dm 500-600B, r 1200-1800B; ❄@🌐; Ⓜ Sukhumvit exit 2, Ⓢ Asok exit 6) This tidy hostel packs 68 plain but more-than-adequate budget rooms, as well as some of the better dorms around with semi-private bathrooms.

★ AriyasomVilla
HOTEL $$$

(Map p90; ✆0 2254 8880; www.ariyasom.com; 65 Soi 1, Th Sukhumvit; r incl breakfast 6300-13,750B; ❄@🌐🏊; Ⓢ Phloen Chit exit 3) Located at the end of Soi 1 behind a virtual wall of fragipani, this renovated 1940s-era villa is one of Bangkok's worst-kept accommodation secrets. If you can score a reservation, you'll be privy to one of 24 spacious rooms, meticulously outfitted with thoughtful Thai design touches and beautiful antique furniture. There's a spa and an inviting tropical pool, and breakfast is vegetarian and served in the villa's stunning glass-encased dining room.

Eugenia
HOTEL $$$

(Map p90; ✆0 2259 9011; www.theeugenia.com; 267 Soi 31, Th Sukhumvit; r incl breakfast 4800-7100B; ❄@🌐🏊; Ⓢ Phrom Phong exit 6 & taxi) A stay in this hotel, decked out in antique furniture and an abundance of animal skins, is like travelling to Burma circa 1936. Don't fear though; you won't have to ask the 'boy' to draw you a bath – modern amenities such as flat-screen TVs and free domestic and international calls are also provided. Ask about the vintage-car airport transfers.

Sheraton Grande Sukhumvit
HOTEL $$$

(Map p90; ✆0 2649 8888; www.luxurycollection.com/bangkok; 250 Th Sukhumvit; incl breakfast r 10,000-12,500B, ste 18,000-55,500B; ❄@🌐🏊; Ⓜ Sukhumvit exit 3, Ⓢ Asok exit 2) This conveniently located, business-oriented hotel offers some of the most spacious rooms in town and fills them with a generous array of amenities. By the time you read this, an impending renovation may have already made what was already a very good hotel an excellent hotel.

Ma Du Zi
HOTEL $$$

(Map p90; ✆0 2615 6400; www.maduzihotel.com; cnr Th Ratchadaphisek & Soi 16, Th Sukhumvit; incl breakfast r 7500-9400B, ste 10,000-14,900B; ❄@🌐; Ⓜ Sukhumvit exit 3, Ⓢ Asok exit 6) The name is Thai for 'come take a look', somewhat of a misnomer for this reservations-only, no walk-ins hotel. If you've gained access, behind the gate you'll find a modern, attractive mid-sized boutique steeped in dark, chic tones and designs. We particularly liked the immense bathrooms, equipped with a walk-in tub and minimalist shower.

Aloft
HOTEL $$$

(Map p90; ☑ 0 2207 7000; www.alofthotels.com/bangkoksukhumvit11; 35 Soi 11, Th Sukhumvit; incl breakfast r 4700-5750B; ste 7700-15,700B; ✳@🛜⌖; Ⓢ Nana exit 5) Fun seems to be the operative term for this new, young-feeling hotel – even down to its strategic location on Soi 11, steps from some of the city's best clubs and bars. The lobby sets the theme with bold colours, a fusball table and lots of TVs, while free wi-fi, a fun bar and generous online specials prove that the sentiment runs more than just skin deep.

Seven
HOTEL $$$

(Map p90; ☑ 0 2662 0951; www.sleepatseven.com; 3/15 Soi 31, Th Sukhumvit; r incl breakfast 3090-4790B; ✳🛜; Ⓢ Phrom Phong exit 5) This tiny hotel somehow manages to be chic and homey, stylish and comfortable, Thai and international all at the same time. Each of the five rooms is decked out in a different colour that corresponds to Thai astrology, and thoughtful amenities and friendly service abound.

S31
HOTEL $$$

(Map p90; ☑ 0 2260 1111; www.s31hotel.com; 545 Soi 31, Th Sukhumvit; incl breakfast r 4000B; ste 6000-7000B; ✳🛜⌖; Ⓢ Phrom Phong exit 5) The bold patterns and graphics of its interior and exterior make the S31 a fun, young-feeling choice. Thoughtful touches such as kitchenettes with large fridge, superhuge beds and free courses (cooking, Thai boxing and yoga) prove that the style also has substance. Branches can also be found on Soi 15 and Soi 33.

Dream
HOTEL $$$

(Map p90; ☑ 0 2254 8500; www.dreambkk.com; 10 Soi 15, Th Sukhumvit; incl breakfast r 2500-3800B; ste 4000-13,00B; ✳@🛜⌖; Ⓜ Sukhumvit exit 3, Ⓢ Asok exit 5) If your idea of interior design involves stuffed tigers, copious mirrors and slick leather, you'll feel at home here. The standard rooms are a tight fit, but like all, include ample and quirky amenities such as the Dream signature blue light to aid in sleeping.

Thewet & Dusit

The area stretching from riverside Thewet inland to Dusit is home to a handful of low-key budget and midrange places.

Taewez Guesthouse
HOTEL $

(Map p95; ☑ 0 2280 8856; www.taewez.com; 23/12 Th Si Ayuthaya; r 290-690B; ✳@🛜; 🚢 Tha Thewet) The cheapest rooms here are plain and share bathrooms, but are good value and looked after by friendly staff. Popular with French travellers.

Hi Baan Thewet
HOTEL $

(Map p95; ☑ 0 2281 0361; baanthewet@tyha.org; 25/2 Th Phitsanulok; r incl breakfast 700-1450B; ✳@🛜; 🚢 Tha Thewet) The rather institutional lobby conceals 14 pleasant, vaguely old-school-themed rooms. Some are on the small side and could use windows, but inviting communal areas and the leafy, quiet, off-the-beaten-track location make up for this.

★ Phra-Nakorn Norn-Len
HOTEL $$

(Map p95; ☑ 0 2628 8188; www.phranakorn-nornlen.com; 46 Soi Thewet 1; r incl breakfast 1800-3600B; ✳@🛜; 🚢 Tha Thewet) Set in an expansive garden compound, this bright and cheery hotel is an atmospheric if not necessarily stupendous-value place to stay. The 31 rooms are attractively furnished with old-timey antiques and wall paintings, and there's massage and endless opportunities for peaceful relaxing.

SSIP Boutique
HOTEL $$$

(Map p95; ☑ 0 2282 6489; www.ssiphotelthailand.com; 42 Th Phitsanulok; incl breakfast r 3500B; ste 4500B; ✳@🛜; 🚢 Tha Thewet) Handsome tiles, heavy wood furniture, antique furnishings: the 20 rooms here have been meticulously recreated to emulate the Bangkok of yesteryear. But modern amenities (TV, fridge, safe) and thoughtful staff ensure a thoroughly contemporary and comfortable stay.

Greater Bangkok

Mystic Place
HOTEL $$

(Map p112; ☑ 0 2270 3344; www.mysticplacebkk.com; 224/5-9 Th Pradiphat; r incl breakfast 1800-2200B; ✳@🛜; Ⓢ Saphan Khwai exit 2 & taxi) This hotel unites 36 rooms, each of which is individually and playfully designed. One room we checked out combined a chair upholstered with stuffed animals and walls covered with graffiti, while another was swathed in eye-contorting op art. Heaps of fun and perpetually popular; book ahead.

★ **Bangkok Tree House** HOTEL **$$$**
(☑08 1453 1100; www.bangkoktreehouse.com; near Wat Bang Nam Pheung Nork; bungalow incl breakfast 6000-10,000B; ❄@🛜❄; Ⓢ Bang Na

exit 2 & taxi) The 12 multilevel bungalows here are stylishly sculpted from sustainable and recycled materials, resulting in a vibe that calls to mind a sophisticated, eco-friendly

A TASTE OF BANGKOK

In Bangkok, the geography of the central plains, influences of the country's predominate minorities and the wealth of the royal palace have all served to shape the local cuisine.

The people of central Thailand are particularly fond of sweet/savoury flavours, and many dishes include freshwater fish, pork, coconut milk and palm sugar – common ingredients in the central Thai plains. Because of their proximity to the Gulf of Thailand, Bangkok eateries also serve a wide variety of seafood. Muslim immigrants introduced a variety of dried spices, and Chinese labourers and vendors introduced a huge variety of noodle and wok-fried dishes to central Thailand as many as 200 years ago. And culinary spillover from the royal court meant that Bangkok's food was particularly refined and sophisticated, often employing unusual and exotic ingredients. It is this version of Thai food, often known as royal Thai cuisine, that has come to define Thai food outside of the country's borders.

You can't say you've tried Bangkok-style Thai food unless you've tasted at least a couple of the following:

➡ *Đôm yam* – Lemon grass, galangal, kaffir lime leaf and lime juice give this soup its characteristic tang; fresh chillies or an oily chilli paste provide it with its legendary sting. Available just about everywhere, but it's hard to beat the version at Krua Apsorn (p113).

➡ *Gŏo•ay đĕe•o reu•a* – Known as boat noodles because they were previously served from small boats along the canals of central Thailand, these intense pork- or beef-based bowls are among the most full-flavoured of Thai noodle dishes. Try a bowl at **Bharani** (Sansab Boat Noodle; Map p90; 96/14 Soi 23, Th Sukhumvit; mains 50-200B; ☺11am-10pm; ❄; Ⓜ Sukhumvit exit 2, Ⓢ Asok exit 3).

➡ *Gŏo•ay đĕe•o kôo•a gài* – Wide rice noodles fried with little more than egg, chicken, preserved squid and garlic oil is a humble but delicious Thai-Chinese dish sold from numerous stalls in Bangkok's Chinatown.

➡ *Kôw mòk* – Biryani, a dish found across the Muslim world, also has a foothold in Bangkok. Here the dish is typically made with chicken and is served with a sweet-and-sour dipping sauce and a bowl of chicken broth. We love the old-school version served at decades-old **Muslim Restaurant** (Map p76; 1354-6 Th Charoen Krung; mains 40-140B; ☺6.30am-5.30pm; 🚤Tha Oriental, Ⓢ Saphan Taksin exit 1).

➡ *Máh hór* – With origins in the palace, this is a Thai appetiser that pairs chunks of mandarin orange or pineapple and a sweet/savoury/peppery topping made from pork, chicken, peanuts, sugar, peppercorns and coriander root. Available as part of the set dinner at nahm (p116).

➡ *Mèe gròrp* – Crispy noodles made the traditional way, with a sweet/sour flavour (a former palace recipe), are a dying breed. Longstanding Banglamphu restaurant **Chote Chitr** (Map p62; 146 Th Phraeng Phuthon; mains 30-200B; ☺11am-10pm; 🚤klorng boat to Tha Phan Fah) serves an excellent version of the dish.

➡ *Pàt tai* – Thin rice noodles stir-fried with dried and/or fresh shrimp, bean sprouts, tofu, egg and seasonings, traditionally served with lime halves and a few stalks of Chinese chives and a sliced banana flower. **Thip Samai** (Map p62; 313 Th Mahachai; mains 25-120B; ☺5.30pm-1.30am; 🚤klorng boat to Tha Phan Fah) is probably Bangkok's most lauded destination for what is arguably Thailand's most famous dish.

➡ *Yen đah foh* – Combining a slightly sweet crimson-coloured broth with a variety of meat balls, cubes of blood and crispy greens, *yen đah foh* is probably both the most intimidating and popular noodle dish in Bangkok. Available at Soi 38 Night Market (p118) as well as at many street stalls.

North Bangkok

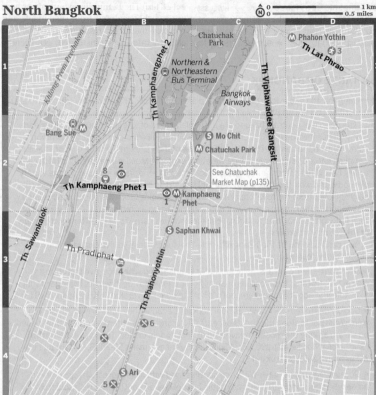

North Bangkok

summer camp. Thoughtful amenities include en suite computers equipped with movies, free mobile phone and bicycle use, and free ice cream.

To get to Bangkok Tree House, take the BTS to Bang Na and jump in a taxi for the short ride to the pier at Wat Bang Na Nork. From there, take the river-crossing ferry (4B, from 5am to 9.30pm), and continue by motorcycle taxi (10B) or on foot (call in advance for directions).

🍴 Eating

Probably the safest of Bangkok's infamous carnal pleasures, food is serious business in this city. Attracting hungry visitors from across the globe, Bangkok's eateries also draw natives from disparate ends of the city, happy to brave traffic or floods for a bowl of noodles or a plate of rice.

The selection is enormous and diverse, with eating places in Bangkok ranging from wheeled carts that set up shop on a daily basis to chic dining rooms in five-star hotels. In our experience the tastiest eats are generally found somewhere in between, at decades old, family-run shophouse restaurants serving a limited repertoire of dishes.

The influences are also vast, and you'll find everything from Chinese-Thai to Muslim-Thai, not to mention most regional domestic cuisines. And if at some point you do tire of *gŏo·ay dĕe·o* (rice noodles) and curries, Bangkok has an ever-expanding selection of high-quality international restaurants, encompassing everything from French cuisine to hole-in-the-wall Japanese ramen houses.

Ko Ratanakosin

Bangkok's royal district has an abundance of sights but a dearth of restaurants – a pity considering the potential riverfront views.

Pa Aew
THAI $
(Map p62; Th Maha Rat, no roman-script sign; mains 20–60B; ☺10am-5pm; ☒; ☒Tha Tien) Yes, it's a bare-bones, open-air curry stall, but if we're talking taste, Pa Aew is our favourite place to eat in this corner of town. Pa Aew is in front of the Krung Thai Bank near Soi Pratu Nokyung.

Coconut Palm
THAI $
(Map p62; www.coconutpalmrestaurant.com; 392/1-2 Th Maha Rat; mains 40–100B; ☺11am-6pm; ☒; ☒Tha Tien) Coconut Palm serves a generous spread of Thai dishes, but most locals come for the Sukhothai-style noodles – thin rice noodles served with pork, ground peanuts and dried chilli.

Khunkung
THAI $$
(Map p62; Navy Club; 77 Th Maha Rat; mains 75–720B; ☺11am-2pm & 6-10pm Mon-Fri, 11am-10pm Sat & Sun; ☒; ☒Tha Chang) The restaurant of the Royal Navy Association has one of the few coveted riverfront locations along this stretch of Mae Nam Chao Phraya. Locals come for the combination of views and cheap and tasty seafood-based eats. The entrance to the restaurant is near the ATM machines at Tha Chang.

Banglamphu

Despite its proximity to the faux *pàt tai* and tame *dôm yam* of Th Khao San, Banglamphu is one of the city's most famous eating areas. Decades-old restaurants and legendary hawkers line the streets in this leafy corner of Old Bangkok, and you could easily spend an entire day grazing the southern end of Th Tanao alone.

Although you'd be wisest to get your domestic nosh away from the main drag, the foreign influence on Th Khao San has led to a few import standouts.

Nang Loeng Market
THAI $
(Off map p62; btwn Soi 8-10, Th Nakhon Sawan; mains 30–80B; ☺10am-2pm Mon-Sat; ☒klorng boat to Tha Phan Fah, ☒Phaya Thai exit 3 & taxi) Dating back to 1899, this atmospheric market, east of Banglamphu, is primarily associated with Thai sweets. Come lunchtime, it's also an excellent place to fill up on savouries.

Likhit Kai Yang
NORTHEASTERN THAI $
(Map p62; off Th Ratchadamnoen Nok; mains 30–150B; ☺10am-10pm; ☒; ☒klorng boat to Tha Phan Fah) Located just behind Ratchadamoen Stadium (avoid the rather grotty branch directly next door to the stadium), this decades-old restaurant is where locals come for a quick northeastern Thai-style meal before a Thai boxing match. The friendly English-speaking owner will coach you through the ordering process, but don't miss the herbal grilled chicken.

★Krua Apsorn
THAI $$
(Map p62; www.kruaapsorn.com; Th Din So; mains 65–350B; ☺10.30am-8pm Mon-Sat; ☒; ☒klorng boat to Tha Phan Fah) This homey dining room has served members of the Thai royal family and, back in 2006, was recognised as Bangkok's Best Restaurant by the *Bangkok Post*. Must-eat dishes include mussels fried with fresh herbs, the decadent crab fried in yellow chilli oil and the *tortilla Española*-like crab omelette.

Shoshana
ISRAELI $$
(Map p62; 88 Th Chakraphong; mains 70–240B; ☺10am-midnight; ☒; ☒Tha Phra Athit (Banglamphu)) Although prices have gone up slightly since it opened in 1982, Shoshana still puts together a cheap and tasty Israeli meal. Feel safe ordering anything deep-fried – they do an excellent job of it – and don't miss the deliciously garlicky eggplant dip.

Poj Spa Kar
THAI $$
(Map p62; 443 Th Tanao; mains 65–200B; ☺12.30-8.30pm; ☒; ☒klorng boat to Tha Phan Fah) Pronounced *pôht sà·pah kahn,* this is allegedly the oldest restaurant in Bangkok, and continues to maintain recipes handed down from a former palace cook. Be sure to order the simple but tasty lemongrass omelette or the deliciously sour/sweet *gaang sôm,* a traditional central Thai soup.

Hemlock
THAI $$

(Map p62; 56 Th Phra Athit; mains 60-220B; ⏰4pm-midnight Mon-Sat; ✻✐; 🚤Tha Phra Athit (Banglamphu)) This white-tablecloth local is a 'safe' intro to Thai food. The vast menu has the usual suspects, but also includes dishes you'd be hard-pressed to find elsewhere, plus a strong vegetarian section.

★ Jay Fai
THAI $$$

(Map p62; 327 Th Mahachai; mains from 400B; ⏰3pm-2am Tue-Sun; 🚤klorng boat to Tha Phan Fah) Despite the bare-bones dining room, Jay Fai is known far and wide for serving Bangkok's priciest – and arguably tastiest – pàt kêe mow (drunkard's noodles). The price is justified by the copious fresh seafood, as well as Jay Fai's distinct frying style that results in a virtually oil-free finished product.

Thonburi

Mangkud Cafe
THAI $$

(Map p62; Club Arts; www.clubartsgallery.com; Soi Wat Rakhang; mains 100-350B; ⏰11am-10pm Tue-Thu, to 11pm Fri-Sun; ✐; 🚤cross-river ferry from Tha Chang) Mangkud is probably the most sophisticated place to eat on this side of Mae Nam Chao Phraya. The river views are unparalleled, and the herb-heavy Thai dishes are tasty; try the 'watermelon with dried fish', a traditional sweet-savoury snack. Look for the sign that says Club Arts.

Chinatown & Phahurat

When you mention Chinatown, most Bangkokians immediately dream of street food. The area is also famous as ground zero for the yearly Vegetarian Festival.

On the western side of the neighbourhood is Phahurat, Bangkok's Little India, filled with small Indian and Nepali restaurants tucked into the tiny soi off Th Chakraphet.

Old Siam Plaza
THAI SWEETS $

(Map p72; cnr Th Phahurat & Th Triphet; mains 30-90B; ⏰6am-7pm; ✻; 🚤Tha Saphan Phut (Memorial Bridge)) Sugar junkies, be sure to include this stop on your Bangkok eating itinerary. The ground floor of this shopping centre is a candyland of traditional Thai sweets and snacks, most made right before your eyes.

Samsara
JAPANESE, THAI $$

(Map p72; 1612 Th Songwat; mains 110-320B; ⏰4pm-midnight Tue-Thu, to 1am Fri-Sun; ✐; 🚤Tha Ratchawong, Ⓜ Hua Lamphong exit 1 & taxi) Combining Thai-Japanese dishes, Belgian beers and a retro/artsy atmosphere, Samsara is easily Chinatown's most eclectic place to eat. It's also very tasty, and the generous riverside breezes and views round out the package. The restaurant is at the end of tiny Soi Khang Wat Pathum Khongkha, just west of the temple of the same name.

VEGGING OUT IN BANGKOK

Vegetarianism is a growing trend among urban Thais, but meat-free restaurants are still generally few and far between.

Banglamphu has the greatest concentration of vegetarian-friendly restaurants, thanks to the preponderance of nonmeat-eating fa·ràng (foreigners). In this part of town, there's longstanding **Arawy Vegetarian Food** (Map p62; 152 Th Din So; mains 20-40B; ⏰7am-8.30pm; ✐; 🚤Tha Phan Fah) and **May Kaidee's** (Map p62; www.maykaidee.com; 33 Th Samsen; mains 50-100B; ⏰9am-10pm; ✻✐; 🚤Tha Phra Athit (Banglamphu)), the latter with a vegetarian cookery school, and restaurants such as Shoshana (p113) and Hemlock (see review above) have lots of meat-free options.

Elsewhere in Bangkok, **Anotai** (Map p90; 976/17 Soi Rama 9 Hospital, Th Phra Ram IX; mains 150-300B; ⏰10am-9pm Thu-Tue; ✻; Ⓜ Phra Ram 9 exit 3 & taxi), **Baan Suan Pai** (Map p112; Banana Family Park, Th Phahonyothin; mains 15-30B; ⏰7am-3pm; ✐; Ⓢ Ari exit 1), **Bonita Cafe & Social Club** (Map p78; 56/3 Th Pan; mains 160-250B; ⏰11am-10pm Wed-Mon; ✻📶✐; Ⓢ Surasak exit 3), Chennai Kitchen (p115) and Saras (p119) are all vegetarian-specific restaurants. As well, Issaya Siamese Club (p116), **Koko** (Map p84; 262/2 Soi 3, Siam Sq; mains 70-220B; ⏰11am-9pm; ✻✐; Ⓢ Siam exit 2), Opposite Mess Hall (p120) and stall C8 at the MBK Food Island (p120) all offer a generous selection of meat-free menu items.

During the Vegetarian Festival in October, the whole city goes mad for tofu. Stalls and restaurants indicate their nonmeat menu with yellow banners; Chinatown has the highest concentration of stalls.

Thanon Phadungdao
Seafood Stalls
THAI $$

(Map p72; cnr Th Phadungdao & Th Yaowarat; mains 100-600B; ⊙4pm-midnight Tue-Sun; ⛴Tha Ratchawong, ⓂHua Lamphong exit 1 & taxi) After sunset, these two opposing open-air restaurants – each of which claims to be the original – become a culinary train wreck of outdoor barbecues, screaming staff, iced seafood trays and messy sidewalk seating. True, the vast majority of diners are foreign tourists, but this has little impact on the cheerful setting, the fun experience and the cheap bill.

Royal India
INDIAN $$

(Map p72; 392/1 Th Chakraphet; mains 70-195B; ⊙10am-10pm; ⧆⚲; ⛴Tha Saphan Phut (Memorial Bridge)) Yes, we're aware that this hole in the wall has been in every edition of our guide since the beginning, but after all these years it's still the most reliable place to eat in Bangkok's Little India. Try any of the delicious breads or rich curries, and don't forget to finish with a homemade Punjabi sweet.

🍴 Silom & Sathon

Th Silom has a bit of everything, from old-school Thai to some of the city's best upscale international dining.

Chennai Kitchen
INDIAN $

(Map p78; 10 Th Pan; mains 70-150B; ⊙10am-3pm & 6-9pm; ⧆⚲; ⓈSurasak exit 3) The arm-length *dosai* (a crispy southern Indian bread) here is always a wise choice, but if you're feeling indecisive, go for the vegetarian *thali* set that seems to incorporate just about everything in the kitchen.

Kalapapruek
THAI $

(Map p78; 27 Th Pramuan; mains 80-150B; ⊙8am-6pm Mon-Sat, to 3pm Sun; ⧆; ⓈSurasak exit 3) This venerable Thai eatery has numerous branches and mall spin-offs around town, but we always go back to this, the free-standing original branch. The diverse menu spans regional Thai specialities from just about every region, daily specials and, occasionally, seasonal treats as well.

Somtam Convent
NORTHEASTERN THAI $

('Hai'; Map p78; 2/4-5 Th Convent; mains 30-100B; ⊙11am-9pm Mon-Fri, to 5pm Sat; ⧆; ⓂSi Lom exit 2, ⓈSala Daeng exit 2) An unintimidating introduction to the wonders of *làhp* (a minced meat 'salad'), *sôm·đam* (spicy green papaya salad) and other Isan delights can be had at this noisy shophouse restaurant.

ℹ️ DAY OFF

Fans of street food be forewarned that all of Bangkok's stalls close on Monday for compulsory street cleaning (the results of which are never entirely evident come Tuesday morning). If you happen to be in the city on this day, take advantage of the lull to visit one of the city's upscale hotel restaurants, which virtually never close.

FooDie
THAI $$

(Map p78; Soi Phiphat 2; mains 80-150B; ⊙11am-11pm; ⧆; ⓈChong Nonsi exit 2) This airy, cafeteria-like restaurant boasts a menu of hard-to-find central- and southern-style Thai dishes. Highlights include the *yam sôm oh* (a spicy/sour/sweet salad of pomelo) and the spicy *prík kĭng ƀlah dòok foo* (catfish fried in a curry paste until crispy).

Sushi Tsukiji
JAPANESE $$

(Map p78; Th Thaniya; sushi per item 60-700B; ⊙10am-11pm; ⧆; ⓂSi Lom exit 2, ⓈSala Daeng exit 1) Th Thaniya is home to tens of host-ess bars catering to visiting Japanese, so the quality of the street's Japanese restaurants is high. Our pick is Tsukiji, named after Tokyo's famous seafood market. Specialising in raw fish, dinner here will leave a significant dent in the wallet, so come for lunch when Tsukiji does sushi sets for as little as 198B.

⭐ Eat Me
INTERNATIONAL $$$

(Map p78; ✆0 2238 0931; www.eatmerestaurant.com; Soi Phiphat 2; mains 340-1200B; ⊙3pm-1am; ⧆⚲; ⓂSi Lom exit 2, ⓈSala Daeng exit 2) The dishes at this longstanding restaurant, with descriptions like 'fig & blue cheese ravioli w/ walnuts, rosemary and brown butter', or 'beef cheek tagine w/ saffron and dates', may sound all over the map or perhaps even somewhat pretentious, but they're actually just plain tasty. A buzzy, casual-yet-sophisticated atmosphere, good cocktails and a handsome wine list, and some of Bangkok's best desserts, are additional reasons why this is one of our favourite places to dine.

D'Sens
FRENCH $$$

(Map p78; ✆0 2200 9000; www.dusit.com; 22nd fl, Dusit Thani Hotel, 946 Th Phra Ram IV; set lunch from 950B, set dinner from 3100B; ⊙11.30am-2pm & 6-10pm Mon-Fri, 6-10pm Sat; ⧆; ⓂSi Lom exit 3, ⓈSala Daeng exit 4) Perched like an air traffic control tower atop the Dusit Thani Hotel,

D'Sens doesn't only offer the best restaurant views in Bangkok, it's also one of the city's best fine dining experiences. The progressive menu draws its influences from the traditions of the south of France, emphasising high-quality imported ingredients.

Somboon Seafood
THAI $$$

(Map p78; ☑ 0 2233 3104; www.somboonseafood. com; cnr Th Surawong & Th Narathiwat Ratchanakharin (Chong Nonsi); mains 120-900B; ⊙ 4-11.30pm; ✿; Ⓢ Chong Nonsi exit 3) Holy seafood factory: ascending the many staircases to a free table might make you nervous about the quality of so much quantity. But Somboon's legendary 'fried curry crab' will make you messy and full. Dainty eaters can opt for the slightly more surgical pursuit of devouring a whole fried fish.

⋇ Lumphini Park & Th Phra Ram IV

Kai Thort Jay Kee
THAI $$

(Map p83; Soi Polo Fried Chicken; 137/1-3 Soi Sanam Khlii (Soi Polo); mains 40-280B; ⊙ 11am-9pm; ✿; Ⓜ Lumphini exit 3) Although the *sôm-đam*, sticky rice and *lâhp* give the impression of a northeastern Thai–style eatery, the restaurant's namesake deep-fried chicken is more southern in origin. Regardless, smothered in a thick layer of crispy deep-fried garlic, it is none other than a truly Bangkok experience.

Issaya Siamese Club
THAI $$

(Map p83; www.issaya.com; 4 Soi Sri Aksorn; mains 150-580B; ⊙ 11.30am-2.30pm & 6-10.30pm; ✿ ✐; Ⓜ Khlong Toei exit 1 & taxi) Housed in a charming 1920s-era villa, Issaya is Thai celebrity chef Ian Kittichai's first effort at a domestic outpost serving the food of his homeland. Dishes alternate between somewhat saucy, meaty items and lighter dishes using produce from the restaurant's organic garden (including lots of vegie options). The restaurant can be a bit tricky to find, and is best approached in a taxi via Soi Ngam Duphli.

Ngwanlee Lung Suan
CHINESE, THAI $$

(Map p83; cnr Soi Lang Suan & Th Sarasin; mains 50-900B; ⊙ 7am-3am; Ⓢ Ratchadamri exit 2) This cavernous food hall is centrally located and open late, making it a perfect postclubbing destination. It's also a great place to try those dishes you never dare to order elsewhere such as *jàp chài* (Chinese-style stewed vegies) or delicious *ɓèt đǔn* (duck braised in Chinese spices).

⭐nahm
THAI $$$

(Map p83; ☑ 0 2625 3388; www.comohotels.com/ metropolitanbangkok/dining/nahm; ground fl, Metropolitan Hotel, 27 Th Sathon Tai (South); set lunch 800-1100B; set dinner 1700B; ⊙ noon-2pm Mon-Fri, 7-10.30pm Mon-Sun; ✿; Ⓜ Lumphini exit 2) Australian chef/author David Thompson is behind what is quite possibly the best Thai restaurant in Bangkok. Using ancient cookbooks as his inspiration, Thompson has given new life to previously extinct and exotic-sounding dishes such as 'smoked fish curry with prawns, chicken livers, cockles and black pepper'. Dinner takes the form of a multicourse set meal, while lunch spans *kà·nŏm jeen*, thin rice noodles served with curries.

If you're expecting bland, gentrified Thai food meant for non-Thais, prepare to be disappointed. Reservations recommended.

⋇ Siam Square & Pratunam

If you find yourself hungry in this part of central Bangkok, you're largely at the mercy of shopping-mall food courts and chain restaurants. However, this is still Thailand, and if you can ignore the prefabricated atmosphere, the food can often be quite good.

Som Tam Nua
NORTHEASTERN THAI $

(Map p84; 392/14 Soi 5, Siam Sq; mains 59-130B; ⊙ 10.45am-9.30pm; ✿; Ⓢ Siam exit 4) It can't compete with the street stalls for flavour and authenticity, but if you need to be seen, particularly while in air-con and trendy surroundings, this is a good place to sample northeastern Thai specialities.

Sanguan Sri
THAI $

(Map p84; 59/1 Th Witthayu (Wireless Rd); mains 40-150B; ⊙ 10am-3pm Mon-Sat; ✿; Ⓢ Phloen Chit exit 5) There's a limited English-language menu at this old-school Thai eatery, but simply pointing to the delicious dishes being consumed around you is probably a better strategy.

New Light Coffee House
INTERNATIONAL $

(Map p84; 426/1-4 Soi Chulalongkorn 64; mains 60-200B; ⊙ 8am-midnight; ✿; Ⓢ Siam exit 2) Travel back in time to 1960s-era Bangkok at this vintage diner popular with students from nearby Chulalongkorn University for its international and Thai dishes.

Food Plus
THAI $

(Map p84; btwn Soi 5 & Soi 6, Siam Sq; mains 30-70B; ⊙ 9am-3pm; Ⓢ Siam exit 2) This claustrophobic alleyway is bursting with the wares

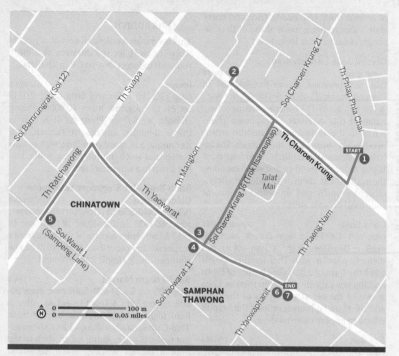

🏃 City Walk
Chinatown Eats Tour

START CNR TH PLAENG NAM & TH CHAROEN KRUNG
FINISH CNR TH YAOWAPHANIT & TH YAOWARAT
DISTANCE APPROXIMATELY 1KM
DURATION TWO TO THREE HOURS

Street food rules in Chinatown, making the area ideal for a culinary adventure. The best time to feast in this area is 7pm to 8pm, but don't try this walk on a Monday when most of the city's street vendors stay at home.

Start at the intersection of Th Plaeng Nam and Th Charoen Krung. Head north along Th Phlap Phla Chai, staying on the east side for about 50m until you reach **❶ Nai Mong Hoi Thod**, a shophouse restaurant renowned for its delicious *or sòo·an* (oysters fried with egg and a sticky batter).

Backtrack to Th Charoen Krung and turn right. Upon reaching Th Mangkon make a right and immediately on your left-hand side you'll see **❷ Jék Pûi** (เจ็กปุ้ย), a table-less stall known for its mild, Chinese-style curries.

Cross Th Charoen Krung again and head east until you reach the market alley that is Soi Charoen Krung 16 (Trok Itsaranuphap). At the opposite end you'll see a gentleman making **❸ gǒo·ay děe·o kôo·a gài** (ก๋วยเตี๋ยวคั่วไก่; rice noodles fried with chicken, egg and garlic oil).

Upon emerging at Th Yaowarat, cross over to the busy market area directly across the street. The first vendor on the right, **❹ Nay Lék Ûan** (นายเล็กอ้วน), sells *gǒo·ay jáp nám sǎi* (a peppery broth containing rice noodles and pork offal).

Go west on Th Yaowarat. Turn left onto Th Ratchawong, where at **❺ Phàt Tai Râht·chá·wong** (ผัดไทยราชวงศ์) an aged Chinese-Thai couple do *pàt tai* fried over coals and served in banana leaf cups.

Backtrack along Th Yaowarat to the corner of Th Yaowaphanit, where you'll see **❻ Mang·korn Khǒw** (มังกรขาว), a stall selling *bà·mèe* (Chinese-style wheat noodles) and barbecued pork.

Adjacent to Mang·korn Khǒw is a no-name **❼ stall** that does Chinese-Thai desserts, including a delicious *boo·a loy nám kǐng* (dumplings stuffed with rich black sesame paste and served in a spicy ginger broth).

of several *ráhn kôw gaang* (rice and curry stalls). Everything is made ahead of time, so simply point to what looks tasty.

Crystal Jade La Mian Xiao Long Bao
CHINESE $$

(Map p84; basement, Erawan Bangkok, 494 Th Ploenchit; mains 115-450B; ⊙11am-10pm; ✶⌁; ⑤Chit Lom exit 8) The tongue-twistingly long name of this excellent Singaporean chain refers to the restaurant's signature wheat noodles (*la mian*) and the famous Shanghainese steamed dumplings (*xiao long pao*). If you order the hand-pulled noodles, allow the staff to cut them with kitchen shears, otherwise you'll end up with evidence of your meal on your shirt.

Coca Suki
CHINESE, THAI $$

(Map p84; 416/3-8 Th Henri Dunant; mains 78-488B; ⊙11am-11pm; ✶⌁; ⑤Siam exit 6) Immensely popular with Thai families, *sù·gêe* takes the form of a bubbling hotpot of broth and the raw ingredients to dip therein. Coca is one of the oldest purveyors of the dish, and the Siam Sq branch reflects the brand's efforts to appear more modern.

Sra Bua
THAI $$$

(Map p84; ⌁02 2162 9000; www.kempinskibangkok. com; ground fl, Siam Kempinski Hotel, 991/9 off Th Phra Ram I; set meal 2700B; ⊙noon-3pm & 6-11pm; ✶; ⑤Siam exits 3 & 5) Helmed by a Thai and a Dane whose Copenhagen restaurant, Kiin Kiin, snagged a Michelin star, Sra Bua takes a correspondingly international approach to Thai food. Putting Thai dishes and ingredients through the wringer of molecular gastronomy, the couple have created dishes with exotic descriptions such as 'frozen red curry with lobster and lychee' and 'snow flaked coconut milk with pickled mushrooms and coriander'.

✗ Sukhumvit

This seemingly endless ribbon of a road is where to go if, for the duration of a meal, you wish to forget that you're in Thailand.

Imoya
JAPANESE $

(Map p90; 3rd fl, Terminal Shop Cabin, 2/17-19 Soi 24, Th Sukhumvit; mains 40-400B; ⊙6pm-midnight; ✶; ⑤Phrom Phong exit 4) A visit to this well-hidden Japanese restaurant, with its antique ads, wood panelling, wall of sake bottles and stuck-in-time prices, is like taking a trip in a time machine.

Boon Tong Kiat Singapore Hainanese Chicken Rice
SINGAPOREAN $

(Map p90; 440/5 Soi 55 (Thong Lor), Th Sukhumvit; mains 60-150B; ⊙10am-10pm; ✶; ⑤Thong Lo exit 3 & taxi) Order a plate of the restaurant's namesake and experience how a dish can be simultaneously simple and profound.

Soi 38 Night Market
THAI $

(Map p90; cnr Soi 38 & Th Sukhumvit; mains 30-60B; ⊙8pm-3am; ⑤Thong Lor exit 4) After a hard night of clubbing, this strip of basic Thai-Chinese stalls will look like a shimmering oasis. If you're going sober, stick to the knot of 'famous' vendors on the right-hand side as you enter the street.

Nasir Al-Masri
MIDDLE EASTERN $$

(Map p90; 4/6 Soi 3/1, Th Sukhumvit; mains 160-370B; ⊙24hr; ✶⌁; ⑤Nana exit 1) One of several Middle Eastern restaurants on Soi 3/1, Nasir Al-Masri is easily recognisable by its thoroughly impressive floor-to-ceiling stainless steel 'theme'. Middle Eastern food generally means meat, meat and more meat, but there are also several delicious vegie-based *mezze*.

WAVING THE YELLOW FLAG

During the annual Vegetarian Festival (p98) in September/October, Bangkok's Chinatown becomes a virtual orgy of nonmeat cuisine. The festivities centre on Chinatown's main street, Th Yaowarat, and the Talat Noi area, but food shops and stalls all over the city post yellow flags to announce their meat-free status.

Celebrating alongside the ethnic Chinese are Thais who look forward to the special dishes that appear during the festival period. Most restaurants put their normal menus on hold and instead prepare soy-based substitutes for standard Thai dishes such as *dôm yam* (spicy, sour soup) and *gaang kĕe·o wăhn* (green curry). Even Thai regional cuisines are sold without the meat.

Along with abstinence from meat, the 10-day festival is celebrated with special visits to a temple, often requiring worshippers to dress in white.

LOCAL KNOWLEDGE

EATING IN BANGKOK

David Thompson is the Head Chef of the award-winning Thai restaurant, nahm (p116). He is also the author of the bestselling books *Thai Food* and *Thai Street Food*.

How Do You Describe the Food of Bangkok?

The food of Bangkok is more urbane, with the rough and rambunctious tastes of the wild and remote regions polished off. There's a huge Chinese influence here because Bangkok was a Chinese city. The central-plains food, which Bangkok is the epitome of, is refined and has the classic four flavours (sweet, sour, salty and spicy).

What Are Some Classic Bangkok-Style Dishes?

I like some of the dishes in Chinatown, whether it be the oyster place I adore (Nai Mong Hoi Thod), or whether it be noodles with fish dumplings or with roast duck. Also *boo pàt pŏng gàrèe* (crab fried with curry powder), when done well, is easy, but is bloody delicious and accessible. And *pàt tai* – well, you can't really escape from the cliché, however delicious it might be.

The Best Food 'Hood?

It depends on what I'm looking for. Chinatown, for smoked duck or noodles. But if you want to eat Thai food, you need to go to the markets. Bangkok still has some remnants of the city or villages that it was. For Muslim food you can go down to the area near Haroon Mosque, near the Oriental Hotel, or for Portuguese cakes, you can go to Santa Cruz. There's still those types of areas.

Your Favourite Restaurant

It changes all the time. I like Krua Apsorn (p113). It's local. It's good. It's unreformed. It's not too precious. They cook for Thais, they feed Thais and it is Thai.

The Best Market

Of course, Or Tor Kor (p135). Even though it's sanitised, its soul has not been expunged from it as it's modernised. There's some great stuff there.

Best Eating Advice for a First-Time Visitor

Just bloody well eat it – don't think about it – just eat it. It's so unlikely you'll get sick, but you will kick yourself for not actually just diving in. Go to places that look busiest, because they're busy for a reason. And a bit of food poisoning, well that adds local colour, doesn't it?

Saras INDIAN **$$**
(Map p90; ww.saras.co.th; Soi 20, Th Sukhumvit; mains 90-200B; ⊙ 8.30am-10.30pm; ⌨ ⍟; Ⓜ Sukhumvit exit 2, Ⓢ Asok exit 4) Describing your restaurant as a 'fast-food feast' may not be the cleverest PR move we've ever encountered, but it's a spot-on description of this Indian restaurant. Order at the counter to be rewarded with crispy *dosai*, meat-free regional set meals or rich curries (dishes are brought to your table). We wish all fast food could be this satisfying.

Supanniga Eating Room THAI **$$**
(Map p90; www.facebook.com/SupannigaEatingRoom; 160/11 Soi 55 (Thong Lor), Th Sukhumvit; mains 120-350B; ⊙11.30am-2.30pm & 5.30-11.30pm Tue-Sun; ⌨; Ⓢ Thong Lo exit 3 & taxi) Thais are finally starting to take a serious interest in their own cuisine, and over the last few years Bangkok has seen an explosion of sophisticated-feeling places serving regional Thai dishes. The best of the lot is probably Supanniga, which focuses on the typically seafood-based, herb-forward dishes of Chanthaburi and Trat in western Thailand.

Snapper INTERNATIONAL **$$**
(Map p90; www.snapper-bangkok.com; 1/20-22 Soi 11, Th Sukhumvit; mains 200-1950B; ⊙5pm-midnight Mon-Fri, noon-midnight Sat-Sun; ⌨; Ⓢ Nana exit 3) Allegedly Bangkok's first restaurant serving New Zealand cuisine, Snapper specialises in Kiwi-style fish and chips. Choose from one of four sustainably harvested fish from New Zealand, your cut of fries, and the delicious homemade tartar sauce or a garlic aioli. A handful of other seafood dishes and salads and a brief wine list round out the selections.

DON'T MISS

BANGKOK'S BEST FOOD COURTS

Every Bangkok mall worth its escalators has some sort of food court. They are a great way to dip your toe in the sea of Thai food as they're generally cheap, clean, air-conditioned and have English-language menus. At most, paying is done by exchanging cash for vouchers or a temporary credit card at one of several counters; your change is refunded at the same desk.

➡ ★ **MBK Food Island** (Map p84; 6th fl, MBK Center, cnr Th Phra Ram I & Th Phayathai; mains 35-150B; ☺10am-10pm; ✳ ⃰; ⑤National Stadium exit 4) The granddaddy of the genre offers tens of vendors selling dishes from virtually every corner of Thailand and beyond. Standouts include a good vegetarian food stall (stall C8) and a very decent Isan food vendor (C22).

➡ **Gourmet Paradise** (Map p84; ground fl, Siam Paragon, 991/1 Th Phra Ram I; mains 35-500B; ☺10am-10pm; ✳; ⑤Siam exits 3 & 5) The perpetually busy Gourmet Paradise unites international fast-food chains, domestic restaurants and food court–style stalls, with a particular emphasis on the sweet stuff.

➡ **Food Republic** (Map p84; 4th fl, Siam Center, cnr Th Phra Ram I & Th Phayathai; mains 30-200B; ☺10am-10pm; ✳ ⃰; ⑤Siam exit 1) The city's newest food court has a good mix of Thai and international (mostly Asian) outlets, all in an open, contemporary-feeling locale. We particularly enjoyed the Thai-Muslim dishes at the stall called 'Curry Rice'.

➡ **Pier 21** (Map p90; 5th fl, Terminal 21, cnr Th Sukhumvit & Soi 21 (Asoke), Th Sukhumvit; mains 39-200B; ☺10am-10pm; ✳ ⃰; Ⓜ Sukhumvit exit 3, ⑤ Asok exit 3) Ascend a seemingly endless number of escalators to arrive at this expansive food court cobbled together from famous vendors across the city. The selection is vast and the dishes exceedingly cheap, even by Thai standards.

➡ **FoodPark** (Map p84; 4th fl, Big C, 97/11 Th Ratchadamri; mains 30-90B; ☺9am-9pm; ✳; ⑤Chit Lom exit 9 to Sky Walk) The selections at this characteristically Thai food court are abundant and inexpensive, and representative of the kind of 'fast food' locals enjoy eating.

Bo.lan
THAI **$$$**

(Map p90; ✆0 2260 2962; www.bolan.co.th; 42 Soi Rongnarong Phichai Songkhram, Soi 26, Th Sukhumvit; set dinner 1980B; ☺6pm-midnight Tue-Sun; ✳; ⑤Phrom Phong exit 4) Upscale Thai is often more garnish than flavour, but Bo.lan, started up by two former chefs of London's Michelin-starred nahm, is the exception. Bo and Dylan (Bo.lan, a play on words that also means 'ancient') take a scholarly approach to Thai cuisine, and generous set meals featuring full flavoured Thai dishes are the results of this tuition. Reservations recommended.

Sukhumvit Plaza
KOREAN **$$$**

(Korean Town; Map p90; Soi 12, Th Sukhumvit; mains 200-1000B; ☺11am-10pm; ✳; Ⓜ Sukhumvit exit 3, ⑤ Asok exit 2) Known around Bangkok as 'Korean Town', this multistorey complex is the city's best destination for authentic 'Seoul' food. Expat Koreans swear by **Mye-ong Ga** (Map p90; ground fl, Sukhumvit Plaza, cnr Soi 12 & Th Sukhumvit; mains 200-950B; ☺11am-10pm Tue-Sun, 4-10pm Mon; ✳; Ⓜ Sukhumvit exit 3, ⑤ Asok exit 2) on the ground floor, although there are slightly cheaper places in the complex as well.

Opposite Mess Hall
INTERNATIONAL **$$$**

(Map p90; www.oppositebangkok.com; 2nd fl, 27/2 Soi 51, Th Sukhumvit; mains 140-350B; ☺7pm-midnight Tue-Sun; ✳ ⃰; ⑤Thong Lo exit 1) Much like the dishes served there (eg 'savoury duck waffle, leg confit, pate, crispy skin & picalily relish'), Opposite can be a bit hard to categorise. But, really, how can you go wrong with a cosy space, food using great local ingredients, and excellent cocktails? There's a menu, but the best strategy is to see what the ever-changing blackboard has to offer.

Soul Food Mahanakorn
THAI **$$$**

(Map p90; ✆0 2714 7708; www.soulfoodmahanakorn.com; 56/10 Soi 55 (Thong Lor), Th Sukhumvit; mains 180-275B; ☺5.30-11pm Sun-Thu, to midnight Fri & Sat; ✳ ⃰; ⑤Thong Lo exit 3) Soul Food gets its interminable buzz from its dual nature as both an inviting restaurant – the menu spans tasty interpretations of rustic Thai dishes – and a bar serving deliciously boozy, Thai-influenced cocktails. Reservations recommended.

Bei Otto

GERMAN **$$$**

(Map p90; www.beiotto.com; 1 Soi 20, Th Sukhumvit; mains 175-590B; ⊙11am-midnight; ❈ ✎; MᴍSukhumvit exit 2, SᴀAsok exit 4) Claiming a Bangkok residence for nearly 20 years, Bei Otto's major culinary bragging point is its pork knuckles, reputedly the best in town. A good selection of German beers and an attached delicatessen with brilliant breads and super sausages make it even more attractive to go Deutsch.

✕ Thewet & Dusit

Kaloang Home Kitchen

THAI **$$**

(Map p95; Th Si Ayuthaya; mains 60-170B; ⊙11am-11pm; ⊕Tha Thewet) Don't be alarmed by the peeling paint and dilapidated deck – Kaloang Home Kitchen certainly isn't. The laid-back atmosphere and seafood-heavy menu will quickly dispel any concerns about sinking into Mae Nam Chao Phraya, and a beer and the breeze will temporarily erase any scarring memories of Bangkok traffic. For the restaurant, follow Th Si Ayuthaya until you reach the river.

✕ Ratchathewi

Pathé

THAI, INTERNATIONAL **$**

(Map p96; www.patherestaurant.com; 507 Th Ratchawithi; mains 85-160B; ⊙2pm-1am; ❈; SᴀVictory Monument exit 4) The modern Thai equivalent of a 1950s-era American diner, this popular place combines solid Thai food, a fun atmosphere and a jukebox playing scratched records. The menu is equally eclectic, and combines Thai and Western dishes and ingredients; be sure to save room for the deep-fried ice cream.

Mallika Restaurant

SOUTHERN THAI **$$**

(Map p96; 21/36 Th Rang Nam; mains 90-500B; ⊙10am-10pm; ❈; SᴀVictory Monument exit 2) A dream come true: authentic regional Thai (southern, in this case), with a legible English menu, good service and a tidy setting. The prices are slightly high for a family Thai joint, but you're paying for quality.

✕ Greater Bangkok

Phat Thai Ari

THAI **$**

(Map p112; Soi Phaholyothin Center, Th Phahonyothin; mains 80-120B; ⊙9am-8pm; SᴀAri exit 4) One of the city's better-known *pàt tai* shops is located a couple of blocks from the eponymous soi. Try the innovative 'noodle-less' version, where strips of crispy green papaya are substituted for the traditional rice noodles.

Salt

INTERNATIONAL **$$$**

(Map p112; www.saltbangkok.com; cnr Soi Ari 4 & Soi 7 (Ari), Th Phahonyothin; mains 180-1450B; ⊙5pm-midnight Mon-Sat; ❈; SᴀAri exit 1) With a DJ booth flashing a conspicuously placed copy of *Larousse Gastronomique*, Salt is the kind of eclectic place that's currently shaping Bangkok's restaurant scene. Appropriately located in Ari, suburban Bangkok's trendiest 'hood, the menu ranges from sushi to pizza, with an emphasis on grilled and smoked dishes. Seating is (loud) indoor or (sweaty) outdoor, and there's draught Belgian beer and house cocktails.

🍸 Drinking & Nightlife

Once infamous as an anything-goes nightlife destination, in recent years Bangkok has been edging towards teetotalism with strict regulations limiting the sale of alcohol and increasingly conservative closing times. Regardless, the city still boasts a diverse and fun bar and club scene, and there are even a few places to go if you find 2am too early to go to bed. Keep in mind that smoking has been outlawed at all indoor (and some quasi-outdoor) entertainment places since 2008. Surprisingly for Thailand, the rule is strictly enforced.

Bangkok's watering holes cover the spectrum from English-style pubs where you can comfortably sit with a pint and the paper to chic dens where the fair and beautiful go to be seen, not to imbibe. But many visitors associate Bangkok with the kind of bars that don't have an address – found just about everywhere in the city. Think streetside seating, plastic chairs, auto exhaust, and tasty dishes that are absent-mindedly nibbled between toasts. Bangkok is also one of the few big cities in the world where nobody seems to mind if you slap a bar on the roof of a skyscraper (see p125).

During the day, Th Khao San is dominated by just about everybody but Thais. At night the natives deem it safe to join the crowds, giving the area an entirely different vibe. In addition to the main strip, Th Rambuttri and Th Phra Athit also draw drinkers and fun seekers from across the city, and the world.

Bangkok's nightclub scene is as fickle as a ripe mango, and that really fun disco you found on your last trip three years ago is most likely history today. To find out what is going on when you're in town, check listings rag BK or the *Bangkok Post*'s Friday supplement, Guru. Alternatively, check in with organisers of hugely popular monthly parties such as **Bangkok Invaders** (www.facebook.com/the.bangkok.invaders), **Club Soma** (www.facebook.com/clubsomaparty), **Dudesweet** (www.dudesweet.org) or the retrothemed Paradise Bangkok/Isan Dancehall DJ events hosted by **ZudRangMa Records** (Map p90; www.zudrangmarecords.com; 7/1 Soi 51, Th Sukhumvit; noon-10pm Tue-Sun; Thong Lo exit 1). Cover charges for nightclubs range from 100B to 800B and usually include a drink or two. Don't even think about showing up before 11pm, and always bring ID. Most clubs close at 2am.

Ko Ratanakosin, Banglamphu & Thonburi

Madame Musur
BAR
(Map p62; 41 Soi Ram Buttri; 8am-1am; Tha Phra Athit (Banglamphu)) Saving you the trip north to Pai, Madame Musur combines the vibes of northern Thailand and Th Khao San all in one locale. Serving a short menu of northern Thai dishes (including what some consider to be one of the city's better bowls of *kôw soy* – a northern-style curry noodle soup), it's also not a bad place to eat.

Hippie de Bar
BAR
(Map p62; www.facebook.com/hippie.debar; 46 Th Khao San; 6pm-2am; Tha Phra Athit (Banglamphu)) Popular with the domestic crowd, Hippie boasts a Thai retro theme and sev-

eral levels of fun, both indoor and outdoor. There's also food, pool tables and a more sophisticated soundtrack than most.

Club
NIGHTCLUB
(Map p62; www.theclubkhaosan.com; 123 Th Khao San; 10pm-3am; Tha Phra Athit (Banglamphu)) Located right in the middle of Th Khao San, this cavernlike dance hall hosts a fun mix of locals and backpackers.

Rolling Bar
BAR
(Map p62; Th Prachathipatai; 5pm-midnight; klorng boat to Tha Phan Fah) An escape from hectic Th Khao San is a good enough excuse to schlep to this quiet canal-side boozer. Tasty bar snacks and live music are excuses to stay.

Taksura
BAR
(Map p62; 156/1 Th Tanao; 5pm-1am; klorng boat to Tha Phan Fah) There's little to indicate the location of this seemingly abandoned century-old mansion in the heart of old Bangkok, which is all the better, according to the cool uni-artsy crowd who frequent the place.

Center Khao Sarn
BAR
(Map p62; Th Khao San; 24hr; Tha Phra Athit (Banglamphu)) Come here for front-row views of the human parade on Th Khao San. The upstairs bar hosts late-night bands.

Silom & Sathon

Tapas Room
NIGHTCLUB
(Map p78; 114/17-18 Soi 4, Th Silom; admission 100B; 9pm-2am; Si Lom exit 2, Sala Daeng exit 1) You won't find gazpacho here, but the

---

THE WHISKY SET

Thai beer is generally more miss than hit, so the next time you're out on the town, why not drink like the Thais do and order a bottle of whisky?

Your first step is to choose a brand. For a particularly decadent night out, the industry standard is a bottle of *blàak* (Johnnie Walker Black Label). Those on a budget can go for the cheaper imported labels such as Red Label or Benmore, and a rock-bottom but fun night can be had on domestic spirits such as 100 Pipers or Sang Som. And it's not unusual to bring your own bottle to many Thai bars, although some might charge a modest corkage fee.

As any Thai can tell you, your next immediate concern is mixers. These will take the form of several bottles of soda water and a bottle or two of Coke, along with a pail of ice. Most waiters will bring these to you as a matter of course.

Mixing is the easiest step and requires little or no initiative on your part; your skilled waiter will fill your glass with ice, followed by a shot of whisky, a splash of soda, a top-off of Coke and, finally, a swirl with the ice tongs to bring it all together.

If you can't finish your bottle, don't fret, as it's perfectly normal to keep it at the bar. Simply tell your trusted waiter, who will write your name and the date on the bottle and keep it for your next visit.

OUT ALL NIGHT

With most pubs and dance clubs closing around 2am, One Night in Bangkok is not quite what it used to be. Thankfully, there are a few places around town that have gained sufficient 'permission' to stay open until the morning hours.

Off Soi Ngam Duphli, **Wong's Place** (Map p83; 27/3 Soi Si Bamphen; ⊙9pm-late Tue-Sun; Ⓜ Lumphini exit 1), a backpacker bar, is so late-night it's best not to show up before midnight. Near Th Khao San, the elevated setting of **Gazebo** (Map p62; www.facebook.com/Gazebo.Club; 3rd fl, 44 Th Chakraphong; ⊙6pm-late; 🚢Tha Phra Athit (Banglamphu)) appears to lend it some leniency with the city's otherwise strict closing times. And in 'new' Bangkok, admittedly cheesy clubs such as **Club Insanity** (Map p90; www.clubinsanitybangkok.com; Soi 12, Th Sukhumvit; admission 200B; ⊙8pm-late; Ⓜ Sukhumvit exit 3, Ⓢ Asok exit 2), **Levels** (www.levelsclub.com; 6th fl, Aloft, 35 Soi 11, Th Sukhumvit; ⊙9pm-late; Ⓢ Nana exit 3), **Mixx** (Map p84; basement, InterContinental Hotel, 973 Th Ploenchit; admission 300B; ⊙10pm-late; Ⓢ Chit Lom exit 7), Narz (p126) and **Scratch Dog** (Map p90; basement, Windsor Suites Hotel, 8-10 Soi 20, Th Sukhumvit; admission 400B; ⊙midnight-late; Ⓜ Sukhumvit exit 2, Ⓢ Asok exit 4) employ a Top 40 and R&B soundtrack to propel partiers into the morning hours.

For something a bit edgier, ask your friendly taxi driver to escort you to any of the following: **Climax**, **Bash**, **Bossy**, **Spicy** or **Shock 39**. These creatively named late-night clubs are all in central Bangkok and stay open until well past sunrise. We'd tell you a bit more about them and put them on our maps, but our experience and research suggest these clubs exist in an alternate late-night reality that only Bangkok taxi drivers can navigate...

---

name is an accurate indicator of the Spanish/Moroccan-inspired vibe of this multilevel den. Come from Wednesday to Saturday when the combination of DJs and live percussion brings the body count to critical level.

Ku Dé Ta NIGHTCLUB
(Map p78; kudeta.com/bangkok/; 38th & 39th fl, Sathorn Square Complex, 98 Th Sathon Neua (North); ⊙11am-1am, to 3am Fri & Sat; Ⓢ Chong Nonsi exit 1) The biggest new thing on Bangkok's club scene – literally and figuratively – the Bangkok branch of Bali's Ku Dé Ta spans seven bars, three restaurants and two clubs. Expect an entry fee of 500B after 10pm on Fridays and Saturdays.

Riverside

Viva & Aviv BAR
(Map p76; www.vivaaviv.com; ground fl, River City, 23 Th Yotha; ⊙11am-midnight; river ferry Tha Si Phraya/River City or shopping centre shuttle boat from Tha Sathon (Central Pier)) An enviable riverside location, casual open-air seating and a funky atmosphere make this restaurant-ish bar a contender for Bangkok's best sunset cocktail destination. Expect a pun-heavy menu (sample item: 'I focaccia name') of pizzas, meaty snacks and salads that really is no joke.

Maggie Choo's BAR
(Map p76; www.facebook.com/maggiechoos; basement, Novotel Bangkok Fenix Silom, 320 Th Silom; ⊙6.30pm-1.30am; Ⓢ Surasak exit 1) A former bank vault with a Chinatown opium den vibe; secret passageways; lounging women in silk dresses; with all this going on, it's easy to forget that the new Maggie Choo's is actually a bar. But creative, yet expensive and somewhat sweet house cocktails, and a crowd that blends selfie-snapping locals and curious tourists are reminders of this.

Siam Square & Pratunam

Co-Co Walk BAR
(Map p84; 87/70 Th Phayathai; ⊙5pm-midnight; Ⓢ Ratchathewi exit 2) This covered compound is a smorgasbord of pubs, bars and live music popular with Thai university students. **Güts** has live acoustic music, **Chilling House Café** has the same and tacks on a few pool tables, **Muay Thai Restaurant** does Thai food and for something confusingly international there's, well, **L'aventure Musical & Frenchy Bar**.

Hyde & Seek BAR
(Map p90; www.hydeandseek.com; ground fl, Athenee Residence, 65/1 Soi Ruam Rudi; ⊙11am-1am; Ⓢ Phloen Chit exit 4) The tasty and comforting English-inspired bar snacks and meals have earned Hyde & Seek the right to call itself a 'gastro bar', but we reckon the real reasons to come here are arguably Bangkok's most well-stocked liquor cabinet and some of the city's best cocktails.

Sukhumvit

★ WTF
BAR

(Map p90; www.wtfbangkok.com; 7 Soi 51, Th Sukhumvit; ⊘6pm-1am Tue-Sun; ⑤Thong Lo exit 3) No, not that WTF; Wonderful Thai Friendship combines a bar and an art gallery in one attractive package. Throw in some of Bangkok's best cocktails, delicious Spanish-influenced bar snacks and a friendly, artsy clientele and as far as we're concerned, you've got Bangkok's best bar.

Badmotel
BAR

(Map p90; www.facebook.com/badmotel; Soi 55 (Thong Lor), Th Sukhumvit; ⊘5pm-1.30am; ⑤Thong Lo exit 3 & taxi) The new Badmotel blends the modern and the kitschy, the cosmopolitan and the Thai, in a way that has struck a (admittedly detached) nerve among Bangkok hipsters. This is manifest in drinks that combine Hale's Blue Boy, a Thai childhood drink staple, with rum, and bar snacks such as 'naam prik ong' a northern-style dip, here served with poppadum.

Tuba
BAR

(34 Room 11-12 A, Soi Ekamai 21, Soi 63 (Ekamai), Th Sukhumvit; ⊘11am-2am; ⑤Ekkamai exit 1 & taxi) Part storage room for over-the-top vintage furniture, part restaurant, part friendly local boozer, this quirky bar certainly doesn't lack in diversity, nor fun. Indulge in a whole bottle (they'll hold onto it if you don't finish it) and don't miss the delicious chicken wings.

Grease
NIGHTCLUB

(Map p90; www.greasebangkok.com; 46/12 Soi 49, Th Sukhumvit; ⊘6pm-4am Mon-Sat; ⑤Phrom Phong exit 3 & taxi) Bangkok's newest, hottest club is also one of its biggest – you could get lost in the four floors of dining venues, lounges and dance floors here.

Cheap Charlie's
BAR

(Map p90; Soi 11, Th Sukhumvit; ⊘4.30-11.45pm Mon-Sat; ⑤Nana exit 3) There's never enough seating, and the design concept is best classified as 'junkyard', but on most nights this chummy open-air beer corner is a great place to meet everybody from package tourists to resident English teachers.

Arena 10
NIGHTCLUB

(Map p90; cnr Soi Ekamai 5 & Soi 63 (Ekamai), Th Sukhumvit; ⑤Ekkamai exit 2 & taxi) This open-air entertainment zone is the destination of choice for Bangkok's young and beautiful – for the moment at least. **Demo** (Map p90; www.facebook.com/demobangkok; admission

---

BANGKOK'S SILVER SCREENS

Movies are a fantastic deal in Bangkok. At 120B, the ticket price is a fraction of what you'd pay for a sticky stool at home, the theatres are almost all new, and best of all, you can drink beer.

But the Thais didn't stop there. With its 16 screens and more than 3000 seats, few cinemas anywhere can rival **Siam Paragon Cineplex** (Map p84; ☑0 2129 4635; www.paragoncineplex.com; 5th fl, Siam Paragon, 991/1 Th Phra Ram I; ⑤Siam exits 3 & 5). In addition to Thailand's largest IMAX screen, options include the Blue Ribbon Screen, a cinema with a maximum of 72 seats, where you're plied with pillows, blankets, complimentary snacks and drinks, and of course, a 15-minute massage; or Enigma, where in addition to a sofa-like love seat designed for couples, you'll be served cocktails and food (in addition to the blankets and a massage).

The retro-inclined can opt for the old-school standalone theatres across the street at Siam Sq, including **Scala** (Map p84; ☑0 2251 2861; Soi 1, Siam Sq; ⑤Siam exit 2) and **Lido** (Map p84; ☑0 2252 6498; www.apexsiam-square.com; btwn Soi 2 & Soi 3, Siam Sq; ⑤Siam exit 2). For something artsy, there's RCA's **House** (www.houserama.com; 3rd fl, RCA Plaza, RCA, off Th Phra Ram IX; ⓂPhra Ram 9 exit 3 & taxi), or for something really cosy, the eight-seat **Friese-Green Club** (FGC; Map p90; ☑08 7000 0795; www.facebook.com/pages/The-Friese-Greene-Club/371737282944797; 259/6 Soi 22, Th Sukhumvit; ⑤Phrom Phong exit 6).

Nearly all movies in Thailand offer screenings with English subtitles – visit **Movie Seer** (www.movieseer.com) for show times. All films are preceded by the Thai royal anthem and everyone is expected to stand respectfully for its duration. And despite the heat and humidity on the streets, keep in mind that all of Bangkok's movie theatres pump the air-con with such vigour that a jumper is an absolute necessity – unless you're going Blue Ribbon class, that is.

UP ON THE ROOF

In previous years, Bangkok's rooftop bars were largely the realm of well-heeled tourists, but nowadays they comprise a diverse spread, with options ranging from basic to formal. Our faves:

→ ★ **Moon Bar** (Map p83; www.banyantree.com; 61st fl, Banyan Tree Hotel, 21/100 Th Sathon (South) Tai; ⊗5pm-1am; Ⓜ Lumphini exit 2) Precariously perched on top of 61 floors of skyscraper, Moon Bar offers a heart-stopping bird's-eye view of central Bangkok. Things can get a bit crowded here come sunset, so be sure to show up a bit early to get the best seats. Note that Moon Bar does not allow entry to those wearing shorts or sandals.

→ **River Vibe** (Map p76; 8th fl, River View Guest House, 768 Soi Phanurangsi, Th Songwat; ⊗7.30-11pm; 🚢Tha Marine Department, Ⓜ Hua Lamphong exit 1 & taxi) Can't afford the drinks and/or have objections to the dress code at Bangkok's other rooftop bars? Slap on some shorts and head to the top floor of the River View Guest House (p104); the casual vibe and stunning river views will hardly feel like a compromise.

→ **Phra Nakorn Bar & Gallery** (Map p62; 58/2 Soi Damnoen Klang Tai; ⊗5pm-1am; 🚢klorng boat to Tha Phan Fah) In addition to charming views of old Bangkok, the breezy rooftop of this artsy bar also offers cheap and tasty Thai food.

→ **Above 11** (Map p90; ☎08 3542 1111; www.aboveeleven.com; 33rd fl, Fraser Suites Sukhumvit, Soi 11, Th Sukhumvit; ⊗6pm-2am; Ⓢ Nana exit 3) Downward glances of Bangkok's most cosmopolitan neighbourhood go best with the Peruvian/Japanese bar snacks at this sophisticated rooftopper.

→ **Sky Bar** (Map p76; www.lebua.com/sky-bar; 63rd fl, State Tower, 1055 Th Silom; ⊗6pm-1am; Ⓢ Saphan Taksin exit 3) Descend the sweeping stairs like a Hollywood diva to the precipice bar of this rooftop restaurant – allegedly the world's highest open-air bar. But leave your shorts and sandals at home.

→ **Amorosa** (Map p62; www.arunresidence.com; rooftop, Arun Residence, 36-38 Soi Pratu Nokyung; ⊗5pm-midnight Mon-Thu, to 1am Fri-Sun; 🚢Tha Tien) Although not as lofty as the others, the riverside Amorosa compensates with what is arguably Bangkok's best view of Wat Arun.

→ **Sky Train Jazz Club** (Map p96; cnr Th Rang Nam & Th Phayathai; ⊗5pm-2am; Ⓢ Victory Monument exit 2) A visit to this comically misnamed bar is more like chilling on the rooftop of your stoner buddy's flat than any jazz club we've ever encountered. But there are indeed views of the BTS, jazz on occasion and a scrappy speakeasy atmosphere.

free; ⊗6pm-2am; Ⓢ Ekkamai exit 2 & taxi) combines blasting beats and a NYC warehouse vibe, while **Funky Villa** (Map p90; www.facebook.com/funkyvillabkk; ⊗7pm-2am; Ⓢ Ekkamai exit 2 & taxi), with its outdoor seating and Top 40 soundtrack, is more chilled. Fridays and Saturdays see a 400B entrance fee for foreigners.

Bar 23
BAR

(Map p90; Soi 16, Th Sukhumvit; ⊗7pm-1am Tue-Sat; Ⓜ Sukhumvit exit 2, Ⓢ Asok exit 6) The foreign NGO crowd and indie Thai types flock to this warehouse-like bar on weekends; cold Beerlao and a retro-rock soundtrack keep them there until the late hours. Bar 23 is about 500m down Soi 16, which is accessible from Th Ratchadaphisek.

Glow
NIGHTCLUB

(Map p90; www.glowbkk.com; 96/415 Soi Prasanmit, Th Sukhumvit; admission from 400B; ⊗7pm-2am; Ⓜ Sukhumvit exit 2, Ⓢ Asok exit 3) Glow is a small venue with a big reputation. Boasting a huge variety of vodkas and a recently upgraded sound system, the tunes range from hip-hop to electronica and just about everything in between.

Iron Fairies
BAR

(Map p90; www.theironfairies.com; 394 Soi 55 (Thong Lor), Th Sukhumvit; ⊗6pm-2am; Ⓢ Thong Lo exit 3 & taxi) Imagine an abandoned fairy factory in Paris c 1912, and you'll get an idea of the design theme at this popular wine bar. If you manage to wrangle one of a handful of seats, the staff claim to serve Bangkok's best burgers and there's live music after 9.30pm.

Bangkok Bar
BAR

(rooftop, The Opus, Soi Thong Lor 10; ☺8pm-1am; Ⓢ Thong Lo exit 3 & taxi) This former indie stomping ground has graduated to a new sophisticated, rooftop home. There's live music (from 9.30pm, Wednesday to Saturday), and the eats are strong enough to make Bangkok Bar a dinner destination in itself. And we double-dog dare you to walk a straight line after two Mad Dogs, the infamous house drink.

Nung-Len
NIGHTCLUB

(Map p90; www.nunglen.net; 217 Soi 63 (Ekamai), Th Sukhumvit; ☺6pm-1am Mon-Sat; Ⓢ Ekkamai exit 1 & taxi) Young, loud and Thai, Nung-Len (literally 'sit and chill') is a ridiculously popular den of dance tunes, live music and uni students on popular Th Ekamai. Make sure you get in before 10pm or you won't get in at all.

Alchemist
BAR

(Map p90; www.thealchemistbkk.com; 1/19 Soi 11, Th Sukhumvit; ☺5pm-midnight Tue-Sun; Ⓢ Nana exit 3) A tiny bar with a big emphasis on cocktails. They claim to do Bangkok's best Old Fashioned, and we don't disagree.

Oskar
BAR

(Map p90; www.oskar-bistro.com; 24 Soi 11, Th Sukhumvit; ☺6pm-2am; Ⓢ Nana exit 3) It touts itself as a bistro, but Oskar is more like a cocktail bar dressed like a club – with food. Correspondingly, the drinks and food are all over the map, but are satisfying and cost less than you'd expect from a place this flashy.

Q Bar
NIGHTCLUB

(Map p90; www.qbarbangkok.com; 34 Soi 11, Th Sukhumvit; admission from 600B; ☺8pm-2am; Ⓢ Nana exit 3) In club years, Q Bar is fast approaching retirement age, but big-name guest DJs and a recent renovation have ensured it still maintains a place in Bangkok's club scene. For something a bit more low-key, consider the attached Parisian-themed absinthe speakeasy, Le Derrière (Map p90; Q Bar, 34 Soi 11, Th Sukhumvit; ☺9pm-3am; Ⓢ Nana exit 3).

Narz
NIGHTCLUB

(Map p90; www.narzclubbangkok.net; 112 Soi Prasanmit, Th Sukhumvit; admission from 600B; ☺9pm-late; Ⓜ Sukhumvit exit 2, Ⓢ Asok exit 3) Like a small clubbing neighbourhood, Narz consists of three vast zones boasting an equal variety of music. It's largely a domestic scene, but the odd guest DJ can pull a large crowd. Open later than most.

▼ Greater Bangkok

RCA
NIGHTCLUB

(Map p90; Royal City Avenue; Royal City Ave, off Th Phra Ram IX; Ⓜ Phra Ram 9 exit 3 & taxi) Formerly a bastion of the teen scene, this Vegas-like strip has finally graduated from high school to become Bangkok's premier clubbing zone, although it must be said that its Top 40 roots still show. Flix/Slim (Map p90; www.facebook.com/slimbkk; Royal City Ave, off Th Phra Ram IX; ☺8pm-2am; Ⓜ Phra Ram 9 exit 3 & taxi) and Route 66 (Map p90; www.route66club.com; 29/33-48 Royal City Ave, off Th Phra Ram IX; ☺8pm-2am; Ⓜ Phra Ram 9 exit 3 & taxi) are the big hitters here, and foreigners must pay a 300B entry fee on Fridays and Saturdays.

☆ Entertainment

Shame on you if you find yourself bored in Bangkok. And even more shame if you think the only entertainment options involve the word 'go-go'. Nowadays Bangkok's nightlife is as diverse as that of virtually any modern city. And even if you're usually in bed by 10pm, Bangkok still offers interesting post-dinner diversions, from flash cinemas to traditional cultural performances.

Gà·teu·i Cabaret

Over the last few years, gà·teu·i (transgender, also spelt *kathoey*) cabaret has emerged to become a staple of the Bangkok tourist circuit. Calypso Bangkok (☏0 2688 1415; www.calypsocabaret.com; Asiatique, Soi 72-76, Th Charoen Krung; admission 1200B; ☺show times 8.15pm & 9.45pm; ⛴shuttle ferry from Tha Sathon (Central Pier)), Mambo Cabaret (☏0 2294 7381; www.mambocabaret.com; 59/28 Yannawa Tat Mai; tickets 800-1000B; ☺show times 7.15pm & 8.30pm; Ⓜ Chong Nonsi exit 2 taxi) and Playhouse Theater Cabaret (Map p84; ☏0 2215 0571; www.playhousethailand.com; basement, Asia Hotel, 296 Th Phayathai; 1200B; ☺show times 8.15pm & 9.45pm; Ⓢ Ratchathewi exit 1) host choreographed stage shows featuring Broadway high kicks and lip-synched pop tunes by the most well-endowed dudes you'll find anywhere.

Go-Go Bars

Although technically illegal, prostitution is fully 'out' in Bangkok, and the influence of organised crime and healthy kickbacks mean that it will be a long while before the existing laws are ever enforced. Yet, despite the image presented by much of the Western media, the underlying atmosphere of Bangkok's red-light districts is not necessarily one of illicitness and exploitation (although these do inevitably exist), but rather an aura of tackiness and boredom. See p719 for background on Thailand's sex industry.

Patpong (Map p78; Soi Patpong 1 & 2, Th Silom; 4pm-2am; Si Lom exit 2, Sala Daeng exit 1), arguably one of the world's most famous red-light districts, earned its notoriety during the 1980s for its wild sex shows involving everything from ping-pong balls to razors to midgets on motorbikes. Today it is more of a circus for curious spectators than sexual deviants; see the boxed text below for more on the history of this street. These days, **Soi Cowboy** (Map p90; btwn Soi 21 (Asoke) & Soi 23, Th Sukhumvit; 4pm-2am; Sukhumvit exit 2, Asok exit 3) and **Nana Entertainment Plaza** (Map p90; Soi 4 (Nana Tai), Th Sukhumvit; 4pm-2am; Nana exit 2) are the real scenes of sex for hire.

PUSSY GALORE

Super Pussy! Pussy Collection! The neon signs leave little doubt about the dominant industry in Patpong, the world's most infamous strip of go-go bars and clubs running 'exotic' shows. There is enough skin on show in Patpong to make Hugh Hefner blush, and a trip to the upstairs clubs could mean you'll never look at a ping-pong ball or a dart the same way again.

For years opinion on Patpong has been polarised between those people who see it as an exploitative, immoral place that is the very definition of sleaze, and others for whom a trip to Bangkok is about little more than immersing themselves in planet Patpong. But Patpong has become such a caricature of itself that in recent times a third group has emerged: the curious tourist. Whatever your opinion, what you see in Patpong or in any of Bangkok's other high-profile 'adult entertainment' areas depends as much on your personal outlook on life as on the quality of your vision.

Prostitution is illegal in Thailand but there are as many as two million sex workers, the vast majority of whom – women and men – cater to Thai men. Many come from poorer regional areas, such as Isan in the northeast, while others might be students helping themselves through university. Sociologists suggest Thais often view sex through a less moralistic or romantic filter than Westerners. That doesn't mean Thai wives like their husbands using prostitutes, but it's only recently that the gradual empowerment of women through education and employment has led to a more vigorous questioning of this very widespread practice.

Patpong occupies two soi that run between Th Silom and Th Surawong in Bangkok's financial district. The two streets are privately owned by – and named for – the Thai-Chinese Patpongpanich family, who bought the land in the 1940s and initially built Patpong Soi 1 and its shophouses; Soi 2 was laid later. During the Vietnam War the first bars and clubs opened to cater to American soldiers on 'R&R'. The scene and its international reputation grew through the '70s and peaked in the '80s, when official Thai tourism campaigns made the sort of 'sights' available in Patpong a pillar of their marketing.

These days Patpong has mellowed considerably, if not matured. Thanks in part to the popular night market that fills the soi after 5pm, it draws so many tourists that it has become a sort of sex theme park. There are still plenty of the stereotypical middle-aged men ogling pole dancers, sitting in dark corners of the so-called 'blow-job bars' and paying 'bar fines' to take girls to hotels that charge by the hour. But you'll also be among other tourists and families who come to see what all the fuss is about.

Most tourists go no further than stolen glances into the ground-floor go-go bars, where women in bikinis drape themselves around stainless-steel poles. Others will be lured to the dimly lit upstairs clubs by men promising sex shows. But it should be said that the so-called 'erotic' shows usually feature bored-looking women performing acts that feel not so much erotic as demeaning to everyone involved. Several of these clubs are also infamous for their scams, usually involving the nonperforming (ie clothed, if just barely) staff descending on wide-eyed tourists like vultures on fresh meat. Before you know it you've bought a dozen drinks, racked up a bill for thousands of baht, and followed up with a loud, aggressive argument flanked by menacing-looking bouncers and threats of 'no money, no pussy!'

By Andrew Burke

GAY & LESBIAN BANGKOK

Bangkok is so gay it makes San Francisco look like rural Texas. With out-and-open night-spots and annual pride events, the city's homosexual community enjoys an unprecedented amount of tolerance considering attitudes in the rest of the region. It should be mentioned, however, that recent years have seen a sharp rise in HIV and other STDs among gay men in Bangkok; when in town, be sure to play it safe.

The website **Utopia** (www.utopia-asia.com) is an evergreen crash-course in Bangkok's gay scene, while local listings mags such as BK (p140) can point you in the direction of the bars and clubs that are hot when you're in town. The **Lesbian Guide to Bangkok** (www.bangkoklesbian.com) is the only English-language tracker of the lesbian scene.

Lower Th Silom is Bangkok's unofficial gaybourhood, and highlights include tiny Soi 2, which is lined with dance clubs such as **DJ Station** (Map p78; www.dj-station.com; 8/6-8 Soi 2, Th Silom; admission from 100B; ☺10.30pm-3am; Ⓜ Si Lom exit 2, Ⓢ Sala Daeng exit 1), the busiest and arguably most famous gay nightclub in Thailand. Virtually next door is Soi 2/1 where bars like **G.O.D** (Guys on Display; Map p78; Soi 2/1; admission 280B; ☺8pm-late; Ⓜ Si Lom exit 2, Ⓢ Sala Daeng exit 1) are not averse to a little shirtless dancing. A more casual scene is found on Soi 4, home to longstanding streetside bars **Balcony** (Map p78; www.balconypub.com; 86-88 Soi 4, Th Silom; ☺5.30pm-1am; ☎; Ⓜ Si Lom exit 2, Ⓢ Sala Daeng exit 1) and **Telephone** (Map p78; www.telephonepub.com; 114/11-13 Soi 4, Th Silom; ☺6pm-1am; ☎; Ⓜ Si Lom exit 2, Ⓢ Sala Daeng exit 1).

Further out of town are a couple smaller gay scenes, including the strip of mostly Thai-frequented bars along Th Kamphaeng Phet such as **Fake Club** (Map p112; www.facebook.com/fakeclub.bangkok; Th Kamphaengphet; ☺8pm-2am; Ⓜ Kamphaeng Phet exit 1); the slightly seedier knot of bars along Soi 8, Th Ratchada, including the infamous **G-Star** (Soi 8, Th Ratchadaphisek; ☺8pm-1am; Ⓜ Phra Ram 9 exit 3); and at RCA, the sleek **Castro** (Map p90; www.facebook.com/Castro.rca.bangkok; Block C, RCA, off Th Phra Ram IX; ☺9.30pm-4.30am; Ⓜ Phra Ram 9 exit 3 & taxi). RCA is also home to Bangkok's only lesbian club, **Zeta** (Map p90; 29/67-69 RCA, off Phra Ram IX; ☺10pm-2am; Ⓜ Phra Ram 9 exit 3 & taxi).

Live Music

Music is an essential element of a Thai night out, and just about every pub worth its salted peanuts has a house band. For the most part this means perky Thai pop covers or tired international standards (if you've left town without having heard a live version of *Hotel California*, you haven't really been to Bangkok), but an increasing number of places are starting to deviate from the norm with quirky and/or inspired bands and performances.

★ **Brick Bar**　　　　LIVE MUSIC
(Map p62; www.brickbarkhaosan.com; basement, Buddy Lodge, 265 Th Khao San; admission 100B; ☺8pm-2am; 🚌 Tha Phra Athit (Banglamphu)) This cavelike pub hosts a nightly revolving cast of live music for an almost exclusively Thai crowd. Come at midnight, wedge yourself into a table a few inches from the horn section, and lose it to Teddy Ska, one of the most energetic live acts in town.

★ **Parking Toys**　　　　LIVE MUSIC
(📞0 2907 2228; 17/22 Soi Mayalap, off Kaset-Navamin Hwy; ☺7pm-2am; Ⓢ Mo Chit exit 3 & taxi) One of Bangkok's best venues for live music, Parking Toys hosts an eclectic revolving cast of fun bands ranging from acoustic/classical ensembles to electro-funk jam acts. Take a taxi heading north from BTS Mo Chit and ask the driver to go to Kaset-Navamin Hwy. Upon passing the second stop light on this road, look for the small Heineken sign on your left.

Cosmic Café　　　　LIVE MUSIC
(Map p90; www.facebook.com/cosmiccafe.bkk; Block C, RCA, off Th Phra Ram IX; ☺8pm-2am Mon-Sat; Ⓜ Phra Ram 9 exit 3 & taxi) Blessedly more low-key than most places on RCA, Cosmic calls itself a cafe but looks like a bar, and in recent years has become one of Bangkok's better destinations for live music. Despite the slight identity crisis, it's a fun place to drink, rock to live music and meet Thai-style.

Titanium LIVE MUSIC

(Map p90; www.titaniumbangkok.com; 2/30 Soi 22, Th Sukhumvit; ⏰8pm-1am; ⓢPhrom Phong exit 6) Some come to this slightly cheesy 'ice bar' for the chill and the flavoured vodka, but we come for Unicorn, the all-female house band.

Living Room LIVE MUSIC

(Map p90; ☎0 2649 8888; www.sheratongrandesukhumvit.com/en/thelivingroom; Level 1, Sheraton Grande Sukhumvit, 250 Th Sukhumvit; ⏰6pm-midnight; ⓜSukhumvit exit 3, ⓢAsok exit 2) Don't let looks deceive you; every night at 8pm this seemingly bland hotel lounge transforms into the city's best venue for live jazz. Contact ahead of time to see which sax master or hide hitter is currently in town.

Raintree LIVE MUSIC

(Map p96; 116/63-64 Th Rang Nam; ⏰8pm-2am; ⓢVictory Monument exit 2) This rustic pub is one of the few remaining places in town where you can hear 'songs for life', Thai folk music with roots in the communist insurgency of the 1960s and '70s.

Sonic LIVE MUSIC

(Map p90; www.facebook.com/SonicBangkok; 90 Soi 63 (Ekamai), Th Sukhumvit; ⏰6pm-2am; ⓢEkkamai exit 4 & taxi) Drawing a mixture of Thai bands, touring indie acts, big-name DJs and a painfully hip crowd, the new Sonic has emerged as Bangkok's hottest venue for live music.

Tawandang German Brewery LIVE MUSIC

(www.tawandang.co.th; cnr Th Phra Ram III & Th Narathiwat Ratchanakharin (Th Chong Nonsi); ⏰5pm-1am; ⓢChong Nonsi exit 2 & taxi) It's Oktoberfest all year-round at this hangar-sized music hall, south of the city. The Thai-German food is tasty, the house-made brews are entirely potable, and the nightly stage shows make singing along a necessity. Music starts at 8.30pm.

Saxophone Pub & Restaurant LIVE MUSIC

(Map p96; www.saxophonepub.com; 3/8 Th Phayathai; ⏰7.30pm-1.30am; ⓢVictory Monument exit 2) Approaching its third decade, Saxophone is a staunch staple of Bangkok's live-music scene. It's a bit too loud for a first date, but the quality and variety of the music makes it a great destination for music-loving buddies on a night out.

Ad Here the 13th LIVE MUSIC

(Map p62; 13 Th Samsen; ⏰6pm-midnight; 🚢Tha Phra Athit (Banglamphu)) This closet-sized pub beside Khlong Banglamphu is everything a neighbourhood joint should be: lots of regulars, cold beer and heart-warming tunes delivered by a masterful house band starting at 10pm.

Brown Sugar LIVE MUSIC

(Map p62; www.brownsugarbangkok.com; 469 Th Phra Sumen; ⏰5pm-1am Mon-Thu, to 2am Sat & Sun; 🚢Tha Phra Athit (Banglamphu)) This long-standing live music staple has found a cosy new home in Old Bangkok.

Bamboo Bar LIVE MUSIC

(Map p76; ☎0 2236 0400; www.mandarinoriental.com/bangkok/fine-dining/the-bamboo-bar; ground fl, Mandarin Oriental, 48 Soi 40, Th Charoen Krung; ⏰9-11.45pm Sun-Thu, to 12.45am Fri & Sat; 🚢Tha Oriental or hotel shuttle boat from Tha Sathon (Central Pier)) The Mandarin Oriental's Bamboo Bar is famous for its live jazz lounge, which holds court inside a colonial-era cabin of lazy fans, broad-leafed palms and rattan decor.

Rock Pub LIVE MUSIC

(Map p84; www.therockpub-bangkok.com; 93/26-28 Th Phayathai; ⏰9.30pm-2am; ⓢRatchathewi exit 2) If you thought the days of heavy metal were long gone, step back in time at this cavelike pub where posters of Iron Maiden pass for interior design and black jeans and long hair are still the unofficial dress code.

Traditional Arts

Sala Chalermkrung THEATRE

(Map p72; ☎0 2222 0434; www.salachalermkrung.com; 66 Th Charoen Krung; tickets 800-1200B; ⏰shows 7.30pm Thu & Fri; 🚢Tha Saphan Phut (Memorial Bridge), ⓜHua Lamphong exit 1 & taxi) In a Thai art deco building at the edge of the Chinatown-Phahurat district, this theatre provides a striking venue for *kŏhn* (masked dance-drama based on stories from the *Ramakian,* the Thai version of the *Ramayana*). Performances are held every Thursday and Friday and last about two hours plus intermission. The theatre requests that patrons dress respectfully, which means no shorts, tank tops or sandals.

National Theatre THEATRE

(Map p62; ☎0 2224 1342; 2 Th Ratchini; tickets 60-100B; 🚢Tha Chang) After a lengthy renovation, the National Theatre is again open for business. Performances of *kŏhn* are held at 2pm on the first and second Sundays of the month from January to March and July to September, and *lá·kon,* Thai dance-dramas, are held at 2pm on the first and second Sundays of the month from April to June and October to December.

Thai Boxing (Moo·ay tai)

Thai boxing's best of the best fight it out at Bangkok's two boxing stadiums: **Ratchadamnoen Stadium** (Map p62; off Th Ratchadamnoen Nok; tickets 3rd class/2nd class/ringside 1000/1500/2000B; ⊠ klorng boat to Tha Phan Fah, ⓢ Phaya Thai exit 3 & taxi) and **Lumpinee Boxing Stadium** (Th Ramintra; tickets 3rd class/2nd class/ringside 1000/2000/3000B; Ⓜ Mo Chit exit 3 & taxi, Ⓜ Chatuchak Park exit 2 & taxi).

You'll note that tickets are not cheap, and these prices are exponentially more than what Thais pay. To add insult to injury, the inflated price offers no special service or seating, and at Ratchadamnoen Stadium foreigners are sometimes corralled into an area with an obstructed view. As long as you are mentally prepared for the financial jabs from the promoters, you'll be better prepared to enjoy the real fight.

Fights are held throughout the week, alternating between the two stadiums. Ratchadamnoen hosts the matches at 6.30pm on Monday, Wednesday, Thursday and Sunday. Lumpinee hosts matches on Tuesday and Friday from 6.30pm to 10.30pm, and Saturday at 4pm to 8pm and 8.30pm to midnight. There is a total of eight to 10 fights of five rounds apiece. The stadiums don't usually fill up until the main events, which normally start around 8pm or 9pm.

There are English-speaking 'staff' standing outside the stadium who will practically tackle you upon arrival. Although there have been a few reports of scamming, most of these assistants help steer visitors to the foreigner ticket windows and hand out a fight roster; they can also be helpful in telling you which fights are the best match-ups between contestants. (Some say that welterweights, between 135lb and 147lb, ie 61.2kg and 66.7kg, are the best.) To keep everyone honest, though, remember to purchase tickets from the ticket window, not from a person outside the stadium.

As a prematch warm-up, grab a plate of *gài yâhng* (grilled chicken) and other northeastern dishes from the restaurants surrounding Ratchadamnoen Stadium.

🔒 Shopping

Welcome to a true buyer's market. Home to one of the world's largest outdoor markets, numerous giant upscale malls, and sidewalk-clogging bazaars on nearly every street, it's impossible not to be awed by the amount of commerce in Bangkok. However, despite the apparent scope and variety, Bangkok really excels in one area when it comes to shopping: cheap stuff. Although luxury items and brand names are indeed available in Bangkok, prices are high, and you'll find much better deals at online warehouses in the US or bargain-basement sales in Hong Kong. Ceramics, dirt-cheap T-shirts, fabric, Asian knick-knackery – and yes, if you can deal with the guilt, pirated items – are Bangkok's bargains.

The difficulty is finding your way around, since the city's intense urban tangle sometimes makes orientation difficult. A good shopping companion is *Nancy Chandler's Map of Bangkok*, with annotations on all sorts of small and out-of-the-way shopping venues and *dà·làht* (markets).

Antiques

Real Thai antiques are rare and costly. Most Bangkok antique shops keep a few authentic pieces for collectors, along with lots of pseudo-antiques or traditionally crafted items that look like antiques.

River City   ANTIQUES
(Map p76; www.rivercity.co.th; 23 Th Yotha; ⊙ 10am-10pm; ⊠ Tha Si Phraya/River City or shopping centre shuttle boat from Tha Sathon (Central Pier)) This multistorey shopping centre is an all-in-one stop for old-world Asiana. Although the quality is high, the prices are too, as many wealthy tourists filter in and out. As is the case with many antique stores in Bangkok, the vast majority of the pieces at River City appear to come from Myanmar, not Thailand. Many stores here close on Sunday.

House of Chao   ANTIQUES
(Map p78; 9/1 Th Decho; ⊙ 9.30am-7pm; ⓢ Chong Nonsi exit 3) This three-storey shop, set, appropriately, in an antique house, has everything necessary to deck out your fantasy colonial-era mansion. Particularly interesting are the various weatherworn doors, doorways, gateways and trellises behind the showroom.

Department Stores & Shopping Centres

Bangkok may be crowded and polluted, but its department stores are modern oases of order. They're also downright frigid, and Sunday afternoons see a significant part of Bangkok's population crowding into the city's indoor malls to take advantage of the air-con. By no accident, the BTS stations also have shaded walkways delivering passengers directly into nearby stores without ever having to set foot on ground level.

ONE NIGHT IN BANGKOK... IS NOT ENOUGH TO HAVE A SUIT MADE

Many tourists arrive in Bangkok with the notion of getting clothes custom-tailored at a bargain price, which is entirely possible. Prices are almost always lower than what you'd pay at home, but common scams ranging from commission-hungry túk-túk (*dúk dúk*) drivers to shoddy workmanship and inferior fabrics make bespoke tailoring in Bangkok a potentially disappointing investment. To maximise your chances of walking away feeling (and looking) good, read on...

➡ **You get what you pay for** If you sign up for a suit, two pants, two shirts and a tie, with silk sarong thrown in for US$169 (a very popular offer in Bangkok), the chances are it will look and fit like a sub-US$200 wardrobe. And although an offer may seem great on the surface, the price may fluctuate significantly depending on the fabric you choose.

➡ **Have a good idea of what you want** If it's a suit you're after, should it be single- or double-breasted? How many buttons? What style trousers? Of course, if you have no idea then the tailor will be more than happy to advise. Alternatively, bring a favourite garment from home and have it copied.

➡ **Set aside a week to get clothes tailored** Shirts and trousers can often be turned around in 48 hours or less with only one fitting, but no matter what a tailor may tell you, it takes more than one and often more than two fittings to create a good suit. Most reliable tailors will ask for two to five sittings. Any tailor who can sew your order in less than 24 hours should be treated with caution.

Reputable tailors include:

➡ **Pinky Tailors** (Map p84; www.pinkytailor.com; 888/40 Mahatun Plaza, Th Ploenchit; ⊙10am-7pm Mon-Sat; Ⓢ Phloen Chit exits 2 & 4) Custom-made shirts and suit jackets have been Mr Pinky's speciality for more than 35 years. Located behind the Mahatun Building.

➡ **July** (Map p78; ☑ 0 2233 0171; www.julytailor.com; 30/6 Th Sala Daeng; ⊙9am-7pm; Ⓜ Si Lom exit 2, Ⓢ Sala Daeng exit 4) Tailor to Thailand's royalty and elite alike, the suits here don't come cheap and the cuts can be somewhat conservative, but the quality is unsurpassed.

➡ **Marco Tailors** (Map p84; 430/33 Soi 7, Siam Sq; ⊙9am-7pm Mon-Fri; Ⓢ Siam exit 2) Dealing solely in men's suits, this longstanding and reliable tailor has a wide selection of banker-sensibility wools and cottons.

➡ **Duly** (Map p90; ☑ 0 2662 6647; www.laladuly.co.th; Soi 49, Th Sukhumvit; ⊙10am-7pm; Ⓢ Phrom Phong exit 1) High-quality Italian fabics and experienced tailors make Duly one of the best places in Bangkok to commission a sharp shirt.

➡ **Raja's Fashions** (Map p90; ☑ 0 2253 8379; www.rajasfashions.com; 160/1 Th Sukhumvit; ⊙10am-8pm Mon-Sat; Ⓢ Nana exit 4) One of Bangkok's more famous tailors, Raja's gets a mixed bag of reviews, but the majority swear by the service and quality.

➡ **Nickermann's** (Map p90; ☑ 0 2252 6682; www.nickermanns.net; basement, Landmark Hotel, 138 Th Sukhumvit; ⊙10am-8.30pm Mon-Sat, noon-6pm Sun; Ⓢ Nana exit 2) Corporate ladies rave about Nickermann's tailor-made power suits: pants and jackets that suit curves and busts. Formal ball gowns are another area of expertise.

The selection is surprisingly good at Bangkok's shopping centres, but don't expect any bargains – most imported items cost more than they would elsewhere. Another quirk is that shop assistants follow you around the store from rack to rack. This is the definition of Thai 'service' rather than an indication that they've sniffed you out as a shoplifter. And be sure you're satisfied with an item, as returns are largely unheard of.

Most shopping centres are open from 10am or 11am to 9pm or 10pm.

★ **MBK Center**   SHOPPING CENTRE
(Map p84; www.mbk-center.com; cnr Th Phra Ram I & Th Phayathai; ⊙10am-10pm; Ⓢ National Stadium exit 4) This colossal mall has become a tourist destination in its own right. Swedish and other languages can be heard as much as Thai, and on any given weekend

half of Bangkok can be found here combing through an inexhaustible range of small stalls and shops.

MBK is the cheapest place to buy mobile phones and accessories (4th floor) and name-brand knock-offs (nearly every other floor). It's also one of the better places to stock up on camera gear (ground floor and 5th floor), and the expansive food court (6th floor) is one of the best in town.

CentralWorld
SHOPPING CENTRE

(Map p84; www.centralworld.co.th; Th Ratchadamri; ⊙10am-10pm; S Chit Lom exit 9 to Sky Walk, Siam exit 6 to Sky Walk) Spanning eight storeys of more than 500 shops and 100 restaurants, CentralWorld is one of Southeast Asia's largest shopping centres. In addition to an ice rink, you'll find an extrahuge branch of bookstore B2S, and you could spend an hour sniffing around the fragrances at Karmakamet (2nd floor).

Siam Paragon
SHOPPING CENTRE

(Map p84; www.siamparagon.co.th; 991/1 Th Phra Ram I; ⊙10am-10pm; S Siam exits 3 & 5) The biggest and glitziest of Bangkok's malls, Siam Paragon is more of an urban park than a shopping centre. Astronomically luxe brands occupy most floors, but there's also Siam Ocean World (p75), Siam Paragon Cineplex (p124), a huge basement-level food court, and on the 3rd floor Kinokuniya, Thailand's largest English-language bookstore.

Siam Center & Siam Discovery Center
SHOPPING CENTRE

(Map p84; cnr Th Phra Ram I & Th Phayathai, Siam Sq; ⊙10am-9pm; S Siam exit 1) Siam Discovery Center excels in home decor, with the whole 3rd floor devoted to Asian-minimalist styles and jewel-toned fabrics; we love the earthy, Thai-influenced designs at Doi Tung. The attached Siam Center has gone under the redesign knife for a younger, hipper look. Youth fashion is its new focus, and several local labels, ranging from anr to senada*, are on the 2nd floor.

Gaysorn Plaza
SHOPPING CENTRE

(Map p84; www.gaysorn.com; cnr Th Ploenchit & Th Ratchadamri; ⊙10am-8pm; S Chit Lom exit 9) A haute couture catwalk, Gaysorn has spiralling staircases, all-white halls and mouthfuls of top-name designers. Local fashion leaders occupy the 2nd floor 'Thai Fashion Chic', while the top floor is a stroll through home decor, highlights of which are the fragrant soaps at Thann and the Asian-influenced ceramics at Lamont.

Pantip Plaza
SHOPPING CENTRE

(Map p84; 604 Th Phetchaburi; ⊙10am-9pm; S Ratchathewi exit 4) Pantip is five storeys of computer and software stores ranging from legit to flea market. Many locals come here to buy 'pirated' software and computer peripherals, but the crowds and touts ('DVD sex? DVD sex?') make it among the more tedious shopping experiences in town.

Central Chidlom
SHOPPING CENTRE

(Map p84; www.central.co.th; 1027 Th Ploenchit; ⊙10am-10pm; S Chit Lom exit 5) Generally regarded as the country's best department store for quality and selection, Central has 13 branches in Bangkok in addition to this chichi flagship.

BARGAINING 101

Many of your purchases in Bangkok will involve an ancient skill that has long been abandoned in the West: bargaining. Contrary to what you'll see on a daily basis on Th Khao San, bargaining (in Thai, *dòr rahkah*) is not a terse exchange of numbers and animosity. Rather, bargaining Thai style is a generally friendly transaction where two people try to agree on a price that is fair to both of them.

The first rule of bargaining is to have a general idea of the price. Ask around at a few vendors to get a rough notion. When you're ready to buy, it's generally a good strategy to start at 50% of the asking price and work up from there. If you're buying several of an item, you have much more leverage to request and receive a lower price. If the seller immediately agrees to your first price you're probably paying too much, but it's bad form to bargain further at this point.

In general, keeping a friendly, flexible demeanour throughout the transaction will almost always work in your favour. And remember, only begin bargaining if you're really planning on buying the item. Most importantly, there's simply no point in getting angry or upset over a few baht. The locals, who probably have less money than you do, never do this.

Fashion & Textiles

In recent years Bangkok has become something of a fashion-conscious and, increasingly, fashion-generating city. Local designers such as senada*, Flynow and Tango have shown that the city harbours a style scene that can compete on the international catwalk. More affordable looks are exhibited by the city's trendy teens who strut their distinctive 'Bangkok' look in the various shopping areas.

★ **Siam Square**   SHOPPING CENTRE
(Map p84; Th Phra Ram I; ⊘11am-9pm; ⓢSiam exits 2, 4 & 6) This open-air shopping zone is ground zero for teenage culture in Bangkok. Pop music blares out of tinny speakers, and gangs of hipsters in various costumes ricochet between fast-food restaurant and closet-sized boutiques. It's a great place to pick up designs you're guaranteed not to find anywhere else, though most outfits require a barely there waist.

It's Happened To Be A Closet   CLOTHING
(Map p84; 1st fl, Siam Paragon, 991/1 Th Phra Ram I; ⊘10am-10pm; ⓢSiam exits 3 & 5) Garbled grammar aside, this is a brilliant place to stock up on locally designed and made togs with a Th Khao San-meets-Siam Paragon vibe.

Flynow   CLOTHING
(Map p84; www.flynowbangkok.com; 2nd fl, Gaysorn Plaza, cnr Th Ploenchit & Th Ratchadamri; ⊘10am-8pm; ⓢChit Lom exit 9) A longstanding leader in Bangkok's home-grown fashion scene, Flynow creates feminine couture that has caught the eyes of several international shows. There are additional branches at Siam Center and CentralWorld.

Tango   ACCESSORIES
(Map p84; www.tango.co.th; 2nd fl, Gaysorn Plaza, cnr Th Ploenchit & Th Ratchadamri; ⊘10am-8pm; ⓢChit Lom exit 9) This home-grown brand specialises in funky leather goods, but you may not even recognise the medium under the layers of bright embroidery and chunky jewels. Also available at Siam Center.

Jim Thompson   TEXTILES
(Map p78; www.jimthompson.com; 9 Th Surawong; ⊘9am-9pm; ⓜSi Lom exit 2, ⓢSala Daeng exit 3) The surviving business of the international promoter of Thai silk, this, the largest Jim Thompson shop, sells colourful silk handkerchiefs, place mats, wraps and pillow cushions. Just up the road is the company's **factory outlet** (Map p78; 149/4-6 Th Surawong; ⊘9am-6pm; ⓢSala Daeng exit 1) that sells discontinued patterns at a significant discount.

Handicrafts, Souvenirs & Decor

The tourist markets have tonnes of factory-made pieces that pop up all along the tourist route. The shopping centres sell products with a little better quality at proportionally higher prices, but the independent shops sell the best items all round.

A bimonthly **Thai Craft Fair** (Map p90; www.thaicraft.org; 3rd fl, Jasmine City Bldg, cnr Soi 23 & Th Sukhumvit; ⊘10am-3pm; ⓜSukhumvit exit 2, ⓢAsok exit 3) is held in Bangkok, featuring the wares of more than 60 Thai artisans.

Nandakwang   HANDICRAFTS
(Map p90; www.nandakwang.com; 108/2-3 Soi Prasanmit, Th Sukhumvit, no roman-script sign; ⊘9am-6.30pm Mon-Sat; ⓜSukhumvit exit 2, ⓢAsok exit 3) The Bangkok satellite of a Chiang Mai–based brand, Nandakwang sells a mix of rustic cloth products. The cheery hand-embroidered pillows and bags are particularly attractive. There is also a branch on the 4th floor of Siam Discovery Center.

Sop Moei Arts   HANDICRAFTS
(Map p90; www.sopmoeiarts.com; Soi 49/9, Th Sukhumvit; ⊘9.30am-5pm Tue-Sat; ⓢPhrom Phong exit 3 & taxi) The Bangkok showroom of this non-profit organisation features the vibrant cloth creations of Karen weavers in Mae Hong Son, northern Thailand. It's near the end of Soi 49/9, in the large Racquet Club complex.

Thai Home Industries   HANDICRAFTS
(Map p76; 35 Soi 40, Th Charoen Krung; ⊘9am-6.30pm Mon-Sat; ⓑTha Oriental) A visit to this temple-like building, a former monks' quarters, is like discovering an abandoned attic of Asian booty. Despite the odd assortment of items (our last visit revealed items ranging from elegant handmade flatware to wooden model ships) and lack of order, it's heaps more fun than the typically faceless Bangkok handicraft shop.

Taekee Taekon   HANDICRAFTS
(Map p62; 118 Th Phra Athit; ⊘9am-6pm Mon-Sat; ⓑTha Phra Athit (Banglamphu)) Representing Thailand's main silk-producing regions, this charming store has a beautiful selection of table runners and wall hangings. Alongside silk products, you will also find small examples of celadon pottery and a vast selection of postcards.

Narai Phand SOUVENIRS
(Map p84; www.naraiphand.com; ground fl, President Tower, 973 Th Ploenchit; ⏰10am-8pm; Ⓢ Chit Lom exit 7) Souvenir-quality handicrafts are given fixed prices and comfortable air-con at this government-run facility. You won't find anything here that you haven't already seen at all of the tourist street markets, but it is a good stop if you're pressed for time or spooked by haggling.

Markets

Although air-conditioned malls have better PR departments, open-air markets are the true face of commercial Bangkok, and are where you'll find the best bargains.

Markets are best approached as sights rather than shopping destinations (see the boxed text for our suggestions).

★**Chatuchak Weekend Market** MARKET
(ตลาดนัดจตุจักร, Talat Nat Jatujak; www.chatuchak.org; Th Phahonyothin; ⏰9am-6pm Sat & Sun; Ⓜ Chatuchak Park exit 1, Kamphaeng Phet exits 1 & 2, Ⓢ Mo Chit exit 1) Among the largest markets in the world, Chatuchak seems to unite everything buyable, from used vintage sneakers to baby squirrels. Plan to spend a full day, as there's plenty to see, do and buy. But come early, ideally around 9am to 10am, to beat the crowds and the heat.

OFF THE BEATEN TRACK

MARKETS AS SIGHTS?

Even if you don't have a shopping list, several of Bangkok's markets are well worth a visit. Here are some of our favourites:

➡ **Talat Rot Fai** (ตลาดรถไฟ; Map p112; www.facebook.com/taradrodfi; Soi 51, Th Srinakharin; ⏰6pm-midnight Wed & Fri-Sun; Ⓢ Udom Suk exit 2 & taxi) Set in a sprawling abandoned rail yard, this market is all about the retro, from antique enamel platters to secondhand Vespas. With mobile snack vendors, VW van-based bars and even a few land-bound pubs, it's also much more than just a shopping destination.

➡ **Pak Khlong Talat** (ปากคลองตลาด, Flower Market; Map p72; Th Chakraphet; ⏰24hr; 🚢Tha Saphan Phut (Memorial Bridge)) Every night this market near Mae Nam Chao Phraya becomes the city's largest depot for wholesale flowers. Arrive as late as you're willing to stay up, and be sure to take a camera, as the technicolour blur of roses, lotuses and daisies on the move is a sight worth capturing. During the day, Pak Khlong is a wholesale vegetable market.

➡ **Nonthaburi Market** (ตลาดนนทบุรี; Tha Nam Nonthaburi, Nonthaburi; ⏰5-9am; 🚢Tha Nonthaburi) Located a short walk from Nonthaburi Pier, the northernmost extent of the Chao Phraya Express Boat, this is one of the most expansive and atmospheric produce markets in the area. Come early, as most vendors are gone by 9am.

➡ **Sampeng Lane** (สำเพ็ง; Map p72; Soi Wanit 1 (Sampeng Lane); ⏰8am-6pm; 🚢Tha Ratchawong, Ⓜ Hua Lamphong exit 1 & taxi) This crowded wholesale market runs roughly parallel to Th Yaowarat, bisecting the two districts of Chinatown and Phahurat. Pick up the narrow artery from Th Ratchawong and follow it through its many manifestations – from handbags, homewares, hair decorations, stickers, Japanese-animation gear and plastic beeping key chains.

➡ **Khlong Toey Market** (ตลาดคลองเตย; Map p90; cnr Th Ratchadaphisek & Th Phra Ram IV; ⏰5-10am; Ⓜ Khlong Toei exit 1) This wholesale market, one of the city's largest, is inevitably the origin of many of the meals you'll eat during your stay in Bangkok. Get there early, and although some corners of the market can't exactly be described as photogenic, be sure to bring a camera to capture the stacks of durians or cheery fishmongers.

➡ **Bang Nam Pheung** (ตลาดบางน้ำผึ้ง; Bang Nam Pheung; ⏰8am-3pm Sat & Sun; Ⓢ Bang Na exit 2 & taxi) An easy escape from the city, this buzzy weekends-only market is on the Phra Pradaeng Peninsula, a vast rural-feeling district often referred to as Bangkok's 'green lung'. The emphasis is on food, and it's a great place for unrestrained outdoor snacking. To get to the market, take the BTS to Bang Na and jump in a taxi for the short ride to the pier at Wat Bang Na Nork. From there, take the river-crossing ferry (4B) followed by a short motorcycle taxi (10B) ride.

Chatuchak Market

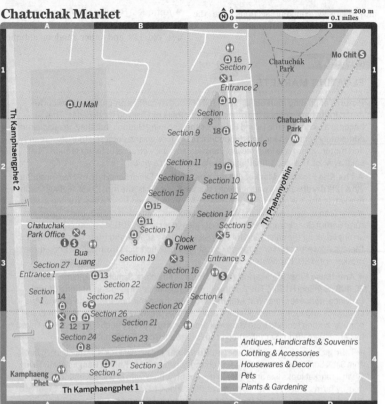

Chatuchak Market

There is an information centre and a bank with ATMs and **foreign-exchange booths** at the **Chatuchak Park office**, near the northern end of the market's Soi 1, Soi 2 and Soi 3. Schematic maps and toilets are located throughout the market.

There are a few vendors on weekday mornings, and a daily vegetable, plant and flower market opposite the market's south-ern side. One section of the latter, known as the **Or Tor Kor Market** (องค์การตลาดเพื่อ เกษตรกร (ตลาด อ.ต.ก.); Map p112; Th Kamphaeng-phet; ☺8am-6pm; Ⓜ Kamphaeng Phet exit 3), sells fantastically gargantuan fruit and sea-food, and has a decent food court as well.

Once you're deep in the bowels of Chatuchak, it will seem like there is no order and no escape, but the market is arranged into relatively coherent sections. Use the clock tower as a handy landmark.

➔ **Antiques, Handicrafts & Souvenirs** Section 1 is the place to go for Buddha statues, old LPs and other random antiques.

WORTH A TRIP

FLOATING MARKETS

Pictures of floating markets jammed full of wooden canoes pregnant with colourful exotic fruits have defined the official tourist profile of Thailand for decades. They've become as iconic as the Grand Palace or the Reclining Buddha, but they are also almost completely contrived for, and dependent upon, foreign and domestic tourists – roads and motorcycles have long moved Bangkokians' daily errands onto dry ground. That said, a few of Thailand's floating markets are worth a visit.

➔ **Tha Kha Floating Market** (ตลาดน้ำท่าคา; Tha Kha, Samut Songkhram; ⊘ 7am–noon, 2nd, 7th & 12th day of waxing & waning moons plus Sat & Sun) This, the most 'real' feeling floating market, is also the most difficult to reach. A handful of vendors coalesce along a narrow *klorng* (canal; also spelt *khlong*) lined with coconut palms and old wooden houses in rural Samut Songkhram Province. Boat rides (per person 20B, 45 minutes) can be arranged along the canal, and there are lots of tasty snacks and fruits for sale. To get there, take a morning *sŏrng·tăa·ou* (passenger pick-up truck) from Samut Songkhram's market area (8B, 10 minutes).

➔ **Amphawa Floating Market** (ตลาดน้ำอัมพวา; Amphawa, Samut Songkhram; dishes 20-40B; ⊘ 4-9pm Fri-Sun) The Amphawa Floating Market, also in Samut Songkhram Province, convenes near Wat Amphawa, the centre of this tiny town. The emphasis is on edibles and tourist knick-knacks, and because the market is only on weekends and is popular among tourists from Bangkok, things can get pretty hectic. Amphawa is linked by *sŏrng·tăa·ou* from Samut Songkhram's market area (8B, 10 minutes).

➔ **Taling Chan Floating Market** (ตลาดน้ำตลิ่งชัน; Khlong Bangkok Noi, Thonburi; ⊘ 7am–4pm Sat & Sun) Just outside Bangkok on the access road to Khlong Bangkok Noi, Taling Chan's market looks like any other in the country, busy with produce vendors from nearby farms. But the twist emerges at the canal, where several floating docks serve as informal dining rooms, and the kitchens are canoes tethered to the docks. Taling Chan is in Thonburi and can be reached via taxi from Wongwian Yai BTS station or via air-con bus 79 (16B, 25 minutes), which makes stops on Th Ratchadamnoen Klang. Long-tail boats from any large Bangkok pier can also be hired for a trip to Taling Chan and the nearby Khlong Chak Phra.

➔ **Damnoen Saduak Floating Market** (ตลาดน้ำดำเนินสะดวก; Damnoen Saduak, Ratchaburi Province; ⊘ 7am–noon) This 100-year old floating market – the country's most famous – is now essentially a floating souvenir stand filled with package tourists. This in itself can be a fascinating insight into Thai culture, as the majority of tourists here are Thais, and watching their approach to this cultural 'theme park' is instructive. But beyond the market, the residential canals are quite peaceful and can be explored by boat (per person 100B). Trips stop at small family businesses including a Thai candy maker, a pomelo farm and a knife crafter. Air-con bus 79, with stops on Th Ratchadamnoen Klang, and minivans from the Victory Monument both connect to the Southern Bus Terminal in Thonburi, from where you can find buses to Damnoen Saduak (80B, two hours, frequent from 6am to 9pm).

➔ **Don Wai Market** (ตลาดดอนหวาย; Don Wai, Nakhon Pathom; ⊘ 6am-6pm) Not technically a swimmer, Don Wai Market claims a riverbank location in Nakhon Pathom Province, having originally started out in the early 20th century as a floating market for pomelo and jackfruit growers and traders. Like many tourist attractions geared towards Thais, the main draw here is food, such as fruit, traditional sweets and *bèt pá·lóh* (five-spice stewed duck), which can be consumed on board large boats that cruise the Nakhon Chaisi River (60B, one hour). The easiest way to reach Don Wai Market is to take a minivan from beside Central Pinklao in Thonburi (45B, 35 minutes).

More secular arts and crafts, such as musical instruments and hill-tribe items, can be found in Sections 25 and 26. **Baan Sin Thai** (Map p135; Section 24, Stall 130, Soi 1; ⊙9am-6pm Sat & Sun) sells a mixture of *kŏhn* masks and old-school Thai toys, all of which make fun souvenirs, and **Kitcharoen Dountri** (Map p135; Section 8, Stall 464, Soi 15; ⊙9am-6pm Sat & Sun) specialises in Thai musical instruments, including flutes, whistles, drums and CDs of classical Thai music. Other quirky gifts include the life-like plastic Thai fruit and vegetables at **Marché** (Map p135; Section 17, Stall 254, Soi 1; ⊙9am-6pm Sat & Sun), or their scaled-down miniature counterparts nearby at **Papachu** (Map p135; Section 17, Stall 23, Soi 1; ⊙9am-6pm Sat & Sun).

➔ Clothing & Accessories

Clothing dominates most of Chatuchak, starting in Section 8 and continuing through the even-numbered sections to 24. Sections 5 and 6 deal in used clothing for every Thai youth subculture, from punks to cowboys, while Soi 7, where it transects Sections 12 and 14, is heavy on the more underground hip-hop and skate fashions. Somewhat more sophisticated independent labels can be found in Sections 2 and 3, while tourist-sized clothes and textiles are in Sections 8 and 10.

For accessories, several shops in Sections 24 and 26, such as **Orange Karen Silver** (Map p135; Section 26, Stall 246, Soi 8; ⊙9am-6pm Sat & Sun), specialise in chunky silver jewellery and semiprecious uncut stones.

➔ Eating & Drinking

Lots of Thai-style snacking will stave off Chatuchak rage (cranky behaviour brought on by dehydration or hunger); numerous food stalls set up shop between Sections 6 and 8. Standouts include **Foon Talop** (Map p135; Section 26, Stall 319, Soi 8; mains 40-100B; ⊙10am-6pm Sat & Sun), a popular Isan restaurant, **Café Ice** (Map p135; Section 7, Stall 267, Soi 3; mains 100-300B; ⊙10am-6pm Sat & Sun), a Western-Thai fusion joint that does good *pàt tai* and fruit shakes, and **Saman Islam** (Map p135; Section 16, Stall 34, Soi 24; mains 40-100B; ⊙10am-6pm Sat & Sun), a Thai-Muslim restaurant that serves a tasty chicken biryani. **Viva 8** (Map p135; www.facebook.com/Viva8JJ; Section 8, Soi 16/1; mains 100-300B; ⊙9am-10pm Sat & Sun) features a DJ and, when we stopped by, a chef making huge platters of paella.

If you need air-con, pop into **Toh-Plue** (Map p135; Section 27; mains 100-250B; ⊙9am-7pm; ✱; ⓂMRT Kamphaeng Phet) for all the Thai standards. As evening draws near,

down a beer at **Viva's** (Map p135; Section 26, Stall 149, Soi 6; ⊙10am-10pm Sat & Sun), a cafebar with live music or, if it's dark, cross to the whisky bars along Th Kamphaeng Phet 2.

➔ Housewares & Decor

The northern and northwestern edge of the market, particularly Sections 8 to 26, specialises in all manner of housewares, from cheap plastic buckets to expensive brass woks. This area is a particularly good place to stock up on inexpensive Thai ceramics, ranging from celadon to the traditional rooster-themed bowls from Lampang.

N & D Tablewares (Map p135; Section 25, Stall 185, Soi 4; ⊙9am-6pm Sat & Sun) has a huge variety of stainless-steel flatware, and **Ton-Tan** (Map p135; Section 8, Stall 460, Soi 15/1; ⊙9am-6pm Sat & Sun) deals in coconut and sugar palm–derived plates, bowls and other utensils.

Those looking to spice up the house should stop by **Spice Boom** (Map p135; Section 26, Stall 246, Soi 8; ⊙9am-6pm), where you can find dried herbs and spices for both consumption and decoration. Other notable olfactory indulgences include the handmade soaps, lotions and scrubs at **D-narn** (Map p135; Section 19, Stall 204, Soi 1; ⊙9am-6pm Sat & Sun) and the fragrant perfumes and essential oils at **AnyaDharu Scent Library** (Map p135; Section 3, Stall 3, Soi 43/2; ⊙9am-6pm Sat & Sun).

For less utilitarian goods, Section 7 is a virtual open-air gallery – we particularly liked **Pariwat A-nantachina's** (Map p135; Section 7, Stall 118, Soi 2; ⊙9am-6pm Sat & Sun) for Bangkok-themed murals. Several shops in Section 10, including **Tuptim Shop** (Map p135; Section 10, Stall 261, Soi 19; ⊙9am-6pm Sat & Sun) sell new and antique Burmese lacquerware. **Meng** (Map p135; Section 26, Stall 195, Soi 8; ⊙9am-6pm Sat & Sun) features a dusty mish-mash of quirky antiques from both Thailand and Burma.

➔ Pets

Possibly the most fun you'll ever have window shopping will be petting puppies and cuddling kittens in Sections 13 and 15. Soi 9 of the former features several shops that deal solely in clothing for pets. This section has, in the past, been associated with the sale of illegal wildlife, although much of this trade has been driven underground.

➔ Plants & Gardening

The interior perimeter of Sections 2 to 4 feature a huge variety of potted plants, flowers, herbs, fruits, and the accessories needed to maintain them. Many of these shops are also open on weekday afternoons.

THE WAR ON THE GEM SCAM

We're begging you, if you aren't a gem trader, don't buy unset stones in Thailand – period. Countless tourists are sucked into the prolific and well-rehearsed gem scam in which they are taken to a store by a helpful stranger and tricked into buying bulk gems that can supposedly be resold in their home country for 100% profit. The expert con artists (part of a well-organised cartel) seem trustworthy and convince tourists they need a citizen of the country to circumvent tricky customs regulations. Guess what, the gem world doesn't work like that, and what most tourists end up with are worthless pieces of glass. By the time you sort all this out, the store has closed, changed names and the police can do little to help.

Want to know more or want to report a scam? Visit 2bangkok.com and navigate down to the 'Gem Scam' page for years' worth of tracking the phenomenon, or go to **Thai Gems Scam Group** (www.oocities.org/thaigemscamgroup/) for photos of touts who troll the temples for victims. The tourist police can also help to resolve some purchase disputes, but don't expect miracles.

Asiatique
MARKET

(www.thaiasiatique.com; Soi 72-76, Th Charoen Krung; ⊘4-11pm; ⛴shuttle boat from Tha Sathon (Central Pier)) At press time Bangkok's buzziest market, Asiatique takes the form of rows of open-air warehouses of commerce next to Mae Nam Chao Phraya. A slightly more upscale version of Chatuchak Market, shoppers can expect clothing, handicrafts, souvenirs and quite a few dining and drinking venues. To get here, take one of the frequent shuttle boats from Tha Sathon (Central Pier) between 4pm and 11.30pm.

Thanon Khao San Market
SOUVENIRS

(Map p62; Th Khao San; ⊘10am-midnight; ⛴Tha Phra Athit (Banglamphu)) The main guesthouse strip in Banglamphu is a day-and-night shopping bazaar for serious baht pinchers, with cheap T-shirts, 'bootleg' CDs, wooden elephants, hemp clothing, fisherman pants and other goods that make backpackers go ga-ga.

Pratunam Market
CLOTHING

(Map p84; cnr Th Phetchaburi & Th Ratchaprarop; ⊘10am-10pm; ⛴klorng boat to Tha Pratunam, ⑤Ratchathewi exit 4) The city's biggest wholesale clothing market, Pratunam is a tight warren of stalls trickling deep into the block. In addition to cheap T-shirts and jeans, luggage, bulk toiletries and souvenirs are also available.

Thanon Sukhumvit Market
SOUVENIRS

(Map p90; btwn Soi 3 & Soi 15, Th Sukhumvit; ⊘11am-11pm Tue-Sun; ⑤Nana exits 1 & 3) Knock-off bags and watches, stacks of skin-flick DVDs, Chinese throwing stars and other questionable gifts dominate at this market peddling to package and sex tourists.

Soi Lalai Sap
CLOTHING

(Map p78; Soi 5, Th Silom; ⊘9am-4pm Mon-Fri; ⓂSi Lom exit 2, ⑤Sala Daeng exit 2) The 'money-melting' street has a number of vendors selling all sorts of cheap clothing, watches and homewares during the day. Regular perusers say that imperfections from name-brand factories often appear in the stacks.

Patpong Night Market
SOUVENIRS

(Map p78; Soi Patpong 1 & 2, Th Silom; ⊘6pm-midnight; ⓂSi Lom exit 2, ⑤Sala Daeng exit 1) Drawing more crowds than the ping-pong shows, this market continues the street's illicit leanings with a deluge of cheap and pirated goods, particularly watches and clothing. Bargain with intensity as first-quoted prices tend to be astronomically high.

ℹ Information

DANGERS & ANNOYANCES

You are more likely to be charmed rather than coerced out of your money in Bangkok. Practised con artists capitalise on Thailand's famous friendliness and a revolving door of clueless tourists. Bangkok's most heavily touristed areas – Wat Phra Kaew, Wat Pho, Jim Thompson House, Th Khao San, Erawan Shrine – are favourite hunting grounds for these scallywags. The best prevention is knowledge, so before hitting the ground, become familiar with the more common local scams.

If you've been scammed, the tourist police can be effective in dealing with some of the 'unethical' business practices and crime. But in general you should enter into every monetary transaction with the understanding that you have no consumer protection or recourse.

CULTURAL CENTRES

Various international cultural centres in Bangkok organise film festivals, lectures, language classes and other educational liaisons.

Alliance Française (☑0 2670 4200; www.afthailande.org; 179 Th Witthayu (Wireless Rd); Ⓜ Lumphini exit 3)

British Council (☑0 2657 5678; www.britishcouncil.or.th; 254 Soi Chulalongkorn 64, Th Phra Ram I; ⊙8.30am-7pm; Ⓢ Siam exit 6)

Foreign Correspondents' Club of Thailand (FCCT; ☑0 2652 0580; www.fccthai.com; Penthouse, Maneeya Center, 518/5 Th Ploenchit; Ⓢ Chit Lom exit 2)

Goethe Institut (☑0 2287 0942; www.goethe.de/ins/th/ban/enindex.htm; 18/1 Soi Goethe; Ⓜ Lumphini exit 2)

EMERGENCY

If you have a medical emergency and need an ambulance, contact the English-speaking hospitals listed below. In case of a police or safety issue, contact the following emergency services:

Fire (☑199) You're unlikely to find an English-speaker at this number, so it's best to use the default ☑191 emergency number.

Police (☑191)

Tourist Police (☑24hr hotline 1155) The best way to deal with most problems requiring police (usually a rip-off or theft) is to contact the tourist police, who are used to dealing with foreigners and can be very helpful in cases of arrest. The English-speaking unit investigates criminal activity involving tourists and can act as a bilingual liaison with the regular police. Although they typically have no jurisdiction over the kinds of cases handled by regular cops, they should be able to help with translation, contacting your embassy and/or arranging a police report you can take to your insurer.

INTERNET & TELEPHONE ACCESS

There's no shortage of internet cafes in Bangkok competing to offer the cheapest and fastest connection. Rates vary depending on the concentration and affluence of net-heads – Banglamphu is cheaper than Sukhumvit or Silom, with rates as low as 15B per hour. Many internet shops have Skype and headsets so that international calls can be made for the price of surfing the web.

A convenient place to take care of your communication needs in the centre of Bangkok is the **TrueMove Shop** (www.truemove.com; Soi 2, Siam Sq; ⊙7am-10pm; Ⓢ Siam exit 4). It has high-speed internet computers equipped with Skype, sells phones and mobile subscriptions, and can also provide information on city-wide wi-fi access for computers and phones.

Wi-fi, provided mostly free of charge, is becoming more and more ubiquitous around Bangkok and is available at more businesses and public hot spots than we have space to list here. For relatively authoritative lists of wi-fi hot spots in Bangkok, go to www.bkkpages.com (under 'Directory') or www.stickmanweekly.com/WiFi/BangkokFreeWirelessInternetWiFi.htm.

ⓘ COMMON BANGKOK SCAMS

Commit these classic rip-offs to memory and join us in our ongoing crusade to outsmart Bangkok's crafty scam artists.

➺ **Closed today** Ignore any 'friendly' local who tells you an attraction is closed for a Buddhist holiday or for cleaning. These are set-ups for trips to a bogus gem sale.

➺ **Túk-túk rides for 10B** Say goodbye to your day's itinerary if you climb aboard this ubiquitous scam. These alleged 'tours' bypass all the sights and instead cruise to all the fly-by-night gem and tailor shops that pay commissions.

➺ **Flat-fare taxi ride** Flatly refuse any driver who quotes a flat fare (usually between 100B and 150B for in-town destinations), which will usually be three times more expensive than the reasonable meter rate. Walking beyond the tourist area will usually help in finding an honest driver. If the driver has 'forgotten' to put the meter on, just say, 'Meter, *kâ/kráp*' (for female/male).

➺ **Tourist buses to the south** On the long journey south, well-organised and connected thieves have hours to comb through your bags, breaking into (and later resealing) locked bags, searching through hiding places and stealing credit cards, electronics and even toiletries. This scam has been running for years but is easy to avoid simply by carrying valuables with you on the bus.

➺ **Friendly strangers** Be wary of smartly dressed men who approach you asking where you're from and where you're going. Their opening gambit is usually followed with: 'Ah, my son/daughter is studying at university in (your city)' – they seem to have an encyclopaedic knowledge of major universities. As the tourist authorities here pointed out, this sort of behaviour is out of character for Thais and should be treated with suspicion.

MEDIA

Daily newspapers are available at streetside newsagents. Monthly magazines are available in most bookstores.

Bangkok 101 (www.bangkok101.com) A monthly city primer with photo essays and reviews of sights, restaurants and entertainment.

Bangkok Post (www.bangkokpost.com) The leading English-language daily with Friday and weekend supplements covering city events.

BK (www.bk.asia-city.com) Free weekly listings mag for the young and hip.

Coconuts Bangkok (bangkok.coconuts.co) News is almost certainly a stretch, so let's just say that Coconuts does a good job at covering... stuff that happens in Bangkok.

Nation (www.nationmultimedia.com) English-language daily with a heavy focus on business.

Not The Nation (www.notthenation.com) Thailand's answer to *The Onion*.

MEDICAL SERVICES

Thanks to its high standard of hospital care, Bangkok is fast becoming a destination for medical tourists shopping for more affordable dental check-ups, elective surgery and cosmetic procedures. Pharmacists (chemists) throughout the city can diagnose and treat most minor ailments (Bangkok belly, sinus and skin infections etc).

The following hospitals offer 24-hour emergency services, and the numbers below should be contacted if you need an ambulance or immediate medical attention. Most of these hospitals also have daily clinics with English-speaking staff.

Bangkok Christian Hospital (☑0 2235 1000; www.bangkokchristianhospital.org; 124 Th Silom; Ⓜ Si Lom exit 2, Ⓢ Sala Daeng exit 1)

BNH (☑0 2686 2700; www.bnhhospital.com; 9 Th Convent; Ⓜ Si Lom exit 2, Ⓢ Sala Daeng exit 2)

Bumrungrad International Hospital (☑0 2667 1000; www.bumrungrad.com; 33 Soi 3, Th Sukhumvit; Ⓢ Phloen Chit exit 3)

Samitivej Hospital (☑0 2711 8000; www.samitivejhospitals.com; 133 Soi 49, Th Sukhumvit; Ⓢ Phrom Phong exit 3 & taxi)

St Louis Hospital (☑0 2210 9999; www.saintlouis.or.th; 215 Th Sathon Tai; Ⓢ Surasak exit)

MONEY

Regular bank hours in Bangkok are generally 8.30am to 3.30pm, although branches in busy areas and shopping malls are open later. ATMs are common in all areas of the city. Many Thai banks also have currency-exchange bureaus; there are also exchange desks within eyeshot of most tourist areas. Go to 7-Eleven shops or other reputable places to break 1000B bills; don't expect a vendor or taxi to be able to change a bill 500B or larger.

POST

Main Post Office (Communications Authority of Thailand, CAT; ☑0 2233 1050; Th Charoen Krung; ⊙8am-8pm Mon-Fri, to 1pm Sat & Sun; ⊠Tha Oriental) Near Soi 35, Th Charoen Krung, services include poste restante and packaging within the main building. Branch post offices throughout the city also offer poste restante and parcel services.

TOILETS

Public toilets in Bangkok are few and far between and your best bet is to head for a shopping centre, fast-food restaurant, or our favourite, a luxury hotel (just waltz in as if you're staying there). Shopping centres might charge 2B to 5B for a visit; some newer shopping centres have toilets for the disabled. Despite what you'll hear, squat toilets are a dying breed in Bangkok.

TOURIST INFORMATION

Official tourist offices distribute maps, brochures and advice on sights and activities. Don't confuse these free services with the licensed travel agents that book tours and transport on a commission basis. Often, travel agencies incorporate elements of the official national tourism organisation name (Tourism Authority of Thailand; TAT) into their own name to purposefully confuse tourists.

Bangkok Information Center (☑0 2225 7612-4; www.bangkoktourist.com; 17/1 Th Phra Athit; ⊙9am-7pm Mon-Fri, 9am-5pm Sat-Sun; ⊠Tha Phra Athit (Banglamphu)) City-specific tourism office that provides maps, brochures and directions. They also operate 26 sporadically staffed **tourist information booths** (⊙ 9am to 5pm Monday to Saturday) in touristed areas.

Tourism Authority of Thailand (TAT; ☑1672; www.tourismthailand.org) Head Office (TAT; ☑0 2250 5500; 1600 Th Phetchaburi Tat Mai; ⊙8.30am-4.30pm; Ⓜ Phetchaburi exit 2); Banglamphu (TAT; ☑0 2283 1500; cnr Th Ratchadamnoen Nork & Th Chakrapatdipong; ⊙8.30am-4.30pm; ⊠Tha Phan Fah); Suvarnabhumi International Airport (TAT; ☑0 2134 0040; 2nd fl, btwn Gates 2 & 5, Suvarnabhumi International Airport; ⊙24hr).

ⓘ Getting There & Away

AIR

Bangkok has two airports. **Suvarnabhumi International Airport** (☑0 2132 1888; www.suvarnabhumiairport.com), 30km east of central Bangkok, began commercial international and domestic service in 2006 after several years of delay. The airport's name is pronounced *sù-wan-ná-poom,* and it inherited the airport code (BKK) previously used by the old airport at Don Muang. The airport website has real-time details of arrivals and departures.

THE INSIDE SCOOP

Several Bangkok residents, local and foreign, have taken their experiences to the 'small screen' and maintain blogs and websites about living in Bangkok. Some of the more informative and/or entertaining include:

➤ **2Bangkok** (www.2bangkok.com) News sleuth and history buff follows the city's headlines from today and yesterday.

➤ **Global Post** (www.globalpost.com/bio/patrick-winn/articles) Patrick Winn, this online news agency's Senior Southeast Asia Correspondent, is based in Bangkok and has a knack for uncovering the wacky things that go on there.

➤ **Greg To Differ** (www.gregtodiffer.com) 'Stories, rants and observations on expat life in Asia's craziest city.'

➤ **Kathy MacLeod** (www.kathymacleod.blogspot.com) A Bangkok life, in comic format.

➤ **Richard Barrow in Thailand** (www.richardbarrow.com) Full time Bangkok-based blogger covering everything from travel to news.

➤ **Still Life in Moving Vehicles** (www.lifeinmovingvehicle.blogspot.com) Photo blog depicting 'Bangkok from the passenger seat'.

Bangkok's former international and domestic **Don Muang International Airport** (DMK; ☑ 0 2535 1111; www.donmuangairportonline.com), 25km north of central Bangkok, was retired from commercial service in September 2006, only to reopen later as Bangkok's de-facto budget hub.

The following carriers service domestic destinations:

Air Asia (☑ nationwide call centre 0 2515 9999; www.airasia.com) Flies between Don Muang International Airport and domestic destinations including Chiang Mai, Chiang Rai, Hat Yai, Khon Kaen, Krabi, Nakhon Phanom, Nakhon Si Thammarat, Narathiwat, Phuket, Surat Thani, Trang, Ubon Ratchathani and Udon Thani, and several international destinations.

Air Asia has three 'service centres' on Th Khao San (127 Th Tanao, Th Khao San; ⊗10am-9.30pm; ⑤ Tha Phra Athit (Banglamphu)), Th Phra Ram I (1st fl, Tesco Lotus, 831 Th Phra Ram I; ⊗10am-8.30pm; ⑤ National Stadium exit 1) and Th Sukhumvit (1st fl, Tesco Lotus, 1710 Th Sukhumvit; ⊗10am-8.30pm; ⑤ On Nut exit 2).

Bangkok Airways (☑1771; www.bangkokair. com; Head Office Suvarnabhumi International Airport) Suvarnabhumi to Chiang Mai, Ko Samui, Krabi, Lampang, Phattaya, Phuket, Sukhothai, Udon Thani and Trat, as well as international destinations.

Happy Air (☑ 0 2134 8000; www.happyair. co.th; Room T1-112, Suvarnabhumi International Airport) Flies between Suvarnabhumi International Airport and Chumphon and Ranong.

Nok Air (☑ nationwide call centre 1318; www. nokair.com) Head Office (☑ 0 2900 9955; 17th fl, Rajanakarn Bldg, 183 Th Sathon Tai (South), ⑤ Chong Nonsi exit 1) Flies from Don Muang International Airport to Buriram, Chiang Mai, Chiang Rai, Chumphon, Hat Yai, Krabi, Loei, Mae Sot, Mukdahan, Nakhom Phanom, Nakhon Si Thammarat, Nan, Phitsanulok, Phrae, Phuket, Ranong, Roi Et, Sakon Nakhon, Surat Thani, Trang, Ubon Ratchathani and Udon Thani.

Orient Thai (☑ nationwide call centre 1126; www.flyorientthai.com) Head Office (☑ 0 2229 4260; 18 Th Ratchadaphisek; ⊗8.30am-6pm Mon-Fri; Ⓜ Sukhumvit exit 3, ⑤ Asok exit 4) Don Muang International Airport to Phuket.

Solar Air (☑ nationwide call centre 0 2535 2456; www.solarair.co.th) Don Muang International Airport (☑ 0 2535 2448; 1st fl, Don Muang International Airport) Solar Air flies 19-seat airplanes between Don Muang International Airport and Chumphon.

Thai Airways International (THAI; ☑ nationwide call centre 0 2356 1111; www.thaiairways. com) Banglamphu (☑ 0 2356 1111; 6 Th Lan Luang, Banglamphu; ⊗8am-5pm Mon-Sat, 9am-1pm Sun; ⑤ Tha Phan Fah); Silom (p766) Operates domestic air services between Suvarnabhumi and Chiang Mai, Chiang Rai, Hat Yai, Khon Kaen, Ko Samui, Krabi, Phuket, Surat Thani, Ubon Ratchathani and Udon Thani.

BUS

Bangkok is the centre for bus services that fan out all over the kingdom. For long-distance journeys to popular tourist destinations it is advisable to buy tickets directly from the bus companies at the bus stations, rather than through travel agents in tourist centres such as Th Khao San. There are three main bus terminals – two of which are an inconvenient distance from the centre of the city – and a terminal at the public transport centre at Suvarnabhumi International Airport with inter-provincial departures. Allow an hour to reach all terminals from most parts of Bangkok.

Eastern Bus Terminal (Ekamai; ☑ 0 2391 2504; Soi 40, Th Sukhumvit; ⑤ Ekkamai exit 2) The departure point for buses to Pattaya, Rayong, Chanthaburi and other points east. Most people call it *sà·tăh·nee èk·gà·mai* (Ekamai station). It's near the Ekamai BTS station.

Northern & Northeastern Bus Terminal (Mor Chit; [J] for northeastern routes 0 2936 2852, ext 602/605, for northern routes 0 2936 2841, ext 325/614; Th Kamphaeng Phet; [M] Kam-phaeng Phet exit 1 & taxi, [S] Mo Chit exit 3 & taxi) Located just north of Chatuchak Park, this hectic bus station is also commonly called *kŏn sòng mŏr chít* (Mo Chit station) – not to be confused with Mo Chit BTS station. Buses depart from here for all northern and north-eastern destinations. To reach the bus station, take BTS to Mo Chit or MRT to Chatuchak Park

TRANSPORT TO/FROM BANGKOK

DESTINATION	AIR	BUS	MINIVAN	TRAIN
Ayuthaya		53-68B; 1½hr; hourly 5am-7pm (from Northern & Northeastern Bus Terminal)	60B; 1hr; every 25min 5.30am-9pm (from Victory Monument)	15-185B; 1½hr; 40 departures 4.20am-11.53pm
Chiang Mai	1750B; 1-1½hr; 20 departures daily (from Don Muang Airport); 1750-2000B; 11 departures daily (from Suvarnabhumi International Airport)	438-876B; 9½-11hr; hourly 5.40am-11pm (from Northern & Northeastern Bus Terminal)		231-1454B; 12-15hr; 5 departures daily 12.45-10pm
Chiang Rai	2135-3590B; 1¼hr/ twice daily (from Don Muang Airport); 2600B; 1¼hr; 3 departures daily (from Suvarnabhumi International Airport)	486-980B; 11-12hr; hourly 7-8am & 7-9.30pm (from Northern & Northeastern Bus Terminal)		
Hat Yai	1700B; 1½hr; 17 departures daily (from Don Muang Airport); 3010B; 1½hr; 4 departures daily (from Suvarnabhumi International Airport)	581-1162B; 13hr; hourly 5-8am & 3-9pm (from Southern Bus Terminal)		259-1590B; 12-15hr; 6 departures 1-10.40Pm
Khon Kaen	1500B; 55 minutes/ twice daily (from Don Muang Airport); 2600B; 55 minutes/ 4 departures daily (from Suvarnabhumi International Airport)	280-560B; 10-11hr; hourly 6.30am-midnight (from Northern & Northeastern Bus Terminal)		77-1168B; 9-11hr; 4 departures 8.20am-8.45pm
Ko Samui	3300B; 1½hr; 19 departures daily (from Suvarnabhumi International Airport)	458-916B; 12hr; every 30min 7-8am & 6-8.30pm (not including ferry transfer; from Southern Bus Terminal)		

and transfer onto city bus 3, 77 or 509, or hop on a motorcycle taxi.

Southern Bus Terminal (Sai Tai Mai; ☏ 0 2894 6122; Th Boromaratchachonanee) The city's newest terminal lies a long way west of the centre of Bangkok. Commonly called *săi đâi mài*, it's among the more pleasant and orderly in the country. Besides serving as the departure point for all buses south of Bangkok, transport to Kanchanaburi and western Thailand also departs from here. The easiest way to reach the station is by taxi, or you can take bus 79, 159, 201 or 516 from Th Ratchadamnoen Klang, or bus 40 or a minivan from the Victory Monument.

TRANSPORT TO/FROM BANGKOK

DESTINATION	AIR	BUS	MINIVAN	TRAIN
Mae Sot	1590B; 65min; 4 departures daily (from Don Muang Airport)	333-666B; 7-8hr; hourly 8.15-10am & 7.15-10.40pm (from Northern & Northeastern Bus Terminal)		
Nong Khai		381-762B; 10hr; hourly 8.30-9.45pm (from Northern & Northeastern Bus Terminal)		213-1317B; 12hr; 3 departures 6.30-8.45pm
Pak Chong (For Khao Yai National Park)		118-150B; 3hr; hourly 5am-7pm (from Northern & Northeastern Bus Terminal)	180B; 2½hr; hourly 6am-6pm (from Victory Monument)	
Phuket	3033B; 75minutes; 9 departures daily (from Don Muang Airport); 3780-5480B; 75minutes; frequent departures daily (from Suvarnabhumi International Airport)	529-1058B; 12-15hr; hourly 5-9pm & 3-9pm (from Southern Bus Terminal)		
Sukhothai	2490B; 1hr; 2 departures daily (from Suvarnabhumi International Airport)	440-454B; 6-7hr; hourly 9am-noon & 10pm (from Northern & Northeastern Bus Terminal)		
Trat	2550B; 1hr; 3 departures daily (from Suvarnabhumi International Airport)	248-275B; 5½hr; frequent 4-9.45am (from Eastern Bus Terminal); 272B; 6hr; 5 departures 11.30am-11.30pm (from Northern & Northeastern Bus Terminal)	300B; 5hr; hourly 5am-5pm (from Victory Monument); 300B; 5hr; hourly 9am-5pm (from Northern & Northeastern Bus Terminal)	
Ubon Ratchathani	1350B; 70min; 7 departures daily (from Don Muang Airport); 2350B; 70min; 2 departures daily (from Suvarnabhumi International Airport)	600-804B; 10-11hr; hourly 6.40am & hourly 7-10pm (from Northern & Northeastern Bus Terminal)		205-1280B; 8½-12hr; 6 departures 5.45am-10.25pm

Suvarnabhumi Public Transport Centre (☎0 2132 1888; Suvarnabhumi Airport) Located 3km from Suvarnabhumi International Airport, this terminal has relatively frequent departures to points east and northeast including Aranya Prathet (for the Cambodian border), Chanthaburi, Ko Chang, Nong Khai (for the Lao border), Pattaya, Rayong, Trat and Udon Thani. It can be reached from the airport by a free shuttle bus.

MINIVAN

Privately run minivans, called *rót dôo*, are a fast and relatively comfortable way to get between Bangkok and its neighbouring provinces. Minivans bound for a number of destinations wait at various points around the Victory Monument (Map p96).

TRAIN

Hualamphong Train Station (☎0 2220 4334, nationwide call centre 1690; www.railway.co.th; off Th Phra Ram IV; Ⓜ Hua Lamphong exit 2) Hualamphong is the terminus for the main rail services to the south, north, northeast and east.

Bookings can be made in person at the advance booking office (just follow the signs; open from 8.30am to 4pm). The other ticket windows are for same-day purchases, mostly 3rd class. From 5am to 8.30am and 4pm to 11pm, advance bookings can also be made at windows 2 to 11. You can obtain a train timetable from the information window. Ignore smiling 'information' staff who try to direct all arrivals to outside travel agencies.

Hualamphong has the following services: shower room, mailing centre, luggage storage, cafes and food courts. To get to the station from Sukhumvit take the MRT to the Hua Lamphong stop. From western points (Banglamphu, Thewet), take bus 53.

Bangkok Noi (off Th Itsaraphap; Ⓢ Wongwian Yai exit 4 & taxi) Bangkok Noi handles infrequent (and overpriced for foreigners) services to Nakhon Pathom and Kanchanaburi. The station can be reached by river ferry to Tha Rot Fai. Tickets can be bought at the station.

Wong Wian Yai (off Th Phra Jao Taksin; Ⓢ Wongwian Yai exit 4 & taxi) This tiny station is the jumping-off point of the Mahachai Short-line commuter line to Samut Sakhon.

ⓘ Getting Around

Although Bangkok's rush-hour traffic is the stuff of nightmares, seemingly random acts of *embouteillage* (gridlock) can impede even the shortest trip, any day, any time. If it's an option, going by river, canal or BTS/MRT is always the best choice; otherwise assume a 45-minute journey for most outings.

A good, up-to-date resource for public transportation in Bangkok is www.transitbangkok. com.

TO/FROM THE AIRPORT

Bangkok is served by two airports; the vast majority of flights are out of Suvarnabhumi International Airport, while the budget airlines operate out of Don Muang International Airport. If you need to transfer between the two, pencil in *at least* an hour, as the two airports are at opposite ends of town. Minivans run between the two airports from 5.30am to 5pm (50B).

Suvarnabhumi International Airport

The following ground transport options leave directly from the Suvarnabhumi terminal to in-town destinations: metered taxis, hotel limousines, airport rail link, private vehicles and some minivans. If there are no metered taxis available kerbside or if the line is too long, you can take the airport shuttle to the taxi stand at the public-transport centre.

Airport Rail Link The elevated train service linking central Bangkok and Suvarnabhumi International Airport is comprised of a local service, which makes six stops before terminating at Phaya Thai station (45B, 30 minutes, every 15 minutes from 6am to midnight), connected by a walkway to BTS at Phaya Thai station, and an express service that runs, without stops, between Phaya Thai and Makkasan stations and the airport (90B, 15 to 17 minutes, hourly from 6am to midnight). Makkasan, also known as Bangkok City Air Terminal, is a short walk from MRT Phetchaburi, and if you arrive

---

INTERNATIONAL BUSES

Bangkok's Northern & Northeastern Bus Terminal (Mor Chit) is now a jumping-off point for a small but growing number of government-run, international bus routes. In particular, the bus to Siem Reap (and a proposed route to Phnom Penh) is a convenient and comfortable alternative to the otherwise hassle-laden crossing at Aranya Prathet.

DESTINATION	COST	DURATION	TIME
Pakse (Laos)	900B	12hr	9pm
Siem Reap (Cambodia; for Angkor Wat)	750B	7hr	9am
Vientiane (Laos)	900B	10hr	8pm

at least three hours before your departure, also has check-in facilities for passengers on Thai Airways International flights departing between 7am and 9pm. Both train lines run from 6am to midnight.

The Airport Rail Link is on floor B1 of Suvarnabhumi International Airport.

Bus & Minivan The public-transport centre is 3km from Suvarnabhumi and includes a public bus terminal, metered taxi stand and long-term parking. A free airport shuttle bus running both an ordinary and express route connects the transport centre with the passenger terminals. Lines that city-bound tourists are likely to use include bus 554, which stops across from Don Muang International Airport (34B, 24 hours), and minivan lines 551 to Victory Monument BTS station (40B, frequent from 5am to 10pm) and 552 to On Nut BTS station (25B, frequent from 5am to 10pm). From these points, you can continue on public transport or by taxi to your hotel. There are also buses and minivans to destinations east including Chanthaburi, Hua Hin, Ko Chang, Pattaya and Trat.

Relatively frequent minivans to Don Muang International Airport wait on floor 1, outside door 8 (50B, 40 minutes, from 5.30am to 5pm).

From town, you can take the BTS to On Nut, then from near the market entrance opposite Tesco Lotus take minivan 552 (25B, frequent from 5am to 10pm), or BTS to Victory Monument, then the **minivan to Suvarnabhumi**

(40B, 30 minutes, every 30 minutes from 5am to 9pm).

Taxi As you exit the terminal, ignore the touts and all the signs pointing you to overpriced 'official airport taxis'; instead, descend to floor 1 to join the generally fast-moving queue for a public taxi. Cabs booked through these desks should always use their meter, but they often try their luck so insist by saying, 'Meter, please'. Typical metered fares from the airport are as follows: 200B to 250B to Th Sukhumvit; 250B to 300B to Th Khao San; 500B to Mo Chit. Toll charges (paid by the passengers) vary between 25B and 45B. Note also that there's an additional 50B surcharge added to all fares departing from the airport, payable directly to the driver.

Don Muang International Airport

Bus & Minivan From outside the arrivals hall, there are two airport bus lines from Don Muang: A1 makes stops at BTS Mo Chit and the Northern and Northeastern Bus Terminal (30B, hourly from 9am to midnight); A2 makes stops at BTS Mo Chit and BTS Victory Monument (30B, hourly from 9am to midnight).

Relatively frequent minivans also departing from outside the arrivals hall link Don Muang International Airport and Suvarnabhumi International Airport (50B, 1 hour, from 5.30am to 5pm).

Public buses stop on the highway in front of the airport. Lines include 29, with a stop at Victory Monument BTS station before

MINIVANS TO/FROM BANGKOK

DESTINATION	COST	DURATION	FREQUENCY
Aranya Prathet (for Cambodian border)	230B	3½hr	every 40min 4.15am-6.30pm
Ayuthaya	60B	1hr	every 25min 5.30am-9pm
Ban Phe (for Ko Samet)	200B	3hr	every 50min 6am-8pm
Cha-am	160B	2½hr	every 30min 5am-7pm
Chanthaburi	200B	3hr	hourly 6am-7.30pm
Hua Hin	180B	3hr	every 30min 5am-7pm
Kanchanaburi	120B	2hr	hourly 5am-8pm
Lopburi	110B	2hr	hourly 4am-8pm
Mae Klong (Samut Songkhram; for Amphawa)	73B	1½hr	frequent 5.30am-9pm
Muak Lek (for Khao Yai)	120B	2hr	hourly 8am-8pm
Nakhon Pathom	60B	1hr	frequent 6am-6pm
Pattaya	100B	2hr	every 40min 5.30am-8pm
Phetchaburi	100B	2hr	every 45min 6.15am-8pm
Southern Bus Terminal	35B	20min	frequent 8am-8pm
Suvarnabhumi International Airport	40B	30min	every 30min 5am-9pm
Trat	300B	4-5hr	hourly 5am-7pm

terminating at Hualamphong Train Station (24 hours); 59, with a stop near Th Khao San (24 hours); line 538, stopping at Victory Monument BTS station (4am to 10pm); and line 555, bound for Suvarhabhumi International Airport (4am to 11pm); fares are approximately 30B.

Taxi As at Suvarnabhumi, public taxis leave from outside the arrivals hall and there is a 50B airport charge added to the meter fare. A trip to Banglamphu, including airport change and tollway fees, will set you back about 400B. The fare will be slightly less for a trip to Sukhumvit or Silom.

Train The walkway that crosses from the airport to the Amari Airport Hotel also provides access to Don Muang train station, which has trains to Hualamphong Train Station every one to 1½ hours from 4am to 11.30am and then roughly every hour from 2pm to 9.30pm (5B to 10B).

BOAT

Once the city's dominant form of transport, public boats still survive along the mighty Mae Nam Chao Phraya and on a few interior *klorng*.

Canal Routes

Over the years boat services along Bangkok and Thonburi's *klorng* have diminished, but with mounting traffic woes there may be plans to revive these water networks. For now, canal taxi boats run along Khlong Saen Saeb (Banglamphu to Ramkhamhaeng) and are an easy way to get from Banglamphu to Jim Thompson House, the Siam Square shopping centres (get off at Tha Saphan Hua Chang for both), and other points further east along Sukhumvit – after a mandatory change of boat at Tha Pratunam. These boats are mostly used by daily commuters and pull into the piers for just a few seconds – jump straight on or you'll be left behind. Fares range from 10B to 20B and boats run from approximately 5.30am to 8.30pm (to 7pm on weekends and holidays).

River Routes

Chao Phraya Express Boat (☎ 0 2623 6001; www.chaophrayaexpressboat.com) provides one of the city's most scenic (and efficient) transport options, running passenger boats along Mae Nam Chao Phraya to destinations both south and north of Bangkok. The central pier is known varyingly as Tha Sathon and Saphan Taksin, and connects to the Saphan Taksin BTS station, at the southern end of the city. Visitors are most likely to go northwards, to the stops designated with an N prefix.

Tickets range from 10B to 40B and are generally purchased on board the boat, although some larger stations have ticket booths. Either way, hold on to your ticket as proof of purchase.

The company operates express (indicated by an orange, yellow or green flag), local (without a flag) and tourist boat (blue flag) services. During rush hour, pay close attention to the flag colours to avoid an unwanted journey to a foreign province. Ask for one of the route maps provided at some of the larger piers.

Local (10-14B; ⊙6.20-8.05am & 3-5.30pm Mon-Fri) The local line (no flag) serves all company piers between Wat Ratchasingkhon, in south-central Bangkok, north to Nonthaburi, stopping frequently.

Orange Express (15B; ⊙6am-7pm) This, the most frequent line, operates between Wat Ratchasingkhon and Nonthaburi with frequent stops.

Yellow Express (20-29B; ⊙6.15-8.30am & 3.30-8pm Mon-Fri) The yellow express line operates between Ratburana and Nonthaburi with stops at major piers.

Green Express (13-32B; ⊙6.15-8.10am & 3.30-6.05pm Mon-Fri) This rush-hour-only boat takes commuters as far north as Pakkret Pier, in Nonthaburi.

Tourist (40B, one-day pass adult/child 150/80B; ⊙9.30am-10pm) The more expensive tourist boat offers heaps of seating and English-language commentary (though it may be hard to comprehend); it operates from Tha Sathon (Central Pier) to 10 major sightseeing piers, only going as far north as Tha Phra Athit (Banglamphu).

River Crossing Boats

There are also flat-bottomed cross-river ferries that connect Thonburi and Bangkok. These piers are usually next door to Chao Phraya Express Boat piers, cost 3B per crossing and run from approximately 7am to 7pm.

BTS & MRT

The elevated **BTS** (Skytrain; ☎ 0 2617 7300; www.bts.co.th), also known as the Skytrain, spans two lines that whisk you through 'new' Bangkok (Th Silom, Th Sukhumvit and Siam Sq). The interchange is at Siam station, and trains run frequently from 6am to midnight. Fares range from 15B to 42B, or 130B for a one-day pass. Most ticket machines only accept coins, but change is available at the information booths.

Bangkok's **MRT** (www.bangkokmetro.co.th), or metro, is helpful for people staying in the Th Sukhumvit or Th Silom area to reach the train station at Hualamphong. Otherwise the system is mainly a suburban commuter line. Fares cost 16B to 40B, or 120B for a one-day pass. The trains run frequently from 6am to midnight.

BUS

The city's public bus system is operated by **Bangkok Mass Transit Authority** (☎ 0 2246 0973; www.bmta.co.th); the website is a great source of information on all bus routes, but this

BANGKOK TAXI TIPS

➡ Never agree to take a taxi that won't use the meter; these drivers park outside hotels and in tourist areas. Simply walk a block or two and get one that's passing by instead.

➡ Bangkok taxi drivers will generally not try to 'take you for a ride' as happens in some other countries; they make more money from passenger turnover.

➡ It's worth keeping in mind that many Bangkok taxi drivers are in fact seasonal labourers fresh from the countryside and may not know their way around.

➡ If a driver refuses to take you somewhere, it may be because he needs to return his rental cab before a certain time, not because he doesn't like you.

➡ Very few Bangkok taxi drivers speak much English; an address written in Thai can help immensely.

➡ Older cabs may be less comfortable but typically have more experienced drivers because they are driver-owned, as opposed to the new cabs, which are usually rented.

doesn't really help the fact that Bangkok's bus system is confusing and generally lacks English. If you're determined, or are pinching pennies, fares for ordinary (fan) buses start at 7B and air-conditioned buses at 10B. Smaller privately operated green buses cost 5B.

Most of the bus lines run between 5am and 10pm or 11pm, except for the 'all-night' buses, which run from 3am or 4am to midmorning.

Bangkok Bus Guide by thinknet, available at Kinokuniya and Asia Books, is the most up-to-date route map available.

CAR

For short-term visitors, you will find driving (and parking) a car in Bangkok far more trouble than it is worth. If you need private transport, consider hiring a car and driver through your hotel or hire a taxi driver that you find trustworthy. One reputable operator is **Julie Taxi** (✆ 08 5115 5455; www.facebook.com/TourWithJulieTaxi), which offers a variety of vehicles and excellent service.

If you're not dissuaded, cars and motorcycles can be rented throughout town, including through such international chains as **Avis** (✆ 0 2251 1131; www.avisthailand.com; 40 Th Sathon Neua (North); ⊙7.30am-7.30pm; Ⓜ Lumphini exit 2) or local chains such as **Thai Rent A Car** (✆ 0 2737 8888; www.thairentacar.com; 2371 Th Petchaburi Tat Mai; Ⓢ Thong Lo exit 3 & taxi), both of which also have branches at/near Suvarnabhumi airport. Rates start at around 1200B per day, excluding insurance. An International Driving Permit and passport are required for all rentals.

MOTORCYCLE TAXI

Forming the backdrop of modern Bangkok, teams of cheeky, numbered and vested motorcycle-taxi drivers can be found at the end of just about every long street. A ride to the end (*sùt soy*) or mouth (*bàhk soy*) of an average soi usually costs 10B to 15B. Longer journeys should

be negotiated in advance, and can range from 20B to 100B.

Helmets are occasionally available upon request, although considering the way some of these guys drive, any body part is at risk. In particular, keep your legs tucked in – the drivers are used to carrying passengers with shorter legs than those of the average Westerner. Women wearing skirts should sit side-saddle and gather any extra cloth to avoid it catching in the wheel or drive chain.

TAXI

Táak-see mee-đêu (metered taxis) were introduced in Bangkok in 1993 and the current flag fare of 35B is only a slight increase from that time, making us wonder how these guys (and there are a lot of them) earn any money. Although many first-time visitors are hesitant to use them, in general, Bangkok's taxis are new and spacious and the drivers are courteous and helpful, making them an excellent way to get around. Fares to most places within central Bangkok cost 60B to 80B, and freeway tolls – 20B to 45B depending where you start – must be paid by the passenger.

Taxi Radio (✆ 1681; www.taxiradio.co.th) and other 24-hour 'phone-a-cab' services are available for 20B above the metered fare. Taxis are usually plentiful except during peak commute hours, when bars are closing (1am to 2am), or when it is raining and your destination requires sitting in too much traffic.

TÚK-TÚK

A ride on Thailand's most emblematic three-wheeled vehicle is an experience particularly sought after by new arrivals, but it only takes a few seconds to realise that most foreigners are too tall to see anything beyond the low-slung roof.

Túk-túk (pronounced *đúk đúk*) drivers also have a knack for smelling crisp bills and can potentially take you and your wallet far away from your desired destination. In particular, beware of drivers who offer to take you on a sightseeing tour for 10B or 20B – it's a touting scheme designed to pressure you into purchasing overpriced goods. A short trip on a túk-túk will cost at least 60B.

AROUND BANGKOK

If you're itching to get out of the capital city, but don't have a lot of time, consider a day trip to one of the neighbouring towns and provinces. On Bangkok's doorstep are all of Thailand's provincial charms – you don't have to go far to find ancient religious monuments, floating markets, architectural treasures and laid-back fishing villages.

Ko Kret เกาะเกร็ด

One of the easiest escapes from Bangkok is to Ko Kret, an artificial island that is the result of dredging a canal in a sharp bend in Mae Nam Chao Praya. The island is home to one of Thailand's oldest settlements of Mon people, who were the dominant culture in central Thailand between the 6th and 10th centuries AD.

◎ Sights & Activities

There are a couple of temples worth peeking into, such as the leaning stupa at **Wat Poramai Yikawat** (Ko Kret; admission free; ⊙9am-5pm; 🚌166 & river-crossing ferry from Wat Sanam Neua), but the real highlight is taking in the bucolic riverside atmosphere. A 6km paved path circles the island, and can be easily completed on food or by bicycle, the latter available for rent from the pier (per day 40B). Alternatively, it's possible to charter a boat for up to 10 people for 500B; the typical **island tour** stops at a batik workshop, a sweets factory and, on weekends, a floating market.

Ko Kret is known for its **hand-thrown terracotta pots**, sold at markets throughout Bangkok; order an iced coffee from just about any vendor on the island and you'll get a small one as a souvenir. From Wat Poramai Yikawa, go in either direction to find both abandoned kilns and working pottery centres on the east and north coasts.

If you come to Ko Kret on a weekday you're likely to be the only visitor. On weekends, things change drastically and Ko Kret is an extremely popular destination for urban Thais.

There's heaps more food, drink and things for sale, but with these come the crowds.

✖ Eating

The northern coast of Ko Kret is home to a row of open-air restaurants, many serving *khâw châa,* an unusual but delicious Mon dish of savoury tit-bits served with chilled fragrant rice.

Pa Ka Lung THAI
(Restaurant Rever Side; Ko Kret; mains 30-60B; ⊙8am-4pm Mon-Fri, to 6pm Sat & Sun; 🚌166 & river-crossing ferry from Wat Sanam Neua) An open-air food court with an English-language menu. This is a good place for *khâw châa* and other local dishes.

❶ Getting There & Away

Ko Kret is in Nonthaburi, about 12km north of central Bangkok. To get there, take bus 33 from Sanam Luang, bus 166 from the Victory Monument or a taxi to Pak Kret, before boarding the cross-river ferry (2B, 5am to 9pm) that leaves from Wat Sanam Neua.

Alternatively, the Chao Phraya Express Boat's 'green flag' express goes as far north as Pak Kret on weekdays between 6.15am and 8.10am, and 3.30pm and 6.05pm (32B).

Amphawa อัมพวา

This canalside village has become a popular destination for city folk who seek out its quintessentially 'Thai' setting. This urban influx has sparked a few signs of gentrification, but the canals, old wooden buildings, atmospheric cafes and quaint waterborne traffic still retain heaps of charm. From Friday to Sunday, Amphawa puts on a floating market. Alternatively, visit on a weekday and you'll probably be the only tourist.

◎ Sights & Activities

Steps from Amphawa's central footbridge is **Wat Amphawan Chetiyaram** (วัดอัมพวัน เจติยาราม; admission free; ⊙daylight hours), a graceful temple believed to be located at the place of the family home of Rama II, and which features accomplished murals. A short walk from the temple is **King Buddhalertla (Phuttha Loet La) Naphalai Memorial Park** (อุทยานพระบรมราชานุสรณ์ พระบาทสมเด็จ พระพุทธเลิศหล้านภาลัย (อุทยาน ร. ๒); admission 20B; ⊙8.30am-5pm), a museum housed in a collection of traditional central Thai houses

Around Bangkok

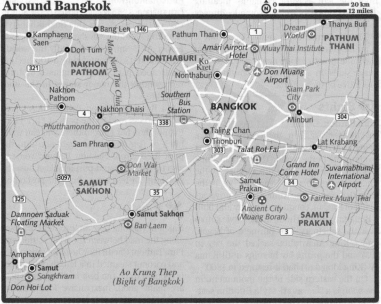

set on 1.5 landscaped hectares. Dedicated to Rama II, the museum contains a library of antiques from early-19th-century Siam.

At night **long-tail boats** zip through Amphawa's sleeping waters to watch the Christmas light–like dance of the *hìng hôy* (fireflies), most populous during the wet season. From Friday to Sunday, operators from several piers lead tours, charging 60B for a seat. Outside of these days, it costs 500B for a two-hour charter.

🛏 Sleeping & Eating

Amphawa is popular with Bangkok's weekend warriors, and it seems like virtually every other house has opened its doors to tourists in the form of homestays. These can range from little more than a mattress on the floor and a mosquito net to upscale guesthouse-style accommodation. Rooms with fan start at about 200B while rooms with air-con, many of which share bathrooms, begin at about 1000B. Prices are half this on weekdays.

If you prefer something a bit more private, consider **Ploen Amphawa Resort** (☑ 08 1458 9411; www.ploenamphawa.com; Th Rim Khlong; r incl breakfast 1400-3000B; ❄ 🛜), or **ChababaanCham Resort** (☑ 08 1984 1000; Th Rim Khlong; r incl breakfast 1500-2400B; ❄ 🛜),

an attractive but somewhat overpriced resort just off the canal. **Baan Ku Pu** (☑ 0 3472 5920; Th Rim Khlong; d 1000B; ❄) is a collection of wooden bungalows.

Amphawa has basic restaurants and a simple **night market** open each evening. If you're in town on a weekend, get your eats at the fun Amphawa Floating Market (p136), where *pàt tai* and other noodle dishes are served directly from boats.

❶ Getting There & Away

From Bangkok's Southern Bus Terminal (p143), board any bus bound for Damnoen Saduak and ask to get off at Amphawa (80B, two hours, frequent 6am to 9pm). Alternatively, from a point north of Bangkok's Victory Monument, frequent **minivans** head for Samut Songkhram (also known as Mae Klong; 73B, 1½ hours, 5.30am to 9pm); from Samut Songkhram's market area, hop on one of the frequent *sŏrng·tăa·ou* to Amphawa (8B, 10 minutes).

Nakhon Pathom   นครปฐม
POP 120,000

Nakhon Pathom is a typical central Thai city, with the Phra Pathom Chedi as a visible link to its claim as the country's oldest settlement. The town's name, which derives from the Pali 'Nagara Pathama' meaning 'First City', appears to lend some legitimacy to this boast.

The modern town is quite sleepy, but it is an easy destination to see everyday Thai ways and practise your newly acquired language skills on a community genuinely appreciative of such efforts.

⊙ Sights

Phra Pathom Chedi BUDDHIST TEMPLE

(พระปฐมเจดีย์) FREE In the centre of town, rising to 127m, is one of the tallest Buddhist monuments in the world. The original stupa was erected in the early 6th century by the Theravada Buddhists of Dvaravati. But, in the early 11th century the Khmer king, Suriyavarman I of Angkor, conquered the city and built a Brahman *prang* (Hindi/Khmer-style stupa) over the sanctuary. The Burmese of Bagan, under King Anawrahta, sacked the city in 1057 and the *prang* lay in ruins until Rama IV (King Mongkut) had it restored in 1860.

On the eastern side of the monument, in the *bòht*, is a Dvaravati-style Buddha seated in a European pose similar to the one in Wat Phra Meru in Ayuthaya. It may, in fact, have come from there.

Also of interest are the many examples of Chinese sculpture carved from a greenish stone that came to Thailand as ballast in the bottom of 19th-century Chinese junks. Opposite the *bòht* is a museum (admission by donation; 9am-4pm Wed-Sun), with some interesting Dvaravati sculpture and lots of old junk. Within the *chedi* complex is Lablae Cave, an artificial tunnel containing the shrine of several Buddha figures.

The *wát* surrounding the stupa enjoys the kingdom's highest temple rank, Rachavoramahavihan; it's one of only six temples so honoured in Thailand. King Rama VI's ashes are interred in the base of the Sukhothai-era Phra Ruang Rochanarit, a large standing Buddha image in the wát's northern *wí·hăhn*.

Phutthamonthon BUDDHIST TEMPLE

(พุทธมณฑล; ⊙daylight hours) FREE Southeast of the city stands this Sukhothai-style standing Buddha designed by Corrado Feroci. At 15.8m, it is reportedly the world's tallest, and it's surrounded by a 400-hectare landscaped park that contains sculptures representing the major stages in the Buddha's life.

All Bangkok-Nakhon Pathom buses pass by the access road to the park at Phra Phutthamonthon Sai 4; from there you can walk, hitch or flag down a *sŏrng·tăa·ou* into the park itself. From Nakhon Pathom you can also take a white-and-purple Salaya bus; the stop is on Th Tesa across from the post office.

✕ Eating

Nakhon Pathom has an excellent market along the road between the train station and Phra Pathom Chedi; its *kôw lähm* (sticky rice and coconut steamed in a length of bamboo) is reputed to be the best in Thailand. There are many good, inexpensive food vendors and restaurants in this area.

ⓘ Getting There & Away

Nakhon Pathom is 64km west of Bangkok. The city doesn't have a central bus station, but most transport arrives and departs from near the market and train station.

The most convenient and fastest way to get to Nakhon Pathom is by minivan from Bangkok's Victory Monument (60B, one hour, frequent 6am to 6pm).

There are also more frequent trains from Bangkok's Hualamphong station (14B to 60B, one hour) throughout the day. Nakhon Pathom is also on the spur rail line that runs from Thonburi's Bangkok Noi station to Kanchanaburi's Nam Tok station, although because of the route's status as a 'tourist line' the fares are exorbitantly high for foreigners.

Central Thailand

Includes ➡

Best Places to Eat

➡ Blue Rice (p177)

➡ Sai Thong (p161)

➡ Baan Mai Rim Nam (p161)

➡ Mangosteen (p177)

➡ Pae Ban Rim Nam (p168)

Best Places to Stay

➡ Baan Lotus Guest House (p160)

➡ Tony's Place (p160)

➡ Noom Guesthouse (p167)

➡ P Guest House (p185)

➡ Sabai@Kan (p176)

Why Go?

The past is never far behind in Central Thailand. Cycle around the temple ruins in Ayuthaya and you can imagine how this former majestic capital must have once looked. Visit the memorials and Death Railway in Kanchanaburi and you can discover new empathy for the WWII prisoners of war who suffered there.

Central Thailand doesn't just do history, though. Nature is a major player here as the jagged mountain ranges that dominate the horizons host spectacular waterfalls, vast national parks and new adventure resorts.

After a few days exploring the war sites in Kanchanaburi, travellers tend to head north to trek or camp in the national parks and maybe catch a glimpse of wild elephants, gibbons or even tigers. Others cycle around Ayuthaya's fabled ruins or browse for bargains at traditional markets. Lopburi tends to combine both nature and history, as dozens of monkeys scamper among the Khmer-style temples in what was once Thailand's second capital.

Head up to the very north of Kanchanaburi to be within touching distance of Burma (Myanmar). Sleep among the tree tops at Thong Pha Phum National Park or visit remote Sangkhlaburi, where volunteer work to help ethnic groups is hugely rewarding.

When to Go

➡ Central Thailand experiences the country's three seasons in equal measure; Kanchanaburi can have baking sunshine while torrential rain buffets Sangkhlaburi. It is hot in the region from February to June, rainy from June to October, and cool (relatively speaking) from October to January: the one constant is the humidity.

➡ Because of altitude, it can be cooler in Sangkhlaburi and surrounding national parks than in other areas. Ayuthaya and Lopburi sit in a wide-open plain that receives similar amounts of rain and heat as Bangkok.

Central Thailand Highlights

1 Clambering up the seven levels at **Erawan** (p179), one of Thailand's most impressive waterfalls

2 Camping in scenic national parks, such as **Si Nakharin** (p182), to look for elusive tigers, elephants and gibbons

3 Visiting the Death Railway and WWII museums in **Kanchanaburi** (p169)

4 Cycling around the temple and palace ruins in **Ayuthaya** (p154)

5 Doing voluntary work with a charity in laid-back **Sangkhlaburi** (p186) and spending time with ethnic groups there

6 Watching monkeys scurrying around the temple ruins in **Lopburi** (p167)

7 Spending a night up high in a tree house then going trekking in **Thong Pha Phum National Park** (p183)

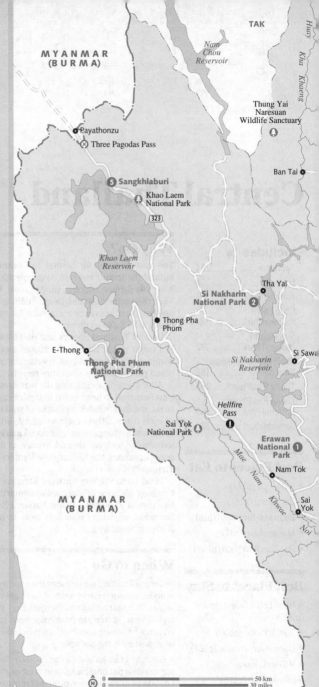

AYUTHAYA PROVINCE

Ayuthaya พระนครศรีอยุธยา

POP 137,553

Once one of the world's leading capitals, Ayuthaya's myriad temples and palaces glittered from miles away. Today the dozens of ruins offer a tantalising glimpse into what was once a glorious city. The most famous sites have been partially restored so it is easy to imagine how they must have looked in their prime, while others remain fully functioning temples.

Between 1350 and 1767 Ayuthaya was the capital of Siam. As a major trading port during the time of the trade winds, international merchants visited and were left in awe by the temples and treasure-laden palaces. At one point the empire ruled over an area larger than England and France combined. Ayuthaya had 33 kings who engaged in more than 70 wars during its 417-year period; however, fine diplomatic skills also ensured no Western power ever ruled Siam.

The last of the empire's battles was in 1767, when an invading Burmese army sacked the city, looting most of its treasures. What was left continued to crumble until major restoration work began. In 1991 Ayuthaya's ruins were designated a Unesco World Heritage Site. The Unesco listing says Ayuthaya's sites 'represent a masterclass of genius', the likes of which cannot be found anywhere else in the world.

Away from the temples, Ayuthaya has a growing number of attractions and markets that focus on locally made produce and handicrafts.

◉ Sights

At its zenith, 400 sparkling temples stood proudly in the heart of Ayuthaya. Today more than a dozen restored ruins can be found around the island, along with several working temples. The headless Buddha images, crumbling columns and battered balustrades recreate images of a once-mighty city.

For simpler navigation, we've divided up the sites into 'on the island' and 'off the island' sections. It is easy to get between the sites by bicycle, and hiring a guide for some historical detail is useful.

Most temples are open from 8am to 4pm; the more famous sites charge an entrance fee. A one-day pass for most sites on the island is available for 220B and can be bought at the museums or ruins.

The ruins are symbols of royalty and religion, two fundamental elements of Thai society, so please show respect.

◉ On the Island

The following sites are in central Ayuthaya.

★ **Wat Phra Si Sanphet** RUIN
(วัดพระศรีสรรเพชญ์; admission 50B; ⊙ 8am-6pm; [P]) The three magnificent *chedi* (stupas) at Wat Phra Si Sanphet are the most iconic image in Ayuthaya. Built in the late 15th century, it was the city's largest temple and was used by several kings. It once contained a 16m-high standing Buddha (Phra Si Sanphet) covered with 250kg of gold, which was melted down by Burmese conquerors.

★ **Ayuthaya Tourist Center** MUSEUM
(☏ 0 3524 6076; www.tourismthailand.org/ayut thaya; ⊙ 8.30am-4.30pm) FREE This should be your first stop in Ayuthaya, as the excellent upstairs exhibition hall puts everything in context and describes the city's erstwhile glories. Also upstairs is the tiny but interesting Ayuthaya National Art Museum. Downstairs, the TAT office has lots of maps and good advice.

Chao Sam Phraya National Museum MUSEUM
(พิพิธภัณฑสถานแห่งชาติเจ้าสามพระยา; cnr Th Rotchana & Th Si Sanphet; adult/child 150B/free; ⊙ 9am-4pm Wed-Sun; [P]) The largest museum in the city has 2400 items on show, ranging from a 2m-high bronze-cast Buddha head to glistening treasures found in the crypts of Wat Phra Mahathat and Wat Ratburana.

Wihaan Phra Mongkhon Bophit BUDDHIST TEMPLE
(วัดพระมงคลบพิตร; ⊙ 8.30am-4.30pm) FREE Next to Wat Phra Si Sanphet is this sanctuary hall, which houses one of the largest bronze Buddha images in Thailand. This 17m-high figure has undergone several facelifts due to lightning strikes and fire.

In 1955 the then Burmese Prime Minister donated 200,000B to restore the building, an act of belated atonement for his country's sacking of the city 200 years before.

Wat Phra Mahathat RUIN
(วัดพระมหาธาตุ; cnr Th Chee Kun & Th Naresuan; admission 50B; ⊙ 8am-6pm) The most photographed image in Ayuthaya is here;

a sandstone Buddha head that lies mysteriously tangled within a tree's entwined roots. Built in 1374 during the reign of King Borom Rachathirat I, Wat Phra Mahathat also has a central *prang* (Khmer-style *chedi*) and rows of headless Buddha images.

Nobody knows how the Buddha head ended up in the tree. Some say the head was abandoned after the Burmese sacked Ayuthaya, and trees subsequently grew around it. Others believe thieves tried to steal the image, but gave up as it was too heavy.

Wat Ratburana RUIN
(วัดราชบูรณะ; admission 50B; ☺8am-6pm) The *prang* in this temple is one of the best extant versions in the city, with detailed carvings of lotus and mythical creatures. The temple, just north of Wat Phra Mahathat, was built in the 15th century by King Borom Rachathirat II on the cremation site for his two brothers who died while fighting each other for the throne.

Looters raided the site in 1957 and stole many treasures. Some of the culprits were arrested and a subsequent official excavation of the site uncovered many rare Buddha images in the crypt.

Wat Thammikarat RUIN
(วัดธรรมิกราช; ☺8am-7pm) FREE To the west of Wat Ratburana, this temple is a pleasant place to sit among the ruins. The most prominent feature is a central *chedi* surrounded by *singha* (guardian lion) sculptures. Local people believe that the temple predated the Ayuthaya period, a claim unsupported by architectural evidence.

Wat Suwannaram RUIN
(วัดสุวรรณาราม; off Th U Thong; ☺8am-7pm) FREE This temple is not one of the most-visited sites but its different architectural styles make it worth seeing. Set in the southeast of the island, King Rama I designed the exterior of the older-style *uposatha* while Rama III was responsible for the interior.

The slightly bowed line along the temple's edge and its plain finish are typical of the late Ayuthaya period. Next to it is a *wí·hǎhn* (sanctuary) from Rama IV's reign, resplendent with a glittering external mosaic.

Ayuthaya Historical Study Centre MUSEUM
(ศูนย์ศึกษาประวัติศาสตร์อยุธยา; Th Rotchana; adult/child 100/50B; ☺9am-4.30pm; P) This well-designed, open-plan museum features a diorama of the city's former glories, replica vessels and an exhibition on how traditional villagers used to survive.

Chantharakasem National Museum MUSEUM
(พิพิธภัณฑสถานแห่งชาติจันทรเกษม; Th U Thong; admission 100B; ☺9am-4pm Wed-Sun) Inside this national museum is a collection of Buddhist art, sculptures, ancient weapons and lacquered cabinets. The museum is within the grounds of Wang Chan Kasem (Chan Kasem Palace), which was built for King Naresuan by his father in 1577.

AYUTHAYA IN...

Two Days
Visit the interactive exhibition at the **Ayutthaya Tourist Center** and discover why the city was once so great. Cycle around **Ayutthaya Historical Park**, then stop at **Lung Lek** for the best noodles in town. The following day hop on an elephant for a short ride among the ruins then finish your visit by sampling locally made produce at the **Ayutthaya Floating Market**.

Four Days
Head out of the city to visit **Bang Pa In Palace** and the nearby **Bang Sai Arts & Crafts Centre**. On the way back, drop by at **Wat Phanan Choeng** to ensure good luck by releasing fish back into the river and return to the island in time to visit the brilliantly nostalgic **Million Toy Museum**.

One Week
A week gives you plenty of time to see the temples and nearby countryside. Cycle to **Wat Yai Chai Mongkhon** and mingle in the neighbouring Muslim markets before returning to the island for a **sunset boat trip** with Ayutthaya Boat and Travel. With a few extra days spare, you can learn how to be a mahout at the **Elephant Stay** (p160).

Ayuthaya

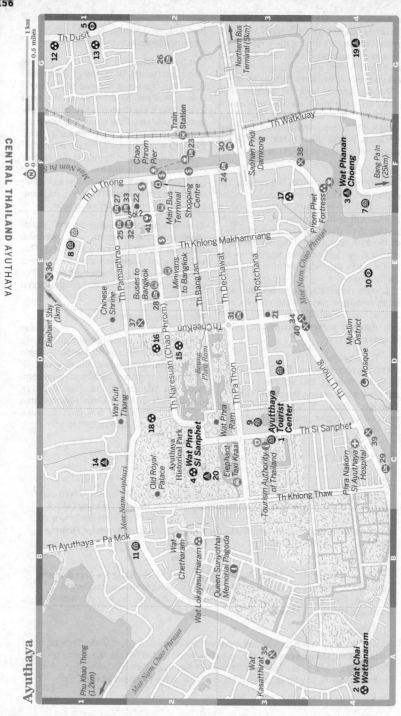

Th Dusit

Mae Nam Pa Sak

Th U Thong

Th Pamaphrao

Chao Phrom Pier

Train Station

Th Watkluay

Northern Bus Terminal (5km)

Chinese Shrine

Buses to Bangkok

Minivans to Bangkok

Th Khlong Makhamriang

Shopping Centre

Main Bus Terminal

Saphan Pridi Damrong

Bang Pa In (25km)

Wat Phanan Choeng

Phom Phet Fortress

Th Khlong Makhamriang

Th Bang Ian

Th Cheekun

Bueng Phra Ram

Th Naresuan (Chao Phrom)

Th Dechawat

Th Rotchana

Mae Nam Chao Phraya

Muslim District

Mosque

Elephant Stay (1km)

Wat Kuti Thong

Th Pa Thon

Th Pa Thon

Wat Phra Ram

Ayuthaya Historical Park

Old Royal Palace

Wat Phra Si Sanphet

Elephant Taxi Kraal

Tourism Authority of Thailand

Ayuthaya Tourist Center

Th Si Sanphet

Phra Nakorn Si Ayuthaya Hospital

Th Khlong Thaw

Th U Thong

Mae Nam Lopburi

Th Ayuthaya – Pa Mok

Wat Chetharam

Wat Lokayasutharam

Queen Suriyothai Memorial Pagoda

Mae Nam Chao Phraya

Phu Khao Thong (1.2km)

Wat Kasatthirat

Wat Chai Wattanaram

0   1 km
0   0.5 miles

Ayuthaya

Million Toy Museum   MUSEUM

(พิพิธภัณฑ์ล้านของเล่นเกริกยุ้นพันธ์; ☑0 3532 8949; www.milliontoymuseum.com; admission 50B; ☺9am-4pm; ℗) Chances are your favourite childhood toy is enjoying retirement here among the tin soldiers, dolls and Godzillas, all lovingly displayed in this two-storey museum by associate professor Krirk Yoonpun. It isn't just toys; the collection of Buddhist amulets and old Thai currency is of interest.

◎ Off the Island

On the opposite side of the water that envelops central Ayuthaya are several famous temples. You can reach some sites by bicycle, but others require a motorbike. Evening boat tours (p159) around the island are another way to see the highlights.

★ Wat Chai Wattanaram   RUIN

(วัดไชยวัฒนาราม; admission 50B; ☺8am-6pm) Just 40 years ago this temple and one-time garrison was immersed in thick jungle. Today it is one of Ayuthaya's most-photographed sites thanks to its impressive 35m-high Khmer-style central *prang*. Built in 1673 by King Prasat Thong, the temple is a great place to watch sunsets. The site is west of the island and can be reached by bicycle via a nearby bridge.

★ Wat Phanan Choeng   BUDDHIST TEMPLE

(วัดพนัญเชิง; admission 20B; ☺8am-7pm) Merit-making ceremonies, firecrackers and ritualistic fish feeding make this a hectic temple. The signature attraction is the 19m-high Phra Phanan Choeng, which was created in 1324 and sits in the *wí·hǎhn*, surrounded by 84,000 Buddha images that line the walls. The statue's broad shape is typical of the U Thong period.

Wat Phanan Choeng, southeast of the old city, can be reached by ferry (5B) from the pier near Phom Phet Fortress. Your bicycle can accompany you across.

Baan Hollanda   MUSEUM

(☑0 3523 5200; www.baanhollanda.org; next to Wat Phanan Choeng; 50B; ☺9am-5pm Wed-Sun; ℗ⓜ) Partly funded by Princess Beatrix, this charming exhibition is based within the grounds of the original Dutch trading post. An upstairs exhibition chronicles Thai-Dutch relations from the time the Dutch East India Company (VOC) arrived in Ayuthaya in 1604. Sip Dutch coffee downstairs then wander back to the main road and admire the adjacent boatyard.

Baan Hollanda is next to Wat Phanan Choeng.

AYUTHAYA'S TOP FIVE SITES

➡ Wat Phra Si Sanphet (p154)

➡ Wat Phanan Choeng (p157)

➡ Wat Chai Wattanaram (p157)

➡ Wat Yai Chai Mongkhon (p159)

➡ Wihaan Phra Mongkhon Bophit (p154)

Ayuthaya Floating Market
MARKET

(ตลาดน้ำอโยธยา; www.ayutthayafloatingmarket. com; ⊙9am-7pm; P) FREE A touch kitsch, but popular with locals and visitors, the floating market sells snacks, artwork and clothes. Set on wooden platforms above the water, long-boats (20B) offer rides through the water-ways. Traditional performances take place throughout the day. Avoid the neighbouring Ayodia Inter Market as it has some dubious animal attractions.

The market is to the east of the old city off Th Dusit, near Wat Kudi Dao.

Foreign Quarter
HISTORICAL SITE

(หมู่บ้านชาวต่างประเทศ) One reason Ayuthaya's rulers lasted so long was that they could talk a good game. As a result of their adroit di-plomacy and tolerance towards other reli-gions and cultures, up to 40 ethnic groups settled here. Today evidence of this remains in the Portuguese Settlement, St Joseph's Church and a Muslim market.

The Portuguese were first to arrive in 1511, followed by the Dutch, British and Japanese. Up to 2000 Portuguese traders and diplo-mats lived in the area and there were three Catholic churches. A small group of Thai Catholics still lives near the site.

TAILOR-MADE TÚK-TÚKS

Túk-túks (pronounced 'dúk dúk'; motorised transport) in Ayuthaya are different from the classic Thai design thanks to their strange dome-shaped fronts. Resembling Darth Vader's iconic mask, they zip around in a variety of colours and designs. One veteran driver remembers these distinctive taxis hav-ing looked the same for more than 50 years. It is thought they may have first been made in Japan, which could ex-plain the samurai-like curved front.

The Portuguese brought guns with them, and this modern weapon helped the Thais defeat the Burmese in 1520. As a result of this victory, the Portuguese were given land on which to build. In 1767 the Burmese in-vaders burned down the settlement and it wasn't until 1985 that a Portuguese founda-tion came to restore the village.

Just south of the island, the **Portuguese Settlement** displays the skeletal remains of 40 Portuguese settlers in an open pit. Look for the unusual spirit house with fig-ures of St Joseph and St Paul. To the west of the Portuguese Settlement is a **Muslim quarter**, where an evening market is held on Wednesdays and Saturdays. The area is picturesque and ideal for cycling. Along the way, stop at **Wat Phutthaii Sawan** to see a reclining Buddha and Khmer-style *prang*.

Japanese Village
MUSEUM

(หมู่บ้านญี่ปุ่น; adult/child 50/20B; ⊙8.30am-4.30pm; P) This interesting exhibition, lo-cated 5km south of the island, details how 1500 Japanese came to settle in Ayuthaya. Some came to trade while others fled the persecution of Christians in their homeland during the 16th century.

The Japanese Village includes a video presentation and a giant electronic image of an oil painting by Dutch artists of the old city at its zenith.

Phu Khao Thong
MONUMENT

(เจดีย์ภูเขาทอง; P) Set northwest of the is-land, it is worth clambering up the *chedi's* 79 steps for splendid views of the city. Origi-nally built by the Burmese during a 15-year occupation, the top section was added later by Thais. The statue at the front is a memo-rial to the all-conquering King Naresuan. Surrounding him are dozens of statues of fighting cockerels.

Legend says that when Naresuan was a hostage in Burma his invincible fighting cockerels secured his fearsome reputation.

Wat Na Phra Meru
BUDDHIST TEMPLE

(วัดหน้าพระเมรุ; admission 20B; P) This temple was one of only a few to escape the wrath of Burma's invading army in 1767 as it was used as their base. Inside the *wí-hähn* is a magnificent 1500-year-old green sandstone Buddha from Sri Lanka. Its prominent facial features and joined eyebrows are typical of the Dvaravati period.

The *bòht* (central sanctuary) houses a carved wooden ceiling showing the Bud-dhist heavens.

Elephant Kraal
ELEPHANT STOCKADE

(เพนียดคล้องช้าง) **FREE** Wild elephants were once rounded up and kept in this *kraal* (stockade). Each year the king would look on as the finest beasts were chosen and either put to work or used as war machines. This restored *kraal*, which has 980 teak logs, is northeast of the island.

During the 2011 floods, elephants from a nearby sanctuary found safety in the top section of the walls. Boats brought them food for several weeks until the water subsided.

Bahn Thanon Dusit
BUDDHIST TEMPLES

(บ้านถนนดุสิต) **FREE** For a scenic side to the city, grab a bicycle and peddle around this rural patch, east of the island. **Wat Maheyong** is a popular weekend meditation retreat in a leafy courtyard. Slightly further down the road is **Wat Kudi Dao** (Baan Th Dusit), which nature has taken hold of, and **Wat Ayuthaya** (Baan Th Dusit), which has a market on Wednesday evenings.

Wat Yai Chai Mongkhon
BUDDHIST TEMPLE

(วัดใหญ่ชัยมงคล; admission 20B) A 7m-long reclining Buddha is the highlight at Wat Yai Chai Mongkhon. If you can get a coin to stick to the Buddha's feet, it is thought good luck will come your way. King U Thong built the monastery in 1357 to house monks from Sri Lanka. The bell-shaped *chedi* was built later to honour King Naresuan's victory over Burma.

Wat Tha Ka Rong
BUDDHIST TEMPLE

(☉6am-5pm; **P**) **FREE** Just to the northwest of the island sits this bizarre temple. If you aren't dazzled by the fairy lights, you may notice the skeleton models that *wai* as you pass by, the room full of life-size monk statues and the super-fancy bathrooms, which are an attraction in themselves.

The display of differing Buddhas from neighbouring countries is worth a look. To the rear is a modest **floating market** that focuses on food.

☞ Tours

You can take brief rides around the historical park by **elephant** (☑0 8066 87727; www.elephantstay.com; 200-500B). The elephants stay at a kraal on Th Pa Thon.

Pedalling around the island is the best way to see the ruins. To see more of the surrounding countryside, guides are available and two-day trips are possible. Try **Tour**

> ### ⓘ AUDIO GUIDES
>
> Audio guides (150B) can be hired at Wat Phra Si Sanphet, Wat Phra Mahathat and Wat Chai Wattanaram. The English-language guides provide excellent background information and vivid detail that help visitors imagine exactly what once stood on these sites.

With Thai (☑0 3523 1084; www.tourwiththai.com; Th Naresuan).

Ayutthaya Boat and Travel (☑08 1733 5687, 0 3524 4558; www.ayutthaya-boat.com) can organise homestays, guided cycling tours or dinner on a teak rice barge.

Boat tours (per hr 150B) can be arranged at the pier near the night market or at guesthouses. Guesthouses offer two-hour sunset tours of the ruins (180B), though these can be cancelled if numbers are too low.

For in-depth coverage of Ayutthaya's history, talk to staff at TAT about hiring a guide.

☆ Festivals & Events

Loi Kratong
CULTURE

(☉Nov) In November, the Bang Sai Arts & Crafts Centre (p164) is the place to be for the Loi Kratong festival. Hundreds of beautiful lotus-shaped vessels containing candles and incense sticks are set afloat from the riverside. In late January, the centre holds its annual fair, showcasing its work.

Swan Boat Races
CULTURE

(☉Sep) The Thailand International Swan Boat Races take place on the Mae Nam Chao Phraya at the Bang Sai Arts and Crafts Centre. It involves long-boats pitting international and domestic crews.

Songkran
NEW YEAR

(☉Apr) Unlike the water mayhem at places such as Bangkok and Chiang Mai, the Thai New Year water festival here is more of a time for merit-making and paying homage to the elderly. It is held around April 12 to 14.

🛏 Sleeping

Backpackers head for Soi 2, Th Naresuan, where there is a handful of guesthouses. Along the river, an increasing number of quality midrange options are appearing. Look for substantial discounts during the low season (April to November).

★ **Baan Lotus Guest House** GUESTHOUSE $
(☎0 3525 1988; 20 Th Pamaphrao; s 200B, d 450-600B; **P**❋☎) The gorgeous, green grounds surrounding this converted teak school-house make staying here a treat. Staff are as charmingly old-school as the building itself.

PU Inn Ubonpon GUESTHOUSE $
(☎0 3525 1213; www.puguesthouse.com; 20/1 Soi Thaw Kaw Saw; s 200-300B, d 400-900B, tr 700B; ❋@☎) Knowledgeable staff and neat, if not spectacular, rooms have made this spot so popular they had to open a sister hotel right opposite. Some staff speak Japanese.

Grandparent's Home GUESTHOUSE $
(☎08 3558 5829; 19/40 Th Naresuan; r 550B; ❋☎) Simple little touches and splashes of colour give the rooms in this deceptively large guesthouse a warm vibe. A good-value place right next to the Historical Park.

Chantana Guest House GUESTHOUSE $
(☎0 3532 3200; chantanahouse@yahoo.com; 12/22 Soi 2, Th Naresuan; r 500-650B; **P**❋☎) Chantana is a well-established guesthouse with sparse but clean rooms. Staff are friendly and the location is excellent. Splash out an extra 50B to snag a room with a balcony.

Baan Khun Pra GUESTHOUSE $
(☎0 3524 1978; www.bannkunpra.com; 48/2 Th U Thong; dm/d 250/600B; ❋@☎) Meaning 'Bureaucrat's Home', this riverside teak property, built around 100 years ago, is in a wonderful charismatic time warp, with antiques dotted everywhere. Dorms sleep up to four.

Baan Are Gong GUESTHOUSE $
(☎0 3523 5592; siriporntan@yahoo.com.sg; off Th Rotchana; s 220B, d 500-600B; ❋☎) Walking distance from the train station, Baan Are Gong is an imposing 100-year-old teak guesthouse, run by a welcoming Thai-Chinese family. The 4B ferry to the island is nearby.

★ **Tony's Place** GUESTHOUSE $$
(☎0 3525 2578; www.tonyplace-ayutthaya.com; 12/18 Soi 2, Th Naresuan; r 300-1200B; ❋☎❋) Tony's remains the flashpackers' top choice thanks to well-renovated rooms, a mini pool and the chance to swap travel trips with fellow visitors. Cheaper rooms have fans and shared bathrooms.

Promtong Mansion GUESTHOUSE $$
(☎0 3524 2459; www.promtong.com; off Th Dechawat; d/tw/f 1090/1090/1690B; ❋☎) Bright rooms and even brighter staff are a big bonus at this four-storey guesthouse. Breakfast included. If full, check out its sister hotel Baan Tebpitak, which is within walking distance and has its own pool.

HELPING AN OLD FRIEND

Elephants helped Thailand win wars, build cities and transport kings. However, today these animals are the ones needing help, as their natural habitat has been slashed back and they are reduced to begging for food in the street. With only 4000 domestic and wild elephants remaining in Thailand, they need all the assistance they can get.

The **Elephant Stay** (☎08 0668 7727; www.elephantstay.com) in Ayuthaya does its part by running a hugely successful breeding program and providing brief tourist rides around the ruins (200B to 500B). This nonprofit organisation protects elephants by buying sick or abused animals, including bulls that have killed villagers.

Laithongrien Meepan opened the centre in 1996 after buying his daughter an elephant as a present. Australians Michelle Reedy, a former zoo keeper, and Ewa Nakiewicz run an Elephant Stay program (12,000B for three days, two nights minimum) where visitors learn how to ride, bathe and earn the trust of the animals.

Paying for a pachyderm is not cheap, as they can munch their way through 150kg of food a day, so the taxi rides and Elephant Stay help cover costs. In turn, some elephants help earn their keep by turning their trunks to art, appearing in movies such as Oliver Stone's *Alexander* and even providing dung, which is made into paper, bookmarks and photo albums. Flooding in 2011 badly damaged the site but it is now fully operational again.

The site is not designed for walk-in tourists; but those who spend time living with the elephants usually come away with a new-found admiration for Thailand's national animal.

Iudia on the River
HOTEL $$$

(☑ 0 3532 3208; www.iudia.com; 11-12 Th U Thong; s 1550B, d 2750-5550B; P ✳ 🕏 ☒) Superbly designed rooms that fuse traditional Thai furnishings with modern finishes make this a fabulous spot. Clever touches include naming the rooms after Ayuthaya's leading erstwhile figures.

Baan Thai House
BOUTIQUE HOTEL $$$

(☑ 0 35245 555; www.baanthaihouse.com; off Th Dusit; r 2400-2800B; P ⊖ ✳ 🕏 ☒) The dozen Thai-style villas, each with their own theme, and well-kept grounds ensure a zenlike stay. The on-site spa is worth a look. A túk-túk (pronounced *'đúk đúk';* motorised transport) to the old city costs 80B.

Krungsri River Hotel
HOTEL $$$

(☑ 0 3524 4333; www.krungsririver.com; 27/2 Th Rotchana; d/ste 1800/5738B; P ✳ @ 🕏 ☒) Splendid river views and more than 200 stylish rooms make this four-star hotel the best spot in town.

Classic Kameo Hotel
HOTEL $$$

(☑ 0 3521 2535; www.kameocollection.com; 148 Moo 5, Th Rotchana; r 2100-3100B; P ✳ @ ☒) Cool white tones throughout this luxury hotel make it a great post-temple place to relax. Facilities include shuttle bus to the island, gym and pool.

✗ Eating

Centuries of mingling with foreign traders has resulted in a rich tapestry of food options. Muslim snacks, fresh seafood and Dutch coffee can all be found here. As well as Western-friendly restaurants on Soi 2, Th Naresuan, try the excellent riverfront restaurants along the southern section of Th U Thong.

★ Sai Thong
THAI $

(Th U Thong; dishes 90-150B; ⊘ 9.30am-10pm; P 🖉 🍴) The number of cars vying for parking spaces each night is testament to how much locals love Sai Thong. The 180 menu items include classics as well as some slight variations, so browse before picking.

Hua Raw Night Market
MARKET $

(Th U Thong) This evening market offers simple riverside seating and a range of Thai and Muslim dishes; for the latter look for the green star and crescent.

Roti Sai Mai Stalls
THAI SWEETS $

(Th U Thong; ⊘ 10am-8pm) The Muslim dessert of *roh-đee săi măi* is famous in these parts. Buy a bag then make your own by by rolling together thin strands of melted palm sugar and wrapping them inside the roti. Stalls can be found opposite Ayuthaya Hospital.

Lung Lek
NOODLES $

(Th Chee Kun; dishes 30-40B; ⊘ 8.30am-4pm) Everybody's favourite noodle emporium, Uncle Lek still serves the most notable noodles in town. Located opposite Wat Ratburana, this is the perfect pit stop between temples.

Baan Mai Rim Nam
SEAFOOD $

(☑ 0 3521 1516; Th U Thong; dishes 150-250B; ⊘ 10am-10pm; P 🖉) One of the livelier restaurants along Th U Thong, this riverfront restaurant specialises in fried and steamed fish.

Tony's Place
WESTERN $

(Soi 2, Th Naresuan; dishes 60-100B; 🖉 🍴) Set at the front of the eponymous guesthouse, this offers simple but tasty Thai/Western dishes, a few veggie nibbles and plenty of fellow travellers to chat with.

★ Baan Watcharachai
THAI $$

(off Th Worachate; dishes 120-250B; P 🍴) Not only do you get to dine on this wooden boat while gazing at the temples across the water, you can also sample great *yam Ƀlah dùk fòo* (crispy catfish salad). Head to Wat Kasatthirat and look for the restaurant at the rear.

Pae Krung Gao
THAI $$

(Th U Thong; dishes 100-200B) A well-established riverside restaurant serving top-notch Thai food. The English-language menu is limited, so if you know what you like, just ask.

🍷 Drinking & Nightlife

Nightlife on the island is limited to Soi 2, Th Naresuan, where visitors listen to live music at **Street Lamp** (⊘ 7am-midnight) or try to answer Toi's infuriating trivia questions at the **Jazz Bar** (⊘ 7pm-midnight).

Off the island, there is a collection of bars along Th Rotchana, near the northern bus terminal. **Khlawng Phleng** (no romanscript sign) is the best, and least salacious, of these with live music and a lively crowd.

162

CENTRAL THAILAND AYUTHAYA

🛍 Shopping

On the island, there is a handicraft, arts and clothes market every Friday to Sunday evening at the junction of Th Rotchana and Th Pridi Banomyong. About 8km south of the island, the Gohng Kohng Market (www.talardkhongkong.com; ⊙ 9am-4pm Thu-Sun) specialises in ceramics and textiles.

ℹ Information

DANGERS & ANNOYANCES

Traffic lights are often absent from road junctions in Ayuthaya where they would seem a prudent choice. This means extra care is needed, especially when on a bicycle. Remember Thailand's unofficial road rules: if you're faster and larger, you have right of way. When cycling, put bags around your body, not in baskets where they could be snatched.

At night several packs of dogs roam the streets. Avoid eye contact and be sure to keep your distance.

EMERGENCY

Tourist Police (☑ emergency 1155; Th Si Sanphet)

INTERNET ACCESS

Several shops on and around Soi 2, Th Naresuan have connections for 30B per hour.

MEDICAL SERVICES

Phra Nakorn Si Ayuthaya Hospital (☑ 0 3532 2555-70, emergency 1669; cnr Th U Thong & Th Si Sanphet) Has an emergency centre and English-speaking doctors.

MONEY

ATMs are plentiful along Th Naresuan, near the Amporn Shopping Centre.
Bank of Ayuthaya (Th U Thong near Th Naresuan)
Kasikorn Bank (Th Naresuan)
Siam City Bank (Th U Thong)
Siam Commercial Bank (Th Naresuan)

POST

Main Post Office (Th U Thong; ⊙ 8.30am-4.30pm Mon-Fri, 9am-noon Sat & Sun) Has an international telephone service, open 8am to 8pm, upstairs.

TOURIST INFORMATION

Tourism Authority of Thailand (TAT; ☑ 0 3524 6076; 108/22 Th Si Sanphet; ⊙ 8.30am-4.30pm Mon-Fri) If you would like in-depth

TRANSPORT TO/FROM AYUTHAYA

Bus

DESTINATION	FARE (B)	DURATION	FREQUENCY
Bang Pa In	20	45min	every 20min (sŏrng·tăa·ou)
Bangkok (Rangsit)	34-50	1hr	every 25min
Bangkok (Victory Monument)	60	1½hr	every 25min (minivan)
Bangkok's Northern (Mo Chit) station	56-60	1½hr	every 25min
Bangkok's Southern (Sai Tai Mai) station	70	1hr	every 30min
Chiang Mai	438-876	8hr	frequent
Lopburi	50	1½hr	every 15min (minivan)
Nan	540-850	10hr	8.45am, 8.20pm
Phitsanulok	304-473	5hr	11am, 1.30pm, 9pm, 11.30pm
Sukhothai	279-387	7hr	frequent
Suphanburi	80	1½hr	every 20min (minivan)

Train

DESTINATION	FARE (B)	DURATION	FREQUENCY
Bang Pa In	3-20	15min	frequent
Bangkok's Bang Sue station	14-345	1½hr	frequent
Bangkok's Hualamphong station	15-345	1½hr	frequent
Chiang Mai	586-1198	8hr	6 departures a day
Khon Kaen	217-315	6hr	4 departures a day
Pak Chong	23-173	4hr	7 departures a day

WORTH A TRIP

SARABURI

Nestled between its more well-known neighbours of Ayuthaya and Lopburi, Saraburi is a small province with a handful of attractions. Fortunately, two of the best spots are next to each other.

Wat Phra Puttachai In this cave temple a silhouette said to be of the Buddha can be seen on one of its hillside walls. Behind six Buddha images are prehistoric paintings dating back 3000 years. If you look closely, chickens and religious images can just be made out. Clamber to the top of the hill and you'll be rewarded with magnificent views of the plains down below. The temple is on Rte 3042, 5km from Hwy 1.

Nam Tok Sam Lan National Park (☑ 0 2562 0760; www.dnp.go.th; adult/child 200/100B) Just 2km down the road from Wat Phra Puttachai is Nam Tok Sam Lan National Park. Covering 44 sq km, the park has a central plain and offers good trekking opportunities and the chance to see pheasants, barking deer, wild boar and butterflies. While the park doesn't quite match its 'three million waterfall' moniker, Nam Tok Sam Lan, Nam Tok Rak Sai and Nam Tok Pho Hin Dat are all near the main entrance and worth a visit. Guides from the main office can lead visitors on a three-hour trek. Tents (200B to 400B) and bungalows (600B to 6000B) are available.

coverage of Ayuthaya history, talk to TAT about hiring a guide. TAT's office at Ayutthaya Tourist Center (p154) is open daily.

ⓘ Getting There & Away

BOAT

Several companies offer boats to Bangkok, though in reality they tend to drop you north of the capital and bus you in.

BUS

Ayuthaya's provincial bus stop is on Th Naresuan, a short walk from the guesthouse area. Minivans and air-con buses depart from down the road. The northern bus terminal is 5km east of the old city, off Th Rotchana. A túk-túk from the terminal to the old city will cost 100B. For Kanchanaburi, transfer at Suphanburi. Buses to Mo Chit can stop at Don Muang Airport.

TRAIN

The train station is east of central Ayuthaya and is accessible by a quick cross-river ferry from the centre of town (4B) or sŏrng·tăa·ou (50B). Pak Chong is the nearest station to Khao Yai National Park. For Bangkok's Th Khao San area, get off at Bang Sue.

ⓘ Getting Around

Săhm·lór (three-wheeled pedicabs; also spelt săamláw) or túk-túk are readily available. Always agree on a price before you get on. For trips on the island, the rate is 30B to 40B.

As most of the ruins are close together, the most environmentally friendly way to see them is by bicycle or elephant. Guesthouses rent bicycles (30B) and motorcycles (200B).

Around Ayuthaya

★ **Bang Pa In Palace**　　PALACE
(บางปะอิน; admission 100B; ⊙ 8am-3.15pm) An eclectic assortment of architectural styles makes this a palace like no other. Built in the 17th century and restored during the reign of Rama V (King Chulalongkorn; 1868–1910), its European, Chinese and Thai buildings reflect the wide influences of Rama V.

Highlights include a replica of the Tiber Bridge in Rome, the stunning Chinese-style Wehut Chamrun, the Victorian-influenced observatory Withun Thatsana and a Thai pavilion in the middle of a pond housing a statue of Rama V.

In 1880, Queen Sunanta drowned during a journey to the palace. Thai law forbid courtiers from touching the queen, and so nobody dared jump in and save her. As a result of the tragedy King Rama V changed the law. A marble obelisk in memory of the queen is in the palace grounds. Self-drive carts (400B for one hour, 100B per hour thereafter) are available. Note the relatively early closing time.

Wat Niwet Thamaprawat, to the rear of the palace car park, is the most unlikely of temples. Designed to resemble a cathedral, its Gothic-style, stained-glass windows and knights in armour stand in contrast to the Buddha images. Take a free, monk-operated cable car to the other side of the water. Recent renovations have made it particularly quaint.

To reach the palace, take a public *sŏrng·tăa·ou* (25B, one hour, frequent) from the provincial bus stop on Th Naresuan in Ayuthaya. Once the *sŏrng·tăa·ou* drops you at the Bang Pa In bus station, jump on a motorbike taxi (30B) to the palace, which is 4km away. Trains run from Ayuthaya (3B, 15 minutes). The train station is closer to the palace than the bus station, but you'll still need a motorbike taxi (20B) to complete the last leg. Or you can charter a túk-túk for about 400B return.

Bang Sai Arts & Crafts Centre
CULTURAL CENTRE

(ศูนย์ศิลปาชีพบางไทร; bird park 20B, aquarium adult/child 100/50B; ☉8am-4.30pm Tue-Sun) Another 17km southwest of the palace is Bang Sai Arts & Crafts Centre. The centre preserves traditional Thai art by offering 30 training courses, ranging from ceramics and silk weaving to mask making. Launched in 1984 with support from Queen Sirikit, this 180-hectare site includes **Sala Phra Ming Kwan** pavilion, which sells a wide range of goods, and an excellent arts and crafts village. A **bird park** and Thailand's largest freshwater fish **aquarium** will keep younger visitors hooked. Avoid coming here on a Monday, when some attractions are closed.

To reach the arts centre, take a train to Bang Pa In then hire a motorbike taxi or *sŏrng·tăa·ou*.

LOPBURI PROVINCE

Lopburi ลพบุรี

Temple ruins and mischievous monkeys – these are the headline attractions in laid-back Lopburi. Beyond this, though, Lopburi hides several natural marvels that are worth exploring and often detain visitors for a few days before they journey north.

Lopburi played a part in the Dvaravati, Khmer, Sukhothai and Ayuthaya empires and the ruins, all within the old part of town, reflect this.

As one of Thailand's oldest cities, Lopburi was first developed during the Dvaravati period (6th to 10th centuries), when it was known as Lavo. The enormous influence of the Khmer empire can still be seen in the architecture and artwork. During the Ayuthaya period, Lopburi was a second capital and hosted many foreign dignitaries, which led to advances in architecture, astronomy and literature.

Today, the monkeys are the main draw as they make their homes among some of the major ruins. These macaques frequently leave their base to zip-line along overhead wires and leap from pole to pole in search of food, so don't be shocked to wake up and see a monkey staring at you through your guesthouse window.

Lopburi, which is 150km north of Bangkok, is renowned for its vast sunflower fields, coconut jelly and rattan furniture, while sugar cane and rice are the main crops.

◉ Sights

★Phra Narai Ratchaniwet
MUSEUM

(วังนารายณ์ราชนิเวศน์; entrance Th Sorasak; admission 150B; ☉gallery 8.30am-4pm Wed-Sun, palace grounds 8am-5pm) Start your tour of Lopburi at this former royal palace. Inside the palace grounds is the **Lopburi Museum** (officially called Somdet Phra Narai National Museum), which houses displays of local history. The museum is divided into three separate buildings. In Phiman Mongkut Pavilion there are sculptures and art from the Lopburi, Khmer, Dvaravati, U Thong and Ayuthaya periods.

The Chantara Phisan Throne Hall contains paintings and artefacts in memory of King Narai, while the European-style Phra Pratiab Building has a small display of traditional handicraft and hunting tools. Built between 1665 and 1677, with help from French and Italian engineers, the palace was used to welcome foreign dignitaries. The main entry point is through Pratu Phayakkha gate, off Th Sorasak. To your left are the remains of the palace reservoir and former reception hall. Ahead of these are the elephant stables and towards the rear of the compound is the Suttha Sawan throne hall, where King Narai died. A 150B one-day pass to the main ruins can be bought here.

★Prang Sam Yot
MONUMENT

(ปรางค์สามยอด; Th Wichayen; admission 50B; ☉6am-6pm) Prang Sam Yot and its resident troop of monkeys are the most famous attraction in Lopburi. The three linked towers originally symbolised the Hindu Trimurti of Shiva, Vishnu and Brahma. Now two of them contain ruined Lopburi-style Buddha images. The towers are accessible and offer relief from the heat and monkeys.

Lopburi

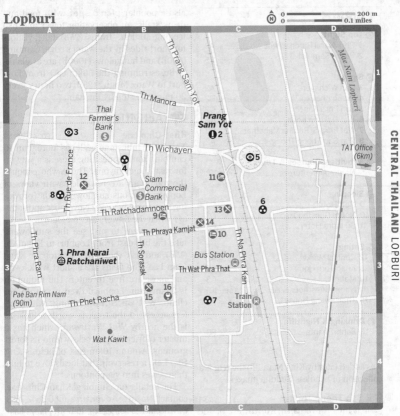

Young guides show visitors around for a small donation and, while their English is minimal, their catapults keep the monkeys at bay. The monument is the best example of Khmer-Lopburi architecture, and looks especially good at night when illuminated.

Wat Phra Si Ratana Mahathat   RUIN
(วัดพระศรีรัตนมหาธาตุ; Th Na Phra Kan; admission 50B; ⊙7am-5pm). Once the town's largest monastery, this 13th-century Khmer wát has been heavily renovated and makes for a great photo opportunity. The central Phra Prang has bas-relief depicting the life of the Buddha while its arched gate has images in the style of the Lawo period.

The northwestern prang has U Thong–style angels; their oblong faces and unusual halos are rare.

Ban Wichayen   HISTORICAL BUILDING
(บ้านวิชาเยนทร์, Chao Phraya Wichayen; Th Wichayen; admission 50B; ⊙9am-4pm) King Narai

built this Thai-European palace as a residence for foreign ambassadors. Greek diplomat and trader Constantine Phaulkon was its most famous resident. What is left today among the scattered ruins includes a Catholic chapel. The palace is across the street and northeast of Wat Sao Thong Thong.

Prang Khaek   RUIN
(ปรางค์แขก) The oldest monument in Lopburi, this 11th-century tower is on a triangular piece of land bordered by Th Wichayen to the north. The structure has Khmer-style brickwork and was possibly once a temple to the Hindu god Shiva.

Wat Nakhon Kosa   RUIN
(วัดนครโกษา; Th Na Phra Kan) Just along from the train station is Wat Nakhon Kosa. Built in the 12th century it may have originally been a Hindu shrine. The main *chedi* was built during the Dvaravati period, while the *wí·hăhn*

was added later by King Narai. To the rear is a collection of headless Buddha images.

Wat Sao Thong Thong   RUIN
(วัดเสาธงทอง; Th Wichayen) Northwest of the palace centre, Wat Sao Thong Thong is remarkable for its unusual Gothic-style windows, which were added by King Narai so it could be used as a Christian chapel.

Wat Khao Wong Kot   BUDDHIST TEMPLE
(วัดเขาวงกต) **FREE** About 30km west of Lopburi is Wat Khao Wong Kot, home to an enormous **bat cave**. At sunset hundreds of thousands of bats emerge for their nocturnal hunt. To find the cave, take the 280 steps to the right of the temple entrance.

The temple can be reached by taking a train (second-/third-class ticket 21/6B) north from Lopburi to Ban Mee station and then catching a motorbike taxi. Buses (25B) also run hourly to Ban Mee. However, the last train to Lopburi departs at 6.12pm while the last bus is at 5.30pm so you will need private transport to witness the bat exodus.

Pa Sak Jolasid Dam   LAKE
(เขื่อนป่าสักชลสิทธิ์; **P**) This 4860m-long dam is the longest of its kind in Thailand. It is

also a popular **picnic spot**, with food and drink stalls, an observation tower and fish feeding station. Trams (25B) take visitors for short rides by the water's edge. Camping (200B) and bungalows (1000B) are available.

Buses running the 50km east from Lopburi to Wang Moung (38B, two hours, every 20 minutes) stop by the dam.

🏃 Activities

Khao Chin Lae   ROCK CLIMBING
This 240m limestone peak has more than 40 climbing routes, meaning there is a way up for just about anyone. Those who conquer the mountain are rewarded with views of Lopburi's famous sunflower fields (providing they come between November and January when the flowers are in bloom).

If you want to just see the sunflowers, take the bus east from Lopburi to Khao Noi (15B) and ask the driver to stop at Khao Chin Lae. The fields are a short walk away, and most are free to enter. The mountain is 20km from Lopburi. Even if you do not climb, **Wat Ba Suwannahong**, which offers access to the trail, is worth a look, as is the nearby **Wat Waruwan**, which has a muster of friendly peacocks within its forest grounds. Around 10km east of here is **Ang Sap Lek**, a reservoir that locals love to hurl themselves into via pontoons.

For details on climbing Khao Chin Lae, contact **Nature Adventure** (✆0 3642 7693; www.noomguesthouse.com; 15-17 Th Phraya Kamjat; half/full-day trip 1000/1800B, renting equipment costs extra) at Noom Guesthouse (p167).

🎉 Festivals & Events

King Narai Festival   CULTURE
(◷16-22 Feb) Held annually at the Phra Narai Ratchaniwet. Locals don traditional clothes and stage a colourful parade that leads to the former palace. Highlights include a demonstration of *lá·kon ling* (a traditional drama performed by monkeys).

Monkey Festival   MONKEYS
(◷Nov) The real macaques take centre stage during the last week of November for their very own Monkey Festival. Thousands gather to watch the simians devour their banquet.

🛏 Sleeping

Budget rooms are the only choice in the old town. A few good midrange options are appearing in the new part of town; local buses offer transport to the attractions.

★ **Noom Guesthouse** GUESTHOUSE $
(☑ 0 3642 7693; www.noomguesthouse.com; 15-17 Th Phraya Kamjat; r 150-500B; ❋ ☎) Easily the most *fa•ràng*-friendly spot in town, Noom's rooms are either bamboo bungalows or simple pads with shared bathrooms. A nearby sister guesthouse takes any overspill.

Nett Hotel GUESTHOUSE $
(☑ 0 3641 1738; netthotel@hotmail.com; 17/1-2 Th Ratchadamnoen; r 260-570B; ❋ ☎) The Nett remains a good option, as rooms are reasonable and you are walking distance from the ruins. Cheaper rooms are fan-only and have cold-water showers.

Benjatara Boutique Place Resort BOUTIQUE RESORT $
(☑ 0 3642 2608; www.benjataralopburi.com; 123/33 M.1 Th Khao Sam Yot; r 550-1200B; P ❋ ☎) This welcome addition to Lopburi has a cosy, boutique feel with quality touches all around. One of the best-value spots in town.

Sri Indra Hotel GUESTHOUSE $
(☑ 0 3641 1261; 3-4 Th Na Phra Kan; r 200-350B; ❋) As long as you don't mind monkeys peering in your room, this is a good, centrally located guesthouse that is near the train station and San Phra Kan. Cheaper options are fan-only.

Lopburi Residence Hotel HOTEL $$
(☑ 0 3661 3410; Th Kanklorngchonbratahn; r 600-1200B; P ❋ ☎ ☀) Not the fanciest of hotels, but it does come with a pool and is a stroll from the bus station. Some rooms lack natural light, so explore before choosing one.

Lopburi Inn Hotel HOTEL $$
(☑ 0 3641 2300; www.lopburiinnhotel.com; 28/9 Th Phra Narai Maharat; r 1200-2000B; P ❋ ☎) If you haven't had enough of monkeys, check out the dozens of simian statues lined up outside or the special Monkey Beer. The top rooms come with enormous bathrooms. Look for off-season discounts.

Lopburi Inn Resort RESORT $$
(☑ 0 3642 0777; www.lopburiinnresort.com; 1144 M.3 Th Pahonyohtin, Tambon Tha Sala; r 1800-2600B; ❋ ☎ ☀) Still Lopburi's best resort, the pool, grounds and facilities ensure it is constantly busy. A minibus makes the 5km run to the old town.

MONKEY MAGIC

Grown men arm their catapults, old women grab 2m-long poles and toy crocodiles peer out from shop windows. Welcome to Lopburi, a town that fights a losing battle to keep its iconic monkeys at bay. Every day the monkeys put on a public performance as they swing, somersault and scamper across town, while residents make up the supporting cast.

The monkeys, a type of macaque, are an integral part of Lopburi's character. Stay in one of the old town's hotels and you will see them scurrying across power cables, pounding over corrugated roofs or squabbling over a tomato.

Their favourite haunts are **San Phra Kan** (Kala Shrine; Th Wichayen) and Prang Sam Yot (p164). While visiting these places, put bottles of water and anything that may be mistaken for food inside your bag. Any bottles on display will be considered fair game. It is also wise to only take your camera, and not its carrying bag.

It may appear that the locals can't stand their simian neighbours, but the monkeys are never harmed due to the Buddhist belief of preserving all life. Some feel the animals are 'descendants' of the Hindu god Kala and so to injure one would be seriously bad karma. Monkey souvenirs are nearly as omnipresent as the real thing; there is even a 'monkey beer' brewed by the Lopburi Inn Hotel and Resort.

A feeding station has been set up to discourage the monkeys from pilfering tourists' food, and so at 10am and 4pm every day heaps of vegetables and fruit are distributed, and quickly scoffed down, next to San Phra Kan.

Things could be about to change, though. A survey in 2012 revealed that many business owners want to restrict the monkeys to the temple ruins, so there are rumours that some troops could be rounded up and taken to an out-of-town location.

Care should be taken when being around the monkeys. They may look cute but they are wild animals, and wherever there is a sweet baby monkey, you can bet a protective mother is not far behind. Take a look at the arms of the young guides who offer to show you around for proof that the monkeys can, and sometimes do, bite.

✗ Eating & Drinking

Street markets and pull-up-a-stool restaurants are the best ways to feast in Lopburi. On Wednesdays a market fills Th Phraya Kamjat, while in the evenings vendors selling noodles and desserts line up along Th Na Phra Kan.

★ Khao Tom Hor
CHINESE-THAI $

(cnr Th Na Phra Kan & Th Ratchadamnoen; dishes 30-80B) Constantly busy Khao Tom Hor offers Thai-Chinese dishes, including *salid tôrd* (deep-fried salted fish) and *pàd gà-prow gài* (chicken with kaprao leaf). Service is speedy and efficient.

Central Market
MARKET $

(off Th Ratchadamnoen & Th Surasongkhram; ⊘6am-5pm) Wander through the narrow alleyways and take in the sights and smells of this local market. Blood-red strawberries, orange prawns and silver fish are laid out alongside *kôw dom mùd* (rice wrapped in coconut leaves), *da·go peu·ak* (taro custard with coconut milk) and *gài tôrt* (fried chicken). In the centre is a vegetarian pavilion.

Pae Ban Rim Nam
SEAFOOD $

(off Th Phet Racha; dishes 100-180B; ⊘10am-10pm; P 🐾) This floating restaurant, specialising in seafood, is the most pleasant eating place in the old town. For post-dinner activities, there is a fish feeding station next door.

Matini
WESTERN $

(www.matinirestaurant.com; Th Phraya Kamjat; dishes 80-130B; ⊘noon-midnight; 🛜 ✏ 🐾) Free pool, a Blues Brothers motif on the wall and great Western food make this Lopburi's hippest place. And though the name may look like a typo, 'Matini' means 'come here' in Thai.

Thaisawang House
THAI $

(Th Sorasak; dishes 60-100B; ⊘8.30am-8pm; ❄) Opposite Phra Narai Ratchaniwet, the menu here is extensive, portions are generous but service is a little slow. Check out the 'shrine' surrounded by toy action figures behind the counter.

Good View
SEAFOOD $

(Th Naresuan; dishes 80-150B; ⊘5pm-1am) One of several trendy, open-air restaurants along this road, Good View has a split-level design and great seafood.

Noom Guesthouse
CAFE $

(Th Phraya Kamjat; 80-130B; 🛜 ✏) Noom's has a good range of breakfasts, including French-style options, along with standard Thai/Western dishes.

Sahai Phanta
BAR

(Th Sorasak) To party with the locals, check out this town-centre venue with its Karabao-style house band.

ℹ Information

There are several banks in the old part of Lopburi and some next to the bus station. Several internet cafes and online game shops sit shoulder to shoulder along Th Na Phra Kan. The going

TRANSPORT TO/FROM LOPBURI

Bus & Minivan

DESTINATION	FARE (B)	DURATION	FREQUENCY
Ayuthaya	38	2hr	2.45pm & noon
Mo Chit	100	1½hr	every 30min
Victory Monument (Bangkok)	120 (minivan)	2hr	every 20min
Khorat (Nakhon Ratchasima)	133-171	3hr	hourly
Suphanburi	60	1hr	12.30pm

Train

DESTINATION	FARE (B)	DURATION	FREQUENCY
Ayuthaya	13-340	1½hr	frequent
Bangkok's Hualamphong Station	28-374	2½hr	frequent
Phitsanulok	49-423	3hr	frequent
Chiang Mai	346-746	12hr	every 4hr

rate is 15B. Free wi-fi is available at the **Zon Coffee Bar** (Th Naresuan).

Communications Authority of Thailand (CAT; Th Phra Narai Maharat; ⊘8.30am-4.30pm)

Muang Narai Hospital (☑0 3661 6300; Th Pahonyothin)

Police (☑0 3678 0042) The police station is 2km west of the old town.

Post Office (Th Phra Narai Maharat)

Tourism Authority of Thailand (TAT; ☑0 3642 2768-9; Th Phra Narai Maharat; ⊘8.30am-6.30pm Mon-Fri) The office is a rather inconvenient 5km east of the old town, along Th Phra Narai Maharat, but is worth finding for TAT's excellent free map.

ℹ Getting There & Away

BUS & MINIVAN

For many, Lopburi is the gateway to the north. If heading to Kanchanaburi, transfer at Suphanburi. Lopburi's bus station is 2km from the old town. Minivans to Bangkok depart from Th Na Phra Kan; big bags require their own ticket. Noom Guesthouse (p168) can arrange buses to Chiang Mai (600B), and will drop you at the pick-up location.

TRAIN

The **train station** (Th Na Phra Kan) is within walking distance of the old town. Luggage can be stored at the station for 20B per bag per day.

ℹ Getting Around

Sŏrng·tăa·ou and city buses run along Th Wichayen and Th Phra Narai Maharat between the old and new towns for 10B per passenger; săhm·lór will go anywhere in the old town for 30B.

KANCHANABURI PROVINCE

Given the jaw-dropping natural beauty around Kanchanaburi, it seems paradoxical that the area is more renowned for the horrors that occurred on the Death Railway in WWII. Visitors often visit the provincial town's WWII memorials before heading northwest to camp in the national parks where tigers, elephants and gibbons roam. Alongside a serrated mountain range that hugs the Burmese border, these vast parks contain tiered waterfalls and crystal-lined caves.

In the north of the province, the tiny towns of Thong Pha Phum and Sangkhlaburi are unspoiled places close to national parks. The parks give visitors the opportunity to explore thick jungle, stay with ethnic groups and visit incredible waterfalls and caves. This is all part of the Western Forest Complex, one of Asia's largest protected areas.

Remote towns in the far northwest, including Sangkhlaburi, are home to ethnic groups who have fled the military regime in Myanmar. An increasing number of foreign visitors now carry out volunteer work in these parts.

Kanchanaburi กาญจนบุรี

The provincial town of Kanchanaburi is an ideal base from which to explore Thailand's wild west.

Today the town is busy and alive but the WWII memorials and museums are a reminder of darker times. Japanese forces used Allied prisoners of war (POWs) and conscripted Southeast Asian labourers to build a rail route to Myanmar. The harrowing story was told in Pierre Boulle's book *The Bridge Over the River Kwai* and the 1957 movie is based on the book. The bridge is one of the main attractions in Kanchanaburi. Roads in the guesthouse area are named after countries that were involved in the conflict.

Sitting in the slightly elevated valley of Mae Nam Mae Klong, the town is surrounded by fields filled with tapioca, sugar cane and corn. Being just 130km from Bangkok, many city folk come here for the weekend, though they prefer to board booming karaoke boats than enjoy the serenity.

Travellers congregate around Th Mae Nam Khwae. The street is centrally located and a 10-minute walk from the train station. Most accommodation is built beside or floating on the river, although it now also has some midrange options. In-town attractions are best covered with the help of a bicycle or motorbike.

◉ Sights

★**Death Railway Bridge (Bridge Over the River Kwai)** HISTORICAL SITE

(สะพานข้ามแม่น้ำแคว; Th Mae Nam Khwae) Bypass the tourist scrum by the entrance, and the famous 300m railway bridge still retains its power and symbolism. The centre was destroyed by Allied bombs in 1945 so only the outer curved spans are original. Every 30 minutes a train rolls over the sleepers –

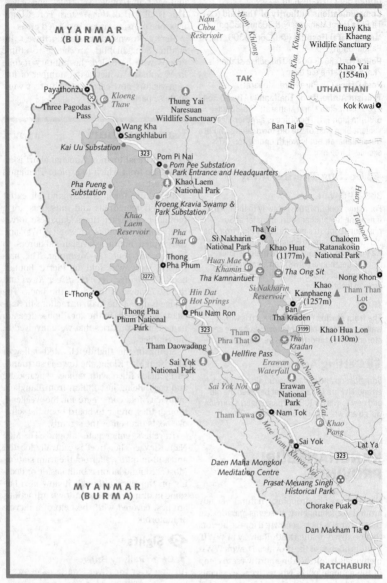

stand in one of the safety points along the bridge when one appears.

On the other side, pop in to the Chinese **temple** on the right and view the bridge from its tranquil garden.

The first version of the bridge, completed in 1943, was wooden and was later replaced by a steel bridge. During the last week of November and first week of December a nightly sound-and-light show marks the Allied attack on the Death Railway in 1945.

a northbound *sŏrng·tăa·ou* (10B) along Th Saengchuto. A mini rainbow-coloured train runs regular trips (20B; 8am to 10am and noon to 2pm) over the bridge from the nearby train station.

★ **Allied War Cemetery**   HISTORICAL SITE
(สุสานทหารพันธมิตรดอนรัก; Th Saengchuto; ⊙24hr) FREE Across the street from the Thailand-Burma Railway Centre is the Allied War Cemetery, which is immaculately maintained by the War Graves Commission. Of the 6982 POWs buried here, nearly half were British; the rest came mainly from Australia and the Netherlands.

It is estimated that at least 100,000 people died while working on the railway, the majority being labourers from nearby Asian countries, though not one of these has an identifiable grave. If you are looking for the resting place of a loved one, a small office to the side has lists of names and their locations within the cemetery. As you stand at the cemetery entrance, the front left area contains Australian graves, the rear left honours Dutch soldiers and the entire right-hand side contains British victims.

As there is no gate, it is possible to visit here anytime.

★ **Thailand-Burma Railway Centre Museum**   MUSEUM
(ศูนย์รถไฟไทย-พม่า; www.tbrconline.com; 73 Th Jaokannun; adult/child 120/60B; ⊙9am-5pm) This informative museum uses video footage, models and detailed displays to explain Kanchanaburi's role in WWII. Nine galleries tell the history of the railway, how prisoners were treated and what happened after the line was completed.

Upstairs is a display of wartime artefacts, including one POW's miniature chess set. A poignant video from POW survivors ensures that the deaths remain a tragedy, not a statistic. Half-/full-day tours (2400/4900B) can be arranged from here.

Jeath War Museum   MUSEUM
(พิพิธภัณฑ์สงคราม; Th Wisuttharangsi; admission 30B; ⊙8am-5pm) This small museum contains cuttings, correspondence and artwork from WWII. Located in bamboo-*ata,* similar to the shelters used for POWs, it details the harsh punishments meted out by Japanese troops.

Jeath is an acronym of the countries involved in the railway: Japan, England, Australia/USA, Thailand and Holland. The war museum is at the west end of Th

Rooms are hard to come by at this time, so book ahead.

The bridge spans Mae Nam Khwae Yai, which is 2.5km from the centre of Kanchanaburi. This means it is walkable from Th Mae Nam Khwae or you can jump on

Kanchanaburi

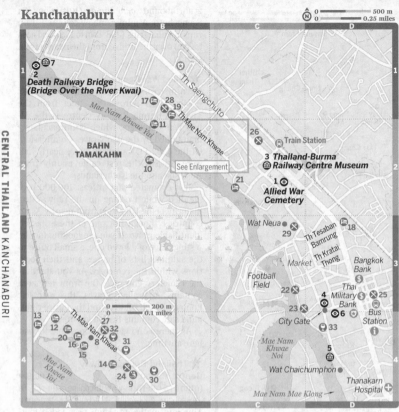

Wisuttharangsi (Visutrangsi). The museum is run by the monks of the adjacent Wat Chaichumphon (Wat Tai). In July 2013 a local man dived in the river outside the temple to retrieve a tourist's wallet – and found a sunken teak boat. The discovery of the vessel, thought to date from WWII, was deemed auspicious and so there is now a shrine in its honour.

Heritage Walking Street   HISTORICAL STREET
Set near the City Gate, this wonderful old street offers a glimpse of a bygone Kanchanaburi. More than 20 yellow signs reveal the history and architecture of this fascinating area. Leave at least an hour to stroll and note the variety of buildings, which include Sino-Portuguese, Thai and Chinese styles. Coffee and art shops are now also here.

Many shops date from the turn of the 20th century and are still owned by the same family. Look out for the erstwhile hotel

that, back in the good old days, charged 1B per night.

Chung Kai Allied War Cemetery   HISTORICAL SITE
(สุสานทหารพันธมิตรช่องไก่; ⊙7am-6pm) FREE Chung Kai was the site of a major prisoner camp during WWII, and Allied prisoners built their own hospital and church close to here. Most graves have brief, touching epitaphs for the 1400 Commonwealth and 300 Dutch soldiers buried here.

The cemetery is 4km south of central Kanchanaburi across the Mae Nam Khwae Noi and can be reached by bicycle.

Lak Meuang   LANDMARK
(ศาลหลักเมือง, City Pillar; Th Lak Meuang; ⊙daylight hours; P) FREE The city pillar is at the centre of the old town and is said to give shelter to local spirits. Just down the road is a statue of King Rama III and the renovated city wall, which used to stretch for more

Kanchanaburi

than 400m and had six fortresses. Three original cannons remain.

Wat Tham Seua & Wat Tham Khao Noi
BUDDHIST TEMPLES

(วัดถ้ำเสือ, วัดถ้ำเขาน้อย; P) FREE These neighbouring hilltop monasteries are of interest due to their vastly different styles. Wat Tham Khao Noi (Little Hill Cave Monastery) has an intricately designed Chinese-style pagoda, while next door the larger Wat Tham Seua (Tiger Cave Monastery) has several styles of *chedi* and an 18m-tall Buddha covered in a golden mosaic.

In front of the Buddha image a conveyor belt has small silver trays into which donations are made and then tipped into a central pot. You can walk to the top or take the easy option and go by cable car (10B).

The temples are around 14km south of the town centre. If coming by motorbike, take the right fork of the highway when you reach Tha Meuang, turn right across the Kheuan Meuang (City Dam) and right again on the other side. By bicycle, avoid the highway by using back roads that follow the river. Follow Th Pak Phraek and cross the bridge towards Wat Tham Mangkon Thong. Once over the bridge, turn left and follow the river for 14km, at which point

you should see the hilltop pagodas on your right. Buses (10B) leave from Kanchanaburi bus station to Ratchaburi every 20 minutes. Get off at Tha Meuang Hospital and hire a motorbike taxi (40B).

WWII Museum
MUSEUM

(พิพิธภัณฑ์สงครามโลกครั้งที่สอง; Th Mae Nam Khwae; admission 40B; ⊗8am-6.30pm) Perhaps the best thing to say about this museum is that the view of the Death Railway Bridge is great. Otherwise, this is an eclectic, ramshackle collection of artefacts. The museum is divided into two buildings. On one side a collection of Japanese vehicles, along with press cuttings and waxwork POWs.

The larger building resembles a Chinese temple and is far more opulent, or garish, depending on your viewpoint, though the collection of weapons and amulets is impressive. The top level is the best place to see the nearby Death Railway Bridge.

Between the two buildings is a pyramid-shaped family shrine with coloured bowls decorating the exterior. The museum is immediately south of the Death Railway Bridge.

Wat Bahn Tham
BUDDHIST TEMPLE

(วัดบ้านถ้ำ; P) FREE The web of hillside caves for which this temple is famous holds many

KANCHANABURI IN...

Two Days

Many of the main attractions are centrally located, so you can see most within 48 hours. Begin at the **Thailand-Burma Railway Centre Museum** before crossing the road to the **Allied War Cemetery**. Spend the afternoon around the **Death Railway Bridge** and then head to the other side of town for a coffee and stroll along the charming **Heritage Walking Street**. For your second day, take a train ride along the Death Railway to **Sai Yok Noi Waterfall** and relish some of the verdant countryside.

Four Days

Head north of the provincial town to visit **Erawan National Park** (p179) and the must-see **Hellfire Pass Memorial** (p179).

One Week

Seven days gives you the opportunity to explore remote towns such as magical **Sangkhlaburi** (p184), where misty morning boat rides and zip-lining await. On the way back down, spend a night in a treetop hut at **Thong Pha Phum National Park** (p183), where giant hornbills are regular visitors.

ancient secrets, according to folklore. Walk up the steps, past the 'dragon's mouth' entrance and check out the five caves near the top. One has a standing Buddha image illuminated by a single shaft of sunlight breaking through the top of the hill.

A stone is said to resemble an innocent woman killed by her husband and is consequently 'dressed' throughout the year while one blocked-off passageway allegedly leads to a village inhabited by giants.

To find the temple, which is 15km south of the town, cross the Kheuan Meuang (City Dam) and go right on the other side of the river. Follow the road parallel to the river and look for the temple on your left.

🏃 Activities

Trekking & Cycling

Whether it is riding on the back of an elephant through the jungle, balancing on a bamboo raft or standing under a cascading waterfall, Thailand's wild west is rich with natural wonders.

All the standard tours can be arranged in Kanchanaburi, along with more adventurous experiences such as cycling tours, canoeing and overnight jungle trekking. As a rule of thumb, the further north you go, the wilder things get. Most of Kanchanaburi's roads are in good condition and perfect for bicycle or motorbike touring, while some off-road routes lead to rarely visited waterfalls and caves. Several trips stay overnight in a Mon or Karen village.

For those with less time, the countryside close to Kanchanaburi is replete with wonderful vistas and a bicycle is an ideal way to see them. One particularly scenic route lies immediately behind the backpacker guesthouses. From the northern end of Th Mae Nam Khwae, cross Sutjai Bridge and head right. Explore Bahn Thamakham and Bahn Hua Hin, where lemon grass, corn, tapioca and teak trees soak up the sun while in the distance mist-covered mountains serve as a breathtaking backdrop.

Some package tours are cancelled if not enough people sign up, so check before booking. The following agencies are reputable.

AS Mixed Travel   TREKKING, CYCLING
(📞 0 3451 2017; www.applenoi-kanchanaburi.com; Apple's Retreat) A well-organised company with knowledgeable staff. Trips can be tailor-made depending on travellers' preferences, and pockets.

Good Times Travel   TREKKING, CYCLING
(📞 0 3462 4441; www.good-times-travel.com; 63/1 Tha Mae Nam Khwae) All the normal day trips are available, plus adventure packages to more remote areas.

Kayaking

Paddle power is one of the most fun ways to get around.

River Kwai Canoe Travel Services   KAYAKING
(📞 0 3451 2346; riverkwaicanoe@yahoo.com; Th Mae Nam Khwae) Arranges one- or two-day trips that include visits to the main attractions.

🍴 Courses

Apple & Noi's Thai Cooking Course
COOKING COURSE

(www.applenoi-kanchanaburi.com; Apple's Retreat, Bahn Tamakahm; course 1550B) If you don't know your *sôm·đam* from your *đôm yam* then Khun Noi can assist. The one-day course starts at the local market and ends, four dishes later, at the dining table.

🛏 Sleeping

Travellers tend to navigate towards a 1km stretch of Th Mae Nam Khwae, where budget guesthouses offer riverfront views on raft houses. In contrast, there are several new boutique midrange spots on this strip and just out of town. The erstwhile backpacker hub along Soi Th Rong Hip Oi has the cheapest beds in town. Check out **Kanchanaburi Info** (www.kanchanaburi-info.com) for more choices.

Blue Star Guest House
GUESTHOUSE **$**

(☑0 3451 2161; bluestar_guesthouse@yahoo.com; 241 Th Mae Nam Khwae; r 200-850B; **P**❄🅟) Arguably the best of the raft house options, nature wraps itself around Blue Star, creating a feeling of remoteness and tranquility. Cheaper rooms have cold showers.

Bamboo House
GUESTHOUSE **$**

(☑0 3462 4470; www.bamboohouse.host.sk; 3-5 Soi Vietnam, Th Mae Nam Khwae; **P**❄🅟) A new block of smart, airy rooms has breathed fresh life into this place. Set in spacious grounds, the cheaper raft rooms have stunning sunset views.

Jolly Frog
GUESTHOUSE **$**

(☑0 3451 4579; 28 Soi China; s 70B, d 150-290B, f 400B; **P**❄🅟) Despite the un-jolly welcome we received, the Frog remains a backpackers' favourite thanks to the hammock-laden garden, lively restaurant and good-value but grungy rooms.

WHY BRIDGE THE RIVER KHWAE?

The construction of the 'Death Railway' was an astonishing feat of engineering. However, the prisoners and conscripted workers who toiled to build it paid a terrible price. Around 100,000 labourers died due to the extreme conditions.

The railway was built during the WWII-era Japanese occupation of Thailand (1942–43) and its objective was to link 415km of rugged terrain between Thailand and Burma (Myanmar) to secure an alternative supply route for the Japanese conquest of other west Asian countries. Some considered the project impossible but the track was completed despite a lack of equipment and appalling conditions.

Construction began on 16 September 1942 at existing stations at Thanbyuzayat in Myanmar and Nong Pladuk (Ban Pong) in Thailand. Japanese engineers estimated it would take five years to link Thailand and Burma by rail. In reality, the Japanese army forced the POWs to complete the 1m-gauge railway in 16 months. Much of the work was done by hand with simple tools used to build bridges and carve cuttings into the sides of the mountains.

As the Japanese demand for faster construction grew, so conditions worsened. The meagre rice supplies were often laced with kerosene, a by-product of Allied bombing raids over rice stocks. Cholera, malaria and dysentery were rife, and Japanese guards employed barbaric punishments for anyone who stepped out of line.

The rails were finally joined 37km south of Three Pagodas Pass; a Japanese brothel train inaugurated the line.

The bridge that spans the River Kwai near Kanchanaburi (dubbed the 'Death Railway Bridge') was used for just 20 months before the Allies bombed it in 1945. Rather than being a supply line, the route quickly became an escape path for Japanese troops. After the war the British took control of the railway on the Burmese side and ripped up 4km of the tracks leading to Three Pagodas Pass for fear of the route being used by Karen separatists.

On the Thai side, the State Railway of Thailand (SRT) assumed control and continues to operate trains on 130km of the original route between Nong Pladuk, south of Kanchanaburi, to Nam Tok.

LOCAL KNOWLEDGE

DON'T BE A BUFFALO

The movie *The Bridge on the River Kwai* made the waterway famous, and also left a generation pronouncing it incorrectly. You should talk about the River Khwae (sounds like 'square' without the 's') and not Kwai (sounds like 'why'). Get it wrong and you'll be referring to the River Buffalo, which the Thais always find amusing.

VN Guest House
GUESTHOUSE $

(☏0 3451 4082; www.vnguesthouse.net; 44 Soi Th Rong Hip Oi; r 280-450B; ✳🛜) One of the few remaining choices along this strip, VN has great river views from its floating raft houses. Prepare for a few passing karaoke boats.

★ Sabai@Kan
HOTEL $$

(☏0 3462 5544; www.sabaiatkan.com; 317/4 Th Mae Nam Khwae; r 1400-1700B; P✳🛜🏊) With the kind of king-size beds you just want to jump on, this pretty boutique resort does everything well. Rooms overlook a swimming pool and have heaps of natural light. Service is excellent.

Ploy Guesthouse
GUESTHOUSE $$

(☏08 2475 3443; www.ploygh.com; 79/2 Th Mae Nam Khwae; r 650-1750B; P✳@🏊) Ploy has stylish rooms with dark-wood flooring and open-air bathrooms. Its family room and river cottage really stand out. Service can be sluggish at times.

Apple's Retreat
GUESTHOUSE $$

(☏0 3451 2017; www.applenoi-kanchanaburi.com; 153/4 Moo 4, Ban Tamakham; r 790-990B; P✳🛜) 🖋 Almost like a chic homestay, the super-friendly Apple and Noi offer simple but stylish rooms, bags of local knowledge and well-maintained grounds. To be ecofriendly, rooms lack a TV and fridge. Cheaper rooms do not include breakfast, but it is worth the extra just for the mango jam.

Pong Phen
GUESTHOUSE $$

(☏0 3451 2981; www.pongphen.com; Th Mae Nam Khwae; r 400-1300B; ✳🛜🏊) Pong Phen has a range of comfortable wooden bungalows and raft houses, plus a restaurant that offers decent Western and Thai dishes – but the real bonus is the pool.

Sam's House
GUESTHOUSE $$

(☏0 3451 5956; www.samsguesthouse.com; 14/2 Moo 1, Th Mae Nam Khwae; d 400-800B; P✳🛜) A walkway beside a bed of hyacinths leads to basic but clean bungalows and raft houses. The A-frame designs and gnarly wood patterns add character.

Good Times Resort
GUESTHOUSE $$

(☏08 7162 4949; good_times_resort@hotmail. com; 265 5-7 Th Mae Nam Khwae; r 850-1500B; P✳🛜🏊) 🖋 This newcomer is set slightly off the main drag, with compact but well-designed rooms, a pool and wonderful host in the form of K.Chalee. A cycling club and cookery class are also based here.

River Kwai Bridge Resort
RESORT $$

(☏0 3451 4522; www.riverkwaibridgeresort.com; 8 Th Vietnam; r Sun-Thu 1500B, Fri-Sat 1600B; P✳🛜🏊) Within walking distance of the Death Railway Bridge is this imposing resort, with sturdy wooden bungalows, a pool and great views. Staff are especially friendly and keen to help out.

U Inchantree Kanchanaburi
HOTEL $$$

(☏0 3452 1584; www.ukanchanaburi.com; 443 Th Mae Nam Khwae; r/ste incl breakfast 3600/4237B; P✳@🛜🏊) Sitting out on the terrace lounge at sunset watching trains rumble over the Death Railway Bridge is just one of the perks of staying here. An iPod in your room, library, gym and free bicycles are some of the other little extras. Rooms are modern but have a few subtle allusions to the nearby bridge.

Felix River Kwai Resort
HOTEL $$$

(☏0 3455 1000; www.felixriverkwai.co.th; 9/1 M.3 Bahn Tamakahm; r 6238B, ste 10,240-45,898B; P✳🛜🏊) Fancy Felix has all the finishings, furnishings and facilities to justify its five-star rating. Set 2km west of the Death Railway Bridge, it boasts two pools, tennis courts, a spa and jogging track.

LEAF IT ALONE

The tapioca fields dotted throughout Kanchanaburi don't look remarkable, yet sometimes they get special attention from travellers. Tour guides have spotted visitors surreptitiously picking the leaves and stuffing them into their bags. The guides then have to patiently explain that while the leaves may closely resemble a marijuana plant, they really are just plain old tapioca.

SINGING THE KARAOKE BLUES

The sounds of a party boat belting out 'My Girl' or 'Dancing Queen' tend to shatter the serene calm that is usually in residence along the Mae Nam Khwae.

Karaoke boats in Kanchanaburi are a regular part of the river scene here as visitors from Bangkok and Korea fill up the boats along Th Song Khwae.

The commotion used to make guesthouses along Soi Rong Hip Oi unappealing, but now the all-nighters have virtually stopped and the boats are a temporary nuisance. Bridges prevent the boats from going too far, so guesthouses along Th Mae Nam Khwae are largely unaffected. If you want to experience the floating karaoke, boats can be hired for 4000B. Food and drink are extra.

River Kwai Hotel
HOTEL $$$

(☑ 0 3451 0111; www.riverkwai.co.th; 284/15-16 Th Saengchuto; r 2200-7000B; P ❄ 🔿 ☎) Look past the somewhat drab exterior, as inside the renovated rooms are plush. A gym, spa and the town's only nightclub make it a good option for those wanting to stay in the town centre.

Royal River Kwai Resort & Spa
HOTEL $$$

(☑ 0 3465 3342; www.royalriverkwairesort.com; 88 Kanchanaburi-Saiyok Rd; r 2450-4650B; P ❄ 🔿 ☎) With vast grounds, a massive pool and more than 60 fabulous rooms, this resort is one of the finest places to stay in Kanchanaburi. Its spa is also renowned for its various treatments. The resort is 4km north of town.

🍴 Eating

Riverside restaurants take top spot when it comes to eating options. Elsewhere, along Th Mae Nam Khwae several Western-style restaurants serve burgers, pizza and pasta. For more authentic food, visit the **night market** (Th Saengchuto; dishes 30-60B; ⊙6-11pm) near the train station, which is packed with stalls serving fried treats and smoothies. Several good-quality **floating restaurants** (Th Song Khwae; dishes 80-200B; ⊙6-11pm) are often full of Korean or Thai package-company tourists. The **market** (Th Saengchuto) near the bus station is well-known for its *hŏy tôrt* (fried mussels in an egg batter).

★ Blue Rice
THAI $

(153/4 M.4 Ban Tamakahm; dishes 95-150B; P 🔿 ✎ 🚶) A perfect riverside setting, brilliant menu and fantastic flavours make this a winner. Chef Apple puts a fresh spin on Thai classics, such as the eponymous rice, *yam sôm oh* (pomelo salad) and chicken soup with banana plant.

★ Mangosteen Cafe
CAFE $

(☑ 08 1793 5814; www.mangosteencafe.net; 13 Th Mae Nam Khwae; dishes 70-150B; ⊙9.30am-10pm; ❄ 🔿 ✎ 🚶) Browse the 1000 or so books on offer while munching through the divine pizza toasties and sipping real coffee.

On's Vegetarian Restaurant
VEGETARIAN $

(☑ 08 7364 2264; www.onsthaiissan.com; Th Mae Nam Khwae; dishes 40B; ⊙10am-10pm; ❄ ✎) If you happen to like the northeastern style veggie food on offer here, On can teach you how to make it. A two-hour, three-dish cookery course costs 600B.

Pai Kan
THAI $

(Th Mae Nam Khwae; dishes 30-50B; ⊙4-10pm) Scribble down your order on scraps of paper, then watch as the cooks go to work in the open kitchen. Thai dishes are simple but flavoursome and authentic; Western dishes are reasonable.

Jukkru
THAI $

(Th Song Khwae; dishes 60-100B) To truly eat like the locals, try this simple but efficiently run restaurant that has a range of Thai dishes. The collection of Burmese artefacts and shrine to the rear is fascinating.

Saisowo
NOODLES $

(Th Chaokunen; dishes 20-30B; ⊙8am-4pm) When a place is this popular with locals, it must be doing something right. This long-established noodle spot has a few surprise options, such as the excellent *gŏoay dĕeo dôm yam kài kem* (noodle soup with salty eggs).

🍷 Drinking & Nightlife

Tourists spend their evenings along Th Mae Nam Khwae, where there are bars, pool tables and a number of prostitutes, though the latter are mainly at the southern end. For true budget drinking, street-side bars offer shots of local spirits for 10B.

Thais head to Th Song Khwae for larger, open-air restaurants. **Tham Naan** is the best of the bars along this strip, with live music and a country vibe.

Sugar Member
BAR
(Th Mae Nam Khwae) Has hip, friendly staff who will sip whisky buckets with you all night.

Buddha Bar
BAR
(Th Mae Nam Khwae) Attracts dreadlocked backpackers.

Pal Bar
BAR
(Th Mae Nam Khwae) Free pool and an easy-going vibe.

ℹ Information

EMERGENCY
Tourist Police (☑ 0 3451 2795, 1155; Th Saengchuto)

INTERNET ACCESS
Internet cafes can be found along Th Mae Nam Khwae for 30B per hour.

MEDICAL SERVICES
Thanakarn Hospital (☑ 0 3462 2366, emergency 0 3462 2811; Th Saengchuto) Near the junction of Th Chukkadon, this is the best-equipped hospital to deal with foreign visitors.

MONEY
Several major Thai banks can be found on Th Saengchuto near the market and the bus terminal. AS Mixed Travel (p174) also offers a foreign-exchange service that is available out of bank hours.
Bangkok Bank (Th U Thong) Near the market.
Krung Thai Bank (Th Saengchuto) Near the River Kwai Bridge.
Thai Military Bank (Th Saengchuto) Near the bus station.

POST
Main Post Office (Th Saengchuto; ⊙ 8.30am-4.30pm Mon-Fri, 9am-noon Sat & Sun)

TELEPHONE
Many private shops along Th Mae Nam Khwae offer long-distance calls.
Communications Authority of Thailand (CAT; ⊙ 8.30am-4.30pm Mon-Fri) This office has an international telephone service.

TOURIST INFORMATION
Tourism Authority of Thailand (TAT; ☑ 0 3451 1200; Th Saengchuto; ⊙ 8.30am-4.30pm) Provides free maps of the town and province, along with advice on what to do and where to stay.

ℹ Getting There & Away

BUS
Kanchanaburi's bus and minivan station is to the south of the town on Th Saengchuto. If heading south, transfer at Ratchaburi. If aiming for Ayuthaya, go to Suphanburi first. Minivans run to Victory Monument and Mo Chit in Bangkok.

Srimongkol Transport (☑ 08 4471 8282; 350B) runs air-conditioned buses to Rayong, stopping at Pattaya.

TRAIN
Kanchanaburi's train station is walking distance from the guesthouse area and 2km northwest of the bus station. Kanchanaburi is on the Bangkok Noi-Nam Tok rail line, which includes a portion of the historic Death Railway built by WWII POWs during the Japanese occupation of Thailand. The SRT promotes this as a historic route, and so charges foreigners 100B for any one-way journey along the line, regardless of the distance. Coming from Bangkok Noi station (located in Thonburi), 100B is reasonable, but for short trips in Kanchanaburi it is steep. The most historic part of the journey begins north of Kanchanaburi as the train crosses the Death Railway Bridge and terminates at Nam Tok station, which is near Sai Yok Noi.
Destinations include:
Nam Tok (100B, two hours, 6.07am, 10.35am, 4.26pm)
Thonburi's Bangkok Noi station (100B, three hours, 7.19am, 2.48pm, 5.41pm)

BUSES TO/FROM KANCHANABURI

DESTINATION	FARE (B)	DURATION	FREQUENCY
Bangkok's Northern (Mo Chit) bus terminal	105-135	2hr	every 90min 6am to 6pm
Bangkok's Southern (Sai Tai Mai) bus terminal	95-110	2hr	frequent 4am to 8pm
Bangkok's Victory Monument	120	2hr	hourly until 8pm
Ratchaburi	50-70	2hr	frequent
Sangkhlaburi	130	4hr	frequent 7.30am to 4.30pm
Suphanburi	50	2hr	frequent

ⓘ Getting Around

BOAT

The river ferry that crosses Mae Nam Mae Klong costs 5B per person for a one-way trip. Long-tail boats offer 1½-hour trips to various attractions by the riverside. Prices start at 800B but are negotiable. Boats leave from the pier off Th Chukkadon or from the Jeath War Museum.

MOTORCYCLE

Motorcycles can be rented at guesthouses and shops along Th Mae Nam Khwae for 200B a day. Bicycle rentals cost 50B.

PUBLIC TRANSPORT

Trips from the bus station to the guesthouse area will cost 50B on a săhm·lór and 30B on a motorcycle taxi. Public sŏrng·tǎa·ou run up and down Th Saengchuto for 10B per passenger (get off at the cemetery if you want the guesthouse area).

Around Kanchanaburi

Many of the main attractions in Kanchanaburi can be seen on day trips from the provincial town but to hit the more remote, rural areas you will need to stay overnight.

Scenic train rides snake their way north through dense forests towards must-see spots such as the Hellfire Pass Memorial and the mighty Erawan National Park. Several national parks around Kanchanaburi give visitors the opportunity to explore thick jungle, stay with ethnic groups and visit spectacular waterfalls and caves.

Entry to the parks is 200B for foreigners. Bungalows and camping facilities are available at most sites, but it is important to book ahead (☑ 0 2562 0760; www.dnp.go.th).

Park headquarters have free booklets and maps, and most have guides that can lead trekking trips. Temperatures range from 8°C to 45°C depending on the time of year, so bring appropriate clothing.

Some tour companies in Kanchanaburi town can arrange tours of the parks with English-speaking guides.

Erawan National Park อุทยานแห่งชาติเอราวัณ

Famed for its impressive seven-tiered waterfall, **Erawan National Park** (admission 200B; ☺8am-4pm) is an extremely popular weekend spot for locals. The **Erawan waterfall** gets its name as the top level is said to resemble Erawan, the three-headed elephant of Hindu mythology. Walking to the first three tiers is easy, but after that good walking shoes and some endurance are needed to complete the 1.5km hike. Bring a bathing costume as you will appreciate the cool water after reaching the top. Levels 2 and 4 are impressive, but be wary of monkeys who may snatch belongings while you're taking a dip.

Elsewhere in this 550-sq-km park, **Tham Phra That** is a cave with a variety of limestone formations. Guides carrying paraffin lamps lead visitors through the gloom, pointing out the translucent rocks, glittering crystals and bat-covered caverns. Geologists find the caves of interest due to a clearly visible fault line. You will need your own transport or a guide to reach the cave, which is 12km northwest of the park entrance, or you can negotiate a ride with park staff. The approach road is a dirt track and there is a stiff walk up to the cave entrance. Another 5km north is the enormous and scenic **Si Nakharin Reservoir**.

Around 80% of Erawan is forest, and many of the park's various trees can be seen along three nature trails, which range from 1km to 2km. Bird-watchers try to spy hornbills, woodpeckers and parakeets from the camping areas and observation trails. Tigers, elephants, cobras and gibbons also call the park home.

Park bungalows (☑ 0 2562 0760; www.dnp.go.th; bungalows 800-5000B, camping 150-300B) sleep between two and 50 people. If you bring your own tent, there is a 30B service fee.

Buses from Kanchanaburi stop by the entrance of the Erawan waterfall (50B, 1½ hours, every 90 minutes from 8am to 5.20pm). The last bus back to Kanchanaburi is at 4pm. Within the park, you can rent bicycles for 20B to 40B per day.

Hellfire Pass Memorial ช่องเขาขาด

The poignant **Hellfire Pass Memorial** (Rte 323; museum admission by donation; ☺grounds 9am-4.30pm, museum to 4pm) **FREE** is a beautifully maintained tribute to those who died while building the Burma-Thailand Railway in WWII.

Start your visit to the memorial at the **museum** on the top level and hire the free audio guide, which has detailed descriptions of the area and fascinating anecdotes from survivors. Gaze out over the contemplation deck, then walk along the trail that runs alongside the original rail bed.

Near the start of the route is the infamous cutting known as **Hellfire Pass** (locally referred to as Konyu Cutting). The area earned its name following the three-month 'Speedo' construction period where shifts of 500 prisoners worked 16 to 18 hours a day. The glow from burning torches cast eerie shadows of the Japanese guards and of the gaunt prisoners' faces, so that the scene was said to resemble Dante's *Inferno*.

Poor hygiene, a lack of medical equipment and the brutal treatment of prisoners claimed the lives of around 15,000 Allied prisoners of war and tens of thousands of civilian labourers from Southeast Asian countries.

Thai officials have blocked off part of the walking route so, at the time of writing, only 2.5km was available, up to the Hin Tok Cutting.

The museum is 80km northwest of Kanchanaburi on Hwy 323 and can be reached by the Sangkhlaburi–Kanchanaburi bus (80B, 1½ hours, frequent departures). The last bus back to Kanchanaburi passes here at 4.45pm. Entry is free but donations are welcomed.

Sai Yok National Park อุทยานแห่งชาติไทรโยค

The 500-sq-km **Sai Yok National Park** (☑0 3468 6024; www.dnp.go.th; admission 200B) is home to limestone mountains, waterfalls, caves – and some extremely rare animals.

The park is well signposted and free leaflets provide information about hiking trails and how to hire canoes, rafts or bicycles. A cycling route is available to the Kitti's hog-nosed bat cave where the eponymous creature, the smallest mammal in the world, was first spotted in 1973. They hang out, literally, at Tham Khang Kow, 2km from the park headquarters. Take a torch.

Near the visitors centre is **Nam Tok Sai Yok Yai** (Sai Yok Yai Waterfall), which is more of a creek than a waterfall. It empties into Mae Nam Khwae Noi near a suspension bridge.

Among the animals to keep an eye out for in the teak forest are elephants, tigers, wild pigs, wreathed hornbills, gibbons, and the red, white and blue queen crab, first discovered in the park in 1983. To see the crabs, head to Mae Nam Noi village, 15km from the park entrance, where a boat and guide can be hired.

Forestry department **bungalows** (☑0 2562 0760; 800-2100B) are available and sleep up to seven. Several raft guesthouses near the suspension bridge offer fantastic views, and there are floating restaurants nearby and rows of food stalls near the visitors centre.

Around 18km south of Sai Yok Noi is **Tham Lawa** (admission 200B), which runs for 500m and has five large caverns with imposing stalactites and stalagmites. To get here private transport is best, or you can take the train to Nam Tok station and try to find a motorcycle taxi.

The entrance to the park is 100km northwest of Kanchanaburi and 5km from Hwy 323. The Sangkhlaburi–Kanchanaburi bus (55B, two hours, frequent departures) goes past the turn-off to the park, and from there a motorcycle taxi is needed to reach the entrance. Tell the driver you want *'nám dòk sai yôhk yài'*. The last bus back to Kanchanaburi passes at 5.10pm.

Long-tail boats near the suspension bridge can be hired for sightseeing trips

---

TIGER SANCTUARY OR TOURIST TRAP?

Perhaps the most controversial tourist attraction in Thailand, the Tiger Temple continues to divide opinion. True, it's one of the few places in the world where you can get so close to these magnificent creatures. On the other hand, numerous allegations about animal welfare continue to dog the temple. In return for the 600B entrance fee (it's the same for adults and children), visitors get to walk the big cats to a canyon, where tourists are then briskly herded around a group of chained-up tigers to have their photos taken. A morning program of events costs a hefty 5000B.

This former sanctuary for abandoned cubs denies allegations that the tigers are ill-treated, drugged or traded and has been planning major developments for years, but progress seems slow. Some tour operators now decline to take visitors to the Tiger Temple, and Lonely Planet no longer recommends visiting.

Reports emerged in August 2013 of a UK student being badly mauled at the Tiger Temple; www.careforthewild.org has a detailed report about alleged abuses.

along the river, and also to **Tham Daowa-dung**. It is wise to take a guide and torch with you before entering the cave. Chartering a long-tail costs about 800B per hour, but rates are negotiable.

Sai Yok Noi is a recreational kind of waterfall as Thais come to paddle and picnic nearby. These gentle falls, within the main park, are a minute's walk from the main road and are popular at weekends, when Thais sit on mats, snack on *sôm-dam* and clamber over the sloping rocks.

The waterfall is 60km northwest from Kanchanaburi on Hwy 323 and can be reached by using the Sangkhlaburi–Kanchanaburi bus (55B, one hour, frequent departures); tell your driver you're going to '*nám dòk sai yôhk nóy*'.

The last bus back is at 4.30pm. Nam Tok train station is 2km away (100B).

Prasat Meuang Singh Historical Park อุทยานประวัติศาสตร์ปราสาทเมืองสิงห์

The **Prasat Meuang Singh Historical Park** (admission 100B; ⊙8.30am-5pm) preserves the remains of a 13th-century Khmer outpost that may have been a relay point for trade along Mae Nam Khwae Noi. The restored ruins show a Bayon style of architecture and cover 73.6 hectares.

All the park's shrines are constructed of laterite bricks and are situated in a huge grassy compound surrounded by layers of laterite ramparts and city walls. Sections of the ramparts show seven additional layers of earthen walls, suggesting cosmological symbolism.

Meuang Singh, or City of the Lion, has two main monuments and two ruins where little more than the bases remain. The principal shrine **Prasat Meuang Singh** is in the centre and faces east (the cardinal direction of most Angkor temples). Walls surrounding the shrine have gates in each of the cardinal directions; the ponds and ditches around it represent the continents and oceans.

Also within the grounds is a **burial site**, excavated in 1986, that shows skeletons and pottery thought to date back 2000 years.

Prasat Meuang Singh is 40km west of Kanchanaburi and is best reached by private transport. Trains heading from Kanchanaburi to Nam Tok stop nearby at Tha Kilen station (100B). From here it is a 1km walk to the entrance, but it's best having some form of transport as the grounds are large.

Daen Maha Mongkol Meditation Centre แดนมหามงคล

If you have ever wondered what your world would be like without an iPad or smartphone, step right up. This **meditation retreat** (⊙8-11am & 1-5pm) is so keen on promoting serenity that a charming old chap runs a metal detector over visitors at the entrance to ensure they haven't got an i-something tucked away.

Women may stay within the main compound; there are rooms for men outside. Because of the strict adherence to calm, you cannot phone or email the centre to make a booking. However, unless you turn up on a public holiday, free rooms will be available (donations are welcomed). Day visitors can drop in from 8am to 11am and 1pm to 5pm – everyone here wears white and appropriate clothes can be hired to the left of the entrance. The impressive stupa at the top of the nearby hill can be climbed in 30 minutes, but is only open at weekends and on holy days.

Entry to the centre, founded in 1986, is via a teak bridge that straddles the Mae Nam Khwae Noi. Inside, the grassy grounds are vast, tranquil and well-kept. About 300 people stay at the centre, most of them permanently. Some staff speak English.

The centre is off Hwy 323, and is well signposted. By train, get off at Maha Mongkol station.

Khao Laem National Park
อุทยานแห่งชาติเขาแหลม

With the mighty Khao Laem Reservoir at its heart, the 1497-sq-km **Khao Laem National Park** (☑0 3453 2099) is a particularly picturesque place.

Ornithologists flock to **Kroeng Kravia Swamp** to see the birdlife, which includes the Asian fairy bluebird and green-billed malkoha. To reach the swamp, go to the Kroeng Kravia substation 45km south of Sangkhlaburi.

More than 260 species of wildlife have been recorded at the park, including gibbons, deer and wild boar. The dam is surrounded by several waterfalls and huge limestone mountains.

Kra Teng Jeng waterfall begins 400m from the park entrance and has a 4km shaded trail leading towards the main falls. A guide is required.

Approximately 1km north from the park entrance is **Pom Pee substation**. From here you can hire long-tail boats to cross the reservoir to Pha Pueng or Kai Uu substations, or head back to the Mon settlement of Wang Kha (or Ka). Hiring a boat with eight people costs around 2000B. Pom Pee also has a campsite and **bungalows** (✆0 2562 0760; www.dnp.go.th; r from 900B), whereas the main park only offers camping facilities.

Approximately 12km south from the park entrance is the 15m-high **Dai Chong Thong** waterfall. The park headquarters are 28km south of Sangkhlaburi. From Thong Pha Phum, *sŏrng·tăa·ou* go to Kroeng Kravia Swamp (35B, one hour, every 45 minutes).

Lake House Adventure (www.visitbeyond. com; dm 13,500B, d from 15,900B) runs four-night trips on its houseboat from Khao Laem. The boat has well-fitted dorms as well as double rooms; prices are seasonal. Park entry fees are included.

Si Nakharin National Park อุทยานแห่งชาติศรีนครินทร์

A new road linking Erawan National Park to Si Nakharin means easy access to the seven-tiered **Huay Mae Khamin** waterfall. The falls, near the **Si Nakharin National Park** (✆0 3451 6667) entrance, are one of Thailand's most beautiful. In addition, the park has hot springs, limestone caves and a hiking route. At the heart of the 1500-sq-km park is the **Si Nakharin Reservoir**, which is fed by surrounding streams and tributaries.

Camping (✆0 2562 0760; www.dnp.go.th; r 150-700B) and **bungalows** (900-2700B) are available.

Chaloem Ratanakosin National Park อุทยานแห่งชาติเฉลิมรัตนโกสินทร์

The area's smallest park, **Chaloem Ratanakosin National Park** (✆0 3451 9606), manages to pack a lot into its 59 sq km, including

HELPING TO NURTURE NATURE

The largest mainland conservation area in Southeast Asia is comprised of **Thung Yai Naresuan Wildlife Sanctuary** and **Huay Kha Khaeng Wildlife Sanctuary**. Designated a Unesco World Heritage Site in 1991, the sanctuaries, which cover 6200 sq km, host an incredible range of fauna and flora.

Set in the northeastern corner of Kanchanaburi and sprawling into neighbouring provinces, the sanctuaries are largely a mountainous wilderness with rivers and streams separating the grassy lowlands and valleys.

The sanctuaries are protected areas, not national parks, and so visitors require prior permission to enter. One way to do this is via P Guest House in Sangkhlaburi.

The sanctuaries are one of the last natural habitats for around 700 tigers, who share space with 400 types of bird, 96 reptiles and 120 mammals, including leopards, gaur, bears and maybe even the Javan rhinoceros.

Thung Yai Naresuan (large field) takes its name from its enormous central grassland plain and the fact that King Naresuan once used the area as a temporary army base. Huay Kha Khaeng has more amenities and camping sites, though there are no restaurants or bungalows. The park includes the Khao Hin Daeng nature study route, which can be reached by private transport via Uthai Thani by following Hwy 333, then Hwy 3438.

There are two camping areas within Huay Kha Khaeng: **Cyber Ranger Station** and **Huay Mae Dee**. Cyber Ranger Station is 7km from the main office and has several waterfalls and valleys within trekking distance. The 37km off-road track to Huay Mae Dee passes a Karen village and is set within thick forest. Thai-speaking guides can be hired from both sites. **Camp sites** (per tent 30B) are available, but you will need to bring all your own equipment.

The main office is best reached by private transport. The closest buses or trains run to Lan Sak, from where it is a 35km drive to the office.

the caves **Tham Than Lot Noi** and **Tham Than Lot Yai**. The former is unremarkable but leads to a pleasant 2.5km nature trail. At the end of the trail is Tham Than Lot Yai, an enormous opening with jagged stalactites.

Sleeping options include **bungalows** (☑ 0 2562 0760; www.dnp.go.th; 2000B) or **tents** (250-600B). Another option is to stay nearby with a friendly Karen family at the solar-powered **Khao Lek Homestay** (r 100-300B). Contact tour agents in Kanchanaburi for details. Most visitors arrive by private transport along Hwy 3086.

Thong Pha Phum   ทองผาภูมิ

Overlooked by mountains – and often tourists – Thong Pha Phum is a tranquil town that enjoys a slower way of life.

The town, used as a stop-off point on the way to Sangkhlaburi, has its own charm and is easy to get around as there is only one main street. Mae Nam Khwae Noi runs parallel to the east of the town. The town lacks any great attractions and therefore tourist facilities are thin on the ground.

The market, at the epicentre of the town, is a great place for breakfast. Browse the dozens of stalls and choose from deep-fried banana, traditional coffee or noodles. Behind the market is the three-tiered **Krua Tom Nam** restaurant, with river views. Other restaurants reflect the large Burmese and ethnic communities that live here; the large metal pots full of tempting curries are typically Mon.

At night the illuminated hilltop **temple** casts an ethereal glow over a town that has long gone to bed. To reach the temple, follow the riverfront road towards the main highway, cross a footbridge and walk up.

As well as being within reach of Sangkhlaburi, the town is close to a growing number of adventure activities. **Phuiyara Resort** (www.phuiyararesort.com; r 1000-1500B) has a zip-line, rope bridge and climbing net course, along with ATV and trekking tours. It can arrange trips to Thung Yai Naresuan Wildlife Sanctuary.

South of Thong Pha Phum town is **Hin Dat Hot Springs** (admission 50B; ⊙ 6am-10pm), which has two soothing geothermal pools and a massage pavilion. The *bòr nám rórn* (hot springs) is accessible via the Sangkhlaburi–Kanchanaburi bus on Hwy 323 (Km 105 marker) and is 1km from the main road.

Along the same road as the hot springs is **Nam Tok Pha That** (admission 200B), a pretty, multi-level waterfall that doesn't get many visitors.

Kheuan Khao Laem, known locally as Vachiralongkorn Dam, is 9km northwest of the town. Some **bungalows** (☑ 0 3459 8030; r 600-800B; ❄) are set within the grounds. Activities include golf, tennis, a shooting range and a boat tour of the dam.

Of the in-town accommodation, **Som Jainuk Hotel** (☑ 0 3459 9001; 29/10 Mu 1; r 250-500B; ❄) is near the market and has simple fan rooms or stone-walled bungalows with balconies. The real bonus is June, the owner, who speaks English and can offer invaluable travel tips. **Baan Puttaraksa** (r 800-1200B), by the town's entrance, has clean rooms and a restaurant.

❶ Getting There & Away

Air-conditioned buses leave from opposite Thanachart Bank on the main road. Tickets are sold at the back of the nearby **Krua Ngobah** (☑ 0 3459 9377) restaurant. Destinations include:

Bangkok's Northern (Mo Chit) terminal (193-248B, five hours, 9.30am, 11am)

Sangkhlaburi (67-86B, two hours, twice daily)

Local buses leave from the market.

❶ Getting Around

You can try your bartering skills on the motorbike taxi drivers at the market, who may let you rent their bikes out for around 300B a day. *Sŏrng·tăa·ou* run up and down the main road and should cost about 10B for rides within town.

Thong Pha Phum National Park   อุทยานแห่งชาติทองผาภูมิ

The **Thong Pha Phum National Park** (☑ 0 3453 2114) is best known for the **Jorgrading** waterfall and its tree-top **accommodation** (☑ 0 2562 0760; www.dnp.go.th; 600-1200B).

The 62km ride from Thong Pha Phum to the park is along a serpentine but well-made road shaded by soaring hillside trees. The main waterfall is 5km from the park entrance.

Keep going for another 8km along the ear-popping Hwy 3272 to visit the frontier village of **E-Thong**, where most of the population is Burmese. The tree-trunk shaped rooms at **Ban Tor Mai** (☑ 08 3614 4432; jikkapompom@gmail.com; r 600-1200B) are functional but fun. Right behind the town is the Burmese border; you can stand with one foot in either country as somewhat bemused guards look on. Entrepreneurial children offer their own brief guided tour of the village, the old Pilok mine and Burmese quarter.

Yellow *sŏrng·tăa·ou* (80B, 1½ hours, 10.30am and 12.30pm) run from Thong Pha Phum's market to E-Thong and the national park. The return trip leaves at 6am and 6.30am.

Sangkhlaburi สังขละบุรี

For many travellers Sangkhlaburi is the end of the line, but for many residents it represents the start of a new journey. Few places in Thailand have such a blend of ethnic identities, with Burmese, Karen, Mon, Thai and some Lao each calling this home.

Many cross the Burmese border driven by economic need or through fear of oppression. The result is a melange of cultures, beliefs and even languages.

Remote Sangkhlaburi overlooks the vast Kheuan Khao Laem (Khao Laem Reservoir),

and owes its existence to the waters. It was founded after an old village, near the confluence of the three rivers that feed the reservoir, was flooded.

Several NGOs in town help the ethnic communities survive and fight for what few rights they have. As a result, there is a constant need for volunteers. Though the town is wonderfully sleepy, there are signs of development – the town now has its first 7-Eleven.

In the last week of July the town is abuzz due to **Mon National Day**.

◉ Sights & Activities

Wang Kha   MON SETTLEMENT
(วังคา) A rickety **wooden bridge** (Saphan Mon), said to be the longest of its kind in Thailand, leads to this Mon settlement. A 70m section of the bridge collapsed due to torrential rain in 2013, making it impassable. While repair work occurs, access to Wang Kha is still possible via a nearby concrete bridge.

WHO ARE THE MON?

The Mon people have a proud history, but today they are in danger of being lost forever. As well as introducing Theravada Buddhism to the region, their Dvaravati kingdom covered much of the central plains of Thailand and Burma between the 6th and 11th centuries.

Many Mon have fled the oppressive regime in Burma and live as refugees around Sangkhlaburi. Less than a million people speak the Mon language and they face a fight to preserve their heritage, beliefs and independence.

For centuries there has been conflict between the Burmese and the Mon. The British exploited this tension during its colonisation of Burma by promising the Mon independence in return for their support. Once Burma achieved independence in 1948, the Mon launched a campaign for self-determination but protests were swiftly crushed, with Mon leaders killed and their villages razed. In 1974 a semi-autonomous state, Monland, was created and a ceasefire was declared in 1996, but clashes continue to this day.

Lai Phipit, who is in his 60s, is one of many who left their homeland due to violence. He said: 'When I was a child, soldiers came and told all the men and boys to come and help carry weapons to fight the communists. Anybody who refused would be shot. My family decided to flee to Thailand.'

Of Sangkhlaburi's 47,000 residents, 23,800 are from ethnic groups. Thailand does little more than tolerate their presence. The Mon are given Thai ID cards that offer virtually no rights, travel is restricted and there are checkpoints all around Sangkhlaburi and Three Pagodas Pass. Many Mon and Karen work for 150B a day or less, below the Thai minimum wage but still more than they would receive in Burma. They fear being fined, deported or even attacked and so often have a self-imposed curfew.

The Mon people in Burma continue to suffer and reports of rape, beatings and arrests are common. They are stuck between a country where they are repressed and a country where they have few rights. Because of this, there are fears their once proud traditions and culture could eventually become completely assimilated and lost forever.

A Mon village close to E-Thong preserves its culture by offering a **homestay** (450B) and performing a traditional show. Contact **Phuiyara Resort** (☑ 0 3468 5632) for details.

The village relocated here after the dam's construction flooded the original settlement. Burma's conflicts forced many Mon into Thailand and now Wang Kha has its own unmistakable character. Children play a form of cricket, women smoke giant cheroots and many wear traditional white face powder.

A day market in the village centre is always busy, while north of this is **Wat Wang Wiwekaram** (Wat Mon), the spiritual centre of the Mon people in Thailand. The temple has two complexes 640m apart. To the right of the T-junction is the multiroofed *wí·hǎhn* with heavy, carved wooden doors and marble banisters. To the left of the T-junction is the **Chedi Luang Phaw Uttama**, constructed in the style of the Mahabodhi *chedi* in Bodhgaya, India. At night the 6kg of gold that cover it are illuminated. Men only may climb to the top. In the same courtyard are an ageing *chedi* and a handicrafts market.

The temple was the home of a highly respected monk, Luang Phaw Uttama. Born in Burma in 1910, he fled to Thailand in 1949 to escape the civil war and was a cornerstone of the Mon community. He helped secure this area after the Mon village's previous location was flooded by the construction of the dam. In 2006 he died aged 97 at Bangkok's Srirat Hospital and his medical bills were covered by the queen.

Be sure to hire a private **boat** (per person 400B) and immerse yourself in the predawn mist that envelops the dam. Trips go under the wooden bridge and past the old Mon temple, which is sometimes submerged depending on the time of year.

Khao Laem Reservoir   LAKE
(เขื่อนเขาแหลม) A morning boat ride out on this gigantic lake is a must. The lake was formed when the Vachiralongkorn Dam (known locally as Khao Laem Dam) was constructed across Mae Nam Khwae Noi in 1983. An entire village at the confluence of the Khwae Noi, Ranti and Sangkhalia Rivers was submerged as a result, however, in the dry season **Wat Sam Prasop** is clearly visible.

Wake up before dawn to witness the ethereal calm on the lake, when the grey and blue mists and sounds of nature envelop the water.

Baan Unrak   VOLUNTEERING
(บ้านอนุรักษ์, House of Joy; www.baanunrak.org) Baan Unrak is a home that cares for around 130 orphaned or abandoned children from

MAKE MINE A SPIRIT

The abandoned Pilok mine in E-Thong gained its name thanks to the supernatural. When an outbreak of malaria hit the tin and wolfram mine, several workers died. Afterwards, villagers began to see strange apparitions near the mine and believed that the spirits of the miners (*pěe*) were playing tricks (*lok*) on them. They would cry out 'pilok' and the name stuck. Pilok is also the name of the subdistrict.

ethnic groups. Most of the children at Baan Unrak are Karen and all follow the home's neohumanist philosophy of vegetarianism, universal love and meditation. The home usually only accepts helpers for six months or longer.

As well as the children's home, Baan Unrak runs a weaving centre to provide an income for local women, helps single mothers, and works with HIV/AIDS patients.

Courses

Scenns   CULTURAL COURSES
(09 1281 6441; www.scenns.com) Classically trained dancer, and thoroughly charming, Scenn runs Thai dance, cookery and language classes. Vegetarians can learn how to make their own tofu. Rooms are available.

Sleeping

At the end of the bridge is **Dok Bua Homestay** (300-500B), which has rafthouses and regular rooms.

★**P Guest House**   GUESTHOUSE $
(0 3459 5061; www.p-guesthouse.com; 81/2 Mu 1; r 250-950B; P✻🔊) You don't normally get

LOCAL KNOWLEDGE

LIVING ON THE EDGE

On the way up the steps of **Chedi Luang Phaw Uttama** in Sangkhlaburi, visitors face a challenge. A footprint of the Buddha is in the middle of the stairs and resting on it are dozens of coins. The task is simple and the reward immense – if you can make your coin balance on its edge, good luck will follow you everywhere.

views like this for 250B. Stone and log-built rooms gaze upon the scenic waters at this family-run spot. Trips out in canoes, on bicycles or by boat can be arranged from here. Fan rooms are simple and come with shared bathrooms. Book a room in advance as this place gets busy.

Oh Dee Hostel HOSTEL $
(☎0 3459 5626; www.ohdee-hostel.com; 147/1 Mu 3; dm 590B, d 1400-1500B; ❄📶) Opened in 2012, this hip hostel has modern dorms and cosy doubles. Downstairs is a cafe/lounge with its own dart board and pool table. Horse-riding can be booked from here.

Nature Club RESORT $$
(☎08 9510 8444; www.thenatureclubresort.com; 207 Mu 3 Nonglu; r 1200-2200B, tents 600B; P❄@) Swim, zip-line or kayak through the jungle, as this action-packed, enormous adventure resort really is at one with nature. Set on the outskirts of Sangkhlaburi, it claims to have Thailand's longest zip-line (at 700m). The waterfront log cabins are immaculate. Nonguests can try out the activities.

Ban Thor Phan RESORT $$$
(☎0 3459 5018; r 2500-36,000B; ❄🏊) Crystal healing, chlorophyll baths and yoga are a few of the holistic treatments on offer in this stunning health retreat. Rooms are cool and calming.

Eating & Drinking

The central market is a fascinating place to stroll and pick up some snacks, especially the delicious Thai and Burmese curries (20B). A handful of bars now exist in town, the best of which is **Garden Home**, which does fantastic homemade burgers.

Baan Unrak Bakery BAKERY $
(snacks 25-90B) Vegetarians will love this meatless cafe, which is part of the Baan Unrak organisation.

Shopping

Visitors interested in Karen weaving can pick up authentic products at the Baan Unrak Bakery; the products are made by the Baan Unrak women's cooperative. Expect to pay 300-600B for a hand-woven souvenir.

Weaving for Women CLOTHING, HANDICRAFTS
(www.weavingforwomen.org) Along the same road as P Guest House, it sells hand-woven goods made by Mon and Karen refugee women.

Information

For money matters go to Siam Commercial Bank (ATM) near the market. Internet shops are also near the market and charge 15B per hour. There is an international phone in front of the post office (located on the main street).

GIVING SOMETHING BACK

Several humanitarian groups do invaluable work in Sangkhlaburi and are always looking for volunteers. Some are happy for short-term assistance; others require a longer commitment. Voluntourism is not without its critics though, so think carefully about what you can contribute, rather than what you will get out of it, before stepping forward. Below are some of the organisations:

- **Children of the Forest** (www.childrenoftheforest.org) This foundation helps stateless Karen and Mon children.
- **Ban Thor Phan** (☎08 1824 3369; banthorphan@gmail.com) Profits from this holistic health resort, based near the main entrance to Sangkhlaburi, go towards a school and home for abused and orphaned Thai and Burmese children. Volunteers at the home and school are welcome.
- **Hilltribe Learning Centre** (ศูนย์การศึกษาตามอัธยาศัยไทยภูเขา) Run by Buddhist nun Pimjai Maneerat, this remote centre for Karen children welcomes short-term helpers or English teachers. Contact P Guest House for details.
- **Thai Animal Sanctuary** (www.thaianimalsanctuary.com) Based at Baan Unrak (p185), this group helps abused or sick animals.

❶ Getting There & Away

Across from the market is a bare patch of land that serves as Sangkhlaburi's local bus station. Tickets for air-con buses are sold opposite 7-Eleven; the minivan office is at the far end of the same street. A motorbike taxi to guesthouses will cost about 15B. Most transport will stop at Thong Pha Phum and Sai Yok. Destinations include:

Bangkok's Northern (Mo Chit) terminal (249B, seven hours, 7.45am, 9.30am)

Kanchanaburi (150-175B, five hours, frequent)

Around Sangkhlaburi

Three Pagodas Pass ด่านเจดีย์สามองค์

The eponymous pagodas *(prá jair·dee săhm ong)* appear on the official Kanchanaburi seal but up close are unremarkable. Nevertheless, this border town is worth visiting for its heavy Burmese influence.

Across the border is the town of Payathonzu, with a **souvenir market** and **teahouses**. For the past few years the border crossing has only been open to Thai nationals and, despite constant whispers, that was still the case at the time of writing. If you want to cross through, ask around locally to check the current situation before setting off.

If there is no way past, then the **market** on the Thai side is full of traders selling Burmese whisky, jewellery, cigars and bizarre health treatments involving goats' heads. At the entrance to one noodle restaurant is a time capsule that was buried in 1995 by Allied POWs to mark the 50th anniversary of the 'Death Railway'. Come here on 20 April 2045 and you can see it being opened.

Should the border be open, foreigners can only obtain one-day passes, not visa extensions. You would need to temporarily surrender your passport and provide a passport photo to the Thai immigration office. At the Myanmar immigration office, a copy of the photo page of your passport and a passport photo is needed, plus 500B or US$10. When you return to Thailand, you will receive your passport back. There is a small photocopy shop near the Thai immigration office.

The pass has a history of violence and smuggling, and even today it is rumoured to be an important drug smuggling route, notably for wood, semiprecious stones and amphetamines.

Green *sŏrng·tăa·ou* leave from Sangkhlaburi's bus station (30B, 40 mintes) every 40 minutes. The border is a short walk from the *sŏrng·tăa·ou* stop in Three Pagodas Pass.

Ko Chang & Eastern Seaboard

Best Places to Eat

➡ Mum Aroi (p199)

➡ Phu-Talay (p224)

➡ Norng Bua (p224)

➡ Cool Corner Cafe (p213)

➡ Pan & David Restaurant (p194)

Best Places to Stay

➡ Keereeta Resort (p221)

➡ Bann Makok (p229)

➡ Rabbit Resort (p198)

➡ Koh Chang Sea Hut (p223)

➡ Tok's (p204)

Why Go?

Bangkok Thais have long escaped the urban grind with weekend escapes to the eastern seaboard. Some of the country's first beach resorts sprang up here, starting a trend that has been replicated wherever sand meets sea. As the country has industrialised, only a few beaches within reach of the capital, such as Ko Samet's, remain spectacular specimens. Further afield, Ko Chang and its sister islands offer a more 'tropical' ambience, but are far from undiscovered.

Just beyond the foothills and the curving coastline is Cambodia, and the east coast provides a cultural link between the two countries. Many of the mainland Thai towns were at some point occupied by the French during the shifting border days of the colonial era. Travellers who take the time to explore these lesser-known spots will find remnants of Old Siam, tasty market meals and an easy-going prosperity that defines ordinary Thai life in this region.

When to Go

➡ The best time to visit is the end of the rainy season (usually around November) but before the start of high season (December to March) when the weather is cool, the landscape green and rates reasonable. Peak season on Ko Chang is the Christmas and New Year holiday period. Crowds thin in March, the start of the hot season.

➡ The rainy season runs from May to October. A few businesses on Ko Chang close and the nearby islands of Ko Kut, Ko Mak and Ko Wai go into hibernation with many places shut. Your best monsoon bet is Ko Samet, which enjoys its own micro-climate and stays relatively dry.

Si Racha ศรีราชา

POP 68,292

A subdued seaside town, Si Racha is a mix of a traditional fishing village and modern industry. Waterfront condo towers eclipse a labyrinth of rickety piers, while the container ships docking at the Laem Chabang port share the shipping channels with wooden, multicoloured fishing boats.

Thai towns are adept at disguising themselves so that they resemble each other. Si Racha, though, is more international than most, thanks to the Japanese car manufacturers based nearby. There are many sushi joints here, as well as Japanese-style bars, and on weekends the impeccably maintained health park is full of Japanese expats jogging and throwing baseballs around.

But Si Racha is most attractive for what it doesn't have; there are no girlie bars or traffic jams and precious few foreign visitors, allowing you to enjoy a taste of small town Thai life.

Best of all, Si Racha is the gateway to the peaceful little island of Ko Si Chang. Once a royal retreat, the island feels like an extended fishing village, only with a palace and some impressive temples scattered around it.

◎ Sights

Si Racha's attractions are limited, but the town itself makes for a pleasant stroll.

Ko Loi   ISLAND

This small rocky island is connected to the mainland by a long jetty at the northern end of Si Racha's waterfront and lauded as a local highlight. It has a festival atmosphere centred around a **Thai-Chinese temple** (⊙daylight hours), decorated by a couple of giant ponds with turtles of every size, from tiny hatchlings to seen-it-all-before seniors. This is also where you can catch the boat to Ko Si Chang.

Health Park   GARDEN

The town's waterfront Health Park is possibly one of the best-maintained municipal parks in the country. There are sea breezes, a playground, a shady coffee shop with wi-fi, a jogging track and a lot of evening activity.

▐ Sleeping

The most authentic (read: basic) places to stay are the wooden hotels on the piers.

Samchai   HOTEL $

(⌨ 0 3831 1800; Soi 10, Th Jermjompol; r 350B; ❋ ⊛ �📶) More comfortable than other pier options, this place seems to ramble forever. The rooms are functional, but clean and acceptable.

Siriwatana Hotel   HOTEL $

(⌨ 0 3831 1037; Soi Siriwatana, Th Jermjompol; r 200B) This wooden stilt hotel sits above the sea – in fact, you can look straight through the squat toilet's hole to the ocean. It's very simple and very cheap.

Seaview Sriracha Hotel   HOTEL $$

(⌨ 0 3831 9000; 50-54 Th Jermjompol; r 990-1900B; ❋ @ 📶) Rooms are large and comfortable; try to score one at the back for views of the sea and piers and to avoid traffic noise.

✕ Eating & Drinking

Unsurprisingly, Si Racha is famous for its seafood and you have the choice of eating it both Thai- and Japanese-style.

Ko Loi Seafood Stalls   SEAFOOD $

(dishes 40-160B; ⊙10am-9pm) Perched on the Ko Loi jetty, these humble spots specialise in fresh seafood. There is no English menu, so just point and pick.

Night Square   MARKET $

(Th Jermjompol & Th Si Racha Nakorn; dishes from 50B; ⊙5pm) This evening market is small, but big enough to feed a street-stall appetite.

Moom Aroy   SEAFOOD $$

(Soi 8, Th Jermjompol; dishes 60-420B; ⊙11am-10pm) Moom Aroy delivers on its name, which means 'delicious corner'. This is *the* place to enjoy a Si Racha seafood meal with views of the pier and squid rigs. It is north of town; turn left at Samitivet Sriracha Hospital and look for the tank with the 2m fish out front.

Asami Sriracha   JAPANESE $$

(Th Jermjompol; sushi from 80B, sashimi from 140B; ⊙11am-11pm; 📶) Authentic and popular eatery that sees a lot of expat Japanese customers. The sushi is as fresh as possible, and there are also ramen and teppanyaki dishes here.

Bang Saen   SEAFOOD $$

(dishes 150-350B; ⊙11am-10pm) Do as the Thais do and judge your beach by its seafood restaurants. This resort, 18km north of town, isn't good for swimming but weekending Bangkokians and local university students love it for its food and views. You'll need private transport to reach it.

Ko Chang & Eastern Seaboard Highlights

1 Beachcombing and jungle trekking on **Ko Chang** (p214)

2 Floating the day away on the crystalline waters of **Ko Kut** (p228)

3 Swimming with the fishes in the gin-clear coves of **Ko Wai** (p226)

4 Cove-hopping on pretty **Ko Samet** (p202), so close to Bangkok but so far away

5 Strolling the old city and watching the gem traders in **Chanthaburi** (p207)

6 Kicking back in **Trat's** (p210) atmospheric wooden shophouse quarter

7 Avoiding Bangkok's hustle and bustle with a day trip to peaceful **Ko Si Chang** (p193) and a layover in **Si Racha** (p189)

8 Admiring the modern masterpiece of Pattaya's **Sanctuary of Truth** (p195), an elaborately carved testament to the artistry of Buddhism and Hinduism

9 Dining on seafood beside the sea everywhere – the principal reason Thais travel to the beach

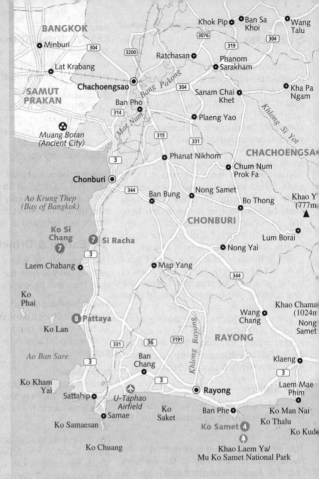

Si Racha

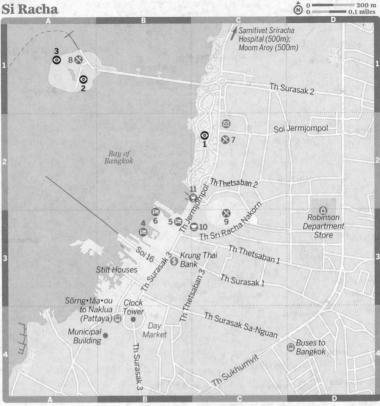

Coffee Tree　　　　　　　　　　CAFE

(Th Jermjompol; ⊙7am-7pm; 🛜) Cute cafe that caters to Si Racha's student hipsters. It offers coffee, juices and tea, as well as snacks.

Pop Pub　　　　　　　　　　　BAR

(Th Jermjompol; dishes 60-220B; ⊙5-11pm) More like 'Rock', this waterfront beer-hall-meets-live music venue boasts a menu ranging from salty snacks to full meals and plenty of liquid sustenance.

ℹ Information

Krung Thai Bank (cnr Th Surasak 1 & Th Jermjompol) Has an ATM and exchange facilities.

Post Office (Th Jermjompol) A few blocks north of the Krung Thai Bank.

Samitivet Sriracha Hospital (☎0 3832 4111; Soi 8, Th Jermjompol) Regarded as Si Racha's best.

CHILI SAUCE BY ANY OTHER NAME

Judging by the phenomenal popularity of Sriracha Hot Chili sauce in the USA, you'd expect the eponymous town to be a veritable sauce temple. But no one in the town of Si Racha seems to know much about the sauce, much less that US haute cuisine chefs are using it on everything from cocktails to marinades and that food magazines are profiling it alongside truffle oil as a must-have condiment. Curiously, the culinary world also mispronounces the name of the sauce: Sriracha, an alternative spelling of 'Si Racha', is pronounced 'see-rach-ah' not 'sir-rach-ah'.

There's a good explanation for all this: the stuff sold in the US was actually invented on home soil. A Vietnamese immigrant living in a Los Angeles suburb concocted a chilli sauce to accompany noodles based on his memory of Vietnamese hot sauces. His first batches were sold out of his car but eventually his business grew into the Huy Fong Foods company.

Today, the company's distinctive rooster logo bottles are distributed in the US and Australia, but not in any Asian countries, according to a company spokesperson. But every now and then you might spot it at a Thai noodle shop. How this US-born, Thai-named, Vietnamese-inspired sauce got here, Huy Fong Foods does not know.

But that doesn't mean Thailand doesn't have its own version of a vinegar-based chilli sauce (*nám prík sĕe rah·chah*). In fact, many believe that the condiment must have originated in Si Racha and then migrated across Asia while undergoing various permutations. In Thailand, Si Racha–style sauces, including such popular brands as Golden Mountain or Sriraja Panich, are used with *kài jee·o* (omelette) and *hŏy tôrt* (fried mussel omelette) and tend to be sweeter and of a thinner consistency than the rooster brand.

ℹ️ Getting There & Around

Si Racha doesn't have a consolidated bus station but all buses stop on Th Sukhumvit (Hwy 3) by Robinson Department Store, or the nearby IT Mall (Tuk Com).

Buses heading north to Bangkok's bus terminals (88B to 97B, two hours) pass by every 30 minutes or so until late. There are also seven buses daily to Suvarnabhumi International Airport (200B, two hours) from an office beside the IT Mall.

Minivans stop in front of Robinson's and have frequent services to Bangkok's various bus stations (100B to 120B, two hours) and Victory Monument (100B, two hours). They head south to Pattaya (40B, 45 minutes) often, too.

White *sŏrng·tăa·ou* (passenger pick-up trucks) leave from near Si Racha's clock tower to Pattaya's Naklua market (25B, 45 minutes).

One daily train from Bangkok's Hua Lamphong station stops at Si Racha (30B, three hours). Si Racha's train station is 3km east of the waterfront.

Motorbike taxis zip around town for 20B to 30B.

Ko Si Chang ✗ เกาะสีชัง

POP 5012

Once a royal beach retreat, Ko Si Chang has a fishing village atmosphere and enough attractions to make it a decent day's excursion from Si Racha, or an overnight stop for those who want to chill out. It gets busier at weekends, when Bangkok Thais come to eat seafood, pose in front of the sea and make merit at the local temples.

◎ Sights

Phra Chudadhut Palace   HISTORICAL SITE
(⊙9am-5pm Tue-Sun) FREE This former royal palace was used by Rama V (King Chulalongkorn) over the summer months, but was abandoned when the French briefly occupied the island in 1893. The main throne hall – a magnificent golden teak structure known as Vimanmek Teak Mansion – was moved to Bangkok in 1910. What's left are subdued Victorian-style buildings set in gardenlike grounds.

Ruen Vadhana and Ruen Mai Rim Talay contain historical displays about the king's visits to the island and his public works programs, including a lecture to the local people on Western tea parties. Up the hill is Wat Asadang Khanimit, a temple containing a small, consecrated chamber where Rama V used to meditate. The Buddha image inside was fashioned more than 50 years ago by a local monk. Nearby is a stone outcrop wrapped in holy cloth, called Bell Rock because it rings like a bell when struck.

As this was a palace, proper attire is technically required (legs and arms should be covered) but the rules aren't enforced here. While some desultory renovations are going on, there is a rather melancholy air to the place and it is far less well-maintained than most royal properties.

Cholatassathan Museum
AQUARIUM

(admission by donation; ⊙ 9am-5pm Tue-Sun) This aquarium has a few marine exhibits and a dash of English-language signage. It's fun to watch the Thais gazing at the outdoor tank and discussing which animals are delicious to eat. The Aquatic Resources Research Institute conducts coral research here.

San Jao Phaw Khao Yai
TEMPLE

(⊙ daylight hours) FREE The most imposing sight on the island, this ornate Chinese temple dates back to the days when Chinese traders anchored in the sheltered waters. During Chinese New Year in February, the island is overrun with tourists from mainland China. There are also shrine caves, multiple platforms and a good view of the ocean. It's east of town.

Wat Tham Yai Phrik
TEMPLE

(วัดถ้ำยายปริก; donation appreciated; ⊙ dawn-dusk) This Buddhist monastery is built around several meditation caves running into the island's central limestone ridge and offers fine views from its hilltop *chedi* (stupa). Monks and *mâa chee* (nuns) from across Thailand come to take advantage of the caves' peaceful environment. Someone is usually around to give informal tours and talk about Buddhism; meditation retreats can also be arranged.

Hat Tham Phang
BEACH

On the southwest side of the island, Hat Tham Phang (Fallen Cave Beach) is the only sandy beach on the island. You can hire kayaks and there is deckchair and umbrella rental. Swimming here isn't recommended, although the Thais plunge in.

🏃 Activities

Several locals run **snorkelling** trips to nearby Koh Khang Khao (Bat Island). Ask at Pan & David Restaurant for details.

Kayaks are available for rent (150B per hour) on Hat Tham Phang. It's a nice paddle down the coast to Koh Khang Khao.

🛏 Sleeping & Eating

There are a smattering of guesthouses and homestays on the island, as well as a fair few restaurants specialising in seafood.

Charlie's Bungalows
GUESTOUSE $$

(☐ 08 5191 3863; www.kosichang.net; Th Makham Thaew; r 1000-1100B; ❄ 🛜) Bright, fresh, all-white bungalows set around a garden. All come with TVs and DVD players. Friendly and helpful staff. Book ahead at weekends and public holidays.

Lek Tha Wang
SEAFOOD $

(dishes 35-420B; ⊙ 10.30am-9pm) This famous, if ramshackle, open-air restaurant is where Thais go to eat conch and other shellfish. For the rest of us, there's always *dôm yam gûng* (spicy and sour prawn soup) and fried fish.

★ Pan & David Restaurant
INTERNATIONAL-THAI $$

(☐ 0 3821 6629; 167 Mu 3 Th Makham Thaew; dishes 60-440B; ⊙ 8am-10pm) With free-range chicken, homemade ice cream, a reasonable wine list and excellent Thai dishes, you can't go wrong here. Phoning ahead for a booking at weekends is recommended. The restaurant is 200m from the palace.

ℹ Information

The island's one small settlement faces the mainland and is the terminus for the ferry. A bumpy road network links the village with all the other sights.

Kasikornbank (99/12 Th Atsadang) Has an ATM and exchange facilities.

Pan & David's Ko Si Chang (www.koh-sichang.com) An excellent source of local information.

Post Office (Th Atsadang) Near the pier.

ℹ Getting There & Around

Boats to Ko Si Chang leave hourly 7am to 8pm from the Ko Loi jetty in Si Racha (one way 50B, 45 minutes). From Ko Si Chang boats shuttle back hourly 6am to 7pm. Boats leave promptly.

Motorbike taxis wait at the pier and will take you anywhere for 30B to 60B.

Motorbikes are available to rent on the pier (250B per day, 80B hourly).

Pattaya พัทยา

POP 215.888

Synonymous with sex tourism, Pattaya is unapologetic about its bread-and-butter industry. Go-go clubs, massage parlours and girlie bars occupy block after block of the central city, making Bangkok's red-light districts look small and provincial. But walking the same streets as the stiletto-wearing ladyboys are ever-increasing numbers of Russian tourists and Chinese tour groups. More than anything, Pattaya today is a schizophrenic experience: part package holiday destination; part prostitution central.

During the day, the city is slightly less seedy as the beach gets crowded out and jet skis and speed boats bounce across the waves. A fair few Thais, too, have adopted Pattaya as a weekend getaway, drawn by the excellent seafood and lower prices than elsewhere on the eastern seaboard. But not even the most enthusiatic Pattaya promoter could claim that the city has changed too much from its original incarnation as an anything-goes sin city for GIs on R & R from the Vietnam War.

The city is built around **Ao Pattaya**, a wide crescent-shaped bay that was one of Thailand's first beach resorts in the 1960s. The surrounding area is now Thailand's manufacturing base, transforming the bay from fishing area and swimming pool into an industrial port. Some provincial Thais still swim here but we don't think you should as the water is dirty. The oceanfront promenade does, however, provide a scenic stroll under shady trees and a lovely coastal view.

Optimists claim that Hat Jomtien, south of the centre, is a family-friendly scene. True, there are fewer girlie bars and the beach is nicer, but Jomtien is about two decades away from being retro and there's a preponderance of mediocre hotels and restaurants. North Pattaya (Pattaya Neua) is fashioning itself as a mini-Bangkok with modern condo towers and respectable corporate hotels. North of the city is **Naklua**, which is glossier than Jomtien and a little more promising for Pattaya's alternative tourists.

◉ Sights & Activities

Sanctuary of Truth   MONUMENT

(ปราสาทสัจธรรม; ☎0 3836 7229; www.sanctuaryoftruth.com; 206/2 Th Naklua; adult/child 500/250B; ⊙8am-6pm) Made entirely of wood (no metal nails) and commanding a celestial view of the ocean, the Sanctuary of Truth is best described as a visionary environment: part art installation, religious shrine and cultural monument. Constructed in four wings dedicated to Thai, Khmer, Chinese and Indian religious iconography, the architecture and setting is impressive.

The ornate temple-like complex was conceived by Lek Viriyaphant, a Thai millionaire who spent his fortune on this and other heritage projects (such as Ancient City near Bangkok) that revived and preserved ancient building techniques and architecture in danger of extinction. In this case, the building will continue to support handhewn woodworking skills because it has been under construction for 30 years and still isn't finished.

Every centimetre of the 20-storey-tall building is covered with wood carvings of Hindu and Buddhist gods and goddesses – an artistic consolidation of centuries of religious myths under one unifying roof for greater spiritual enlightenment. For non-Buddhists the experience may be more educational than transcendent as much of the symbolism will be unfamiliar.

Compulsory tours are led through the building every half hour. Thai dancing is on display at 11.30am and 3.30pm. Motorcycle taxis can be hired from Pattaya for 50B to 70B. The sanctuary is 1km down Soi 12 off Th Naklua, about 3km from the centre of town.

Anek Kusala Sala (Viharn Sien)   MUSEUM

(อเนกกุศลศาลา (วิหารเซียน); ☎0 3823 5250; off Th Sukhumvit; admission 50B; ⊙9am-5pm) A popular stop for tour groups, this museum contains more than 300 very impressive pieces of Chinese artwork, mainly bronze and brass statues depicting historical figures as well as Buddhist, Confucian and Taoist deities. Founded by Sa-nga Kulkobkiat, a Thai national who grew up in China, the museum was intended as a friendship-building project between the two countries.

The 1st floor is a crowded pavilion of Chinese immortals, from Pangu, the cosmic giant, to Guan Yin, the goddess of mercy. The 2nd-floor terrace is the museum's most dramatic, with larger-than-life-sized statues of Shaolin monks depicting different martial arts poses. Nearby, is a touching collection of daily life statues (a fortune teller, dress maker, liquor seller) that visitors place 1 baht coins on.

Pattaya & Naklua

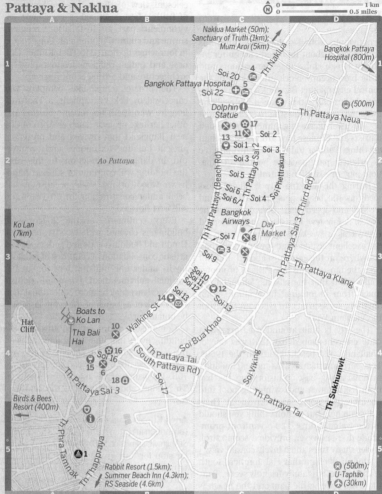

KO CHANG & EASTERN SEABOARD PATTAYA

The museum is 16km south of central Pattaya; take Th Sukhumvit to the turn-off for Wat Yan Sangwararam. There is a Pattaya–Sattahip *sŏrng·tǎa·ou* (25B) that will take you to the turn-off; from there you can hire a motorcycle the remaining 3km to the museum (50B) but finding a ride back to the main road is difficult. You can either negotiate with the driver to wait or come with your own transport.

Hat Ko Lan   BEACH

(เกาะล้าน) Day-trippers flock to this small island, 7km offshore of central Pattaya. On weekends, its five beaches are crowded and the aquamarine sea is busy with banana boats and other marine merriment. Overcrowded ferries leave Pattaya's Bali Hai pier (30B, five daily departures) at the southern end of Walking St. The last boat back from Ko Lan is at 6pm.

Khao Phra Tamnak   BUDDHIST SITE

(เขาพระตำหนัก; ☼ daylight hours) **FREE** A giant golden Buddha sits atop this forested hill between Jomtien and South Pattaya, proof perhaps that religion has not forsaken this modern-day Gomorrah. The serene Buddha

Pattaya & Naklua

figure of Wat Phra Yai dates back to when Pattaya was a small fishing village, long before mini-skirts, high heels and happy hours arrived. You can walk here from the southern end of Walking St.

Flight of the Gibbon   ZIP LINING
(⌕08 9970 5511; www.treetopasia.com; tours from 3000B) This zip-line course extends 3km with 26 platforms through the forest canopy of Khao Kheeo Open Safari in Chonburi, 50 minutes from Pattaya. It is an all-day tour with additional add-on activities, like a jungle obstacle course and a visit to the neighbouring animal zoo. Children 1m tall can do the zip line independently, while nippers can ride tandem with adults.

Fairtex Sports Club   FITNESS, MOO·AY TAI
(⌕0 3825 3888; www.fairtex-muaythai.com; 179/185-212 Th Pattaya Neua; per session 800-1200B) Burned-out professionals, martial arts fans and adventurous athletes flock to this resort-style sports camp for *moo·ay tai* (Thai boxing; also spelled *muay thai*) training and a sweat-inducing vacation. Accommodation packages are available and use of the club's pool and other sports facilities are included.

Fairtex has been training *moo·ay tai* fighters for 40 years. In 2005, the company opened this sports club to provide Western-style comfort for international visitors interested in fighting and fitness courses.

Daily sessions include pad work, sparring and clinching, exercise drills and body sculpting work. There are also occasional brushes with fame: domestically famous *moo·ay tai* champions and international mixed martial arts fighters also train here.

✱ Festivals

Pattaya International Music Festival   MUSIC
(www.pattayamusicfest.com; ⊙mid-Mar) In mid-March, Pattaya's oceanfront esplanade is transformed into an outdoor concert venue running for three days of live music. Local musicians, as well as bands from across Asia, take to the stages playing everything from hip-hop to rock.

⊟ Sleeping

If you're an 'alternative' Pattaya tourist (meaning you aren't a sex tourist or a package tourist), then you can avoid staying in central Pattaya and opt instead for Naklua, Jomtien or parts of Pattaya Neua. Even if you have no desire to visit Pattaya, you might consider an overnight here if you're transiting to Suvarnabhumi International Airport, 110km away, and don't want to layover in Bangkok.

RS Seaside   HOTEL $
(⌕0 3823 1867; www.rs-seaside.com; Th Hat Jomtien; r 660-1400B; ❄🗣☲) Opposite the beach and popular with Thais, RS has small-ish rooms but remains a good-value spot in the package-tour part of town. Two breakfasts are included in the room rate.

Bella Vista   HOTEL $
(⌕0 3836 2132; www.eastinypattaya.com; 217/29 Moo 9 Th Pattaya Beach, Soi 7 ; r 750-900B; ❄🗣) If you want to stay in the belly of the beast, then the Bella Vista is a comfortable and reasonably priced place to rest your head. Solid rooms, pleasant staff.

CHARITY SQUAD

A natural counterpoint to the city's prominent debauchery is the city's solid network of charitable organisations. Among the many benevolent servants in Pattaya, Father Ray Brennan, an American priest with the Redemptorist Order who died in 2003, established a lasting and inspiring legacy that today includes six charitable programs under the umbrella of the Redemptorist Foundation. He also founded the Pattaya Orphanage and School for the Deaf, both of which are now operated by the Catholic diocese. All of them succeed thanks to the generosity of benefactors and volunteers.

Pattaya Orphanage (☑ 0 3842 3468; www.thepattayaorphanage.org; Th Sukhumvit, North Pattaya) was founded in the 1970s when Father Ray was given a baby by a parishioner who could not care for the child. This first child led to many more as word spread that the priest could care for the unintended consequences of the US military presence in the area during the Vietnam War. Today the orphanage cares for children orphaned by modern misfortunes (poverty, drug abuse, HIV/AIDS) and helps find adoptive parents. Those interested in helping the orphanage can sponsor a meal, donate useful items and volunteer for an extended period of time.

Redemptorist Foundation (☑ 0 3871 6628; www.fr-ray.org) operates schools for the blind and disabled and a home and drop-in centre for street children, many of whom may be involved in Pattaya's child-sex industry. The foundation also runs a day-care centre for children of labourers who would otherwise accompany their parents to dangerous work sites. Volunteers rotate through the different centres, teaching English, playing with the children and leading art projects. A six-month commitment is required; contact the foundation for a volunteer handbook that outlines the application process.

If you don't have the time to commit to volunteering, stop by **Thais 4 Life** (www.thais 4life.com; Soi Yen Sabai Condotel, Th Phra Tamnak; ☺noon-6pm Mon-Sat), a charity bookstore whose proceeds go to medical treatments for destitute patients, orphanages and school uniform scholarships.

Garden Lodge Hotel HOTEL $$
(☑ 0 3842 9109; www.gardenlodgepattaya.net; cnr Soi 20 & Th Naklua; r 1250-2500B; ❄ 🛜 🏊) Rather old-fashioned rooms, but they're a good size and come with balconies, set around a landscaped garden and large swimming pool.

Summer Beach Inn HOTEL $$
(☑ 0 3823 1777; Th Hat Jomtien; r 700-900B; ❄ @ 🛜) Uninspired but fair-enough rooms in an anonymous high-rise hotel far from Pattaya's vice.

★ Rabbit Resort HOTEL $$$
(☑ 0 3825 1730; www.rabbitresort.com; Hat Dongtan; r 3700-11,000B; ❄ @ 🛜 🏊) Rabbit Resort has stunning, stylish and secluded bungalows and villas that showcase Thai design and art, all set in beachfront forest hidden between Jomtien and Pattaya Tai. There are no rabbits here, but it's a perfect choice for families with a couple of swimming pools and easy beach access.

Birds & Bees Resort HOTEL $$$
(☑ 0 3825 0556; www.cabbagesandcondoms.co.th; Soi 4, Th Phra Tamnak; r 2000-12,000B; ❄ @ 🛜 🏊)

Retreat into a tropical garden resort bisected by meandering paths and decorated with tongue-in-cheek artwork. The cheaper rooms are a little drab for the price, but there's a semi-private beach and an incongruous wholesomeness for a resort affiliated with PDA, the Thai family planning NGO that promotes condom use.

Woodlands Resort HOTEL $$$
(☑ 0 3842 1707; www.woodland-resort.com; cnr Soi 22, 164/1 Th Naklua; r 2500-5200B; ❄ @ 🛜 🏊) A surprisingly affordable quality resort, marred only by the 300B per day fee for wi-fi; Woodlands Resort is low-key and professional with light, airy rooms, a tropical garden and two swimming pools.

🍴 Eating

Pattaya is a package holiday town, so there are a lot of overpriced, mediocre restaurants. But the seafood is always good.

Leng Kee THAI-CHINESE $
(Th Pattaya Klang; dishes 100-300B; ☺24hr) Pattaya has a thriving Chinatown run by families who expertly balance their Thai

and Chinese heritage. Leng Kee specialises in duck dishes, but is city-renowned during Chinese New Year when the menu goes vegetarian and includes golden good-luck noodles.

Mae Sai Tong   THAI $
(Th Pattaya Klang; dishes 50B) Next to the day market, a fine spot for cheap fried rice and noodle dishes, this stand is famous for selling *kôw nĕe·o má·môo·ang* (ripe mango with sticky rice) all year round. Everyone else has to wait for the hot-dry season to compete.

★ Mum Aroi   THAI $$
(☑0 3822 3252; 83/4 Soi 4, Th Naklua; dishes 180-380B; ⊙5-10pm) 'Delicious corner' is a contemporary glass-and-concrete restaurant perched beside the sea in the fishing village end of Naklua. Old fishing boats sit marooned offshore and crisp ocean breezes envelop diners as they greedily devour fantastic Thai food. Try *sôm·đam ʰboo* (spicy papaya salad with crab) and *ʰblah mèuk nêung ma-now* (squid steamed in lime juice). You'll need to charter a baht bus to get here (one way 100B).

Nang Nual   THAI $$
(☑0 3842 8478; Walking St; dishes 80-500B; ⊙11am-11pm) Pattaya's most famous seafood restaurant now spreads across both sides of Walking St. The dishes are pleasant, if not spectacular, and the fish are all on display.

The section of the restaurant on the waterfront has an outdoor deck offering bay views.

Abu Saeed   MIDDLE EASTERN $$
(363/13 Soi 16, off Walking St; dishes 60-300B; ⊙8am-midnight) Soi 16 is Pattaya's Arab quarter, home to shisha cafes and authentic Middle Eastern cuisine. This long-established, alcohol-free place is always busy. The house speciality is couscous royale and the menu ranges across the Middle East.

Ban Amphur   THAI $$
(dishes 100-380B; ⊙11am-11pm) This fishing village 15km south of Pattaya is a dinner destination for Thais. A half-dozen seafood restaurants line the beach road and some are so large the waiters use walkie-talkies. Pick one that doesn't seem lonely or overwhelmed and order all the seafood specialities. You'll have to hire transport to get here.

Sketch Book Art Cafe   INTERNATIONAL-THAI $$
(Th Tha Phraya; dishes 90-640B; ⊙8am-11pm; 🛜) A cool, surprising place to find in Jomtien. There's a pleasant garden, while inside the walls are covered with paintings by customers; kids will like it. Decent steaks, as well as Western and Thai faves. They sell art supplies, too.

La Baguette   BAKERY $$
(☑0 3842 1707; 164/1 Th Naklua; dishes 210-360B; ⊙8am-midnight; 🛜) This posh cafe is a favourite of upmarket Thais. Great salads, yummy pastries and crepes and lots of coffee options.

PATTAYA – GLOBAL RETIREMENT HOME

Pattaya! The very name conjures up images of aged sex tourists walking seedy streets lined with scantily clad women trying to entice them into beer bars and go-go shows.

Yet, despite the very obvious sex industry here, there's no question that Pattaya is Thailand's only truly international city after Bangkok. From its beginnings as a quiet fishing village transformed by the arrival of US servicemen on leave from the Vietnam War, to the booming metropolis it is now, Pattaya has always attracted visitors from all over the world.

Russians and Chinese are a huge presence, but there's also a thriving Arab community centred around Soi 16 at the south end of Walking St. In contrast, Naklua is home to many Germans and Scandinavians.

In their wake have come increasing numbers of shops offering specialist services and goods for foreigners, whether it's South American coffee or French cheese.

It's the presence of those amenities, as well as the climate and cheap cost of living compared to the West, that has helped turn sleazy Pattaya into one of the world's most popular retirement havens.

Accurate figures are hard to come by, but it's likely that over 50,000 foreigners call Pattaya home now, with many more spending part of the year here. And as the city continues to adapt to their presence, those numbers are set to increase.

Traktirr Zaharovna RUSSIAN $$

(Th Pattaya Sai btwn Soi 1 & 2; dishes 120-400B; ⏲11am-midnight) With so many Russians in Pattaya now, there are a growing number of places offering food from the old country. This one is Russian-run and serves up classic dishes like borscht, as well as a good range of salads.

Mantra INTERNATIONAL $$$

(☑0 3842 9591; Th Hat Pattaya; dishes 160-1240B; ⏲5pm-midnight Mon-Sat, 11am-2pm & 5pm-midnight Sun; ☎) Industrial cool and rather posh for Pattaya, Mantra is fun even if you can only afford a classy cocktail (from 180B). The menu combines Japanese, Thai and Western dishes and it's a popular spot for Sunday brunch.

🍷 Drinking & Nightlife

Despite the profusion of identikit beer bars, there are still some good places for a no-strings-attached drink.

Hopf Brew House BAR

(☑0 3871 0650; 219 Th Hat Pattaya; beers from 90B; ⏲3pm-late) Moodily authentic in dark wood, the Hopf Brew House gets packed at weekends when there is live music. Beers and pizza (from 160B) are brewed and wood-fired on-site.

Green Bottle BAR

(☑0 3842 9675; 216/6-20 Th Pattaya Sai 2; beers from 65B) Cheap beer, pool and sport on the TV at this laid-back, dressed-down, wood-themed bar.

Gulliver's BAR

(☑0 3871 0641; Th Hat Pattaya; beers from 90B; ⏲3pm-2am) The neo-colonial facade belies the sports bar inside. There are lots of screens for watching the football.

ℹ BYPASSING BANGKOK

An expanding network of bus and minivan services now connects the eastern seaboard with Suvarnabhumi airport, meaning that you don't have to transit through Bangkok for a flight arrival or departure. This is especially alluring to winter-weary visitors eager to reach a beach fast. Ko Samet is the closest prettiest beach to the airport and its southeastern beaches are serene enough for honeymooners. From the airport bus terminal, check the schedule for Rayong-bound buses and then catch a *sŏrng·tăa·ou* to reach the ferry pier to Ko Samet.

Lima Lima NIGHTCLUB

(Walking St; ⏲7pm-late) International DJs, sometimes, and a mix of Russian and Western tourists, locals and expats. Free entry but the drinks are pricey.

⭐ Entertainment

Tiffany's THEATRE

(☑0 3842 1700; www.tiffany-show.co.th; 464 Th Pattaya Sai 2; admission 800-1200B; ⏲6pm, 7.30pm & 9pm) Family-friendly ladyboy show (lots of sequins, satin and sentimental songs) and madly popular with Chinese tour groups and Russians.

Blues Factory LIVE MUSIC

(☑0 3830 0180; www.thebluesfactorypattaya.com; Soi Lucky Star, Walking St; ⏲8.30pm-late) Classic rock (think '70s Americana) is performed every night at this long-running venue.

ℹ Information

DANGERS & ANNOYANCES

So many people are so drunk in this town that all sorts of mayhem ensues (fighting, pickpocketing and reckless driving) after dark. Keep your wits about you and leave the passport and credit cards at your hotel.

EMERGENCY

Tourist Police (☑emergency 1155; tourist@police.go.th) The head office is beside the Tourism Authority of Thailand office on Th Phra Tamnak with police boxes along Pattaya and Jomtien beaches.

MEDIA

Pattaya Mail (www.pattayamail.com) is the city's English-language weekly. **Pattaya One** (www.pattayaone.net) is a website that offers an intriguing insight into the darker side of the city.

MEDICAL SERVICES

Bangkok Pattaya Hospital (☑0 3842 9999; www.bph.co.th; 301 Th Sukhumvit, Naklua; ⏲24hr) For first-class health care.

MONEY

There are banks and ATMs throughout the city.

POST

Post Office (Soi 13/2, Th Pattaya Sai 2)

TOURIST INFORMATION

Tourism Authority of Thailand (TAT; ☑0 3842 8750; 609 Th Phra Tamnak; ⏲8.30am-4.30pm) Located at the northwestern edge of Rama IX Park. The helpful staff have brochures and maps.

ⓘ Getting There & Away

Pattaya's airport is **U-Taphao Airfield** (☎0 3824 5599), 33km south of town. **Bangkok Airways** (☎0 3841 2382; www.bangkokair.com; 179/85-212 Th Pattaya Sai 2) flies from here.

The main bus station is on Th Pattaya Neua.

Minivans heading north to Bangkok leave from the corner of Th Sukhumvit and Th Pattaya Klang.

Pattaya Train Station (☎0 3842 9285) is off Th Sukhumvit south of town.

ⓘ Getting Around

Locally known as 'baht buses', *sŏrng·tăa·ou* do a loop along the major roads; just hop on and pay 10B when you get off. If you're going all the way to or from Jomtien to Naklua, you might have to change vehicles at the dolphin roundabout in Pattaya Neua and the price goes up to 20B. Baht buses run to the bus station from the dolphin roundabout as well. If you're going further afield, you can charter a baht bus; establish the price beforehand.

Motorbikes can be hired around town for 200B a day.

Rayong & Ban Phe ระยอง/บ้านเพ

POP 106,737/16,717

You're most likely to transit through these towns en route to Ko Samet. Rayong has frequent bus connections to elsewhere and the little port of Ban Phe has ferry services to Ko Samet. Blue *sŏrng·tăa·ou* link the two towns (25B, 45 minutes, every 15 minutes).

🛏 Sleeping

Rayong President Hotel   HOTEL **$**
(☎0 3861 1307; www.rayongpresident.com; Th Sukhumvit, Rayong; d & tw 400B; ❄ ☎) From the bus station, cross to the other side of Th Sukhumvit and walk to the right. The hotel is down a side street that starts next to the Siam Commercial Bank; look for the sign.

Christie's Guesthouse   GUESTHOUSE **$**
(☎0 3865 1976; 280/92 Soi 1, Ban Phe; r 600B; ❄ ☎) Christie's is a comfortable place near the pier if you need a room, meal or a book.

ⓘ Getting There & Away

Minivans from Rayong's bus station go to Bangkok's eastern (Ekamai) and northern (Mo Chit)

TRANSPORT TO/FROM PATTAYA

DESTINATION	BUS	MINIVAN	TRAIN	AIR
Bangkok's Eastern Bus Terminal	124B; 2hr; every 30min 4.30am-11pm	40B; 2hr; frequent		
Bangkok Suvarnabhumi International Airport	250B; 2hr; 7 daily 6pm-7pm	140B; 2hr; frequent		
Bangkok Northern Bus Terminal	133B; 2½hr; every 30min 4.30am-9pm	140B; 2½hr; frequent		
Bangkok Southern Bus Terminal	124B; 2½hr; hourly 6am-6.30pm			
Bangkok Hua Lamphong		38B; 3½hr; 1 daily		
Ko Chang		300B; 3½hr; 3 daily		
Ko Samet		200B; 2hr; 4 daily		
Ko Samui				from 3890B; 13½hr; daily
Phuket				from 2590B; 14hr; daily
Rayong	90B; 1½hr; frequent	100B; 1½hr; frequent		
Si Racha	40B; 45min; frequent	40B; 50min; frequent	30B; 1¼hr; 1 daily	

ⓘ BEACH ADMISSION FEE

Ko Samet is part of the Mu Ko Samet National Park and charges all visitors an entrance fee (adult/child 200/100B) upon arrival. If you can prove that you live and work in Thailand, you'll get in for 40B, the price Thais pay. The fee is collected at the national parks office (p207) in Hat Sai Kaew; *sŏrng·tăa·ou* from the pier will stop at the gates for payment. Hold on to your ticket for later inspections.

bus terminals, as well as Suvarnabhumi Airport (160B, 3½ hours, frequently 5am to 8pm).

There are also minivans to Chanthaburi (120B, 2½ hours, frequent) and Pattaya (100B, 1½ hours, frequent).

Buses from Ban Phe's bus station (near Tha Thetsaban) go to/from Bangkok's Eastern (Ekamai) station (173B, four hours, hourly 6am to 6pm).

Ban Phe also has minivan services to Laem Ngop for boats to Ko Chang (300B, four hours, three daily), Pattaya (230B, two hours, three daily) and Bangkok's Victory Monument (250B, four hours, hourly 7am to 6pm.

There are also boats to/from Ko Samet.

Ko Samet   เกาะเสม็ด

An idyll island, Ko Samet bobs in the sea with a whole lot of scenery: small sandy bays bathed by clear aquamarine water. You'll have to share all this prettiness with other beach lovers as it's an easy weekend escape from Bangkok, as well as a major package-tour destination.

But considering its proximity and popularity, Ko Samet is surprisingly underdeveloped with a thick jungle interior crouching beside the low-rise hotels. There are, though, plans in place to redevelop the main street that runs from the pier to Hat Sai Kaew, so expect some changes. The interior road around the island remains rutted and largely unpaved, however most beach-hopping is done the old-fashioned way, by foot along wooded trails skirting the coastline.

◉ Sights & Activities

On some islands you beach-hop, but on Ko Samet you cove-hop. The coastal footpath traverses rocky headlands, cicada-serenaded forests and one stunning bay after another. The mood becomes successively more mellow the further south you go.

Hat Sai Kaew   BEACH
Starting in the island's northeastern corner, Hat Sai Kaew, or 'Diamond Sand', is the island's widest and whitest stretch of sand, as well as its busiest beach. With sunbathers, sarong-sellers, speedboats, jet-skis, resorts and restaurants galore, the people-watching here is part of the appeal. At night, the scene is equally rambunctious with late-night parties and karaoke sessions.

At the southern end of Hat Sai Kaew are the prince and **mermaid statues** that memorialise Samet's literary role in *Phra Aphaimani,* the great Thai epic by Sunthorn Phu. The story follows the travails of a prince exiled to an undersea kingdom ruled by a lovesick female giant (who has her own lonely statue in Hat Puak Tian in Phetchaburi). A mermaid aids the prince in his escape to Ko Samet, where he defeats the giant by playing a magic flute.

Ao Hin Khok & Ao Phai   BEACH
Less frenetic than their northern neighbour, Ao Hin Khok and Ao Phai are two gorgeous bays separated by rocky headlands. The crowd here tends to be younger and more stylish than the tour groups who gather in Hat Sai Kaew; these two beaches are the traditional backpacker party centres of the island.

Ao Phutsa (Ao Tub Tim)   BEACH
Further still is wide and sandy Ao Phutsa (Ao Tub Tim), a favourite for solitude seekers, families and couples who need access to 'civilisation' but not a lot of other stimulation.

Ao Wong Deuan   BEACH
A smaller sister to Hat Sai Kaew, Ao Wong Deuan is a lovely crescent-shaped bay. Busy at the weekends, it's much more relaxed during the week.

Ao Thian   BEACH
Ao Thian (Candlelight Beach) is punctuated by big boulders that shelter small sandy spots creating a castaway ambience. More developed than it once was, it's still one of Samet's most easy-going beaches and is deliciously lonely on weekdays. On weekends, Bangkok university students serenade the stars with all-night guitar sessions.

Ko Samet

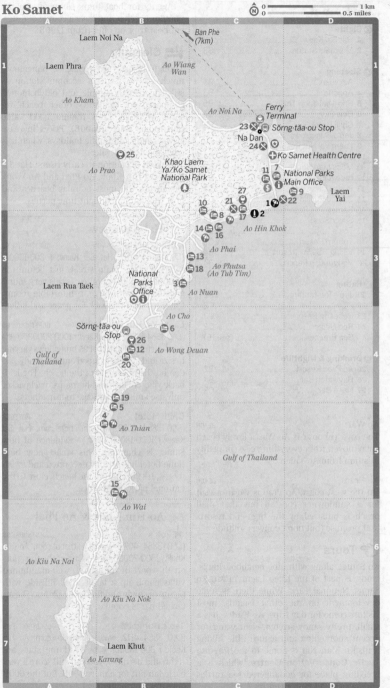

Laem Noi Na

Laem Phra

Ao Kham

Ao Wiang Wan

Ao Noi Na

Ban Phe (7km)

Ferry Terminal

23 Na Dan

Sŏrng·tǎa·ou Stop

24

Ko Samet Health Centre

25

Ao Prao

Khao Laem Ya/Ko Samet National Park

11

7

National Parks Main Office

9

27

1

22

Laem Yai

10

21

17

8

2

14

16

Ao Hin Khok

Ao Phai

13

Ao Phutsa (Ao Tub Tim)

18

National Parks Office

3

Ao Nuan

Laem Rua Taek

Ao Cho

Sŏrng·tǎa·ou Stop

6

26

12

Ao Wong Deuan

20

Gulf of Thailand

19

5

4

Ao Thian

Gulf of Thailand

15

Ao Wai

Ao Kiu Na Nai

Ao Kiu Na Nok

Laem Khut

Ao Karang

Ko Samet

Ao Wai　　　　　　　　　　　　BEACH
The cove 'caboose' is Ao Wai, a lovely beach far removed from everything else (in reality it is 1km from Ao Thian).

Ao Prao　　　　　　　　　　　　BEACH
On the west coast, Ao Prao is worth a visit for a sundowner cocktail but the small beach is outsized by the high-end resorts that promise (but don't deliver) solitude.

☞ Tours

Ko Samet, along with nine neighbouring islands, is part of the Khao Laem Ya/Mu Ko Samet National Park. While there is some development on the other islands, most visitors come for day trips. **Ko Kudee** has a small, pretty sandy stretch, clear water for decent snorkelling and a nice little hiking trail. Ko Man Nai is home to the **Rayong Turtle Conservation Centre**, which is a breeding place for endangered sea turtles and has a small visitor centre.

Agents for boat tours camp out on the popular beaches and have a couple of different boat trips on offer (from 1200B).

🛏 Sleeping

Though resorts are replacing bungalows, much of Ko Samet's accommodation is still surprisingly simple and old-fashioned compared to Thailand's other beach resorts. Weekday rates remain good value (fan rooms start at 600B). Prices increase at weekends and public holidays, when it is advisable to book ahead.

A word of caution to early risers: Hat Sai Kaew, Ao Hin Khok, Ao Phai and Ao Wong Deuan are the most popular beaches and host well-amplified night-time parties.

Hat Sai Kaew

Moss Man House　　　　GUESTHOUSE $$
(☎0 3864 4017; Hat Sai Kaew; r 800-1000B; ❄️@) On the main street, just before the national park ticket office, is this very sound guesthouse, with large, comfortable rooms. Choose one at the back for peace and quiet.

Laem Yai Hut Resort　　GUESTHOUSE $$
(☎0 3864 4282; Hat Sai Kaew; r 1000-2000B; ❄️@) A colourful collection of 25 bungalows varying in size and age are camped out in a shady garden on the north end of the beach. The laid-back vibe creates an alternative backpacker universe amid the package tour madness.

Chilli Hotel　　　　　　　　HOTEL $$
(☎0 3864 4039; www.chilli-hotel.com; Hat Sai Kaew; r 1000-1800B; ❄️@) Evidence of how Samet is changing, this smart new boutique hotel has artfully decorated and swish rooms. It's 200m from the beach, close to the national park ticket office.

Ao Hin Khok & Ao Phai

★ Tok's　　　　　　　　　GUESTHOUSE $$
(☎0 3864 4073; www.tok-littlehut.com; Ao Hin Khok; r 1500-2000B; ❄️@) One of the top spots on this part of the island, well-maintained villas climb up a landscaped hillside with plenty of shade and flowering plants. The attached bar is popular.

Jep's Bungalows　　　　GUESTHOUSE $$
(☎0 3864 4112; www.jepbungalow.com; Ao Hin Khok; r 300-1800B; ❄️@@) If the stars are right, and it's quiet, you can still score a very basic fan hut for a mere 300B. But the 600B ones are a far better deal.

Le Blanc
GUESTHOUSE $$

(📞0 3861 1646; www.leblancsamed.com; Ao Hin Khok; r 1500-2500B; ❄🌐) Formerly known as Ao Pai, this place has gone upmarket and re-branded itself with smart, all-white bungalows. They're perched amid trees and there's enough space between them for proper privacy.

Silver Sand
HOTEL $$

(📞0 3864 4300; www.silversandsamed.com; Ao Phai; r 2000-4000B; ❄@🌐) An ever-expanding empire, Silver Sand is a mini-resort, complete with bar, restaurant and shops. It's a little impersonal but the rooms are flashpacker quality and on a super strip of beach.

Samed Pavilion Resort
HOTEL $$$

(📞0 3864 4420; www.samedpavilionresort.com; Ao Phai; r 3000-5000B; ❄🌐🌐) Part of the Jep family (the posh branch), this new-ish boutique resort comes with all the trimmings and has elegant, sizeable rooms.

🏖 Ao Phutsa & Ao Nuan

Tubtim Resort
HOTEL $$

(📞0 3864 4025; www.tubtimresort.com; Ao Phutsa; r 600-3600B; ❄@🌐) Well-organised place with great, nightly barbecues and a range of solid, spacious bungalows of varying quality all close to the same dreamy beach. It's popular with upmarket Thais.

Ao Nuan
GUESTHOUSE $$

(Ao Nuan; r 600-2500B; ❄) The inventor of chillaxin' on Ko Samet, quirky Ao Nuan has both very simple wooden bungalows and a few posh ones with air-con and sea views. No reservations. Nor is there any internet access; you hang out in the attached restaurant and talk to people. Old school!

Pudsa Bungalow
GUESTHOUSE $$

(📞0 3864 4030; Ao Phutsa; r 600-1700B; ❄🌐) The nicer bungalows with beach views are trimmed with driftwood, and look their age now, but this is still a good place to kick back and listen to the sound of the sea.

🏖 Ao Wong Deuan & Ao Thian (Candlelight Beach)

Ferries run between Ao Wong Deuan and Ban Phe (140B return), with increased services at the weekend.

To get to Ao Thian, catch a ferry to Ao Wong Deuan and walk south over the headland. It's also a quick walk from here to the west side of the island – look for the marked trail on Ao Thian.

Blue Sky
GUESTHOUSE $

(📞08 9936 0842; Ao Wong Deuan; r 800-1200B; ❄) A rare budget spot on Ao Wong Deuan, Blue Sky has beaten-up bungalows set on a rocky headland. Though we love cheapies, budgeteers will get better value on other beaches.

Apache
GUESTHOUSE $

(📞08 1452 9472; www.apachesamed.com; Ao Thian; r 800-1300B; ❄) Still one of the most chilled spots on Samet, Apache's bungalows have seen better days but are good enough. The bar/restaurant is popular with people who like to roll their own cigarettes.

Nice & Easy
HOTEL $$

(📞0 3864 4370; nice.easy_samed.island@hotmail. com; Ao Wong Deuan; r 1200-2000B; ❄🌐) As the name suggests, a very amenable place with comfortable, modern and big bungalows set around a garden behind the beach. A decent deal for this part of Samet.

Viking Holiday Resort
HOTEL $$

(📞0 3864 4353; www.sametvikingresort.com; Ao Thian; r 1200-2000B; ❄@🌐) Ao Thian's most upscale spot with comfortable, if not very modern, rooms. There are only nine of them so book ahead. Pleasant staff and OK restaurant.

AO PRAO OIL SPILL

In late July 2013, the east coast of Ko Samet was severely affected by the fourth-largest oil spill in Thailand's history. Around 50,000 litres of crude oil gushed out of a pipeline operated by PTT Global Chemical, a subsidiary of Thailand's largest energy company, into the Gulf of Thailand close to Samet.

Worst hit was the beach of Ao Prao, where an estimated 20% of the oil ended up. After a massive clean-up operation, the beach has been restored to its usual, sandy state. Less certain, though, is the condition of the ocean, with reports in the Thai media stating that the number of fish being caught in the area has plummeted since the spill.

For now, we don't advise swimming off Ao Prao. But check with the locals to ascertain the current situation.

GETTING TO CAMBODIA: BAN PAKARD TO PSAR PRUHM

Getting to the Border Minivans (☎08 1949 0455) depart from a stop across the river from River Guest House in Chanthaburi to Ban Pakard/Pong Nam Ron (150B, 1½ hours, two daily).

At the Border This is a far less busy and more pleasant crossing than Poipet further north. You need a passport photo and US$20 for the visa fee.

Moving On Hop on a motorbike taxi to Pailin. From there, you can catch frequent shared taxis ($5 per person, 1½ hours) to scenic Battambang. After that, you can move on to Siem Reap by boat, or Phnom Penh by bus.

Ban Thai Sang Thain HOTEL $$
(☎08 1305 9408; www.bathaisangthain.com; Ao Thian; r 1000-2000B; ❄📶) Think of traditional Thai architecture with a tree-house twist and you'll sum up this family-run place, which offers rooms rather than bungalows. It's slap in the centre of the beach.

Vongdeuan Resort HOTEL $$$
(☎0 3864 4171; www.vongdeuan.com; Ao Wong Deuan; r 2500-4500B; ❄📶) This sprawling resort occupies much of the southern part of Ao Wong Deuan with its gardenlike setting. Popular with families and efficiently run, the smart bungalows come with the best bathrooms in this part of the world.

Ao Wai

Ao Wai is about 1km from Ao Thian but can be reached from Ban Phe by chartered speedboat.

Samet Ville Resort HOTEL $$$
(☎0 3865 1682; www.sametvilleresort.com; Ao Wai; r 1080-4500B; ❄📶) Under a forest canopy, it's a case of 'spot the sky' at the only resort at this secluded bay. It is an unpretentious place with a range of rooms and cottages that suit most budgets. Plus, the beach is great.

🍴 Eating

Most hotels and guesthouses have restaurants that moonlight as bars after sunset. The food and the service won't blow you away, but there aren't many alternatives. Nightly beach barbecues are an island favourite but pick one that looks professionally run and popular. There are cheapie Thai places in town.

Rabeang Baan THAI $
(Na Dan; dishes 70-120B; ⏲8am-10pm) Right by the ferry terminal, this spot has food so good you'll forget you have to leave the island. It's busier at lunch than dinner.

Jep's Restaurant INTERNATIONAL $
(Ao Hin Khok; mains 60-150B; ⏲7am-11pm) Canopied by the branches of an arching tree decorated with lights, this pretty place does a little of everything. It's right on the beach.

Red Ginger INTERNATIONAL-THAI $$
(Na dan; dishes 125-285B; ⏲11am-10pm) Small but select menu of the French-Canadian chef's favourite dishes at this atmospheric eatery in between the pier and Hat Saw Kaew. Good salads, great oven-baked ribs. There's Thai food, too.

Sea Breeze SEAFOOD $$
(Ao Phai; dishes 80-500B; ⏲11am-11pm) Appropriately named: you can dine on a wide range of seafood right on Ao Phai's pretty beach here. There's some Western food on the menu as well.

Ploy SEAFOOD $$
(Hat Sai Kaew; dishes 50-400B; ⏲11am-11pm) Long-established, massive operation that's packed most nights with Thais crunching crabs and lobster. Huge array of dishes and a humming bar too.

🍷 Drinking & Nightlife

On weekends, Ko Samet is a boisterous night-owl with provincial tour groups crooning away on karaoke machines or the young ones slurping down beer and buckets to a techno beat. The bar scene changes depending on who is around but there is usually a crowd on Hat Sai Khao, Ao Hin Khok, Ao Phai and Ao Wong Deuan.

Baywatch Bar BAR
(Ao Wong Deuan; beers from 80B) A good spot for after-dark beach-gazing, with a fun crowd and strong cocktails.

Naga Bar BAR
(Ao Hin Khok; beers from 70B) This busy beachfront bar comes with a *moo·ay tai* ring, although the days of drunk foreigners getting battered by the locals are long gone. Instead, you get DJs and lots of whisky and vodka/Red Bull buckets.

Ao Prao Resort BAR
(Ao Prao; drinks from 90B; 🛜) On the sunset-side of the island, there's a lovely sea-view restaurant perfect for a sundowner. You'll need private transport to reach it.

ⓘ Information

There are several ATMs on Ko Samet, including those near the Na Dan pier, Ao Wong Deuan and Ao Thian.

Ko Samet Health Centre (🗷 0 3861 1123; ⏰8.30am-9pm Mon-Fri, 8.30am-4.30pm Sat & Sun) On the main road between Na Dan and Hat Sai Kaew. On-call mobile numbers are posted for after-hours emergencies.

National Parks Main Office (btwn Na Dan & Hat Sai Kaew; ⏰sunrise-sunset) Has another office on Ao Wong Deuan.

Police Station (🗷1155) On the main road between Na Dan and Hat Sai Kaew. There's a substation on Ao Wong Deuan.

ⓘ Getting There & Away

Ko Samet is accessed via the mainland piers in Ban Phe. There are dozens of piers each used by different ferry companies, but they all charge the same fares (one way/return 70/100B, 40 minutes, hourly 8am to 5pm) and dock at Na Dan, the main pier on Ko Samet. The last boat back to the mainland leaves at 6pm.

If you're staying at Ao Wong Deuan or further south, catch a ferry from the mainland directly to the beach (one way/return 90/140B, one hour, three daily departures).

Speedboats charge 200B one way and will drop you at the beach of your choice, but they only leave when they have enough passengers.

ⓘ Getting Around

Ko Samet's small size makes it a great place to explore on foot. A network of dirt roads connects most of the western side of the island.

Green *sŏrng·tăa·ou* meet arriving boats at the pier and provide drop-offs at the various beaches (100B to 400B, depending on the beach). The same fares apply no matter how many people are on board.

You can rent motorcycles nearly everywhere along the northern half of the island. Expect to pay 300B per day. The dirt roads are rough and hazardous, and larger vehicles can leave behind blinding dust clouds. Test the brakes before you drive off and exercise caution.

Chanthaburi จันทบุรี
POP 99,819

Chanthaburi is proof that all that glitters is not gold. Here, gemstones do the sparkling, attracting international traders, including many South Asians, dealing in sapphires, rubies, emeralds, agate and jade. Thanks to the gem market and Chanthaburi's multicultural history (French, Vietnamese and Chinese), the so-called 'City of the Moon' is surprisingly diverse for a regional Thai town. It's well worth visiting for an appreciation of the economic and religious sanctuary Thailand has long provided in the region.

WORTH A TRIP

NATIONAL PARKS NEAR CHANTHABURI

Two small national parks are easily reached from Chanthaburi, and make good day trips. Both are malarial, so take the usual precautions.

Khao Khitchakut National Park (อุทยานแห่งชาติเขาคิชฌกูฏ; 🗷 0 3945 2074; admission 200B; ⏰6am-6pm) is 28km northeast of town. The cascade of **Nam Tok Krathing** is the main attraction; though it is only worth a visit just after the rainy season.

To get to Khao Khitchakut, take a *sŏrng·tăa·ou* from next to the post office, near the northern side of the market in Chanthaburi (35B, 45 minutes). The *sŏrng·tăa·ou* stops 1km from the park headquarters on Rte 3249, from which point you'll have to walk. Returning transport is scarce so expect to wait or hitch.

Nam Tok Phlio National Park (อุทยานแห่ง ชาติน้ำตกพลิ้ว; 🗷 0 3943 4528; admission 200B; ⏰8.30am-4.30pm), off Hwy 3, is 14km to the southeast of Chanthaburi and is much more popular. A pleasant, 1km nature trail loops around the waterfalls, which teem with soro brook carp. To get to the park, catch a *sŏrng·tăa·ou* from the northern side of the market in Chanthaburi to the park entrance (50B, 30 minutes). You'll get dropped off about 1km from the entrance.

Accommodation is available at both parks; book with the **park reservation system** (🗷 0 2562 0760; www.dnp.go.th).

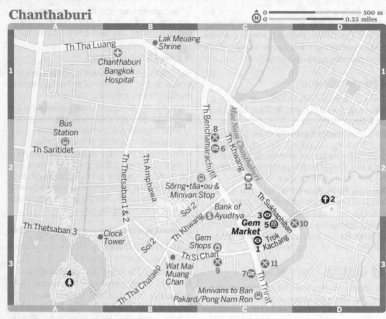

The old city (also known as the Chantaboon Waterfront Community) is the best place to chart the course of immigration and international involvement in the city. The Vietnamese began arriving in the 19th century when Christian refugees escaped religious and political persecution in Cochin China (southern Vietnam). A second wave of Vietnamese refugees followed in the 1920s and 1940s, fleeing French rule, and a third arrived after the 1975 communist takeover of southern Vietnam. The French occupied Chanthaburi from 1893 to 1905, a consequence of a dispute over the border between Siam and Indochina.

◉ Sights & Activities

★ Gem Market
MARKET

(ตลาดพลอย; Th Si Chan & Trok Kachang; ⊙ Fri, Sat & Sun) On weekends, the streets and side streets near Th Si Chan (or 'Gem Rd') overflow with the banter and intrigue of the hard sell. Incongruously humble considering the value of the commodities on offer, people cluster around makeshift tables or even a trader's outstretched palm, examining small piles of unset stones.

In the more formal shops, hard-eyed staff examine the gemstones under magnifying glasses looking for quality and authenticity.

Buying and selling gems here is not recommended for the uninitiated, but it is a fascinating glimpse at a relatively private trade.

In the hills surrounding Chanthaburi, several sapphire and ruby mines once supplied the palace with fine ornaments prior to the mid-19th century when the mines were developed into commercial operations by Shan (Burmese) traders. These days, locally mined gems are of inferior international quality but the resourceful Chanthaburi traders roam the globe acquiring precious and semi-precious stones, which are in turn traded here to other globetrotters.

The last remaining mine in the area is **Khao Phloi Waen**, 6km from town, which is famous locally for its 'Mekong Whiskey' yellow-coloured sapphire.

Chantaboon Waterfront Community
HISTORICAL SITE

(Th Sukhaphiban) Along the banks of Mae Nam Chanthaburi is a 1km stretch of old wooden houses that are valiantly being preserved. It makes for an atmospheric stroll with a typical Thai twist: food features more prominently than facts. Stop by the **Learning House** (☑ 08 1945 5761; ⊙ 9am-5pm), which displays historic photos, paintings and architectural drawings that reveal the community's history.

Of especial interest are the drawings of the homes' beautifully carved ventilation panels. Much of the community's immigrant past is revealed in these unique panels: there are carvings of Chinese characters and even French fleurs-de-lis.

Farmers and merchants first settled on the fertile river banks some 300 years ago, establishing the area as an agricultural trading post. Chinese traders and economic migrants sought refuge here, thus diversifying the local population. Vietnamese Catholics fled from religious persecution in their home country. And before long the different groups had intermarried until everyone claimed a little bit of each culture.

Today, the older generation remains in the rickety old houses but increasing numbers of domestic tourists are coming for weekend outings to eat Chinese, Thai and Vietnamese specialities and listen to all the old stories.

Cathedral CHURCH

(east bank of Mae Nam Chanthaburi; ⌚ daylight hours) This French-style cathedral, across a footbridge from Th Sukhaphiban, is the town's architectural highlight. A small missionary chapel was built here in 1711, when Vietnamese Catholics and a French priest arrived. The original has undergone four reconstructions between 1712 and 1906 and is now the largest building of its kind in Thailand.

Chanthaburi

Top Sights
1 Gem Market C3

Sights
2 Cathedral D2
3 Chantaboon Waterfront Community C2
4 King Taksin Park A3
5 Learning House C3

Sleeping
6 Kasemsarn Hotel C2
7 River Guest House C3

Eating
8 Chanthorn Phochana C2
9 Muslim Restaurant C3
10 Seafood Noodle Shop D3
11 Sony Yaday C3

Drinking & Nightlife
12 Sweet Moon C2

King Taksin Park PARK

(สวนสาธารณะสมเด็จพระเจ้าตากสิน; Th Tha Chalaep; ⌚ daylight hours) The town's main oasis is filled with picnicking families and joggers. It's a pleasant spot for an evening stroll.

Festivals

Fruit Festival FOOD

(⌚ May or Jun) At the end of May, or beginning of June, Chanthaburi's annual fruit

LIVING WITH HISTORY

Pratapan Chatmalai is the community leader of the Chantaboon Waterfront Community Association. She grew up here and fondly remembers Chantaboon's tight-knit community of culturally diverse people. Today, she works to save the stories and the character of this community in Chanthaburi.

What Does Your Organisation Do?

Now this community is a 'grandma' city. The old city is losing life and the young people have moved away. I want to keep the culture for the next generation to learn about and I'm trying to help the people in the area have a good life. We run the Learning House so that people can come look at the daily life of the past.

What Do You Recommend Tourists See or Do in the Old City?

There is unique history and lifestyle of the past here. Come look at the cathedral, Chinese shrines and old houses. Each house is different and mixes Thai, Chinese and Western styles. Eat at the local restaurants. There are seafood noodles, old-style ice cream and dim sum. If you get tired, you can have a massage in an old Thai-style house.

What Is Your Favourite Part of the Old City?

I love the whole place because it is a living museum and I can walk along and talk to the people about the past and make them happy.

As told to China Williams

festival is a great opportunity to sample the region's superb produce, especially rambutans, mangosteens and the ever-pungent durian.

Sleeping

Accommodation can get busy at weekends when the gem traders are in town.

River Guest House
HOTEL $

(☑ 0 3932 8211; 3/5-8 Th Si Chan; r 190-490B; ✴ @ 🛜) Lumpy beds, boxlike rooms and tiny bathrooms, but this is as good as it gets in the budget range. The relaxed outdoor terrace is a plus. Try to score a room away from the highway.

Kasemsarn Hotel
HOTEL $$

(☑ 0 3931 1100; www.hotelkasemsarn.com; 98/1 Th Benchamarachutit ; r 1300-4300B; ✴ @ 🛜) Good enough for visiting Bangkokians, Kasemsarn has modern rooms and friendly staff. Discounts of 30% are standard during the week.

Eating & Drinking

Seafood Noodle Shop
THAI $

(Th Sukhaphiban; dishes 50-70B; ⊘ 10.30am-9pm) The old city, along Mae Nam Chanthaburi, is where you'll find most sightseeing Thais eating this Chanthaburi variation of the basic rice-noodle theme; nearby are other homemade snacks.

Muslim Restaurant
MUSLIM-THAI $

(☑ 08 1353 5174; cnr Soi 4, Th Si Chan; dishes 40-200B; ⊘ 9.30am-9pm) Run by Thai Muslims, this place has excellent paratha, biryani, curries and chai tea. Most dishes are under 100B.

Sony Yaday
INDIAN $

(Th Si Chan; dishes 50-100B; ⊘ 8am-10pm; ☑) Hole-in-the-wall Muslim vegetarian restaurant patronised by visiting South Asian gem traders.

Chanthorn Phochana
THAI-CHINESE $$

(☑ 0 3931 2339; 102/5-8 Th Benchamarachutit; dishes 80-300B; ⊘ 8am-10pm) The Thai-Chinese menu includes such specialities as stir-fried papaya and mangosteen wine. The soft-shell crab with black pepper is delicious. Pick up a bag of local durian chips (tastier than you think) for your next bus ride.

Sweet Moon
CAFE

(Th Sukhaphibon; coffee from 35B; 🛜) Cool spot to sip a coffee or a fruit juice right by the river. Decent cakes, too.

ℹ Information

Banks with change facilities and ATMs can be found across town.

Bank of Ayudhya (Th Khwang)

Chanthaburi Bangkok Hospital (☑ 0 3935 1467; Th Tha Luang; ⊘ 6am-9pm) Part of the Bangkok group; handles emergencies.

ℹ Getting There & Around

Chanthaburi's bus station is west of the river. Minivans leave from near the market.

Motorbike taxis charge 20B to 30B for trips around town.

Trat
ตราด

POP 21,590

A major transit point for Ko Chang and coastal Cambodia, Trat's provincial charms are underappreciated. The guesthouse neighbourhood occupies an atmospheric wooden shophouse district, bisected by winding sois and filled with typical Thai street life: kids riding bikes, housewives running errands, small businesses selling trinkets and necessities. Since your destination is still far away, stay a little longer and enjoy all the things you can't get on the islands: fresh, affordable fruit, tasty noodles and tonnes of people-watching.

TRANSPORT TO/FROM CHANTHABURI

DESTINATION	BUS	MINIVAN
Bangkok Eastern (Ekamai) Bus Terminal	250B; 4hr; 25 daily	
Bangkok Northern (Mo Chit) Bus Terminal	214B; 4hr; 2 daily	
Khorat	292B; 4hr; hourly	
Rayong		100B; 2½hr; frequent
Sa Kaew	150B; 2hr; hourly	
Trat	74B; 1hr; every 30min	70B; 50min; frequent

Trat's signature product is a medicinal herbal oil (known in Thai as *nám·man lĕu·ang*), touted as a remedy for everything from arthritis to bug bites and available at local pharmacies. It's produced by resident Mae Ang-Ki (Somthawin Pasananon), using a secret pharmaceutical recipe that has been handed down through her Chinese-Thai family for generations. It's said that if you leave Trat without a couple of bottles of *nám·man lĕu·ang*, then you really haven't been here.

Sights

One booming business in the city is **swiftlet farming**. Walk down Th Lak Meuang and you'll soon figure out that the top floors of a shophouse have been purposefully converted into a nesting site for a flock of birds who produce the edible nests considered a delicacy among the Chinese. Swiflets' nests were quite rare (and expensive) because they were only harvested from precipitous sea caves by trained, daring climbers. But in the 1990s, entrepreneurs figured out how to replicate the cave atmosphere in multistorey shophouses and the business has become a key operation throughout Southeast Asia and here in Trat. Now many municipalities are dealing with the noise pollution of these moneymakers; have a listen for yourself.

Indoor Market MARKET

The indoor market sprawls east from Th Sukhumvit to Th Tat Mai and has a little bit of everything, especially all the things that you forgot to pack. Without really noticing the difference you will stumble upon the **day market**, selling fresh fruit, vegetables and takeaway food.

Sleeping

Trat has many budget hotels housed in traditional wooden houses on and around Th Thana Charoen.

Ban Jaidee Guest House GUESTHOUSE $

(08 3589 0839; banjaideehouse@yahoo.com; 6 Th Chaimongkol; r 200B;) In a charming neighbourhood, this relaxed traditional wooden house has simple rooms with shared bathrooms (hot-water showers). Paintings and objets d'art made by the artistically inclined owners decorate the common spaces. It's very popular and booking ahead is essential.

Trat Province

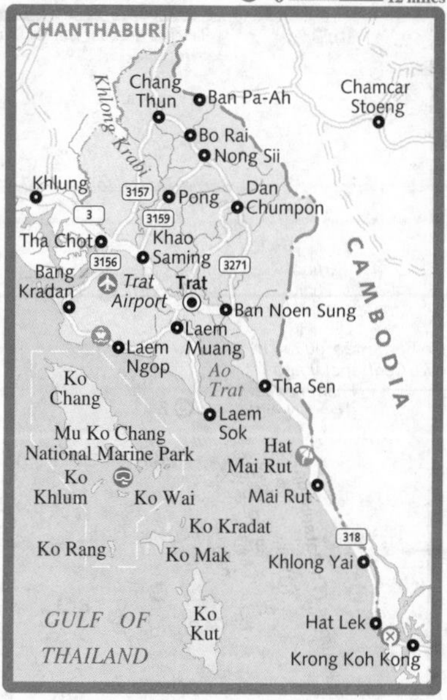

Pop Guest House GUESTHOUSE $

(0 3951 2392; 1/1 Th Thana Charoen; r 150-600B;) The owner isn't the most popular man in Trat, thanks to his aggressive touting for guests which puts some travellers off, but Pop is an efficient and expanding – if bland – operation. There are many rooms here, all well-maintained, and the restaurant is OK, too.

NP Guest House GUESTHOUSE $

(0 3951 2270; Soi Yai On; r 150-400;) Tucked down a quiet soi running between Th Lak Meuang and Th Thana Charoen, this newcomer offers simple rooms with a few nice, decorative touches. The cheapest rooms have shared bathrooms.

Orchid GUESTHOUSE $

(0 3953 0474; orchidguesthouse@gmail.com; 92 Th Lak Meuang; r 150-600B;) Big, slightly battered rooms in a house with a large garden. The cheapest rooms are fan-only and share bathrooms. The excessively laid-back owner sometimes opens her attached restaurant, which serves rather good pizzas.

Trat

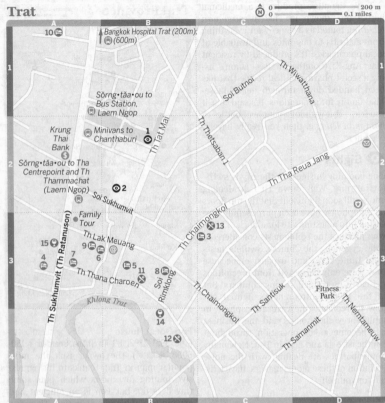

Trat

Sawadee GUESTHOUSE $
(☎0 3953 0063; sawadee_23000@hotmail.com; 94 Th Lak Meuang; r 100-300B; ☜) Located above an internet cafe in a converted shophouse, this simple family-run place has boxlike fan rooms with shared bathrooms.

Garden Guest House GUESTHOUSE $
(☎0 3952 1018; 87/1 Th Sukhumvit; r 150-350B) A cheerful grandmotherly type runs this guesthouse festooned with flowers and the flotsam of Thai life. Of the eight basic rooms, only one has a private bathroom.

Rimklong HOTEL $$
(☎0 3952 3388; soirimklong@hotmail.co.th; 194 Th Lak Meuang; r 800-900B; ❄☜) Trat's only boutique hotel occupies both ends of the soi. Rooms are bright and welcoming, if a little small. There's a pleasant, attached cafe.

Trat Center Hotel HOTEL $$
(☑ 0 3953 1234; www.tratcenterhotel.com; 45/65
Th Tasaban 5; r 900B; ☺❄☎) Spotless, mod-
ern rooms with comfy beds at this decent
mid-range option. It's a 10-minute walk
north of the day market.

✗ Eating & Drinking

Trat is all about market eating: head to the
day market on Th Tat Mai for *gah·faa bo-
hrahn* (ancient coffee), the indoor market
for lunchtime noodles, or the night market
for a stir-fried dinner. Food stalls line Th Su-
khumvit come nightfall.

★ Cool Corner Cafe INTERNATIONAL-THAI $
(☑ 08 4159 2030; 49-51 Th Thana Charoen; dishes
60-160B; ☺8am-10pm) Run by Khun Morn, a
modern Renaissance woman (writer, artist
and traveller) from Bangkok, Cool Corner is
an anchor for Trat's expats. The cafe has a
degree of sophistication that you don't usu-
ally find in provincial towns and serves up
a great mix of Thai and Western dishes with
an Indian influence, as well as beers, coffee
and lassies.

Story House INTERNATIONAL-THAI $
(61-65 Th Chaimongkol; dishes 50-150B; ☺9.30am-
9.30pm) Bright and cheerful restaurant serv-
ing up Thai and Western classics, as well
as sandwiches. It makes for a good coffee/
smoothie stop as well.

Pier 112 THAI $$
(132/1 Th Thana Charoen; dishes 80-250B;
☺10.30am-10.30pm; ☑) Large selection of

vegetarian dishes here, as well as reliable
curries, and you can eat outside in a plant-
festooned garden.

Cafe Oscar BAR
(Th Thana Charoen; beers from 55B; ☺9am-2am)
A very eclectic crew of locals and expats
gather at this cubbyhole corner bar, with
wooden furniture and a retro 1970s and '80s
soundtrack. In low season, it opens in the
evening only.

Gru BAR
(Th Sukhumvit; beers from 75B; ☺6pm-late) Key
local hang-out that sees few foreigners, with
live music most nights and football on the
TV at weekends.

ℹ Information

Th Sukhumvit runs through town, though it's
often referred to as Th Ratanuson.

Bangkok Hospital Trat (☑ 0 3953 2735;
www.bangkoktrathospital.com; 376 Moo 2, Th
Sukhumvit; ☺24hr) Best health care in the
region. It's 400m north of the town centre.

Krung Thai Bank (Th Sukhumvit) Has an ATM
and currency-exchange facilities.

Police Station (☑1155; cnr Th Santisuk & Th
Wiwatthana) A short walk from Trat's centre.

Post Office (Th Tha Reua Jang) East of Trat's
commercial centre.

Sawadee@Cafe Net (☑ 0 3952 0075; Th Lak
Meuang; per min 1B; ☺10am-10pm)

Trat Map (www.Tratmap.com) An online directory of businesses and attractions in Trat.

TRANSPORT TO/FROM TRAT

DESTINATION	BUS	MINIVAN	AIR
Bangkok Suvarnabhumi International Airport	272B; 5-6hr; 5 daily		from 2550B; 1hr; 3 daily
Bangkok Eastern (Ekamai) Bus Terminal	265B; 5hr; 17 daily		
Bangkok Northern (Mo Chit) Bus Terminal	272B; 5-6hr; 5 daily		
Chanthaburi	80B; 1hr; hourly 7.30am-11.30pm	70B; 50min; frequent 5am-7pm	
Hat Lek (for Cambodia)		120B; 1½hr; hourly 5am-6pm	
Pattaya	245B; 4hr; 1 daily	300B; 3½hr; hourly 7am-4pm	
Rayong/Ban Phe (for Ko Samet)		200B; 2½hr; hourly 5am-7pm	

WORTH A TRIP

SCRATCHING THE BEACH ITCH

If you're going through coastal withdrawal, the sliver of Trat Province that extends southeast towards Cambodia is fringed by sandy beaches. One of the easiest beaches to reach is **Hat Mai Rut**, roughly halfway between Trat and the border crossing of Hat Lek. Nearby is a traditional fishing village filled with colourful wooden boats and the sights and smells of a small-scale industry carried on by generations of families. **Mairood Resort** (⏺ 08 9841 4858; www.mairood-resort.com; Km 53; r from 1300B; ❄ @ ☎) is a lovely spot to stay overnight, with slick cottages by the sea and in the mangroves.

You can get to Hat Mai Rut from the Trat bus station via Hat Lek-bound *sŏrng·tǎa·ou*. The resort is 3km from the Km 53 highway marker.

ⓘ Getting There & Around

Trat's bus station is 2km out of town.

Minivans leave from various points along Th Sukhumvit. **Family Tour** (⏺ 08 1940 7380; Th Sukhumvit cnr Th Lak Meuang) has minivans to Bangkok's Victory Monument and northern (Mo Chit) bus terminal.

The three piers that handle boat traffic to Ko Chang, Ko Kut, Ko Mak and Ko Wai are located in Laem Ngop, about 30km southwest of Trat. For prices and departure times to the islands, see the section for each island.

Sŏrng·tǎa·ou to Laem Ngop (50B per person for six passengers, 200B for the whole vehicle, 35 to 50 minutes) leave from Th Sukhumvit just past the market.

Bangkok Airways (⏺ Trat airport 0 3955 1654/5, in Bangkok 0 2265 5555; www.bangkokair.com) operates flights from the airport, which is 40km from town. Taxis to Trat cost a ridiculous 600B.

Motorbike taxis charge 20B to 30B for local hops.

Motorbikes can be rented for 200B a day along Th Sukhumvit near the guesthouse area.

Ko Chang เกาะช้าง

POP 7033

With steep, jungle-covered peaks, picturesque Ko Chang (Elephant Island) retains its remote and rugged spirit despite its current status as a package-tour resort akin to Phuket. The island's swathes of sand are girl-next-door pretty but not beauty-queen gorgeous. What it lacks in sand, it makes up for in an unlikely combination: accessible wilderness with a thriving party scene. Convenient forays into a verdant jungle or underwater coral gardens can be enthusiastically toasted at one of Lonely Beach's many beer and bucket parties.

A little more than a decade ago, Ko Chang didn't have 24-hour electricity, was still considered malarial, had few paved roads and only a handful of motorised vehicles. Today, it is still a slog to get here, but there is a constant migration of visitors: Russian package tourists, Cambodia-bound backpackers and beach-hopping couples funnelling through to more remote islands in the Mu Ko Chang National Marine Park. Along the populous west coast are virtual mini-cities with a standard of living that has noticeably outpaced the island's infrastructure, a common problem on many Thai islands. Ko Chang struggles to provide decent sanitation and

---

KO CHANG IN...

Four Days

Lie on the beach, rotate your body and repeat, with occasional forays into the ocean. Do this until you get sunburned or bored and then rouse yourself out of your sun-induced stupor to explore the island. Do a **day hike** (p218) through the jungle or view the island from aboard a **kayak** (p217). Catch a *sŏrng·tǎa·ou* to **Ban Bang Bao** for lunch or an early dinner and work off your meal with some souvenir shopping. The next day rent a motorbike and explore the **east coast** (p217).

One Week

Migrate to the nearby islands of **Ko Wai** (p226) or **Ko Kut** (p228) for a little sightseeing, or devote a day or two giving back to the island by volunteering at **Koh Chang Animal Project**.

0 _____ 5 km
0 _____ 3 miles

Tha Thammachat
(Laem Ngop; 5.6km)
Tha Centrepoint
(Laem Ngop; 8km)
Laem Ngop
(10km)

Chang Noi Peninsula
Ao Khlong Son
Ban Khlong Son
Ao Sapparot
Tha Sapparot
Khlong Son Valley
Sai Thong
Ao Dan Kao
Ko Chang Hospital & Police Headquarters
Ban Kwan Chang
Nam Tok Chao Luang
Nam Tok Nonsi
Ban Dan Mai
Hat Sai Khao
(White Sand Beach)
Ko Chang International Clinic
National Park Headquarters
Hat Kai Mook
(Pearl Beach)
Khlong Prao
Nam Tok Khlong Plu
Khlong Mayom
Ban Than Mayom
Laem Chaichet
Nam Tok Than Mayom
Ao Khlong Prao
Ban Khlong Prao
Ao Nam Khun
GULF OF THAILAND
Khao Salak Phet
(744m)
Ao Salak Kok
Ban Salak Kok
Nam Tok Khiri Phet
Hat Kaibae
Lonely Beach
Bailan Bay
Ban Bailan
Ban Salak Phet
Ao Salak Phet
Ban Jekbae
Ruang Tan
Ko Maphrao Nai
Lookout Point
Ban Bang Bao
Ko Maphrao Nok
Laem Bang Bao
Ao Bang Bao
Hat Yao
(Long Beach)
Ko Wai (9km);
Ko Mak (18km); Ko Kut (32km)

KO CHANG & EASTERN SEABOARD KO CHANG

alternative means of transport to an ever-expanding nonresident population.

Sights

Although Thailand's second-largest island has accelerated into the modern world with some understandable growing pains, Ko Chang still has tropically hued seas, critter-filled jungles and a variety of water sports for athletic beach bums.

West Coast

The west coast has the island's widest and sandiest beaches and the greatest amount of development. Frequent public *sŏrng·tăa·ou* make beach-hopping easy and affordable. It is a good idea to bring swim shoes, especially for children, as many of the beaches are rocky in spots. These shallow, gentle seas are great for inexperienced swimmers, but be careful of riptides during storms and the rainy season (May to September).

Hat Sai Khao   BEACH

(หาดทรายขาว, White Sand Beach) The longest, most luxurious stretch of sand on the island is packed with package-tour hotels and serious sunbathers. Finding a towel's-worth of sand can be tough during the high season; try the more low-key backpacker area in the far northern section of the beach. Along the main road, the village is busy and brash – but comes with all the necessary amenities.

Hat Kai Mook   BEACH

(หาดไข่มุก, Pearl Beach) The pearls here are large pebbles that pack the shore and culminate in fish-friendly headlands. Swimming and sunbathing are out but there's good snorkelling.

GETTING TO CAMBODIA: HAT LEK TO KRONG KOH KONG

Getting to the border From Trat, the closest Thai–Cambodia crossing is from Hat Lek to the Cambodian town of Krong Koh Kong. Minivans run to Hat Lek hourly 5am to 6pm (120B, 1½ hours) from Trat's bus station.

At the border This is the most expensive place to cross into Cambodia from Thailand. Visas are a steep 1500B (they are US$20 at other crossings) and payment is only accepted in baht. You'll need a passport photo, too. Avoid anyone who says you require a 'medical certificate' or other paperwork. The border closes at 8pm.

Moving on Take a taxi (US$10) or moto (US$3) to Koh Kong where you can catch onward transport to Sihanoukville (four hours, one or two departures per day) and Phonm Penh (five hours, two or three departures until 11.30am).

Thai visas can be renewed here, but note that the visas issued at land borders have been shortened to 15 days.

Ao Khlong Prao
BEACH

(อ่าวคลองพร้าว) Khlong Prao's beach is a pretty sweep of sand pinned between hulking mountainous headlands and bisected by two estuaries. At low tide, beachcombers stroll the rippled sand eyeing the critters left naked by the receding water. Sprawling luxury resorts dominate here and the primary pasttime is sunbathing by the pool, as high tide gobbles up much of the beach.

With hired transport, you can head in to the interior of the island for some waterfall-spotting. The island's biggest is **Nam Tok Khlong Plu**, a three-tiered cascade with a swimmable pool. It is reached via a 600m jungle path and is most stunning just after the rainy season months. Best viewed in the morning before the crowds arrive.

Hat Kaibae
BEACH

(หาดไก่แบ้) A companion beach to Khlong Prao, Hat Kaibae is a good spot for families and thirty-something couples. A slim strip of sand unfurls around an island-dotted bay far enough removed from the package tour scene that you'll feel self-righteously independent. There's kayaking to the outlying island and low tide provides hours of beachcombing.

Lonely Beach
BEACH

There's nothing very lonely about this beach anymore, especially not in high season. Ko Chang's backpacker enclave is the most social place on the island come nightfall, when the music is loud, the drinks strong and the young crowd have shaken off the previous night's hangovers. The beach itself is a bit scruffy, but still a decent strip of sand.

Tree Top Adventure Park
PARK

(www.treetopadventurepark.com; Bailan Bay; admission 1100B; ⊙9am-5pm) Swing through the jungle like Tarzan, walk rope bridges, or ride the zip lines, flying skateboards and carpets at this popular attraction. Close to Bailan Bay, it's a three-hour adventure, and the price includes transport there and back. All tour agencies around Ko Chang can book it.

Ban Bang Bao
VILLAGE

(บ้านบางเบ้า) A former fishing community built in the traditional fashion of interconnected piers, the villagers of Bang Bao have swapped their nets for renting out portions of their homes to souvenir shops and restaurants. Most visitors come for the excellent seafood and a bit of shopping.

While Bang Bao isn't a very traditional experience, the commercialisation of Bang Bao has been done the Thai way. It's much like a mainland market, with every possible space dedicated to selling something. Follow the pier all the way to the end, though, and you'll find a big blue ocean and boats waiting to take you past the horizon. There are some fine places to stay here, but if you're heading back up the coast, finish your visit before sunset, as taxis become scarcer and more expensive after dark.

Hat Khlong Kloi
BEACH

At the eastern end of Ao Bang Bao, Khlong Kloi is a sandy beach that feels a lot like a secret though there are other people here and all the requisite amenities (beer, fruit, food, massage) and a few guesthouses if you want the place to yourself. You'll need private transport to get out here.

Northern Interior

Ko Chang's mountainous interior is mostly protected as a national park. The forest is lush and alive with wildlife and threaded by silvery waterfalls.

Ban Kwan Chang ELEPHANT CAMP
(บ้านควาญช้าง; ☎08 1919 3995; changtone@ yahoo.com; ☺8am-5pm) In a beautiful forested setting, this is the best of the three elephant camps on the island; deeper in the jungle and you get more time riding the beasts. Tours range from 1½ to three hours (500/900B) and involve feeding, bathing and riding a pachyderm. Transport to and from the camp is included in the price. Be sure to apply mozzie spray.

Pittaya Homkrailas is the camp owner, a well-regarded conservation enthusiast who works to preserve a humane relationship between the elephant and mahout. His interest in environmental and community issues also includes efforts to preserve the southeastern mangroves in Ao Salak Kok on the island's east coast.

East Coast

The east coast is still peaceful and undeveloped, mainly undulating hills of coconut and palm trees and low-key fishing villages that have resisted the resort rush of the west coast. You'll need private transport to explore this lost coast of scenic bays and mangrove forests.

Nam Tok Than Mayom WATERFALL
(น้ำตกธารมะยม; park fee 200B; ☺8am-5pm) A series of three falls along the stream of Khlong Mayom can be reached via the park office near Tha Than Mayom. The view from the top is superb and nearby there are inscribed stones bearing the initials of Rama V, Rama VI and Rama VII.

Ao Salak Kok MANGROVE BAY
(อ่าวสลักคอก) From a developers' perspective, this thick tangle of mangroves is an unprofitable wasteland. But the local population of fisherfolk recognises that its beauty and profit are in its environmental fertility. Mangroves are the ocean's nurseries, fostering the next generation of marine species, as well as resident birds and crustaceans, and this bay is now Ko Chang's prime ecotourism site.

Villagers, working in conjunction with Khun Pittaya, of Ban Kwan Chang elephant camp, operate an award-winning program to preserve the environment and the traditional way of life. They rent kayaks through the Salak Kok Kayak Station and run an affiliated restaurant.

Ban Salak Phet VILLAGE
(บ้านสลักเพชร) In the southeast pocket of the island is Ban Salak Phet, a surprisingly bustling community of fisherfolk and merchants plus lots of bike-riding kids and yawning dogs. This is what most of Ko Chang looked like less than a generation ago. Most visitors come for the seafood restaurants, or to cruise the lonely byways for a secluded beach.

Beyond the commercial heart of the village is **Ao Salak Phet**, a beautiful blue bay serenely guarded by humpbacked islands.

Nam Tok Khiri Phet WATERFALL
(น้ำตกคีรีเพชร) This small waterfall, 2km from Ban Salak Phet, is a 15-minute walk from the road and rewards you with a small, deep plunge pool. It's usually less crowded than many of the larger falls and is easily reached if you're in the neighbourhood of Ao Salak Phet.

🏃 Activities

Kayaking
Ko Chang cuts an impressive and heroic profile when viewed from the sea aboard a kayak. The water is generally calm and offshore islands provide a paddling destination that is closer than the horizon. Most hotels rent open-top kayaks (from 300B per day) that are convenient for near-shore outings and noncommittal kayakers.

KayakChang KAYAKING
(☎0 3955 2000; www.kayakchang.com; Amari Emerald Cove Resort, Khlong Prao) For more serious paddlers, KayakChang rents high-end, closed-top kayaks (from 1000B per day) that handle better and travel faster. They also lead one-day and multiday trips (from 2200B) to other islands in the archipelago.

Salak Kok Kayak Station KAYAKING
(☎08 1919 3995; kayak rentals per hr 100B) On the east side of the island, explore the mangrove swamps of Ao Salak Kok, while supporting an award-winning eco-tour program. Salak Kok Kayak Station rents self-guided kayaks and is a village-work project designed to promote tourism without affecting the traditional

way of life. They can also help arrange village homestays and hiking tours.

Hiking

Ko Chang is unusual for a Thai island in that is has a well-developed trekking scene. The island is blessed with lush forests filled with birds, monkeys, lizards and beautiful flowers. Best of all there are a handful of guides who know and love the forest and can speak English so that it can be shared with tourists.

Mr Tan from **Evolution Tour** (☑ 0 3955 7078; www.evolutiontour.com) or Lek from **Jungle Way** (☑ 08 9247 3161; www.jungleway.com) lead one-day treks (700B to 1400B) through Khlong Son Valley. The trip works up a sweat and then rewards with a waterfall swim and a stop at the Ban Kwan Chang elephant camp organisations. Multiday trips can be arranged through both. Mr Tan also has family-friendly treks and a hike that heads west from Khlong Son to Hat Sai Khao.

Koh Chang Trekking HIKING, BIRDWATCHING (☑ 08 1588 3324; www.kohchangtrekking.info) Bird-watchers should contact Koh Chang Trekking which runs one- and two-day trips (1200B to 1500B) into Mu Ko Chang National Marine Park and hikes to the top of Khao Chom Prasat, two nearby rocky tipped peaks. Prices are for a group of four people.

Salak Phet Kayak Station HIKING (☑ 08 7834 9489; from 1500B) Guides overnight treks on Khao Salak Phet, Ko Chang's highest peak, which rises 744m into the heavens and provides a sunrise and sunset view. This is one of the few places in Thailand where you can combine such serious exertion with a coastal landscape; you can choose to sleep in a tent or under the stars.

Volunteering

Koh Chang Animal Project VOLUNTEERING (☑ 08 9042 2347; www.kohchanganimalproject. org; Ban Khlong Son) Abused, injured or abandoned animals receive medical care and refuge at this nonprofit centre, established in 2002 by American Lisa McAlonie. The centre also works with local people on spaying, neutering and general veterinarian services, and Lisa is well-known to concerned pet owners and flea-ridden dogs on the island. Volunteers, especially travelling vets and vet nurses, are welcome to donate a bit of TLC and elbow grease for the cause. Call to make an appointment. Most *sŏrng·tăa·ou* drivers know how to get here; tell them you're going to 'Ban Lisa' (Lisa's House) in Khlong Son.

Massage

Sima Massage MASSAGE (☑ 08 1489 5171; main road, Khlong Prao; massage per hr 250B; ◷ 8am-10pm) Across from Tropicana Resort, and regarded by locals as the best massage on the island – quite an accolade in a place where a massage is easier to find than a 7-Eleven.

Bailan Herbal Sauna SAUNA (☑ 0 3955 8077; www.bailan-kohchang.com; Ban Bailan; sauna from 250B; ◷ 3-9pm) Sweating on purpose might seem like a free and unintended consequence of tropical living but, just south of Lonely Beach, Bailan continues an old-fashioned Southeast Asian tradition of the village sauna. Set amid lush greenery, the earthen huts are heated with a health-promoting stew of herbs. There's also massage, facial treatments and a post-steam juice bar.

🐾 Courses

Break up your lazy days with classes designed to enhance mind and body. Khlong Prao hosts a well-regarded culinary school. Classes are typically four to five hours, include a market tour and cost 1200B per person; book ahead.

Koh Chang Thai Cookery School COOKING (☑ 0 3955 7243; Blue Lagoon Bungalows, Khlong Prao) Slices, dices and sautées in a shady open-air kitchen beside the estuary.

ⓘ NATIONAL PARK STATUS

Some areas of Ko Chang are protected and maintained as part of the Mu Ko Chang National Marine Park. Conservation efforts are a bit haphazard, but you will be required to pay a 200B park entrance fee when visiting some of the waterfalls (entrance fees are stated in the reviews and payable at the site). **National Park headquarters** (☑ 0 3955 5080; Ban Than Mayom; ◷ 8am-5pm) is on the eastern side of the island near Nam Tok Than Mayom.

Be aware also that nudity and topless sunbathing are forbidden by law in Mu Ko Chang National Marine Park; this includes all beaches on Ko Chang, Ko Kut, Ko Mak and Ko Wai.

DIVING & SNORKELLING

The dive sites near Ko Chang offer a variety of coral, fish and beginner-friendly shallow waters on par with other Gulf of Thailand dive sites.

The seamounts off the southern tip of the island within the Mu Ko Chang National Marine Park are reached within a 30-minute cruise. Popular spots include **Hin Luk Bat** and **Hin Rap**, rocky, coral-encrusted seamounts with depths of around 18m to 20m. These are havens for schooling fish and some turtles.

By far the most pristine diving in the area is around **Ko Rang** (boat from Ko Chang), an uninhabited island protected from fishing by its marine park status. Visibility here is much better than near Ko Chang and averages between 10m and 20m. Everyone's favourite dive is **Hin Gadeng**, spectacular rock pinnacles with coral visible to around 28m. On the eastern side of Ko Rang, **Hin Kuak Maa** (also known as Three Finger Reef) is another top dive spot and is home to a coral-encrusted wall sloping from 2m to 14m and attracting swarms of marine life.

Ko Yak, **Ko Tong Lang** and **Ko Laun** are shallow dives perfect for both beginners and advanced divers. These small rocky islands can be circumnavigated and have lots of coral, schooling fish, puffer fish, morays, barracuda, rays and the occasional turtle.

About 7km offshore from Ban Bang Bao (p216) there's a popular dive to the wreck of the **HTMS Chang**, a 100m-long former Thai naval vessel which was purposely sunk in 2012 to form an artifical reef and now sits 30m beneath the surface.

Reef-fringed **Ko Wai** features a good variety of colourful hard and soft corals and is great for snorkelling. It is a popular day-tripping island but has simple overnight accommodation for more alone time with the reef.

The snorkelling on **Ko Mak** is not as good as elsewhere, but the island offers some decent dives even if the reefs don't see as many fish.

One-day diving trips typically start at 2500B. PADI Open Water certification costs 14,500B per person. Many dive shops remain open during the rainy season (June to September) but visibility and sea conditions are generally poor. The following are recommended dive operators:

➡ **BB Divers** (☎ 0 3955 8040; www.bbdivers.com) Based at Bang Bao with branches in Lonely Beach, Khlong Prao and Hat Sai Khao, as well as outposts on Ko Kut and Ko Wai (high season only).

➡ **Lonely Beach Divers** (☎ 08 0619 0704; www.lonelybeachdivers.com) Operating out of Lonely Beach, this place offers multilingual instructors.

➡ **Paradise Divers** (☎ 08 7144 5945) Branches on Ko Mak and Ko Kut.

🛏 Sleeping

Ko Chang's package-tour industry has distorted accommodation pricing. In general, rates have risen while quality has not, partly because hotels catering to group tours are guaranteed occupancy and don't have to maintain standards to woo repeat visitors or walk-ins. There is also a lot of copy-cat pricing giving value-oriented visitors little to choose from.

A few places close down during the wet season (April to October) and rates drop precipitously. Consider booking ahead and shopping for online discounts during peak season (November to March), weekends and holidays.

On the west coast, Lonely Beach is still the best budget option, Hat Kai Bae is the best-value option and Hat Sai Khao is the most overpriced; you will also find accommodation on the east coast at Ao Salak Kok and Ao Dan Kao.

🛏 Hat Sai Khao

The island's prettiest beach is also its most expensive. The northern and southern extremities have some budget and midrange options worth considering if you need proximity to the finest sand. There's a groovy backpacker enclave north of KC Grande Resort accessible only via the beach. There are more further north.

At the southern end, you can find some good-value budget and midrange places but this end of the beach is rocky and lacking sand during high tide.

If you want to splash out, don't do it on Hat Sai Khao where good money will be wasted.

Independent Bo's
GUESTHOUSE $

(✆08 5283 5581; Hat Sai Khao; r 400-850B; ❄ 🛜) Despite the eccentric Scottish owner (no reservations accepted here) this place on the jungle hillside exudes a creative, hippy-ish vibe that Ko Chang used to be famous for. Each bungalow is funky and different.

Starbeach Bungalows
GUESTHOUSE $

(✆09 2575 7238; Hat Sai Khao; bungalows 700B; 🛜) Ramshackle in appearance, the simple bungalows here wind up the hillside and are solid enough. You're very close to the prime part of the beach.

Arunee Resort
GUESTHOUSE $

(✆0 3955 1075; aruneeresorttour@hotmail.com; Hat Sai Khao; r 250-500B; 🛜) Digs don't come much cheaper than this anywhere on the island, and you're a 50m walk from the beach. But, the rooms are basic and cramped. Strong wi-fi signal, though.

Rock Sand Beach Resort
GUESTHOUSE $$

(✆08 4781 0550; www.rocksand-resort.com; r 550-3750B; ❄🛜) Touting itself as a flashpacker destination, this place isn't really a resort. But the sea-view rooms are decent and come wth shared balconies. Cheaper rooms are plainer. Be prepared to wade here when it's high tide.

Sai Khao Inn
GUESTHOUSE $$

(✆0 3955 1584; www.saikhaoinn.com; r 1200-1800B; ❄🛜) A garden setting on the interior side of the road and good value in the land of resorts, Sai Khao Inn has a little bit of everything – bungalows on stilts and more ordinary rooms. It's up an alley off the main road.

Koh Chang Hut Hotel
HOTEL $$

(✆08 9831 4851; www.kohchanghut.com; r 450-1800B; ❄🛜) At the southern end of the beach, this cliff-side hotel was being extensively refurbished at the time of writing. A pleasant, breezy spot, you're within walking distance of the beach without spending a lot of baht. The cheaper street-side rooms are noisier.

Palm Garden Hotel
HOTEL $$

(✆0 3955 1095; www.15palms.com; r 1200-1500B; ❄🛜) Across the road from the attached beachfront restaurant are plain-ish but clean midrange rooms very close to the most popular part of the beach. You have to use the wi-fi in the restaurant.

Keereeelé
HOTEL $$

(✆0 3955 1285; www.keereeele.com; r 2200-2600B; ❄🛜❄) An excess of 'e's in the name doesn't detract from the merits of this multistorey hotel on the interior side of the road. The rooms are modern and comfortable with beds raised off the floor Chinese-style. Some have views of the verdant mountains behind. The beach is 300m away.

🏖 Ao Khlong Prao

Ao Khlong Prao is dominated by high-end resorts, with just a few budget spots peppered in between. There are a handful of cheapies on the main road that are within walking distance to the beach, though traffic can be treacherous and noisy.

Tiger Huts
GUESTHOUSE $

(✆08 4109 9660; Ao Khlong Prao; r 300-600B) Basic wooden huts, rock-hard beds and cold-water showers, but this is the prettiest part of the beach. You'll need the attached restaurant; it's over 1km to the main road from here.

Blue Lagoon Bungalows
GUESTHOUSE $$

(✆0 3955 7243; www.kohchangbluelagoon.com; Ao Khlong Prao; r 650-1300B; ❄🛜) An exceedingly friendly garden spot with a range of bungalows to suit different budgets beside a peaceful estuary. A wooden walkway leads to the beach. All sorts of amenities, including yoga, cooking school, kids' playground and activities, are on offer, too.

Lin Bungalow
GUESTHOUSE $$

(✆08 4120 1483; lin.bungalow@gmail.com; r 1300B; ❄🛜) Ten sturdy and sizeable bungalows right on the beach. A good midrange choice.

Baan Rim Nam
GUESTHOUSE $$

(✆08 7005 8575; www.iamkohchang.com; r 1200-1600B; ❄🛜) Converted fisherman's-house-turned-guesthouse teeters over a mangrove-lined river; kayaks and dialled-in advice free of charge.

Sofia Resort
HOTEL $$

(✆08 1191 9205; www.jussinhotel.com; r 790-1190B; ❄🛜❄) Great price for the comfort factor, but not a lot of character to the rooms and the location is on the main road without direct beach access.

★ **Keereeta Resort**   GUESTHOUSE $$$
(⏻0 3955 1304; www.keereeta.com; r 3500B;
❄🛜) Only five very special rooms here; all
individually colour-themed, huge, secluded
and oh so stylish. Free kayaks for guests to
paddle to the beach or the restaurants op-
posite. Book ahead.

Aana   HOTEL $$$
(⏻0 3955 1137; www.aanaresort.com; r 3500-
6500B; ❄@🛜) Private villas perch prettily
above the forest and Khlong Prao, kayaking
distance from the beach. The cheaper rooms
are a little faded for the price.

🛏 Hat Kaibae

Hat Kaibae has some of the island's best
variety of accommodation, from boutique
hotels to budget huts and midrange bungalows. The trade-off is that the beach is only
sandy in parts.

Porn's Bungalows   GUESTHOUSE $
(⏻08 0613 9266; www.pornsbungalows-kohchang.
com; Hat Kaibae; r 550-1500B) Very chilled spot
at the far western end of the beach. All bungalows are fan-only. The 900B beachfront
bungalows are a great deal.

Buzza's Bungalows   GUESTHOUSE $
(⏻08 7823 6674; Hat Kaibae; r 400-450B; 🛜)
Simple fan-only bungalows with porches
that face each other, creating a laid-back
travellers ambience. However, this is the
rocky part of the beach.

KB Resort   HOTEL $$
(⏻0 3955 7125; www.kbresort.com; r 1250-5000B;
❄@🛜) Lemon-yellow bungalows have
cheery bathrooms and pose peacefully be-
side the sea. Listen to the gentle lapping
surf while the kids construct mega-cities in
the sand. The fan bungalows are overpriced.
Sleepy staff.

Kaibae Hut Resort   HOTEL $$
(⏻08 1862 8426; www.kaibaehutresort.com; r
700-2500B; ❄🛜) Sprawling across a scenic
stretch of beach, Kaibae Hut has a variety of
lodging options – slightly worn fan huts, fan-
cier concrete bungalows and modern hotel-
style rooms. A large open-air restaurant fires
up nightly barbecues and there's plenty of
room for free-ranging kids.

Garden Resort   HOTEL $$
(⏻0 3955 7260; www.gardenresortkohchang.
com; r 2200-2600B; ❄@🛜) On the interior
side of the main road, Garden Resort has
large and well-kept bungalows blossoming
in a shady garden with a salt-water swim-
ming pool. A sandy stretch of beach is 150m
away.

GajaPuri Resort & Spa   HOTEL $$$
(⏻0 3969 6918; www.gajapuri.com; r 4350-
19,000B; ❄🛜) Polished wooden cottages
gleam with quintessential Thai touches so
that you have a sense of place and pampering. Oversized beds with crisp linens, sun-
drenched reading decks and a pretty beach
are even more luxurious if you score an online discount.

🛏 Lonely Beach

A backpacker party fave, Lonely Beach is one
of the cheapest places to sleep on the island,
though oceanfront living has mostly moved
upmarket, pushing the penny-pinchers into
the interior village. If you've been flashpack-
erised, there are several creative midrangers
that will save you from carbon-copy resorts.
This end of the island is less developed and
the jungle broods just over the squatty commercial strip.

Little Eden   GUESTHOUSE $
(⏻08 4867 7459; www.littleedenkohchang.com;
Lonely Beach; r 600-1100B; ❄🛜) Fifteen bungalows here, all connected by an intricate
series of wooden walkways, and a decent
size with better bathrooms than the price
indicates. Pleasant communal area and staff.

Siam Hut   GUESTHOUSE $
(⏻0 3961 9012; Lonely Beach; r 480-680B; ❄🛜)
Raucous, a bit random and party central
for backpackers. This is the only budget option right on the sandy stretch of the beach.
Small-ish wooden huts, but then you won't
be spending much time in them.

Paradise Cottages   HOTEL $
(⏻08 1773 9337; www.paradisecottagekochang.
com; Lonely Beach; r 400-1000B; ❄🛜) Stylishly
minimalist rooms and a mellow atmosphere
with hammocks for guests to swing their
worries away. It's oceanfront, but the beach
is too rocky for swimming.

KLKL Hostel   GUESTHOUSE $
(⏻08 3088 3808; r 500-700B; ❄@🛜) Not a
true hostel – no dorms here. Instead, rather
pleasant blue-, green- and pink-themed
rooms at a reasonable price. Cheaper rooms
are fan only, but all have hot water.

Oasis Bungalows GUESTHOUSE $$
(☑ 08 1721 2547; www.oasis-kohchang.com; r 500-1300B; ❄ 🗢) Sitting up a steep hill that offers sea views, Oasis has roomy, midrange bungalows in a pretty fruit and flower garden. But even the cheaper, fan bungalows come with cute outdoor bathrooms. It's a fair walk to the beach from here.

Warapura Resort HOTEL $$
(☑ 0 3955 8123; www.warapuraresort.com; r 1400-3300B; ❄ @ 🗢 🛋) Chic for relatively cheap prices, Warapura has a collection of adorable cottages tucked in between the village and a mangrove beach. The oceanfront pool is perfect for people who would rather gaze at the ocean than frolic in it.

Lonely Beach Resort GUESTHOUSE $$
(☑ 08 1279 5120; www.lonelybeach.net; r 1300B; ❄ 🗢) The bungalows here slope downhill amid a leafy garden. They're plain but a good size and comfortable enough. The attached restaurant is a bizarre, albeit tasty, mix of Danish and Thai dishes.

🏠 Ban Bang Bao

Despite its touristy veneer, Ban Bang Bao is still a charming place to stay for folks who pre-

---

GETTING TO CAMBODIA: ARANYA PRATHET TO POIPET

Getting to the Border The easiest way to get from Bangkok to Siem Reap overland is the direct bus departing from the Northern (Mo Chit) Bus Terminal. The through-service bus trips sold on Th Khao San and elsewhere in Bangkok seem cheap and convenient, but they haven't been nicknamed 'scam buses' for nothing, and you will be most likely hassled and ripped off, often quite aggressively.

If you choose to do it in stages (much cheaper than the direct Mo Chit bus), you can get from Bangkok to the border town of Aranya Prathet (aka Aran) by bus from Mo Chit, by bus or minivan from the Eastern (Ekamai) Bus Terminal, by bus from Suvarnabhumi International Airport bus station, by minivan from Victory Monument or by 3rd-class train (only the 5.55am departure will get you there early enough to reach Siem Reap the same day) from Hualamphong. Aran also has bus service about every one or two hours from other cities in the area including Khorat, Surin and Chanthaburi. All minivans, plus some buses, go all the way to the Rong Kluea Market next to the border, so there's no need to stop in Aranya Prathet city. Otherwise, you'll need to take a *sŏrng·tăa·ou* (15B), motorcycle taxi (60B) or túk-túk (pronounced *dúk dúk;* 80B) the final 7km to the border.

At the Border The border is open 7am to 8pm daily. There are many persistent scammers on the Thai side trying to get you to buy your Cambodia visa through them, but no matter what they might tell you, there's absolutely no good reason to get visas anywhere except the border. Buying them elsewhere costs more and takes longer. Don't even show your passport to anyone before you reach Thai immigration and don't change money.

After getting stamped out of Thailand – an easy and completely straightforward process – follow the throng to Cambodian immigration and find the 'Visa on Arrival' sign if you don't already have a visa. Weekday mornings you might finish everything in 10 to 20 minutes, but if you arrive after midday it could take an hour or more. Weekends and holidays, when many Thais arrive to gamble and foreign workers do visa runs, are also very busy. You will probably be offered the opportunity to pay a special 'VIP fee' (aka a bribe) of 200B to jump to the front of the queue. You will almost certainly be asked to pay another small bribe, which will be called a 'stamping' or 'overtime' fee. You should refuse, though doing so might mean you have to wait a few extra minutes.

Moving On There are frequent buses and share taxis from Poipet to Siem Reap along a good sealed road from the main bus station, which is about 1km away (2000r by motorcycle taxi) around the main market, one block north of Canadia Bank off NH5. Poipet also has a second 'international' bus station 9km east of town where tickets cost double and which is only used by uninformed or gullible foreigners who get swept into the free shuttle that takes travellers out there. Lonely Planet's *Cambodia* guide has full details for travel on this side of the border.

fer scenery to swimming. Accommodation is mainly converted pier houses overlooking the sea with easy access to inter-island ferries. Daytime transport to a swimmable beach is regular thanks to the steady arrival and departure of day-trippers. Night owls should either hire a motorbike or stay elsewhere, as *sŏrng·tăa·ou* become rare and expensive after dinnertime.

Bang Bao Paradise GUESTHOUSE $
(☑08 8838 0040; r 500-700B; ✸) Six mini-huts perched over the water, all in bright, fresh colours and all sharing bathrooms.

Bang Bao Cliff Cottage GUESTHOUSE $
(☑08 5904 6706; www.cliff-cottage.com; r 400-1200B; ✸⊚) Partially hidden on a verdant hillside west of the pier are a few dozen simple thatch huts overlooking a rocky cove. Most have sea views and a couple offer spectacular vistas. The cheaper rooms share bathrooms.

★Koh Chang Sea Hut HOTEL $$
(☑08 1285 0570; www.kohchang-seahut.com; r 2500B; ✸⊚) With seven luxurious bungalows built on the edge of Bang Bao's pier, this is one of Ko Chang's most unusual places to stay, offering near panoramic views of the bay. Each bungalow is surrounded by a private deck where breakfast is served. There are five rooms here, too.

Buddha View GUESTHOUSE $$
(☑0 3955 8157; www.thebuddhaview.com; Ban Bang Bao; r 800-1200B; ⊜✸⊚) Swish pier guesthouse popular with Bangkok Thais. Only seven thoughtfully designed rooms, four of which come with private bathrooms. The restaurant is also excellent.

Nirvana HOTEL $$$
(☑0 3955 8061; www.nirvanakohchang.com; r 2500-8500B; ✸⊚⊠) Super-deluxe, Balinese-style bungalows hidden away on a rocky, jungle-filled peninsula. Come to get away from it all, including everything else on the island, and to enjoy the stunning sea views. The adjacent beach is scenic but not swimmable.

🛏 **Northern Interior & East Coast**

The northern and eastern part of the island is less developed than the west coast and much more isolated. You'll need your own transport and maybe even a posse not to feel lonely out here, but you'll be rewarded with a quieter, calmer experience.

Jungle Way GUESTHOUSE $
(☑08 9247 3161; www.jungleway.com; Khlong Son Valley; r 300-500B) Ko Chang's un-sung attribute is its jungle interior and the English-speaking guides who grew up playing in it. Lek, a local guide, and his family run this friendly guesthouse, deep in the woods and beside a babbling brook. Bungalows are simple but adequate and the on-site restaurant will keep you well fed. Free pier pick-up.

Souk GUESTHOUSE $$
(☑08 1553 3194; www.thesoukkohchang.com; Ao Dan Kao; r 700B; ✸⊚⊚) This cool spot has seven pop-art bungalows at a pleasant price. There are lots of chill-out spaces and an open-deck restaurant and cocktail bar, just in front of the red-sand beach. There's good snorkelling 150m offshore and free kayaks.

Amber Sands HOTEL $$
(☑0 3958 6177; www.ambersandsbeachresort.com; Ao Dan Kao; r 1800-4250B; ✸⊚⊚⊠) Sandwiched between mangroves and a quiet red-sand beach, Amber Sands has smart bungalows and great sea views. The location feels a world away but it is only 15 minutes from the pier. Closes low season.

Spa Koh Chang Resort HOTEL $$$
(☑0 3955 3091; www.thespakohchang.com; Ao Salak Kok; r 3178-4060B; ✸⊚⊠) In a lush garden setting embraced by the bay's mangrove forests, this spa resort specialises in all the popular health treatments (yoga, meditation, fasting etc) that burned-out professionals need. Elegantly decorated bungalows scramble up a flower-filled hillside providing a peaceful getaway for some quality 'me' time. No beach access.

🍴 **Eating & Drinking**

Virtually all of the island's accommodation has attached restaurants with adequate but not outstanding fare. Parties abound on the beaches and range from the older, more restrained scene on Hat Sai Khao, to the younger and sloppier fiestas on Lonely Beach.

🍴 **West Coast**

Porn's Bungalows Restaurant THAI $
(Hat Kaibae; dishes 80-180B; ⊙11am-11pm) This laid-back, dark-wood restaurant is the quintessential beachside lounge. Great barbecue. Feel free to have your drinks out-size your meal and don't worry about dressing for dinner.

Nid's Kitchen
THAI $

(nidkitchen@hotmail.com; Hat Kaibae; dishes 50-150B; ⊕6pm-midnight) Nid's does all the Thai standards like a wok wizard in a hut festooned with rasta imagery. Equally fine for a drink or three.

Baan Mai
THAI $

(dishes 50-160B; ⊕9am-11pm) Extensive Thai menu, with a vague Chinese influence, at this two-floor converted house that sits in a strategic spot on the main road through Lonely Beach.

Magic Garden
THAI $

(✑0 3955 8027; Lonely Beach; dishes 60-220B; ⊕11am-late) Still a popular Lonely Beach hangout, but better for a drink than a meal. The menu covers Thai and Western standards.

★ Norng Bua
THAI $$

(Hat Sai Khao; dishes 40-300B; ⊕8am-11pm) Once a stir-fry hut, now a fully fledged restaurant that makes everything fast and fresh and with chillies and fish sauce (praise the culinary gods). Always crowded with visiting Thais, a good sign indeed.

★ Phu-Talay
SEAFOOD $$

(Khlong Prao; 100-320B; ⊕10am-10pm) Cute, homey feel at this wooden-floored, blue and white decorated place perched over the lagoon. Sensible menu of Ko Chang classics (lots of fish) and far more reasonably priced than many other seafood places.

Oodie's Place
INTERNATIONAL-THAI $$

(✑0 3955 1193; Hat Sai Khao; dishes 80-390B; ⊕11am-midnight) Local musician Oodie runs a nicely diverse operation with excellent French food, tasty Thai specialities and live music from 10pm. After all these years, it is still beloved by expats.

Ruan Thai
SEAFOOD $$

(Ban Bang Bao; dishes 80-400B; ⊕9.30am-10pm) It's about as fresh as it gets (note your future dinner greeting you in tanks as you enter) and the portions are large. The doting service is beyond excellent – they'll even help you crack your crabs.

Ton Sai
THAI $$

(Khlong Prao; dishes 80-350B; ⊕11am-10pm) A favourite of locals, visiting Thais and foreigners, paintings adorn this hut of a restaurant. A mix of well-prepared, creative Thai and Western dishes are on the menu. Closed low season.

Saffron on the Sea
THAI $$

(✑0 3955 1253; Hat Kai Mook; dishes 120-350B; ⊕8am-10pm; 🕾) Owned by an arty escapee from Bangkok, this friendly boutique hotel has a generous portion of oceanfront dining and a relaxed, romantic atmosphere. All the Thai dishes are prepared in the island style, more sweet than spicy.

Iyara Seafood
SEAFOOD $$

(✑0 3955 1353; Khlong Prao; dishes 180-1250B; ⊕11am-10pm) Iyara isn't your standard island seafood warehouse: after dining in the lovely bamboo pavilion, guests are invited to kayak along the nearby estuary.

Chowlay
SEAFOOD $$

(Ban Bang Bao; dishes 100-450B; ⊕10am-10pm) Fine bay views at this pier restaurant and enough fresh fish to start your own aquarium.

Kaotha
INTERNATIONAL-THAI $$

(Lonely Beach; dishes 50-300B; ⊕9am-midnight; 🕾) One of the hot spots on the Lonely Beach dining scene, with an excellent selection of pizzas and nice and spicy Thai dishes, this airy venue is a popular hang-out for coffee, too. There's live music on Saturdays.

KaTi Culinary
THAI $$

(✑08 1903 0408; Khlong Prao; dishes 120-550B; ⊕11am-10pm) Seafood, and a few Isan dishes and their famous, homemade curry sauce. The menu features creative smoothies, such as lychee, lemon and peppermint, and there's a kid's menu as well.

Invito Al Cibo
ITALIAN $$$

(✑0 3955 1326; Koh Chang Hut, Hat Sai Khao; dishes 190-609B; ⊕11am-11pm) Popular with *fa•ràng* visitors who come for the top pizzas, homemade pasta and stunning sea views.

✖ Northern Interior & East Coast

Blues Blues Restaurant
THAI $

(✑08 5839 3524; Ban Khlong Son; dishes 40-150B; ⊕10am-9pm) Through the green screen of tropical plants is an arty stir-fry hut that is beloved for expertise, efficiency and economy. The owner's delicate watercolour paintings are on display too. Take the road to Ban Kwan Chang and it's 600m ahead on the right.

Jungle Way Restaurant
THAI $

(✑08 9247 3161; Ban Khlong Son; dishes 70-120B; ⊕8am-9pm; ✑) Enjoy the natural setting and home-style cooking of this guesthouse restaurant. Meal preparation takes a leisurely pace so climb up to the elevated wildlife-viewing platform to spot some jungle creatures while the wok is sizzling.

Paradise Behind the Sea
Restaurant
THAI $$

(📞08 1900 2388; Ban Hat Sai Daeng; dishes 120-320B; ⏰10am-10pm) If you're cruising the east coast for scenery, stop in for a view and a meal at this cliff-side restaurant. Vietnamese and Thai dishes crowd the tables and cool breezes provide refreshment. In Thai, it's called 'Lang Talay'.

❶ Information

DANGERS & ANNOYANCES

It is not recommended to drive between Ban Khlong Son south to Hat Sai Khao, as the road is steep and treacherous with several hairpin turns. There are mud slides and poor conditions during storms. If you do rent a motorbike, stick to the west coast beaches and take care when travelling between Hat Kaibae and Lonely Beach. Wear protective clothing when riding or driving a motorcycle.

The police conduct regular drug raids on the island's accommodation. If you get caught with narcotics, you could face heavy fines or imprisonment.

Be aware of the cheap minibus tickets from Siem Reap to Ko Chang; these usually involve some sort of time- and money-wasting commission scam.

Ko Chang is considered a low-risk malarial zone, meaning that liberal use of mosquito repellent is probably an adequate precaution.

EMERGENCY

Police Station (📞0 3958 6191; Ban Dan Mai)

Tourist Police Office (📞1155) Based north of Ban Khlong Prao. Also has smaller police boxes in Hat Sai Khao and Hat Kaibae.

MEDICAL SERVICES

Bang Bao Health Centre (📞0 3955 8088; Ban Bang Bao; ⏰8.30am-6pm) For the basics.

Ko Chang Hospital (📞0 3952 1657; Ban Dan Mai) Public hospital with a good reputation and affordably priced care; south of the ferry terminal.

Ko Chang International Clinic (📞0 3955 1151; Hat Sai Khao; ⏰24hr) Related to the Bangkok Hospital Group; accepts most health insurances and has expensive rates.

MONEY

There are banks with ATMs and exchange facilities along all the west coast beaches.

POST

Ko Chang Post Office (📞0 3955 1240; Hat Sai Khao) At the far southern end of Hat Sai Khao.

TOURIST INFORMATION

The free magazine **Koh Chang Guide** (www.koh-chang-guide.com) is widely available on the island and has handy beach maps.

The comprehensive website **I Am Koh Chang** (www.iamkohchang.com) is a labour of love by an irreverent Brit living on the island. It's jam-packed with opinion and information.

❶ Getting There & Away

Whether originating from Bangkok or Cambodia, it is an all-day haul to reach Ko Chang.

Ferries from the mainland leave from either Tha Thammachat, operated by **Koh Chang Ferry** (📞0 3955 5188), or Tha Centrepoint (Laem Ngop) with **Centrepoint Ferry** (📞0 3953 8196). Boats from Tha Thammachat arrive at Tha Sapparot; Centrepoint ferries at a pier down the road.

The inter-island ferry **Bang Bao Boats** (www.bangbaoboat.com) connects Ko Chang with Ko Mak, Ko Kut and Ko Wai during the high season. The boats leave from Bang Bao in the southwest of the island.

TRANSPORT TO/FROM KO CHANG

ORIGIN	DESTINATION	BOAT	BUS
Bangkok Eastern (Ekamai) Bus Terminal	Tha Thammachat		275B; 7hr; 3 daily
Ko Chang	Ko Kut	900B; 5hr; 1 daily	
Ko Chang	Ko Mak	550B; 2hr; 1 daily	
Ko Chang	Ko Wai	300B; 1hr; 1 daily	
Ko Chang	Bangkok Airport		550B; 6-7hr; 3 daily
Tha Centrepoint	Ko Chang	80B; 45min; hourly 6.30am-7pm	
Tha Thammachat	Ko Chang	80B; 30min; every 30min 6.30am-7pm	

Speedboats travel between the islands during high season.

It's possible to go direct to and from Ko Chang from both Bangkok's Eastern (Ekamai) bus terminal and Bangkok's Suvarnabhumi International Airport, via Chanthaburi and Trat.

ⓘ Getting Around

Shared *sŏrng·tăa·ou* meet arriving boats to shuttle passengers to the various beaches (Hat Sai Khao 100B, Khlong Prao 150B and Lonely Beach 200B). Hops between neighbouring beaches range from 50B to 200B but prices rise dramatically after dark, when it can cost 500B to travel to Bang Bao to Hat Sai Khao.

Motorbikes can be hired from 200B per day. Ko Chang's hilly and winding roads are quite dangerous; make sure the bike is in good working order. Remember that if you crash, you'll be paying for the bike repairs as well as your medical bills.

Ko Wai   เกาะหวาย

Stunning Ko Wai is teensy and primitive, but endowed with gin-clear waters, excellent coral reefs for snorkelling and a handsome view across to Ko Chang. Expect to share the bulk of your afternoons with day-trippers but have the remainder of your time in peace.

Most bungalows close during the May-to-September low season when seas are rough and flooding is common.

🛏 Sleeping

Good Feeling   GUESTHOUSE $
(☑ 08 1850 3410; r 400-500B) Twelve wooden bungalows, all but one with private bathroom, spread out along a rocky headland interspersed with private, sandy coves.

Ko Wai Paradise   GUESTHOUSE $
(☑ 08 1762 2548; r 300-500B) Simple wooden bungalows (with shared bathrooms and no electricity) on a postcard-perfect beach. You'll share the coral out front with day-trippers.

Grandma Hut   GUESTHOUSE $
(☑ 08 1841 3011; r 350-500B) On the rocky northeastern tip of the island is this basic and remote place; speedboat operators know it by the nearby bay of Ao Yai Ma.

Ko Wai Pakarang   GUESTHOUSE $$
(☑ 08 4113 8946; www.kohwaipakarang.com; r 600-2200B; ❋ @ 🛜) Wooden and concrete bungalows, the cheaper ones fan-only, an OK attached restaurant and helpful, English-speaking staff.

Koh Wai Beach Resort   HOTEL $$$
(☑ 08 1306 4053; www.kohwaibeachresort.com; r 2100-5400B; ❋ 🛜) Upscale collection of spacious bungalows with all mod cons just a few steps from the beach and on the southern side of the island.

ⓘ Getting There & Around

Boats will drop you off at the nearest pier to your guesthouse; otherwise you'll have to walk 15 to 30 minutes along a narrow forest trail.

Bang Bao Boat (www.bangbaoboat.com) is the archipelago's inter-island ferry running a daily loop from Ko Chang to Ko Kut. Boats depart Ko Chang at 9am and arrive at Ko Wai (one way 300B, one hour) and continue on to Ko Mak (one way 400B, one hour) and Ko Kut (700B, three hours).

During high season, speedboats run from Ko Wai to the following destinations:

Ko Mak   เกาะหมาก

Little Ko Mak measures only 16 sq km and doesn't have speeding traffic, wall-to-wall development, noisy beer bars or crowded beaches. The palm-fringed bays are bathed by gently lapping water and there's a relaxed vibe. But Ko Mak is not destined for island super-stardom: the interior is a utilitarian landscape of coconut and rubber plantations and reports of sand flies make visitors a little nervous. The vast majority of tourists are Scandinavian and German families, but a growing number of independent travellers congregate here, too.

Visiting the island is easier in the high season; during the low season (May to September) many boats stop running and bungalow operations wind down. Storms

SPEEDBOAT TRANSPORT FROM KO WAI

DESTINATION	PRICE	DURATION	FREQUENCY
Ko Chang	one way 400B	15min	2 daily
Ko Kut	one way 800B	1hr	2 daily
Ko Mak	one way 450B	30min	2 daily
Laem Ngop	450B	2-3hr	1 daily

also deposit uninvited litter on the exposed southern beaches.

◉ Sights & Activities

The best beach on the island is **Ao Pra** in the west, but it's completely undeveloped and hard to reach. For now, swimming and beach strolling are best on the northwestern bay of **Ao Suan Yai**, which is a wide arc of sand and looking-glass-clear water that gets fewer sand flies than the beaches on the southern side of the island. It is easily accessible by bicycle or motorbike if you stay elsewhere.

Offshore is **Ko Kham**, a private island that was sold in 2008 for a reported 200 million baht. It used to be a popular day-trippers' beach but is currently being developed into a superluxury resort.

Koh Mak Divers   DIVING
(☑ 08 3297 7724; www.kohmakdivers.com; dive trips from 2400B) Koh Mak Divers runs dive trips to the Mu Ko Chang National Marine Park, about 45 minutes away.

🛏 Sleeping & Eating

Most budget guesthouses are on Ao Khao, a decent strip of sand on the southwestern side of the island, while the resorts sprawl on the more scenic northwestern bay of Ao Suan Yai.

There are a handful of family-run restaurants on the main road between Monkey Island and Makathanee Resort. And if you feel like a journey, use a meal or a sundowner as an excuse to explore different bays.

Koh Mak Cottage   GUESTHOUSE $
(☑ 08 1910 2723; Ao Khao; r 400-500B; @) Eighteen small and rustic bungalows. No frills, but you're right on the beach.

Monkey Island   GUESTHOUSE $$
(☑ 08 5389 0949; www.monkeyislandkohmak.com; Ao Khao; r 350-2000B; ✳@🛜) The troop leader of guesthouses, Monkey Island has earthen or wooden bungalows in three creatively named models – Baboon, Chimpanzee and Gorilla – with various amenities (shared or private

bathroom or private deck). All have fun design touches and the hip restaurant does respectable Thai cuisine in a leisurely fashion. In true Thai beach style, the affiliated bar rouses the dead with its nightly parties.

Bann Chailay   GUESTHOUSE $$
(☑ 08 0101 4763; Ao Khao; r 800-1600B; ✳🛜) A cross between a homestay and a guesthouse, you can stay in bungalows on the beach, or rooms in the family house at this friendly place at the eastern, less busy, end of Ao Khao. Fine for barbecues on the beach, too.

Makathanee Resort   HOTEL $$
(☑ 08 7600 00374; www.makathanee.com; Ao Khao; r 1500-5200B; ✳🛜) Floor-to-ceiling windows are open to sea views in these plush bungalows, which have deliciously soft mattresses and lots of breathing room. Behind them are rooms in a hotel block, some of which offer sea views. Kayaks for rent (400B per day) and professional service.

Baan Koh Mak   GUESTHOUSE $$
(☑ 08 9895 7592; www.baan-koh-mak.com; Ao Khao; r 1000-1900B; ✳🛜) Bright and funky, Baan Koh Mak provides a respectable flashpacker abode with colourful paint jobs and soft mattresses.

Ao Kao Resort   GUESTHOUSE $$
(☑ 08 3152 6564; www.aokaoresort.com; Ao Khao; r 2500-3000B; ✳🛜) In a pretty crook of the bay, Ao Kao has an assortment of stylish bungalows. Opt for a traditional Thai-style house complete with carved wood flourishes and handsome balconies. Families congregate here as there is front-yard swimming and the rocky headland harbours sea creatures.

Lazy Day Resort   GUESTHOUSE $$
(☑ 08 1882 4002; www.kohmaklazyday.com; r 2250-2700B; ✳🛜) This professionally run operation has big bungalows stationed around an attractive garden; rates include breakfast.

Koh Mak Resort   HOTEL $$$
(☑ 0 3950 1013; www.kohmakresort.com; Ao Suan Yai; r 2800-6800B; ✳🛜🏊) A self-contained resort, with restaurants, a direct speedboat to and

SPEEDBOAT TRANSPORT FROM KO MAK

DESTINATION	PRICE	DURATION	FREQUENCY
Ko Chang	one way 600B	45min	3 daily
Ko Kut	one way 500B	45min	2 daily
Ko Wai	one way 400B	30min	2 daily
Laem Ngop (mainland pier)	one way 500B	1hr	4 daily

from the mainland (450B), and an amenable bar. The best bungalows come with Jacuzzis and they line a stretch of pretty beach.

ℹ Information

There are no banks or ATMs on the island, so stock up on cash before visiting.

Ball's Cafe (☑08 1925 6591; Ao Nid Pier; ☺9am-6pm) Has internet access, travel agent and coffee shop. Khun Ball is an active island promoter and runs www.kohmak.com as well as environmental initiatives.

Ko Mak Health Centre (☑08 9403 5986; ☺8.30am-4.30pm) Can handle basic first-aid emergencies and illnesses. It's on the cross-island road near Ao Nid Pier.

Police (☑0 3952 5741) Near the health centre.

ℹ Getting There & Around

Speedboats (450B one way, 50 minutes) arrive at the pier on Ao Suan Yai or at Makathanee Resort on Ao Khao.

A fast speedboat instead of a ferry now runs to Ao Nid (450B one way, four daily, 50 minutes), the main port on the eastern side of the island. There are only two boats daily in low season. Guesthouses and hotels pick people up free of charge.

Bang Bao Boat (www.bangbaoboat.com) is the archipelago's inter-island ferry running a daily loop from Ko Chang to Ko Kut. Boats depart Ko Chang at 9am and arrive at Ko Mak (one way 400B, 1½ to two hours) and continue on to Ko Kut (one way 300B, one to two hours, departs 1pm). In the opposite direction, you can catch it to Ko Wai (one way 300B, 45 minutes) and Ko Chang (400B, 2½ hours).

In high season, speedboats run from Ko Mak to various destinations. Once on the island, you can pedal (40B per hour) or motorbike (200B per day) your way around.

Ko Kut   เกาะกูด

All the paradise descriptions apply to Ko Kut: the beaches are graceful arcs of sand, the water clear, coconut palms outnumber buildings, and a secluded, unhurried atmosphere embraces you upon arrival. Far less busy than Ko Chang, there's nothing in the form of nightlife, or even dining really, but those are the reasons for visiting.

Half as big as Ko Chang and the fourth-largest island in Thailand, Ko Kut (also known as Koh Kood) has long been the domain of package-tour resorts and a seclusion-seeking elite. But the island is becoming more egalitarian and independent travellers, especially families and couples, will find home sweet home here.

◉ Sights & Activities

Beaches   BEACHES
White sand beaches with gorgeous aquamarine water are strewn along the western side of the island. Hat Khlong Chao is the island's best and could easily compete with Samui's Hat Chaweng in a beach beauty contest. Ao Noi is a pretty boulder-strewn beach with a steep drop-off and steady waves for strong swimmers. Ao Prao is another lovely sweep of sand.

There is no public transport on Ko Kut but you can rent motorbikes for exploring the west coast beaches. Traffic is minimal and the road is mostly paved from Khlong Hin in the southwest to Ao Noi in the northeast.

With its quiet rocky coves and mangrove estuaries, Ko Kut is great for snorkelling and kayaking. Most resorts have equipment on offer.

Nam Tok Khlong Chao   WATERFALL
Two waterfalls on the island make good short hiking destinations. The larger and more popular Nam Tok Khlong Chao is wide and pretty with a massive plunge pool. It's a quick jungle walk to the base, or you can kayak up Khlong Chao. Further north is Nam Tok Khlong Yai Ki, which is smaller but also has a large pool to cool off in.

🛏 Sleeping & Eating

During low season (May to September) many boats stop running and bungalow operations wind down. On weekends and holidays during the high season, vacationing Thais fill the resorts. Call ahead during busy periods so you can be dropped off at the appropriate pier by the speedboat operators.

You can scrimp your way into the neighbourhood of beautiful Hat Khlong Chao by staying at one of the village guesthouses, which are a five- to 15-minute walk to the beach. Families might like the midrange and budget options on Ao Ngam Kho, which has a small sandy section in the far northern corner of the bay, though the rest is an old coral reef and very rocky. Bring swim shoes.

Ao Ngam Khao is also a popular spot for independent travellers, thanks to its good choice of accommodation options.

If you're itching to splurge, Ko Kut is the place to do it.

Cozy House   GUESTHOUSE $
(☑08 5101 4838; www.kohkoodcozy.com; Khlong Yai; r 250-600B; ❄ ☎) The go-to place for back-

packers, Cozy is just a 10-minute walk from delightful Hat Khlong Yai. There are cheap and cheerful rooms with shared bathrooms, or more comfortable wooden bungalows.

Koh Kood Ngamkho Resort   GUESTHOUSE $
(☑ 08 1825 7076; www.kohkood-ngamkho.com; Ao Ngam Kho; r 750B; @ 🛜) One the best budget options around. Agreeably rustic huts perch on a forested hillside over a reasonable beach. Some are bigger than others. They rent kayaks (250B per day) and the restaurant is fabulous.

Happy Days Guesthouse   GUESTHOUSE $
(☑ 08 7144 5945; www.kohkood-happydays.com; r 450-750B; ❄ 🛜) Laidback joint halfway between Hat Khlong Yao and Ao Ngam Khao. Rooms are spread over two floors, there are hammocks to swing in, lots of dogs and a couple of resident monkeys.

Koh Kood Boutique House   HOTEL $$
(☑ 08 4524 4321; www.kohkoodboutiquehouse. com; Ao Prao; r 1200-2800B; ❄ 🛜) Almost at the southernmost point of the island is this secluded, very peaceful hotel that was converted from two traditional houses on stilts. Reservations are required.

Dusita   HOTEL $$
(☑ 08 1707 4546; Ao Ngam Kho; r 1290-2190B; ❄) Justifiably popular with families, whose kids can run wild in the huge oceanfront garden. For everyone else, solid well-spaced-out bungalows provide a perfect retreat from the real world. Closed low season.

Siam Beach   GUESTHOUSE $$
(☑ 08 4332 0788; www.siambeachkohkood.net; Ao Bang Bao; r 1400-2000B; ❄ @ 🛜) With a monopoly on the sandiest part of the beach, Siam Beach has adequate, if unremarkable, bungalows. But location is what you get.

Mark House Bungalows   GUESTHOUSE $$
(☑ 08 6133 0402; www.markhousebungalow.com; Ban Khlong Chao; r 1200B; ❄ 🛜) Right behind the beachside resorts, Mark House is the closest cheapie to the beach. The bungalows sit beside the canal and it feels like you're halfway through a nap all the time you stay here.

★ Bann Makok   HOTEL $$$
(☑ 08 1643 9488; www.bannmakok.com; Khlong Yai Ki; r 2800-4000B; ❄ @ 🛜) Be the envy of the speedboat patrons when you get dropped off at this boutique hotel tucked into the mangroves. Recycled timbers painted in vintage colours have been constructed into a maze

of eight rooms designed to look like a traditional pier fishing village. Common decks and reading nooks provide a peaceful space to listen to birdsong or get lost in a book.

Tinkerbell Resort   HOTEL $$$
(☑ 08 1826 1188; www.tinkerbellresort.com; Hat Khlong Chao; r 9900B; ❄ @ 🛜 🛖) Natural materials, like towering bamboo privacy fences and thatched roof villas, blend this resort seamlessly into the landscape. The bungalows are smack dab on the prettiest beach you've ever seen; the rooms behind come with plunge pools. The bar is a great spot for a sundowner. Expect 40% discounts in low season.

Homefood Restaurant   THAI $$
(Khlong Yai; dishes 60-350B; ⏱ 8.30am-9.30pm; 🛜) A few independent restaurants are scattered across the island. This is the most pleasant of them; family-run with an outdoor eating area and an alluring selection of seafood and salads, as well as Western breakfasts.

ⓘ Information

There are no banks or ATMs, though major resorts can exchange money. A small **hospital** (☑ 0 3952 5748; ⏱ 8.30am-4.30pm) can handle minor emergencies and is located inland at Ban Khlong Hin Dam. The **police station** (☑ 0 3952 5741) is nearby. Almost all hotels and guesthouses have wi-fi now.

ⓘ Getting There & Around

Ko Kut is accessible from the mainland pier of Laem Sok, 22km southeast of Trat, the nearest bus transfer point.

Koh Kood Princess (☑ 08 6126 7860; www. kohkoodprincess.com) runs an air-con boat (one way 350B, one daily, one hour 40 minutes) that docks at Ao Salad, in the northeastern corner of the island. There's free land transfer on your arrival.

Speedboats also make the crossing to/from Laem Sok (one way 600B, 1½ hours) during high season and will drop you off at your hotel's pier.

Bang Bao Boat (www.bangbaoboat.com) is the archipelago's inter-island ferry running a daily loop from Ko Chang, departing at 9am, to Ko Kut (one way 900B, five to six hours). In the opposite direction, you can catch it to Ko Mak (one way 300B, one to two hours) and Ko Wai (one way 400B, 2½ hours).

Ko Kut's roads are steep, ruling out renting a push bike unless you are a champion cyclist. Motorbikes can be rented for 250B per day.

Chiang Mai Province

Best Places to Eat

➡ Kow Soy Siri Soy (p263)

➡ Pun Pun (p267)

➡ Salsa Kitchen (p268)

➡ New Delhi (p265)

➡ Chiang Dao Nest (p283)

Best Places to Stay

➡ Villa Duang Champa
(p257)

➡ Awanahouse (p256)

➡ Riverside House (p261)

➡ Sakulchai (p261)

➡ Baan Orapin (p261)

Why Go?

The province of Chiang Mai, with its mist-shrouded mountains and temple-filled capital city, has long been a darling on the travellers' trail. The laid-back city of Chiang Mai is an endearing mix of old and new: the moated, partially walled old quarter shelters celebrated temples that reflect the forest-inspired aesthetics of the bygone teak trade and the ethnic mixing pot born during the caravan era. A traveller-friendly scene caters to the party set, the holiday learner, families and sightseers. There's something for everybody, and many decide to call the city home for as long as possible.

Just a short jaunt outside of the city is a stunning landscape of rural farms, forested mountains and minority villages. Two of Thailand's highest peaks – Doi Inthanon (2565m) and Doi Chiang Dao (2195m) – are a few hours' drive out of Chiang Mai. And the province's extensive forest cover provides plenty of athletic escapes.

When to Go

➡ The weather in Chiang Mai is best for travel during the cool season, roughly from November to February, when temperatures are mild and rain is scarce.

➡ The hot season, from March until June, is just that and hazy from agricultural fires.

CHIANG MAI

เชียงใหม่

POP 200,000

Nestled into the foothills of northern Thailand, Chiang Mai is a sanctuary. The pace is laid-back, the accoutrements are international and the landscape is picturesque. It is a fine urban specimen with a much-celebrated traditional culture ideal for sightseers, nature buffs and city connoisseurs.

The Lanna kings who ruled the north from ancient Chiang Mai built a moated quarter filled with a multitude of temples. These houses of worship are adorned with mirrored mosaics, tinkling bells and gabled rooftops soaring skyward as if in communication with the heavens. Wandering around these sacred spaces you'll find art, architecture and enlightenment, as many offer monk chats and meditation courses to tourists who are willing to do more than just look.

Beyond the historic centre is a dynamic and modern place with lots of down-to-earth charm. Bangkok refugees, artists, international NGO-workers and hip university students mix together, carving out creative spaces amid Thailand's ubiquitous concrete shophouses, many of which are being abandoned for the spacious suburbs. Head down to Th Nimmanhaemin and you'll glimpse the city's future movers and shakers, intent now on moving and shaking it in the nightclubs and bars.

Maintaining an ever-watchful pose over the metropolis, the mountains of Doi Suthep and Doi Pui are constant and scenic reminders of the city's mythical beginnings. A journey from the steamy plains into the mountains' cloud belt is a winding and meditative escape.

The city can easily consume a week with sightseeing, holiday courses, outdoor activities and, of course, eating. Cuisine specialities of the city include sushi bars around the university, Myanmarese curries, Thai street food and vegetarian health food.

History

Chiang Mai and Thailand's other northern provinces share more of their early development with the Shan state of present-day Myanmar, neighbouring parts of Laos and even the southern mountains of China than with Bangkok and Thailand's central plains.

King Phaya Mengrai (also spelt Mangrai) is credited for founding the Lanna kingdom in Chiang Saen and expanding it into the Ping River valley. Once he reached the valley, he built a temporary capital at Wiang Kum Kam. Around 1296, King Mengrai relocated the Lanna capital to a more picturesque spot between Doi Suthep and the Ping River and named the auspicious city Nopburi Si Nakhon Ping Chiang Mai (shortened to Chiang Mai, meaning the 'New Walled City'). Traces of the original 1296 earthen ramparts can still be seen today along Th Kamphaeng Din in Chiang Mai.

In the 14th and 15th centuries, the Lanna kingdom expanded as far south as Kamphaeng Phet and as far north as Luang Prabang in Laos. During this time, Chiang Mai became an important religious and cultural centre, and the eighth world synod of Theravada Buddhism was held here in 1477.

The Lanna kingdom was soon confronted by challenges from Ayuthaya, the powerful city-state that had flourished in Thailand's central plains and that would later consolidate the region under Siamese control and help shape the broader 'Thai' identity. But it was Myanmar that would overtake the city and the kingdom in 1556, an occupation that lasted 200 years.

The fall of Ayuthaya in 1767 to Myanmar marked another turning point in Chiang Mai's history. The defeated Thai army reunited under Phraya Taksin south of Ayuthaya in present-day Bangkok and began a campaign to push out the occupying forces from Myanmar. Chao Kavila, a chieftain (known as *jôw meu·ang*) from nearby Lampang principality, helped 'liberate' northern Thailand from Myanmarese control, which led to the eventual integration of the Lanna kingdom into the expanding Thai kingdom based in Bangkok.

Under Kavila, Chiang Mai became an important regional trade centre. In 1800 Kavila built the monumental brick walls around Chiang Mai's inner city and expanded the city in southerly and easterly directions, establishing a river port at the end of what is today Th Tha Phae (*tha phae* means 'raft pier'). Many of the later Shan- and Burmese-style temples were built by wealthy teak merchants who emigrated from Myanmar during this period.

There were many political and technological factors that ultimately led to the demise of an independent Lanna state. The Bangkok-based government designated Chiang Mai as an administrative unit in 1892 during the expansion of colonial rule in neighbour-

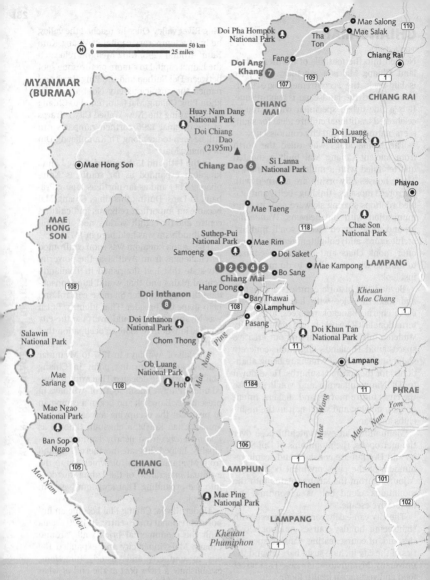

Chiang Mai Highlights

1 Doing a temple tour of sacred **Wat Phra Singh,** (p233) **Wat Chedi Luang** (p233) and **Wat Phra That Doi Suthep** (p245)

2 Learning how to make a tasty curry at a **cooking class** (p252)

3 Joining the human shopping parade at the **Saturday Walking Street** (p239) and **Sunday Walking Street** (p237)

4 Plunging into the commercial beehive of **Talat Warorot** (p238)

5 Tapping into your inner peace with a **meditation course** (p252)

6 Exploring the mystical **Chiang Dao cave** (p281)

7 Ascending into the highlands of **Doi Ang Khang** (p283) which makes the rest of Thailand seems like a foreign country

8 Scaling the heights of **Doi Inthanon** (p289), and posing for pics among the conifers and rhododendrons

ing Myanmar and Laos. The completion of the northern railway to Chiang Mai in 1921 finally linked the north with central Thailand. In 1927, King Rama VII and Queen Rambaibani rode into the city at the head of an 84-elephant caravan, becoming the first central Thai monarchs to visit the north. In 1933, Chiang Mai officially became a province of Siam.

In 2001, then prime minister and Chiang Mai native Thaksin Shinawatra sought to make Chiang Mai one of the nation's primary centres of information technology by expanding the airport and building superhighways. Though the prime minister's grand vision for Chiang Mai was interrupted by his ouster in 2006, the restoration of his political proxies, including his prime minister sister, has seen renewed promises of a new high-speed rail system linking Bangkok to Chiang Mai, a municipal transit system and additional investment. The city is undergoing a rapid expansion as middle-class families relocate to the suburbs, and tourism, especially from China, is increasing exponentially.

◉ Sights

Temples, museums, markets and neighbourhoods make up the bulk of Chiang Mai's attractions.

◉ Old City เมืองเก่า

Chiang Mai's historic quarter is hemmed in by a brick rampart and a moat, old-fashioned defences that now repulse the traffic and urban chaos of modern Thai life. Within the old city, temples dominate the skyline, orange-robed monks weave in and out of the tourist crowds and morning temple bells awaken before the motorcycle engines. The area is a charming remnant of the past but it is changing: the municipal offices have moved out and have been replaced by museums and other tourist attractions, decrepit shophouses are being replaced by modern arcade malls, and boutique hotels and guesthouses have infiltrated every quiet residential corner.

★ **Wat Phra Singh**   BUDDHIST TEMPLE
(วัดพระสิงห์; Map p240; Th Singharat; 20B; ⊗6am-6pm) Chiang Mai's most revered temple, Wat Phra Singh draws pilgrims and sightseers for its resident Buddha and its classic Lanna art and architecture. Visitors should dress modestly (clothing covering shoulders and knees).

Phra Singh (Lion Buddha), the temple's famous image, is housed in Wihan Lai Kham, a small chapel to the rear of the temple grounds next to the *chedi* (stupa). The building boasts a Lanna-style three-tiered roof and carved gables. Inside are sumptuous *lai·krahm* (gold-pattern stencilling) and murals.

Despite Phra Singh's exalted status, very little is actually known about the image. It is considered one of the most beautiful examples of Lanna religious art thanks to its thick human-like features and lotus-shaped topknot. Because there are two nearly identical images in Nakhon Si Thammarat and Bangkok, no one knows if this is the real one, nor can anyone document its place of origin. Regardless, this Phra Singh image came to reside here around the 1360s, and is now a fixture in the religious ceremonies of the Songkran festival.

Other features include the temple's main *chedi,* which is a classic Lanna-style octagonal base. It was built by King Pa Yo in 1345 in honour of his father. The main *wi·hǎhn* (sanctuary), which sits right at the entrance, houses a bigger but less important Buddha known as Thong Thip.

★ **Wat Chedi Luang**   BUDDHIST TEMPLE
(วัดเจดีย์หลวง; Map p240; Th Phra Pokklao; donations appreciated; ⊗6am-6pm) An historic and venerable temple, Wat Chedi Luang is built around a crumbling Lanna-style *chedi* (built in 1441) that was one of the tallest structures in ancient Chiang Mai.

The famed Phra Kaew (Emerald Buddha), now held in Bangkok's Wat Phra Kaew, resided in the eastern niche in 1475. Today there is a jade replica, given as a gift from the Thai king in 1995 to celebrate the 600th anniversary of the *chedi* and the 700th anniversary of the city.

Stories say that the *chedi* was damaged by either a 16th-century earthquake or by the cannon fire of King Taksin in 1775 during the recapture of Chiang Mai from Myanmar. A restoration was financed by Unesco and the Japanese government in the 1990s. The restoration work is easily spotted: new porticoes and *naga* (mythical serpent) and new Buddha images in three of the four directional niches. On the southern side of the monument, five elephant sculptures in the pediment can be seen. Four are cement restorations; only the one on the far right – without ears and trunk – is original brick and stucco. The restoration efforts also

Chiang Mai

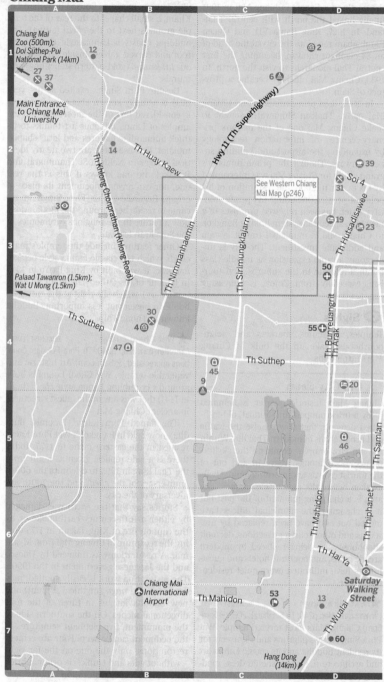

Chiang Mai
Zoo (500m);
Doi Suthep-Pui
National Park (14km)

12

27
37

Main Entrance
to Chiang Mai
University

2

6

14

Th Huay Kaew

Hwy 11 (Th Superhighway)

39

See Western Chiang
Mai Map (p246)

31

3

Palaad Tawanron (1.5km);
Wat U Mong (1.5km)

Th Suthep

Th Khlong Chonprathan (Khlong Road)

Th Nimmanhaemin

Th Sirimungklajarn

19

23

Th Hutsadisawee

50

55

Th Bunreuangrit

Th Arak

30

4

47

45

9

Th Suthep

20

46

Th Mahidon

Th Samlan

Th Thiphanet

Chiang Mai
International
Airport

Th Mahidon

53

13

Th Hai Ya

Saturday
Walking
Street

1

Th Wualai

60

Hang Dong
(14km)

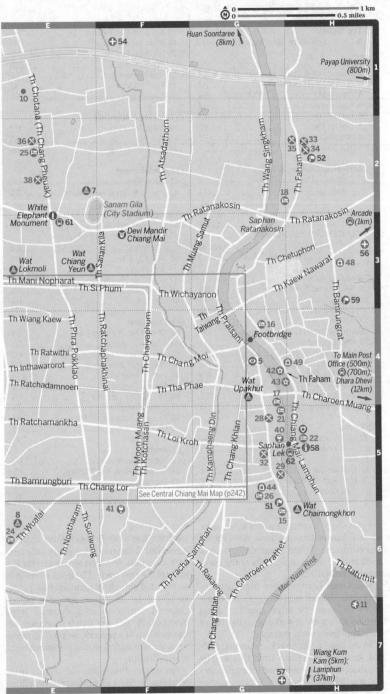

Chiang Mai

stopped short of creating a new spire, since no one knows for sure how the original superstructure looked. Regardless, a slow stroll around the massive walls of the *chedi* is quite meditative.

Wat Chedi Luang's other prominent attraction is the *làk meu·ang* (city pillar, believed to house the city's guardian deity) enshrined in a small building to the left of the compound's main entrance.

In the main *wí·hăhn* is the standing Buddha, known as Phra Chao Attarot, flanked by two disciples, both renowned for meditation and mysticism.

Wat Phan Tao   BUDDHIST TEMPLE
(วัดพันเถา; Map p240; Th Phra Pokklao; donations appreciated; ☉6am-6pm) This pretty little temple evokes mist-shrouded forests and the largesse of the teak trade. The main *wí·hăhn* is constructed entirely of moulded teak panels supported by 28 gargantuan teak pillars. Coloured mirror mosaics decorate *naga* bargeboards, and the facade's primary ornamentation of a peacock over a dog, represents the astrological year of the former royal resident's birth.

On display inside are old temple bells, ceramics, a few old northern-style gilded wooden Buddha statues, and antique cabinets stacked with old palm-leaf manuscripts.

★ **Sunday Walking Street** MARKET
(ถนนเดินวันอาทิตย์; Map p240; Th Ratchadamnoen; ◷4pm-midnight Sun) The old city's central avenue is closed to traffic for the weekly Sunday Walking Street, a convergence of provincial culture, commerce and people-watching. It is also a resurrection of the itinerant merchant tradition from the ancient caravan days.

Vendors line the length of Th Ratchadamnoen. The temples host food stalls selling northern Thai cuisine and other shopping-stamina boosts. The market gets very crowded, so come early. There is also a Saturday Walking Street (p239).

Chiang Mai City Arts & Cultural Centre MUSEUM
(หอศิลปวัฒนธรรมเชียงใหม่; Map p240; ☑0 5321 7793; Th Phra Pokklao; adult/child 90/40B; ◷8.30am-5pm Tue-Sun) This museum offers a fine primer on Chiang Mai history. The 1st floor has engaging and informative historical and cultural displays. The 2nd floor rooms have life-sized exhibits of bygone eras, including an early Lanna village.

Nearby are two sister museums: Chiang Mai Historical Centre and Lanna Folklife Museum. A combination ticket for all three costs 180B.

The Arts & Cultural Centre is housed in a lovely 1920s building that used to be Chiang Mai's former Provincial Hall.

★ **Lanna Folklife Museum** MUSEUM
(พิพิธภัณฑ์พื้นถิ่นล้านนา; Map p240; Th Phra Pokklao; adult/child 90/40B; ◷8.30am-5pm Tue-Sun) This new and professional museum is a sister site to the other cultural attractions near Anusawari Sam Kasat (Three Kings Monument). Life-size dioramas explain northern Thai religious beliefs and customs, temple paraphernalia and symbolism, traditional crafts and other features of ordinary life. The displays have artistic merit and informative English signage and the atmospheric building, once a former royal residence and later used by the court system, is a pleasure to stroll around. Combination tickets to nearby museums are available.

Chiang Mai Historical Centre MUSEUM
(หอประวัติศาสตร์เมืองเชียงใหม่; Map p240; Th Ratwithi; 8.30am-5pm Tue-Sun; ◷adult/child 90/40B) This new museum covers the area's history

with professional and well-signed displays. Topics cover the founding of the capital, the occupation by Myanmar and the modern era of trade and unification with Bangkok. The bottom floor contains an archaeological dig of an ancient temple wall. Combination tickets (180B) to nearby museums are available.

Anusawari Sam Kasat MONUMENT
(อนุสาวรีย์สามกษัตริย์; Map p240; Th Phra Pokklao) A focal point of the old city, the bronze Three Kings Monument commemorates the alliance forged between the three northern Thai kings (Phaya Ngam Meuang of Phayao, Phaya Mengrai of Chiang Mai and Phaya Khun Ramkhamhaeng of Sukhothai) in the founding of Chiang Mai. The monument is a shrine for local residents, who regularly leave devotional offerings.

Wat Chiang Man BUDDHIST TEMPLE
(วัดเชียงมั่น; Map p240; Th Ratchaphakhinai; donations appreciated; ◷6am-6pm) Chiang Mai's oldest temple, Wat Chiang Man, was established by the city's founder, Phaya Mengrai, sometime around 1296. The temple contains two famous Buddhas, which reside in the small sanctuary to the right of the main chapel. **Phra Sila** is a marble bas-relief Buddha that stands about 30cm high and reportedly came from Sri Lanka or India. **Phra Sae Tang Khamani**, a 10cm high, crystal image, is thought to have come from Lavo (Lopburi) 1800 years ago.

In front of the *bòht* (ordination hall), a stone slab, engraved in 1581, bears the earliest known reference to the city's founding.

Museum of World Insects & Natural Wonders MUSEUM
(Map p240; Th Ratchadamnoen; admission 100B; ◷9am-5pm) Bugs, butterflies and creepy crawlies are showcased at this quirky museum operated by a malaria researcher and his entomologist wife. Their personal collection of insects and rocks as well as their philosophical musings occupy three floors in this second and central location. The primary location is west of the old city and charges a heftier entrance fee.

◉ **East of the Old City**

Passing through Pratu Tha Phae leads to a standard-issue commercial neighbourhood of concrete shophouses and busy multi-laned roads. Amid the clutter are old heritage houses built by the British and teak merchants from Myanmar. Shopping and dining are the primary pastimes in this part

DON'T MISS

DOKMAI GARDEN

Chiang Mai is often referred to as the rose of the north, in part because the cool highlands can grow these temperate flowers and also because the city itself is regarded to be as beautiful. The north is famous for its flowers, both native and commercially grown varieties introduced as cash crops to replace opium production. February is the celebrated blooming season but flowers adorn gardens, forests and roadsides throughout the year.

For flower enthusiasts and plant geeks who collect floral trivia, **Dokmai Garden** (☑ 08 7187 5787; Hang Dong; admission 300B, tour 1200-1900B; ⊙ Jan-Jun) is a private botanical garden south of Chiang Mai that preserves and propagates native flora and floral knowledge. The garden contains over 1000 plants and their friends, including bees, birds and butterflies. Basic admission allows visitors to wander around the garden reading the informative signs that give the plants' scientific names and cultural applications. Guided tours offer more in-depth discussions. Dokmai Gardens is also involved with Thailand's Orchid Ark program, a conservation effort to protect the country's endangered orchids threatened by illegal logging in the national parks. The program propagates native species in a woodland setting in order to maintain genetic diversity, fragrance and other naturally occurring factors, in the hopes that these specimens can be returned to the forest when poaching is no longer a threat. The garden is run by the Seehamongkol family, a Thai gardening team, and Eric Danell, an academic plant researcher. Call ahead to make an appointment. The garden is about 30 minutes south of Chiang Mai airport and can be reached by chartered transport (about 300B); you may need to contact the garden for specific directions.

of town. Further east, Mae Ping River carves out a meandering path once populated on the eastern bank by foreign missionaries.

★ **Talat Warorot**　MARKET
(ตลาดวโรรส; Map p240; cnr Th Chang Moi & Th Praisani; ⊙ 6am-5pm) Chiang Mai's oldest and most famous market, Talat Warorot, excels in every category: day market, souvenir shopping, people-watching and snacking. It is locally known as 'gàht lŏo·ang', which is northern Thai for 'great market'. There are two multistorey buildings, a beehive of outdoor vendors and several disorienting lanes filled with additional commerce. It is a smaller and less hectic version of Bangkok's Chatuchak Market.

You'll know you've arrived at the market when traffic comes to a stand-still and carts laden with merchandise weave in between the cars. The market is orbited by fruit and vegetable vendors selling highland produce considered exotic in central Thailand. Just beyond these vendors are two multistorey buildings specialising in northern Thai products from foodstuffs, such as *kâap mŏo* (pork rinds), to handicrafts and ordinary necessities. The adjacent streets do a bustling trade in bolts of fabrics, market fashion, handicrafts and knick-knacks. Parked near the fruit vendors are an endangered mode of

travel: the three-wheeled bicycle rickshaw, known as săhm·lór (also spelt săamláw), which shuttles home shoppers burdened with produce. Across the road from the săhm·lór is the river, the historic thoroughfare for delivering farm goods to the commercial centres.

Talat Tonlamyai　MARKET
(Map p234; Th Praisani; ⊙ 24hr) Facing the river, the city's main fresh **flower market** (gàht dòrk mái) offers a bouquet of tropical and temperate flowers that are brought to market at night to avoid the wilting daytime heat. Cool-weather varieties, including daisies and roses, are grown in the nearby highlands. Catch the flower market during citywide festivals, such as Loi Krathong and the Flower Festival.

Chinatown　HISTORICAL DISTRICT
(Th Chang Moi) The city's small Chinatown is marked by a flamboyant **Chinese-style arch** and the typical two-storey shophouses of Thailand's mercantile districts. It is an interesting stroll en route to Talat Warorot. There are old-style apothecaries, two Chinese **temples** and clan houses that host an annual Chinese New Year parade. A small population of Sikhs worships at the **Namdhari Sikh Temple** (Map p240; Th Ratchawong).

Wat Bupparam TEMPLE

(วัดบุปผาราม; Map p240; Th Tha Phae; donations appreciated; 6am-6pm) This highly ornate temple is an example of Shan and Myanmarese influences on Chiang Mai's temple architecture. It is one of three temples (including Wat Chetawan and Wat Mahawan) along Th Tha Phae financed by teak merchants from Myanmar who immigrated to Chiang Mai a century or more ago.

No two guardian deity sculptures are alike; the whimsical forms include animals playing and various mythical creatures. Wat Bupparam contains a charming little *bòht* constructed of teak and decorated in pure Lanna style.

Wiang Kum Kam HISTORICAL RUINS

(เวียงกุมกาม; 8am-5pm) Pre-dating Chiang Mai, Wiang Kum Kam served as the Lanna capital for 10 years from 1286. The city was abandoned in the 16th century due to flooding when Mae Ping changed its course. Today the excavated ruins cover 3 sq km. The actual ruins have more historical importance than spectacle; the horse-drawn carriages for visitors and the bucolic setting add to the ancient ambience.

It is about 5km southeast of town off Th Chiang Mai-Lamphun (Rte 106).

Wiang Kum Kam was originally established by the Mon as a satellite town for the Hariphunchai kingdom and its capital in Lamphun. It later was adopted by the Lanna king Phaya Mengrai. Over 1300 inscribed stone slabs, bricks, bells and *chedi* have been excavated at the site. The most important archaeological discovery has been a four-piece inscribed stone slab, now on display in the Chiang Mai National Museum. The early- 11th-century inscriptions on this slab indicate that the Thai script predates King Ramkhamhaeng's famous Sukhothai inscription (introduced in 1293) by 100 or more years.

South of the Old City

The southern part of the city is a mix of quaint antique houses and impersonal modern spaces. Th Wualai is renowned for its silver shops and is often filled with the tapping sound of a decorative pattern being imprinted onto a plate of silver (or, more often, aluminium). One of the best ways to observe Th Wualai is to come for the Saturday Walking Street.

Saturday Walking Street MARKET

(ถนนเดินวันเสาร์; Map p234; Th Wualai; 4pm-midnight Sat) On Saturdays, Th Wualai is closed to traffic and mobbed by pedestrians parading past food and souvenir vendors. Come early to shop as it does get crowded. There are additional food stalls across the street near Talat Pratu Chiang Mai.

Wat Sisuphan BUDDHIST TEMPLE

(วัดศรีสุพรรณ; Map p234; Soi 2, Th Wualai; donations appreciated; 6am-6pm) The district's silver craftsmanship is given a spectacular setting at this neighbourhood temple. The prime attraction is the 'silver' *ubosot* (ordination hall), covered entirely with silver, nickel and aluminium embossed panels. The temple also hosts local silver artisans, monk chat, meditation courses and the Poy Luang Festival (a Shan ordination in March).

The temple was founded in 1502, but little remains of the original structures except for some teak pillars and roof beams in the *wí·hǎhn*. The murals inside show an interesting mix of Taoist, Zen and Theravada Buddhist elements.

West of the Old City

'Modern' Chiang Mai resides west of the old city. It is a mix of ho-hum shophouses, Chiang Mai University, and fashionable Th Nimmanhaemin which is known for its dining and nightlife.

CHIANG MAI PROVINCE CHIANG MAI

MONK CHAT

If you're curious about Buddhism, many Chiang Mai temples offer 'monk chat', in which monks get to practise their English by fielding questions from visitors about religion, rituals and life in the monastery. Remember that it is respectful to dress modestly: cover your shoulders and knees. Women should take care not to touch the monks or their belongings, or to pass anything directly to them.

Wat Suan Dok (p242) has a dedicated room just beyond the main sanctuary hall and holds its chats from 5pm to 7pm, Monday, Wednesday and Friday. Wat Sisuphan (p239) holds its sessions from 5.30pm to 7pm just before its meditation course. Wat Chedi Luang (p233) has a table under a shady tree where monks chat from 9am to 6pm daily.

Central Chiang Mai

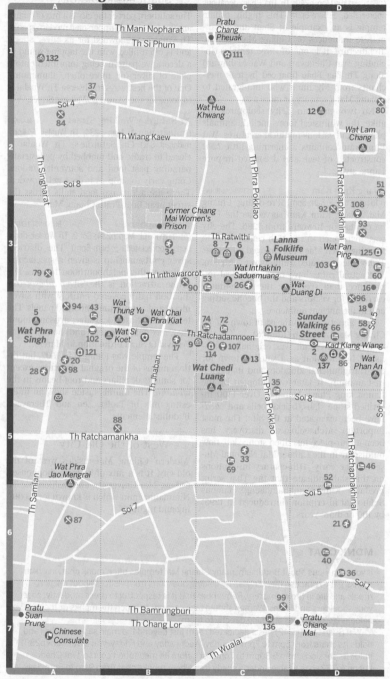

400 m
0.2 miles

Th Muang Samut
Th Wichayanon
US Consulate
Mae
Nam
Ping
Th Charoenrat
30
Th Kaew Nawarat
Nakhon Ping Bridge
Th Taiwang
Th Praisani

44
65
32
Soi 9
Soi 1
39
Soi 8
54
Soi 7
63
Th Chaiyaphum
110
Soi 1
100
Soi 6
Soi 2
135
Wat Chompu
Th Chang Moi Kao
Soi 2
Chinese-Style Arch
Th Ratchawong
138
3
Talat Warorot
10

106
Wat Dokaueng
31
Soi 5
134
76
42
56
70
91
27
73
38
75
Wat U Sai Kham
97
105
Th Chang Moi
Soi 2
Wat Saen Fang
83
Th Khang Mehn
130

49
Pratu Tha Phae
45
113
117
59
95
Wat Chetawan
116
Th Tha Phae
124
128
127
11
Th Kamphaeng Din

14
25
78
48
22
109
133
64
57
67
Wat Mahawan
Soi 4
Soi 5
Soi 3
41
29
71
24
47
Th Chang Khlan
119
Soi 1
85
61
104
82
Soi 2
123
118
Soi 6
19
131
139
89
23
Soi 1
81
122
Wat Phan Tawng
Wat Loi Khroh
115
Soi 6
55
68
Soi 1
Th Moon Muang
Th Kotchasan
Th Loi Kroh
62
Wat Chang Khong
50
15
77
112
Soi Anusan
Wat Sai Moon Myanmar
126
101
Th Si Donchai
129
Wat Muang Mang
Wat Phuak Chang

Central Chiang Mai

Wat Suan Dok   BUDDHIST TEMPLE
(วัดสวนดอก; Map p234; Th Suthep; donations appreciated; ⊙6am-6pm) Built on a former flower garden in 1373, this plain-jane temple has a photogenic collection of whitewashed *chedi* that pose in front of the blue peaks of Doi Suthep and Doi Pui.

According to legend, a relic was brought to Wat Suan Dok, miraculously duplicated itself and was then used as a 'guide' for the founding of Wat Doi Suthep. The relic is enshrined in the temple's central *chedi*.

The main *chedi* is a textbook example of the Lanna period that began to be influenced by Sukhothai. The other *chedi* on the grounds contain the ashes of various members of the Lanna royal family.

Mahachulalongkorn Buddhist University is located on the same grounds and is home to a large population of resident monks and novices. Foreigners often come to Wat Suan Dok for the popular monk chat and the English-language meditation retreats.

CHIANG MAI PROVINCE CHIANG MAI

Wat U Mong   BUDDHIST TEMPLE
(วัดอุโมงค์; Soi Wat U Mong, Th Khlong Chonprathan; donations appreciated; ⊙6am-6pm) This **forest wát** is best known for its secluded sylvan setting and a series of interconnecting brick **tunnels** built around 1380 for the clairvoyant monk Thera Jan. A marvellously grisly fasting Buddha sits on top of the tunnel hill, along with a large and venerated *chedi*.

Wat U Mong is off Th Suthep near Chiang Mai University. Note that there is another Wat U Mong in town, so to clearly instruct a driver ask for 'Wat U Mong Thera Jan'.

The temple was first used during Phaya Mengrai's rule in the 14th century. The monastery was abandoned at a later date and wasn't reactivated until a local Thai prince sponsored a restoration in the late 1940s. The since-deceased Ajan Buddhadasa Bhikkhu, a well-known monk and teacher at southern Thailand's Wat Suanmok (a famous meditation temple), sent a number of monks to re-establish a monastic community at Wat U Mong in the 1960s.

Also on the grounds is a small artificial lake, surrounded by *gù•dì* (monastic cottages).

Chiang Mai University   UNIVERSITY

(มหาวิทยาลัยเชียงใหม่ ; CMU; Map p234; Th Huay Kaew & Th Suthep) The city's principal public university was established in 1964. The main campus occupies a 2.9 sq km wedge of land, about 2km west of the city centre, that has preserved much of its original forest character. There are bike lanes throughout the campus and cafes for pit-stops.

The area around the university on Th Huay Kaew is referred to as 'nâh mor' (in front of the university), and on Th Suthep as 'lăng mor' (behind the university).

Chiang Mai University Art Museum   MUSEUM

(Map p234; www.cmumuseum.org; Th Nimmanhaemin; ⊙9am-5pm Tue-Sun) FREE The museum displays temporary exhibitions of contemporary Thai and international artists. There's no permanent collection and the museum collaborates with established and emerging artists so the special shows can be a bit hit and miss.

Chiang Mai Night Safari   ZOO

(เชียงใหม่ไนท์ซาฟารี; ☑0 5399 9000; www.chiangmainightsafari.com; Rte 121/Th Klorng Chonprathan; safari adult/child 800/400B; ⊙11am-10pm) This attraction is open during the day, but the real action happens at night when an open-sided tram transports visitors through the park. The Predator Prowl and Savannah Safari are the two zones visited during these night safaris and English-language trams leave at 7.45pm and 9.30pm, and 8.30pm and 10.15pm, respectively.

Non-human-eating animals – including wildebeest, giraffe, rhinoceros and zebra – come right up to the tram. In the Predator Prowl section, the tigers, lions, Asiatic black bears and crocodiles are kept at a safe distance by deep trenches.

Arrive around dusk so that the kids have enough time to play at the playground. There are also day safaris and a walking trail called **Jaguar Trail** (adult/child 100/50B) encircling Swan Lake, a 1.2km walk where over 50 species (ranging from rabbits to cranes) are generally not in cages, except of course the trail's namesake animal.

The Night Safari is 12km from central Chiang Mai. Most bookings are made through a tour agency that handles hotel transfers.

Chiang Mai Zoo   ZOO

(สวนสัตว์เชียงใหม่; ☑0 5322 1179; www.chiangmaizoo.com; 100 Th Huay Kaew; adult/child 100/50B; ⊙8am-5pm) The Chiang Mai Zoo occupies a park setting at the foot of Doi Suthep which is often crowded with Thai families and school groups. The zoo has the usual menagerie and several special exhibits requiring separate admission, including the **aquarium** (adult/child 450/350B) and the

---

SOI BAN HAW

Chiang Mai straddled one of Asia's famous crossroads: the southern spur of the Silk Road. Dating from the 15th century, Chinese-Muslim traders from Yunnan Province (China) drove their horse-drawn caravans south through the mountains to the Indian Ocean to buy and sell goods through the international sea trade. To the Thais of Chiang Mai, these caravans were a remarkable sight and the traders were nicknamed *jeen hor* (galloping Chinese), a reference to their strange beasts of burden.

The caravans exported silk, opium, tea, dried fruit, lacquerware, musk, ponies and mules – a mix of luxury and necessity goods. Imports included gold, copper, cotton, edible bird's nest, betel nut, tobacco and ivory. In the 19th century, artisans from China, northern Myanmar and Laos settled in Chiang Mai to produce crafts for the steady flow of regional trade.

Though the conveyances and the fashions have changed, some of these goods are still bought and sold along these very same trade routes. The city's original transhipment point was a market district known as **Ban Haw**, near the present night bazaar, which sells silk, cotton and plastic goods from China.

The 100-year-old **Matsayit Chiang Mai** (Soi 1, Th Charoen Khlan), also known as Ban Haw Mosque, was founded by *jeen hor*. Within the past two centuries, the city's Muslim community has also grown to include ethnic Yunnanese Muslims escaping unrest in Laos and Myanmar. Along the soi there are a number of simple restaurants and vendors selling Thai-Muslim-style food, including curries, *kôw soy* (curried chicken and noodles), *kôw mòk gài* (chicken biriani) and *néu·a òp hŏrm* ('fragrant' dried beef).

panda house (adult/child 110/50B). A shuttle bus and monorail (adult/child 100/50B) make a loop around the grounds.

It is a pleasant, traffic-free zone for children to roam, though the facilities are ageing and under-populated by animals, especially the exhibits that are further up the mountain.

Doi Suthep-Pui National Park   PARK
(อุทยานแห่งชาติดอยสุเทพ – ปุย; ☑ 0 5321 0244; Th Huay Kaew; adult/child 100/50B, car 30B; ⊘ 8am-sunset) Often bearing a crown of clouds, Doi Suthep (1676m) and Doi Pui (1685m) are Chiang Mai's sacred peaks. The mountains ascend from the humid lowlands into the cool (and even cold) cloud belt where moss and ferns thrive. Portions of the mountains form a 265-sq-km national park that is home to famous Wat Doi Suthep and other attractions. There is also park accommodation (www.dnp.go.th; camping 60B, bungalows 400-2500B).

The park is 16km northwest of central Chiang Mai. Shared rót daang (taxis) leave from Chiang Mai University (Th Huay Kaew entrance) to various points within the national park. One-way fares start at 40B to Wat Doi Suthep and 70B to Phra Tamnak Bhu Bhing. You can also charter a sŏrng·tăa·ou (pick-up minibus) for about 600B.

The diverse climate fosters more than 300 bird species and nearly 2000 species of ferns and flowering plants. During the rainy season, butterflies bloom as abundantly as the flowers. The eastern side of the mountain stays green and cool almost year-round.

The natural attractions include Nam Tok Monthathon (the park admission fee is collected here), 2.5km off the paved road. Pools beneath the falls hold water year-round, although swimming is best during or just after the monsoon. Close to the base of the mountain, Nam Tok Wang Bua Bahn is free, and full of frolicking locals, although it is more of a series of rapids than falls.

For off-road mountain biking, the park has technical single-track trails that were old hunting and transport routes used by hilltribe villagers. The routes are never crowded and provide hours of downhill. Because the trails aren't well marked it is advisable to join a guided mountain-biking tour.

★ Wat Phra That Doi Suthep   BUDDHIST TEMPLE
(วัดพระธาตุดอยสุเทพ; Th Huay Kaew, Doi Suthep; admission 30B; ⊘ 6am-6pm) Overlooking the

THE LONG WALK

At the start of every academic year in July, the freshman class from Chiang Mai University makes the annual pilgrimage on foot to Wat Suthep. It is a long-time tradition that fills the winding mountain road with close to 10,000 exuberant students and faculty members. The purpose of the trek is to introduce the new students to the spirit of the city, believed to reside in the mountain, and to make merit to the revered Buddha relic at Wat Suthep. But it is also a chance for the students to introduce themselves to each other and make friendships that can last a lifetime.

city from its mountain throne, Wat Suthep is one of the north's most sacred temples.

The temple was established in 1383 under King Keu Naone and enjoys a mystical birth story. A visiting Sukhothai monk instructed the Lanna king to establish a temple with the twin of a miraculous Buddha relic (enshrined at Wat Suan Dok). The relic was mounted on a white elephant, which wandered the mountain until it died at this spot, interpreted as the 'chosen' location.

The temple is reached by a strenuous, 306-step staircase, the climb is intended as an act of meditation. (For the less fit, there's a tram for 20B.)

The 1st-floor terrace documents this history of the temple with a shrine to Sudeva, the hermit who lived on the mountain, and a statue of the white elephant which carried the Buddha relic up the mountain. On the 2nd-floor terrace is the picturesque golden chedi that enshrines the relic; it is topped by a five-tiered umbrella in honour of the city's independence from Myanmar and its union with Thailand

Within the monastery compound, the International Buddhism Center conducts a variety of religious outreach programs for visitors.

Phra Tamnak Bhu Bhing   GARDENS
(พระตำหนักภูพิงค์ ; Bhu Bhing Palace; Th Huay Kaew, Doi Suthep; admission 50B; ⊘ 8.30-11.30am & 1-3.30pm) The grounds of the royal family's winter palace are open to the public (when the royals aren't visiting). Thanks to Doi Suthep's cool climate, the gardens specialise in exotic species such as roses. More interesting is

Western Chiang Mai

the **water reservoir** brought to life by dancing fountains and the king's musical compositions. Though not a must, 'nature sightseers' might like the paved footpaths.

Hmong Villages
VILLAGE

(Doi Suthep; museum 10B) Near the summit of Doi Pui are two Hmong villages. **Ban Doi Pui** is off of the main road and is basically a tourist market at altitude. A more interesting stop is **Ban Kun Chang Kian**, 500m down a dirt track just past the Doi Pui campground. It is best to park at the campground's visitor centre and walk from there. The village runs a coffee house, surrounded by coffee plants that are harvested in January.

◉ North of the Old City

Sights north of the old city through Pratu Chang Pheuak (the 'white elephant gate', a reference to the elephant which carried the sacred relic to Doi Suthep) are less of a tourist draw, which is a draw in itself for some. These sights tend to be too spread out to visit on foot; it is advisable to hire your own transport.

Wat Jet Yot
BUDDHIST TEMPLE

(วัดเจ็ดยอด; Map p234; Th Superhighway; ⊙6am-6pm) Dedicated temple-spotters are the prime candidates for this out-of-town temple. It was built to host the eighth World Buddhist Council in 1477, a momentous occasion for the Lanna capital. In the back of the compound, the old *wí·hăhn* is still topped by *jèt yôrt* (seven spires) that represent the seven weeks Buddha spent in Bodhgaya after his enlightenment.

The *wí·hăhn* was supposed to be a replica of the Mahabodhi Temple in Bodhgaya, India, but the proportions don't match up. Some scholars assume that the blueprint for the temple must have come from a small votive tablet depicting the Mahabodhi in distorted perspective.

Of the original stucco relief, a few intact Bodhisattva (Buddhist saints, usually associated with Mahayana Buddhism) depictions remain on the outer walls.

Wat Ku Tao
BUDDHIST TEMPLE

(วัดกู่เต้า; Map p234; Soi 6, Th Chang Pheuak; ⊙6am-6pm) North of the old city, Wat Ku Tao dates from 1613 and has a distinctive Tai Lü–style *chedi,* in the shape of a pile of diminishing spheres. The *chedi* contains the ashes of Tharawadi Min, a son of king Bayinnaung from Myanmar, ruler of Lanna from 1578 to 1607. The temple is a quiet, untouristed place with photographic merit.

Western Chiang Mai

Chiang Mai National Museum MUSEUM
(พิพิธภัณฑสถานแห่งชาติเชียงใหม่; Map p234; ☎0 5322 1308; www.thailandmuseum.com; off Th Superhighway; admission 100B; ☺9am-4pm Wed-Sun) Operated by the Fine Arts Department, this museum is the primary caretaker of Lanna artefacts and northern Thai history. This museum is a nice complement to the municipally run Chiang Mai City Arts & Cultural Centre with more art and artefacts that extend beyond the city limits. The best curated section is Lanna art, which displays a selection of Buddha images in all styles. Apart from this exhibit, the museum is a bit lacklustre.

Huay Teung Thao Reservoir RESERVOIR
(อ่างเก็บน้ำห้วยตึงเฒ่า; admission 20B; ☺8am-sunset) Thais embrace reservoirs as recreational retreats, not just as pieces of infrastructure. A common reservoir activity is to lounge by the water in floating bamboo huts and snack on fried bugs. Huay Teung Thao is about 12km northwest of the city off Rte 107 (follow signs towards Mae Rim).

Darapirom Palace MUSEUM
(☎0 2218 3635; Mae Rim; admission 20B; ☺9am-5pm Tue-Sat) The last chapter of Lanna history has a comfortable home in this former royal residence outside of Chiang Mai, in the northern suburb of Mae Rim. This stately teak house built in the neocolonial style of the early 20th century was the home of Princess Dara Rasmee, the daughter of the last Lanna king. Her personal effects and furnishings along with English signs describing her life are on display. Catch a *sŏrng·tăa·ou* to Mae Rim police station and follow the signs from there; it is about 1.5km from the main road on the grounds of a Thai military base.

🏃 Activities

Outdoor escapes are easy in Chiang Mai: scenic countryside and lush forests are within an hour's drive or less of the city, and a variety of outfitters tackle the byways, waterways and jungle tracks.

The city's closest green space is Doi Suthep with hiking and mountain-biking trails. The Mae Sa–Samoeng loop is the closest and most stunning escape into the mountains and a popular getaway for motorcycling.

Rock climbers head to Crazy Horse Buttress, an impressive set of limestone cliffs located behind Tham Meuang On, near Sankamphaeng, 45km east of Chiang Mai. While the scenery isn't as stunning as Krabi's

PRINCESS BRIDE

Much like a Brothers Grimm tale, the life story of Princess Dara Rasmee is rich with political intrigue, surprise twists and even a happily ever after. She was born in 1873 when Chiang Mai was still part of the independent Lanna kingdom; her father was Phra Chao Inthawichayanon, the last Lanna king. As a gesture of alliance, her father sent her at the age of 13 to Bangkok to live in the court of King Chulalongkorn. She participated in the topknot ceremony along with the other royal children, but was taken as a consort by the king at the age of 14. The engagement was viewed as a political move to unite the two royal houses against potential British intrusion, based upon rumours that the British monarch approached the Lanna king with interest in his daughter.

She was described as being very beautiful and was regarded as one of the king's favourite consorts (he had more than 100). Unlike other female residents in the royal compound, Dara Rasmee did not dress in Siamese fashion but continued to be a Lanna woman, wearing her long hair in a bun and dressing in northern textiles. She also continued to speak the northern dialect with her entourage and was the inspiration for a Thai adaptation of *Madame Butterfly* in which a Siamese man falls in love with a Lanna woman. Dara Rasmee gave birth to a daughter in 1886 but the child did not live past the age of three.

Prior to his death in 1910, King Chula gave Dara Rasmee the honorific title of Phra Raj Jaya, which elevated her to the status of an official royal wife, the only royal consort to receive such an honour. She is regarded by historians as being a vital cultural and personal bridge between what were then two foreign groups: central and northern Thais.

She returned to the north in 1914 and lived out her days at Darapirom Palace (p247). During her 'retirement', she cultivated roses in her garden, revitalised Lanna arts and culture, and helped establish the local longan industry. She died of consumption at the age of 60 in 1933.

seaside cliffs, the ascents reward with pastoral views.

White-water rafting tackles the wild and frothy Mae Taeng, which carves a path through the Doi Chiang Dao National Park and the Huai Nam Dang National Park. It has a surprisingly long white-water season (roughly from July to March). The 10km rafting route travels through grade II to grade IV, and some grade V, rapids. In one particularly thrilling stretch, the river drops almost 60m in about 1.5km. Following a heavy rain, especially in September, the river can become swollen and ferocious and drownings do occur. When choosing a white-water outfitter, ask about their safety standards and training (and check your travel insurance).

Chiang Mai is one of Thailand's most famous destinations for **elephant encounters**. In the past, most elephant attractions were circus-like sideshows with poor animal-safety standards. But conservation-minded operations have expanded to include nature preserves and mahout-training schools, with more concern for the animals' health and welfare. We get many readers' letters ranging from impassioned condemnation of elephant domestication to more practical requests for determining which camps treat their elephants kindly. Based on our interviews and observations, we see elephant tourism as one of the most practical ways to ensure that the 3200 domesticated elephants living in Thailand can live a 'good' life: meaning that they are social, well fed and receive daily health assessments as well as periodic veterinary check-ups. We encourage our readers to exercise their collective consumer will to hold the industry to the highest standards possible.

Book directly with tour providers, either at their offices (listed here) or online, to avoid agent commissions.

Flight of the Gibbon   ZIPLINING
(Map p240; ☑ 0 5301 0660; www.treetopasia.com; 29/4-5 Th Kotchasan; 3hr tour 3400B) ✪ This adventure outfit in Chiang Mai started the zipline craze a few years ago. Nearly 5km of wire with 33 staging platforms are strung up through the forest canopy some 1300m above sea level. Multiday, multi-activity tours include a night at a homestay in Mae Kampong, a high-altitude village an hour's drive east from Chiang Mai.

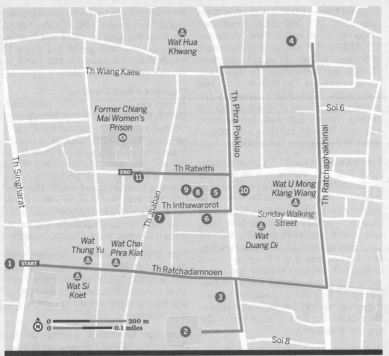

City Walk
Old City Temple Tour

START WAT PHRA SINGH
END VOCATIONAL TRAINING CENTER OF CHIANG MAI WOMEN'S CORRECTIONAL INSTITUTION
LENGTH 2.5KM; THREE TO FOUR HOURS

No visit to Chiang Mai is complete without spending a sweaty day temple-spotting. Starting with the best, **1 Wat Phra Singh** (p233) is home to the city's most revered Buddha image (Phra Singh) and is an excellent example of Lanna architecture. Trot down Th Ratchadamnoen and turn right on Th Phra Pokklao to **2 Wat Chedi Luang** (p233), another venerable temple. If you're curious about Buddhism, go to the 'monk chat' table in front of the *chedi*. Backtrack to **3 Wat Phan Tao** (p236), a teak temple that is all looks. If it isn't too hot, squeeze in one more temple by turning right on Th Ratchadamnoen and left on Th Ratchaphakhinai to **4 Wat Chiang Man** (p237), the oldest in the city.

Backtrack south and turn right on Th Wiang Kaew and left on Th Phra Pokklao. Just past **5 Anusawari Sam Kasat** (p237) (Three Kings Monument), turn right at Th Inthawarorot. Snap a few pics of newly refurbished **6 Wat Inthakhin Saduemuang**, a gilded teak temple of petite proportions. Just beyond the temple is a row of local lunch spots known for *kôw man gài* and *kôw soy*; **7 Kow Soy Siri Soy** (p263) is great.

Backtrack on Th Phra Pokklao to the informative and air-conditioned **8 Chiang Mai City Arts & Cultural Centre** (p237). If you're feeling clever, buy a combination ticket to **9 Chiang Mai Historical Centre** (p237) next door and the **10 Lanna Folklife Museum** (p237) (across the street).

Finally, reward yourself with a Thai massage at the **11 Vocational Training Center of the Chiang Mai Women's Correctional Institution** (p253) along Th Ratwithi. The centre provides job training in Thai massage for the female inmates. Doing good never took so little work.

Elephant Nature Park ELEPHANT ENCOUNTER (Map p240; ☑ 0 5381 8754; www.elephant naturepark.org; 1 Th Ratchamankha; 1-/2-day tour 2500/5800B) A pioneer in the new wave of elephant tourism, Khun Lek (Sangduen Chailert) runs this sanctuary for injured and rescued elephants. The park is in the Mae Taeng valley, 60km from Chiang Mai, and provides a semi-wild environment for the animals. Visitors help wash the elephants and watch the herd, but there is no show or riding. Volunteering is also available.

Patara Elephant Farm ELEPHANT ENCOUNTER (☑ 08 1992 2551; www.pataraelephantfarm.com; day tour 5800B) Khun Pat is a passionate and thoughtful player in Chiang Mai's elephant-conservation tourism industry. His primary focus is to support the mother-baby bond, and combat Thailand's declining domesti-cated elephant population through tourism. His elephant farm is in a beautiful forested setting and offers an intimate and educa-tional elephant encounter. Guests become 'caretakers' for a day by conducting a health inspection, feeding, bathing, and exercising the animals. The farm is 30km west of Chi-ang Mai in Samoeng.

Baan Chang Elephant Park ELEPHANT ENCOUNTER (Map p240; ☑ 0 5381 4174; www.baanchang elephantpark.com; 147/1 Th Ratchadamnoen; tours 2400-4200B) Educating visitors about el-ephants and their preservation, Baan Chang is a solid choice in the conservation tourism model. Tours involve a day of mahout train-ing, including guiding, riding and bathing. Less expensive tours are for two people to one elephant. It is located in Mae Taeng, 50 minutes north of Chiang Mai.

Chiang Mai Rock Climbing Adventures ROCK CLIMBING (CMRCA; Map p240; ☑ 08 6911 1470; www.thailand climbing.com; 55/3 Th Ratchaphakhinai; climb-ing course 3000-4000B) CMRCA maintains many of the climbing routes at Crazy Horse Buttress (also known as 'The Crack'). Tours teach introductory and fundamental rock climbing, bouldering and caving. The office sells and rents gear, has an indoor climb-ing wall (adult/child 300/200B) and other climbing services, a partner-finding service and a bouldering wall for practice sessions.

Peak Adventure Tour ADVENTURE SPORTS (Map p240; ☑ 0 5380 0567; www.thepeakadventure. com; tours 1800-2500B) The Peak offers a vari-ety of adventure trips, including quad biking, abseiling, trekking, white-water rafting and rock climbing.

Siam River Adventures WHITE-WATER RAFTING (Map p240; ☑ 08 9515 1917; www.siamrivers.com; 17 Th Ratwithi; tours from 1800B) With more than a decade of experience, this white-wa-ter rafting outfit has a well-regarded safety reputation. The guides have swiftwater res-cue training and additional staff are located at dangerous parts of the river with throw

---

TREKKING IN CHIANG MAI

Thousands of visitors trek into the hills of northern Thailand each year hoping to see fantastic mountain scenery, interact with primitive cultures and ride elephants. Most come with an Indiana Jones sense of adventure but leave with disappointment: the actual walk through the jungle lasted less than an hour, the hill-tribe villagers were unin-terested in the lowlanders, and the other trekkers were boring.

Chiang Mai is not the only base for hill-tribe treks but it is the most accessible and one of the cheapest. Most companies operating out of Chiang Mai offer the same type of tour: a one-hour minibus ride to Mae Taeng or Mae Wang (depending on the duration of the trip), a brief hike to an elephant camp, a one-hour elephant ride to a waterfall, another hour rafting down a river and, for multiday tours, an overnight stay in or near a hill-tribe village. The day goes by pretty quickly and is perfectly suited for travellers who want a little bit of everything at an affordable price; day tours typically start at 1000B, which is shockingly cheap and is only sustainable if the trips are sold in great quantities and a lot of corners are cut. Most guesthouses in Chiang Mai act as booking agents in exchange for a commission, which in turn subsidises the cheap room rates.

For those looking for something different, Chiang Dao and Tha Ton are two scenic towns north of Chiang Mai that have fewer tourists and a variety of small-scale trek-king options. The drawback is that less well-known places have higher lodging and tour prices. These are the economic trade-offs.

THE ELEPHANT DEBATE

Thailand's emblematic animal is one of its strongest tourism draws. But the quality of the encounters and the welfare of the animals vary greatly. Government regulations offer little to no oversight, as they still classify elephants as modes of transport.

Without regulations, elephant welfare is left to consumers and other business owners, resulting in disagreements about what is safe and profitable. One of the biggest critics of elephant tourism is Sangduen (Lek) Chailert, whose Elephant Nature Park offers a successful alternative to the traditional elephant-as-entertainment model.

Khun Lek questions the safety and dignity of such popular elephant entertainment as riding. At her park, elephant riding is expressly excluded because many of her elephants suffer from mental illness and she feels that it is not a natural activity for the animals.

'Most of our elephants are rescued from traumatising situations, from injuries that have caused them to be handicapped, and more. It is one of the reasons I never want them to be disturbed again', explains Khun Lek. 'There are many ways to enjoy these beautiful giants with soft adventures [feeding and bathing]. I think it is not necessary for humans to be entertained by riding.'

The wider elephant tourism community recognises the need to curtail abuses at irresponsible facilities, but they don't always agree with Khun Lek about her specific examples of abuse. Patara (Pat) Trungprakan of Patara Elephant Farm, sees elephant riding as part of a health regimen.

'Elephants need exercise. They need to sink into the mud and sand to file their nails. Foot infection is one of the primary causes of death in captive elephants', says Khun Pat.

He gives the following tips to ensure safety of the creature during riding. 'The elephant should be fitted with a custom wooden seat; there should be special padding between the seat and the hide to prevent chafing and the elephant should be bathed beforehand to prevent skin irritation.'

Khun Pat's best practices for elephant welfare includes reproduction. 'Elephants have the right to be mother and father. If they have babies, they are doing what nature wants', says Khun Pat. 'Ask the camps how many elephant babies they have. Do they have a high birth rate, low death rate? Then they are taking care of the elephants.'

The other problem area for Khun Lek is the process of training elephants. 'I support many ways of the mahouts and the ways they are in terms of the traditional dress, the traditional ceremonies that bless, but nothing that includes animal abuse. I don't support the part of training animals by violence', says Khun Lek. The metal instrument (often referred to as a 'hook') used by mahouts to steer, communicate and reprimand elephants is seen by Khun Lek and other animal rights activists as an instrument of abuse.

'Many places in Thailand now don't use the hook and now use a bamboo stick, which is a good start. Before, no one believed they could control elephants without a hook, but today when they visit ENP [Elephant Nature Park] they can see that some things can be changed.'

Khun Pat doesn't see the hook as an inherently evil tool, but says that the degree to which it is used depends on the mahout. 'This tool is needed to keep elephants and humans safe. These are 5-tonne animals and one small man. If the elephant tries to grab vines growing on electricity lines, the mahout uses the hook to keep the elephant from electrocuting itself.' He also explains that food is often a more effective motivator in elephant training.

Proper medical treatment is another vital component of elephant welfare from Khun Pat's perspective. At some facilities, it isn't profitable to adequately address the elephants' health needs or to retire sick elephants from service. 'The animals also have the right to be restored to the best health possible as soon as possible. Keeping an elephant sick is unacceptable.'

The dialogue about what is safe for elephants, economically viable for their caretakers and entertaining for visitors continues, and will hopefully result in a more humane industry.

ropes. Trips can be combined with elephant trekking and village overnight stays. It also operates kayak trips.

Chiang Mai Mountain Biking & Kayaking
MOUNTAIN BIKING

(Map p240; ☑ 08 1024 7046, 0 5381 4207; www. chiangmaikayaking.com; 1 Th Samlan; tours 1550-2000B) A variety of guided mountain biking and kayaking trips head into the jungles and rivers, respectively, for fresh air, a good workout and mountain scenery. Tours are suited for all levels and adjusted for the seasons. There is a second branch (Map p240; 28 Th Kamphaeng Din) near the night market.

Gymkhana Club
SPORTS CLUB

(Map p234; ☑ 0 5324 1035; www.chiengmaigymkhana.com; Th Ratuthit) One of Thailand's oldest, this sports club was founded in 1898 by teak merchants and boasts many heritage-style features. Sport facilities include tennis courts, and golf and driving ranges that are open to nonmembers for a daily fee. It's southeast of the Nawarat Bridge just off Th Chiang Mai–Lamphun.

Namo
YOGA

(Map p240; ☑ 0 5332 6648; www.namochiangmai. com; 109/1 Th Moon Muang; classes 220B; ⊙10am & 6pm Mon-Sat) Tucked away down a quiet lane near Tha Pae Gate, Namo has drop-in yoga classes as well as workshops in chanting, qigong and massage.

🐾 Courses

Buddhist Meditation

The following temples offer *vipassana* meditation courses and retreats to English-language speakers. Participants should dress in modest white clothes, which can typically be purchased from the temple. Following Buddhist precepts, there is no set fee but donations are appreciated. Peruse the various websites for course descriptions and daily routines.

International Buddhism Center
MEDITATION

(IBC; ☑ 0 5329 5012; www.fivethousandyears.org; Wat Phra That Doi Suthep) Headquartered within the temple grounds on Doi Suthep, this centre offers beginner to advanced meditation retreats, lasting from three to 21 days.

Northern Insight Meditation Centre
MEDITATION

(☑ 0 5327 8620 ext 13; www.watrampoeng.net; Wat Ram Poeng) This intensive 26-day or longer course is best suited for serious meditation students. Days start at 4am and meals are taken in silence. See the website for a complete introduction to the strict rules of participation. The formal name for Wat Ram Poeng is Wat Tapotaram and it is located 4km south of Chiang Mai.

Wat Sisuphan
MEDITATION

(Map p234; ☑ 0 5320 0332; 100 Th Wualai; ⊙ 5.30-9pm Tue, Thu & Sat) This temple south of the old city offers an introduction to meditation using the four postures: standing, walking, sitting and lying down.

Wat Suan Dok Meditation Retreat
MEDITATION

(Map p234; ☑ 08 4609 1357; www.monkchat.net; Th Suthep; ⊙ Tue & Wed) The Buddhist university affiliated with Wat Suan Dok conducts a two-day meditation retreat. Participants should register in advance and meet at Wat Suan Dok for transfer to the meditation centre, 15km northeast of Chiang Mai. Check the website for more details.

Cooking

Cooking courses in Thai cuisine are another staple of Chiang Mai's holiday learning scene. Dozens of schools offer classes, typically costing around 900B to 1100B a day, either in town, such as at an atmospheric old house, or out of town in a garden or farm setting. For out-of-town schools, there is usually a city booking office. Classes are usually day or half-day programs. Students learn about Thai culinary herbs and spices, tour a local market and prepare a set menu, which might vary per season or day. Of course, you also get to eat the Thai food and travel home with a recipe booklet. When booking your course, ask about the student-to-teacher ratio as this will affect the quality of the experience.

Asia Scenic Thai Cooking
COOKING

(Map p240; ☑ 0 5341 8657; www.asiascenic.com; 31 Soi 5, Th Ratchadamnoen; courses 900-1000B) Khun Gayray's cooking school has expanded to include an out-of-town farm location as well as its original in-town spot for those with less time. The city classroom has a kitchen garden so you'll still see the food source.

Chiang Mai Thai Cookery School
COOKING

(Map p240; ☑ 0 5320 6388; www.thaicookery-school.com; 47/2 Th Moon Muang; course 1450B) One of Chiang Mai's first cooking schools holds classes in a rural setting outside of

Chiang Mai. The school also has a master-class with a northern Thai menu and it is run by TV chef Sompon Nabnian.

Gap's Thai Culinary Art School　COOKING
(Map p240; ☑ 0 5327 8140; www.gaps-house.com; 3 Soi 4, Th Ratchadamnoen; course 900B; ☺ closed Sun) Affiliated with the guesthouse Gap's House, classes are held out of town at the owner's house. The student-to-teacher ratio is an intimate 6:1.

Thai Farm Cooking School　COOKING
(Map p240; ☑ 08 7174 9285, 08 1288 5989; www.thaifarmcooking.com; Soi 9, Th Moon Muang; course 1100B) Teaches cooking classes at its organic farm, 17km outside of Chiang Mai.

Baan Thai　COOKING
(Map p240; ☑ 0 5335 7339; www.baanthaicookery.com; 11 Soi 5, Th Ratchadamnoen; course 900B)

Has an in-town location; prior to the class you select which dishes you would like to prepare and you are then grouped with people who made similar selections.

Language

Being a university town, Chiang Mai is an affordable and affable place for continuing education opportunities in Thai language.

American University Alumni　LANGUAGE
(AUA; Map p240; ☑ 0 5327 8407; www.learnthai-inchiangmai.com; 73 Th Ratchadamnoen; group course 4800B) Conducts six-week and eight-week Thai courses that work on mastering tones, small talk and basic reading and writing. Classes meet for two hours, Monday to Friday. Private instruction is also available.

MASSAGE: STRAIGHT UP, NO CHASER

Before there were spas in every corner of Thailand, there was just massage: a few mattresses on the floor and a surprisingly strong practitioner who could bend, stretch and pummel knotted bodies into jelly without a painful price tag. Thankfully Chiang Mai still has loads of these modest massage centres, many of which can be found on the temple grounds in simple *săh·lah* (open-air pavilion, often spelt *sala*), continuing an ancient tradition of the monasteries being a repository for traditional knowledge and healing. Here are a few recommendations to work out the kinks of the road without causing injury to the wallet:

Vocational Training Center of the Chiang Mai Women's Correctional Institution (Map p240; 100 Th Ratwithi; foot/traditional massage 150/180B; ☺ 8am-4.30pm Mon-Fri, 9am-4.30pm Sat & Sun) offers fantastic massages performed by female inmates participating in the prison's job-training rehabilitation program. Despite their incarceration, the ladies aren't career criminals but eager to turn their lives around with these new job skills. Those working in the centre are due for release within six months, and the money they earn is used after their release. The cafe next door sells other rehabilitation initiatives, including baked goods.

Ban Hom Samunphrai (☑ 0 5381 7362; www.homprang.com; Saraphi; steam bath 200B, massage 600-1300B) is a unique time capsule of old folk ways, 9km from Chiang Mai near the McKean Institute. Maw Hom (Herbal Doctor) is a licensed herb practitioner and massage therapist. She runs a traditional herbal steam bath, recreating what was once a common feature of rural villages. Traditional Thai massage is also available.

Thai Massage Conservation Club (Map p240; 99 Th Ratchamankha; massages 150-250B) employs only blind masseuses who are considered to be expert practitioners because of their heightened sense of touch.

Lila Thai Massage (Map p240; Th Phra Pokklao ; massage 200-600B; ☺ 10am-10pm) was established by the director of the Chiang Mai women's prison and offers post-release employment to the inmates who participated in the prison's massage training program. There are now five branches in the old city and a full menu of massage treatments.

Oasis Spa (Map p240; ☑ 0 5392 0111; www.oasisspa.net; 4 Th Samlan; treatments from 1700B) has a tranquil garden setting navigated by elevated walkways to private villas for single or couples treatments. If you've had a spa experience elsewhere in Thailand, the Oasis will be a familiar friend, offering scrubs, wraps, massage and Ayurvedic treatments.

Payap University LANGUAGE
(http://ic.payap.ac.th; Th Kaew Nawarat, Kaew Nawarat Campus; classes from 8000B) A private university founded by the Church of Christ of Thailand; offers intensive Thai language courses in 60-hour or 120-hour modules. There is also a three-day course in Thai language, culture and professional ethics (5000B) offered to foreign teachers.

Thai Boxing

Chiang Mai has several established gyms that have trained national champions, and the city's cost of living makes it an affordable place for extended stays.

Lanna Muay Thai Boxing Camp MARTIAL ARTS

(Kiatbusaba; Map p234; ☑ 0 5389 2102; www.lanna muaythai.com; 161 Soi Chang Khian, Th Huay Kaew; day/month 400/8000B) Offers *moo·ay tai* (also spelt *muay thai*) instruction to foreigners and Thais. The gym is famous for having trained the title-winning, transvestite boxer Parinya Kiatbusaba.

Chai Yai Gym MARTIAL ARTS

(☑ 08 2938 1364; www.chaiyaigym.com; 30/17 Th Sunpiliang, Nong Hoi; day/month 550/8000B) This 30-year veteran trains Thai and foreign fighters of all levels. It also offer children's courses and cardio-workout sessions. The gym is southeast of town.

Santai Muay Thai MARTIAL ARTS

(☑ 08 2528 6059; www.muay-thai-santai.com; 79 Moo 9, Sankamphaeng; day/month 400/8000B) Run by former prize fighters, Santai specialises in training *moo·ay tai* students to advance their skill sets and reach competitive levels. The gym is east of town.

Thai Massage

Some of these schools are government-accredited programs that will provide students with the fundamentals to practise Thai massage professionally. Some programs are also recognised as continuing education options by international body-work organisations.

Thai Massage School of Chiang Mai MASSAGE, YOGA

(TMC; ☑ 0 5385 4330; www.tmcschool.com; 203/6 Th Chiang Mai-Mae Jo; basic courses 6500-7500B) Northeast of town, this well-known school offers a government-licensed massage curriculum. There are three foundation levels and an intensive teacher-training program.

Old Medicine Hospital MASSAGE
(OMH; Map p234; ☑ 0 5327 5085; www.thaimassage-school.ac.th;78/1SoiSiwakaKomarat,ThWualai;courses 5000-6000B) Old Medicine's government-accredited curriculum is very traditional, with a northern-Thai slant, and it was one of the first to develop massage training for foreigners. There are two 10-day massage courses a month, as well as shorter foot and oil massage courses.

Chetawan Thai Traditional Massage School MASSAGE

(Map p234; ☑ 0 5341 0360; www.watpomassage. com; 7/1-2 Soi Samud Lanna, Th Pracha Uthit; general course 9500B) Bangkok's Wat Pho massage school established this Chiang Mai branch outside of town near Rajabhat University. Courses range from traditional to infant and child.

Lek Chaiya MASSAGE

(Map p240; ☑ 0 5327 8325; www.nervetouch.com; 27-29 Th Ratchadamnoen; courses 5000-7000B) Khun Lek learned *jàp sên* (literally 'nerve touch'), a northern Thai massage technique akin to acupressure, from her mother and became a well-known practitioner. Her son Jack carries on the business and the profession. Courses run from two to three days and cover about 50% of a traditional Thai massage course, with the remainder dedicated to the nerve-touch technique and herbal therapies. To experience *jàp sên*, stop in for a massage (550B to 1200B).

Art of Massage MASSAGE

(Map p240; ☑ 08 3866 2901; www.artofmassage. webs.com; Soi 3, Th Loi Kroh; courses 1200-2900B) Khun Wanna gets rave reviews for her practical training sessions, limited to a maximum of two people. Courses are typically two to three days, ideal for students looking for quick hands-on experience.

TEFL Training

A crummy job market back home has helped spur many recent graduates to turn their backpacking sojourn through Southeast Asia into a working abroad commitment, thanks to their accidental luck of being native English speakers. English teaching jobs are widely available throughout Thailand. Most schools don't require specialised degrees or certificates for native speakers, but coursework in teaching English as a foreign language (TEFL) prepares first-time teachers to have more success in the classroom through activities designed to engage students in a subject that is second nature for the native speaker.

TEFL courses come in varying degrees of legitimacy and have become, in recent years, a way to circumvent visa regulations in Thailand. For those truly interested in preparing for an English teaching job, quality TEFL schools should offer the following: trainers with several years of experience and a training diploma, accreditation from one of the international governing boards (either CELTA or TEFL International), a final exam and school practicums.

There are tonnes of TEFL schools in Chiang Mai, thanks to its reputation as an affordable and easy place to live. Most TEFL programs run for one month and issue certificates to teach English as a second language in Thailand and other countries.

Here are a few long-running programs with solid credentials.

UniTEFL International   TEFL
(Map p234; ☑08 8402 8217; www.unitefl.com; 123/1 Th Huay Kaew; certificate program 45,000B) Offers 120-hour certificate program with six practicums in Thai schools; uses TEFL International (TI) standards with access to other TI centres and job networks.

International House   TEFL
(www.ihbangkok.com; Vdara Resort & Spa, Mae Hia; certificate program 48,000B) International network of schools using CELTA standards; the school is headquartered in Bangkok with branches in Chiang Mai and Phuket. Classes in Chiang Mai are held at Vdara Resort & Spa (www.vdararesortandspa.com), 7km south of Chiang Mai.

⛳ Tours

Segway Gibbon   GUIDED TOUR
(☑08 4614 4004; www.segwaygibbon.com; 29/4-5 Th Kotchasan; tours 1599-1999B) Why march between Chiang Mai's temples and other cultural attractions, when you can glide through the old city on your own Segway? Guided two-hour tours take in the most popular sites; three-hour tours dive into the neighbourhoods and backstreets. This is the latest tour concept from Flight of the Gibbon company and shares a booking office.

Click & Travel   CYCLING
(☑0 5328 1553; www.clickandtravelonline.com; tours 1050-1200B; ♠) Click & Travel offers a pedal-powered, cultural trip with full- and half-day tours, visiting temples and attrac-

tions outside of the city centre. Routes and bikes suited for children are also available.

Chiang Mai Street Food Tours   FOOD
(☑08 5033 8161; www.chiangmaistreetfoodtours.com; tours 700B) Cooking schools are all the rage in Chiang Mai but for the rest of us who would rather eat than work, this tour comes to the rescue. Morning and evening tours take curious appetites through the old city to sample hallmark dishes. The evening market tour is a good introduction to this classic Thai dining experience.

✯ Festivals & Events

Chiang Mai is famous for the Flower Festival, Songkran and Loi Krathong; make your travel arrangements far in advance during these periods.

Chiang Mai Red Cross & Winter Fair   CULTURE
This 10-day festival assumes a country-fair atmosphere, with food booths purveying northern Thai cuisine and cultural displays. It is held at the Chiang Mai City Arts & Cultural Centre from late December to early January.

Flower Festival   FLOWERS
This agricultural celebration (called *têt·sà·gahn mái dòrk mái ʰbrà·dàp*) is held over a three-day period in early February and includes displays of flower arrangements, cultural performances and beauty pageants. The festival highlight is the parade that starts at Saphan Nawarat, travelling down Th Tha Phae and then all the way to Suan Buak Hat.

Chiang Mai Chinese New Year   NEW YEAR
The city's Chinatown heralds its cultural new year in February with a spotlight on Chinese food and cultural displays.

Songkran   NEW YEAR
The traditional Thai New Year (12 to 14 April) is celebrated in Chiang Mai with boozy enthusiasm. Thousands of revellers line up along all sides of the moat to throw water on passersby (and each other) in the city. It is virtually impossible to stay dry during the five days of this festival. Prior to the start of the pandemonium, more traditional Songkran rituals are held at Wat Phra Singh.

Poy Sang Long (Poy Luang)   RELIGIOUS
Young boys with Shan (Tai Yai) heritage participate in this three-day ordination ceremony (usually in April). Novices are dressed in

makeup and garish costumes to represent the time when Buddha was a prince, prior to his search for enlightenment. Wat Pa Pao, Wat Ku Tao and Wat Sisuphan host this ceremony.

Intakin Festival
RELIGIOUS

Held at Wat Chedi Luang in mid-May, this religious festival (known as *ngahn tam bun sǒw in·tá·gin*) is centred on the *làk meu·ang* (city pillar) and propitiates the city's guardian deity to ensure that the annual monsoon will arrive on time.

Loi Krathong
RELIGIOUS

This lunar holiday (usually October or November) is celebrated along Mae Ping with small lotus-shaped boats honouring the spirit of the river. Northern Thais call it Yi Peng, which is traditionally celebrated by launching illuminated lanterns into the night sky.

🛏 Sleeping

With the influx of Chinese tourists, Chiang Mai's hotel scene is changing rapidly. New hotels and guesthouses have sprung up all over the city and are often full, even during the traditional low season. Be prepared to do some hunting if you arrive without a hotel booking, and make reservations in advance if visiting during Chinese New Year, Songkran and other international holiday periods.

Accommodation prices in the city have also increased, with 1000B or less being the new budget category. Dorms and hostels have sprung up to fill in the disappearing backpacker cheapies, though communal sleeping doesn't offer great value when single rooms can still be found for only 50B to 100B more than dorms; some travellers do prefer the social aspect of hostels over the privacy of single occupancy. Be aware that sometimes hotels will call themselves 'hostels'. For long-term visitors there are a handful of places that offer weekly and monthly discounts or a flat monthly rate with additional electricity and water usage fees. Free wi-fi is standard in Chiang Mai accommodation.

Many budget guesthouses subsidise their room rates through commissions from booking treks and tours. Most expect that their guests will take a trek, and will give them priority if vacancies are limited. Staff usually inform nontrekkers that the room is available for a limited period.

The top-end range is dominated mainly by huge corporate-style hotels. The more interesting ones are the intimate boutique hotels that tend to marry antique Lanna elements with modern amenities. At the summit of the scale are the destination resorts that have recreated a village setting complete with rice fields and historic architecture.

🏛 Old City

There are heaps of guesthouses in the northeast and southeast corners of the old city.

★ Awanahouse
GUESTHOUSE $

(Map p240; ☑ 0 5341 9005; www.awanahouse. com; 7 Soi 1, Th Ratchadamnoen; r 375-1000B; ❄ 🐱 🅿) Popular with families, this multi-storey building has bright and well-decorated rooms, ranging from basic to just right. The ground-level pool and the rooftop chill-out area are added bonuses.

Gap's House
GUESTHOUSE $

(Map p240; ☑ 0 5327 8140; www.gaps-house.com; 3 Soi 4, Th Ratchadamnoen; r 550-850B; ❄ 🐱) A matron among guesthouses, good old Gap's still has a jungle-like garden and budget rooms in old-fashioned wooden houses. Bring your mozzie spray. No advance reservations. Gap's is also famous for its Thai cooking course and nightly vegetarian buffet.

Nice Apartments
GUESTHOUSE $

(Map p240; ☑ 0 5321 8290; 15 Soi 1, Th Ratchadamnoen; r 400-500B; ❄) This low-rise is a decent deal with clean rooms and a central location. The service is friendly and the shaded outdoor seating is a perfect perch from which to plot the day.

Aoi Garden Home
GUESTHOUSE $

(Map p240; ☑ 08 3574 8174; 51/1 Soi 4, Th Singharat; dm 150, r 300-380B; ❄ 🐱) This self-described 'homey hostel' is set in a traditional wooden house with an ample garden and lots of shady nooks. Five-bed dorms are mixed; private rooms share bathrooms.

Lamchang House
GUESTHOUSE $

(Map p240; ☑ 0 5321 0586; 24 Soi 7, Th Moon Muang; r 200-300B) One of Chiang Mai's cheapest, this old wooden house has basic fan rooms with shared bathrooms and simple, ascetic charm.

The downstairs rooms are a little dark but there's a pleasant front garden and attached restaurant.

Julie Guesthouse   GUESTHOUSE $
(Map p240; ☎ 0 5327 4355; www.julieguesthouse.
com; 7 Soi 5, Th Phra Pokklao; dm 80B, r 100-350B;
@) Ever popular Julie is Chiang Mai's sleep
and be-seen scene. Rooms boast little to no
mod cons (shared bathrooms, cold showers)
but the cafe is full of enthusiastic first-timers.

In the evenings, folks retire to the covered
roof terrace strung up with hammocks.

Thong Ran's House   GUESTHOUSE $
(Map p240; ☎ 0 532 77307; www.thongranhouse.
com; 105 Th Ratchamankha; r 600B; ✳@) This
new guesthouse has cosy, stylish rooms in a
quiet soi off of the main road. The location is
slightly removed from the usual tourist hub-
bub but still central.

Diva Guesthouse   GUESTHOUSE $
(Map p240; ☎ 0 5327 3851; www.divaguesthouse.
com; 84/13 Th Ratchaphakhinai; dm 110B, r 250-
800B; ✳@@) One of many new hostels in
town, Diva does communal sleeping with
a hip attitude. Rooms range from dorms to
family suites. The downstairs cafe is a happening scene.

Smile House 1   GUESTHOUSE $
(Map p240; ☎ 0 5320 8661; www.smilehousechi-
angmai.com; 5 Soi 2, Th Ratchamankha; r 300-
1000B; ✳@≋) A little backpacker village
flourishes around this old house tucked
away on a tranquil soi. The rooms are basic
boxes popular with young backpackers and
families because of the lounge-worthy pool.

The atmosphere is friendly and the owner
confirmed that the old house once served
as the 'safe house' of Kun Sa, the infamous
Shan-Chinese opium warlord.

Rendezvous Guest House   GUESTHOUSE $
(Map p240; ☎ 0 5321 3763; 3/1 Soi 5, Th Ratchadamnoen; r 350-900B; ✳@) On a soi filled
with budget options, Rendezvous stands out
from the pack with clean, adequate rooms.
It flaunts its backpacker credentials with
handy traveller info.

Jonadda Guest House   GUESTHOUSE $
(Map p240; ☎ 0 5322 7281; 23/1 Soi 2, Th Ratwithi; r
250-450B; ✳) This reliable cheapie has spotless basic rooms.

Siri Guesthouse   GUESTHOUSE $
(Map p240; ☎ 0 5332 6550; 31/3 Soi 5, Th Moon
Muang; r 350-450B; ✳) This low-key guesthouse has an assortment of quality budget
rooms in a central location. The upstairs
rooms are more spacious and airy than the
cheaper ground-floor rooms.

Thapae Gate Lodge   GUESTHOUSE $
(Map p240; ☎ 0 5320 7134; www.thapaegatelodge.
com; 38/7 Soi 2, Th Moon Muang; r 300-600B;
✳@) This German-Thai guesthouse has basic bunkers with a sliding scale of amenities,
from air-con to extra space and balconies.
The beds can be a little saggy.

Banjai Garden   GUESTHOUSE $
(Map p240; ☎ 08 5716 1635; 43 Soi 3, Th Phra
Pokklao; r 350-450B; @) This pretty wooden
house has a homey appeal and a pleasant
garden for hanging out. The simple rooms
have shared bathrooms and better-than-
average beds. There's also a shared mini-
kitchen.

Boonthavon   GUESTHOUSE $
(Map p240; ☎ 0 5322 6700; www.bonnthavon.com;
Soi 1, Th Ratchadamnoen; r 550B; ✳@@) This
multistorey building won't impress from
the outside, but the recently updated rooms
(fresh tiled floors and bathrooms) are un-
beatable value. Here's hoping the mattresses
get an upgrade soon.

60 Blue House   GUESTHOUSE $
(Map p240; ☎ 0 8691 9277; www.60bluehouse.com;
32-33 Th Ratchaphakhinai; dm 200-500B; @) This
ladies-only hostel has four-bed dorms and
private rooms (all shared bathroom). Khun
Tao treats everyone like a friend, making
sure they know where to go and what to do.

VIP House   GUESTHOUSE $
(Map p240; ☎ 08 1366 5625; Soi 1, Th Ratchadamnoen; r 250-500B; ✳@) What VIP lacks in
personality it makes up for in budget value:
rooms are basic and clean with en suites.

Supreme House   GUESTHOUSE $
(Map p240; ☎ 0 5322 2480; 44/1 Soi 9, Th Moon
Muang; r 350-550B; ✳@) Multistorey building
with a relaxed atmosphere and rooms with
fan or air-con.

★ **Sri Pat Guest House**   GUESTHOUSE $$
(Map p240; ☎ 0 5321 8716; 16 Soi 7, Th Moon
Muang; r 1000-1400B; ✳@≋) A standout in
the flashpacker category, Sri Pat has just the
right dose of personality. Rooms have sunny
dispositions, celadon-coloured tiles, folksy
cotton drapes and balconies.

★ **Villa Duang Champa**   HOTEL $$
(Map p240; ☎ 0 5332 7199; http://duangchampa.
com; 82 Th Ratchadamnoen; r from 1500B; ✳@)
Duang Champa is an excellent small hotel in
a heritage-style building. Rooms are pretty
enough to be in a design magazine, with

minimalist modern furnishings. Stick to the hotel as the dark, cramped guesthouse rooms are not a good deal.

TJR Boutique House
HOTEL $$

(Map p240; ☑ 0 5332 6525; Soi 1, Th Moon Muang; r 1000-1200B; ❋@☎) A new apartment-style hotel, TJR has huge rooms, huge beds and bathrooms with tubs. Street-facing rooms get views of the mountain. It is often booked as the desk clerk speaks Chinese and English.

Mini Cost
HOTEL $$

(Map p240; ☑ 0 5341 8787; www.minicostcm.com; 19/4 Soi 1, Th Ratchadamnoen; r 1000B; ❋@☎) This apartment-style building has contemporary rooms, comfy beds and more couches and chaise longues than you could ever sit on. It delivers solid midrange comfort at a modest price.

3 Sis
HOTEL $$

(Map p240; ☑ 0 5327 3243; www.the3sis.com; 1 Soi 8, Th Phra Pokklao; d 1500-1800B; ❋☎) A mini hotel empire occupies this corner spot. Rooms are well proportioned with plenty of flashpacker appeal. The 'vacation lodge' building has more flair than the 'front' building, with lovely wooden floors and additional mod cons. The breezy lobby provides a communal space, and rates include breakfast.

Koko Palm Inn
HOTEL $$

(Map p240; ☑ 08 6428 0495; www.kokopalminn. com; Soi 6, Th Ratchadamnoen; r 1200-1400B; ❋☎) This new boutique has only eight rooms facing a garden filled with ponds and palms. The rooms are compact yet cute, and bathrooms are big enough for serious grooming.

Baan Hanibah Bed & Breakfast
HOTEL $$

(Map p240; ☑ 0 5328 7524; www.baanhanibah. com; 6 Soi 8, Th Moon Muang; r 900-1400B; ❋☎) Protected by a garden of fragrant frangipani trees, Baan Hanibah is a relaxed boutique escape in the heart of the old city. The converted teak house retains its traditional ambience while providing small yet stylish rooms.

Charcoa House
HOTEL $$

(Map p240; ☑ 0 5321 2681; www.charcoa.com; 4 Soi 1, Th Si Phum; r 1400-2600B; ❋@☎) Like a petit four, this boutique hotel has small but pretty rooms that rely on an imported heritage style of exposed timbers and white-washed walls. The attached bakery and cafe gets rave reviews.

Hotel M
HOTEL $$

(Map p240; ☑ 0 5321 1069; www.hotelmchiang-mai.com; 2-6 Th Ratchadamnoen; r 1450-2100B; ❋) Recently rebranded, Hotel M is a multi-storey affair centrally located next to Pratu Tha Phae (Tha Phae gate). It has modern, well-sized rooms for guests looking for convenience and comfort, though it lacks some of the flash and flourish of its peers. If only it had a pool, then we would be smitten.

Buri Gallery
GUESTHOUSE $$

(Map p240; ☑ 0 5341 6500; www.burigallery.com; 102 Th Ratchadamnoen; r 1600-2400B; ❋☎❊) Buri Gallery occupies a converted teak building decorated with Lanna handicrafts. Skip the cramped ground-floor superior rooms with walls too thin to block out noise. The upstairs deluxe rooms are quieter and have small terraces, and the new villa building offers more privacy. Though the rates are a tad high, the location near Wat Phra Singh is a bonus.

Top North Hotel
HOTEL $$

(Map p240; ☑ 0 5327 9623; www.topnorthgroup. com; 41 Th Moon Muang; r 900-1500B; ❋☎❊) Right in the old city, this place sprawls like a resort but the rates remain reasonable. Standard and superior rooms in the older building are a bit of a mixed bag (en suites get a little musty). The spiffy new wing is a much better option. The real pull is the salt-water swimming pool. Rates include breakfast.

Tamarind Village
HOTEL $$$

(Map p240; ☑ 0 5341 8896-9; www.tamarindvil-lage.com; 50/1 Th Ratchadamnoen; r from 7000B; ❋☎❊) One of the first of the 'Lanna revival' hotels in Chiang Mai, Tamarind Village recreates the quiet spaces of a temple on the grounds of an old tamarind orchard. The bamboo-shrouded walkway and white-washed perimeter wall shut out the distractions of the modern world, while the garden courtyards create an intimate space for some serious self-indulgence.

Vieng Mantra
HOTEL $$$

(Map p240; ☑ 0 5332 6640; www.viengmantra. com; 9 Soi 1, Th Ratchadamnoen; r 1500-4500B; ❋@☎❊) A small hotel tucked into modest Soi 1, Vieng Mantra creates an oasis with its courtyard pool and landscaped gardens. Rooms boast Lanna-style decor and pool-

COUNTRY ESCAPES

Becoming acclimatised to Chiang Mai's laid-back pace and then finding it too hectic is a common affliction. To escape from your escape, there are many scenic country resorts just beyond the superhighways and the sun-stroked suburbs where you can adore misty mountains, green fields and tropical forests. The following are less than two hours' drive from Chiang Mai.

Kaomai Lanna Resort (☎05383 4470; www.kaomailanna.com; Th Chiang Mai-Hot/Rte 108, Km 29, San Pa Thong; r from 3500B; ❄ ☀) has turned many of the property's abandoned tobacco-curing sheds into comfortable lodgings amid a lush garden. This used to be one of many northern Thai tobacco farms supplying the international cigarette market before China supplanted the local growers. The resort also arranges tours to the nearby handicraft villages (which are truly villages instead of souvenir markets). The yoga studio, spa and swimming pool mean you can easily spend a few relaxing days here. Even if you don't stay here, the outdoor restaurant serves superb Thai food. The resort is south of Chiang Mai on the outskirts of San Pa Thong and can be used as a base for exploring Doi Inthanon.

Rabeang Pasak Tree House (☎08 7660 1243; ChiangmaiTreehouse@gmail.com; Rd 4031, Baan Pasak Ngam , Doi Saket; r from 2000B) is a kid's fantasy come true: wooden huts are built high among the tree branches. Lodging is simple – open-air bathrooms and basic beds – but far from ordinary. A small creek runs through the wooded property and jungle insects gossip nonstop. Bicycles are available for exploring the nearby village, and tours can be arranged to a to bat cave and waterfall. Online booking is available through its Facebook page. It is 75km north of Chiang Mai in the Doi Saket area.

Chai Lai Orchid (☎0 86923 0867; www.chailaiorchid.com; 202 Moo 9, Tambon Mae Win, Mae Wang; r 1200-2250B; ❄ ☀) is a nature resort planted in the middle of the forest, across the Mae Wang river via a suspended footbridge, and shares space with an elephant camp. Huts range from rustic to resort-ish. Jungle critters and trumpeting elephants serenade visitors, and a variety of activities (elephant bathing, bamboo rafting, Thai cooking) are offered. The resort also partners with a social welfare group that provides educational and professional development training to at-risk women. It is 45km southwest of Chiang Mai.

Stonefree House (☎0 8503 17332; 7/4 Moo 7, Yuwa, San Pa Thong; r from 400B) redefines easygoing with its backpacker country 'resort'. This down-home operation has four rustic bungalows that squat beside a rice field and longan trees. The price is modest and the vibe is rasta. It is 21km south of Chiang Mai.

Tharnthong Lodge (☎08 6420 5354; www.tharnthonglodges.com; r 1200-4000B) is the Thai version of the idyllic alpine chalet tucked into a jungle embrace. A pebble-strewn stream bisects the garden-filled property that backs up against a dense jungle. Resident bunnies hop among the sitting areas and the flowers delighting the visiting children. The spacious bungalows sized for couples and families have porches and patios for watching all the natural solitude. The restaurant is a popular weekend stop for Thais who stroll the grounds posing for pictures. The lodge has become an anti-gravity-yoga training centre. It is 50km east of Chiang Mai in the Mae Kampong area.

view balconies, though sizes and standards vary. Walk-in rates are cheaper if it's not busy.

Rachamankha HOTEL $$$
(Map p234; ☎0 5390 4111; www.rachamankha.com; off Soi 1, Th Samlan; r from 8000B; ❄ @ ☎ ☀) The encore effort by architect Ong-ard Satrabhandu after Tamarind Village, Rachamankha imitates an ancient monastery in Lampang. Rooms are understated opulent and the superiors are quite small. The deluxe rooms are more generous, with four-poster beds and bathrooms that double the living space. The highlight is the hotel's light-strewn library smelling of polished wood and musty paper.

U Chiang Mai HOTEL $$$
(Map p240; ☎0 5332 7000; www.uhotelsresorts.com; 70 Th Ratchadamnoen; r 4500-6000B; ❄ ☎ ☀) Briefcases and golf clubs are shuttled out of this corporate-friendly hotel.

The central courtyard infinity pool creates a resort-like escape in the heart of the old city. And the 24-hour checkout policy (you leave at the same time you arrived) is handy for late departures.

East of the Old City

While it isn't as quaint as the old city, Th Tha Phae is just as convenient for sightseeing and nightlife and is even closer to the night bazaar. Corporate hotels with business centres and conference capacity occupy the area near the Chiang Mai Night Bazaar.

★ Baan Kaew Guest House
GUESTHOUSE $

(Map p234; ☑ 0 5327 1606; www.baankaew-guesthouse.com; 142 Th Charoen Prathet; r 680-800B; ❋ 🛜) This two-storey, apartment-style place is a good honest deal in a quiet part of town. Rooms have all the basics plus small balconies to enjoy the spacious garden. The setting, away from the road and slightly removed from the touristy night bazaar, will make you feel like a local instead of a visitor.

Soho Hostel
HOSTEL $

(Map p240; ☑ 0 5320 6360; 64/2 Th Loi Kroh; dm 200-300B, r 1000-1800; ❋ 🛜) Loi Kroh is better known for girly bars than backpacker bunks, but that hasn't prevented this huge hostel from winning fans. It has six- to 12-bed dorms and private rooms.

Daret's House
GUESTHOUSE $

(Map p240; ☑ 0 5323 5440; 4/5 Th Chaiyaphum; s/d 170/220B) Dependable Daret's has stacks of basic, well-worn but clean rooms at a smidge more than what dorms charge for herd sleeping. You can even splurge for hot-water showers.

Roong Ruang Hotel
HOTEL $

(Map p240; ☑ 0 5323 4746; www.roongruang.com; 398 Th Tha Phae; r 600-900B; ❋ @) With a prime location near Pratu Tha Phae, Roong Ruang is a great deal for an older-style hotel.

Rooms are dated but still adequate for the price. Cheaper rooms are fine to crash, just a bit cell-like and dark.

Stay With Me Guesthouse
GUESTHOUSE $

(Map p240; ☑ 0 5320 8077; 4 Soi 6, Th Tha Phae; r 350-650B; ❋ 🛜) The former Tawan guesthouse now sports a new name and a cheery coat of paint. Rooms are basic (fans, shared bathrooms) but there's a lovely garden and a hipster vibe.

★ Mo Rooms
HOTEL $$

(Map p240; ☑ 0 5328 0789; www.morooms.com; 263/1-2 Th Tha Phae; r 2800-3500B; ❋ @ 🛜) This art-concept hotel has 12 rooms, individually decorated by local artists according to the Chinese zodiac. For an auspicious stay, pick the room that matches your birth year. The rooms are quirky endeavours with funky beds, angular windows and 'art you can live in', though many of the bathrooms are not self-contained, turning a toilet trip into performance art.

Thapae Boutique House
HOTEL $$

(Map p240; ☑ 0 5328 4295; www.thapaeboutiquehouse.com; 4 Soi 5, Th Tha Phae; r 1000-1400B; ❋ @) This reliable flashpacker hotel has colourful rooms and tiled bathrooms. Superior rooms are the best deal. Rates include breakfast.

Imperial Mae Ping Hotel
HOTEL $$

(Map p240; ☑ 0 5328 3900; www.imperialhotels.com; Th Loi Kroh & Th Kamphaeng Din; r 2000-4000B; ❋ @ 🛜) Though it has its shortcomings, this older specimen is the best of a bunch of lacklustre hotels around the night bazaar. The rooms are unspectacular but the pool is a redemption. Superior rooms are better value than deluxe.

Banthai Village
HOTEL $$$

(Map p240; ☑ 0 5325 2789; www.banthaivillage.com; 19 Soi 3, Th Tha Phae; r 6000-8000B; ❋ @ 🛜) This boutique 'rice-village' strikes the right balance between intimacy and privacy. Several terraced houses shelter a central swimming pool framed by birds-of-paradise flowers. The 33 rooms have funky fittings, huge stone bath-tubs and dinner-plate-sized showerheads. Hunt for discounted rates online as published rates are too high for what you get.

DusitD2 Chiang Mai
HOTEL $$$

(Map p240; ☑ 0 5399 9999; www.dusit.com; 100 Th Chang Khlan; r from 3500B; ❋ @ 🛜) One of Chiang Mai's only 'cool' corporate hotels, DusitD2 does minimalism with intelligent design. The rooms are comfortable and functional as well as slick and spare. Mountain views are available from the 6th floor up, and the view from the fitness room makes repetitive exercise more tolerable. It is also smack bang in the night bazaar area.

Yaang Come Village
BOUTIQUE HOTEL $$$

(Map p234; ☑ 0 5323 7222; www.yaangcome.com; 90/3 Th Si Donchai; r 7000-10,000B; ❋ @ 🛜)

A clever twist on the Lanna-style hotel is this homage to a Tai Lue village, based on the owner's travels to the Yunnan region of China. All rooms are spacious with murals, textiles and teak furniture, and have balconies. For what you actually get the rooms are a tad overpriced, but walk-in rates are heavily discounted.

Le Meridien Chiang Mai HOTEL $$$
(Map p240; ☏ 0 5325 2666; www.lemeridien.com/chiangmai; 108 Th Chang Khlan; r from 3000B; ❄ 🛜 ☒) This corporate hotel delivers a sleek and modern package in the middle of the night bazaar. Rooms are spacious and contemporary, with the ever-popular see-through bathroom. But the infinity pool with mountain views is a much better place to be seen.

🛏 Riverside

The neighbourhoods on either bank of the riverside are less touristy, but are still accessible to the night market and other attractions. It is an ideal 'opt-out' spot for Chiang Mai veterans.

★ Riverside House GUESTHOUSE $
(Map p234; ☏ 0 5324 1860; www.riversidehouse-chiangmai.com; 101 Th Chiang Mai–Lamphun; r 550-1500B; ❄ @ 🛜 ☒) Near the Saphan Lek (Iron Bridge), this guesthouse is low-key but high-powered. Clean and spacious rooms populate a pretty garden with pool. Rates rise with amenities, including TV and fridge.

Hollanda Montri GUESTHOUSE $
(Map p234; ☏ 0 5324 2450; www.hollandamontri.com; 365 Th Charoenrat; r 450-550B; ❄ @) Readers often recommend this place. It's a bit out of town, north of Saphan Ratanakosin, and the accommodation is fairly rudimentary but the riverside setting is nice.

★ Baan Orapin B&B $$
(Map p234; ☏ 0 5324 3677; www.baanorapin.com; 150 Th Charoenrat; r from 2400-3600B; ❄ @ ☒) It's a family affair at Baan Orapin, a pretty garden compound anchored by a stately teak house, which has been in the family since 1914. Luxurious guest residences (a total of 15 rooms) are in separate and modern buildings spread throughout the property.

River View Lodge HOTEL $$
(Map p234; ☏ 0 5327 1109; www.riverviewlodgch.com; 25 Soi 4, Th Charoen Prathet; r 1800-2200B;

❄ @ ☒) This breezy lodge is the perfect antidote to the hustle of the night bazaar area. Its quiet riverside setting is enhanced by a lush garden and pool. The rooms are a tad lacklustre but many don't mind when a chirping red bul-bul volunteers as a morning alarm clock.

Galare Guest House GUESTHOUSE $$
(Map p234; ☏ 0 5381 8887; www.galare.com; 7 Soi 2, Th Charoen Prathet; r 1100B; ❄) This quiet riverside lodge is close, but not too close, to the night bazaar. It has slightly dated but comfortable rooms with shared verandah, and the river-facing restaurant is a pleasant spot to start the morning.

🛏 West of the Old City

There are a mix of options in this part of town ranging from long-term hotels to hip boutiques. Staying west of the old city puts you close to Chiang Mai University and Th Nimmanhaemin's bars and restaurants.

★ Sakulchai HOTEL $
(Map p246; ☏ 0 5321 1982; Soi Plubpueng, Th Huay Kaew; r 590-790B; ❄ 🛜) The neighbourhood has zero ambience but this multistorey hotel is excellent value: midrange standards at budget prices. Rooms are large and new with all the mod cons.

It is at the end of a quiet soi just north of Kad Suan Kaew.

Spicythai Backpackers HOSTEL $
(Map p234; ☏ 08 3477 9467; www.spicyhostels.com; 14 Th Hutsadisawee; dm 250B; ❄ @ 🛜) Recommended by readers, this place offers single-sex dorms in a converted residence. It is north of the city and has a garden with hammocks, and offers a free continental breakfast and a homey setting.

Misoland Room & Tour GUESTHOUSE $
(Map p246; ☏ 0 5389 4989; 9 Soi 7, Th Nimmanhaemin; d 150B, r 500B) One of Nimman's few budget spots, Misoland is really a Korean restaurant and travel agent with a side business in renting dorms and private rooms. It's pretty basic but clean.

Long-term stays are also available.

Uniserv-International Center Hostel HOTEL $
(Map p246; ☏ 0 5394 2881; 239 Th Nimmanhaemin; r 690-790B; ❄ @) Can't get much closer to the university than this campus hotel.

Rooms are large and dated but some have views of the mountain.

There are no dorms despite the errant 's' in the name.

International Hotel Chiangmai HOTEL $

(Map p234; ☑ 0 5322 1819; www.ymcachiangmai. org; 11 Soi Sermsak, Th Hutsadisawee; r 500-700B; ✳ @ ☎ ☲) This local YMCA branch has well-priced, if slightly worn, rooms. On the 6th floor and higher, you get great mountain views.

To get here, turn onto Th Hutsadisawee from the corner of Th Huay Kaew and Th Mani Nopharat and then take your first left.

Dome HOTEL $$

(Map p246; ☑ 0 5340 5400; www.thedomechiang-mai.com; 1 Soi Plubpueng, Th Huay Kaew; r 800-1200B; ✳ ☎) A sleeper hit, the Dome has basic but modern rooms with lots of natural light, generous floor plans and views of the mountain on the 8th floor and higher.

Weekly and monthly rates are available, making it a popular long-term residence.

Baan Say-La GUESTHOUSE $$

(Map p246; ☑ 08 5618 1110; www.baansaylaguest-house.com; Soi 5, Th Nimmanhaemin; r 600-900B; ✳ ☎) This bohemian-chic guesthouse has basic but stylish rooms with shared bathrooms, four-poster beds and rattan furnishing. It isn't the best bargain but Th Nimman doesn't do budget well.

Nimman Boutique Resort HOTEL $$

(Map p246; ☑ 0 5322 2638; www.nimmanresort. com; 29 Soi 17, Th Nimmanhaemin; r from 1200B; ✳ ☎) This well-priced hotel does smart and efficient rooms in the otherwise overpriced Nimman neighbourhood. Standards are modern if a bit small. Paths wind through a small garden and there are many stylish restaurants and bars nearby.

Pann Malee Home GUESTHOUSE $$

(Map p246; ☑ 0 5328 9147; off Soi 17, Th Nim-manhaemin; r 1000-1600B; ✳) This converted townhouse feels like you're sleeping over at an arty friend's house. The rooms are eclectically furnished, reflecting the personalities of the owner's family members.

Yesterday Hotel BOUTIQUE HOTEL $$

(Map p246; ☑ 0 5321 3809; www.yesterday.co.th; 24 Th Nimmanhaemin; r from 2000B; ✳ @) Yesterday does a quick trip backwards to the near past. The common spaces of the converted apartment building are decorated with vintage prints, old phonographs and the soon-to-be-extinct tube televisions. Rooms are plush, bathroom fittings impressive, and superior rooms come with balcony but no view; deluxe rooms are a better deal.

🛏 Elsewhere

Viangbua Mansion HOTEL $$

(Map p234; ☑ 0 5341 1202; www.viangbua-chi-angmai.com; 3/1 Soi Viangbua, Th Chang Pheuak; r from 750B, per week 5600-8400B; ✳ @ ☎) North of Pratu Chang Pheuak, this serviced-apartment hotel doesn't have the best location for sightseers but it has plenty of amenities and comfort for long-term guests. The rooms have contemporary furnishings, fridge, small lounge, and some have kitchens. Monthly rates are also available.

Tri Yaan Na Ros BOUTIQUE HOTEL $$$

(Map p234; ☑ 0 5327 3174; www.triyaannaros.com; 156 Th Wualai; r from 3675B; ✳ ☎) A superb honeymoon candidate, this boutique hotel creates a romantic reconstruction of the past with its artfully restored house, galleried chambers and narrow walkways. Rooms are intimate and old-fashioned, with four-poster beds. There are only eight rooms and the owner is a charming host.

Four Seasons Chiang Mai RESORT $$$

(☑ 0 5329 8181; www.fourseasons.com; Th Mae Rim-Samoeng Kao; r from 25,000B; ✳ @ ☎ ☲) Chiang Mai's first destination resort features vaulted pavilion suites and residences spread amid 8 hectares of landscaped gardens and rice terraces worked by water buffalo. The resort is north of the city in the forested foothills and includes all the necessary self-contained distractions: cooking school, award-winning spa, swimming pool and tennis courts.

Dhara Dhevi RESORT $$$

(☑ 0 5388 8888; www.dharadhevi.com; 51/4 Th Chiang Mai-San Kamphaeng; r from 18,500B; ✳ @ ☎ ☲) A kingdom unto itself, the Dhara Dhevi has recreated a royal Lanna village with footpaths through walled residences and terraced rice fields. So much architectural history has been reproduced here that the resort fancies itself a cultural attraction, offering guided tours to guests. The rooms are, of course, regal and there is a slightly cheaper colonial wing.

It's 5km east of the old city.

STIMULATING BREWS

Chiang Mai's creative and sociable temperament has eagerly adopted the global phenomenon of cafe culture. There are so many coffeeshops in town that they appear to outnumber the ubiquitous 7-Elevens. Many shops serve Arabica beans grown in the surrounding highlands, introduced as a replacement crop for opium. Thai coffee tends to be lighter than the brawny Starbucks beverages but most people opt for the dessert-in-a-cup drinks, such as iced coffee. For drinks that require steamed milk, Thais take great artistic expression in foam art. Courting a cafe is a common Chiang Mai pastime and here are a few introductory dates:

Libernard Cafe (Map p240; 36 Th Chaiyaphum; dishes 50-110B; ⊗8am-5pm Tue-Sun) Unassuming Libernard Cafe is run by Pong who roasts her own beans daily, making adjustments based on the day's climate. She brews a smooth latte, which hardly needs to be spiked with sugar, and her banana pancakes will make you a fan of this often-derided dish.

Ristr8to (Map p246; Th Nimmanhaemin; coffee 60-120B; ⊗7am-8pm) This high-octane cafe transforms a cup of coffee into a tasting experience. The complicated menu requires selecting coffee strength (beans to water ratio), bean origin and then coffee type (coffee to cream ratio). Your drink comes with tasting notes (juicy with hints of berries) and is easily the best cup of mud in town.

Akha Ama Cafe (Map p234; 9/1 Soi 3, Th Hutsadisawee, Mata Apartment; coffee drinks from 50B; ⊗9am-9pm) Organic, fair trade coffee is the centrepiece of this cafe, the brainchild of an enterprising Akha who was the first in his village to graduate from college. His personal story adds sweetness to each cup. There is a second branch (Map p240; www.akhaama.com; 175/1 Th Ratchadamnoen; ⊗8am-8pm; 🛜) in the old city.

Raming Tea House (Map p240; Th Tha Phae; drinks 50-100B; ⊗9.30am-6pm) The northern mountains also produce Assam tea, served in this Victorian-era cafe within the Siam Celadon shop. It's a beautiful setting for a cuppa and a snack.

🍴 Eating

The restaurant scene in Chiang Mai is surprisingly down to earth and wholesome with an emphasis on healthy ingredients. It is the kind of town that will turn devoted carnivores into vegetarians. Modest family-run establishments and open-air food courts dominate the city's hot dining spots. As the sun sets, evening food stalls emerge, peddling all sorts of delicious stir-fried wonders. Northern specialities include *kôw soy* (sometimes written as *khao soi*), a curried noodle dish claiming Shan-Yunnanese heritage, accompanied by pickled vegetables and a thick red chilli sauce, which can be found in the markets and simple shopfront restaurants.

🍴 Old City

Residents pick up *gàp kôw* (pre-made food served with rice) from evening vendors lining the stretch of Th Samlan south of Th Ratchadamnoen. Night markets set up in front of Talat Pratu Chiang Mai and on Th Mani Nopharat near Pratu Chang Pheuak.

★ Kow Soy Siri Soy — THAI $

(Map p240; Th Inthawarorot; mains 40-50B; ⊗7am-3pm Mon-Fri) Well-known among locals, this is an easy and tasty lunch stop for *kôw soy*. Order *kôw man gài* (chicken and rice) for children and the chilli-averse.

Angel's Secrets — INTERNATIONAL $

(Map p240; Soi 1, Th Ratchadamnoen; mains 90-150B; ⊗Tue-Sun 7am-4pm; 🛜🖋) True to its name, this sweet little restaurant is shielded by a fence of greenery from peeping appetites. Inside you'll find creative and wholesome Western breakfasts, including crusty homemade bread, crepes and omelettes, and made-to-order vegetarian Thai food.

Safe House Court — THAI $

(Map p240; 178 Th Ratchaphakhinai; mains 60-100B; ⊗7am-10pm; 🛜🖋) Guesthouse restaurants usually excel in convenience over cuisine but this one is an exception. Thai dishes – including regional specialities, spicy salads and vegetarian options – are well prepared and served in a pleasant garden.

MARKET MEALS

Foodies will love Chiang Mai's markets, which offer everything from morning noodles to daytime snacking and evening supping. To impress a Thai friend, pick up a bag of *man gâa·ou*, a roasted acorn-like nut harvested at the end of the rainy season.

Talat Warorot (p238) is the grandmother of Chiang Mai markets and has northern Thai food stalls tucked in all sorts of corners. Just squeeze in and act like you belong.

North of the Th Ratwithi intersection, **Talat Somphet** (Somphet Market; Map p240; Soi 6, Th Moon Muang; ☉ 6am-6pm) sells all the fixings for a takeaway feast: fried chicken, fresh juices, sweets and fruit. Many of the cooking schools do their market tours here.

In the early morning, **Talat Pratu Chiang Mai** (Map p240; Th Bamrungburi; ☉ 4am-noon & 6pm-midnight) is the city's communal larder, selling foodstuffs and ready-made dishes. Things quieten down by lunchtime, but the burners are re-ignited for a large and popular night market that sets up across the road. The evening market is a popular dinner spot during Th Wualai's Saturday Walking Street.

Market aficionados will be impressed by **Talat Thanin** (Map p234; off Th Chang Pheuak; ☉ 5am-early evening), an efficient and clean covered market. The meat vendors are segregated into their own glass-enclosed area preventing an accidental tour by sensitive stomachs. The fruit and vegetable section is a beautiful display of tropical bounty. In the prepared food section you'll find Chiang Mai's recent food trends – make-your-own salads and sushi rolls. Continue deeper to the covered food centre for made-to-order noodles and stir-fries. It is north of the old city just off Th Chang Pheuak.

Talat Ton Phayom (Map p234; Th Suthep) acts as both a local market and a souvenir stop for Thais visiting from other provinces. Take a look at the packaged food area to see the kinds of edible gifts (such as bags of *kâap mǒo* and *sâi òo·a*) that make a visit to Chiang Mai complete. Prices tend to be low because CMU students make up a good portion of the clientele. This place is just off Th Suthep near the corner of Th Khlorng Chonprathan.

Talat Na Mor (Map p234; Malin Plaza, Th Huay Kaew; dishes from 60B; ☉ 5-10pm) is a night market filled with food and fashion for the teeny-boppers. Cruise the stalls and restaurants to see what is hip with the new generation – sushi, K-pop, crepes and nerd glasses.

Dada Kafe
VEGETARIAN $

(Map p240; Th Ratchamankha; mains 60-100B; ☉ 8am-10pm; ☏ ✎) Tasty health food marches from the kitchen to the dining room of this busy restaurant. Cure-all fruit juices, hearty breakfasts and stir fries with tofu and brown rice become daily rituals for many visitors.

AUM Vegetarian Food
VEGETARIAN $

(Map p240; 66 Th Moon Muang; mains 75-150B; ☉ 8am-5pm; ☏ ✎) One of the original health-food peddlers, AUM (pronounced 'om') creates a meditative space to enjoy fresh and original vegetarian dishes.

There's organic coffee from Laos, refreshing lemon-mint juices, fried tempeh and sushi-style vegie rolls. On the 2nd floor there are floor cushions and low tables for a nearly reclined meal.

Baan Nok Noodle
THAI $

(Map p240; Th Singharat; mains 35-45B; ☉ 2-8pm Thu-Tue) North of Wat Phra Singh, this noodle joint is well hidden by a screen of vines and potted plants. The signature dish is a spicy *gǒo·ay đěe·o tom yum baan nok*.

Lert Ros
NORTHEASTERN THAI $

(Map p240; Soi 1, Th Ratchadamnoen; mains 30-100B; ☉ 11am-10pm) As you go to sit down, you'll pass the main course, whole fish grilled on an open fire, accompanied by various northeastern-style side dishes, such as *sôm·đam* (spicy green papaya salad).

With only five items on its menu, Lert Ros takes the indecision out of a meal.

Pak Do Restaurant
THAI $

(Map p240; Th Samlan; mains 30-55B; ☉ 7am-early afternoon) Across the street from Wat Phra Singh, this morning curry shop displays its dishes in big metal bowls out front.

Do as the Thais do and lift the lids to survey the contents. If your stomach has developed a hankering for rice in the morning, you'll be glad you peeked into the pots.

Nayok Fa
THAI $

(Map p240; Th Ratchaphakhinai; mains 40-50B; ⊘10am-6pm) This ma-and-pa place cooks up fresh food in the massive woks out front. Try pàt see·éw (wide noodles stir-fried with a choice of beef, pork or chicken) or the suckling pig and rice.

Fern Forest Cafe
DESSERTS $

(Map p240; 2/2 Soi 4, Th Singharat; mains 70-100B; ⊘8.30am-8.30pm; 🛜) Festooned with ferns and babbling water features, this cafe does delectable desserts, coffees and fruit juices. The lush garden provides a respite from the heat of the day.

Blue Diamond
VEGETARIAN $

(Map p240; 35/1 Soi 9, Th Moon Muang; mains 70-150B; ⊘7am-9pm Mon-Sat; 🛜🍴) Chock-full of fresh produce and baked goods, this backpacker kitchen is a jack-of-all-health-trends: big salads sopped up with slices of bread, veg stir-fries, and 'inter' food such as fish-sauce spaghetti.

Good Morning Chiang Mai
INTERNATIONAL $

(Map p240; 29/5 Soi 6, Th Ratchamankha; mains 75-95B; ⊘8am-4pm; 🛜) A favourite among expats, this hip cafe near Wat Phra Jao Mengrai does breakfasts, standard Thai curries and stir-fries, and sandwiches.

The shady garden with shabby-chic bric-a-brac provides a stylish backdrop for chit-chat and hanging out.

Juicy 4U
VEGETARIAN $

(Map p240; 5 Th Ratchamankha; mains 90-120B; ⊘8.30am-5.30pm; 🛜🍴) This funky cafe does vegan and veg dishes, hangover-fighting juices and make-your-own vegetarian sandwiches – all to a cool techno soundtrack.

Taa Peng
CAFE $

(Map p240; 16 Th Samlan; mains 40-180B; ⊘8am-4pm; 🛜) South of Wat Phra Singh, this cute cafe does panini, coffee, cakes and other treats that will give you the stamina to conquer one more temple.

Swan
MYANMARESE $

(Map p240; Th Chaiyaphum; mains 70-150B; ⊘11am-10pm; 🍴) This grubby restaurant east of the old city offers a trip across the border with its menu of cuisine from Myanmar. The backyard courtyard provides an escape from the moat traffic.

Girasole
ITALIAN $

(Map p240; ☑0 5327 6388; Kad Klang Wiang, Th Ratchadamnoen; mains 90-150B; ⊘11am-9pm;

✳) Kad Klang Wiang, the garden arcade at the corner of Th Ratchadamanoen and Th Ratchaphakhinai, is a hub for dining and people-watching. Adding to its appeal is this small Italian restaurant with fantastic pizzas: crispy crust, tangy sauce and imported cheeses. Pizza Hut can't compete.

★New Delhi
INDIAN $$

(Map p240; Th Ratwithi; mains 150-280B; ⊘11am-10pm; ✳) This basic eatery serves up some of Chiang Mai's best Indian food – lots of complex flavours without an oily afterglow. The handi dishes, among other northern Indian fare, are the restaurant's specialities.

Heuan Phen
NORTHERN THAI $$

(Map p240; ☑0 5327 7103; 112 Th Ratchamankha; mains 80-200B; ⊘11am-10pm; ✳) True northern food is difficult to find in a restaurant setting, but this tourist-friendly place does its best to introduce visitors to regional specialities. During the day, pre-made dishes are set up in a large canteen out front. In the evenings, an antique-cluttered dining room offers more of a culinary experience.

✕ East of the Old City

Chiang Mai's small Chinatown, along Th Chang Moi, is a tasty quarter to investigate early in the morning for stalls selling nám đow·hôo (soy milk) and baton-shaped Chinese-style doughnuts. Talat Warorot is an unassuming but authentic place to sample northern dishes.

Just Khao Soy
THAI $

(Map p234; 108/2 Th Charoen Prathet; mains 100-150B; ⊘11am-9pm; ✳) This restaurant is a confidence builder: it offers a primer on northern Thailand's signature dish of kôw soy.

First you order your meat (or vegies), then level of spice, type of noodles and sauce, and a delicious, hearty broth is born. The food is beautifully presented but it's a bit overpriced. Nevertheless now you can kôw soy wherever you want.

Ratana's Kitchen
THAI $

(Map p240; 320-322 Th Tha Phae; mains 50-190B; ⊘7.30am-11.30pm; ✳) Jump out of the daytime oven and into Ratana's kitchen. It isn't a culinary legend but the dishes are affordable and it's close to Pratu Tha Phae for wilting tourists.

Chez Marco Restaurant & Bar
FRENCH $$

(Map p240; ☑ 0 5320 7032; 15/7 Th Loi Kroh; mains 150-350B; ☺ 5.30pm-midnight Mon-Sat; ✱) It is surprising to find such a beloved restaurant in the middle of Loi Kroh's girlie bar scene. But Chez Marco catapults past the ho-hum tourist joints with top-notch French fare and reasonable prices. Homemade bread, duck dishes and tuna carpaccio are just some of the specialities. Kids menu too.

Antique House
THAI $$

(Map p234; 71 Th Charoen Prathet; mains 100-250B; ☺ 11am-10pm) Set in a quaint teak house with an antique-filled garden, this touristy restaurant does a much better job with ambience than it does food. Regardless, it remains a popular place to entertain out-of-towners, and the grilled fish dishes won't disappoint.

Whole Earth Restaurant
THAI, INDIAN $$

(88 Th Si Donchai; mains 150-350B; ☺ 11am-10pm; ✱) This confectionery-coloured teak house wears a garden of hanging vines and orchids growing in the crooks of tree limbs. It is the sort of place Thais take someone special – where the staff will treat you like royalty and the dishes seem exotic (Thai, Indian and vegetarian) without being demanding.

Anusan Food Centre
MARKET $$

(Map p240; Th Chang Khlan, Anusan Night Bazaar; mains 80-350B; ☺ 5-10pm) Anusan is a buzzing food market best known for Thai-Chinese seafood. There is a market stall section with communal seating and stand-alone restaurants. Try Lena Restaurant, where 1kg of succulent grilled prawns will set you back 300B, a splash-out meal for Thai.

Tianzi Tea House
THAI $$

(Map p240; Th Kamphaeng Din; mains 80-250B; ☺ 10am-10pm) Such hard-core health food is usually found in dirt-floor hippy shacks, but Tianzi has adopted the ascetic's meal to an aesthetic surrounding. Pretty open-air pavilions are decorated with flowers and dappled with sunlight. Diners can enjoy a range of organic and macrobiotic dishes, such as Yunnanese tofu cheese.

✗ Riverside & Elsewhere

Past Saphan Nakhon Ping is Th Faham, known as Chiang Mai's *kôw soy* ghetto. Situated here are **Khao Soi Lam Duan** (Map p234; Th Faham; dishes 50-70B), which also serves *kà·nŏm rang pêung* (literally beehive pastry, a coconut-flavoured waffle), **Khao Soi Samoe Jai** (Map p234; Th Faham; dishes 50-70B) and **Khao Soi Ban Faham** (Map p234; Th Faham; dishes 45-55B). Foodies sometimes spend the day sampling a bowl at each place to select their favourite.

Huan Soontaree
THAI $

(☑ 0 5387 2707; 208 Th Paton; mains 160-200B; ☺ 4pm-midnight; ✱) Visiting Bangkok Thais make the pilgrimage to this rustic restaurant, partly for the food but mainly for the owner, Soontaree Vechanont, a famous northern singer popular in the 1970s. She performs at the restaurant from 8.30pm to 9.30pm Monday to Saturday. The menu is a pleasant blend of northern, northeastern and central Thai specialities. It is 8km north of town beyond the superhighway along the west side of the river.

Spirit House
INTERNATIONAL $$

(Map p234; Soi Viangbua, Th Chang Pheuak; mains 150-230B; ☺ 5-11pm, Mon-Sat; ✱) North of the old city, this antique-filled dining room is the creative outlet for the owner, a former chef in New Orleans and self-described 'nut about food'. He builds the daily menu around what looks interesting at the market. The restaurant also hosts concerts and cultural events.

Cuisine de Gardin
INTERNATIONAL $$

(☑ 0 5344 1599; 99 Moo11, Th Nong Kwai, Hang Dong; mains 200-500B; ☺ 11am-2pm & 4-10pm; ✱) Outside of town, this innovative restaurant turns haute cuisine into edible art through the techniques of molecular gastronomy. The Thai chef is self-taught and prepares snail prawns (a shrimp cocktail served in a snail shell) and smoke-infused terrarium salad among other such frothy concoctions.

Chedi
INTERNATIONAL $$$

(Map p234; ☑ 0 5325 3385; 123 Th Charoen Prathet; mains 500-1000B; ☺ 7am-10pm; ✱) Decor and design are the main ingredients at this luxury hotel's restaurant. The property transformed the former British consulate into an experiment in minimalism with geometric grounds and spare common spaces. Come to dine on a gorgeous riverside view with a side order of slightly overpriced Vietnamese, Indian, Thai and international dishes.

⚔ West of the Old City

The area west of Wat Suan Dok on Th Suthep has several simple vegetarian restaurants. Th Nimmanhaemin and the surrounding soi excel in international cuisine, especially Japanese; new restaurants and cafes pop up every month here, but turnover is high so we've stuck to proven winners. In the evenings, CMU students head to the market that sets up in front of the university entrance on Th Huay Kaew for cheap sushi, ice cream and other hip eats.

★ Pun Pun   VEGETARIAN $
(Map p234; Th Suthep, Wat Suan Dok; mains 50-65B; ⊙9am-5pm; ✍) 🍃 This simple spot practises all of the popular health-food trends without any of the marketing. Meatless and vegan meals use little-known herbs and vegetables, whole grains and no refined sugars.

Most ingredients are sourced from the restaurant's farm, a project in sustainable agriculture and seed preservation. The restaurant is behind the 'monk chat' office. Pun Pun also conducts workshops in organic farming, cooking, and even mud-hut building. There is another branch called **Imm Aim Vegetarian Restaurant** (Map p234; 10 Th Santhitham ; ⊙10am-9pm).

Khun Churn   VEGETARIAN $
(Map p246; Soi 17, Th Nimmanhaemin; buffet 129B; ⊙8am-10pm; ✍) The 'professor' of vegetarian, Khun Churn is best known for its all-you-can-eat meatless buffet (11am to 2pm) boasting dozens of dishes, salads, herbal drinks and Thai-style desserts. Dining with the Churn is a Chiang Mai ritual for expats and Thais.

NinjaRamen & Japanese Food   JAPANESE $
(Map p246; Th Sirimungklajarn; mains 80-160B; ⊙11am-3pm & 4-10pm; ❄) This cramped Japanese noodle house does ramen every which way, plus soba and udon noodles, sashimi and sushi. The medium size is big enough for non-practising ninjas. Pat yourself on the back when a Japanese family arrives; you're dining among those who know.

Din Dee Cafe   ASIAN FUSION $
(Map p234; Th Nimmanhaemin; mains 70-120B; ⊙9am-6pm Tue-Sun; ❄) In the middle of the parking lot of Chiang Mai University Art Center is this outpost of healthy living, housed in a mud hut. Japanese-owned Din Dee does fresh baked bread, herbal salads and bean curries, plus coffee and fruit shakes.

Barfry   INTERNATIONAL $
(Map p246; Soi 15, Th Nimmanhaemin; mains from 60B; ⊙5-11pm Mon-Sat; ❄) French fries get an attitude adjustment at this upscale fry shack with a menu of toppings, ranging from restrained mayonnaise to the 'pimp my fries' option. Next door is a wine bar and a sushi restaurant should you want to migrate to another trough.

I-Berry   DESSERTS $
(Map p246; off Soi 17, Th Nimmanhaemin; mains from 60B; ⊙11am-9pm; ❄ 🔊) An ice-cream shop with star power, I-Berry is owned by Thai comedian Udom Taepanich (nicknamed 'Nose' for his signature feature). If he's not around, celebrity hunters settle for the huge yellow sculpture out front, said to resemble the star.

Why Not? Mediterranean Restaurant   MEDITERRANEAN $$
(Map p246; 14 Soi 11, Th Nimmanhaemin; mains 180-300B; ⊙5-11pm) Why not? 'Of course yes' is the answer at this al fresco restaurant serving authentic pizzas, pastas and imported seafood. Keep an eye out for their weekend wine buffets.

FOR THE LOVE OF PORK

Chiang Mai reveals its Chinese heritage with its devotion to pork products, most obvious in the northern Thai speciality of *sâi òo·a* (pork sausage). Good quality *sâi òo·a* should be zesty and spicy with discernible flavours of lemongrass, ginger and turmeric. Here are a few well known purveyors.

The sign is in Thai but you'll know **Dom Rong** (Map p240; Talat Warorot; dishes from 80B; ⊙8am-8pm), a famous sausage stall in Talat Warorot's dried goods section, by the crowd of people gathered around it. Further out of town are **Mengrai Sai Ua** (Th Chiang Mai–Lamphun), near the Holiday Inn on the east bank of the river, and our favourite **Sai Ua Gao Makham** (Rte 121), a small stall in Talat Mae Huay (Mae Huay market), which is a few kilometres south of the Night Safari on the way to Hang Dong.

100% Isan Restaurant
NORTHERN THAI **$**

(Map p234; Th Huay Kaew; mains 60-200B; ⊙11am-9pm) Directly in front of CMU's main gate, this fluorescent-lit shop does a bumping business of northeastern standards: *sôm·đam*, *kôw něe·o* and *gài yâhng*. From the looks of it, everyone who leaves the university gets hungry when they hear the mortar-and-pestle music of *sôm·đam*.

Salad Concept
INTERNATIONAL **$**

(Map p246; Th Nimmanhaemin; mains 50-160B; ⊙11am-9pm; ※🖉) Watch Thais eat like rabbits at this salad buffet, which consists of chemical-free greens, toppings and dressings. The restaurant was born out of the owners' interest in healing foods during their father's battle with cancer.

Lemontree
THAI **$**

(Map p246; Th Huay Kaew; mains 70-110B; ⊙11am-10pm; ※) The well-worn dining room tells you it's been around for a long time and it still garners praise for its cheap, quick and generous portions of Thai standards.

★ Salsa Kitchen
MEXICAN **$$**

(Map p246; Th Huay Kaew; mains 150-220B; ⊙11am-11pm; ※) Baja-style Mexican earns high praise for its fresh and zesty dishes served in super-sized portions. It's an expat favourite but Thais dig it too, and it's often busy in the evening.

Sumo Sushi
JAPANESE **$$**

(Map p246; 28/7 Soi 11, Th Nimmanhaemin; mains 120-250B; ⊙11am-9pm; ※) Chiang Mai has a serious sushi addiction and everyone claims to know *the* best in town. We ascribe to the 'love the one you're with' theory, meaning that where you are now is good too. If you're in the neighbourhood, Sumo does American-style rolls along with sashimi and sets.

Hong Tauw Inn
THAI **$$**

(Map p246; 95/17-18 Nantawan Arcade, Th Nimmanhaemin; mains 120-220B; ⊙11am-11pm; ※) Decked out in an old-fashioned costume of antiques, pendulum clocks and stained glass, Hong Tauw is a quaint diner with reliable standards. It is a user-friendly experience that ticks off a lot of boxes for newbies thanks to its extensive menu, including *sai ou*, *kà·nŏ m jeen* and other regional specialities.

Amazing Sandwich
AMERICAN **$$**

(Map p246; 20/2 Th Huay Kaew; mains 100-200B; ⊙8.30am-8pm; ※) Bringing bread to the wheat-deprived masses, Amazing Sandwich is beloved for its make-your-own sandwiches, but it also does breakfasts claiming international pedigree (Dover, Idaho, etc), burgers and pizzas.

Smoothie Blues
WESTERN **$$**

(Map p246; 32 Th Nimmanhaemin; mains 100-180B; ⊙7.30am-9pm; ※) This expat favourite is known for its breakfasts, as well as its sandwiches, baguettes and the namesake drink.

Palaad Tawanron
THAI **$$**

(🖉0 5321 6039; Th Suthep; mains 160-320B; ⊙lunch, dinner) Set into a rocky ravine near Doi Suthep, this restaurant inhabits a magical spot overlooking the twinkling city below. Everyone loves the ambience but the food, mainly Thai seafood, receives mediocre reviews. Follow the signs at the end of Th Suthep.

Green Table Restaurant
INTERNATIONAL **$$**

(Map p246; 44/12 Th Nimmanhaemin, 2nd fl, Kantary Terrace; mains 160-400B; ⊙11am-midnight; ※) Posh and professional, this Mediterranean restaurant is preferred by Chiang Mai's sophisticated set for its light lunch fare of grilled fish salads and hearty dinners of high-end steaks.

LOCAL KNOWLEDGE

HOW TO SURVIVE SONGKRAN

This is my favourite holiday. First, if you don't like being wet all day, stay out of Thailand for Songkran. But it is a loving and fun holiday; be sure to keep your phone and wallet in a waterproof bag, wear colourful flowered clothing, buy a huge water gun and then prepare to blast and get blasted with water from around 10am to dark. Songkran goes on for about five days straight and if you like to drink all day this is your chance to do it style. The action takes place around the moat and along Th Huay Kaew, near Kad Suan Kaew shopping centre. Soho Bar (p269) is right smack in the middle of it all and is one huge gay party.

Shauna Pugh is co-owner of Soho Bar & Guesthouse.

Royal Project Restaurant
THAI **$$**

(Th Huay Kaew; mains 70-300B; ⊘9am-6pm; ❄)

🍲 Fine dining Thai-style features products from the Queen's royal agricultural projects. It's popular with Thais for a special occasion. Rainbow trout and other seasonal northern Thai specialities are the highlights of the menu. It is across from the zoo.

🍷 Drinking & Nightlife

Chiang Mai has two primary areas for watering holes: the old city and Th Nimmanhaemin. The old city tends to be more touristy, while Nimmanhaemin is popular with CMU students and hi-so (high society) Thais. Keep an eye out for wine and beer 'buffets' that are sponsored by beverage suppliers at bars in and around Th Nimmanhaemin.

🍷 Old City

Zoe In Yellow
BAR

(Map p240; 40/12 Th Rathwithi; ⊘5pm-2am) Everybody's party pal, Zoe is a beer garden, club and live music venue. Start off in the garden for sobriety cure-alls then stumble over to the dance floor with your new found confidence.

Writer's Club & Wine Bar
BAR

(Map p240; 141/3 Th Ratchadamnoen; ⊘10am-midnight) Run by a former foreign correspondent, this bar and restaurant is popular with expats, including current and retired writers, and anybody else who wanders by. There's also English pub grub to help anchor a liquid meal.

UN Irish Pub
PUB

(Map p240; 24/1 Th Ratwithi; ⊘10am-midnight) Chiang Mai's leading pub ambassador, this is *the* place for international sport matches and Thursday quiz nights. There's Guinness on tap, a backyard garden and a bakery.

John's Place
BAR

(Map p240; Th Moon Muang; ⊘10am-midnight) This old-school spot dominates the triangular wedge of Th Ratchamankha and Soi 2 with neon and beer bellies. Climb the stairs to the roof deck where a cold beer is good company at sunset.

Archers
BAR

(Map p240; 33/4 Th Ratchaphakhinai; ⊘8am-midnight; 🐾) Come to this chilled-out restaurant-bar for the cold beer, the people-watching and the pub-away-from-home atmosphere. The Sunday roast gets rave reviews.

🍷 East & South of the Old City

Bus Bar
BAR

(Map p234; Th Charoen Prathet; ⊘5pm-midnight) Parked beside Saphan Lek (Iron Bridge), the Bus Bar is the cheapest and most chic place to party by the river. Drinks and food are served al fresco from the eponymous vehicle.

Pinte Blues Pub
BAR

(Map p234; 9 Soi 1,Th Ratcha Chiangsaen; ⊘4pm-midnight) Just when you think nothing ever changes, this veteran bar up and quits the old city. They've got a new location but everything else is the same: espresso, beer and blues in a Thai 'country' setting.

🍷 West of the Old City

Beer Republic
BAR

(Map p246; Soi 11, Th Nimmanhaemin; ⊘5pm-midnight Tue-Sun) Fifteen draft beers keep the hop-sippers happy at this upscale beer bar in trendy Nimman. It is packed and chummy.

Pub
PUB

(Map p246; 189 Th Huay Kaew; ⊘7am-midnight) In an old Tudor-style house surrounded by a big garden, this venerable institution recreates the atmosphere of an English country pub with history to boot. It's a couple of hundred metres past Th Nimmanhaemin on the west side of Th Huay Kaew.

Soho Bar
BAR

(Map p246; www.sohochiangmai.com; 20/3 Th Huay Kaew; ⊘5pm-midnight) Personality is on tap at this cosy shopfront bar. It is gay-friendly and all-inclusive and the affable owners attract a steady supply of regulars and newcomers with cheerful chats and cold drinks.

Small House Kafe
BAR

(Map p246; 18/1 Th Sermsuk; ⊘5pm-midnight Tue-Sat) A groovy place to howl at the moon with expats and Thais alike. Hip hop on Friday nights, periodic book swaps and lots of built-in friends.

Blar Blar Bar
BAR

(Map p246; Soi 5, Th Nimmanhaemin; ⊘5pm-2am) Lots of Thai drinking culture flows at Blar Blar, a big and boozy beer garden popular with uni students and other youthful punters.

That's Wine
BAR

(Map p246; Soi 9, Th Nimmanhaemin; ⊘5pm-1am) Wine, wine, wine (and water, if you must)

THE MOVIE THAT LAUNCHED MILLIONS OF SUITCASES

The low-budget Chinese comedy, *Lost in Thailand* (2011), is a feel-good story about two mismatched travelling companions who learn, through a series of misadventures set in Chiang Mai and northern Thailand, that human relationships are more important than money. It became the highest-grossing domestic film in China, giving competition to massively popular Hollywood hits such as *Titanic* and *Avatar*. But its influence has extended beyond the silver screen, inspiring middle-class Chinese tourists to travel to Thailand in search of the temples and forests depicted in the movie.

More than two million Chinese tourists visited Thailand each year in 2012 and 2013, and TAT estimates nearly five million visitors per year in the coming years. Not only have the numbers increased but the demographics have changed. A larger number are independent travellers, both young couples and families who come for weekend breaks, thanks to direct flights linking Chiang Mai to China's major cities, or for weeklong holidays. Chiang Mai's tourism industry is struggling to meet demand; it is estimated that the area's 40,000 hotel rooms have an 80% to 90% occupancy rate, according to the Chiang Mai Tourism & Business Association.

In these early days, the Chinese tourists fit into the existing tourism model designed for Westerners. But businesses are re-calibrating to suit Chinese tastes: fruit-shake stands have proliferated, signs and menus are now written in Chinese, and Thai drivers repress their anger as Chinese tourists stop in the middle of the street to consult a map. These new arrivals take some of the pressure off clueless *fa·ràng* and are a reminder that we are all strangers in a strange land.

is the tipple of choice at this contemporary Nimman bar, owned by a former porn star.

Monkey Club NIGHTCLUB
(Map p246; 7 Soi 9, Th Nimmanhaemin; ⊙5pm-2am) This all-purpose club does dinner, drinks and dancing for a tribe of affluent Thai students and expats who might migrate from the garden seats to the glassed-in, all-white bar and club. It's a very happening place for the younger set.

Warm-Up NIGHTCLUB
(Map p246; ☑0 5340 0676; 40 Th Nimmanhaemin; ⊙9pm-2am) Still going strong, this hi-so dance club attracts the young and the beautiful. Hip hop is spun in the main room, electronic house reverberates in the lounge, and rock/indie bands jam in the garden.

☆ Entertainment

★Sudsanan LIVE MUSIC
(Map p246; Th Huay Kaew; ⊙5pm-2am) Down a dark driveway near Kad Suan Kaew, this old wooden house is filled with characters and songs. Mainly acoustic bands jog from samba to *pleng pêu·a chee·wít* (songs for life) and the eclectic crowd bows solemnly during tear-jerking songs.

North Gate Jazz Co-Op LIVE MUSIC
(Map p240; Th Si Phum) This tight little jazz club packs in more musicians, both local and foreign, than patrons, especially for its Tuesday open-mic night.

Inter LIVE MUSIC
(Map p240; 271 Th Tha Phae; ⊙5pm-midnight) You don't have to go far to find good music. This small wooden house packs in a rockin' house band and a crowd of backpackers and travellers. It has new millennial attitudes, using crowdsourcing for musical talent.

Riverside Bar & Restaurant LIVE MUSIC
(Map p234; 9-11 Th Charoenrat; ⊙noon-midnight) Long-running Riverside does dining, drinking and music with a view of the twinkly Mae Ping. Bands range from classic-rock, jazz and even pop and a recent expansion across the road adds more elbow room.

Sangdee Gallery LIVE MUSIC
(Map p246; Soi 5, Th Sirimungklajarn; ⊙11am-midnight) It is hard to classify Sangdee: art gallery, live music club, bar and cafe. It isn't one thing, it is many, but mainly it is a cool hang-out for Chiang Mai's creative set. The week's roster features a rotating menu of live music and art exhibits, including a Thai country-and-western band and the ever-popular open-mic nights.

Good View   LIVE MUSIC
(Map p234; 13 Th Charoenrat; ⊙5pm-2am) Cover bands, 20-somethings and a pretty riverside location keeps Good View in everyone's good graces.

Le Brasserie   LIVE MUSIC
(Map p240; Th Chaiyaphum; ⊙5pm-2am) The popular late-night spot has recently moved from its riverside location to this convenient spot near Pratu Tha Phae. Devotees come to hear local guitarist Took pay homage to all the rock and blues legends.

Thapae Boxing Stadium   BOXING
(Map p240; ☑08 6187 7655; Th Moon Muang; tickets 400-600B; ⊙9pm-midnight) Right in the heart of the backpacker scene, this stadium hosts *moo·ay tai* matches for entertainment rather than as proving grounds for the sport. There's also a cabaret to add to the spectacle.

🛍 Shopping

Chiang Mai is Thailand's handicraft centre, or at least it used to be. There are still some small cottage factories and workshops dotting the outskirts of town, though modernisation is taking its toll. Despite the economic tides, shopping continues to thrive with corridors and markets sprinkled throughout the city: the Chiang Mai Night Bazaar, Saturday Walking Street on Th Wualai, Sunday Walking Street on Th Ratchadamnoen, Th Tha Phae and Th Charoenrat. Th Nimmanhaemin, west of the old city near Chiang Mai University, has a handful of contemporary boutiques visited by trend-conscious Thais. Handicraft 'villages', more a marketing term,

lie just outside of the city to the south and to the east.

🏛 Old City

Mengrai Kilns   CERAMICS
(Map p234; ☑0 5327 2063; www.mengraikilns.com; 79/2 Th Arak; ⊙10am-6pm) In the southwestern corner of the old city, Mengrai Kilns keeps the tradition of Thai celadon pottery alive with a showroom full of table settings, decorative items and even Thai- and Western-style nativity scenes.

HQ Paper Maker   PAPER
(Map p240; ☑0 5381 4718; www.hqpapermaker.com; 3/31 Th Samlan; ⊙8.30am-5.30pm Mon-Sat) Handmade mulberry paper *(săh)*, a Chiang Mai speciality, is sold in a variety of colours and designs at this friendly shop. It also conducts paper-making classes and donate a portion of profits to a nearby elephant hospital.

Herb Basics   SOAP
(Map p240; ☑0 5323 4585; Th Ratchadamnoen; ⊙9am-6pm Mon-Sat, 2-9pm Sun) All of these good-smelling products – such as herbal lip balm, soap and shampoo – are made in Chiang Mai with natural ingredients.

Lost Book Shop   BOOKSTORE
(Map p240; 34/3 Th Ratchamankha; ⊙9am-9pm) Secondhand books are free of plastic wrap for easy browsing at this long-running shop.

On the Road Books   BOOKSTORE
(Map p240; 38/1 Th Ratwithi; ⊙10am-9pm) Good-quality reads fill the shelves at this reliable book seller.

NIGHT-TIME SHOPPING

Chiang Mai Night Bazaar (Map p240; Th Chang Khlan; ⊙7pm-midnight) is one of the city's main night-time attractions, especially for families, and is the modern legacy of the original Yunnanese trading caravans that stopped here along the ancient trade route between Simao (in China) and Mawlamyaing (on Myanmar's Gulf of Martaban coast). Today the night bazaar sells the usual tourist souvenirs, like what you'll find at Bangkok's street markets. In true market fashion, vendors form a gauntlet along the footpath of Th Chang Khlan from Th Tha Phae to Th Loi Kroh. In between are dedicated shopping buildings: the Chiang Mai Night Bazaar Building is filled mainly with antique and handicraft shops. Across the street is the **Galare Night Bazaar** (Map p240) selling upmarket clothes and home decor. Behind the collection of shops is the **Galare Food Centre** (Map p240; Th Chang Khlan; dishes 50-80B; ⊙6pm-midnight). The **Anusan Night Bazaar** (Anusan Night Market; Map p240; Th Chang Khlan; ⊙5-10pm) is less claustrophobic and filled with tables of vendors selling knitted caps, carved soaps and other cottage-industry goods. Deeper into the market is the Anusan Food Centre (p266).

    The quality and bargains aren't especially impressive, but the allure is the variety and concentration of stuff, and the dexterity and patience it takes to trawl through it all.

CHIANG MAI'S SHOPPING BOOM

Chiang Mai is fast becoming an alternative to Bangkok for global brand names, and the city is in the middle of a mall invasion that is capitalising on two major societal changes: expansion of the city's middle-class suburbs and growth of Chinese tourists on shopping holidays. During mid-2013 there were three major shopping centre projects in a town that has mostly kept faith with two low-key, provincial shopping centres (Kad Suan Kaew and Central Airport Plaza). The new projects are big, modern and heavily marketed as 'lifestyle' malls, a concept popular in Bangkok.

The most ambitious project is the **Promenada Resort Mall**, 5km east of town just off the Superhighway near the Don Chan intersection. Its anchor tenant is the discount fashion house Uniqlo, and it is located near new housing estates and condominiums that have moved middle-class families out of the central city. On weekends, the mall is packed with families enjoying a clean air-conditioned space, eating at the ever-popular Fuji Japanese restaurant and window shopping. Nearby, the **Central Festival** is touted as a 'happiness hub' intended to replicate the success of Central Festival in Pattaya.

In town there are several small arcade malls that have replaced ageing shophouses. The old city now hosts two such centres that have ushered in gentrification of the area. The Frank Gehry–style building at the corner of Th Nimmanhaemin and Th Huay Kaew is the new **Maya Mall**, another concept mall. The growth in retail represents the city's new-found affluence, be it home-grown or imported.

Chiang Mai Cotton
CLOTHING

(Map p240; Th Ratchadamnoen; ⊙10am-6pm) The old city has sprouted several cute boutiques, including this clothing shop selling high-quality natural cotton cut for modern tropical living.

East of the Old City

Wander the sois in between Th Tha Phae and Talat Warorot for a plethora of textile shops selling Thai and imported handicrafts.

Elements
JEWELLERY

(Red Ruby; Map p240; 400-402 Th Tha Phae; ⊙10am-9pm) An eclectic and fun collection of sterling silver and stone jewellery and other trinkets fill this unsigned store near Pratu Tha Phae. Its shop next door sells silks and decorative items.

Nova
JEWELLERY

(Map p240; www.nova-collection.com; 201 Th Tha Phae; ⊙10am-8pm Mon-Sat, 12.30-8.30pm Sun) For contemporary jewellery, this studio makes high-quality rings, pendants and earrings using silver, gold and precious stones. Pieces can be custom made and are very classy.

Dee Dee Pan Pan
JEWELLERY

(Map p240; 33 Th Tha Phae; ⊙10am-6pm) Murano-glass beaded necklaces and other pieces of handmade jewellery decorate this pleasant shop.

Kesorn
HANDICRAFTS

(Map p240; 154-156 Th Tha Phae) A collector's best friend, this cluttered shop has been trading old stuff for years. It specialises mainly in hill-tribe textiles, beads and crafts.

Siam Celadon
CERAMICS

(Map p240; www.siamceladon.com; 158 Th Tha Phae; ⊙8am-6pm) This established company sells its fine collection of cracked-glazed celadon ceramics in a lovely teak building. Enjoy the Victorian-era structure and its dainty fretwork for longer with a proper English tea at the attached Raming Tea House (p263).

Praewphun Thai Silk
TEXTILES

(Map p240; 83-85 Th Pha Phae; ⊙10am-6pm) This 50-year-old shop sells silks of all ilks, and the octogenerian owner is a spry and dedicated saleswoman.

KukWan Gallery
TEXTILES

(Map p240; 37 Th Loi Kroh; ⊙9am-6pm) Set slightly back from the road, this charming teak building sells natural cotton and silk by the metre. It's a great place to shop for better-than-market quality scarves and bedspreads available in subtle colours.

Pantip Plaza
ELECTRONICS

(Map p240; Th Chang Khlan; ⊙10am-9pm) Near the night bazaar, this shiny shopping centre is a more legitimate version than its grey-market counterpart in Bangkok. Mainly licensed suppliers of electronic hardware, such as computers and cameras, fill the space without a single bootleg software vendor in sight.

Suriwong Book Centre BOOKSTORE
(Map p240; 54 Th Si Donchai; ☉8am-8pm) A Chiang Mai institution carrying mainly magazines and Thai titles with a small but sturdy English-language section of Thai and Southeast Asian nonfiction.

Backstreet Books BOOKSTORE
(Map p240; 2/8 Th Chang Moi Kao; ☉9am-8pm) Backstreet has a good selection of crime and thriller novels in a rambling shop along 'book alley'.

Chilli Antiques & Arts ANTIQUES
(Map p234; Th Si Donchai; ☉10am-6pm) A reliable purveyor of antiques and reproductions, Chilli's has this in-town studio and a larger showroom in Hang Dong.

Riverside

Vila Cini TEXTILES
(Map p234; ☑0 5324 6246; www.vilacini.com; 30-34 Th Charoenrat; ☉10am-6pm) Vila Cini sells high-end handmade silks and cotton textiles that are reminiscent of the Jim Thompson brand. Perhaps the real draw is the store's atmospheric teak house with marble floors and a narrow, rickety staircase that leads to a galleried courtyard. It's on the eastern side of the road about 400m north of Saphan Nawarat.

Sop Moei Arts TEXTILES, HANDICRAFTS
(Map p234; ☑0 5330 6123; www.sopmoeiarts.com; 150/10 Th Charoenrat; ☉10am-6pm) High-end hill-tribe crafts, from textiles to baskets, are sold at this economic-development shop. The shop's directors began working with Pwo Karen village in Mae Hong Son province people some 30 years ago, and have since harnessed their craft traditions into the modern marketplace.

Thai Tribal Crafts TEXTILES
(Map p234; ☑0 5324 1043; www.ttcrafts.co.th; 208 Th Bamrungrat; ☉10am-6pm) Peruse the ornate needlework of the various hill tribes at this missionary-backed, fair trade shop near the McCormick Hospital. There is an old town branch called **Fair Trade** (Map p240; 25/9 Th Moon Muang).

West of the Old City

Trendy and cosmopolitan boutiques can be found around affluent Th Nimmanhaemin. There is a lot of turnover here so we've stuck with reliable standards.

Elephants HANDICRAFTS
(Map p246; 8 Soi 1, Th Nimmanhaemin; ☉10am-6pm) Elephant carvings by master woodworker Phet Wiriya are sold in this in-town showroom. He is known for his use of traditional methods, unique poses and local cassia wood. His workshop, Baan Jang Nak, is in San Kamphaeng.

Hill-Tribe Products Promotion Centre TEXTILES, HANDICRAFTS
(Map p234; 21/17 Th Suthep; ☉10am-6pm) Hill-tribe crafts and souvenirs from the royally sponsored economic development program are sold at this and other shops around the moat. There are tribal costumes available from six hill tribes. All the profits go to hill-tribe welfare programs.

SHOPPING FOR A CAUSE

Chiang Mai is Thailand's conscience, in part because the city is the de facto caretaker of hill-tribe villagers and struggling immigrants from Myanmar. Both groups lack the proper citizenship to get an education, well-paid jobs and medical care. This close proximity to poverty prods the average resident out of complacency and into action, resulting in a myriad NGOs that help develop legitimate sources of income. Adorn with Studio Naenna is the in-town showroom of a village weaving project that gives young women in the Chom Thong district of Chiang Mai a viable economic income without having to leave their families and migrate to the city for work. It also preserves traditional weaving techniques and aims for a softer environmental footprint through the use of natural fibres and dyes. Other handicraft outlets for village-weaving projects include KukWan Gallery, Sop Moei Arts, Thai Tribal Crafts and the Hill-Tribe Products Promotion Centre.

Srisanpanmai
TEXTILES

(Map p246; 6 Soi 1, Th Nimmanhaemin; ⊙10am-6pm) The display cases here show a visual textbook of the textiles of the Lanna people. From the technicolour rainbow patterns of Myanmar to the wide-hem panel style of Chiang Mai, Srisanpanmai specialises in silks made in the old tradition.

Adorn with Studio Naenna
TEXTILES

(Map p246; 22 Soi 1, Th Nimmanhaemin; ⊙10am-6pm) The pensive colours of the mountains have been woven into these naturally dyed silks and cottons, part of a village weaving project pioneered by Patricia Cheeseman, an expert and author on Thai-Lao textiles. You can see the production process at the out-of-town workshop, Studio Naenna. This is one of the best places in Chiang Mai for textiles.

Studio Naenna
TEXTILES

(Map p246; www.studio-naenna.com; 138/8 Soi Chang Khian, Th Huay Kaew; ⊙9am-4pm Wed) If you liked what you saw at Adorn with Studio Naenna, then head out of town to the main gallery of this textile cooperative. It's about 1km northwest of the intersection of Th Huay Kaew and Th Khlorng Chonprathan, along Soi Chang Khian.

Shinawatra
TEXTILES

(Map p246; www.shinawatrathaisilk.co.th; 18 Th Huay Kaew; ⊙10am-6pm) This venerable family-owned silk shop was already a household name before the owners' nephew, Thaksin Shinawatra, became the now-exiled prime minister. The colours and styles are a little dowdy for foreign tastes, but reconsider the selection should you happen to be elected mayor of Chiang Mai.

Gongdee Gallery
ART

(Map p246; www.gongdeegallery.com; 30 Soi 1, Th Nimmanhaemin; ⊙10am-6pm) With one of the largest showrooms on the block, Gongdee is the soi's primary incubator for young artistic talent. There's a mix of home decor, furniture and paintings. Keep an eye out for the Byzantine icon-like Buddhas and altars painted by Chiang Mai artist Barinya.

Chabaa
CLOTHING

(Map p246; www.atchabaa.com; 14/32 Th Nimmanhaemin, Nimman Promenade; ⊙10am-6pm) If Putumayo put out clothes instead of music, you'd have Chabaa, which specialises in global ethno-chic. You'll find brightly coloured embroidered tops and skirts plus big-statement jewellery.

Ginger
CLOTHING, ACCESSORIES

(Map p246; 6/21 Th Nimmanhaemin; ⊙10am-6pm) For something more night-on-the-townish, check out the shimmery dresses, sparkly mules, fabulous jewellery and colourful accessories offered in this place.

ⓘ Information

DANGERS & ANNOYANCES

Compared to Bangkok, Chiang Mai is a breeze for tourists. The hassles from *sŏrng·tăa·ou* and túk-túk drivers are minimal.

A major annoyance is the traffic, but if you've just come from Bangkok you'll probably find it a relief as it's nowhere near as bad, and although very busy, the main arteries do generally flow pretty well, except during rush hour.

In March and April, Chiang Mai can be enveloped in a smoky, dusty haze caused in large part by farmers burning off their fields in nearby districts. During the rainy season, dengue is a concern as the mosquito population increases with the monsoons; Chiang Mai province ranks as one of the highest risk places for dengue fever in the country.

Inexpensive guesthouses in Chiang Mai will sometimes evict guests who don't engage trekking tours. Most places are pretty forthcoming with their policies on this and will usually offer rooms to nontrekking guests for a limited period.

EMERGENCY

Tourist Police (Map p234; ☏0 5324 7318, 24hr emergency 1155; Th Faham; ⊙6am-midnight) Has a volunteer staff of foreign nationals who speak a variety of languages. It's on the eastern side of the river, just south of the superhighway.

INTERNET ACCESS

Guesthouses, restaurants and cafes in Chiang Mai have free wi-fi access. A few guesthouses and cafes still have internet-enabled terminals though these are quickly disappearing. Data connections on mobile devices that are not wi-fi can vary in speed and reliability.

MEDIA

Chiangmai Mail (www.chiangmai-mail.com) Weekly English-language newspaper covering local and regional news and politics.

Citylife (www.chiangmainews.com) Lifestyle magazine profiling restaurants, bars, local culture, politics and people; also has a classified section.

Compass A bi-lingual monthly magazine covering city trends, business profiles and tourist attractions.

INVISIBLE MIGRANT WORKERS

Construction workers, hotel cleaning staff, a middle-class family's nanny: many of Thailand's low-wage, low-skill jobs are now filled by the people of Myanmar who have either crossed over the border for economic opportunity or who have escaped their home country due to armed conflict between ethnic groups and Myanmar's central government. Thailand hosts about three million Myanmarese migrants living and working in Thai cities and about 150,000 refugees and asylum-seekers in nine camps along the two countries' border. The recent liberalisation in Myanmar's central government has brought about ceasefires in some ethnic areas and optimism that there can be repatriation or stabilisation of displaced people.

But the strength of the Thai economy means that outward migration from Myanmar to Thailand will continue. The current Thai government has sought to remedy the situation through its nationality verification process, which qualifies migrants for legal status and the newly instated minimum wage of 300B. It is estimated that about 500,000 migrants (of various nationalities) have registered, according to figures from Thailand's office of foreign workers administration. Many undocumented workers have missed the deadlines, are uninformed about the process or can't afford the associated application fees. Without the proper paperwork, these workers can be arrested and deported, are paid less and are vulnerable to other exploitation by their employers and by the police.

The majority of migrant workers in Chiang Mai – an estimated 150,000 to 200,000 people – are from the neighbouring Shan State of Myanmar. A variety of NGOs work on social welfare, labour rights, education, health care and other issues related to displaced people. These groups have volunteer opportunities for those who would like to get involved:

➜ **Best Friend Library** (Map p246; 302/2 Soi 13, Th Nimmanhaemin; ⊙11.30am-8pm Mon-Sat) is a community space that offers English-language courses to migrants, maintains a lending library to educate the international community about Myanmar and works on positive change within Myanmar.

➜ **Thai Freedom House** (www.thaifreedomhouse.org) offers education programs.

➜ **We Women Foundation** (www.wewomenfoundation.org) assists the women of Myanmar to be leaders within their country and communities through scholarships and career development.

➜ **MAP Foundation** (www.mapfoundationcm.org) is an advocacy group working on labour rights, immigration policies and legal representation for the migrant population from Myanmar.

Guidelines Living (www.guidelineschiangmai.com) Monthly lifestyle magazine that features business profiles plus respectable historical essays and bi-lingual (Thai and English) articles.

Irrawaddy News Magazine (www.irrawaddy.org) A well-respected journal covering news in Myanmar, northern Thailand and other parts of Southeast Asia.

MEDICAL SERVICES

Chiang Mai Ram Hospital (Map p234; ☑0 5322 4880; www.chiangmairam.com; 8 Th Bunreuangrit) The most modern hospital in town though expats often complain that prices are inflated for travel insurance plans.

Lanna Hospital (Map p234; ☑0 5399 9777; www.lanna-hospital.com; Th Superhighway) One of the better hospitals in town and less expensive than Chiang Mai Ram.

Malaria Centre (Map p234; ☑0 5322 1529; 18 Th Bunreuangrit) Offers blood checks for malaria.

McCormick Hospital (Map p234; ☑0 5392 1777; www.mccormick.in.th; 133 Th Kaew Nawarat) Former missionary hospital; good for minor treatments.

Mungkala Traditional Medicine Clinic (Map p240; ☑0 5327 8494; 21-27 Th Ratchamankha; ⊙9am-12.30pm & 2.30-7pm) Government-licensed clinic using acupuncture, massage and Chinese herbal remedies.

Rajavej Hospital (Map p234; ☑0 5380 1999; 36/1 Th Chiang Mai-Lamphun) Affordable hospital with international standards and English-speaking staff. Pronounced 'racha-vet'.

MONEY

All major Thai banks have several branches and ATMs throughout Chiang Mai; many of them along Th Tha Phae.

Western Union (Map p246; ☑ 0 5322 4979; Th Huay Kaew) Send or receive money by wire. There are counters at Central Airport Plaza, Kad Suan Kaew shopping centre, Th Huay Kaew and also available at any post office.

POST

A private **postal shop** (Map p240) on Th Ratchadamnoen is a good place to organise packages home.

Main Post Office (☑ 0 5324 1070; Th Charoen Muang; ⊙ 8.30am-4.30pm Mon-Fri, 9am-noon Sat & Sun) Other convenient branches on Th Singharat/Samlan, Th Mahidon at Chiang Mai International Airport, Th Charoen Prathet, Th Phra Pokklao, Th Chotana and Chiang Mai University.

TOURIST INFORMATION

Chiang Mai Municipal Tourist Information Centre (Map p240; ☑ 0 5325 2557; Th Tha Phae; ⊙ 8.30-11.30am & 1-4.30pm) Small city-run tourist information centre near the night bazaar.

Tourism Authority of Thailand (TAT; Map p234; ☑ 0 5327 6140; www.tourismthailand. org; Th Chiang Mai-Lamphun; ⊙ 8.30am-4.30pm) English-speaking staff provide maps and recommendations for tour guides; TAT doesn't make hotel reservations. It's just over

TRANSPORT TO/FROM CHIANG MAI

DESTINATION	AIR	BUS	TRAIN
Bangkok	Don Muang Airport: Air Asia & Nok Air, 1750B, 1½hr, daily; Suvarnabhumi: Thai Airways & Bangkok Airways, 1½hr, 1750-2000B, daily	438-876B, 9-10hr, frequent	fan 231-391B, air-con 541-611B, sleeper 491-881B, 12hr, 5-6 daily
Chiang Dao		40B, 2hr, 6 daily; minibus 80B, 1½hr, 6 daily	
Chiang Khong		190-351B, 6½hr, 2 daily	
Chiang Rai		144-288B, 3-4hrs, every hour	
Chiang Saen		232B, 4hr, 1 daily	
Khon Kaen		621B, 12hr, 10 daily	
Khorat (Nakhorn Ratchasima)		600-700B, 12hr, 11 daily	
Lamphun		32-38B, 1hr, hourly	
Luang Prabang	Lao Airlines: 5000B, 6 weekly	1200B, 20hr, 2 daily	
Mae Hong Son (via Pai)	Kan Air & Nok Air: 1500B, 35min, daily	138B, 7-8hr, hourly; minivan 250B, 6hr, hourly	
Mae Hong Son (via Mae Sariang)		192-346B, 5-6hr, 6 daily	
Mae Sai		182-364B, 5hr, 2-3 daily	
Mae Sariang		100-200B, 4-5hr, 6 daily	
Mae Sot	Nok Air: 1200B, 1hr, daily	259-330B, 6hr, 2 daily	
Nan	Kan Air: 1900B, 45min, 2 weekly	225-451B, 6hr, 10 daily	
Pai	Kan Air: 1900B, 1½hr, 3 weekly	138B, 4hr, hourly; minivan 150B, 3hr, hourly	
Phayao		125-249B, 3hr, 8 daily	
Phrae		151-302B, 4hr, 10 daily	
Sukhothai		239-308B, 5-6hr, 6 daily	
Tha Ton		90B, 4hr, 6 daily	
Udon Thani	Nok Air: 2500B 1½hr daily	444-666B, 12hr, 2 daily	

Saphan Lek on the eastern side of the river. At the time of writing the office had temporarily relocated to 164/94-95 Th Chang Khlan while a new building was being constructed on the original site.

USEFUL WEBSITES

1 Stop Chiang Mai (www.1stopchiangmai.com) Comprehensive website covering tourist attractions and amenities.

Chiang Mai Sawadee (http://chiangmai. sawadee.com) Hotel booking site.

Getting There & Away

AIR

Regularly scheduled flights arrive and depart from **Chiang Mai International Airport** (Map p234; www.chiangmaiairportonline.com), which is 3km south of the old city. International and domestic routes and frequencies vary with the seasons and tourist demand. Direct flights linking Chiang Mai to Chinese cities are expanding rapidly.

Air Asia (0 2515 9999; www.airasia.com) Flies to Bangkok (Don Muang Airport), Kuala Lumpur, Phuket and Macau.

Air Bagan (0 5328 4985; www.airbagan. com) Flies twice a week to Yangon.

Air China (0 2134 2452; www.airchina.com) Flies to Beijing daily.

Bangkok Airways (1771; www.bangkokair. com) Flies daily to Bangkok (Suvarnabhumi Airport) and continues to Samui.

China Eastern (0 2636 6980; www.flychina eastern.com) Flies to Kunming three days a week.

Dragon Air (0 2263 0606; www.dragonair. com) Flies to Hong Kong four days a week.

Hong Kong Airlines (www.hongkongairlines. com) Flies to Hong Kong daily.

Jin Air (0 2168 7495; www.jinair.com) Flies to Seoul three days a week.

Kan Air (02 551 6111; www.kanairlines.com) Flies to Mae Hong Son, Pai, Phitsanulok and Nan.

Korean Air (0 2620 6900; www.koreanair. com)

Lao Airlines (0 5322 3401; www.laoairlines. com) Flies to Luang Prabang six days a week.

Nok Air (1318; www.nokair.com) Flies to Bangkok (Don Muang Airport), Mae Hong Son, Mae Sot and Udon Thani; note that Nok Air is a subsidiary of Thai Airways.

Silk Air (0 5390 4985; www.silkair.com) Flies to Singapore five days a week.

Thai Airways International (0 5321 1047, 0 5321 1044; www.thaiair.com) Flies to Bangkok (Suvarnabhumi Airport).

Tiger Air (www.tigerair.com; from 2000B) Flies to Singapore four days weekly

BUS

Chiang Mai has two bus stations (long distance and provincial) as well as several sŏrng·tăaou (pick-up minibus) stops (for nearby destinations).

Arcade Bus Station (Th Kaew Nawarat) is Chiang Mai's long-distance station and is about 3km from the old city. From the town centre, a túk-túk shoud cost 80B to 100B; rót daang (shared taxis), about 60B. There are three terminal buildings serving specific geographic areas (though there is overlap in coverage between buildings 2 and 3):

Building 1 Nakornchai Air to Phuket and southern Thailand.

Building 2 Various companies to towns north of Chiang Mai.

Building 3 Various companies to towns south and east of Chiang Mai.

There is a new shopping centre next door to Building 3, providing an air-conditioned place to wait for a departing bus. Do note that from Bangkok, the most reliable companies use Bangkok's Northern and Northeastern bus terminal (Mo Chit). It is not advisable to go north with a bus company that leaves from Bangkok's tourist centres such as Th Khao San. These invariably over-promise and under-deliver.

Thanks to the new Mekong River bridge at Chiang Khong–Huay Xai border crossing, bus services to/from Laos has increased. There is now a bus that links Luang Prabang, Bokeo, Luang Nam Tha, Udom Xai to Chiang Mai.

Chang Pheuak Bus Terminal (Map p234; Th Chang Pheuak) is just north of the old city and serves destinations within Chiang Mai province, including Chiang Dao, Fang, Tha Ton, Chom Thong and Hot. Minibuses to Chiang Dao leave from Soi Sanam Gila, which is behind the bus terminal.

Talat Warorot sŏrng·tăaou stop (Map p240; Th Praisani) serves nearby towns, such as Lamphun, Bo Sang, San Kamphaeng, Mae Jo and Mae Rim. Fares cost about 20B and run frequently throughout the day.

Saphan Lek sŏrng·tăaou stop (Map p234; Th Chiang Mai-Lamphun) serves Lamphun and Lampang.

Pratu Chiang Mai sŏrng·tăaou (Map p240; Th Bamrungburi) stop serves Hang Dong and points south.

TRAIN

Chiang Mai's **train station** (Th Charoen Muang) is about 2.5km east of the old city. The train station has an ATM, a left-luggage room (20B per piece) and an advance-booking counter at the regular ticket window. For information on schedules and fares contact the **State Railway of Thailand** (free hotline 1690; www.railway. co.th) or grab a timetable from the station. Local transport to the train station from the old city should cost 40B to 60B.

All Chiang Mai–bound trains originate from Bangkok's Hua Lamphong station. There are four different types of trains (rapid, express, sprinter and special express) with different classes of cars. Sleeping berths (fan and air-con) and seats (2nd and 3rd class, air-con and fan) are available on most trains, except Sprinters, which don't have sleeper cars. Sleeping berths are increasingly hard to reserve without booking well in advance.

Though the overnight journey between Bangkok and Chiang Mai is a classic Thailand experience, train service has been suffering in the last several years with frequent delays and derailments. In 2013, there were 13 derailments along a section of track between Uttaradit and Chiang Mai. As of 13 September, SRT closed this portion of the line for repairs. Repairs have met with delays and it was unclear when the line would be fully operational. In the meantime, SRT has arranged bus transport to cover the closed portion.

Since 1992, passenger traffic on Thailand's national rail system has fallen by 40%, according to an article in the *Bangkok Post*, and maintenance of the tracks has suffered due to the system's accumulated financial losses. A total of 114 derailments occurred in 2013 throughout the rail system, and the national government has since promised a 1.12 trillion baht package for rail upgrades. Part of the infrastructure investment includes plans for a new high-speed rail project linking Bangkok and Chiang Mai but, at the time of writing, it was unclear how feasible and profitable the project would be.

Getting Around

TO/FROM AIRPORT

There is only one licensed airport taxi service, charging a flat 120B fare. Public bus number 6 (15B) goes from the airport to points west en route to Chiang Mai University; it isn't a convenient option if you're staying in the old city. Many guesthouses and hotels also provide airport transfers.

From any point within the city, you can charter a túk-túk or *rót daang* to the airport for about 60B to 80B; you can usually get one from the airport into the old city too, although you may have to wait around for a while until one shows up.

BICYCLE

Cycling is a good way to get around Chiang Mai. Rickety cruiser bikes with a fixed gear can be rented for around 60B a day from guesthouses. Check the bike carefully before you hire – brakes in particular can be dodgy. Chiang Mai Mountain Biking (p252) rents mountain bikes and city bikes (80B to 150B) for the day. **Cacti Bike** (Map p240; 0 5321 2979; 94/1 Th Singharat; bike hire 80-350B) also offers reliable bike hire, from simple cruisers to serious mountain bikes with all the accessories. For the really good mountain bikes a deposit of US$250 or passport is required. An alternative, **SM Travel** (Map p240; 0 5320 6844; 87 Th Ratchadamnoen; mountain bikes 100-200B) also hires bikes and is a bit cheaper, reflective of the quality of their bikes.

GETTING AROUND LIKE A PRO

Chiang Mai is a very manageable city to navigate. Most of the cultural attractions are within the old city, which is easily covered on foot or by bike.

Directions outside of the old city are often given in relationship to the old city's four cardinal gates. The easternmost gate is Pratu Tha Phae, which leads to Th Tha Phae, a main drag that links to the riverside area. This is where you'll find Chiang Mai's bustling day market (Talat Warorot) and the night bazaar.

Pratu Suan Dok exits the western moat and connects to the leafy environs of Chiang Mai University, modern metropolis of fashionable Th Nimmanhaemin. Further west is Doi Suthep, the city's picturesque peak. The northern gate is Pratu Chang Pheuak; and the southern gate is Pratu Chiang Mai. Sights beyond the old city are easily reached by *rót daang* (shared taxis).

Outside of the central city, the highway system has a variety of names that confuses visitors. The innermost beltway is often referred to as the Superhighway or the 700 Year Stadium Road. Then there are the first and second ring roads.

A copy of Nancy Chandler's *Map of Chiang Mai*, available in bookshops, is a worthwhile investment. It shows the city's main points of interest, shopping venues and oddities that you will be pleased to stumble upon. This schematic map will help you wander with confidence.

CAR & TRUCK

Private transport is available from rental agencies throughout the city, mainly along Th Moon Muang. Be sure that the vehicle you rent has insurance (liability) coverage, which usually includes a 5000B excess. This does not cover personal injury and medical payments of anyone injured in a traffic accident. Ask to take a look at the terms of the insurance policy so you're clear on what is and isn't included. Standard rental rates for small 1.5L cars, such as Toyota Vios or Honda Jazz, start at 1500B. Weekly and monthly rates are available and petrol is not included in the price. Unlimited kilometres should be included.

One of the most well-regarded agencies is **North Wheels** (Map p240; ☐ 0 5387 4478; www.northwheels.com; 70/4-8 Th Chaiyaphum), which offers hotel pick-up and delivery, 24-hour emergency road service, and comprehensive insurance. Another good bet is **Thai Rent a Car** (Petchburee Car Rent; ☐ 0 5390 4188; www. thairentacar.com; Chiang Mai International Airport), located at the airport. Other car-rental agencies in town include **Budget Car Rental** (Map p234; ☐ 0 5320 2871; 201/2 Th Mahidol), across from Central Airport Plaza.

MOTORCYCLE

One of the most popular options for getting about on your own is to rent a motorcycle. Agencies along Th Moon Muang and even some guesthouses rent Honda Dream 100cc step-through manual and automatic bikes for about 200B a day; more powerful bikes, such as the Honda or Yamaha 125cc to 150cc, rent for 250B to 300B a day. A few places rent 400cc motorcycles (600B to 900B), while a 650cc can go for 1500B. The small bikes are good for city touring but if you plan on going outside of town along mountain roads, consider upgrading to a stronger machine. By law, you must wear a helmet, and police frequently set up checkpoints to enforce this.

Most agencies include motorcycle insurance in the price, but always ask if insurance is included and what it covers. Some policies will cover free repairs if the bike breaks down, but will charge a 1500B excess in case of accident and a 10,000B excess if the motorbike is stolen. Often bike hire places will ask for your passport as a security deposit; while it is unnerving to surrender such an important document, it is usually returned when you return the bike.

If you're renting a motorcycle for touring the countryside around Chiang Mai, check out the tips and routes at **Golden Triangle Rider** (www. gt-rider.com).

Here are some of the more established and reliable outlets:

Mr Mechanic (Map p240; ☐ 0 5321 4708; www.mr-mechanic1994.com; 4 Soi 5, Th Moon Muang) There are also two other branches in the old city; new, well-maintained fleet and comprehensive insurance.

Tony's Big Bikes (Map p240; ☐ 0 5320 7124; 17 Th Ratchamankha) Rents well-maintained 125cc to 400cc motorbikes that all have license plates. Also offers riding lessons, gives touring advice and repairs motorcycles.

Dang Bike Hire (Map p240; ☐ 0 5327 1524; 23 Th Kotchasan; ☺9am-5pm daily) Fleet quality varies so inspect the bike before committing.

PUBLIC & CHARTERED TRANSPORT

Chiang Mai residents who don't have their own wheels rely on the ubiquitous *rót daang* (literally 'red truck'), *sŏrng·tăaou*) or túk-túk.

Rót daang are shared taxis: you can flag them down, tell them your destination and if they are going that way they'll nod (ever so slightly). Along the way they might pick up other passengers if the stops are en route or close by. Short trips should cost 20B per person (eg around the old city) and longer trips from 40B per person (eg from the old city to Th Nimmanhaemin), and more depending on the distance and your negotiation skills. If you travel from the riverside area to Th Nimmahaemin you'll probably have to pay around 40B. By and large you shouldn't have a problem with *rót daang* drivers being too greedy about fares. Most quote honest prices and it seems to be something of a tradition for the drivers to scoot around town in the evenings and on weekends with their wives in the front seat for company. If a *rót daang* is parked alongside the road, the driver prefers to charter the vehicle for trips to attractions, such as Doi Suthep, or to tourist attractions that pay a commission (animal shows, San Kamphaeng etc) instead of running a shared taxi route.

Túk-túk work only on a charter basis and are more expensive than *rót daang*. Rates start at 60B to 80B for most trips and creep up to 100B at night when people are returning home from the bars. The benefit of túk-túk is that it takes you directly to your destination and the driver usually speaks passable English. The drawback is that the drivers can be a little more aggressive about fares and prefer to steer their customers to attractions that pay commissions. Regardless, this is the best option for trips to/from the bus station, train station and airport when you're burdened with baggage and don't know your way around.

Chiang Mai still has a few săhm·lór (pedicabs), typically parked at Talat Warorot. Săhm·lór cost around 20B to 30B for short trips near the market.

TAXI

It is very rare to see a metered taxi to flag down in Chiang Mai. Call **Taxi Meter** (✆ 0 5326 2878; www.taxichiangmai.com) for a pick-up if you want one – most fares within greater Chiang Mai are no more than 150B. You can also organise tours in and around the city.

NORTHERN CHIANG MAI PROVINCE

North of Chiang Mai the province becomes mountainous and rugged as it bumps against Myanmar's frontier. Among the highlights are the beautiful Mae Sa Valley and the forested peaks around Chiang Dao.

Mae Sa Valley & Samoeng
แม่สา/สะเมิง

One of the easiest mountain escapes, the Mae Sa–Samoeng loop travels from the lowland's concrete expanse into the highlands' forested frontier. The 100km route makes a good day trip with private transport or a country getaway with an overnight in Samoeng. Golden Triangle Rider (p279) publishes a detailed map of the area and provides trip reports.

Head north of Chiang Mai on Rte 107 (Th Chang Pheuak) toward Mae Rim, then left onto Rte 1096. The road becomes more rural but there's a steady supply of tour-bus attractions: orchid farms, butterfly parks, snake farms, you name it. Also lots of all-terrain vehicle (ATV) and off-road buggy hire.

Only 6km from the Mae Rim turn-off, **Nam Tok Mae Sa** (adult/child 100/50B, car 30B) is part of the Doi Suthep-Pui National Park. The falls are more of a series of pools than a full-blown cascade but it is a picturesque spot to picnic or tramp around in the woods for a bit. It is also a great place to take a plunge, especially during the hot season. You could bring your swimsuit or do as the Thais and frolic in your street clothes. It is a favourite weekend getaway for locals so get there early and stake out your waterhole.

The road starts to climb and twist after the waterfall entrance. Catch your breath at **Mae Sa Elephant Camp** (✆ 0 5320 6247; www.maesaelephantcamp.com; Rte 1096; shows adult/child 200/100B, ride for 2 people 800B; ⊙ shows 8am, 9.40am & 1.30pm), one of the north's largest. Mae Sa is a bit old-fashioned in its attitudes towards elephant entertain-

ment, but it enjoys a good reputation for the general welfare of the herd. The camp has a high fertility rate, which is a good sign that the elephants are mentally and socially healthy. The camp attracts criticism from animal rights activists because they still offer old-fashioned circus shows with balancing acts, considered dangerous because of the crippling effects a fall could cause. Mae Sa also pioneered the 'artist' elephant, in which the elephant holds a paint brush in its trunk to paint; it is a perennial hit with tourists, though it is another sore point with activists. There is also elephant riding and mahout training. The camp is in a lovely wooded setting and you can skip the shows (held three times daily) and just wander the grounds feeding, petting and posing with the creatures.

Two kilometres past the elephant camp is the **Queen Sirikit Botanic Gardens** (✆ 0 5384 1333; www.qsbg.org; Rte 1096; adult/child 100/50B; ⊙ 8.30am-4.30pm), a shorn mountainside displaying 227 hectares of various exotic and local flora for conservation and research purposes. Near the administration building, the orchid collection contains over 400 species, the nation's largest display. The highlight of the garden is the **glasshouse complex** sitting near the mountain peak. There are waterlily and lotus collections and the rainforest house, recreating a southern Thai jungle complete with indoor waterfall and canopy platforms.

After the botanic gardens the road climbs up into the fertile Mae Sa Valley, once a high-altitude basin for growing opium poppies. Now the valley's hill-tribe farmers have re-seeded their terraced fields with sweet peppers, cabbage, flowers and fruits – which are then sold to the royal agriculture projects under the Doi Kham label. The royal project at the Hmong village of **Nong Hoi** sits some 1200m above sea level and is accessible by a turn-off road in the village of Pong Yeang. Continue on this road to **Mon Cham** (Nong Hoi Mai; mains from 60-150B; ⊙ 9am-7pm), a collection of bamboo huts teetering on the ridgeline. The restaurant serves tasty Thai food using the royal project's produce but the food takes second spoon to the panoramic view. The last 100m to the restaurant is a steep gravel climb that is difficult to ascend on a motorbike.

Sitting at the western wedge of the valley, **Proud Phu Fah** (✆ 0 5387 9389; www.proudphu-fah.com; Rte 1096, Km 17; r 2500-4000B; ❄ @ 🛜 ☎) is a small boutique hotel with creature-

SUPERHIGHWAY OF YORE: MAE PING RIVER

In ancient times, Thai cities were intimately tied to the waterways for sustenance and transportation. The fundamental role of rivers in everyday life often elevated them from thoroughfares to revered entities honoured by such festivals as Loi Krathong.

Chiang Mai's exalted river, **Mae Ping**, connects the forested highlands and fertile agricultural valleys to the commercial centres on its 569km course before it merges with Chao Phraya River. It feeds a vast agricultural system of rice paddies, coffee plantations, lam yai orchards, strawberry fields and flower gardens, and was the primary thoroughfare for the teak trade in the 19th century.

The river's historical role can still be observed in the area known as **Wat Ket**, which runs along the city's eastern riverbank, originally settled by Chinese merchants and Western missionaries. Today there are still old-fashioned wooden shophouses and missionary-sponsored schools and hospitals along Th Charoenrat. For more river history, hop aboard a traditional watercraft affiliated with **Scorpion Tailed River Cruise** (Map p240; 08 1960 9398; www.scorpiontailedrivercruise.com; Th Charoenrat; ticket 500B). Tours depart from Wat Srikhong pier near Rim Ping Condo. The river along this stretch is wide and muddy with a mix of urban and rustic scenery.

North of Chiang Mai, the river carves a windy path out of the mountains through a jungle canopy and rural landscape. Kayak tours led by Chiang Mai Mountain Biking & Kayaking (p252) explore these scenic bits of the river and offer the added benefit of nature sightseeing without as much sweat.

comfort villas designed to give the illusion of sleeping amid the great outdoors. Each villa also has a patio area right on the water's edge. The open-air restaurant serves healthy Thai food (dishes 150B to 250B) with a view of the valley.

After Proud Phu Fah, the road swings around the mountain ridge and starts to rise and dip until it reaches the conifer zone. Beyond, the landscape unfolds in a cascade of mountains. Eventually the road spirals down into **Samoeng**, a pretty village. If you want to stay overnight, **Samoeng Resort** (0 5348 7074; Rte 6033; r 500-800B;) is not a resort at all but rather a bunch of OK concrete bungalows in a bushy setting, about 2.5km outside the village; but it is one of the most affordable options around. To get here take Rte 1349 from Samoeng (a right-hand turn in the town). There are prettier and more expensive resorts on Rte 1269 between Samoeng and Chiang Mai. To return to Chiang Mai, stay on Rte 1269 all the way to the Th Khlong Chonprathan (canal road).

Getting There & Away

Only part of the route is accessible via public transport. Sŏrng·tăaou go to Samoeng (70B, 2¾ hours, two morning departures) from the Chang Pheuak bus terminal in Chiang Mai. In Samoeng, the vehicles stop near the market, across from Samoeng Hospital.

Chiang Dao เชียงดาว

In a lush, jungle setting in the shadow of a mighty limestone mountain, Chiang Dao is a popular country escape from the steaming urban plains of Chiang Mai. Families and 30-something travellers come to relax and wander, enjoying the area's rural character. The star attraction is Doi Chiang Dao, allegedly Thailand's highest limestone mountain. It is a thickly forested peak with a revered cave shrine burrowed into the base, and trails popular with birders and trekkers.

Sights & Activities

Chiang Dao town isn't much but a dusty crossroad that hosts a colourful twice monthly morning market, when hill tribes come to sell their wares. The more charming part of town is 5km west along the road that leads to Tham Chiang Dao (Chiang Dao Cave).

From the main four-way junction at Chiang Dao, those with their own wheels can head eastwards to visit hill-tribe villages, many of which have become multi-ethnic villages due to cultural assimilation over the generations has occurred. Roughly 13.5km east from Rte 107 is the Lisu village of Lisu Huay Ko, where rustic accommodation is available. Without independent transport, you can arrange hill-tribe treks through the guesthouses at Chiang Dao. Some guesthouses rent mountain bikes for 150B a day – not much of a bargain but an improvement on two feet. They can also help you arrange motorbike hire (300B to 400B) so you've got more freedom.

Tham Chiang Dao
CAVE

(ถ้ำเชียงดาว, Chiang Dao Cave; admission 40B) In the heat of the day, the coolest place in town is the Chiang Dao Cave, a complex said to extend some 10km to 14km into Doi Chiang Dao. There are four interconnected caverns that are open to the public. Tham Phra Non (360m) is the initial segment and is electrically illuminated and can be explored on your own.

It contains several religious shrines, a common feature of Thailand's caves, which are regarded as holy meditation sites. There are also some surreal-looking stalactites reminiscent of a Salvador Dali painting.

To explore the other caves – Tham Mah (735m), Tham Kaew (474m) and Tham Nam (660m) – we recommend that you hire a guide with a pressurised gas lantern (100B for up to five people), not because you aren't intrepid enough to go solo but because the guide service provides income for the local villagers. The guides point out the interior cave formations that have been named, yet another Thai cave tradition.

Local legend says this cave complex was the home of a *reu·sĕe* (holy man) for a thousand years, and that the sage was on such intimate terms with the deities that he convinced some *tair·wá·dah* (the Buddhist equivalent of angels) to create several magic wonders inside the caverns: a stream flowing from the pedestal of a solid-gold Buddha; a storehouse of divine textiles; a mystical lake; a city of *naga* (mythical serpents); a sacred immortal elephant; and the hermit's tomb. Such fantastical wonders are said to be much deeper inside the mountain, beyond the last of the illuminated caverns.

There is a temple complex outside the cavern, and a stream with huge carp and catfish you can feed (which handily counts as making merit via a donation). Vendors by the parking lot sell medicinal roots and herbs harvested in the nearby forests.

Doi Chiang Dao
MOUNTAIN

(ดอยเชียงดาว, Doi Luang) Part of the Doi Chiang Dao National Park, Doi Chiang Dao pokes into the heavens at 2195m above sea level. From the summit, reachable by a two-day hike, the views are spectacular. The southern side of the mountain is believed to be one of the most accessible spots in the world to see the giant nuthatch and Hume's pheasant. **Birdwatching** and **overnight treks** can be arranged through local guesthouses.

If you just want to wander by yourself, continue to the end of the cave road to Samnak Song Tham Pha Plong (Tham Pha Plong Hermitage), where the famous meditation master Luang Pu Sim once resided. A long, steep stairway leads up the mountain to a large *chedi* framed by forest and limestone cliffs.

Elephant Training Center of Chiang Dao
ELEPHANT ENCOUNTER

(☑0 5329 8553; www.chiangdaoelephantcamp.com; show 100B; ☺shows 9am & 10am) In a lovely wooded setting near the highway, this elephant camp enjoys a good reputation. It hosts educational training exhibitions in which visitors are offered a rare insight into how young elephants are taught to obey mahout commands, work with other elephants and accept mahouts on their backs. The camp also has a 'joy ride' program (8000B for two people), in which visitors spend two hours riding, bathing, feeding and caring for

---

ONE MILLION RICE FIELDS

Once upon a time, northern Thailand was as distinct and foreign to Bangkok and the central plains as Cambodia or Laos is today. The northern kingdom of Lanna (meaning 'one million rice fields') had its own dialect, writing system, customs and tribal ethnicity. Even after the decline of an independent Lanna state, the north was still viewed as the 'other' by Bangkok Thais. A concerted effort to unite the country's different ethnicities into one unified national identity began after WWII. Now with the national educational system and a modern transient workforce, Thai culture is much more homogenised. The northern Thai dialect continues to be spoken by *'kun meu·ang'* (people of the north) and elements of Lanna culture are embraced by Thais from outside the region with romantic nostalgia. For a guide to the northern Thai dialect and northern food, see the Northern Thailand chapter (p291).

the elephants. There are also one-hour riding tours along the river and river rafting.

🛏 Sleeping

Many of the guesthouses are spread out along the road leading to Tham Chiang Dao and enjoy a view of the mountain and butterfly-filled gardens. They can arrange trekking tours, give sightseeing advice and rent bicycles and motorbikes.

Hobby Hut   GUESTHOUSE $
(☑08 0034 4153; r from 250B) Chiang Dao's cheapest backpacker choice, Hobby Hut has simple A-frame huts with shared bathrooms surrounded by rice fields. Meals with the family are available.

Chiang Dao Hut   GUESTHOUSE $
(☑0 5345 6384; www.chiangdaohut.com; r 350-750B) This cute collection of bungalows has a 'central' location near the cave. Some bungalows practically kiss the mountain, while others are closer to the road. There are just eight huts with varying sizes and amenities.

★Chiang Dao Nest   GUESTHOUSE $$
(☑08 6017 1985; http://nest.chiangdao.com; r 895-1500B; @🛜🞲) The guesthouse that put Chiang Dao on the travellers' map creates an inviting rural retreat. Simple bungalows get the basics right – comfy beds, privacy and immaculate interiors. Those closest to the restaurant have terrific views from the rickety rear porches.

There's a secluded, forested swimming pool with mountain views. The garden has lots of chill-out spaces, including a pavilion filled with kids' toys. Goats from a nearby farm come for daily visits to tame the grass and be petted by guests. The owners are knowledgeable about the area and can arrange a variety of intimate trekking tours. But the primary reason for the Nest's success is the sensational restaurant known among Chiang Mai expats as a dining destination.

Nature Guest House   GUESTHOUSE $$
(☑08 9955 9074; r 650-900B; @🛜) This quiet place is set in a fruit orchard with mountain views. The fan-cooled wooden huts are well-maintained and have generous porches; modern air-con bungalows are newer and have more 'bells'. Chickens wander the grounds, longan litter the pathways, and all that fresh air makes an irresistible sleep aid.

Malee's Nature Lovers Bungalows   GUESTHOUSE $$
(☑08 1961 8387; www.maleenature.com; r 350-1500B; @🞲) Malee's has a rustic traveller vibe with its collection of variously priced and sized bungalows. The cheapest share bathrooms, while the 'honeymoon bungalows' have privacy and wrap-around porches, and one is set high off the ground for birders to watch the canopy activity. There is also a family cabin, which has an extra sleeping room. The owner is an orchid collector and has over 82 varieties on-site.

Yang Tone Farmstay   GUESTHOUSE $$
(☑0 5312 1626; www.yantongfarmstay.com; r from 690-900B) Tucked down a country road, Yangtone's 12 bamboo bungalows have funky finishings and balconies with fantastic mountain views centred on a common campfire pit.

Chiang Dao Nest 2   GUESTHOUSE $$
(☑0 5345 6242; www.nest.chiangdao.com; r 895B; @) The original Chiang Dao Nest was so popular that it has opened this second location closer to the cave. The grounds are just as lovely with almost touchable views of the mountain, and the bungalows have better-than-average beds.

🍴 Eating

Chiang Dao has a lovely assortment of farm-fresh produce – mostly chemical-free – thanks to the nearby royal agriculture projects.

There is a **daily food market** off the main street through Chiang Dao. The **Tuesday Morning Market** (⊙7am-noon 1st & 3rd Tue of the month) is the most colourful, with hill tribes bringing wares to sell.

Chiang Dao Saloon   INTERNATIONAL $$
(mains 150-250B; ⊙10am-9pm Sep-May) The former Mon & Kurt Restaurant has been re-fashioned into a bar and restaurant serving Thai and Western food.

★Chiang Dao Nest   INTERNATIONAL $$$
(☑0 6017 1985; mains 300-500B; ⊙6am-10pm) The Nest's restaurant serves sophisticated fusion-European food in a relaxed garden setting. Wicha, the owner and chef, received her culinary training in the UK and creates a menu that reflects the seasons. Double-baked cheese soufflé with spinach cream and roasted-veg salad and baked passion-fruit cheesecake are just a few of the dinner

options. The food ain't cheap but definitely comes with the wow factor.

ⓘ Getting There & Around

Chiang Dao is 72km north of Chiang Mai along Rte 107. Buses to Chiang Dao (40B, 1½ hours, six daily) leave from Chiang Mai's Chang Pheuak terminal. The buses arrive and depart from Chiang Dao's bus station; from there, hire a *sŏrng·tăaou* (100B) to your guesthouse. Most drivers charge 150B to deliver passengers to guesthouses on the cave road. Buses also travel to Fang (60B) and Tha Ton (70B). Most accommodation hires mountain bikes, and some organise scooters and cars. Or, you can hire a *sŏrng·tăaou* for about 1000B a day to drive you round the area.

Doi Ang Khang   ดอยอ่างขาง

Welcome to Thailand's 'Little Switzerland', so called for its cool climate and mountain scenery. A visit here is like entering a different world: you leave the tropical heat of the plains, following the narrow switchback road up the mountain with its expansive views of the towns and fields below, until you reach the cloud belt where villagers are bundled up in winter jackets and speak languages imported from faraway places. The winter phenomenon of frost (occurring usually in January) adds to Doi Ang Khang's exoticism. Thais often make the pilgrimage here during the New Year's holiday period to shiver from cold for amusement. Doi Ang Khang (1300m) also borders Myanmar and offers the illusion of peeping over the border into that country's vast frontier.

The main road to the summit is via Rte 1249 with lots of looping hairpin turns. There are about four minority villages situated along the ridgelines of Doi Ang Khang. As you approach the summit, look for the turnoff to **Ban Luang**, a Yunnanese village just south of the campground. **Ran Ahlee** (Ban Luang; mains 45B) (no romanscript sign; look for the sign with the Muslim crescent) serves Yunnanese-style *kôw soy* and is a good excuse to drive through town. Most villagers make their living through farming.

Near the summit of Doi Ang Khang is the **Royal Agricultural Station** (admission 50B), showcasing fruit orchards, tea plantations, a bonsai garden and other flora. The mountain sits at an altitude of 1300m and supports the cultivation of many temperate species that are considered exotic in Thailand. These crops were introduced as substitutes

for opium poppies. The station's restaurant serves Thai standards, using local produce.

There are several places to stay near the station's entrance in the village of **Ban Khum**, a mix of Myanmarese and hill-tribe people, who make their living off the tourist trade. Marketing itself as an ecoresort, **Angkhang Nature Resort** (ⓓ0 5345 0110; www.mosaic-collection.com; r from 2500B; ✳@) has large bungalows set in a slope behind the main reception building. They are quite plush and the best feature is the small, wooden outdoor porches with lovely garden views. In the resort itself, the attractive restaurant features royal project produce, and the lobby boasts stone fireplaces to complete the winter-lodge atmosphere. A portion of its staffing is dedicated to hiring from local hill tribes, providing a much needed job source. The hotel can arrange lots of outdoor activities: mountain biking, trekking and mule riding (a traditional form of transport on the mountain). It also distributes a thematic map showing hill-tribe villages, walking trails and birdwatching spots, though geographic details are a little lean. A more detailed description of birdwatching trails can be found at **Thai Birding** (www.thaibirding.com).

Other villages include **Ban Khop Dong**, a Lahu settlement, and **Ban Nor Lae**, a Palong settlement; both are involved in farming for the royal project. Residents of Nor Lae crossed the border into Thailand from Myanmar about 30 years ago and the village is within site of a border patrol station.

ⓘ Getting There & Away

Leaving the mountain, you can take the scenic back road of Rte 1178, which winds along a ridge to the mountain's western slopes. Doi Ang Khang is about 25km from the intersection of Rte 107 and 1249; from this turnoff it's a further 13km to Fang. If you're travelling by motorbike you'll need a 250cc machine to make the climb.

Fang & Tha Ton   ฝาง/ท่าตอน

The northernmost towns in Chiang Mai province feel light-years removed from the provincial capital and its sophisticated ways. Few foreigners stop in at Fang, which was originally founded by Phaya Mengrai in the 13th century, although the locale dates back at least 1000 years as a stop for *jeen hor* caravans. The odd foreigners who do wander into town do so to catch a bus elsewhere. While here they might wander around the Shan-style **Wat Jong Paen** (near the New

Wiang Kaew Hotel), which has an impressive stacked-roof *wí·hǎhn*, Fang's other source of notoriety comes from its proximity to Myanmar, and the surrounding district is an 'underground' conduit for *yah bâh* (methamphetamine). Police checkpoints along the highways are typically inspecting vehicles for contraband.

More charming is Tha Ton, a petite settlement planted on a pretty bend along Mae Nam Kok. Travellers come here to catch the river boat to Chiang Rai, but recently new guesthouses have been enticing visitors to stay a little longer and explore the wild corners of the province and enjoy the river views. It is easy to cycle around the town, exploring rice fields and small villages, or take a day trip to the high-altitude village of Mae Salong or the hot springs at Doi Pha Hompok National park. You can also charter a boat to various points along the river, including the Myanmarese border or small hill-tribe villages.

⊙ Sights & Activities

Wat Tha Ton   BUDDHIST TEMPLE
(✐0 5345 9309; www.wat-thaton.org) In Tha Ton, this temple sprawls up the side of a wooded hill. There are nine different levels and each level affords stunning views of the mountainous valley towards Myanmar, the plains of Tha Ton and the winding river.

From the base to the ninth level, it is about 3km or a 30-minute walk. The first level has a statue of Kuan Yin, the Chinese goddess of compassion; the international liaison monk has his office here too. The large white Buddha peeping out from the trees is on level three. On level eight is the recently constructed Chedi Kaew, featuring a colourful almost Arabic-influenced stupa.

Hilltribe Trekking   ADVENTURE SPORTS
(tours from 1000B) Tha Ton has a very low-key personality and does little to promote itself as a tourism destination, but within 20km of the town, there are six hill-tribe villages inhabited by Palaung, Black Lahu, Akha, Karen and Yunnanese. These villages see fewer foreign visitors than those around Chiang Mai. Treks can be arranged through any of Tha Ton's guesthouses.

Boat Trip to Chiang Rai   BOAT RIDE
(✐0 5305 3727; ticket 350B; ⊙departs 12.30pm) Long-tail boats make the journey between Chiang Rai and Tha Ton daily. It is a scenic,

forested route past thatch-hut villages and fisherfolk casting nets in the shallows.

The boat takes up to 12 passengers and makes pit stops along the way. The best time to go is at the end of the rainy season in November when the river level is high. The travel time depends on river conditions, taking anywhere from three to five hours.

Some travellers make the trip in two or three stages, stopping first in Mae Salak, a large Lahu village, or Ban Ruammit, a Karen village. Both are well touristed, but you can get off the path by joining a trek from here to Shan, Thai and hill-tribe villages. Doi Wawi, south of Mae Salak, is a large multi-ethnic community of *jeen hor,* hill-tribe and Thai peoples known for its coffee and tea plantations; Chiang Mai's Wawee coffeeshops get their beans from this district. The Wawi area has dozens of hill-tribe villages of various ethnicities, including Thailand's largest Akha community (Saen Charoen) and the oldest Lisu settlement (Doi Chang).

You can also make the trip (much more slowly) upriver from Chiang Rai; this is possible despite the rapids. The boats are also available for charter hire (2200B, six people).

🛏 Sleeping

Tha Ton's guesthouses enjoy a peaceful setting beside the river. Guesthouses can arrange motorcycle and bicycle hire, trekking and tourist information. Unless otherwise noted in the review, these guesthouses are located across the bridge opposite the boat launch.

Sappaya Guesthouse   GUESTHOUSE $
(✐08 0792 8725; r 400-500B) This newcomer is a friendly and breezy spot with simple, shared bathrooms in a two-storey terraced house. There are shared kitchen facilities, lots of local information and an outgoing host.

Thaton Garden Riverside   GUESTHOUSE $
(✐0 5345 9286; r 400-600B) You don't get a lot of personality at this old-school establishment but it is one of Tha Ton's best-priced options. You could go for a cheap fan room and at least get a private bathroom or step up to the air-con rooms and spend your day hanging out in your riverside terrace.

★Old Tree's House   HOTEL $$
(✐08 5722 9002; www.oldtreeshouse.net; bungalows 1200-1400B; ❄ 🛜 ☲) Nestled into a forested hillside, this French-Thai operation provides reason enough to come to Tha

Ton. It's a cleverly designed mini-resort, up a steep driveway, with luxury bungalows sitting in a pretty garden with lots of nooks and crannies. The nerve centre of the property is the central swimming pool and treetop pavilion from which you can enjoy the mountain and river views while drying off from the pool. It is a good fit for families. It's 400m past Tha Ton, and well signed off the road.

Apple Resort GUESTHOUSE **$$**
(☑ 0 5337 3144; r 500-1200B; ❋) Tha Ton's hippest hang-out, Apple has made the most of its riverside setting. Cheap garden bungalows are basic but roomy while the upscale riverfront bungalows are bright and breezy with fantastic front porches. There is a friendly and vibrant riverside restaurant for enjoying Tha Ton's best feature: the river by moonlight. Rates include breakfast.

Garden Home GUESTHOUSE **$$**
(☑ 0 5337 3015; r 300-1800B) Thatch-roofed bungalows are spaced among lychee trees and bougainvillea at this tranquil riverside spot. There are also a few stone bungalows, and three larger, more luxurious bungalows on the river, with lovely verandahs, TV and fridge.

Thaton River View HOTEL **$$**
(☑ 0 5337 3173; thatonriverview@hotmail.com; r 1700B; ❋) On the plus side, this hotel has the best riverside setting, with completely forested views, and waterfront bungalows connected by wooden walkways. The common sitting areas teetering over the water make sipping a cool drink all the more enjoyable. The bad news is that it is rundown. Ageing rooms with blah bathrooms are slightly saved by stylish wooden floors. But for a night or two you won't notice these wrinkles.

Areeya Phuree GUESTHOUSE **$$**
(☑ 0 5305 3658; www.areeyaphuree-resort.com; r 200-2000B; ❋) This sprawling hotel has a quiet riverside location about 200m from town on the boat-launch side of the river. Lodging spans every budget category from stylish bungalows to budget digs. The dorm wing with private sleeping quarters and shared common area is one Tha Ton's cheapest. There are also cute rooms with jungle bathrooms decorated with plants and river rocks. It is still a work in progress after undergoing a change of ownership

two years ago, but the owner is very enthusiastic about Tha Ton's merits as a tourist attraction and has big ideas, if not a big budget.

✗ Eating

In Tha Ton, riverside restaurants provide food and views. A small night market sets up a few metres before the bridge. There is a row of basic huts selling stir-fry by the boat dock.

Chankasen THAI **$**
(209 Rimnumkok; mains 60-80B; ⊙10am-8pm) The food is fine at this friendly, entrepreneurial Thai spot, but the real puller is the seating right on the river. It is conveniently located right alongside the boat dock.

Sunshine Cafe CAFE **$**
(mains 60-110B; ⊙8am-3pm) This is the place to come for freshly brewed coffee in the morning. It also does a wide selection of Western breakfasts including muesli, fresh fruit and yoghurt. It is located on the main road, just before the bridge.

❶ Getting There & Away

BUS
The bus stop in Tha Ton is across the bridge from town; the following destinations are served:
Bangkok (600B, 14 hours, four daily)
Chiang Dao (63B, two hours, seven daily)
Chiang Mai (90B, four hours, seven daily)
Fang (30B, 30 minutes, seven daily)
For more frequent service or more routes, head to Fang. Buses go to Chiang Rai (200B, one afternoon departure).

Across the street from Tha Ton's bus stop is a *sǒrng·tǎaou* stop, with service to the following:
Fang (25B, frequent between 5.30am and 5.30pm)
Mae Salong (60B, 1½ hours, three daily)
From Mae Salong you can continue on to Chiang Rai without having to backtrack.

MOTORCYCLE
Motorcycle trekkers can travel between Tha Ton and Doi Mae Salong, 48km northeast, over a fully paved but sometimes treacherous mountain road. There are a couple of Lisu and Akha villages on the way. The 27km or so between the village of Muang Ngam and Doi Mae Salong are very steep and winding – take care, especially in the rainy season. When conditions are good, the trip can be done in 1½ hours.

SOUTHERN CHIANG MAI PROVINCE

To the immediate south of Chiang Mai is the Ping Valley, a fertile agricultural plain that has also grown some noteworthy handicraft villages. Further to the southwest is Thailand's highest peak, Doi Inthanon (2565m).

Bo Sang & San Kamphaeng   บ่อสร้าง/สันกำแพง

Southeast of Chiang Mai is **Bo Sang**, known throughout the country as the 'umbrella village'. It is mainly a tourist market filled with craft shops selling painted umbrellas, fans, silverware, statuary, celadon pottery and lacquerware. Vendors do demonstrations of traditional crafts – assembling and painting paper umbrellas and making mulberry paper – though the majority of the goods are produced in factories elsewhere. It is moderately interesting for the craft demos but the products themselves can just as easily be found at the Chiang Mai Night Bazaar.

In late January the **Bo Sang Umbrella Festival** (*têt·sà·gahn rôm*) features a colourful umbrella procession during the day and a night-time lantern procession. Although it sounds touristy, this festival is actually a very Thai affair; a highlight is the many northern-Thai music ensembles that perform in shopfronts along Bo Sang's main street.

Further down Rte 1006 is **San Kamphaeng**, once known as a production centre for cotton, silk and other handicrafts. There are still some small-scale factories here, but the area is changing with the globalisation of manufacturing and the downturn in Western tourism. Today the stores sell mainly luxury goods – silk, jewellery, leather – to tourists who are in the mood to shop. The stores also have demonstration rooms where workers show the traditional manufacturing of textiles on hand looms, though their efforts in no way represent the bulk of the items for sale in the showroom.

The quality and the prices aren't especially remarkable, but the stores still make enough to hand out attractive commissions to *sŏrng·tăaou* drivers, thus ensuring a steady supply of clients. Most stores will pay the drivers 30B to 'park', while a customer shops, and also give them a percentage of whatever sale is made. If the customer spends big, the drivers often refer to their windfall as 'winning the lottery'. In Thailand, commissions are similar to taking out an advertisement in local media – an accepted form of promoting one's business. But the cost of paying commissions is often passed on to the customer, meaning that prices here aren't as competitive as more centrally located places. It also means that there is more pressure to make a sale, since each customer who walks in the door already costs the company. This results in a somewhat unscrupulous sales climate. One Persian rug dealer told us that all of the rugs were made on-site by Thai workers, were decorated with Thai symbolism, and came with a certificate documenting authenticity. If you decide to shop in San Kamphaeng, do so with a healthy dose of scepticism.

ℹ Getting There & Away

White *sŏrng·tăaou* to Bo Sang (20B) and San Kamphaeng (20B) leave Chiang Mai frequently during the day from the Talat Warorot *sŏrng·tăaou* stop on Th Praisani. Bo Sang is 10km from Chiang Mai and San Kamphaeng is 14km.

Mae Kampong   แม่กำปอง

If you plough across the Ping Valley on Rte 1317 past the housing developments and the rice fields to Mae On district, the road begins to narrow and climb into the forested hills of Mae Kampong, one of Chiang Mai's closest and most accessible high-altitude villages. Most visitors are first introduced to the area on day trips with Flight of the Gibbon (p248), a zipline canopy tour.

Sitting at an altitude of about 1300m, **Ban Mae Kampong** is a Thai village that produces *mêeang* (pickled tea leaves), the northern Thai equivalent of betel nut. Most villagers make their living in this small-scale industry (an average annual salary for a farming family is 35,000B). Recently though, the villagers have expanded into coffee production, as demand for *mêeang* has declined. In the early mornings the pickers stop by the local temple where the monk has prepared a restorative brew of medicinal herbs before they head out into the fields to collect the tea leaves. The village itself is a gravity-defying collection of maze-like huts hugging the steep hillside. Flowers bow in the cool breezes and the jungle insects screech at each other.

DON'T MISS

A CHANCE TO SOAK YOUR CARES AWAY

Doi Pha Hompok National Park (Doi Fang or Mae Fang National Park; ☑ 0 5345 3517; adult/child 200/100B) is a picturesque spot known for its hot springs (*bòr nám rórn; bor nâam hórn* in northern Thai). Trails wind through a boulder-strewn field punctuated by some 40 geothermal springs, pools and steam vents sometimes shooting water 30m high. A small bath complex pipes the heated water (50°C and 87°C) into public and private bathing pools (20B to 50B). There is no time limit in the public pools so you can take advantage of the water's curative powers for as long as you like. Just remember to wear modest swimming attire, as provincial Thais are easily embarrassed about Western-style bathing suits. Once you've turned yourself into a prune, you can get a massage or enjoy or fruit drink or snack. Rather than boiling themselves, Thai visitors opt to boil eggs in the hot water instead. The park is very tranquil during the week once the tour buses have evacuated.

The rest of the park is forested and mountainous with hiking trails and **camping** (www.dnp.go.th; mountain campsite 60B). A popular local activity is to camp at one of the mountain campgrounds and then hike to the summit of Doi Pha Hompok (one of Thailand's highest peaks) just in time for sunrise. At the top of the mountain, average temperatures are a mere 2°C during winter and 14°C during summer. From November to February average temperatures in the park are 14°C to 19°C.

The park lies about 10km west of Fang at Ban Meuang Chom, near the agricultural station, off Rte 107 at the end of Rte 5054.

The community has banded together to develop a tourism initiative to encourage visitors to experience their traditional lifestyle. Several families participate in a **homestay program** (☑ 08 9559 4797; r 580B) that includes three meals and basic lodging. It is estimated that homestay families earn about 10,000B to 15,000B per year through the program, and 10% of the income enters a village development fund that has been used for infrastructure and forest conservation. A similar homestay set-up is **Baan Chom Nok Chom Mai** (☑ 08 9559 9371; r 600B). You can arrange tours of the village through **Khun Sukanya** (☑ 08 1951 4797).

The narrow road through the village summits the hill and winds down into **Chae Son National Park**, where you'll find waterfalls and hot springs.

If you visit Mae Kampong as a day trip from Chiang Mai, stop in at the restaurant of Tharnthong Lodge, south of Ban Mae Kampong, for a bite to eat and wander around its photo-op garden.

Mae Kampong is 48km east of Chiang Mai and can be reached by following Rte 1317 towards San Kamphaeng. At the T-junction at Ban Huay Kaew, turn right towards the signs for Ban Mae Kampong. There is no public transport to the village but it can be reached via motorcycle or car.

Hang Dong & Ban Thawai

หางดง/บ้านถวาย

Of Chiang Mai's two handicraft centres, the area south of the city still retains its reputation as a 'furniture highway' where stores and workshops specialise in decorative arts, woodcarving, antiques and contemporary furniture. The area is 15km south of Chiang Mai accessible by private transport via Rte 108.

The greatest concentration of shops can be found on Th Thakhilek, the first left turn after Talat Hang Dong. A cluster of stores near the intersection sells antique reproductions using new wood; in times past they used salvaged teak but most of that is now gone. Further down the road is **Chili Antiques & Arts** (☑ 08 9952 7898; www.chilianti ques.com; 125 Th Thakhilek), a massive showroom of bronze and wooden Buddhas, sculptures, woodcarvings and fine decor. Across the street is **Piak Antiques** (☑ 0 5344 1157; www.piakantique.com; Th Thakhilek) selling reclaimed, chunky wooden furniture. **Crossroads Asia** (☑ 0 5343 4650; 214/7 Th Thakhilek, Chaiyo Plaza) sells ethnic art and textiles from 26 countries, with an international clientele. Better-than-average souvenirs can be found at **World Port Services** (☑ 0 5343 4200; Th Thakhilek) with its quirky collection of folk art, bronze statues and Buddhas. If you're after something for the kids, pop into **Kala**

Design ([✆] 08 1034 5495; Th Thakhilek). It's a bit more downmarket but there are some wonderful animal interpretations in wood: the goggle-eyed owls are adorable. When you need a break from the browsing, call into Pana Botanicals, which has a small cafe set in a converted wooden house.

Continue towards the right fork in the road to **Ban Thawai Tourism Village**, which is a pedestrian-friendly market with 3km of shops selling all sorts of home decor, knick-knacks and other souvenir market goodies, if you haven't yet gotten your fill of souvenir shopping. Past Zone 5 is Sriboonmuang's workshop, an example of what made Ban Thawai famous in the first place. In the factory's covered sheds, workers sand and polish small armies of wooden elephants, hobby horses and dolls.

Many of the shops here deal in wholesale as well as retail, and shipping can be arranged.

It is advisable to come with private transport, but you can catch a *sŏrng·tǎaou* from Pratu Chiang Mai to Hang Dong (20B) and to Ban Thawai (30B).

Doi Inthanon National Park อุทยานแห่งชาติดอยอินทนนท์

Thailand's highest peak is Doi Inthanon (often abbreviated to Doi In), which measures 2565m above sea level, an impressive altitude for the kingdom, but a tad diminutive compared to its cousins in the Himalayan range. The 1000-sq-km **national park** ([✆] 0 5328 6730; adult/child 200/100B, car/motorbike 30/20B; ☺ 8am-sunset) surrounding the peak has hiking trails, waterfalls and two monumental stupas erected in honour of the king and queen. It is a popular day trip from Chiang Mai for tourists and locals, especially during the New Year holiday when there's the rarely seen phenomenon of frost.

◉ Sights & Activities

There are eight waterfalls that dive off the mountain. Nam Tok Mae Klang (at Km 8) is the largest and the easiest to get to. Nam Tok Wachiratan (at Km 20.8) is another popular stop with food vendors at its base and a huge frothy mane that plummets 50m. If you'd rather be a part of the cascade, try abseiling with Peak Adventure Tour (p250). Nam Tok Siriphum (at Km 30) looks like a river of silver from the vantage point of Ban Mong Khun Klang, a Hmong village. In February the village builds and races wooden carts down a steep incline. Along the road to the top are terraced rice fields and covered greenhouses tended by Hmong and Karen tribespeople.

About 3km before the summit of Doi Inthanon, **Phra Mahathat Naphamethanidon and Nophamethanidon** (Km 41-42; admission to both 40B) are two *chedi* built by the Royal Thai Air Force to commemorate the king's and queen's 60th birthdays in 1989 and 1992, respectively. In the base of the octagonal *chedi* is a hall containing a stone Buddha image.

The whole point of the park is to get as high as you can to see life in a colder climate, and the coolness is such a relief from the sweltering plains below. Thais relish bundling up in hats and jackets and posing for pictures among conifers and rhododendrons. Almost at the exact summit there's a *chedi* dedicated to one of the last Lanna kings (Inthawichayanon). From there, a lovely boardwalk through the thick, cool forest leads to a cafe, obligatory souvenir shop and the start of the Ang Ka nature trail, a 360m platform walkway through a moss-festooned bog. Walking through the forest on the nature trail is an enchanting experience (if devoid of crowds).

The views from Doi Inthanon are best in the cool dry season from November to February. But don't expect a rewarding view from the summit, as for most of the year a mist, formed by the condensation of warm humid air below, hangs around the top of the mountain creating an eerie effect. You can expect the air to be quite chilly towards the top, so take a jacket. The views on the way to the summit are much better.

The park is one of the top destinations in Southeast Asia for naturalists and birdwatchers. The mist-shrouded upper slopes produce abundant orchids, lichen, moss and epiphytes, while supporting nearly 400 bird species, more than any other habitat in Thailand. Most of the park's bird species are found between 1500m and 2000m; the best birdwatching season is from February to April, and the best spots are the beung (bogs) near the top. The mountain is also home to Assamese macaques, Phayre's leaf monkeys, and a selection of other rare and not-so-rare monkeys and gibbons, as well as the more common Indian civet, barking deer and giant flying squirrel – around 75 mammal species in all.

🛏 Sleeping & Eating

Park **accommodation** (www.dnp.go.th; camping 60-600B, bungalows 1500-3000B) is available in comfortable bungalows located next to the information centre (the best ones overlook the water), and camping in front of the information centre or at Nam Tok Mae Pan. At Km 31 there's a restaurant that has decent Thai mains but is really a dining hall for tour-bus patrons. Most accommodation options have an attached restaurant.

Outside the park there is a number of accommodation options lining Rte 1009, none of which is outstanding but all perfectly OK for a night or two.

Ratchaphruek Hotel　　　　　HOTEL **$**
(☏ 0 5334 1901; www.ratchaphruekhotel.com; r 500-950B; ❄ ☂) Close to the turn-off with Rte 108, this hotel has comfortable and no-fuss rooms. Warning: karaoke bar on-site.

Little Home Inthanon Resort　　BUNGALOWS **$**
(☏ 0 5303 3555; www.littlehomeinthanonresort. com; r 450-600B; ❄) These boxy bungalows are good value for the price, although a bit dark inside. You can park your car right alongside, like at a motel.

Touch Star Resort　　　　　HOTEL **$$$**
(☏ 08 0589 9168; www.touchstarresort.com; r 1600-2200B; ❄) A step up in comfort and luxury, the cheapest bungalows here are fairly small and rudimentary inside but have lovely little outside porches overlooking the extensive gardens, which are the best feature of this place. It's well signed down a small lane off Rte 1009, just before entry into the park. Good restaurant serving Thai standards on-site.

❶ Getting There & Away

Most visitors come with private transport or on a tour from Chiang Mai. You can reach the park via public transport but be prepared for an adventure. Public transport to Chom Thong (70B), the closest town to the park, leave from Chang Pheuak terminal and from the Pratu Chiang Mai *sŏrng·tăaou* stop. Some buses go directly to the park's entrance gate near Nam Tok Mae Klang, and some are bound for Hot and will drop you off in Chom Thong.

From Chom Thong there are regular *sŏrng·tăaou* to the park's entrance gate at Nam Tok Mae Klang (50B), about 8km north. *Sŏrng·tăaou* from the turn-off to Mae Klang, just outside the park gates, to the summit of Doi Inthanon (100B) leave almost hourly until late afternoon.

Northern Thailand

Best Places to Eat

➡ Larp Khom Huay Poo (p388)

➡ Khaomao-Khaofang (p374)

➡ Lung Eed (p311)

➡ Ban Mai (p352)

Best Places to Stay

➡ Fern Resort (p398)

➡ Boklua View (p347)

➡ Phu Chaisai Resort & Spa (p317)

➡ Riverside Guest House (p300)

Why Go?

What can't you do in northern Thailand?

The region's premier draw is its nature, and northern Thailand's rugged geography is a playground for outdoor pursuits ranging from rafting in Um Phang to hiking among wild orchids in Mae Hong Son.

For those drawn to the human side of things, there's also northern Thailand's buffet of cultural attractions and experiences. The region is regarded as the birthplace of much of what is often associated with Thai culture, and is a great place to take part in activities ranging from exploring a Buddhist temple in Phrae to taking part in a homestay in rural Sukhothai or sampling a local dish at Lampang's evening market.

In the north, even niche players are catered for: intrepid explorers can head off on a hill-tribe trek in Mae Sariang or on a road trip to Phayao, history buffs can travel back in time at Sukhothai Historical Park, and we suspect that even the most devout beach bum could be converted by the inland party scene in Pai.

When to Go

➡ Winter (from November to January) is the time to head to northern Thailand, when daytime temperatures at the higher elevations are a relatively comfortable 20°C to 23°C. Nighttime temperatures can, in some places, dip perilously close to freezing.

➡ From March to May, the hottest time of year, daytime temperatures climb close to 40°C and smoke from slash-and-burn agriculture can fill the skies.

➡ The rainy season, June to October, should generally be avoided if you plan to do any trekking.

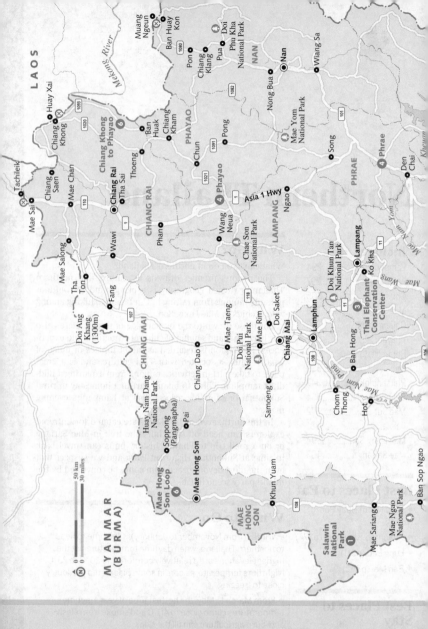

Northern Thailand Highlights

1 Exploring nature reserves such as Phitsanulok's **Phu Hin Rong Kla National Park** (p353) or Mae Hong Son's **Salawin National Park** (p406)

2 Hiking and rafting in remote Um Phang, where the end of the road leads to **Nam Tok Thilawsu** (p377), Thailand's most beautiful waterfall

3 Learning to be a mahout (elephant caretaker) at Lampang's **Thai Elephant Conservation Center** (p304)

4 Investigating little-visited cities such as **Phayao** (p332) or **Phrae** (p335)

5 Cycling around the ruins of Thailand's golden age at

LAOS

Mekong River

MYANMAR (BURMA)

Muang Ngeun

Ban Huay Kon

Doi Phu Kha National Park

NAN

Tachileik

Mae Sai

Huay Xai

Chiang Khong

Pon

Chiang Klang

Pua

Chiang Saen

Mae Chan

Thoeng

Ban Huak

Chiang Kham

Nan

Wiang Sa

6 Chiang Khong to Phayao

Mae Salong

110

4 Chiang Rai

Chiang Rai

Tha Sai

Chun

PHAYAO

Nong Bua

Mae Yom National Park

Tha Ton

Fang

Wawi

Phan

Pong

4 Phayao

Phayao

101

Doi Ang Khang (1300m)

107

CHIANG MAI

Wang Neua

Asia 1 Hwy

1

Song

Chae Son National Park

LAMPANG

4 Phrae

Phrae

Ngao

Den Chai

Chiang Dao

Mae Taeng

Doi Pui National Park

Mae Rim

Doi Saket

Doi Khun Tan National Park

Lampang

Ko Kha

11

Huay Nam Dang National Park

Pai

Soppong (Pangmapha)

118

Chiang Mai

Lamphun

Ban Hong

3 Thai Elephant Conservation Center

Mae Hong Son

6 Mae Hong Son Loop

Samoeng

108

Mae Nam Ping

Chom Thong

Hot

Khun Yuam

MAE HONG SON

108

Salawin National Park

1 Mae Sariang

Mae Ngao National Park

Ban Sop Ngao

Mae Nam

Mae Wang

Yom

Mae Nam

Khwae

PHRAE

106

N

0   50 km
0   30 miles

History

Northern Thailand's history has been characterised by the shifting powers of various independent principalities. One of the most significant early cultural influences in the north was the Mon kingdom of Hariphunchai (based in contemporary Lamphun), which held sway from the late 8th century until the 13th century. Hariphunchai art and Buddha images are particularly distinctive, and many good examples can be found at the Hariphunchai National Museum in Lamphun.

The Thais, who are thought to have migrated south from China around the 7th century, united various principalities in the 13th century – this resulted in the creation of Sukhothai and the taking of Hariphunchai from the Mon. In 1238 Sukhothai declared itself an independent kingdom under King Si Intharathit and quickly expanded its sphere of influence. Because of this, and the significant influence the kingdom had on Thai art and culture, Sukhothai is considered by Thais to be the first true Thai kingdom.

In 1296 King Mengrai established Chiang Mai after conquering Hariphunchai. Later, in the 14th and 15th centuries, Chiang Mai, in an alliance with Sukhothai, became a part of the larger kingdom of Lan Na Thai (Million Thai Rice Fields), popularly referred to as Lanna. This empire extended as far south as Kamphaeng Phet and as far north as Luang Prabang in Laos. The golden age of Lanna was in the 15th century, and for a short time during this period, the Sukhothai capital was moved to Phitsanulok, and Chiang Mai increased in influence as a religious and cultural centre. However, during the 16th century, many of Lan Na Thai's important alliances weakened or fell apart, ultimately leading to the Burmese capturing Chiang Mai in 1556. Burmese control of Lanna lasted for the next two centuries. The northern Thais ultimately regrouped after the Burmese took Ayuthaya in 1767, and under King Kawila, Chiang Mai was recaptured in 1774 and the Burmese were pushed north.

In the late 19th century, Rama V of Bangkok made efforts to integrate the northern region with the centre to ward off the colonial threat. The completion of the northern railway to Chiang Mai in 1921 strengthened those links until the northern provinces finally became part of the kingdom of Siam in the early part of the 20th century.

Language

Thailand's regional dialects vary greatly and can even be unintelligible to native speakers of Thai not familiar with the vernacular being spoken. *Găm méuang,* the northern Thai dialect, is no exception and, in addition to an entirely different set of tones to master, possesses a wealth of vocabulary specific to the north. The northern dialect also has a slower rhythm than Thailand's three other main dialects, an attribute reflected in the relaxed, easygoing manner of the people who speak it.

Northern Thai also has its own writing system, based on an old Mon script that was originally used only for Buddhist scripture. The script became so popular during the Lanna period that it was exported for use by the Thai Lü in China, the Khün in the eastern Shan State and other Thai–Kadai-speaking groups living between Lanna and China. Although few northerners nowadays can read the northern Thai script – often referred to as 'Lanna script' – it is mostly used in signage to add a northern Thai cultural flavour.

LAMPHUN PROVINCE

This tiny province southeast of Chiang Mai consists of little more than a small city surrounded by farms and villages.

Lamphun ลำพูน
POP 14,000

Essentially a culture stop for Chiang Mai sightseers, this provincial capital sits quietly along the banks of Mae Kuang, a tributary of Mae Ping. There's not much fanfare regarding its superlative as one of Thailand's oldest cities. The old fortress wall and ancient temples are surviving examples of Lamphun's former life as the northernmost outpost of the ancient Mon Dvaravati kingdom, then known as Hariphunchai (AD 750–1281). During part of this period, the city was ruled by Chama Thewi, a Mon queen who has earned legendary status among Thailand's constellation of historic rulers.

The 26km voyage along a former highway between Chiang Mai and Lamphun is one of the city's primary attractions. It's a beautiful country road, stretches of which are canopied by tall dipterocarp trees.

SPEAKING NORTHERN THAI

Northerners used to take offence when outsiders tried speaking *găm méuang* (the colloquial name for the northern dialect) to them, an attitude that dates back to a time when central Thais considered northerners to be very backward and made fun of their dialect. Nowadays, most northerners are proud of their native language, and speaking a few words of the local lingo will go a long way in getting them to open up. The following words and phrases will help you talk to, flirt with or perhaps just win some smiles from the locals.

Ôo găm méuang bòr jâhng I can't speak northern Thai

A yăng gór? What did you say?

An née tôw dai? How much is this?

Mee kôw nêung bòr? Do you have sticky rice?

Lám đáa đáa Delicious

Mâan lâ Yes/That's right

Bòr mâan No

Gàht Market

Jôw (A polite word used by women; equivalent to the central Thai *ka*)

Ďàht só! Nôrng née ngáhm kànàht! Hey, you're really cute!

⊙ Sights

Wat Phra That Hariphunchai
BUDDHIST TEMPLE

(วัดพระธาตุหริภุญชัย; Th Inthayongyot; admission 20B; ⊙ daylight hours) This temple spans back to the Mon period, having originally been built on the site of Queen Chama Thewi's palace in 1044 (or 1108 or 1157 according to some datings).

Behind the temple is **Kad Khua Moong Tha Sing** (⊙ 9am-6pm), a souvenir market selling local items such as dried *lam yai* (longan fruit) and silk.

The temple boasts some interesting architecture, a couple of fine Buddha images and two old *chedi* (stupas) in the original Hariphunchai style. The compound lay derelict until Khru Ba Sriwichai, a famous northern Thai monk, ordered renovations in the 1930s.

The tallest of the ancient *chedi*, Chedi Suwan, is a narrow brick spire dating from 1418 that sits 21m high. The newer *chedi*, 46m-high Phra Maha That Chedi, is regarded as a textbook example of 15th-century Lanna architecture with its square pedestal rising to a rounded bell shape.

Hariphunchai National Museum
MUSEUM

(พิพิธภัณฑสถานแห่งชาติหริภุญไชย; Th Inthayongyot; admission 100B; ⊙ 9am-4pm Wed-Sun) Across the street from Wat Phra That Hariphunchai is the informative Hariphunchai National Museum. Inside is a collection of Mon and Lanna artefacts and Buddhas from the Dvaravati kingdom, as well as a stone inscription gallery with Mon and Thai Lanna scripts. There is a small bookshop with some English titles.

Wat Chama Thewi
BUDDHIST TEMPLE

(วัดจามเทวี; Th Chamadevi; ⊙ daylight hours) FREE An unusual Hariphunchai *chedi* can be seen at Wat Chama Thewi. The structure dates to around the 13th century, but has been restored many times since then and is now a mixture of several schools of architecture.

Wat Chama Thewi is about 1.5km from Wat Phra That Hariphunchai; you can take a motorcycle taxi (20B) from the museum.

Each side of the *chedi* has five rows of three Buddha figures, diminishing in size on each higher level. The standing Buddhas, although sculpted recently, are in Dvaravati style.

✦ Festivals & Events

Songkran
WATER FESTIVAL

Should Chiang Mai's water fight be too wet and wild for your taste, Lamphun hosts a milder, more traditional affair. In mid-April.

Lam Yai Festival
CULINARY

During the second week of August, Lamphun hosts the annual festival spotlighting its primary agricultural product. The festival features floats made of fruit and, of course, a Miss Lam Yai contest.

🛏 Sleeping & Eating

You're unlikely to stay overnight as Lamphun is so close to Chiang Mai. But in a pinch, try the very capable **Lamphun Will Hotel** (✆ 0 5353 4865; www.lamphunwillhotel.com; 204/10 Th Chamadevi; r incl breakfast 1200-1500B, ste incl breakfast 2500-3000B; ❄ 🛜 ☕), directly opposite Wat Chama Thewi. There is a string of decent **noodle shops** (Th Inthayongyut;

mains 30-90B) on Lamphun's main street, just south of Wat Phra That.

ℹ Getting There & Away

Frequent blue *sŏrng·tăa·ou* (passenger pick-up trucks) and purple buses bound for Lamphun leave Chiang Mai from Chiang Mai's Chang Pheuak terminal, from a stop on Th Praisani in front of Talat Warorot, and from another stop on the east side of the river on Th Chiang Mai-Lamphun, just

---

ℹ TRANSPORT IN THE NORTH

Public Transport

Going by train is the most comfortable way to get up north, although there's only one main northern line and it is comparatively quite slow. Just about everywhere in the region is accessible by bus and increasingly minivan, except among the communities along the Myanmar border, where the *sŏrng·tăa·ou* (pasenger pick-up truck, also spelt *songthaew*) is the transport of choice.

Car & Motorcycle

An increasingly popular way of exploring northern Thailand is from a hired vehicle. Despite the obvious risks of driving in Thailand, hiring is the best way to explore the countryside at your own pace, and provides the opportunity to leave the beaten track at any moment. Car and motorcycle hire are available at most urban centres.

For motorcycle hire, unless you're intending to go off-road or plan on crossing unpaved roads during the wet season, it's highly unlikely you'll need one of the large dirt bikes you'll see for rent in Chiang Mai. The automatic transmission 110cc to 150cc scooterlike motorcycles found across Thailand are fast and powerful enough for most roads. If you want something a bit larger and more comfortable on those long straightways, an alternative is the 200cc Honda Phantom, a Thai-made chopper wannabe. For general hire information and safety considerations, see p768.

A good introduction to motorcycle touring in northern Thailand is the 100km Samoeng loop, which can be tackled in half a day. The route extends north from Chiang Mai and follows Rtes 107, 1096 and 1269, passing through excellent scenery and ample curves, and providing a taste of what a longer ride up north will be like. The 470km Chiang Rai loop, which passes through scenic Fang and Tha Ton along Rtes 107, 1089 and 118, is another popular ride that can be broken up with a stay in Chiang Rai. The classic northern route is the Mae Hong Son loop, a 600km ride that begins in Chiang Mai and takes in Rte 1095's 1864 curves with possible stays in Pai, Mae Hong Son and Mae Sariang, before looping back to Chiang Mai via Rte 108. A lesser known but equally fun ride is to follow Rtes 1155 and 1093 from Chiang Khong in Chiang Rai Province to the little-visited city of Phayao, a day trip that passes through some of the most dramatic mountain scenery in the country.

The best source of information on motorcycle touring in the north is **Golden Triangle Rider** (GT Rider; www.gt-rider.com). Publishers of a series of terrific motorcycle touring-based maps, their website includes heaps of information on hiring bikes (including recommended hire shops in Chiang Mai and Chiang Rai) and bike insurance, plus a variety of suggested tours with maps and an interactive forum.

Air

For those in a hurry, northern Thailand's air links are surprisingly good. At research time, **Nok Air** (✆ 1318; www.nokair.co.th), a subsidiary of THAI, had the most expansive network, with flights connecting several provincial capitals in the region with Bangkok or Chiang Mai. Other domestic airlines that cover the north include **Bangkok Airways** (✆ 1771; www.bangkokair.com), **Kan Air** (✆ 0 2551 6111; www.kanairlines.com) and **THAI** (✆ 0 2356 1111; www.thaiair.com).

south of the Tourist Authority of Thailand (TAT) office, during daylight hours (20B, 30 minutes). Both can drop you off on Th Inthayongyot at the stop in front of the national museum and Wat Phra That Hariphunchai. Minibuses and *sŏrng·tăa·ou* (20B, 30 minutes) return to Chiang Mai from the stop in front of the national museum or from the city's bus terminal on Th Sanam.

Doi Khun Tan National Park อุทยานแห่งชาติดอยขุนตาล

This 225-sq-km **national park** (☏ 0 5354 6335, Royal Forest Department accommodation booking centre 0 2562 0760; www.dnp.go.th; admission 200B; ⊗8am-5pm) straddles the mountains between Lamphun and Lampang Provinces. It ranges in elevation from 350m at the bamboo forest lowlands to 1363m at the pine-studded summit of Doi Khun Tan. Wildflowers, including orchids, ginger and lilies, are abundant. At the park headquarters there are maps of well-marked trails that range from short walks around the headquarters' vicinity to trails covering the mountain's four peaks; there's also a trail to **Nam Tok Tat Moei** (7km round trip). Intersecting the mountain slopes is Thailand's longest train tunnel (1352m), which opened in 1921 after six years of manual labour by thousands of Lao workers (several of whom are said to have been killed by tigers).

Bungalows (☏ 0 2562 0760; www.dnp.go.th; bungalows 1500-2700B) sleeping between two and nine people are available near the park headquarters, where there's also a restaurant. The park is very popular on cool-season weekends.

The main access to the park is from the Khun Tan train station. To check timetables and prices from various destinations, call the **State Railway of Thailand** (☏1690; www.railway.co.th) or look at its website. Once at the Khun Tan station, cross the tracks and follow a steep, marked path 1.3km to the park headquarters. By car, take the Chiang Mai–Lampang highway to the Mae Tha turn-off then follow the signs along a steep unpaved road for 18km.

LAMPANG PROVINCE

Formerly associated with the logging trade, today Lampang is more closely linked to industries such as mining and ceramics. It's a vast, mountainous province known for its natural beauty, a pleasant provincial capital, and some of northern Thailand's most emblematic Buddhist temples.

Lampang ลำปาง
POP 59,000

Boasting lumbering elephants, the elegant mansions of former lumber barons and impressive (and in many cases, timber-based) Lanna-era temples, Lampang seems to unite every northern Thai cliché – but in a good way. Despite all this, the city sees relatively few visitors, giving it more of an 'undiscovered' feel than some of the more touristed destinations in the north.

History

Although Lampang Province was inhabited as far back as the 7th century in the Dvaravati period, legend has it that Lampang city was founded by the son of Hariphunchai's Queen Chama Thewi, and the city played an important part in the history of the Hariphunchai Kingdom.

Like Chiang Mai, Phrae and other older northern cities, modern Lampang was built as a walled rectangle alongside a river (in this case, Mae Wang). At the end of the 19th and beginning of the 20th century, Lampang, along with nearby Phrae, became an important centre for the domestic and international teak trade. A large British-owned timber company brought in Burmese supervisors familiar with the teak industry in Burma to train Burmese and Thai loggers in the area. These well-paid supervisors, along with independent Burmese teak merchants who plied their trade in Lampang, sponsored the construction of more than a dozen temples in the city, a legacy that lives on in several of Lampang's most impressive wáts and the beautiful antique homes along Th Talad Gao.

⊙ Sights & Activities

Wat Phra Kaew Don Tao   BUDDHIST TEMPLE (วัดพระแก้วดอนเต้า; off Th Phra Kaew; admission 20B; ⊗daylight hours) The main *chedi* shows Hariphunchai influence, while the adjacent *mon·dòp* (small square-sided building with a spire) was built in 1909. A display of Lanna artefacts can be viewed in the wát's **Lanna Museum** (admission by donation; ⊗7am-6pm).

Adjacent to the temple complex, **Wat Suchadaram** dates back to 1809 and is named after Mae Suchada, the central figure in a local legend (see the boxed text on p303).

Wat Phra Kaew Don Tao's *mon·dòp*, decorated with glass mosaic in typical Burmese style, contains a Mandalay-style Buddha image. From 1436 to 1468, Wat Phra Kaew

NORTHERN THAILAND LAMPANG

Lampang

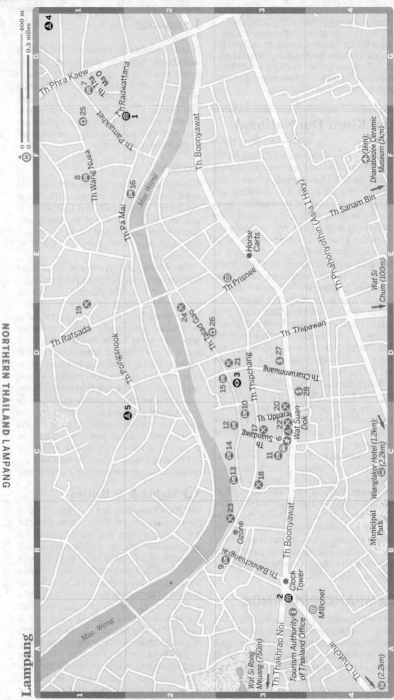

0 400 m
0 0.2 miles

Th Phra Kaew
Th The
Ma 0
Th Panakhet
Th Radwattana
25
1
7
Th Wang Nuea
8
Th Pa Mai
Mae Wang
16
Th Boonyawat
Horse Carts
Th Prisnee
19
Th Ratsada
24
Th Pongsnook
Th Gao Dtai
26
Th Thipawan
5
15
3
21
Th Thipchang
Th Charuenmuang
27
10
20
28
Th Upparat
12
Wat Suan Dok
17
6 22
14
Th Suandawg
11
13
18
Th Boonyawat
23
Ozone
9
Th Bahnchiangrai
Municipal Park
Clock Tower
2
M@cnet
Tourism Authority
of Thailand Office
Th Thakhrao Noi
Th Chatchai

Wat Si Rong Meuang (750m)

Dhanabadee Ceramic Museum (1km)
Th Sanam Bin
Th Phahonyothin (Asia 1 Hwy)
Wat Si Chum (100m)
Wianglakor Hotel (1.2km) (2.2km)
(2.2km)

Mae Wang

Lampang

Don Tao was among four wát in northern Thailand to have housed the Emerald Buddha (now in Bangkok's Wat Phra Kaew).

Thanon Talad Gao　　　　NEIGHBOURHOOD
(ถนนตลาดเก่า;) Lampang's multi-cultural history can be seen along this riverside street, which is lined with old homes, temples and shophouses showcasing Thai, English, Chinese and Burmese architectural styles. It's also where the town's weekly Walking Street (p302) market is held.

Wat Pongsanuk Tai　　　BUDDHIST TEMPLE
(วัดปงสนุกใต้; Th Pongsnook; ⊘daylight hours) FREE Despite having lost much of its character in a recent renovation, the *mon·dòp* at Wat Pongsanuk is still one of the few remaining local examples of original Lanna-style temple architecture, which emphasised open-sided wooden buildings. To get an idea of what it was like previously, look at the carved wooden gateway at the entrance to the north stairway. There are a couple of informal museums on the temple grounds displaying local artefacts, but they include little English explanation.

Baan Sao Nak　　　　　　　MUSEUM
(บ้านเสานัก; 85 Th Radwattana; admission 50B; ⊘10am-5pm) A huge Lanna-style house built in 1895 and supported by 116 square teak pillars, Baan Sao Nak was once owned by a local *kun·yǐng* (a title equivalent to 'Lady' in England); it now serves as a local museum. The entire house is furnished with mildly interesting Burmese and Thai antiques, but the structure itself and its manicured garden are the highlights.

Dhanabadee Ceramic Museum　　MUSEUM
(พิพิธภัณฑ์เซรามิคธนบดี; www.dhanabadeeceramic museum.com; off Soi 1, Th Phrabat; admission 100B; ⊘9am-5pm) Dhanabadee claims to be the first producer of the emblematic 'chicken bowls' used across Thailand. In 2013, the company opened its doors to visitors and began running guided tours that span a history of the chicken bowl in Thailand and the various steps involved in making them. At press time the tour was only available in Thai, but there is some written English-language explanation.

Wat Chedi Sao　　　　　BUDDHIST TEMPLE
(วัดเจดีย์ซาว; Th Pratuma; ⊘daylight hours) FREE This temple is named for the 20 (*sow* in northern Thai) whitewashed Lanna-style *chedi* on its grounds. But the wát's real treasure is a solid-gold, 15th-century seated Buddha on display in a glassed-in pavilion, built over a square pond.

The Buddha image is said to contain a piece of the Buddha's skull in its head and an ancient Pali-inscribed golden palm leaf in its chest; precious stones decorate the image's hairline and robe. A farmer reportedly found the figure next to the ruins of nearby Wat Khu Kao in 1983.

Monks stationed at Wat Chedi Sao make and sell herbal medicines; the popular *yah mòrng* is similar to Tiger Balm.

Wat Chedi Sao is about 6km north of town, via Th Pamaikhet; a round-trip motorcycle taxi here should cost about 60B.

Phum Lakhon Museum
MUSEUM

(พิพิธภัณฑ์เมืองของชาวลำปาง; cnr Th Chatchai & Th Thakhrao Noi; ⊙10am-6pm Wed-Sun) FREE A small but engaging museum that employs multimedia displays to tell the story of the history, people and culture of Lampang.

Wat Si Rong Meuang & Wat Si Chum
BUDDHIST TEMPLES

(วัดศรีรองเมือง/วัดศรีชุม; ⊙daylight hours) FREE Wat Si Rong Meuang, on Th Thakhrao Noi, and Wat Si Chum, on Th Thipawan, were built in the late 19th century by Burmese artisans. The temple buildings are constructed in the Burmese 'layered' style, with tin roofs gabled by intricate woodcarvings.

Horse Carts
GUIDED TOUR

(Th Suandawg; 30-/60-minute tours 200/300B; ⊙5am-9pm) Lampang is the only town in Thailand where horse carts are still found. Now fully relegated to tourists, you can't miss the brightly coloured carts that drip with plastic flowers and are handled by Stetson-wearing drivers. A 30-minute tour goes along Mae Wang while a one-hour tour stops at Wat Phra Kaew Don Tao and Wat Si Rong Meuang.

Horse carts can be found waiting on Th Suandawg, near the Pin Hotel, and just east of the market on Th Boonyawat.

🛏 Sleeping

Akhamsiri Home
HOTEL $

(☑0 5422 8791; www.akhamsirihome.com; 54/1 Th Pamaikhet; r 590B; ❉@🛜) The tagline here ought to be 'Midrange amenities at a budget price'. The large cool rooms are located in a tidy residential compound and all have TV, fridge and a garden or balcony.

Tip Inn Guest House
GUESTHOUSE $

(☑0 5422 1821; Th Talad Gao; r 450-550B; ❉🛜) Tip Inn consists of four fan-cooled, shared-bathroom rooms in a 100-year old house and two air-con rooms in a newer structure out back. A garden area and an old-school vibe are the unifying elements.

Chita Coffee & Guesthouse
GUESTHOUSE $

(www.facebook.com/chitacoffeeguesthouse; 143 Th Talad Gao; r 400-700B; ❉🛜) Smack-dab in the middle of historic Th Talad Gao, Chita offers relatively bright and stylish budget rooms

above a cafe. The cheapest are closet-sized, fan-cooled and share a bathroom.

TT&T Back Packers Guesthouse
GUESTHOUSE $

(☑0 5422 1303; 82 Th Pa Mai; r 250-450B; ❉🛜) This long-standing place has an appropriately old-school backpacker vibe. Rooms are simple and bathrooms are shared, but this is made up for by a pleasant riverfront location and expansive chill-out areas.

★ Riverside Guest House
GUESTHOUSE $$

(☑0 5422 7005; www.theriverselampang.com; 286 Th Talad Gao; r 350-900B; ste 1800-2000B; ❉🛜) Although still within budget range, this leafy compound of refurbished wooden houses is one of the more pleasant places to stay in Lampang, if not all of northern Thailand. It couldn't be any nearer the river, shaded tables for chatting or eating abound, and motorcycle rental and other tourist amenities are available.

Try to score one of the two upstairs rooms in the main structure that feature vast balconies overlooking Mae Wang, or the huge two-room suite.

Auangkham Resort
GUESTHOUSE $$

(☑0 5422 1305; www.auangkhamlampang.com; 49-51 Th Wang Nuea; r 1000-1250B; ❉🛜) Not a resort at all, but rather an exceptionally well done, boutique-style guesthouse. The 14 rooms are bright and airy, and all have balconies overlooking an attractive garden. The homey service complements the peaceful vibe, and there are bonus perks such as free use of bicycles and a location steps from Friday's Cultural Street market.

R-Lampang
GUESTHOUSE $$

(☑0 5422 5278; www.r-lampang.com; 278 Th Talad Gao; r 250-1000B; ❉🛜) Cute is the underlying aesthetic at this compound next to Mae Wang. Wind through brightly coloured halls decked with teddy bears to emerge at spacious air-con rooms and rather tight fan-cooled, shared-bathroom budget rooms. An attached shop sells snacks, drinks and souvenirs.

Pin Hotel
HOTEL $$

(☑0 5422 1509; pin.hotel@yahoo.com; 8 Th Suandawg; r incl breakfast 600-900B; ste incl breakfast 1300-1800B; ❉@🛜) Spotless, spacious and secluded, the vast rooms here come decked out with cable TV, minibar and large bathrooms, but not a lot of character. Making up for this is the fact that the Pin is within walking distance of most sights in 'downtown' Lampang, and is also close to both the horse cart and taxi stalls.

Prink
HOTEL $$

(☎ 08 3589 6921; 262-264 Th Talad Gao, no roman-script sign; r 500-1000B; ❄️🛜) One of Th Talad Gao's noblest historic buildings has been turned into a stylish boutique hotel. The eight rooms, located above a cafe and ice cream shop, share a fun retro design theme and bathrooms, although some lack windows and feel somewhat claustrophobic. Avoid this by requesting one of the more expensive balcony rooms.

Baan Chiangrai
HOTEL $$

(☎ 0 5422 1961; 336/9 Th Bahnchiengrai; r incl breakfast 750B; ❄️🛜) Seven stylish and contemporary-feeling rooms above a coffee shop. All have balcony, flat-screen TV and vast desks. Good value.

Wienglakor Hotel
HOTEL $$$

(☎ 0 5431 6430-5; www.wienglakor.com; 138/35 Th Phahonyothin; r incl breakfast 1000-1700B, ste incl breakfast 3000B; ❄️@🛜) If you're going upscale, this is Lampang's best choice. The lobby is tastefully decorated in a teak and northern Thai temple theme, a design that continues into the rooms. Deluxe rooms feature an added sitting area and walk-in closet, and the hotel's attractive outdoor dining area with carp pond is a classy, natural touch.

🍴 Eating & Drinking

For a relatively small town, Lampang boasts a pretty decent repertoire of restaurants, ranging from good northern Thai to acceptable Western fare, and a few things in between.

It has an equally vibrant drinking scene, and the strip of Th Thipchang near Riverside is Lampang's nightlife district. There you'll find a string of friendly open-air restaurant-pubs that seem to change ownership and name each time we're in town.

Aroy One Baht
THAI $

(cnr Th Suandawg & Th Thipchang; mains 15-80B; ⊙4pm-midnight) Some nights it can seem like everybody in Lampang is here, and understandably so: the food is tasty and embarrassingly cheap, and the setting in a wooden house is heaps of fun.

> **DON'T MISS**
>
> ### KHUN MANEE
>
> Lampang is known for its addictive *kôw dǎan*, deep-fried rice cakes seasoned with watermelon juice and drizzled with palm sugar. You can pick up a few bags or even watch the sweets being made at this homey **factory** (35 Th Ratsada; ⊙daylight hours) just off Th Ratsada – look for the yellow arrow.

Niyom Sen
NORTHERN THAI $

(125 Th Talad Gao; mains 30-40B; ⊙9am-7pm Tue-Sun) Be sure to stop by this popular local haunt serving *kà·nǒm jeen*, fresh rice noodles topped with curries. The house speciality is *kà·nǒm jeen nám ngée·o*, a northern-style broth of pork and tomato.

Mae Hae
NORTHERN THAI $

(1017 Th Upparaj, no roman-script sign; mains 20-50B; ⊙11am-7pm) Boost your Lampang foodie street cred by eating at this unassuming and long-standing northern Thai–style restaurant. There's no menu, so simply point to the soup, curry, dip or salad that looks tastiest.

Phat Thai Yay Fong
THAI $

(Th Boonyawat, no roman-script sign; mains 35-60B; ⊙5-10pm) How do northern Thais take their *pàt tai*? With minced pork and pork rinds, of course. This popular stall is located just east of Wat Suan Dok.

Grandma's Café
THAI $

(361 Th Thipchang; mains 30-70B; ⊙10am-9pm; ❄️) Stop by this contemporary-feeling cafe for decent java and a menu of rice dishes that rarely exceeds the 50B barrier.

Vegetarian Food
VEGETARIAN, THAI $

(Th Talad Gao; mains 25-35B; ⊙8am-6pm Mon-Sat; 🍃) A wide selection of Thai-style veggie dishes is served at this shophouse restaurant.

Riverside
INTERNATIONAL-THAI $$

(328 Th Thipchang; mains 80-210B; ⊙10am-10pm) This wooden shack that appears to be on the verge of tumbling into Mae Wang is extremely popular with both visiting and resident foreigners. Live music, a full bar and an expansive menu of local and Western dishes bring in the crowds. You'd be wise to plan your visit around the homemade pizza nights (Tuesday, Thursday, Saturday and Sunday).

🛍 Shopping

Walking Street MARKET

(Th Talad Gao; ⊗4-10pm Sat & Sun) Lampang now has its own walking street market along charming Th Talad Gao. On Saturday and Sunday evenings, the usual traffic is replaced by souvenir, handicraft and food stalls. A similar **Cultural Street** (Th Wang Nuea; ⊗6-9pm Fri) is also held across the river on Th Wang Nuea every Friday evening.

ℹ Information

Several banks with ATMs can be found along Th Boonyawat.

M@cnet (Th Chatchai; per hour 15B; ⊗9am-10pm) Internet access.

Post Office (Th Prisnee; ⊗8.30am-4.30pm Mon-Fri, 9am-noon Sat)

Sanuksabai (☎0 5421 9398; 8 Th Suandawg; ⊗8am-5pm Mon-Sat) Next door to the Pin Hotel, this agency can arrange air tickets, saving you the trouble of a trip to the airport.

Tourism Authority of Thailand Office (TAT; ☎0 5423 7229, nationwide 1672; Th Thakhrao Noi; ⊗8.30am-5pm Mon-Fri) The helpful folks here can provide a decent map of the area and details about local sights and activities. The office hours extend to weekends from October to December.

ℹ Getting There & Away

Lampang's airport is about 1.5km south of the centre of town, at the east end of Th Phahonyothin (Asia 1 Hwy). At research time, **Bangkok Airways** (☎0 5482 1522, 1771; www.bangkokair.com; Lampang Airport; ⊗7.30-11.30am & 12.30-6.30pm), with flights to/from Bangkok, was the only airline operating out of Lampang. *Sŏrng·tăa·ou* from the airport to downtown cost 50B; taxis charge 200B.

Lampang's **bus and minivan terminal** is nearly 2km south of the centre of town, at the corner of Th Phahonyothin (Asia 1 Hwy) and Th Chantarasurin – frequent *sŏrng·tăa·ou* run between the station and town from 3am to 9pm (20B, 15 minutes).

Lampang's historic **train station** (☎0 5421 7024, 1690; www.railway.co.th; Th Phahonyothin) dates back to 1916 and is a fair hike from most accommodation; a túk-túk between here and the centre of town should run around 80B.

ℹ Getting Around

Getting around central Lampang is possible on foot. The Tourism Authority of Thailand office has free bicycle rental from 10am to 4pm; bring your passport. Both bicycles (per day 60B) and motorcycles (per day 200B) are available for rent at **Ozone** (395 Th Thipchang; ⊗9am-8pm). For destinations outside of town, there is a **taxi stall** (☎0 5421 7233; Th Suandawg; ⊗6.30am-5pm) near the Pin Hotel.

TRANSPORT TO/FROM LAMPANG

DESTINATION	AIR	BUS	MINIVAN	TRAIN
Bangkok	2340B; 1½hr; 2 daily (to Suvarnabhumi International Airport)	378-756B; 9hr; frequent 7.30-11.30am & 6.30-9pm		256-1872B; 12hr; 6 daily
Chiang Mai		53-140B; 2hr; half-hourly 2am-8.30pm	70B; 1½hr; hourly 6.30am-5.30pm	23-413B; 3hr; 6 daily
Chiang Rai		111-153B; 4hr; frequent 6.30am-3pm		
Mae Sai		138B; 6hr; 10.30am & 12.30pm		
Mae Sot		199-265B; 4hr; 1pm & 2.30pm		
Nan		165-330B; 4hr; hourly 8am-midnight		
Phitsanulok		171-256B; 4½hr; hourly 5am-10.30pm		48-1542B; 5hr; 6 daily
Phrae		78-175B; 2hr; hourly 9am-midnight	85B; 2hr; half-hourly 7.10am-4.30pm	
Sukhothai		178B; 3½hr; hourly 5am-7pm		

Around Lampang

Wat Phra That Lampang Luang
วัดพระธาตุลำปางหลวง

This ancient **Buddhist temple compound** (⊙ daylight hours) **FREE** houses several interesting religious structures, including what is arguably the most beautiful wooden Lanna temple in northern Thailand, the open-sided **Wihan Luang**. Dating back to 1476 and thought to be the oldest-standing wooden structure in the country, the impressive *wí·hǎhn* (sanctuary) features a triple-tiered wooden roof supported by immense teak pillars and early 19th-century *jataka* murals (stories of the Buddha's previous lives) painted on wooden panels around the inside upper perimeter. A huge, gilded *mon·dòp* in the back of the *wí·hǎhn* contains a Buddha image cast in 1563.

The small and simple **Wihan Ton Kaew**, to the north of the main *wí·hǎhn,* was built in 1476, while the tall Lanna-style *chedi* behind the main *wí·hǎhn,* raised in 1449 and restored in 1496, is 45m high.

The *wí·hǎhn* to the north of the *chedi,* **Wihan Nam Taem**, was built in the early 16th century and, amazingly, still contains traces of the original murals, making them among the oldest in the country.

Wihan Phra Phut, which is south of the main *chedi,* dates back to the 13th century and is the oldest structure in the compound.

Unfortunately, only men are allowed to see a camera obscura image of the *wí·hǎhn* and *chedi* in the **Haw Phra Phutthabaht**, a small white building behind the *chedi.* The image is projected (upside down) onto a white cloth, and clearly depicts the colours of the structures outside.

The lintel over the entrance to the compound features an impressive dragon relief, once common in northern Thai temples but rarely seen today. This gate supposedly dates to the 15th century.

In the arboretum outside the southern gate of the *wát,* there are now three **museums**. One displays mostly festival paraphernalia and some Buddha figures. Another, called 'House of the Emerald Buddha', contains a miscellany of coins, banknotes, Buddha figures, silver betel-nut cases, lacquerware and other ethnographic artefacts, along with three small heavily gold-leafed Buddhas placed on an altar behind an enormous repoussé silver bowl. The third, a small museum, features shelves of Buddha figures, lacquered boxes, manuscripts and ceramics, all well labelled in Thai and English.

ⓘ Getting There & Away

Wat Phra That Lampang Luang is 18km southwest of Lampang in Ko Kha. To get there by public transport from Lampang, flag a blue eastbound *sǒrng·tǎa·ou* (20B) on Th Boonyawat. From the Ko Kha *sǒrng·tǎa·ou* stop, it's a 3km chartered motorcycle taxi ride to the temple (40B). Alternatively, you can charter a *sǒrng·tǎa·ou* from Lampang's bus station for around 350B, or taxis will take you there and back for 500B.

If you're driving or cycling from Lampang, head south on Th Phahonyothin (Asia 1 Hwy) and take the Ko Kha exit, then follow the road over a bridge and bear right. Follow the signs and continue for 3km over another bridge until you see the temple on the left.

Thai Elephant Conservation Center & Around ศูนย์อนุรักษ์ช้างไทย

Hang Chat, 33km southeast of Lampang via Rte 11, is home to a few attractions, the centrepiece of which are two separate centres dedicated to elephants.

About 5km southeast of the TECC, the **Thung Kwiang Market** (ตลาดทุ่งเกวียน; Rte 11; ⊙ 7am-6pm) is a crash course in northern Thai food and handicrafts, with everything from rót dòo·an (deep-fried worms, a northern speciality) to the distinctive rooster bowls made in Lampang.

★ **Thai Elephant Conservation Center**   ELEPHANT ENCOUNTER
(TECC; ✆ 0 5482 9333; www.thailandelephant.org; Rte 11; admission adult/child 170/110B; ⊙ elephant bathing 9.45am & 1.15pm, public shows 10am, 11am & 1.30pm) This popular centre promotes the role of the Asian elephant in ecotourism.

In addition to elephant shows, there is an exhibit on the history and culture of elephants, an elephant art gallery, an elephant graveyard, and **elephant rides** (10/30/60min 200/500/1000B; ⊙ 8am-3.30pm) through the surrounding forest.

For those keen on delving deeper into pachyderm culture, the TECC's **Mahout Training School** (✆ 0 5424 7875; www.thailandelephant.org; programs 3500–100,000B) offers an array of programs ranging in duration from one day to one month.

The popular one-day course involves learning a few simple commands for leading an elephant, experimenting with dung paper, riding an elephant in the jungle and a tour of the elephant hospital. A more in-volved three-day, two-night homestay program includes all meals, a night's lodging in a well-equipped wood-and-bamboo bungalow and another night at a jungle camp, plus a general introduction to elephant care and training.

All proceeds from the entrance fee and souvenir shops go to the elephant hospital on-site, which cares for old, abandoned and sick elephants from all over Thailand, as well as working for the preservation of elephants through various research and breeding programs.

FAE's Elephant Hospital   ELEPHANT HOSPITAL
(Friends of the Asian Elephant; ✆ 08 1914 6113; www.elephant-soraida.com; off Rte 11; admission by donation; ⊙ 8am-5pm) Located next door to the TECC (but not affiliated) is this hospital, which claims to be the first of its kind in the world. In June 2008 the centre reached another first when it successfully provided an elephant with a prosthetic leg. Although visitors are appreciated and provided for, keep in mind that this is a functioning medical facility: there are no guided tours and certainly no elephant art. Donations are greatly appreciated.

🛏 Sleeping & Eating

In addition to accommodation, there are three restaurants on the TECC grounds.

Homestay   HOTEL **$**
(✆ 0 5482 9333; TECC; 500B; @) Those enrolled in the TECC's multiday homestay programs live and eat with a mahout at these basic fan-cooled bungalows; accommodation and food are included in the price of tuition. Rooms – exclusive of meals – are also available for non-students.

Chang Thai Resort   RESORT **$$**
(✆ 0 5482 9338; changthairesort@gmail.com; TECC; bungalows 1000-1500B; ❋ ❀ 🤶) The TECC's one- and two-room bungalows are modern and comfortable, and a stay allows free admission to elephant shows.

ⓘ Getting There & Away

Both facilities can be reached by Chiang Mai–bound minivan bus or sŏrng·tăa·ou (30B to 70B, 40 minutes) from Lampang's bus station. Let the driver know where you are headed and get off at the Km 37 marker. TECC is 1.5km from the highway, and shuttle buses will take you inside. Alternatively, you can charter a blue sŏrng·tăa·ou for 600B at Lampang's bus station or a taxi for about 1000B.

OFF THE BEATEN TRACK

WAT LAI HIN

If you're visiting Wat Phra That Lampang Luang and you've got your own transport, you might also consider a visit to beautiful **Wat Lai Hin** (วัดไหล่หิน; ⊙ daylight hours) FREE, also near Ko Kha. Built by artists from Kengtung (also known as Chiang Tung), Myanmar, the tiny temple is one of the most characteristically Lanna temples around, and was a significant influence on the design of the Mandarin Oriental Dhara Dhevi hotel in Chiang Mai, not to mention a set for the 2001 Thai blockbuster, *Suriyothai*. There's an interesting **folk museum** on the grounds that the monks can unlock for you.

If coming from Ko Kha, the temple is located about 6km down a road that turns off 1km before reaching Wat Phra That Lampang Luang.

CHIANG RAI PROVINCE

Chiang Rai, Thailand's northernmost province, has a bit of everything: the mountains in the far east are among the most dramatic in the country, the lowland Mekong River floodplains to the northeast are not unlike those one would find much further south in Isan, and the province shares borders with Myanmar and Laos. In terms of people, it's among Thailand's most ethnically diverse provinces and home to a significant minority of hill tribes, Shan and other Tai groups, and more recent Chinese immigrants.

Chiang Rai

เชียงราย

POP 68,000

Chiang Rai Province has such a diversity of attractions that its capital is often overlooked. This small delightful city is worth getting to know, however, with its relaxed atmosphere, good-value accommodation and great local food. It's also the logical base from which to plan excursions to the more remote corners of the province.

Founded by Phaya Mengrai in 1262 as part of the Lao-Thai Lanna kingdom, Chiang Rai didn't become a Siamese territory until 1786 and a province until 1910.

◉ Sights

Oub Kham Museum   MUSEUM
(พิพิธภัณฑ์อูบคำ; www.oubkhammuseum.com; Th Nakhai; adult/child 300/100B; ◉8am-5pm) This slightly zany museum houses an impressive collection of paraphernalia from virtually every corner of the former Lanna kingdom. The items, some of which truly are one of a kind, range from a monkey-bone food taster used by Lanna royalty to an impressive carved throne from Chiang Tung, Myanmar.

Guided tours (available in English) are obligatory and include a walk through a gilded artificial cave holding several Buddha statues, complete with disco lights and fake torches! The grounds of the museum are equally kitschy, and include a huge golden *naga* (a mythical serpentlike being with magical powers) statue and countless waterfalls and fountains. Truly an equal parts bizarre and enlightening experience.

The Oub Kham Museum is 2km west of the town centre and can be a bit tricky to find; túk-túk will go here for about 50B.

Mae Fah Luang Art & Culture Park   MUSEUM
(ไร่แม่ฟ้าหลวง; www.maefahluang.org/rmfl; 313 Moo 7, Ban Pa Ngiw; admission 200B; ◉8.30am-4.30pm Tue-Sun) In addition to a museum that houses one of Thailand's biggest collections of Lanna artefacts, this meticulously landscaped compound includes antique and contemporary Buddhist temples, art and other structures.

Haw Kaew, the park's museum, has a permanent collection of mostly teak-based artefacts and art from across the former Lanna region, as well as a temporary exhibition room.

Haw Kham, a temple-like tower built in 1984 from the remains of 32 wooden houses, is arguably the park's centrepiece. The immense size of the structure – allegedly influenced by Lanna-era Wat Pongsanuk in Lampang – with its Buddha image seemingly hovering over white sand (the latter imported from Ko Samet), and sacred, candle-lit aura culminate in a vibe not unlike the place of worship of an indigenous cult.

You'll probably have to ask staff to open up **Haw Kham Noi**, a structure housing folksy but beautiful Buddhist murals taken from a dismantled teak temple in Phrae.

Mae Fah Luang Art & Culture Park is located about 4km west of the centre of Chiang Rai; a túk-túk or taxi here will run around 100B.

Hilltribe Museum & Education Center   MUSEUM
(พิพิธภัณฑ์และศูนย์การศึกษาชาวเขา; www.pdacr. org; 3rd fl, 620/25 Th Thanalai; admission 50B; ◉9am-6pm Mon-Fri, 10am-6pm Sat & Sun) This museum and cultural centre is a good place to visit before undertaking any hilltribe trek. Run by the nonprofit Population & Community Development Association (PDA), the displays are underwhelming in their visual presentation, but contain a wealth of information on Thailand's various tribes and the issues that surround them.

A visit begins with a 20-minute slide show on Thailand's hill tribes, followed by self-guided exploration among exhibits that include typical clothing for six major tribes, examples of bamboo usage, folk implements and other anthropological objects. The curator is passionate about his museum and, if present, will talk about the different hill tribes, their histories, recent trends and the community projects that the museum helps fund.

The PDA also runs highly recommended treks.

Chiang Rai

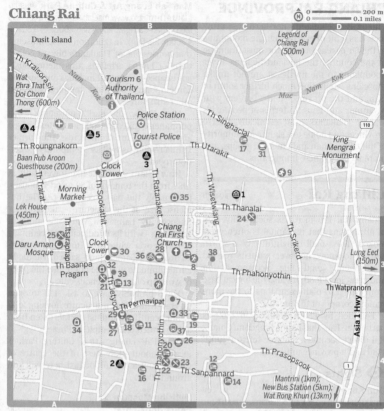

Wat Phra Kaew
BUDDHIST TEMPLE

(วัดพระแก้ว; Th Trairat; ⊙temple 7am-7pm, museum 9am-5pm) **FREE** Originally called Wat Pa Yia (Bamboo Forest Monastery) in the local dialect, this is the city's most revered Buddhist temple. The main prayer hall is a medium-sized, well-preserved wooden structure. The octagonal *chedi* behind it dates from the late 14th century and is in typical Lanna style. The adjacent two-storey wooden building is a **museum** housing various Lanna artefacts.

Legend has it that in 1434 lightning struck the temple's *chedi*, which fell apart to reveal the Phra Kaew Morakot, or Emerald Buddha (actually made of jade). After a long journey that included a lengthy stopover in Vientiane, Laos, this national talisman is now ensconced in the temple of the same name in Bangkok.

In 1990, Chiang Rai commissioned a Chinese artist to sculpt a new image from Canadian jade. Named the Phra Yok Chiang Rai (Chiang Rai Jade Buddha), it was intentionally a very close but not exact replica of the Phra Kaew Morakot in Bangkok, with dimensions of 48.3cm across the base and 65.9cm in height, just 0.1cm shorter than the original. The image is housed in the impressive Haw Phra Yoke, the walls of which are decorated with beautiful modern murals, some depicting the journey of the original Phra Kaew Morakot, as well as the elaborate ceremony that saw the current image arrive at its new home in Chiang Rai.

Tham Tu Pu & Buddha Cave
BUDDHIST TEMPLE

(ถ้ำตุ๊ปู่/ถ้ำพระ; ⊙daylight hours) **FREE** If you follow Th Winitchaikul across the bridge to the northern side of Mae Nam Kok, you'll come to a turn-off for both Tham Tu Pu and the Buddha Cave.

Chiang Rai

Neither attraction is particularly amazing on its own, but the surrounding country is beautiful and would make an ideal destination for a lazy bike ride.

Follow the road 1km, then turn off onto a dirt path 200m to the base of a limestone cliff where there is a steep set of stairs leading to a main chamber holding a dusty Buddha statue; this is **Tham Tu Pu**.

Continue along the same road for 3km more (the sign says 'Buddha Images Cave') and you'll reach **Buddha Cave**, a cavern by Mae Nam Kok containing a tiny but active Buddhist temple, a lone monk and several cats. The temple was one of several destinations on a visit to the region by King Rama V in the early 20th century.

Wat Phra Singh　　　BUDDHIST TEMPLE
(วัดพระสิงห์; Th Singhaclai; ⊙ daylight hours) FREE This temple dates back to the late 14th century, and its oldest surviving original buildings are typical northern Thai–style wood structures with low, sweeping roofs. The main *wí·hăhn* (sanctuary) houses impressive wooden doors thought to have been carved by local artists, as well as a copy of Chiang Mai's sacred Phra Singh Buddha.

Wat Jet Yot　　　BUDDHIST TEMPLE
(วัดเจ็ดยอด; Th Jetyod; ⊙ daylight hours) FREE The seven-spired *chedi* at Wat Jet Yot is similar to that of its Chiang Mai namesake, but without stucco ornamentation. Of more aesthetic interest is the wooden ceiling of the front verandah of the main *wí·hăhn*, which features a unique Thai astrological fresco.

Wat Klang Wiang　　　BUDDHIST TEMPLE
(วัดกลางเวียง; cnr Th Ratanaket & Th Utarakit; ⊙ daylight hours) FREE This temple appears contemporary, but probably dates back at least 500 years. Extensive remodelling in the early 1990s has left several structures in the temple with a unique 'modern Lanna' style, but the elegant *hŏr drai* (manuscript depository) appears to have retained its original form.

Wat Phra That Doi Chom Thong　　　BUDDHIST TEMPLE
(วัดพระธาตุดอยจอมทอง; off Th Kraisorasit; ⊙ daylight hours) FREE King Mengrai, Chiang Rai's founder, first surveyed the site for the city from this peak. The Lanna-style *chedi* found at the top most likely dates from the 14th to 16th centuries and may cover an earlier Mon

chedi inside. The hilltop compound is also home to Chiang Rai's 'city navel'.

⚡ Activities

Nearly every guesthouse and hotel in Chiang Rai offers trekking excursions in hill tribe country. Many of the local travel agencies merely act as brokers for guides associated with one of the local guesthouses, so it may be cheaper to book directly through the guesthouses themselves. As elsewhere in northern Thailand, you're more assured of a quality experience if you use a TAT-licensed guide.

Trek pricing depends on the type of activities and the number of days and participants. Rates, per person, for two people for a two-night trek range from 2500B to 6500B. Generally everything from accommodation to transport and food is included in this price.

Mirror Foundation
TREKKING

(☑0 5373 7616; www.thailandecotour.org) Although its rates are higher, trekking with this nonprofit NGO helps support the training of its local guides. Treks range from one to three days and traverse the Akha, Karen and Lahu villages of Mae Yao District, north of Chiang Rai.

PDA Tours & Travel
TREKKING

(☑0 5374 0088; www.pda.or.th/chiangrai/package_tour.htm; 3rd fl, Hilltribe Museum & Education Center, 620/25 Th Thanalai; ☺9am-6pm Mon-Fri, 10am-6pm Sat & Sun) One- to three-day treks are available through this NGO. Profits go back into community projects that include HIV/AIDS education, mobile health clinics, education scholarships and the establishment of village-owned banks.

Rai Pian Karuna
TREKKING

(☑08 7186 7858, 08 2195 5645; www.facebook.com/raipiankaruna) This new, community-based social enterprise conducts one- and multi-day treks and homestays at Akha, Lahu and Lua villages in Mae Chan, north of Chiang Rai. Other activities, from week-long volunteering stints to cooking courses, are also on offer.

Eagle Adventure Tour
TREKKING

(☑08 7265 0527; www.thaieagletour.com; off Th Phahonyothin; ☺8.30am-9pm) A Chiang Rai-based outfit offering the usual variety of treks and guided tours.

Dragon Sabaii Tours
TREKKING

(☑08 5548 0884; www.thailandhilltribeholidays.com) Guided tours in and around Chiang Rai.

Akha Hill House
TREKKING

(☑08 9997 5505; www.akhahill.com; Akha River House, Th Ratanaket; ☺9am-7pm) This outfit leads one- to seven-day treks. They begin with a long-tail boat trip up the river before trekking to and around the Akha Hill House, located about 23km from Chiang Rai at a height of 1500m. Enquiries can be made at Akha River House, their Chiang Rai–based accommodation.

Golden Triangle Tours
TREKKING

(☑0 5374 0478; www.goldenchiangrai.com; Golden Triangle Inn, 590 Th Phahonyothin; ☺9am-6pm) Offers two-day treks that include a half-day 'elephant safari'.

Si La Lang Tour
TREKKING, TOURS

(☑0 5375 2219; www.silalangtour.com; 541 Th Phahonyothin; ☺9am-9pm) Offers a variety of treks and tours; Paul, a guide here, is experienced and comes recommended.

Suwannee
COOKING

(☑08 4740 7119; www.chiangraicookingclass.com; lessons 1250B; ☺courses 9.30am-2pm) Suwannee offers nearly day-long cooking courses that involve a visit to a local market and instruction in cooking four dishes. Suwanee's house is about 3km outside the city centre, but she can pick you up at most centrally located hotels and guesthouses.

Jao Nang Studio
PORTRAIT STUDIO

(645/7 Th Utarakit; ☺10am-7pm) Dress up like a member of Lanna royalty and have your portrait taken for posterity – a must-do activity for Thai visitors to Chiang Mai and Chiang Rai. Has a huge array of costumes and backdrops.

🛏 Sleeping

Chiang Rai has a good selection of places to stay, and price increases have been incremental in the past several years, making accommodation in the town good value. The two main areas for hotels are in the centre, clustered around Th Jetyod and off Th Phahonyothin.

HEAVEN & HELL

Lying just outside Chiang Rai are two of the province's most touted – and bizarre – destinations.

Whereas most of Thailand's Buddhist temples have centuries of history, construction of **Wat Rong Khun** (White Temple | วัดร่องขุ่น; off Asia 1 Hwy; ⊙8am-5pm Mon-Fri, 8am-5.30pm Sat- & Sun) FREE, brainchild of noted Thai painter-turned-architect Chalermchai Kositpipat, began in 1997. Seen from a distance, the temple appears to be made of glittering porcelain; a closer look reveals that the appearance is due to a combination of whitewash and clear-mirrored chips. To enter the temple, one must walk over a bridge and pool of reaching arms (symbolising desire), where inside, instead of the traditional Buddha life scenarios, the artist has painted contemporary scenes representing samsara (the realm of rebirth and delusion). Images such as a plane smashing into the Twin Towers and, oddly enough, Keanu Reeves as Neo from *The Matrix* (not to mention Elvis, Hello Kitty and Superman, among others), dominate the one finished wall of this work in progress.

Wat Rong Khun is located about 13km south of Chiang Rai. To get to the temple, hop on one of the regular buses that run from Chiang Rai to Chiang Mai or Phayao (20B).

The bizarre brainchild of Thai National Artist Thawan Duchanee, and a rather sinister counterpoint to Wat Rong Khun, **Baan Dum** (Black House; off Asia 1 Hwy; ⊙9am-noon & 1-5pm) FREE unites several quasi-traditional structures, most of which are stained black and ominously decked out with animal pelts and bones.

The centrepiece is a black, cavernous temple-like building holding a long wooden dining table and chairs made from deer antlers – a virtual Satan's dining room. Other buildings include white, breast-shaped bedrooms, dark phallus-decked bathrooms, and a bone- and fur-lined 'chapel'. The structures have undeniably discernible northern Thai influences, but the dark tones, flagrant flourishes and all those dead animals coalesce in a way that is more fantasy than reality.

Baan Dum is located 13km north of Chiang Rai in Nang Lae; any Mae Sai–bound bus will drop you off here for around 20B.

🛏 In Town

Baan Warabordee　　　　　HOTEL $
(☑0 5375 4488; baanwarabordee@hotmail.com; 59/1 Th Sanpannard; r 500-600B; ❋🛜) A delightful small hotel has been made from this modern three-storey Thai villa. Rooms come decked out in dark woods and light cloths, and are equipped with air-con, fridge and hot water.

Moon & Sun Hotel　　　　HOTEL $
(☑0 5371 9279; www.moonandsun-hotel.com; 632 Th Singhaclai; r incl breakfast 500-600B, ste incl breakfast 800B; ❋🛜) Bright and sparkling clean, this little hotel offers large modern rooms. Some feature four-poster beds, while all come with desk, cable TV and refrigerator. Suites have a separate, spacious sitting area.

Jansom House　　　　　　HOTEL $
(☑0 5371 4552; 897/2 Th Jetyod; r incl breakfast 450-500B; ❋🛜) This three-storey hotel offers tidy rooms set around a small courtyard filled with plants. Go for the slightly more expensive air-con rooms, as the ground-floor fan rooms can be a bit musty.

Baan Bua Guest House　　GUESTHOUSE $
(☑0 5371 8880; www.baanbua-guesthouse.com; 879/2 Th Jetyod; r 300-500B; ❋@🛜) This quiet guesthouse consists of a strip of 17 bright green rooms surrounding an inviting garden. Rooms are simple, but clean and cosy.

The North　　　　　　　　HOTEL $
(☑0 5371 9873; www.thenorth.co.th; 612/100-101 Sirikon Market; dm 200B, r with fan/air-con 350/450B; ❋@🛜) This hotel has provided the drab market/bus station area with a bit of colour. The 15 rooms combine both Thai and modern design; some are attached to inviting chill-out areas.

Orchids Guest House　　GUESTHOUSE $
(☑0 5371 8361; www.orchidsguesthouse.com; 1012/3 Th Jetyod; r 450-500B; ❋@🛜) This collection of spotless rooms in a residential compound is a good budget catch. In addition to accommodation, various services are available here, including internet, laundry, taxi transfer and trekking.

Chook Dee Guest House
GUESTHOUSE $

(☑08 6027 8529; Th Jetyod; dm 100B, r 200-250B) The rooms are basic, and the hyper-chilled reggae vibe doesn't exactly suggest sky-high standards of service, but for those who fancy a social backpacker scene, this is your place.

Baan Rub Aroon
GUESTHOUSE $$

(☑0 5371 1827; www.baanrubaroon.net; 893 Th Ngam Meuang; r incl breakfast 550-1000B; ❋@✶) The rooms in this handsome villa, located just west of the city centre, aren't as charming as the exterior suggests, and most share bathrooms, but it's a good choice if you're looking for a quiet homey stay.

Lek House
GUESTHOUSE $$

(☑0 5371 1550; lekhousehotel@live.co.uk; cnr Th Ratyotha & Th Baanpa Pragarn; r incl breakfast 450-750B; ❋@✶✹) This purple compound is home to a handful of tight but attractive air-con rooms, although there's little separating the bathrooms. The fan-cooled rooms are much simpler, and everybody gets to use the pool. Lek House is near the corner of Th Ratyotha (the continuation of Th Thanalai) and Th Baanpa Pragarn.

Diamond Park Inn
HOTEL $$

(☑0 5375 4960; www.diamondparkinn.com; 74/6 Th Sanpannard; r incl breakfast 1100B, ste incl breakfast 1400-1500B; ❋@✶✹) Aggressive marketing strategy aside ('When ever you are at Chiang Rai. Stay at The Diamond Park Inn'), this vast hotel is a safe midrange choice. Rooms are attractive, with modern furniture and beds on an elevated platform. The more expensive rooms have bath-tubs, wide balconies, and are big enough to feel slightly empty.

Golden Triangle Inn
HOTEL $$

(☑0 5371 1339; www.goldentriangleinn.com; 590 Th Phahonyothin; s/d incl breakfast 700/800B; ❋✶) Resembling an expansive Thai home (including the occasional lived-in untidiness this can entail), the 31 rooms here have tile or wood floors, wooden furniture and twin beds. The compound includes a restaurant, a Budget car-rental office and an efficient travel agency.

Wiang Inn
HOTEL $$$

(☑0 5371 1533; www.wianginn.com; 893 Th Phahonyothin; r incl breakfast 2000-2400B, ste incl breakfast 6000-10,000B; ❋@✶✹) The large modern lobby sets the stage for this centrally located, business-class hotel. Despite the hotel's 30-plus years, the rooms are well maintained and include a few Thai decorative touches.

🛏 Outside of Town

★ Bamboo Nest de Chiang Rai
GUESTHOUSE $$

(☑08 9953 2330, 08 1531 6897; www.bamboo-est-chiangrai.com; bungalows incl breakfast 650-1300B) The Lahu village that's home to this unique accommodation is only 23km from Chiang Rai but feels a world away. Bamboo Nest takes the form of simple but spacious bamboo huts perched on a hill overlooking tiered rice fields. The only electricity is provided by solar panels, so leave your laptops in the city and instead take part in activities that range from birdwatching to hiking.

Free transport to/from Chiang Rai is available for those staying two nights or more.

Ben Guesthouse
GUESTHOUSE $$

(☑0 5371 6775; www.benguesthousechiangrai.com; 351/10 Soi 4, Th Sankhongnoi; r 350-850B, ste 1500-3000B; ❋@✶✹) Ben is one of the best budget-to-midrange places we've encountered in the north. The absolutely spotless compound has a bit of everything, from fan-cooled cheapies to immense suites, not to mention a pool. It's 1.2km from the centre of town, at the end of Soi 4 on Th Sankhongnoi (the street is called Th Sathanpayabarn where it intersects with Th Phahonyothin) – a 60B túk-túk ride.

Chezmoi
GUESTHOUSE $$

(☑08 9747 5683; www.chezmoimyhome.com; 34/2 Th Sankhongnoi; r incl breakfast 550-1200B; ❋✶) The seven rooms in this home/studio are fashionably sparse with clean shared bathrooms, and are looked after by a friendly, welcoming family. Chezmoi is about 1.5km from the centre of town at the western end of Th Sankhongnoi (the street is called Th Sathanpayabarn where it intersects with Th Phahonyothin) – a 60B túk-túk ride.

Legend of Chiang Rai
HOTEL $$$

(☑0 5391 0400; www.thelegend-chiangrai.com; 124/15 Th Kohloy; r incl breakfast 3900-5900B, bungalows incl breakfast 8100-12,900B; ❋@✶✹) One of the few Chiang Rai hotels to boast a riverside location, this upscale resort feels like a traditional Lanna village. Rooms are romantic and luxuriously understated with furniture in calming creams and rattan. The riverside infinity pool and spa

CAFE CULTURE, CHIANG RAI STYLE

For a relatively small town, Chiang Rai has an enviable spread of high-quality, Western-style cafes. This is largely due to the fact that many of Thailand's best coffee beans are grown in the more remote corners of the province. Some of the town's better cups can be found at the following:

BaanChivitMai Bakery (www.baanchivitmai.com; Th Prasopsook; ⊙8am-9pm Mon-Sat; 🛜) In addition to a proper cup of joe made from local beans, you can snack on amazingly authentic Swedish-style sweets and Western-style meals and sandwiches at this popular bakery. Profits go to BaanChivitMai, an organisation that runs homes and education projects for vulnerable, orphaned or AIDS-affected children.

Doi Chaang (542/2 Th Ratanaket; ⊙7am-10pm; 🛜) Doi Chaang is the leading brand among Chiang Rai coffees, and its beans are now sold as far abroad as Canada and Europe.

Wawee Coffee (cnr Th Singhaclai & Th Srikerd; ⊙7am-9pm; 🛜) Another local brand done well, this contemporary-feeling cafe serves a variety of creative coffee drinks using Chiang Rai–grown beans.

Pangkhon Coffee (Th Sookathit; ⊙7am-10pm; 🛜) Combine coffee brewed from local beans with views of Chiang Rai's gilded clock tower.

are the icing on the comfort-filled cake. The resort is about 500m north of Th Singhaclai.

Le Meridien Chiang Rai Resort   HOTEL **$$$**
(☏0 5360 3333; www.lemeridien.com; 221/2 Th Kwaewai; r incl breakfast 3800-4300B, ste incl breakfast 5300-16,000B; ❄@🛜☲) Chiang Rai's newest upscale resort is about 2km outside of the city centre on a beautiful stretch of Mae Nam Kok. Rooms are immense and decked out in greys, whites and blacks, and the compound includes two restaurants and an infinity pool, in addition to the usual amenities of a hotel in this price range.

Mantrini   HOTEL **$$$**
(☏0 5360 1555; www.mantrini.com; Rte 1; r incl breakfast 2300-2800B, ste incl breakfast 7500B; ❄@🛜☲) The standard rooms here are modern and spacious, if a bit plain. Consider instead one of the two Designer Suites, which are decked out in a faux-Victorian motif that somehow successfully combines disparate elements such as an African mask and a rocking horse. The hotel is about 1km south of the city centre near Central Plaza.

🍴 Eating

Come mealtime, you'll almost certainly be pointed in the direction of Chiang Rai's night bazaar, but the food there is generally pretty dire – don't say we didn't warn you! Instead, if you're in town on a weekend, hit the vendors at Chiang Rai's open-air markets, Thanon Khon Muan and the Walking Street, which feature a good selection of local dishes.

★ Lung Eed   NORTHERN THAI **$**
(Th Watpranorn; mains 40-100B; ⊙11.30am-9pm Mon-Sat) One of Chiang Rai's most delicious dishes is available at this rustic but yummy northern-style food shack. There's an English-language menu on the wall, but don't miss the sublime *lâhp gài*, minced chicken fried with herbs and topped with crispy deep-fried chicken skin, shallots and garlic. The restaurant is on Th Watpranorn about 100m from the intersection with the Superhighway.

Khao Soi Phor Jai   NORTHERN THAI **$**
(Th Jetyod, no roman-script sign; mains 30-60B; ⊙7.30am-5pm) Phor Jai serves mild but tasty bowls of the eponymous curry noodle dish, as well as a few other northern Thai staples.

Paa Suk   NORTHERN THAI **$**
(Th Sankhongnoi, no roman-script sign; mains 10-25B; ⊙8am-3pm) Paa Suk does rich bowls of *kà·nŏm jeen nám ngée·o*, a broth of pork or beef and tomatoes served over fresh rice noodles. The restaurant is between Soi 4 and Soi 5 on Th Sankhongnoi (the street is called Th Sathanpayabarn where it intersects with the southern end of Th Phahonyothin); look for the yellow sign.

Nam Ngiaw Paa Nuan VIETNAMESE-THAI $
(Vietnamese Restaurant; Th Sanpannard, no roman-
script sign; mains 10-120B; ⊘9am-5pm) This
quasi-concealed place serves a unique mix
of Vietnamese and northern Thai dishes.
Tasty food, friendly service and a fun barn-
like atmosphere make us wish it was open
for dinner as well.

Muang Thong CHINESE-THAI $
(cnr Th Sanpannard & Th Phahonyothin; mains 30-
100B; ⊘24hr) Comfort food for Thais and
travellers alike: this long-standing open-air
place serves the usual repertoire of satisfy-
ingly salty and spicy Chinese-Thai dishes.

TRANSPORT TO/FROM CHIANG RAI

DESTINATION	AIR	BOAT
Bangkok	2135-3590B; 1¼hr; 2 daily (to Don Muang Airport); 2600B; 1¼hr; 3 daily (to Suvarnabhumi International Airport)	
Ban Huay Khrai (for Doi Tung)		
Ban Pasang (for Doi Mae Salong)		
Ban Ruammit		80B; 1hr; 10.30am
Chiang Khong		
Chiang Mai		
Chiang Saen		
Fang		
Khon Kaen		
Kunming (China)	7500B; 1hr; 3 weekly	
Lampang		
Luang Prabang (Laos)		
Mae Sai		
Mae Sot		
Nakhon Ratchasima (Khorat)		
Nan		
Phayao		
Phitsanulok		
Phrae		
Sob Ruak (Golden Triangle)		
Sukhothai		
Tha Ton		350B; 4hr; 10.30am

Rosprasert Muslim Food   MUSLIM-THAI **$**
(Th Itsaraphap; mains 25-50B; ⊘ 7am-8pm) This
open-air restaurant next to the mosque on
Th Itsaraphap dishes up delicious Thai-
Muslim favourites, including *kôw mòk gài*,
the Thai version of chicken biryani.

Phu-Lae   NORTHERN THAI **$$**
(673/1 Th Thanalai; mains 80-320B; ⊘ 11.30am-
3pm & 5.30-11pm; ❄) This air-conditioned
restaurant is exceedingly popular with Thai
tourists for its tasty, but somewhat gentri-
fied northern Thai fare. Recommended local
dishes include the *gaang hang·lair* (pork
belly in a rich Burmese-style curry, here

BUS	MINIVAN
487-980B; 11-12hr; hourly 7-9.40am & 5-7.30pm (new bus station)	
23B; 30min; frequent 6am-8pm (inter-provincial bus station)	
25B; 30min; frequent 6am-8pm (inter-provincial bus station)	
65B; 2hr; frequent 6am-5pm (inter-provincial bus station)	
144-288B; 3-7hr; hourly 6.30am-7.30pm (new bus station); 144-288B; 7hr; frequent 6.30am-noon (inter-provincial bus station)	
39B; 1½hr; frequent 6.20am-7pm (inter-provincial bus station)	45B; 1½hr; hourly 6.20am-5.40pm (inter-provincial bus station)
92B; 2½hr; 8am (new bus station)	
486-601B; 11-12hr; 9am, frequent 2-8pm (new bus station)	
112-157B; 4-5hr; hourly 9.30am-4.30pm (new bus station); 102-157B; 5hr; frequent 6.30am-noon (inter-provincial bus station)	
950B; 16hr; 1pm (new bus station)	
39B; 1½hr; frequent 6am-8pm (inter-provincial bus station)	46B; 1½hr; frequent 6.30am-6pm (inter-provincial bus station)
384-493B; 12hr; 8.15am & 8.45am (new bus station)	
514-771B; 12-13hr; 6.30am, 11.30am, 1.15pm, 3.30pm, 5.30pm, 7.20pm (new bus station)	
164B; 6hr; 9.30am (inter-provincial bus station)	
49B; 1½-2hr; hourly 10am-3.30pm (new bus station); 49B; 2hr; frequent 6am-4.30pm (inter-provincial bus station)	62B; 1hr; frequent 6am-7.30pm (new bus station)
273-410B; 6-7hr; hourly 6.30am-10.30pm (new bus station)	
164-267B; 4hr; half-hourly, 6am-6pm (new bus station)	150B; 3½hr; frequent 6am-5pm (new bus station)
	50B; 2hr; hourly 6.20am-5.40pm (inter-provincial bus station)
300B; 8hr; hourly 7.30am-2.30pm (new bus station)	

served with pickled garlic), and *sâi òo·a* (herb-packed pork sausages).

🍷 Drinking & Entertainment

Th Jetyod is Chiang Rai's somewhat tacky drinking strip. Standouts include Cat Bar (1013/1 Th Jetyod; ⊙5pm-1am), which has a pool table and live music from 10.30pm, and Easy House (cnr Th Jetyod & Th Pemavipat; ⊙5pm-midnight), with a friendly, open-air vibe and a dinner menu.

🔒 Shopping

Walking Street   MARKET
(Th Thanalai; ⊙4-10pm Sat) If you're around on a Saturday evening be sure not to miss the open-air Walking Street, an expansive street market focusing on all things Chiang Rai, from handicrafts to local dishes. The market spans Th Thanalai from the Hilltribe Museum to the morning market.

Thanon Khon Muan   MARKET
(Th Sankhongnoi; ⊙6-9pm Sun) Come Sunday evening, the stretch of Th Sankhongnoi from Soi 2 heading west is closed to traffic, and in its place are vendors selling clothes, handicrafts and local food. Th Sankhongnoi is called Th Sathanpayabarn where it intersects with the southern end of Th Phahonyothin.

Fair Trade Shop   HANDICRAFTS
(www.ttcrafts.co.th; Th Jetyod; ⊙9am-5pm Mon-Sat) Bright hill-tribe cloths and knick-knacks are available at this shop, the profits of which go to various development projects.

Orn's Bookshop   BOOKSTORE
(off Soi 1, Th Jetyod; ⊙8am-8pm) Although Orn's feels like the private library of a conspiracy theorist, the general selection is decent and spans many languages.

Night Bazaar   MARKET
(off Th Phahonyothin; ⊙6-11pm) Adjacent to the bus station off Th Phahonyothin is Chiang Rai's night market. On a much smaller scale than the one in Chiang Mai, it is nevertheless an OK place to find an assortment of handicrafts and touristy souvenirs.

ℹ️ Information

There are several banks with foreign exchange and ATMs on both Th Phahonyothin and Th Thanalai.

Internet access is readily available around town and costs about 30B per hour. It's especially abundant near the night market.

Overbrook Hospital (☑0 5371 1366; www.overbrookhospital.com; Th Singhaclai) English is spoken at this modern hospital.

Tourism Authority of Thailand (TAT; ☑0 5374 4674, nationwide 1672; tatchrai@tat.or.th; Th Singhaclai; ⊙8.30am-4.30pm) English is limited, but staff here do their best to give advice and can provide a small selection of maps and brochures.

Tourist Police (☑0 5374 0249, nationwide 1155; Th Utarakit; ⊙24hr) English is spoken and police are on stand-by 24 hours a day.

ℹ️ Getting There & Away

Chiang Rai International Airport, also known as Mae Fah Luang, is approximately 8km north of the city. **Air Asia** (☑0 5379 3543, nationwide 02 515 9999; www.airasia.com; ⊙8am-9pm) and **Nok Air** (☑0 5379 3000, nationwide 1318; www.nokair.co.th; ⊙8am-7pm) fly to Bangkok's Don Muang Airport, while **THAI** (☑0 5379 8202, nationwide 0 2356 1111; www.thaiair.com; ⊙8am-8pm) flies to Suvarnabhumi. At research time, the airport's only international destination was Kunming, China, on **China Eastern** (☑0 5379 3688; www.flychinaeastern.com; ⊙8.30am-5pm). Taxis run into town from the airport for 200B. From town, a metered trip with Chiang Rai Taxi will cost around 120B. The terminal has airline offices, restaurants, a money exchange, a post office and several car-rental booths.

Passenger boats ply Mae Nam Kok between Chiang Rai and Tha Ton, in Chiang Mai, departing from **CR Pier** (☑0 5375 0009; ⊙6am-4.30pm), 2km northwest of town, via Th Kraisorasit; a túk-túk to the pier should cost about 60B.

Buses bound for destinations within Chiang Rai Province, as well as a couple of minivans and mostly slow fan-cooled buses bound for a handful of destinations in northern Thailand, depart from the **inter-provincial bus station** (Th Prasopsook) in the centre of town. If you're heading beyond Chiang Rai (or are in a hurry), you'll have to go to the **new bus station** (☑0 5377 3989), 5km south of town on Asia 1 Hwy; frequent *sŏrng·tǎa·ou* linking it and the inter-provincial station run from 6am to 6.30pm (15B, 15 minutes).

ℹ️ Getting Around

Chiang Rai Taxi (☑0 5377 3477) operates inexpensive metered taxis in and around town.

A túk-túk ride anywhere within central Chiang Rai should cost around 60B.

Bicycle hire can be arranged at **Fat Free** (☑0 5375 2532; 542/2 Th Baanpa Pragarn; per day 80–450B; ☺9am-6pm). Motorcycles can be hired at **ST Motorcycle** (☏0 5371 3652; 1025/34-35 Th Jetyod; per day 150-1000B; ☺8am-7pm) – they take good care of their bikes. Many guesthouses also rent out motorcycles and bikes.

The following car rental companies have offices in Chiang Rai:

Avis Rent-A-Car (☏0 5379 3827; www. avisthailand.com; Chiang Rai International Airport (Mae Fah Luang); ☺7.30am-9pm)

Budget Rent-A-Car (☏0 5374 0442/3; www. budget.co.th; Golden Triangle Inn, 590 Th Phahonyothin; ☺8am-6pm)

North Wheels (☏0 5374 0585; www.north-wheels.com; 591 Th Phahonyothin; ☺8am-7pm)

Thai Rent A Car (☏0 5379 3393; www.thai rentacar.com; Chiang Rai International Airport (Mae Fah Luang); ☺8am-8pm)

Mae Salong (Santikhiri) แม่สลอง (สันติคีรี)

POP 20,000

For a taste of China without crossing any international borders, head to this atmospheric village perched on the back hills of Chiang Rai.

Mae Salong was originally settled by the 93rd Regiment of the Kuomintang (KMT), who had fled to Myanmar from China after the establishment of communist rule in 1949. The renegades were forced to leave Myanmar in 1961 when the then Rangoon-based government decided it wouldn't allow the KMT to legally remain in northern Myanmar. Crossing into northern Thailand with their pony caravans, the ex-soldiers and their families settled into mountain villages and re-created a society like the one they'd left behind in Yunnan.

A generation later, this unique community persists, and today the Yunnanese dialect of Chinese still remains the lingua franca, residents tend to watch Chinese, rather than Thai, TV, and you'll find more Chinese than Thai food. And although Mae Salong is now thoroughly on the beaten track, the distinctly Chinese vibe, hilltop setting and abundance of hill tribes and tea plantations converge in a destination quite unlike anywhere else in Thailand. It's a great place to kick back for a couple of days, and the surrounding area is ripe for self-guided exploration.

◎ Sights

A tiny but quite interesting **morning market** convenes from 6am to 8am at the T-intersection near Shin Sane Guest House. The market attracts town residents and tribespeople from the surrounding districts. An **all-day market** forms at the southern end of town and unites vendors selling hill-tribe handicrafts, shops selling tea and a few basic restaurants.

To soak up the great views from **Wat Santikhiri** go past the market and ascend 718 steps (or drive if you have a car). The wát is of the Mahayana tradition and Chinese in style.

Past Khumnaiphol Resort and further up the hill is a **viewpoint** with some teashops, and a famous KMT general's **tomb**. It is sometimes guarded by a former soldier who will describe (in Thai or Yunnanese) the history of the KMT in the area. In the same vein and south of the tomb is the **Chinese Martyr's Memorial Museum** (admission 20B; ☺8am-6pm), an elaborate Chinese-style building that houses displays on the KMT experience – battles, migration, culture – in Thailand.

🏃 Activities

Shin Sane Guest House and Little Home Guesthouse have free maps showing approximate trekking routes to Akha, Lisu, Mien, Lahu and Shan villages in the area. Nearby Akha and Lisu villages are less than half a day's walk away.

The best hikes are north of Mae Salong between Ban Thoet Thai and the Myanmar border. Ask first about political conditions before heading off in this direction; Shan and Wa armies competing for control over this section of the Thailand–Myanmar border do occasionally clash in the area. A steady trade in methamphetamine and, to a lesser extent, heroin, flows across the border via several conduit villages.

Shin Sane Guest House leads **horseback treks** to four nearby villages for 500B for about three or four hours.

🛏 Sleeping

Since the road from Mae Salong to Tha Ton opened, fewer visitors are opting to stay overnight in Mae Salong. The resulting surplus of accommodation often makes prices negotiable, except during the high season (November to January).

NORTHERN THAILAND MAE SALONG (SANTIKHIRI)

BAN THOET THAI

In a narrow river valley about 20km north of Mae Salong, **Ban Thoet Thai** (บ้าน
เทอดไทย) is a multi-ethnic village with a remote, border-town vibe and an interesting
back story.

The village is probably most famous for having formerly served as the base of Khun
Sa, the Shan narco-warlord known as the 'Opium King'. Until the early 1980s, proximity
to the Golden Triangle, rough mountainous terrain and lack of sealed roads meant that
the outside world was essentially cut off from Ban Thoet Thai (then known as Ban Hin
Taek – Broken Stone Village), allowing Khun Sa to establish a virtual monopoly on the
world opium trade (for more on the Golden Triangle and Khun Sa, see p329). Displays on
the man (don't miss the VIP Living Room that boasts a creepy life-sized model of Khun
Sa) and on Shan culture and history can be seen at the **Khunsa Museum** (☉8am-5pm)
FREE, located in his former headquarters, about 500m north of the market area.

Ban Thoet Thai was also allegedly the first settlement of Akha in Thailand, and today
is also home to many Shan and Chinese, not to mention other groups including Thai Lü,
Lahu, Hmong, Lua and Liso. Approximately 6km northwest of town along a very steep
road is **Ban Ah Hai**, a picturesque Akha village that's also home to a unique adobe Buddhist temple. The owner of Rim Taan Guest House can provide directions or even lead an
informal tour.

The best place to stay is **Rim Taan Guest House** (☏0 5373 0209; r & bungalows
350-2000B; ❄ ☎), located roughly in the middle of town, with basic fan bungalows and
air-con rooms in an attractive stream-side garden. Next door, **Restaurant Ting Ting**
(mains 40-150B; ☉7am-9pm) has a thick English-language menu of tasty Chinese dishes.
There are ATMs at the town's 7-Eleven and an **internet cafe** (per hour 20B; ☉9am-11pm)
nearby.

To Ban Thoet Thai, sŏrng·tăa·ou depart when full from Ban Pasang, just off Asia 1
Hwy; in the opposite direction, trucks depart from Ban Thoet Thai's market area from
6am to 5pm (60B, one hour). It's also possible to hop on a sŏrng·tăa·ou at the crossroads village of Samyaek, 12km east of Mae Salong.

🛏 In Town

All accommodation is located on, or just off,
the main road.

Saeng A Roon Hotel GUESTHOUSE $
(☏0 5376 5029; r 300-400B; ❄ ☎) Next to the
teashop of the same name, this new hotel
has friendly staff, spacious tiled-floor rooms
and great views of the hills. The cheaper
rooms share spick-and-span hot-water bathrooms.

Shin Sane Guest House GUESTHOUSE $
(☏0 5376 5026; www.maesalong-shinsane.blog-
spot.com; r 100B, bungalows 300B; @ ☎) The
rooms at Mae Salong's oldest hotel are bare
but spacious with shared bathrooms, while
the bungalows are much more comfortable
and have bathrooms and TV. Located near
the morning market intersection.

Little Home Guesthouse GUESTHOUSE $$
(☏0 5376 5389; www.maesalonglittlehome.com;
bungalows 800B; @ ☎) Behind a wooden
house near the market intersection is this
handful of attractive, great-value bunga-
lows. Rooms are tidy and sunny, and the
owners are extremely friendly. They have
put together one of the more accurate maps
of the area.

Baan Hom Muen Li HOTEL $$
(☏0 5376 5271; osmanhouse@hotmail.com; no
roman-script sign; r incl breakfast 1000-2000B;
❄ ☎) Located in the middle of town, across
from Sweet Maesalong cafe, this stylish
place consists of 14 rooms artfully decked
out in modern and classic Chinese themes.
Go for the upstairs rooms in the new structure, which have huge windows with views
over the surrounding tea plantations.

Khumnaiphol Resort HOTEL $$
(☏0 5376 5001; https://th-th.facebook.com/
khumnaiphol.chiangrai; no roman-script sign; r incl
breakfast 800B, bungalows incl breakfast 1200-
1500B; ☎) Located 1km south of town near
the afternoon market intersection, this
resort has comfortable but rather tackily-

decorated bungalows perched on a hillside. The covered porches give great views of the tea plantations below. Cheaper rooms are also available.

Outside of Town

Maesalong Mountain Home   HOTEL $$
(☑ 08 4611 9508; www.maesalongmountainhome. com; bungalows 1000-2500B; ☎) Down a dirt road 1km east of Mae Salong's town centre (look for the orange sign), this boutique-feeling place is a great choice if you've got your own wheels or don't mind walking. The 10 bungalows are in the middle of a working farm and are bright and airy, with wide balconies and huge bathrooms.

Maesalong Flower Hills Resort   RESORT $$
(☑ 0 5376 5496; www.maesalongflowerhills.com; r incl breakfast 1100B, bungalows incl breakfast 1500-7000B; ✴☎☒) Located 2km east of Mae Salong's town centre, you can't miss this monument to flower-based landscaping. There's a variety of rooms and bungalows, and the huge pool and larger bungalows make this the logical choice for families.

★ Phu Chaisai Resort & Spa   RESORT $$$
(☑ 0 5391 0500; www.phu-chaisai.com; bungalows incl breakfast 4708-25,894B; ✴☎☒) Approximately 7km from Ban Pasang (the turn-off for Doi Mae Salong) on a remote bamboo-covered hilltop, this resort is the most unique place to stay in the area. The decidedly rustic adobe/bamboo bungalows fittingly lack TV, but have amazing views of the surrounding mountains and include access to a host of activities (including spa treatment, massage, yoga, day hikes and swimming) to keep you occupied.

Transport from Chiang Rai is available for 900B.

✕ Eating

The very Chinese breakfast of *ʉah·tôrng·gŏh* (deep-fried dough sticks) and hot soybean milk at the morning market is a great way to start the day.

In fact, many Thai tourists come to Mae Salong simply to eat Yunnanese dishes such as *màn·tŏh* (steamed Chinese buns) served with braised pork leg and pickled vegetables, or black chicken braised with Chinese-style herbs. Homemade wheat and egg noodles are another speciality of Mae Salong, and are served with a local broth that combines

pork and a spicy chilli paste. They're available at several places in town.

Countless teahouses sell locally grown teas (mostly oolong and jasmine) and offer complimentary tastings.

Sweet Maesalong   CAFE $
(mains 45-155B; ⊙ 8.30am-5pm; ☎) If you require more caffeine than the local tea leaves can provide, stop by this modern cafe with an extensive menu of coffee drinks made using local beans. Surprisingly sophisticated baked goods and one-plate dishes are also available. Located more or less in the middle of town.

Sue Hai   CHINESE $
(mains 40-250B; ⊙ 7am-9pm) This simple family-run teashop-cum-Yunnanese place has an English-language menu of local specialities including local mushroom fried with soy sauce, or the delicious air-dried pork fried with fresh chilli. It's roughly in the middle of town.

Salema Restaurant   MUSLIM-CHINESE $$
(mains 30-250B; ⊙ 7am-8pm) One of the friendliest restaurants in town also happens to be the most delicious. Salema does tasty Muslim-Chinese dishes including a rich 'Beef curry Yunnan style' or a deliciously tart 'Tuna & tea leaves spicy salad'. The noodle dishes are equally worthwhile, and include a beef *kôw soy* (northern Thai curry noodle soup). Salema is situated at the southern end of town.

ℹ Information

There is an ATM at the Thai Military Bank opposite Khumnaiphol Resort, at the southern end of town. An **internet cafe** (per hour 20B; ⊙ 9am-11pm) can be found nearby.

ℹ Getting There & Away

Mae Salong is accessible via two routes. The original road, Rte 1130, winds west from Ban Pasang. Newer Rte 1234 approaches from the south, allowing easier access from Chiang Mai. The older route is more spectacular.

To get to Mae Salong, take a *sŏrng·tăa·ou* or Mae Sai–bound bus from Chiang Rai to Ban Pasang (20B to 25B, 30 minutes, every 20 minutes from 6am to 8pm). From Ban Pasang, blue *sŏrng·tăa·ou* head up the mountain to Mae Salong when full (60B, one hour, from 6am to 5pm). To get back to Ban Pasang, *sŏrng·tăa·ou* park near Mae Salong's 7-Eleven. *Sŏrng·tăa·ou* stop running at around 5pm but you can charter one in either direction for about 500B.

You can also reach Mae Salong by road from Tha Ton, in Chiang Mai. Yellow *sŏrng·tăa·ou* bound for Tha Ton stop near Little Home Guesthouse at 8.20am, 10.20am, 12.20pm and 1.50pm (60B, one hour).

Mae Sai
แม่สาย

POP 22,000

At first glance, Thailand's northernmost town appears to be little more than a large open-air market. But Mae Sai serves as a convenient base for exploring the Golden Triangle, Doi Tung and Mae Salong, and its position across from Myanmar also makes it a jumping-off point for those wishing to explore some of the more remote parts of Shan State.

Because occasional fighting within Myanmar or disputes between the Thai and Myanmar governments can lead to the border being closed temporarily, it's always a good idea to check the current situation before travelling to Mae Sai.

◉ Sights

Wat Phra That Doi Wao   BUDDHIST TEMPLE
(วัดพระธาตุดอยเวา; Soi 1; ⊙ daylight hours) FREE
Take the steps up the hill near the border to Wat Phra That Doi Wao for superb views over Mae Sai and Myanmar. This *wát* was re-

portedly constructed in memory of a couple of thousand Burmese soldiers who died fighting the KMT here in 1965 (you'll hear differing stories around town, including a version wherein the KMT are the heroes).

🛏 Sleeping

Maesai Guest House   HOTEL $
(☎ 0 5373 2021; 688 Th Wiengpangkam; bungalows 200-600B; 🛜) This collection of A-frame bungalows ranges from simple rooms with shared cold-water showers to bungalows on the river with terraces and private bathrooms.

Yeesun Guesthouse   HOTEL $
(☎ 0 5373 3455; www.yeesunguesthouse.com; 816/13 Th Sailomjoy; r 400B; ❄🛜) This four-storey family-run hotel has great-value, if rather characterless, rooms with comfortable furniture and beds.

S-House Hotel   HOTEL $
(☎ 0 5373 3811; www.s-house-hotel-maesai.com; 384 Th Sailomjoy; r with fan/air-con 500/600B; ❄) At the end of the covered part of Th Sailomjoy, a short walk from the border crossing, this budget place has spacious rooms with balconies overlooking the hills.

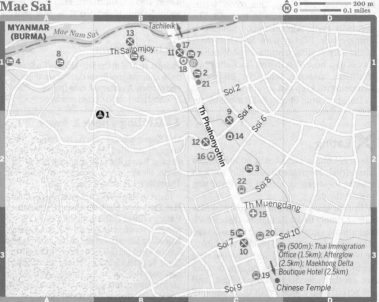

Mae Sai

Little Bear   HOTEL **$**
(☑ 053640933; www.littlebear-house.com; off Soi 6, Th Phahonyothin; r 280-480B; ❄@🛜) The basic but tidy rooms here are given a bit of life by the attached lobby that also functions as a bar-cafe.

Khanthongkham Hotel   HOTEL **$$**
(☑ 5373 4222; www.kthotel.com; 7 Th Phahonyothin; r incl breakfast 800-900B, ste incl breakfast 1200-1650B; ❄🛜) This hotel features huge rooms that have been tastefully decorated in light woods and brown cloths. Suites are exceptionally vast, and like all rooms have flat-screen TVs and spacious and inviting bathrooms. A downside is that many rooms don't have windows.

Afterglow   HOTEL **$$**
(☑ 0 5373 4188; www.afterglowhostel.com; 139/5 Th Phahonyothin; r incl breakfast 600-800B, bungalows incl breakfast 600B; ❄🛜) Boasting a ground-floor cafe and rooms with a minimalist feel, Afterglow is probably the hippest place to stay in Mae Sai. A new addition sees a few equally stylish bungalows out back. Inconveniently located about 4km from the border.

Maekhong Delta Boutique Hotel   HOTEL **$$**
(☑ 0 5364 2517; www.maekhonghotel.com; 230/5-6 Th Phahonyothin; r incl breakfast 900-1200B; ❄@🛜) It's an odd name, considering that the Mekong delta is way down in Vietnam. Odder still that the rooms here are somehow reminiscent of a ski lodge. Regardless, they're both modern and attractive, albeit nearly 4km from the centre of town.

Piyaporn Place Hotel   HOTEL **$$**
(☑ 0 5373 4511; www.piyaporn-place.com; 77/1 Th Phahonyothin; r incl breakfast 800B, ste incl breakfast 1800B; ❄@🛜) On the main road by Soi 7, this seven-storey business hotel is good value. The large, contemporary-styled rooms have wooden floors, a small sofa and the usual four-/five-star amenities like bathroom, cable TV and minibar.

Wang Thong Hotel   HOTEL **$$**
(☑ 0 5373 3389; wangthong_maesai@hotmail.com; 299 Th Phahonyothin; r incl breakfast 550-950B, ste incl breakfast 2500B; ❄@🛜⊠) The nine-storey Wang Thong is a comfortable business-class hotel located steps from the border crossing. The rooms are nothing special, but they're spacious and well equipped. Discounts available in the low season.

✖ Eating

An expansive **night market** (Th Phahonyothin; mains 30-60B; ⊙5-11pm) unfolds every evening along Th Phahonyothin. During the day, several **snack and drink vendors** (Th Phahonyothin; ⊙8am-5pm) can be found in front of the police station.

Bismillah Halal Food   MUSLIM-THAI **$**
(Soi 4, Th Phahonyothin; mains 30-60B; ⊙5am-5pm) This tiny restaurant does an excellent biryani, not to mention virtually everything else Muslim, from roti to samosa.

Sukhothai Cuisine   THAI **$**
(399/9 Th Sailomjoy; mains 30-40B; ⊙7am-4pm) This open-air restaurant serves the namesake noodles from Sukhothai, as well as satay and a few other basic dishes.

Kik Kok Restaurant   THAI $
(Th Phahonyothin; mains 30-120B; ⊘6am-8pm;
🖋) Kik Kok has a fat English-language
menu of Thai dishes, including several vegetarian options.

🛍 Shopping

Commerce is ubiquitous in Mae Sai, although most of the offerings are of little
interest to Western travellers. One particularly popular commodity is gems, and a walk
down Soi 4 will reveal several open-air **gem
dealers** (Soi 4, Th Phahonyothin) diligently
counting hundreds of tiny semiprecious
stones on the side of the street.

ℹ Information

There are several banks with ATMs near the
border.

Immigration Main Office (☑ 0 5373 1008;
Th Phahonyothin; ⊘8.30am-4.30pm Mon-Fri)
About 3km from the border, near Soi 17.

Immigration Border Office (Th Phahonyothin;
⊘6.30am-6.30pm) At the entrance to the
border bridge.

Internet Cafe (Th Phahonyothin; per hour 20B;
⊘8am-11pm) Behind the Wang Thong Hotel by
the car park.

Overbrook Clinic (☑0 5373 4422; 20/7 Th
Phahonyothin; ⊘8am-5pm) Connected to the
modern hospital in Chiang Rai, this small clinic
on the main road has doctors who can speak
English.

Tourist Police (☑115; Th Phahonyothin;
⊘8.30am-6pm) Has a booth in front of the
border crossing before immigration.

ℹ Getting There & Away

Mae Sai's **bus station** (☑0 5371 1224; Rte 110)
is 1.5km from the border; shared *sŏrng·tăa·ou*
ply the route between the bus station and a stop
on Soi 2, Th Phahonyothin (15B, five minutes,
from 6am to 9pm). Alternatively, it's a 50B motorcycle taxi ride to/from the stand at the corner
of Th Phahonyothin and Soi 4.

If you're headed to Bangkok, you can avoid
going all the way to the bus station by buying
your tickets at **Chok-Roong Tawee Tour** (☑0
5364 0123; near cnr Soi 9 & Th Phahonyothin, no
roman-script sign; ⊘8am-5.30pm) – it's near
Soi 9, Th Phahonyothin, next door to the motorcycle dealership.

TRANSPORT TO/FROM MAE SAI

DESTINATION	BUS	MINIVAN	SŎRNG·TĂA·OU
Bangkok	673-943B; 12hr; frequent 4-5.45pm		
Ban Huay Khrai (for Doi Tung)			25B; 35min; frequent 6.30am-5pm
Chiang Mai	182-364B; 5hr; 9 departures 6.15am-4.30pm		
Chiang Rai	39-69B; 1½hr; frequent 5.45am-6pm	46B; 1hr; frequent 6am-5.30pm	
Chiang Saen			50B; 1hr; frequent 8am-1pm
Fang	88B; 3hr; 7am		
Mae Sot	420-540B; 12hr; 6.15am & 6.45am		
Nakhon Ratchasima (Khorat)	707-825B; 15hr; 6 departures 5.15am-6pm		
Phayao	139-162B; 3hr; 6 departures 5.15am-6pm		
Phitsanulok	398-464B; 8hr; 6 departures 5.15am-6pm		
Phrae	257-300B; 5hr; 6 departures 5.15am-6pm		
Sop Ruak (Golden Triangle)			40B; 45min; frequent 8am-1pm
Tha Ton	74B; 2hr; 7am		

On Th Phahonyothin, by Soi 8, is a sign saying 'bus stop'; this is where you'll find the stop for *sŏrng·tăa·ou* bound for Sop Ruak and Chiang Saen. *Sŏrng·tăa·ou* to Ban Huay Khrai (the turn-off to Doi Tung) park at a stop (Th Phahonyothin) by Soi 10.

ⓘ Getting Around

Sŏrng·tăa·ou around town cost 15B. Motorcycle taxis cost 20B to 40B.

Motorcycles can be rented at **Pornchai** (☏ 0 5373 1136; 4/7 Th Phahonyothin, no roman-script sign; per day 250B; ⊗ 8am-5pm), located near Soi 9, Th Phahonyothin.

GETTING TO MYANMAR (BURMA): MAE SAI TO TACHILEIK

As of 2013, Tachileik is one of a handful of Myanmar's newly 'open' land borders for foreign tourists. But there are a few caveats in crossing here, and the following information is liable to change, so be sure to check the situation locally before you travel.

Getting to the Border The border and Thai immigration office are a short walk from most accommodation in Mae Sai.

At the Border The Thai immigration office is open from 6.30am to 6.30pm. After taking care of the usual formalities, cross the bridge and head to the Myanmar immigration office. If you've already procured a Myanmar visa, you'll be allowed to proceed by land to Kyaingtong (also known as Kengtung) or Mong La, or via air to other points in Myanmar.

If you haven't already obtained a Myanmar visa, it's relatively straightforward to cross to Tachileik for the day and slightly more complicated to get a two-week border pass to visit Kyaingtong and/or Mong La.

Day-trippers must pay a fee of 500B for a temporary ID card; your passport will be kept at the border. There is little to do in Tachileik apart from sample Burmese food and shop – the prices are about the same as on the Thai side and everyone accepts baht. There's an interesting morning market and it can be fun to hang about in the teashops.

Moving On If you'd like to visit Kyaingtong and/or Mong La, but haven't already received a Myanmar visa, proceed directly to the Myanmar Travels & Tours (MTT) office. There you'll need to inform the authorities exactly where you're headed, and you'll need three photos and US$10 or 500B to process a border pass valid for 14 days; your passport will be kept at the border ensuring that you return the way you came. It's also obligatory to hire a guide for the duration of your stay. Guides cost 1000B per day, and if you haven't already arranged for a Kyaingtong-based guide to meet you at the border, you'll be as-signed one by MTT and will also have to pay for your guide's food and accommodation during your stay. Recommended Kyaingtong-based guides include Leng (☏ +95 9490 31470; sairoctor.htunleng@gmail.com), **Freddie** (Sai Yot; ☏ +95 9490 31934; yotkham@gmail.com) and **Paul** (Sai Lon; ☏ +95 842 2812, +95 9490 30464).

Kyaingtong is a sleepy but historic capital for the Shan State's Khün culture – the Khün speak a northern Thai language related to Shan and Thai Lü, and use a writing script similar to the ancient Lanna script. Places to stay include the **Princess Hotel** (☏ +95 842 1319; kengtung@mail4u.com.mm; 21 Zaydankalay Rd; r incl breakfast $50; ❄) and the budget-oriented **Harry's Trekking House** (☏ +95 842 1418; harry.guesthouse@gmail.com; 132 Mai Yang Rd; r incl breakfast $7-20; ❄).

Mong La, on the Chinese border and under the control of the United Wa State Army, was formerly associated with the drug trade, casinos and prostitution. At press time, foreigners were not allowed to cross to China from Mong La. In Mong La, the **Kai Xuan Hotel** (☏ +86 691 556 8555; no roman-script sign; r Y220-260, ste Y580-680; ❄ @) is the town's least grubby accommodation option.

Buses bound for Kyaingtong (K10,000, five hours, 7.30am and 12.30pm) depart from Tachileik's bus station, which is 2km and a 20B *sŏrng·tăa·ou* ride or a 50B motorcycle taxi ride from the border. Alternatively, you can charter a taxi from the same station for about K50,000, or if you're willing to wait until it's full, get a front/back seat in a share taxi for K15,000/12,000.

There are no direct buses from Tachileik to Mong La.

For more details on Kyaingtong and Mong La, refer to Lonely Planet's *Myanmar (Burma)* guidebook.

Doi Tung ดอยตุง

About halfway between Mae Chan and Mae Sai on Rte 110 is the turn-off (west) for Doi Tung. The name means 'Flag Peak', from the northern Thai word for flag (*dung*). King Achutarat of Chiang Saen ordered a giant flag to be flown from the peak to mark the spot where two *chedi* were constructed in AD 911; the *chedi* are still there, and the site is a pilgrimage for Thai, Shan and Chinese Buddhists.

But Doi Tung's main attraction is the journey. The 'easy' way is via Rte 1149, which is mostly paved to the peak of Doi Tung. But it's winding, steep and narrow, so if you're driving or riding a motorcycle, take it slowly.

◉ Sights

Doi Tung Royal Villa   NOTABLE BUILDING
(☏ 0 5376 7011; www.doitung.org; admission 90B; ⊙ 7-11.40am & 12.30-5.30pm) On the theory that local hill tribes would be so honoured by a royal presence that they would stop cultivating opium, the late Princess Mother (the current king's mother) built the Doi Tung Royal Villa, a summer palace on the slopes of Doi Tung near Pa Kluay Reservoir, which is now open to the public as a museum.

The royal initiative also provided education on new agricultural methods to stop slash-and-burn practices. Opium has now been replaced by crops such as coffee, macadamia nuts and various fruits. The rest of the property, including the Mae Fah Luang Garden and **Mae Fah Luang Arboretum** (admission 90B; ⊙ 7am-5.30pm), is also open to the public. There is also a hotel, restaurant, coffee kiosk and craft shop up here. Near the parking lot, the Doi Tung Bazaar is a small open-air market with local agricultural products, prepared food and hill-tribe handicrafts. This entire complex is popular with bus tour groups.

Wat Phra That Doi Tung   BUDDHIST TEMPLE
(⊙ daylight hours) FREE At the peak, 1800m above sea level, Wat Phra That Doi Tung is built around the twin Lanna-style *chedi*. The *chedi* were renovated by Chiang Mai monk Khruba Siwichai, famous for his prodigious building projects, early in the 20th century.

Pilgrims bang on the usual row of temple bells to gain merit. Although the wát isn't that impressive, the forested setting will make the trip worthwhile. From the walled edge of the temple you can get an aerial view of the snaky road you've just climbed. A walking path next to the wát leads to a spring and there are other short walking trails in the vicinity.

A bit below the peak is the smaller **Wat Noi Doi Tung**, where food and beverages are available from vendors.

🛏 Sleeping & Eating

If you want to spend the night in the area, try **Ban Ton Nam 31** (☏ 0 5376 7015; www.doitung.org; r incl breakfast 2500-3000B; ✳ 🖎). Located near Doi Tung Royal Villa, it consists of 46 comfortable rooms that formerly served as the living quarters of the Princess Mother's staff. The more expensive rooms have better views. A self-service **restaurant** (dishes 80-250B; ⊙ 7am-9pm) offers meals made with local produce, and there's also a Doi Tung cafe.

ℹ Getting There & Away

To reach Doi Tung, it's necessary to charter a *sŏrng·tăa·ou* from Ban Huay Khrai (600B, 30 minutes, from 6am to 5pm).

Alternatively, if you've got your own wheels, you can travel 24km between Doi Tung and Mae Sai along the even more challenging sealed but narrow Rte 1149. From Doi Tung Royal Villa simply follow the signs to Wat Phra That Doi Tung. The road hugs the Thai–Myanmar border behind the large limestone mountains you may have seen from Rte 110, and emerges at Soi 7 in Mae Sai. There are at least three military checkpoints along the way, so be sure to bring ID.

If you want to do a full loop from Mae Sai, ride or drive via Rte 110 south of Mae Sai, then Rte 1149 up to Doi Tung. Once you've had a look around the summit, return to Mae Sai via aforementioned roads; this means you'll be travelling downhill much of the way.

If you're coming from Mae Salong, Rte 1334 weaves from steep hills to a lush valley, before climbing again to Rte 1149 and Doi Tung. The road is fully sealed and in good shape, although it can be quite steep and windy in parts.

Chiang Saen เชียงแสน
POP 11,000

The dictionary definition of a sleepy river town, Chiang Saen is the site of a former Thai kingdom thought to date back to as early as the 7th century. Scattered throughout the modern town are the ruins of this empire – surviving architecture includes several *chedi*, Buddha images, *wí·hăhn*

Chiang Saen

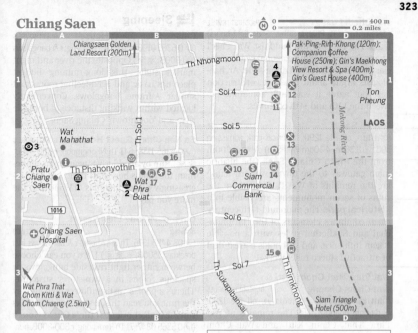

pillars and earthen city ramparts. Chiang Saen later became loosely affiliated with various northern Thai kingdoms, as well as 18th-century Myanmar, but didn't become a Siamese possession until the 1880s.

Today huge river barges from China moor at Chiang Saen, carrying fruit, engine parts and all manner of other imports, keeping the old China–Siam trade route open. Despite this trade, the town hasn't changed too much over the last decade, and because of this is a pleasanter base than nearby Sop Ruak.

Chiang Saen lies across the Mekong River from the Lao town of Ton Pheung, but only locals are allowed to cross here.

◉ Sights & Activities

Wat Phra That Pha Ngao   BUDDHIST TEMPLE
(วัดพระธาตุผาเงา; off Rte 1129; ☉ daylight hours)
FREE Located 3km south of town in the village of Sop Kham, this Buddhist temple complex contains a large prayer hall built to cover a partially excavated Chiang Saen-era Buddha statue. There is a beautiful golden teak *hŏr đrai* (manuscript depository) and a steep road leads to a hilltop pagoda and temple with views over the area and the Mekong River.

Chiang Saen

Wat Chedi Luang
BUDDHIST TEMPLE

(วัดเจดีย์หลวง; Th Phahonyothin; ⊙ daylight hours) FREE The ruins of the Buddhist Wat Chedi Luang feature an 18m octagonal *chedi* in the classic Chiang Saen or Lanna style. Archaeologists argue about its exact construction date but agree it was built sometime between the 12th and 14th centuries.

Wat Pa Sak
HISTORICAL SITE

(วัดป่าสัก; off Rte 1290; historical park admission 50B; ⊙ 8.30am-4.30pm Wed-Sun) About 200m from the **Pratu Chiang Saen** (the historic main gateway to the town's western flank) are the remains of Wat Pa Sak, where the ruins of seven monuments are visible in a historical park. The main mid-14th-century *chedi* combines elements of the Hariphunchai and Sukhothai styles with a possible Bagan influence, and still holds a great deal of attractive stucco relief work.

Wat Phra That Chom Kitti & Wat Chom Chaeng
BUDDHIST TEMPLES

(วัดพระธาตุจอมกิตติ / วัดจอมแจ้ง; off Rte 1290; ⊙ daylight hours) FREE The remains of Wat Phra That Chom Kitti and Wat Chom Chaeng can be found about 2.5km northwest of town on a hilltop. The round *chedi* of Wat Phra That Chom Kitti is thought to have been constructed before the founding of the kingdom.

Wat Pha Khao Pan
BUDDHIST TEMPLE

(วัดผ้าขาวป้าน; Th Rimkhong; ⊙ daylight hrs) FREE Inside the grounds of this living *wát* near the river stands a magnificent Lanna-period *chedi*. The large square base contains Lanna-style walking Buddhas in niches on all four sides. The Buddha facing east is sculpted in the *mudra* ('calling for rain') pose, with both hands held pointing down at the image's sides – a pose common in Laos but not so common in Thailand.

Chiang Saen National Museum
MUSEUM

(พิพิธภัณฑสถานแห่งชาติเชียงแสน; 702 Th Phahonyothin; admission 100B; ⊙ 8.30am-4.30pm Wed-Sun) This museum is a great source of local information considering its relatively small size.

Mekong River Trips
RIVER CRUISE

(Th Rimkhong; ⊙ 8am-3pm) Five-passenger speedboats leave from the waterfront jetty to Sop Ruak (per boat one way/return 500/600B, one hour), or all the way to Chiang Khong (per boat one way/return 2500/3000B, 1½ hours).

🛏 Sleeping

Chiang Saen Guest House
GUESTHOUSE $

(☑ 0 5365 0196; 45/2 Th Rimkhong; r & bungalows 100-500B; ❄ 🛜) Opposite the river and night market stalls, this long-running budget place has basic and aged-feeling rooms and similar A-frame bungalows. Conveniently located within walking distance of both the river and 'downtown' Chiang Saen.

Sa Nae Charn Guest House
GUESTHOUSE $

(☑ 0 5365 1138; 641 Th Nhongmoon; r 300-450B; ❄ 🛜) Run by an elderly Singaporean gentleman, the rooms here start basic, but have increasingly nicer amenities (TV, air-con) the more you pay.

Gin's Maekhong View Resort & Spa
HOTEL $$

(☑ 08 4485 1376; Th Rimkhong; r & bungalows incl breakfast 1500B; ❄ 🛜 🏊) Here you can choose between rather tight riverside bungalows or spacious rooms in a two-storey structure. There's a pool, a vast sunflower field and, by the time you read this, a spa. The same folks run the budget-oriented **Gin's Guest House** (☑ 0 5365 0847; 71 Th Rimkhong; r 300-800B, bungalows 500B; ❄ 🛜), just across the road. Gin's is located about 1km north of the centre of Chiang Saen, near the reconstructed city walls.

Pak-Ping-Rim-Khong
GUESTHOUSE $$

(☑ 0 5365 0151; www.facebook.com/pakpingrimkhong; 484 Th Rimkhong; r incl breakfast 800-1400B; ❄ 🛜) A new and tidy villa compound just north of town. Rooms feel spacious and come equipped with air-con, TV and fridge.

Chiengsaen Golden Land Resort
HOTEL $$

(☑ 0 5365 1100; www.chengsanresort.com; 663 Th Sai 1; r incl breakfast 800B, bungalows incl breakfast 1200-2000B; ❄ 🛜 🏊) At this resort-feeling hotel you can choose from large well-equipped rooms in a two-storey building or several attractive wooden bungalows surrounding a garden and a covered swimming pool. There is another branch with 10 similarly priced bungalows in the village of Sop Kham, 3km south along the Mekong.

Viang Yonok
GUESTHOUSE $$$

(☑ 0 5365 0444; www.viangyonok.com; off Rte 1016; bungalows incl breakfast 2400-2950B; ❄ @ 🛜 🏊) The emphasis at this well-manicured compound of seven comfortable, modern bungalows is activities, and if a swimming pool, sauna, weight room, bicycles, kayaks and birdwatching aren't enough, well, you're a pretty tough customer. Viang Yonok is approximately 5km west of Chiang Saen; follow the yellow signs that appear about 1km after the Esso station.

Siam Triangle Hotel HOTEL $$$
(☑ 0 5365 1115; www.siamtriangle.com; 267 Th Rimkhong; r incl breakfast 1800-3000B; ste incl breakfast 6000B; ✿@🕿🏊) Chiang Saen's newest and biggest hotel lacks charm, but the gigantic suites with river-view hot tubs are pretty impressive. The hotel is just outside Chiang Saen, about 400m south of the former city wall.

🍴 Eating & Drinking

Cheap noodle and rice dishes are available at **food stalls** (Th Phahonyothin; mains 30-60B) near the bus stop. Come nightfall, **evening food vendors** (Th Phahonyothin; mains 30-60B; ⏰4-10pm) set up just west of here. Every Saturday evening, a section of Th Rimkhong is closed to vehicle traffic for the busy **Walking Street** (Th Rimkhong; mains 20-60B; ⏰4-9pm Sat), which has lots of food.

Riverside Food Vendors THAI $
(Th Rimkhong; mains 30-60B; ⏰4-11pm) During the dry months, riverside vendors set up mats and sell rustic food such as fish or chicken barbecued inside thick joints of bamboo, along with sticky rice and *sôm·dam* (spicy green papaya salad).

Jinda's Kitchen NORTHERN THAI $
(Rte 1290; mains 25-99B; ⏰8am-9pm) This home-bound roadside restaurant has been serving up local dishes for more than 50 years. Jinda's Kitchen is roughly halfway between Chiang Saen and Sop Ruak.

Kiaw Siang Hai CHINESE $$
(44 Th Rimkhong, no roman-script sign; mains 50-200B; ⏰8am-8pm) Serving the workers of Chinese boats that dock at Chiang Saen, this authentic Chinese restaurant prepares a huge menu of dishes in addition to the namesake noodles. Try the spicy Sichuan-style fried tofu or one of the Chinese herbal soups. The restaurant can be identified by the giant ceramic jars out front.

2 be 1 BAR
(Th Rimkhong; ⏰5.30pm-midnight) By the river is this tiny bar with indoor and outdoor seating and a pool table.

ℹ️ Information

Chiang Saen Hospital (☑ 0 5377 7017; Rte 1016) Government hospital just south of Wat Pa Sak.
Companion Coffee House (Th Rimkhong; ⏰8am-7pm; 🕿) This coffee shop also has a computer and wi-fi. Located north of town near Soi 2.
Visitors Centre (☑ 0 5377 7084; Th Phahonyothin; ⏰8.30am-4.30pm Mon-Sat) Has a good relief display showing the major ruin sites as well as photos of various *chedi* before, during and after restoration.

ℹ️ Getting There & Away

Blue *sŏrng·tǎa·ou* bound for Sop Ruak (20B) and Mae Sai (50B) wait at a stall (Th Phahonyothin) at the eastern end of Th Phahonyothin from 7.20am to noon. The green *sŏrng·tǎa·ou* bound for Chiang Khong park at a stall (Th Rimkhong) on Th Rimkhong, south of the riverside immigration office, from 9am to noon (80B, two hours). This trip involves a transfer in Ban Hat Bai, and after noon it's only possible to charter the entire vehicle, which costs 1000B.

ℹ️ DAY BOAT TO JINGHONG (CHINA)

It was previously possible to take a passenger boat along the Mekong River from Chiang Saen to Jinghong in China's Xishuangbanna, a trip of 15 hours when conditions are right. However, this service was halted in 2011, when a violent shooting incident led to the death of 13 Chinese sailors.

If reinstated, boats usually depart from Chiang Saen on Monday, Wednesday and Friday at 5am, but this is not set in stone and it's important to call ahead before you make plans. During the drier months (typically March to May) boats don't run, as rocks and shallows can hamper the way.

To do this trip you must already have your visa for China – several guesthouses in town can arrange this for you, but it's quicker to arrange from Chiang Mai or Bangkok. If you already have a visa, tickets can be arranged through **Chiang Saen Tour and Travel** (☑ 08 1993 2425; 64 Th Rimkhong; ⏰9am-7pm) or **Maekhong Delta Travel** (☑ 0 5364 2517; www.maekhongtravel.com; Maekhong Delta Boutique Hotel, 230/5-6 Th Phaholyothin; one way 3500B or Y820; ⏰9am-5pm), the latter in Mae Sai.

Chiang Saen has no proper bus terminal, rather there is a covered bus shelter at the eastern end of Th Phahonyothin where buses pick up and drop off passengers. From this stop there are frequent buses to Chiang Rai (37B, 1½ hours, from 5.30am to 5.30pm) and a daily bus to Chiang Mai (232B, five hours, 9am).

Sombat Tour (☑ 08 1595 4616; Th Phahonyothin; ⊙ 8am-5.30pm) operates two daily VIP buses to Bangkok (999B, 12 hours, 5pm and 5.30pm), departing from a small office adjacent to Krung Thai Bank.

ⓘ Getting Around

Motorbike taxis will do short trips around town for 20B. They congregate near and across from the bus stop.

A good way to see the Chiang Saen area is on two wheels. Mountain bikes and motorcycles can be rented at a **motorcycle hire** shop (☑ 08 9429 5798; 247/1 Th Phahonyothin, no roman-script sign; per 24hr bike/motorcycle 80/200B; ⊙ 8am-7pm) shop near a barber shop on Th Phahonyothin, and **Angpao Chiangsaen Tour** (☑ 0 5365 0143; www.angpaotour.com; 121/2 Th Phahonyothin; motorcycle per 24hr 200B; ⊙ 8am-5pm). The latter can also provide a vehicle with driver and conducts a variety of local tours.

Sop Ruak   สบรวก

The borders of Myanmar, Thailand and Laos meet at Sop Ruak, the so-called centre of the Golden Triangle, at the confluence of Nam Ruak and the Mekong River. The town's two opium-related museums, the House of Opium and Hall of Opium, are both worth a visit, and a boat trip is an enjoyable way to pass an hour. But the only reason to overnight here is if you've already booked a room in one of the area's outstanding luxury hotels.

⊙ Sights & Activities

Hall of Opium   MUSEUM
(หอฝิ่น; Rte 1290; admission 200B; ⊙ 8.30am-4pm Tue-Sun) One kilometre north of Sop Ruak on a 40-hectare plot opposite the Anantara Golden Triangle Resort & Spa, the Mae Fah Luang Foundation has established the 5600-sq-metre Hall of Opium. The multimedia exhibitions include a fascinating history of opium, as well as engaging and informative displays on the effects of abuse on individuals and society. Well balanced and worth seeing.

House of Opium   MUSEUM
(บ้านฝิ่น; www.houseofopium.com; Rte 1290; admission 50B; ⊙ 7am-7pm) This small museum

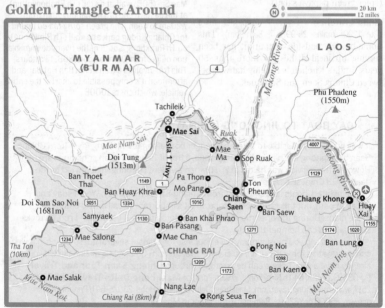

Golden Triangle & Around

20 km
12 miles

with historical displays pertaining to opium culture is worth a peek. Exhibits include all the various implements used in the planting, harvest, use and trade of the *Papaver somniferum* resin, including pipes, weights, scales and so on, plus photos and maps with labels in English. The museum is at the southeastern end of Sop Ruak, virtually across from Phra Chiang Saen Si Phaendin.

Phra Chiang Saen Si Phaendin
BUDDHIST TEMPLE

(พระเชียงแสนสี่แผ่นดิน; Rte 1290; ⊙7am-9pm) FREE The first sight you'll inevitably see in Sop Ruak is Phra Chiang Saen Si Phaendin, a giant Buddha statue financed by a Thai-Chinese foundation. The statue straddles a boat-like platform, and visitors are encouraged to donate by rolling coins from an elevated platform behind the statue.

Wat Prathat Pukhao
BUDDHIST TEMPLE

(วัดพระธาตุภูเข้า; Rte 1290; ⊙daylight hours) FREE Next to the House of Opium are some steps up to the Buddhist Wat Prathat Pukhao, from where you get the best viewpoint of the Mekong meeting of Laos, Myanmar and Thailand.

Mekong River Cruises
RIVER CRUISE

(1hr cruise max 5 people per boat 400B; ⊙6am-6pm) Long-tail boat trips on the Mekong River can be arranged at one of various piers. The typical trip involves a circuit upriver for a view of Myanmar's casino hotel and a stop at the Lao island of **Don Sao**, roughly halfway between Sop Ruak and Chiang Saen. Upon arrival in Laos, a 30B tax is collected from each visitor.

🍴 Sleeping & Eating

The only reason to stay in or around Sop Ruak is to take advantage of some of northern Thailand's best upscale lodgings; those on a budget are advised to go to Chiang Saen. There are several tourist-oriented restaurants overlooking the Mekong River.

Four Seasons Tented Camp
HOTEL $$$

(☑0 5391 0200; www.fourseasons.com; tents per night, all-inclusive 79,000-89,000B; ❄@🛰🏊) If you can fit it into your schedule (and budget), this safari-inspired resort is among the most truly unique accommodation experiences in Thailand. The 'tents' are appropriately luxurious and decked out in colonial-era safari paraphernalia. A minimum stay of at least two nights is required, and guests take part in daily activities ranging from mahout training to spa treatment.

Anantara Golden Triangle Resort & Spa
HOTEL $$$

(☑0 5378 4084; www.anantara.com; Rte 1290; r & ste per night all-inclusive 36,500-44,000B; ❄@🛰🏊) This award-winning resort takes up a large patch of beautifully landscaped ground directly opposite the Hall of Opium. The rooms combine Thai and international themes, and all have balconies looking over the Mekong River. Squash and tennis courts, gym, sauna and spa round out the luxury amenities, and activities, ranging from elephant training to cooking courses, are included in most packages.

ℹ️ Getting There & Away

There are frequent *sŏrng·tǎa·ou* to Chiang Saen (20B, from 7am to noon) and Mae Sai (45B, every 40 minutes from 8am to 1pm), both of which can be flagged down along the main strip. Minivans to Chiang Rai (50B, one hour, hourly from 6am to 5pm) wait in the parking lot west of Phra Chiang Saen Si Phaendin. It's an easy bicycle ride of 9km from Chiang Saen to Sop Ruak.

Chiang Khong
เชียงของ

POP 12,000

More remote yet livelier than its neighbour Chiang Saen, Chiang Khong is historically an important market town for local hill tribes and for trade with northern Laos. At one time the city was part of a small *meu·ang* (city-state) called Juon, founded in AD 701 by King Mahathai. Over the centuries Juon paid tribute to Chiang Rai, then Chiang Saen and finally Nan before being occupied by the Siamese in the 1880s. The territory of Chiang Khong extended all the way to Yunnan Province in China until the French turned much of the Mekong's northern bank into French Indochina in 1893.

Today, the riverside town is a popular travellers' gateway into Laos. At press time, crossing to Laos was still done by boat, but a bridge over Mae Nam Khong was set to open in December 2013, which will inevitably facilitate transport links to Laos and China. From Huay Xai, on the opposite side of the Mekong, it's a two-day slow boat trip to Luang Prabang. And for those who have set their sights even further, Huay Xai is only an eight-hour bus ride from Boten, a border crossing to and from China.

Chiang Khong

🛏 Sleeping

The vast majority of accommodation in Chiang Khong is geared towards the budget market.

🛏 In Town

PP Home
GUESTHOUSE $

(Baan Pak Pon; ☎ 0 5365 5092; baanpakpon@hotmail.co.th; off Th Sai Klang; r 350-600B; ❄ @ 🖤) One of a dwindling number of accommodation options still owned by locals, this rambling wooden house features large rooms with wood panelling and a couple of new rooms in an adjacent cement add-on.

Ban Tammila
HOTEL $

(☎ 0 5379 1234; www.baantammila.com; 113 Th Sai Klang; r & bungalows 400-650B; ❄ 🖤) Although the exterior looks a bit ragged, the rooms and bungalows here are neat and decorated in warm colours. A new addition sees rooms with wide balconies and hammocks; room

12 in particular has breezy views over to Laos.

Baan-Fai Guest House
GUESTHOUSE $

(☎ 0 5379 1394; 108 Th Sai Klang; r 150-700B; ❄ 🖤) A recent renovation has this inviting wooden house looking better than ever. The six rooms in the main structure are new and have air-con, while the original fan rooms are still awaiting an update.

Funky Box
HOSTEL $

(☎ 08 2765 1839; Soi 2, Th Sai Klang; dm 100; ❄ 🖤) In addition to 16 dorm beds, this new and lively hostel also has a bicycle-themed pub and museum.

Rimnaum Guest House
HOTEL $

(☎ 0 5365 5680; abu_bumpbump@sanook.com; off Th Sai Klang; r 350-500B; ❄ 🖤) This riverside place unites 20 mostly identical, spacious and clean budget rooms, the more expensive of which have air-con.

Chiang Khong Green Inn HOTEL $
(☑ 0 5379 1009; www.chiangkhong-greeninn.com; 89/4 Th Sai Klang; r 200-500B; ❋ @ 🛜) The cheaper rooms in this modern-feeling backpacker joint are tight, fan-cooled and share bathrooms, but the rooms with air-con have a bit more legroom and TVs.

Portside Hotel HOTEL $
(☑ 0 5365 5238; portsidehotel@hotmail.com; 546 Th Sai Klang; r with fan/air-con 300/500B; ❋ 🛜) This good-value hotel features two floors of tidy but cramped rooms. The rooms can't claim river views, but a communal rooftop area makes up for this.

THE GOLDEN TRIANGLE, YESTERDAY & TODAY

In historical terms, the Golden Triangle refers to an area stretching thousands of square kilometres into Myanmar, Laos and Thailand, within which the opium trade was once prevalent. From the early 20th century to the 1980s, the Golden Triangle was the world's biggest grower of *Papaver somniferum*, the poppy that produces opium. Poverty and lack of infrastructure and governance in the largely rebel-controlled areas meant that growing poppies and transporting opium proceeded virtually unchecked, eventually making its way around the world as refined heroin.

Undoubtedly the single most significant player in the Golden Triangle drug trade was Khun Sa, a Shan-Chinese warlord dubbed the 'Opium King' by the press. Starting in the mid-1970s from his headquarters in Chiang Rai Province, Khun Sa, his Shan United Army (SUA), ex-Kuomintang (KMT; Chinese Nationalist Party) fighters in Mae Salong and other cohorts in the region formed a partnership that would eventually claim a virtual monopoly of the world's opium trade.

In 1988, after having been the victim of two unsuccessful assassination attempts, Khun Sa offered to sell his entire crop of opium to the Australian government for AUS$50 million a year, claiming that this would essentially end the world's entire illegal trade in heroin. He made a similar offer to the US, but was dismissed by both. With a US Drug Enforcement Authority (DEA) bounty of US$2 million on his head, in 1996 Khun Sa surrendered to Burmese officials. They refused to extradite him to the US, and Khun Sa eventually died in Yangon in 2007.

Khun Sa's surrender seemed to be the last nail in the coffin of the Golden Triangle opium trade – land dedicated to poppy cultivation in the region hit an all time low in 1998 – and since the early 21st century, Afghanistan's Golden Crescent has replaced the region as the world's preeminent producer of opium. But a recent report by the United Nations Office on Drugs and Crime claims that the trade has yet again spiked – most likely due to increased demand from China – and in 2012 Myanmar alone was thought to have produced 10% of the world's opium.

However, most agree that the contemporary Golden Triangle drug trade has shifted from opium to methamphetamines. Manufactured in Myanmar in factories with alleged links to the United Wa State Army, the drug, known in Thai as *yah bâh* (crazy drug) has become the new scourge of the region, and footage of tweaked-out users holding hostages was a Thai news staple in the early 2000s. Although recent efforts to eradicate methamphetamines by Thai authorities have led to higher prices, trafficking and use are thought to have increased.

The area's opium days are (mostly) long gone, but hoteliers and tour operators in Chiang Rai have been quick to cash in on the name by rebranding the tiny village of Sop Ruak as 'the Golden Triangle'. The name is undoubtedly meant to conjure up images of illicit adventure, exotic border areas and opium caravans, but these days the only caravan you're likely to see is the endless parade of buses carrying package tourists. Sop Ruak's opium is fully relegated to museums, and even the once beautiful natural setting has largely been obscured by ATMs, stalls selling tourist tat and the seemingly never-ending loud announcements from the various temples. And perhaps most tellingly, Khun Sa's formerly impenetrable headquarters in Ban Thoet Thai are today a low-key tourist attraction.

THE MEKONG'S GIANT CATFISH

The Mekong River stretch that passes Chiang Khong is a traditional habitat for the *blah bèuk* (giant Mekong catfish, *Pangasianodon gigas* to ichthyologists), among the largest freshwater fish in the world. A *blah bèuk* takes at least six and possibly 12 years (no one's really sure) to reach full size, when it will measure 2m to 3m in length and weigh up to 300kg. Although the adult fish have only been found in certain stretches of the Mekong, it's thought that the fish originate in China's Qinghai Province (where the river originates) on the Tibetan Plateau and swim all the way to the middle Mekong, where they spend much of their adult lives.

In Thailand and Laos the mild-tasting flesh is revered as a delicacy, and the fish are taken between late April and June when the river depth is just 3m to 4m and the fish are swimming upriver. Ban Hat Khrai, 1.5km from Chiang Khong, is famous as being one of the few places where *blah bèuk* are still occasionally caught. Before netting them, Thai and Lao fishermen hold a special annual ceremony to propitiate Chao Mae Pla Beuk, a female deity thought to preside over the giant catfish. Among the rituals comprising the ceremony are chicken sacrifices performed aboard the fishing boats. After the ceremony is completed, fishing teams draw lots to see who casts the first net, and then take turns casting.

In recent years only a few catfish have been captured in a typical season (some years have resulted in no catches at all). The catfish hunters' guild is limited to natives of Ban Hat Khrai, and the fishermen sell the meat on the spot for up to 500B or more per kilo (a single fish can bring 100,000B in Bangkok); most of it ends up in Bangkok, since local restaurants in Huay Xai and Chiang Khong can't afford such prices.

Although the *blah bèuk* is on the Convention on International Trade in Endangered Species (CITES) list of endangered species, there is some debate as to just how endangered it is. Because of the danger of extinction, in 1983 Thailand's Inland Fisheries Department developed a program to breed the fish in captivity. Every time a female was caught, it was kept alive until a male was netted, then the eggs were removed (by massaging the female's ovaries) and put into a pan; the male was then milked for sperm and the eggs fertilised in the pan. The program was largely unsuccessful until 2001 when 70,000 hatchlings survived. The fish were distributed to fishery centres elsewhere in the country, some of which have had moderate success breeding the fish, mostly in ponds in the central Thai province of Suphanburi. Because of this, *blah bèuk* is again being seen on menus around the country.

At the moment the greatest threats to the wild Mekong catfish's survival are dams: there are three in existence and eight more proposed along the Mekong River, posing potential obstacles to the fish's migration. Another threat is the blasting of Mekong River rapids in China, done to allow the passage of large ships, which is robbing the fish of important breeding grounds.

Boom House HOTEL $
(☑ 0 5365 5136; 406/1 Th Sai Klang; dm 100B, r 250-400B; ❄ ☎) This multilevel place has a spread of plain but tidy rooms, the more expensive of which have air-con, TV and fridge.

River House HOTEL $$
(☑ 0 5379 2022; theriverhouse_chiangkhong@ hotmail.com; 419 Th Sai Klang; dm 150B, r 300-800B; ❄ @ ☎) This homey white house overlooking the Mekong River represents a great budget/midrange choice. The cheaper rooms are small, fan-cooled and share bathrooms, while the more expensive rooms are spacious and come equipped with air-con, fridge, TV and balcony.

Namkhong Riverside Hotel HOTEL $$
(☑ 0 5379 1796; www.namkhongriverside.com; 174-176 Th Sai Klang; r incl breakfast 1000B; ❄ @ ☎) This modern and popular three-storey hotel holds heaps of clean, neat rooms, most with private balconies overlooking the river. It's a great midrange catch, the only downside being the noise from nightly karaoke parties.

Chiang Khong Teak Garden Hotel HOTEL $$$
(☑ 0 5379 2008; www.chiangkhongteakgarden. com; 666 Th Sai Klang; r incl breakfast 1500-1800B; ❄ @ ☎) The modern duplex bungalows at

Chiang Khong's newest, most expensive digs are well outfitted and cosy, if somewhat sterile. The price depends on garden or river view.

Outside of Town

Baanrimtaling GUESTHOUSE $
(☑ 0 5379 1613; maleewan_th@yahoo.com; 99/2 Soi 19, Th Sai Klang; dm 100-120B; r 150-450B; @ 🛜) The rooms here are pretty run-of-the-mill for this price range, and the location isn't exactly ideal, but the homelike atmosphere and gentle service may have you staying a bit longer than you planned.

Rai Saeng Arun RESORT $$$
(☑ 08 1900 4300, 0 5391 8255; www.raisaengarun. com; Rte 4007; bungalows incl breakfast 3900B; ❄ 🛜) Located 22km from Chiang Khong on Rte 4007, which leads to Chiang Saen, this beautiful resort brings together 14 bungalows in a rural setting adjacent to the Mekong River. All are stylish and comfortable, feature balconies and open-air showers, and are connected by bridged walkways over rice fields. Considerable discounts are available during the low season.

Eating & Drinking

On Wednesdays and Saturdays during the tourist season (approximately November to May), Chiang Khong's main drag hosts a **Walking Street** (Th Sai Klang; mains 30-60B; ⊙ 6-10pm Wed & Sat, Nov-May), which has a decent selection of local eats.

Khao Soi Pa Orn NORTHERN THAI $
(Soi 6, Th Sai Klang, no roman-script sign; mains 15-30B; ⊙ 8am-4pm) You may think you know *kôw soy*, the famous northern curry noodle soup, but the version served in Chiang Khong forgoes the coconut milk and replaces it with a rich minced pork and tomato mixture.

Nangnuan THAI $
(Ban Hat Khrai; mains 30-150B; ⊙ 8am-9pm) Freshwater fish from the Mekong is the emphasis here, and it's prepared in a variety of ways, as the extensive English-language menu describes.

Baan Pheung Rim Khong THAI $
(Ban Hat Khrai, no roman-script sign; mains 40-150B; ⊙ 10am-10pm) A scruffy but tasty riverside shack where locals go to eat fish-based dishes. Located at the end of the road that leads to Ban Hat Khrai, about 1km south of town.

Bamboo Mexican House INTERNATIONAL $$
(Th Sai Klang; mains 70-250B; ⊙ 7.30am-8.30pm; 🖋) Run by the manager of a now-defunct guesthouse, where the chef of this tiny restaurant and bakery learned to make Mexican dishes from her American and Mexican guests. To be honest, though, we never got past the coffee and delicious homemade breads and cakes. Opens early, and boxed lunches can be assembled for the boat ride to Luang Prabang.

Hub BAR
(Soi 2, Th Sai Klang; ⊙ noon-midnight) After cycling around the world in record time, Brit Alan Bate decided to plant roots in Chiang Khong and opened this fun cycling-themed pub. If cheap beer isn't enough to hold your interest, the compound also includes a small **museum** (⊙ noon-10pm) FREE dedicated to bicycles and cycling.

ℹ Information

A handful of banks along Th Sai Klang have ATMs and foreign-exchange services.

BUSES TO/FROM CHIANG KHONG

Chiang Khong has no central bus terminal; buses pick up and drop off passengers at various points near the market, south of the centre of town. If you're bound for Bangkok, arrive at the stop at least 30 minutes early or buy tickets in advance from the office or from Easy Trip. The daily *sŏrng·tăa·ou* bound for Chiang Saen (80B, two hours, 8.30am), which involves a brief transfer in Ban Hat Bai, also departs from a stall in this area.

DESTINATION	PRICE (B)	DURATION (HR)	DEPARTURES
Bangkok	688-963	14	several buses between 3pm and 4pm
Chiang Mai	144-288	3	frequent 8am-5.30pm
Chiang Rai	65	2½	half-hourly 4.30am-3.45pm
Phayao	122	3	7.15am & 10.30am

GETTING TO LAOS: CHIANG KHONG TO HUAY XAI

Chiang Khong is a convenient and popular crossing point to Laos. At press time, work was nearly finished on a bridge over the Mekong River, which will inevitably change some of the details below.

Getting to the Border The jumping-off point is Tha Bak, a 1km, 30B sǎhm·lór (three-wheeled pedicab)or motorcycle ride from Chiang Khong's bus stops.

At the Border The Thai immigration office (✆0 5379 1332) is open from 8am to 4pm.

Long-tail boats crossing the Mekong River to Huay Xai leave frequently from 8am to 5pm (40B). A vehicle ferry also crosses a few times daily between the main Thai immigration point and the slow-boat landing in Huay Xai, costing 500B for motorcycles and 1000B for cars.

Foreigners can purchase a 30-day visa for Laos upon arrival in Huay Xai for US$30 to US$42, depending on nationality. There is an extra US$1 charge after 4pm and on weekends, and if you don't have a passport-style mugshot they'll charge 40B extra. On your return to Thailand, unless you've already received a Thai visa, immigration grant you permission to stay in the country for 15 days.

Moving On Once on the Lao side, bus destinations from Huay Xai include Luang Nam Tha (350B, 4½ hours, 9am and 12.30pm), Luang Prabang (700B to 900B, 12 hours, 2pm and 5pm), Udomxai (500B to 700B, nine hours, 3pm) and Vientiane (1800B, 24 hours, 3pm).

If time is on your side, the daily slow boat (950B, 10.30am) to Luang Prabang takes two days, including a night in the village of Pak Beng. Avoid the noisy fast boats (1600B, six to seven hours, frequent from 9am to 11am) as there have been reports of bad accidents. Booking tickets through a Chiang Khong–based agent such as Easy Trip costs slightly more, but they arrange tickets for you and provide transport from your guest-house and across the Mekong River, as well as a boxed lunch for the boat ride.

Lao Airlines (✆local +856 8421 1026, nationwide +856 2121 2051; www.laoairlines.com) operates a flight from Huay Xai to Vientiane every Wednesday for US$100.

If you already hold a Chinese visa, it's also possible to go directly to China from Chiang Khong. After obtaining a 30-day Lao visa on arrival in Huay Xai, simply board one of the buses bound for Mengla (1900B, eight hours, 10am from Monday to Saturday) or Kunming (2500B, 18 hours, 10am from Monday to Saturday), which are both in China's Yunnan Province.

Easy Trip (✆0 5365 5174, 08 6997 7246; www.discoverylaos.com; 183 Th Sai Klang; ⊙8.30am-6pm) This professional travel agency organises boats and buses to Laos, as well as private minivans to destinations in northern Thailand and flights in Thailand and to Laos.

Internet (Th Sai Klang; per hour 30B; ⊙10am-10pm) On the main street roughly across from Bamboo Mexican House.

ℹ Getting Around

A sǎhm·lór or motorcycle between the bus station and Tha Reua Bak, the border crossing to Laos, costs 30B.

PHAYAO PROVINCE

Phayao
พะเยา

POP 20,000

Few people, including many Thais, are aware of this quiet but attractive northern city. Perhaps in an overzealous effort to remedy this, a tourist brochure we came across described Phayao as 'the Vienna of South East Asia'. Although this is just *slightly* stretching the truth, Phayao is certainly one of the pleasanter towns in northern Thailand. Its setting on Kwan Phayao, a vast wetland, gives the town a back-to-nature feel that's utterly lacking in most Thai cities, and the tree-lined streets, temples and old wooden houses of 'downtown' Phayao provide a pleasing old-school Thai touch.

The little-visited town is the perfect place to break up your journey to/from Chiang Rai, and can also serve as a bookend to our suggested driving trip (see the boxed text) from Chiang Khong.

Sights & Activities

★ **Kwan Phayao**   LANDMARK
(กว๊านพะเยา; Th Chaykawan) This vast body of water is the largest swamp in northern Thailand and a symbol of Phayao. Although naturally occurring, the water level is artificially controlled, otherwise the wetlands would tend to go dry outside of the wet season. Framed by mountains, the swamp is in fact more scenic than the name suggests, and is the setting for what must be among the most beautiful sunsets in Thailand.

Rowing crews can be seen practising in the evenings, and there's a pier at the southern end of Th Chai Kwan where there are **boat rides** (per person 20B; ⏱8am-6pm) to what remains of **Wat Tiloke Aram**, a submerged 500-year-old temple. There are ambitious plans to rebuild the temple, one of many submerged religious structures in Kwan Phayao.

In addition to lost Buddhist artefacts, there are at least 50 types of fish native to these waters, and there's a **small fish breeding area** where for 5B you can feed the fish.

Wat Sri Khom Kham   BUDDHIST TEMPLE
(วัดศรีโคมคำ; Th Chaykawan; ⏱daylight hours) FREE Phayao's most important temple is thought to date back to 1491, but its present structure was finished in 1923. The immense prayer hall holds the Phra Jao Ton Luang, the largest Chiang Saen–era Buddha statue in the country. Standing 18m high, legend has it that the construction of the statue took more than 30 years. It's not the most beautiful or well-proportioned Buddha image in Thailand, but it certainly is impressive.

The ordination hall that is elevated over Kwan Phayao features graceful modern wall paintings. Also on the grounds of the wát is a Buddhist sculpture garden that includes gory, larger-than-life depictions of Buddhist hell.

The temple is about 2km from the northern end of Th Chaykawan.

OFF THE BEATEN TRACK

THE LONG WAY TO PHAYAO

If you're in Chiang Khong and happen to have your own wheels, we have an excellent suggestion for a drive. Rtes 1155 and 1093 are among Thailand's most dramatic roads, hugging steep mountainsides along the Thailand–Laos border and passing waterfalls, incredible vistas and national parks. If you need a destination you can continue all the way to Phayao, a little-visited town with ample accommodation and good food.

From Chiang Khong, the trip is as straightforward as heading south on Rte 1020 and following the signs to **Phu Chi Fa**, a national park near the Lao border. The signs are surprisingly clear for Thailand, but a good companion is the *Golden Triangle* map produced by **Golden Triangle Rider** (GT Rider; www.gt-rider.com).

At the mountaintop village of Doi Pha Tang, consider a quick detour to **Pratu Siam** (1653m), one of Thailand's most impressive viewpoints. There is basic lodging and food here.

Rte 1093 narrows and the roadside becomes markedly less populated as you approach Phu Chi Fa, a mountaintop that offers high-altitude views into Laos. There are a few different ways to approach the peak, the most popular being via Ban Rom Fah Thai. There is a variety of accommodation and some basic restaurants on either side of Phu Chi Fa.

Upon passing Phu Chi Fa, stay on Rte 1093 and follow the signs to **Ban Huak**. This is a picturesque village in Phayao Province, 2km from the Lao border. There's a border market on the 10th and 30th of every month, and homestay-style accommodation in the town, and nearby **Nam Tok Phu Sang** is a unique waterfall of thermally heated water.

From Ban Huak, follow signs to Chiang Kham, then take Rte 1021 to Chun, from where it's a straight shot to Phayao (via Dok Kham Tai).

If you do the drive in one go, allow at least six hours, including stops for taking photos, coffee and a meal.

Phayao Cultural Exhibition Hall   MUSEUM
(หอวัฒนธรรมนิทัศน์; Th Chaykawan; admission 40B; ⊙8.30am-4.30pm) This is a two-storey museum packed with artefacts and a good amount of information on local history and culture in English. Standout items include a unique 'black' Buddha statue and a fossil of two embracing crabs labelled 'Wonder Lover'.

The museum is next door to Wat Sri Khom Kham, about 2km from the northern end of Th Chaykawan.

Wat Li   BUDDHIST TEMPLE
(วัดลี; off Hwy 1 Asia; ⊙temple daylight hours, museum 9am-3pm) FREE Just off Rte 1 opposite the turn-off to Phayao, Wat Li features a small museum with a decent variety of items from the Chiang Saen era.

Wat Phra That Jom Thong   BUDDHIST TEMPLE
(วัดพระธาตุจอมทอง; off Th Chaykawan; ⊙daylight hrs) FREE An attractive chedi on a wooded hilltop 3km from the centre of town.

🛏 Sleeping

Huean Phak Jum Jai   GUESTHOUSE $
(☎0 5448 2659; 37/5-6 Th Phrasart; r 600B; ✳🛜) Rooms here are spacious, clean and decked out in handsome wood. The sign says 'Home Stay & Guest House'; it's just off Th Chaykawan, a short walk from the waterfront.

Tharn Thong Hotel   HOTEL $
(☎0 5443 1302; 56-59 Th Donsanam; r 200-340B; ✳🛜) Stark fan-cooled rooms are available in the main building, while more comfortable air-con rooms can be found in the complex behind it. It's near Phayao's police station.

Gateway Hotel   HOTEL $$
(☎0 5441 1333; 7/36 Soi 2, Th Pratu Khlong; r incl breakfast 900-1100B, ste incl breakfast 2000-2500B; ✳🛜🏊) Despite being the city's most upmarket hotel, the rooms here are a bit on the tired side, although the 'sea view' rooms on the upper floors do boast great views of Kwan Phayao. It's located next door to the bus station.

🍴 Eating

For such a small town, Phayao has an amazing abundance of food, much of which is pretty good. There are literally dozens of lakefront restaurants at the edge of Kwan Phayao, beginning at Th Thakawan and extending all the way to the public park. Kaat Boran (Th Chaykawan; mains 30-60B; ⊙6-10pm), a largely food-based night market, sets up every evening near the King Ngam Muang monument. And another extensive night market (Th Rob Wiang; mains 30-60B; ⊙6-10pm) convenes along the north side of Th Rob Wiang every evening.

Khao Soi Saeng Phian   NORTHERN THAI $
(Th Thakawan, no roman-script sign; mains 25-40B; ⊙9am-3pm) One of the better bowls of kôw soy in this neck of the north is available at this family-run restaurant, a block from the waterfront.

Chue Chan   THAI $$
(Th Chaykawan; mains 50-250B; ⊙10am-10.30pm; ✳) Of all the waterfront restaurants, this place has received the most acclaim from the various Thai food authorities. The lengthy menu, which has both pictures and English, spans dishes you won't find elsewhere, such as 'Stuffed pig leg' or 'Sour fish fried with egg'. The restaurant is the tallest building on the busy restaurant stretch of Th Chaykawan.

BUSES TO/FROM PHAYAO
In addition to the buses listed here, there are also minivans to Chiang Rai (62B, one hour, hourly 6.20am to 8pm) and Phrae (106B, two hours, hourly 6.20am to 8pm).

DESTINATION	PRICE (B)	DURATION (HR)	DEPARTURES
Bangkok	435-871	11	frequent 7.30-8am & 3.30-8.20pm
Chiang Khong	122	3½	12.10pm & 4.40pm
Chiang Mai	182-364	5	9 departures 6.15am-4.30pm
Chiang Rai	25-249	3	frequent 7.45am-6.15pm
Lampang	99	3	hourly 6.10am-5.30pm
Mae Sai	49	3	three departures 11.30am-3pm
Nan	134	4	1.20pm

ⓘ Information

There are several banks along Th Donsanam, near the town's morning market, many with ATM and exchange services.

Internet@Cafe (Th Pratu Khlong; per hour 20B; ⊘10am-10pm) Other shops offering internet access dot Th Donsanam.

ⓘ Getting There & Away

Phayao's bus and minivan station, at the northern end of Th Chaykawan, is quite busy, primarily because the city lies on the main north–south highway. Because of this, if you're bound for Bangkok, it's possible to hop on one of the 40 or so buses that pass through the station from points further north.

PHRAE PROVINCE

Phrae is a rural, mountainous province most often associated with teak. Despite a nationwide ban on logging, there's not a whole lot of the hardwood left, and the little that does exist is under threat.

Phrae แพร่

POP 18,000

Walking around the older parts of Phrae one is struck by similarities with the historic Lao city of Luang Prabang: ample greenery, traditional wood buildings and scenic temples dominate the scenery, and monks form a significant part of the traffic. The city's residents must be among the friendliest folks in Thailand, and Phrae's location on the banks of Mae Nam Yom and its ancient wall also invite comparisons with Chiang Mai. Despite all this, Phrae is a little-visited city and a great destination for those who require little more than a few low-key attractions, good local food and cheery company.

◉ Sights

◎ In Town

Wat Luang BUDDHIST TEMPLE
(วัดหลวง; Soi 1, Th Kham Leu; ⊘daylight hours) **FREE** This is the oldest wát in Phrae, probably dating from the founding of the city in the 12th or 13th century.

NORTHERN THAILAND PHRAE

DON'T MISS

PHRAE'S ANTIQUE HOUSES

The lucrative teak trade led to Phrae being home to more than its fair share of beautiful antique mansions. Some that visitors can peek inside include:

Vongburi House (บ้านวงศ์บุรี; 50 Th Kham Leu; admission 30B; ⊘9am-5pm) The two-storey teak house of the last prince of Phrae has been converted into a private museum. It was constructed between 1897 and 1907 for Luang Phongphibun and his wife Chao Sunantha, who once held a profitable teak concession in the city. Inside, many of the house's 20 rooms display late 19th-century teak antiques, documents (including early 20th-century slave concessions), photos and other artefacts from the bygone teak-dynasty era.

Pratubjai House (บ้านประทับใจ; admission 40B; ⊘8am-5pm) Known in Thai as Baan Pratubjai (Impressive House), this is a large northern Thai–style teak house that was built using more than 130 teak logs, each over 300 years old. It's rather tackily decorated, so don't take the moniker 'impressive' too seriously. Pratubjai House is somewhat difficult to find; your best bet is to exit at the west gate of the former city wall and follow the signs, turning right after the school. A sǎhm·lór here should cost about 60B.

Wichairacha House (8 Th Wichai Racha; ⊘daylight hours) **FREE** This beautiful teak mansion is thought to have been built in 1898 by Cantonese artisans. Efforts are being made to turn the house into a museum, although at research time the work was far from complete.

Khum Jao Luang (คุ้มเจ้าหลวง; Th Khum Doem; ⊘8.30am-5pm) **FREE** Built in 1892, this imposing building, sporting a mixture of Thai and European architectural styles, was the home of the final Lord, or Chao Luang, of Phrae. The structure subsequently served as a governor's residence, and is today a museum on local history, although there's no English. Ask to see the basement, which was used to punish and house slaves and prisoners.

Phrae

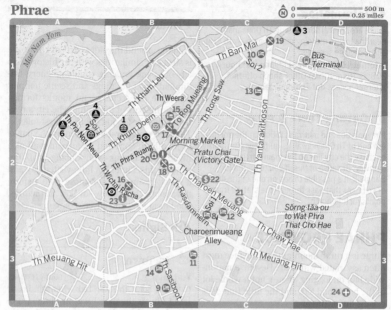

Also on the temple grounds is a **museum** displaying temple antiques, ceramics and religious art dating from the Lanna, Nan, Bago and Mon periods.

The verandah of the main *wí·hǎhn* (sanctuary) is in the classic Luang Prabang–Lan Xang style but has unfortunately been bricked in with laterite. Opposite the front of the *wí·hǎhn* is Pratu Khong, part of the city's original entrance gate. No longer used as a gate, it now contains a statue of Chao Pu, an early Lanna ruler.

Phra That Luang Chang Kham, the large octagonal Lanna-style *chedi*, sits on a square base with elephants supporting it on all four sides. As is sometimes seen in Phrae and Nan, the *chedi* is occasionally swathed in Thai Lü fabric.

The museum's 16th-century Phrae-made sitting Buddha on the 2nd floor is particularly exquisite. There are also some 19th-century photos with English labels on display, including some gruesome shots of a beheading. The museum is usually open weekends only, but the monks will sometimes open it on weekdays on request.

Wat Phra Non
BUDDHIST TEMPLE

(วัดพระนอน; Th Phra Non Neua; ☉daylight hours) FREE Located west of Wat Luang is a 300-year-old *wát* named after its highly revered reclining Buddha image. The *bòht*

(chapel) was built around 200 years ago and has an impressive roof with a separate, two-tiered portico and gilded, carved, wooden facade with Ramayana scenes. The adjacent *wí·hǎhn* contains the Buddha image, swathed in Thai Lü cloth with bead and foil decoration.

Wat Jom Sawan
BUDDHIST TEMPLE

(วัดจอมสวรรค์; Th Ban Mai; ☉daylight hours) FREE Outside the old city on Th Ban Mai, this temple was built by local Shan in the late 19th and early 20th centuries, and shows Shan and Burmese influences throughout. An adjacent copper-crowned *chedi* has lost most of its stucco to reveal the artful brickwork beneath. Since a recent renovation, Wat Jom Sawan is more of a museum piece than a functioning temple.

Wat Phra Baht Ming Meuang
BUDDHIST TEMPLE

(วัดพระบาทมิ่งเมือง; Th Charoen Meuang; ☉daylight hrs) FREE Across from the post office within the old city, Wat Phra Baht Ming Meuang combines two formerly separate temple compounds (one of which contains a **museum** that is sporadically open), a Buddhist school, an old' *chedi*, an unusual octagonal drum tower made entirely of teak and the highly revered Phra Kosai, which closely resembles the Phra Chinnarat in Phitsanulok.

Outside of Town

Phae Meuang Phi NATURE RESERVE
(แพะเมืองผี; off Rte 101; ⊙6am-6pm) FREE The name Phae Meuang Phi means 'Ghost-Land', a reference to a strange geological phenomenon in which erosion has created bizarre pillars of soil and rock that look like giant fungi.

The park is located approximately 18km northeast of Phrae off Rte 101; getting there by public transport is not an option. You can charter a *sŏrng·tăa·ou* for about 600B or talk to Khun Kung at Nok Bin for alternatives.

The area has been made a provincial park; a few walking trails and viewpoints are recent additions. There are picnic pavilions in the park and food vendors selling *gài yâhng* (grilled chicken), *sôm·đam* (spicy green papaya salad) and sticky rice near the entrance.

Wat Phra That Cho Hae BUDDHIST TEMPLE
(วัดพระธาตุช่อแฮ; Rte 1022; ⊙daylight hours) FREE Named for the cloth that worshippers wrap around it, this hilltop *wát* is famous for its 33m-high gilded *chedi*. Like Chiang Mai's Wat Doi Suthep, it is an important pilgrimage site for Thais living in the north.

Tiered naga stairs lead to the temple compound. The interior of the *bòht* is rather tackily decorated with a gilded wooden ceiling, rococo pillars and walls with lotus-bud mosaics. The Phra Jao Than Jai Buddha image here, which resembles the Phra Chinnarat in Phitsanulok, is reputed to impart fertility to women who make offerings to it.

The temple is 9km southeast of town off Rte 1022. The scenery along the road leading to the *wát* is picturesque and there is also an abundance of restaurants serving local dishes. *Sŏrng·tăa·ou* between Phrae and Phra That Cho Hae (20B) depart from a stop near Talat Phrae Preeda, on Th Chaw Hae, from 6am to 4.30pm; outside of these hours a *sŏrng·tăa·ou* can be chartered for 400B.

🛏 Sleeping

Bua Khao HOTEL $
(⌨0 5451 1372; 8 Soi 1, Th Charoen Meuang, no roman-script sign; r 350-600B; ❄🤙) Tucked just off the main road, this flagrant teak compound has mostly small rooms and hard beds, but the service is friendly and it has heaps of character.

Phrae

⊙ Sights
1 Khum Jao Luang..................................B2
2 Vongburi House..................................A2
3 Wat Jom Sawan..................................D1
4 Wat Luang..A1
5 Wat Phra Baht Ming Meuang.............B2
6 Wat Phra Non.....................................A2
7 Wichairacha House............................B2

🛏 Sleeping
8 Bua Khao...C3
9 Huern na na.......................................B3
10 Maeyom Palace Hotel........................C1
11 Nakhon Phrae Tower..........................B3
12 Nana...C3
13 Paradorn Hotel...................................C1
14 Phoomthai Garden.............................B3
15 Priwan's Homestay............................B2

🍴 Eating
16 Khao Soi Klang Wiang........................B2
    Night Market...............................(see 20)
17 Pan Jai...B2
18 Saeng Fah Laep..................................B2
19 Sod Cheon..C1

🛍 Shopping
20 Maw Hawm Anian...............................B2

ℹ Information
21 Bangkok Bank.....................................C2
    Government Savings Bank........(see 18)
22 Krung Thai Bank.................................C2
23 Nok Bin...B2
24 Phrae Hospital....................................D3

Paradorn Hotel HOTEL $
(⌨0 5451 1177; kanthatham@hotmail.com; 177 Th Yantarakitkoson; r incl breakfast 330-800B; ste incl breakfast 900B; ❄❄🤙) A decent budget choice a short walk from the bus terminal. The fan-cooled rooms here have private balconies.

Nana HOTEL $
(⌨0 5452 1985; 346/2 Th Charoen Meuang, no roman-script sign; r 400-500B; ❄🤙) The vast rooms here are outfitted with appropriately huge TVs and fridges; the more expensive rooms pack in even more furniture. Nana is on the tiny side street labelled Charoen-meuang Alley; look for the yellow sign.

Priwan's Homestay GUESTHOUSE $
(⌨08 1764 8447; 1 Th Weera; s/d 150/200B) This enterprising local language teacher has opened up her vast wooden house to foreign guests. The six rooms are simply furnished and share a bathroom and a rambling vegetarian restaurant.

Phoomthai Garden
HOTEL $$

(☎ 0 5462 7359; www.phoomthaitravel.com; 31 Th Sasiboot; r incl breakfast 1000-1700B; ❄@🛜) Although it's a bit of a hike from the old town, this boutique hotel is the best all-around choice in Phrae. The rooms are attractive, modern and comfortable, and all have balconies overlooking the hotel's garden. The hotel is about 300m south of the former town wall on Th Sasiboot.

Nakhon Phrae Tower
HOTEL $$

(☎ 0 5452 1321; www.nakornphraetower.com; 3 Th Meuang Hit; r incl breakfast 650-800B; ste incl breakfast 1800-2500B; ❄🛜) A large business-class hotel, Nakhon Phrae Tower lies just outside the old city. Expect the usual bland-but-functional amenities of a provincial Thai hotel of this price range.

Huern na na
HOTEL $$$

(☎ 0 5452 4800; 7/9 Th Sasiboot; r incl breakfast 4500B, ste incl breakfast 7000-8000B; ❄@🛜) Opened in 2012, it didn't take long for this Lanna-style compound to become Phrae's most sophisticated hotel. Rooms are spacious and come decked out in both contemporary and northern Thai-style themes. Suites throw in a hot tub, and executive suites can boast a functional kitchenette. Huern na na is located off Th Sasiboot, about 250m south of Th Meuang Hit.

Maeyom Palace Hotel
HOTEL $$$

(☎ 0 5452 1028-34; wccphrae@hotmail.com; 181/6 Th Yantarakitkoson; r incl breakfast 1600-2000B, ste incl breakfast 3500-4000B; ❄@🛜) Opposite the bus terminal, Phrae's top-end staple has all the modern amenities – carpeted rooms with cable TV and a pool – in a somewhat aged package. Discounts of up to 30% are typical during the low season.

✖ Eating & Drinking

A small but fun **night market** (Th Rop Mueang; mains 30-60B; ⏱6-10pm) convenes around the Pratu Chai (Victory Gate) intersection every evening.

TRANSPORT TO/FROM PHRAE

DESTINATION	AIR	BUS	MINIVAN	TRAIN
Bangkok	1590B; 1hr; 4 weekly (to Don Muang Airport)	346-692B; 8hr; frequent 9.30am-noon & 6.30-9pm		155-1291B; 9-11hr; 8 daily
Ban Huay Kon (border with Laos)			180B; 5hr; 4 departures 3am-7.10pm	
Chiang Mai		151-194B; 4hr; frequent 6am-5pm		72-549B; 4-6hr; 7 daily
Chiang Rai		150-320B; 4hr; frequent 10.20am-3.50am	150B; 4½hr; half-hourly 5am-6pm	
Lampang		87-112B; 2hr; frequent 10.20am-3.50am	80B; 2hr; hourly 6am-4.50pm	50-968B; 2hr; 4 daily
Mae Sai		200-300B; 5hr; frequent 10.20am-3.50am		
Nan			78B; 2hr; frequent 3am-6.50pm	
Phayao			100B; 2hr; half-hourly 5am-6pm	
Phitsanulok		127B; 3hr; frequent 6am-3.45pm		30-348B; 3½hr; 8 daily
Sukhothai		120B; 3hr; 3 departures 11.20am-2.20pm		

Phrae's entertainment zone is the dusty road leading to the bus station; there you'll fine several loud bars and karaoke joints.

Pan Jai
NORTHERN THAI $

(2 Th Weera, no roman-script sign; mains 20-40B; ⊙7am-10pm) During the day, the emphasis here is on *kà·nŏm jeen,* fresh rice noodles served with various curries and herbs. At night, locals come for *mŏo gà·tá,* DIY northern-style barbecue.

Khao Soi Klang Wiang
NORTHERN THAI $

(Th Wichai Racha, no roman-script sign; mains 35-50B; ⊙10am-2pm) This place does just one dish: fat bowls of *kôw soy.* Order a regular or 'jumbo' bowl supplemented with beef, pork or chicken. It's the bright orange place just opposite Nok Bin.

Saeng Fah Laep
THAI $

(Th Charoen Meuang, no roman-script sign; mains 10-40B; ⊙9am-7pm) This friendly family sells Thai sweets, including a tasty *kôw nĕe·o má·môo·ang* (mango sticky rice). There's no English sign, but it's the old shophouse just west of the police station.

Sod Cheon
CHINESE-THAI $

(Th Yantarakitkoson, no roman-script sign; mains 30-120B; ⊙11am-4am) At the crossroads 50m north of the Maeyom Palace Hotel is this simple but very popular Chinese-Thai restaurant. Choose from big pots of Chinese-style soups or go for the Thai standards.

🔒 Shopping

Phrae is known for the distinctive *sêua môr hôrm,* the indigo-dyed cotton farmer's shirt seen all over northern Thailand. The cloth is made in Ban Thung Hong, just outside of the city. In town, a good place to pick one us is **Maw Hawm Anian** (36 Th Charoen Meuang, no roman-script sign; ⊙7am-8.30pm).

ℹ Information

Nok Bin (☎08 1423 5599; 24 Th Wichai Racha; ⊙10am-5pm) Khun Kung, a local journalist, and her husband have created a cheery cafe that also functions as an informal information centre for visitors. The couple prints a tourist map of Phrae that is updated regularly and can also arrange bicycle or motorcycle hire.

Phrae Hospital (☎0 5452 2444) Just east of Th Chaw Hae, southeast of town.

ℹ Getting There & Away

At research time, the only airline operating out of Phrae's airport was **Nok Air** (☎0 5452 2189, nationwide 1318; www.nokair.com; ⊙8am-5pm), with flights to/from Bangkok. From the airport, 2.5km east of the city centre, **Pikun** (☎0 5452 3233; pikun2514@hotmail.com; Phrae Airport; ⊙8am-5pm Mon-Sat) can provide transport to your hotel (50B to 100B).

Unlike most cities in Thailand, Phrae's **bus and minivan terminal** is located within walking distance of a few accommodation options.

Phrae's closest rail link, **Den Chai station** (☎0 5461 3260, nationwide 1690; www.railway. co.th), is 23km south. There are frequent blue *sŏrng·tăa·ou* between Phrae's bus station and Den Chai (40B, 40 minutes, from 6.30am to 5.30pm), or you can charter one for 400B.

ℹ Getting Around

A *săhm·lór* within the old town costs around 40B. Motorcycle taxis are available at the bus terminal; a trip from here to Pratu Chai should cost around 40B. Khun Kung at Nok Bin can arrange motorcycle rental, and car hire can be arranged at Pikun (per day 1700B).

NAN PROVINCE

Tucked into Thailand's northeastern corner, Nan is a remote province to be explored for its natural beauty. Nan's ethnic groups are another highlight and differ significantly from those in other northern provinces. Outside the Mae Nam Nan Valley, the predominant hill tribes are Mien, with smaller numbers of Hmong, while dispersed throughout Nan are four lesser-known groups seldom seen outside this province: the Thai Lü, Mabri, Htin and Khamu.

Nan
น่าน

POP 20,000

Due to its remote location, Nan is not the kind of destination most travellers are going to stumble upon. And its largely featureless downtown isn't going to inspire many postcards home. But if you've taken the time to get here, you'll be rewarded by a city rich in both culture and history. Many of Nan's residents are Thai Lü, the ancestors of immigrants from Xishuangbanna, in southwestern China. This cultural legacy is seen in the city's art and architecture, particularly in its

Nan

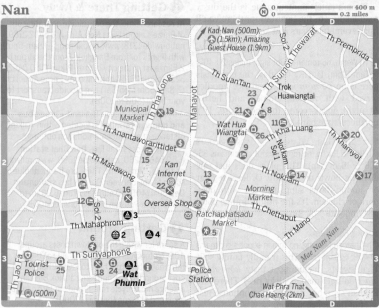

exquisite temples. A Lanna influence on the town can also be seen in the remains of the old city wall and several early wát.

History

For centuries Nan was an isolated, independent kingdom with few ties to the outside world. Ample evidence of prehistoric habitation exists, but it wasn't until several small *meu·ang* (city-states) consolidated to form Nanthaburi in the mid-14th century that the city became a power to contend with. Towards the end of the 14th century Nan became one of the nine northern Thai-Lao principalities that comprised Lan Na Thai. The city-state flourished throughout the 15th century under the name Chiang Klang (Middle City), a reference to its position approximately midway between Chiang Mai (New City) and Chiang Thong (Golden City, today's Luang Prabang). The Burmese took control of the kingdom in 1558 and transferred many of the inhabitants to Burma as slaves; the city was all but abandoned until western Thailand was wrested from the Burmese in 1786. The local dynasty then regained local sovereignty and it remained semi-autonomous until 1931, when Nan finally (and reluctantly) accepted full Bangkok sponsorship.

◉ Sights

★ Wat Phumin
BUDDHIST TEMPLE

(วัดภูมินทร์; cnr Th Suriyaphong & Th Pha Kong; ⊙ daylight hours) FREE Nan's most famous Buddhist temple is celebrated for its exquisite murals that were executed during the late 19th century by a Thai Lü artist named Thit Buaphan. For an insight into the historical significance of the murals, see the boxed text (p342).

The exterior of the temple takes the form of a cruciform *bòht* (chapel) that was constructed in 1596 and restored during the reign of Chao Anantavorapitthidet (1867–74). The ornate altar in the centre of the *bòht* has four sides, with four Sukhothai-style sitting Buddhas facing in each direction.

Nan National Museum
MUSEUM

(พิพิธภัณฑสถานแห่งชาติน่าน; Th Pha Kong; admission 100B; ⊙ 9am-4pm Wed-Sun) Housed in the 1903 vintage palace of Nan's last two feudal lords, this museum first opened its doors in 1973. In terms of collection and content, it's one of the country's better provincial museums, with English labels for most items.

The ground floor has ethnological exhibits covering the various ethnic groups found in the province. Among the items on display are silverwork, textiles, folk utensils and tribal costumes.

On the 2nd floor are exhibits on Nan history, archaeology, local architecture, royal regalia, weapons, ceramics and religious art. Of the latter, the museum's collection of Buddha images includes some rare Lanna styles as well as the floppy-eared local styles. Also on display on the 2nd floor is a rare 'black' elephant tusk said to have been presented to a Nan lord over 300 years ago by the Khün ruler of Chiang Tung (Kyaingtong).

Wat Phra That Chae Haeng BUDDHIST TEMPLE
(วัดพระธาตุแช่แห้ง; off Rte 1168; ⊙ daylight hours)
FREE Two kilometres past the bridge that spans Mae Nam Nan, heading southeast out of town, this Buddhist temple dating from 1355 is the most sacred wát in Nan Province. It's set in a square walled enclosure on top of a hill with a view of Nan and the valley.

A round-trip motorcycle taxi here from the centre of Nan will run about 100B.

The Thai Lü-influenced *bòht* features a triple-tiered roof with carved wooden eaves and dragon reliefs over the doors. A gilded Lanna-style *chedi* sits on a large square base next to the *bòht*; visit late in the day and the structure practically glows in the afternoon light.

Wat Phra That Chang Kham BUDDHIST TEMPLE
(วัดพระธาตุช้างค้ำ; cnr Th Suriyaphong & Th Pha Kong; ⊙ daylight hours) FREE This is the second-most important temple in the city after Wat Phra That Chae Haeng. The founding date is unknown, but the main *wí·hǎhn* (sanctuary), reconstructed in 1458, has a huge seated Buddha image and faint murals that have been partially recovered.

The *chedi* behind the *wí·hǎhn* is thought to date to around the same time as the temple was founded, and features elephant supports similar to those seen in Sukhothai and Si Satchanalai.

Next to the *chedi* is a small, undistinguished *bòht* from the same era. Wat Phr That Chang Kham's current abbot tells an interesting story involving the *bòht* and a Buddha image that was once kept inside. According to the abbot, in 1955 art historian AB Griswold offered to purchase the 145cm-tall Buddha inside the small *bòht*. The image appeared to be a crude Sukhothai-style walking Buddha moulded of plaster. After agreeing to pay the abbot 25,000B for the image, Griswold began removing the image – but as he did it fell and the plaster around

the statue broke away to reveal an original Sukhothai Buddha of pure gold underneath. Needless to say, the abbot made Griswold give it back, much to the latter's chagrin. Did Griswold suspect what lay beneath the plaster? The abbot refuses to say. The image is now kept behind a glass partition in the *hŏr drai* (Tripitaka library) adjacent to the *wí·hǎhn*, the former the largest of its type in Thailand, and was in the process of being renovated when we were in town.

Wat Hua Khuang BUDDHIST TEMPLE
(วัดหัวข่วง; cnr Th Mahaphrom & Th Pha Kong; ⊙ daylight hours) FREE This temple features a distinctive Lanna/Lan Xang–style *chedi* with

DON'T MISS

THE MURALS OF WAT PHUMIN

Wat Phumin is northern Thailand's Sistine Chapel, and the images on its walls are now found on everything from knick-knacks at Chiang Mai's night bazaar to postcards sold in Bangkok. Yet despite the seemingly happy scenes depicted, the murals were executed during a period that saw the end of Nan as a semi-independent kingdom. This resulted in several examples of political and social commentary manifesting themselves in the murals – rarities in Thai religious art.

The murals commissioned by Jao Suliyaphong, the last king of Nan, include the *Khaddhana Jataka*, a relatively obscure story of one of the Buddha's lives that, according to Thai historian David K Wyatt in his excellent book, *Reading Thai Murals,* has never been illustrated elsewhere in the Buddhist world. The story, which is on the left side of the temple's northern wall, depicts an orphan in search of his parents. Wyatt argues that this particular tale was chosen as a metaphor for the kingdom of Nan, which also had been abandoned by a succession of 'parents', the Thai kingdoms of Sukhothai, Chiang Mai and Ayuthaya. At roughly the same time as the murals were painted, Nan was fully incorporated into Siam by King Rama V, and much of its territory was allotted to France. Apparent discontent with this decision can be seen in a scene on the west wall that shows two male monkeys attempting to copulate against a background that, not coincidentally, according to Wyatt, resembles the French flag.

The murals are also valuable purely for their artistic beauty, something that is even more remarkable if one steps back and considers the limited palette of colours that the artist, Thit Buaphan, had to work with. The paintings are also fascinating for their fly-on-the-wall depictions of local life in Nan during the end of the 19th century. A depiction of three members of a hill tribe on the west wall includes such details as a man's immense goitre and a barking dog, suggesting this group's place as outsiders. Multiple depictions of a man wearing a feminine shawl, often seen performing traditionally female-only duties, are among the earliest depictions of a *gà·teu·i* (transsexual). And in what must be one of the art world's most superfluous cameos, the artist painted himself on the west wall, flirting with a woman. Considering that the murals took Thit Buaphan more than 20 years to complete, we'll allow him this excess.

four Buddha niches, an attractive wooden *hŏr drai* and a noteworthy *bòht* with a Luang Prabang–style carved wooden veranda. Inside is a carved wooden ceiling and a huge *naga* altar. The temple's founding date is unknown, but stylistic cues suggest this may be one of the city's oldest *wát*.

🏃 Activities

Nan has nothing like the organised trekking industry found in Chiang Rai and Chiang Mai, and many visitors, particularly Thais, opt to float rather than walk. White-water rafting along Mae Nam Wa, in northern Nan, is only possible when the water level is high (September to December), and is said to be best during the early part of the rainy season. The rapids span from classes I to IV, and pass through intact jungle and remote villages.

Nan Touring RAFTING
(☑08 1961 7711; www.nantouring.com; 11/12 Th Suriyaphong; 3 days & 2 nights per person 5500B; ⊘9am-5pm) This outfit offers a variety of rafting trips for groups of at least five people.

Fhu Travel TREKKING
(☑0 5471 0636, 08 1287 7209; www.fhutravel.com; 453/4 Th Sumon Thewarat; trekking per person 1/2/3 days 1700/3000/4000B; ⊘9am-6pm) Offers treks (two-person minimum) to Mabri, Hmong, Mien, Thai Lü and Htin villages, and can also arrange elephant trekking, rafting and kayaking trips and city tours. The operators have been leading tours for more than 20 years; the guide Noi gets good reviews, the occasional foreign trekking guides less so.

Nan Seeing Tour TOURS
(☑08 1472 4131; www.nanseeingtour.com; Th Sumon Thewarat; bike tours per person 2/3 days 2250/4550B; ⊘8am-7pm) This locally owned

outfit conducts two-wheeled expeditions in and around Nan. A three-day package starts with mountain bikes in Nan city and finishes with dirt bikes in the countryside. Prices are all-inclusive, and Nan Coffee functions as the office. Four-person minimum.

🛏 Sleeping

Fah Place HOTEL $
(📞 0 5471 0222; 237/8 Th Sumon Thewarat; r 350-500B; ❄️🛜) The rooms here are spacious and have been decorated with attractive teak furniture, including the kind of puffy inviting beds you'd expect at places that charge several times this much.

The same people also run the similar **Sukkasem Hotel** (📞 0 5477 2555; sukksasem-nan@gmail.com; 119-121 Th Anantaworarittidet; r 400-1000B; ❄️🛜).

Nan Guest House HOTEL $
(📞 08 1288 8484; www.nanguesthouse.net; 57/15 Soi 2, Th Mahaphrom; r 250-430B; ❄️@🛜) In a quiet residential area a short walk from Nan's most famous temples, this long-standing and well-maintained place has spotless spacious rooms, half of which have private hot-water bathrooms, air-con, TV and fridge.

Huen Muan Jai
Boutique Guest House GUESTHOUSE $
(📞 08 2765 8730; muanjai_nan@hotmail.com; off Th Mahaphrom, no roman-script sign; r 350-500B; 🛜) This place unites seven rooms in a 60-year-old wooden house. Accommodation is basic, edging on rustic, but for charming atmosphere, there's probably no better place in Nan.

Huan Gum Gin GUESTHOUSE $
(📞 08 1472 4131; www.huangumgin.com; 309 Th Sumon Thewarat; r incl breakfast 450-800B; ❄️🛜) Six cosy rooms in a house decked out in subtle Nan-themed cloths and patterns. A restaurant, tourist advice and (free) coffee are available on the ground floor.

Amazing Guest House GUESTHOUSE $
(📞 0 5471 0893; 23/7 Th Rat Amnuay/Suntisuk; r 300-450B; ❄️🛜) Rooms in the main building have wooden floors, clean beds and shared hot-water showers, while rooms in the concrete structures out the back have private bathrooms. Amazing is about 1km north of town; if heading north on Th Mahayot, turn right on Th Prempracharat then left on Th Rat Amnuay, which is also labelled as Th Suntisuk.

Nan Noble House HOTEL $$
(📞 08 1796 9029; www.nannoblehouse.com; off Rte 1080; r 1200B; ❄️🛜❄️) Approximately 3km northwest of Nan is this orchard, which is also home to five dome-like duplex bungalows. Rooms are simple but clean and comfy, and a stay here is more about taking in the rural setting and chilling by the pool than contemplating interior design. Transfer to/from the bus station, airport and downtown are available for free.

Srinual Lodge HOTEL $$
(📞 0 5471 0174; www.facebook.com/srinuallodge-fanpage; 40/5 Th Nokham; r/ste 600/1800B; ❄️🛜) This two-storey brick structure holds a couple dozen rooms decked out in a *faux rustique* style with logs, bamboo and local textiles. Despite the earthy design theme, the rooms look comfortable and it's about as close as you'll get to sleeping near Mae Nam Nan.

Dhevaraj Hotel HOTEL $$
(📞 0 5475 1577; www.dhevarajhotel.com; 466 Th Sumon Thewarat; r incl breakfast 900-1500B, ste incl breakfast 4000B; ❄️@🛜❄️) Not all the rooms here live up to the retro-yet-tidy exterior, with some of the cheaper ones feeling somewhat aged and musty. But with a convenient location and one of Nan's only hotel pools, the Dhevaraj represents an OK value.

★ Pukha Nanfa Hotel HOTEL $$$
(📞 0 5477 1111; www.pukhananfahotel.com; 369 Th Sumon Thewarat; r 2500-4600B; ❄️@🛜) The former and forgettable Nan Fah Hotel has been meticulously transformed into this charming boutique. Rooms are cosy and classy, with aged wood accentuated by touches such as local cloth, handicrafts and art. Antique adverts and pictures add to the old-world feel, and to top it off, the place is conveniently located and has more-than-capable staff.

Nan Boutique Hotel HOTEL $$$
(📞 0 5477 5532; www.nanboutiquehotel.com; 1/11 Th Kha Luang; r incl breakfast 1800-3200B; ❄️🛜) This super-tidy suburban-feeling compound lacks the character of some of Nan's other choices, but makes up for it with some of the city's most modern and well-equipped rooms, free pickup and drop-off, free bicycles, and an on-site spa.

NORTHERN THAILAND NAN

✕ Eating & Drinking

Despite its other charms, Nan has one of the least inspiring dining scenes in northern Thailand.

The town's **night market** (Th Pha Kong; mains 30-60B; ⊘ 5-11pm) provides a few decent food stall offerings. Better is Nan's Saturday Walking Street (p344), where dishes and tables are provided for the takeaway northern Thai–style food.

Pu Som Restaurant   NORTHERN THAI $
(203/1 Th Khamyot, no roman-script sign; mains 35-90B; ⊘ 10am-10pm) The emphasis here is on meat, served in the local style as *lâhp* (a type of minced meat 'salad') or *néu·a nêung* (beef steamed over herbs and served with an incredibly delicious galangal-based dip). There's no English-language sign; look for the 'est cola' banner.

Hot Bread   INTERNATIONAL-THAI $
(38/1-2 Th Suriyaphong; mains 25-130B; ⊘ 7am-4pm; ☑) This retro-themed cafe and restaurant has a generous menu of Western-style breakfast dishes – including the eponymous and delicious homemade bread – and other Western and Thai items. Come for *kôw soy* in the mornings.

Som Tam Thawt   THAI $
(Th Sumon Thewarat, no roman-script sign; mains 35-60B; ⊘ 10am-9pm Tue-Sun) This tiny restaurant is known for its *sôm·đam tôrt:* deep-fried *sôm·đam* (papaya salad), an equal parts crunchy and refreshing snack. It also does great fruit smoothies and other basic dishes. Located roughly across from Fah Place hotel.

Fasai   THAI $
(Th Pha Kong, no roman-script sign; mains 25-50B; ⊘ 7am-7.30pm) A young, friendly Thai couple are behind this old-school-themed cafe. A great breakfast destination, start the day with *kài gà·tá*, described on the menu as 'Egg pan breakfast', and a Thai-style coffee drink.

Good View Nan   THAI $
(203/1 Th Mano; dishes 35-150B; ⊘ 11am-11pm) One of the few places in town to take advantage of the views over Mae Nam Nan, this place works equally well as a dinner-date locale or a riverside pub.

Yota Vegetarian Restaurant VEGETARIAN-THAI $
(Th Mahawong; mains 10-35B; ⊘ 7am-3pm; ☑) Run by the friendliest lady in town who will not let you leave hungry, this is perhaps the best deal in Nan. It's popular and once the food is gone after lunch, that's it for the day.

Nan Coffee   CAFE
(Th Sumon Thewarat; ⊘ 7.30am-7pm; 🖥) This conveniently located cafe does good coffee in floral and light meals. There are a few souvenirs for sale and the restaurant is also the unofficial headquarters for Nan Seeing Tour (p342).

🛍 Shopping

Nan is one of the best places in northern Thailand to pick up some souvenirs, and good buys include local textiles, especially the Thai Lü weaving styles, which typically feature red and black designs on white cotton in floral, geometric and animal designs. A favourite is the *lai nám lǎi* (flowing-water design) that shows stepped patterns representing streams, rivers and waterfalls. Local Hmong appliqué and Mien embroidery are of excellent quality. Htin grass-and-bamboo baskets and mats are worth a look, too.

Walking Street   MARKET
(Th Sumon Thewarat; ⊘ 5-10pm Sat) Every Saturday afternoon the stretch of Th Sumon Thewarat from Wat Hua Wiangtai to Th Premprida is closed and vendors selling food, textiles and clothing, and local handicrafts set up shop.

Kad-Nan   MARKET
(www.kad-nan.com; 43 Th Mahayot; ⊘ 10am-10pm) This open-air mall is Nan's answer to Bangkok's Chatuchak Weekend Market. Here you'll find shops selling local knick-knacks, art, clothing, restaurants, coffee shops and bars. The market is technically open from 10am, but evening, when most shops and restaurants are open and live music gives the place a fair-like atmosphere, is the best time to visit.

Amnouy Porn & Jangtrakoon HANDICRAFTS
(Th Sumon Thewarat, no roman-script sign; ⊘ 8am-7pm) These adjacent shops sell a variety of local goods with an emphasis on textiles and clothing.

OTOP   HANDICRAFTS
(Th Suriyaphong; ⊘ 8.30am-6pm) The showroom of this government-funded development initiative has everything from local snacks to silverware.

Peera HANDICRAFTS
(26 Th Suriyaphong; ☺8am-7pm) A short walk from Wat Phumin, this place offers high-quality local textiles, mostly consisting of women's skirts and blouses.

Nan Silver HANDICRAFTS
(430/1 Th Sumon Thewarat; ☺7.30am-7pm) This small but classy shop sells a huge variety of locally designed and produced silver items.

ℹ Information

Kan Internet (Th Mahayot; per hour 15B; ☺9am-10pm) Other places offering internet services can be found around town for about 20B per hour.

Tourist Information Centre (☎0 5475 1169; Th Pha Kong; ☺8.30am-noon & 1-4.30pm) Opposite Wat Phumin, this helpful information centre is hidden behind vendors and coffee shops.

ℹ Getting There & Away

Nok Air (☎08 8263 2012, nationwide 1318; www.nokair.co.th; Nan Airport; ☺7.30am-7pm) is the only airline operating out of Nan, with flights to Bangkok. **Nan Taxi** (☎08 4617 0777) does airport transfers for about 100B per person.

From Nan, all buses, minivans and *sŏrng·tăa·o* leave from the bus station at the southwestern edge of town. A motorcycle taxi between the station and the centre of town costs 30B.

If you're connecting to the train station at Den Chai in Phrae, you can hop on any bus bound for Chiang Mai or Bangkok.

ℹ Getting Around

Săhm·lór around town cost 30B to 40B. Taxis can be hailed via Nan Taxi.

Several businesses, including Amazing Guest House, Fah Place, **Oversea Shop** (☎0 5471 0258; 488 Th Sumon Thewarat; ☺8.30am-5.30pm) and Nan Guest House hire bikes (per day from 60B to 100B), and motorcycles (from 180B to 300B).

TRANSPORT TO/FROM NAN

DESTINATION	AIR	BUS	MINIVAN	SŎRNG·TĂA·OU
Bangkok	2190B; 1½hr; 2 daily (to Don Muang Airport)	420-820B; 10-11hr; frequent 8-10am & 7-7.30pm		
Ban Huay Kon (border with Laos)			100B; 3hr; 4 departures 5-9.30am	
Chiang Mai		225-451B; 6hr; frequent 8am-10.30pm		
Chiang Rai		181B; 6hr; 9am		
Lampang		212-330B; 4hr; frequent 8am-10.30pm		
Phayao		223B; 4hr; frequent 8am-10.30pm		
Phitsanulok		204B; 4hr; frequent 8-10am & 7-7.30pm		
Phrae		54-84B; 2½hr; hourly 6am-5pm	78B; 2hr; half-hourly 5.30am-6pm	
Pon (border with Laos)		85B; 2½hr; hourly 6am-6pm		
Pua (for Doi Phu Kha National Park)				50B; 2hr; hourly 7am-5pm

NORTHERN THAILAND NAN

Around Nan

Nan Riverside Gallery   หอศิลป์ริมน่าน

Twenty kilometres north of Nan on Rte 1080, this private **art gallery** (www.nanart-gallery.com; Km 20, Rte 1080; admission 20B; ⊙9am-5pm Thu-Tue) exhibits contemporary Nan-influenced art in a peaceful setting. Established in 2004 by Nan artist Winai Prabipoo, the two-storey building holds the more interesting temporary exhibitions downstairs – sculpture, ceramics and drawings – as well as a permanent painting collection upstairs (which seems to be mainly inspired by the Wat Phumin murals). The unusual building is a light-filled converted rice barn with an arrow-shaped turret. The shop and cafe have seats right on the Mae Nam Nan and the beautiful manicured gardens are nice to wander around.

From Nan, take any northbound bus or *sŏrng·tăa·ou* (30B) to the gallery.

Wat Nong Bua   วัดหนองบัว

The neat and tidy Thai Lü village of Nong Bua, near the town of Tha Wang Pha, approximately 30km north of Nan, is famous for the Lü-style **Wat Nong Bua** (⊙day-

light hours) `FREE`. Featuring a typical two-tiered roof and carved wooden portico, the *wí·hăhn* design is simple yet striking – note the carved *naga* heads at the roof corners. Inside the *wí·hăhn* are rustic but beautiful *jataka* murals thought to have been painted by Thit Buaphan, the same mural artist whose work can be seen at Wat Phumin. Be sure to leave a donation at the altar for the temple's upkeep and restoration.

There is a model Thai Lü house directly behind the wát where weaving is done and you can buy attractive local textiles.

Nong Bua is about 30km north of Nan. To get there, take a northbound bus or *sŏrng·tăa·ou* (35B) to Tha Wang Pha. Get off at Samyaek Longbom, walk west to a bridge over Mae Nam Nan and turn left. Continue until you reach another small bridge, after which Wat Nong Bua will be on your right. It's a long 3km from the highway to the wát.

Doi Phu Kha National Park   อุทยานแห่งชาติดอยภูคา

This **national park** (☑0 2562 0760, 08 2194 1349; www.dnp.go.th; admission 200B) is centred on 2000m-high Doi Phu Kha, the province's highest peak, in Amphoe Pua and Amphoe Bo Kleua, about 75km northeast of Nan. There are several Htin, Mien, Hmong and

---

GETTING TO LAOS: BAN HUAY KON TO MUANG NGEUN

Located 140km north of Nan, Ban Huay Kon is a sleepy village in the mountains near the Lao border. There's a fun border market on Saturday mornings, but most will come here because of the town's status as an international border crossing to Laos.

Getting to the Border To Ban Huay Kon, there are four daily minivans originating in Phrae and stopping in Nan at 5am, 6.50am, 8am and 9.30am (100B, three hours). If you miss one of these, the only other option is to hop on a bus from Nan to Pon (85B, 2½ hours, hourly from 6am to 6pm), at which point you'll need to transfer to the infrequent *sŏrng·tăa·ou* that go the remaining 30km to Ban Huay Kon (100B, one hour, from 9am to 6pm). In the opposite direction, minivans bound for Nan (100B, three hours) and Phrae (180B, five hours) leave Ban Huay Kon at 9.45am, 11.45am, 12.45pm and 2.15pm, while the only scheduled *sŏrng·tăa·ou* back to Pon departs at 1pm (100B, one hour).

At the Border After passing the **Thai immigration booth** (☑0 5469 3530; ⊙8am-6pm), foreigners can purchase a 30-day visa for Laos for US$30 to US$42, depending on nationality. There is an extra US$1 or 50B charge after 4pm and on weekends.

Moving On You can then proceed 2.5km to the Lao village of Muang Ngeun, where you could stay at the **Phouxay Guesthouse** (☑020-2214 2826; r 60,000K), or, if you're heading onward, to the tiny **Passenger Car Station** (☑020-244 4130, 020-245 0145) beside the market, from where *sŏrng·tăa·ou* leave for Hongsa (40,000K, 1½ hours) between 2pm and 4pm, and to Pak Kaen (35,000K, one hour) at around 7.30am and 2pm arriving in time for the Mekong slow boats to Huay Xai and Pak Beng respectively. Once the new bridge north of Pakbeng is open, there will also be a bus service and ostensibly, more frequent transport links.

Thai Lü villages in the park and vicinity, as well as a couple of caves and waterfalls, and endless opportunities for forest walks. The park headquarters has a basic map and staff can arrange a local guide for walks or more extended excursions around the area, as well as rafting on Nam Wa. The park is often cold in the cool season and especially wet in the wet season.

There is a variety of bungalows (✆ 0 2562 0760; www.dnp.go.th; bungalow 2-7 people 300-2500B) in the park, and there is a nearby restaurant and basic shop.

To reach the national park by public transport you must first take a bus or sŏrng·tăa·ou north of Nan to Pua (50B, two hours, hourly from 7am to 5pm). Get off at the 7-Eleven then cross the highway to board one of the three daily sŏrng·tăa·ou that depart at 7.30am, 9.30am and 11.30am (50B, 30 minutes).

Ban Bo Luang   บ้านบ่อหลวง

Ban Bo Luang (also known as Ban Bo Kleua, or Salt Well Village) is a picturesque Htin village southeast of Doi Phu Kha National Park where the long-standing occupation has been the extraction of salt from local salt wells. It's easy to find the main community salt wells, which are more or less in the centre of the village.

If you have your own transport, the village is a good base for exploring the nearby national parks, Doi Phu Kha and Khun Nan National Park (อุทยานแห่งชาติขุนน่าน; ✆ 0 5477 8140; admission adult/child 100/50B; ⏰ 8am-4.30pm). The latter is located a few kilometres north of Ban Bo Luang, and has a 2km walk from the visitor centre that ends in a viewpoint looking over local villages and nearby Laos. Accommodation (bungalows 800B to 1600B) and a basic restaurant are available.

There is a handful of places to stay in Ban Bo Luang. By far the best of these is Boklua View (✆ 08 1809 6392; www.bokluaview. com; r & bungalows incl breakfast 1850B; ❄ 🌐), an attractive and well-run hillside resort overlooking the village and the river, Nam Mang, that runs through it. The resort has its own garden and serves good food (be sure to try Chef Toun's chicken deep-fried with northern Thai spices). If Boklua View is full or beyond your budget, Oon Ai Mang (✆ 08 1374 7994; no roman-script sign; bungalows incl breakfast 600-1500B; 🌐), just downhill, has some very basic tents and bamboo bungalows with shared bathrooms at the edge of Nam Mang. There are a handful of similar 'homestay' set-ups outside of the town.

A few small restaurants serve basic dishes in Ban Bo Luang. At press time, Bo Luang's only ATM did not accept foreign cards, so be sure to bring cash.

To reach Ban Bo Luang from Nan, take a bus or sŏrng·tăa·ou north of Nan to Pua (50B, two hours, hourly from 7am to 5pm). Get off at the 7-Eleven and cross the highway to take the sŏrng·tăa·ou that terminates in the village, departing at 7.30am, 9.30am and 11.30am (80B, one hour). To Pua, sŏrng·tăa·ou leave from near Bo Luang's T-intersection at 9am, 10.30am and 12.30pm.

PHITSANULOK PROVINCE

Phitsanulok   พิษณุโลก
POP 83,000

Phitsanulok sees relatively few independent travellers but a fair amount of package tourists, probably because the city is a convenient base from which to explore the attractions of historical Sukhothai, Si Satchanalai and Kamphaeng Phet. The vibrant and extremely friendly city also boasts some interesting sites and museums, chief of which is Wat Phra Si Ratana Mahathat, which contains one of the country's most revered Buddha images.

Those willing to forge their own path can also use the city as a base to visit the nearby national parks and wildlife sanctuaries of Thung Salaeng Luang and Phu Hin Rong Kla, the former strategic headquarters of the Communist Party of Thailand (CPT).

◉ Sights

★ Wat Phra Si Ratana Mahathat   BUDDHIST TEMPLE
(วัดพระศรีรัตนมหาธาตุ; Th Phutta Bucha; ⏰ 6am-9pm, museum 9am-5.30pm Wed-Sun) FREE The main wí·hăhn at this temple, known by locals as Wat Yai, appears small from the outside, but houses the Phra Phuttha Chinnarat, one of Thailand's most revered and copied Buddha images. This famous bronze statue is probably second in importance only to the Emerald Buddha in Bangkok's Wat Phra Kaew.

NORTHERN THAILAND PHITSANULOK

Phitsanulok

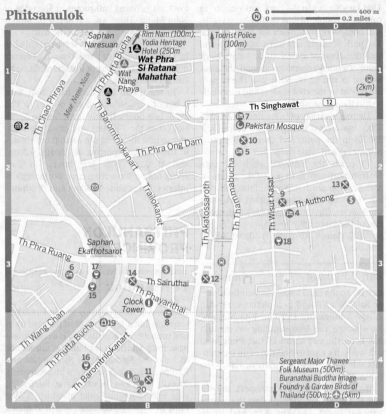

The story goes that construction of this wát was commissioned under the reign of King Li Thai in 1357. When it was completed, King Li Thai wanted it to contain three high-quality bronze images, so he sent for well-known sculptors from Si Satchanalai, Chiang Saen and Hariphunchai (Lamphun), as well as five Brahman priests. The first two castings worked well, but the third required three attempts before it was decreed the best of all. Legend has it that a white-robed sage appeared from nowhere to assist in the final casting, then disappeared. This last image was named the Chinnarat (Victorious King) Buddha and it became the centrepiece in the wí·hǎhn. The other two images, Phra Chinnasi and Phra Si Satsada, were later moved to the royal temple of Wat Bowonniwet in Bangkok.

The image was cast in the late Sukhothai style, but what makes it strikingly unique is the flamelike halo around the head and torso that turns up at the bottom to become dragon-serpent heads on either side of the image. The head of this Buddha is a little wider than standard Sukhothai, giving the statue a very solid feel.

Another sanctuary to one side has been converted to a free **museum**, displaying antique Buddha images, ceramics and other historic artefacts.

Despite the holiness of the temple, endless loud broadcasts asking for donations, Thai musicians, a strip of vendors hawking everything from herbs to lottery tickets, several ATM machines and hundreds of visitors all contribute to a relentlessly hectic atmosphere. Come early (ideally before 7am) if you're looking for quiet contemplation or simply wish to take photos, and regardless of the time be sure to dress appropriately – no shorts or sleeveless tops.

Wat Ratburana
BUDDHIST TEMPLE

(วัดราชบูรณะ; Th Phutta Bucha; ☉ daylight hours)
FREE Across the street from Wat Phra Si Ra-tana Mahathat, Wat Ratburana draws fewer visitors but in some ways is more interesting than its famous neighbour. In addition to a *wí·hǎhn* with a 700-year-old gold Buddha, there's an *ùbohsòt* with beautiful murals thought to date back to the mid-19th cen-tury and two wooden *hǒr đrai* (manuscript libraries).

The temple is also home to a few quirky attractions that offer a fascinating insight into the practices of Thai Buddhism. The most obvious of these is a large wooden boat decked with garlands that originally served to transport King Rama V on an official visit to Phitsanulok. Today the boat is thought to grant wishes to those who make an offering and crawl under its entire length three or nine times. Next to the *wí·hǎhn* is a sacred tree with ladders on either side that visitors climb up, leave an offering, then ring a bell and descend, again repeating the action a total of three or nine times. And directly ad-jacent to the tree is an immense gong that, when rubbed the right way, creates a unique ringing sound. Near each of these attrac-tions you'll find somebody stationed who, in addition to selling the coins, incense and flowers used in offerings, will also instruct visitors in exactly how to conduct each par-ticular ritual, including how many times to pass, what to offer and what prayer to say.

Museum of Phitsanulok
MUSEUM

(พิพิธภัณฑ์เมืองพิษณุโลก; Pibulsongkram Rajab-hat University, Th Wang Chan; ☉ 8.30am-4.30pm)
FREE A new but bare-bones museum with mostly text-based displays on local history and culture. Upstairs are additional displays on the five southernmost provinces of north-ern Thailand – Phetchabun, Phichit, Tak, Phitsanulok and Uttaradit – but virtually none of the information is in English.

🛏 Sleeping

Kraisaeng Place
HOTEL **$**

(☎ 0 5521 0509; www.facebook.com/kraisaeng-place45; 45 Th Thammabucha; r incl breakfast 400-450B; ❄ 🛜) Having more in common with a small apartment building than a hotel, the well-equipped rooms here are a super bar-gain, although traffic noise can be an issue.

Lithai Guest House
HOTEL **$**

(☎ 0 5521 9626; 73/1-5 Th Phayarithai; r incl break-fast 300-580B; ❄ @ 🛜) The light-filled 60 or

so rooms here don't have much character but they are clean. Air-con rooms include perks such as large private bathrooms with hot water, cable TV, fridge and breakfast.

Golden Grand Hotel
HOTEL **$$**

(☎ 0 5521 0234; www.goldengrandhotel.com; 66 Th Thammabucha; r incl breakfast 690-850B, ste incl breakfast 2500B; ❄ @ 🛜) The funky mint-green furniture, carpet and curtains date this 1970s-era business-class hotel. But rooms are spacious and clean, and an on-going renovation will hopefully impart the suites with the colour schemes and furniture of the current era.

Pattara Resort & Spa
HOTEL **$$$**

(☎ 0 5528 2966; www.pattararesort.com; 349/40 Th Chaiyanupap; r incl breakfast 3500-4000B, villa incl breakfast 7500-9000B; ❄ @ 🛜 ≋) This natural-feeling resort about 1.5km east from the centre of Phitsanulok has a lot going for it. Rooms feel big and all have equally huge bathrooms with tubs, as well as wide balconies that look out over lotus ponds and

FOLK MUSEUM, BUDDHA-CASTING FOUNDRY & BIRD GARDEN

A nationally acclaimed expert on Thai folkways, former military cartographer, Buddha statue caster and apparent bird aficionado, Sergeant Major Thawee Buranakhet has taken from his diverse experiences and interests to create three very worthwhile attractions in Phitsanulok.

The **Sergeant Major Thawee Folk Museum** (พิพิธภัณฑ์พื้นบ้านจ่าทวี; 26/43 Th Wisut Kasat; adult/child 50/25B; ☉8.30am-4.30pm) displays a remarkable collection of tools, textiles and photographs from Phitsanulok Province. This fascinating museum is spread throughout five traditional-style Thai buildings with well-groomed gardens, and the displays are all accompanied by informative and legible English descriptions. Those interested in cooking will find much of interest in the display of a traditional Thai kitchen and the various traps used to catch game. Male visitors will feel twinges of empathetic pain upon seeing the display that describes traditional bull castration – a process that apparently involves no sharp tools.

In the same compound is a basic **aquarium** featuring fish native to Phitsanulok.

Across the street and also belonging to Sergeant Major Thawee is the small **Buranathai Buddha Image Foundry** (โรงหล่อพระบูรณะไทย; Th Wisut Kasat; ☉8am-5pm) `FREE`, where bronze Buddha images of all sizes are cast. Visitors are welcome to watch the process, and there are even detailed photo exhibits demonstrating the lost-wax method of metal casting. Some of the larger images take a year or more to complete. There is a small gift shop at the foundry where you can purchase bronze images of various sizes.

In addition to the Buddha foundry, there is also a display of fighting cocks, which are bred and sold all over the country. (The official English name for this part of the facility is 'The Centre of Conservative Folk Cock'.)

Attached to the foundry is **Garden Birds of Thailand** (สวนนกไทย; Th Wisut Kasat; adult/child 50B/free; ☉8am-5pm), a collection of cages containing indigenous Thai birds, including some endangered species such as the very pretty pink-chested jamu fruit-dove and the prehistoric-looking helmeted hornbill. Unfortunately, the cages are generally rather small and don't reflect the birds' natural environments.

The museums are on Th Wisut Kasat, about 1km south of Phitsanulok's train station; a túk-túk here should cost around 80B.

a pool. Better yet, go for one of the two pool villas with private pool, or the two floating villas built over the lotus pond.

Yodia Heritage Hotel　BOUTIQUE HOTEL **$$$**
(☎0 5521 4677; www.yodiaheritage.com; 89/1 Th Phutta Bucha; r incl breakfast 3200-4200B, ste incl breakfast 8900B; ✳@☎) This boutique hotel, located along a quiet stretch of the Mae Nam Nan, takes the crown as Phitsanulok's most upscale accommodation. Suites are huge and feature similarly large tubs and a semi-private swimming pool.

Grand Riverside Hotel　HOTEL **$$$**
(☎0 5524 8333; www.tgrhotel.com; 59 Th Phra Ruang; r incl breakfast 1600-1800B, ste incl breakfast 3000B; ✳@☎) Overlooking Mae Nam Nan from its west bank, the Grand Riverside offers all the amenities you'd expect in a relatively new top-end hotel, and represents

solid value. Deluxe rooms offer an additional sitting area and river views.

Ayara Grand Palace　HOTEL **$$$**
(☎0 5590 9993; www.ayaragrand.com; Th Authong; r incl breakfast 1800B, ste incl breakfast 2200-3500B; ✳@☎✳) The '90s-era pastels and relentless flower theme of this new hotel give it an undeniably cheesy feel. But it's all in good fun, and the vast suites – the most expensive of which is decked out with an electric massage chair – are pretty good value.

✗ Eating

Phitsanulok takes its cuisine seriously. The city is particularly obsessive about night markets, and there are no fewer than three dotted in various locations around town. The most touted, Phitsanulok's night bazaar (p353), focuses mainly on clothing, but the southernmost restaurant along the strip specialises in *pàk bûng loy fáh* (literally 'floating-in-the-sky morning glory'), in which the cook fires up a batch of *pàk bûng* in the wok and then flings it through the air to a waiting server who catches it on a plate. If you're lucky, you'll be here when a tour group is trying to catch the flying vegetables, but actually dropping *pàk bûng* all over the place. Another **night market** (Th Phra Ong Dam; mains 30-60B; ⊙ 5pm-midnight) lines either side of Th Phra Ong Dam north of Th Authong, and there's a very busy **night market** (off Th Akatossaroth; mains 30-60B; ⊙ 4-8pm) just south of the train station that features mostly takeaway items including *kôw něe·o hòr*, tiny banana-leaf parcels of sticky rice with various toppings. There are two vendors opposite each other near the Th Akatossaroth entrance to the market.

Another dish associated with Phitsanulok is *gǒo·ay děe·o hôy kàh* (literally meaning,

'legs-hanging' noodles). The name comes from the way customers sit on the floor facing the river, with their legs dangling below. **Rim Nan** (5/4 Th Phutta Bucha, no roman-script sign; mains 20-35B; ⊙ 9am-4pm), north of Wat Phra Si Ratana Mahathat, is one of a few similar restaurants along Th Phutta Bucha that offer noodles and 'alternative' seating.

Paknang CHINESE-THAI **$**
(Th Sairuthai; mains 40-280B; ⊙ 10am-10pm) This corner of old Phitsanulok has a distinctly old-world Chinese feel – an excellent pairing with the tasty Chinese-style dishes at this long-standing restaurant.

Fah-Ke-Rah MUSLIM-THAI **$**
(786 Th Phra Ong Dam, no roman-script sign; mains 20-60B; ⊙ 6am-9pm) There are several Thai-Muslim cafes near the Pakistan Mosque on Th Phra Ong Dam, and this is one of the better ones. Thick *roh·đee* (crispy dough 'pancakes') is served up with *gaang mát·sà·màn*

THE GREEN ROUTE

Rte 12, which runs along the scenic, rapid-studded Lam Nam Khek between Phitsanulok and Lom Sak, is known as the 'Green Route'. Off this road are waterfalls, resorts and the Phu Hin Rong Kla and Thung Salaeng Luang National Parks.

The Phitsanulok TAT office distributes a good map of the attractions along this 130km stretch of road. You may want to bypass the first two waterfalls, **Nam Tok Sakhunothayan** (at the Km 33 marker) and **Kaeng Song** (at the Km 45 marker), which on weekends can be overwhelmed with visitors. The third, **Kaeng Sopha** (at the Km 72 marker), is a larger area of small falls and rapids where you can walk from rock formation to rock formation – there are more or fewer rocks depending on rainfall. When there's enough water (typically from September to November) any of the resorts along this section can organise **white-water rafting** trips on Lam Nam Khek.

Further east along the road is the 1262-sq-km **Thung Salaeng Luang National Park** (☑ 0 5526 8019, accommodation 0 2562 0760; www.dnp.go.th; admission 200B; ⊙ 8am-5pm), one of Thailand's largest and most important wildlife sanctuaries. The entrance is at the Km 80 marker, where the park headquarters has information on walks and accommodation.

If you have your own wheels, you can turn south at the Km 100 marker onto Rte 2196 and head for **Khao Kho** (Khow Khor), another mountain lair used by the CPT during the 1970s.

If you've made the side trip to Khao Kho you can choose either to return to the Phitsanulok–Lom Sak highway, or take Rte 2258, off Rte 2196, until it terminates at Rte 203. On Rte 203 you can continue north to Lom Sak or south to Phetchabun.

Resort-style accommodation can be found along most of the Green Route, with budget accommodation clumping near Kaeng Song, around Km 45, and at the various **national parks** (☑ 0 2562 0760; www.dnp.go.th; tent sites 30B, 2-8 person tents 150-600B, bungalows 300-5000B). Several **restaurants** are located on the banks of Nam Khek, most taking full advantage of the views and breezes.

Buses between Phitsanulok and Lom Sak cost between 68B and 95B, and run from 6am to 6pm. For more freedom it's best to do this route with your own wheels; cars can be hired via Budget (p353) in Phitsanulok.

(Muslim curry) and fresh yoghurt is made daily.

Jaroen Tham VEGETARIAN-THAI $

(Th Sithamatraipidok, no roman-script sign; mains 15-40B; ⏰8am-3pm; 🖊) This simple place serves a choice of vegetarian dishes paired with husky brown rice. There are at least three other similar places along the same strip – look for the yellow banners.

★ Ban Mai THAI $$

(93/30 Th Authong, no roman-script sign; mains 100-200B; ⏰11am-10pm; ❄) Dinner at this local favourite is like a meal at your grandparents' place: opinionated conversation resounds, frumpy furniture abounds and an overfed cat appears to rule the dining room. The likewise homey dishes include *gaeng phed ped yang* (a curry of grilled duck), and *yam tra krai* (a herbal lemongrass 'salad'). Look for the yellow compound across from Ayara Grand Palace Hotel.

 Drinking & Entertainment

Wood Stock BAR

(148/22-23 Th Wisut Kasat; ⏰7pm-midnight) It's, like, 1969 all over again, man. Wood Stock combines funky '60s- and '70s-era furniture, live music and a brief and cheap menu of *gàp glâam* (Thai-style nibbles). Groovy.

TRANSPORT TO/FROM PHITSANULOK

DESTINATION	AIR	BUS	MINIVAN	TRAIN
Bangkok	520-2699B; 55min; 6 daily (to Don Muang Airport)	304-416B; 5-6hr; hourly 6.20am-12.30am		69-1664B; 5-7hr; 10 daily
Chiang Mai		299-349B; 6hr; hourly 5.40am-1.30am		65-1645B; 7-9hr; 6 daily
Chiang Rai		273-410B; 7-8hr; hourly 8am-12.40am		
Kamphaeng Phet		59-83B; 3hr; hourly 5am-6pm		
Lampang		220-265B; 4hr; hourly 8am-midnight		158-1042B; 5hr; 5 daily
Lom Sak (for Green Route)		68-95B; 1-2hr; frequent 6am-6pm		
Mae Sai		398-464B; 7hr; hourly 11.30am-11.55pm		
Mae Sot		168B; 4hr; hourly 7am-3pm	163B; 4hr; 4 departures 8am-3pm	
Nakhon Thai (for Phu Hin Rong Kla National Park)		52-94B; 2hr; hourly 5am-6pm		
Nan		204B; 6hr; 5 departures 7.30am-1.30pm		
Phayao		218-303B; 4hr; hourly 11.20am-2am		
Phrae		127-191B; 4hr; frequent 6am-12.40am		
Sukhothai		43-56B; 1hr; hourly 7.20am-6.15pm	60B; 1hr; half-hourly 5am-6pm	
Sukhothai Historical Park			70B; 1½hr; half-hourly 5am-6pm	

Camper
BAR

(Th Baromtrilokanart; ⊙7pm-midnight) An open-air, ramshackle convocation of falling-apart retro furniture, local hipsters, draft beer and live music, Camper is as loose and fun as it sounds.

Calito
BAR

(84/1 Th Wang Chan; ⊙6.30pm-midnight) This wooden riverside balcony has a short menu of Thai drinking snacks, cold draught beer and live music every night after 7pm.

Paradise
BAR

(Food & Drink; off Th Wang Chan; ⊙7pm-midnight) As the only remaining floating pub in Mae Nam Nan, Paradise is a dying breed. Snacks and more substantial Thai dishes are available.

🛍 Shopping

Night Bazaar
MARKET

(Th Phutta Bucha; ⊙7pm-midnight) Distinctly more workday and less crafty than northern Thailand's other night markets, Phitsanulok's night bazaar is worth a visit if you need some cheap clothes or a foot massage.

❶ Information

Several banks in town offer foreign-exchange services and ATMs. There are also several ATMs inside the Wat Phra Si Ratana Mahathat compound.

@net (off Th Baromtrilokanart; per hour 10B; ⊙24hr) 24hr Internet access.

Golden House Tour (✉0 5525 9973; 55/37-38 Th Baromtrilokanart; ⊙7am-7pm Mon-Sat) This experienced travel agency can book airline tickets and arrange ground transport in and around Phitsanulok.

Tourism Authority of Thailand Office (TAT; ✉0 5525 2742, nationwide 1672; tatphlok@tat. or.th; 209/7-8 Th Baromtrilokanart; ⊙8.30am-4.30pm) Off Th Baromtrilokanart, with helpful staff who hand out free maps of the town and a walking-tour sheet. This office also oversees the provinces of Uttaradit, Phichit and Phetchabun.

Tourist Police (✉1155; Th Akatossaroth)

❶ Getting There & Away

Air Asia (✉0 2515 9999; www.airasia.com; Phitsanulok Airport) and **Nok Air** (✉0 5530 1051; www.nokair.co.th; Phitsanulok Airport; ⊙8am-5pm) operate out of Phitsanulok, with flights to/from Bangkok. The **airport** (✉0 5530 1002) is about 5km south of town; Golden House Tour provides car/minivan

service from the airport to hotels (300B to 500B).

Phitsanulok's **bus station** (✉0 5521 2090; Rte 12) is 2km east of town on Hwy 12; túk-túk and motorcycle taxis to/from town cost 60B. Transport options out of Phitsanulok are good as it's a junction for several bus and minivan routes.

The **train station** (✉0 5525 8005, nationwide 1690; www.railway.co.th; Th Akatossaroth) is within walking distance of accommodation and offers a left-luggage service. The station is a significant train terminal and virtually every northbound and southbound train stops here.

❶ Getting Around

Rides on the town's Darth Vader–like sǎhm·lór start at about 60B. Outside the train station there's a sign indicating prices for different destinations around town.

Phitsanulok now has a small **taxi** (✉0 5533 8888) fleet.

Budget (✉0 5530 1020; www.budget.co.th; Phitsanulok Airport; ⊙7am-8pm) has a car-hire office at the airport (per day from 1500B).

Phu Hin Rong Kla National Park อุทยานแห่งชาติภูหิน ร่องกล้า

Between 1967 and 1982, the mountain that is known as **Phu Hin Rong Kla** (✉0 5523 3527, accommodation 0 2562 0760; www.dnp.go.th; admission 200B; ⊙8.30am-5pm) served as the strategic headquarters for the Communist Party of Thailand (CPT) and its tactical arm, the People's Liberation Army of Thailand (PLAT). The remote, easily defended summit was perfect for an insurgent army. China's Yunnan Province is only 300km away and it was here that CPT cadres received their training in revolutionary tactics. (This was until the 1979 split between the Chinese and Vietnamese communists, when the CPT sided with Vietnam.)

For nearly 20 years the area around Phu Hin Rong Kla served as a battlefield for Thai troops and the communists. In 1972 the Thai government launched an unsuccessful major offensive against the PLAT. The CPT camp at Phu Hin Rong Kla became especially active after the Thai military killed hundreds of students in Bangkok during the October 1976 student-worker uprising. Many students subsequently fled here to join the CPT, setting up a hospital and a school of political and military tactics. By 1978 the PLAT ranks here had swelled to 4000. In 1980 and 1981 the Thai armed forces tried again and were able to recapture some parts of CPT territory. But the decisive blow to the CPT came in 1982, when the government declared an amnesty for all the students who had joined the communists after 1976. The departure of most of the students broke the spine of the movement, which had become dependent on their membership. A final military push in late 1982 resulted in the surrender of the PLAT, and Phu Hin Rong Kla was declared a national park in 1984.

◉ Sights & Activities

The park covers about 307 sq km of rugged mountains and forest. The elevation at park headquarters is about 1000m, so the area is refreshingly cool even in the hot season. The main attractions don't tend to stray too far from the main road through the park and include the remains of the CPT stronghold – a rustic meeting hall, the school of political and military tactics – and the CPT administration building. Across the road from the school is a water wheel designed by exiled engineering students.

Phu Hin Rong Kla can become quite crowded on weekends and holidays; schedule a more peaceful visit for midweek.

Pha Chu Thong   HISTORICAL SITE
A 1km trail leads to Pha Chu Thong (Flag Raising Cliff, sometimes called Red Flag Cliff), where the communists would raise the red flag to announce a military victory. Also in this area is an air-raid shelter, a lookout and the remains of the main CPT headquarters – the most inaccessible point in the territory before a road was constructed by the Thai government.

The buildings in the park are made out of wood and bamboo and have no plumbing or electricity – a testament to how primitive the living conditions were.

There is a small museum at the park headquarters that displays relics from CPT days, although there's not a whole lot of English explanation. At the end of the road into the park is a small White Hmong village.

Walking Trails   HIKING
(⊙8.30am-4.30pm) If you're not interested in the modern history of Phu Hin Rong Kla, there are waterfalls, hiking trails and scenic views, as well as some interesting rock formations – jutting boulders called Lan Hin Pum and an area of deep rocky crevices

where PLAT troops would hide during air raids, called Lan Hin Taek. Ask at the visitor centre for maps.

🛏 Sleeping & Eating

Golden House Tour, near the TAT office in Phitsanulok, can help book accommodation.

Thailand's Royal Forest Department   CAMPING GROUND $
(✎0 2562 0760; www.dnp.go.th; 2-8 person tents 150-600B, bungalows 300-2100B) Bungalows for three to 15 people, in three different zones of the park, must be booked in advance via this organisation. You can also pitch a tent or rent one, and rent sleeping bags (60B). Near the camping ground and bungalows are restaurants and food vendors. The best are Duang Jai Cafeteria – try its famous carrot sôm-đam – and Rang Thong.

ℹ Getting There & Away

The park headquarters is about 125km from Phitsanulok. To get here, first take an early bus to Nakhon Thai (52B to 94B, two hours, every hour from 5am to 6pm). From there you can charter a sŏrng-tăa-ou to the park (700B) from near the market. As a day trip from Phitsanulok, Golden House Tour charges 1700B for car and driver; petrol is extra. This is a delightful trip if you're on a motorcycle since there's not much traffic along the way, but a strong engine is necessary to conquer the hills to Phu Hin Rong Kla.

SUKHOTHAI PROVINCE

Sukhothai   สุโขทัย
POP 37,000
The Sukhothai (Rising of Happiness) kingdom flourished from the mid-13th century to the late 14th century. This period is often viewed as the golden age of Thai civilisation, and the religious art and architecture of the era are considered to be the most classic of Thai styles. The remains of the kingdom, today known as meu-ang gòw (old city), feature around 45 sq km of partially rebuilt ruins, which are one of the most visited ancient sites in Thailand.

Located 12km east of the historical park on Mae Nam Yom, the market town of New Sukhothai is not particularly interesting. Yet its friendly atmosphere, good transport links and excellent-value accommodation make it a logical base from which to explore the old city ruins.

Sukhothai Historical Park

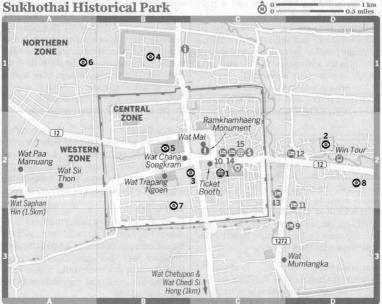

History

Sukhothai is typically regarded as the first capital of Siam, although this is not entirely accurate. The area was previously the site of a Khmer empire until 1238, when two Thai rulers, Pho Khun Pha Muang and Pho Khun Bang Klang Hao, decided to unite and form a new Thai kingdom.

Sukhothai's dynasty lasted 200 years and spanned nine kings. The most famous was King Ramkhamhaeng, who reigned from 1275 to 1317 and is credited with developing the first Thai script – his inscriptions are also considered the first Thai literature. Ramkhamhaeng eventually expanded his kingdom to include an area even larger than that of present-day Thailand. But a few kings later in 1438, Sukhothai was absorbed by Ayuthaya.

◉ Sights

The **Sukhothai Historical Park** (อุทยาน ประวัติศาสตร์สุโขทัย) ruins are one of Thailand's most impressive World Heritage Sites. The park includes the remains of 21 historical sites and four large ponds within the old walls, with an additional 70 sites within a 5km radius.

The architecture of Sukhothai temples is most typified by the classic lotus-bud *chedi*,

featuring a conical spire topping a square-sided structure on a three-tiered base. Some sites exhibit other rich architectural forms introduced and modified during the period, such as bell-shaped Sinhalese and double-tiered Srivijaya *chedi.*

Despite the popularity of the park, it's quite expansive and solitary exploration is generally possible. Some of the most impressive ruins are well outside the city walls, so a bicycle or motorcycle is essential.

The ruins are divided into five zones. The central, northern and western zones each have a separate 100B admission fee.

Central Zone

This is the historical park's main **zone** (admission 100B, plus per bicycle/motorcycle/car 10/30/50B; ⊙ 6.30am-7pm Sun-Fri, to 9pm Sat) and is home to what are arguably some of the park's most well-preserved and impressive ruins. An audio tour, available in English, Japanese or Thai, can be rented at the ticket booth for 150B.

Wat Mahathat   HISTORICAL SITE
(วัดมหาธาตุ) Completed in the 13th century, the largest wát in Sukhothai is surrounded by brick walls (206m long and 200m wide) and a moat that is believed to represent the outer wall of the universe and the cosmic ocean.

The *chedi* spires feature the famous lotus-bud motif, and some of the original stately Buddha figures still sit among the ruined columns of the old *wí·hǎhn* (sanctuary). There are 198 *chedi* within the monastery walls – a lot to explore in what is believed to be the former spiritual and administrative centre of the old capital.

THE FIRST KINGDOM?

The establishment of Sukhothai in 1238 is often described as the formation of the first Thai kingdom. But the kingdom of Chiang Saen had already been established 500 years earlier, and at the time of Sukhothai's founding, other Thai kingdoms such as Lanna and Phayao also existed. Sukhothai's profound influence on the art, language, literature and religion of modern Thai society, not to mention the immense size of the kingdom at its peak in the early 13th century, are doubtlessly reasons for the proliferation of this convenient, but technically incorrect, historical fact.

Ramkhamhaeng National Museum   MUSEUM
(พิพิธภัณฑสถานแห่งชาติรามคำแหง; admission 150B; ⊙ 9am-4pm) A good starting point for exploring the historical park ruins is this museum. A replica of the famous Ramkhamhaeng inscription, said to be the earliest example of Thai writing, is kept here among an impressive collection of Sukhothai artefacts. Admission to the museum is not included in the ticket to the central zone.

Wat Si Sawai   HISTORICAL SITE
(วัดศรีสวาย) Just south of Wat Mahathat, this Buddhist shrine (dating from the 12th and 13th centuries) features three Khmer-style towers and a picturesque moat. It was originally built by the Khmers as a Hindu temple.

Wat Sa Si   HISTORICAL SITE
(วัดสระศรี) Also known as 'Sacred Pond Monastery', Wat Sa Si sits on an island west of the bronze monument of King Ramkhamhaeng (the third Sukhothai king). It's a simple, classic Sukhothai-style wát containing a large Buddha, one *chedi* and the columns of the ruined *wí·hǎhn.*

Wat Trapang Thong   BUDDHIST TEMPLE
(วัดตระพังทอง) Next to the museum, this small, still-inhabited wát with its fine stucco reliefs is reached by a footbridge across the large lotus-filled pond that surrounds it. This reservoir, the original site of Thailand's Loi Krathong festival, supplies the Sukhothai community with most of its water.

Northern Zone

This **zone** (admission 100B, plus per bicycle/motorcycle/car 10/30/50B; ⊙ 7.30am-5.30pm), 500m north of the old city walls, is easily reached by bicycle.

Wat Si Chum   HISTORICAL SITE
(วัดศรีชุม) This wát is northwest of the old city and contains an impressive *mon·dòp* with a 15m, brick-and-stucco seated Buddha. This Buddha's elegant, tapered fingers are much photographed. Archaeologists theorise that this image is the 'Phra Atchana' mentioned in the famous Ramkhamhaeng inscription. A passage in the *mon·dòp* wall that leads to the top has been blocked so that it's no longer possible to view the *jataka* inscriptions that line the tunnel ceiling.

TOP SPOTS IN SUKHOTHAI

Ronny Hanquart, manager of Cycling Sukhothai (p358), told us his top tips for visiting Sukhothai.

Best Temples Wat Mahathat and the majestic Buddha statue at Wat Si Chum are two temples you should not miss.

Best Museum If you are visiting Si Satchanalai Historical Park, then I recommend the excavated kilns along Mae Nam Yom.

Best Time to Visit Early in the morning is cooler and there are fewer visitors. After a siesta under one of the big trees in the park, you can continue till evening. Sukhothai is green during the monsoon (May to October) and nice and cool during the cool season (December to February).

Best Place to Escape the Crowds The western zone is quite large and has a beautiful natural background. Few tourists go there.

Best Sunset Wat Sa Si in the central zone is a good spot for sunset.

Secret Spot Wat Tawet, where Buddhist and Hindu morals are explained through a display of about 200 statues, is an interesting place for people who like art and kitsch.

Wat Phra Phai Luang   HISTORICAL SITE
(วัดพระพายหลวง) Outside the city walls in the northern zone, this somewhat isolated wát features three 12th-century Khmer-style towers, bigger than those at Wat Si Sawai. This may have been the centre of Sukhothai when it was ruled by the Khmers of Angkor prior to the 13th century.

◉ Western Zone

This **zone** (admission 100B, plus per bicycle/motorcycle/car 10/30/50B; ⊗ 8am-4.30pm), at its furthest extent 2km west of the old city walls, is the most expansive. In addition to Wat Saphan Hin, several mostly featureless ruins can be found. A bicycle or motorcycle is necessary to explore this zone.

Wat Saphan Hin   HISTORICAL SITE
(วัดสะพานหิน) Located on the crest of a hill that rises about 200m above the plain, the name of the wát, which means 'stone bridge', is a reference to the slate path and staircase that leads up to the temple, which are still in place.

All that remains of the original temple are a few chedi and the ruined wí·hăhn, consisting of two rows of laterite columns flanking a 12.5m-high standing Buddha image on a brick terrace. The site is 3km west of the former city wall and gives a good view of the Sukhothai ruins to the southeast and the mountains to the north and south.

Other Sites

A few more worthwhile destinations lie outside the more popular paid zones.

Sangkhalok Museum   MUSEUM
(พิพิธภัณฑ์สังคโลก; Rte 1293; adult/child 100/50B; ⊗ 8am-5pm) This small but comprehensive museum is an excellent introduction to ancient Sukhothai's most famous product and export, its ceramics.

The ground floor displays an impressive collection of original Thai pottery found in the area, plus some pieces traded from Vietnam, Myanmar and China. The 2nd floor features examples of non-utilitarian pottery made as art, including some beautiful and rare ceramic Buddha statues.

The museum is about 2.5km east of the centre of New Sukhothai; a túk-túk here will run about 100B.

Wat Chang Lom   HISTORICAL SITE
(วัดช้างล้อม; off Rte 12) FREE Off Rte 12 in the east zone, Wat Chang Lom (Elephant Circled Monastery) is about 1km east of the main park entrance. A large bell-shaped *chedi* is supported by 36 elephants sculpted into its base.

Wat Chetupon   HISTORICAL SITE
(วัดเชตุพน) FREE Located 1.4km south of the old city walls, this temple once held a four-sided *mon·dòp* featuring the four classic poses of the Buddha (sitting, reclining, standing and walking). The graceful lines of

the walking Buddha can still be made out today.

Wat Chedi Si Hong
HISTORICAL SITE

(วัดเจดีย์สี่ห้อง) **FREE** Directly across from Wat Chetupon, the main *chedi* here has retained much of its original stucco relief work, which shows still vivid depictions of elephants, lions and humans.

🏃 Activities

Cycling Sukhothai
BICYCLE TOURS

(☎08 5083 1864, 0 5561 2519; www.cycling-sukhothai.com; off Th Jarot Withithong; half-/full day 650/750B, sunset tour 350B) A resident of Sukhothai for nearly 20 years, Belgian cycling enthusiast Ronny Hanquart offers rides following themed itineraries such as the Historical Park Tour, which includes stops at lesser-seen *wát* and villages.

Cycling Sukhothai is based about 1.2km west of Mae Nam Yom, in New Sukhothai, and free transport can be arranged.

✨ Festivals & Events

Loi Krathong
TRADITIONAL

Sukhothai Historical Park is one of the most popular destinations for this holiday, celebrated over five days in November. In addition to the magical floating lights, there are fireworks, folk-dance performances and a light-and-sound production.

🛏 Sleeping

Most accommodation is in New Sukhothai, which is home to some of the best-value budget-level accommodation in northern Thailand. Clean, cheerful hotels and guesthouses abound, with many places offering attractive bungalows, free pick-up from the bus station and free use of bicycles.

There are an increasing number of options near the park, many of them in the upscale bracket. Prices tend to go up during the Loi Krathong festival.

🛏 New Sukhothai

TR Room & Bungalow
GUESTHOUSE $

(☎0 5561 1663; www.sukhothaibudgetguesthouse.com; 27/5 Th Prawet Nakhon; r 250-450B, bungalows 400-550B; ❄@🖥) The rooms here are basic and lack character, but figure among the tidiest we've encountered in northern Thailand. For those needing legroom, there are five wooden bungalows out back.

Sabaidee House
HOTEL $

(☎0 5561 6303; www.sabaideehouse.com; 81/7 Th Jarot Withithong; r 200-600B; ❄🖥) This cheery guesthouse in a semi-rural setting spans seven attractive bungalows and rooms in the main structure. Sabaidee is off Th Jarot Withithong about 200m before the intersection with Rte 101; look for the sign.

J&J Guest House
GUESTHOUSE $

(☎0 5562 0095; jjguest-house@hotmail.com; 12 Th Kuhasuwan; bungalows 500-600B; ❄@🖥) Located in a manicured garden by the river, the eight bungalows here are attractive, cool and relatively spacious. They're also identical, and price depends on whether you go with fan or air-con.

Hangjeng
GUESTHOUSE $

(☎0 5561 0585; viyada_sethvanich@hotmail.com; 44/10 Th Prawet Nakhon; r 200-400B; ❄🖥) A sign here reads 'Welcome with open arms', and one gets the impression they really mean it. Maintained by an exceptionally lovely family, the basic rooms are in a rambling house and share toilets and balconies.

Ban Thai
HOTEL $

(☎0 5561 0163; banthai_guesthouse@yahoo.com; 38 Th Prawet Nakhon; r 200-500B, bungalows 350-550B; ❄🖥) None of the rooms here are particularly remarkable, but the convergence a friendly atmosphere, an attractive garden setting and low prices result in a winner.

Baan Thit
GUESTHOUSE $

(☎08 1532 6400; www.baantit.com; 31/6 Th Jarot Withithong; r incl breakfast 450-600B; ❄@🖥) The modern-feeling home of a former English teacher has been turned into this comfortable guesthouse. The four rooms are basic but stylish, and most feature quasi-outdoor bathrooms and small balconies.

4T Guesthouse
HOTEL $

(☎0 5561 4679; fourthouse@yahoo.com; 122 Soi Mae Ramphan; r 300-400B, bungalows 600-700B; ❄@🖥🏊) Hardly a leaf is out of place at this expansive budget resort. There's a smorgasbord of bungalows and spacious rooms to consider, and the swimming pool makes the decision even easier.

Lotus Village
HOTEL $$

(☎0 5562 1484; www.lotus-village.com; 170 Th Ratchathani; r incl breakfast 720-1200B, bungalows incl breakfast 1000-2850B; ❄@🖥) Village is an apt label for this peaceful compound of wooden bungalows that sit elevated over lo-

NORTHERN NOSH

Much like the language, Thailand's food seems to take a slightly different form every time you cross a provincial border. The cuisine of Thailand's northern provinces is no exception and is indicative of the region's seasonal and relatively cool climate, not to mention a love for pork, veggies and all things deep-fried. Traditionally, the residents of Thailand's north ate almost exclusively *kôw něe·o* (sticky rice) known in the local dialect as *kôw nêung*. Coconut milk rarely makes its way into the northern kitchen, and northern Thai cuisine is probably the most seasonal and least spicy of Thailand's regional schools of cooking, often relying on bitter or other dried spice flavours.

Paradoxically (and unfortunately), it can be quite difficult to find authentic local food in northern Thailand. Outside of Chiang Mai and the other large cities in northern Thailand, there are relatively few restaurants serving northern-style dishes, and the vast majority of authentic local food is sold from stalls in 'to go' bags. However, if you manage to come across a restaurant serving northern-style food, some must-try dishes include:

➡ *Gaang hang·lair* – Burmese in origin (*hang* is a corruption of the Burmese *hin*, meaning curry), this rich pork curry is often seen at festivals and ceremonies. Try a bowl at Mae Si Bua (p398) in Mae Hong Son.

➡ *Kâap mǒo* – Deep-fried pork crackling is a common, delicious side dish in northern Thailand.

➡ *Kôw gân jǐn* – Banana-leaf packets of rice mixed with blood, steamed and served with garlic oil. A popular snack in Mae Hong Son.

➡ *Kôw soy* – This popular curry-based noodle dish is possibly Burmese in origin and was probably introduced to northern Thailand by travelling Chinese merchants. A mild but tasty version is available at Khao Soi Phor Jai (p311) in Chiang Rai.

➡ *Kà·nǒm jeen nám ngée·o* – Fresh rice noodles served with a meaty and tart pork- and tomato-based broth. An excellent bowl can be got at Paa Suk (p311), in Chiang Rai.

➡ *Lâhp kôo·a* – Literally 'fried *lâhp*', this dish takes the famous Thai minced-meat 'salad' and fries it with a mixture of unique dried spices. Try the version at Pu Som Restaurant (p344) in Nan.

➡ *Lôo* – Raw blood mixed with a curry paste and served over deep-fried intestines and crispy noodles – the most hardcore northern dish of all, and one often associated with Phrae Province.

➡ *Nǎam* – Fermented raw pork, a sour delicacy that tastes much better than it sounds.

➡ *Nám prík nùm* – Green chillies, shallots and garlic that are grilled then mashed into a stringy and spicy paste served with sticky rice, parboiled veggies and deep-fried pork crackling. Try it at Phu-Lae (p313), in Chiang Rai.

➡ *Nám prík òrng* – A chilli dip of Shan origin made from tomatoes and minced pork – a northern Thai bolognese of sorts. Available at Banpleng (p398), in Mae Hong Son.

➡ *Sâi òo·a* – A grilled pork sausage seasoned with copious fresh herbs. Available at Jinda's Kitchen (p325), outside Chiang Saen.

➡ *Đam sôm oh* – The northern Thai version of *sôm·đam* substitutes pomelo for green papaya.

➡ *Đôm yam* – The northern Thai version of this Thai soup staple is flavoured with some of the same dried spices that feature in *lâhp kôo·a*.

tus ponds. Smaller, mostly fan-cooled rooms in a wooden building are also available, and an attractive Burmese/Indian design theme runs through the entire place. Both the breakfast and staff get great reports, and an on-site spa offers a variety of services.

At Home Sukhothai GUESTHOUSE $$
(☎ 0 5561 0172; www.athomesukhothai.com; 184/1 Th Vichien Chamnong; r incl breakfast 400-800B; ❄ @ ☎) Located in the 50-year-old childhood home of the proprietor, the simple but comfortable rooms here – both those

New Sukhothai

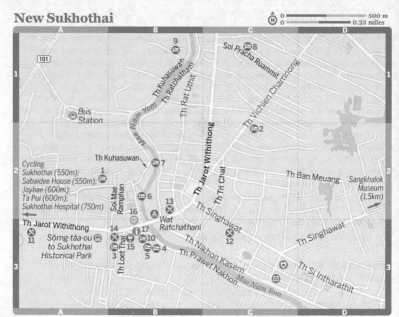

New Sukhothai

🛏 Sleeping

1	4T Guesthouse	A2
2	At Home Sukhothai	C2
3	Baan Thit	B3
4	Ban Thai	B3
5	Hangjeng	B3
6	J&J Guest House	B2
7	Lotus Village	B2
8	Ruean Thai Hotel	C1
9	Sila Resort	B1
10	TR Room & Bungalow	B3

🍽 Eating

11	Chula	A3
12	Dream Café	C3
13	Night Market	B2
14	Poo Restaurant	B3

🍸 Drinking & Nightlife

15	Chopper Bar	B3

ⓘ Information

	Kasikorn Bank	(see 17)
16	Tawan Hi-Speed	B3
17	Tourism Authority of Thailand	B3

fan-cooled in the original structure and the newer air-con ones – here really do feel like home. The only downside is the relative distance from 'downtown' Sukhothai.

Sila Resort HOTEL **$$**
(☎ 0 5562 0344; www.silaresortsukhothai.com; 3/49 Th Kuhasuwan; r 250-450B, bungalows 700-1200B; ❄ @ ☎) We couldn't help but think of Disneyland when we first encountered this compound of flowering trees, a gingerbread Thai villa, wood bungalows, statues, resortlike A-frames and a restaurant. And like Disneyland, it comes together in a cheerful, colourful package looked after by smiling people. The only downside is that it's a fair hike from the centre of New Sukhothai.

★ Ruean Thai Hotel HOTEL **$$$**
(☎ 0 5561 2444; www.rueanthaihotel.com; 181/20 Soi Pracha Ruammit; r incl breakfast 1480-4200B; ❄ @ ☎ ☲) At first glance, you may mistake this eye-catching complex for a Buddhist temple or a traditional Thai house. The rooms on the upper level follow a distinct Thai theme, while the poolside rooms are slightly more modern, and there's a concrete building with simple air-con rooms out the back. Service is both friendly and flawless, and the whole place boasts a resort-like feel. Call for free pick-up from the bus station.

Sukhothai Historical Park

Vitoon Guesthouse GUESTHOUSE $
(📞 0 5569 7045; www.vitoonguesthouse.com; 49 Rte 12; r 300-900B; ❋@☎) The better of the two budget options within walking distance of the old city, the fan rooms here are starkly bare, but the air-con rooms, in a newer building, are spotless and represent a good deal.

Old City Guest House GUESTHOUSE $
(📞 0 5569 7515; 28/7 Rte 12; r 200-700B; ❋☎) This vast budget complex features heaps of rooms in a variety of styles, most with air-con and TV; ask to see a few before you make a decision.

Orchid Hibiscus Guest House HOTEL $$
(📞 0 5563 3284; orchid_hibiscus_guest_house@yahoo.com; 407/2 Rte 1272; r/bungalows 900/1300B; ❋@☎❀) This collection of rooms and bungalows is set in relaxing, manicured grounds with a swimming pool as a centrepiece and the self-professed 'amazing breakfast' (100B) as a highlight. Rooms are spotless and fun, featuring colourful design details and accents. Orchid Hibiscus is on Rte 1272 about 500m off Rte 12 – the turn-off is between the Km 48 and Km 49 markers.

Wake Up @ Muang Kao GUESTHOUSE $$
(📞 0 5569 7153; 1/1 Rte 12; r incl breakfast 1000-1500B; ❋@☎) If there's a homestay equivalent to flashpacker, Wake Up has nailed it. The five rooms here are spacious and tasteful, come decked out with local touches and are looked after by a friendly local couple. A breath of fresh air in Old Sukhothai.

Thai Thai HOTEL $$
(📞 08 4932 1006; www.thaithaisukhothai.com; 95/8 Rte 1272; r incl breakfast 800-2400B; bungalows incl breakfast 1200-1800B; ❋☎) As the name brings home, Thai Thai takes the form of an indigenously inspired compound. There's a string of 10 wooden bungalows in an attractive garden and 10 rooms in a few larger structures out back. All come fully outfitted with TV, fridge, hot water and air-con.

PinPao Guest House HOTEL $$
(📞 0 5563 3284; orchid_hibiscus_guest_house@hotmail.com; Rte 12; r 900B; ❋@☎❀) PinPao is home to 10 of the most gaily coloured rooms we've seen anywhere, although many lack windows and can be rather dark. The invit-

BAN NA TON CHAN

The residents of Ban Na Ton Chan, a picturesque village in rural Sukhothai, have formed a worthwhile and award-winning **homestay program** (📞 08 9885 1639; http://homestaynatonchan.blogspot.com; per person 350B). Approximately 20 households are involved, and the fee includes breakfast and dinner (for lunch you can try *kôw ɓòep*, a local noodle dish), and involvement in daily activities such as cooking, furniture making and weaving. The locals are keen to open their homes and share their knowledge, but it must be noted that the level of English ability among the villagers is low.

The village is 15km east of Rte 101, down a signed turn-off north of Ban Hat Siaw. A motorcycle taxi from near the 7-Eleven in Ban Hat Siaw will take people here for 150B; a sǎhm-lór costs 350B.

ing pool and sunbathing area go quite a distance in making up for this. PinPao is on Rte 12, directly opposite the turn-off to Rte 1272.

Tharaburi Resort HOTEL $$$
(📞 0 5569 7132; www.tharaburiresort.com; 321/3 Rte 1272; r incl breakfast 3600-4200B, villa/ste incl breakfast 5000/6000B; ❋@☎❀) This sumptuous boutique hotel features three traditional-feeling structures divided into 13 rooms and suites. Rooms are themed (Moroccan, Japanese, Chinese), using faux antiques and silks, while the suites feel like a small home, and there is also a couple of two-floor family rooms. A stylish, if somewhat overpriced, choice.

Le Charme Sukhothai HOTEL $$$
(📞 0 5563 3333; www.lecharmesukhothai.com; 9/9 Rte 1272; r & bungalow incl breakfast 1500-4500B; ❋☎❀) It may not look like much from a distance, but a closer look reveals an inviting cluster of bright bungalows linked by an elevated wooden walkway, lush gardens and lotus ponds. Rooms are large and simply but tastefully decorated, with inviting balconies looking out over all that water.

✖ Eating & Drinking

✖ New Sukhothai

Sukhothai's signature dish is *gŏo·ay đĕe·o sù·kŏh·tai* (Sukhothai-style noodles), which features a slightly sweet broth with different types of pork, ground peanuts and thinly sliced green beans. The dish is available at **Jayhae** (Th Jarot Withithong; dishes 25-40B; ☉8am-4pm) and **Ta Pui** (Th Jarot Withithong, no roman-script sign; dishes 25-35B; ☉7am-3pm), located across from each other on Th Jarot Withithong, about 1.3km west of Mae Nam Yom.

A wise choice for cheap eats is New Sukhothai's tiny **night market** (Th Jarot Withithong; mains 30-60B; ☉6-11pm). Most vendors here are accustomed to accommodating foreigners and even provide bilingual menus.

Chula   CHINESE-THAI $
(Th Jarot Withithong; dishes 30-120B; ☉10am-11pm) It has all the charm of an airport hangar, but the food at this local favourite is solid. Pick and choose from prepared dishes, or do the same with the raw ingredients displayed out front.

Poo Restaurant   INTERNATIONAL-THAI $
(24/3 Th Jarot Withithong; mains 30-150B; ☉11am-midnight; 🛜) Unfortunately named and deceptively simple, Poo does mediocre food but has an impressive selection of Belgian beers.

Dream Café   THAI $$
(86/1 Th Singhawat; mains 120-250B; ☉5-11pm; ✸🖉) A meal at Dream Café is like dining in an antique shop. Eclectic but tasteful furnishings and knick-knackery abound, staff are equal parts competent and friendly, and most importantly of all, the food is good. Try one of the well-executed *yam* (Thai-style 'salads'), or one of the dishes that feature freshwater fish, a local speciality.

Chopper Bar   BAR
(Th Prawet Nakhon; mains 30-150B; ☉10am-12.30am; 🛜) Both travellers and locals congregate at this restaurant-bar from morning till hangover for food, drinks and live music. Take advantage of Sukhothai's cool evenings on the rooftop terrace.

✖ Sukhothai Historical Park

Along the road that leads to the historical park is a string of food stalls and simple shophouse restaurants.

Coffee Cup   INTERNATIONAL-THAI $
(Rte 12; dishes 30-150B; ☉7am-10pm; 🛜) If you're staying in the old city or are an early riser, come here for breakfast; the coffee is strong and the bread is fresh.

ⓘ Information

There are banks with ATMs scattered all around the central part of New Sukhothai, particularly in the area west of Mae Nam Yom, and several in Old Sukhothai as well.

WORTH A TRIP

FARMER FOR A DAY

Sukhothai's **Organic Agriculture Project** (📞08 6202 3757; www.khaohomsukhothai.in.th; 850B; ☉9am-noon & 1-4pm) allows visitors to take part in a half-day's worth of traditional Thai farm activities.

Taking place at Sukhothai Airport's organic farm, the half-day begins by donning the outfit of a Thai rice farmer and riding an *ee đáan* (a traditional utility vehicle) to gather duck eggs. This is followed by riding a buffalo, checking into an orchid farm, witnessing the stages of rice production and, ultimately, planting or gathering rice. The session ends with an informal cooking lesson and meal using organic produce from the farm.

Up to this point, the project has primarily hosted Thai visitors, and non-Thai speakers will most likely need to bring or hire a translator. This can be arranged via the concierge at the nearby Sukhothai Heritage Resort (p366).

The compound is also home to a **restaurant** serving dishes made from the farm's organic produce (from 8am to 5pm, mains from 50B to 120B).

The project is located on the same road as Sukhothai's airport, 27km from New Sukhothai off Rte 1195, and is not accessible by public transport. If you don't have your own wheels, you can arrange a ride with the Sukhothai Airport's minivan service.

Smile Internet Cafe (Rte 12; per hour 25B; ⊙9am-11pm) Internet access in Old Sukhothai; located across from Wat Trapang Thong.

Tawan Hi-Speed (Th Jarot Withithong, no roman-script sign; per hour 10B; ⊙9.30am-midnight) Internet cafe near the bridge in New Sukhothai.

Sukhothai Hospital (✆0 5561 0280; Th Jarot Withithong) Located just west of New Sukhothai.

Tourism Authority of Thailand (TAT; ✆0 5561 6228, nationwide 1672; Th Jarot Withithong; ⊙8.30am-4.30pm) Near the bridge in New Sukhothai, this new office has a pretty good selection of maps and brochures.

Tourist Police (✆1155; Rte 12)

❶ Getting There & Away

Sukhothai's airport is located a whopping 27km from town off Rte 1195. **Bangkok Airways** (✆0 5564 7224, nationwide 1771; www.bangkokair. com; Sukhothai Airport; ⊙7.30am-5.30pm) is the only airline operating here, with flights to Bangkok. There is a **minivan service** (✆0 5564 7220; Sukhothai Airport; 180B) between the airport and New Sukhothai.

Sukhothai's **minivan and bus station** (✆0 5561 4529; Rte 101) is almost 1km northwest of the centre of New Sukhothai; a motorcycle taxi between here and central New Sukhothai should cost around 50B, or you can hop on any *sörng·tăa·ou* bound for Sukhothai Historical Park, which make a stop at the bus station on their way out of town (30B, 10 minutes, frequent from 6am to 5.30pm).

TRANSPORT TO/FROM SUKHOTHAI

DESTINATION	AIR	BUS	MINIVAN	SÖRNG·TĂA·OU
Bangkok	2490B; 1hr; 2 daily (to Suvarnabhumi International Airport)	279-416B; 6-7hr; half-hourly 7.50am-10.40pm		
Chiang Mai		239-308B; 5-6hr; half-hourly 6.15am-5.30pm		
Chiang Rai		266B; 9hr; 4 departures 6.40-11.30am		
Kamphaeng Phet		60-77B; 1½hr; frequent 7.50am-11pm		43B; 2hr; frequent 7am-4.30pm
Khon Kaen		255-374B; 7hr; frequent 8.30am-10pm		
Lampang		178-229B; 3hr; half-hourly 7.15am-4.30pm		
Mae Sot			130B; 3hr; 4 departures 9.15am-4.15pm	
Nan		202B; 4hr; 3pm & 4pm		
Phitsanulok		43B; 1hr; hourly 6am-6pm	43B; 1hr; hourly 8am-6pm	
Sawankhalok		29-38B; 1hr; hourly 6.40am-6pm	85B; 2hr; half-hourly 7.10am-4.30pm	
Si Satchanalai		50B; 1½hr; 11am		
Sukhothai Historical Park				30B; 30min; frequent 6am-5.30pm

Alternatively, if you're staying near the historical park, **Win Tour** (Rte 12; ⊘6am-9.40pm) has an office roughly opposite Wat Trapang Thong, where you can board buses to Bangkok (356B, six hours, 8.20pm, 12.30pm and 9.40pm) and Chiang Mai (239B, five hours, hourly from 6.30am to 1.40pm).

ⓘ Getting Around

A *săhm·lór* ride within New Sukhothai should cost no more than 40B.

Relatively frequent *sŏrng·tǎa·ou* run between New Sukhothai and Sukhothai Historical Park (30B, 30 minutes, from 6am to 5.30pm), leaving from a stop on Th Jarot Withithong just west of Poo Restaurant. Motorcycle taxis go between the town or bus station and the park for 120B.

The best way to get around the historical park is by bicycle, which can be rented at shops outside the park entrance for 30B per day (6am to 6pm). The park operates a tram service (40B, one hour, from 8am to 5pm) that stops at three temples in the central zone, although explanation is in Thai only.

Motorbikes can be rented starting at about 250B for 24 hours and are available at Poo Restaurant and nearly every guesthouse in New Sukhothai.

Si Satchanalai-Chaliang Historical Park
อุทยาน
ประวัติศาสตร์ศรีสัชนาลัย

Set among hills, the 13th- to 15th-century ruins of the old cities of Si Satchanalai and Chaliang, 50km north of Sukhothai, are in the same basic style as those in the Sukhothai Historical Park, but the setting is more rural and arguably more peaceful. The park covers roughly 720 hectares and is surrounded by a 12m-wide moat. Chaliang, 1km southeast, is an older city site (dating to the 11th century), though its two temples date to the 14th century.

The nearby towns of Ban Hat Siaw and Sawankhalok are the main centres for the area.

ⓘ GOOD DEAL

An admission fee of 220B allows entry to Si Satchanalai, Wat Chao Chan (at Chaliang) and the Si Satchanalai Centre for Study & Preservation of Sangkalok Kilns.

Si Satchanalai

This zone (admission 100B, plus car 50B; ⊘8am-5pm) contains the majority of ruins. An information centre (⊘8.30am-5pm) at the park distributes free maps and has a small exhibit outlining the history and attractions. Bike hire (per day 30B; ⊘8am-5pm) is available near the entrance gate.

Wat Chang Lom   HISTORICAL SITE

(วัดช้างล้อม) This fine temple, marking the centre of the old city of Si Satchanalai, has elephants surrounding a bell-shaped *chedi* that is somewhat better preserved than its counterpart in Sukhothai. An inscription states that the temple was built by King Ramkhamhaeng between 1285 and 1291.

Wat Khao Phanom Phloeng   HISTORICAL SITE

(วัดเขาพนมเพลิง) On the hill overlooking Wat Chang Lom are the remains of Wat Khao Phanom Phloeng, including a *chedi*, a large seated Buddha and stone columns that once supported the roof of the *wí·hǎhn*.

From this hill you can make out the general design of the once-great city. The slightly higher hill west of Phanom Phloeng is capped by a large Sukhothai-style *chedi* – all that remains of **Wat Khao Suwan Khiri**.

Wat Chedi Jet Thaew   HISTORICAL SITE

(วัดเจดีย์เจ็ดแถว) Next to Wat Chang Lom, these ruins contain seven rows of *chedi,* the largest of which is a copy of one at Wat Mahathat in Sukhothai. An interesting brick-and-plaster *wí·hǎhn* features barred windows designed to look like lathed wood (an ancient Indian technique used all over Southeast Asia).

Wat Nang Phaya   HISTORICAL SITE

(วัดนางพญา) South of Wat Chedi Jet Thaew, this *chedi* is Sinhalese in style and was built in the 15th or 16th century, a bit later than the other monuments at Si Satchanalai. Stucco reliefs on the large laterite *wí·hǎhn* in front of the *chedi* – now sheltered by a tin roof – date from the Ayuthaya period when Si Satchanalai was known as Sawankhalok. Goldsmiths in the district still craft a design known as *nahng pá·yah*, modelled after these reliefs.

Chaliang

This older site, a short bike ride from Si Satchanalai, has two temples of note. Admission isn't always collected at Wat Chao Chan.

Si Satchanalai-Chaliang Historical Park

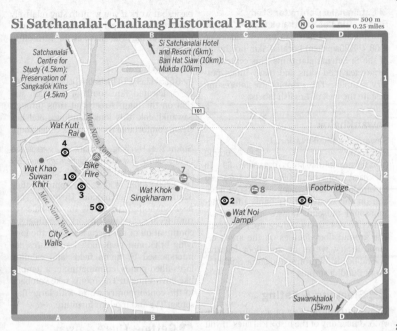

Si Satchanalai-Chaliang Historical Park

Wat Phra Si Ratana Mahathat
HISTORICAL SITE

(วัดพระศรีรัตนมหาธาตุ; admission 20B; ⊙8am-4.30pm) These ruins consist of a large laterite *chedi* (dating back to 1448–88) between two *wí·hǎhn*. One of the *wí·hǎhn* holds a large seated Sukhothai Buddha image, a smaller standing image and a bas-relief of the famous walking Buddha, exemplary of the flowing, boneless Sukhothai style. The other *wí·hǎhn* contains some less distinguished images.

Wat Chao Chan
HISTORICAL SITE

(วัดเจ้าจันทร์; admission 100B; ⊙8am-5pm) The central attraction here is a large Khmer-style tower similar to later towers built in Lopburi and probably constructed during the reign of Khmer King Jayavarman VII (1181–1217). The tower has been restored and is in fairly good shape. The roofless *wí·hǎhn*

on the right contains the laterite outlines of a large standing Buddha that has all but melted away from exposure and weathering.

Sawankhalok Kilns

At one time, more than 200 huge pottery kilns lined the banks of Mae Nam Yom in the area around Si Satchanalai. In China – the biggest importer of Thai pottery during the Sukhothai and Ayuthaya periods – the pieces produced here came to be called 'Sangkalok', a mispronunciation of Sawankhalok. Today, several barely recognisable kiln sites can be found along the road that runs north of Si Satchanalai. Ceramics are still made in the area, and at least one local ceramic artist even continues to fire his pieces in an underground wood-burning oven.

Si Satchanalai Centre for Study & Preservation of Sangkalok Kilns   MUSEUM

(ศูนย์ศึกษาและอนุรักษ์เตาสังคโลก; admission 100B; ⊙8.30am-5pm) Located 5km northwest of the Si Satchanalai ruins, this centre has large excavated kilns and many intact pottery samples. The exhibits are interesting despite the lack of English labels.

Sawankhalok

Sawanworanayok National Museum   MUSEUM

(พิพิธภัณฑสถานแห่งชาติสวรรควรนายก; 69 Th Phracharat; admission 50B; ⊙9am-4pm) In Sawankhalok town, near Wat Sawankhalam on the western river bank, this state-sponsored museum houses an impressive collection of 12th- to 15th-century artefacts. The ground floor focuses on the area's ceramic legacy, while the 2nd floor features several beautiful bronze and stone Sukhothai-era Buddha statues.

🛏 Sleeping & Eating

There's little in the way of accommodation or food near any of the historical sites. If you have your own transport, a better alternative is to be based in Sawankhalok, 15km to the south, or Ban Hat Siaw, about 9km north of the park.

Homestay   GUESTHOUSE $

(☑ 08 4048 8595, 0 5563 1063; r 500B; ❄) A local artist has opened her family's home/studio to guests. A single room, separate from the house, is equipped with private bath and air-con. Look for the 'Homestay' sign directly across from Wat Khok Singkharam, near the entrance to Si Satchanalai.

Papong Homestay   GUESTHOUSE $

(☑ 08 7313 4782, 0 5563 1557; r 500B; ❄) A locally run outfit near the historical park, the three rooms here include private bathrooms and are tidy and comfortable.

Si Satchanalai Hotel and Resort   HOTEL $

(☑ 0 5567 2666; 247 Rte 101, no roman-script sign; r & bungalows 400-600B; ❄ ⬮) The rooms here are featureless but tidy, and the expansive bungalows would be great for families. There's no English-language sign, but you can't miss the bright pink buildings 6km north of the park on the west side of Rte 101.

Mukda   HOTEL $

(☑ 0 5567 1024; Rte 101, Ban Hat Siaw, no roman-script sign; r 200-500B; ❄) The rooms here are basic, but work if you want to stay relatively close to the historical park. It's at the northern end of Ban Hat Siaw, at the turn-off to Uttaradit.

Saengsin Hotel   HOTEL $

(☑ 0 5564 1259; 2 Th Thetsaban Damri; r 220-320B; ❄ ⬮) Located 1km south of the train station on the main street that runs through Sawankhalok, this long-standing hotel has clean, comfortable rooms and a coffee shop.

Sukhothai Heritage Resort   RESORT $$$

(☑ 0 5564 7564; www.sukhothaiheritage.com; 999 Moo 2; r incl breakfast 3200-4200B, ste incl breakfast 6200-8200B; ❄ @ ⬮ ⬮) Approximately 32km from Si Satchanalai Historical Park near Sukhothai Airport is this upscale yet rural-feeling, isolated resort. Seemingly a continuation of the historical park, the low-lying brick and peak-roofed structures are interspersed by green fields and calming lotus-filled ponds, culminating in a temple-like environment. The rooms take you back to the contemporary world with large flat-screen TVs and modern furniture.

❶ Getting There & Away

BUS

Si Satchanalai-Chaliang Historical Park is off Rte 101 between Sawankhalok and Ban Hat Siaw. From New Sukhothai, take a Si Satchanalai bus (50B, 1½ hours, 11am) or one of three buses to Chiang Rai at 6.40am, 9am and 11.30am (46B), and ask to get off at 'meu·ang gòw' (old city). The last bus back to New Sukhothai leaves at 4.30pm.

To get to the park from Sawankhalok, you can hop on just about any north-bound line from the town's roadside bus terminal (24B to 50B, 30 minutes, frequent from 7am to 5pm).

TRAIN

Sawankhalok's original train station is one of the local sights. King Rama VI built a 60km railway spur from Ban Dara (a small town on the main northern trunk) to Sawankhalok just so that he could visit the ruins. Amazingly, there's a daily special express from Bangkok to Sawankhalok (482B, seven hours, 10.50am). The train heads back to Bangkok at 7.40pm, arriving in the city at 3.30am. You can also take this train to Phitsanulok (328B, 3½ hours, 5.55pm). It's a 'Sprinter' – 2nd class air-con and no sleepers. The fare includes dinner and breakfast.

❶ Getting Around

You can hire bicycles (p364) from near the food stalls at the entrance to the historical park.

KAMPHAENG PHET PROVINCE

Kamphaeng Phet กำแพงเพชร

POP 30,000

Located halfway between Bangkok and Chiang Mai, Kamphaeng Phet translates as 'Diamond Wall', a reference to the apparent strength of this formerly walled city's protective barrier. This level of security was necessary, as the city helped to protect the Sukhothai and later Ayuthaya kingdoms against attacks from Burma or Lanna. Parts of the wall can still be seen today, as well as impressive ruins of several religious structures. The modern city stretches along a shallow section of Mae Nam Ping and is one of Thailand's nicer provincial capitals.

◉ Sights & Activities

A Unesco World Heritage Site, the **Kamphaeng Phet Historical Park** (อุทยานประวัติศาสตร์กำแพงเพชร; ⊘ 8am-6pm) features the ruins of structures dating back to the 14th century, roughly the same time as the better-known kingdom of Sukhothai. Kamphaeng Phet's Buddhist monuments continued to be built up until the Ayuthaya period, nearly 200 years later, and thus possess elements of both Sukhothai and Ayuthaya styles, resulting in a school of Buddhist art quite unlike anywhere else in Thailand. In general, the ruins are not nearly as well restored as those of Sukhothai, but they are smaller, more intimate and less visited.

The park consists of two distinct sections: a formerly walled city just north of modern Kamphaeng Phet, and a larger compound about 1.5km further north.

⊙ Walled City

Just north of modern Kamphaeng Phet, this walled **zone** (admission 100B; ⊘ 8am-4pm) is the origin of the city's name, and was formerly inhabited by monks of the *gamavasi* ('living in the community') sect.

It's a long walk or an approximately 40B motorcycle taxi ride from the centre of town.

Wat Phra Kaew   HISTORICAL SITE
(วัดพระแก้ว) This former temple, adjacent to what is believed to have been the royal palace (now in ruins), dominates the walled city. There's an immense reclining Buddha

and several smaller, weather-corroded Buddha statues that have assumed slender, porous forms, reminding some visitors of the sculptures of Alberto Giacometti.

Wat Phra That   HISTORICAL SITE
(วัดพระธาตุ) The ruins of this temple are distinguished by a large round-based brick and laterite Kamphaeng Phet–style *chedi* surrounded by columns.

◉ Outside of Town

The majority of Kamphaeng Phet's ruins are found in this expansive **zone** (admission 100B; ⊘ 8am-6pm), located about 1.5km north of the city walls. The area was previously home to monks of the *arani* ('living in forests') sect, and in addition to the two temple compounds mentioned here, contains more than 40 other former compounds, although most are not much more than flat brick foundations with the occasional weather-worn Buddha image.

There is an excellent **visitor centre** (⊘ 8am-4.30pm) at the entrance where **bicycle hire** (per day 30B) can be arranged.

A motorcycle taxi from central Kamphaeng Phet to the entrance will run about 80B.

Wat Phra Si Iriyabot   HISTORICAL SITE
(วัดพระสี่อิริยาบถ) The highlight here is a towering *mon·dòp* (the small square building with a spire in a *wát*) that contains the shattered remains of standing, sitting, walking and reclining Buddha images all sculpted in the classic Sukhothai style.

Wat Chang Rob   HISTORICAL SITE
(วัดช้างรอบ) With a name meaning 'elephant-encircled temple', this ruin is just that – a temple buttressed with 68 stucco-covered elephants.

Other Sights
Kamphaeng Phet
National Museum   MUSEUM
(พิพิธภัณฑสถานแห่งชาติกำแพงเพชร; Th Pindamri; admission 100B; ⊘ 9am-noon & 1-4.30pm Wed-Sun) Kamphaeng Phet's visit-worthy

Kamphaeng Phet

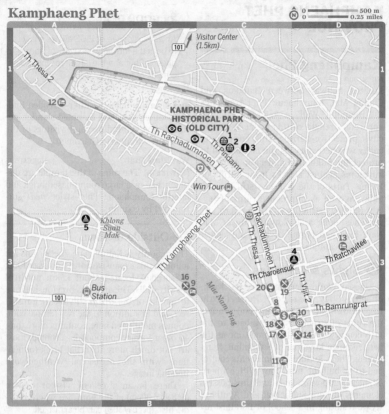

Kamphaeng Phet

◎ Sights

⊜ Sleeping

⊗ Eating

◎ Drinking & Nightlife

museum was being renovated when we stopped by. Previously, the museum has been home to an expansive collection of artefacts from the Kamphaeng Phet area, including an immense Shiva statue that is the largest bronze Hindu sculpture in the country.

The image was formerly located at the nearby **Shiva Shrine** `FREE` until a German missionary stole the idol's hands and head in 1886 (they were later returned). Today a replica stands in its place.

Kamphaeng Phet Regional Museum MUSEUM
(พิพิธภัณฑ์เฉลิมพระเกียรติกำแพงเพชร; Th Pindamri; admission 10B; ⏲9am-4.30pm) The regional museum is a series of Thai-style wooden structures on stilts set among nicely landscaped grounds. There are three main buildings in the museum featuring displays ranging from history and prehistory to the various ethnic groups that inhabit the province.

Wat Phra Borommathat BUDDHIST TEMPLE
(วัดพระบรมธาตุ; off Rte 1078; ⏲daylight hours) FREE Across Mae Nam Ping are the ruins of Wat Phra Borommathat, located in an area that was settled long before Kamphaeng Phet's heyday although visible remains are post-classical Sukhothai. The compound has a few small *chedi* and one larger *chedi* of the late Sukhothai period which is now crowned with a Burmese-style umbrella added early in the 20th century.

Wat Khu Yang BUDDHIST TEMPLE
(วัดคูยาง; Soi 4, Th Rachadumnoen 1; ⏲daylight hours) FREE Located just north of central Kamphaeng Phet, this Buddhist temple contains a handsome wooden *hŏr đrai* dating back to the 19th century.

Phra Ruang Hot Springs HOT SPRINGS
(บ่อน้ำร้อนพระร่วง; admission 30B; ⏲8.30am-6pm) Along the road to Sukhothai, 20km from Kamphaeng Phet, this complex of hot springs is the Thai version of a rural health retreat. The reputedly therapeutic hot waters have been diverged into seven private bathing rooms (50B), and there's also several places offering traditional Thai massage. There is no public transport to the hot springs, but transport can be arranged at Three J Guest House.

Sleeping

Three J Guest House GUESTHOUSE $
(☎08 1887 4189, 0 5571 3129; www.threejguesthouse.com; 79 Th Rachavitee; r 250-800B; ❄@📶) The cheapest bungalows at this welcoming guesthouse are fan-cooled and share a clean bathroom while the more expensive have air-con. There's heaps of local information, and bicycles and motorcycles are available for hire.

Grand View Resort HOTEL $
(☎0 5572 1104; 34/4 Moo 2, Nakhon Chum; r & bungalows incl breakfast 290-590B; ❄📶) One of a handful of semirural 'resorts' on the west bank of Mae Nam Pings, the highlight here is the six floating raft bungalows.

Ko Chokchai Hotel HOTEL $
(☎0 5571 1531; 19-43 Soi 8, Th Ratchadumnoen 1; r 280-340B; ❄📶) This egg-carton-like building with smallish but tidy rooms is a good budget choice.

Navarat Hotel HOTEL $$
(☎0 5571 1211; 2 Soi 21, Th Tesa 1; r incl breakfast 700-1400B; ❄📶) The '70s-era Navarat has undergone a recent renovation, erasing some but not all signs of the hotel's true age. The rooms are slightly overpriced, but clean and cosy, some boasting nice views of the river.

Chakungrao Riverview HOTEL $$
(☎0 5571 4900; www.chankungraoriverview.com; 149 Th Thesa 1; r incl breakfast 1000-1300B, ste incl breakfast 3500B; ❄@📶) At Kamphaeng Phet's poshest digs, rooms are tastefully decked out in dark woods and forest green and feature balconies with river or city views. Suites are huge and generally available at a considerable discount.

Scenic Riverside Resort HOTEL $$$
(☎0 5572 2009; www.scenicriversideresort.com; 325/16 Th Tesa 2; r & bungalow incl breakfast 1500-3500B; ❄📶🏊) Picture a Greek fishing village in which the interior design has been overseen by a teenaged Thai girl, and you start to get an idea of this wacky but fun resort. The eight dome-shaped, whitewashed villas here are decked out with stuffed dolls

BRICKS & MORTAR

The primary building material of many of the religious structures of Kamphaeng Phet and Sukhothai is laterite (*sì·lah laang* in Thai), a claylike substance found over much of Southeast Asia. When still in the ground, laterite is soft and pliable, but when exposed to light and air, it hardens. The early builders discovered this and shaped the clay into bricks before drying it in the sun. As is evident today, laterite is extremely porous and must be coated with plaster to give it a smooth look. The new and helpful 'Reconstructed' placards near most ruins give an idea of what the structures originally looked like.

and other kitsch, but are spacious and share a pool and a pleasant riverside location.

✖ Eating & Drinking

Kamphaeng Phet is not a culinary destination, but there are a few mildly interesting offerings. For cheap Thai eats, a busy **night market** (Th Thesa 1; mains 30-60B; ☉4-10pm) sets up every evening near the river just north of the Navarat Hotel.

There's a knot of mostly local bars at the corner of Th Bamrungrat and Soi 2, Th Charoensuk.

★ Bamee Chakangrao   THAI $

(Th Ratchadamnoen 1, no roman-script sign; mains 25-30B; ☉8.30am-3pm) Thin wheat and egg noodles *(bà·mèe)* are a speciality of Kamphaeng Phet, and this famous restaurant is one of the best places to try them. The noodles are made fresh every day behind the restaurant, and pork satay is also available. There's no English-language sign; look for the green banners on the corner.

Piggy   THAI $

(cnr Th Rachadumnoen 1 & Soi 5, no roman-script sign; per person 70B; ☉6-11pm) *Mŏo gà·tá*, DIY grilled pork, is one of the more popular dining traditions in these parts. Simply choose your ingredients from the buffet, then grill your meats, adding your veggies and other ingredients to the broth.

Phayao Bakery   INTERNATIONAL-THAI $

(Th Thesa 1; mains 45-120B; ☉9am-8pm; ✳) This air-conditioned cafe, with real coffee, a variety of baked goods and ice cream, is a clever place to escape from the heat.

Mae Ping Riverside   THAI $

(50/1 Moo 2, Nakhon Chum, no roman-script sign; mains 40-120B; ☉lunch & dinner) Decent eats, draught beer and live music can be found here, on the west bank of Mae Nam Ping. There are a few other similar riverside places along this strip.

Kitti   CHINESE-THAI $$

(cnr Th Vijit 2 & Th Bamrungrat, no roman-script sign; mains 50-350B; ☉10am-2pm & 4-10pm; ✳) Long-standing Kitti excels at seafood-forward, Chinese-style dining. Try the unusual but delicious fried chicken with cashew nut, which also includes pickled garlic and slices of sweet pork.

Rong Tiam   BAR

(Soi 9, Th Thesa 1, no roman-script sign; ☉6pm-1am) Live music (from 8.30pm), snacks and beer are available at this friendly pub located in a converted antique shophouse.

ⓘ Information

Most of the major banks also have branches with ATMs along the main streets near the river and on Th Charoensuk.

Internet Cafe (Soi 8, Th Rachadumnoen 1; per hour 15B; ☉10am-9pm)

ⓘ Getting There & Away

Kamphaeng Phet's **bus station** (✆0 5579 9844; Rte 101) is about 1km west of Mae Nam Ping. Motorcycles (50B) and *sŏrng·tăa·ou* (20B, frequent from 7.30am to 5pm) run between the station and town. If coming from Sukhothai or Phitsanulok, get off in the old city or at the roundabout on Th Thesa 1 to save yourself the

BUSES TO/FROM KAMPHAENG PHET

In addition to the buses listed here, there are minivans to Mae Sot (140B, three hours, frequent 8am to 6pm) and Sukhothai (65B, one hour, 8.30am and 2.30pm), and *sŏrng·tăa·ou* to Sukhothai (39B, two hours, hourly 1pm to 8pm).

DESTINATION	PRICE (B)	DURATION (HR)	DEPARTURES
Bangkok	230-344	5	frequent 8.30am-1.30am
Chiang Mai	228-342	5	8 departures 11.30am-1am
Chiang Rai	305-773	7	frequent noon-10.30pm
Lampang	168	4	8 departures 11.30am-1am
Mae Hong Son	509-905	11	10pm & 11pm
Nan	251	6	1.30pm
Phitsanulok	59-83	2½	hourly 6am-6pm
Phrae	176	4	1.30pm
Sukhothai	77	1	hourly 10.50am-8.30pm

trouble of having to get a *sŏrng·tăa·ou* back into town.

Alternatively, if you're bound for Bangkok you can circumvent the bus station altogether by buying tickets (295B for the five-hour trip) and boarding a bus at **Win Tour** ([📞] 0 5571 3971; Th Kamphaeng Phet), near the roundabout. Services run frequently from 9am to 11pm.

ℹ Getting Around

There are very few motorcycle taxis or túk-túk or in Kamphaeng Phet. As such it's wise to consider hiring a bicycle or motorbike – Three J Guest House has both (bicycle/motorcycle per day 50/200B).

TAK PROVINCE

Tak is a vast, mountainous province whose proximity to Myanmar has resulted in a complex history and unique cultural mix. There are Hmong, Musoe (Lahu), Lisu and White and Red Karen settlements throughout the west and north, while western Tak in particular has always been in distinct con-trast with other parts of Thailand because of strong Karen and Burmese cultural influences. Today, the Thailand–Myanmar border districts of Mae Ramat, Tha Song Yang and Mae Sot are dotted with refugee camps, an outcome of years of fighting between the Karen National Union (KNU) and the Burmese government.

Perhaps due its relative isolation, much of Tak still remains quite wild. The linked Um Phang Wildlife Sanctuary, Thung Yai Naresuan National Park, Huay Kha Kaeng Wildlife Sanctuary and Khlong Lan and Mae Wong National Parks together form one Thailand's largest wildlife corridors and one of the largest intact natural forests in Southeast Asia.

Yet with the opening of Myanmar's first land border at Mae Sot/Myawaddy in 2013, Tak is no longer isolated, and it remains to be seen how its new role as an increasingly important crossroads will change the province.

Around Tak & Mae Sot

Mae Sot
แม่สอด

POP 120,000

Despite its remote location and relatively small size, Mae Sot is among the most culturally diverse cities in Thailand. Walking through the streets of the town, you'll see a fascinating ethnic mix of Burmese men in their *longyi* (sarongs), Hmong and Karen women in traditional hill-tribe dress, bearded Muslims, Thai army rangers and foreign NGO workers. Burmese and Karen are spoken as much as Thai, shop signs along the streets are in Thai, Burmese and Chinese, and most of the temple architecture is Burmese. Mae Sot has also become the most important jade and gem centre along the border, with much of the trade controlled by Chinese and Muslim immigrants from Myanmar.

Although there aren't many formal sights in Mae Sot, and many visitors come simply for a visa run, many end up staying longer than expected. A vibrant market, several good restaurants and a fun nightlife scene have become attractions in their own right.

◉ Sights & Activities

Border Market   MARKET
(ตลาดริมน้ำเมย; Rte 105; ⊙7am-7pm) Alongside Mae Nam Moei on the Thai side is an expansive market that sells a mixture of workaday Burmese goods, black-market clothes, cheap Chinese electronics and food, among other things.

The market is 5km west of Mae Sot; *sŏrng·tăa·ou* depart from a spot on Th Bun Khun between approximately 6am and 6pm (20B).

Herbal Sauna   SAUNA
(Wat Mani, Th Intharakhiri; admission 20B; ⊙3-7pm) Wat Mani has separate herbal sauna facilities for men and women. The sauna is towards the back of the monastery grounds, past the monks' *gù·dì* (living quarters).

Cookery Course   COOKING
(☑0 5554 6584; borderlineshop@yahoo.com; Borderline, 674/14 Th Intharakhiri; lessons 1000B; ⊙lessons 8.30am-noon & 1-4pm Tue-Sun) Held at Borderline Shop (p375), this course teaches how to make Shan, Burmese and Karen dishes, and includes a trip to the market, food and drink preparation, a cookbook, and sharing the results in the adjoining cafe. Courses decrease in price with bigger groups.

✦✦ Festivals & Events

Thai Boxing Competition   THAI BOXING
Around April, Thai and Burmese boxers meet for a competition in the traditional style, held somewhere outside town. Five-round matches are fought in a circular ring; the first four rounds last three minutes, the fifth has no time limit. With their hands bound in hemp, boxers fight till first blood or knockout. You'll have to ask around to find the changing venue for this annual slugfest.

🛏 Sleeping

Many places in Mae Sot are in the budget range and cater to NGO workers who tend to stay for the long-term.

Phan Nu House   GUESTHOUSE $
(☑08 1972 4467; 563/3 Th Intharakhiri; r 250-500B; ❄🛜) This place consists of 29 large rooms in a residential strip just off the street. Most are equipped with air-con, TV, fridge and hot water, making them a good deal.

Ban Pruk Sa Guesthouse   GUESTHOUSE $
(☑0 5553 2656; www.banpruksa.com; 740 Th Intharakhiri; r 200-800B; ❄🛜) This tidy villa unites a handful of unassuming but spacious and comfortable budget rooms.

@ Baan Tung   GUESTHOUSE $
(☑0 5553 3277; www.baantungguesthouse.com; 63/4 Soi Ban Tung; r 350-500; ❄@🛜) Located on a quiet street, this place features vast rooms in polished concrete, beds on an elevated platform and tight, round-shaped bathrooms. The price depends on whether you opt for fan or air-con.

Bai Fern Guesthouse   HOTEL $
(☑0 5553 1349; www.bai-fern.com; 660 Th Intharakhiri; r 150-350B; ❄@) Set just off the road in a large house, the shared-bathroom budget rooms here are tidy but plain. Service is friendly, and a stay includes use of a kitchen, fridge and wireless internet in the communal area.

Ban Thai Guest House   HOTEL $$
(☑0 5553 1590; banthai_mth@hotmail.com; 740 Th Intharakhiri; r 250-1000B; ❄@🛜) This tiny neighbourhood of converted Thai houses includes spacious, stylish air-con rooms with Thai-style furniture, axe lounging pillows and Thai textiles, and nine fan-cooled, shared-bathroom rooms in the main structure. The whole package is neat, homey and

Mae Sot

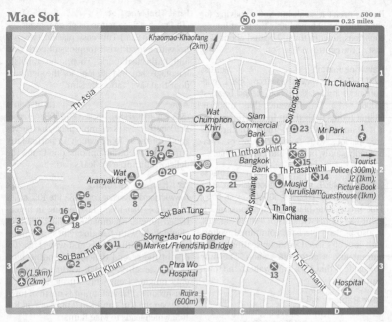

Mae Sot

Activities, Courses & Tours
Cookery Course .... (see 19)
1 Herbal Sauna D2

Sleeping
2 @ Baan Tung A3
3 Baan Rabiangmai A3
4 Bai Fern Guesthouse B2
5 Ban Pruk Sa Guesthouse A2
6 Ban Thai Guest House A2
7 Irawadee Resort A3
8 Phan Nu House B2

Eating
9 Aiya C2
10 Casa Mia A3
11 Famous Ray's B3

12 Khrua Canadian D2
13 Lucky Tea Garden C3
14 Night Market D2
15 Phat Thai Mae Sot D2

Drinking & Nightlife
16 Mali Bar A3
17 Pizza Mickey @ngelo B2
18 Water Bar A2

Shopping
19 Borderline Shop B2
20 Fair Trade Shop B2
21 Gem Shops C2
22 Municipal Market C2
23 Walking Street D2

comfortable, not to mention popular with long-stay NGO workers, so booking ahead is a good idea.

Picturebook Guesthouse HOTEL **$$**
(☎09 0459 6990; www.picturebookthailand.org; 125/4-6 Soi 19, Th Intharakihiri; r incl breakfast 500-700B; ❈🖵) This new compound is already one of the more charming hotels in northern Thailand. Located in an attractive garden, the 10 rooms here call to mind trendy dorms, with their smooth concrete, artsy details and custom wood furniture. Staff are friendly and keen to help, and are part of a not-for-profit training program.

It's located in unmarked Soi 19, directly behind J2 Hotel, about 1km east of Mae Sot.

J2 HOTEL **$$**
(☎0 5554 6999; www.facebook.com/j2hotel; 149/8 Th Intharakhiri; r incl breakfast 780-1800B; ❈@🖵) The bright new J2 has large rooms decked out in an intriguing minimalist-retro theme – think repro '60s- and '70s-era furniture.

Rooms aren't a steal, but you're paying for style, and the J2 is probably the most image-conscious hotel in town. Located about 1km east of the centre of Mae Sot.

Irawadee Resort
HOTEL $$

(📷 0 5553 5430; www.irawadee.com; 758/1 Th In-tharakhiri; r incl breakfast 950B, ste incl breakfast 1800B; 🕸🎘) The Irawadee has modern-feeling rooms decked out in a Burmese – or is it an imperial Chinese – theme. Bathrooms are spacious with open-air showers. Una-bashedly gaudy, but fun and comfortable.

Rujira
HOTEL $$

(📷0 5554 4969; rujira_tom@hotmail.com; 3/18 Th Buakjoon; r incl breakfast 500-1000B; 🕸@🎘) This great-value place has spacious, apart-ment-like rooms with lots of homey touches. It also packs a pleasant communal feeling, with lots of shaded outdoor seating, a res-taurant and a cute coffee shop. The only downside is that it's a long walk to the town centre.

Baan Rabiangmai
HOTEL $$

(📷0 5553 2144; www.baanrabiangmai.in.th; 3/3 Th Don Kaew; r incl breakfast 950-1600B; 🕸🎘) Baan Rabiangmai is the type of clean, homey, no-fuss hotel every town should have. The 19 rooms aren't huge, but come thoughtfully equipped with kitchenette, big fridge, sitting area, flat-screen TV and a small balcony.

🍴 Eating

Mae Sot is a virtual culinary crossroads with a buffet of cuisines not seen in other Thai towns. For a fun breakfast head to the area directly south of the Musjit Nurulislam, where several busy **Muslim restaurants** serve sweet tea, roti and *nanbya,* tandoor-style bread. The town's vibrant day market (p375) is the place to try Burmese dishes such as *mohinga,* Myanmar's unofficial na-tional dish, or Burmese-style curries served over rice. Mae Sot's **night market** (Th Prasat-withhi; mains 30-60B; ⊙6-11pm) features mostly Thai–Chinese-style dishes.

Lucky Tea Garden
BURMESE $

(Th Bun Khun; mains 10-50B; ⊙6am-6pm) For the authentic Burmese teashop experience without crossing over to Myawaddy, visit this friendly cafe equipped with sweet tea, tasty snacks and, of course, bad Burmese pop music.

Phat Thai Mae Sot
THAI $

(Th Prasatwithi, no roman-script sign; mains 25-45B; ⊙noon-9pm) This cosy place serves *pàt tai* with a local twist: toppings of pork rind and barbecued pork. There's no English-language sign, instead look for the sign next door that says 'Tattoo By Kim'.

Aiya
BURMESE-THAI $

(533 Th Intharakhiri; mains 50-250B; ⊙noon-11.30pm; 📷) Aiya is a simple place that serves good Burmese food, which is particularly strong on vegetarian options; don't miss the delicious Burmese tea-leaf salad.

★ Khaomao-Khaofang
THAI $$

(www.khaomaokhaofang.com; 382 Rte 105; mains 90-320B; ⊙11am-10pm) Like dining in a gen-trified jungle, Khaomao-Khaofang replaces chandeliers with hanging vines, and inte-rior design with orchids and waterfalls. Try one of the several delicious-sounding *yam* (Thai-style spicy salads), featuring ingredi-ents ranging from white turmeric to local mushrooms. The restaurant is north of town between the Km 1 and Km 2 markers on Rte 105, which leads to Mae Ramat.

Casa Mia
INTERNATIONAL-THAI $$

(Th Don Kaew; mains 50-200B; ⊙8am-10pm Sun-Fri; 📷) Tucked down a side street, this simple restaurant serves what must be the cheapest homemade Italian pasta dishes in the universe. And better yet, they're right tasty. It also does Thai and Burmese, and some great desserts, including a wicked banoffee pie.

Famous Ray's
AMERICAN $$

(Th Ban Thung; mains 100-300B; ⊙noon-10.30pm) Just burgers here, including crea-tive variations such as Thai (with *pàt tai* seasoning and sautéed morning glory) or Burmese (with curry spices and topped with Burmese-style tomato salad).

Khrua Canadian
INTERNATIONAL-THAI $$

(3 Th Sri Phanit; dishes 40-280B; ⊙7am-10pm; 🎘📷) This is the place to go if you want to forget you're in Asia for one meal. Dave, the Canadian, brews his own coffee and also offers homemade bagels, deli meats and cheeses. The servings are large, the menu is varied, and when you finally remember you're in Thailand again, local information is also available.

🍸 Drinking & Nightlife

The strip of Th Intharakhiri that runs west from Wat Aranyakhet is where a handful of open-air bars are located.

Mali Bar BAR
(Th Intharakhiri; ⏰ 6pm-midnight) Staffed by Burmese and popular with the NGO set, this rather dark bar has a pool table and a world music soundtrack.

Pizza Mickey @ngelo BAR
(674/15 Th Intharakhiri; ⏰ 11am-midnight; 📶) We still can't get behind the combination of office furniture, a clubby soundtrack and assertive art, but who can argue with pizza, cold beer and water pipes?

Water Bar BAR
(Th Intharakhiri; ⏰ 7pm-midnight) More of a Thai scene, this place has open-air tables, draught beer, snacks and a big screen for the big game.

🛍 Shopping

Mae Sot is most famous for its gems trade and is the most important jade and gem centre along the border. Check out the hustle and bustle among the glittering treasures in the **gem shops** (⏰ 8am-6pm) along Th Prasatwithi, just east of the morning market.

Municipal Market MARKET
(off Th Prasatwithi; ⏰ 6am-6pm) Mae Sot's municipal market is among the largest and most vibrant we've encountered anywhere in Thailand. There's heaps of exotic stuff from Myanmar, including Burmese bookshops, sticks of *thanaka* (the source of the yellow powder you see on many faces), bags of pickled tea leaves and velvet thong slippers from Mandalay.

Borderline Shop HANDICRAFTS
(www.borderlinecollective.org; 674/14 Th Intharakhiri; ⏰ 10am-6pm Tue-Sat, 2-6pm Sun, tea garden 9am-6pm Tue-Sun) Selling arts and crafts items made by refugee women, the profits from this shop go back into a women's collective and a child-assistance foundation. Upstairs, a gallery sells paintings and the house is also home to tea garden and cookery course.

Walking Street MARKET
(Soi Rong Chak; ⏰ 5-9pm Sat) Every Saturday evening the small street by the police station is closed to traffic, and in its place are vendors selling handicrafts, clothes and food.

Fair Trade Shop HANDICRAFTS
(www.weave-women.org; 656 Th Intharakhiri; ⏰ 9am-5pm Mon-Sat) One of three branches in northern Thailand, this shop specialises in bright handcrafted cloth goods created by displaced women from Myanmar.

ℹ Information

Several centrally located banks have ATMs. There is no official tourist office in Mae Sot, but Khrua Canadian is a good source of local information.

Immigration (📞 0 5556 3000; Th Intharakhiri; ⏰ 8.30am-4.30pm) Located next to the Friendship Bridge, this office can do visa extensions.

net @ all (Th Intharakhiri; per hr 15B; ⏰ 9am-10pm)

Tourist Police (📞 1155; 738/1 Th Intharakhiri) Located east of the centre of town.

ℹ Getting There & Away

Mae Sot's tiny **airport** (📞 0 5556 4056; Th Intharakhiri) is about 2km west of town. At research time, **Nok Air** (📞 0 5556 3883, nationwide 1318; www.nokair.co.th; Mae Sot Airport, Th Intharakhiri; ⏰ 8am-5pm) was the only airline operating out of Mae Sot, with domestic flights to/from Bangkok and Chiang Mai, and international flights to/from Mawlamyine and Yangon, both in Myanmar. There's no local taxi service, so you'll have to arrange pick-up in advance with your hotel.

All long-distance *sŏrng·tăa·ou*, minivans and buses leave from Mae Sot's **bus station** (📞 0 5553 2949; Th Intharakhiri), located 1.5km west of town; a motorcycle taxi to/from here should cost about 50B.

ℹ Getting Around

Most of central Mae Sot can be navigated on foot. Motorcycle taxis and săhm·lór charge 40B for trips within the centre of town.

Sŏrng·tăa·ou to the Friendship Bridge leave from a stop on Th Bun Khun (20B, 15 minutes, frequent from 6am to 6pm) .

Many guesthouses hire motorbikes for around 250B for 24 hours.

Mr Park (📞 0 5553 3900; 304-304/1 Th Intharakhiri; ⏰ 8am-5pm) This retail shop rents motorbikes for 150B to 200B per 24 hours.

Mae Sot to Um Phang

Rte 1090 goes south from Mae Sot to Um Phang, 150km away. This stretch of road used to be called the 'Death Highway' because of the guerrilla activity in the area that hindered highway development. Those days ended in the 1980s, but lives are still lost because of brake failure or treacherous turns on this steep, winding road through incredible mountain scenery.

Along the way there are two waterfalls, **Nam Tok Thararak** (น้ำตกธารารักษ์; ⊘ 6am-6pm) **FREE**, 26km from Mae Sot, and **Nam Tok Pha Charoen** (น้ำตกพาเจริญ; ⊘ 6am-6pm) **FREE**, 41km from Mae Sot. Nam Tok Thararak streams beside a picturesque *chedi* and over limestone cliffs and calcified rocks with a rough texture that makes climbing the falls easy. It's been made into a park of sorts, with benches right in the stream at the base of the falls for cooling off and a couple of outhouse toilets nearby; on weekends food vendors set up here. The turn-off isn't clear; look for the sign indicating Chedi Kho.

Just beyond Ban Rom Klao 4 – roughly midway between Mae Sot and Um Phang – is **Um Piam**, a very large Karen and Burmese refugee village with around 20,000 refugees that were moved here from camps around Rim Moei. There are also several Hmong villages in the area.

Sŏrng·tăa·ou to Um Phang depart from Mae Sot's bus station hourly from 7am to 3pm (120B, four hours).

Um Phang & Around อุ้มผาง

Sitting at the junction of Mae Nam Klong and Huay Um Phang, Um Phang is a remote village populated mostly by Karen. Many of the Karen villages in this area are quite traditional, and elephants are a common sight, especially in Palatha, a traditional Karen village 25km south of Um Phang. *Yaeng* (elephant saddles) and other tack used for elephant wrangling are a common sight on the verandahs of the houses in this village.

Yet the majority of visitors come to Um Phang for nature, not culture. The area borders the Um Phang Wildlife Sanctuary, a popular destination for rafting, trekking and elephant rides that is also home Nam Tok Thilawsu, the largest waterfall in Thailand.

TRANSPORT TO/FROM MAE SOT

DESTINATION	AIR	BUS	MINIVAN	SŎRNG·TĂA·OU
Bangkok	1590B; 65min; 4 daily (Don Muang Airport)	333-666B; 7-8hr; frequent 8am-9.45pm		
Chiang Mai	1290B; 40min; 1 daily	259-333B; 5-6hr; 6am & 8am		
Chiang Rai		356-493B; 9hr; 6am & 8am		
Kamphaeng Phet		140B; 3hr; frequent 8am-3.30pm		
Lampang		199-256B; 4hr; 6am & 8am		
Mae Sai		420-540B; 12hr; 6am-8am		
Mae Sariang				200B; 6hr; hourly 6am-noon
Mawlamyine (Myanmar)	1590B; 30min; 9.45am			
Phitsanulok			185B; 4hr; 4 departures 7am-1pm	
Sukhothai			150B; 3hr; 4 departures 7am-1pm	
Um Phang				120B; 4hr; hourly 7am-3pm
Yangon (Myanmar)	1590B; 55min; 11.35am			

◉ Sights

Nam Tok Thilawsu NATURE RESERVE
(น้ำตกทีลอซู) Located in the **Um Phang Wild-life Sanctuary** (เขตรักษาพันธุ์สัตว์ป่าอุ้มผาง; ☏0 5557 7318; admission 200B, plus car 30B; ⊙8am-4.30pm), this waterfall is Thailand's largest, measuring an estimated 200m high and up to 400m wide during the rainy season.

You can camp (30B) at the sanctuary headquarters, although you'll have to bring your own tent, and it's best to book ahead from November to January. This is also the only time of year the sanctuary's basic restaurant is guaranteed to be open.

Thais, particularly fanatical about such things, consider Nam Tok Thilawsu to be the most beautiful waterfall in the country. There's a shallow cave behind the falls and several levels of pools suitable for swimming. The best time to visit is after the rainy season (November and December) when the 200m to 400m limestone cliffs alongside Mae Nam Klong are streaming with water and Nam Tok Thilawsu is at its best.

The easy 1.5km path between the sanctuary headquarters and falls has been transformed into a self-guided nature tour. Surrounding the falls on both sides of the river are Thailand's thickest stands of natural forest, and the hiking in the vicinity of Nam Tok Thilawsu can be superb. The forest here is said to contain more than 1300 varieties of palm; giant bamboo and strangler figs are also commonplace.

The vast majority of people visit the falls as part of an organised tour, but it's also possible to go more or less independently. If you've got your own wheels, take the turn-off to Rte 1167 just north of Um Phang. After 12km, turn left at the police checkpoint onto Rte 1288. Continue 6km until you reach the sanctuary checkpoint, where you're expected to pay the entry fee. It's another 25km along a recently paved road to the sanctuary headquarters.

It's easy to book a truck just about anywhere in Um Phang (round trip 1500B). Alternatively, you can take a Poeng Kloeng-bound sŏrng·tăa·ou to the sanctuary checkpoint (30B, every hour from 6.30am to 3.30pm), and organise transport from there.

Tham Ta Khu Bi CAVE
(ถ้ำตะโค๊ะบิ) From Ban Mae Klong Mai, just a few kilometres north of Um Phang via the highway to Mae Sot, Rte 1167 heads southwest along the Thai–Myanmar border.

Along the way is the extensive cave system of Tham Ta Khu Bi, which in Karen allegedly means 'Flat Mango'. There are no guides here, so be sure to bring your own torch.

Poeng Kloeng & Letongkhu VILLAGES
(บ้านเปิ่งเคลิ่ง/เลตองคุ) Rte 1288, which leads to the checkpoint for Um Phang Wildlife Sanctuary, continues more than 70km, terminating in Poeng Kloeng – a Karen, Burmese, Talaku and Thai trading village on the Myanmar border.

Poeng Kloeng is a pretty nondescript border town where the main occupations appear to be selling black-market cigarettes from Myanmar and the production of betel nut. The real reason to make the schlep here is to visit the neighbouring village of Letongkhu, 12km south of Poeng Kloeng along a rough uphill track.

According to what little anthropological information is available, the villagers belong to the Lagu or Talaku sect, said to represent a form of Buddhism mixed with shamanism and animism. Each village has a spiritual and temporal leader called a *pu chaik* (whom the Thais call *reu·sĕe* – rishi, or sage) who wears his hair long – usually tied in a topknot – and dresses in white, yellow or brown robes, depending on the subsect.

Evangelistic Christian missionaries have infiltrated the area and have tried to convert the Talaku, thus making them sensitive to outside visits. If you do visit Letongkhu, take care not to enter any village structures without permission or invitation. Likewise, do not take photographs without permission. Overnight stays are not generally permitted.

From the *sŏrng·tăa·ou* station in Um Phang there are *sŏrng·tăa·ou* to Poeng Kloeng approximately every hour from 6.30am to 3.30pm (100B, 2½ hours). There's no regular transport to Letongkhu, and if you're not willing to walk or hitch from Poeng Kloeng or organise a guided visit to the village, a 4WD will do the trip from Um Phang for about 5000B.

✦ Activities

Virtually every guesthouse in Um Phang can arrange combination trekking and rafting trips in the area. Yet because Um Phang is dominated by Thai tourists, only a handful of guides have experience in dealing with foreign visitors.

A typical three-day, two-night trip involves both rafting and hiking, with a popular optional activity being elephant rides.

The majority involve trips to Nam Tok Thilawsu and beyond, and longer or shorter trips, and trips to other destinations, may also be arranged.

Rafting trips range from one-day excursions along Mae Klong, from Um Phang to Nam Tok Thilawsu, to three-day trips from Palatha to Nam Tok Thi Lo Re, another impressive waterfall. Most rafting is only possible between November and January.

Um Phang Khi is a 'new' area for rafting, northeast of Um Phang. Officially there are 47 (some rafting companies claim 67) sets of rapids rated at class III (moderate) and class IV (difficult) during the height of the rainy season. The rafting season for Um Phang Khi is short – August to October only – as at other times of the year the water level isn't high enough.

Costs are all-inclusive and start at about 4000B per person (for two people) for a three-day rafting and trekking excursion. Elephant rides and other extras will bring the price up.

Trekker Hill
TREKKING, RAFTING

(☑ 0 5556 1090; off Th Pravatpriwan) This recommended outfit has the greatest number of English-speaking guides and offers a variety of treks running from one to four days.

BC Adventure Tour
TREKKING, RAFTING

(☑ 08 1379 2591, 0 5556 1020; www.boonchuaytour.com; Th Pravatpriwan; ⊙ 1-6pm) Mr Boonchuay offers a variety of treks and rafting trips led by guides who can speak English and who have experience in dealing with foreign trekkers.

Umphang House
TREKKING, RAFTING

(☑ 08 9568 5273, 0 5556 1511; www.umphanghouse.webs.com; Soi 4, Th Sukhumwattana; ⊙ 8am-5pm) This outfit offers a variety of tours led by English-speaking guides, many with a focus on elephants.

Napa Tour
TREKKING, RAFTING

(☑ 0 5556 1287; off Th Pravatpriwan) Napa has an emphasis on rafting and offers a variety of programs and English-speaking guides.

Tu Ka Su Cottage
TREKKING, RAFTING

(☑ 0 5556 1295; www.tukasu.net; off Rte 1090; ⊙ 8am-5pm) This resort can arrange a variety of tours with its English-speaking guides.

🛏 Sleeping

Most places in Um Phang cater to large groups of Thai visitors, so individual foreign travellers can be met with a bit of confusion. Likewise, many of the rooms in town are designed for four or more people, but singles or couples can usually negotiate lower rates, especially in the wet season.

Um Phang

Se Heng Chai Resort
HOTEL $

(☑ 0 5556 1605; Rte 1090, no roman-script sign; r 450B; ✳ 🛜) Just east of town, this 'resort' has 13 clean, modern-feeling rooms in a two-storey building. There's no English-language sign, but it's the tallest building on the hill.

K & K Guest House
GUESTHOUSE $

(☑ 08 7846 1087; Th Sukhumwattana; r 350–600B; ✳ 🛜) Five tiny rooms in a brand new shophouse right in the middle of the hustle and bustle of 'downtown' Um Phang.

Phudoi Camp Site & Resort
HOTEL $

(☑ 0 5556 1049; www.phudoi.com; Th Ratpattana; tent 150B, bungalows 400-500B; ✳ @ 🛜) Primarily catering to its prebooked tour clients, Phudoi has bungalows set on a well-landscaped hillside near the village centre. The log cabin–style bungalows are spacious and have verandahs. There's also a camping area and a restaurant with the same name.

Trekker Hill
HOTEL $

(☑ 0 5556 1090; off Th Pravatpriwan; dm 100B, r 300-500B; 🛜) This rustic collection of huts on a steep hillside is a good place to stay, and rooms have hot water and views of the valley and Um Phang.

Tu Ka Su Cottage
HOTEL $$

(☑ 0 5556 1295; www.tukasu.net; off Rte 1090; r 600-2200B; ✳ 🛜) This is the most comfortable and best-run accommodation in Um Phang. The attractive collection of brick-and-stone multiroom cottages is surrounded by flower and exotic fruit gardens, and all rooms come equipped with air-con, hot water, TV, fridge and quasi-outdoor bathrooms. The owner is a great source of local information and tours can be arranged here.

Baan Farang
HOTEL $$

(☑ 08 0115 5678; off Rte 1090; r incl breakfast 700-1200B; 🛜) Located 3km from Um Phang, off Rte 1090 near the intersection that leads to Thilawsu, this attractive plot of land unites seven cosy huts, the more expensive of which are riverside.

Umphang Country Hut
HOTEL $$

(☑ 0 5556 1079; www.umphangcountryhut.com; off Rte 1090; r incl breakfast 700-4000B; 🛜) The wooded hilly setting is more of a draw here then the basic accommodation, although some of the rooms in the middle price range have inviting balconies looking out over a stream. The resort is 2km from Um Phang; if approaching from Mae Sot, turn right just after Um Phang's wooden district gate, then right again at the smaller wooden gate.

Garden Huts
HOTEL $$

(☑ 0 5556 1093; www.boonyapornresort.com; Rte 1090; r 300-1500B; 🛜) Operated by a sweet older lady, this collection of budget bungalows of varying degrees of comfort and size fronts the river. It features pleasant sitting areas and a well-cared-for garden. A newer building has several spacious rooms with TV.

Ban Phurkchaya
HOTEL $$

(☑ 0 5556 1308; www.banphurkchaya.com; Rte 1090, no roman-script sign; r incl breakfast 700B; ✳ 🛜) A cute compound of rooms in and around a modern villa, all of which appear clean and comfortable. There's no English sign here, but you'd have to struggle to miss the huge flower-decked letters out front.

🍴 Eating & Drinking

Um Phang has several simple restaurants, a minuscule **evening market** (Th Pravatpriwan; mains 20-60B; ⏲ 6-9pm) and a couple of small shops.

Ban Kru Sun
CAFE $

(Th Sukhumwattana; mains 20-35B; ⏲ 6.30am-8.30pm; 🛜) Owned by a Thai musician, this souvenir shop and cafe also does decent coffee and other drinks.

ℹ Information

There are now four ATMs in Um Phang. **Internet** (Th Pravatpriwan, no roman-script sign; per hour 15B; ⏲ 8am-10pm) is available at a cafe near the 7-Eleven.

ℹ Getting There & Away

Sŏrng·tăa·ou to Mae Sot depart from a stop at the northern end of Th Pravatpriwan (120B, four hours, hourly from 6.30am to 12.30pm). *Sŏrng·tăa·ou* Poeng Kloeng depart from a stop on Th Ratpattana, opposite the hospital (100B, 2½ hours, hourly from 6.30am to 3.30pm).

Mae Sot to Mae Sariang

Rte 105 runs north along the Thailand–Myanmar border from Mae Sot all the way to Mae Sariang (226km) in Mae Hong Son Province. The winding, paved road passes through the small communities of Mae Ramat, Mae Salit, Ban Tha Song Yang and Ban Sop Ngao (Mae Ngao). The thick forest in these parts still has a few stands of teak and

GETTING TO MYANMAR: MAE SOT TO MYAWADDY

The 420m Friendship Bridge that links Mae Sot and Myawaddy, in Myanmar's Kayin State, is one of a handful of newly open land borders between the two countries.

Getting to the Border *Sŏrng·tăa·ou* make frequent trips between Mae Sot and the Friendship Bridge from 6am to 6pm (20B).

At the border Immigration procedures are taken care of at the **Thai immigration booth** (☑ 0 5556 3004; ⊙ 6.30am-6.30pm) at the Friendship Bridge. Cross to the Myanmar immigration booth, where, if you've already procured a Myanmar visa in Bangkok or elsewhere, you'll be allowed to proceed to other destinations. Otherwise you must pay a fee of 500B for a temporary ID card at the **Myanmar immigration booth** (☑ 95 0585 0100; ⊙ 6am-6pm), which allows you to stay in Myawaddy until 6pm the same day; your passport will be kept at the border.

Myawaddy is a fairly typical Burmese town, with a number of monasteries, schools, shops and so on. The most important temple is Shwe Muay Wan (Dar Tu Kalair St) a traditional bell-shaped *chedi* gilded with many kilos of gold and topped by more than 1600 precious and semiprecious gems. Another noted Buddhist temple is Myikyaungon (Nat Shin Naung St) called Wat Don Jarakhe in Thai and named for its gaudy, crocodile-shaped sanctuary. Myawaddy's 1000-year-old earthen city walls, probably erected by the area's original Mon inhabitants, can be seen along the southern side of town.

Moving On About 200m from the border, on the corner with Pattamyar St, is a glut of white share taxis (called 'vans' by the Burmese). Cars depart when full between 6am and 5pm – on even-numbered days only; destinations include Mawlamyine (10,000K to 15,000K, six hours), Hpa-an (10,000K to 15,000K, six hours) and Yangon (40,000K, 14 hours). There's also a bus to Yangon (12,000K, 16 hour), departing from a small office on Pattamyar St at 5am daily.

---

the Karen villages continue to use the occasional work elephant.

Nam Tok Mae Kasa, between the Km 13 and Km 14 markers, is an attractive waterfall fronting a cave. There's also a hot spring in the nearby village of Mae Kasa.

In **Mae Ramat**, don't miss **Wat Don Kaew**, behind the district office, which houses a large Mandalay-style marble Buddha.

At Km 58, after a series of roadblocks, you'll pass **Mae La**, where it's estimated that 60,000 Burmese refugees live. The village is at least 3km long and takes a couple of minutes to drive past, bringing home the significant refugee problem that Thailand faces.

There are extensive limestone caverns at **Tham Mae Usu**, at Km 94 near Ban Tha Song Yang (not to be confused with the village of the same name further north). From the highway it's a 2km walk to Tham Mae Usu; note that it's closed in the rainy season, when the river running through the cave seals off the mouth.

At the northern end of Tak Province, you'll reach **Ban Tha Song Yang**, a Karen village attractively set at the edge of limestone cliffs by Mae Nam Moei. This is the last significant settlement in Tak before you begin climbing uphill and into the dense jungle and mountains of Mae Ngao National Park, in Mae Hong Son Province.

Ban Sop Ngao, little more than a roadside village that is home to the park headquarters, is the first town you'll come to in Mae Hong Son. From there it's another 40km to Mae Sariang, where there's ample food and accommodation.

🛏 Sleeping & Eating

There aren't too many places to stay and eat along this route. The most convenient base is Tha Song Yang (the town near Km 90, not the village of the same name at the northern edge of Tak Province), as there are a few restaurants in town. Mae Salit, slightly further north, also has basic accommodation and food.

Thasongyang Hill Resort HOTEL $
(☑ 0 5558 9088; www.thasongyanghill.9nha.com; Rte 105, Ban Tha Song Yang, Km 85; r 300-500B; ❄ 🛜) North of Ban Tha Song Yang, accommodation here takes the form of either large modern rooms in a long building or attractive bungalows in a flower-lined garden. There are a couple of similar hotels in the area, but this place is the nicest.

Per-pron Resort HOTEL $
(☑ 08 1774 5624; 110 Moo 2; bungalows 300-350B)
Just south of Mae Salit, this place has a few rustic bungalows looking over Mae Nam Moei.

❶ Getting There & Away

Sŏrng·tăa·ou to Mae Sariang depart from Mae Sot's bus station (200B, six hours, hourly from 6am to noon).

MAE HONG SON PROVINCE

Accessible only by incredibly windy mountain roads or a dodgy flight to the provincial capital, Mae Hong Son is arguably Thailand's remotest province. Thickly forested and mountainous, and far from the influence of sea winds, the temperature seldom rises above 40°C, while in January the temperature can drop to 2°C. The air is often misty with ground fog in the winter and smoke from slash-and-burn agriculture during the hot season. Mae Hong Son's location along the border with Myanmar means that it is also a crossroads for ethnic minorities (mostly Karen, with some Hmong, Lisu and Lahu), Shan and Burmese immigrants.

Although the province is firmly on the tourist trail, with many resorts opening in the area around the capital, the vast majority of visitors don't seem to make it much further than Pai.

Pai ปาย

POP 2000

Spend enough time in northern Thailand and eventually you'll hear the comparisons between Pai and Bangkok's Khao San Road. Although this is definitely a stretch, in recent years the small town has started to resemble something of a Thai island getaway without the beaches. Guesthouses appear to outnumber private residences in the 'downtown' area, the internet is never more than a few steps away and the nights buzz with the sound of live music and partying.

However, unlike Khao San or the islands, Pai (pronounced more like the English 'bye', not 'pie') is just as popular among Thais as foreigners. During the peak of the cool

Mae Hong Son Province

season (December and January), thousands of Thais from Bangkok crowd into the town, making parts of it feel more like the Chatuchak Weekend Market than a remote village in Mae Hong Son. Traffic jams aren't unusual during this time of year, and accommodation becomes so scarce that many are forced to rough it in tents.

Despite all this, the town's popularity has yet to negatively impact its nearly picture-perfect setting in a mountain valley. There's heaps of quiet accommodation outside the main drag, a host of natural, lazy activities to keep visitors entertained, a vibrant art and music scene, and the town's Shan roots can still be seen in its temples, quiet back streets and fun afternoon market.

◉ Sights

Most of Pai's sights are found outside the city centre, making hiring a motorcycle a necessity. Motorcycle and bike hire are available at several guesthouses, as well as at aYa Service (p390).

Pai

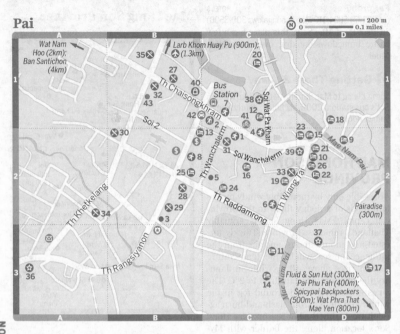

Pai

Buddhist Temples

Wat Phra That Mae Yen
BUDDHIST TEMPLE

(วัดพระธาตุแม่เย็น; ☉daylight hours) FREE This temple sits atop a hill and has good views overlooking the valley. To get here, walk 1km east from the main intersection in town to get to the stairs (353 steps) that lead to the top. Or, if you've got wheels, take the 400m sealed road that follows a different route.

Wat Nam Hoo
BUDDHIST TEMPLE

(วัดน้ำฮู; Ban Nam Hoo; ☉daylight hours) FREE Wat Nam Hoo is about 2km west of Pai and houses a sacred Buddha image said to have once emitted holy water from its head. The place is popular with visiting Thais and there's a small market on the grounds.

Waterfalls

There are a few waterfalls around Pai that are worth visiting, particularly after the rainy season (October to early December). The closest and the most popular, **Nam Tok Mo Paeng**, has a couple of pools that are suitable for swimming. The waterfall is about 8km from Pai along the road that also leads to Wat Nam Hoo – a long walk indeed, but suitable for a bike ride or short motorcycle trip. Roughly the same distance in the opposite direction is **Nam Tok Pembok**, just off the road to Chiang Mai. The most remote is **Nam Tok Mae Yen**, a couple of hours' walk down the rough road east of Pai, just before the turn-off to Fluid.

Other Sights

Ban Santichon
VILLAGE

(บ้านสันติชน) FREE About 4km outside of Pai, a small market, restaurants serving Yunnanese food, tea tasting, pony rides, a tacky recreation of the Great Wall of China and a **mountaintop viewpoint** (admission 20B; ☉4.30am-6pm) make the former KMT village of Ban Santichon not unlike a Chinese-themed Disneyland.

Tha Pai Hot Springs
HOT SPRINGS

(บ่อน้ำร้อนท่าปาย; adult/child 200/100B; ☉7am-6pm) Across Mae Nam Pai and 7km southeast of town via a paved road is this well-kept local park. A scenic stream flows through the park mixing with the hot springs in places to make pleasant bathing areas. The water is also diverted to a couple of nearby spas.

Pai Canyon
NATURE RESERVE

(กองแลนปาย) FREE Located 8km from Pai along the road to Chiang Mai, a paved stairway here culminates in an elevated lookout over high rock cliffs and the Pai valley. The

---

LOCAL KNOWLEDGE

PAI BEFORE THE BUZZ

Today, Pai is an established stop on the backpacker trail and one of northern Thailand's most talked about destinations. Yet according to Joe Cummings, author of the original edition of this guidebook, Pai in the early '80s was little more than 'a string of wooden houses, shophouses and two wats'. Since those days, Joe has continued to live in Thailand, contributing to more than 30 books on the region, and maintains a home in Pai.

When did you first go to Pai? In early 1981 I rented a 250cc dirt bike in Chiang Mai and set out for Mae Hong Son. I was researching the first edition of Lonely Planet *Thailand* and was warned not to be on the road after 5pm because 'communists and bandits' came out after dark.

What do you remember of that visit? I stayed at the only place that rented rooms, Wiang Pai Hotel, a two-storey teakwood building with six rooms, a shared toilet and shower, and a one-room opium den out back. I liked Pai but throughout the 1980s I assumed it would always be just a one-night stopover for people on the way to Mae Hong Son.

What do you think of the Pai of today? Have you ever regretted including it in the guidebook? Pai got popular for a good reason. It's the most beautiful valley in Thailand, for my tastes at least (and by now I've seen most of them), it's still pretty chill and there's lots to do in the area. [I have] no regrets writing about Pai. Word of mouth travels much faster than guidebook prose anyway, so there was no way to keep it a secret.

What are some worthwhile things to do, see or eat in Pai? I still like hiking around Nam Tok Pembok. And the Yunnanese cuisine in Ban Santichon makes a nice change from the Thai and *fa·ràng* (Westerner) food in town.

latter can be followed by a dirt trail, but lacking shade, is best tackled in the morning or afternoon.

Memorial Bridge   LANDMARK
(สพานประวัติศาสตร์ท่าปาย; Rte 1095) `FREE` It may look like no more than an antiquated bridge to foreigners, but to thousands of Thai tourists who stop here during the tourist season it's one of several crucial photo ops along the '762 curves' to Pai. Located 9km from Pai along the road to Chiang Mai, the bridge was originally built by Japanese soldiers during WWII.

🏃 Activities

Massage & Spa Treatments

There are plenty of traditional Thai massage places charging from around 150B an hour. Reiki, crystal healing, acupuncture, reflexology and other non-indigenous methods of healing are also available; keep your eyes open for signs or refer to the monthly *Pai Events Planner*. In addition to this, a few local businesses near Tha Pai Hot Springs have taken advantage of the area's healing thermal waters.

Pai Traditional Thai Massage   MASSAGE
(PTTM; ☑0 5369 9121; www.pttm1989.com; 68/3 Soi 1, Th Wiang Tai; massage per 1/1½/2hr 180/270/350B, sauna per visit 100B, 3-day massage course 2500B; ⊙9am-9pm) This longstanding and locally owned outfit offers very good northern Thai massage, as well as a sauna (cool season only) where you can steam yourself in *sà·mŭn·prai* (medicinal herbs). Three-day massage courses begin every Monday and Friday and last three hours per day. The friendly couple that do the massages and teach the course are accredited and are graduates of Chiang Mai's Old Medicine Hospital.

Spa Exotic   SPA
(☑08 1917 9351; www.spaexotic.com; 86 Moo 2, Ban Mae Hi; thermal water soak 80B; ⊙7am-10pm) This resort channels the hot water into its bungalow bathrooms and an open-air pool.

Pai Hotsprings Spa Resort   SPA
(☑0 5306 5748; www.paihotspringsparesort.com; 84-84/1 Moo 2, Ban Mae Hi; thermal water soak 100B, 1hr massage 300B; ⊙8am-6.30pm) A resort-style hotel that also offers massages and thermal water soaks.

Aroma Pai Spa   SPA
(☑0 5306 5745; www.aromapaispa.com; 110 Moo 2, Ban Mae Hi; thermal water soak 100B, spa treatments 650-2000B; ⊙7am-9pm) Offers soaks in private rooms and in a communal pool, as well as a variety of spa treatments.

Rafting & Kayaking

Rafting along Mae Nam Pai during the wet season (approximately June to February) is also a popular activity. The most popular trip runs from Pai to Mae Hong Son, which, depending on the amount of water, can traverse rapids in scale from class I to class V. Rates are all-inclusive (rafting equipment, camping gear, dry bags, insurance and food) and run from 1200B to 1500B per person for a one-day trip and from 1800B to 2700B per person for two days.

Pai Adventure   RAFTING
(☑0 5369 9385; www.thailandpai.net; 28 Th Chaisongkhram; ⊙8am-10pm) The one- to two-day white-water rafting trips offered by this recommended outfit can be combined with trekking and other activities. Also offers a jungle survival course upon request.

Thai Adventure Rafting   RAFTING
(☑0 5369 9111; www.thairafting.com; Th Chaisongkhram; ⊙8am-5pm) This French-run outfit leads one- and two-day rafting excursions. On the way, rafters visit a waterfall, a fossil reef and hot springs; one night is spent at the company's permanent riverside camp.

Back-Trax   RAFTING
(☑0 5369 9739; backtraxinpai@yahoo.com; Th Chaisongkhram; ⊙8am-10pm) With more than a decade of experience, this company offers multiday rafting excursions, inner-tubing trips and, of course, reiki lessons.

Trekking

Guided treks range in cost from about 800B to 1000B per person per day, in groups of two or more, and are all-inclusive. Most treks focus on the Lisu, Lahu and Karen villages in and around neighbouring Soppong (Pangmapha). Treks can be booked through guesthouse-based agencies such as the longstanding **Duang Trekking** (☑0 5369 9101; http://sites.google.com/site/lungtangtrekking; Duang Guest House, Th Chaisongkhram; ⊙8am-8pm), or through specific outfitters, including all of the rafting outfits listed earlier.

Other Activities

Fluid
GYM

(Ban Mae Yen; admission 60B; ⊙9am-6pm) This pool and gym complex is just outside of town, roughly across from Sun Hut.

Thom's Pai Elephant Camp
ELEPHANT ENCOUNTERS

(☑0 5369 9286; www.thomelephant.com; Th Rangsiyanon; elephant rides per person 500-2000B; ⊙9am-6pm) Pai's most established elephant outfitter has an office in town. You can choose between riding bareback or in a seat, and some rides include swimming with the elephants – a barrel of laughs on a bouncing elephant in the river. Rides include a soak in the hot-spring-fed tubs afterwards.

Courses

The type of courses available in Pai range from drumming to circus arts; check listings rags such as the *Pai Events Planner* (PEP) or **Pai Explorer** (www.paiexplorer.com) to see what's on when you're in town. In addition to what's listed here, lessons in Thai massage are available at Pai Traditional Thai Massage, and Thai cooking lessons are also available at Sipsongpanna guesthouse.

Pai Cookery School
COOKING

(☑08 1706 3799; Th Wanchalerm; lessons 600-750B; ⊙lessons 11am-1.30pm & 2-6.30pm) With a decade of experience, this outfit offers a variety of courses spanning three to five dishes. The afternoon course involves a trip to the market for ingredients. Contact a day in advance.

Taste of Pai
COOKING

(☑08 5620 9918; Th Chaisongkhram; lessons 600-700B; ⊙courses 9.30am-12.30pm & 4.30-8.30pm) Full-day classes here involve a visit to the market and instruction in six dishes, while half-day courses cover four dishes.

Mam Yoga House
YOGA

(☑08 9954 4981; www.mamyoga.paiexplorer.com; 27 Th Rangsiyanon; lessons 200-550B; ⊙10am-noon & 3-5pm) Just north of the police station, Mam offers Hatha yoga classes and courses in small groups.

S. Wisarut
THAI BOXING

(☑08 3321 2230; www.wirasutmuaythai.com; lessons 500B; ⊙lessons 8-10am & 3-5pm) Wanachai and Emanuel lead instruction in Thai boxing at this rustic gym about 1km outside of town, on the turn-off just before Fluid.

🛌 Sleeping

Despite several years of growth, Pai's accommodation boom continues, and the rumour on the ground during our visit was that there were more than 500 hotels, guesthouses and resorts. Although 'downtown' Pai has seen relatively little change in this respect over the last few years, on our last visit there were dozens of new resorts in an approximate 3km circle around the town. Yet despite the glut of accommodation, during the height of the Thai tourist season (December and January), accommodation in Pai can be nearly impossible to come by, although tents are available for about 100B.

Keep in mind that prices fluctuate significantly in Pai, and nearly all the midrange and top-end accommodation cut their prices, sometimes by as much as 60%, during the off season. We've listed high-season walk-in rates here.

🛏 In Town

Pai used to be an exceedingly inexpensive place to stay and we still recall the days of the 50B riverside bungalow. But a flood in 2005 demolished many of the truly cheap places, most of which have been replaced by upper-budget or midrange choices. There are still some cheap rooms just outside the centre of town, which is where you should base yourself if you're coming to Pai with preconceived notions of an idyllic, rural stay.

Tayai's Guest House
GUESTHOUSE $

(☑0 5369 9579; off Th Raddamrong; r & bungalows 200-500B; ❄️🖥️) Simple but clean fan and air-con rooms and bungalows in a leafy compound just off the main drag.

Pai Country Hut
HOTEL $

(☑08 7779 6541; www.facebook.com/paicountry-bungalows; Ban Mae Hi; bungalows incl breakfast 200-500B; 🖥️) The bamboo bungalows here are utterly simple, but are tidy and most have bathrooms and inviting hammocks. Although it's not exactly riverside, it's the most appealing of several similar budget places in the area.

TTK
GUESTHOUSE $

(☑0 5369 8093; 8/10 Th Raddamrong; r 350-450B; ❄️🖥️) Set behind the Israeli restaurant of the same name, the rooms here lack both natural light and any attempt at interior design, but are spotless and conveniently located.

NORTHERN THAILAND PAI

Charlie's House
GUESTHOUSE $

(☑0 5369 9039; Th Rangsiyanon; r 150-600B; ✷ ☏) This long-standing, locally run place offers a range of options in a clean, suburban-feeling compound.

Giant Guest House
GUESTHOUSE $

(☑0 5369 8059; www.giantguesthouse.com; Th Wiang Tai; bungalows 300-500B; ☏) It isn't the most comfortable or service-minded accommodation Pai has to offer, but nobody else comes close to Giant for that old-school hippy, authentic Pai vibe.

Baan Pai Village
HOTEL $$

(☑0 5369 8152; www.baanpaivillage.com; 88 Th Wiang Tai; bungalows incl breakfast 1000-1900B; ✷@☏) This well-maintained place has a collection of 21 wooden bungalows set among winding garden pathways. The rooms don't leave heaps of room to stretch, but have floor-to-ceiling sliding windows, and large quite plush bathrooms, as well as spacious terraces with rattan mats and axe cushions to best enjoy the greenery. Huge off-season discounts available.

Breeze of Pai Guesthouse
HOTEL $$

(☑08 1998 4597; suthasinee.svp@gmail.com; Soi Wat Pa Kham; r 400B, bungalows 800B; ✷☏) This well-groomed compound near the river consists of nine attractive and spacious rooms and six large A-frame bungalows. It's close to the action without the noise pollution. A loyal customer base means you'll probably have to book ahead.

Baan Pai Riverside
HOTEL $$

(☑08 8404 9211; www.baanpairiverside.net; bungalows incl breakfast 1000-1200B; ☏) Choose from pastel-coloured mobile-home-like bungalows or their bamboo counterparts. All are similarly equipped with fan, hot-water showers and the same furniture; riverside bungalows cost more. Baan Pai Riverside is located east of town, just across Mae Nam Pai.

Pai Fah
HOTEL $$

(☑08 8409 1151; www.paifahhotel.com; 77 Th Wiang Tai; r 900-1500B; ✷@☏) This self-professed 'boutique house' takes the form of simple but bright and clean rooms in a two-storey villa steps from all the action. Rooms with air-con are more expensive.

Kanoon House
GUESTHOUSE $$

(☑0 5369 9453; www.baankanoonpai.com; 33 Soi Wanchalerm; bungalows 600B; ☏) Consisting of 14 bright duplex and free-standing bungalows around a 100 year-old *kà·nŭn* (jackfruit) tree, this locally owned place is quiet, clean and cosy.

Villa De Pai
HOTEL $$

(☑0 5369 9109; www.villadepai.com; 87/1 Th Wiang Tai; bungalows incl breakfast 600-1200B; ☏) Slightly aged but clean and conveniently located riverside bungalows.

★ Rim Pai Cottage
HOTEL $$$

(☑0 5369 9133; www.rimpaicottage.com; Th Chaisongkhram; bungalows 1200-4000B; ✷☏) The home-like bungalows (incl breakfast only from October to February), here are spread out along a secluded and beautifully wooded section of Mae Nam Pai. There are countless cosy riverside corners to relax in and a palpable village-like vibe about the whole place. The interiors have a romantic feel with their lacy mosquito nets and attractive Thai decorating details, and the open bathrooms are particularly nice.

Rim Pai is an excellent deal in the low season when the prices drop dramatically.

Hotel des Artists
HOTEL $$$

(☑0 5369 9539; www.hotelartists.com; 99 Th Chaisongkhram; r incl breakfast 3600-4000B; ✷☏) This former Shan mansion has been turned into an attractive boutique hotel. The 14 slightly crowded rooms mingle pan-Asian and Western design elements in a tasteful, attractive package. Twin beds are on an elevated platform and all rooms have balconies, those with riverside views being slightly larger and more expensive.

Baan Tawan Guest House
HOTEL $$$

(☑0 5369 8116; www.baantawan-pai.com; 117 Th Wiang Tai; r 1000-3000B, bungalows 2000-3000B; ✷@☏) The older and more charming two-storey riverside bungalows made with salvaged teak are the reason to stay here, but there are also spacious (and less expensive) rooms in a large two-storey building. Service is first-rate, and Baan Tawan is located on a relatively isolated stretch of the river. Breakfast included.

Pai River Villa
HOTEL $$$

(☑0 5369 9796; pairivervilla@gmail.com; 7 Th Wiang Tai; bungalows incl breakfast 1200-2500B; ✷☏) This place boasts some of the more attractive riverside bungalows in town. The air-con bungalows are spacious and stylish, and have wide balconies that encourage lazy riverside relaxing and mountain viewing, while the fan bungalows are a significantly tighter fit.

Pai RiverCorner
HOTEL $$$

(☏0 5369 9049; www.pairivercorner.com; 94 Th Chaisongkhram; r incl breakfast 3400-6400B; ✳@⊛✸) A no-brainer for the design-conscious traveller, the nine rooms here include beautiful Thai furniture, gorgeous colours and lots of deluxe details. All rooms have river-facing balconies and some have lounges and interior spa pools.

Pai Vimaan Resort
HOTEL $$$

(☏0 5369 9403; wwww.paivimaan.com; 73 Th Wiang Tai; r 1000-1800B, bungalows 4000-7000B; ✳⊛) The highlight here is the five riverside tented bungalows. Huge and equipped with air-con, hot tubs, TV and other modern amenities, they redefine camping. The resort's two-storey bungalows are bright and airy, with the top-floor rooms allowing great views of the river, and there are also rooms in the main wooden structure. Breakfast included.

🛏 Outside of Town

If you've got your own wheels, there are far more options outside of the centre of Pai than we have room to list here. The vast majority are targeted towards domestic rather than foreign tourists, which means they fall in the mid- and upper-range of the price spectrum, and typically take the form of air-con-equipped bungalow compounds.

Spicypai Backpackers
HOTEL $

(☏08 5263 5147; Ban Mae Yen; dm 100-150B, bungalows 500B; ✳@⊛) The bamboo dorms here look like they could have featured in an episode of *Survivor*. Communal areas ranging from kitchen to fire pit continue the rustic feel, and there are a few air-con bungalows for those with loftier standards. It's about 750m east of Mae Nam Pai, just off the road that leads to Thai Pai Hot Springs.

★ Bueng Pai Farm
GUESTHOUSE $$

(☏08 9265 4768; www.paifarm.com; Ban Mae Hi; bungalows 500-2000B; ⊛✸) Uniting yoga enthusiasts and fisherfolk, the 12 simple bungalows here are strategically and attractively positioned between a functioning farm and a vast pond stocked with freshwater fish. During the tourist season, Run and Orn serve meals made with their own organic produce; there's a campfire during the winter months, and a pool, communal kitchen and fishing equipment are available year round.

Bueng Pai is 2.5km from Pai, off the road that leads to Tha Pai Hot Springs; look for the sign.

★ Pairadise
HOTEL $$

(☏0 5369 8065; www.pairadise.com; Ban Mae Hi; bungalows 800-1400B; ✳✸) This neat resort looks over the Pai Valley from atop a ridge just outside of town. The bungalows are stylish, spacious and include gold leaf lotus murals, beautiful rustic bathrooms and terraces with hammocks. All surround a spring-fed pond that is suitable for swimming. The hotel is about 750m east of Mae Nam Pai; look for the sign just after the bridge.

Sipsongpanna
HOTEL $$

(☏0 5369 8259; www.facebook.com/paisipsongpanna; Wiang Nua; bungalows incl breakfast 1300-1500B; @✸) The four adobe-style riverside bungalows here are rustic and quirky with a mix of bright colours, beds on elevated platforms and sliding-glass doors opening to wide balconies. There are also still a few original wooden bungalows, although these are being phased out.

The hotel is about 2.5km from the centre of town off the road to Mae Hong Son; look for the well-posted turn-off, about 1km from Pai.

Sun Hut
HOTEL $$

(☏0 5369 9730; www.thesunhut.com; Ban Mae Yen; bungalows incl breakfast 900-1900B; ✸) Located in a jungle-like setting with a stream running through it, this long-standing and rustic resort is one of the more unique places in the area. Bungalows are nicely spaced apart and more expensive ones have porches and lots of charm. The hotel is 500m east of Mae Nam Pai along the road that leads to Tha Pai Hot Springs.

Pai Chan
HOTEL $$

(☏08 1180 3064; www.paichan.com; Ban Mae Hi; bungalows incl breakfast 600-2000B; ✸⊛) Pai Chan doesn't look like much from the parking lot, but closer inspection reveals attractive and comfortable heavy wooden bungalows, each with a spacious balcony overlooking rice fields or an inviting pool. Located about 200m east of Mae Nam Pai.

PuraVida
HOTEL $$

(☏08 9635 7556; www.puravidapai.com; Wiang Nua; bungalows incl breakfast 1425B; ✳⊛) A friendly Dutch-Thai couple look after these eight cute bungalows on a well-manicured hillside in the quiet Wiang Nua area. The honeymoon bungalow offers a bit more privacy, and all rooms are equipped with aircon, TV, fridge and hot water. PuraVida is about 4km from the centre of town off the road to Mae Hong Son; look for the well-posted turn-off about 1km from Pai.

Lychee Garden Bungalow GUESTHOUSE $$
(☑08 5471 9220; Wiang Nua; bungalows 500-1500B; ❄⑧) The four bungalows here, located in an overflowing garden shaded by lychee trees, may not represent the most luxurious accommodation in the area, but they're clean and have good mattresses, TV, air-con and hot water. The hotel is about 2.5km from the centre of town off the road to Mae Hong Son; look for the well-posted turn-off about 1km from Pai.

Pai Phu Fah HOTEL $$
(☑08 1906 2718; www.paiphufah.com; Ban Mae Hi; r & bungalows 300-1500B; ❄⑧) There's a decent range of accommodation here, from bungalows to rooms; it's all in a quiet, rural setting. It's about 650m east of Mae Nam Pai along the road to Thai Pai Hot Springs.

Bulunburi HOTEL $$$
(☑0 5369 8302; www.bulunburi.com; Ban Pong; bungalows incl breakfast 600-4000B; ❄@⑧) Set in a tiny secluded valley of rice fields and streams, the seductively bucolic location is as much a reason to stay here as the attractive accommodation. The 11 bungalows, which range from tight fan-cooled rooms to huge two-bedroom houses, are well equipped and stylish.

Bulunburi is about 2.5km from the centre of town along the road to Mae Hong Son; look for the well-posted turn-off, about 1km from Pai.

Phu Pai HOTEL $$$
(☑0 5306 5111; www.phupai.com; Mae Na Theung; bungalows incl breakfast 2000-3500B; ❄⑧) This self-professed 'Art Resort' is an attractive, remote-feeling gathering of 40 locally styled luxury bungalows. Views are the focus here, with most bungalows edging rice fields and an infinity pool framing the Pai Valley. The hotel is about 4km from the centre of town off the road to Mae Hong Son; look for the well-posted turn-off just after the airport runway, about 1.3km from Pai.

Pai Treehouse HOTEL $$$
(☑08 1911 3640; www.paitreehouse.com; Ban Mae Hi; bungalows incl breakfast 1000-6500B; ❄⑧) Even if you can't score one of the three tree-

house rooms here (they're popular), there are several other attractive bungalows, many near the river. On the vast grounds you'll also find elephants and floating decks on Mae Nam Pai, all culminating in a family-friendly atmosphere. The resort is 6km east of Pai, just before Tha Pai Hot Springs.

Pai à Ars HOTEL $$$
(☑08 9763 2444; Ban Mae Khong; bungalows incl breakfast 1500-2000B; ❄⑧⑧) The gleaming white, two-storey tube-like structures here are meant to resemble wombs – according to Pai à Ars, the epitome of comfortable accommodation. If it's too oedipal for you, there are also more conventional air-con bungalows by a stream. The hotel is about 4km from the centre of town off the road to Mae Hong Son; look for the well-posted turn-off just after the airport runway.

✗ Eating

At first glance, Pai has a seemingly impressive range of restaurants for such a small town, but a few meals will reveal that the quality of food is generally pretty mediocre.

During the morning, there's takeaway food at **Saengthongaram market** (Th Khetkelang; mains 30-60B; ⊙6-11am). For tasty take-home local-style eats, try the **evening market** (Th Raddamrong; mains 30-60B; ⊙3-7pm) that unfolds every afternoon from about 3pm to sunset. And every evening during the tourist season several vendors set up along Th Chaisongkhram and Th Rangsiyanon, selling all manner of food and drink from stalls and refurbished VW vans.

★**Larp Khom Huay Poo** NORTHERN THAI $
(Ban Huay Pu; mains 30-70B; ⊙9am-8pm) Escape the wheat grass and tofu crowd and get your meat on at this unabashedly carnivorous local eatery. The house special (and the dish you must order) is *lâhp kôo·a*, minced meat (beef or pork) fried with local herbs and spices. Accompanied by a basket of sticky rice, a plate of bitter herbs and an ice-cold Singha, it's the best meal in Pai.

The restaurant is on the road to Mae Hong Son, about 1km north of town, just past the well-posted turn-off to Sipsongpanna.

★**Yunnanese Restaurant** CHINESE $
(no roman-script sign; mains 30-180B; ⊙8am-8pm) This open-air place in the Chinese village of Ban Santichon serves the traditional dishes of the town's Yunnanese residents. Standouts include *màntŏ* (steamed buns),

here served with pork leg stewed with Chinese herbs. There are several dishes using unique local crops and other dishes involving exotic ingredients such as black chicken.

Or you could always go for the excellent noodles, made by hand and topped with a delicious mixture of minced pork, garlic and sesame. The restaurant is in an open-air adobe building behind the giant rock in Ban Santichon, about 4km west of Pai.

Witching Well　　　　INTERNATIONAL $
(www.witchingwellrestaurant.com; Th Wiang Tai; mains 75-140B; ⊙7am-11pm; 🛜🍴) This buzzy foreigner-run place is where to come if you're looking for authentic sandwiches, pasta, cakes and pastries. It also does good coffee and the kind of sophisticated breakfasts you're not going to find elsewhere in Pai.

Ping's Burger Queen　　　　AMERICAN $
(Th Wiang Tai; mains 60-80B; ⊙2-10pm) Burgers are huge in Pai, and of the various vendors, we're certain that Ping does the best job. Everything is homemade, from the soft, slightly sweet buns to the rich garlic mayo that accompanies the thick-cut fries.

Thai Style BBQ Buffet　　　　THAI $
(Th Khetkelang; per person 139B; ⊙4-10pm) As the name suggests, this is *mǒo gàtà*, the DIY barbecue so beloved by northern Thais. Yet unlike most places, the meat and veg here are of good quality and there's live music.

TTK　　　　ISRAELI $
(The Thai Kebab; Th Raddamrong; mains 70-150B; ⊙8.30am-8.30pm; 🛜🍴) The expansive menu here spans Israeli dishes from standards to surprises, with breakfast options and Thai vegetarian dishes thrown in for good measure.

Good Life　　　　INTERNATIONAL $
(Th Wiang Tai; mains 40-170B; 🛜🍴) Trays of wheatgrass and secondhand books (sample title: *The Aloe Answer*) function as interior design at this eclectic and popular cafe.

Khanom Jeen Nang Yong　　　　THAI $
(Th Chaisongkhram, no roman-script sign; mains 20B; ⊙10am-9pm) This place specialises in *kà·nǒm jeen*, thin rice noodles served with a curry-like broth. It's in the same building as Pai Adventure.

Nong Beer　　　　THAI $
(cnr Th Khetkalang & Th Chaisongkhram; mains 20-150B; ⊙8am-8pm) A good place for cheap and

---

ⓘ DRINKING IN PAI 101

As a general guide to downtown Pai's drinking scene, most of the open-air and VW-van-based cocktail bars are along Th Chaisongkhram; Th Wiang Tai is where you'll find the largely indoor, live music places; Th Rangsiyanon is where most of the 'guesthouse' style restaurant-bars with a diverse soundtrack and a dinner menu are located. A knot of open-air reggae-style bars can be found at the eastern end of Th Raddamrong, just across the bridge.

---

authentic Thai eats ranging from *kôw soy* to curries ladled over rice.

All About Coffee　　　　INTERNATIONAL $
(Th Chaisongkhram; mains 70-99B; ⊙8am-5pm; 🛜🍴) Come here for eye-opening coffee drinks and the best French toast in town. Yummy open sandwiches are made with homemade bread.

Mama Falafel　　　　ISRAELI $
(Soi Wanchalerm; set meals 80-90B; ⊙11am-8pm Mon-Sat; 🍴) This friendly native of Pai has been cooking up tasty felafel, hummus, schnitzel and other Jewish and Israeli faves since 2002; the set meals win in both quality and quantity.

Charlie & Lek Health Restaurant　　　　THAI $
(Th Rangsiyanon; mains 35-180B; ⊙11am-10pm; 🍴) This popular place does central Thai-style fare for foreigners: lots of veggie options and light on the flavours.

Amido's Pizza Garden　　　　PIZZA $$
(Th Raddamrong; pizzas 160-350B; ⊙11am-11pm; 🍴) For the record, we never said that Amido's does 'the best pizza in the world', but given how far Pai is from Naples, we reckon they're doing a pretty good job.

🍷 Drinking & Entertainment

There are dozens of bars in Pai – too many to list here – and given the fickleness of the local drinking scene, few would still be around by the time this goes to print. Instead, we've listed some of the more interesting and long-standing live music places in and around town.

Edible Jazz
LIVE MUSIC

(www.ediblejazz.com; Soi Wat Pa Kham; ⊗8.30-11pm) Probably Pai's cosiest place for live music. Stroke a cat and nurse a beer while listening to acoustic guitar performances. Depending on who's in town, the open-mike nights on Thursdays and Sundays can be surprisingly good.

Bebop
LIVE MUSIC

(Th Rangsiyanon; ⊗8pm-1am) This legendary box is popular with both locals and travellers and has live music nightly (from about 10pm), emphasising blues, R&B and rock.

Lun Laa Bar
LIVE MUSIC

(Th Wiang Tai; ⊗7pm-midnight) The nightly jam sessions at this tiny bar start at 9pm.

Don't Cry
BAR

(Th Raddamrong; ⊗6pm-late) Located just across the river, this is the kind of reggae bar you thought you left behind on Ko Pha Ngan. Soporifically chilled out and open until the last guy goes home.

Shopping

Every evening during the tourist season, from November to February, a **Walking Street** (Th Chaisongkhram & Th Rangsiyanon; ⊗6-10pm) forms in the centre of town.

Information

There are plenty of places around town, especially at the western end of Th Raddamrong, that offer internet services (20B to 30B per hour).

Several foreign exchange booths and ATMs can be found along Th Rangsiyanon and Th Chaisongkhram.

Pai Explorer (www.paiexplorer.com) is the free local English-language map. The *Pai Events Planner* (PEP) is a free monthly map that covers cultural events, travel destinations and some restaurant and bar openings; you can find it around town.

Getting There & Away

Pai's airport is around 1.5km north of town along Rte 1095. At research time, **Kan Air** (✆0 5369 9955, nationwide 02 551 6111; www.kanairlines.com; Pai Airport; ⊗8.30am-5pm) was the only airline operating out of the town, with a daily connection to Chiang Mai.

Pai's tiny **bus station** (Th Chaisongkhram) is the place to catch slow, fan-cooled buses and more efficient minivans to Chiang Mai and destinations in Mae Hong Son.

AYa Service also runs air-con minivan buses to Chiang Mai (150B, three hours, hourly from 8am to 4.30pm) as well as destinations in Chiang Rai province including Chiang Rai (550B, six hours, 5.30am), Mae Sai (600B, six hours, 5.30am) and Chiang Khong (650B, seven hours, 6pm).

Getting Around

Most of Pai is accessible on foot. Motorcycle taxis wait at the **taxi stand** across from the bus station. Sample fares are 50B to Ban Santichon and 80B to Nam Tok Mo Paeng.

For local excursions you can hire bicycles or motorcycles at several locations around town.
aYa Service (✆0 5369 9888; www.ayaservice.com; 22/1 Th Chaisongkhram; bikes per 24hr 100-400B; ⊗8am-9pm) This busy outfit has more than 100 bikes. There are a couple of similar places in the immediate vicinity.
North Wheels (✆0 5369 8066; www.north-wheels.com; Th Khetkelang; motorcycle/car per 24hr 140/1500B; ⊗8am-6pm) Both motorcycles and cars can be hired here.

Soppong
สบป่อง

Soppong (also sometimes known as Pang-mapha, actually the name of the entire district) is a small market village a couple of hours northwest of Pai and about 70km from Mae Hong Son. There's not much to see in town, but the surrounding area is defined by dense forests, rushing rivers and dramatic limestone outcrops and is *the* place in northern Thailand for caving. The best source of information on caving and trekking in the area is the owner of Cave Lodge in nearby Tham Lot, the most accessible cave in the area.

TRANSPORT TO/FROM PAI

DESTINATION	AIR	BUS	MINIVAN
Chiang Mai	1990B; 20min; daily	80B; 3-4hr; noon	150B; 3hr; hourly 7am-4.30pm
Mae Hong Son		75B; 3-4hr; 11am	150B; 2½hr; 8.30am
Soppong (Pangmapha)		45B; 1½hr; 11am	100B; 1hr; 8.30am

There are also several Shan, Lisu, Karen and Lahu villages that can easily be visited on foot.

If you're here on Tuesday morning, check out the town's rustic **market**.

✴ Activities

Cave Lodge has experienced local guides and arranges recommended kayaking, trekking and caving trips in the area. It is located near Tham Lot, 9km from Soppong.

Poodoi Namfaa Tour & Trekking

TREKKING, RAFTING

(☎ 08 4372 5295; ⊙ 8am-8pm) This outfit can arrange various outdoor pursuits, all led by local Musoe, Lisu and Karen guides. The emphasis is on two-day rafting trips along the Nam Khong and Nam Pai rivers (1500B per person, at least four people, all-inclusive). Two-day treks start at 800B per person (at least two people). The office is at the far western edge of town.

🛏 Sleeping & Eating

All accommodation, much of which is found along Soppong's main road, is clearly marked by signs. There's little in the way of food in Soppong, but virtually every guesthouse has a restaurant attached.

★ Soppong River Inn

HOTEL **$$**

(☎ 0 5361 7107; www.soppong.com; r & bungalows 200-2450B; ❄ @ 🛜) Combining rooms in a couple of rambling riverside structures and a handful of free-standing basic bungalows, this is the most attractive place in Soppong. Set among lush gardens with winding paths, the rooms have heaps of character and are all slightly different; the River Rim Cottage, with a private balcony situated right over the river, is our fave. Soppong River Inn is at the western edge of town, within walking distance of the bus station.

Little Eden Guesthouse

HOTEL **$$**

(☎ 0 5361 7054; www.littleeden-guesthouse.com; r & bungalows 400-1800B; ❄ @ 🛜 ⊜) The five A-frame bungalows around a pleasant pool are well kept with hot-water showers. And the four rooms in the new building are spacious and attractive. Yet, it's the beautiful two-storey 'houses' that make this place special. Perfect for families or a group of friends, they are stylishly decorated with living rooms, interesting nooks and crannies, and terraces with hammocks.

Baan Café

HOTEL **$$**

(☎ 0 5361 7081; khunjui@yahoo.com; r 600B, bungalows 1200B; 🛜) Located near the bridge, about 750m west of Soppong's bus stop, this place combines spotless rooms and house-like bungalows in a park setting by Nam Lang. The bungalows include fireplaces, have balconies looking over the river and are terrific value. Baan Café is also one of the better restaurants in town (open from 7.30am to 7.30pm) and serving locally grown coffee.

Northern Hill Guest House

GUESTHOUSE **$$**

(☎ 0 5361 7136; www.northernhillgh.com; r & bungalows 350-1200B) This place combines several cramped but tidy bungalows on a hill looking over Soppong. Some rooms include TV and fridge. Northern Hill is at the eastern extent of town, opposite the turn-off to Tham Lot.

Rim Doi

GUESTHOUSE **$$**

(☎ 08 1952 3570; r & bungalows incl breakfast 500-2000B) About 2km from Soppong along the road to Tham Lot, this place unites bamboo huts and more permanent-feeling rooms on a grassy hillside. Rooms are large and comfortably furnished.

Lemon Hill Garden

GUESTHOUSE **$$**

(☎ 0 5361 7039; r & bungalows 300-2500B; ❄ 🛜) Due to its location across from the town bus stop, this guesthouse is probably the most popular place in town, although it must be said that there are nicer places to stay. There's a mishmash of accommodation ranging from rooms to bungalows – check out a few before coming to a decision – and a restaurant (open 7am to 6pm).

Rock

RESORT **$$$**

(☎ 0 5361 7134; www.therockresort.com; r & bungalows incl breakfast 1500-5000B; ❄ 🛜) Located about 1.5km west of town, you can't miss this place. The new bungalows are scattered across a manicured riverbank pockmarked with rock formations, and there are also a few rooms equipped with TV, fridge and aircon. A suspension bridge links the grounds with adjacent flower gardens. Rock is geared towards Thai tourists and communicating in English might be a problem.

Coffee Cottage

THAI **$**

(dishes 40-160B; ⊙ 8am-6pm; 🛜) Good food and real coffee can be had at this wooden house along the road to Tham Lot. Early-morning breakfasts and late dinners can be arranged in advance.

NORTHERN THAILAND SOPPONG

ℹ️ Information

Soppong's police station is 1.5km west of the town. There are a couple of ATMs in the centre of town near Lemon Hill Garden.

ℹ️ Getting There & Around

Motorcycle taxis stationed at the bus stop in Soppong will take passengers to Tham Lot or the Cave Lodge for 70B per person; private pick-up trucks will take you and up to five other people for 300B.

Motorcycles can be hired at **Castrol Bike Point** (📞 0 5361 7185; ⏰ 7am-6pm), at the western edge of town, for 250B per day.

Buses and minivans stop near the town's market.

Around Soppong

Tham Lot
ถ้ำลอด

About 9km north of Soppong is Tham Lot (pronounced *tâm lôrt* and also known as *tâm nám lôrt*), a large limestone cave with impressive stalagmites, 'coffin caves' and a wide stream running through it. Along with Tham Nam Lang further west, it's one of the largest known caves in Thailand. The total length of the cave is 1600m, and the stream runs through it for 600m.

At the entrance, you must hire a gas lantern and guide for 150B (one guide leads one to three people) to take you through the caverns; visitors are not permitted to tour the caves alone. From the entrance to the exit and taking in the Column Cavern, Doll Cave and Coffin Cave, the rafts (up to three people) cost 400B return, or 300B one way. If going one way you can walk back from outside the cave (20 minutes), but only during the dry season (from approximately November to May). In the dry season it may be possible to wade to the Doll Cave and then take a raft through to the exit (300B return, 200B one way). Try to be at the exit at sunset when hundreds of thousands of swifts pour into Tham Lot and cling to their bedtime stalagmites.

Apart from the main chamber there are also three side chambers – Column Cavern, Doll Cave and Coffin Cave – that can be reached by ladders. It takes around two hours to explore the whole thing. Depending on the time of year, it is necessary to take a bamboo raft for some or all of the journey through the caves. Access to parts of the cave may be limited between August and October because of water levels.

A **Nature Education Centre** (⏰ 8am-5.30pm) on the grounds has basic displays on the area as well as displays of pottery remains found in the cave.

🛏️ Sleeping & Eating

A row of **outdoor restaurants** (mains 20-60B; ⏰ 9am-6pm) outside the Tham Lot park entrance offer simple Thai fare.

★ **Cave Lodge**   HOTEL $$
(📞 0 5361 7203; www.cavelodge.com; dm 120B, r 250B, bungalows 300-1500B; 📶) Open since 1986, this is one of the more legendary places to stay in northern Thailand (and probably the first guesthouse in Mae Hong Son). Run by the unofficial expert on the area, John Spies, the 19 rooms here are basic but unique and varied. The setting on a wooded hillside above the Nam Lang is beautiful and options for adventure abound.

Choose from caving and kayaking trips (the latter possible from approximately February to May), guided or unguided treks (good maps are available), or just hang out in the beautiful communal area. The traditional Shan herbal sauna is an experience and the custom ovens bake bread and other treats. Tham Lot is a short walk away.

Mae La-Na
แม่ละนา

Set in a jaw-droppingly picturesque mountain valley located 6km off Rte 1095, this tiny, remote Shan village feels like a lost corner of the world. The most famous local attraction is **Tham Mae La-Na**, a 12km-long cavern with a stream running through it. Although local guides are willing to take

TRANSPORT TO/FROM SOPPONG

DESTINATION	BUS	MINIVAN
Chiang Mai	105B; 6hr; 10.30am	250B; 5hr; hourly from 8.30am to 5.30pm
Mae Hong Son	45B; 2hr; 1pm	150B; 1½hr; hourly from 9.30am to 6.30pm
Pai	45B; 1½ hr; 10.30am	100B; 1hr; hourly from 8.30am to 5.30pm

THE CAVES OF PANGMAPHA

The 900-sq-km area of Pangmapha district is famous for its high concentration of cave systems – over 200 have been found. Apart from Tham Lot, one of its most famous is **Tham Nam Lang**, which is 20km northwest of Soppong near Ban Nam Khong. It's 8.5km long and said to be one of the largest caves in the world in terms of volume.

Many of the caves are essentially underground river systems, some of which boast waterfalls, lakes and sandy 'beaches'. *Cryptotora thamicola,* an eyeless, waterfall-climbing troglobitic fish that forms its own genus, is found in only two caves in the world, both of which are in Pangmapha. Other caves contain little or no life, due to an abundance of noxious gases or very little oxygen.

More than 85 of the district's 200 limestone caverns are known to contain ancient teak coffins carved from solid teak logs. Up to 9m long, the coffins are typically suspended on wooden scaffolds inside the caves. The coffins have been carbon-dated and shown to be between 1200 and 2200 years old. The ends are usually carved and Thai archaeologists have identified at least 50 different design schemes.

The local Shans know these burial caves as *tâm pĕe* (spirit caves) or *tâm pĕe maan* (coffin caves). It is not known who made them or why they were placed in the caves, but as most caves have fewer than 10 coffins it indicates that not everyone was accorded such an elaborate burial. Similar coffins have been found in karst areas west of Bangkok and also in Borneo, China and the Philippines, but the highest concentration of coffin caves from this period is in Pangmapha.

The easiest coffins to visit are in the **coffin cave** (admission 20B; ⊗ 8.30am-5pm) just past Pangmapha Hospital, 2km west of Soppong, and the coffin caves in Tham Lot, 9km northeast of Soppong. Several caves that scientists are investigating at the moment are off limits to the public, but John Spies at Cave Lodge may know which caves are possible to explore. His book, *Wild Times,* is also a great informal guide to the area's caves.

people inside, in reality the cave lacks the appropriate infrastructure to support visitors, who run a serious risk of permanently damaging delicate cave formations and disturbing the habitat of sensitive cave fish. A better bet is to check out the nearby **Tham Pakarang** (Coral Cave) and **Tham Phet** (Diamond Cave), both of which feature good wall formations. Guides (200B) can be arranged at the main village shop and petrol station. Some of the caves may not be accessible during the rainy season.

Mae La-Na is also a good base for some inspiring **walks**. Some of Mae Hong Son's most beautiful scenery is within a day's ramble, and there are several Red and Black Lahu villages nearby. It's also possible to walk a 15km half-loop all the way from Mae La-Na to Tham Lot and Soppong. Khun Ampha at Maelana Garden Home can provide a basic map.

The Mae La-Na junction is 13km west of Soppong. A motorcycle taxi here from Soppong costs 200B. Along the way you'll pass the Black Lahu village of Jabo, which also has a coffin cave.

🛏 Sleeping & Eating

A dozen homes in Mae La-Na have collaborated to form a **homestay program** (per person per night 100B); fees go back into a community fund. Meals can be prepared for 70B per person. Enquire at the sporadically staffed wooden office at the entrance to town or at any home with a 'home stay' sign.

Maelana Garden Home GUESTHOUSE **$**
(☑ 08 1706 6021; r & bungalows 200-500B) At the edge of town towards Tham Mae La-Na, this beautiful farmlike compound combines rooms in two wooden houses and a few A-frame bamboo bungalows. Authentic Shan meals can be prepared (100B per person). Call ahead – transport can be arranged for 100B from Rte 1095 or from Soppong for 400B – or ask for Khun Ampha at the village shop and petrol station.

Mae Hong Son แม่ฮ่องสอน
POP 7000

With its remote setting and surrounding mountains, Mae Hong Son fits many travellers' preconceived notion of how a northern

Mae Hong Son

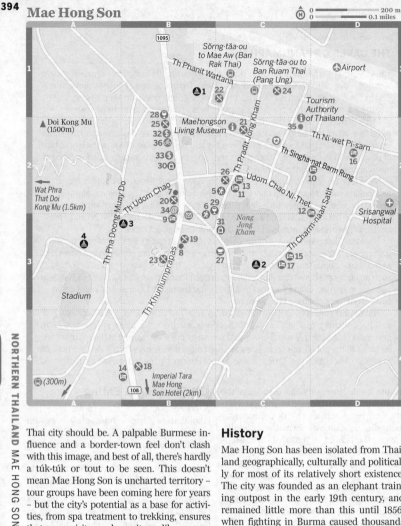

Thai city should be. A palpable Burmese influence and a border-town feel don't clash with this image, and best of all, there's hardly a túk-túk or tout to be seen. This doesn't mean Mae Hong Son is uncharted territory – tour groups have been coming here for years – but the city's potential as a base for activities, from spa treatment to trekking, ensures that your visit can be quite unlike anyone else's.

Mae Hong Son is best visited between November and February when the town is at its coolest and most beautiful. During the rainy season (June to October), travel to the more remote corners of the province can be difficult because there are few paved roads. During the hot season (approximately February to May), the Mae Nam Pai valley fills with smoke from swidden agriculture. The only problem with going in the cool season is that the nights are downright cold – you'll need at least one sweater and a thick pair of socks for mornings and evenings.

History

Mae Hong Son has been isolated from Thailand geographically, culturally and politically for most of its relatively short existence. The city was founded as an elephant training outpost in the early 19th century, and remained little more than this until 1856, when fighting in Burma caused thousands of Shan to pour into the area. In the years that followed, Mae Hong Son prospered as a centre for logging and remained an independent kingdom until 1900, when King Rama V incorporated the area into the Thai kingdom.

◉ Sights

With their bright colours, whitewashed stupas and glittering zinc fretwork, Mae Hong Son's Burmese- and Shan-style temples will have you scratching your head wondering which country you're in.

Mae Hong Son

NORTHERN THAILAND MAE HONG SON

Wat Jong Kham & Wat Jong Klang
BUDDHIST TEMPLE
(วัดจองคำ/วัดจองกลาง; Th Charm-naan Satit; museum ⊙ daylight hours) FREE Wat Jong Kham was built nearly 200 years ago by Thai Yai (Shan) people, who make up about half of the population of the Mae Hong Son Province.

Next door, Wat Jong Klang houses 100-year-old glass *jataka* paintings and a **museum** (admission by donation; ⊙ 8am-6pm) with 150-year-old wooden dolls from Mandalay that depict some of the more gruesome aspects of the wheel of life.

Both temples are lit at night and reflected in Nong Jong Kham – a popular photo op for visitors.

Wat Hua Wiang
BUDDHIST TEMPLE
(วัดหัวเวียง; Th Phanit Wattana; ⊙ daylight hours) FREE This wát, just east of Mae Hong Son's main street, is recognised for its *bòht* boasting an elaborate tiered wooden roof and a revered bronze Buddha statue from Mandalay.

Other Temples
BUDDHIST TEMPLE
Other notable temples include **Wat Kam Kor** (วัดก้ำก่อ; Th Pha Doong Muay Do; ⊙ daylight hours) FREE, known for its unique covered walkway, and **Wat Phra Non** (วัดพระนอน; Th Pha Doong Muay Do; ⊙ daylight hours) FREE home to the largest reclining Buddha in town.

🏃 Activities

Trekking
Mae Hong Son's location at the edge of mountainous jungle makes it an excellent base for trekking into the countryside. Trekking here is not quite the large-scale industry it is elsewhere, and visitors willing to get their boots muddy can expect to find relatively untouched nature and isolated villages. Trekking excursions can be arranged at several guesthouses and travel agencies.

Multiday treks in groups of two people range from 1200B to 3000B per person, per day. As is the case elsewhere in Thailand, the per-day rates drop significantly with a larger group and a longer trek.

Nature Walks
TREKKING
(☎ 08 9552 6899, 0 5361 1040; www.trekkingthailand.com) Although the treks here cost more than elsewhere, John, a native of Mae Hong Son, is the best guide in town. Treks range from day-long nature walks to multiday journeys across the province. John can also arrange custom nature-based tours, such as

the orchid-viewing tours he conducts from March to May.

John does not have an office; email and phone are the only ways to get in touch with him.

Friend Tour   TREKKING

(☑0 5361 1647; PA Motor, 21 Th Pradit Jong Kham; ☉7.30am-7.30pm) With nearly 20 years' experience, this recommended outfit offers trekking, elephant riding and rafting, as well as day tours. Located at PA Motor.

Namrin Tour   TREKKING

(☑0 5361 4454; 21 Th Pradit Jong Kham; ☉9am-7pm) Mr Dam advertises 'Bad sleep, bad jokes', but his treks get good reports.

Boat Trips

Long-tail boat trips on the nearby Mae Nam Pai are popular, and the same guesthouses and trekking agencies that organise treks from Mae Hong Son can arrange river excursions. The most common trip sets off from Tha Pong Daeng, 4km southwest of Mae Hong Son. Boats travel 15km downstream to the 'long-neck' village of Huay Pu Keng (700B, one hour), or all the way to the border village of Ban Nam Phiang Din (900B, 1½ hours), 20km from the pier, before returning. Boats can accommodate a maximum of eight passengers.

Mud Spa

Pooklon Country Club   SPA

(☑0 5328 2579; www.pooklon.com; mud treatments from 60B, massage per hour 200-400B; ☉8am-6.30pm) This self-professed country club is touted as Thailand's only mud treatment spa.

Discovered by a team of geologists in 1995, the mud here is pasteurised and blended with herbs before being employed in various treatments (facial 60B). There's thermal mineral water for soaking (60B), and on weekends, massage.

Pooklon is 16km north of Mae Hong Son in Mok Champae. If you haven't got your own wheels, you can take the daily Ban Ruam Thai– or Mae Aw–bound *sŏrng·tăa·ou* (25B), but this means you might have to find your own way back.

⛱ Tours

Rosegarden Tours   TOURS

(☑0 5361 1681; www.rosegarden-tours.com; 86/4 Th Khunlumprapas; tours from 600B; ☉8.30am-10pm) The English- and French-speaking guides at this long-standing agency focus on cultural and sightseeing tours.

Tour Merng Tai   TOURS

(☑0 5361 1979; www.tourmerngtai.com; 89 Th Khunlumprapas) This outfit mostly does city-based van tours and cycling tours, but can also arrange treks.

🎎 Festivals & Events

Poi Sang Long Festival   ORDINATION CEREMONY

Wat Jong Klang and Wat Jong Kham are the focal point of this March festival, where young Shan boys are ordained as novice monks in the ceremony known as *boò·at lôok gâa·ou*. As part of the Shan custom, the boys are dressed in ornate costumes (rather than simple white robes) and wear flower headdresses and facial make-up.

Jong Para Festival   BUDDHIST

Another important local event, this festival is held towards the end of the Buddhist Rains Retreat around October – it's three days before the full moon of the 11th lunar month, so it varies from year to year. The festival begins with local Shan bringing offerings to monks in the temples in a procession marked by the carrying of models of castles on poles.

An important part of the festival is the folk theatre and dance, which is performed on the *wát* grounds, some of it unique to northwest Thailand.

Loi Krathong   TRADITIONAL

During this national holiday in November – usually celebrated by floating *grà·tong* (small lotus floats) on the nearest pond, lake or river – Mae Hong Son residents launch balloons called *grà·tong sà·wăn* (heaven *grà·tong*) from Doi Kong Mu.

🛏 Sleeping

Mae Hong Son generally lacks inspiring accommodation, although there are a couple of standout midrange options. Because it's a tourist town, accommodation prices fluctuate with the seasons; outside of the high season (November to January) it's worth pursuing a discount.

🏚 In Town

Coffee Morning   HOTEL $

(☑0 5361 2234; 78 Th Singha-nat Barm Rung; r 500-600B; @🛜) This old wooden house unites a cafe-bookshop and three basic rooms. Considering that bathrooms are shared, the rates aren't exactly a steal, but free internet and an artsy atmosphere make up for it.

Kiang Doi House
GUESTHOUSE $

(☎0 5361 1167; 10 Th Udom Chao Ni-Thet; r 300-1000B, bungalows 400-500B; ❄️🛜) A jumble of tight rooms – some with attached bathroom – and bungalows in a lakeside residential compound. Cafe and massage are available on-site.

Palm House
GUESTHOUSE $

(☎0 5361 4022; 22/1 Th Charm-naan Satit; r 350-700B; ❄️🛜) This two-storey cement building offers several characterless but clean rooms with TV, fridge, hot water and fan/air-con. The helpful owner speaks English and can arrange transport when he's not napping.

Friend House
GUESTHOUSE $

(☎0 5362 0119; 20 Th Pradit Jong Kham; r 150-500B; 🛜) The super-clean though characterless rooms here run from the ultra-basic, which share hot-water bathrooms, to larger rooms with private bathrooms.

Romtai House
GUESTHOUSE $$

(☎0 5361 2437; www.maehongson-romtai.com; Th Charm-naan Satit; r 500-700B, bungalows 800-1000B; ❄️🛜) Hidden behind both the lakeside temples and a bland-looking reception area, this place has a huge variety of accommodation ranging from spacious, clean rooms to bungalows looking over a lush garden with fish ponds.

Jongkham Place
GUESTHOUSE $$

(☎0 5361 4294; 4/2 Th Udom Chao Ni-Thet; bungalows/ste 800/1500B; ❄️🛜) This family-run place by the lake has four attractive bungalows and two penthouse-like suites. All accommodation includes TV, fridge and air-con.

Residence@MaeHongSon
HOTEL $$$

(☎0 5361 4100; www.theresidence-mhs.com; 41/4 Th Ni-wet Pi-sarn; r 1300-1900B; ❄️🛜) A cheery yellow building with 10 inviting rooms that boast TV, air-con, fridge, teak furnishings and lots of windows ensuring ample natural light. There's also a sunny communal rooftop area, a friendly English-speaking owner and bicycles provided free of charge.

Baiyoke Chalet Hotel
HOTEL $$$

(☎0 5361 3132; www.baiyokehotel.com; 90 Th Khunlumprapas; r incl breakfast 1280-1800B; ❄️🛜)

This place intertwines convenient location and comfortable lodging. As established in the lobby, the rooms are tastefully outfitted in hardwood and local themes. A downside is that the restaurant-lounge downstairs can get quite loud, so request a room away from the street or on an upper level. Low-season rates are almost 50% less.

Mountain Inn & Resort
HOTEL $$$

(☎0 5361 1803; www.mhsmountaininn.com; 112/2 Th Khunlumprapas; r incl breakfast 2400-2800B, ste incl breakfast 4500B; ❄️@🛜🏊) Clean, cosy rooms with Thai decorative touches are the standard here. There is a pretty courtyard garden with small ponds, a pool, and benches and parasols. Standard rooms are a better deal than deluxe as they include a terrace overlooking the garden.

Outside of Town

Sang Tong Huts
HOTEL $$

(☎0 5361 1680; www.sangtonghuts.com; Th Maka Santi; bungalows 800-3000B; @🛜🏊) This clutch of rustic bungalows in a wooded area just outside of town is one of Mae Hong Son's more character-filled places to stay. Accommodation is spacious, comfortable and well designed, and the tasty baked goods and pool make up for the distance from the centre of town. It's popular among repeat

DON'T MISS

WAT PHRA THAT DOI KONG MU

Climb the hill west of town, Doi Kong Mu (1500m), to visit this **temple compound** (วัดพระธาตุดอยกองมู; ☉daylight hours), also known as Wat Plai Doi. Two Shan *chedi*, erected in 1860 and 1874, enshrine the ashes of monks from Myanmar's Shan State. Around the back of the *wát* you can see a tall, slender, standing Buddha and catch views west of the ridge. There's also a cafe and a small tourist market. The view of the sea of fog that collects in the valley each morning is impressive; at other times you get wonderful views of the town and surrounding valleys.

On Th Pha Doong Muay Do is a long stairway leading to the top of Wat Phra That Doi Kong Mu, otherwise a motorcycle taxi costs 120B return.

visitors to Mae Hong Son, so it pays to book ahead.

Sang Tong Huts is about 1km northeast of Th Khunlumprapas, just off Th Maka Santi – if going towards Pai, turn left at the intersection before the town's northernmost stoplight and follow the signs.

Pana Huts
GUESTHOUSE $$

(☑ 0 5361 4331; www.panahuts.com; 293/9 Th Maka Santi; r & bungalows 600-800B; 🛜) Set in a wooded area outside of town, the four bamboo huts here all have terraces and hot-water bathrooms. The inviting communal area is equally rustic, with its thatched teak leaf roof, wooden benches and enclosed campfire for chilly nights.

Pana Huts is about 1km northeast of Th Khunlum Praphat, just off Th Maka Santi – if going towards Pai, turn left at the intersection just before the town's northernmost stoplight and follow the signs.

★ Fern Resort
RESORT $$$

(☑ 0 5368 6110; www.fernresort.info; off Rte 108; bungalows incl breakfast 2500-3500B; ✳@🛜🏊) This longstanding ecofriendly resort is one of the pleasanter places to stay in northern Thailand. The 40 wooden bungalows are set among tiered rice paddies and streams and feature stylishly decorated interiors. Nearby nature trails lead to the adjacent Mae Surin National Park.

The downside is that the resort is 7km south of town, but free pick-up is available from the airport and bus terminal, and regular shuttles run to/from town, stopping at Fern Restaurant.

Imperial Tara Mae Hong Son Hotel
HOTEL $$$

(☑ 0 5368 4444-9; www.imperialhotels.com; Rte 108; r incl breakfast 3800B; ste incl breakfast 5000-6600B; ✳@🛜🏊) Rooms in this upmarket, 104-room hotel all have wooden floors and balconies and are tastefully decorated. French windows that open onto a terrace make a pleasant change from the standard business hotel layout. Facilities include a sauna, swimming pool and fitness centre. It's about 2km south of town.

✗ Eating & Drinking

Mae Hong Son's morning market (off Th Phanit Wattana; mains 10-30B; ⊘6-9am) is a fun place to have breakfast. Several vendors at the north end of the market sell unusual dishes such as tòo·a ɔ̀on, a Burmese noodle dish supplemented with thick chickpea porridge and deep-fried chickpea flour cakes and tofu. Other vendors along the same strip sell a local version of kà·nŏm jeen nám ngée·o (thin rice noodles served with a pork-and-tomato-based broth) often topped with kàhng pòrng, a Shan snack of battered-and-deep-fried vegetables.

The city also has two good night markets: the night market (Th Phanit Wattana; mains 20-60B; ⊘4-8pm) near the airport offers mostly takeaway northern Thai–style food, while the night market (Th Khunlumprapas; mains 10-60B; ⊘4-9pm) at the southern end of Th Khunlumpras has more generic Thai food. Several vendors at Mae Hong Son's Walking Street (p399) also sell a variety of dishes, some local.

Chom Mai Restaurant
THAI $

(www.sesamebar.com; off Rte 108, no roman-script sign; mains 35-180B; ⊘8.30am-3.30pm; 🛜🅿) The English-language menu here is limited, but don't miss the deliciously rich kôw soy or the Khaw mok kai, the latter the Thai version of biryani. Chom Mai is located about 4km south of Mae Hong Son along the road that leads to Tha Pong Daeng – look for the Doi Chaang coffee sign.

Banpleng Restaurant
NORTHERN THAI $

(108 Th Khunlumprapas; mains 30-150B; ⊘8am-10pm Mon-Sat) This popular open-air restaurant does a handful of tasty local dishes – you're safe going with anything that says 'Maehongson style' on the English-language menu.

Mae Si Bua
NORTHERN THAI $

(cnr Th Pradit Jong Kham & Th Singha-nat Barm Rung, no roman-script sign; mains 20-30B; ⊘lunch) Like the Shan grandma you never had, Auntie Bua prepares a huge variety of curries, soups and dips on a daily basis.

Salween River Restaurant & Bar
INTERNATIONAL-THAI $

(www.salweenriver.com; 23 Th Pradit Jong Kham; mains 40-240B; ⊘8am-10pm; 🛜🅿) Salween is your typical traveller's cafe: a few old guidebooks, free wi-fi and a menu ranging from burgers to Burmese. Yet unlike most traveller's cafes, the food here is good; don't miss the Burmese green tea salad.

Baan Tua Lek
CAFE $

(51 Th Singha-nat Barm Rung; mains 20-30B; ⊘7am-9pm; 🛜) This tiny modern cafe serves

good coffee drinks and a few sweets and cakes.

No-Name Restaurant — THAI $$

(Th Khunlumprapas, no roman-script sign; mains 30-170B; ☺11am-10pm) There really is no name here (it's a tax thing, we were told), but this has no negative repercussions on the central Thai–style dishes which are delicious. Near the corner with Th Singha-nat Barm Rung.

Fern Restaurant — INTERNATIONAL-THAI $$

(Th Khunlumprapas; mains 65-285B; ☺10.30am-10pm; ☺🖧) The Fern is almost certainly Mae Hong Son's most upscale restaurant, but remember, this is Mae Hong Son. Nonetheless, service is professional and the food is decent. The expansive menu covers Thai, local and even European dishes. There is live lounge music some nights.

La Tasca — ITALIAN $$

(Th Khunlumprapas; mains 149-209B; ☺11am-10pm; ✳🖧) This cosy place has been serving homemade pasta, pizza and calzone for as long as we can remember and is one of the few places in town to do relatively authentic Western food.

Crossroads — BAR

(61 Th Khunlumprapas; ☺8am-1am) This friendly bar-restaurant is a crossroads in every sense, from its location at one of Mae Hong Son's main intersections to its clientele that ranges from wet-behind-the-ears backpackers to hardened locals. And there's steak.

Sunflower Café — BAR

(Th Pradit Jong Kham; ☺7.30am-10pm) This open-air place combines draught beer, live lounge music and views of the lake. Sunflower also does meals (mains 35B to 180B) and runs tours.

🛍 Shopping

From October to February the roads around the Jong Kham Lake becomes a lively **Walking Street** (Th Pradit Jong Kham; ☺5-10pm Oct-Feb), with handicrafts and food vendors.

LONG-NECKED KAYAN VILLAGES

These villages are Mae Hong Son's most touted – and most controversial – tourist attraction. The 'long-necked' moniker originates from the habit of some Kayan women (sometimes also referred to as Padaung, a Shan term) of wearing heavy brass coils around their necks. The coils depress the collarbone and rib cage, which makes their necks look unnaturally stretched. A common myth claims if the coils are removed, a woman's neck will fall over and she will suffocate. In fact, the women attach and remove the coils at will and there is no evidence that this deformation impairs their health at all.

Nobody knows for sure how the coil custom got started. One theory is that it was meant to make the women unattractive to men from other tribes. Another story says it was so tigers wouldn't carry the women off by their throats. Most likely it is nothing more than a simple fashion accessory. Until relatively recently the custom was largely dying out, but money from tourism, and undoubtedly the influence of local authorities eager to cash in on the Kayan, have reinvigorated it.

Regardless of the origin, the villages are now on every group tour's itinerary, and have become a significant tourist draw for Mae Hong Son. The villages are often derided as human zoos, and there are certainly elements of this, but we find them more like bizarre rural markets, with the women earning much of their money by selling tacky souvenirs and drinks. The Kayan we've talked to claim to be happy with their current situation, but the stateless position they share with all Burmese refugees is nothing to be envied, and these formerly independent farmers are now reliant on aid and tourists to survive. A report on the villages by journalist Patrick Winn can be seen at www.globalpost.com/dispatch/thailand/110128/thailand-tourism-burma-refugee-chiang-mai.

Any of the three Kayan settlements outside Mae Hong Son can be visited independently, if you have transportation, or any travel agency in Mae Hong Son can arrange a tour. The most-touted Kayan village is **Huai Seua Thao**, about 7km from Mae Hong Son. More remote, but definitely not off the beaten track, is **Kayan Tayar**, near the Shan village of Ban Nai Soi, 35km northwest of Mae Hong Son. Another 'long-necked' community is based at **Huay Pu Keng** and is included on long-tail boat tours departing from Tha Pong Daeng. All collect an entry fee from non-Thais of 250B per person.

A few well-stocked souvenir shops can be found near the southern end of Th Khunlumprapas, including **Maneerat** (80 Th Khunlumprapas, no roman-script sign; ⊘8am-9pm), which features an extensive array of Shan and Burmese clothing, as well as Burmese lacquerware boxes.

ⓘ Information

Most of the banks at the southern end of Th Khunlumprapas have ATMs.

Mae Hong Son Internet (88 Th Khunlumprapas; per hour 30B; ⊘8.30am-10pm)

Maehongson Living Museum (27 Th Singhanat Barm Rung; ⊘7am-5pm; 🛜) An attractive wooden building – actually Mae Hong Son's former bus depot – has been turned into a museum on local culture, food and architecture, although the bulk of information is only in Thai. There are a few maps and brochures in English, and there's also free wi-fi and bike rental for only 15B per day.

Tourism Authority of Thailand (TAT; 📞0 5361 2982, nationwide 1672; www.travelmaehongson.org; Th Ni-wet Pi-sarn; ⊘8.30am-4.30pm) Basic tourist brochures and maps can be picked up here.

Tourist Police (📞0 5361 1812, nationwide 1155; Th Singhanat Bamrung; ⊘8.30am-4.30pm)

ⓘ Getting There & Away

For many people the time saved flying from Chiang Mai to Mae Hong Son versus bus travel is worth the extra baht. At research time, **Nok Air** (📞0 5361 2057, nationwide 1318; www.nokair.co.th; Mae Hong Son Airport; ⊘9am-5pm) was the only airline operating out of Mae Hong Song's **airport** (📞08 5361 2057). A túk-túk into town costs about 80B.

Mae Hong Son's bus and minivan station is 1km south of the city; a túk-túk or motorcycle ride to/from here costs 60B. **Prempracha Tour** (📞0 5368 4100; Mae Hong Son Bus Station) runs bus services within the province; **Sombat Tour** (📞0 5361 3211; Mae Hong Son Bus Station) operates connections between Mae Hong Son and Bangkok.

ⓘ Getting Around

The centre of Mae Hong Son can easily be covered on foot, and it's one of the few towns in Thailand that doesn't seem to have a motorcycle taxi at every corner. A few can be found near the entrance to the morning market, and charge 20B to 40B for trips within town. There are also a few túk-túk who charge from 40B per trip within town.

Because most of Mae Hong Son's attractions are outside of town, renting a motorcycle or bicycle is a wise move.

PA Motor (📞0 5361 1647; 21 Th Pradit Jong Kham; ⊘8am-6.30pm) Next to Friend House,

TRANSPORT TO/FROM MAE HONG SON

DESTINATION	AIR	BUS	MINIVAN	SÖRNG·TÄA·OU
Bangkok		796-905B; 15hr; 3 departures 2-4pm		
Ban Ruam Thai (Pang Ung)				80B; 1hr; 9am & 3.30pm
Chiang Mai	1590B; 35min; 3 daily	145B; 8hr; 8.30am & 12.30pm (northern route); 178-319B; 9hr; frequent 6am-9pm (southern route)	250B; 6hr; hourly 7am-3pm	
Khun Yuam		55-90B; 2hr; frequent 6am-9pm		
Mae Aw (Ban Rak Thai)				80B; 1hr; noon & 3pm
Mae Sariang		95-187B; 4hr; frequent 6am-9pm		
Pai		80B; 4½hr; 8.30am & 4pm	150B; 2½hr; hourly 7am-4pm	
Soppong (Pangmapha)		45B; 2hr; hourly 7am-4pm	150B; 1½hr; hourly 7am-4pm	

rents motorbikes (150B to 250B per day) and trucks (2500B to 3000B per day).

PJ (☑08 4372 6967; Th Ni-wet Pi-sarn; ⊙8am-6.30pm) Rents motorbikes (150B to 200B per day).

Titan (Th Khunlumprapas; ⊙9am-9pm) Rents good-quality mountain bikes (100B per day).

Around Mae Hong Son

Pha Bong Hot Springs   บ่อน้ำร้อนผาบ่อง

Eleven kilometres south of the capital in the Shan village of Pha Bong is this public park with **hot springs** (private bath/bathing room 50/400B; ⊙8am-sunset). You can take a private bath or rent a room, and there's also massage (per hour 150B). The springs can be reached on any southbound bus.

Tham Pla National Park   อุทยานแห่งชาติถ้ำปลา

The most touted attraction of this **national park** (adult/child 100/50; ⊙6am-6pm) is Tham Pla (Fish Cave), a water-filled cavern where hundreds of soro brook carp thrive. A 450m path leads from the park entrance to a suspension bridge that crosses a stream and continues to the cave. A statue of a Hindu *rishi* (sage) called Nara, said to protect the holy fish from danger, stands nearby. The fish grow up to 1m long and are found only in the provinces of Mae Hong Son, Ranong, Chiang Mai, Rayong, Chanthaburi and Kanchanaburi. They eat vegetables and insects, although the locals believe them to be vegetarian and feed them only fruit and vegetables, which can be purchased at the park entrance. It's all a bit anticlimactic, but the park grounds are a bucolic, shady place to hang out. Food and picnic tables are available.

The park is 16km north of Mae Hong Son; to get there, hop on any northbound bus.

Mae Aw (Ban Rak Thai) & Around   แม่ออ

A worthwhile day trip from the provincial capital is to **Mae Aw**, also known as Ban Rak Thai, an atmospheric Chinese outpost right at the Myanmar border, 43km north of Mae Hong Son.

The road to Mae Aw is a beautiful route that passes through tidy riverside Shan communities such as **Mok Champae** before suddenly climbing through impressive mountain scenery. Stops can be made at **Pha Sua Waterfall**, about 5km up the mountain, and **Pang Tong Summer Palace**, a rarely used royal compound a few kilometres past the waterfall.

For an interesting detour, at Ban Na Pa Paek take a left and continue 6km to the Shan village of **Ban Ruam Thai**. There are several basic places to stay and eat here, and the road ends 500m further at **Pang Ung**, a peaceful mountain reservoir surrounded by pines that is immensely popular among Thai day-trippers in search of a domestic Switzerland.

From Ban Na Pa Paek it is 6km further to Mae Aw. Located on the edge of a reservoir and surrounded by tea plantations, the town was established by Yunnanese KMT fighters who originally fled from communist rule in 1949; the town's faces and architecture remain very Chinese. The main industries are tourism and tea, and there are numerous places to taste the local brew, as well as several restaurants serving Yunnanese cuisine.

There's a brief dirt road to a border crossing (for locals only), but it's not advisable to do any unaccompanied trekking here, as the area is an occasional conflict zone and an infamous drug smuggling route.

🍴 Sleeping & Eating

Ping Ping Guest House   GUESTHOUSE $
(☑08 44481 9707; Mae Aw (Ban Rak Thai); r 300-400B) This place and other similar outfits ringing Mae Aw's reservoir offer basic accommodation in adobe-style bungalows.

Guest House and Home Stay   GUESTHOUSE $$
(☑08 3571 6668; Ban Ruam Thai; r 500-2000B) The first guesthouse in Ban Ruam Thai (there are now numerous 'homestays' offering accommodation from 200B to 400B), this place consists of several simple brick huts positioned on a slope surrounded by coffee plants, tea plants and fruit trees.

Gee Lee Restaurant   CHINESE $$
(Mae Aw, no roman-script sign; mains 60-180B; ⊙8am-7pm) This was one of the first places in Mae Aw to serve the town's Yunnanese-style Chinese dishes to visitors. Stewed pork leg and stir-fried local veggies are the specialities. It's at the corner of the lake, just before the intersection that leads to the centre of the village.

ℹ Getting There & Away

There are four daily *sŏrng·tăa·ou* that head towards Mae Aw: two depart from a stall east of the market that only go as far as Ban Ruam Thai (80B, one hour, 9am and 3.30pm), and two depart from a stall opposite the market that terminate in Mae Aw (80B, one hour, noon and 3pm). Both depart only when full, which can sometimes be a couple of hours after the scheduled departure time. Because of this, it's probably worth getting a group of people together and chartering a vehicle; the *sŏrng·tăa·ou* drivers we talked to quoted from 1200B to 1600B for either destination, while any tour agency in Mae Hong Son will arrange a vehicle for around 1500B. Heading back to Mae Hong Son, *sŏrng·tăa·ou* leave Ban Ruam Thai at 5.30am and 11am, and Mae Aw at 8am.

Alternatively, the route also makes a brilliant motorcycle ride – just make sure you have enough petrol, as the only station is in Ban Na Pa Paek, at the end of a very long climb.

Khun Yuam ขุนยวม

Between Mae Sariang and Mae Hong Son, where all northbound buses make their halfway stop, is the quiet hillside town of Khun Yuam. There are a couple of places to stay and a few notable sights, and this little-visited town is a nice break from more 'experienced' destinations nearby.

◎ Sights

Khun Yuam's sights are located outside of town and you'll need private transport to reach them.

★ Thai-Japan Friendship Memorial Hall   MUSEUM

(adult/child 50/30B; ⊙8.30am-5pm) At the northern end of town is the recently renovated Thai-Japan Friendship Memorial Hall. After watching a brief film on the history of Khun Yuam, you'll find displays and artefacts that document the period when the Japanese occupied Khun Yuam in the closing weeks of the war with Burma, as well as local history. After they had recovered, some of the Japanese soldiers stayed in Khun Yuam and married; the last Japanese soldier who settled in the area died in 2000.

Wat To Phae   TEMPLE

(วัดต่อแพ; ⊙daylight hours) **FREE** About 6km to the west of Khun Yuam, the atmospheric Wat To Phae sits alongside a country stream and boasts a Mon-style *chedi* and an immac-

ulate Burmese-style *wí·hăhn* (sanctuary). Inside the latter, take a look at the large, 150-year-old Burmese *kalaga* (embroidered and sequined tapestry) that's kept behind curtains to one side of the main altar.

The tapestry depicts a scene from the Vessantara Jataka, one of the stories of the Buddha's previous lives, and local devotees believe one accrues merit simply by viewing it.

Ban Mae U Khaw   VILLAGE

(บ้านแม่อูคอ) On the slopes of Doi Mae U Khaw, 25km from Khun Yuam via Rte 1263, is the Hmong village of Ban Mae U Khaw. During late November the area blooms with scenic Mexican sunflowers, known locally as *dòrk booa torng*. This event is incredibly popular among Thais and accommodation in the town is booked out.

Nam Tok Mae Surin   NATURE RESERVE

(น้ำตกแม่สุรินทร์; admission 200B) Approximately 50km from Khun Yam is the 100m-high Nam Tok Mae Surin, part of the Mae Surin National Park and reportedly Thailand's highest waterfall.

🛏 Sleeping & Eating

There are also a few homestay options in Ban To Phae.

In Khun Yuam you'll find a collection of modest rice and noodle shops along the east side of Rte 108, towards the southern end of town. Most of these close by 5pm or 6pm.

Mithkhoonyoum Hotel   HOTEL $

(☏0 5369 1057; 61 Rte 108; r 200-1000; ❄) On the main road through the town centre, Mithkhoonyoum Hotel has simple, clean rooms with private bathrooms, the cheapest of which were about to be renovated when we passed through.

Ban Farang   HOTEL $$

(☏0 5369 1505; www.banfarang-guesthouse.com; 499 Th Ratburana; dm incl breakfast 150B, r & bungalows incl breakfast 700-1600B; ❄🛜) Off the main road towards the north end of town (look for the signs near the bus stop), the tidy bungalows here are set on a wooded hillside. The cheaper fan rooms are plain and dark but have a terrace, while the more expensive ones come with air-con, fridge and TV.

Yoont   HOTEL $$

(☏0 5369 1531; yoontkhunyuam@hotmail.com; 92 Rte 108; r incl breakfast 700-900B; ❄@🛜) The newest place in Khun Yuam, Yoont is comprises 12 rooms in a tall concrete building more or less in the centre of town. Rooms are relatively spacious and stylish – if slightly overpriced – and there's an inviting rooftop chill-out area.

ℹ Information

There are a couple of banks with ATMs along the main strip.

Mae Sariang   แม่สะเรียง

Little-visited Mae Sariang is gaining a low-key buzz for its attractive riverside setting and potential as a launching pad for sustainable tourism and trekking opportunities. There are several hill-tribe settlements nearby, particularly around Mae La Noi, 30km north of the city, and the area south of Mae Sariang is largely mountainous jungle encompassing both Salawin and Mae Ngao National Parks.

◉ Sights

Mae Sariang Museum   MUSEUM
(พิพิธภัณฑ์แม่สะเรียง; Th Wiang Mai; ⊙8.30am-4.30pm) FREE Located in the imposing, temple-like structure near the highway junction is this museum dedicated to local culture. There's no explanation in English, but the life-sized dioramas that depict the customs of Mae Sariang's northern Thai, Shan, Karen and Lua inhabitants are worth a look.

Wat Jong Sung &
Wat Si Bunruang   TEMPLES
(วัดจองสูง/วัดศรีบุญเรือง; off Th Wiang Mai; ⊙daylight hours) FREE These two adjacent Burmese-Shan temples, Wat Jong Sung and Wat Si Bunruang, are located just off Mae Sariang's main street. Built in 1896, Wat Jong Sung is the more interesting of the two and has slender, Shan-style *chedi* and wooden monastic buildings.

☂ Activities

The area surrounding Mae Sariang is probably one of the best in northern Thailand for trekking and nature tours. This is due not only to the area's natural beauty and cultural diversity, but also because of a new breed of responsible and community-based touring and trekking outfits that have sprung up here. Prices for the following range from 1200B to 3400B per day, per person, for groups of at least two people.

Mae Sariang Tours   TREKKING, RAFTING
(☎08 8404 8402; www.maesariangtours.com) Mae Sariang Man, as the owner of this company prefers to be known, is an experienced trekker who leads environmentally conscious and community-based treks and rafting trips in the jungles and national parks surrounding his native city and in Sop Moei, further south. He has no office in town; call or look at his website to arrange an excursion.

Dragon Sabaii Tours   TREKKING
(☎08 9555 8715, 08 9956 9897; www.thailandhill-tribeholidays.com; Th Mongkolchai) This outfit emphasises eco- and cultural tourism primarily in the Mae La Noi area just north of Mae Sariang. Activities range from non-intrusive tours of hill-tribe villages to homestays, 'volunteerism', and cooking and farming with hill tribes, all of which are designed to benefit local communities directly.

Salawin Tour & Trekking   TREKKING, RAFTING
(☎08 1024 6146; River Bank Guesthouse, Th Laeng Phanit) Mr Salawin and his brothers have been leading tours in the area for years. Their trips typically involve activities such as elephant riding, rafting and hiking. Mr Salawin can be found at River Bank Guest House.

Northwest Tour   TREKKING
(☎0 5368 2860; Northwest Guest House, 81 Th Laeng Phanit) Out of Northwest Guest House, this outfit can arrange treks to natural areas and Karen villages in Sop Moei District.

NORTHERN THAILAND MAE SARIANG

BUSES TO/FROM KHUN YUAM
Buses stop regularly at Khun Yuam on their runs between Mae Sariang and Mae Hong Son. The bus station is at the northern end of town.

DESTINATION	PRICE (B)	DURATION (HR)	DEPARTURES
Chiang Mai	160-282	7-8	frequent 6.30am-10.30pm
Mae Hong Son	60-90	1½-2	6 departures 3am-5.30pm
Mae Sariang	70-120	3-4	frequent 6.30am-10.30pm

Mae Sariang

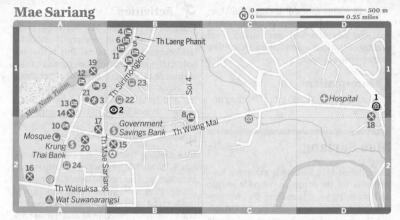

Mae Sariang

🛏 Sleeping

Pang Sariang   GUESTHOUSE $

(📞 0 5368 2333; 2 Th Laeng Phanit, no roman-script sign; r 300B; ❄ @ 🛜) A villa with four homey-feeling yet simple rooms. Look for the sign that says 'Guest House & Restaurant'.

Northwest Guest House   GUESTHOUSE $

(📞 08 9700 9928; www.northwestgh.blogspot. com; 81 Th Laeng Phanit; r 250-450B; ❄ @ 🛜) The rooms in this cosy wooden house are mattress-on-the-floor simple, but get natural light and are relatively spacious.

Riverhouse Hotel   HOTEL $$

(📞 0 5362 1201; www.riverhousehotels.com; 77 Th Laeng Phanit; r incl breakfast 1000-1300B; ❄ @ 🛜) The combination of teak and stylish decor – not to mention the riverside location – make

this boutique hotel the best spot in town. Most 2nd-floor rooms have air-con, huge verandahs overlooking the river, as well as floor-to-ceiling windows. The same folks also run the more expensive but slightly less charming **Riverhouse Resort** (📞 0 5368 3066; r incl breakfast 1500-2800B; ❄ @ 🛜), just south on Th Laeng Phanit.

Mae Loe Gyi   GUESTHOUSE $$

(📞 08 3564 4767; www.maeloegyi.com; Soi 4, Th Wiang Mai; bungalows incl breakfast 800B; ❄ 🛜) Four spacious bungalows in a quiet compound, each equipped with separate sleeping, TV and kitchen areas. Breakfast and the food served in the attached cafe-restaurant is vegetarian, and work on an adjacent garden was underway when we visited.

Black Ant Resort · HOTEL $$
(☑0 5368 2123; www.blackantcoffee.net; 113 Th Laeng Phanit; r incl breakfast 1000-1200B; ❄@🛜) Black Ant has rooms on each side of Th Laeng Phanit. All are large and well-outfitted, with some boasting unique quirks such as a tree growing in the middle of the room.

Huen-Kham-Kong · HOTEL $$
(☑0 5368 2416; www.huenkhamkong.com; 102 Th Laeng Phanit; bungalows 800B; ❄🛜) The six cutesy bungalows here appear comfortable, come equipped with TV, fridge and air-con, and are looked after by some friendly folks.

River Bank Guest House · GUESTHOUSE $$
(☑0 5368 2787; Th Laeng Phanit; r 700-900B; ❄🛜) Rooms in this attractive riverside house are decked out in hardwood and have lots of natural light. It's worth shelling out 200B more for the rooms on the upper floor as the cheaper rooms feel cramped and have comically small TVs. A highlight here is the stylish and inviting riverside balcony.

Chok Wasana · GUESTHOUSE $$
(☑0 5368 2132; www.chok-wasana.com; 104 Th Laeng Phanit; r 800-1000B; ❄🛜) Six new, spacious and well-equipped rooms in a large concrete home.

Good View Guest House · GUESTHOUSE $$
(☑0 5368 3100; thauscrong@gmail.com; 103 Th Laeng Phanit; r incl breakfast 300-1000B; ❄🛜) New but largely characterless rooms, equipped with air-con, TV and fridge, in a riverside teak structure.

🍴 Eating & Drinking

If you're in Mae Sariang on a Sunday, don't miss the town's tiny but worthwhile **Sunday market** (Th Wiang Mai; mains 20-60B; ⊗3-8pm), where you'll find a good selection of local-style dishes.

Muu Thup · NORTHERN THAI $
(Th Wiang Mai, no roman-script sign; mains 30-60B; ⊗8am-7pm) An authentic northern Thai-style grilled meat shack; you can't go wrong with the eponymous *mǒo túp*, pork that's been grilled then tenderised with a mallet. Located roughly across from Mae Sariang Museum.

Inthira Restaurant · THAI $
(Th Wiang Mai; mains 30-150B; ⊗8am-10pm) Probably the town's best allround restaurant, this place features a thick menu of dishes using unusual ingredients such as locally grown shiitake mushrooms and fish from Mae Nam Moei.

Kai Yang Rai Khwan · THAI $
(Th Waisuksa, no roman-script sign; mains 30-180B; ⊗9am-2pm Tue-Sun) Head here for the Isan holy trinity of grilled chicken, papaya salad and sticky rice. This simple place is at the foot of the bridge crossing.

Lee Lawadee · THAI $
(cnr Th Wiang Mai & Th Mae Sariang; mains 40-180B; ⊗7am-9pm; 🛜) This friendly place has an English-language menu of both one-dish meals and mains, as well as real coffee and free wi-fi.

TRANSPORT TO/FROM MAE SARIANG

DESTINATION	BUS	MINIVAN	SÖRNG·TÄA·OU
Bangkok	482-722B; 12hr; 4 departures 4pm-7.30pm		
Chiang Mai	105-187B; 4-5hr; 5 departures 7am-3pm	200B; 3½hr; 5 departures 8am-5pm	
Khun Yuam	70-120B; 2-3hr; 6 departures 7am-5.30pm		
Mae Hong Son	105-187B; 3-4hr; 6 departures 7am-1am		
Mae Sam Laep			70B; 1½hr; frequent 6.30am-3.30pm
Mae Sot			200B; 6hr; frequent 6.30am-12.30pm

NORTHERN THAILAND MAE SARIANG

Ban Rao
THAI $

(Th Laeng Phanit, no roman-script sign; mains 30-140B; ⊙ 5-10pm) For an authentic Thai dinner minus the spice, head to this homey riverside restaurant. The English-language menu touches on just about everything, from familiar curries to the more exotic *yam sôm oh,* a Thai-style pomelo salad.

Sawaddee Restaurant & Bar
THAI $

(Th Laeng Phanit; mains 40-150B; ⊙ 7am-10pm; 📶 🖉) Like a beachside bar, this is a great place to recline with a beer and watch the water (in this case Mae Nam Yuam). There's a lengthy menu with lots of options for vegetarians.

Coriander in Redwood
INTERNATIONAL-THAI $$

(Th Laeng Phanit; dishes 70-250B; ⊙ 10am-10pm Mon-Sat) The city's poshest restaurant, this attractive wooden structure makes a big deal of its steaks, but we'd suggest sticking with Thai dishes such as the various *nám prík* (chilli-based dips). There's also ice cream and iced coffee drinks for an afternoon cooler.

ⓘ Information

Mae Sariang has several banks with ATMs, mostly along the west end of Th Wiang Mai. **Internet** (Th Laeng Phanit; per hour 10B; ⊙ 9am-10pm) is available at the southern end of Th Laeng Phanit.

ⓘ Getting There & Away

Located at the bus station, **Prempracha Tour** (🖉 0 5368 1347) conducts buses between Mae Sariang and Mae Hong Son. With an office just north of the bus station, **Sombat Tour** (🖉 0 5368 1532; Th Mae Sariang) handles buses to Bangkok.

Sŏrng·tăa·ou to Mae Sam Laep (70B, 1½ hours, frequent from 6.30am to 3.30pm) depart from a stop on Th Laeng Phanit near the morning market.

ⓘ Getting Around

Motorcycles and bicycles are available for hire at a **rental shop** (🖉 08 1181 3695; off Th Laeng Phanit; bike/motorcycle hire per 24hour 50/200B; ⊙ 7am-7pm) near Th Laeng Phanit, as well as at the Northwest Guest House.

Salawin National Park & Mae Sam Laep
อุทยานแห่งชาติสาละวิน/แม่สามแลบ

This **national park** (🖉 0 5307 1429, accommodation 0 2562 0760; www.dnp.go.th; 200B) covers 722 sq km of protected land in Mae Sariang and Sop Moei districts. The park is heavily forested with teak and Asian redwood and is home to what is thought to be the second-largest teak tree in Thailand. There are numerous hiking trails, and it's also possible to travel by boat along Mae Nam Salawin to the park's outstation at Tha Ta Fang.

The main headquarters are 6km from Mae Sariang and have bungalow-style accommodation (300B to 1200B), which can be booked via the **Royal Forest Department** (🖉 0 2562 0760; www.dnp.go.th).

The riverside trading village of **Mae Sam Laep** is nearly at the end of a 50km winding mountain road from Mae Sariang, within the park boundaries. Populated by Burmese refugees, the town has a raw, border-town feel and is a launching point for **boat trips** along Mae Nam Salawin. The trips pass through untouched jungle, unusual rock formations along the river and, occasionally, enter Myanmar.

From the pier at Mae Sam Laep it's possible to charter boats south to Sop Moei (1500B, 1½ hours), 25km from Mae Sam Laep, and north to the Salawin National Park station at Tha Ta Fang (1200B, one hour), 18km north of Mae Sam Laep. There are passenger boats as well, but departures are infrequent and, unless you speak Thai, difficult to negotiate.

Sŏrng·tăa·ou from Mae Sariang to Mae Sam Laep (70B, 1½ hours, frequent from 6.30am to 3.30pm) depart from Th Laeng Phanit near the morning market.

Northeastern Thailand

Best Places to Eat

➡ Baan Yai (p468)

➡ Bao Pradit (p487)

➡ Turm-Rom (p445)

Best Places to Stay

➡ Ban Kham Pia (p475)

➡ Baan Chang Ton (p427)

➡ Mut Mee Garden
Guesthouse (p461)

➡ Bouy Guesthouse (p466)

➡ Huean Yai Bab Pa (p471)

Why Go?

For travellers and Thais alike, the northeast is Thailand's forgotten backyard. Isan (ee·săhn), as it's called, offers a glimpse of the Thailand of old: rice fields run to the horizon, water buffalo wade in muddy ponds, silk weavers work looms under their homes, and pedal-rickshaw drivers pull passengers down city streets. If you have a penchant for authentic experiences, it will surely be satisfied here.

Spend even a little time in this colossal corner of the country and you'll discover as many differences as similarities to the rest of Thailand. The language, food and culture are more Lao than Thai, with hearty helpings of Khmer and Vietnamese thrown into the mix. And spend time here you should, because it's home to some of Thailand's best historic sites, national parks and festivals. Thailand's tourist trail is at its bumpiest here (English is rarely spoken), but the fantastic attractions and daily interactions could end up being highlights of your entire trip.

When to Go

➡ Only 1% of foreign travellers who come to Thailand visit Isan, so you don't need to worry about high and low seasons.

➡ The relatively cool dry season from November through February is the most comfortable time to visit, and the Surin Elephant Round-up in November is one festival worth planning your travels around.

➡ As the hot season (March to May, when temperatures can climb over 40°C) comes to a close, towns and villages across the region, most famously Yasothon, launch giant homemade rockets into the sky to call for rain.

➡ Isan is at its most beautiful during the rainy season (June to October) when the forests and rice paddies turn green and the waterfalls run wild. Dan Sai's Phi Ta Khon Festival (June) and Ubon Ratchathani's Candle Parade (July) attract hordes of Thai tourists.

North-eastern Thailand Highlights

1 Getting awestruck by the scenery in **Pha Taem National Park** (p440)

2 Having a blast at a **Rocket Festival**

3 Looking for elephants, tigers, pythons, monkeys and more in **Khao Yai National Park** (p419)

4 Stepping back in time at the restored Angkor-era temple complexes of **Phanom Rung Historical Park** (p423) and **Phimai** (p417)

5 Climbing the rickety walkways up the mountain at **Wat Phu Tok** (p475)

6 Travelling along the **Mekong River**.

7 Making friends with elephants in **Ban Ta Klang** (p429)

8 Eating *sôm·dam* (spicy papaya salad) and **drinking** *lôw kŏw* (rice whisky) with the locals

9 Succumbing to the surreal at **Wat Pa Non Sawan** (p492)

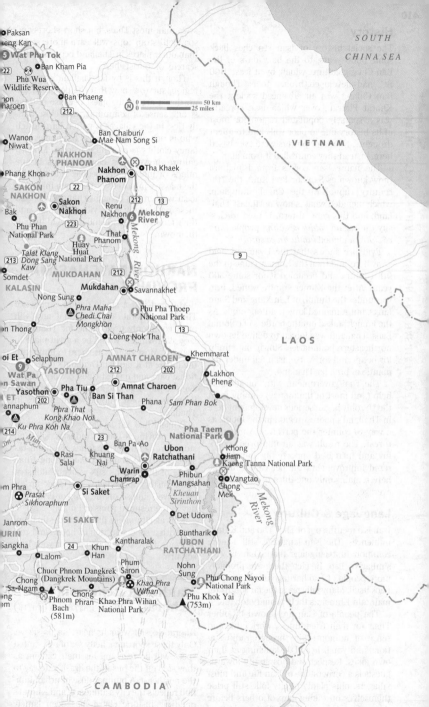

History

The social history of Isan stretches back some 5600 years, to the hazy days of the Ban Chiang culture, which, by at least 2100 BC, had developed bronze tools. Though Ban Chiang was an advanced society, the Khorat Plateau, over which Isan spreads, was a sparsely populated region for most of its history due to poor soils and frequent droughts. No major powers were ever based here, instead they controlled it from afar.

The name Isan comes from Isanapura (now known as Sambor Prei Kuk), the 7th-century capital of the Chenla kingdom, which included what is now northeast Thailand, and this general term is used to classify the region *(pâhk ee·săhn)*, people *(kon ee·săhn)* and food *(ah·hăhn ee·săhn)*.

Evidence shows that the Dvaravati held sway here, and then the Khmers came in the 9th century and occupied it for some 500 years. After the Khmer empire waned, Isan was under the thumb of Lan Xang and Siam kings, but remained largely autonomous. As the French staked out the borders of colonial Laos, Thailand was forced to define its own northeastern boundaries. Slowly but surely, for better and for worse, Isan fell under the mantle of broader Thailand.

The Thai government, with considerable help (and most of the money) coming from the US, only began serious development here in Thailand's poorest region in the 1960s, as a way to counter the perceived communist threat. The result was an improved economy and increased opportunity, but despite rapid improvement, the per capita income here remains only one-third of the national average.

Language & Culture

Isan is a melting pot of Thai, Lao and Khmer influences. The Isan language, still a more common first language than Thai, is very similar to Lao. In fact, there are probably more people of Lao heritage in Isan than in Laos itself. Many villages in the far south still maintain Khmer as their primary tongue.

The people of Isan are known by other Thais for their friendliness, work ethic and sense of humour: flip through radio stations and you'll hear DJs laughing at their own jokes. Respect and hospitality towards guests is a cornerstone of Isan life and most villagers, plus plenty of city folk, still pride themselves on taking care of others before themselves. Isan people are far less conserv-ative than most Thais, but short shorts and spaghetti-strap tops will earn more stares than other places in Thailand because of the scarcity of tourists here.

Though this is by far Thailand's poorest region, surveys show that the people of the northeast are the happiest because of their strong sense of community and close family ties. In the villages it's often hard to tell who is rich or poor because big homes and fancy clothes garner little respect. Modern culture, however, is changing this in the minds of most young people. Additionally, the massive influx of Western men marrying local women has brought changes too, and these days many Isan village women and their families hope to land a foreign man of their own.

NAKHON RATCHASIMA PROVINCE

If you had just a single day to experience Thailand, Khorat – the original and still most commonly used name for Thailand's largest province – would be a great place to spend it. Most visitors are here to jump into the jungle at Khao Yai, Thailand's oldest national park and newest Unesco World Heritage site. Its large size and easy access make it one of the best wildlife-watching sites in Thailand.

While Khao Yai is the soaring pinnacle of the province's tourist industry, silk and stone are solid cornerstones. Fashionistas should hit the shops in Pak Thong Chai, home of the region's silk-weaving industry, while history aficionados can soak up an evocative glimpse of the Angkor-era's heyday at the restored ruins at Phimai.

Khorat city offers little as a destination, but with a solid selection of hotels and restaurants, it makes a good base for your Isan sojourn.

Nakhon Ratchasima (Khorat) นครราชสีมา (โคราช)

POP 209,881

Khorat doesn't wear its heart on its sleeve. Only those sporting a hefty set of rose-tinted specs will be reaching for their camera as they step off the bus in the brash gateway to the northeast. A bumper dose of urban hub-bub reflects the city's affluence, and Khorat's one-time historic charm has been largely smothered under a duvet of homogenous development.

Khorat is however, a city that grows on you. It has a strong sense of regional identity (people call themselves *kon koh·râht* instead of *kon ee·săhn*) and is at its best in its quieter nooks, such as inside the east side of the historic moat, where local life goes on in a fairly traditional way.

Sights & Activities

Thao Suranari Monument   MONUMENT
(อนุสาวรีย์ท้าวสุรนารี; Th Rajadamnern) **FREE**
Thao Suranari, wife of the city's assistant governor during the reign of Rama III, is something of a wonder woman in these parts. Ya Mo (Grandma Mo), as she's affectionately called, became a hero in 1826 by organising a successful prisoner revolt after Chao Anou of Vientiane had conquered Khorat during his rebellion against Siam. As one version of the legend has it, Ya Mo convinced the women to seduce the Lao soldiers and then the Thai men launched a surprise attack, which saved the city.

Her exploits have probably been greatly exaggerated or completely concocted (some scholars suggest that she didn't even exist) to instil a sense of Thai-ness in the ethnically Lao people of the province, but locals and visiting Thais dismiss all of this entirely and flock to the monument in adoring droves to burn incense and leave offerings of flowers and food. Those whose supplications have been honoured hire singers to perform *pleng koh·râht* (Khorat folk song) on small stages.

Ya Mo's monument sits photogenically in front of **Chumphon Gate**, the only original gate left standing: the other three are recent rebuilds. It was a part of the city walls erected in 1656 by French technicians on the orders of Ayuthaya King Narai. The little white building north of this gate that resembles the old fortifications is **Suranari Hall** (Th Chumphon; **FREE**; ☉ 9am-6pm Tue-Sun) a museum of sorts with a cool diorama and even cooler sculpted mural creatively depicting the famous battle.

Wat Salaloi   BUDDHIST TEMPLE
(วัดศาลาลอย; Soi 1, Th Thaosura; ☉ dawn-dusk)
FREE The city's most interesting temple was supposedly founded by Thao Suranari and her husband in 1827. Half of her ashes are interred in a small stupa (the other half is at her monument), so there are also singing troupes on hire to perform for her

spirit here. A small statue of the heroine sits praying in the pond in front of the temple's award-winning *bòht* (chapel).

Built in 1967, it resembles a Chinese junk and holds a large gleaming white Buddha image in 'calming the ocean' pose. It, and other buildings, are decorated with Dan Kwian pottery. Elsewhere around the grounds are a variety of spirit shrines that have nothing to do with Buddhism.

Wat Phayap   BUDDHIST TEMPLE
(วัดพายัพ; Th Polsaen; ☉ dawn-dusk) **FREE** When the abbot of Wat Phayap learned that blasting for a quarry in Saraburi Province was destroying a beautiful cave, he rescued pieces of it and plastered the stalactites, stalagmites and other incredible rocks all over a room below his residence, creating a shrine like no other.

Wat Phra Narai Maharat   BUDDHIST TEMPLE
(วัดพระนารายณ์มหาราช; Th Chomphon; ☉ dawn-dusk) **FREE** This large temple is of interest because of three holy Khmer sandstone sculptures that were unearthed here, of which Phra Narai (Vishnu) is the holiest. To see them, follow the signs with red arrows back to the special **Naranya Temple** (☉ 10am-6pm) at the southeast corner. The temple's *bòht* sits on an island and there are some enormous monitor lizards living in the pond.

Maha Viravong National Museum   MUSEUM
(พิพิธภัณฑสถานแห่งชาติมหาวีรวงศ์; Th Rajadamnern; admission 50B; ☉ 9am-4pm Wed-Sun) Though the collection at this seldom-visited museum is very small, it's also very good. There's ancient pottery (don't miss sneaking a peak at what's stored in the back) and a variety of Buddha images spanning the Dvaravati to Rattanakosin eras.

Festivals

Khorat explodes into life during the **Thao Suranari Festival** (23 March to 3 April), when the city celebrates the namesake heroine. It features parades, theatre and other events along Rajadamnern Rd.

During Khao Phansaa in July, Khorat has a **Candle Parade**, smaller than but similar to that in Ubon Ratchathani.

Sleeping

⭐ **Sansabai House**   HOTEL $
(☎ 0 4425 5144; www.sansabai-korat.com; Th Suranaree; r 300-550B; P ❄ ✱ ☎) Walk into the

Nakhon Ratchasima (Khorat)

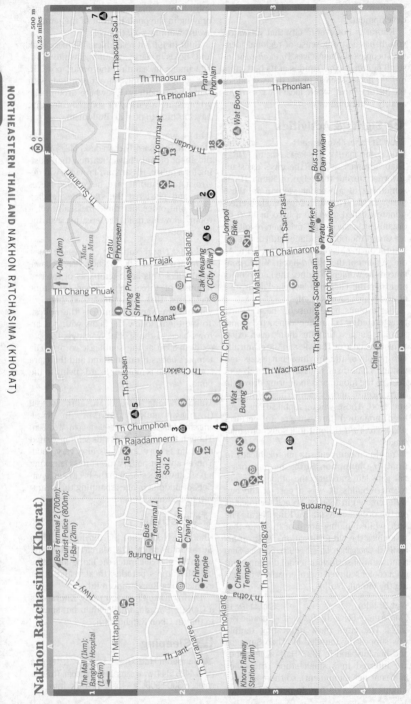

500 m
0.25 miles

Th Thaosura Soi 1
7

Th Thaosura
Th Phonlan
Pratu Phonlan
Th Phonlan
Wat Boon
Th Yommarat
18
13
Th Kudan
17

2

Th Assadang
6
Jompol Bike
19
Th San-Prasit
Market
Pratu Chainarong
Lak Meuang (City Pillar)
Th Prajak
Pratu Phonsaen
V-One (1km)
Mae Nam Mun
Chang Prueak Shrine
Th Chang Phuak
Th Chainarong
Th Mahat Thai
Th Manat
8
20
Th Kamhaeng Songkhram
Th Ratchanikun
Th Chomphon
Th Suranari

Th Polsaen
Th Chakri
Th Wacharasrit
Chira

5
Wat Bueng
Th Chumphon
3
4
Th Rajadamnern
1
16
Th Buarong
15
12
Vatmung Soi 2
9
14
Bus Terminal 2 (700m); Tourist Police (800m); U-Bar (2km)
Bus Terminal 1
Euro Karm Chang
Th Buring
11
Chinese Temple
Chinese Temple
Th Yotha
Th Jomsurangyat
Hwy 2
10
The Mall (1km); Bangkok Hospital (1.6km)
Th Mittaphap
Th Suranaree
Th Jant
Th Phoklang
Khorat Railway Station (1km)

welcoming lobby and you half expect the posted prices to be a bait-and-switch ploy. But no, all rooms are bright and cheerful and come with good mattresses, mini-fridges and little balconies.

Assadang Hotel HOTEL $
(☑ 0 4424 2514; Th Assadang; r 400-500B; P❋☎) There's no escaping the fact that this is just an old concrete box with small rooms, but a two-tone paint job and various little decorations boost it past the jailhouse vibe endemic in so many Thai hotels in this price range, as does the friendly owner. Wi-fi only reaches the 500B rooms.

Sri Ratna Hotel HOTEL $
(☑ 0 4424 3116; Th Suranaree; r 200-350B; P) The centrally located Sri Ratna has the ambience of an insane asylum, but the owners run it with the care and efficiency of a four-star resort. The 200B fan rooms have cold-water showers, squat toilets and a fair price. If you want air-con, choose another hotel.

Thai Inter Hotel HOTEL $$
(☑ 0 4424 7700; www.thaiinterhotel.com; Th Yommarat; r incl breakfast 750-850B; P❋@☎) This little hotel tries to be hip by patching together an odd mix of styles, and it pretty much pulls it off. The lobby is homey and the rooms are comfy. It's got a good (though not so quiet) location near decent restaurants and bars.

Chaophaya Inn HOTEL $$
(☑ 0 4426 0555; www.chaophayainn.com; Th Jomsurangyat; r 550-1100B; P❋@☎) This centrally located place was once pretty classy, but that was sufficiently long ago that the rooms are now retro. Facilities include massage, karaoke and 24-hour room service.

Rachaphruk Grand Hotel HOTEL $$
(☑ 0 4426 1222; www.rachaphrukgrandhotel.com; Th Mittaphap; r incl breakfast 1200-1500B; ste 4500; P⊖❋@☎☒) 'Grand' is laying it on pretty thick, but this 10-storey tower in the city centre is still a decent top-end choice after all these years. The most recent renovation added furnishings that accentuate rather than hide its age. There's a fitness centre with a sauna, a yoga room and many entertainment options.

V-One HOTEL $$$
(☑ 0 4434 2444; www.v-onehotelkorat.com; Th Chang Phuak; r incl breakfast 1500-7950B; P⊖❋@☎☒) The self-proclaimed 'Trendy

& Boutique Hotel' is a brash mixture of colours and styles that sometimes feels more like a children's playroom than a three-star hotel. But, in trying to be different (does anybody really want a Britney Spears–themed room?) they certainly earn an A for effort. All rooms have safes and other little amenities and *most* are more tasteful than tacky.

Sima Thani HOTEL $$$
(☑ 0 4421 3100; www.simathani.com; Th Mittaphap; r incl breakfast 1200-2800B; ste 4600-17,550B; P⊖❋@☎☒) If V-One isn't your style, this place west of the city centre offers a more standard variety of luxury.

🍴 Eating

There's abundant *fa·ràng* food at The Mall (p415).

Wawee Coffee COFFEESHOP $
(Th Mahat Thai; espresso 50B; ☉7am-9pm; ☎) From the lattes to the brownies and the patio to the couches, this stylish place is pretty much perfect.

Wat Boon Night Bazaar THAI $
(Th Chomphon; ⊙ 5-9.30pm) This night market
is less popular than Night Bazaar Korat, but
it's the better choice for eating. Offers Thai,
as well as northeastern Thai food.

EATING ISAN

Isan's culinary creations are a blend of Lao and Thai cooking styles that make use of local ingredients. The holy trinity of northeastern cuisine, *gài yâhng* (grilled chicken), *sôm·đam* (spicy papaya salad) and *kôw něe·o* (sticky rice), is integral to the culture. Also crucial are chillies, and a fistful of potent peppers find their way into most dishes. Outsiders, including most other Thais, are rarely fans of *b̃lah ráh,* a fermented fish sauce (that looks like rotten mud), but Isan people consider it almost essential for good cooking. If your *sôm·đam* doesn't have this, it's not real *sôm·đam.*

Fish dominates Isan menus, with *b̃lah dùk* (catfish), *b̃lah chôrn* (striped snake-head) and *b̃lah boo* (sand goby) among the most popular. These are mostly caught in the Mekong and other large rivers. Fish that families catch themselves are usually small (sometimes so tiny they're eaten bones and all) because they come from streams and rice paddies, as do crabs, frogs and eels. The most famous fish associated with the northeast is *b̃lah bèuk* (giant Mekong catfish), but it's seldom eaten here because it's expensive. Fish farming, however, is slowly bringing it back to menus.

To both Westerners and other Thais, nothing stands out in Isan cuisine as much as insects. Even as recently as the 1970s insects comprised a large part of the typical family's diet, though it became a fading tradition when the government promoted chicken and pig farming, thus lowering the prices of these now popular meats. Insects are still very common as snacks and chilli-sauce ingredients. Purple lights shining out in the countryside are for catching giant water bugs, which, along with crickets, grasshoppers, cicadas, *nŏrn mái pài* (bamboo worms), and more, are sold in most night markets. In fact, there's still enough demand that imports come from Cambodia. Thailand has no shortage of silkworm larvae, which, after they're dropped into boiling water to remove the silk threads from the cocoon, are popped into the mouth. If they stay in the water long enough to get crispy on the outside, you're in for a literal taste explosion: try one when you visit a weaving village and you'll see what we mean.

Along with the *gài yâhng*, *sôm·đam*, *kôw něe·o* and insects mentioned above, the following foods will provide a well-rounded introduction to Isan food.

lâhp Thailand's famous minced-meat 'salad' is actually an Isan dish, and if eaten here, it's one of the spiciest foods in Thailand. Sometimes the meat (it can be made with almost anything as a base, including mushrooms) is raw, but this is not recommended due to bacteria and parasites.

nám đòk Essentially the same as *lâhp*, but with the meat sliced and grilled rather than diced and boiled.

đôm sâap The Isan version of *đôm yam*. Usually full of innards and tendons, the soft parts of an animal left over after making *lâhp*.

súp nòr·mái Usually translated as bamboo shoot 'salad', it uses 'yanang' leaves for flavour. It's much less spicy than *sôm·đam*.

gaang òrm This prototypical Isan curry is heavy on herbs and only mildly spicy. Like all Isan curries, there's no coconut milk.

gaang hèt Another common northeastern curry, it is the tamarind that makes it a little sour. The mix is often seasonal depending on what mushrooms have been just been picked in the forest.

sâi gròrk ee·sǎhn 'Isan sausage' uses fermented pork for a sour taste. Sticky rice, garlic and salt also go inside the skin.

b̃lah pŏw Grilled fish (several freshwater species are used) coated in salt and its stomach stuffed with pandanus leaves and lemongrass.

Ming Ter VEGAN $
(Th Rajadamnern; dishes 35-80B; ⊗7.30am-6pm; 🍴) There's little English at this homey vegan affair, but since it does mock-meat versions of Thai and Chinese standards you can just order your favourites and the message will get through. Or, just point to something in the buffet tray.

Gai Yang Saang Thai NORTHEASTERN THAI $
(Th Rajadamnern; whole free-range chicken 150B; ⊗7.30am-8pm) Has served some of the best *gài yâhng* (grilled chicken) in Khorat for half a century.

★**Rabieng Kaew** THAI $$
(Th Yommarat; dishes 80-300B; ⊗11am-5pm; 🅿) This lovely spot has an antique-filled dining room and a leafy garden in back, but it's not all about the atmosphere. The food, all big dishes meant to be shared, is simply excellent.

Anego JAPANESE $$$
(Th Jomsurangyat; dishes 60-600B; ⊗5pm-midnight; 🅿) Popular little place with a huge menu of Japanese dishes, plus one page of Italian pastas.

🍷 Drinking & Nightlife

Khorat has a glut of good Thai-style pubs. Th Mahat Thai and Th San-Prasit around their junctions with Th Chainarong is a good bar-hopping district.

U-Bar (Hwy 2), 2.5km north of the centre, and the less-popular but more convenient **Bar Nana** (Th Mittaphap), at the Rachaphruk Grand Hotel, have student-filled dance floors. Both get hopping around 10pm.

🛍 Shopping

Night Bazaar Korat MARKET
(Th Manat; ⊗5-10pm) While it's got nothing on Chiang Mai's version, this night market, selling mostly clothes, attracts a youthful crowd and is fun to stroll.

100 Year Meuang Ya Market MARKET
(Th Mukhamontri; ⊗4-10pm) Similar to Night Bazaar Khorat, but full of kitsch. It's pretty quiet on weekdays.

The Mall MALL
(Th Mittaphap; ⊗10.30am-9pm Mon-Fri, 10am-9pm Sat & Sun) This is Isan's largest and glossiest mall. It has a small branch of Asia Books selling English-language books.

DON'T MISS

PÀT MÈE KOH·RÂHT

One speciality you must try once is *pàt mèe koh·râht*. It's similar to *pát tai*, but boasts more flavour and is made with a local style of rice noodle (*mèe koh·râht*). It's widely available in Khorat Province, but very rare everywhere else.

ℹ Information

The Mall has many banks with extended opening hours, and an AEON ATM.

Bangkok Hospital (🕿0 4442 9999; Th Mittaphap)

Immigration (🕿0 4437 5138; ⊗8.30am-noon & 1-4pm Mon-Fri) Located in Dan Kwian village.

Klang Plaza 2 (Th Jomsurangyat) This shopping centre has a Bangkok Bank open 10.30am to 7pm daily, and an AEON ATM outside by the alley entrance.

Post Office (Th Jomsurangyat; ⊗8.30am-10.30pm Mon-Fri, 9am-noon & 4-10.30pm Sat, 4-10.30pm Sun & holidays)

Tourism Authority of Thailand (TAT; 🕿0 4421 3666; tatsima@tat.or.th; Th Mittaphap; ⊗8.30am-4.30pm) Next to Sima Thani Hotel.

ℹ Getting There & Away

BUS

Khorat has two bus terminals. **Terminal 1** (🕿0 4424 2899; Th Burin) in the city centre, serves Bangkok (1st-class only) and most towns within Khorat Province, including Pak Chong (60B, 1½ hours, every 20 minutes). Buses to other destinations, plus more Bangkok buses and minivans, use **Terminal 2** (*bor kör sör sŏrng*; 🕿0 4429 5271; Hwy 2) north of downtown. You never have to wait long for a bus to Bangkok (171B to 320B, 3½ hours) since buses from most cities in Isan pass through Khorat on their way to the capital.

There are minivans to/from Ayuthaya (132B, four hours, every 30 minutes) and Lopburi (120B, 3½ hours, hourly) from Bus Terminal 2.

TRAIN

Many trains pass through **Khorat Railway Station** (🕿0 4424 2044), but buses are much faster. Nine daily trains go to/from Bangkok (50B to 1010B, five to seven hours), via Ayuthaya, and Ubon Ratchathani (58B to 1068B, five to six hours). There are also three Khon Kaen (38B to 170B, 3½ hours) and one Nong Khai (64B to 301B, 6½ hours) trains.

Khorat's smaller **Chira Railway Station** is closer to the old city, so it may be more convenient to get off there.

ⓘ Getting Around

There are fixed *sŏrng·tăa·ou* (shared taxi; 8B) routes through the city, but even locals find it hard to figure them out because of the dizzying array of numbers and colours representing them. Most pass the junction of Th Suranaree and Th Rajadamnern, so if you want to go somewhere just head there and ask around; someone will put you on the right one. Heading west on Suranaree, yellow *sŏrng·tăa·ou* 1 with white and green stripes will take you past the train station, the tourism office and The Mall. Heading north on Rajadamnern the white 6 with red and yellow stripes passes The Mall more directly and the white 15 with purple stripes goes to Bus Terminal 2.

Túk-túk cost between 40B and 70B to most places in town. Motorcycle taxis and *săhm·lór* (pedicabs), both of which are common, always cost less. **Metered taxis** (☏ 0 4492 8678) are found only at Bus Terminal 2 and The Mall, but there's almost no chance of getting them to use the meter.

Korat Car Rental (☏ 08 1877 3198; www.koratcarrental.com) is a local firm with a stellar reputation. The Sima Thani Hotel also arranges cars with drivers, some of whom speak English.

Euro Karn Chang (☏ 08 8355 9393; 239-241 Th Suranaree; ⊘ 8am-5pm Mon-Sat) near Bus Terminal 1 hires motorcycles for 300/1400B per day/week, and **Jompol Bike** (☏ 08 1955 2838; Th Chomphon; ⊘ 8am-5.30pm) hires bicycles for 100B/day.

Around Nakhon Ratchasima

Dan Kwian   ด่านเกวียน

If you have even a small interest in ceramics, you should pay Dan Kwian a visit. Just a quick trip out of Khorat, this village has been producing pottery for hundreds of years and its creations are famous for their rough texture and rust-like hue. Only kaolin sourced from this district produces such results. Most of what's made and sold these days are cheap lawn ornaments, but there's also some attractive modern pottery plus cast sandstone reproductions of ancient Khmer sculpture. If you walk through the village proper, south of the myriad shops lining the highway (turn east at the school), you'll find some families with small workshops and kilns at their houses. There's also a large workshop behind the DinPao shop on the north end of the highway, near the pedestrian bridge.

To get here from Khorat, hop on a bus (14B, 30 minutes) from near the southern city gate (or catch it along Th Mahat Thai), or another route from Terminal 2 (25B, 45 minutes).

Pak Thong Chai   ปักธงชัย

Amphoe Pak Thong Chai became one of Thailand's most famous silk-weaving centres when Jim Thompson started buying

BUSES FROM NAKHON RATCHASIMA'S TERMINAL 2

DESTINATION	DURATION (HR)	PRICE (B)	DEPARTURES
Aranya Prathet (Rong Kluea Market)	4	165	5.30am-5.30pm (5 daily)
Ayuthaya (minivan)	4	132	6am-7pm (frequent)
Chiang Mai	12-13	473-710	3am-8.30pm (11 daily)
Khon Kaen	3-4	120-250	6am-11pm (frequent)
Khon Kaen (minivan)	2½	129	7am-5pm (hourly)
Lopburi (minivan)	3½	120	6am-7pm (every 30 minutes)
Nang Rong	2	75-95	all day (frequent)
Nang Rong (minivan)	1½	75	5am-8pm (every 30 minutes)
Nong Khai	6	220-435	all day (hourly)
Surin	4	136-175	7am-7.20pm (6 daily)
Trat	8	324	1am
Ubon Ratchathani	5-6	286-445	8am-1am (14 daily)
Vientiane	Laos (must have Lao visa already)	6½	540

silk here. Today there are almost a dozen large silk factories in the district and thousands of families still work hand looms at home in every village. Pak Thong Chai is known for following the latest trends, but some shops stock traditional styles such as *mát-mèe*, most of which are woven in other provinces.

Because Pak Thong Chai is a fairly large town, it's not nearly as fun a place to visit as other Isan silk centres such as Chonnabot or Ban Tha Sawang, but **Macchada** (⊙8am-5pm), a shop at the city's southern end, where you can watch weavers working, is worth seeking out if you do come. There are highway signs directing you to a Silk Cultural Center, but it's been closed for years.

Pak Thong Chai is 30km south of Khorat on Rte 304. Buses (21B, one hour, frequent, leaves from Terminal 1.

Ban Prasat
บ้านปราสาท

About 3000 years ago, a primitive agricultural culture, closely related to Ban Chiang, put down roots at Ban Prasat, near the banks of the Than Prasat River. It survived some 1500 years, planting rice, domesticating animals, fashioning coloured pottery, weaving cloth and, in later years, forging tools out of bronze. The secrets of this early civilisation were revealed during extensive archaeological digs completed in 1991.

Three **excavation pits** FREE with skeletons (most are replicas) and pottery left in situ are on display in the village, and a small but good **museum** (⊙8am-4.30pm) FREE houses some of the discoveries. It also explains what life was like in those days and in the village today. South of the museum, one family still does **silk weaving**, including raising their own worms and spinning their own thread. They welcome visitors to come by for a look.

Many families (some speak a little English) are part of an award-winning **homestay program** (☑08 1725 0791; per person incl 2 meals 400B) where villagers put up visitors in their homes and show them daily activities including basketry and farming. Reservations should be made at least a day in advance.

Ban Prasat is 45km northeast of Khorat, off Hwy 2, and buses (35B, one hour) heading to Phimai will drop you off at the highway. A motorcycle taxi will zip you around to all the sites for 50B per person,

but note that sometimes only one driver is working.

Phimai
พิมาย

The otherwise mundane little town of Phimai has one of Thailand's finest surviving Khmer temple complexes right at its heart. Reminiscent of Cambodia's Angkor Wat, Prasat Phimai once stood on an important trade route linking the Khmer capital of Angkor with the northern reaches of the realm. Phimai is an easy day trip out of Khorat, but if you prefer the quiet life, you could always make Khorat a day trip out of Phimai instead.

⊙ Sights

★**Phimai Historical Park**   HISTORICAL SITE
(อุทยานประวัติศาสตร์พิมาย; ☑0 4447 1568; Th Anantajinda; admission 100B; ⊙7.30am-6pm) Started by Khmer King Jayavarman V (AD 968–1001) during the late 10th century and finished by his successor King Suriyavarman I (1002–49), Phimai is the largest Khmer ruin in Thailand and is also one of the most impressive and beautiful. Though built as a Mahayana Buddhist temple, the carvings also feature many Hindu deities and, as explained in the **visitor center** (⊙8.30am-4.30pm), design elements at Prasat Phimai influenced Angkor Wat.

You enter over a cruciform **naga bridge**, which symbolically represents the passage from earth to heaven, and then through the **southern gate** (which is unusual since most Khmer temples face east) of the outer wall, which stretches 565m by 1030m. A raised passageway, formerly covered by a tiled roof, leads to the inner sanctum and the 28m-tall **main shrine** built of white sandstone and covered in superb carvings. At the centre of the **Prang Brahmathat**, in front of the main shrine, is a replica stone sculpture of Angkor King Jayavarman VII sitting cross-legged and looking very much like a sitting Buddha. The original is in the Phimai National Museum.

Knowledgeable local students sometimes act as guides, but few speak English. Luckily, a free brochure provides a good overview of the complex.

Phimai National Museum   MUSEUM
(พิพิธภัณฑสถานแห่งชาติพิมาย; Th Tha Songkhran; admission 100B; ⊙9am-4pm Wed-Sun) Situated on the banks of Sa Kwan, a 12th-century Khmer reservoir, this museum houses a fine

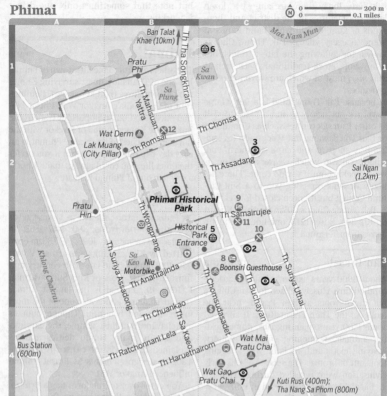

Phimai

collection of Khmer sculptures from Prasat Phimai, including many exquisite lintels, and other ruins around Lower Isan. There's also some distinctive black Phimai pottery (500 BC–AD 500) and even older ceramics from nearby Ban Prasat. At the time of writing, this museum was closed for renovations and wasn't due to reopen until April 2016.

Sai Ngam   PARK
(ไทรงาม; ⊙dawn-dusk) A bit east of town is Thailand's largest and oldest banyan tree, a 350-plus-year-old megaflorum spread over an island. The extensive system of interlocking branches and gnarled trunks makes the 'Beautiful Banyon' look like a small forest.

Other Historic Sites
Meru Bhramathat (Th Buchayan) **FREE** is a toppled brick *chedi* dating back to the late Ayuthaya period (18th century). Its name is derived from a folk tale that refers to it as the cremation site of King Bhramathat.

Three city gates remain. **Pratu Chai** (Victory Gate) `FREE`, the one that served the road to Angkor, is the most intact. The mounded dirt ridge alongside it shows what the ramparts formerly surrounding the entire city looked like. These city walls went up in the 13th century, as did what's now known as **Kuti Rusi** (Hermit's Quarters; ⊙ dawn-dusk) `FREE`, a healing station built by Jayavarman VII, and **Tha Nang Sa Phom** (⊙ dawn-dusk) `FREE`, a laterite landing platform on the grounds of the Fine Arts Department compound; turn right immediately after entering the gate.

✸ Festivals & Events

Staged in mid-November, the **Phimai Festival** celebrates the town's history, with cultural performances, sound-and-light shows (tickets 200B to 600B) and long-boat races.

🛏 Sleeping

Phimai Paradise   HOTEL $
(📞 0 4428 7565; www.phimaiparadise.com; Th Samairujee; r 450-650B; 🅿 ❄ ✳ @ 🛜 🏊) Nothing too fancy, but this newish tower has by far the best rooms in town.

Khru Pom   GUESTHOUSE $
(📞 08 6648 9383; Th Anantajinda; s w/o bath 150B, r 350-450B; 🅿 ❄ ✳ 🛜) This quiet and immaculate little place in the centre of the block won't excite you, but it won't let you down either. The friendly owners speak English.

Moon River Homestay   GUESTHOUSE $
(📞 08 5633 7097; www.moon-river-phimai.com; Ban Sai Ngam Patana Soi 2; r 400-600B, f 1200B; 🅿 ❄ ✳ 🛜) This German–Thai run guesthouse is in an almost rural location on the north bank of the river (you can swim here) and features mostly simple but good wooden cabins, some with air-con and some with fan. They're surrounded by greenery and connected by a cool boardwalk.

🍴 Eating

The string of vendors next to Sai Ngam, open for breakfast and lunch, serve Thai and Isan basics including *pàt pímai,* which is the same as *pàt mèe koh râht* except it uses a softer noodle. A few restaurants in town have it on their menus, too.

Vimaya Purapat Place   THAI $
(Th Romsai; dishes 40-220B; ⊙ 11am-10pm; 🛜) On the north side of the historical park, this large, all-wood spot is a lovely mix of modern and traditional. The large menu features a few out-of-the-ordinary dishes such as their delicious 'Vimaya special friend noodles' (stir-fried egg noodles with vegetables, sesame seeds and chicken or tofu) and prices are very reasonable.

Rabiang Mai   THAI $
(Th Samairujee; dishes 50-250B; ⊙ 5pm-midnight; 🛜) This semifancy place is a tad on the pricey side, but the food (mostly Thai, plus some Isan and *fa·ràng* options) is quite good.

Night Bazaar   NORTHEASTERN THAI $
(Th Anantajinda; ⊙ 4-9pm) More of a fresh-food market than a dining destination, this small street market still warrants a stroll.

ℹ Getting There & Away

Phimai has a bus station, but there's no need to use it since all buses pass near Pratu Chai, the clock tower and the museum on their way in and out of town.

Buses and minivans for Phimai leave Khorat's Bus Terminal 2 (50B, 1½ hours) about every 20 minutes throughout the day. If you're heading north, take the Khorat bus to Ban Talat Khae (13B, 15 minutes) on the highway and catch a connection there.

ℹ Getting Around

Phimai is small enough to stroll, but to travel further, hire a bike from **Boonsiri Guesthouse** (Th Chomsudasadet; per day 100B) or a motorcycle from **Niu Motorbike** (📞 0 4447 1694; Th Anantajinda; 200B/day; ⊙ 8am-5pm Mon-Sat).

Khao Yai National Park
อุทยานแห่งชาติเขาใหญ่

Up there on the podium with some of the world's greatest parks, **Khao Yai** (📞 08 6092 6529; adult/child 400/200B, car 50B) is Thailand's oldest and most visited reserve. Covering 2168 sq km, Khao Yai incorporates one of the largest intact monsoon forests remaining in mainland Asia, which is why it was named a Unesco World Heritage site (as part of the Dong Phayayen-Khao Yai Forest Complex). Visiting independently is quite easy, as the mostly English-speaking staff at the **visitor centre** (📞 08 6092 6529; ⊙ 8am-9pm) are very helpful.

Rising to 1351m at the summit of Khao Rom, the park's terrain covers five vegetation zones: evergreen rainforest (100m to

BEYOND THE FOREST

The greater Pak Chong region is a very popular escape for Bangkokians, and for many of them the national park is beside the point. The roads approaching Khao Yai from the north are lined with enough BB-gun shooting ranges, sweet-corn stands, shopping malls and other tourist traps for families to stay busy all weekend without ever thinking about nature.

An almost mandatory stop is **Farm Chokchai** (☑ 0 4432 8386; www.farmchokchai. com; Mittaphap Hwy, Km159; ⊗ 9am-7pm), a 32-sq-km dairy farm overflowing with cowboy kitsch. The expanding empire now includes an ice-cream parlour, steakhouse, a souvenir shop and a safari-style tented camp (weekday/weekend per adult from 2490/2990B). There are 2½-hour **tours** (adult/child 300/150B; ⊗ 10am & 2pm Tue-Fri, every 20min 9-11.40am 1-3.40pm Sat, Sun & holidays, reservations essential) of the milking parlour, petting zoo and cowboy show.

For some actual Thai culture, there's the excellent **Khao Yai Art Museum** (☑ 0 4475 6060; www.khaoyaiartmuseum.com; ⊗ 9am-6pm) `FREE`, which has three rooms of modern art from some of Thailand's top artists including Anupong Chantorn and Lampu Kansanoh. It's 4km east of Th Thanarat at Km 15; turn at the police box.

Thailand is the pioneer of 'New Latitude Wines' and with over a dozen wineries in the area, the Khao Yai area is now the epicentre of this increasingly respectable industry. Two of the leaders, **PB Valley** (☑ 0 3622 6415; www.khaoyaiwinery.com; tour 200B; ⊗ tours 10.30am, 1.30pm & 3.30pm), which corked its first bottle in 1998, and **GranMonte** (☑ 0 4400 9544; www.granmonte.com; ⊗ tours 11am, 1pm & 3pm Sat, Sun & holidays), which got into the game three years later) lie along Muak Lek road (exit Km 144), the direct route from Bangkok to Khao Yai. Both are scenically set and offer tours (book in advance), tastings, luxury lodging and classy restaurants for lunch and dinner. They're 22.5km and 16km respectively from the park gate.

Life Park (Km19.5; per activity 160-640B; ⊗ 9am-6pm), near the park gate at the Greenery Resort, is Khao Yai's biggest adventure park. It has go-karts, paintball, a giant swing and more.

400m); semi-evergreen rainforest (400m to 900m); mixed deciduous forest (northern slopes at 400m to 600m); hill evergreen forest (over 1000m); and savannah and secondary-growth forest in areas where agriculture and logging occurred before the park was protected.

Some 200 elephants tramp the park's boundaries. Other mammals include tigers, leopards, bears, gaur, barking deer, otters, various gibbons and macaques, and some rather large pythons. Khao Yai's bird list boasts 392 species, and one of Thailand's largest populations of hornbills lives here, including the great hornbill (*nók gòk* or *nók gah·hang*).

The main entrance is south of Pak Chong, but there's a second, seldom-used southern entrance in Prachinburi Province.

◉ Sights & Activities

Waterfalls

Khao Yai has many waterfalls. Little **Nam Tok Kong Kaew**, sits right behind the visitor centre while **Nam Tok Haew Narok** in the far south of the park (an 800m walk from the parking area), whose three levels combine to form a 150m drop, is the biggest. The beauty award, however, goes to 25m **Nam Tok Haew Suwat**, which scooped a starring role in Danny Boyle's film *The Beach*. It has water year-round, and you can walk down to the bottom, but swimming isn't allowed. Though easily reached by car, Haew Suwat can also be accessed by a couple of footpaths including the Kong Kaew-Haew Suwat Trail.

Wildlife

There are several **viewpoints** and **salt licks** (often attracting elephants in the early morning and evening) along the roads through the park. There's a good chance of seeing gibbons and hornbills on the Kong Kaew-Haew Suwat Trail, and it's probably the best footpath for spotting elephants, though encounters here are unlikely; the roads are better for elephant-spotting.

The **Nong Phak Chi observation tower** overlooks a little lake and a salt lick, and is one of the best wildlife-spotting spots in the park. This is the most likely place you'll see a tiger, but you have to be very lucky (like lottery-winner lucky) to do so. In the early evening, deer congregate at the visitor centre and campgrounds.

Hiking

The Nong Phak Chi observation tower can be reached via a couple of walking trails; the shortest way (900m) to the tower starts 1.8km north of the visitor centre, and it's a wide, well-maintained path. Trekkers can also get to the observation tower either by a 5.4km trail from the visitor centre or a 3km path starting at Km 33. The latter is better for seeing wildlife along the way and is one of Khao Yai's best birdwatching walks. To get to the Nam Tok Haew Suwat waterfall, try the mildly challenging, 8km-long **Kong Kaew-Haew Suwat Trail** (Trail 1), which starts behind the visitor centre.

While the Kong Kaew-Haew Suwat Trail and walks to the tower don't require a guide, hiring one is highly recommended (except for the short route to the observation tower) because the trails aren't well trodden or well marked. We've heard from travellers who got lost and were forced to sleep in the forest overnight. Park rangers can be hired as guides (half-/full day 500/1000B per group) through the visitor centre. They can also lead you on longer off-trail treks.

No matter where you hike, you should wear boots and long trousers. During the rainy season leeches are a problem; mosquito repellent helps keep them away, but the leech socks sold in the visitor centre are much better.

Tours

Most hotels and resorts around Khao Yai arrange **park tours** and this is really the ideal way to visit: a good guide will show you creatures you never would have seen on your own. The typical day-long program (1300B to 1900B per person) includes some easy morning walks looking for wildlife and a visit to Haew Suwat waterfall. Lunch, snacks, water and, in the rainy season, 'leech socks' are always included, but sometimes the park entry fee isn't, so do some comparison shopping. Half-day trips (450B to 600B) typically stay outside the park to visit a cave, swim in a spring and watch a million or so rare wrinkle-lipped bats disgorge from a mountain-top cave. Birdwatching, camping, trekking and other speciality tours are also available. Greenleaf Guesthouse (p421)

and Khaoyai Garden Lodge (p422) have long earned enthusiastic praise for their tours, as has the relative newcomer **Bobby's Apartments & Jungle Tours** (☑08 6262 7006; www.bobbysjungletourkhaoyai.com) based near Tesco-Lotus in Pak Chong.

Khao Yai is one of Thailand's top **birdwatching** sites. Two noted birdwatching guides are Tony, who owns **Khao Yai Nature Life Resort** (☑08 1827 8391; www.khaoyai naturelifetours.com), and **Nang** (☑08 9427 1823; www.thailandyourway.com), who is one of Khao Yai's few female guides. Both also lead standard park tours.

The park itself offers one-hour **night safaris** (☑08 1063 9241; per vehicle 500B; ☉7pm & 8pm), which use spotlights to look for animals. There are often so many vehicles during the safari that it ruins the experience. Reservations are a must, and if you're sleeping outside the park, you can only do the 7pm trip. On all Saturdays and any Sunday that precedes a public-holiday Monday, you can join with others (50B per person) rather than hiring the whole vehicle.

Sleeping & Eating

There are dozens of places to stay on and near Th Thanarat (Rte 2090), the road leading to the park, and plenty more in the not-so-pleasant gateway city of Pak Chong. Budget and some midrange places offer free transport to/from town, though usually only if you book a tour with them. All but the cheapies do weekday and off-season (April to October) discounts of up to 40%.

The best setting for sleeping is, of course, in the park itself. There are **campsites** (per person with own tent 30B, 3-person tent 225B) and a variety of **lodgings** (☑0 2562 0760; www. dnp.go.th/parkreserve; tents 150-400B, r & bungalows 800-3500B, 30% discount Mon-Thu) available around the park, all pretty far from the visitor centre.

Each of the lodges reviewed serves food, and there are many more restaurants along Th Thanarat; a surprising number serve Italian. The park itself has restaurants at all busy locations, including the visitor centre, campsites and some waterfalls, but even the campsite restaurants close around 6pm, so plan ahead.

★ **Greenleaf Guesthouse**   GUESTHOUSE **$**
(☑0 4436 5073; www.greenleaftour.com; Th Thanarat, Km 7.5; r 200-300B; **P**☎) Step past the slightly chaotic common areas and you'll be surprised by the good-value rooms (with

cold-water private bathrooms) at the back of this family-owned place. Note that they'll probably be 'full' if you don't book a tour.

Palm Garden Lodge $

(☏ 08 9989 4470; www.palmgalo.com; r 400-650B, bungalows 1200B; P ❄ ✺ @ ☎) A relaxing and welcoming place set in a quiet garden 10km outside the southern park gate in Ban Khon Kwang, Prachinburi Province. It has homey fan and air-con rooms, motorcycles for hire (250B per day) and park tours are available, though because of its location it's unlikely you'll be able to share tour costs with other travellers. Note that food is expensive.

Khao Yai Villa HOTEL $$

(☏ 08 3365 8588; www.khaoyaivilla.com; Th Thanarat, Km 12; r 790B; P ❄ ☎ ☎) What these simple new rooms lack in charm, they more than make up for in value. The price is very low by Khao Yai standards.

Khaoyai Garden Lodge HOTEL $$

(☏ 0 4436 5178; www.khaoyaigardenlodgekm7. com; Th Thanarat, Km 7; r 250-2500B, f 2800B; P ❄ ✺ @ ☎ ✺) This friendly, family-run place offers a variety of rooms (the cheapest are sterile, have shared hot water bathrooms and fans), all spread out around a garden. It's a bit worn, but it's still good value and the restaurant-lounge in front encourages interaction with your fellow guests. There's a Thai dance show on Friday nights.

★ Hotel des Artists HOTEL $$$

(☏ 0 4429 7444; www.hotelartists.com; Th Thanarat, Km 22; r/bungalow incl breakfast 5000/6000B; P ❄ ✺ @ ☎ ✺) Breaking from the Khao Yai norm, this tasteful hotel goes for French-colonial chic rather than a nature theme; though with its gorgeous mountain views out the back you won't forget where you are. The villas sit right on the large swimming pool. The only knockback is that rooms are quite small.

Balios HOTEL $$$

(☏ 0 4436 5971; www.balioskhaoyai.com; Th Thanarat, Km 17; r incl breakfast 3600-4400B; P ❄ ✺ @ ☎ ✺) Khao Yai's original luxury lodge has kept up with the times and has recently had a full remodel in an attractive, vaguely Italian threme. There are pleasant gardens in back around the pool.

Kirimaya HOTEL $$$

(☏ 0 4442 6000; www.kirimaya.com; Rte 3052; r incl breakfast 10,530-11,700B, ste 20,475-23,400B, pool villas 25,895B, tented villas 38,610B; P ❄ ✺ @ ☎ ✺) This luxury resort-spa makes an awesome first impression. Step 'through' the wooden front doors and you're greeted by a towering stilted restaurant and other Thai-Balinese fusion buildings rising from a lotus- and reed-filled pond and backed by the mountains. Rooms have genuine style and lots of little luxuries. We're not keen on having a golf course on the edge of the park (even one designed by Jack Nicklaus), but there's no denying this place is special. It's 7km east of the park gate. Ask about discounts; we've seen promotional prices of over 50% off.

Jungle House HOTEL $$$

(☏ 0 4429 7183; www.junglehousehotel.com; Th Thanarat, Km 19.5; r 1400-2200B; P ✺ ☎ ☎) The humdrum rooms won't wow you (unless you're really into loft sitting areas), but from its own little patch of untamed forest to an abundance of reptiles, this older place has got the jungle vibe down pat. It even has its own elephants (30-minute rides 300B).

ⓘ Getting There & Away

Sŏrng·tăa·ou cover the 30km from Pak Chong down Th Thanarat to the park's northern gate (40B, 45 minutes) every 30 minutes from 6am to 5pm. They start their journey in front of the 7-Eleven near the artistic deer (they look like giraffes) statue. It's another 14km to the visitor centre, and park guards are used to talking drivers into hauling people up there. Some also do a side business hiring motorcycles for 500B per day. Several motorcycle shops on Pak Chong's main road do rentals for 300B per 24 hours including **Petch Motor** (☏ 08 1718 2400; Th Mittaphap, at Th Tesabarn 13), a bit southwest of the stoplight (look for the diamond in the window).

Only 2nd-class buses to Bangkok (128B, three hours) use the bus station, which is southwest of the traffic light at Th Thesabarn 8. Frequent 2nd-class buses and minivans to Khorat (60B, 1½ hours) stop about 500m northeast of the deer statue near *dà·làht kàak*. Minivans to Bangkok's Victory Monument (180B, 2½ hours, hourly) park near the deer statue. You can also catch minivans (departing from Khorat) to Ayuthaya (100B, 2½ hours) and Lopburi (80B, two hours) across the street from *dà·l àht kàak*, if they have empty seats when they pass through, and they usually do. Board 1st-class buses to both Bangkok (150B, 2½ hours) and Khorat (80B, one hour) across the highway from the deer statue.

You can also get to Pak Chong by train from Bangkok and Khorat, but it's much faster to go by bus or minivan. Ayuthaya, on the other hand, has no direct bus service and not many minivans, so the train (23B to 363B, two to three hours, nine daily) can be a good option.

BURIRAM PROVINCE

Buriram is not a province for urban exploration. Despite hanging on to half of its historic moat, Mueang Buriram, the provincial capital and only large town, is a tough sell as a tourist destination. Buriram Province is best as a place to get a glimpse of the past. The countryside is chock-a-block with tradition and peppered with dozens of Khmer ruins. The crowning glory is Phanom Rung, a beautifully restored complex climbing to the summit of an extinct volcano. The most spectacular Angkor monument in Thailand, Phanom Rung is well worth the journey and should impress even those who've already experienced Angkor Wat in Cambodia.

Nang Rong

นางรอง

POP 23,778

This workaday city is even more forgettable than the capital city, 45km to the north, but it's the most convenient base for visiting Phanom Rung, and a full range of services and a good selection of hotels make it a friendly and comfortable starting point.

Sleeping & Eating

★P California Inter Hostel GUESTHOUSE $

(☎08 1808 3347; www.pcalifornianangrong.webs.com; Th Sangkakrit; s 250-500B, d 300-600B; P⊜❄☜) This great place, which isn't actually a hostel, on the east side of town offers bright, nicely decorated rooms with good value in all price ranges, including the cheapest, which have fans and cold-water showers. English-speaking owner Khun Wicha is a wealth of knowledge about the area and leads tours. Bikes are free of charge. A motorcycle taxi from the bus station costs 50B.

Honey Inn GUESTHOUSE $

(☎08 1264 7144; Soi Si Kun; r 250-350B; ❄@☜) This family-run Nang Rong veteran 1km from the bus station is a bit older and cheaper than P California, but still a fine choice. Motorcycle hire and guided tours are also available. To find it, walk north from the bus station, cross the main road and head east until you see the sign.

The Park HOTEL $$

(☎0 4463 3778; www.theparknangrong.com; Th Praditpana; r 590-1000; P⊜❄☜) One of several new, midrange hotels in Nang Rong, The Park is the lovliest, with all of its fairly priced rooms around a quiet, lovely garden. It's southeast of the bus station, next to the lake.

Cabbages & Condoms HOTEL $$

(☎0 4465 7145; Hwy 24; r 240-1500B; P⊜❄@☜) The cheapest (shared bathroom) rooms at this Population & Community Development Association–run resort, set in a garden, are pretty limp. But move up the price scale (where you get large rooms with stone floors) and this is a pleasant place to stay. There's a clothing and shoe factory on-site, opened to bring work normally found in the city to the surrounding villages. It's 6.5km west of town.

Phob Suk THAI $$

(Hwy 24; dishes 40-360B; ⊙9am-9.30pm; P☜) The picture menu at this well-known restaurant near the bus station presents the typical mix of Thai, Isan and Chinese, but we recommend the city's famous *kăh mŏo* (pork-rump roast).

Getting There & Around

Nang Rong's **bus station** (☎0 4463 1517) is on the west side of town. Most buses running to the Phanom Rung Historical Park stop in Nang Rong.

Both P California and Honey Inn hire motorcycles, starting at 250B per day, and the former also has mountain bikes for 100B per day.

Phanom Rung Historical Park

อุทยานประวัติศาสตร์เขาพนมรุ้ง

The largest and best-restored Khmer monument in Thailand, **Phanom Rung** (☎0 4466 6251; admission 100B, combined ticket with Prasat Muang Tam 150B; ⊙6am-6pm) has a knock-'em-dead location. Crowning the summit of a spent volcano (the name is derived from the Khmer words for 'big mountain'), this sanctuary sits 200m above the paddy fields.

The temple was erected as a Hindu monument to Shiva between the 10th and 13th centuries, the bulk of it during the reign of King Suriyavarman II (r AD 1113–50), which was the prime period of Angkor architecture. The complex faces east, and four times a year the sun shines through all 15 sanctuary doorways. The correct solar alignment happens during sunrise from 3 to 5 April and 8 to 10 September, and sunset from 5 to 7 March and 5 to 7 October (some years are one day earlier.). The park extends its hours during these events, and locals celebrate the

Phanom Rung Festival around the April alignment, with ancient Brahmin ceremonies and modern sound-and-light shows.

◉ Sights

Below the main sanctuary, above the long row of gift shops, an **information centre** (◷ 8.30am-4.30pm) houses artefacts found at the site and displays about both the construction and 17-year restoration. You can pick up a free informative brochure or arrange a Thai-speaking guide (free, but tips are expected) here. Those who don't want to climb can use an upper parking lot (50B per car), but the brochure isn't available there.

One of the most remarkable aspects of Phanom Rung is the **promenade** leading to the main gate. It begins on a slope 400m east of the main tower with three earthen **terraces**. Next comes a cruciform base for what may have been a wooden pavilion. To the right of this is the **changing pavilion** (Phlab Phla) where royalty bathed and changed clothes before entering the temple complex. You then step down to a 160m-long **processional walkway** flanked by sandstone pillars with early Angkor style (AD 1100–80) lotus-bud tops. This walkway ends at the first and largest of three **naga bridges**, flanked by 16 five-headed *naga* (mythical serpents) in the classic Angkor style. As at all Khmer temple, these represent the passing from the earthly realm to the heavenly.

After crossing this bridge and climbing the stairs you come to the magnificent **east gallery** leading into the main sanctuary. The **main tower** has a gallery on each of its four sides and the entrance to each gallery is itself a smaller version of the main tower.

The craftsmanship at Phanom Rung represents the pinnacle of Khmer artistic achievement, on par with the reliefs at Angkor Wat in Cambodia. Excellent sculptures of both Shaiva and Vaishnava deities can be seen in the lintels and pediments over the doorways to the central monuments, and in various other key points on the sanctuary exterior. On the east portico of the *mon·dòp* is a Nataraja (Dancing Shiva), which is late Baphuon or early Angkor style, while on the south entrance are the remains of Shiva and Uma riding their bull mount, Nandi. The central cell of the *brah·sàht* contains a Shivalingam (phallus image) and in front of it is an evocative Nandi statue.

ⓘ Getting There & Away

Sŏrng·tăa·ou (25B, 30 minutes, every half-hour) from in front of the old market (*nâh dà·làht sòt*) on the east end of town in Nang Rong and Chanthaburi-bound buses from the bus station (p423) on the west side of town go to Ban Ta Pek where motorcycle taxi drivers charge 200B to Phanom Rung, including waiting time.

Coming from or heading to Ubon Ratchathani (263B, 4½ hours, hourly), Surin (80B, two hours, every half-hour), Khorat (75-95B, two hours, hourly), Pak Chong (122B, 2½ hours, hourly) or Bangkok (231-275B, five hours, hourly), you have the option of getting off at Ban Tako, a well-marked turn-off about 14km east of Nang Rong, and waiting for one of the vehicles from Nang Rong; or just taking a motorcycle taxi (300B return) direct to Phanom Rung.

P California Inter Hostel's standard one-day tour (2736B, for four people) is a good choice because as well as Phanom Rung, Muang Tam and Wat Khao Angkhan, you'll get to visit a silk-weaving village.

VISHNU & THE KING OF POP

Phanom Rung's most famous carving is the **Narai Bandhomsindhu lintel**, which depicts a reclining Vishnu ('Phra Narai' in Thai) in the Hindu creation myth. Growing from his navel is a lotus that branches into several blossoms, on one of which sits the creator god, Brahma. Vishnu is asleep on the milky sea of eternity, here represented by a *naga* and alongside him are heads of Kala, the god of time and death. This lintel sits above the eastern gate (the main entrance) beneath the impressive dancing Shiva relief.

Its fame stems not from its beauty, but from its role in a quarter-century-long whodunnit-cum-David-versus-Goliath tale that began in 1965 when it was discovered to have been stolen. (It likely went missing several years earlier, but nobody noticed.) In 1972 it was found on display at the Art Institute of Chicago and Thailand pressed for its return. Superstars Carabao helped the cause with their song 'Thaplang' (Lintel) featuring the line 'Take back Michael Jackson, Give us Phra Narai'. Phra Narai finally came home in 1988, the year the Phanom Rung restoration was finished.

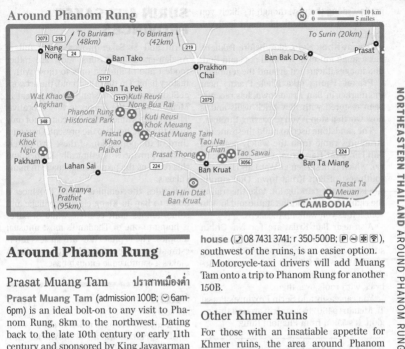

Around Phanom Rung

Prasat Muang Tam   ปราสาทเมืองต่ำ

Prasat Muang Tam (admission 100B; ☉6am-6pm) is an ideal bolt-on to any visit to Phanom Rung, 8km to the northwest. Dating back to the late 10th century or early 11th century and sponsored by King Jayavarman V, 'Lower City' is Isan's third most interesting Khmer temple complex (after Phanom Rung and Phimai) in terms of size, atmosphere and quality of restoration work. Also, making it worth a visit are the many superb carvings still in situ, including one lintel depicting Shiva and his consort Uma riding the sacred bull, Nandi.

The complex, built as a shrine to Shiva, has an unusual layout. Most significantly, the five *prang* are grouped three in front and two in back rather than the typical quincunx cross shape. The principal *prang*, likely representing Mt Kailasa, Shiva's home, could not be rebuilt. Four lotus-filled L-shaped ponds, representing the oceans, ring the *prang* and are themselves surrounded by whimsical five-headed *naga*. Muang Tam is the only Khmer temple with this particular arrangement.

Begin your visit across the road in the small **information centre** (☉6am-6pm) FREE, next to **Barai Muang Tam** (a 510m-by-1090m reservoir dug by the Khmer), which has good displays about the site. The village has a **homestay** (☏08 9070 8889; per person with 3 meals 500B) program, but for independent travellers the private **Tanyaporn Guesthouse** (☏08 7431 3741; r 350-500B; P🐕❄🛜), southwest of the ruins, is an easier option.

Motorcycle-taxi drivers will add Muang Tam onto a trip to Phanom Rung for another 150B.

Other Khmer Ruins

For those with an insatiable appetite for Khmer ruins, the area around Phanom Rung offers a smorgasbord of lesser-known sites that, taken together, create a picture of the crucial role this region once played in the Khmer empire. Most people find these places of only minor interest, but driving through this rice-growing region offers an unvarnished look at village life and will surely make for an enlightening trip. All of the following sites, restored to some degree by the Fine Arts Department, are free of charge and open during daylight hours.

Kuti Reusi Nong Bua Rai sits right below Phanom Rung, and the similar but more atmospheric **Kuti Reusi Khok Meuang** is just northwest of Prasat Muang Tam.

Little of **Prasat Khao Plaibat** is left standing. But the adventure of finding it, along with cool views of both Phanom Rung and the Dangrek Mountains on the Cambodian border, makes it worth seeking out. The seldom-used trail starts at Wat Khao Plaibat, 3km from Prasat Muang Tam. Pass the gate next to the giant Buddha image, veer right at the *gù·dì* (monks' quarters) and slip through the barbed-wire fence. From here take the path to the right, and then a quick left up the hill and follow the strips of orange cloth tied to trees. The walk up the hill should take less than 30 minutes if you don't get lost along the way, though it's likely you will. If you ask a monk he might lead you there.

Prasat Khok Ngio, 3km before Pakham, has a small museum with old pots and Buddha images unearthed around the temple.

Prasat Thong (aka Khok Prasat) near the market in Ban Kruat town, has recently been restored with new brick walls and is now worth a stop if you're passing through.

The sandstone used to build these ancient structures came from the widely scattered **Lan Hin Dtat Ban Kruat** (Ban Kruat Quarry), which is best seen at Wat Lan Hin Dtat, southwest of Ban Kruat town. One cutting site is near the parking lot: take the trail to the right after the Buddha statue and look to your left as you walk up the steps.

Also near Ban Kruat are **Tao Nai Chian** and the larger **Tao Sawai**, two kilns that supplied pottery to much of the Khmer empire between the 9th and 13th centuries. Today they're little more than piles of dirt and brick with roofs over them.

You can easily add Surin Province's Prasat Ta Meuan (p430) to your trip around this region. It's 55km from Phanom Rung.

Wat Khao Angkhan   วัดเขาอังคาร

Although this peaceful **temple** (วัดเขาอังคาร; ☺dawn-dusk; FREE) atop an extinct volcano has an ancient past, as evidenced by the 8th- or 9th-century Dvaravati sandstone boundary markers, it's the modern constructions that make Wat Khao Angkhan worth a visit. The flamboyant *bòht* was erected in 1982 in an unusual nouveau-Khmer style that sort of hearkens back to the age of empire. The *wát* also hosts a Chinese-style pagoda, a 29m reclining Buddha and beautiful views of the surrounding forest. If you're up for a little adventure, a trail lets you walk or mountain bike down the hill to Ban Khwao village. Though there's a map posted at the temple and signs along the way, it would be best to seek advice from P California in Nang Rong.

The temple is about 20km from either Nang Rong or Phanom Rung, with both roads horribly potholed, and there's no public transport. The route is pretty well signposted, but if you're driving you'll have to ask directions at some junctions. A motorcycle taxi should cost 200B from Ban Ta Pek and 300B from Nang Rong.

SURIN & SI SAKET PROVINCES

Surin and Si Saket provinces are full of Angkor-era Khmer ruins. Most are rather modest and of interest only to those with a history habit. On the other hand, the artwork at Sikhoraphum is outstanding and Prasat Ta Meuan, out in the jungle, is very evocative. The region's Khmer influence comes not only from the past, but also the present. Over one-third of the population of these two closely related provinces is ethnically Khmer and this remains the principal language in many villages.

Besides the temples, Surin Province is home to Ban Ta Klang elephant village and some famous craft centres, while Si Saket is home to one of Thailand's most unusual temples. The capital cities are far less interesting than the countryside, although Surin makes a comfortable enough base.

Surin   สุรินทร์

POP 40,169

Surin city doesn't have much to say for itself until November, when the provincial capital explodes into life for the Surin Elephant Round-up and the city hosts giant scrums of pachyderm. You've surely never seen so many well-dressed tuskers!

◉ Sights & Activities

Surin National Museum   MUSEUM
(พิพิธภัณฑสถานแห่งชาติสุรินทร์; ☑0 4451 3358; Th Surin-Prasat; ☺9am-4pm Wed-Sun) FREE Displays at this well-executed museum focus on the province's Khmer ruins and Surin's three ethnic groups: Lao, Khmer and Suai, the region's renowned elephant herders. It's 4km south of town on Rte 214; catch pink *sŏrng·tǎa·ou* 1 (10B) in front of the bus station or the clock tower by the fresh market (*dà·làht sòt*).

Queen Sirikit Sericulture
Center   CRAFT WORKSHOP
(ศูนย์หม่อนไหมเฉลิมพระเกียรติสมเด็จพระนางเจ้า สิริกิติ์ พระบรมราชินีนาถ (สุรินทร์); ☑0 4451 1393; Rte 226; ☺8am-4.30pm) FREE The easiest place to see the entire silk-making process, from larva to loom, is at this research centre 4km west of town. Various displays can be seen any time, but the silk makers only work on weekdays.

San Lak Meuang

MONUMENT

(ศาลหลักเมือง; Th Lak Meuang) Surin's gorgeous city pillar shrine, just west of Th Thansarn, is a Khmer-style *prang* with copies of Pha-nom Rung's famous Narai Bandhomsindhu lintel above the doors.

LemonGrass

VOLUNTEERING

(📋 08 1977 5300; www.lemongrass-volunteering. com) A well-run Surin-based outfit places native English-speakers in local primary schools where they work alongside the regular teachers.

🎉 Festivals

Surin Elephant Round-up

CULTURAL

Surin celebrates its famous festival for 11 days, but the massive crowds come on just the last weekend for the main event, which features 300 elephants showing their skills and taking part in battle reenactments. Arguably the festival's best event is the elephant buffet on the Friday before the big show. Tickets for the battle reenactment start at 40B, but VIP seats, which get you closest to the action, guaranteed shade and (sometimes) English commentary, cost 500B and 1000B.

👉 Tours

Saren Travel

(📋 0 4452 0174; 202/1-4 Th The-saban 2; ⊗ 8.30am-5pm Mon-Sat) and, more expensively, Pirom-Aree's House offer tours in and around Surin Province.

🛏 Sleeping

Prices skyrocket during the Elephant Round-up and hotels fill up fast, so book as far in advance as possible.

★ Baan Chang Ton

HOMESTAY $

(📋 08 7459 8962; www.baanchangton.com; Th Suri-yarart; r 400-500B; 🅿 ➆ ✳ @ 🛜) The friendly owners have rescued an old wooden house and created one of Isan's most charming places to stay. It's quite simple (shared bathrooms, mattresses on the floor, and air-conditioning in only one room) but the atmosphere makes it special. Guests can use the kitchen or, if arranged in advance, join the family for dinner. Bring your own towel. It's on a mostly quiet side street south of *săh·lah glahng* (provincial hall).

Maneerote Hotel

HOTEL $

(📋 0 4453 9477; www.maneerotehotel.com; Soi Poi Tunggor, Th Krungsri Nai; r 400-450B; 🅿 ✳ @ 🛜) This quiet hotel southwest of the fresh market scores off the charts in the high-quality-to-low-price ratio, though it's a little out of the way.

Pirom-Aree's House

GUESTHOUSE $

(📋 0 4451 5140; Soi Arunee; s/d 120/200B; 🅿 ➆ 🛜) The location for this long-time budget favourite, 1km west of the city on the other side of the tracks, is inconvenient but peaceful. Simple wooden rooms with shared bathrooms, and a shady garden overlooking a rice paddy. Aree cooks some pretty good food and Pirom is one of the best sources

---

GETTING TO CAMBODIA: SURIN & SI SAKET

Chong Chom to O Smach

Getting To The Border Because of the Cambodian casinos, there are plenty of mini-buses (60B, 1½ hours, frequent) from Surin's bus terminal to the Cambodian border at Chong Chom.

At The Border The border is open 7am to 8pm and Cambodian visas are available on the spot. Don't let anyone assist you getting the visa as this will just cost you extra money for what you can easily do on your own at the counter.

Moving On Taxi agents wait on the Thai side of the border, but it's cheaper to deal directly with the actual drivers who congregate near the visa office in Cambodia. You still have to bargain, though, as no prices are fixed. One seat for the two-hour ride will cost anywhere from 350B to 500B. You can also charter the whole car for 1500B to 1800B, which after around 9pm, when few people travel, might be your only option.

Chong Sa-Ngam to Choam

This border crossing in Sri Saket province sees very little traffic – despite the road to Siem Reap being in excellent shape – because it can't be done by public transport. Visas are available on arrival.

of information in the region. A túk-túk from the train/bus station costs 60/70B.

Sang Thong Hotel
HOTEL $

(⊘0 4451 2099; Th Tanasan; s 100-350B, d 100-500B; P❀❀🛜) Though it's just an ordinary ageing cheapie, this hotel (aka Siri Surin) is run with jet-engine precision by an army of attentive staff. Wi-fi reaches some rooms. It's a short walk south of the train station, just past the fountain.

Surin Majestic Hotel
HOTEL $$

(⊘0 4471 3980; www.surinmajestic.com; Th Jitrbumrung; r incl breakfast 1200-1400B, ste 2200-4500B; P⊖❀@🛜🛋) The rooms here are nothing special, but they can fetch these high prices because they're the best in town and there are also plenty of extras, including a swimming pool and fitness room. It's next to the bus station in the heart of town.

✖ Eating & Drinking

Surin's surprisingly exuberant nightlife mostly revolves around the Thong Tarin Hotel east of the bus station.

Tang Lak
THAI $

(Th Sirirat; dishes 49-300B; ⊙11am-11pm; 🛜) This cute little place, popular with both Thai and fa·ràng, mixes fake wood and real antiques to create an old-time feel. But it's not all about the style; the food is delicious. It's north of the Thong Tarin Hotel at the end of the road.

Petmanee 2
NORTHEASTERN THAI $

(Th Murasart; dishes 20-80B; ⊙9am-3pm) This simple spot south of Ruampaet Hospital by Wat Salaloi (look for the large chicken grill) is Surin's most famous purveyor of sôm·đam and gài yâhng. The súp nòr mái (bamboo-shoot salad) is good too. There's little English, spoken or written, but the food is so good it's worth stumbling through an order.

Night Market
NORTHEASTERN THAI $

(Th Krungsri Nai; ⊙5-10pm) A block south of the fountain, this good night market whips up a wide selection of Thai and Isan dishes.

Kit Teung
COFFEESHOP, BAKERY $

(Th Sanit Nikomrut; espresso 40B; ⊙7.30am-8.30pm; P🛜) This bright modern place just southeast of the train station has some of the best coffee in town, but it really sets itself apart with a fun selection of Thai baked goods.

Larn Chang
NORTHEASTERN THAI $

(Th Siphathai Saman; dishes 35-280B; ⊙10am-midnight; 🛜) Tasty and low-priced Thai and Isan food is served in and around an old wooden house that overlooks a surviving stretch of the city moat called Sŭan Rák (Love Park). The food and the setting are lovely, especially at sunset. It's a longish walk south of the centre, on the east side of the park.

Surin Chai Kit
THAI $

(297 Th Tanasan; dishes 25-55B; ⊙7am-2pm Mon-Sat) This no-frills spot whips up tasty pan-egg breakfasts and stir-fried lunches. The owners wear welcoming permagrins and give fa·ràng customers a handy city map. It's just to the right of the Sang Thong Hotel.

Sydney Steak
INTERNATIONAL, THAI $$

(Th Lak Meuang; dishes 50-1100B; ⊙11am-10pm; 🛜) By far our favourite choice for fa·ràng food is this Thai-owned spot west of the city pillar shrine, not far from Maneerote Hotel. The Australian-trained chef does a variety of dishes including chicken lasagna and duck breast fillet with orange sauce, plus some Thai and Japanese, too.

ⓘ Information

Banks in the Surin Plaza Mall are open evenings and weekends and there's an AEON ATM outside the back entrance of Petchkasem Plaza. They are both located on Th Thesaban 1, two

BUSES FROM SURIN

DESTINATION	FARE (B)	DURATION (HR)	FREQUENCY
Aranya Prathet	234	6	5 daily
Khon Kaen	182	4	hourly
Khorat	125-175	4	every 30min
Roi Et	104	2½	hourly
Ubon Ratchathani	105-200	3	every 2hr

blocks west and one block east of the fountain respectively.

Ruampaet Hospital (☏ 0 4451 3192; Th Thesaban 1)

Tourism Authority of Thailand (TAT; ☏ 0 4451 4447; tatsurin@tat.or.th; Th Thesaban 1; ⏲ 8.30am-4.30pm) Across from Ruampaet Hospital.

ℹ️ Getting There & Away

BUS

Frequent buses from Surin's **bus terminal** (☏ 0 4451 1756; Th Jitrbumrung) head to/from Bangkok (272B to 543B, seven hours), though the best service is **Nakhonchai Air** (☏ 0 4451 5151) which has VIP buses (407B, nine daily) from their own terminal 1km north of the train station; though if coming from Bangkok, you can get off at the main bus terminal.

TRAIN

Surin Railway Station (☏ 0 4451 1295) is on the line between Bangkok (73B to 1146B, seven to nine hours, nine daily) and Ubon Ratchathani (31B to 382B, two to four hours, 10 daily).

ℹ️ Getting Around

Surin is very convenient for travellers; virtually everything you'll want or need is within a few blocks of the bus and train stations. If you don't want to walk, túk-túk charge 40B to 50B for a trip within the centre. Surin also still has many cheaper pedicabs.

Saren Travel and Surin Chai Kit restaurant hire cars, and some of the fa·ràng bars on the soi behind the bus station hire motorcycles.

Around Surin

Ban Ta Klang   บ้านตากลาง

To see Surin's elephants outside festival time, visit the **Elephant Study Centre** (☏ 0 4414 5050; admission 100B; ⏲ 8.30am-4pm) in the Suai village of Ban Ta Klang where people and pachyderms live side by side. The main attraction is the half-hour **talent show** (⏲ 10am & 2pm) with painting and basketball among the many tusker tricks. There's also a little **museum**, **elephant rides** (per 20min 200B) and a **cobra show** (ticket 20B). During Visakha Bucha day (usually in May) all Suai villages in the area host **Elephant Parades**, with brightly painted pachyderms carrying the men who will enter the monkhood.

If you'd like to spend some quality time with elephants, sign up for activities with the excellent **Surin Project** (☏ 08 4482 1210; www.surinproject.org), which works to improve elephants' living conditions by, among other things, letting the elephants roam inside large enclosures so they don't need to be chained. You'll work side by side with the mahouts caring for the elephants, cutting food, doing construction, and more. Activities, available Monday to Saturday, include walking with the elephants for an hour when they go to bathe in the river (400B per person), one day of volunteering (2000B including meals), and one week of volunteering (13,000B including lodging and meals). While it's best to book ahead, if space and staff are available you can sometimes just show up and join in. The information centre is near the showgrounds. They also offer a **homestay** (per person 200B, meals 50-100B) program.

Sŏrng·tăa·ou run from Surin's bus terminal (60B, 1½ hours, hourly) with the last one returning at 4pm. If you're driving, take Rte 214 north for 40km and follow the elephant signs down Rte 3027 for 22km more.

Craft Villages

There are many craft villages in easy striking distance of Surin town and many of the products, including *pâh hohl* fabric (a geometric pattern that bears a slight resemblence to *mát·mèe*, but isn't tye died) have a Cambodian influence. Surin silks, which often use natural dyes, aren't readily available in other parts of Thailand and prices are much cheaper here.

The most famous weaving centre is Ban Tha Sawang.

Ban Khwao Sinarin and **Ban Chok**, nextdoor neighbours 18km north of Surin via Rte 214 and Rte 3036, are known for silk (now mostly synthetic) and silver. One of the weaving specialities is *yók dòrk*, a simpler brocade style than what's made in Ban Tha Sawang, but it still requires up to 50 foot pedals on the looms. The silver standout is *brà keuam,* a Cambodian style of bead brought to Thailand by Ban Chok's ancestors many centuries ago. You can see it, and other jewellery, being made in the **OTOP handicrafts mall** (Th Jitrbumrung; ⏲ 8am-5.30pm Mon-Fri, 8am-5pm Sat) at the east end of the villages. Big blue *sŏrng·tăa·ou* to Ban Khwao Sinarin (25B, 30 minutes, hourly) park on an unnamed soi between the fountain and Surin Railway Station: look for the 'Osram' signs.

The residents of Ban Buthom (14km east of Surin on Rte 226 on the way to Sikhoraphum) weave sturdy, rattan baskets, including some flat ones that pack well.

Prasat Ta Meuan ปราสาททาเมือน

The most atmospheric of Surin's Khmer ruins is a series of three sites known collectively as Prasat Ta Meuan (☉dawn-dusk) FREE in the forest on the Cambodian border. They line the ancient route linking Angkor Wat to Phimai and this is where the road crossed the Dongrek Mountains.

The first site, Prasat Ta Meuan proper, was built in the Jayavarman VII period (AD 1181–1210) as a rest stop for pilgrims. It's a fairly small monument with a two-door, five-window sanctuary constructed completely of laterite blocks; one sandstone lintel, of a meditating Buddha, remains.

Just 300m south, Prasat Ta Meuan Toht, which was the chapel for a 'healing station', is a bit larger. Also built by Jayavarman VII, the ruins consist of a gopura, mon·dòp and main prang, all surrounded by a laterite wall.

Nearly 1km further on, next to the army base at the end of the road, is the largest site, Prasat Ta Meuan Thom. This Shiva shrine, built around a natural rock linga, pre-dates the others by as much as two centuries. Despite a somewhat haphazard reconstruction (and major damage from the years in the 1980s when it was occupied by the Khmer Rouge), this one justifies the effort it takes to get here. Three prang and a large hall are built of sandstone blocks on a laterite base and several smaller buildings still stand inside the boundary wall. No significant carvings remain. A stairway on the southern end (like Phimai, this temple faces south) drops

to Cambodian territory, which begins at the tree line.

The sites begin 10.3km south of Ban Ta Miang (on Rte 224, 23km east of Ban Kruat) via a winding road used more by cows than cars. You need your own transport to get here and a visit is just as convenient from Phanom Rung as from Surin town.

Other Khmer Temple Ruins

The 11th-century Prasat Ban Phluang (admission 50B; ☉7am-6pm), 33km south of Surin, is just a solitary sandstone prang without its top, but the wonderful carvings (including Indra riding his elephant Airavata, Erawan in Thai, with just a single head rather than the usual three) make it worth a stop. The prang was probably never completed, but some speculate it may have had a wooden top. The site sits 600m off Rte 214; the turn-off is 2.5km south of Hwy 24. Any vehicle bound for Kap Choeng or the border can drop you nearby (30B, 30 minutes).

Prasat Sikhoraphum (admission 50B; ☉7.30am-6pm) is a larger and more rewarding Khmer site 30km northeast of Surin. Built in the 12th century, Sikhoraphum features five brick prang, two of which still hold their tops, including the 32m-tall central one. Only one lintel remains, but it's a stunner. Featuring a dancing 10-armed Shiva, it's in excellent condition and one of the most beautiful pieces of Khmer art ever carved. Below it are the only two apsara (celestial dancers) carvings in Thailand. There's a sound-and-light show here during the Elephant Round-up. Sikhoraphum can be reached by minivan (30B, one hour, hourly) or train (7B to 50B, 30 minutes, frequent) from Surin town.

WORTH A TRIP

BAN THA SAWANG

Chansoma (☉8am-5pm) has made Ban Tha Sawang one of the most renowned silk villages in Thailand. Its exquisite brocade fabrics (pâh yók torng) incorporate threads made of real gold and silver, but the weaving process is even more impressive than the finished cloth. Four women, including one sitting a floor below the others, work the loom simultaneously and collectively manage over 1000 heddles. Not surprisingly, they produce just a few centimetres per day. Many of the finished products are destined for the royal court, but you can custom order your own at an average price of 30,000B per metre. Other shops around Chansoma sell typical silks to a steady stream of Thai visitors. The village is 8km west of Surin via Rte 4026. Sŏrng·tăa·ou (15B, 20 minutes) run regularly from the north side of Surin's fresh market (don't wait for a return vehicle in the village, walk out to the main road), and a túk-túk should cost about 200B.

If you happen to be driving to Sikho-raphum, you may as well take a 400m detour off Rte 226 for a peep at **Prasat Muang Thi** (🕐dawn-dusk) FREE. The three remaining brick *prang* are in sad shape (one looks like it's ready to topple), but they're so small they're kind of cute.

Si Saket

Officially it's Wat Pa Maha Chedi Kaeo, but these days nearly everyone calls it **Wat Lan Khuat** (🕐dawn-dusk; FREE), the 'Million Bottle Temple'. In 1982 the abbot dreamt of a *brah·sàht* in heaven made of diamonds and gems. Realising that this symbolised the need for clarity of purpose in one's life, he decided to replicate the idea as best he could on earth by covering nearly every surface of every building of his temple with glass bottles. The project would, he believed, have many benefits, including fostering cooperation within the community, encouraging younger people to come to the temple, and saving money on paint. The more you look around, the less the name seems like an exaggeration. He took the theme one step further by using bottle caps to create much of the adornment. It's in Khun Han, 11km south of Hwy 24 via Rte 2111. Turn west at the roundabout in the centre of Si Saket town.

Thirty kilometres west of Si Saket town on Rte 226, **Prasat Sa Kamphaeng Yai** (🕐dawn-dusk) FREE, built as a shrine to Shiva, features four 11th-century *prang* and two *wí·hǎhn*. The *prang,* including the main one, which was built of sandstone but restored with brick, have lost their tops, but several lintels and other Baphuon-style carvings remain. Behind the modern temple buildings are some amusing statues depicting what punishments may await people in the Buddhist version of Hell as a result of various misdeeds in this life. Hit your parents, for example, and you'll have enormous hands. Buses from Surin (55B, 1½ hours) can drop you there.

UBON RATCHATHANI PROVINCE

Though it hosts relatively few visitors, Thai or foreign, Ubon Ratchathani is one of the Thailand's most interesting provinces. The capital city has plenty of history and charm, and rustic rovers will really enjoy themselves here. The scenery along the Mekong River is often as bizarre as it is gorgeous and Pha Taem National Park has so much to see that it warrants a couple of days. Even more remote is the jungle-clad intersection of Thailand, Laos and Cambodia, now known as the 'Emerald Triangle' (inspired by northern Thailand's 'Golden Triangle') due to the magnificent jungle landscape of Phu Chong Nayoi National Park.

Ubon Ratchathani อุบลราชธานี

POP 83,173

Few cities in Thailand reward aimless wandering as richly as Ubon. Survive the usual knot of choked access roads, and the 'Royal City of the Lotus' will reveal an altogether more attractive face. Racked up against Mae Nam Mun, Thailand's second-longest river, the historic heart of the city, south of Th Kueuan Thani, has a sluggish character rarely found in the region's big conurbations. And throughout the city there are many interesting temples that even people suffering acute temple overload will enjoy.

Ubon grew prosperous as a US air base during the Vietnam War and is now a financial, educational and agricultural market centre. It's not a busy tourist destination, though the nearby Thai–Lao border crossing at Chong Mek generates a small but steady stream of travellers who, by and large, enjoy their stay here.

◎ Sights & Activities

⭐**Wat Thung Si Meuang**　　BUDDHIST TEMPLE
(วัดทุ่งศรีเมือง; Th Luang; 🕐dawn-dusk) FREE Wat Thung Si Meuang was built during the reign of Rama III (1824–51) and has a classic *hŏr drai* (Tripitaka hall) in excellent shape. Like many *hŏr drai,* it rests on tall, angled stilts in the middle of a pond to protect the precious scriptures (written on palm-leaf paper) from termites. It's kept open so you can look inside. The original murals in the little *bòht* beside the *hŏr drai* show life in Rama III's era and are in remarkably good condition.

Ubon Ratchathani National Museum　　MUSEUM
(พิพิธภัณฑสถานแห่งชาติอุบลราชธานี; Th Kheuan Thani; admission 100B; 🕐9am-4pm Wed-Sun) Occupying the former city hall, this is a very informative museum with plenty on show, from Dvaravati-era Buddhist

ordination-precinct stones and a 2500-year-old Dong Son bronze drum to Ubon textiles. The museum's most prized possession is a 9th-century Ardhanarisvara, a composite statue combining Shiva and his consort Uma into one being; one of just two ever found in Thailand.

Wat Si Ubon Rattanaram
BUDDHIST TEMPLE

(วัดศรีอุบลรัตนาราม; Th Uparat; ☺dawn-dusk) FREE The **bòht** (☺8am-4pm) at this important temple resembles Bangkok's Wat Benchamabophit, but it's the 7cm-tall topaz Buddha inside that most Thais come to see. Phra Kaew Butsarakham, as it's known, was reportedly brought here from Vientiane at Ubon's founding and is one of the city's holiest possessions. It sits behind glass high up the back wall, all but out of sight. The image directly in front of the largest Buddha is a copy and actual-sized replicas are for sale.

The temple has turned a beautiful old wooden *săh·lah* into a **museum** (☺9am-4pm Wed-Sun) FREE of religious items. The highlight is the collection of 18th-century *doô prá đrai'bìdòk*, gorgeous boxes used for storing sacred palm-leaf texts.

Wat Ban Na Meuang
BUDDHIST TEMPLE

(วัดบ้านนาเมือง; ☺dawn-dusk) FREE Wat Sa Prasan Suk, as it's also known, stands out from other temples in many ways. Most famously, the *bòht* sits on a boat: a ceramic-encrusted replica of King Rama IX's royal barge *Suphannahong,* complete with crew. The *wí·hăhn* also has a boat-shaped base, this one resembling the second-most important royal barge, *Anantanagaraj;* and it's surrounded by an actual pond. These were not just artistic endeavours: the water represents our desires and the boats represent staying above them.

The commissioner of these creations, Luang Pu Boon Mi, died in 2001 and his body is on display (they're waiting to finish building a museum before cremating him) in the *săh·lah* next to the boat *bòht.*

Finally, to reach all of these you pass under an immense statue of Airavata (Erawan in Thai), Hindu god Indra's three-headed elephant mount. The temple is north of the airport. *Sŏrng·tăa·ou* 8 passes it, but you need to tell the driver you're going here or he won't make the turn down the little road.

Wat Phra That Nong Bua
BUDDHIST TEMPLE

(วัดพระธาตุหนองบัว; Th Thammawithi; ☺dawn-dusk) FREE The gleaming gold and white *chedi* at this temple loosely resembles the Mahabodhi stupa in Bodhgaya, India, and inside is another beautiful golden *chedi* (open 8am to 6pm). The latter was built in 1956 to honor of 2500 years of Buddhism, and the 55m exterior went up over it 12 years later. It's the only square stupa in Ubon Province unless you count the four similar but smaller ones at the corners. The adjacent *wihan* vaguely resembles the Mahaparinirvana temple in Kushinagar, India, where the Buddha died. It's on the outskirts of town; to get there, take *sŏrng·tăa·ou* 10.

Ubon Ratchathani Art & Culture Centre
MUSEUM

(ศูนย์ศิลปวัฒนธรรมกาญจนาภิเษกฯ; Th Jaeng Sanit; ☺8.30am-4.30pm Mon-Sat) FREE The museum in the lower level of this striking contemporary Isan-design tower at Rajabhat University is more scattershot than the National Museum, but there are some interesting cultural displays, particularly of houses and handicrafts. There's also a lot of wax sculpture.

Wat Jaeng
BUDDHIST TEMPLE

(วัดแจ้ง; Th Nakhonban; ☺dawn-dusk) Founded around the same time as the city, Wat Jaeng has an adorable Lan Xang–style *bòht* (built in 1887) with large *naga*-eave brackets on the sides, crocodiles along the stairs and Airavata with two mythical lions atop the carved wooden facade. A travelling market fills up the wàt grounds every Wednesday.

Thung Si Meuang
PARK

(ทุ่งศรีเมือง) The highlight of this city-centre park is a huge concrete **Candle Parade statue** of a float. The humble brick obelisk in the northeast corner is the **Monument of Merit**, erected by former allied forces POWs (brought here for forced labour by the Japanese, who occupied Thailand during WWII) in gratitude for the secret assistance they received from ordinary Thai citizens while in the prison camps. The **City Pillar Shrine** (San Lak Meuang) is to the south.

Wat Tai
BUDDHIST TEMPLE

(วัดใต้; Th Kheuan Thani; ☺dawn-dusk) FREE The myriad sculptures covering the grounds of Wat Tai comprise a fairly complete who's who of Thai deities and make it a fun place to visit.

Wat Supatanaram
BUDDHIST TEMPLE

(วัดสุปัฏนาราม; Th Supat; ☺dawn-dusk) FREE Called Wat Supat for short, the unique *bòht* at this riverside temple, built between 1920 and 1936, features a Thai roof, European

Ubon Ratchathani

Ubon Ratchathani

◎ Top Sights

1 Wat Thung Si Meuang	B3

◎ Sights

2 Candle Parade statue	A3
3 City Pillar Shrine	C3
4 Monument of Merit	B2
Thung Si Meuang	(see 2)
5 Ubon Ratchathani National Museum	C4
6 Wat Jaeng	B1
7 Wat Si Ubon Rattanaram	A3
8 Wat Supatanaram	A4
9 Wat Tai	C3

⊨ Sleeping

10 New Nakornluang Hotel	D4
11 Phadaeng Mansion	B2
12 Ratchathani	D4
13 Sri Isan Hotel	B4
14 T3 House	B2

⊗ Eating

15 Boon Niyon Uthayan	C3
16 Chiokee	D4
17 Gway-tiao Gai Boran	C4
18 Jumpa-Hom	D2
19 Krua Ruen Pae	B4
20 Moon Lover	B4
21 Night Market	D4
22 Peppers Bakery & Cafe	A1
23 Porntip Gai Yang Wat Jaeng	B1
24 Risotto	C2
25 Rung Roj	B1

⊝ Drinking & Nightlife

26 Saduak Duem	B2
27 U-Bar	C2

⊜ Shopping

Ban Khampun	(see 11)
28 Camp Fai Ubon	C2
29 Grass-Root	D4
30 Maybe	C3
31 Punchard	D4
32 Punchard	A2
33 Rawang Thang	D4
34 Walking Street Market	D4

KHAO PHRA WIHAN NATIONAL PARK

อุทยานแห่งชาติเขาพระวิหาร

The main attraction of this 130-sq-km **national park** (☏ 0 4581 8021; admission 100B) is **Khao Phra Wihan** ('Preah Vihear' in Khmer), one of the region's great Angkor-period monuments. Though this Khmer ruin sits just inside Cambodia, it's normally easiest to reach via Thailand. Hugging the edge of a cliff on the brow of the Dangrek escarpment and accessed via a series of steep stepped *naga* approaches, the large temple complex, which the Cambodian government chooses not to restore, towers 500m above the plains below offering both evocative ruins and stunning views.

Claimed by both countries because of a misdrawn French map (which went unchallenged by Thailand for decades), the temple was awarded to Cambodia in a 1962 World Court ruling. Thailand's bruised pride never healed. In June 2008, as the Cambodian government sought Unesco World Heritage status for the complex, a border conflict over 4.6 sq km of land in front of the temple flared and has since led to several deadly clashes between the nations' armies and become a cause célèbre of Thailand's ultra-nationalist 'yellow-shirts'. The situation remains unresolved and Thailand has shut its land border that lies within the park; for the time being, the temple itself can no longer be reached via Thailand.

Renewed access to the Khmer ruin is likely years away (previously the Cambodians charged 200B and the Thais collected another 5B) though the small core section of the national park – full of razor wire, bomb shelters and soldiers – above **Pha Mo-E-Daeng** cliff has reopened. There are some fabulous views of Cambodia below and you can also see Khao Phra Wihan in the distance. Also here, accessible by a short stairway, is the oldest bas-relief in Thailand. The 1000-plus-year-old carving depicts three figures whose identities are an enigma to archaeologists and art historians.

Landmines have been laid during the present conflict and others may remain from the Khmer Rouge era, so it's important not to stray from any well-worn path.

You'll need your own wheels to visit as there's no public transport here and hitching is not advised (and also not easy) due to the political situation. The nearest town is little Phum Saron; if you ask around you can probably find someone to drive you on the 22km roundtrip for 250B on a motorcycle and twice this in a truck. Most visitors include it as a stop on a day-long tour, in which case Ubon Ratchathani is the most convenient departure point to hire a car and driver.

---

arches, a Khmer base and also some Chinese design elements. And, in contrast to other temple structures of the region, it's made entirely of stone. In front is a wooden bell that the monks say is the largest in Thailand, though we're certain we've seen bigger.

🎆 Festivals & Events

Ubon's famous **Candle Parade** (Kabuan Hae Tian) began during the reign of King Rama V when the appointed governor decided the rocket festival was too dangerous. The original simple designs have since grown (with the help of internal frames) to gigantic elaborately carved wax sculptures. The parade is part of **Khao Phansaa**, which usually happens in July.

Prize-winning candles go on display along Th Srinarong next to Thung Si Meuang for three days after the parade and most of them will be parked at the city's temples

for several months after. Construction, also done on temple grounds, begins about a month before the parade. The festival is very popular with Thai tourists and the city's hotels are booked out long in advance.

Ubon also has Lái Reua Fai (p477) during **Ork Phansaa**, but it's a much smaller affair than that in Nakhon Phanom.

🛏 Sleeping

★ **Sri Isan Hotel**   HOTEL $

(☏ 0 4526 1011; www.sriisanhotel.com; Th Ratchabut; r incl breakfast 450-800B; P ⊖ ✿ @ ☏) The exception to the rule of Isan's typically uninspired budget hotels, the bright, cheerful lobby of this hotel is full of natural light streaming down through the atrium. The rooms are small, and rather ordinary compared to the lobby (look at several before deciding), and the air-conditioning takes a while to cool them down, but Sri Isan has a great location for exploration and overall it's good for the price.

Phadaeng Mansion HOTEL $
(☎0 4525 4600; www.thephadaeng.com; Th Phadaeng; r 500B; P ⊖ ❄ @ 🛜) One of the best values in Ubon, the Phadaeng has well-maintained rooms with good furnishings (including large TVs) just minutes from Thung Si Meuang park. The hotel is filled with copies of classic paintings, a very nice touch that livens it up. Bike hire costs 50B per day.

Ratchathani HOTEL $
(☎0 4524 4388; www.theratchathani.com; Th Kheuan Thani; r 400-700; P ⊖ ❄ 🛜) The Ratchathani is an old hotel that has had some style slapped onto it (except in the bland standard rooms) and though the rooms aren't as attractive as the lobby and restaurant, overall they're quite good. It's got a great location in the thick of the action, though this makes it a bit noisy, especially for rooms in the front.

New Nakornluang Hotel HOTEL $
(☎0 4525 4768; Th Yutthaphan; r 170-350B; ❄) This place is so past its prime the name is now ironic, but, if you want to spend as little as possible and still be in the city centre, the cheap fan rooms are clean enough.

★ **Outside Inn** GUESTHOUSE $$
(☎08 8581 2069; www.theoutsideinnubon.com; Th Suriyat; r incl breakfast 450-790B; P ⊖ ❄ 🛜) A nice little garden lounge area sets the relaxed, communal vibe at this new hotel. The rooms are large and comfy, though the 450B rate only gets you ceiling fans instead of air-con, and noise from outside the rooms drift in easily. The Thai-American owners are great hosts and cook some good food, both Thai and Mexican. It's a long walk to the town's main attractions, but bikes (50B per day) and motorcycles (250B to 300B per day) can be hired and *sŏrng·tăa·ou* 10 can deliver you from the bus station.

T3 House HOTEL $$
(☎0 4524 4911; Th Saphasit; r 600-700B; P ⊖ ❄ 🛜) This new hotel isn't exactly beautiful, but it doesn't follow the cookie-cutter design you expect in Thailand, and the rooms have plenty of nice little touches: the owners particularly proud of the 'rain shower'. Solid all around except for one glaring design flaw to note...watch your head going up the stairs.

Tohsang Hotel HOTEL $$
(☎0 4524 5531; www.tohsang.com; Th Palochai; r incl breakfast 1200-1800B, ste 4000B; P ⊖ ❄ @ 🛜) The tasteful decor here almost manages to hide Tohsang's age. The lobby

WARIN CHAMRAP TEMPLES

The famous monk and meditation master Luang Pu Chah Subhaddo, a former disciple of Luang Pu Man, known for his simple and direct teaching method, was born in this area. During his exemplary life, Ajahn Chah, as he's best known, founded the following two famous forest monasteries and hundreds more around the world.

Peaceful **Wat Nong Pa Phong** (⊙dawn-dusk), his home for most of his monastic life, is known for its quiet discipline and daily routine of work and meditation, and some Thai-speaking Westerners live here. Spread around the huge and healthy forest are the golden *chedi* where his relics are interred; an interesting modern, open-sided *bòht*; and a three-storey **museum** (⊙8am-4.30pm) FREE displaying an odd assortment of items, from his worldly possessions to sea shells to ancient artefacts to world currencies. The temple is about 10km past the river. *Sŏrng·tăa·ou* 3 will take you there, if you tell the the driver where you're going.

A Western-oriented wát opened in 1975 specifically for non-Thais; English is the primary language at **Wat Pa Nanachat** (www.watpahnanachat.org; ⊙dawn-dusk) FREE. There's nothing really to see here, but visitors, if they dress and act respectfully, are welcome to drop by and chat with a senior monk most days between 10am and noon and can join in other regular teaching activities. Those with previous meditation experience are welcome to apply to stay here (write to: Guest Monk, Wat Pa Nanachat, Ban Bung Wai, Amphoe Warin Chamrap, Ubon Ratchathani 34310). Guests must follow all temple rules including eating just one meal a day and rising at 3am, and after three days men must shave their heads. A *sŏrng·tăa·ou* from Warin Market or any Si Saket bus can drop you on Rte 226, 400m from the entrance. The wát is in the forest behind the rice fields.

is downright elegant while the rooms are as comfortable as they should be at these prices. They'll pick you up for free when you arrive.

Sunee Grand Hotel HOTEL $$$
(☑0 4535 2900; www.suneegrandhotel.com; Th Chayangkun; r incl breakfast 1800-3000B, ste 4250-12,500B; P❄✳@❤☀) The Sunee Grand is Ubon's best, and far less expensive than anything similar outside Isan. From the stylish light fixtures to the at-a-snap service, it will meet expectations. There's a large business centre, and a piano player in the lobby, and the adjacent shopping mall has a kid-sized rooftop water park. They sometimes discount rooms down to 1100B.

✖ Eating

★ Rung Roj THAI $
(Th Nakhonban; dishes 45-280B; ⊙9.30am-8.30pm; ☀) What this Ubon institution lacks in service, it more than makes up for with excellent food using family recipes and only fresh ingredients: the meals look like they are straight out of a foodie magazine photo shoot. Many people swear by the ox-tongue stew. It's the restaurant with the bold plate, fork and spoon sign.

Night Market THAI, VIETNAMESE $
(Th Kheuan Thani; ⊙4-11pm) Though it's smaller than you'd expect, Ubon's city-centre night market makes an excellent dining destination; especially when paired with the weekend Walking Street Market. Vendors sell Thai, Isan and Vietnamese food.

Porntip Gai Yang
Wat Jaeng NORTHEASTERN THAI $
(Th Saphasit; dishes 20-130B; ⊙8am-8pm) It looks like a tornado has whipped through this no-frills spot, but the chefs cook up a storm of their own. This is considered by many to be Ubon's premier purveyor of *gài yâhng, sôm·đam*, sausages and other classic Isan foods.

Moon Lover COFFEESHOP $
(Th Rimmun; espresso 40B; ⊙9am-9pm Tue-Sun; P☀) While most coffeeshops in Thailand follow a design-by-the-numbers formula, this vivid place down by the river has actual style. Enjoy delicious coffees, teas, waffles and smoothies (we recommend the 'Good Morning Monkey': pineapple, banana, coconut and walnut) with a jazz soundtrack.

Outside Inn INTERNATIONAL, THAI $
(Th Suriyat; dishes 50-215B; ⊙11am-2.30pm & 5-9pm Wed-Mon; P❤☀) This hotel restaurant sets itself apart with good (by Thailand standards) Mexican meals, but the Thai food is delicious, too. The menu also features sandwiches and a full roster of cocktails.

Krua Ruen Pae THAI $
(dishes 40-300B; ⊙10am-11pm; P❤) One of several floating restaurants on the Mun River, Krua Ruen Pae serves up tasty Thai and Isan food and a relaxed atmosphere. The *đôm kàh gài* (chicken with galangal in coconut milk) is lovely. If you are driving here, exit to the west and then go under the bridge.

Gway-tiao Gai Boran THAI $
(Th Phrommarat; 30-50B; ⊙8.30am-3pm) Yes, the *gŏo·ay·đĕe·ăo* (noodle soup) here is delicious, but we love it most for it's old-time feel. It's part of the revival of the old city centre.

Chiokee THAI $
(307-317 Th Kheuan Thani; dishes 30-150B; ⊙6am-6pm) A steady stream of old-timers linger over congee, tea and newspapers at this classic spot to have breakfast. Although it's less popular during the rest of the day, the menu has all your Thai favourites.

Boon Niyon Uthayan VEGETARIAN $
(Th Srinarong; per plate 10-20B; ⊙6am-2pm Tue-Sun; ☑) 🍽 Run by Ratchathani Asoke, the local branch of a non-mainstream Buddhist sect preaching a curious mix of asceticism and right-wing politics, this restaurant has an impressive vegetarian buffet under a giant roof. Most of the food is grown organically just outside the city.

★ Jumpa-Hom THAI $$
(Th Phichitrangsan; dishes 65-325B; ⊙5pm-midnight; ☀) One of the loveliest and most delicious restaurants in Isan, Jumpa-Hom has a large menu featuring some less-common dishes. You can dine on a water-and-plant-filled wooden deck or in the air-con dining room, which offers a choice of tables and chairs or cushions for floor seating.

Risotto ITALIAN $$
(Th Phichitrangsan; dishes 100-350B; ⊙11am-10pm; ☀) The dining room can't quite pull off an Italian vibe, but the kitchen offers a dash of *la dolce vita*. The menu has a full roster of pasta, plus salmon steak and one of the best pizzas in Isan. They will, in the lifetime of

this book, likely move out to Th Chayangkun Soi 30, 5km northwest of their current location, on the way to the bus station.

Peppers Bakery & Cafe
INTERNATIONAL, BAKERY **$$**

(Th Upalisan; dishes 75-450B; ⊗8am-9pm; 🛜) Peppers, popular with both *fa·ràng* and Thai, features a broad international menu with everything from nachos to chicken Kiev to pub pies to *đôm yam gûng* and all-day breakfast. As far as we can tell it's all pretty good, while the bakery offerings, their real speciality, are downright delicious.

🍷 Drinking & Nightlife

U-Bar
NIGHTCLUB

(Th Phichitrangsan) While other clubs have come and gone over the years, U-Bar has long remained at the top of the heap for the college crowd, partly because the best bands from Bangkok often play here when they visit Ubon. If you go, try a Blue Kamikaze, served out of a sinister-looking slushy machine behind the bar.

Saduak Duem
BAR

(Th Saphasit) This is a small, fairly chill place with a pool table (20B per game) and very trendy Thai decor.

🛍 Shopping

Isan may be silk country, but Ubon is a cotton town and there are several good shops selling handwoven fabric, clothing, bags etc. **Camp Fai Ubon** (Th Thepyothi; ⊗8.30am-5pm), signed as Peaceland, has a good variety and some of their products are made with natural dyes. **Grass-Root** (Th Yutthaphan; ⊗10am-5pm) sells mostly unfinished fabric, almost all naturally dyed. **Maybe** (Th Si Narong; ⊗8am-7pm) has the biggest clothing selection, though none of it's naturally dyed.

★ Rawang Thang
HANDICRAFTS

(Th Kheuan Thani; ⊗8am-8pm Mon-Thu, 8am-9pm Fri-Sun) There's also Ubon cotton at this Isan-themed shop, which sells fun and funky T-shirts, pillows, postcards, picture frames and assorted bric-a-brac, most made and designed by the friendly husband-and-wife owners. They can fill you in on all things Ubon.

Ban Khampun
HANDICRAFTS

(Th Phadaeng; ⊗8am-6pm) Ubon's famous silk specialist makes some exquisite fabrics using many patterns and styles not found elsewhere. For two days before the Candle Festival, the owner hosts a mini cultural festival at his gorgeous home-workshop just outside town.

Walking Street Market
MARKET

(Th Ratchabut; ⊗6-11pm Fri-Sun) This fun, youthful market takes over Th Ratchabut on weekends.

Punchard
HANDICRAFTS

(Th Phadaeng; ⊗9am-7pm) Though pricey, this is the best all-round handicrafts shop in Ubon. Many of their products are a merging of old methods and designs in modern products. The smaller **Th Ratchabut branch** (Th Ratchabut; ⊗8am-7pm) across from the night market is mostly home decor.

ℹ Information

Ying Charoen Park, near Rajabhat University, has the extended-hours banks nearest to downtown. There are AEON ATMs at Tesco-Lotus and City Mall, both on the way to the bus station.

Tourism Authority of Thailand (TAT; ☑0 4524 3770; tatubon@tat.or.th; Th Kheuan Thani; ⊗8.30am-4.30pm) Has helpful staff.

Ubonrak Thonburi Hospital (☑0 4526 0285; Th Phalorangrit) Has a 24-hour casualty department.

ℹ Getting There & Away

AIR

Air Asia (☑0 2515 9999; www.airasia.com) and **Nok Air** (☑0 2900 9955; www.nokair.com) fly to Bangkok's Don Mueang airport two and five times daily respectively for about 1350B one way. **Thai Airways** (☑0 4531 3340; www.thaiairways.com) flies twice a day to Bangkok's Suvarnaphumi Airport for about 1000B more.

Many travel agencies, including **Sakda Travel World** (☑0 4525 4333; www.sakdatour.com; Th Phalorangrit; ⊗9am-6pm Mon-Sat), sell tickets.

BUS

Ubon's **bus terminal** (☑0 4531 6085) is north of town; take *sŏrng·tăa·ou* 2, 3 or 10 to the city centre. Several buses link Ubon with Bangkok: the top VIP service (804B) is offered by **999 VIP** (☑0 4531 4299), departing at 6.30pm, and **Nakhonchai Air** (☑0 4526 9777) at 10.15am, 9.45pm and 10.45pm.

BUSES FROM UBON RATCHATHANI

DESTINATION	FARE (B)	DURATION (HR)	FREQUENCY
Bangkok	420-603	8½-10	morning, evening & midday
Khon Kaen	180-277	4½	every 30min
Mukdahan	75-135	3½	every 30min
Nakhon Ratchasima	286-445	5-6	14 daily
Nang Rong	263	4½	hourly
Pakse (Laos)	200	3	9.30am & 3.30pm
Surin	105-200	3	every 2hr

TRAIN

Ubon's **railway station** (☑ 0 4532 1588) is in Warin Chamrap; take *sŏrng·tăa·ou* 2. There's an overnight express train to/from Bangkok (2nd-class sleeper upper/lower 641/691B, 1st-class sleeper upper/lower 1080/1280B, 11½ hours) at 6.30pm. The five other departures (95B to 581B) take from 8½ to 12 hours. All trains also stop in Si Saket, Surin and Khorat.

ⓘ Getting Around

Numbered *sŏrng·tăa·ou* (10B) run throughout town. TAT's free city map marks the routes, most of which pass near its office. A túk-túk trip within the centre should cost from 30B to 50B. Ubon also has a few **metered taxis** (☑ 0 4526 5999; flagfall 30B, call fee 20B) that park at the bus station and airport. They're unlikely to use their meters, and charge 100B for rides into town.

Car-hire companies include the long-running **Chow Watana** (☑ 0 4524 2202). You can hire bicycles from **Nam Sai Art & Decor** (Th Ratchabut; ⊙ 10am-10.30pm), a peculiar (in a good way) little coffee shop, and **Ubon Rental Cycle** (115 Th Srinarong; ⊙ 8am-8pm), a laundromat, for 100B per day. If nobody is around at the latter, ask at the house in back.

Around Ubon Ratchathani

Ban Pa-Ao   บ้านผาอ่าว

Ban Pa-Ao village is famous for producing brass and bronze items using a unique lost-wax casting method involving long strands of wax. This is the only place in Thailand

that still does it. You can watch workers creating bells, bowls and more at **Soon Thorng Leuang Ban Pa-Ao** (⊙ 7am-5pm) on the far side of the village. Ban Pa-Ao is also a silk-weaving village and there's a **silk centre** (⊙ 8am-5pm) at the entrance to the town with a shop (the quality of the *mát·mèe* here is excellent) and a couple of looms, but most weaving is done at home.

Wat Burapa Pa-Ao Nuea has just opened a gorgeous **museum** (⊙ 8am-5pm) FREE holding various historical artefacts and local handicrafts; unfortunately, there are very few labels.

Ban Pa-Ao is 3.5km off Hwy 23. Buses to/from Yasothon pass the turn-off (20B, 20 minutes), and a motorcycle taxi from the highway costs 20B each way.

Phibun Mangsahan   พิบูลมังสาหาร

Thais often stop in the dusty town of Phibun Mangsahan to see a set of rapids called **Kaeng Sapheu**, just downstream of the Mun River bridge. The rocky islets make 'Python Rapids' rise between February and May, but the shady park here is a pleasant stop year-round.

The tile-encrusted *bòht* at **Wat Phu Khao Kaew** (⊙ dawn-dusk) on the west side of town is covered with Khmer symbols including *apsara* and dancing Shivas on the outside, while the interior walls have reliefs of important stupas from around Thailand.

Villages past the bridge as you drive toward Khong Jiam are famed for forging iron and bronze **gongs**, both for temples and classical Thai-music ensembles. You can watch the gong-makers hammering the flat metal discs and tempering them in rustic fires at many roadside workshops. People make drums, bells, and cymbals here, too.

Visa extensions are available at Phibun Mangsahan's **immigration office** (☑ 0 4544 1108; ⊙ 8.30am-noon & 1-4.30pm Mon-Fri), 1km south of the bridge on the way to Chong Mek.

🛏 Sleeping & Eating

In the centre of town, between the bus park and the bridge, the friendly and clean **Phiboonkit Hotel** (☑ 0 4544 1201; Th Phiboon; r 250-300B; P 🕸 🕾) is your usual, slightly chaotic, old-time budget hotel.

Phibun is famous for *sah·lah·bow* (Chinese buns; 5B each). Three ramshackle shops near the bridge sell them, as do many more out on the highway. Deep-fried frog

SAM PHAN BOK สามพันโบก

Visit Sam Phan Bok (3000 Holes) and you'll feel as much like you're on another planet as in another country. Eons of erosion have made Swiss cheese of this narrow, rocky Mekong bend, creating one of the most stunning moments of the river's epic journey. Water drowns it during the rainy season, but when it's fully exposed (usually between December and May) you can explore for hours. Even in the shoulder months, when it only partly protrudes, it's worth the trip. There's no shade out here, so early-morning and late-afternoon visits are best. Boat rides beyond Sam Phan Bok are also very rewarding for the bucolic scenery.

Sam Phan Bok is north of Pha Taem National Park, and there's no public transport. You can camp there, and a few people even hire tents in the busy season. There's now accommodation, but we prefer the simple and friendly **Song Khon Resort** (☑08 7256 1696; www.songkhonresort.com; r 500-700B; P ❀ ☎) overlooking Hat Salung, a lovely stretch of river in its own right, in the nearby in the village of Ban Song Khon. Where ever you stay, definitely book ahead on weekends and holidays during Sam Phan Bok season.

skins *(năng gòp tôrt)* are the speciality of the many simple restaurants at Kaeng Sapheu.

ℹ️ Getting There & Away

Phibun's bus stop behind the market serves ordinary buses (35B, one hour, every 20 minutes) to Ubon's bus station (these stop to pick up passengers at Warin Market across the river) and *sŏrng·tăa·ou* to Chong Mek (35B, one hour, every 30 minutes).

Minivans between Ubon (50B) and Chong Mek (50B) stop every 30 minutes in Phibun one block behind the bus stop in front of an auto-parts store.

Sŏrng·tăa·ou (40B, 1½ hours, every 30 minutes) to Talat Ban Du (Ban Du Market), in Ubon's city centre, and Khong Jiam (40B, one hour, two each morning) park near the bridge.

Kaeng Tana National Park อุทยาน แห่งชาติแก่งตะนะ

Five kilometres before Khong Jiam you can cross the Pak Mun Dam to **Kaeng Tana National Park** (☑0 4540 6888; admission 100B). After circling thickly forested Don Tana (Tana Island), linked to the mainland by two long suspension bridges, the Mun River roils through the park's beautiful namesake rapids and passes below some photogenic cliffs. In the rainy season the rapids lie under water, and towards the end of the dry season, naturally cut holes in the rock, similar to those at Sam Phan Bok, emerge. There are several good short walks from the **visitor centre** (⊙8am-4pm): the 1.5km clifftop trail to **Lan Pha Phueng** viewpoint is especially serene. **Nam Tok Tad Ton** is a wide and lovely waterfall in the far south of the park, just 300m off the main road.

There's a **campsite** (per person with own tent 30B, 4-/8-person tent hire 150/225B) and four **bungalows** (☑0 2562 0760; www.dnp.go.th/parkreserve; 6/10 people 1000/2000B). The simple restaurant opens during the day only.

By road, the park is 14km from Khong Jiam. There's no public transport, but boats in town will take you upriver and drop you at the park for a quick look around for 600B.

Khong Jiam โขงเจียม

Khong Jiam sits on a picturesque peninsula at the confluence of the reddish Mekong and bluish Mun rivers, which is known as **Mae Nam Song Si** (Two-Colour River) because of the contrasting colours at the junction. The multicoloured merger is usually visible from the shore, but it's best seen from a boat. When the rivers are high (June to October) the blending waters create small whirlpools and a strange bubbling that resembles boiling lava. A trip in a large boat that can carry 30 people, with a sunshade and life-jackets, costs 350B, while you'll pay 200B in a tiny boat that holds three. The big boats can also take you to Kaeng Tana and Pha Taem national parks or elsewhere along the Mekong River.

Above the town is **Wat Tham Khuha Sawan** (⊙dawn-dusk) The awesome views (best from above the minimart) alone are worth the trip, but this well-known temple also has a unique nine-pointed *chedi*, an all-white *bòht,* an impressive orchid garden (blooming in the cold season) and the body of the late abbot, Luang Pu Kam, on display in a glass case atop a flamboyant altar.

Naga fireballs began appearing at Khong Jiam in 2005 (see p464), but they don't occur every year.

🛏 Sleeping & Eating

Khong Jiam doesn't get many *fa·ràng* visitors, but it's popular with Thais, so there's an abundance of lodging. There are several pricey restaurants near the Mae Nam Song Si, including two floating on the Mekong.

Banpak Mongkhon HOTEL $
(☏0 4535 1352; www.banmongkhon.com; Th Kaewpradit; r 250-1000B; f 1500-2500B; P➋❄@⛵) From the simple fan rooms to the four cute stilted wooden cottages, this place near the highway has friendly, clued-in owners and lots of character, making it a great choice for any budget.

Khong Jiam Place HOTEL $
(☏0 4535 1046; Th Phookhamchai; r 350B; P➋❄⛵) Rooms are small and simple, but they're very clean, and overall this striking yellow hotel offers very good value. It's one block south of the main road, near Banpak Mongkhon.

Apple Guesthouse GUESTHOUSE $
(☏0 4535 1160; Th Kaewpradit; r 200-300B; P❄⛵) Behind a general store, the spruced up Apple has wooden buildings with concrete rooms below. It's the cheapest place in town and good enough for the price. The 200B rooms have fans.

Baansuan Rimnam Resort HOTEL $$
(☏08 5493 3521; Th Rimmoon; r incl breakfast 700-1000B; P➋❄⛵) This quiet spot sits in a small patch of forest along the Mun River. The most expensive bungalows have terraces looking at the water through a line of trees. These aren't the best rooms in Khong Jiam at this price, but combined with the location the whole package is highly recommended.

★ Tohsang Khongjiam Resort HOTEL $$$
(☏0 4535 1174; www.tohsang.com; r incl breakfast 2500-3890B, villas 2500-7060B, Sedhapura pool villas 12,500-14,500B; P➋❄@⛵⛲) The glitz and gloss at this large resort-spa are somewhat incongruous for this stretch of rural Thailand, but it holds all the aces in the posh-accommodation stakes, and the prices for the rooms are fair for what you get. The 3rd-floor rooms have the best views. There's

a good restaurant and a spa, and bikes and kayaks are for hire. It's 3.5km from town on the south bank of the river.

ℹ Getting There & Away

All transport to town stops at the highway junction. The only direct bus to Ubon (80B, 2½ hours) leaves at 6am and departs to Khong Jiam at 2pm. You can also take the morning *sŏrng·tăa·ou* to Phibun Mangsahan (40B, one hour, 6am and 8am) and continue from there. Buses to Bangkok leave at 7.30am (2nd class 435B) and 4.30pm (1st class 560B).

Apple Guesthouse and Banpak Mongkon rent bicycles (100B per day) and motorcycles (200B and 300B per day).

Pha Taem National Park อุทยานแห่งชาติผาแต้ม

Up the Mekong from Khong Jiam is a long cliff named Pha Taem, the centrepiece of awesome but unheralded **Pha Taem National Park** (☏0 4531 8026; admission 200B). From the top you get a bird's-eye view across the river into Laos and down below a trail passes prehistoric rock paintings dating to at least 1000 BC. Mural subjects include *blah bèuk* (giant Mekong catfish), elephants, human hands, geometric designs and fish traps that look much like the huge ones still used today. The second viewing platform fronts the most impressive batch. A **visitor centre** (⏰5am-6pm) here contains exhibits pertaining to the paintings and local ecology.

North of the cliff is **Nam Tok Soi Sawan**, a 25m-tall waterfall flowing from June to December, the same period as all the park's waterfalls. It's a 19km drive from the visitor centre and then a 500m walk, or you can hike (with a ranger) for about 15km along the top of the cliff if you arrange it in advance. What the park calls **Thailand's largest flower field** (blooming November to February) lies near the falls.

The northern half of the park holds more waterfalls, ancient art and wonderful views. **Pa Cha Na Dai** cliff offers Thailand's first sunrise view (Pha Taem is about one minute behind and also has the first sunset view), and amazing **Nam Tok Saeng Chan** waterfall flows through a hole cut naturally into the overhanging rock. Scattered across the 340-sq-km park are many oddly eroded rocks, including four sites known as **Sao Chaliang**, which are mushroom-shaped stone formations similar to those found in Mukdahan's Phu Pha Thoep National Park.

Pha Taem has **campsites** (per person with own tent 30B, 2-/3-/4-person tent hire 150/225/300B) and five **bungalows** (✆ 0 2562 0760; www.dnp.go.th/parkreserve; 6-person bungalows with fan 1200B, 5-person with air-con 2000B; ❊) and vendors sell snacks and fast food until about sunset.

Pha Taem is 18km from Khong Jiam via Rte 2112. There's no public transport, so the best way to get there is to hire a motorcycle in Khong Jiam.

Chong Mek ช่องเม็ก

South of Khong Jiam, at the end of Rte 217, is the small border town of Chong Mek. The new bridges over the Mekong further north have reduced traffic on this route and stolen much of the bustle from the Chong Mek Market, which used to be a big hit with Thai tourists. If you get stuck here after hours, there are cheap guesthouses north of the market.

There's no public transport between Chong Mek and Khong Jiam; either go through Phibun or hire a motorcycle taxi/túk-túk/pickup truck for 250/300/500B.

Phu Chong Nayoi National Park
อุทยานแห่งชาติภูจองนายอย

Sitting at the heart of the 'Emerald Triangle' is the little-known **Phu Chong Nayoi National Park** (✆ 0 4541 1515; admission 200B), one of Thailand's wildest corners and healthiest forests. Resident fauna includes elephants, tigers, Malayan sun bears, barking deer, gibbons, black hornbills and endangered white-winged ducks; though you won't likely see them.

The 686-sq-km park's primary attraction is **Namtok Huay Luang**, a waterfall that plunges 45m over a cliff in two parallel streams and has at least a little water all year. A short trail leads to a viewpoint and you can walk down 274 steps to the bottom where you can swim, though the water dries up around March. About 150m downstream is **Namtok Praon La-or**, also a pretty picture. Rangers love taking visitors on short bamboo-raft trips (300B for six people) above the falls, though for various reasons, this activity is intermittent. Between the waterfall and the lodging/visitor centre is **Pa-lan Pachad**, a rocky field that features many wildflowers.

At the far end of the park, from atop **Phu Hin Dang**, there are superb views of the forest in Laos more than 300m below. It's a 55km drive from the main park area and then about a 3km hike. Because of land mines and poachers, this trip needs to be done with armed rangers. This is easiest to arrange at the main visitor center, but sometimes can be done on the road to the cliff.

Stargazing is superb here, so consider spending the night. There are six well-worn **bungalows** (✆ 0 2562 0760; www.dnp.go.th/parkreserve; 3-/6-/8-bed bungalows 600/1200/1600B) plus a **campsite** (per person with own tent 30B, 3-person tent hire 150B) 2km from Huay Luang. A restaurant opens at least 9am to 4pm daily at the waterfall, and snacks and drinks are sold at the lodging area.

There's no public transport to the park and not much traffic in the park, so hitching requires patience.

GETTING TO LAOS: CHONG MEK TO VANGTAO

Getting to the border Almost every traveller uses the direct Ubon Ratchathani–Pakse buses, which wait long enough to buy Lao visas at the border. Otherwise, Chong Mek's little bus terminal serves *sŏrng·tăa·ou* from Phibun Mangsahan (35B, one hour, frequent), minivans from Ubon (100B, 1¼ hours, every 30 minutes) via Phibun (50B) and buses from Bangkok (547B to 638B, 10 hours, five daily). It's nearly 1km from the bus station to the border: motorcycle taxis and túk-túk charge 20B.

At the border The border is open from 6am to 8pm and the crossing, involving walking though an underground tunnel, is largely hassle-free. Lao officials sometimes try to extract additional 'stamping fees', but they're usually not too insistent.

Moving on Pakse is about an hour away in one of the frequent *sŏrng·tăa·ou* (10,000K).

KHON KAEN PROVINCE

Khon Kaen Province, the gateway to Isan for those arriving from northern Thailand, serves up an interesting mix of old and new. Farming and textiles still dominate life in the countryside, while things are booming in the increasingly modern capital city.

Khon Kaen ขอนแก่น

POP 116,157

As the site of the northeast's largest university and an important hub for all things commercial, Khon Kaen is youthful, educated and on the move. Khon Kaen has ridden Isan's economic boom for all it's worth and a glut of new condos and malls are transforming the skyline, but the modernisation hasn't come close to wiping out its Isan pride. While it's the kind of city that's more likely to land on a best-places-to-live list than a traveller's itinerary, there are more than enough interesting attractions and good facilities to make a stop rewarding.

⊙ Sights

⊙ Bueng Kaen Nakhon บึงแก่นนคร

This 100-hectare lake is the most pleasant place in town to spend some time, and the paths hugging its shore link quite a few interesting places. There's bike hire at the market and down along the west shore across from Wat Klang Muang Kao; the latter has two- and three-seaters (30B per hour per seat).

★ Wat Nong Wang   BUDDHIST TEMPLE

(วัดหนองแวง; Th Robbung; ⊙daylight hours) FREE Down at the south end of the lake, **Phra Mahathat Kaen Nakhon** (⊙7am-5pm), the stunning stupa at the heart of this important temple, is Khon Kaen's one must-see. It features enlightening murals depicting Isan culture; various historical

Khon Kaen

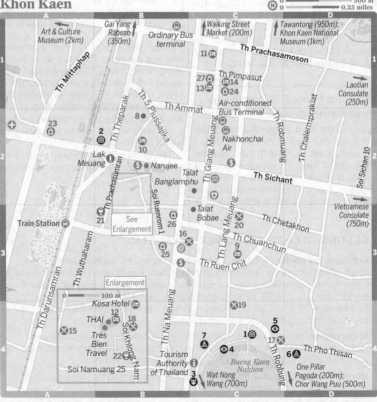

displays, including a collection of rare Buddha images on the 4th floor; and a 9th-floor observation deck.

Mahesak Shrine HINDU TEMPLE
(ศาลเจ้าพ่อมเหศักดิ์; Th Robbung; **FREE**) This modern Khmer-style *prang* is dedicated to the Hindu god Indra. It's almost spooky at night.

Wat That BUDDHIST TEMPLE
(วัดธาตุ; Th Robbung; ⊙dawn-dusk, *chedi* 8am-6pm) This old temple has a soaring *bòht* and *chedi*. The latter, built in 1789, is surrounded by a cloister featuring many Buddha images and you can go inside.

Rim Bueng Market MARKET
(ตลาดริมบึง; Th Robbung; ⊙4-9pm) This fun little market, in the shadow of Wat That, features food, secondhand clothing and paint-your-own pottery stalls. During the day there are paddleboats (40B per half-hour after 5pm; 50B for any length of time that ends before 5pm) for hire.

Hong Moon Mung MUSEUM
(โฮงมูนมังเมืองขอนแก่น; Th Robbung; admission 90B; ⊙9am-5pm Mon-Sat) Inside the amphitheatre, this excellent museum about Khon Kaen provides a good introduction to Isan with dioramas and displays going back to the Jurassic period.

Sanjao Bueng Tao Gong Ma TEMPLE
(ศาลเจ้าปึงเถ่ากงม่า; Th Robbung) Sometimes called Sanjao Bueng Kaen Nakhon, this is Khon Kaen's biggest and most beautiful Chinese temple. There's a large Guan-Im (Chinese Goddess of Mercy) statue in the park across the street.

Wat Pho Ban Nontan BUDDHIST TEMPLE
(วัดโพธิ์โนนทัน; Th Pho Thisan; ⊙dawn-dusk) Just off the lake, this peaceful tree-filled temple and noted meditation centre predates the city and has a *săh·lah* like no other in Thailand. The ground floor is covered with ingeniously sculpted trees, animals and village scenes of people acting out old Isan proverbs. There's also a small museum under the *bòht* (though it's often locked) and this is a great place for a Thai massage.

One Pillar Pagoda SHRINE
(ศาลเจ้าเสาเดียว; Th Robbung) This replica of Hanoi's iconic temple was built by Khon Kaen's sizeable Vietnamese community. It's a good sunset-watching spot.

⊙ **Elsewhere in Khon Kaen**

Khon Kaen National Museum MUSEUM
(พิพิธภัณฑสถานแห่งชาติขอนแก่น; Th Lang Sunratchakan; admission 100B; ⊙9am-4pm Wed-Sun) This interesting collection of artefacts spans prehistoric times to the present. Highlights are Ban Chiang pottery and a beautiful Dvaravati *săir·mah* (temple boundary marker) depicting Princess Pimpa cleaning Lord Buddha's feet with her hair. The household and agricultural displays shed light on what you will see out in the countryside.

Wat Pa Thama Uthayan BUDDHIST TEMPLE
(วัดธรรมอุทยาน; Th Mittaphap; ⊙dawn-dusk)
This peaceful temple, 10km north of the
city, has many beautiful monuments, including a 23m-tall white walking Buddha
image, spread across its vast grounds. It
has become a well-known meditation centre because, rather than teaching a formal
method, Luang Po Gluai encourages people
to find their own path to inner peace. Take
sŏrng·tăa·ou 4 (15B) from Na Muang or
Prachasamoson streets; be sure to tell the
driver where you are going since not all go
that far.

🐾 Courses

Centrum Health Center MASSAGE
(☑0 4333 2113; veenasspa@gmail.com; Soi
Supatheera) Teaches Thai massage in English
and Thai.

👉 Tours

Several tour companies based in Khon Kaen
can show you around town or take you
across Isan.

Thai Dream Tours COOKING, MEDITATION
(☑0 4333 2113; www.thaidreamtours.com) Gre-
garious owner-guide Veena has made meditation tours her speciality, but she does all
kinds of trips. She also arranges casual cooking classes (1500B per person) on Thursdays
(Isan food) and Fridays (Thai food).

**Khon Kaen Education & Travel
Programs** TOURS
(☑08 3359 9115; www.kketp.com) Aimed mostly
at leisure travellers. Offers quiet-water kayaking on the Nam Phong River near Ubon-
rat Dam.

✪ Festivals

The **Silk Fair** and **Phuk Siaw Festival** are
held simultaneously over 12 days starting
in late November. Centred on the *săh·lah
glahng,* the festival celebrates and seeks to
preserve the tradition of 'phuk siaw' (friend
bonding), a ritual union of friends during
which *fâi pòok kăan* (sacred threads) are
tied around one's wrists. More than just a
symbolic act, the friends gain a standing on
par with siblings in each other's families.
Other activities include a parade, Isan music
and lots of shopping.

🛏 Sleeping

Chonlada HOTEL $
(☑08 1873 1387; Soi Supatheera; r 300-400B;
❄️❋☎) A small, simple spot with decent
new rooms at an excellent price. The soi is
pretty quiet and the ever-smiling owners
round out the experience.

Saen Samran Hotel HOTEL $
(☑0 4323 9611; Th Glang Meuang; r 220-340B;
❄️@☎) The city's oldest hotel is also its
most charismatic, with the wooden upper
floor clinging to its once-upon-a-time glory.
The rooms are worn but clean and the owner is a good source of Khon Kaen advice.

Charoenchit House HOTEL $
(☑0 4322 7300; Th Chuanchun; r incl breakfast 500-600B; P❄️❋@☎) A solid budget
choice, just north of the lake. The rooms
are attractively decorated and have a fair
amount of va-va-voom for the price.

Roma Hotel HOTEL $
(☑0 4333 4444; Th Glang Meuang; r 230-1000B;
P❄️❋☎) A simple but effective renovation
has cheered up what would otherwise be a

THE KHON KAEN ART SCENE

To the surprise of many, Thais and travellers alike, Khon Kaen has an active and growing contemporary art scene. You can start to uncover it at the following galleries. Also,
Chocolate Bar (p446) has ocassional exhibitions.

Art & Culture Museum (หอศิลปวัฒนธรรม มหาวิทยาลัยขอนแก่น; ⊙10am-7pm) Khon
Kaen's leading arts showcase is this two-storey gallery at Khon Kaen University that
features monthly installations of mostly professional artists.

Ton Tann Art Space & Gallery (หอศิลป์ต้นตาล; Hwy 2; ⊙4-10pm) In the stilted building
in Ton Tann Green Market.

Lak Muang Gallery (หอศิลป์หลักเมือง; Th Sichant; ⊙10am-6pm) Hidden behind FedEx.

Khon Kaen Faculty of Fine & Applied Arts Gallery (หอศิลป์คณะศิลปกรรมศาสตร์
มหาวิทยาลัยขอนแก่น; ⊙9am-7pm Mon-Fri) Mostly promotes student work, but sometimes
artists from elsewhere exhibit here. Some months have no exhibits.

depressing old building, making the cheaper rooms good value. The extra 100B for a 'boutique' room only gets you a brighter paint job, and at the upper prices you're better off staying elsewhere.

★**Piman Garden** HOTEL $$
(☏0 4333 4111; www.pimangardenhotel.com; Th Glang Meuang; r 850-1250B, ste 1450B; P❄@☎) Set back off the road around an attractive garden, Piman offers serenity and privacy despite its city-centre location. All rooms come with safes and fridges plus most have balconies or porches. Due to its age, it's no longer the great bargain it used to be, but it still outshines it's competition in the price range.

★**KK Centrum** HOTEL $$
(☏08 1574 0507; www.kk-centrum.com; 33/17-18 Soi Supatheera; r incl breakfast 650-850B; P❄@☎) What seems like an ordinary small Thai hotel sets itself apart in the details. All rooms have high-quality furnishings and the owner, who lives on-site, is serious about service and cleanliness. And it's quiet because it's built in the back of the block. Bikes are available for guest use.

Reuan Kanyarat HOTEL $$
(☏0 4332 1999; www.rueankanyarathotel.com; Th Robbung; r incl breakfast 960-1050B; P❄@☎) With a good lakeside location (the pricier rooms are worth it for the sunset view.), and stylish, comfortable rooms, this relatively new hotel makes for a relaxing night. The staff are attentive, though English is limited.

BB Hotel HOTEL $$
(☏0 4332 2999; Th Robbung; r 590-800B; P❄☎) If you're in Khon Kaen to relax rather than live it up, then BB (which stands for Biggie & Biggoe) at the foot of the lake is a good bet. Rooms are rather bland, but good overall.

Pullman Raja Orchid HOTEL $$$
(☏0 4332 2155; www.pullmanhotels.com; off Th Prachasumran; r incl breakfast 2950-3450B, ste 3950-5450B; P❄@☎≋) A stunning lobby sets the tone for Khon Kaen's top hotel. Though it's definitely not the five-star property it claims to be, this Accor-run place in the heart of the city has plenty of razzle dazzle, including a luxurious spa and gym, a microbrewery and well-equipped rooms. Definitely pay the little extra to move up from Standard to Superior level, which gets you a renovated room and a better view.

And insist on a room at the front, unless you want to listen to music drift out of the nearby nightclubs.

Supanniga Home HOTEL $$$
(☏08 9944 4880; www.supannigahome.com; Th Pho Tisan; ste incl breakfast 4800-12,000B; P❄☎) A place that actually deserves its 'boutique' label, Supanniga boasts three large, lovely villas, one with an outdoor Jacuzzi. They're in a beautiful 6.5-hectare estate technically still in the city, but far from the centre, so it's best to stay here if you have your own transport or don't mind long waits for taxis. There's a restaurant on-site.

✗ Eating

Khon Kaen has a good **night market** (Th Reunrom; ☺5pm-midnight) and the eastern-most block of the Saturday Walking Street Market (p446) is an awesome noshing destination. There are also food vendors at Rim Bueng Market (p443), though people generally come here more for the atmosphere than the cuisine.

★**Turm-Rom** THAI $
(Th Chetakhon; dishes 40-159B; ☺5.30pm-1am; ☎) This superb place combines one of the best kitchens in town with a covered garden to create the perfect place for a night out. The *hòr mòk tá·lair* (seafood curry served in a coconut) is especially good, but in our many visits we've never had a dud dish.

★**Slove U** CAFE $
(Th Sri Nual; green-tea latte 40B; ☺6am-6pm; ☎) Khon Kaen's youthful population has spawned many good coffee shops and this friendly closet-sized one, attractively cluttered with knick-knacks, is one of our favourites.

Gai Yang Rabeab NORTHEASTERN THAI $
(Th Theparak; dishes 30-150B; ☺9am-3pm) Most Thais believe Khon Kaen Province makes Thailand's best *gài yâhng* and this simple joint, serving an all-Isan menu, gets the most nods as best of the best in the city, since both the owners and the chickens come from Khao Suan Kwang, the most famous *gài yâhng* town.

Tawantong VEGAN $
(Th Lang Sunratchakan; dishes 25-35B; ☺6.30am-2pm; P) This large, all-vegie, health-food buffet sits across from the National Museum. The food is so good it also gets carnivorous diners.

Chocolate Bar
INTERNATIONAL $

(Th Robbung; 80-140B; ⊙5pm-late Mon-Sat; 🕿) A chill place with a mostly young *fa·ràng* crowd, fresh food, good music, and good cocktails. The most recent incarnation of the ever-evolving menu featured mostly Mexican and sandwiches plus a tasty Japanese curry.

Plapanoy
NORTHEASTERN THAI $

(Th Robbung; dishes 30-350B; ⊙10am-10pm; 🅿🕿) Though they serve a lot of Thai food, this large, simple spot near Bueng Kaen Nakhon makes a good choice to sample Isan food for the sole reason that some dishes, such as mushroom curry and the Thai-Isan fusion stir-fried frog with basil leaf, are written in English.

Chor Wang Puu
THAI $$

(Th Robbung; dishes 60-400B; ⊙11am-midnight; 🅿) With wood-and-thatch dining areas spread around a large pond, the 'Crab Palace' vaguely resembles a fishing village. Naturally, seafood features prominently on the menu. It's a beautiful spot at night, and you can even catch a little sunset view way back behind the lake.

Pomodoro
ITALIAN $$

(Soi Khlong Nam; dishes 150-330B; ⊙5-11pm; 🕿) The best Italian in town, by far.

Didines
INTERNATIONAL $$

(Th Prachasumran; dishes 60-380B; ⊙kitchen 5-10.30pm, bar until midnight; 🕿) Far more successful behind the bar than in the kitchen, this stylish restaurant nonetheless has the biggest selection of *faràng* food in town including chicken cordon bleu, salmon ravioli, and black-bean quesadillas. The real reason to go, however, is the selection of American microbrews and the pool table.

Pavilion Café
INTERNATIONAL $$$

(Th Prachasumran; breakfast/lunch/dinner 450/550/700B; ⊙6-10am, 11.30am-2pm, 6-10.30pm; 🅿🕿) The principal restaurant of the Pullman Raja Orchid (p445) hotel features an excellent international buffet; though it's not available for lunch every day. The nearby Kosa Hotel has a smaller but similar set-up for breakfast and lunch at half the price.

Tasty Chocolat
CHOCOLATE

(📱08 9572 7997; Khon Kaen Ram Hospital Shopping Arcade; ⊙9am-8pm Mon-Fri, 8am-8pm Sat & Sun; 🅿) Isan's very own gourmet chocolate shop.

🍷 Drinking & Nightlife

Several chill, open-air Thai-style pubs, where groups of friends come to eat, drink and eat some more, have sprung up around the intersection of Th Reunrom and Th Prachasumran. The fast growing Lang Mor neighborhood way out of town behind Khon Kaen University has more of the same with a mostly student clientele.

Rad
NIGHTCLUB

(Th Prachasumran) The exuberant anchor of Khon Kaen's nightlife, this is a multifaceted place with live music, DJs, karaoke, 'coyote' dancers and an al fresco restaurant.

U-Bar
NIGHTCLUB

(Soi Khlong Nam) Smaller than Rad, but just as loud and crowded, U-Bar hosts more big-name bands from Bangkok.

☆ Entertainment

Central Plaza
CINEMA

(Th Sichant) Khon Kaen's glossiest shopping mall screens movies in English and has a bowling alley.

🛍 Shopping

Because of the variety available, Khon Kaen is arguably the best place to buy Isan handicrafts.

★ Walking Street Market
MARKET

(Th Na Soon Ratchakan; ⊙5.30-10.30pm Sat) In the spirit of Chiang Mai's street markets, hundreds of vendors, many of them students, gather to sell handmade handbags, T-shirts, postcards, picture frames and more. Dancers, musicians and other buskers work strategic corners.

Prathammakant
HANDICRAFTS

(Th Reunrom; ⊙9am-7pm) With by far the largest and best selection of handicrafts in town, including an impressively large choice of silk, this well-known shop makes a perfect one-stop shop.

Ton Tann Green Market
MARKET

(Hwy 2; ⊙4-11pm) Half market, half mall, Ton Tann is an attractive open space where, like the Walking Street Market, many of the vendors sell modern handmade crafts. There's also a fashion zone and many restaurants.

Sueb San
SOUVENIRS

(Th Glang Meuang; ⊙8am-6.30pm Mon-Sat) A small shop stocking a few natural-dyed fabrics plus some creative handmade note-books, handbags and other souvenirs.

Rin Thai Silk
HANDICRAFTS

(Th Na Meuang) Many locals, especially brides-to-be, looking for top-quality silk shop here.

Naemnueng Lablae
FOOD & DRINK

(Th Glang Meuang; ⊗6.30am-9pm Mon-Thu, 6.30am-9.30pm Fri-Sun) Few Thai visitors leave Khon Kaen without stuffing their suitcase full of local foods: *gun chee·ang* (red pork sausages) are especially popular and this family-owned shop has been making their own for decades. *Kà·nŏm tùa* (sweets made with peanuts) and *kà·nŏm tan·yá·pêut* (sweets made with seeds) are another delicious local speciality.

Central Plaza
SHOPPING CENTRE

(Th Sichant; ⊗10.30am-9pm Mon-Thu, 10am-9pm Fri-Sun) One of the biggest shopping malls in Isan. Has a branch of the English-language Asia Books.

ⓘ Information

Khon Kaen's three largest shopping malls, Central Plaza, TukCom and Fairy Plaza have extended-hours banks. Central and Fairy have AEON ATMs.

Immigration (☑0 4346 5242; Hwy 2; ⊗8.30am-noon & 1-4.30pm Mon-Fri) North of town, near the entrance to Khon Kaen University.

Khon Kaen Ram Hospital (☑0 4333 3800; Th Sichant) Has a 24-hour emergency room.

Tourism Authority of Thailand (TAT; ☑0 4322 7714; tatkhkn@tat.or.th; Th Prachasamoson; ⊗8.30am-4.30pm) Distributes maps of the city and can answer questions about surrounding provinces, too.

Très Bien Travel (☑0 4332 2155; Pullman Raja Orchid Hotel; ⊗8.30am-5.30pm Mon-Fri, 8.30am-2pm Sat) A reliable spot for booking plane tickets.

ⓘ Getting There & Away

AIR

Thai Airways (☑0 4322 7701; www.thaiairways. com; Pullman Raja Orchid Hotel, off Th Prachas-umran; ⊗8am-5pm Mon-Fri) operates four daily flights between Khon Kaen and Suvarnabhumi Airport in Bangkok (2600B one way) while **Air Asia** (☑0 2515 9999; www.airasia.com) flies twice daily to Bangkok's Don Muang Airport (1500B).

Several hotels, including the Pullman, send shuttles (70B) to meet flights at Khon Kaen Airport and you don't need to be staying at the hotels to use them. Taxis at the airport don't use their meters.

BUS

Khon Kaen is a busy transport hub and you can ride directly to nearly all cities in Isan and many beyond. A new bus terminal has been built on the ring road south of town and though it's opening has been delayed for years, it's likely that within the life time of this book all buses will move out there. When that happens, the plan is to keep ticket offices at the current bus stations and to have shuttle vans take people to the new station.

For now, buses and most minivans use the central and convenient **ordinary bus terminal** (☑0 4333 3388; Th Prachasamoson) and **air-conditioned bus terminal** (☑0 4023 9910; Th Glang Meuang). The names no longer accurately describe them. The former serves all variety of buses to almost everywhere, including all destinations within the province, while the latter is mostly for 1st-class and VIP buses departing at night. Some minivans also depart from Central Plaza.

The best service to Bangkok is with **Nakhon-chai Air** (☑0 2790 0009), departing frequently throughout the day from the air-con terminal. Their 'First-Class' VIP service (560B) departs at 11.15am, 11.15pm and 12.15am.

TRAIN

There's one morning and two evening express trains (seat 77B to 399B, 1st-class sleeper upper/lower 968/1168B, 8½ to nine hours) between Bangkok and **Khon Kaen Railway Station** (☑0 4322 1112). There's also a cheaper evening rapid train. Three trains go to Nakhon Ratchasima (38B to 170B, 3½ hours) and six go to Udon Thani (25B to 267B, two hours) with four continuing north to Nong Khai (35B to 290B, three hours).

ⓘ Getting Around

Sŏrng·tăa·ou (9B) ply regular routes across the city. Some of the handiest (all of which pass the air-con terminal on Th Glang Meuang) are line 4, which passes immigration and the Lao consulate; line 8, which goes to Wat Nong Wang and also northwest through the university; line 10 (going north), which passes near and sometimes in front of the Vietnamese consulate; and line 21, which goes out to the National Museum.

For individual rides, *túk-túk* are the most expensive way to get around (40B to 60B to most places in the centre), but they're the method most people use because it's rare to find **metered taxis** (☑0 4334 2800, 0 4346 5777; flagfall 30B, call fee 20B) on the street, and when you call for one you usually have to wait a long time. About the only place you're likely to find taxis or motorcycle taxis (within town 20B

BUSES FROM KHON KAEN

DESTINATION	PRICE (B)	DURATION (HR)	TERMINAL	DEPARTURES
Bangkok (2nd-class only)	280	7	ordinary	6.40am-9pm (hourly)
Bangkok	360-560	6-7	air-con	6.30am-12.30am (frequent)
Chiang Mai	427-949	12	ordinary	3.45am-7.15pm (10 daily)
Chiang Mai	549-949	12	air-con	3.30am-9pm (7 daily)
Khorat	120	3-4	ordinary	5am-7.30pm (frequent)
Khorat	166-250	3-3½	air-con	8.30am-11.30pm (frequent)
Khorat (minivan)	129	2½	ordinary	7am-5pm (hourly)
Loei	143	3½	ordinary	3.40am-6.30pm (hourly)
Mukdahan	170-220	4½	ordinary	4am-6.30pm (every 30min)
Mukdahan	230	4	air-con	2.45am & 4.30am
Nakhon Phanom	243	5	ordinary	7.30-pm (5 daily)
Nakhon Phanom	243	5	air-con	7.30am-4pm (5 daily)
Nong Khai	119	3½	ordinary	9am-8pm (hourly)
Nong Khai	176	3½	air-con	12.20-8pm (4 daily)
Phitsanulok	221-386	6	ordinary	6am-8.30pm (15 daily)
Phitsanulok	323	6	air-con	12.30-10pm (8 daily)
Roi Et	80	2½	ordinary	5am-7.30pm (frequent)
Roi Et	104-122	2	air-con	9am-3pm (9 daily)
Suvarnabhumi Airport	365	6½	air-con	10.50pm
Surin	182	4	ordinary	4am-3pm (hourly)
Ubon Ratchathani	185-277	4½	ordinary	4.40am-5pm (every 30min)
Ubon Ratchathani	180-277	4½	air-con	1am-8pm (16 daily)
Udon Thani	84	2	ordinary	5am-2am (frequent)
Udon Thani	126-180	2	air-con	5am-7pm (hourly)
Udon Thani (minivan)	100	1½	ordinary	6am-8.30pm (every 30min)
Udon Thani (minivan)	100	1½	Central Plaza	6.10am-7.40pm (every 30min)
Vientiane (must already have a Lao visa)	180	4	air-con	8am & 3pm

to 30B) parked is at the bus stations and Central Plaza, and the taxis here won't use their meters.

There are many car-hire outlets around TukCom; **Narujee** (☑ 08 1729 6139; Soi Kosa), which charges from 1200B for a car and 200B for a motorcycle, is a reliable choice.

Around Khon Kaen

Chonnabot   ชนบท

This small town located 55km southwest of Khon Kaen is one of Thailand's most successful silk villages and is famous for producing top-quality *mát·mèe*. The **Sala Mai Thai** (☑ 0 4328 6160; ⊙ 8am-5pm) **FREE** is a silk-weaving museum 1km west of town where you can learn about the entire silk-making process, and even take a turn at a loom. Out back is an exhibition hall showing the wooden contraptions devised to spin, tie, dye and weave silk by hand, and a large machine used in factories. A pair of mock-Isan houses hold various traditional household items, and a room upstairs catalogues traditional *mát·mèe* patterns.

The museum sells silk too, but most people buy from the myriad shops on Th Sriboonruang, aka **Silk Road**, some of which also stock attractive cotton fabrics made in the nearby village of Ban Lawaan. If you get away from the centre of town, particularly to the north near the temple and school, you'll sometimes see women working looms under their houses and they rarely mind if you stop by to take a look.

Most people visit as part of a tour so they can be sure to see silk weaving and thread making, but it's possible to go by public transport. Buses bound for Nakhon Sawan, departing from Khon Kaen's ordinary bus terminal, will drop you in Chonnabot (42B, one hour, six daily). Or take a bus (35B, one hour, every 30 minutes) or train (9B, 30 minutes, 8am and 8.30am) to Ban Phai, where you can get a bus to Chonnabot (20B, 20 minutes, hourly).

Prasat Puay Noi ปราสาทเปือยน้อย

The 12th-century **Prasat Puay Noi** (⊙dawn-dusk) FREE is the largest and most interesting Khmer ruin in northern Isan, though it can't compete with even some of the not-so-famous ruins further south. About the size of Buriram's Prasat Muang Tam, but less grand, the east-facing monument comprises a large central sandstone sanctuary surmounted by three partially collapsed *prang* and surrounded by laterite walls. There are still some excellent carvings intact, including Shiva riding his bull Nandi, on the pediment on the back of the 'library' and some almost lifelike *naga* on the corner of the main entrance.

By public transport from Khon Kaen, catch a bus (35B, one hour, every 30 minutes) or train (9B, 30 minutes, 8am and 8.30am) to Ban Phai, then catch a *sŏrng·tăa·ou* to Puay Noi (35B, one hour). The last *sŏrng·tăa·ou* back to Ban Phai departs at 2pm. If you have your own wheels, head east of Ban Phai on Hwy 23 (signposted to Borabu) for 11km to Rte 2301. Follow it and Rte 2297 for 24km.

Phu Wiang National Park อุทยานแห่ง ชาติภูเวียง

A geologist looking for uranium discovered a giant patella bone here in 1976, and the palaeontologists who were called to investigate then unearthed a fossilised 15m-long herbivore, later named *Phuwianggosaurus sirindhornae* after Princess Sirindhorn. Dinosaur fever followed (explaining the myriad model dinosaurs in Khon Kaen city),

more remains were uncovered and **Phu Wiang National Park** (☑ 0 4335 8073; admission 200B) was born.

Enclosed **excavation sites** (⊙8.30am-4.30pm), including one that contains a partial skeleton of *Siamotyrannus isanensis*, an early ancestor of *Tyrannosaurus rex*, can be easily reached by trails from the visitor centre or nearby parking areas. Those who want to explore further (best done by 4WD or mountain bike) will find dinosaur footprints, waterfalls and a superb viewpoint.

Phu Wiang Museum (☑08 7246 1134; adult/child 60/30B; ⊙8.30am-4.30pm Tue-Sun), 5km before the park, has palaeontology and geology displays, including full-size models of the dinosaur species that once lived in the area. Kids will love it. They'll also go ape over the giant photogenic dinosaur statues in nearby **Si Wiang Dinosaur Park**. Wiang Kao, the district inside the horseshoe-shaped mountains that comprise the park, is a fruit-growing area and a great place to explore by car, if you want to look at traditional village life.

The park has one 12-person **bungalow** (☑ 0 2562 0760; www.dnp.go.th/parkreserve; bungalows 1200B) and a **campsite** (per person with own tent 30B, 3-/6-person tent hire 225/450B). Simple food is available during the day only.

The park entrance is 90km west of Khon Kaen. Buses and minivans from Khon Kaen's ordinary bus terminal go to Phu Wiang town (40B to 1000B, 1½ hours, every 30 minutes) where you can hire a túk-túk (500B return) or motorbike taxi (300B) for the remaining 19km to the park.

Nam Nao National Park อุทยานแห่ง ชาติน้ำหนาว

One of Thailand's most valuable nature preserves, **Nam Nao National Park** (☑08 1962 6236; admission 200B) covers 966 sq km across the Phetchabun Mountains of Chaiyaphum and Phetchabun Provinces, just beyond Khon Kaen Province. Although it covers remote territory (this remained a People's Liberation Army of Thailand stronghold until the early 1980s), Hwy 12 makes access easy.

With an average elevation of 800m, temperatures are fairly cool year-round (*nám nŏw* means 'the water feels cold') and frost can occur in December and January. There are both evergreen and deciduous forest mixed with some vast bamboo groves. Nam

Nao lies at the heart of the Western Isaan Forest Complex, a 6000-sq-km block of eight connected preserves (including Phu Kradueng National Park (p473) and **Phu Khiaw Wildlife Sanctuary**; permits much be acquired in advance to visit the latter), so wildlife is particularly abundant. Elephant encounters are common enough that there's an electric fence around the campground. Lucky visitors might also spot Malayan sun bears, *banteng* (wild cattle), Asian jackals, barking deer, gibbons, pangolins and flying squirrels. There are even a few tigers. More than 200 species of bird, including great hornbill and silver pheasant, fly through the forest, and the exceptional visibility makes this one of Thailand's best birdwatching sites.

A fair system of hiking **trails** branches out from the visitor centre to several scenic overlooks. **Haewsai Waterfall** is 17km east of the visitor centre, while to the west lie the the best sunrise/morning fog (5km) and sunset (11km) **viewpoints**. When the park is busy, vehicles (70B per person) deliver people to the viewpoints; reserve a seat at the visitor centre.

There are **campsites** (per person with own tent 30B, 2-6 person tent hire 250-300B), a variety of **bungalows** (☑ 0 2562 0760; www.dnp.go.th/parkreserve; 4-12 person bungalows 1500-4000B) and some simple restaurants around the visitor centre.

Most buses heading west to Lom Sak or Phitsanulok from the ordinary bus terminal in Khon Kaen (120B, 2½ hours) will stop in the park. The visitor centre is 1.5km from the highway.

Ban Khok Sa-Nga Cobra Village
หมู่บ้านงูจงอางบ้านโคกสง่า

The self-styled 'King Cobra Village' of Ban Khok Sa-Nga has a thing about snakes. Locals rear hundreds of the reptiles, and most families have some in boxes under their houses.

The custom began in 1951 when a travelling medicinal herb salesman, Ken Yongla, began putting on snake shows to attract customers. His plan was a success, and the art of breeding and training snakes has been nurtured in this village ever since. Today the King Cobra Club of Thailand puts on **snake shows** where handlers taunt snakes and tempt fate; they often lose, as the many missing fingers show. Medicinal herbs are still sold in the village.

The village is located 50km northeast of Khon Kaen via Hwy 2 and Rte 2039. Take a Kranuan bus or minivan from Khon Kaen's ordinary bus terminal to the turn-off for Ban Khok Sa-Nga (30B, one hour, every 30 minutes) and then take a túk-túk (40B) to the showgrounds. If you're driving from Khon Kaen, consider taking the rural route that passes **Phra That Kham Kaen**, a revered *chedi* situated in the village of Ban Kham.

UDON THANI PROVINCE

Udon Thani
อุดรธานี

POP 169,073

Udon Thani has one foot on the highway and the other off the beaten track. The city boomed on the back of the Vietnam War as the site of one of the largest US air bases, and it subsequently became the region's primary transport hub and commercial centre. Today you have to dig deep behind its prosperous concrete veneer to find any flashes of its past. Udon sees relatively few foreign travellers, its main selling point being the abundance of Western foods and facilities preventing Isan's largest expat community from getting too homesick.

⊙ Sights

Sanjao Pu-Ya   TEMPLE
(ศาลเจ้าปู่ย่า; Th Nittayo; ⊙ dawn-dusk) FREE This large, brash Chinese temple on the southern shore of Nong Bua attests to the wealth of the local Thai-Chinese merchant class. At its heart, the Pu-Ya Shrine houses small images of the Chinese gods Pu (Grandpa) and Ya (Grandma).

In front of the temple is the gorgeous **Udon Thani Thai-Chinese Cultural Center** (XXX; Th Nittayo; ⊙ 9am-7pm) FREE. It features a large **garden** and the **Moral Museum**, which has excellent displays about the history of the Chinese Community in Udon Thani, Chinese culture and Confucius. The **Pu-Ya Chinese Orchestra** plays Wednesday and Friday from 5pm, and a smaller group performs Saturday and Sunday at 1pm.

Udorn Sunshine Nursery   GARDEN
(สวนกล้วยไม้หอมอุดรซันไฌน์; ☑ 08 5747 4144; Th Udorn-Nong Samrong; ⊙ 8am-5pm) FREE Ever seen a plant dance? Well, you can here. Originally earning notoriety for producing the first perfume made from an orchid, the

Udorn Sunshine Nursery, just northwest of town, has since developed a hybrid of *Codariocalyx motorius ohashi leguminosae* that 'dances' to music. The mature gyrant has long oval leaves, plus smaller ones of a similar shape. If you sing or talk to the plant in a high-pitched voice (saxophone or violin works even better), a few of the smaller leaves will shift back and forth. It's no hype; we've seen it ourselves, although it's much more of a waltz than a jig. The plants are most active from November to February, the cool season, and from 7am to 9.30am and 4.30pm to 6.30pm.

The plants aren't for sale. You can, however, buy Udorn Dancing Tea (now very popular for its supposed medical benefits; each batch sells out quickly), made from the plant, along with the Miss Udorn Sunshine orchids and perfumes. The nursery's newest product is Udorn Toob Moob Maeng Kaeng, a perfume derived from brown stink bugs.

To get here, go to the Welcome to Nongsamrong Community sign on Rte 2024, then after 150m follow the Udorn Sunshine Fragrant Orchid sign. *Sŏrng·tăa·ou 6* and the 'yellow bus' get you close to it. A túk-túk from Udon's city centre should cost 60B to 70B.

Udon Thani Provincial Museum
MUSEUM

(พิพิธภัณฑ์เมืองอุดรธานี; Th Phosri; ◷8.30am-4.30pm Mon-Fri, 8am-4pm Sat & Sun) FREE Filling a 1920s colonial-style building that used to be a girls' school, this museum has an interesting catch-all collection ranging from geology to handicrafts.

Nong Prajak Park
PARK

(หนองประจักษ์) Udon's most popular park starts to rev up as the afternoon winds down. Much of the action takes place on the sunset-watching side of the lake, along Th Thesa. Dozens of streetside massage (Th Thesa; ◷10am-10pm) artists do rubdowns starting around 10am, and paint-your-own pottery shops join in around 4pm. There's a bike hire (1-/2-/3-seaters per hr 20/40/50B; ◷8am-8pm) shop on the northeast shore.

Wat Phothisomphon
BUDDHIST TEMPLE

(วัดโพธิสมภรณ์; Th Poniyom; ◷dawn-dusk) FREE The centrepiece of this historic temple, built during the reign of King Rama V, is a modern *chedi*, built to honor several revered monks. The mural paintings inside are excellent.

Festivals & Events

For the first 15 days of December, Udon celebrates the **Thung Si Meuang Fair**, with Isan cultural performances and all the usual shopping and eating. The Pu and Ya statues from Sanjao Pu-Ya spend the first 10 days in a temporary temple in City Field. The statues' transfers on the 1st and 10th are grand processions accompanied by a 99m dragon; there's also dragon dancing on the 5th.

Sleeping

The One
HOTEL $

(☏0 4224 4330; www.theoneud.com; Th Prajak Sinlapacom; s/d 550/600B; P✪❄⊛) This new place delivers what you expect at this price: good, comfortable rooms with a splash of style. But, its location – central and near the action, but away from the sleaze – is its best feature.

Top Mansion
HOTEL $

(☏0 4234 5015; topmansion@yahoo.com; Th Sampanthamit; r 450-750B; P✪❄@⊛) This popular hotel is so impressively spick-and-span that it warrants consideration despite being on 'Soi Falang'.

P & Mo Guesthouse
GUESTHOUSE $

(☏08 1380 1952; www.pmo-udon.com; Th Rung Sun; r 390B; ❄@⊛) Rooms are simple, but this friendly place is better-than-average value and the best of the budget hotels near the bus station. Despite its location, most rooms are in the back of the building and thus quiet.

Ban Pannarai
HOTEL $

(☏0 4230 4001; Th Poniyom; r 440B; ❄⊛) In contrast to most older hotels in Thailand, this unmissable yellow building has some actual character. It could use some new mattresses, but it you want to stay near the lake on a budget, this is a good choice. Very little English is spoken.

Lotus Condotel
HOTEL $

(☏0 4234 0777; Th Thepburi; r 299-399B; P❄⊛) It looks like a grain silo on the outside and feels like a hospital in the hallways; but the rooms are what matter most, and these are big, clean and priced right. The best feature is the neighbourhood full of university students.

★Much-che Manta
HOTEL $$

(☏0 4224 5222; www.much-chemanta.com; Th Makkang; r incl breakfast 900-1600B; ste 5000B; P✪❄@⊛✪) A lovely boutique hotel that,

Udon Thani

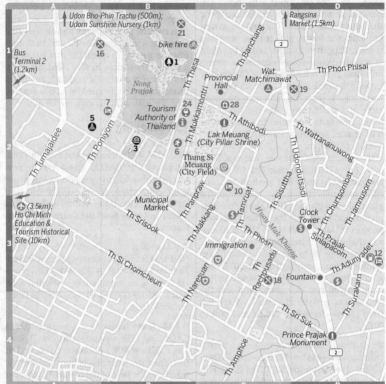

Udon Thani

for our money, tops the better-known and higher-priced Prajaktra, with which it's often compared. Creative lighting, liberal use of real wood and random splashes of colour craft a unique design, while the lovely and relaxing backyard restaurant features wood-fired pizzas as part of an international menu.

Centara   HOTEL $$$

(☎0 4234 3555; www.centarahotelsresorts.com; Th Prajak Sinlapacom; r 2000-2300B, ste 4800-6950B; P❄☀@🛜🏊) Long Udon's flagship hotel, the former Charoensri Grand has undergone a major renovation to keep it on top of the pack. Rooms are very good, except for those at the standard level, which are windowless and musty, and the full range of facilities (including a sauna, spa and fitness centre) are top-notch. Breakfast is included.

✖️ Eating & Drinking

Udonites take their night markets very seriously. The three adjoining markets in front of the train station, **Centre Point** (☺4-10pm), **Precha** (☺4-10pm) and **UD Bazaar** (Th Prajak Silpakorn; ☺11am-11pm), offer an impressive spread of food and large beer gardens.

Rabiang Phatchanee   THAI $

(Th Suppakitchanya; dishes 50-320B; ☺10am-11pm; 🛜) This place on the lake's east shore offers all the usual Thai dishes, but also many you've probably never tried before, such as fish-stomach salad. Eat outdoors on the deck or in air-conditioned dining rooms.

Maeya   THAI $

(Th Rachpusadu; dishes 55-355B; ☺10am-10.30pm; P) One part Thai restaurant and three parts English tearoom, this labyrinth has waiters dressed in black tie, and a menu stretching from grilled cheese to wild boar in red-curry sauce. The English menu can be a little cryptic: the 'rice with spit in sauce' is really 'rice with liver in sauce'.

Chai Dun   THAI $

(539/14 Th Nittayo; buffet 75B; ☺9am-10pm) The crowds are exhibit A for how tasty (and cheap) this all-you-can-eat buffet is.

Papagallo   ITALIAN $$

(Th Udondutsadi; 170-250B; ☺11am-11pm; 🛜) There are several Italian eateries in the Central Plaza/Soi Farang area, but we prefer this slightly less convenient place. The pizza is especially good.

Irish Clock   INTERNATIONAL $$

(Th Sampanthamit; dishes 60-360B; ☺8.30am-11pm; 🛜) This wood-trimmed, Guinness-infused pub is an island of class in a sea of pick-up joints. The menu has *fa·ràng*, Indian and Thai food.

Good Everything   INTERNATIONAL, THAI $$$

(Th Poniyom; dishes 150-580B; ☺8am-10pm; P🛜) This little white cottage and garden transported from the English countryside is the polar opposite of the Soi Falang experience. It features fresh and healthy cuisine, such as lamb served with Texas-style chilli, Polish mushroom soup, both Thai- and *fa·ràng*-style salads, plus quality coffees and teas. It's one of Udon's most expensive restaurants, but the many regulars consider it money well spent.

Gib Shop
JUICE BAR

(Th Prajak Sinlapacom; juice 30-70B; ⏰ 10.30am-9pm Mon-Fri, 10am-9pm Sat & Sun) 🍴 Not all juice is created equal, and this shop on the ground floor of Central Plaza proves it. Most of the fruits and vegies are organic and you can choose to have no added sugar. There's another branch (Th Thesa; juice 20-50B; ⏰ 9am-9pm) at Nong Prajak.

☆ Entertainment

The three night markets in front of the train station offer a range of diversions. Besides dining you can shop for clothes, sing karaoke, play snooker, get a tattoo and have your fortune told. On some weekends you can watch football games on the big screen or listen to live bands.

Central Plaza occassionally screens movies in their original English and also has a bowling alley.

Udon has the largest and most in-your-face sex tourism scene in Isan, and the 'Soi Falang' (Th Sampanthamit) area is rather sleazy at night, and even in the daytime you'll have to endure "Hallo, massaaaage". That said, not everyone out for a night here is looking for extracurricular activities.

🛍 Shopping

Central Plaza (Th Prajak; ⏰ 10.30am-9pm Mon-Fri, 10am-9pm Sat & Sun) is Udon's biggest shopping centre and has a branch of the English-language bookstore Asia Books, though strolling the open-air **UD Town** (Th Thongyai; ⏰ 10am-10pm Mon-Fri, 9am-10pm Sat-Sun) is more fun.

Udon Bho-Phin Trachu
HANDICRAFTS

(Th Poniyom; ⏰ 7am-6pm) There's a great selection of silk and cotton, including some natural-dyed fabrics, at this large spot northwest of Nong Prajak Lake. Look for the sign with the wooden roof.

Udon City Walking Street
MARKET

(Th Athibodi; ⏰ 5-10pm Fri & Sat) With just a handful of vendors selling handmade items, Udon's Walking Street pales in comparison to the markets in Chiang Mai and Khon Kaen that inspired it.

Fuzzy Ken's
BOOKS

(302/10 Th Prajak Sinlapacom; ⏰ 10am-11pm Mon-Fri, noon-11pm Sat) Good selection of second-hand books.

ℹ Information

Central Plaza and Tesco-Lotus have AEON ATMs and extended-hour banks.

Aek Udon International Hospital (📞 in Thailand 0066 4234 2555; Th Phosri) Has a 24-hour casualty department.

Immigration (📞 0 4224 9982; Th Phosri; ⏰ 8.30am-noon & 1-4.30pm) Does visa extensions.

Tourism Authority of Thailand (TAT; 📞 0 4232 5406; tatudon@tat.or.th; Th Thesa; ⏰ 8.30am-4.30pm)

Udon Thani Map (www.udonmap.com) This map and its companion magazine the *Udon Thani Guide* are mostly geared towards expats, but helpful for travellers, too. They're available free at *fa-ràng*-focused businesses.

ℹ Getting There & Away

AIR

Thai Airways (📞 0 4531 3340; www.thaiairways.com) connects Udon Thani to Bangkok through Suvarnaphumi airport four times daily, while **Nok Air** (📞 0 2900 9955; www.nokair.com) and **Air Asia** (📞 0 2515 9999; www.airasia.com) use Don Muang airport six and three times daily respectively. The latter two charge from about 1500B; Thai Airways is always more expensive. Air Asia also has a daily direct flight to Phuket (1800B) and Nok Air goes thrice daily direct to Chiang Mai (1900B).

Buy tickets at **On Time** (📞 0 4224 7792; Th Sai Uthit; ⏰ 8am-5pm Mon-Sat, 9am-3pm Sun), one of several travel agencies near Bus Terminal 1.

BUS

Buses to most destinations, including Bangkok (350B to 450B, eight to nine hours, every 30 minutes), use the downtown **Bus Terminal 1** (📞 0 4222 2916; Th Sai Uthit). **Chan Tour** (📞 0 4234 3403; ticket 525B; ⏰ 7 daily) and **999 VIP** (📞 0 4222 1489; ticket 700B; ⏰ 9pm) have VIP service to Bangkok. Other destinations include Sakon Nakhon (110B to 140B, three hours, every 30 minutes), Khon Kaen (84B to 180B, two hours, every 30 minutes), Pattaya (511B to 636B, 11 hours, 10 daily) and Suvarnabhumi International Airport (455B, eight hours, 9pm). If you already have a Lao visa you can take the bus to Vientiane (80B, two hours, eight daily; the 6pm departure has an additional 5B fee.) and Vang Vieng (320B, seven hours, 8.30am).

Bus Terminal 2 (📞 0 4221 4914), on the western ring road, serves many of the same destinations, plus it's the only station for western cities such as Loei (100B, three hours, every 30 minutes), Phitsanulok (238B to 306B, seven hours, 13 daily) and Chiang Mai (666B to 888B, 12 hours, 10 daily).

There are buses to Nong Khai (40B to 45B, one hour) from both terminals, but the most frequent departures are from Rangsina Market; the last departs at 9pm. There are also Nong Khai minivans (50B, 45 minutes, hourly from 6.30am to 6.30pm) from Central Plaza.

TRAIN

There are two express trains (seat 95B to 479B, 1st-class sleeper upper/lower 1077/1277B, 10½ hours) each evening and one each morning between Bangkok and Udon Thani Railway Station. There's also a cheaper evening rapid train. Four morning trains head to Nong Khai (11B to 55B, one hour).

🛈 Getting Around

Sŏrng·tăa·ou (10B) run regular routes across town. Route 6 (white) is handy since it runs up and down Th Udondutsadi (with a convenient detour to the Th Prajak-Surakarn junction), past Rangsina Market and out to Bus Terminal 2. There are also two city buses (10B). The White Bus follows Th Udondutsadi while the Yellow Bus tracks Th Phosri-Nittayo, connecting the two bus terminals in the process. *The Udon Thani Map* shows all bus and *sŏrng·tăa·ou* routes.

You can rarely flag a **taxi** (📞 0 4234 3239; call fee 30B) down on the street, but they park at Bus Terminal 1 and Central Plaza; drivers don't use meters. Túk-túk (called 'skylab' here) are seemingly everywhere. The cost from Central Plaza to Nong Prajak Park is usually 50B. Cheaper pedicabs are also still common in Udon.

Many hotels pick guests up at the airport for free, otherwise shuttle vans to downtown cost 80B per person. **Lek Car Rental** (📞 08 6059 3028; www.lekcarrentaludonthani.com) is a reputable company and there are also many smaller car-hire outlets around Central Plaza.

Around Udon Thani

Ban Chiang   บ้านเชียง

This was once an important centre of the ancient Ban Chiang civilisation, an agricultural society that thrived in northeastern Thailand for thousands of years. Archaeological digs in this village have uncovered a treasure trove of artefacts dating back to 3600 BC that overturned the prevailing theory that Southeast Asia was a cultural backwater compared to China and India at the time.

What's now one of Southeast Asia's most important archaeological sites was discovered accidentally in 1966. Stephen Young, an anthropology student from Harvard doing surveys in rural Isan on political opinions, tripped while walking through the area and found the rim of a buried pot right under his nose. Looking around he noticed many more and speculated that this might be a burial site. He was right. Serious excavations began soon after and over a million pottery pieces and dozens of human skeletons were unearthed. The now iconic burnt-ochre swirl-design pottery (made between 300 BC and AD 200) is just one of many styles these people created over the years. Researchers also found the earliest evidence of the manufacture of metal tools (people here began working bronze around 2000 BC) in the region. The area was declared a Unesco World Heritage site in 1992.

👁 Sights

Ban Chiang National Museum   MUSEUM
(พิพิธภัณฑสถานแห่งชาติบ้านเชียง; admission 150B; ⏰ 9am-4pm Tue-Sun) This excellent museum exhibits a wealth of pottery from all Ban Chiang periods, plus myriad spearheads, sickles, fish hooks, ladles, neck rings and other metal objects. The displays (with English labels) offer excellent insight into the region's distant past and, just as interestingly, how its mysteries were unravelled. Hidden in back is a room showcasing the culture of the Tai Phuan people, who migrated here about 200 years ago and founded the present town. One kilometre east, at **Wat Pho Si Nai**, is an original **burial ground excavation pit** (⏰ 8.30am-6pm), with a cluster of 52 individual burial sites dating to 300 BC. It shows how bodies were laid to rest with pottery. It's included in the museum ticket, though it's free on Mondays.

Phuan Thai House   HISTORIC SITE
(บ้านไทพวน) About 300m southwest of the burial site (follow the signs for 'Phuan House which the King and Queen visited in 1972'), this traditional Isan house is promoted as an attraction, but the still-lived-in houses throughout the village are more interesting.

Wat Pa Lelai   BUDDHIST TEMPLE
(วัดป่าเลไลยก์; ⏰ dawn-dusk) `FREE` For something completely different, visit this temple 500m north of the burial site, across the little bridge. The awesome childlike murals in the two-storey building at the back are both enlightening and entertaining.

BAN CHIANG CRAFTS

Rice farming remains the town's primary livelihood, but selling souvenirs now comes a close second. Some of the items, including Ban Chiang–style pottery, are made in the area. Walk down the road facing the museum to find a couple of **pottery workshops**. Just south of the Phuan Thai House is a small **women's weaving group** that mostly weaves indigo cotton.

Most pottery is made in **Ban Kham Or**. If you're lucky you'll find someone making large pots using the ancient paddle-and-anvil method, though they only work when they have an order. It's on the highway south of Ban Chiang. If you are travelling by public transport save your visit here for after the museum because it's not very easy to find a lift to Ban Chiang.

Sticky-rice baskets are woven by nearly every household in the village of **Ban Dong Yen** east of Ban Chiang.

Sleeping & Eating

There are several restaurants on the road fronting the museum, one of which stays open for dinner.

Lakeside Sunrise Guesthouse GUESTHOUSE $
(☎08 0193 4300; suppawat2508@gmail.com; r 300B; P❄☺🛜) In a countryside setting, yet within easy striking distance of the museum, this old wooden house is reason enough to spend the night in town. The simple rooms share bathrooms downstairs and a spacious verandah. It's best to call ahead because the joyful owner, who speaks good English, isn't always at home.

Getting There & Around

From Udon Thani, take a bus bound for Sakon Nakhon or Nakhon Phanom and get off at Ban Nong Mek (35B, 45 minutes, every 30 minutes), where túk-túk will take one or two people the 8km to Ban Chiang and bring you back for 100B.

With a lack of hills and traffic, the countryside around Ban Chiang is a great place to explore by bike. You can rent bikes for 10B per day from the shops next to the police box east of the museum.

Ban Na Kha   บ้านนาข่า

Na Kha village is one of the best fabric shopping destinations in Thailand. Downtown is a covered market with dozens of shops selling a great variety of silk and cotton from Thailand and Laos. Except at the large shops on the highway, much of the fabric is handmade. **Mae Bah Pah Fai** (☺6.30am-6pm), across from the temple entrance, has as good a selection as any, including some century-old *kít* hanging in the back.

Before leaving, take a peek at **Wat Na Ka Taewee** (☺dawn-dusk), founded by a wandering monk who found a hole from which bellowed the sound and smoke of a *naga*. It's right behind the small *bòht*. Pottery and human skeletons unearthed during various construction projects at the temple are on display under the giant Buddha.

Udon's White Bus runs to the village, 16km north of Udon.

Phu Phrabat Historical Park อุทยาน ประวัติศาสตร์ภูพระบาท

Steeped in mythical intrigue and peppered with bizarre rock formations, **Phu Phrabat** (☎0 4291 8619; admission 100B; ☺8am-4.30pm) is one of Isan's highlights. Sometime around the turn of the millennium, during the Dvaravati era, local people built Hindu and Buddhist shrines alongside the many spires, whale-sized boulders and improbably balanced rocks here. But prehistoric paintings on several rock overhangs, best seen at side-by-side **Tham Woau** and **Tham Khon**, show this was probably regarded as a holy site at least 1500 years earlier. A climb beyond these rock formations to **Pha Sa Dej**, at the edge of the escarpment, ends with vast views of the farms and forest beyond. A web of trails meanders past all these sites and you can see them in a leisurely two hours, but it's worth spending several more. A remoter northern loop is lovely, but not well marked so it's easy to get lost.

Many of the rock formations feature in a fairy tale about a king (Phaya Kong Phan), his stunningly beautiful daughter (Nang U-sa), a hermit (Ruesi Chanta) and a love-struck prince (Tao Baros) from another kingdom. The most striking rock formation, **Hor Nang U-sa**, an overturned boot-shaped outcrop with a shrine built into it, is said to be the tower where the beautiful princess was forced to live by her overprotective father. Many of these rock formations are signposted with names in Thai and English alluding to the legend, a short version of which can be read in the museum. If you're staying at the Mut Mee Garden Guesthouse in Nong Khai, you can read the entire tale there.

South of the entrance is **Wat Phra Phutthabaht Bua Bok**, with its namesake Lao-style *chedi* covering a Buddha footprint. It also has many rocks like those in the park.

There are **campsites** (per tent with own tent 20B, 2-/8-person tent hire 50B/200B) and three lovely **bungalows** (2/4/6 people 300/600/1200B) with rock-hard mattresses.

❶ Getting There & Away

The park is 65km from Udon Thani and Nong Khai and can be visited as a day trip from either city. *Sŏrng·tăa·ou* from Nong Khai's bus station to Ban Pheu (55B, 1½ hours) travel via Tha Bo. Vehicles from Udon's Rangsina Market continue past Ban Pheu to Ban Tiu (*sŏrng·tăa·ou*/minivans 35/100B, one hour/45 minutes), the village at the base of the hill where a motorcycle taxi costs 100B return for the final 5km climb. Túk-túk from Ban Pheu cost around 250B return and motorcycle taxis (they're illegal, but a few usually hang around where the buses stop) cost half that. The last vehicle back to Nong Khai leaves at 4pm and the last to Udon at 3pm.

Wat Pho Chai Sri วัดโพธิ์ชัยศรี

With brightly painted statuary that's even more bizarre than Nong Khai's Sala Kaew Ku, this *wát* is a perfect add-on to Phu Phrabat. The life-size figures around the temple grounds are acting out scenes from Isan fables and demonstrating the punishment awaiting the wicked in the Buddhist Hell.

The temple is also home to **Luang Po Naak**, a very holy 1200-year-old Buddha image shaded by a seven-headed *naga* that locals believe is responsible for many miracles.

Also known as Wat Ban Waeng, the temple is about 5km out of Ban Pheu. A túk-túk costs about 100B round trip with waiting time.

NONG KHAI PROVINCE

Lady Luck certainly smiles on the location. Occupying a narrow sweep along the banks of the Mekong, Nong Khai Province is a beautiful region. Being on the travel route to/from Vientiane, Laos – just a short hop across the river via the Friendship Bridge – it's also one of northeastern Thailand's most popular destinations. The surreal Sala Kaew Ku sculpture park is a must-see on any jaunt through the region, while the towns and temples along the Mekong west of the capital encourage travellers to slow down.

Nong Khai หนองคาย

POP 61,500

As a major staging post for those on their way from Laos, Nong Khai is the only Isan town with a fully fledged backpacker scene, albeit a modest one. But Nong Khai's popularity is about more than just its proximity to Vientiane and bounty of banana pancakes. Seduced by its dreamy pink sunsets and sluggish pace of life, many visitors who mean to stay one night end up bedding down for many more.

History

Crammed between nations, Nong Khai is both a historic and physical bridgehead between Thailand and Laos. Nong Khai once fell within the boundaries of the Vientiane (Wiang Chan) kingdom, which itself vacillated between independence and tribute to Lan Xang and Siam. In 1827 Rama III gave a Thai lord, Thao Suwothamma, the rights to establish Meuang Nong Khai at the present city site, which he chose because the surrounding swamps (*nong*) would aid in the city's defence.

In 1891, under Rama V, Nong Khai became the capital of *monthon* Lao Phuan, an early Isan satellite state that included what are now Udon, Loei, Khon Kaen, Sakon Nakhon, Nakhon Phanom and Nong Khai Provinces, as well as Vientiane. But, when western Laos was partitioned off from Thailand by the French in 1893, the French demanded that Thailand have no soldiers within 25km of the border and so the capital was moved to Udon Thani, leaving Nong Khai's fortunes to fade.

One hundred and one years later, the opening of the US$30 million, 1174m-long Saphan Mittaphap Thai-Lao (Thai-Lao Friendship Bridge) marked a new era of development for Nong Khai as a regional trade and transport centre. The skyline has been creeping slowly upwards ever since.

Central Nong Khai

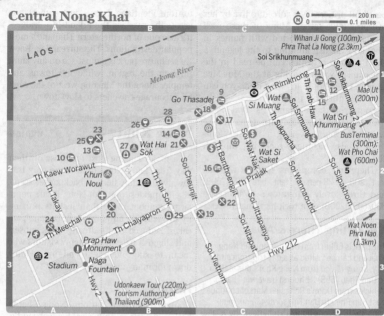

Central Nong Khai

◎ Sights

Wat Pho Chai
BUDDHIST TEMPLE
(วัดโพธิ์ชัย; Th Phochai; ⊙7am-7.30pm) FREE
Luang Po Phra Sai, a large Lan Xang–era
Buddha image awash with gold, bronze
and precious stones, sits at the hub of Nong
Khai's holiest temple. The head of the image is pure gold, the body is bronze and the
ùt·sà·nít (flame-shaped head ornament) is
set with rubies. Due to a great number of
dubious miracles people attribute to it, this
royal temple is a mandatory stop for most
visiting Thais.

Luang Po Phra Sai was one of three similar statues made for each of the daughters of Lao King Setthathirat, and they were taken as bounty after King Rama I sacked Vientiane in 1778. The awesome murals in the *bòht* depict their travels from the interior of Laos to the banks of the Mekong, where they were put on rafts. A storm sent one of the statues to the bottom of the river where it remains today. It was never recovered because, according to one monk at the temple, the *naga* like having it. The third statue, Phra Soem, is at Wat Patum Wanaram next to Siam Paragon in Bangkok. Phra Sai was supposed to accompany it, but, as the murals show you, the cart carrying it broke down here, and so this was taken as a sign that it wished to remain in Nong Khai.

Tha Sadet Market   MARKET
(ตลาดท่าเสด็จ; Th Rimkhong; ⊗8.30am-6pm) It is the most popular destination in town, and almost everyone loves a stroll through this covered market. It offers the usual mix of clothes, electronic equipment, food and assorted bric-a-brac, most of it imported from Laos and China, but there are also a few shops selling quirky quality stuff.

Village Vocational Training Center   WORKSHOP
(ศูนย์ฝึกอบรมอาชีพชนบทหนองคาย; ⊗8am-5pm) FREE Run by the Good Shepherd Sisters, this workshop 7km south of town (take Hwy 2 and turn east just after the Km 2 pillar) provides training and jobs for locals. Most of the time you can see women weaving *mát-mèe*, and it also has a pottery workshop and mushroom farm.

Wat Noen Phra Nao   BUDDHIST TEMPLE
(วัดเนินพระนาวนาราม; ⊗dawn-dusk) FREE This forest *wát* on the south side of town is a respected *vipassana* (insight meditation) centre on pleasant, tree-shaded grounds. Some extremely ornate temple architecture, including perhaps the most rococo bell tower we've ever seen, stands in contrast with the usual ascetic tone of forest monasteries. There are many Vietnamese graves here and some of the statuary wouldn't be out of place at Sala Kaew Ku.

Phra That Klang Nam   STUPA
(พระธาตุกลางน้ำ; Th Rimkhong) The 'Holy Reliquary in the Middle of the River' (sometimes called Phra That Nong Khai) is a ruined Lao-style *chedi* submerged in the middle of the river that can only be seen in the dry season when the water is low: the river rises and falls about 13m annually. The *chedi* was gobbled up by the meandering Mekong in the middle of the 18th century and it toppled over in 1847. The *chedi* is still holy and when it's exposed, people attach coloured flags to it. **Phra That La Nong**, a replica erected on land, glows brightly at night.

Nong Khai Aquarium   AQUARIUM
(พิพิธภัณฑ์สัตว์น้ำจังหวัดหนองคาย; admission 100B; ⊗10am-6pm Tue-Sun) This big green building displays freshwater and ocean-dwelling fish from Thailand and beyond, with the giant Mekong catfish in the 'giant tank' being the star attraction. It's a fun place to visit, though it's far out of town on the Khon Kaen University campus and not served by public transport.

Wat Lam Duan   BUDDHIST TEMPLE
(วัดลำดวน; Th Rimkhong; ⊗dawn-dusk) FREE You can easily pick out this temple on the skyline because an immense Buddha image sits atop the *bòht*. You're welcome to climb up (shoes off) and gaze over the Mekong alongside it.

Wat Tung Sawang   BUDDHIST TEMPLE
(วัดทุ่งสว่าง; Soi Silpakhom; ⊗dawn-dusk) FREE The *bòht* here is one of the Thailand's smallest, but the artistic flair makes it one of the prettiest. Nine sculptures of celestial deities sit on fanciful pedestals alongside it.

Wihan Ji Gong   CHINESE TEMPLE
(วิหารจี้กง, Sanjao Tekka Chee; Th Rimkhong) FREE The city's newest Chinese temple is dedicated to Ji Gong, an eccentric and heavy-drinking Chinese monk (he's usually depicted with a bottle of wine) now worshipped as a deity who assists and heals people in need. It features an eye-catching octagonal tower with murals creatively done in black and white.

THE MEKONG EXPLORER

Mekong River Cruises (www.cruise mekong.com) and its gorgeous boat, the *Mekong Explorer*, offer a new way to explore the Mekong River in Isan. Its weeklong voyages starting in Nong Khai sail November to March, and sightseeing while lounging on the deck can be as rewarding as the onshore excursions.

SALA KAEW KU ศาลาแก้วกู่

One of Thailand's most enigmatic attractions, this **sculpture park** (admission 20B; ◷8am-6pm) is a surreal journey into the mind of a mystic shaman. Built over a period of 20 years by Luang Pu Boun Leua Sourirat, who died in 1996, the park features a weird and wonderful array of gigantic sculptures that merge Hindu and Buddhist imagery.

As he tells his own story, Luang Pu tumbled into a hole as a child and met an ascetic named Kaewkoo, who introduced him to the manifold mysteries of the underworld and set him on course to become a Brahmanic-yogi-priest-shaman. Shaking up his own unique blend of Hindu and Buddhist philosophy, mythology and iconography, Luang Pu developed a large following on both sides of the Mekong in this region. In fact, his original project was on the Lao side of the river where he had been living until the 1975 communist takeover in Laos.

The park is a smorgasbord of large and bizarre cement statues of Buddha, Shiva, Vishnu and other celestial deities born of Luang Pu's dreams and cast by workers under his direction. Some of the sculptures are quite amusing. If you're travelling with kids, they'll enjoy the serene elephant wading though a pack of anthropomorphic dogs (which teaches people to not be bothered by gossip). The tallest sculpture, a Buddha seated on a coiled *naga* with a spectacular seven-headed hood, is 25m high. Also of interest is the Wheel of Life, which you enter through a giant mouth. An explanation is available on the back side of the handy map to the sculpture park provided by Mut Mee Garden Guesthouse.

The main shrine building, almost as strange as the sculptures, is full of images of every description and provenance (guaranteed to throw an art historian into a state of disorientation), photos of Luang Pu at various ages and Luang Pu's corpse lying under a glass dome ringed by flashing lights.

All buses headed east pass the road leading to Sala Kaew Ku (10B), which is also known as Wat Kaek. It's about a five-minute walk from the highway. Chartered túk-túk cost 150B return with a one-hour wait, or you can reach it by bike in about 30 minutes. The Mut Mee map shows the scenic route. Near the entrance is a touristy **crocodile show**.

Governor's Mansion Museum   MUSEUM
(จวนผู้ว่าราชการจังหวัดหนองคาย; Th Meechai; ◷8.30am-6pm) FREE The renovated 1929 French-colonial mansion has more shine outside than in. It's lovely when lit up at night.

Nong Khai Museum   MUSEUM
(พิพิธภัณฑ์จังหวัดหนองคาย; Th Meechai; ◷8.30am-4pm Mon-Fri) FREE This little museum in the former city hall has little more than old photographs, but there's enough English labelling to make it worth a few minutes of your time; and the price is right.

🏃 Activities

Thailand-wide organisations Isara (p753) and Open Mind Projects (p753) are based in Nong Khai and have many volunteering opportunities available in the area. Isara sometimes has short-term projects in Nong Khai city.

Khao Niao Tours   TOURS
(☎09 0452 3620; www.nongkhaitours.com; Th Rimkhong) Offers tours around Nong Khai and beyond and is a good source of local info and advice. Intends to offer cooking classes in the near future. There's a desk inside Smile Bar.

🎉 Festivals & Events

During Songkran the priceless image of Luang Po Phra Sai from Wat Pho Chai (p458) is paraded around town.

Like many other cities in the northeast, Nong Khai has a **Rocket Festival**, which begins on Visakha Bucha day in late May/ early June.

At the end of Buddhist Lent (Ork Phansaa) in late October/early November, there are **long-boat races** on the Mekong. These correspond with the October full moon, which is when **naga fireballs** can be seen.

One particularly fun event is Nong Khai's version of the **Chinese Dragon Festival**, held over 10 days usually in November, with dragon dancing, acrobatics, Chinese opera and lots of firecrackers.

The **Anu Sahwaree Prap Haw Festival** (5 to 15 March) boasts the city's biggest street fair.

🛏 Sleeping

Catering to the steady flow of backpackers, Nong Khai's budget lodging selection is the best in Isan.

★Mut Mee Garden Guesthouse
GUESTHOUSE $

(📞0 4246 0717; www.mutmee.com; Soi Mutmee; r 180-1500B; ☕✳🗨) Occupying a sleepy stretch of the Mekong, Nong Khai's budget old-timer has a garden so relaxing it's intoxicating, and most nights it's packed with travellers. A huge variety of rooms (the cheapest with shared bathroom, the most expensive with an awesome balcony) are clustered around a thatched-roof restaurant where the owner, Julian, holds court with his grip on local legend and his passion for all things Isan. Because nobody will ever be required to vacate their room (people often stay longer than planned), only a few reservations are taken per day. There's a yoga studio in front.

Joomemalee Guesthouse
GUESTHOUSE $

(📞08 5010 2540; Soi Srikhunmuang; s 200-300B; d 300-450B; q 800B; P☕✳🗨) Filling two old wooden houses, Joomemalee is less lovely but more homey than its neighbour the E-San, and all rooms here have a private bathroom. The family runs the business to honour the wishes of their parents that the house never be sold. Use of bikes is free.

E-San Guesthouse
GUESTHOUSE $

(📞08 6242 1860; 538 Soi Srikhunmuang; r 250-450B; P☕✳🗨) Just off the river in a small, beautifully restored wooden house ringed by a long verandah, this is an atmospheric place to stay. The cheapest rooms share bathrooms and there are also rooms in a new building. Bikes are free.

Ruan Thai Guesthouse
GUESTHOUSE $

(📞0 4241 2519; Th Rimkhong; r 300-400B; f 1200B; P☕✳@🗨) Long popular due to its good prices, convenient location, regular maintenance and friendly vibe. There's a mix of fan and air-con rooms plus one wooden cottage and some flower-filled garden greenery.

Khiangkhong Guesthouse
HOTEL $

(📞0 4242 2870; Th Rimkhong; r 300-400B; ☕✳🗨) You can catch a refreshing breeze and snag some river views from the 3rd-floor terrace (and some of the rooms) at this family-run concrete tower that falls between guesthouse and hotel.

Sawasdee Guesthouse
GUESTHOUSE $

(📞0 4241 2502; www.sawasdeeguesthouse.com; Th Meechai; s 180B, d 200-450B; P✳@🗨) If you could judge a hotel by its cover, this charismatic guesthouse in an old Franco-Chinese shophouse would come up trumps. The tidy rooms (the fan options share bathrooms) mostly lack the old-school veneer of the exterior and lobby, but they're tidy and fairly priced. The owner is quite a character.

Thai Nongkhai Guesthouse
GUESTHOUSE $

(📞0 4241 3155; www.thainongkhai.com; Th Banthoengjit; tw 400B, d 500B; P☕✳@🗨) The seven rooms and bungalows here are fairly humdrum, but they are gleaming clean and the backyard location makes it pretty peaceful.

Baan Mae Rim Nam
HOTEL $$

(📞0 4242 0256; www.baanmaerimnam.com; Mekong Promenade; d 500-700B; tr 800-1000B; ☕✳🗨) Right on the riverfront, this bright yellow building has great rooms with balconies and river views. The cheaper standard rooms in back, however, are less inviting.

Baan Sabai Rimkhong
HOTEL $$

(📞0 4241 3545; www.baansabairimkhong.com; Th Kaew Worawut; r 490-1200B; P☕✳🗨) This new riverside place is a tad odd, but the prices are fair for what you get. And, because it's a new building, it doesn't suffer the quirks of many older properties. Rooms with river views start at 690B.

Sofa Gallery
HOTEL $$$

(📞08 0279 8789; www.sofagalleryhotel.com; Th Kaew Worawut; r 1500-1900B; P☕✳🗨) A lovely boutique hotel with an odd but effective mix of concrete and panache that, along with the riverside garden, makes for a relaxing place to stay. Unfortunately, it's a small jaunt from the city centre.

Budsabong Fine Resort
HOTEL $$$

(📞08 1666 5111; www.budsabongfineresort.com; Th Donsawan-Wattad; r incl breakfast 1600-1800B, ste 3800-4400B; P☕✳@🗨🏊) The stark white exterior won't inspire love at first sight, but get inside and you'll find large, attractive and well-appointed rooms, many with terraces stepping right into the enormous pool. It's out in the country, beyond Sala Kaew Ku.

✕ Eating

There are many restaurants in the Tha Sadet Market, and elsewhere along the promenade, that serve big river views.

★ **Dee Dee Pohchanah**   THAI $
(Th Prajak; dishes 45-250B; ⊙10.30am-2am) How good is Dee Dee? Just look at the dinnertime crowds – but don't be put off by them. Despite having a full house every night, this simple place is a well-oiled machine and you won't be waiting long.

★ **Saap Lah**   NORTHEASTERN THAI $
(Th Meechai; dishes 25-150B; ⊙7am-8pm) For excellent *gài yâhng*, *sôm·dam* and other Isan foods, follow your nose to this no-frills shop.

Mae Ut   VIETNAMESE $
(Th Meechai; dishes 30-50B; ⊙10am-6pm) While Daeng Namnuang operates as much like a factory as a restaurant, this little place, serving just four items including spring rolls and *khâo gee·ab 'bahk mŏr* (fresh noodles with pork), is essentially grandma's kitchen. Look for the orange building with tables under a bright blue awning. English is limited.

Daeng Namnuang   VIETNAMESE $
(Th Rimkhong; dishes 60-130B; ⊙8am-8pm; P🅿🖥) This massive river restaurant has grown into an Isan institution, and hordes of out-of-towners head home with car boots and carry-on bags (there's an outlet at Udon Thani's airport) stuffed with *năam neu·ang* (pork spring rolls).

Khao Soi Chiang Mai   NORTHERN THAI $
(949 Th Meechai; 35-50B; ⊙8am-3pm) If you're missing the flavours of northern Thailand, this hole-in-the-wall will satisfy your cravings.

Mariam Restaurant   INDIAN, THAI $
(Th Prajak; dishes 30-120B; ⊙7am-9pm; 🖥) This Muslim restaurant serves Indian (Pakistani, actually) and southern Thai food. For 140B you get three dishes, two roti and one drink.

Hospital Food Court   THAI $
(Th Meechai; ⊙7am-3pm) A dozen cooks here whip up the standards at low prices. The food is delicious, there's plenty of choice and it is conveniently located near the most popular guesthouses in town.

Nagarina   THAI $$
(📞0 4241 2211; Th Rimkhong; dishes 40-400B; ⊙10am-9pm; 🖥📶) As with nearly all *fa·ràng*-focused guesthouses in Thailand, the Thai food at Mut Mee Garden Guesthouse is toned down and not recommended. (The Western breakfasts, on the other hand, are fine.) But the kitchen of its floating restaurant, which specialises in fish, turns out the real deal. There's a sunset cruise (100B) most nights around 5pm; order food at least 30 minutes before departure.

Café Thasadej   INTERNATIONAL $$
(Th Bunterngjit; dishes 60-375B; ⊙8am-late) Sophistication oozes out of this little restaurant. Both the menu and liquor list, the latter among the best in town, go global. Gyros, Weiner schnitzel, fish and chips, lasagne, tuna salad and smoked salmon are some of the most popular options.

🍷 Drinking & Nightlife

For something completely Thai, follow the Mekong-hugging Th Rimkhong east past Tha Sadet Market and you'll pass a bevy of restaurants and bars, some earthy, some fashionable, churning out dinner and drinks. There are some expat-owned bars around here, too.

Gaia   BAR
(Th Rimkhong; ⊙7pm-late) Much of the Mut Mee crowd and many resident *fa·ràng* fill this laid-back lounge on the Mekong. There's a great drinks list, a chilled vibe and sometimes live music. It often hosts fundraisers for local charitable projects.

Warm Up   BAR
(Th Rimkhong) This little place rises above, both figuratively and literally, the other bars at this end of Th Rimkhong. It looks out over the river, has a pool table and is popular with both locals and travellers.

🛍 Shopping

Nong Khai Walking Street Market   MARKET
(⊙4-10pm Sat) This street festival featuring music, handmade items, and food takes over the promenade every Saturday night.

Village Weaver Handicrafts   HANDICRAFTS
(Th Prajak) This place sells high-quality, hand-woven fabrics and clothing (ready-made or made to order) that help fund development projects around Nong Khai. The *mát·mèe* cotton is particularly good here.

GETTING TO LAOS: NONG KHAI TO VIENTIANE

This is one of the busiest Thai border crossings. For more information on visas, see p764.

Getting To the Border If you already have your Lao visa, the easiest way to Vientiane is the direct bus from Nong Khai's bus terminal (55B, one hour, six daily). There's also a bus to Vang Vieng (270B, four hours, 10am). The 5B surcharge for tickets to Laos on weekends, holidays and 7.30am and 6pm weekdays is genuine.

If you plan to get your visa at the border (6am to 10pm), take a túk-túk there; expect to pay 100B from the bus station, but you can pay 50B from the town centre. Unless you're travelling in a large group, there's no good reason to use a visa service agency, so don't let a driver take you to one.

You can also go to Laos by train (there are immigration booths at both stations) though not to Vientiane, so we strongly recommended against doing it. The 15-minute ride (20B to 30B, departs 9am and 2.45pm) drops you in Thanaleng (aka Dongphasay) station just over the bridge, leaving you at the mercy of túk-túk drivers who charge extortionate prices.

At the Border After getting stamped out of Thailand, you can take the minibuses (weekdays/weekends 20/30B) that carry passengers across the bridge to the hassle-free, but sometimes busy, Lao immigration checkpoint where 30-day visas are available.

Moving On It's about 20km to Vientiane. Plenty of buses, túk-túk and taxis will be waiting for you and it's easy to find fellow travellers to share the costs.

Hornbill Books BOOKS
(Soi Mut Mee; ⊘10am-7pm Mon-Sat) Buys, sells and trades English-language books. Has internet access, too.

ⓘ Information

There are banks with extended opening hours and AEON ATMs at **Asawann** (Hwy 2; ⊘10am-9pm) shopping centre.

Go Thasadej (☑08 1592 0164; www.gotha sadej.com; Mekong Promenade; ⊘10am-7pm) One of the most reliable all-round travel agents in Thailand.

Immigration (☑0 4299 0935; ⊘8.30am-noon & 1-4.30pm Mon-Fri) South of the Friendship Bridge. Offers Thai visa extensions.

Nong Khai Hospital (☑0 4241 3456; Th Meechai) Has a 24-hour casualty department.

Tourism Authority of Thailand (TAT; ☑0 4242 1326; tat_nongkhai@yahoo.com; Hwy 2; ⊘8.30am-4.30pm) Inconveniently located outside of town.

ⓘ Getting There & Away

AIR

The nearest airport is 55km south in Udon Thani. **Udonkaew Tour** (☑0 4241 1530; Th Pranang Cholpratan; ⊘8.30am-5.30pm) travel agency runs minivans (150B per person) to/from the airport. Coming into town they'll drop you at your hotel or the bridge; going back you need to get yourself to their office. It's best to buy tickets in advance.

BUS

Nong Khai bus terminal (☑0 4242 1264) is located just off Th Prajak, about 1.5km from the main pack of riverside guesthouses. Udon Thani (40B to 45B, one hour, every 30 minutes) is the most frequent destination. For those travelling west along the Mekong, there are buses to Sangkhom (60B, three hours, 7.30am, 11am, 3pm) with the 7.30am bus continuing all the way to Loei (130B, 6½ hours). There are also buses to Khon Kaen (119B to 176B, 3½ hours, hourly), Nakhon Phanom (210B, 6½ hours, four daily until noon), and Kanchanaburi (855B, 10 hours, 8am) and minivans to Udon Thani (50B, 45 minutes, hourly) and Bueng Kan (100B to 150B, 2½ hours, eight daily). Many people headed to Udon Thai catch buses at the junction of Hwy 2 and Hwy 212, though you may not get a seat if you board here.

Bangkok (380B to 490B, 11 hours) buses are frequent in the late afternoon and early evening, but less so during the day. **Nakhonchai Air** (☑0 4242 0285; ticket 762B; ⊘departs 8.30pm), **Chan Tour** (☑0 4246 0205; ticket 620B; ⊘departs 7.45am, 10.15am, 7.30pm, 8.45pm) and **999 VIP** (☑0 4241 2679; ticket 762B; ⊘8pm) offer VIP buses. There's also one bus direct to Suvarnabhumi (Airport) bus station (495B, nine hours, 8pm). For Chiang Mai, you have to change at Udon's Bus Terminal 2.

TRAIN

Two express trains, one in the morning and the other in the afternoon, connect Bangkok (seat 103B to 498B, 1st-class sleeper upper/lower 1117/1317B, 11½ hours) and Nong Khai Railway Station, which is 2km west of downtown. There's also one cheaper evening rapid train.

ℹ Getting Around

Nong Khai is a great place for cycling due to the limited traffic and the nearby countryside. Many guesthouses let you use their bikes for free. If you need to hire one, **Khun Noui** (☏ 08 1975 4863; Th Kaew Worawut; ⊙ 8am-4pm), who sets up on the roadside across from the entrance to Mut Mee, has reliable bikes (50B per day) and motorcycles (200B). Khao Niao Tours (p460) rents real mountain bikes for 70/40B per adult/child.

You can find metered taxis at the bus station and the bridge. Generally people agree on a price rather than use the meter; but if you do use it there's an initial fee of 50B, which gets you 2km and then each additional kilometre costs 4B. A túk-túk between the Mut Mee area and either the bus station or bridge should be 40B to 50B.

West of Nong Khai

The people living west of Nong Khai are obsessed with **topiary**, and along Rte 211 you'll pass hedges and bushes sculpted by ambitious gardeners into everything from elephants to boxing matches. The river road (Th Kaew Worawut), lined with floodplain fields of tobacco, tomatoes and chillies, is another option for the first stretch of the route west, though cyclists should note that it has no shoulder.

GREAT BALLS OF FIRE

Methane gas? Drunken Lao soldiers? Clever monks? Or perhaps the fiery breath of the sacred *naga*, a serpent-like being that populates folkloric waterways throughout Southeast Asia. Since 1983 (or for ages, depending on who you ask), the sighting of the *bâng fai pá yah nâhk* (loosely translated, '*naga* fireballs') has been an annual event along the Mekong River. Sometime in the early evening, at the end of the Buddhist Rains Retreat (October), which coincides with the 15th waxing moon of the 11th lunar month, small reddish balls of fire shoot from the Mekong River and float a hundred or so metres into the air before vanishing without a trace. Most claim the *naga* fireballs are soundless, but others say a hissing can be heard if one is close enough to where they emerge from the surface of the river. Most Thai and Lao see the event as a sign that resident *naga* are celebrating the end of the holiday.

There are many theories about the fireballs. One, which aired on a Thai exposé-style TV program, claimed that Lao soldiers taking part in festivities on the other side of the Mekong were firing their rifles into the air. Interestingly, the reaction to the TV program was a storm of protest from both sides of the river. Some suggest that a mixture of methane gas and phosphane, trapped below the mud on the river bottom, somehow reaches a certain temperature at exactly that time of year and is released. Many simply assume that some monks have found a way to make a 'miracle'. The latter was the premise behind a 2002 comedy film entitled *Sìp Hâh Kâm Deuan Sìp èt* (Fifteenth Waxing Moon of the Eleventh Lunar Month), released with English subtitles under the peculiar title *Mekhong Full Moon Party*.

Naga fireballs have become big business in Nong Khai Province, and curious Thais from across the country converge at various spots on the banks of the Mekong for the annual show. Little Phon Phisai, the locus of fireball-watching, hosts some 40,000 guests. Special buses (cheap or free) make the return trip to Nong Khai city, and several hotels run their own buses where you'll get a guaranteed seat. Mut Mee Garden Guesthouse sails its boat there and back (2800B, including lunch and dinner).

If you don't come with the right mindset, you'll likely be disappointed. The fireball experience is more than just watching a few small lights rise from the river; it's mostly about watching Thais watching a few small lights rise from the river. And even if the *naga* doesn't send his annual greeting on the day you come (it's sometimes delayed by a day due to the vagaries of calculating the arrival of the full moon), it'll be an interesting experience.

Around Nong Khai

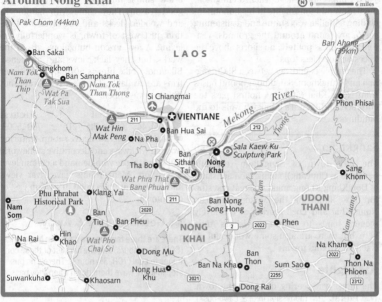

Wat Phra That Bang Phuan วัดพระ ธาตุบังพวน

Boasting a beautiful *chedi* that locals believe holds 29 Buddha relics, **Wat Phra That Bang Phuan** (วัดพระธาตุบังพวน; admission free; ☉dawn-dusk) is one of the region's most sacred temples. Nobody knows when the first stupa was erected here, but after moving his capital from Luang Prabang to Vientiane in 1560, Lan Xang King Setthathirat commissioned grand temples to be built all around his kingdom, including a new stupa built here over an older one. Rain caused it to lean precariously and in 1970 it toppled. It was rebuilt in 1976–77. The current one stands 34m high on a 17-sq-metre base and has many unsurfaced *chedi* around it, giving the temple an ancient atmosphere; and it's this, much more than the main stupa, that makes a trip here rewarding.

The temple is 22km from Nong Khai on Rte 211. Take a Pak Chom–bound bus (20B, 45 minutes).

Tha Bo ท่าบ่อ

Prosperous Tha Bo is the most important commercial centre between Nong Khai and Loei, and the covered market, which spills out to the surrounding streets, is full of local products. A large Vietnamese population lives here, and they've cornered the market on noodle production. You'll see masses of *sên lék* (small rice noodles) drying in the sun on the west side of town. From about 5am to 10am you can watch people at the factories making the noodles, and then at around 2pm they start the cutting, all by hand.

Production used to be mostly spring-roll wrappers laid out on the bamboo racks, but noodles are easier to make and sell so locals have made the switch. Ban Hua Sai, 10km upriver just before Si Chiangmai, is now the area's spring-roll-wrapper capital.

Tha Bo is mostly a day-trip destination, but there are some guesthouses, if you want to spend the night.

The Yellow Bus runs regularly between Nong Khai and Tha Bo (27B, one hour, every 30 minutes), taking the scenic riverside route. Pick it up in Nong Khai at the bus station or near the hospital on Th Meechai.

Wat Hin Mak Peng วัดหินหมากเป้ง

Overlooking a lovely stretch of the Mekong, this vast forest **temple** (วัดหินหมากเป้ง; admission free; ☉6am-7pm) is centred on a cliff rising out of the river. The very peaceful temple is respected by Thais because of their reverence for the founding abbot, Luang Pu

Thet, whom they believe reached enlightenment. Several monuments in his honour, including a lifelike wax statue and a glistening *chedi*, are found around the grounds. Visitors must dress politely: no shorts above the knees or sleeveless tops.

The temple is midway between Si Chiangmai and Sangkhom. Sangkhom-bound buses from Nong Khai (50B, 2¼ hours) pass the entrance, and then it's a longish walk to the buildings.

Sangkhom   สังคม

The little town of Sangkhom (officially named Ban Chueang), facing the Lao island of Don Klang Khong, makes a great rest stop for those following the Mekong between Nong Khai and Loei. Staring at the lovely scenery tends to dominate visitors' time here, but there are also some wonderful attractions around town.

◉ Sights

The forest wát peering down on the town, **Wat Pa Tak Sua** (admission free; ☉ dawn-dusk), lies just 2km away as the crow flies, but it's 19km to drive. It has the most amazing Mekong views we know of except for Pha Taem National Park; you might see the valley filled with fog on early mornings during the cold season. The footpath used by the monks every morning begins east of town just before the Km 81 pillar (look for the faded green sign with white letters). Follow Soi 5 past the last house, then veer right by the mango and papaya trees.

Three-tiered **Nam Tok Than Thip** (admission free) waterfall, 13km west of Sangkhom (2km off Rte 211), is the largest waterfall in the area. The lower level drops 30m and the second, easily reached via stairs, falls 100m. The 70m top drop is only barely visible through the lush forest. **Nam Tok Than Thong** (admission free) waterfall, 12km east of Sangkhom, is a wider but shorter drop. Than Thong is more accessible than Than Thip, but can be rather crowded on weekends and holidays. Both are at full flow around July to September and dry up by February.

⌂ Sleeping

★ **Bouy Guesthouse**   GUESTHOUSE $
(☎0 4244 1065; toy_bgh@hotmail.com; Rte 211; s 250-280B, d 280-300B, r with air-con 500B; ▣❄@⬆) As the ever-smiling owners will tell you, Sangkhom's veteran lodge has just

a few 'simple huts', but they're popular for good reason. They come with hammocks and wooden decks and the riverside location, just west of town, is wonderfully relaxing. A few air-con bungalows are in the works, but they lack views and ambience. Bike/motorbike hire is 50B/200B and river trips are available. There's a restaurant, but it's not always open.

Poopae Ruenmaithai   HOTEL $$
(☎0 4244 1088; Rte 211; r 700-1500B; ▣❄❄@⬆) This attractive set-up, featuring wooden walkways and decorative stonework, will satisfy those who demand a certain level of comfort. Many rooms have river views and the restaurant is good. It's 1.5km east of downtown.

❶ Getting There & Away

There are three fan buses a day from Nong Khai (60B, three hours) and the earliest of those continues to Loei (70B, 3½ hours). There's no bus stop in town; wave them down when they pass.

LOEI PROVINCE

Stretching south from the sleepy arc of the Mekong River at Chiang Khan to the vast mountain plateau of Phu Kradueng National Park, Loei (meaning 'to the extreme') is a diverse, beautiful province untouched by mass tourism, despite all it has to offer. This isn't the wildest place in Thailand, but the region's tranquil national parks and nature reserves can lead you to some splendid isolation. And, if you have the luck to arrive at the right time, you can balance the hush of nature with the hubbub of Dan Sai's incredible Phi Ta Khon Festival.

The terrain here is mountainous and temperatures fluctuate from one extreme to the other: it's hotter than elsewhere in Thailand during the hot season, though it's also one of the few provinces in Thailand where temperatures drop below 0°C, and in December and January the crisp air paints leaves red and yellow at high elevations.

Loei   เลย

POP 33,000

Arrive here after a sojourn in the region's remote countryside and the capital city is little more than a reminder that concrete and congestion still exist. Not that it's a bad

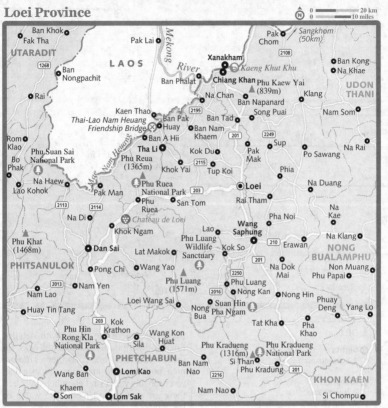

place, but, as the Tourism Authority of Thailand itself used to say, 'the city of Loei has little to hold the traveller's interest'. Still, it's likely you'll end up passing through here if you're travelling in the region.

Sights

Loei's small museums aren't worth a special trip, but if you won't be visiting Dan Sai, there are Phi Ta Khon festival masks and photos (plus pottery, fabrics and other artefacts) to see at the **Loei Museum** (Th Charoenrat; admission free; ⊙8.30am-4.30pm), above the TAT office, and the **Loei Cultural Centre** (Rte 201; admission free; ⊙8.30am-4pm) 5km north of town at Rajabhat University.

Sleeping

Sugar Guesthouse GUESTHOUSE $
(☎08 9711 1975; www.sugarguesthouse.blog.com; Soi 2, Th Wisut Titep; r 200-380B; P ⊖ ✳ @ 🛜) This genuine guesthouse has simple (the fan rooms share a bathroom) clean rooms and a friendly English-speaking owner.

King Hotel HOTEL $
(☎0 4281 1701; Th Chumsai; r 399-750B; P ✳ 🛜) Fit for a king? No; though a major modernisation has given the rooms a simple but attractive style and made it a pleasant place to stay. The restaurant is good too.

Baan Sabai HOTEL $
(☎0 4281 1132; www.baansabailoei.com; off Th Nok Kaew; 350-400B; P ⊖ ✳ 🛜) The bright new hotel is plain, but offers good-value rooms (even the cheap ones feature fridges and quality mattresses) in a quiet, convenient location.

Loei Village HOTEL $$
(☎0 4283 3599; www.loeivillages.com; Th Nok Kaew Soi 3; r incl breakfast 800-1400B; P ⊖ ✳ @ 🛜) Though it's just a concrete block, like most small Thai hotels, this spiffy new place adds

Loei

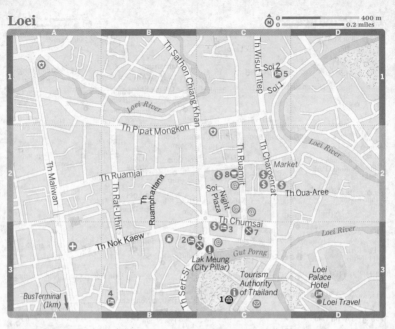

enough small details (such as decorative lamps and a proper breakfast) to make it the city's top lodging choice.

✕ Eating & Drinking

A handful of bars on Th Ruamphattana comprise Loei's meager attempt at a trendy nightlife scene.

★ Baan Yai   NORTHEASTERN THAI $
(Th Sert-Si; dishes 25-150B; ⊙11am-11pm; 🛜) This big, leafy place with a funky variety of wooden tables and chairs is a genuine Isan restaurant where the menu (with detailed English descriptions) features ant eggs, insects, rattan and frogs. It also serves *dtòhng mŏo* (pork in a sour-and-spicy sauce), a dish you probably won't find elsewhere. At night there are movies and football to watch or live music.

Walking Street   NORTHEASTERN THAI $
(Th Ruamjit; ⊙4-11pm) Loei's grandly named, but otherwise typical, night market is a good dining destination.

Phuloei Coffee   CAFE
(Th Ruamjit; coffee 35B; ⊙8am-8.30pm; 🛜) This little spot serves good locally grown coffee and delicious bakery goods.

❶ Information

The **Tourism Authority of Thailand** (TAT; 🖉 0 4281 2812; tatloei@tat.or.th; Th Charoenrat; ⊙8.30am-4.30pm) provides a good map and has helpful staff.

There are extended-hour banks and an AEON ATM in the Big C department store on the highway.

❶ Getting There & Away

AIR

Nok Air (🖉 0 2900 9955; www.nokair.com) connects Loei to Bangkok's Don Muang Airport

Foreigners can get Lao visas at the seldom-used **Thai-Lao Nam Heuang Friendship Bridge** (⊘6am-6pm) in Amphoe Tha Li, 60km northwest of Loei. But the road from Kaen Thao to Luang Prabang is rough and public transport is scarce.

once daily with prices starting around 1700B. **Loei Travel** (☑08 5010 2426; www.loeitravel. com; ⊘10-5 Mon-Fri, 10.30am-4pm Sat), inside Loei Palace Hotel, sells tickets.

BUS

The most frequent service from Loei's **bus terminal** (☑0 4283 3586) is to Udon Thani (100B, three hours, every 30 minutes). There are also buses to Khon Kaen (143B, 3½ hours, hourly), Khorat (290B, six hours, hourly), Phitsanulok (154B, four hours, four daily) and Chiang Mai (409B to 570B, 10 hours, four daily). The only bus to Nong Khai (130B, 6½ hours) leaves at 6am, and it's worth catching because it follows the scenic Mekong River route. It's faster, however, to go via Udon Thani.

First-class buses to Bangkok (440B, 11 hours) are frequent and there are VIP buses (697B) each evening with **Air Muang Loei** (☑0 4283 2042) and **999 VIP** (☑0 4281 1706).

ⓘ Getting Around

Sŏrng·tăa·ou (10B) run from the bus station through town or you can take a túk-túk for about 40B.

Sugar Guesthouse rents bicycles (50B per day) and motorcycles (250B per day) and leads reasonably priced trips around the area. Loei Palace Hotel rents bikes (50/80B per half-/full day).

Chiang Khan เชียงคาน

What was once a sleepy, little-known riverside town full of traditional timber houses is now a trendy destination for Thais, full of tacky gift shops. That said, it's far from ruined and we still think it's a good place to visit. The photogenic views of the river and the Lao mountains beyond are still there and things remain fairly peaceful in the daytime, before the evening shopping stampede begins.

◉ Sights

Kaeng Khut Khu VIEWPOINT

(admission free) With the mountains making an attractive backdrop, this famous bend in the Mekong and its small set of rapids is a popular stop. The surrounding park has a bevy of vendors selling *má·prów gàaw* (coconut candy), the local speciality. This is also a good place to try *gûng-paa* (crispy fried shrimp), which looks a little like a frisbee, and *gûng đên* (dancing shrimp), little bowls of live shrimp. It's 5km downstream from town; túk-túk drivers charge 100B per person.

Phu Tok VIEWPOINT

In the cool season, people head to nearby Phu Tok mountain for sunrise and 'sea of fog' views. If you don't have your own vehicle, ask your hotel to arrange a ride. Túk-túk charge 100B per person and then you have to ride the *sŏrng·tăa·ou* (25B per person) to the top.

Wat Si Khun Mueang BUDDHIST TEMPLE

(Th Chai Khong; ⊘dawn-dusk) The *bòt* at Wat Si Khun Mueang, which probably dates to the Rama III era, is mostly Lao-style (in particular, note the sweeping roof), but it also freely mixes central (the lotus pillars) and northern (the guardian lions) Thai stylings. It's fronted by a superb mural of the Jataka tales.

Wat Mahathat BUDDHIST TEMPLE

(Th Srichiang Khan; ⊘daylight hours) Wat Mahathat, in the centre of town, is Chiang Khan's oldest temple. The *bòt*, constructed in 1654, has a new roof over old walls with the faded original mural on the front.

CELEBRATING THE BOVINE AT BUN BÂNG FAI

The little-known **Phi Kon Nam** festival in Ban Na Sao, 7km south of Chiang Khan, is part of the village's rain-inducing Bun Bâng Fai, and coincides with Visakha Bucha in May or June. Locals believe that the souls of their cows and buffaloes wander around the village after they die, so to show respect, the villagers don wild bovine-inspired masks and colourful costumes to commune with them.

Chiang Khan

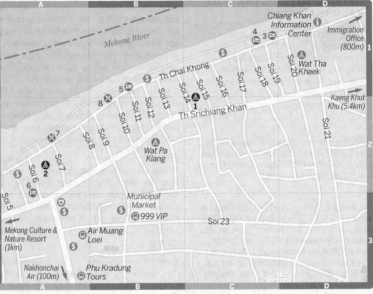

Chiang Khan

◉ Sights

1 Wat Mahathat	C2
2 Wat Si Khun Mueang	A2

🛏 Sleeping

3 Chiang Khan Guesthouse	C1
4 Chiangkhan Riverview Guesthouse	C1
5 Huean Yai Bab Pa	B1
6 Torng Sai Homestay	A2

❌ Eating

7 Ban-Jerd-Loei	A2
8 Rabiang Kong	B2

🏃 Activities

Most guesthouses arrange boat trips to Kaeng Khut Khu or further afield, and the mountain scenery makes them highly recommended. Rates swing with petrol prices, but the typical 1½-hour trip costs around 1000B for up to 10 people.

Another option is to kayak the river with **Mekong Culture & Nature Resort** (☑0 4282 1457; per person 1600-2000B, minimum 4 people), 1km upstream from town. They also have accommodation.

🛏 Sleeping

Chiang Khan's popularity means hotel owners don't need to price their rooms reasonably. But, most places are quick to discount on weekdays and in the low season. You can also usually save money by staying on a soi (Soi 11 has many choices) rather than along the river road. And note that preserving the historic character of buildings means shared bathrooms (unless stated otherwise) and thin walls.

Chiangkhan Riverview Guesthouse GUESTHOUSE **$**
(☑08 0741 8055; 277 Th Chai Khong; r 300-800B; ⊖✴🗟) This diverse riverside spot has rooms with fan and air-conditioning, shared and private bathrooms, and a mix of old and new construction. Some rooms have river views, the terrace is very inviting, and the owners friendly.

Chiang Khan Guesthouse GUESTHOUSE **$**
(☑0 4282 1691; www.thailandunplugged.com; 282 Th Chai Khong; s/d/tr/f 300/400/600/1000B; ⊖🗟) This traditional-style place is all creaking timber and tin roofing, and the terrace sits really close to the river. Owner Pim will make you feel at home. Must love cats and dogs.

Torng Sai Homestay

GUESTHOUSE $

(☑08 6227 2667; 129/3 Soi 6; s/d/tr 200/300/450B; ☺) This old wooden shophouse hasn't been gussied up like those on the riverfront. You get just a mattress on the floor, a fan and a warm welcome. If the owners aren't around, they're probably at the temple: just call and they'll rush over.

Norn-Nab-Dao

HOTEL $$

(☑08 6792 0215; Th Chai Khong; r incl breakfast 800-1000B; P☺✳☎) A brand new place without any history, but a bit of charm nonetheless. The cutely painted rooms lie around a central terrace.

★Huean Yai Bab Pa

HOTEL $$$

(☑0 4282 1705; 340 Th Chai Khong; r incl breakfast 1500-1800B; P☺✳☎) The friendly owners of this seven-room spot have combined historic touches with modern stylings, and the results are impressive. All rooms have private bathrooms. The river views cost extra.

Chiang Khan Hill Resort

HOTEL $$$

(☑0 4282 1285; www.chiangkhanhill.com; r 900-3800B; P✳☎☺) The best views of Kaeng Khut Khu are from the town's original resort, which overlooks the rapids east of town. Rooms are nice for the price and the restaurant is quite good.

✖ Eating

Ban-Jerd-Loei

THAI $

(Th Chai Khong; dishes 35-150B; ☺10am-10pm) Mekong fish (try the 'black pepper fried river fish') is the speciality of this well-hidden riverside place (look for the Coke sign), but its other Thai dishes are good, too.

Rabiang Kong

THAI $

(Th Chai Khong; dishes 50-200B; ☺10am-10pm) Popular with locals long before the tourism boom, the prices have risen a bit but the quality has not dropped.

ⓘ Information

There are some full-service banks in town that exchange money including Krungthai.

Bike hire generally costs 50B per day while motorcycles are 250B. Most hotels have free bikes for their guests.

Chiang Khan Information Center (Soi 21, Th Chai Khong; ☺10am-5pm)

Immigration Office (☑0 4282 1911; Soi 26, Th Chai Khong; ☺8.30am-4.30pm Mon-Fri) For visa extensions.

ⓘ Getting There & Away

Sŏrng·tăa·ou to Loei (35B, 1¼ hours) depart about every 15 minutes in the early morning, and then whenever there are enough passengers, from a stop on Th Srichiang Khan (at Soi 26). They also pick up passengers at the market and Rte 201 along the way. Eight 1st-class buses (38B, 45 minutes) leave from the **Nakhonchai Air** (☑0 4282 1905) terminal on Rte 201. They continue to Khorat (326B, seven hours) via Chaiyaphum.

Three companies, departing from their own offices, make the run to Bangkok (10 hours) in the morning and early evening: **Air Muang Loei** (☑0 4282 1390; Th Srichiang Kan Soi 23; ticket 486B); **999 VIP** (☑0 4282 1002; Soi 9; 351-756B) and **Phu Kradung Tours** (☑08 9842 1524; Old Shell Petrol Station, Rte 201; ticket 486B).

No transport runs to Nong Khai. The quickest way there is via Loei and Udon Thani, but for the scenic river route take a Loei-bound sŏrng·tăa·ou south to Ban Tad (20B, 30 minutes) where you can catch the bus to Nong Khai that leaves Loei at 6am. Another option is to hire a car to take you to Pak Chom (about 700B) where there are buses to Nong Khai (80B, four hours) at 10am and 3pm.

If you're heading west and you've got your own wheels, consider following the seldom-seen back roads along Mae Nam Heuang; they'll eventually deposit you in Dan Sai.

Phu Ruea National Park

อุทยานแห่งชาติภูเรือ

Phu Ruea means 'Boat Mountain', a moniker stemming from a cliff jutting out of the peak that's sort of in the shape of a Chinese junk. The 121-sq-km **Phu Ruea National Park** (☑0 4280 7624; admission 200B) isn't one of Thailand's most impressive reserves, but it does offer vast views from the summit (1365m), reached by either a sŏrng·tăa·ou or a 1km footpath. For a longer hike to the top, take the easy (but usually overgrown) 2.5km trail from the lower visitor centre to 30m-tall **Nam Tok Huai Phai**, arguably the park's most scenic waterfall, and then keep going another 5.5km.

There are two campgrounds. The **upper campground** (per person with own tent 30B, tent hire 305-450B; r 500-700B) is informal and facilities are poor, but the campsites and rough bucket-shower rooms put you pretty close to the summit for sunrise and sunset. There's hot water, all-day electricity and wi-fi at the more attractive **lower**

THE GARDEN OF ISAN

The Phu Ruea region is famous for its flower farms and there's a riot of colours along the roadside. The cool, dry climate allows farmers to grow a variety of crops not common in Isan, such as strawberries, coffee (the Coffee Bun chain is based here and their blend includes Loei-grown beans), macadamia nuts, petunias and persimmon.

One stop that most travellers with their own wheels make is **Chateau de Loei** (☑ 0 4280 9521; www.chateaudeloei. com; Rte 203, Km 61; ☾8am-5pm), which released the first commercially produced Thai wine in 1995. It's a penny-ante operation compared to the attractive and well-managed wineries around Khao Yai, but visitors are welcome to taste its wines and brandies way back in the utilitarian main building.

campsite (per person with own tent 30B, tent hire 540B, bungalows 4/6 people 2000/3000B), which also has six comfortable bungalows with TV and fridge. There are restaurants at the campsites (those at the upper site aren't always open), and many small resorts below the park with cheaper prices. Night-time temperatures can drop to near freezing in December and January, so come prepared.

The park is 50km west of Loei on Rte 203 and buses can drop you in the town of Phu Ruea (55B, one hour) where you'll have to hitch or charter a truck (around 800B, including a few hours' wait) to the park itself. The summit is 8km from the highway.

Dan Sai   ด่านซ้าย

For 362 days a year, Dan Sai is an innocuous little town where life revolves around a small market and a dusty main street. For the remaining three days, however, it's the site of one of the country's liveliest and loudest festivals. As its normal, peaceful self, the town won't appeal to everyone; but for people who appreciate slow travel and want a good look at local life, Dan Sai (in large part because of its homestay program) delivers in spades.

⊙ Sights & Activities

Phi Ta Kon Museum   MUSEUM
(พิพิธภัณฑ์ผีตาโขน; Th Kaew Asa; ☾8.30am-4.30pm) FREE Wat Phon Chai, the temple behind the big white gate, plays a major role in the Phi Ta Khon festivities, so it's an appropriate home for this museum. It has a collection of costumes worn during the celebrations and a display showing how the masks are made.

Wat Neramit Wiphatsana   BUDDHIST TEMPLE
(วัดเนรมิตวิปัสสนา; ☾dawn-dusk) FREE Built on a wooded hill just outside town, this gorgeous meditation temple features buildings made of unplastered laterite blocks. The massive *bòht,* hosts a faithful copy of Phitsanulok's Chinnarat Buddha and wonderful murals. The temple is dedicated to the memory of the late Luang Pu Mahaphan, a much-revered local monk.

Phra That Si Songrak   STUPA
(พระธาตุศรีสองรัก; Rte 2113; museum free; ☾7am-5pm) The most highly revered stupa in Loei Province, this whitewashed Lao-style *chedi* stands 20m high and was built in 1560–63 on what was then the Thai–Lao border as a gesture of unity between the Lao kingdom of Wiang Chan (Vientiane) and the Thai kingdom of Ayuthaya in their resistance against the Burmese. Despite use of the name Phra That, there are no Buddha relics here. You can't wear shoes, hats or the colour red, or carry food or open umbrellas if you climb up to the *chedi*. Down below is a modest museum with random artefacts donated by locals.

🛏 Sleeping & Eating

Homestay   HOMESTAY $
(☑08 9077 2080; dm/tw/tr 150/550/700B, meals 70B) Several villages near town have been running a successful homestay program for many years, and the families dote on *fa·ràng* guests. When not at work (most of the English-speaking hosts are teachers) they'll take you out to share typical daily activities. Everything can be arranged at Kawinthip Hattakham.

Dansai Resort Hotel   HOTEL $
(☑0 4289 2281; Rte 2013; r 300-700B; P ❋ 🛜) Dan Sai's most centrally located lodging has rooms ranging from past-their-prime fan rooms to big new cottages.

★**Phunacome**   HOTEL $$$
(☑0 4289 2005; www.phunacomeresort.com; Rte 2013; r 2500-4500B; P ➠ ❋ @ 🛜 ⌘) 🌿 This

DON'T MISS

DAN SAI'S PHI TA KHON FESTIVAL

Falling during the fourth lunar month, Dan Sai's **Phi Ta Khon Festival** (also called Bun Phra Wet) combines the Phra Wet Festival – during which recitations of the Mahavessantara Jataka (a story about one of the Buddha's past lives) are supposed to enhance the listener's chance of being reborn in the lifetime of the next Buddha – with Bun Bâng Fai (Rocket Festival). For those wishing to plunge headlong into Isan life, this curious cross between the drunken revelry of Carnival and the spooky imagery of Halloween is a must-see.

The origins of the Phi Ta Khon Festival are shrouded in ambiguity, but some aspects appear to be related to tribal Tai (possibly Tai Dam) spirit cults. The dates for the festival (usually June) are divined by Jao Phaw Kuan, a local spirit medium who channels the information from the town's guardian deity. On the first day Jao Phaw Kuan performs a sacrifice to invite Phra Upakud (an enlightened monk with supernatural powers who chose to transform himself into a block of white marble to live eternally on the bottom of the Man River) to come to town. Locals then don wild costumes and masks for two days of dancing that's fuelled by *lôw kŏw* (rice whisky) and is full of sexual innuendo, before launching the rockets and heading to the temple to listen to sermons on the third day.

luxury resort makes the most of its country location, and the kitchen makes use of the organic rice and vegies grown on the grounds. (They make their own low-impact soaps and detergents too.) Standard hotel rooms and some cool wood-and-thatch Isan-inspired cottages line a row of ponds. Both are plush and lovely with nice views.

The lobby has a library, massage service and restaurant with Thai and Western food, and free bikes are available. Its mascot is the buffalo and three real ones roam the grounds.

🛍 Shopping

Night Market THAI $
(Th Kaew Asa; ⊘4.30-9.30pm) On the main road across from the municipal market.

Kawinthip Hattakham SOUVENIRS
(กวินทิพย์หัตถกรรม; Th Kaew Asa; ⊘8am-7pm) This shop selling Phi Ta Khon masks and other festival-related souvenirs makes for a fun browse. It also has bike hire (100B per day) and coffee.

ⓘ Information

The main road through town is Th Kaew Asa. At its north end, is the municipal market; the **library** (⊘8am-4.30pm Mon-Fri), which has free internet and festival displays, and **city hall** (têt·sà·bahn; ☑0 4289 1231; www.tessaban dansai.com; Th Kaew Asa; ⊘8.30am-4.30pm Mon-Fri), where English-speaking staff enjoy answering questions.

ⓘ Getting There & Away

Buses between Loei (65B to 79B, 1½ hours) and Phitsanulok (73B to 102B, three hours) stop in Dan Sai near the junction of Th Kaew Asa and Rte 2013 every couple of hours.

Phu Kradueng National Park อุทยานแห่งชาติภูกระดึง

Capped off by its eponymous peak, **Phu Kradueng National Park** (☑0 4287 1333; admission 400B; ⊘trail to summit 7am-2pm Oct-May) covers a high-altitude plateau, cut through with trails and peppered with cliffs and waterfalls. Rising to 1316m, Thailand's second national park is always cool at its highest reaches (average year-round temperature is 20°C), where its flora is a mix of pine forest and savannah. Various forest animals, including elephants, Asian jackals, Asiatic black bears, sambar deer, serows and white-handed gibbons inhabit the 348-sq-km park.

There's a small visitor centre at the base of the mountain, but almost everything else is up top. The main trail scaling Phu Kradueng is 5.5km long and takes about three to four hours to climb. It's strenuous, but not too challenging (unless it's wet) since there are steps at most of the steep parts. The hike is quite scenic and there are rest stops with food vendors about every kilometre. Once on top, it's another 3km to the main visitor centre. You can hire porters to carry your

WORTH A TRIP

SUAN HIN PHA NGAM
สวนหินผางาม

With intriguingly warped and eroded limestone outcroppings, 'Beautiful Rock Garden' is an apt name for this hidden oasis; though Thais know it as **Kunming Mueang Thai** (Thailand's Kunming; 📞 0 4289 4254; per group 100B, per person tractor ride 15B; ⏰ 8.30am-5.30pm), due to its resemblance with the Stone Forest in Kunming, China. Most people just ride a tractor up to the easy-to-reach viewpoint for a quick look, but the best thing to do is walk back with your guide through the labyrinthine paths. At times the hour-long route is a little rough and you need to duck through some small passageways, but it's not difficult.

A second site in the same forest, recently reopened, is a bit more adventurous. The path through **Suan Sawan** (Heavenly Garden; 📞 08 4952 0591; per group 100B, per person tractor ride 15B; ⏰ 8.30am-4pm) follows a series of metal walkways over the rocks and through some caves. The trip takes about 90 minutes.

The sites are about 15km and 18km respectively southwest of Nong Hin. There's no public transport and hitching is highly impractical.

gear balanced on bamboo poles for 30B per kilogram.

The 5.5km trail that passes six waterfalls in a forested valley is the most beautiful destination, even after November, when the water has largely dried up. There are also many **clifftop viewpoints**, some ideal for sunrise and sunset, scattered around the mountain.

Spending the night atop Phu Kradueng is a rite of passage for many students, so the park gets unbelievably crowded during school holidays (March–May and especially New Year). The park is closed June to September.

🛏 Sleeping & Eating

Atop the mountain there's space for 5000 people to **camp** (per person with own tent 30B, 3-person-tent hire 225B), a variety of large **bungalows** (📞 0 2562 0760; www.dnp.go.th/parkreserve; bungalows 900-3600B) and many open-air restaurants. If you're arriving late, there's also camping and bungalows at the bottom.

ℹ Getting There & Away

Buses between Loei (56B, 1½ hours, every 30 minutes) and Khon Kaen (75B, two hours) stop in Phu Kradueng town where *sŏrng·tăa·ou* (20B per person, charters 300B) take people to the base of the mountain, 10km away.

BUENG KAN PROVINCE

Thailand's newest province split off from Nong Khai in 2011. It's remote and often lovely territory, and though most people travelling along the Mekong River out of Nong Khai head west, there are some real rewards for bucking the trend and heading east, including one of Thailand's most amazing temples and best homestay programs.

Bueng Kan
บึงกาฬ

Little Bueng Kan is growing fast, but it's the rubber industry (40% of the province's land is now rubber-tree plantation) driving the boom rather than its new capital-city status. The only thing that qualifies as an attraction is the **Thai-Lao Market** that takes place on Tuesday and Friday mornings. Some of the products sold by the Lao traders, such as herbs and mushrooms, are gathered in the forest. It's also interesting to take a gander at the river during the dry season since it recedes far from Bueng Kan and reaches one of its narrowest points along the Thai–Lao border.

Not surprisingly, most travellers only stop long enough to catch connecting transport to Wat Phu Tok. If you do decide to stay, the Mekong-facing **Maenam Hotel** (📞 0 4249 1051; Th Chansin; r 400-450B; 🅿 ➹ ❄ @ 🛜) is the best located place in town. **The One** (📞 0 4249 2234; www.theonehotel-bk.com/; Nakhon Phanom Rd; r 790-1700B, ste 2500B; 🅿 ➹ ❄ @ 🛜 🛎), out on the highway, is the top hotel in town. Many restaurant set up tables along the riverside promenade at dinner time, making this the best place to eat.

Buses to Nong Khai (100B to 150B, 3½ hours, eight daily), Nakhon Phanom (140B, 3½ hours, four daily) and Udon Thani (130B to 150B, 4½ hours, 12 daily) park near the old clock tower. The last departures for Nong Khai and Nakhon Phaonm are at 3pm, and for Udon Thani at 4pm. You you could also take one of the later Bangkok buses to Nong Khao or Udon Thani, but you'll probably need to pay the full fare.

Wat Phu Tok วัดภูทอก

With its network of rickety staircases and walkways built in, on and around a giant sandstone outcrop, **Wat Phu Tok** (Isolated Mountain Temple; admission free; ☻6am-5pm, closed 10-16 April) is one of the region's wonders. The precarious paths lead past shrines and *gù·dì* that are scattered around the mountain on cliffs and in caves, and provide fabulous views over the surrounding countryside. A final scramble up roots and rocks takes you to the forest on the summit, which is considered the seventh level. If you hustle and take all the short cuts you can be up and down in about an hour, but we advise against it: this is a climb that should be savoured. The quiet isolation entices monks and *mâa chee* (nuns) from across Thailand to come meditate, so be quiet and respectful as you explore.

This forest temple used to be the domain of the famous meditation master Luang Pu Juan, a disciple of Luang Pu Man. He died in a plane crash in 1980 along with several other highly revered forest monks who were flying to Bangkok for Queen Sirikit's birthday celebration. A marble *chedi* containing Luang Pu Juan's belongings, some bone relics and fantastic exterior sculptures sits below the mountain amid a gorgeous garden.

❶ Getting There & Away

Túk-túk in Bueng Kan charge 800B for the return journey to Wat Phu Tok, including a few hours waiting time. It's cheaper to take a bus from Bueng Kan to Ban Siwilai (30B, 45 minutes), where túk-túk drivers will do the trip for 350B. If you catch an early bus to Bueng Kan, Wat Phu Tok can be visited as a day trip from Nong Khai, although there's no need to backtrack since buses from Siwilai go to Udon Thani (140B, four hours, last bus 4.45pm).

If you're driving or pedalling, continue past Bueng Kan for 27km until you reach Chaiyapon, then turn right at Rte 3024, the road signed for Chet Si, and several other waterfalls. (These are in the Phu Wua Wildlife Reserve and make worthy detours, as much for the weird rocky landscape as the cascades. There's only water

mid-May through December.) After 17.5km make a right and continue 4km more.

Ban Kham Pia บ้านขามเปี้ย

Isan is flush with village homestay programs that let you delve deep into rural life; however most are aimed at Thai tour groups. But, thanks to the help of Open Mind Projects and English-speaking village-head Khun Bunleud, **Ban Kham Pia** (☏08 7861 0601; www.thailandwildelephanttrekking.com; r 200-300B, meals 50-90B) really knows how to welcome *fa·ràng*.

Another great thing about this homestay is that it's within walking distance of the 186-sq-km **Phu Wua Wildlife Reserve**, so you can add some superb treks (including sleeping in a cave) to your trip. The forest is flush with waterfalls and home to about three-dozen elephants. They're sometimes encountered on day walks from the village during the rainy season and seen almost daily from January to April during overnight stays in the 'treehouses' (not for the fainthearted). These are in the middle of a forest clearing where monks bring sugarcane to discourage the elephants from raiding farm fields. It's about an hour's drive from the village. The standard guide fee in and around the village is 300B per day and motorcycles cost 200B per day.

Buses between Nong Khai (150B, 3½ hours) and Nakhon Phanom (130B, three hours) will drop you at Ban Don Chik, 3km away.

GETTING TO LAOS: BUENG KAN TO PAKSAN

Although it's very rarely done, you can cross the Mekong here to Paksan, but only if you already have your Lao visa.

Getting To the Border Immigration (8am to 6pm) is 2.5km northwest of town. A túk-túk will cost about 60B.

At the Border Boats cross the river between 8.30am and noon and between 1 and 4.30pm when they have about 20 passengers. During lunch and after 4.30pm you'll probably need to charter the whole boat for 1000B.

Moving On Túk-túk wait on the Lao shore, though the highway and a few hotels are an easy walk from the landing.

NAKHON PHANOM PROVINCE

Lao and Vietnamese influences are strong in Nakhon Phanom, a province bordered by the Mekong and full of highly revered temples. It's a region of subtleties rather than can't-miss attractions, but there are plenty of fine river views and interesting historic sites, and the colossal Wat Phra That Phanom is an enchanting talisman of Isan culture.

Nakhon Phanom   นครพนม

POP 31,700

Nakhon Phanom means 'City of Mountains', but the undulating sugarloaf peaks all lie across the river in Laos, so you'll be admiring rather than climbing them. The views are stunning, though, especially during a hazy sunrise. Nothing else in the peaceful, clean and proud city is quite as appealing as the distant row of hills, though there's plenty more to see and do for those who've come all the way out here.

Nakhon Phanom's temples have a distinctive style. This was once an important town in the Lan Xang Empire, and after that Thai kings sent their best artisans to create new buildings. Later a vivid French influence crossed the Mekong and jumped into the mix.

◎ Sights & Activities

Ho Chi Minh's House   MUSEUM
(บ้านโฮจิมินห์; ☑ 0 4252 2430; entry by donation; ⊙ dawn-dusk) The Vietnamese community in Ban Na Chok village, about 3.5km west of town, has built a replica of Udon Thani's **Uncle Ho's House**, the simple wooden house where Ho Chi Minh sometimes stayed (1928–29) while planning his resistance movement. There are more displays, some labelled in English, in the **Ho Chi Minh Museum** (☑ 08 0315 4630; admission free; ⊙ 8am-4pm), a bit to the northwest at the community centre. His birthday is celebrated here every 19 May.

Wat Okat   BUDDHIST TEMPLE
(วัดโอกาส; Th Sunthon Wijit; ⊙ dawn-dusk) Predating the town, Wak Okat is home to Phra Teaw and Phra Tiam, two sacred wooden Buddha images covered in gold that sit on the highest pedestal in the *wí·hǎhn*. The current Tiam (on the right) is a replica because the original was stolen in 2010. (Theft of Buddha images is a growing problem

in Thailand.) The amazing mural is one of our favourites in Thailand (it's like a Thai *Where's Wally?*; try to find the backpackers), and shows the story of Phra Tiew and Phra Tiam floating across the Mekong from Laos. The temple is beautifully illuminated at night.

Wat Si Thep   BUDDHIST TEMPLE
(วัดศรีเทพประดิษฐาราม; Th Si Thep; ⊙ dawn-dusk) This historic temple's *bòht* has a lot of flair. It's surrounded by statues of *têp* (angels) and has a colourful triptych on the back wall. The interior murals show the life of the Buddha around the upper portion and kings of the Chakri dynasty below. The abbot's residence was built in 1921 in French Colonial style.

Former Governor's Residence Museum   MUSEUM
(จวนผู้ว่าราชการจังหวัดนครพนม (หลังเก่า); Th Sunthon Wijit; ⊙ 9am-5pm Wed-Sun) **FREE** This museum fills a beautifully restored 1925 mansion with photos of old Nakhon Phanom, many labelled in English, while in the back are displays about the Illuminated Boat Procession.

Mekong Underwater World   AQUARIUM
(สถานที่จัดแสดงโลกของปลาแม่น้ำโขง; Rte 2033; admission 30B; ⊙ 8.30am-4pm Mon-Fri) If you like fish, you'll like this aquarium housing Mekong River species, including *blah bèuk* (giant Mekong catfish). It's 6km west of town along Hwy 22. *Sǒrng·tǎa·ou* to Na Kae (20B, 15 minutes) pass by.

Wat Maha That   BUDDHIST TEMPLE
(วัดมหาธาตุ; Th Sunthon Wijit; ⊙ dawn-dusk) **FREE** The 24m-tall, gold-and-white Phra That Nakhon *chedi* here resembles the previous *chedi* built at That Phanom.

Mekong Walking Street   MARKET
(⊙ 4.30-9.30pm Fri & Sat) This street market features little of interest for shopping, but it does make a fun stroll.

Chom Khong Park   PARK
(สวนชมโขง; Th Ratchathan; ⊙ 5am-8pm) **FREE** This park used to be a prison, and models of prisoners sit in some of the old cells. You can also climb the guard towers.

Sunset Cruise   BOAT TRIP
(☑ 0 4251 4436; per person 50B) The city runs this hour-long Mekong River cruise on *Thesaban*, which docks across from the Indochina Market. Snacks and drinks are served.

Nakhon Phanom

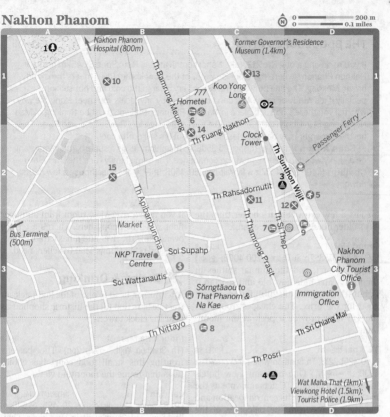

NORTHEASTERN THAILAND NAKHON PHANOM

✶ Festivals & Events

Nakhon Phanom is famous for its illuminated boat procession, **Lái Reua Fai** (illuminated boats; ⊙ late Oct/early Nov), during **Ork Phansaa** (the end of Buddhist Lent). It's a modern twist on the ancient tradition of sending rafts loaded with food, flowers and candles down the Mekong as offerings for the *naga*. Today's giant bamboo rafts hold up to 20,000 handmade lanterns, and some designers add animation to the scenes. Boat races, music competitions and other festivities run for a week, but the boats are launched only on the night of the full moon.

⌷ Sleeping

SP Residence   HOTEL **$**
(⌨ 0 4251 3500; Th Nittayo; r 450-800B; P ⊖ ❋ @ ☎) Plain but modern, the rooms here are less institutional than the exterior and hallways would lead you to believe, and

Nakhon Phanom

◉ Sights
1 Chom Khong Park	A1
2 Mekong Walking Street	C1
3 Wat Okat	C2
4 Wat Si Thep	C4

◔ Activities, Courses & Tours
5 Sunset Cruise	D2

⌷ Sleeping
6 777 Hometel	C1
7 Grand Hotel	C3
8 SP Residence	C4
9 TC Apartment	D3

⊗ Eating
10 Baa Nang	B1
11 Good Morning Vietnam & Coffee	C2
12 Indochina Market	D2
13 Khun Kaew Steak Corner	C1
14 Luk Tan	C2
15 Night Market	B2

THE BI-COLOURED RIVER แม่น้ำสองสี

If you're driving along Rte 212, take a short break at Mae Nam Song Si, 45km north of Nakhon Phanom, where the greenish water of the Songkhram River meets the muddy brown Mekong. The line between the two is very clear in the cold and hot seasons, especially if it's windy or rainy. And don't be swayed by any locals you meet along the way who tell you there's no such place in Nakhon Phanom, that you must be thinking of Mae Nam Song Si in Ubon Ratchathani. Just turn at the sign for 'The Bi-Coloured River.' This northern merger may be much less famous, but it's still pretty cool.

Suan Ahahn Paknam (dishes 25-350B; ⏰10am-9pm; P) is a superb little restaurant on a shaky wooden deck right at the confluence. The same family runs the **Ban Nam Chaiburi** (☑08 1974 4227; r w fan/air-con 150/450B; P ⊖ ❀ 🛜) guesthouse a few doors down.

for just a few extra baht it's better than the city's older hotels in this price range.

Grand Hotel HOTEL $
(☑0 4251 3788; Th Si Thep; r 200-400B; P❀) 'Grand' it ain't, and the animal statues in the lobby can't hide how old and spartan it is, but it's clean and the 200B fan rooms are good for the price. The cheapest rooms on the 4th floor provide a peek at the mountains.

TC Apartment HOTEL $$
(☑0 4251 2212; Th Sunthon Wijit; r incl breakfast 690B; P⊖❀🛜) One of many new hotels in Nakhon Phanom, TC gets our vote as the best of the bunch for its central location and big river views from the balconies of the front-facing rooms.

777 Hometel HOTEL $$
(☑0 4251 4777; www.777hometel.com; Th Thamrong Prasit; r 590-790B; P⊖❀@🛜) Don't let the boxy exterior fool you, inside this is Nakhon Phanom's most stylish hotel. And it doesn't just get by on looks alone. It's well managed and has some of the friendliest, most helpful staff in town. It's called *dorng jet* in Thai.

iHotel HOTEL $$
(☑0 4254 3355; Th That Phanom; r incl breakfast 550-1000B; P⊖❀@🛜) The stylish 'i' mixes good mattresses, 'power showers', a backyard garden and attentive staff. It's only knock is that it's 5km south of town.

Viewkong Hotel HOTEL $$
(☑0 4251 3564; www.viewkonghotel.com; Th Sunthon Wijit; r incl breakfast 600-700B; ste 2500B; P⊖❀@🛜) The town's former chart-topping hotel has little pizzazz and quite a bit of wear and tear, but it's priced right and

if you take a river-view room from an upper floor you'll be happy here. There's a terrace overlooking the river and it has karaoke, massage and other things Thai travellers need.

✗ Eating & Drinking

After dinner, head to one of the laid-back, attractive bars that fill the historic shophouses near the clock tower.

Indochina Market THAI $
(Th Sunthon Wijit; ⏰7am-7pn) The balcony fronting this small food court has choice seats that frame the mountain views.

Luk Tan INTERNATIONAL, THAI $
(Th Bamrung Meuang; dishes 39-149B; ⏰5-10pm Wed-Sun) This quirky little spot does Thai-style steaks and *fa·ràng* favourites including some delicious mashed potatoes. Owner Bai-Tong is a great source of local advice.

Night Market THAI $
(Th Fuang Nakhon; ⏰4-9pm) Large and diverse, but few places to sit.

Good Morning Vietnam & Coffee VIETNAMESE $
(Th Thamrong Prasit; dishes 30-150B; ⏰6am-8pm) This little corner shop has modernised with bright colours and a coffee bar, but it still serves the same family recipes, including *năam new·ang* (assemble-it-yourself pork spring rolls) and spicy Thai salads, that it has through four generations.

Baa Nang NORTHEASTERN THAI $
(Th Apibanbuncha; dishes 30-150B; ⏰7am-4pm) This corrugated-roof shack across from Anuban Nakhon Phanom school attracts the masses for *gài yâhng, sôm·đam* and other down-home Isan food.

Khun Kaew Steak Corner INTERNATIONAL, THAI $$
(Th Sunthon Wijit; dishes 65-475B; ☺4-10pm Mon-Sat) Funky from the decor to the the Thai-fusion pastas, this little riverside spot, owned by a dedicated Thai chef who has worked for some years in Texas, makes a nice night; especially if you can get one of the tables with a view.

ℹ Information

Bangkok Bank (Tesco-Lotus, Th Nittayo; ☺10.30am-7pm) Keeps late hours.
Immigration Office (☎0 4251 1235; Th Sunthon Wijit; ☺8.30am-noon & 1-4.30pm Mon-Fri) For visa extensions.
Tourism Authority of Thailand (TAT; ☎0 4251 3490; tatphnom@tat.or.th; Th Sunthon Wijit; ☺8.30am-4.30pm) Covers Nakhon Phanom, Sakon Nakhon and Mukdahan provinces.

ℹ Getting There & Away

AIR

Nok Air (☎0 2900 9955; www.nokair.com) and **Air Asia** (☎0 2515 9999; www.airasia.com) each fly daily to/from Bangkok's Don Muang Airport with one-way prices from 1000B. Agencies such as **NKP Travel Centre** (☎0 4252 0999; Th Apibanbuncha; ☺8am-6pm Mon-Sat, 9am-5pm Sun) sell tickets. An airport shuttle drops passengers at any in-town hotel for 100B per person.

BUS

Nakhon Phanom's **bus terminal** (☎0 4251 3444; Th Fuang Nakhon) is west of the town centre. From here buses head to Nong Khai (210B, 6½ hours, four daily); Udon Thani (170B to 220B, 4½ hours, frequent) via Sakon Nakhon (70B to 88B, 1½ hours); and Ubon Ratchathani (229B, 4½ hours, 7am). For Ubon, most people use minivans (162B, four hours, seven daily) which go via Mukdahan (80B, 2½ hours) and That Phanom (40B, one hour). Most Bangkok (447B to 574B, 11 to 12 hours) buses depart between 7am to 8am and 5pm to 7pm. VIP service is offered by **999 VIP** (☎0 4251 1403) for 893B.

Sŏrng·tăa·ou to That Phanom (40B, 90 minutes, frequent until 5pm) park near Kasikornbank.

ℹ Getting Around

Túk-túk drivers quote 20B to 30B per person from the bus station to most places in town, and 200B for the round trip to Ban Na Chok.

Nakhon Phanom's sparse traffic makes it a good place for biking. **Koo Yong Long** (☎0 4251 1118; 363 Th Sunthon Wijit; per hr/day 10/70B; ☺8am-5pm) and **777 Hometel** (☎0 4251 4777; bikes 50B/day motorcycles 200B/day; ☺24hr) hire bikes.

That Phanom ธาตุพนม

Towering over this small, peaceful town, the spire of the colossal *chedi* at Wat Phra That Phanom is one of the region's most emblematic symbols and one of the great flagpoles of Isan identity. Some historic buildings in the Mekong-hugging half of town can round out a pleasant visit.

◉ Sights

Wat Phra That Phanom BUDDHIST TEMPLE
(วัดพระธาตุพนม; Th Chayangkun; ☺5am-8pm)
FREE This temple is a potent and beautiful place; even if you're feeling templed-out, you'll likely be impressed. At its hub is a *tâht,* more impressive than any in present-day Laos and highly revered by Buddhists from both countries. The *tâht* is 53.6m high, and a 16kg real gold umbrella laden with precious gems adds 4m more to the top.

Though the story doesn't appear in Buddhist texts, many Thais believe that the Lord Buddha travelled to Thailand and directed that one of his breast-bone relics be enshrined in a *chedi* to be built on this very site; and so it was in 535 BC, eight years after his death. Historians date the first construction, a short stupa (there's a replica of how it may have looked in a pond in front of the temple), to around the 9th century AD and modifications have been routine since then. In 1690 it was raised to 47m and you'll find

---

GETTING TO LAOS: NAKHON PHANOM TO THA KHAEK

Getting to the Border Passenger ferries cross the Mekong to Tha Khaek in Laos, but they're for Thai and Lao only. All travellers must use the Thai-Lao Friendship Bridge 3, north of the city. Buses to Tha Khaek (70/75B weekdays/weekends, eight daily) run between 8am and 5pm.

At the Border All immigration formalities are handled at the bridge, and Lao visas are available on arrival. Things get pretty chaotic when droves of Vietnamese workers, who don't appreciate the value of a queue, are passing through.

Moving On The bus tends to wait a long time to get more passengers, so total travel time to Tha Khaek often takes over two hours.

That Phanom

⊙ Sights

replicas of this *tâht* all over Isan. The current design went up in 1941, but it toppled during heavy rains in 1975 and was rebuilt in 1978.

Behind the surrounding cloister is a shady little park and **museum** (admission free; ⊙8.30am-4pm), which tells the legend (not the history) of the *tâht* and also displays a collection of pottery, gongs and some rare Buddha images.

Kong Gate MONUMENT

(ประตูโขง) Standing tall on the road in front of Phra That Phanom is an arch that symbolically connects the *tâht* to the Mekong. The block of French Indochinese architecture between the arch and the river is reminiscent of old Saigon, and a few shops sell Vietnamese food.

Wat Hua Wiang Rangsi BUDDHIST TEMPLE

(วัดหัวเวียงรังสี; ⊙dawn-dusk) This riverside temple has a *bòht* built in 1921, and the paintings inside are in excellent condition for their age, though they're central Thai rather than Isan style.

A **Tai-Lao Open-Border Market** takes place in front of the temple every Monday and Thursday (7am to 2pm). It's mostly the same tat found in other Thai markets, but some of the Lao traders sell roots, honey, bats and other forest products.

**Wat Phra That Renu
Nakhon** BUDDHIST TEMPLE

(เรณูนคร; ⊙dawn-dusk) The Phu Thai town of Renu Nakhon, 15km northwest of That Phanom, hosts a 35m-tall *tâht* that closely resembles the previous *chedi* built in That Phanom and is considered very holy. The temple also hosts a good **textiles market** with locally made fabrics and clothes as well as silk and cotton from Laos and elsewhere in Thailand. There's no public transport. Túk-túk drivers in That Phanom ask 300B round trip.

✹✹ Festivals

During the **That Phanom Festival** in late January or early February, visitors descend from all over Thailand and Laos to make merit and pay respect to the *tâht*. The streets fill with market stalls, many top *mŏr lam* troupes perform and the town hardly sleeps for nine days.

On the morning of **Ork Phansaa**, the Phu Tai perform their 'peacock dance' in front of That Phanom.

🛏 Sleeping

During the That Phanom Festival, rates soar and rooms are booked out well in advance.

Kritsada Rimkhong Hotel HOTEL $

(📞08 1262 4111; www.ksdrimkhong-resort.com; Th Rimkhong; r 400-600B; P⊛❄@🛜) Rooms range from plain to very attractive, but all are comfy. If the friendly English-speaking owner is around when you call, he'll pick you up at the bus station for free. Note that the nearby Kritsada 2 is OK, but it's not as good as the original.

Baan-Ing-Oon Guesthouse HOTEL $
(☑ 0 4254 0111; Th Phanom Phanarak; r 450-550B; ❸ 🕸 🔞) Though the rooms are a little plain, this new place a block off the river offers comfort for a good price and solid service.

Chaivon Hotel HOTEL $
(☑ 08 9622 4545; Th Phanom Phanarak; r 250B; 🕸) This green wooden hotel is pretty shabby and definitely not for everyone, but some people may enjoy a night here as it's a genuine historic relic. All rooms have fans and shared bathrooms.

That Phanom Riverview Hotel HOTEL $$
(☑ 0 4254 1555; www.thatphanomriverviewhotel. com; Th Rimkhong; r 850-1300B; 🅿 ❸ 🕸 @ 🔞) Rooms at That Phanom's biggest and best lodge are pretty plain for the price, but being large and bright helps compensate. Note that, despite the name, most rooms have little or no view.

✖️ Eating

Krua Kritsada Rimkhong NORTHEASTERN THAI $
(Th Rimkhong; dishes 40-200B; ⊘ 9.30am-10pm; 🅿 🔞) The service is lacking, but the food is good and it's quieter than most of the many other riverside spots. In season, they use their own-grown organic vegies and herbs.

Night Market NORTHEASTERN THAI $
(⊘ 4-10pm) That Phanom's night market is much bigger than you'd expect for a town this size. It has a good variety of food, but few places to sit.

ℹ️ Information

There are several regular banks in the centre of town. For weekends and evenings, there's a **Bangkok Bank** (⊘ 10.30am-7pm) north of town in the Tesco-Lotus shopping centre, which also has an AEON ATM.

ℹ️ Getting There & Around

From That Phanom's new **bus station**, inconveniently located west of town (a túk-túk to the river should cost 30B), there are services to Ubon Ratchathani (bus/minivan 185/150B, 4½/4 hours, 14 daily) via Mukdahan (47B/50B, one hour), Udon Thani (168B to 200B, four hours, six daily) via Sakon Nakhon (55B to 70B, 1¼ hours) and Nakhon Phanom (40B to 50B, one hour, seven daily). For Nakhon Phanom you can also take one of the *sŏrng·tǎa·ou* (40B, 90 minutes,

frequent until 4pm) that park north of the *tâht*. There are a few morning buses to Bangkok (435B to 871B, 10 to 11 hours), but most depart between 5pm and 7pm. One Bangkok-bound company still departs from the old bus station in town.

Poo Gam Phra (☑ 08 1431 5096; Soi 8) gift shop rents bikes (100B to 200B per day) and motorcycles (300B per day) and can arrange day-long kayak trips down the Mekong to Kaeng Kaboa.

SAKON NAKHON PROVINCE

Many famous forest temples sit deep in the Phu Phan mountain range that runs across Sakon Nakhon Province, and among Sakon Nakhon's famous sons are several of the most highly revered monks in Thai history, including Ajahn Man Bhuridatto, who was born in Ubon Ratchathani but died here. He was a revolutionary ascetic *tú·dong* monk who attained a high level of proficiency in *vipassana* meditation and is widely recognised among Thais as having been an *arahant* (fully enlightened being). But, despite the province's reputation, few visitors – Thai or foreign – visit.

Sakon Nakhon สกลนคร

POP 53,877

Workaday Sakon Nakhon is an important market town, and though the city centre is the usual concrete mess, quiet neighbourhoods on the fringes are full of old wooden houses, and this is where you'll find the main attractions.

◉ Sights

Wat Phra That Choeng Chum BUDDHIST TEMPLE
(วัดพระธาตุเชิงชุม; Th Ruangsawat; ⊘ dawn-dusk) **FREE** The most visible highlight at Wat Phra That Choeng Chum is the 24m-high Lao-style *chedi*, which was erected in the 17th century over a smaller 11th-century Khmer *prang* and is now topped by a solid-gold umbrella. The name means 'Stupa of the Gathering of the Footprints Temple' because it was built above four Buddha footprints, which many Thais believe were left by four incarnations of the Buddha.

Also on the grounds are a gorgeous modern Lan Xang–style *bòht,* a simple century-old

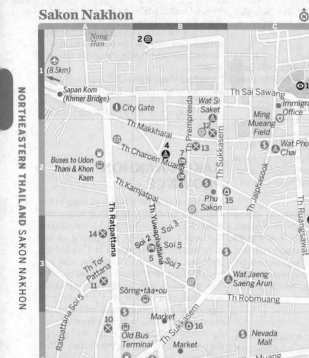

Sakon Nakhon

Isan-style *bòht*, and an octagonal *hŏr đrai* that now houses a little **museum**: If you want to look inside, ask a monk to get the key. The top of the western gate resembles the wax castles carved for Ork Phansaa.

Wat Saphan Kham　　　　BUDDHIST TEMPLE
(วัดสะพานคำ; Th Charoen Muang; ⊙dawn-dusk) **FREE** Beautiful in its simplicity, the small, recently restored *bòht* here is estimated to be about a century old and is fronted by two unintentionally adorable *naga*.

Wat Pa Sutthawat　　　　BUDDHIST TEMPLE
(วัดป่าสุทธาวาส; ⊙5am-9pm) **FREE** The grounds of Wat Pa Sutthawat, on the southwestern outskirts of town, is essentially a shrine to one of Thailand's best-known monks, Ajahn Man Bhuridatto, who helped found the temple but didn't live here until just before his death in 1949. The final resting place of his personal effects, the **Ajahn Man Museum** (6am to 7pm), looks a bit like

a modern Christian church, with arches and etched-glass windows. A bronze image of Ajahn Man sits on a pedestal at the back and relics that remained after his cremation are in a glass box in front. Signs are in English.

Ajahn Lui Chanthasaro, who died in 1989, was one of Ajahn Man's most famous students, and King Rama IX designed the *chedi* that holds the **Ajahn Lui Museum**. Ajahn Lui is represented in wax.

Wat Phra That Narai Cheng Weng
BUDDHIST TEMPLE

(วัดพระธาตุนารายณ์แจงแวง) FREE About 5km west of town at Ban That is an 11th-century Khmer *prang* (known as Phra That Nawaeng, a contraction of the words Narai Cheng Weng) in the early Bapuan style. Originally part of a Khmer-Hindu complex, it's missing much of its top, but still features several good carvings including a Krishna fighting a lion over its northern portico and a dancing Shiva (with 12 arms instead of the normal 10) over its eastern one. It's not very impressive or evocative, but it's the most complete Khmer ruin in the province.

To get here by public transport take *sŏrng·tăa·ou* 3 (10B) from near the market or catch it heading north on Th Ratpattana. Get off at Ban That Market and walk 500m south.

Phu Phan Museum
MUSEUM

(พิพิธภัณฑ์ภูพาน; ⏰9am-5pm Tue-Sun) FREE Though displays are only signed in Thai, this well-done museum still warrants a visit. Displays cover dinosaurs, Buddhism and Sakon Nakhon's six tribes.

Nong Han
LAKE

(หนองหาน) Rimming the eastern and northern edges of town is 123-sq-km Nong Han, Isan's largest natural lake. Fishermen, who tie up their boats just east of Srinakarin Park, will take you out sightseeing, including a stop to visit **Ko Don Sawan** (Paradise Island), the lake's largest island which serves as a meditation retreat for monks. The going rate is around 400B for three people. Don't copy the fishermen and swim in the lake: it's infested with liver flukes, which can cause a nasty infection known as opisthorchiasis.

The nearby Fishery Station has an **aquarium** (Th Sai Sawang; admission free; ⏰8.30am-4.30pm Mon-Sat) with fish from the lake as well as the Mekong and Songkhram rivers.

✤✤ Festivals

Ork Phansaa, the end of the Buddhist lent (late October or early November), is fervently celebrated in Sakon. There's a parade featuring **wax castles**, which are then put on display in Ming Mueang Field. They can also be seen at each of the city's temples for about a month after the event. A smaller wax-candle parade happens during **Khao Phansaa**.

🛏 Sleeping

Dusit Hotel
HOTEL $

(☏0 4271 1198; Th Yuwaphattana; r 370-890B, ste 3000B; P❄☀@🖧) This reborn old-timer has the loveliest lobby and cheeriest staff in town. As for the rooms, the more you pay the more atmosphere you get, but each price category offers fair value. The restaurant is very expensive but good, and the owner, Fiat, is a great source of local info.

LP Mansion
HOTEL $

(☏0 4271 5356; Th Prempreeda; r 270-420B; P❄☀@🖧) LP is cheap, but not a cheapskate. Rooms are good for the price and even the 270B fan rooms get free coffee, Oreos and a minifridge. Rates at its **older sister sleeper** around the corner are a little lower.

NH The Elegant Hotel
HOTEL $$

(☏0 4271 3338; www.nheleganthotel.com; Th Robmuang; s/d & tw incl half-board 650/700B; P❄☀@🖧) Smart sums it up better than elegant, but that's really beside the point. What matters is that these well-appointed rooms are rock solid for the price. Except those on the 1st floor, which have no windows.

✗ Eating

Mit Uppatam
THAI $

(Th Sukkasem; dishes 30-200B; ⏰7am-2pm & 4.30-9pm) This traditional place is a popular breakfast stop (with great omelettes) but it also has a big menu of curries, fish and more. The food is so good that word reached Princess Sirindhorn, who dropped in to dine in 2008. Nobody here speaks English.

Kam Hawm
COFFEESHOP $

(Th Ratpattana Soi 5; ⏰8am-8pm; P🖧) A relaxing little coffeeshop in a lovely wooden building. Not only are the coffees and cakes good, but you can order lunch and dinner off the Thai-*fa·ràng* menu (55B to 180B) from the adjacent restaurant.

Saban Ngaa
NORTHEASTERN THAI **$**

(Th Ratpattana; dishes 40-120B; ⊙10am-10pm; 🐾) Famous for its Isan food (but also serving Thai and Chinese), this is a great place to try local dishes such as *gaang wǎi* (rattan curry), and vegetarians have the rare chance to eat *lâhp wún sên* (spicy glass noodles). The atmosphere is terrible but the food is terrific.

Prachachuen
THAI **$**

(Th Makkhalai; dishes 49-369B; ⊙5pm-midnight; 🐾) This lovely, youthful place in an old wooden house is one of Sakon's trendiest restaurants, but it doesn't slack on the food. Whether it's the fried rice or *blah chôrn sá·mǔn·prai* (snake-head fish with herbs in chilli sauce with mango) it will be delicious.

11 Brothers & Sisters Night Market
NORTHEASTERN THAI **$**

(Th Sukkasem; ⊙5pm-1am) A variety of food actually sold by the titular 11 siblings, plus many other relatives.

Green Corner
INTERNATIONAL, THAI **$$**

(Th Ratpattana; dishes 45-420B; ⊙7am-10pm; P) This long-time favourite has a huge menu of *fa·ràng*, Thai and Isan dishes, though many of the latter, such as fried cicadas and ants'-egg omelettes, aren't written in English on the menu. There are also good breads and cakes in the bakery.

🔒 Shopping

Mann Craft (Th Sukkasem; ⊙8.30am-6pm) has some beautiful clothes and bags, mostly dyed with indigo and other natural colorants. The **OTOP Center** (Th Sukkasem; ⊙8.30am-5pm) also sells good indigo fabrics plus maoberry and black-ginger wines.

ℹ️ Information

Most banks are found along Th Sukkasem and Th Ratpattana. Branches of Bangkok Bank at Big C and Tesco-Lotus shopping centres open 10.30am to 7pm daily and there's an AEON ATM in the Nevada Mall across from Big C.

Immigration Office (☎0 4271 5219; Th Jaiphasook; ⊙8.30am-noon & 1-4.30pm Mon-Fri) For visa extensions.

ℹ️ Getting There & Away

AIR

Nok Air (☎0 2900 9955; www.nokair.com) flies once daily to/from Bangkok's Don Muang Airport (one way from 1400B). **Phu Sakon** (☎0 4271 2259; Th Sukkasem; ⊙8.30am-5pm Mon-Sat) sells tickets and can arrange an airport shuttle for 150B per person.

BUS

Sakon's **old bus terminal** (Th Ratpattana) serves Ubon Ratchathani (180B to 232B, five hours, nine daily), That Phanom (55B to 70B, 1¼ hours, frequent), Nakhon Phanom (70B to 88B, 1½ hours, every 30 minutes), Udon Thani (110B to 140B, three hours, every 30 minutes), Khon Kaen (173B, four hours, five daily) and Bangkok (392B to 588B, 11 hours, morning and early-evening departures only).

Buses for Khon Kaen and Udon Thani can also be boarded at the Esso petrol station in the city.

There are VIP bus services to Bangkok (784B, 7.30pm and 7.45pm) with **999 VIP** (☎0 4271 2860). Tickets are sold its office on Th Sukkasem and they also have an 8.30am 1st-class bus (504B) departing from this office.

ℹ️ Getting Around

The bus terminal is 4km west of town. You can get downtown with a taxi (20B per kilometre), motorcycle taxi (60B) and *sǒrng·tǎa·ou* 3 or 1422 (10B). Heading to the terminal, *sǒrng·tǎa·ou* park near the market and then head north along Th Ratpattana.

Phu Phan Mountains

Highway 213 south from Sakon Nakhon towards Kalasin crawls over the Phu Phan mountain range, which has some interesting sites on its slopes. Some buses to Kalasin and Mahasarakham will drop off and pick up passengers along the way, but most won't. It's best to use *sǒrng·tǎa•ou* from Sakon Nakhon's old bus terminal (p484).

Phu Phan Rajaniwet Palace พระ ตำหนักภูพานราชนิเวศน์

The grounds of the royal family's Isan home (พระตำหนักภูพานราชนิเวศน์; ☎0 4271 1550; admission free; ⊙8.30am-4pm), 14km south of Sakon Nakhon, are open to the public when not in use. It's quite a modest residence compared to some of their other palaces, but the gardens are beautiful and peaceful. Only walking is allowed around the main grounds, but cars can go to the elephant corral. Visitors are not permitted to wear shorts above the knees, short dresses or revealing tops. *Sǒrng·tǎa·ou* cost 20B and take 30 minutes from town.

Phu Phan National Park อุทยานแห่ง
ชาติภูพาน

This **national park** (☎08 1263 5029; admission free) remains relatively undeveloped and isolated. It's no surprise that the area once provided cover for the Seri Thai resistance fighters in WWII and People's Liberation Army of Thailand (PLAT) guerrillas in the 1970s. The former used **Tham Seri Thai** cave as an arsenal and mess hall. The 664-sq-km park is now a stomping ground for barking deer, monitor lizards, slow loris, many monkeys and a few elephants.

There are two main areas to visit. Near the visitor centre there are nice views at **Nang Mern Cliff** and you can climb down a further 1.5km to **Lan Sao Aee** plateau, which is even better for sunsets. **Nam Tok Kam Hom**, a stretch of four petite waterfalls, is 8.5km north of the visitor centre, at a wild bend in the road called **Khong Ping Ngu Curve** (named after the stacked shape that snakes make when put on a skewer for grilling) that has Thailand's largest kilometre pillar. Water only runs from July to October.

Accommodation options include **campsites** (per person with own tent 30B, 3-person tent 150B) and **bungalows** (☎0 2562 0760; www. dnp.go.th/parkreserve; 4-person bungalows 500-600B; ✿).

Sŏrng·tǎa·ou to the visitor centre cost 25B and take 45 minutes.

MUKDAHAN PROVINCE

Mukdahan มุกดาหาร

POP 31,565

On the banks of the Mekong, directly opposite the Lao city of Savannakhet, Mukdahan sees few visitors, despite being home of the Thai-Lao Friendship Bridge 2 connecting Thailand to Vietnam by road. It's not an exciting place, but there's enough of interest to fill a relaxing day, and the countryside near the city has plenty of low-key attractions worth exploring for people who love culture and nature.

◉ Sights

Talat Indojin MARKET
(ตลาดอินโดจีน; ◷8am-6pm) Other than the bridge, Mukdahan is best known for this riverside market, which stretches along and under the promenade. Most Thai tour groups on their way to Laos and Vietnam make a shopping stop for cheap food, clothing, and assorted trinkets from China and Vietnam, and silk and cotton fabrics made in Isan.

Hor Kaew Mukdahan MUSEUM
(หอแก้วมุกดาหาร; Th Samut Sakdarak; admission 50B; ◷8am-6pm) This eye-catching 65m-tall tower was built for the 50th anniversary of King Rama IX's ascension to the throne. The nine-sided base has a good museum with displays (labelled in English) on the eight ethnic groups of the province. There are great views and a few more historical displays in 'The 360° of Pleasure in Mukdahan by the Mekong' room up at the 50m level. The ball on the top holds a locally revered Buddha image supposedly made of solid silver.

Phu Manorom VIEWPOINT
(ภูมโนรมย์; ◷6am-7pm) You can get a more organic view of Laos and the Mekong from this mountain further south. The temple here has a small garden and is constructing a massive 84m-tall Buddha image. Tourism officials try to promote sunrise-watching here, but odds are it'll be just you and the monks.

Wat Si Mongkhon Tai BUDDHIST TEMPLE
(วัดศรีมงคลใต้; Th Samran Chaikhongthi; ◷dawn-dusk) **FREE** According to one of the many legends associated with it, this temple's 2m-tall Phra Chao Ong Luang Buddha image is older than the city itself and was unearthed during Mukdahan's construction. It sits in a simple but lovely *bòht*. The ceramic-encrusted northern gate was built as a gesture of friendship by the city's large Vietnamese community in 1954.

Wat Yod Kaeo Sivichai BUDDHIST TEMPLE
(วัดยอดแก้วศรีวิชัย; Th Samran Chaikhongthi; ◷dawn-dusk) **FREE** This temple stands out for having an enormous Buddha inside a glass-walled *wí·hǎhn,* and not one, but two small *chedi* modelled on Phra That Phanom.

Wat Pa Silawiwet BUDDHIST TEMPLE
(วัดป่าศิลาวิเวก; Th Damrongmukda; ◷dawn-dusk) **FREE** It's the hundred or so resident monkeys rather than anything religious or artistic that makes this forest temple on the edge of town worth a visit.

Mukdahan

0 ——— 200 m
0 ——— 0.1 miles

Mukdahan

◎ Sights

⊜ Sleeping

⊗ Eating

🎊 Festivals

Besides the ordinary activities, the **Mukdahan Thai Tribal Festival**, better known as the Red Cross Fair, held 9 to 17 January in the field fronting the *săh·lah glahng*, features dancing and other cultural activities from Mukdahan's eight ethnic groups.

🛏 Sleeping

Ban Rim Suan   HOTEL $
(📞0 4263 2980; www.banrimsuan.weebly.com; Th Samut Sakdarak; r 350B; P⊜❄@🛜) You can't call it lovely, but the owners have made some effort to liven things up here and that helps makes this the best budget deal in town; it is why it's almost always full by mid-afternoon. It's a tad south of the centre, but that makes it convenient for dinner and drinks along the river.

Submukda Grand Hotel   HOTEL $
(📞0 4263 3444; www.submukdagrandhotel.com; Th Samut Sakdarak; r 400-500B; P⊜❄@🛜) Although it doesn't come close to Ban Rim Suan's value, the rooms are pretty similar, and you can even squeeze out a river view from upper-floor balconies. They shut-off the wi-fi in the middle of the day and late at night.

Huanum Hotel   HOTEL $
(📞0 4261 1137; Th Samut Sakdarak; r 180-350B; P❄@🛜) A friendly old-timer that's been spruced up, this is the first choice of most backpackers. The cheapest rooms have shared cold-water showers.

★Riverview Maekhong Hotel   HOTEL $$
(📞0 4263 3323; Th Samran Chaikhongthi; r 650B; P⊜❄@🛜) Not to be confused with the pricier Riverfront Hotel, this funky place situated south of Talat Indojin has good rooms and a great location. Add the friendly staff, free bikes and wooden terrance overlooking the river and it's our favourite place in Mukdahan. Be sure to request a river view.

River City Hotel   HOTEL $$
(📞0 4261 5444; Th Samut Sakdarak; r incl breakfast 750-960B; ste 3200-25,000B; P⊜❄🛜) This large tower, topped by a 16th-floor revolving restaurant, is now tops in town. But, we can only recommend the 960B rooms, especially those with river views. The cheaper rooms are in the old block and are downright bad while the suites are just too expensive for what's on offer. The pool has been shut down and staff was skeptical that it would ever reopen.

🍴 Eating

Most downtown restaurants shut their doors early, but many out along Th Phitak Phanomkhet keep the woks sizzling late into the night.

★ Bao Pradit NORTHEASTERN THAI $

(Th Samran Chaikhongthi; dishes 30-280B; ◔10am-10pm; 🖥) It's a bit of a trek south of the centre (look for the Coke sign), but this is a real Isan restaurant with dishes including *gôry kài mót daang* (raw beef with lemon, chilli, fish sauce and extra blood with red ant eggs) and *gaang wǎi* (rattan curry). It's all served on a peaceful riverside deck. Though the English menu is a bit mysterious, it's rare that a restaurant of this sort has any English at all.

Wine Wild Why? NORTHEASTERN THAI $

(Th Samran Chaikhongthi; dishes 40-150B; ◔9am-10pm; P🖥) Housed in an atmospheric wooden building next to the river, this relaxing spot has character and delicious Thai and Isan food, though it no longer serves wine.

Night Market THAI, VIETNAMESE $

(Th Song Nang Sathit; ◔4-9pm) Mukdahan's night market has all the Thai and Isan classics, but it's the Vietnamese vendors that set it apart. A few sell *bǎhn dah* (the vendors will tell you it's 'Vietnamese pizza'), which combines soft noodles, pork, spring onions and an optional egg served on a crispy cracker.

Kufad VIETNAMESE $

(Th Samut Sakdarak; dishes 40-130B; ◔7am-6pm; 🖥) This family-run Vietnamese cafe is rightly popular and a good choice for breakfast – if you're not in a rush. The picture menu takes the guesswork out of ordering, but leaves you clueless about the prices.

Goodmook* INTERNATIONAL, THAI $$

(Th Song Nang Sathit; dishes 70-450B; ◔9am-10pm Tue-Sun; 🖥) This fun place has all the ingredients of a travellers' cafe – a mix of Thai and Western food, art on the walls, chill music, good coffee – except a room full of travellers, though many of those who do stop in Mukdahan longer than is needed to change buses do cosy up here at some point.

ⓘ Information

Immigration Office (☎0 4267 4274; ◔8.30am-4.30pm Mon-Fri) The office for visa extensions is north of town by the bridge.
Krung Thai Bank (Th Song Nong Satit; ◔10am-7pm) The only extended-hours bank downtown.
Tourism Information Center (Th Phitak Phanomkhet; ◔9am-4.30pm Mon-Fri) You can pick up maps and brochures here, but don't expect staff to be able to answer your questions. There's also Thai massage and a crafts shop.

ⓘ Getting There & Away

Mukdahan's **bus terminal** (☎0 4263 0486) is on Rte 212, west of town. To get there from the centre catch a yellow *sŏrng·tǎa·ou* (10B, 6am to 5pm) running west along Th Phitak Phanomkhet. There are minivans to Nakhon Phanom (80B, two hours, every 30 minutes) via That Phanom (40B, 45 minutes), Yasothon (84B, two hours, every 30 minutes) and Ubon Ratchathani (105B, 2½ hours, every 30 minutes). Buses go to Khon Kaen (170B to 230B, 4½ hours, every 30 minutes) and Ubon Ratchathani (75B to 135B, 3½ hours, every 30 minutes). A few Bangkok buses (420B to 533B, 10 hours) leave during the day, but most depart between 5pm and 8pm, including **999 VIP** (☎0 4261 1478; 829B), with luxury buses at 8.30am, 8pm and 8.15pm.

If you're driving to Ubon Ratchathani, Rte 212 will zip you there in three hours, but if you have a whole day, take the Mekong-hugging back roads through a gorgeous stretch of rural Thailand.

ⓘ Getting Around

Rides with **Taxi Mukdahan** (☎0 4261 3666; ◔6am-midnight) start at 30B plus a 20B call fee, if the driver uses the meter.

Goodmook* restaurant hires bikes for 100B per day.

Phu Pha Thoep National Park อุทยานแห่งชาติภูผาเทิบ

Despite only covering 48 sq km, hilly **Phu Pha Thoep National Park** (☎08 9619 7741; admission 100B) has a host of beautiful attractions; most famously large mushroom-

GETTING TO LAOS: MUKDAHAN TO SAVANNAKHET

Thais and Lao can use the boats that cross the Mekong from the city centre while everyone else must use the bridge. Buses to Savannakhet, Laos (45B, hourly 7.30am to 7pm) depart Mukdahan's bus station and the trip will take from one to two hours depending on the length of the immigration queues. A 5B surcharge applies before 8.30am, between noon and 1pm, and after 4.30pm weekdays, and all day weekends and holidays.

shaped rock formations. The main rock groups sits right behind the visitor centre, and wildflowers bloom around them October through December. Besides the weird rocks there are several clifftop viewpoints and **Nam Tok Phu Tham Phra**, a scenic waterfall (May to November only) with a grotto atop it holding hundreds of small Buddha images. It only takes a few hours on the well-marked trails to see all these sights. **Tham Fa Mue Daeng**, a cave with 5000-year-old hand paintings, is an 8km drive from the main park area and then a 1.5km walk.

For accommodation, there's **camping** (per person with own tent 30B, 4-/8-person tent hire 300/600B) and a three-bedroom **bungalow** (⊘0 2562 0760; www.dnp.go.th/parkreserve; bungalow 1800B).

The park is 15km south of Mukdahan via Rte 2034. *Sŏrng·tăa·ou* (20B, 30 minutes, every 30 minutes) to Don Tan, departing from Porn Pet Market, 300m north of Hor Kaew Mukdahan, pass the turn-off to the park. Hitching the last 1.3km to the visitor centre isn't tough, or you can ask the *sŏrng·tăa·ou* driver to detour off their route and take you; they'll probably do it for 100B. Be back at the junction by 4.30pm to guarantee finding a *sŏrng·tăa·ou* back to town.

North along the Mekong

Travelling north along the Mekong offers a lovely look at village life and makes a fantastic bike trip. Leaving the city on Samranchaikong Rd you'll follow a long line of fish farms for 6km before ducking under the 1.6km-long **Thai-Lao Friendship Bridge 2**. At this point you can get off the main road and use the tiny, mostly paved roads closer to the river, although at times the main road (by this point no longer full of traffic) is the only road.

Two and a half kilometres after the bridge you'll meet a **troop of monkeys** that resides next to Wat Ban Sai Yai. Here, you must use the main road as it has the only bridge over the small river. You can get back to the river at the first *big* dirt road you meet.

After another 9.5km, where the greenish Mae Nam Chanot meets the muddy Mekong, is **Wat Mano Phirom** (admission free; ⊘dawn-dusk), one of Mukdahan Province's oldest temples. The original *bòht*, now a *wí·hăhn*, was built in 1756 in Lan Xang style

with an elaborately carved wooden facade and large painted eave brackets. The creatures guarding the staircase are too incredible for words.

Wat Srimahapo (admission free; ⊘dawn-dusk), sometimes called Wat Pho Si, is another 4.5km north in Ban Wan Yai. You may not expect its tiny *bòht*, built in 1916, to be worth a look, but inside, elaborately carved beams hold up the tin roof and well-preserved murals cover the walls. The monks' residence is French-colonial style.

After a further 8km you'll pass the modern, glass-walled **Our Lady of the Martyrs of Thailand Shrine** (admission free; ⊘8am-5pm, Mass 7am Sun), locally called Wat Song Khon and often incorrectly described as the largest church in Southeast Asia. It was built in 1995 to commemorate seven Thai Catholics killed by the police in 1940 for refusing to renounce their faith. Wax sculptures of the martyrs and their ashes lie under glass at the back.

Three and a half kilometres after the church is **Kaeng Kabao**, a stretch of rocky shore and islets emerging during the dry season. Several rustic restaurants have set up along the river here, making this a good place to refuel before heading back to Mukdahan, or continuing for another 17km to That Phanom.

YASOTHON & ROI ET PROVINCES

Yasothon and Roi Et, two of Thailand's most rural provinces, have little of interest to fast-track travellers, but they do show a side of Thailand that few people (including other Thais) ever see.

People looking to nose deeper into Isan culture will want to take a peek at Phra That Kong Khao Noi and purchase some pillows in Ban Si Than in Yasothon Province. Yasothon city saves all its gusto for the annual Rocket Festival, which completes a trifecta of Isan icons. Roi Et Province, whose capital city is the far more pleasant of the two, has a few enormous off-beat attractions, including a serious contender for Thailand's strangest temple.

Yasothon   ยโสธร

POP 20,675

Yasothon has little to offer visitors outside the official whizz-bang period of mid-May, and it neither looks nor acts like a capital city. In fact, sometimes, it barely feels like a city at all.

◉ Sights

Yasothon has two attractions, though neither is worth a special trip.

The centrepiece of **Wat Mahathat** (Th Wariratchadet; admission free; ☉ dawn-dusk) is a highly venerated Lao-style *chedi* said to date from AD 695 and to enshrine holy relics of Phra Anan (Ananda), the Buddha's personal attendant monk. Much more interesting, however, is the restored *hŏr drai* (a building for storing Tripitaka Buddhist scriptures), dating to the 1830s, that sits on stilts in a pond to protect the sacred scripts from termites. It's kept open so people can go inside.

The heart of the **Ban Singha Tha** neighbourhood, just below Wat Mahathat, has several classic French Indochinese shophouses, trimmed with artistic flourishes that are evidence of Yasothon's former wealth. They were built for Chinese merchants by Vietnamese labourers almost a century ago at what was then Yasothon's port, and with their historic value recently recognised, restoration work has begun.

♨♨ Festivals

Rocket Festival CULTURAL
(Bun Bâng Fai) Rocket Festivals are held across Isan in May and June to tell Phaya Thaen, a pre-Buddhist rain god, that it's time for him to send rain; but no place celebrates as fervently as Yasothon, where the largest rockets are 3m long and, according to the rocket-makers we talked to, packed with 500kg of gunpowder. The three-day event, held on the second weekend of May, features traditional local dances, parades, rocket contests and a lot of bawdy, drunken revelry.

⌂ Sleeping

BM Grand HOTEL $
(☑ 0 4571 4262; Th Rattanakhet; s/d 400/450; ᴘ☉❄❅) This city-centre place near the night market has nicely decorated and well-appointed rooms that provide the best value in town.

JP Emerald Hotel HOTEL $
(☑ 0 4572 4848; www.jpemeraldhotel.com; Th Prapa; r 550B, incl breakfast 700-2300B; ᴘ❄@❅) Yasothon's only full-service three-star hotel. The rooms won't excite you, but unlike many older hotels, they do keep up on maintenance pretty well here making them a good value. Night-time diversions include snooker and coyote dancers in the disco. It's at the Roi Et end of town.

In Town Hotel HOTEL $
(☑ 0 4571 3007; 614 Th Jangsanit; r 220-380B; ᴘ❄❅) This place, on the main road, is so far south that it almost loses the rights to its name, but for Yasothon it's better than the budget average. The Warotohn Hotel next door is even cheaper.

Green Park Grand HOTEL $$
(☑ 0 4571 4700; www.thegreenparkgrand.com; Th Wariratchadet; r 800-1200B, f 1500-2500B; ᴘ☉❄@❅❆) Though the hotel lacks panache, Green Park's big, bright and sparking clean rooms are the best in Yasothon. You can use the adjacent health club for free. It's 1km east of the centre on the way to Mukdahan.

✗ Eating

Rim Chi Riverside NORTHEASTERN THAI $
(dishes 40-450B; ☉ 9am-9pm; ᴘ) Enjoy superb Isan and Thai food from either the tree-filled terrace or your own thatched-roof raft on the Chi River. This is an English-free zone, but you can't go wrong ordering *sôm-dam* or *blah nin lui sŏo-an* (fried tilapia 'run through the garden'). It's 900m west of Krung Thai Bank.

Hippy Cafe THAI $
(Th Rattanakhet; dishes 50-90B; ☉ 10am-9pm; ᴘ❅) This Thai-trendy cafe in the old bus station (by the clock tower) serves the expected coffee and cakes, but surprises with fresh and delicious salads and Thai dishes, albeit in very small portions. We really like their unique version of tofu *laap*, though you'll have to tell them to make it spicy.

Night Market THAI $
(Th Wariratchadet; ☉ 4-10pm) East of Wat Mahathat, this small market is as good a place as any to sample Yasothon's famous dessert, *kà·nom wăhn lôrt chôrng* (rice noodles made with pandan served in coconut milk).

ⓘ Getting There & Away

Yasothon's **bus terminal** (☑ 0 4571 4500) is north of the city on the bypass road. A motorcycle taxi to the centre costs 50B. It's best to get your driver's phone number for the return trip because finding a motorcycle taxi in town is difficult.

The main destinations are Ubon Ratchathani (73B to 109B, 1½ hours, every 30 minutes), Khorat (175B to 230B, four hours, hourly), Mukdahan (minivans 84B, two hours, every 30 minutes) and Khon Kaen (126B to 189B, 3½ hours, every 30 minutes) via Roi Et (52B to 78B, one hour).

Bangkok (360B to 419B, eight to nine hours) buses leave approximately hourly during the day, and frequently from 7pm to 10pm. There are VIP buses to Bangkok with **999** (☑ 0 4571 2965; ticket 652B) and **Chan Tour** (☑ 08 5309 2079; ticket 463B).

Around Yasothon

Phra That Kong Khao Noi   พระธาตุ ก่องข้าวน้อย

A rather sinister myth surrounds the **Phra That Kong Khao Noi** (⊙ dawn-dusk), which translates as 'Small Sticky Rice Basket Stupa', a brick-and-stucco *chedi* dating from the late Ayuthaya period 5km outside town towards Ubon Ratchathani. According to one legend (which is taught to school children as an example of why it's important to keep your emotions in check) a young, ravenously hungry farmer, who had toiled all morning in the hot sun, murdered his mother here when she brought his lunch to the fields late and in a small sticky-rice basket. The farmer, eating his lunch over his mother's dead body, realised that there was actually more food than he could eat. To atone for his misdeed, he built this *chedi*.

Or perhaps not. Others say it was built by people who were travelling to Phra That Phanom to enshrine gold and gems, but got to Ban Tat Thong and learned they were too late; so they built this *chedi* instead. Some locals combine the myths and say that the repentant son was unable to build a *chedi* of his own and so joined forces with the pilgrims and they built it together.

Further complicating matters, most Yasothonians claim the real Small Sticky Rice Basket Stupa is at Ban Sadao village (7km east of Yasothon on Rte 202) in the back of **Wat Tung Sadoa**. All that remains is the base; when the original tumbled over shortly after the redeemed son's death, locals built another petite *chedi* next to it. When we asked a monk here why Thai tourists

visit the other *chedi,* he simply answered, '*Gahn meuang*' (It's politics).

Ban Si Than   บ้านศรีฐาน

Residents of Ban Si Than can't leave their work behind when they go to sleep: this is a pillow-making village. All around the village (and most villages surrounding it) you'll see people sewing, stuffing or selling *mŏrn lai kít* (pillows decorated with diamond-grid *kít* patterns). The most famous style is a stiff triangle-shaped pillow *(mŏrn săhm lĕeam)* used as an arm support while sitting on the floor. Prices here are far lower than you'll pay elsewhere in Thailand, and this is also one of the few places you can buy them unstuffed (*yang mâi sài nûn;* literally 'no kapok inserted'), which makes the big ones viable as souvenirs.

If you want to see monkeys, have someone point you to **Don Ling**, 5km out of town at Ban Tao Hi.

The village is 20km from Yasothon on Rte 202, then 2.5km south of Ban Nikom. Any Amnat Charoen-bound bus can drop you at the junction (20B to 25B, 45 minutes) where a motorcycle taxi will zip you in for 20B.

Roi Et   ร้อยเอ็ด

POP 34,557

There has been a settlement at this spot for at least 2800 years, making this one of Isan's oldest cities. At one point, legend says, it had 11 city gates, and in ancient writing '11' was expressed as '10-plus-1'. Somehow this morphed into the city's name, which means 'one hundred one'.

Except for extensive stretches of the old city moat, Roi Et's long history hasn't followed it into the 21st century. Still, the city retains a charm and sense of identity all its own. You can't call Roi Et sleepy, but, perhaps taking its cue from the beloved walking Buddha on the island in the city-centre lake, it does seem to move to its own urban beat.

◉ Sights

Wat Burapha   BUDDHIST TEMPLE
(วัดบูรพา; Th Phadung Phanit; ⊙ dawn-dusk) FREE
The enormous standing Buddha towering above Roi Et's squat skyline is **Phra Phuttha Ratana Mongkon Mahamuni** (Luang Po Yai for short), the main attraction at this temple. Despite being of little artistic significance, it's hard to ignore. Head to toe he

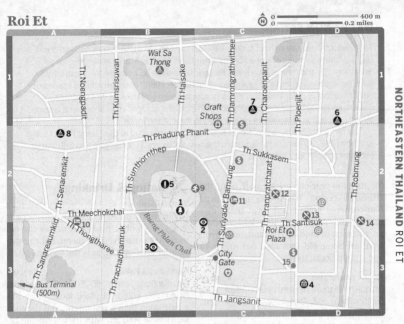

Roi Et

stands 59.2m, and from the ground to the tip of the *ùt·sà·nít* it's 67.8m. You can climb up the stairs behind him.

Roi Et National Museum MUSEUM
(พิพิธภัณฑสถานแห่งชาติร้อยเอ็ด; Th Ploenjit; admission 100B; ⊘9am-4pm Wed-Sun) This interesting museum gives equal billing to ancient artefacts and Isan culture. The 3rd floor features silk weaving, including a good display showing the materials used to produce natural-dye fabrics.

Bueng Phlan Chai PARK
(บึงพลาญชัย) Walking paths criss-cross the attractive, shady island and attract the usual crowd of doting couples, students, joggers and picnickers. The beloved **walking Buddha statue** is on the north side and the **lak meuang** (city pillar) is to the south.

Wat Klang Ming Muang BUDDHIST TEMPLE
(วัดกลางมิ่งเมือง; Th Phadung Phanit; ⊘dawn-dusk)
FREE The first thing most people notice about this old temple, which dates to the late Ayuthaya era, is the unusual four-storey tower at the back, but the real gems here are the old Isan-style paintings on the exterior of the *bòht*, which mostly recount the Jataka tales.

Roi Et

Wat Neua BUDDHIST TEMPLE
(วัดเหนือ; Th Phadung Phanit; ⊘dawn-dusk)
FREE This temple in the northern quarter of town has a peaceful ambience. It's known

DON'T MISS

WAT PA NON SAWAN

Thirty kilometres east of Roi Et, **Wat Pa Non Sawan** (วัดป่าโนนสวรรค์; ☉ dawn-dusk) **FREE** is home to hundreds of colourful sculptures ranging from merely peculiar to 'what-the...?!', and makes Sala Kaew Ku (p460) feel like a Thomas Kinkade product. Whether it's the immense dragons, greeting turtles, Hindu gods, gruesome scenes of hell or the lonely polar bear, this place is sure to make you think as well as smile.

Be sure to say sà·wà·dee to Lungpu Khampan, the octogenarian abbot who inspired it all. He lives and greets visitors on the ground floor of the tower.

The temple is 30km east of Roi Et and buses can drop you at the Thung Khao Luang junction (25B, 30 minutes), 8km from the temple, where a motorcycle taxi will charge 150B for a two-hour round-trip.

for its 1200-year-old brick *chedi* from the Dvaravati period, which has an unusual four-cornered bell-shaped form that's rare in Thailand. Also inside the cloister (these are common in most of Thailand, but rare in Isan) are some old Dvaravati *bai săir·mah* and a giant bodhi tree.

Roi Et Aquarium AQUARIUM
(สถานแสดงพันธุ์สัตว์น้ำเทศบาลเมืองร้อยเอ็ด; Th Sunthornthep; ☉ 8.30am-4.30pm) **FREE** This little aquarium with a walk-through tunnel houses fish found around Isan.

🛏 Sleeping

City Home Place HOTEL $
(🗐 0 4351 6079; Th Thongtharee; s/d 400/440B; P ✳ 🛜) There isn't really anything special about this hotel west of the lake, and the rooms have the feel of a student dorm, but this is currently the only hotel in the city centre that isn't old and rundown.

Saithip Hotel HOTEL $
(🗐 0 4351 5515; Th Suriyadet Bamrung; r 240-320B; P ✳ 🛜) The architect added a bit of decoration to the facade and some rooms have sit-down toilets, but this is otherwise your ordinary cold-water cheapie.

Thanintorn Green Park HOTEL $$
(🗐 0 4351 8393; www.thanintorn-greenpark.com; Roi Et–Yasothon Rd; r 690-790 ste 2300-2600; P ➴ ✳ @ 🛜) This boxy hotel 1km east of town is Roi Et's best, but this is entirely due to lack of competition. Room are thoroughly clean and comfortable, but Green Park lacks even a lick of character and the service should be better.

🍴 Eating & Drinking

White Elephant INTERNATIONAL, THAI $
(Th Robmuang; dishes 60-350B; ☉ 4pm-midnight; P 🛜) This public place just across the old moat has a massive Thai menu, but the specialities are German, as is the owner.

Rishi India Food INDIAN $
(Th Santisuk; dishes 50-250B; ☉ 10am-10pm; 🛜 ✎) This colourful place looks more like a hair salon than a restaurant, and the food won't wow you, but with Indian cuisine being so rare in Isan, you take what you can get.

Cafe & Gallery COFFEESHOP $
(Th Ronnachai Chanyut; espresso 30B; ☉ 9am-6.30pm; 🛜) Owned by a photographer, and full of his framed prints (for sale starting at 500B), this small coffee shop brings a welcome bit of culture to Roi Et. For a snack, try the 'spicy cake': chocolate with chilli peppers. The cafe's 1km south of the lake, across the street from Roi Et Hospital.

Night Market NORTHEASTERN THAI $
(Th Pranpratcharat; ☉ 3-11pm) By day, this big roof hosts Roi Et's municipal market, but at night it shifts gears to become the city's main night market.

ⓘ Getting There & Away

Nok Air (🗐 0 2900 9955; www.nokair.com) has one morning and one evening flight to/from Bangkok's Don Muang Airport with fares from about 1800B. **ST Travel** (🗐 08 1974 3438; Th Ploenjit; ☉ 8.30am-6pm Mon-Sat) sells tickets. The airport is 13km north of town.

Buses depart at least hourly from Roi Et's **bus terminal** (🗐 0 4351 1939; Th Jangsanit) to Bangkok (320B to 678B, eight hours), Khon Kaen (bus and minivan 80B to 122B, 2½ hours), Ubon Ratchathani (118B to 176B, three hours), and Surin (104B, 2½ hours). The bus terminal is 1km west of the city centre. Túk-túk charge 60B to anywhere near the lake.

Hua Hin & the Upper Gulf

Best Places to Eat

➡ Rang Yen Garden (p501)

➡ Hua Hin Koti (p510)

➡ Prikhorm (p524)

➡ * Rim Lom (p519)

➡ Rabieng Rim Nam (p498)

Best Places to Stay

➡ Baan Bayan (p508)

➡ Brassiere Beach (p514)

➡ Away Hua Hin (p513)

➡ NaNa Chart Baan Krut (p521)

➡ House 73 (p518)

Why Go?

Known as the 'royal' coast, the upper gulf has long been the favoured playground of the Bangkok monarchy and elite. Every Thai king from Rama IV on has found an agreeable spot to build a royal getaway. Today, domestic tourists flock to this coast in the same pursuit of leisure, as well as to pay homage to the revered kings whose summer palaces are now open to the public.

Culture meets the coast here, with historic sites, national parks and long sandy beaches ideal for swimming all an easy commute from Bangkok. And while Thais have long known of the region's delights, increasing numbers of Western travellers are now falling for the combination of an unspoiled coastline and the easy pace of provincial life on offer. There's little diving or snorkelling, but kiteboarders will be in paradise as this region is by far the best place in Thailand to jump the waves.

When to Go

➡ The best time to visit is during the hot and dry season (February to June). From July to October (southwest monsoon) and October to January (northeast monsoon) there is occasional rain and strong winds; but the region tends to stay drier than the rest of the country because of a geographic anomaly.

➡ During stormy periods, jellyfish are often carried close to shore making swimming hazardous. The Thais get around this by swimming fully clothed.

Hua Hin & the Upper Gulf Highlights

1 Motorcycling between curvaceous bays and limestone peaks in **Prachuap Khiri Khan** (p516)

2 Strolling the long blonde coastline of **Hua Hin** (p502) dotted with wave-jumping kiteboarders

3 Eating and shopping (and eating some more) at Hua Hin's **night market** (p509)

4 Escaping into the depths of **Kaeng Krachan National Park** (p499) and spotting gibbons and wild elephants

5 Being a beach bum on laid-back **Hat Thung Wua Laen** (p522)

6 Exploring the hilltop palace and underground caves, while dodging monkeys, in **Phetchaburi** (p495)

7 Making the popular pilgrimage to **Khao Sam Roi Yot National Park** (p514) to see the illuminated cave shrine of Tham Phraya Nakhon

8 Letting the kids run around all day in their bathing suits at **Dolphin Bay** (p513)

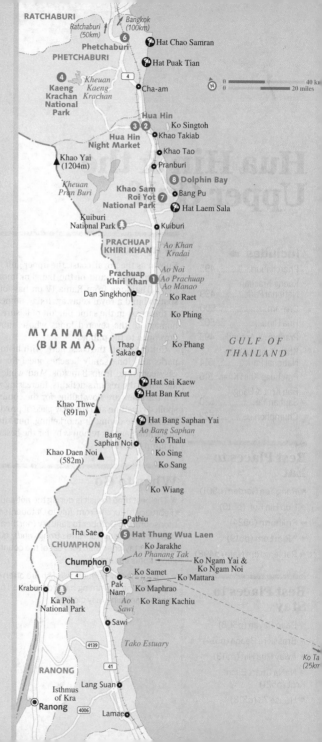

Phetchaburi (Phetburi)

เพชรบุรี

POP 46,600

An easy escape from Bangkok, Phetchaburi should be on every cultural traveller's itinerary. It has temples and palaces, outlying jungles and cave shrines, as well as easy access to the coast. Best of all, Phetchaburi remains a sleepy provincial town, complete with markets and old teak shophouses. Relatively few foreigners make it here; instead it is visiting groups of Thai students who can be found touring the sites and working up the courage to say 'hello' to any wandering Westerners.

Historically, Phetchaburi is a visible timeline of kingdoms that have migrated across Southeast Asia. During the 11th century the Khmer empire settled in, although their control was relatively short-lived. As Khmer power diminished, Phetchaburi became a strategic royal fort during the Thai-based Sukhothai and Ayuthaya kingdoms. During the stable Ayuthaya period, the upper gulf flourished and Phetchaburi thrived as a 17th-century trading post between Myanmar and Ayuthaya. The town is often referred to as a 'Living Ayuthaya', since the equivalent of the many relics that were destroyed in the former kingdom's capital are still intact here.

◎ Sights & Activities

For such a small town, Phetchaburi has enough historic temples to keep anyone busy for the day.

Phra Nakhon Khiri
Historical Park   HISTORICAL SITE

(อุทยานประวัติศาสตร์พระนครคีรี; ✆ 0 3240 1006; admission 150B; tram return adult/child 40B/free; ◷ 8.30am-4.30pm, tram 8.30am-4.30pm) This national historical park sits regally atop Khao Wang (Palace Hill) surveying the city with subdued opulence. Rama IV (King Mongkut) built the palace, in a mix of European and Chinese styles, and surrounding temples in 1859 as a retreat from Bangkok. The hilltop location allowed the king to pursue his interest in astronomy and stargazing.

Each breezy hall of the palace is furnished with royal belongings. Cobblestone paths lead from the palace through the forested hill to three summits, each topped by a *chedi* (stupa). The white spire of **Phra That Chom Phet** skewers the sky and can be spotted from the city below.

There are two entrances to the site. The front entrance is across from Th Ratwithi and involves a strenuous footpath that passes a troop of unpredictable monkeys. The back entrance is on the opposite side of the hill and has a **tram** that glides up and down the summit. This place is a popular school-group outing, and you'll be as much a photo-op as the historic buildings.

A **Monday night market** lines the street in front of Khao Wang with the usual food and clothing stalls.

Wat Mahathat Worawihan   BUDDHIST TEMPLE

(วัดมหาธาตุวรวิหาร; Th Damnoen Kasem) FREE Centrally located, gleaming white Wat Mahathat is a lovely example of an everyday temple with as much hustle and bustle as the busy commercial district around it. The showpiece is a five-tiered Khmer-style *prang* (stupa) decorated in stucco relief, a speciality of Phetchaburi's local artisans, while inside the main *wí·hăhn* (shrine hall or sanctuary) are contemporary murals.

The tempo of the temple is further heightened with the steady beat from traditional musicians and dancers who perform for merit-making services.

After visiting here, follow Th Suwanmunee through the old teak-house district filled with the smells of incense from religious paraphernalia shops.

Tham Khao Luang   CAVE

(ถ้ำเขาหลวง; ◷ 8am-6pm) FREE About 4km north of town is Tham Khao Luang, a dramatic stalactite-stuffed chamber that is one of Thailand's most impressive cave shrines and a favourite of Rama IV. Accessed via a steep set of stairs, its central Buddha figure is often illuminated with a heavenly glow when sunlight filters in through the heart-shaped skylight.

At the opposite end of the chamber are a row of sitting Buddhas casting repetitive shadows on the undulating cavern wall.

PHETCHABURI SIGHTSEEING

Some of the city's best sights are outside town, but don't let the distance deter you. Hire a *sŏrng·tăa·ou* (passenger pick-up truck) for the day (usually around 500B) to hit all the highlights. Alternatively, you can rent a motorbike (200B to 300B) or a bicycle (100B).

Phetchaburi (Phetburi)

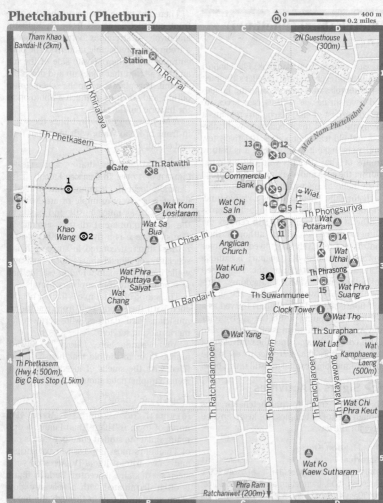

The story is that Rama IV built the stone gate that separates the main chamber from a second chamber as a security measure for a couple who once lived in the cave. A figure of a prostrate body in the third chamber is said to represent the cycle of life and death but it hasn't experienced a peaceful resting place as bandits destroyed much of it in search of hidden treasures. Deeper in the cave is supposedly a rock formation that looks like Christ on the cross but our literal eyes couldn't spot it. (Thais are especially imaginative at spotting familiar forms in cave stalactites.)

Around the entrance to the cave you'll meet brazen monkeys looking for handouts. Guides lurk in the car park, but they're not essential and aren't always forthcoming about their fees (usually 100B per person). You'll need to arrange transport here from town (around 150B round-trip).

Phra Ram Ratchaniwet   HISTORICAL SITE
(พระรามราชนิเวศน์; ☏0 3242 8083; Ban Peun Palace; admission 50B; ⏱8.30am-4.30pm Mon-Fri) An incredible art nouveau creation, construction of this elegant summer palace began in 1910 at the behest of Rama V (who

Phetchaburi (Phetburi)

◎ Sights
1 Phra Nakhon Khiri Historical
   Park..A2
2 Phra That Chom Phet......................A3
3 Wat Mahathat Worawihan................C3

🛏 Sleeping
4 J.J. Home...C2
5 Sabaidee Resort...............................C2
6 Sun Hotel...A2

🍽 Eating
7 Day Market......................................D3
8 Jek Meng..B2
9 Ne & Nal..C2
10 Night Market...................................C2
11 Rabieng Rim Nam............................C3

ℹ Transport
12 Air-con Buses to Bangkok................C2
13 Minivans to Bangkok........................C2
14 Ordinary Buses to Cha-am &
   Hua Hin..D3
15 Sŏrng·tǎa·ou to Kaeng
   Krachan National Park....................D3

died just after the project was started). Designed by German architects, who used the opportunity to showcase contemporary design innovations, inside there are spacious sun-drenched rooms decorated with exquisite glazed tiles, stained glass, parquet floors and plenty of wrought-iron details.

While the structure is typical of early 20th century Thailand, a period that saw a local passion for erecting European-style buildings in an effort to keep up with the 'modern' architecture of Thailand's colonised neighbours, the scale of the palace is impressive. Check out the double-spiral staircase, which provides a classic debutante's debut, and the state-of-the-art, for the time, personal bathroom of the king. The palace is on a military base 1km south of town; you may be required to show your passport.

Wat Kamphaeng Laeng   BUDDHIST TEMPLE
(วัดกำแพงแลง; Th Phokarang) FREE A 12th-century remnant of the time when the Angkor (Khmer) kingdom stretched from present-day Cambodia all the way to the Malay peninsula, this ancient and once ornate shrine was originally Hindu before Thailand's conversion to Buddhism. There is one intact sanctuary, flanked by two smaller shrines and crumbling sandstone walls, making for intriguing photo opportunities.

Tham Khao Bandai-It   CAVE
(ถ้ำเขาบันไดอิฐ; donation appreciated; ⏱9am-4pm) This hillside monastery, 2km west of town, sprawls through several large caverns converted into simple Buddha shrines and meditation rooms. English-speaking guides (tip appreciated) lead tours, mainly as a precaution against the monkeys. One cavern contains a significant population of bats, and guides will instruct you not to look up with your mouth open (a good rule for everyday life).

Hat Puak Tian   BEACH
(หาดปึกเตียน) Locals come to this dark-sands beach, 20km southeast of Phetchaburi and famed for its role in Thai literature, on weekends to eat seafood and frolic in the surf. You'll need private transport to get here.

The beach is mentioned in the Thai epic poem *Phra Aphaimani*, written by Sunthorn Phu. A partially submerged statue of a giant woman standing offshore with an outstretched hand and a forlorn expression depicts a character from the poem who disguised herself as a beautiful temptress to win the love of the hero and imprison him on this beach. But he discovers her treachery (and her true ugliness) and with the help of a mermaid escapes to Ko Samet (which has nicer beaches so maybe he was onto something).

🎊 Festivals & Events

Phra Nakhon Khiri Fair   CULTURAL
(⏱Apr) Centred on Khao Wang, this provincial-style celebration takes place in early April and lasts nine days. Phra Nakhon Khiri is festooned with lights, there are traditional dance performances, craft and food displays and a beauty contest.

🛏 Sleeping

Once bereft of guesthouses, Phetchaburi's accommodation options have improved significantly in the last couple of years. But there aren't many places, so it's worth booking ahead, especially in high season.

2N Guesthouse   GUESTHOUSE $
(☑0 3240 1309; two_nguesthouse@hotmail.com; 98/3 Moo 2, Tambol Bankoom; d & tw 580B; ❄🐾📶) There are only six big and bright rooms, all with small balconies. The friendly staff are a solid source of information and they offer free pick-ups and bicycles.

...ee Resort GUESTHOUSE $

...3240 0194; sabai2505@gmail.com; 65-67 ...longkrachang; r 250-500B; 🌂 @ 🛜) Basic ...ut well-kept bungalows and rooms, some fan only and all with shared bathrooms, set around a small garden. Pleasant staff and a popular spot for breakfast.

J.J. Home GUESTHOUSE $

(📱 08 1880 9286; a.sirapassorn@hotmail.com; 2 Th Chisa-In; r 200-500B; 🌂 🛜) By the road, so a little noisy, but the rooms here are spacious and clean and a decent deal. The more expensive options have private bathrooms and air-con.

Sun Hotel HOTEL $$

(📱 0 3240 1000; www.sunhotelthailand.com; 43/33 Soi Phetkasem; r 900-1150B; 🌂 @ 🛜) The only realistic midrange option in town, the Sun Hotel sits opposite the back entrance to Phra Nakhon Khiri. It has large, modern but uninspired rooms with professional staff. There's a pleasant cafe downstairs and you can rent bikes for 20B per hour.

🍴 Eating

Surrounded by palm sugar plantations, Phetchaburi is famous for Thai sweets, including *kà·nŏm môr gaang* (egg custard) and the various 'golden' desserts made from egg yolks to portend good fortune. Nearby fruit orchards produce refreshingly aromatic *chom·pôo Phet* (Phetchaburi rose apple), pineapples and golden bananas.

⭐ Rabieng Rim Nam INTERNATIONAL-THAI $

(📱 0 3242 5707; 1 Th Chisa-In; dishes 45-80B; ⏱ 7am-10pm; 🛜) This riverside restaurant serves up terrific food and the English-speaking owner is a fount of tourist infor-

mation. The affiliated guesthouse has a few run-down but bearable rooms, all with shared bathrooms.

Jek Meng THAI $

(www.jekmeng-noodle.com; 85 Th Ratwithi; dishes 50-150B; ⏱ 7am-5pm) A cut above your average hole-in-the-wall joint, you can find curries and dumplings here, as well as fried rice and noodles. It's opposite the Shell petrol station. Look for the black-and-white checked tablecloths.

Ne & Nai THAI $

(Th Damnoen Kasem; dishes 40-60B; ⏱ 8am-5pm) Great slow-cooked soups in claypots are the signature dishes at this casual place. The *gŏo·ay dĕe·o gài* (chicken noodles) comes southern style with a whole chicken drumstick.

Night Market THAI $

(Th Ratwithi; ⏱ 4pm-10pm) Big and bustling from the late afternoon, head here for all the standard Thai fast food favourites and decent barbecue.

Day Market THAI $

(⏱ 6am-6pm) A good spot for people-watching, the day market, north of the clock tower, has food stalls on the perimeter serving the usual noodle dishes as well as specialities such as *kà·nŏm jeen tôrt man* (thin noodles with fried spicy fishcake) and the hot-season favourite *kôw châa pét·bù·ree* (moist chilled rice served with sweetmeats).

ℹ️ Information

There's no formal information source in town, but 2N Guesthouse and Rabieng Rim Nam are both good for traveller tips.

Main Post Office (cnr Th Ratwithi & Th Damnoen Kasem)

Police Station (📱 0 3242 5500; Th Ratwithi) Near the intersection of Th Ratchadamnoen.

Siam Commercial Bank (2 Th Damnoen Kasem) Other nearby banks also offer foreign exchange and ATMs.

ℹ️ Getting There & Away

The stop for buses to Bangkok is at the back of the night market. Across the street is a minivan stop with services to Bangkok. Minivans for Kaen Krachan National Park also leave from opposite the night market.

Ordinary buses to Cha-am and Hua Hin stop in town near Th Matayawong.

Most southbound air-conditioned buses and minivans stop out of town on Th Phetkasem in

---

ℹ️ MONKEY BUSINESS

Phetchaburi is full of macaque monkeys who know no shame or fear. Having once just congregated on Khao Wang (Palace Hill), they have now spread to the surrounding streets, as well as to the road leading to Tham Khao Luang. There they lurk by food stands, or eye up pedestrians as potential mugging victims. These apes love plastic bags – regarding them as a signal that you are carrying food – so be wary about displaying them. Keep a tight hold on camera bags too. Above all, don't feed or bait the monkeys. They do bite.

TRANSPORT TO/FROM PHETCHABURI

DESTINATION	BUS	MINIVAN	TRAIN
Bangkok Hua Lamphong			84-388B; 3-4hr; 12 daily 1.53am-4.47pm
Bangkok southern bus terminal	120B; 2-3hr; 8.30am & 10.30am	100B; 2hr; hourly 7am-6pm	
Bangkok Victory Monument		100B; 2hr; every 45min 5am-6pm	
Chaam from Th Matayawong	30B; 40min; frequent		
Hua Hin from Th Matayawong	40B; 1½ hours; frequent		12 daily
Kaeng Krachan National Park		100B; 1hr; hourly 6.30am-6pm	

front of the Big C department store. Destinations include Cha-am and Hua Hin. Motorcycle taxis await and can take you into town for around 50B.

Frequent rail services run to/from Bangkok's Hua Lamphong station. Fares vary depending on the train and class.

ⓘ Getting Around

Motorcycle taxis go anywhere in the town centre for 40B to 50B. *Sŏrng·tăa·ou* (pick-up trucks) cost about the same. It's a 20-minute walk (1km) from the train station to the town centre.

Rabieng Rim Nam restaurant hires out bicycles (100B per day) and motorbikes (200B to 300B per day).

Kaeng Krachan National Park อุทยานแห่งชาติแก่งกระจาน

Wake to an eerie symphony of gibbon calls as the early morning mist hangs limply above the forest canopy. Hike through lush forests in search of elephant herds and other wildlife at the communal watering holes. Or sweat through your clothes as you summit the park's highest peak. At 3000 sq km, Thailand's largest national park (⌨ 0 3245 9293; www.dnp.go.th; admission 200B; ⏱ visitors centre 8.30am-4.30pm) is surprisingly close to civilisation but shelters an intense tangle of wilderness that sees few tourists. Two rivers (Mae Nam Phetchaburi and Mae Nam Pranburi), a large lake and abundant rainfall keep the place green year-round. Animal life is prolific and includes wild elephants, deer, gibbons, boars, dusky langurs and wild cattle.

This park also occupies an interesting, overlapping biozone for birds as the southernmost spot for the northern species and the northernmost for the southern species. There are about 400 species of birds, including hornbills as well as pheasants and other ground dwellers.

🏃 Activities

Hiking is the best way to explore the park. Most of the trails are signed and branch off the main road. The **Nam Tok Tho Thip** trail starts at the Km 36 marker and continues for 4km to an 18-tiered waterfall. **Phanoen Thung** (1112m) is the park's highest point and can be summited via a 6km hike that starts at the Km 27 marker. Note that most trails, including the one to Phanoen Thung, are closed during the rainy season (August to October).

The twin waterfalls of **Pa La-U Yai** and **Pa La-U Noi** in the southern section of the park are popular with day-trippers on tours from Hua Hin and stay open in the rainy season, when they are in full flow. It's also possible to organise mountain biking in the park from Hua Hin.

Tourist infrastructure in Kaeng Krachan is somewhat limited and the roads can be rough. The park rangers can help arrange camping-gear rental, food and transport. There are crowds on weekends and holidays but weekdays should be people free. The best months to visit are between November and April.

🛏 Sleeping & Eating

There are various **bungalows** (📞0 2562 0760; www.dnp.go.th/parkreserve; bungalows from 1200B) within the park, mainly near the reservoir. These sleep from four to six people and are simple affairs with fans and fridges. There are also **campsites** (per person 60-90B), including a pleasant grassy one near the reservoir at the visitors centre, and a modest restaurant. Tents can be rented at the visitors centre. Bear in mind that you can't stay overnight during the rainy season.

On the road leading to the park entrance are several simple resorts and bungalows. About 3.5km before reaching the visitors centre, **A&B Bungalows** (📞08 9891 2328; r from 700B) is scenic and popular with bird-watching groups. There is a good restaurant here that can provide you with a packed lunch.

ⓘ Getting There & Away

Kaeng Krachan is 52km southwest of Phetchaburi, with the southern edge of the park 35km from Hua Hin. If you have your own vehicle, drive 20km south from Phetchaburi on Hwy 4 to the town of Tha Yang. Turn right (west) and after 38km you'll reach the visitors centre. You use the same access road from Tha Yang if coming south from Hua Hin.

You can also reach the park by **minivan** (📞08 9231 5810; one-way 100B; ⊙ hourly 6.30am-6pm) from Phetchaburi. Alternatively you can catch a *sŏrng·tăa·ou* (80B, 1½ hours, 6am to 2pm) from Phetchaburi (near the clock tower) to the village of Ban Kaeng Krachan, 4km before the park. From the village, you can charter transport to the park. You can also hire your own *sŏrng·tăa·ou* all the way to the park; expect to pay around 1500B for the return trip.

Minivan tours also operate from Hua Hin.

Cha-am   ชะอำ

POP 72,341

Cheap and cheerful Cha-am has long been a popular beach getaway for working-class families and Bangkok students. On weekends and public holidays, neon-painted buses (called '*chor ching cha*'), their sound systems pumping, deliver groups of holiday-makers. It is a very Thai-style beach party with eating and drinking marathons held around umbrella-shaded beach chairs and tables. Entertainment is provided by the banana boats that zip back and forth, eventually making a final jack-knife turn that throws the passengers into the sea. Applause

and giggles usually follow from the beachside audience.

Cha-am doesn't see many foreigners; visitors are usually older Europeans who winter here instead of more expensive Hua Hin. And there are even fewer bathing suits on display as most Thais frolic in the ocean fully clothed. This isn't the spot to meet a lot of young travellers or even a good option for families of young children who might be overwhelmed by paparazzi-like Thais in holiday mode. But for everyone else, Cha-am's beach is long, wide and sandy, the grey-blue water is clean and calm, the seafood is superb, the people-watching entertaining and the prices are some of the most affordable anywhere on the coast.

✪ Festivals & Events

Crab Festival   FOOD
(⊙Feb) In February, Cha-am celebrates one of its local marine delicacies: blue crabs. Food stalls, concerts, and lots of neon turn the beachfront into a pedestrian party.

Gin Hoy, Do Nok, Tuk Meuk   FOOD
(⊙Sep) You really can do it all at this annual festival held in September. The English translation means 'Eat Shellfish, Watch Birds, Catch Squid' and is a catchy slogan for all of Cha-am's local attractions and fishing traditions. Mainly it is a food festival showcasing a variety of shellfish but there are also bird-watching events at nearby sanctuaries and squid-fishing demonstrations.

🛏 Sleeping

Cha-am has two basic types of accommodation: hotels along the beach road (Th Ruamjit) and more expensive 'condotel' developments (condominiums with a kitchen and operating under a rental program). Expect a discount on posted rates for weekday stays. For guesthouses, head to Soi 1 North off Th Ruamjit or raucous Soi Bus Station, a few hundred metres south of Soi 1 North.

The northern end of the beach (known as Long Beach) has a wider, blonder strip of sand and sees more foreign tourists, while the southern end is more Thai. Th Narathip divides the beach into north and south and the soi off Th Ruamjit are numbered in ascending order in both directions from this intersection.

Charlie House   GUESTHOUSE **$**
(📞0 3243 3799; www.charlie-chaam.com; 241/60-61, Soi 1 North, Th Ruamjit; r 650-800B; 🌐❄) This

ANIMAL ENCOUNTERS

sensibilities have turned away from circuslike animal attractions but many well-intentioned animal lovers curious to see Thailand's iconic creatures (such as elephants, monkeys and tigers) unwittingly contribute to an industry that is poorly regulated and exploitative. Animals are often illegally captured from the wild and disfigured to be less dangerous (tigers often have their claws and teeth removed), they are acquired as pets and then neglected or inhumanely confined, or abandoned when they are too sick or infirm to work.

Wildlife Friends Foundation Thailand runs a **wildlife rescue centre** (☏ 0 3245 8135; www.wfft.org; Wat Khao Luk Chang), 35km northwest of Cha-am, that adopts and cares for abused and abandoned animals. Most of these animals are creatures that can't return to the wild due to injuries or lack of survival skills. The centre cares for 400 animals, including bears, tigers, gibbons, macaques, loris and birds. There is also an affiliated elephant rescue program that buys and shelters animals being used as street beggars.

The centre offers a **full access tour** (5000B for six people) that introduces the animals and discusses their rescue histories. The tour includes a visit with the elephants (but no rides are offered) and hotel transfer from Hua Hin or Cha-am.

Those looking for a more intimate connection with the animals can volunteer to help at the centre. An average day could involve chopping fruits and vegetables to feed sun bears, cleaning enclosures and rowing out to the gibbon islands with a daily meal. Volunteers are required to stay a minimum of one week and have to make a compulsory donation (from US$455/14,368B) to the centre. Contact the centre or visit the **volunteer website** (www.wildlifevolunteer.org) for details.

---

cheery place boasts a lime-green lobby and modern, comfortable and colourful rooms. Don't confuse it with the institutional Charlie Place or Charlie TV on the same soi.

Cha-am Mathong Guesthouse GUESTHOUSE $
(☏ 0 3247 2528; www.chaammathong.com; 263/47-48 Th Ruamjit; r 600-700B; ❋ 🛜) No frills here, but the rooms are clean and you're right across from the beach. Better rooms have sea views and small balconies. The attached restaurant does brisk business during the day.

Sala Thai Guest House GUESTHOUSE $
(☏ 0 3243 3505; www.guesthousesalathai.com; Soi 1 North, Th Ruamjit; r 600-800B; ❋ 🛜) Run by two slightly grumpy ladies (their bark is worse than their bite), this place has a cool wooden exterior and large rooms. Not much English spoken.

Baan Pantai Resort HOTEL $$
(☏ 0 3243 3111; www.baanpantai.com; 247/58 Th Ruamjit; r from 2000B; ❀❋🛜❋) Rather more upmarket than most hotels in Cha-am, this family-friendly place has a huge pool and small fitness centre. It's in the heart of all the action, but the rooms towards the back are quiet.

🍴 Eating

From your beach chair you can wave down the itinerant vendors selling barbecued and fried seafood, or order from the many nearby beachfront restaurants. At the far northern end of the beach, seafood restaurants with reasonable prices can be found at the fishing pier. There's also a large night market on Th Narathip close to the train station.

★ Rang Yen Garden THAI $
(☏ 0 3247 1267; 259/40 Th Ruamjit; dishes 60-180B; ⏰11am-10pm Nov-Apr) This lush garden restaurant is a cosy and friendly spot to feel at home after a day of feeling like a foreigner. It serves up Thai favourites and is only open in the high season.

Didine INTERNATIONAL-THAI $$
(Soi Bus Station, Th Ruamjit; dishes 80-350B; ⏰10am-11pm; 🛜) There are two chefs here, one French, one Thai, and the menu spans continental Europe, as well as offering a very solid selection of seafood and local favourites.

Bella Pizza ITALIAN $$
(☏ 0 3247 0980; 328/19 Th Nongjiang; pizzas from 155B; ⏰4pm-midnight) Now relocated to the southern end of town, this popular pizza place has a large, quiet outdoor terrace. Thai food is on offer as well and they deliver free if you're feeling lazy.

ℹ Information

Phetkasem Hwy runs through Cha-am's busy town centre, which is about 1km away from the beach. The town centre is where you'll find the main bus stop, banks, the main post office, an outdoor market and the train station.

You'll find plenty of banks along Th Ruamjit with ATMs and exchange services.

Only Chaam (www.onlychaam.com) An online blog and website about visiting Cha-am.

Post Office (Th Ruamjit) On the main beach strip.

Tourism Authority of Thailand (TAT; ☑ 0 3247 1005; tatphet@tat.or.th; 500/51 Th Phetkasem; ⊙ 8.30am-4.30pm) On Phetkasem Hwy, 500m south of town. The staff speak good English.

ℹ Getting There & Away

Buses stop on Phetkasem Hwy near the 7-Eleven store at the intersection of Th Narathip. Frequent bus services operating to/from Cha-am include Bangkok, Phetchaburi and Hua Hin.

Minivans to Bangkok's Victory Monument leave from Soi Bus Station, in between Th Ruamjit and Th Chao Lay. Buses to Bangkok's southern bus terminal also leave from Soi Bus Station. Other minivan destinations include Hua Hin and Phetchaburi. A private taxi to Hua Hin will cost 500B.

The **train station** (Th Narathip) is west of Phetkasem Hwy. From Bangkok's Hua Lamphong station trains go to Cha-am and continue on to Hua Hin. Note that Cha-am is listed in the timetable only in Thai as 'Ban Cha-am'.

ℹ Getting Around

From the city centre to the beach it's a quick motorcycle ride (40B). Some drivers may try to take you to hotels that offer commissions instead of the one you requested.

You can hire motorcycles for 200B to 300B per day all along Th Ruamjit. Cruisy bicycles are available everywhere for 20B per hour or 100B per day, and are a good way to get around.

Hua Hin หัวหิน

POP 98,896

Thailand's original beach resort is no palm-fringed castaway island and, arguably, is better for it. Instead, it is a delightful mix of city and sea with a cosmopolitan ambience, lively markets, tasty street eats, long beaches and fully functional city services (meaning no septic streams bisect the beach like those *other* places).

Hua Hin traces its aristocratic roots to the 1920s when Rama VI (King Vajiravudh) and Rama VII (King Prajadhipok) built summer residences here to escape Bangkok's stifling climate. The more famous of the two is **Phra Ratchawang Klai Kangwon** (Far from Worries Palace), 3km north of town, which is still a royal residence today and so poetically named that Thais often invoke it as a city slogan. Rama VII's endorsement of Hua Hin and the construction of the southern railway made the town *the* place to be for Thai nobility, who built their own summer residences beside the sea.

In the 1980s, the luxury hotel group Sofitel renovated the town's grand dame hotel and foreign tourists started arriving. Today, all the international hotel chains have properties in Hua Hin, and a growing number of wealthy expats retire to the nearby housing estates and condominiums. Middle-class and high-society Thais from Bangkok swoop into town on weekends, making parts of the city look a lot like upper Sukhumvit.

There's a lot of money swirling around but because this is a bustling Thai town, seafood is plentiful and affordable, there's cheap public transport for beach-hopping and it takes a lot less effort (and money) to get here from Bangkok than to the southern islands. So, stop wasting your time elsewhere, and grab a spot on the beach!

TRANSPORT TO/FROM CHA-AM

DESTINATION	BUS	MINIVAN	TRAIN
Bangkok Hua Lamphong			40-90B; 4½hr; 4.55am & 2.33pm daily
Bangkok southern bus terminal	150B; 3hr; frequent	160B; 2½hr; hourly 7am-6pm	
Bangkok Victory Monument		160B; 2½hr; every 30min 7am-6.30pm	
Hua Hin	30B; 30min; frequent	40B; frequent	30-40B; 1½hr; 2 daily
Phetchaburi	30B; 40min; frequent	50B; frequent	20-30B; 1hr; 3 daily

◉ Sights

The city's beaches are numerous, wide and long; swimming is safe, and Hua Hin continues to enjoy some of the peninsula's driest weather. During stormy weather, watch out for jellyfish.

◉ Hua Hin Town เมืองหัวหิน

A former fishing village, Hua Hin town retains its roots with an old teak shophouse district bisected by narrow soi, pier houses that have been converted into restaurants or guesthouses and a busy fishing pier still in use today. South of the harbour is a rocky headland that inspired the name 'Hua Hin', meaning 'Stone Head'. In the commercial heart are busy markets and all the modern conveniences you forgot to pack.

Hat Hua Hin   BEACH

(หาดหัวหิน; public access via eastern end of Th Damnoen Kasem) When viewed from the main public entrance, Hua Hin's beach is a pleasant but not stunning stretch of sand punctuated by round, smooth boulders. Don't be dismayed; this is the people-watching spot. If you're after swimming and sunbathing continue south where the sand is a fine white powder and the sea a calm grey-green.

The 5km-long beach stretches to a Buddha-adorned headland (Khao Takiab). The north end is where Thais come to photograph their friends wading ankle-deep in the sea, and pony rides are offered to anyone standing still. Further south, resort towers rather than coconut trees line the interior of the beach, but that's a minor distraction if you're splashing around in the surf. Access roads lead to Th Phetkasem, where you can catch a green *sŏrng·tăa·ou* back to town.

Hua Hin Train Station   HISTORICAL SITE

(สถานีรถไฟหัวหิน; Th Liap Thang Rot Fai) An iconic piece of local architecture, the red-and-white pavilion that sits beside Hua Hin's train station once served as the royal waiting room during Rama VI's reign. Cutting the journey time from Bangkok to a mere four hours, the arrival of the railway made Hua Hin a tourist destination for the Bangkok-based monarchy and the city's elite.

One hundred years later even speeding minivan drivers fuelled by energy drinks can't do it much quicker.

◉ North Hua Hin

The summer residences of the royal family and minor nobility dot the coast northwards from Hua Hin's fishing pier towards Cha-am.

Hat Hua Hin Neua   BEACH

(หาดหัวหินเหนือ; North Hua Hin Beach; ⊗ grounds 5.30-7.30am & 4-7pm) While the northern end of Hua Hin's beach is not its most spectacular section, it is lined with genteel Thai-Victorian garden estates bestowed with ocean-inspired names such as 'Listening to the Sea House'. The current monarchy's palace lies about 3km north of town but visitors are only allowed on the **grounds** (ID required).

There are public access paths to the beach off Th Naebkehardt. On weekends, Th Naebkehardt is the preferred getaway for Bangkok Thais, some of whom still summer in the old-fashioned residences while others come to dine in the houses that have been converted into restaurants (p509).

Plearn Wan   NOTABLE BUILDING

(เพลินวาน; ☑ 0 3252 0311; www.plearnwan.com; Th Phetkasem btwn Soi 38 & Soi 40; ⊗ 9am-9pm) **FREE** As much an art installation as a commercial enterprise, Plearn Wan is a vintage village containing stylised versions of the old-fashioned shophouses which once occupied the Thai-Chinese districts of Bangkok and Hua Hin. There's a pharmacy selling (well actually displaying) roots, powders and other concoctions that Thai grandmothers once used, as well as music and clothes stores.

It would be a tourist trap if it charged an admission fee but the mostly Thai visitors just wander the grounds snapping photos without making any impulse purchases. If you want to support this bit of nostalgia, there are retro souvenirs and snack shops.

Phra Ratchaniwet
Mrigadayavan   HISTORICAL SITE

(พระราชนิเวศน์มฤคทายวัน; ☑ 0 3250 8443; admission 30B; ⊗ 8.30am-4pm) With a breezy seaside location 12km north of Hua Hin, this summer palace was built in 1923 during the reign of Rama VI. Set in a beautiful garden with statuesque trees and stunning sea views, it's a series of interlinked teak houses with tall shuttered windows and patterned fretwork built upon stilts forming a shaded ground-level boardwalk.

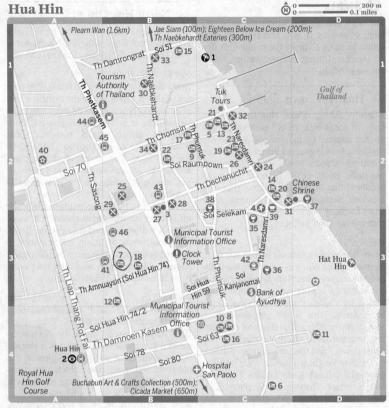

The functional but elegant style of the palace was a result of Rama VI suffering from rheumatoid arthritis; the court's Italian architect designed it to maximise air circulation and make the most of the seaside location. There's not a huge amount to see (a small selection of royal photos is on display), but it's a tranquil spot and Thais flock here to pay their respects.

The palace is within the grounds of Camp Rama VI, a military base, and you may need to show ID. It is easiest to get here with private transport but you can also catch a Hua Hin to Cha-am bus and ask to be dropped off opposite the camp's front gate. Motorcycle taxis are sometimes waiting to take you the remaining 2km. As this is a royal palace, legs and arms should be covered, otherwise you'll be given a sarong-like garment to hide your limbs.

⊙ Inland from Hua Hin

Baan Silapin ART GALLERY
(บ้านศิลปิน; ☑ 0 3253 4830; www.huahinartistvillage.com; Th Hua Hin-Pa Lu-U; art classes adult/child 150/100B; ⊙ 10am-5pm Tue-Sun, art classes 9.30-11.30am) Local painter Tawee Kasengam established this artist collective in a shady grove 4km west of Th Phetkasem. The galleries and studio spaces showcase the works of 19 artists, many of whom opted out of Bangkok's fast-paced art world in favour of Hua Hin's more relaxed atmosphere and scenic landscape of mountains and sea.

There are rotating exhibitions, while outlying clay huts shelter the playful sculptures. **Art classes** are available for adults on Tuesday and Thursday and for kids on Saturday.

Hua Hin Hills Vineyard VINEYARD
(ไร่องุ่นหัวหินฮิลล์ วินยาร์ด; ☑ 08 1701 0222; www.huahinhillsvineyard.com; Th Hua Hin-Pa Lu-U; vine-

Hua Hin

yard tour 1500-2100B, wine tasting 3 glasses 290B; ⊗9am-7pm) Part of the New Latitudes wine movement (p510), this vineyard is nestled in a scenic mountain valley 45km west of Hua Hin. The loamy sand and slate soil feeds several Rhone grape varieties that are used in its Monsoon Valley wine label. Daily **vineyard tours** start at 1500B, including return transport, wine and a three-course meal. Alternatively you can just do the **wine tasting**.

There is also a pétanque course, mountain-biking trails and the picturesque **Sala Wine Bar & Bistro** (dishes from 300B; ⊗11am-6.30pm).

A vineyard shuttle leaves the affiliated **Hua Hin Hills Wine Cellar store** (☑0 3252 6351; Market Village, Th Phetkasem, South Hua Hin) at 10.30am and 3pm and returns at 1.30pm and 6pm; a return ticket is 300B.

⊙ Khao Takiab เขาตะเกียบ

About 7km south of Hua Hin, Monumental Chopstick Mountain guards the southern end of Hua Hin beach and is adorned with a giant standing Buddha. Atop the 272m mountain is a Thai-Chinese temple (**Wat Khao Lat**) and many resident monkeys who are not to be trusted – but the views are great.

On the southern side of Khao Takiab is **Suan Son Pradipath** (Sea Pine Garden), a muddy beach maintained by the army and popular with weekending Thais. Green *sŏrng∙tăa∙ou* go all the way from Hua Hin to Khao Takiab village, where you'll find loads of simple Thai eateries serving fish straight off the fishing boats that dock here.

The nearby **Cicada Market** (Th Phetkasem; dishes 45-120B; ⊗4-11pm Fri & Sat, 4-10pm Sun) hosts lots of outdoor food stalls at the weekend and is a pleasant, mellow spot with live music from 7pm. It's just before Khao Takiab on the left-hand side of the road. You can catch a green *sŏrng∙tăa∙ou* (20B, from 6am to 9pm) from Hua Hin's night market; a hired túk-túk (pronounced *đúk đúk;* motorised three-wheeled taxi) will cost 150B one-way.

🏃 Activities

With nine courses scattered around its environs, Hua Hin continues to be an international and domestic golfing destination.

Cycling is a scenic and affordable option for touring Hua Hin's outlying attractions, especially since hiring a taxi to cover the same ground is ridiculously expensive. Don't be spooked by the busy thoroughfares; there are plenty of quiet byways where you can enjoy the scenery.

Kiteboarders flock to Hua Hin for the strong winds that blow almost all year round.

Kiteboarding Asia　　　KITEBOARDING
(☑ 08 1591 4593; www.kiteboardingasia.com; South Hua Hin; beginner courses 11,000B) This long-established company operates three beachside shops that rent kite-boarding equipment and offer lessons. The three-day introductory course teaches beginners the physical mechanics of the sport, and the instructor recommends newbies come when the winds are blowing from the southeast (January to March) and the sea is less choppy.

Hua Hin Golf Centre　　　GOLF
(☑ 0 3253 0476; www.huahingolf.com; Th Selakam; ⊙noon-9pm) The friendly staff at this pro shop can steer you to the most affordable, well-maintained courses where the monkeys won't try to run off with your balls. The company also organises golf tours and rents sets of clubs (500B to 700B per day).

Black Mountain Golf Course　　　GOLF
(☑ 0 3261 8666; www.bmghuahin.com; green fees 2100-3600B) The most popular course in Hua Hin, and one that has hosted Asian PGA tournaments. About 10km west of Hua Hin, its 18 holes are carved out of jungle and an old pineapple plantation and it retains some natural creeks as water hazards.

👉 Tours

There are many travel agencies in town offering day trips to nearby national parks. Unless you're in a group, you may have to wait until enough people sign up for the trip of your choice.

Hua Hin Adventure Tour　　　ADVENTURE TOURS
(☑ 0 3253 0314; www.huahinadventuretour.com; 69/8 Th Naebkehardt) Hua Hin Adventure Tour offers somewhat more active excursions including kayaking trips in the Khao Sam Roi Yot National Park and mountain biking in Kaeng Krachan National Park.

Hua Hin Bike Tours　　　CYCLING
(☑ 08 1173 4469; www.huahinbiketours.com; 15/120 Th Phetkasem btwn Soi 27 & 29; tours 1500-2750B) A husband-and-wife team operates this cycling company that leads half-, full- and multiday tours to a variety of attractions in and around Hua Hin. Pedal to the Hua Hin Hills Vineyard for some well-earned refreshment, tour the coastal byways south of Hua Hin, or ride among the limestone mountains of Khao Sam Roi Yot National Park. They also rent premium bicycles (500B per day) for independent cyclists and can

---

KITE CRAZY

Adding to the beauty of Hua Hin's beach are the kiteboarders flying and jumping above the ocean. Hua Hin is Thailand's kiteboarding, or kitesurfing, capital, blessed with strong, gusty winds, shallow water and a long, long beach off which to practise your moves.

From here down to Pranburi, the winds blow from the northeast October to December, and then from the southeast January to May: perfect for kitesurfing. Even during the May to October rainy season, there are plenty of days when the wind is fine for taking the waves. In fact, this stretch of coast is so good for kiteboarding that Hua Hin hosted the Kiteboarding World Cup in 2010.

This is also the best place in Thailand to learn how to kiteboard, with a number of schools in Hua Hin offering tuition. After three days with them, you can be leaping into the air too. The schools also cater for more advanced students, and you can qualify as an instructor here as well.

But if you prefer to stay on the ground while flying a kite, then check out the **Hua Hin International Kite Festival**. Staged every two years in March, 12km north of town at the Rama VI military base, it's a chance to see stunt kiters in action, as well as kites of every conceivable size and colour.

recommend routes. The same couple also leads long-distance charity and corporate bike tours across Thailand; visit the parent company **Tour de Asia** (www.tourdeasia.org) for more information.

⚡ Courses

Buchabun Art & Crafts Collection COOKING
(☑ 08 1572 3805; www.thai-cookingcourse.com; 19/95 Th Phetkasem; courses 1500B) Aspiring chefs should sign up for a half-day Thai cooking class that includes a market visit and recipe book. The course runs only if there are a minimum of four people.

✦✦ Festivals & Events

**King's Cup Elephant Polo
Tournament** CULTURAL
(⊘ Aug & Sep) Polo with a Thai twist, this annual tournament involving elephant mounts instead of horses takes place on the scenic grounds of the Anantara Hua Hin resort in late August and early September. It might not be as fast-paced as its British cousin but it is a charitable event that raises money for elephant-welfare issues.

Hua Hin Jazz Festival MUSIC
(⊘ May or Jun) In honour of the king's personal interest in the genre, the city that hosts royal getaways also hosts an annual jazz festival featuring Thai and international performers. All events are free and usually occur in May or June.

Fringe Festival THEATRE
(⊘ Jan-Mar) Organised by the Patravadi Theatre, a renowned avant-garde performance space in Bangkok, this modern arts festival is held at its sister location, **Vic Hua Hin** (☑ 0 3282 7814; www.vichuahin.com; 62/70 Soi Hua Na Nong Khae, South Hua Hin). Running from January to March, there are a host of dance, music and comedy performances from local and international artists as well as multinational collaborations.

🛏 Sleeping

Most budget and midrange options are in town occupying multistorey buildings in the old shophouse district. It is an atmospheric setting with cheap tasty food nearby but you'll have to 'commute' to the beach, either by walking to north Hat Hua Hin (best at low tide) or catching a *sŏrng·tǎa·ou* to the southern end of Hat Hua Hin.

The top-end options are beachfront resorts sprawling south from the Sofitel. All the international brands have a presence in Hua Hin but we've only listed special local options for a more intimate experience.

🛏 Hua Hin Town

Victor Guest House GUESTHOUSE $
(☑ 0 3251 1564; victorguesthouse@gmail.com; 60 Th Naresdamri; r 390-790B; ❄ @ 🖤) Popular with both Thais and foreigners, this new-ish guesthouse has solid rooms, a small garden and a central location. Helpful staff and a good source of travel tips.

Fulay Guesthouse GUESTHOUSE $
(☑ 0 3251 3145; www.fulayhuahin.net; 110/1 Th Naresdamri; r 550-900B; ❄ 🖤) With the waves crashing underneath and the floorboards creaking, this is a fine old-school pier guesthouse. Good beds, OK bathrooms and flowering plants in the common area.

Pattana Guest House GUESTHOUSE $
(☑ 0 3251 3393; 52 Th Naresdamri; r 390-590B; ❄ 🖤) Located in a simple teak house tucked away down a soi. There's a lovely garden here filled with little reading nooks. The rooms are small and basic, but the more expensive ones have private bathroom.

Euro-Hua Hin City Hotel YHA HOSTEL $
(☑ 0 3251 3130; www.huahineuro.com; 5/15 Th Sasong; r 179-999B; ❄ @ 🖤) Some dorms are fan-only, all are cramped and it feels a tad institutional, but the price is right for Hua Hin and the staff are helpful. The private rooms are sizeable, though the bathrooms could do with an overhaul. Add 50B to these prices if you don't belong to HI. It's off the road; look for the sign.

Sirima GUESTHOUSE $
(☑ 0 3251 1060; www.sirimaguesthouse.blogspot. com; Th Naresdamri; r 450-1000B; ❄ 🖤) A classic pier guesthouse, Sirima has a pretty exterior with lots of polished wood and a common deck overlooking the water. The cheaper rooms are small and fan-only but good value for Hua Hin.

Tong-Mee House GUESTHOUSE $$
(☑ 0 3253 0725; tongmeehuahin@hotmail.com; 1 Soi Raumpown, Th Naebkehardt; r 550-950B; ❄ @ 🖤) Hidden away in a quiet residential soi, this smart guesthouse has cosy and clean rooms with balconies. Book ahead here.

King's Home GUESTHOUSE $$
(☑ 08 9052 0490; huahinkingshome@gmail. com; off Th Phunsuk; 550-1200; ❄ 🖤 🖤)

Family-run guesthouse with loads of character; it's crammed with antiques and artefacts from the owners' travels across Southeast Asia. Decent-sized rooms, and it even has a small splash pool out back. It gets a lot of repeat guests, which says it all.

Baan Chalelarn Hotel HOTEL $$
(☑ 0 3253 1288; www.chalelarnhotel.com; 11 Th Chomsin; r 1200-1600B; ❋ @ 🛜) Chalelarn has a beautiful lobby with wooden floors, while the 12 big rooms are equipped with king-size beds. Verandahs and breakfast are all part of the perks. Book ahead here.

Tai Tai Guest House GUESTHOUSE $$
(☑ 0 3251 2891; 1/8 Th Chomsin; r 800B; ❋ @ 🛜) Formerly known as the Supasuda, the large rooms come with excellent beds, mermaid murals and hot showers. The more expensive ones have verandahs and a bit of road noise. There's a cosy communal roof terrace.

Fat Cat Guesthouse GUESTHOUSE $$
(☑ 08 6206 2455; www.thefatcathuahin.com; 8/3 Th Naresdamri; r 300-950B; ❋ 🛜) The air-con rooms for 650B are a great deal and go quick. The cheaper rooms with fan occupy a separate building and some have fantastic views of the city. They do a decent breakfast.

Ban Somboon GUESTHOUSE $$
(☑ 0 3251 1538; www.baansomboon.com; 13/4 Soi Hua Hin 63, Th Phetkasem; r 900-1000B; ❋ 🛜) With family photos decorating the walls and a compact garden, this place on a very quiet centrally located soi is like staying at your favourite Thai auntie's house. The rooms, though, are showing their age and could do with an upgrade.

Hotel Alley HOTEL $$
(☑ 0 3251 1787; www.hotelalleyhuahin.com; 13/5 Soi Hua Hin 63, Th Phetkasem; r 1200-1400B; ⊜ ❋ 🛜) New hotel in a quiet soi with spacious rooms decorated in pastel colours. Most have balconies and breakfast is included.

Baan Oum-or Hotel HOTEL $$
(☑ 08 1944 9390; baan_oum-or@hotmail.com; 77/18-19 Soi 63, Th Phetkasem; r 1000-1200B; ❋) The rooms are big and bright, and there are only seven of them so book ahead.

Baan Manthana HOTEL $$
(☑ 0 3251 4223; www.manthanahouse.com; 24/10 Th Sasong; r 800-1200B; ❋ @ 🛜 ⊠) With three separate wings, there's always space here even during public holidays. Rooms are anonymous but comfortable and proper-

sized and there's a pool too. The rooms at the back are quieter.

Baan Tawee Suk GUESTHOUSE $$
(☑ 08 9459 2618; 43/8 Th Phunsuk; r 800-1000B; ❋ @ 🛜) This efficient guesthouse has clean and modern rooms on both sides of the soi. They are cramped, so leave the super-sized luggage at home.

My Place Hua Hin HOTEL $$$
(☑ 0 3251 4111; www.myplacehuahin.com; 17 Th Amnuaysin, Th Phetkasem; r 1850-6500B; ❋ @ 🛜 ⊠) A smart, amiable and efficient place in the heart of the city with stylish, good-sized rooms that qualify it for boutique status. There's a rooftop swimming pool.

🛏 Hua Hin Beaches

Rahmahyah Hotel GUESTHOUSE $$
(☑ 0 3253 2106; Rahmahyah@yahoo.co.uk; 113/10 Soi Hua Hin 67, Th Phetkasem, South Hua Hin; r 800-1200B; ❋ 🛜 ⊠) Across the street from Market Village, about 1km south of town, is a small guesthouse enclave tucked between the high-end resorts, with beach access. The Rahmahyah is the best of the bunch with clean, functional rooms. Guests can use the communal swimming pool opposite.

★ Baan Bayan HOTEL $$$
(☑ 0 3253 3540; www.baanbayan.com; 119 Th Phetkasem, South Hua Hin; r 3300-9000B; ❋ 🛜 ⊠) A colonial beach house built in the early 20th century, Baan Bayan is perfect for travellers seeking a luxury experience without the overkill of a big resort. Airy, high-ceilinged rooms, attentive staff – and the location is absolute beachfront.

Green Gallery HOTEL $$$
(☑ 0 3253 0487; www.greenhuahin.com; 3/1 Soi Hua Hin 51, Th Naebkehardt, North Hua Hin; r 2500-8500B; ❋ 🛜 ⊠) As cute as candy, this small hotel occupies a converted colonial-style beach house that was once the vacation home of a princess. Individually decorated rooms reflect a hip artiness that defines urban Thai style. The attached restaurant is recommended.

Baan Laksasubha HOTEL $$$
(☑ 0 3251 4525; www.baanlaksasubha.com; Th 53/7 Naresdamri; r 2999-13,275B; ❋ 🛜 ⊠) Sixteen much-in-demand cottages are on offer at this petite resort, owned by a Bangkok aristocrat. The decor is crisp and subdued, meandering garden paths lead to the beach

and there's a dedicated kid's room with toys and books. The taxi drivers will understand you better if you say 'baan lak-su-pah'.

Centara Grand Resort and Villas   HOTEL **$$$**
(☑ 0 3251 2021; www.centarahotelsresorts.com; 1 Th Damnoen Kasem; r 7600-27,000B; ❋@◈≋) The historic Railway Hotel, Hua Hin's first seaside hotel, still has a colonial vibe but has been restored to world-class levels. Fantastic grounds, great pool, beach access, huge rooms, many restaurants and super-smooth staff.

Veranda Lodge   HOTEL **$$$**
(☑ 0 3253 3678; www.verandalodge.com; 113 Soi Hua Hin 67, Th Phetkasem, South Hua Hin; r 3400-5500B; ❋◈≋) Beachfront without the whopping price tag, the garden bungalows are very pleasant; the rooms are a little plain for the price. Noisy parrots live next to the lobby.

✗ Eating

Night Market   THAI **$**
(Th Dechanuchit btwn Th Phetkasem & Th Sasong; dishes from 50B; ◷5pm-midnight) An attraction that rivals the beach, Hua Hin's night market tops locals' lists of favourite spots to eat. Ice-packed displays of spiny lobsters and king prawns appeal to the big spenders but the simple stir-fry stalls are just as tasty. Try *pàt pŏng gà·rèe bòo* (crab curry), *gûng tôrt* (fried shrimp) and *hŏy tôrt* (fried mussel omelette). In between, souvenir stalls cater to the Thai favourite digestive activity: shopping.

Jek Pia Coffeeshop   THAI **$**
(51/6 Th Dechanuchit; dishes 80-160B; ◷9am-1pm & 5.30-8.30pm) More than just a coffee shop, this 50-year-old restaurant is a culinary destination specialising in an extensive array of stir-fried seafood dishes. It's wildly popular with the locals and they stick rigidly to their serving hours; get here after 7.30pm and you won't be able to order.

Thanon Chomsin Food Stalls   THAI **$**
(cnr Th Chomsin & Th Naebkehardt; dishes 30-40B; ◷9am-9pm) If you're after 100% authentic eats, check out the food stalls that congregate at this popular lunch corner. Though the setting is humble, Thais are fastidious eaters and use a fork (or their fingers with a pinch of *kôw nĕe·o*) to remove the meat from the bones of *gài tôrt* (fried chicken) rather than putting teeth directly to flesh.

Chatchai Market   THAI **$**
(Th Phetkasem; dishes from 30B; ◷daylight hours) The city's day market resides in a historic

---

WEEKENDS EATING WITH BANGKOK'S THAIS

On weekends, a different kind of tidal system occurs in Hua Hin. Bangkok professionals flow in, filling up hotels and restaurants on Th Naebkehardt, washing over the night market or crowding into nightclubs. And then come Sunday they clog the roadways heading north, obeying the pull of the upcoming work week.

Their presence is so pronounced that there is an irresistible urge to join them. And because of restaurant features on Thai TV or food magazines, everyone goes to the same places. So don your designer sunglasses and elbow your way to a table at one of these popular spots in North Hua Hin:

➡ **Sôm·dam Stand** (Th Naebkehardt; dishes 25-70B; ◷10am-2pm) Across from Iammeuang Hotel is a *sôm·dam* stand that easily wipes out the country's supply of green papayas in one weekend. Great grilled chicken too. On the other side of the road are other food stalls.

➡ **Eighteen Below Ice Cream** (Th Naebkehardt; ice cream from 69B; ◷11am-5pm, closed Tue) At the end of the road behind Baan Talay Chine Hotel, this gourmet ice-cream shop is run by a trained chef and specialises in rich and creamy flavours.

➡ **Ratama** (12/10 Th Naebkehardt; dishes 50-390B; ◷10am-10pm) New spot for visiting hipsters, with a menu that runs from simple noodle dishes to great, spicy seafood curries. If you're feeling very Thai, go for the hot and sour chicken-feet soup.

➡ **Jae Siam** (Th Naebkehardt; dishes 35-60B; ◷9am-10pm) If you've lost track of the days of the week, cruise by this open-air noodle shop, just before the Evergreen Hotel, where Hua Hin civil servants pack in on weekdays and Bangkok Thais come on weekends. The shop is famous for *gŏo·ay dĕe·o mŏo dŭn* (stewed pork noodles) and *gŏo·ay dĕe·o gài dŭn* (stewed chicken noodles).

building built in 1926 with a distinctive seven-eaved roof in honour of Rama VII. There are the usual market refreshments: morning vendors selling *bah·tôrng·gŏh* (Chinese-style doughnuts) and *gah·faa boh·rahn* (ancient-style coffee spiked with sweetened condensed milk); as well as all-day noodles with freshly made wontons; and the full assortment of fresh tropical fruit.

★ Hua Hin Koti THAI $$
(☑ 0 3251 1252; 16/1 Th Dechanuchit; dishes 120-300B; ⊙11am-10pm) Across from the night market, this Thai-Chinese restaurant is a national culinary luminary. Thais adore the fried crab balls, while foreigners swoon over *dôm yam gûng* (shrimp soup with lemon grass). And everyone loves the spicy seafood salad *(yam tá·lair)* and deep-fried fish with ginger. Be prepared to queue for a table.

Sang Thai Restaurant SEAFOOD $$
(Th Naresdamri; dishes 100-300B; ⊙10am-11pm) One of many beloved pier-side restaurants, Sang Thai is a Hua Hin institution and a massive operation. There's a vast choice of seafood housed in giant tanks awaiting your decision. You can eat very well for not much, or spend lots.

Chaolay SEAFOOD $$
(15 Th Naresdamri; dishes 100-700B; ⊙10.30am-11pm) Another Hua Hin old-time pier restaurant and always busy. There's a big open kitchen on the ground floor enabling you to see the chefs preparing your seafood selection. Ascend the stairs to find a table.

Cool Breeze MEDITERRANEAN $$
(62 Th Naresdamri; tapas from 100B; ⊙11am-midnight) Popular tapas joint spread over two floors. Decent wine list and an amiable spot for a drink.

Sadko RUSSIAN $$
(Th Naresdamri; dishes 100-300B; ⊙9am-11pm, closed Sun) More and more Russians are visiting Hua Hin, and this friendly place caters to them with authentic dishes cooked by a Russian chef. Top dumplings and borscht, and vodka as well. Good for a Western or Russian breakfast (pancakes and sour cream) too.

🍷 Drinking & Entertainment

Drinking destinations in Hua Hin are stuck in a time warp: sports bars or hostess bars – and sometimes you can't tell the difference. But the onslaught of weekending Bangkok Thais has kicked up the sophistication factor.

No Name Bar BAR
(Th Naresdamri) Past the Chinese shrine that sits on the rocky headland is this cliff-side bar. It feels miles away from the lurid and loud hostess bars and is perfect for a chilled beer; sit and listen to the waves slapping against the rocks below.

NEW ATTITUDES TOWARDS WINE

Common wisdom would tell you that tasty wine grapes don't grow alongside coconut trees. But advances in plant sciences and a global palate for wines has ushered in the geographic experiment dubbed New Latitude Wines, produced from grapes grown outside the traditional 30- to 50-degree parallels.

The New Latitudes' main challenge is to replicate the wine-producing grapes' preferred climate as best as possible. That means introducing a false dormancy or winter period through pruning, regulated irrigation and companion planting of grasses to prevent soil loss during the rainy season. If you're familiar with viticulture in the Old World, you'll be shocked to see all the cultivation rules Thai vineyards successfully break.

Wine experts have yet to crown a New Latitude that surpasses the grand dames, but they do fill a local niche. Siam Winery, the parent company of Hua Hin Hills Vineyard (p504), aims to produce wines that pair with the complex flavours of Thai food. The vineyard grows columbard, chenin blanc, muscat, shiraz and sangiovese grapes, among others, and typically the citrus-leaning whites are a refreshing complement to the fireworks of most Thai dishes.

Because of the hot climate, a wine drinker's palate is often altered. The thinner wines produced in Thailand tend to have a more satisfying effect than the bold chewy reds that pair well with a chilly spring day. Drinking red wine in Thailand has always been a challenge because the heat turns otherwise leathery notes straight into vinegar. To counteract the tropical factor, break yet another wine rule and chill reds in the refrigerator to replicate 'cellar' temperature as close as possible.

Mai Tai Cocktail & Beer Garden   BAR
(33/12 Th Naresdamri) Recession-era prices are on tap at this convivial, always crowded outdoor terrace made for people-watching and beer-drinking.

O'Neill's Irish Pub   BAR
(5 Th Phunsuk) Reasonably authentic for being so far from the Blarney Stone, O'Neill's has a pool table and a fine wooden bar to sit around. Cheap draught specials and live sport on several TVs.

World News Coffee   CAFE
(130/2 Th Naresdamri; coffee from 90B, sandwiches from 180B; ⊘ 8am-11pm) This Starbucks-esque cafe serves many varieties of coffee and tea, as well as Western breakfasts, hefty sandwiches and tasty bagels, You can surf the web for 150B per hour. Wi-fi is free if you spend over 300B. Otherwise, it's 75B for 30 minutes.

El Murphy's Mexican Grill & Steakhouse   BAR
(25 Soi Selakam, Th Phunsuk) Every sports bar has an international gimmick and this comfy spot marries Mexico and Ireland. There's a big menu, live music sometimes and a pleasant vibe, although the beers aren't cheap.

Bang Bar   LIVE MUSIC
(Th Liap Thang Rot Fai) North of Soi 70 along Railway Road are a string of Thai music bars, nearly all foreigner-free. This one stays packed into the early hours, with rotating singers and bands.

🛈 Information

EMERGENCY
Tourist Police (☑ 0 3251 5995; Th Damnoen Kasem) At the eastern end of the street.

INTERNET ACCESS
Internet access is available all over Hua Hin, in guesthouses and cafes.

MEDICAL SERVICES
Bangkok Hospital Hua Hin (☑ 0 3261 6800; www.bangkokhospital.com/huahin; Th Phetkasem btwn Soi Hua Hin 94 & 106) The latest outpost of the luxury hospital chain; it's in South Hua Hin.
Hospital San Paolo (☑ 0 3253 2576; 222 Th Phetkasem) Just south of town with emergency facilities.

MONEY
There are exchange booths and ATMs on Th Naresdamri and banks on Th Phetkasem.

POST & TELEPHONE
Main Post Office (Th Damnoen Kasem)

TOURIST INFORMATION
Municipal Tourist Information Office (☑ 0 3251 1047; cnr Th Phetkasem & Th Damnoen Kasem; ⊘ 8.30am-4.30pm Mon-Fri) Provides maps and information about Hua Hin. There's another branch (☑ 0 3252 2797; Th Naebkehardt; ⊘ 9am-7.30pm Mon-Fri, 9.30am-5pm Sat & Sun) near the clock tower.
Tourism Authority of Thailand (TAT; ☑ 0 3251 3885; 39/4 Th Phetkasem; ⊘ 8.30am-4.30pm) Staff here speak English and are quite helpful; the office is north of town near Soi Hua Hin 70.

TRAVEL AGENCIES
Tuk Tours (☑ 0 3251 4281; www.tuktours. com; 2/1 Th Chomsin) Helpful, no-pressure place that can book activities and transport all around Thailand.

WEBSITES
Hua Hin Observer (www.observergroup.net) An online expat-published magazine.
Tourism Hua Hin (www.tourismhuahin.com) A cursory intro to the city with a good rundown on the outlying area.

🛈 Getting There & Away

The **airport** (www.huahinairport.com) is 6km north of town, but only has charter services through **Nok Mini** (☑ 0 2641 4190; www.nokair. com).

Hua Hin's **long-distance bus station** (Th Phetkasem btwn Soi Hua Hin 94 & 98) is south of town and goes to Chiang Mai, Prachuap Khiri Khan, Phuket, Surat Thani and Ubon Ratchathani. Buses to Bangkok leave from a bus company's in-town **office** (Th Sasong), near the night market. Buses to Bangkok Suvarnabhumi International Airport leave from the long-distance bus station.

Ordinary buses depart from north of the market on Th Phetkasem, and destinations include Cha-am and Phetchaburi.

Lomprayah offers a bus-boat combination from Hua Hin to Ko Tao (1000B, 8½ hours, one morning and one night departure).

Minivans go to Bangkok's Sai Tai Mai (southern) bus terminal and Victory Monument. A direct service to Victory Monument leaves from an office on the corner of Th Phetkasem and Th Chomsin.

There are frequent trains running to/from Bangkok's Hua Lamphong station and other stations on the southern railway line (see table p512).

TRANSPORT TO/FROM HUA HIN

DESTINATION	BUS	MINIVAN	TRAIN	AIR
Bangkok Don Muang Airport				from 1500B Nok Air; 1hr; 3 weekly
Bangkok Hua Lamphong			44-421B; 5-6hr; 13 daily 12.45am-4.01pm	
Bangkok southern bus terminal	175B; 4½hr; 8 daily 3am-9pm			
Bangkok Suvarn-abhumi Airport	305B; 5hr; 6 daily 7am-6pm			
Bangkok Victory Monument		180B; 4hr; every 30min 6am-7pm		
Cha-am	30B; 30min; frequent		20-30B; 2 daily	
Chiang Mai	851B; 12hr; 3 daily 8am, 5pm & 6pm			
Ko Tao	1000B; 8½hr; 1 daily			
Phetchaburi	40B; 1½hr; frequent		30-40B; 12 daily	
Phuket	823B; 9-10hr; 3 nightly			
Surat Thani	413-829B; 7-8hr; 4 daily			
Ubon Ratcha-thani	1005B; 13hr; 3 nightly			

ℹ Getting Around

Green *sŏrng·tăa·ou* depart from the corner of Th Sasong & Th Dechanuchit, near the night market and travel south on Th Phetkasem to Khao Takiab (20B). Pranburi-bound buses (20B) depart from the same stop.

Túk-túk fares in Hua Hin are outrageous and start at a whopping 100B and barely budge from there. Motorcycle taxis are much more reasonable (40B to 50B) for short hops.

Motorcycles (250B to 500B per day) can be hired from shops on Th Damnoen Kasem and Th Chomsin. **Thai Rent A Car** (☏ 0 2737 8888; www.thairentacar.com) is a professional car-rental agency with competitive prices, a well-maintained fleet and hotel drop-offs.

Hua Hin to Pranburi

South of Hua Hin are a series of beaches framed by dramatic headlands that make great day trips when Hua Hin beach feels too urban.

Hat Khao Tao   หาดเขาเต่า

About 13km south of Hua Hin, a barely inhabited beach stretches several kilome-tres south from Khao Takiab to Khao Tao (Turtle Mountain). It's far quieter and less-developed than Hua Hin's beach: there are no high-rises, no beach chairs, no sarong sellers and no horseback riders.

The mountain has a sprawling temple dedicated to almost every imaginable deity: Buddha, Guan Yin (Chinese goddess of Mercy), Vishnu and even the Thai kings. Follow the trail towards the oceanfront to hike up to the Buddha on the hill.

To get here, take a Pranburi-bound bus from Hua Hin and ask to be dropped off at the turn-off for Khao Tao (20B); a motorbike taxi can take you to the temple (20B). A motorbike from Hua Hin will cost 200B one-way. Return transport is rare; you can always walk or flag down a ride as people are usually coming and going from the temple.

Hat Sai Noi   หาดทรายน้อย

About 20km south of Hua Hin, a scenic cove, Hat Sai Noi, drops off quickly into the sea, providing a rare opportunity for deep-water swimming. Mostly patronised by Thais, nearby are all the amenities: simple seafood restaurants and even small guesthouses.

For ideal seclusion, come on a weekday. The beach is south of Khao Tao on a lovely road that passes a reservoir and is lined with bougainvillea and limestone cliffs. To get there take a Pranburi-bound bus from Hua Hin and ask to be dropped off at the turn-off for Khao Tao (20B); then ask a motorcycle taxi to take you to Hat Sai Noi (60B). Getting back to the highway will be difficult but inquire at one of the restaurants for assistance.

Pranburi & Around

POP 75,571

Continuing along the highway south from Hua Hin leads to the country 'suburb' of Pranburi district, which has become the in-the-know coastal alternative for Bangkok Thais. Ever-more popular, some even go so far as to call it the 'Thai Riveria'. Yet locally the fishing village and nearby beaches are known by a more humble name: **Pak Nam Pran** (mouth of the Pranburi River), which designates its geographic location only.

A coastal road separates a string of small villa-style resorts, and an increasing number of condo developments, from the beach. With each successive rainy season, the ocean claims more sand than its fair share and a breakwater is being constructed along parts of the coastline. Since most of the visitors are Thai, the disappearing beach is of minor consequence. Instead, most domestic tourists come for sea views and the village's primary product: dried squid. Every morning, the squid boats dock in the river, unload their catch and begin the process of sun-drying. It is a pungent but interesting affair with large drying racks spread out across town.

Bordering the river is an extensive mangrove forest, protected by the **Pranburi Forest Park** (✆0 3262 1608) FREE. Within the park is a wooden walkway that explores the mangroves from the perspective of a mud-dweller, a sea-pine lined beach and accommodation facilities. The park also offers boat trips along the river and small canals.

The coastal road provides a pleasant trip to **Khao Kalok** (Skull Mountain), a mammoth headland that shelters a beautiful bay on the southern side. This southern beach is wide and sandy and far removed from the hubbub of Hua Hin and even from Pak Nam Pran for that matter, though it does get busy on weekends. Lazing along this stretch are several secluded boutique resorts that are ideal for honeymooners or folks looking to 'get away from it all' without having to go too far.

The next southern bay is often called **Dolphin Bay**, because of the seasonal visit from bottlenose dolphins and finless porpoise from February to May. Sculpted, jungle-covered islands sit scenically offshore and the beach is a lovely, wide strip of powdery sand. This area is a family favourite because the resorts are value-oriented, traffic is minimal and nightlife is nonexistent. You're also a few kilometres from the northern entrance to Khao Sam Roi Yot National Park.

Sleeping & Eating

It is mainly high-end here but not all of the beach resorts earn the price tag so be discerning when making online reservations for places not listed below. That said, this area has some of the best seaside boutique hotels in Thailand, making it a fine place to splash out.

Beach House　　　GUESTHOUSE $$
(✆08 7164 6307; karl@beachhousepranburi.com; Pak Nam Pran; r 700-1200B; ❄️🛜🏊) One of the cheapest options around, this affable, English-run guesthouse has comfortable, decent-sized rooms. It caters mainly to young kiteboarders; you can learn to kitesurf here and the wind is as good, if not better, than Hua Hin.

Palm Beach Resort & Hotel　　HOTEL $$
(✆0 3263 1304; www.palmbeachpranburi.com; Pak Nam Pran; r 1800-2500B; ❄️🛜🏊) Right by the beach. Although the spacious rooms are a little under-maintained, the staff are nice and breakfast is included.

★ **Away Hua Hin**　　　HOTEL $$$
(✆08 9144 6833; www.away-huahin.com; south of Khao Kalok; r 3500-4500B; ❄️🛜🏊) A boutique resort without pretence, and one of the more affordable in the area, seven antique teak houses have been transported to this coastal patch of paradise and outfitted with large comfy beds and stylish bathrooms.

The amiable owners, a Thai–Australian family, set a homey mood where breakfast is enjoyed at a common table in the 'big' house providing instant camaraderie. Some villas offer extreme privacy while others accommodate families. The beach is just across the road.

South of Hua Hin

Each villa is extremely private but evocative of traditional rustic lifestyles with living quarters on the ground floor and often steep, ladderlike stairs leading to the sleeping area. And then there's the semi-private beach right on your doorstep.

Dolphin Bay Resort
HOTEL $$$

(0 3255 9333; www.dolphinbayresort.com; Dolphin Bay; r 1790-14,300B; ✽@☎☲) The resort that defined Dolphin Bay as a family-friendly retreat offers a low-key holiday camp ambience with a variety of standard-issue, value-oriented bungalows and apartments, as well as a few very expensive ones. The grounds are large enough for kids to roam safely, there are two big pools and there's a great sandy beach opposite.

Khao Kalok Restaurant
THAI $$

(dishes 80-300B; ⊙11am-10pm) At the southern base of the mountain, this open-air restaurant provides a front-row view of the moored fishing boats. Tasty dishes, like *gaang kĕe·o wăhn* (green curry), *blah mèuk gà·prow* (squid stir-fried with basil) and even the standard *pàt pàk roo·am* (stir-fried vegetables) arrive at a leisurely pace.

❶ Getting There & Around

Pranburi is about 35km south of Hua Hin and accessible by ordinary bus from Hua Hin's night market (20B). You'll be dropped off on the highway where you can catch a *sŏrng·tăa·ou* to Pak Nam Pran.

There is also a minivan service from Bangkok's Victory Monument to Pranburi (200B); if you're going to Dolphin Bay (sometimes referred to as Khao Sam Roi Yot Beach), you'll have to negotiate an additional fare with the driver (usually 100B).

If you want to explore the area, you'll need to rent a motorbike; public transport isn't an option.

★ Brassiere Beach
HOTEL $$$

(0 3263 0554; www.brassierebeach.com; Dolphin Bay; r 4000-5000B; ✽☎☲) A delicious combination of privacy and personality; these 12 stucco villas abut the mountains of Khao Sam Roi Yot National Park and face a secluded beach, 100m from the nearest paved road. The rooms have an uncluttered Spanish colonial feel, some with roof decks and most with open-air showers. You might mispronounce its name, but Brassiere Beach deserves your support.

La a natu Bed & Bakery
HOTEL $$$

(0 3268 9941; www.laanatu.com; south of Khao Kalok; r 4488-15,888B; ✽☎☲) Turning the humble Thai rice village into a luxury experience is all the rage in the boutique hotel world but La a natu does it with more panache than most. The thatched roof villas growing on stilts from cultivated rice paddies have rounded modern corners and a Flintstone-esque playfulness to their design.

Khao Sam Roi Yot National Park

อุทยานแห่งชาติเขาสามร้อยยอด

Towering limestone outcrops form a rocky jigsaw-puzzled landscape at this 98-sq-km **park** (0 3282 1568; www.dnp.go.th; adult/child 200/100B), which means Three Hundred Mountain Peaks. There are also caves, beaches and coastal marshlands to explore for outdoor enthusiasts and bird-watchers.

With its proximity to Hua Hin, the park is well travelled by day-trippers and contains a mix of public conservation land and private shrimp farms, so don't come expecting remote virgin territory.

Rama IV and a large entourage of Thai and European guests came here on 18 August 1868 to see a total solar eclipse (apparently predicted by the monarch himself) and to enjoy a feast prepared by a French chef. Two months later the king died from malaria, contracted from mosquito bites inflicted here. Today the risk of malaria in the park is low but the mosquitoes can be pesky, especially during the rainy season.

The **Khao Daeng Visitors Centre** in the southern end of the park has the largest collection of tourist information, and English-speaking rangers. Maps are handed out at the entrance gates.

Travel agencies in Hua Hin run day trips to the park. Hua Hin Bike Tours (p506) offers cycling and hiking tours.

◉ Sights & Activities

Maps provided at the park checkpoints are often in Thai. The following sites are listed in geographical order from north to south.

Tham Kaew
CAVE

(ถ้ำแก้ว) Tham Kaew is a series of underground chambers and narrow passageways accessed by a steep scramble 128m up the mountain. It's not a popular stop, even though the stalactites and limestone formations here glitter with calcite crystals (hence the cave's name, 'Jewel Cave'). You can hire lamps from the booth at the footpath's entrance. The path can be slippery and dangerous.

Tham Phraya Nakhon & Hat Laem Sala
CAVE

(ถ้ำพระยานคร/หาดแหลมศาลา) The park's most-visited attraction is this revered cave sheltering a royal săh·lah (meeting hall; often spelled sala) built for Rama V in 1890 that is often bathed in streams of light. It's accessed via a walking trail from the picturesque sandy beach of **Hat Laem Sala**, flanked on three sides by limestone hills and casuarinas.

The beach hosts a small visitors centre, restaurant, bungalows and campsites. The cave trail is 450m long and is steep, rocky and at times slick so don't wear your ballet flats. Once there you'll find two large caverns with sinkholes – the meeting hall is the second of the two.

Reaching Laem Sala requires alternative travel since there is no road connection. It is reached by boat from Bang Pu (300B return), which sits beachfront from the turn-off from Tham Kaew. Alternatively, you can follow the steep footpath from Bang Pu for a 20-minute hike to the beach.

Tham Sai
CAVE

(ถ้ำไทร) Sitting at the end of a 280m hillside trail, Tham Sai features a large single cavern filled with stalactites and stalagmites. Be careful of steep drop-offs inside and slippery footings. Usually, only more adventurous types undertake this one. Villagers rent out lamps near the cave mouth. It is just north of Hat Sam Phraya.

Hat Sam Phraya
BEACH

(หาดสามพระยา) This shady casuarina-lined beach is about 1km long and is a pleasant stop for a swim after a sweaty hike. There is a restaurant and toilets.

Khao Daeng
HIKING

(เขาแดง) The turn-off to the trail winds through towering mountains promising a rewarding hike. The 30-minute steep trail that leads to the top of Khao Daeng delivers

---

BIRDS OF A FEATHER

At the intersection of the East Asian and Australian migration routes, Thung Sam Roi Yot National Park is home to as many as 300 migratory and resident bird species, including yellow bitterns, cinnamon bitterns, purple swamp hens, water rails, ruddy-breasted crakes, bronze-winged jacanas, grey herons, painted storks, whistling ducks, spotted eagles and black-headed ibises. The park is one of only two places in the country where the purple heron breeds.

Waterfowl are most commonly seen in the cool season from November to March. The birds come from as far as Siberia, China and northern Europe to winter here. Common places for bird-watchers are the Mangrove Centre, Khlong Khao Daeng and even some of the beaches.

Thai Birding (www.thaibirding.com) provides more in-depth information about the park's bird species and where to spot them.

WHERE THE ELEPHANTS ARE

Want to see herds of wild elephants enjoying an evening bath surrounded by the sounds of the jungle? Although urbanised Thailand seems hundreds of kilometres away from such a natural state, **Kuiburi National Park** (☑ 0 3264 6292; Hwy 3217; adult/child 200/100B), southwest of Khao Sam Roi Yot National Park, shelters one of the country's largest herds of wild elephants (estimated at 230 animals). The park provides an important habitat link between the rugged Myanmar border and Kaeng Krachan National Park, forming one of the largest intact forest tracts in Southeast Asia. The herds can frequently be found bathing at the watering ponds near the Pa Yang substation, which is equipped with wildlife-viewing platforms.

Trekking and elephant-spotting tours include English-speaking guides and transport and can be arranged through the park headquarters.

Bungalow **accommodation** (☑ 0 2562 0760; www.dnp.th.go/parkreserve; bungalows 1800B) is available for overnight stays with advance reservations.

---

spectacular views of limestone cliffs against a jagged coastline.

Khlong Khao Daeng
BIRD WATCHING

(คลองเขาแดง) You can hire a boat at Wat Khao Daeng for a cruise (500B, 50 minutes) along the canal in the morning or afternoon. Before heading out, chat with your prospective guide to see how well they speak English. Better guides will know the English names of common waterfowl and point them out to you.

Thung Sam Roi Yot
BIRD WATCHING

(ทุ่งสามร้อยยอด) The country's largest freshwater marsh is recognised as a natural treasure and provides an important habitat for songbirds and water birds, amphibians and other wetland species. It sits in the western corner of the park accessible from Hwy 4 (Th Phetkasem) at the Km 275.6 marker; hold on to your entrance fee ticket to avoid having to pay again.

Mangrove Walk
NATURE TRAIL

Located behind the visitors centre in the southern end of the park is a 900m wooden boardwalk that circumnavigates a mangrove swamp popular for bird-watching and crab spotting. There are guides for hire from the centre, depending on availability and English-language skills.

🛏 Sleeping & Eating

There are private resorts within 4km of the park at Dolphin Bay.

National Parks Department
CAMPING GROUND $

(☑ 0 2562 0760; www.dnp.go.th/parkreserve; tent sites 160-225B, bungalows at visitors centre 1200-1400B, bungalows at Hat Laem Sala 1600-3000B)

The National Parks Department hires out bungalows (sleeping up to six people) at Hat Laem Sala and at the visitors centre; advance reservations are required. You can pitch a tent at campsites near the Khao Daeng viewpoint, Hat Laem Sala or Hat Sam Phraya. There are basic restaurants at all these locations.

ℹ Getting There & Away

The park is about 40km south of Hua Hin, and best visited by vehicle. There are two main entrances into the park. The turn-off for the northern entrance is at Km 256 marker on Hwy 4 (Th Phetkasem). The southern entrance is off the Km 286.5 marker.

If there's a group of you, a taxi from Hua Hin is 1800B return. You can also come on day tours from there. Alternatively, you can catch a minivan from Bangkok's Victory Monument to Pranburi (200B) and then hire a motorcycle to tour the park independently. You can also negotiate with the minivan driver to drop you off at the entrance to the park but then you won't have transport into the park.

Prachuap Khiri Khan
ประจวบคีรีขันธ์

POP 86,870

A sleepy seaside town, Prachuap Khiri Khan is a delightfully relaxed place; one of the real jewels of this part of Thailand. The broad bay is a tropical blue punctuated by bobbing fishing boats and there are tremendous beaches close by, all overlooked by honeycombed limestone mountains – scenery that you usually have to travel to the southern Andaman to find.

In recent years, expats have discovered Prachuap's charms and begun defecting here from the overdeveloped Samui archipelago. But their numbers are still small, leaving plenty of room on the beaches, at the hilltop temples and the many excellent seafood restaurants.

◉ Sights & Activities

Khao Chong Krajok VIEWPOINT
(เขาช่องกระจก) At the northern end of town, Khao Chong Krajok ('Mirror Tunnel Mountain', so named for the mountain-side hole that seemingly reflects the sky) provides a beloved Prachuap tradition: climbing to the **temple** at the top, dodging ill-behaved monkeys and enjoying a cascading view of a curlicue coastline.

A long flight of stairs soiled by the partly wild monkeys leads to a mountaintop temple established by Rama VI. From here there are perfect views of the town and the bay and even the border with Myanmar, just 11km away. Don't bring food, drink or plastic bags with you as the monkeys will assume it is a prize worth having.

Ao Prachuap BAY
(อ่าวประจวบ) The town's crowning feature is Ao Prachuap (Prachuap Bay), a gracefully curving bay outlined by an oceanfront esplanade. In the cool hours of the morning and evening, locals run, shuffle or promenade along this route enjoying the ocean breezes and sea music.

On Friday and Saturday evenings, the esplanade hosts a **Walking Street market**, selling food, souvenirs and clothes.

North of Khao Chong Krajok, just over the bridge, the bay stretches peacefully to a toothy mountain scraper with less commercial activity than its in-town counterpart. There is a good sandy beach here though it does lack privacy due to its proximity to passing motorists. Nonetheless, weekending Thais often visit because there is no breakwater and it is a pleasant beachcombing spot. At the far northern end is a traditional fishing village decorated with colourful wooden trawlers and a visible sense of a hard-working life.

Wat Ao Noi BUDDHIST TEMPLE
(วัดอ่าวน้อย) From Ao Prachuap, follow the coastal road 8km north as it skirts through the fishing village to reach this beautiful teak temple that straddles two bays (Ao Noi and Ao Khan Kradai). Limestone mountains

Prachuap Khiri Khan

Prachuap Khiri Khan

pose photogenically in the background, while a dramatic nine-headed naga protects the temple's exterior. Inside are unique bas-relief murals depicting the *jataka* (stories of Buddha's previous lives).

The temple grounds are forested with a variety of fruit trees (jackfruit, pomegranate, mango and rose apple) and a lotus pond filled with ravenous fish, eager to be fed by merit-makers. You'll catch an unpleasant odour nearby indicating that the temple is in the business of raising swiftlets for the profitable edible bird's nest industry; the punishment for stealing nests or eggs is severe (five years' imprisonment and 500,000B).

A craggy limestone mountain (Khao Khan Kradai) shelters the temple from the coast and contains a locally famous cave temple, known as Tham Phra Nawn (Sleeping Buddha Cave). The cave is accessible via a concrete trail that leads up and around the side of the hill providing scenic views of Ao Khan Kradai and the foothills beyond. It is blissfully quiet and the forested hill is dotted with blooming cactus clinging to the craggy rocks. Inside the cave is a small cavern leading to a larger one that contains the eponymous reclining Buddha. If you have a torch (flashlight) you can proceed to a larger second chamber also containing Buddha images.

Ao Manao   SWIMMING
(อ่าวมะนาว) On weekends, locals head to Ao Manao, 4km south of town, an island-dotted bay ringed by a clean sandy beach. It is within Wing 5 of a Thai air-force base and

each and every week the beach is given a military-grade clean up.

There are the usual beach amenities: a restaurant and beach chairs, umbrellas and inner tubes for hire. En route to the beach you'll pass Thailand's Top Guns relaxing on a nearby golf course and driving range. You enter the base through a checkpoint on Th Suseuk from town; you may need to show your passport. The beach closes at 8pm.

🛌 Sleeping

There are a number of oceanfront options, ranging from guesthouses to hotels. It's rare that you can't find a cosy spot to lay your head.

In Town

Maggie's Homestay   GUESTHOUSE $
(☏08 7597 9720; 5 Soi Tampramuk; r 180-550B; ✴@☎) In the old-fashioned backpacker tradition, lovely owner Maggie oversees an eclectic collection of travellers who call her house home. Comfortable rooms, all with shared bathrooms, occupy a converted house with a shady garden and shared kitchen facilities.

Yuttichai Hotel   GUESTHOUSE $
(☏0 3261 1055; 115 Th Kong Kiat; r 160-350B; @☎) Yuttichai has simple budget rooms (with cold-water showers) close to the train station. The cheapest rooms are cell-like and share OK bathrooms. Their old-school Thai-Chinese cafe is decent and patronised by the local fuzz.

★House 73   GUESTHOUSE $$
(☏08 6046 3923; www.house73prachuab.com; 73 Th Suseuk; r 800-1300B; ⊖✴☎) Lovingly designed to within an inch of its life, this modernist boutique guesthouse is the most eye-catching building in town. There are only four big rooms here, all painted in pastel colours, with huge beds. There's a communal lounge and, best of all, a fantastic roof terrace with commanding views across the bay.

Sun Beach Guesthouse   GUESTHOUSE $$
(☏0 3260 4770; www.sunbeach-guesthouse.com; 160 Th Chai Thaleh; r 700-1100B; ✴@☎⊛) With hotel amenities and guesthouse hospitality, Sun Beach is a superb midranger. Its neo-classical styling and bright-yellow paint liven things up, while the rooms are super-clean and come with large verandahs.

PRACHUAP KHIRI KHAN IN WORLD WAR II

Prachuap, and specifically Ao Manao, was one of seven points on the gulf coast where Japanese troops landed on 8 December 1941 during their invasion of Thailand. The air-force base at Ao Manao was the site of fierce skirmishes, with the Japanese unable to capture it until the Thai government ordered its soldiers to stop fighting as an armistice had been arranged.

Several street names around town refer to that time, such as Phithak Chat (Defend Country), Salachip (Sacrifice Life) and Suseuk (Fight Battle), and an annual memorial service commemorates the soldiers and civilians who died in the battle.

DAN SINGKHON BORDER MARKET

A mere 12km southwest of Prachuap Khiri Khan is the Myanmar border town of Dan Singkhon. Once a strategic military point, Dan Singkhon now hosts a lively border **market** beloved by locals for its many bargains.

Beginning at dawn on Saturday mornings, locals from Myanmar appear from a bend in the road just beyond the checkpoint, pushing handcarts piled high with the usual trinkets, market goods and plants. Short-term tourists might be befuddled as to what will fit in a suitcase, but locals and expats make frequent buying trips here for orchids, the market's speciality, and hardwood furniture. Even if you come to window-shop, the market has a festive vibe, with music blaring, colourful umbrellas lining the road and thatched 'sales booths' hidden under palms. You'll need to arrive well before noon to enjoy it, as the market closes at midday.

To get to Dan Singkhon from Prachuap Khiri Khan with your own vehicle, head south on Hwy 4. After several kilometres you'll see a sign for Dan Singkhon; from there head west about 15km to reach the border.

Prachuap Beach Hotel　　HOTEL **$$**
(☑ 0 3260 1288; www.prachuapbeach.com; 123 Th Suseuk; r 700-1200B; ❄ ☎) Crisp white linens and modern, comfortable rooms at this multistorey number. One side has fabulous sea views, while the other has decent, though not exciting, mountain views.

Out of Town

Natural Home　　GUESTHOUSE **$**
(☑ 0 3260 2082; 149-151 Th Suanson; r 250-600B; ❄ ☎) About 1km north of town, these small bungalows (with closetlike bathrooms and cold-water showers) are simple, but you are right across the road from Ao Prachuap's beach. Pleasant staff.

Aow Noi Sea View　　HOTEL **$$**
(☑ 0 3260 4440; www.aownoiseaview.com; Ao Noi; r 800-1200B; ❄ ☎) North of town, this secluded three-storey hotel is Prachuap's best beachfront choice. With pretty Ao Noi beach at your doorstep, you'll enjoy sea breezes, spacious rooms with balconies and a homey ambience.

Golden Beach Hotel　　HOTEL **$$**
(☑ 0 3260 1626; www.goldenbeachprachuap.com; 113-115 Th Suanson; r 500-1000B; ❄ ☎) A comfortable midrange option opposite Ao Prachuap's beach, and a decent deal these days for a sea view. The rooms are plain and a little old-fashioned, but clean.

Eating & Drinking

Restaurants in Prachuap are cheap and offer excellent seafood, while Western dishes are popping up more frequently. The **day market** (Th Maitri Ngam; ☺daylight hours) is the place to get pineapples fresh from the orchards; ask the vendor to cut it for you. The **night market** (Th Kong Kiat; ☺5-9pm) is small and has the usual stir-fry stalls.

Suan Krua　　VEGETARIAN **$**
(Soi Tampramuk; dishes 20-60B; ☺6.30am-3pm; ✿) Super vegetarian, buffet-style eatery. Choose from an array of dishes, but they go fast and then it shuts. Be here promptly and with an appetite.

★**Rim Lom**　　SEAFOOD **$$**
(5 Th Suanson; dishes 120-290B; ☺10am-10pm) Still the go-to place in town for the locals, the *pàt pŏng gà·rèe ʬoo* (crab curry) comes with big chunks of sweet crab meat and the *yam ta-lair* (seafood salad) is spicy and zesty. It's 200m past the bridge on the left.

Phloen Samut　　SEAFOOD **$$**
(44 Th Chai Thaleh; dishes 120-250B; ☺10am-10pm) One of a few seafood restaurants along the promenade, Phloen Samut is a big, bustling operation. The dishes are tasty, especially if you can handle spicy.

Ma Prow　　INTERNATIONAL-THAI **$$**
(48 Th Chai Thaleh; dishes 120-395B; ☺10am-10pm) An airy wooden pavilion, Ma Prow is more foreigner-orientated than other places on the promenade. This is the best option in town if you're craving a steak rather than seafood, although the tamarind fish here goes down a treat.

Ciao Pizza　　ITALIAN **$$**
(Th Suseuk; pizzas from 170B; ☺11am-10pm) Italian-owned, come here for fine pizzas,

homemade pasta and gelato, as well as fresh bread baked daily and a takeaway selection of cheese, sausage and salami.

Jim's Bar & Restaurant BAR
(53 Th Chai Thaleh; beers from 60B; ⊙4pm-1am)
Prachuap is an early to bed town, but at Jim's you can sip a libation till late while gazing out at the winking lights of the fishing boats in the bay.

ℹ Information

Bangkok Bank (cnr Th Maitri Ngam & Th Sarachip)
Police Station (Th Kong Kiat) Just west of Th Sarachip.
Post Office (cnr Th Maitri Ngam & Th Suseuk)
Thai Farmers Bank (Th Phitak Chat) Just north of Th Maitri Ngam.
Tourist Office (📞0 3261 1491; Th Chai Thaleh; ⊙8.30am-4.30pm) At the northern end of town. The staff speak English and are helpful.

ℹ Getting There & Away

Seven air-conditioned buses run daily to Bangkok's southern terminal from Th Phitak Chat. Buses also leave from here for Ban Krut and Bang Saphan Yai.

Minivans leave from the corner of Th Thetsaban Bamrung and Th Phitak Chat

Long-distance buses to southern destinations (such as Phuket and Krabi) stop at the new bus station, 2km northwest of town on the main highway; motorcycle taxis will take you for 40B to 50B.

The train station is on Th Maharat; there are frequent services to/from Bangkok.

ℹ Getting Around

Prachuap is small enough to get around on foot, but you can hop on a motorcycle taxi for 30B. A bike to Ao Noi and Ao Manao is 100B to 150B.

You can hire motorbikes for 250B per day. The roads in the area are very good and it's a great way to see the surrounding beaches.

Ban Krut & Bang Saphan Yai บ้านกรูด/บางสะพานใหญ่

POP 4275/ 68,344

What a nice surprise to find these lovely, low-key beaches (80km to 100km south of Prachuap Khiri Khan, respectively) so close to civilisation, yet so bucolic. Dusk falls softly through the coconut trees and the sea is a crystalline blue lapping at a long sandy coastline. No high-rises, no late-night discos and no speeding traffic to distract you from a serious regimen of reading, swimming, eating and biking.

Although both beaches are pleasantly subdued, they are also well known to Thais. Ban Krut, in particular, hosts bus tours as well as weekending families. During the week you'll have the beaches largely to yourself and a few long-tail boats.

Check out the websites **Ban Krut Info** (www.bankrutinfo.com) and **Bang Saphan Guide** (www.bangsaphanguide.com) for local information on the area.

◉ Sights & Activities

Ban Krut is divided into two beaches by a temple-topped headland. To the north is **Hat Sai Kaew**, which is remote and private with only a few resorts in between a lot of

TRANSPORT TO/FROM PRACHUAP KHIRI KHAN

DESTINATION	BUS	MINIVAN	TRAIN
Ban Krut		70B; 1hr; hourly 6am-5pm	1 daily
Bang Saphan Yai		80B; 1½hr; hourly 6am-5pm	8 daily
Bangkok Hua Lamphong			168-455B; 7-8hr; 8 daily 2.41am-11.26pm
Bangkok southern bus terminal	200B; 6-7hr; 7 daily 9am-1am	200B; 5-6hr; hourly 7am-5pm	
Bangkok Victory Monument		240B; 6hr; hourly 6am-5pm	
Cha-am		120B; 2hr; hourly 6am-5pm	1 daily
Hua Hin		80B; 1½hr; hourly 6am-5pm	8 daily
Phetchaburi		150B; 3hr; hourly 6am-5pm	8 daily

jungle. To the south is **Hat Ban Krut**, with a string of bungalow-style resorts and restaurants sitting opposite the beach. Both are golden-sand beaches with clear, calm water but Hat Ban Krut is more social and developed (you'll find ATMs here) and easier to get around without private transport.

Bang Saphan Yai, 20km south of Ban Krut, fits that most famous beach cliché: it is Thailand 15 years ago before pool villas and package tourists pushed out all the beach bums. Once you settle into a simple beachfront hut, you probably won't find shoes and the days will just melt away. Islands off the coast, including **Ko Thalu** and **Ko Sing**, offer good **snorkelling** and **diving** from the end of January to mid-May.

🛏 Sleeping & Eating

🛏 Ban Krut

You'll struggle to find true budget options here, but if you visit on a weekday you should secure a discount. In Hat Ban Krut, bicycles (100B per day) and motorcycles (300B per day) can be hired to run errands in town, and most accommodation options arrange snorkelling trips to nearby islands. If you stay in Hat Sai Kaew you'll need private transport.

★ NaNa Chart Baan Krut HOTEL $$
(📞 0 3269 5525; www.thailandhostel.com; 123 Th Ban Krut-Kohktahom; dm 400B, r 600-2900B; ❄@🛜🏊) Technically it is a hostel – and it does have dorms – but NaNa Chart easily qualifies as a resort with a variety of bungalows on a barely inhabited, superb stretch of beach. The cheapest are wooden huts with fans, while the ritzy beachfront ones have all the mod cons. The resort caters to large groups so expect some company at peak times; in low season it's much quieter. Hostel members receive discounted rates.

Proud Thai Beach Resort GUESTHOUSE $$
(📞 08 9682 4484; www.proudthairesort.com; Hat Ban Krut; r 800-1200B; ❄🛜) Well-maintained bungalows in a flower-filled garden have porches, and morning coffee delivered by the affable owner. Prices rise at weekends and on public holidays.

Bayview Beach Resort HOTEL $$$
(📞 0 3269 5566; www.bayviewbeachresort.com; Hat Ban Krut; r 1600-5400B; ❄🛜🏊) A great choice for families, Bayview has handsome bungalows with large verandahs amid shady grounds. There's a beachside pool and a kid-friendly wading pool as well as a small playground. The resort also offers snorkelling and diving trips and rents kayaks and bikes.

Kasama's Pizza ITALIAN $$
(Hat Ban Krut; pizza from 180B; ⊙7.30am-11pm, closed Thu; 🛜) Substantial, succulent baguettes (from 90B) for beach-snacking, and it's fine for breakfast or a New York-style pizza in the evening.

🛏 Bang Saphan Yai

The beach is 6km south of the town of Bang Saphan Yai. It's not as idyllic a strip of sand as Ban Krut, but there's both budget accommodation and high-end pool villas here. Walk north of the Why Not Bar for the cheaper places.

Roytawan GUESTHOUSE $
(📞08 7670 8943; Hat Bang Saphan Yai; r from 300B) Smack dab on the beach, this bare-bones operation is run by a friendly local Muslim family. The bungalows are simple but adequate and the resident roosters kindly sleep until daybreak. The restaurant is fab too.

Suan Luang Resort GUESTHOUSE $
(📞0 3269 1663; www.suanluangresort.com; Hat Bang Saphan Yai; bungalows 480-680B; ❄🛜) Run by a laid-back family, Suan Long is the most professional of the guesthouses with rustic wooden bungalows set around an interior garden. The air-con ones are a big step up from the fan rooms, but you're 700m from the beach. The excellent restaurant serves Thai and French food, and motorbikes are available for rent (300B per day).

Patty Hut GUESTHOUSE $
(📞08 6171 1907; Hat Bang Saphan Yai; r 300-700B) The most basic option (mattress on the floor, fan and cold-water showers), but you're just 300m from the beach.

Coral Hotel HOTEL $$$
(📞0 3281 7121; www.coral-hotel.com; Hat Bang Saphan Yai; r 2385-6890B; ❄@🛜🏊) Catering mostly to French tourists – the restaurant is decent – this upmarket hotel is right on the beach and has all the resort amenities, including organised diving and snorkelling tours. The tastefully decorated rooms are very comfortable and the pool is big.

ⓘ Getting There & Around

Public transport is either nonexistent or limited. When booking transport, don't confuse Bang Saphan Yai with Bang Saphan Noi, which is a fishermen's village 15km further south.

From Bangkok's southern (Sai Tai Mai) terminal buses go to Bang Saphan Yai (275B, hourly, six hours); in Bangkok, use **Bangsaphan Tour** (☑ 08 7829 7752).

Frequent minivans run from Prachuap Khiri Khan to Ban Krut (70B) and Bang Saphan Yai (80B). Most minivans to Ban Krut will stop on the highway, a 100B motorbike ride from the beach.

Many seasoned visitors prefer to take the train for closer proximity to the beaches. There are several daily options but the sprinter train (special express No 43) is one of the fastest. It leaves Bangkok's Hua Lamphong station at 8.05am and arrives in Ban Krut (445B) at 1.07pm and Bang Saphan Yai (450B) at 1.20pm. You can also hop on an afternoon train to Chumphon with plenty of time to spare before the ferry to Ko Tao.

A motorcycle taxi from town to Bang Saphan Yai is 70B. Talk to your hotel or guesthouse about arranging transport back to town for your onward travel.

Chumphon   ชุมพร

POP 55,835

A transit town funnelling travellers to and from Ko Tao or westwards to Ranong or Phuket, Chumphon is also where the south of Thailand starts proper; Muslim headscarves are a common sight here.

While there's not a lot to do while you wait for your ferry, there's good seafood in town and the surrounding beaches are great places to step off the backpacker bandwagon for a few days. **Hat Thung Wua Laen** (15km north of town) is an excellent beach with plenty of traveller amenities and during the week you'll have it mostly to yourself.

For a transit hub, Chumphon is surprisingly unconsolidated: the main bus station and piers for boats to Ko Tao, Ko Samui and Ko Pha-Ngan are some distance from town. Travel agencies and guesthouses can book tickets, provide timetables and point you to the right bus stop; fortunately agents in Chumphon are a dedicated lot.

✦✦ Festivals & Events

Chumphon Marine Festival   CULTURAL
(☉Mar) Normally held in mid-March, Hat Thung Wua Laen hosts a variety of events including folk-art exhibits, shadow-puppet performances and a food display.

Chumphon Traditional Boat Race   CULTURAL
(☉Oct) To mark the end of Buddhist Lent in October (Ork Phansaa), traditional long-tail boats race each other on the Mae Nam Lang Suan (Lang Suan River), about 60km south of Chumphon. Other merit-making activities coincide with the festival.

🛏 Sleeping

As most people overnighting in Chumphon are backpackers, accommodation is priced accordingly. Th Tha Taphao is the local Th Khao San, with many guesthouses and travel agencies.

★ Suda Guest House   GUESTHOUSE $
(☑08 0144 2079; 8 Soi Sala Daeng 3; r 250-650B; ❄@☞) Suda, the friendly English-speaking owner, maintains her impeccable standards with six rooms, all with wooden floors and a few nice touches that you wouldn't expect for the price. It's very popular so phone ahead.

Salsa Hostel   HOSTEL $
(☑0 7750 5005; www.salsachumphon.com; 25/42 Th Krom Luang Chumphon; dm/d 230/700B; ❄@☞) Helpful hostel (the owner speaks good English) with cramped but clean and modern dorms. The private rooms are big and bright, even if they are overpriced for this town.

Fame Guest House   GUESTHOUSE $
(☑0 7757 1077; 188/20-21 Th Sala Daeng; r 200-300B; @☞) A *fa•ràng* (Westerner) depot, Fame does a little bit of everything, from providing basic but OK rooms to booking tickets and renting motorbikes. The attached restaurant is a key backpacker hang-out, staying open until midnight and offering a wide range of Thai, Indian and Western food.

San Tavee New Rest House   GUESTHOUSE $
(☑0 7750 2147; 4 Soi Sala Daeng 3; r 250-300B) Only four rooms, all with shared bathrooms. They're small, well-kept and set around a garden. It feels more like a homestay than a guesthouse.

View Resort   BUNGALOW $
(☑0 7756 0214; Hat Thung Wua Laen; r 650-1100B; ❄☞) Sleepy bungalow operation outside town that's right on the beach. The restaurant is pretty good too.

Chumphon

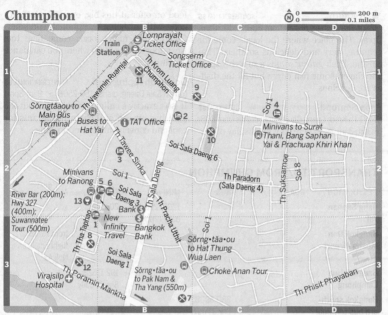

N 0 — 200 m
0 — 0.1 miles

Chumphon Gardens Hotel HOTEL $$
(0 7750 6888; www.chumphongarden.com; 66/1
Th Tha Taphao; r 730B;) Sports a 1970s-
style design but has large, comfortable
rooms and the bathrooms are a cut above
the local competition.

Morakot Hotel HOTEL $$
(0 7750 2999; www.morakothotel.com; 102-112
Th Tawee Sinka; r 490-890B;) Spread across
two buildings, the rooms here are characterless but modern and clean, making it a solid
midrange option.

**Chumphon Cabana Resort &
Diving Centre** HOTEL $$$
(0 7756 0245; www.cabana.co.th; Hat Thung Wua
Laen; r 1650-3000B;) The most pleas-
ant resort on the beach, despite the rather
plain bungalows, Chumphon Cabana has
done a great job upgrading its environmental
profile. Inspired by the King's environmental
sustainability speech, the owner reconfigured
the resort to look to the past for instructions
on how to be green. Now, the grounds are de-
voted to raising the resort's own food with rice
fields, hydroponic vegetable gardens and a
chicken farm. Waste water is recycled through
water-hyacinth ponds. If you don't stay here,
at least try the homegrown food at **Rabieng
Talay**, the resort's affiliated restaurant.

Chumphon

Sleeping
1 Chumphon Gardens Hotel	A2
2 Fame Guest House	B1
3 Morakot Hotel	B2
4 Salsa Hostel	C1
5 San Tavee New Rest House	B2
6 Suda Guest House	B2

Eating
7 Day Market	B3
8 Day Market	A3
9 Night Market	C1
10 Ocean Shopping Mall	C2
11 Papa Seafood	B1
12 Prikhorm	A3

Drinking & Nightlife
13 Farang Bar	A2

Eating & Drinking

Chumphon's **night market** (Th Krom Luang
Chumphon) is excellent, with a huge variety
of food options and good people-watching.
There are **day markets** along **Th Tha
Taphao** (Th Tha Taphao) and **Th Pracha Uthit**
(Th Pracha Uthit), and Th Sala Daeng and Th
Pracha Uthit are both lined with hole-in-the-
wall noodle joints.

★ **Prikhorm** SOUTHERN THAI $$
(32 Th Tha Taphao; dishes from 80B; ⏱10.30am-11pm) The place where the locals come for genuine, fiery and delicious southern Thai cuisine. Their *gaang som* is a superbly spicy and flavoursome fish curry, but all the dishes are delicious.

Papa Seafood SEAFOOD $$
(2-2/1 Th Krom Luang Chumphon; dishes from 80B; ⏱3pm-3am; ☎) There's a wide display of seafood on offer at this big, open-air place; it's good without being exceptional. Foreigner-friendly, but many locals come here too. Next door is Papa 2000 where you can dance off dinner.

Ocean Shopping Mall INTERNATIONAL $$
(off Th Sala Daeng; dishes 150-250B; ⏱9am-8pm) It isn't exactly a culinary destination but the mall has air-con and chain restaurants for cool and convenient layover noshing.

TRANSPORT TO/FROM CHUMPHON

DESTINATION	BOAT	BUS	MINIVAN	TRAIN	AIR
Bang Saphan Yai			120B; 2hr; 1 daily (2pm)	20B; 2hr; 12 daily	
Bangkok Don Muang Airport					from 1674B; 2 flights daily on Nok Air
Bangkok Hua Lamphong				192-1162B; 8hr; 11 daily	
Bangkok southern bus terminal		380-590B; 8hr; 11 daily			
Hat Yai		400B; 4 daily; 7hr		6 daily	
Ko Pha-Ngan via Lomprayah	1000B; 3¼hr; 2 daily (7am & 1pm)				
Ko Pha-Ngan via Songserm	900B; 5½hr; 1 daily (7am)				
Ko Samui via Lomprayah	1100B; 4½hr; 2 daily (7am & 1pm)				
Ko Samui via Songserm	1000B; 7hr; 1 daily (7am)				
Ko Tao via car ferry	400B; 6hr; 1 daily (11pm Mon-Sat)				
Ko Tao via Lomprayah	600B; 1½hr; 2 daily (7am & 1pm)				
Ko Tao via slow boat	250B; 6hr; 1 daily (midnight)				
Ko Tao via Songserm	500B; 3hr; 1 daily (7am)				
Phetchaburi		210B; 5 daily; 6hr		11 daily	
Phuket		350B; 4 daily; 3½hr			
Prachuap Khiri Khan			180B; 1 daily (3pm); 4hr	10 daily	
Ranong		120B; 4 daily; 2½hr	130B; frequent; 2hr		
Surat Thani			170B; hourly 6am-5pm; 3hr	12 daily	

River
BAR

(4/9 Th Poramin Mankha; ⊙ 4pm-1am; 🛜) Perched over the Taphao River, this bar has live music every night. It's a fine spot for a sundowner; it gets more lively later on. The menu is a mix of classic Thai and Western dishes.

Farang Bar
BAR

(☑ 0 7750 1003; www.farangbarchumphon.com; 69/36 Th Tha Taphao; beers from 80B; ⊙ 11am-midnight; 🛜) An agreeable hang-out for expat English teachers and passing travellers, the Farang Bar is an easy place to while away a few hours over a drink. The menu mixes Thai and Western dishes; the local ones are better. There are also basic rooms here (250B) and day-use showers (20B).

❶ Information

There are banks along Th Sala Daeng with exchange facilities and ATMs.

Bangkok Bank (Th Sala Daeng) Has an ATM.

Main Post Office (Th Poramin Mankha) In the southeastern part of town.

New Infinity Travel (☑ 0 7757 0176; 68/2 Th Tha Taphao; ⊙ 8am-10pm; 🛜) A great travel agency with knowledgeable and friendly staff; they'll also sell you paperbacks and rent you one of four rooms (250B).

Tourism Authority of Thailand (TAT; ☑ 0 7750 1831; 111/11-12 Th Tawee Sinka; ⊙ 8.30am-4.30pm) Hands out maps and brochures but not always up-to-date on transport information.

Virajsilp Hospital (☑ 0 7750 3238; Th Poramin Mankha) Privately owned; handles emergencies.

❶ Getting There & Away

Boats leave from different piers; bus transfer is sometimes included in the ticket price. Otherwise, you pay an extra 50B for transport to the pier. During low season, the car ferry and slow boat don't always run.

BOAT

You have many boat options for getting to Ko Tao, though departure times are limited to mainly morning and night. Most ticket prices include pier transfer. If you buy a combination ticket, make sure you have a ticket for both the bus and the boat.

Slow boat – the cheapest, slowest and most scenic option as everyone stretches out on the open deck of the fishing boat with the stars twinkling overhead. This boat doesn't run in rough seas or inclement weather.

Car ferry – a more comfortable ride with bunk or mattress options available on board.

Songserm (☑ 0 7750 6205; www.songserm-expressboat.com; ⊙ 9am-8pm) express boat – faster, morning option leaving from Tha Talaysub, about 10km from town, but the company has a growing reputation for being poorly organised and for not providing promised free transport into town if you are coming from the islands. The ticket office doesn't seem to open often; book tickets through guesthouses.

Lomprayah (☑ 0 7755 8214; www.lomprayah. com; ⊙ 5am-9pm) catamaran – the best and most popular bus-boat combination that leaves from Tha Tummakam, 25km from town; the ticket office is beside Chumphon train station.

BUS

The main bus terminal is on the highway, an inconvenient 16km from Chumphon. To get there you can catch a *sŏrng·tăa·ou* (50B) from Th Nawamin Ruamjai. You'll have to haggle with the opportunistic taxi drivers for night transit to/from the station; no matter what they tell you, it shouldn't cost more than 200B.

There are several in-town bus stops to save you a trip out to the main bus station. **Choke Anan Tour** (☑ 0 7751 1757; soi off of Th Pracha Uthit), in the centre of town, has departures to Bangkok, Phuket and Ranong. **Suwannatee Tour** (☑ 0 7750 4901), 700m southeast of train station road, serves Bangkok, Phetchaburi and Prachuap Khiri Khan. Buses to Hat Yai depart from near the petrol station on Th Nawamin Ruamjai.

All minivans for Surat Thani, Bang Saphan Yai and Prachuap Khiri Khan leave from the unnamed soi opposite Salsa Guesthouse.

TRAIN

There are frequent services to/from Bangkok (2nd class 292B to 382B, 3rd class 235B, 7½ hours). Overnight sleepers range from 440B to 770B.

Southbound rapid and express trains – the only trains with 1st and 2nd class – are less frequent and can be difficult to book out of Chumphon from November to February.

❶ Getting Around

Sŏrng·tăa·ou and motorcycle taxis around town cost 40B and 20B respectively per trip. *Sŏrng·tăa·ou* to Hat Thung Wua Laen cost 30B.

Motorcycles can be rented at travel agencies and guesthouses for 200B to 350B per day.

Ko Samui & the Lower Gulf

Includes ➡

Best Places to Eat

➡ Dining On The Rocks (p543)

➡ 69 (p543)

➡ Ging Pagarang (p544)

➡ Fisherman's Restaurant (p561)

➡ Baraccuda (p575)

Best Places to Stay

➡ Six Senses Samui (p537)

➡ Divine Comedie (p555)

➡ Viewpoint Resort (p574)

➡ Samui-Ley (p538)

➡ Sanctuary (p560)

Why Go?

The Lower Gulf features Thailand's ultimate island trifecta: Ko Samui, Ko Pha-Ngan and Ko Tao. This family of spectacular islands lures millions of tourists every year with their powder-soft sands and emerald waters. Ko Samui is the oldest sibling, who has made it big. Here, high-class resorts operate with Swiss efficiency as uniformed butlers cater to every whim. Ko Pha-Ngan is the slacker middle child with tangled dreadlocks and a penchant for hammock-lazing and all-night parties. Meanwhile Ko Tao is the outdoorsy, fun-loving kid with plenty of spirit and spunk – the island specialises in high-adrenalin activities, including world-class diving and snorkelling.

The mainland coast beyond the islands sees few foreign visitors. From the pink dolphins and waterfalls of sleepy Ao Khanom to the Thai Muslim flavours of kite-flying, beach strolling Songkhla, this region will convince any naysayer that Thailand still holds a bevy of off-the-beaten-track wonders.

When to Go

➡ February to April celebrates endless sunshine after the monsoon rains have cleared. June to August, conveniently coinciding with the northern hemisphere's summer holidays, are among the most inviting months, with relatively short drizzle spells.

➡ October to December is when torrential monsoon rains rattle hot-tin roofs, and room rates drop significantly to lure optimistic beach goers.

GULF ISLANDS

Ko Samui
เกาะสมุย

POP 50,000

Ko Samui is like a well-established Hollywood celebrity: she's outrageously manicured, has lovely blonde tresses and has gracefully removed all of her wrinkles without more than a peep in the tabloids. She's been in the tourism business longer than almost any other Thai island, but rather than becoming passe, she's embraced a new generation of resort goers, many of them upscale and Russian. Academy Award–winning holidays here include fine stretches of sand clogged with beach loungers, rubbish-free roads, world-class international cuisine, luxurious spas and beach bar parties for scantily clad 20-somethings that start at noon.

Behind the glossy veneer there's still a glimmer of the girl from the country. Look for steaming street-side food stalls beyond the beach, backpacker shanties plunked down on quiet stretches of sand and secreted Buddhist temples along the backstreets. It's then that you remember you're in Thailand and not a globalisation-induced trance of a Photoshopped beach vacation. To really get away, head to the south or the west of the island, where you'll find authentic Samui family-run seafood restaurants, tourist-free towns buzzing with descendents of the original Chinese merchant settlers and long stretches of refreshingly wild and shaggy coconut palms.

◉ Sights

Ko Samui is quite large – the island's ring road is almost 100km total.

Hin-Ta & Hin-Yai   LANDMARK

At the south end of **Hat Lamai**, the second-largest beach, you'll find these infamous stone formations (also known as Grandfather and Grandmother Rocks). These rocks, shaped like genitalia, provide endless mirth for giggling Thai tourists.

Ban Hua Thanon   NEIGHBOURHOOD

Just beyond Hat Lamai, Hua Thanon is home to a vibrant Muslim community, and its anchorage of high-bowed fishing vessels is a veritable gallery of intricate designs.

Nam Tok Na Muang   WATERFALL

At 30m, this is the tallest waterfall on Samui and lies in the centre of the island about 12km from Na Thon. The water cascades over ethereal purple rocks, and there's a great pool for swimming at the base. This is the most scenic – and somewhat less frequented – of Samui's falls.

There are two other waterfalls in the vicinity: a smaller waterfall called **Na Muang 2**, and the high drop at **Nam Tok Wang Saotong**, which, thanks to recently improved road conditions, is now accessible. These chutes are just north of the ring road near Ban Hua Thanon. There's a great fried chicken and *sôm·đam* (spicy green papaya salad)

GULF ISLANDS IN...

One Week

First, shed a tear that you have but one week to explore these idyllic islands. Then start on one of **Ko Pha-Ngan's** (p549) secluded beaches in the west or east to live out your ultimate castaway fantasies. For the second half of the week choose between partying in **Hat Rin** (p553), pampering on **Ko Samui** (p527) or diving on little **Ko Tao** (p565).

Two Weeks

Start on **Ko Tao** (p565) with a 3½-day Open Water certification course, or sign up for a few fun dives. Slide over to **Ko Pha-Ngan** (p549) and soak up the sociable vibe in party-prone Hat Rin. Then, grab a long-tail and make your way to one of the island's hidden coves for a few days of detoxing and quiet contemplation. **Ko Samui** is next. Try **Bo Phut** (p538) for boutique sleeps or live it up like a rock star on Chaweng or Choeng Mon beach. If you have time, do a day trip to **Ang Thong National Marine Park** (p580).

One Month

Follow the two-week itinerary at a more relaxed pace, infusing many extra beach-book-and-blanket days on all three islands. Be sure to plan your schedule around the Full Moon Party, which takes place at Hat Rin's Sunrise Beach on **Ko Pha-Ngan** (p549).

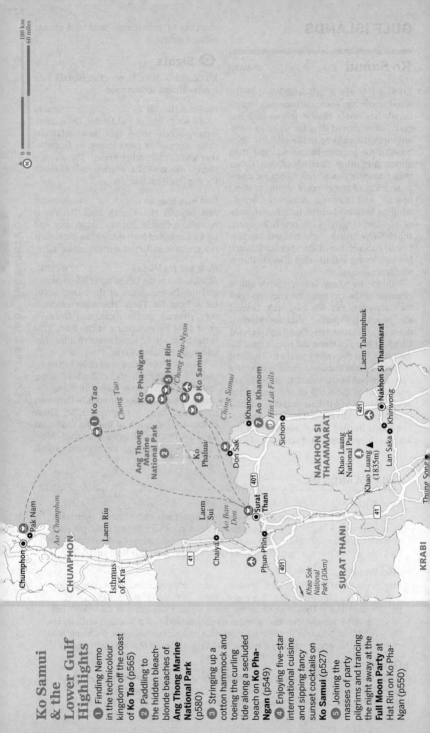

GULF ISLANDS

Ko Samui

Ko Samui is like a well-oiled tourist machine that's learned how to cater to every flavour of traveller. Budget backpackers can still buy a cheap bungalow, while jet-setters who never fly economy can charter private planes to the island's newly expanded airport. Each spot along the sandy shores has a distinct personality, so it's worth shopping around for the right vibe.

Despite the constant flow of tourism, much of the local magic still remains. Behind the glitzy resorts and beachfront wine bars, the island's spirit lives on in its
aboriginal fishing villages. Ko Samui turns 'sultry' into an artform.

Sights

Ko Samui is quite large – it's the second-biggest island in Thailand.

Ring Rd (Rte 4169) circles the island's perimeter and all of these beach towns with their myriad mini-malls and convenience stores are linked together like a strand of Christmas lights. Chaweng and Lamai are the main beaches on the island's east side; the pushy port village of Na Thon is situated in the middle of the west coast.

Ko Samui & the Lower Gulf Highlights

1 Finding Nemo in the technicolour kingdom off the coast of **Ko Tao** (p565)

2 Paddling to the hidden bleach-blonde beaches of **Ang Thong Marine National Park** (p580)

3 Stringing up a cotton hammock and toeing the curling tide along a secluded beach on **Ko Pha-Ngan** (p549)

4 Enjoying five-star international cuisine and sipping fancy sunset cocktails on **Ko Samui** (p527)

5 Joining the masses of party pilgrims and trancing the night away at the **Full Moon Party** at Hat Rin on Ko Pha-Ngan (p550)

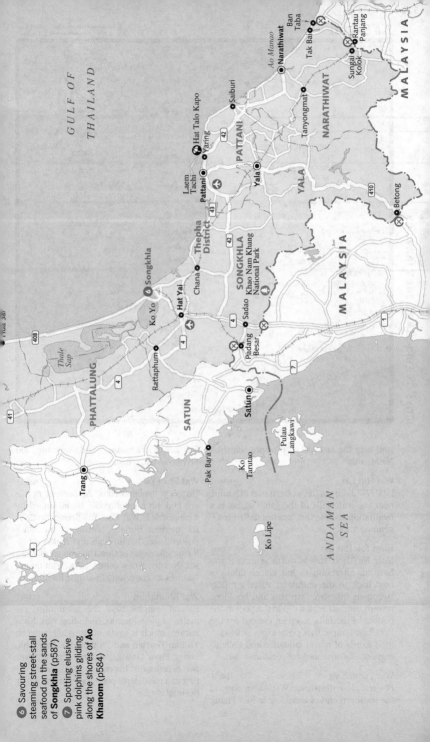

GULF OF THAILAND

ANDAMAN SEA

MALAYSIA

6 Savouring steaming street-stall seafood on the sands of **Songkhla** (p587)

7 Spotting elusive pink dolphins gliding along the shores of **Ao Khanom** (p584)

Ko Samui

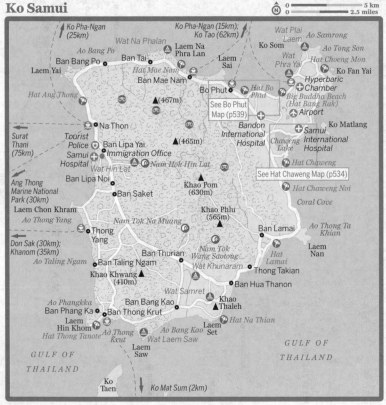

stall near the last rest stop before Nam Tok Na Muang.

Wat Hin Lat
TEMPLE

(☎ 0 7742 3146) On the western part of Samui, near the waterfalls of the same name, is a meditation temple that teaches daily *vipassana* courses.

Nam Tok Hin Lat
WATERFALL

Near Na Thon, this is worth visiting if you have an afternoon to kill before taking a boat back to the mainland. After a mildly strenuous hike over streams and boulders, reward yourself with a dip in the pool at the bottom of the falls. Keep an eye out for the Buddhist temple that posts signs with spiritual words of moral guidance and enlightenment. Sturdy shoes are recommended.

Wat Laem Saw
TEMPLE

For temple enthusiasts, Wat Laem Saw, at the southern end of Samui near Ban Phang Ka, has an interesting, highly venerated old Srivijaya-style stupa.

Wat Phra Yai
TEMPLE

(Temple of the Big Buddha) At Samui's northern end, on a small rocky island linked by a causeway, is Wat Phra Yai. Erected in 1972, the modern Buddha (sitting in the Mara posture) stands 15m high and makes an alluring silhouette against the tropical sky and sea. Nearby, a new temple, **Wat Plai Laem**, features an enormous 18-armed Buddha.

Wat Khunaram
TEMPLE

Several temples have the mummified remains of pious monks, including Wak Khunaram, which is south of Rte 4169 between Th Ban Thurian and Th Ban Hua. Its monk, Luang Phaw Daeng, has been dead for over two decades but his corpse is preserved sitting in a meditative pose and sporting a pair of sunglasses.

Wat Samret   BUDDHIST TEMPLE

At Wat Samret, near Th Ban Hua, you can see a typical Mandalay sitting Buddha carved from solid marble – a common sight in India and northern Thailand, but not so common in the south.

🏃 Activities

Ko Samui is an excellent choice for families travelling with kids as there are many activities especially geared to the little ones.

Blue Stars   KAYAKING, SNORKELLING

(Map p534; ☑ 0 7741 3231; www.bluestars.info; Hat Chaweng; kayak & snorkelling tours 2200B) There are many choices for snorkelling and kayak tours to Ang Thong Marine National Park, but Blue Stars has the best reputation and the coolest boat. Even if you don't go with this company, don't miss taking a trip to these islands.

Naish SUP   WATERSPORTS

(Map p534; ☑ 08 6947 7233; Hat Chaweng; SUP rental per hr/day 200/500B) Paddle it like a boat (although you're standing up) or try to surf it; popular stand up paddle boards have reached Ko Samui and you can rent them here. Take an hour-long lesson in the sandy shallows if it's your first time for 300B.

Football Golf   FOOTBALL GOLF

(☑ 08 9771 7498; ⊙ 9am-6.30pm) At Hat Choeng Mon there's a strange combustion called 'football golf' where you 'putt' your football into a rubbish-bin-sized hole. It's great for the kids and each game (350B) comes with a complimentary soft drink. It's a par 66.

Magic Alambic   RUM TASTING

(www.rumdistillerie.com; Ban Bang Kao; tasting shots 50-75B; ⊙ noon-6pm) The only rum distillery in Thailand produces Caribbean agricole style (distilled from fresh, fermented sugar cane juice) in a variety of all natural flavours including a delectable coconut rum obtained from soaking coconut meat in the rum for several months. There's a video about the production process, a tasting area and shop in beautiful palm-shaded surrounds. It's on Samui's southern coast.

Aquapark   SEA PARK

(Map p534; Hat Chaweng; hourly/half-day 200/350B; ⊙ 10am-6pm) Let the kids loose on these gigantic green, climbable, slip-off-able and all-around-fun inflatables (including a UFO, an iceberg climbing wall and trampolines) anchored to a corded-off area of Ao Chaweng. All participants are required to wear lifejackets. Meanwhile you can lounge on the beach and watch, or join them as many parents are enticed to do.

Coco Splash Waterpark   WATER PARK

(Ban Lamai; admission 200B; ⊙ 10.30am-5.30pm) Kids under 10 will love this small park of fun painted concrete water slides. Towel hire is 60B and there's mediocre food available. Note that if you're planning on watching the kids and not going in the water yourself, you get in for free. Arrive after 4pm and the price drops to 60B.

Samui Dog & Cat Rescue Centre   VOLUNTEERING

(Map p534; ☑ 0 7741 3490; www.samuidog.org; Soi 3, Chaweng Beach Rd; ⊙ 9am-6pm) Donations of time and/or money are hugely appreciated at the aptly named Samui Dog & Cat Rescue Centre. Volunteers are always needed to take care of the animals at either of the kennel/clinics (in Hat Chaweng and Ban Taling Ngam). Call the centre for volunteering details or swing by for additional info.

The organisation has played an integral role in keeping the island's dog population under control through an active spaying and neutering program. The centre also vaccinates dogs against rabies.

Diving

If you're serious about diving, head to Ko Tao and base yourself there for the duration of your diving adventure. If you're short on time and don't want to leave Samui, there are plenty of operators who will take you to the same dive sites (at a greater fee, of course). Try to book with a company that has its own boat (or leases a boat) – it's slightly more expensive, but you'll be glad you did it. Companies without boats often shuttle divers on the passenger catamaran to Ko Tao, where you board a second boat to reach your dive site. These trips are arduous, meal-less and rather impersonal.

Certification courses tend to be twice as expensive on Ko Samui as they are on Ko Tao, due largely to use of extra petrol, since tiny Tao is significantly closer to the preferred diving locations. You'll spend between 14,000B and 22,000B on an Open Water certification, and figure on between 4500B and 6200B for a diving day trip including two dives, depending on the location of the site.

Ko Samui's hyperbaric chamber is at Big Buddha Beach (Hat Bang Rak).

WORTH A TRIP

KO TAH

Tired of tours and busy beaches? For the intrepid DIY traveller there's no better way to spend a day on Ko Samui than with a trip to the white sands of Ko Tah. Hire a long-tail boat from the boatmen who beach their boats alongside the strip of seafood restaurants on Hat Thong Tanote on Ko Samui's south coast; a boat for up to six people should cost 1500B to 2000B for a four-hour trip. The island itself is only about 15 minutes from Ko Samui. While the snorkelling isn't that great, the white-sand beach is empty aside from the occasional visit by charter boats and local fishermen, and the views and swimming are sublime.

100 Degrees East   DIVING
(✆0 7742 5936; www.100degreeseast.com; Hat Bang Rak) Highly recommended.

Samui Planet Scuba   DIVING
(SIDS; Map p534; ✆0 7723 1606; samuiplanetscuba@planetscuba.net; Hat Chaweng)

Spas & Yoga
Competition for Samui's five-star accommodation is fierce, which means that the spas are of the highest calibre. For top-notch pampering, try the spa at Anantara (p538) in Bo Phut, or the Hideaway Spa at the Six Senses Samui (p537). The Spa Resort (p536) in Lamai is the island's original health destination, and is still known for its effective 'clean me out' fasting regime.

Yoga Thailand   YOGA, SPA
(✆0 7792 0090; www.yoga-thailand.com; Phang Ka; retreats around €840) Secreted away along the southern shores, Yoga Thailand is ushering in a new era of therapeutic holidaying with its state-of-the-art facilities and dedicated team of trainers. Accommodation is in a comfy apartment block up the street while yoga studios, wellness centres and a breezy cafe sit calmly along the shore.

Tamarind Retreat   THAI MASSAGE
(✆0 7723 0571; www.tamarindretreat.com) Tucked far away from the beach within a silent coconut-palm plantation, Tamarind's small collection of villas and massage studios is seamlessly incorporated into nature: some have granite boulders built into walls and floors, while others offer private ponds or creative outdoor baths.

Absolute Sanctuary   YOGA, SPA
(✆0 7760 1190; www.absolutesanctuary.com) What was once a friendly yoga studio has blossomed into a gargantuan wellness complex featuring plenty of accommodation and an exhaustive menu of detox and wellness programs. Located a few kilometres north of Chaweng.

Courses

Samui Institute of Thai Culinary Arts   COOKING
(SITCA; Map p534; ✆0 7741 3434; www.sitca.net; Hat Chaweng; one-day course 1950B) If you're contemplating a Thai cooking course, SITCA is the place to do it. It has daily Thai-cooking classes and courses in the aristocratic Thai art of carving fruits and vegetables into intricate floral designs. Lunchtime classes begin at 11am, while dinner starts at 4pm (both are three-hour courses with three or more dishes).

Included is an excellent tutorial about procuring ingredients in your home country. Of course, you get to eat your projects, and you can even invite a friend along for the meal. Complimentary DVDs with Thai cooking instruction are also available so you can practise at home.

Lamai Muay Thai Camp   THAI BOXING
(✆08 7082 6970; www.lamaimuaythaicamp.com; 82/2 Moo3, Lamai; 1-day/1-week training sessions 250/1250B; ⏰7am-8pm) The island's best *moo-ay tai* (also spelt *muay thai*) training (best for the seriously serious) is at this place catering to beginners as well as those wanting to hone their skills. There's also a well-equipped gym for boxers and non-boxers who want to up their fitness levels.

Kiteboarding Asia   KITEBOARDING
(✆08 3643 1627; www.kiteboardingasia.com; 1-/3-day courses 4000/11,000B) With two locations – one on Hua Thanon in the south of the island for May to October winds and the other at Na Thon on the west side for November to March winds – this pro place will get you kitesurfing on flat shallow water. The instructors here claim that Ko Samui is the best place in the country to learn the sport.

Sleeping
The island's array of sleeping options is overwhelming. If you're looking to splurge, there

is definitely no shortage of top-end resorts sporting extravagant bungalows, charming spas, private infinity pools and first-class dining. Bo Phut, on the island's northern coast, has a charming collection of boutique lodging – the perfect choice for midrange travellers. Backpack-toting tourists will have to look a little harder, but budget digs do pop up once in a while along all of the island's beaches.

Most visitors arrive having prebooked their resort but outside of peak season most midrange and budget places offer discounted walk-in rates equal or better to what you'll find online. Calling around in advance rather than surfing the web is the best way to find a deal if you don't want to schlep your stuff on foot from place to place. We've compiled a list of our favourite places to stay but the following inventory is by no means exhaustive.

Private villa services have become quite popular in recent years; www.gosamuivillas.com is a good place to book the luxury variety.

🛏 Hat Chaweng

Busy, bodaciously flaxen Chaweng is packed wall-to-wall with every level of accommodation from cheap backpacker pads advertised with cardboard signs (some as low as 300B for a double) to futuristic villas with private swimming pools – and these might be just across the street from each other. The northern half of the beach is the biggest party zone and resorts in this region will be in earshot of the thumping bass emanating from Ark Bar at the centre of it all. If you're hoping for early nights, pick a resort near the southern half of the beach or bring earplugs.

Lucky Mother GUESTHOUSE $
(Map p534; ☑ 0 7723 0931; 60 Moo 2; r & bungalows 800-1500B; ❋ 🛜) First, let's take a moment to giggle at the name. OK now let's appreciate the action-filled beachfront location, clean, bright, polished cement detailed rooms and popular bar out front that's prime for mingling with your toes in the sand. In all it's a great deal if you avoid the sour lemons on staff.

P Chaweng HOTEL $
(Map p534; ☑ 0 7723 0684; r from 600B; ste 1000B; ❋ @ 🛜) Off the main drag and a short walk to the beach, this vine-covered cheapie has extra-clean, pink-tiled or wood-floored spacious rooms, all decked out with air-con, hot water, TVs and fridges. It's a 10-minute walk to the bar zone and not particularly hip, but good luck finding a better room in the area for this price.

Loft Samui HOSTEL $
(Map p534; ☑ 0 7741 3420; www.theloftsmaui.com; r 700-1500B; ❋ @ 🛜) The row house doubles and deluxe rooms in the new building have a warm, butter-yellow, near-Mexican style, but avoid the darker, mustier bungalows across from reception. All walls are thin and despite the distance from the 'scene' (about 10 minutes' walking) this place is popular with partiers, so bring earplugs if you're an early sleeper.

Queen Boutique Resort HOTEL $
(Map p534; ☑ 0 7741 3148; queensamui@yahoo.com; r 700-1500B; ❋ @ 🛜) The Queen offers up boutique sleeps at backpacker prices. Reception is friendly and the clean well-equipped (with air-con, TVs and DVD) rooms get style points from colourful throw pillows and modern Asian art on the walls. However, most are boxy and many of them windowless.

Pott Guesthouse GUESTHOUSE $
(Map p534; r fan/air-con 300/500B; ❋ 🛜) The big, bright cement rooms all with attached hot-water bathrooms in this nondescript apartment block are a steal. Reception is at an unnamed restaurant on the main drag across the alley.

Akwa GUESTHOUSE $
(Map p534; ☑ 08 4660 0551; www.akwaguesthouse.com; r from 700B; ❋ @ 🛜) Akwa has a few funky rooms decorated with bright colours but there's little natural light and everything is a bit past its prime. There's no shortage of character, however, with teddy bears adorning each bed, quirky bookshelves stocked with DVDs and cartoon paintings all over.

Samui Hostel HOSTEL $
(Map p534; ☑ 08 9874 3737; dm 200B; ❋ @) It doesn't look like much from the front, but the three dorm rooms here are surprisingly spic and span and each has its own hot water bathroom and air-conditioning. The staff are sweet too.

★ Jungle Club BUNGALOW $$
(☑ 08 1894 2327; www.jungleclubsamui.com; huts 800-1800B, houses 2700-4500B; ❋ @ 🛜 ☒) The perilous drive up the slithering road

Hat Chaweng

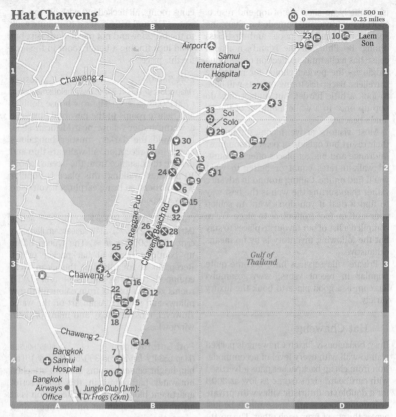

is totally worthwhile once you take in the incredible views from the top. This isolated mountain getaway is a huge hit among locals and tourists alike. There's a relaxed back-to-nature vibe – guests chill around the stunning horizon pool or catnap under the canopied roofs of an open-air *săh·lah* (often spelt as *sala*).

Call ahead for a pick-up – you don't want to spend your precious jungle vacation in a body cast.

Chaweng Garden Beach RESORT $$
(Map p534; ☎0 7796 0394; www.chawenggarden. com; r 2300-9500B; ❄@☎☲) There's a large variety of room types here from rather bland standards to a private beachfront pool villa. The best value is found in those such as the modern Asian-inspired 'Shinto' rooms and polished wood bungalows. The whole place is hidden in foliage and serviced by an extra-smiley staff.

Pandora Boutique Hotel RESORT $$
(Map p534; ☎0 7741 3801; www.pandora-samui. com; r 2940-4470B; ❄☎☲) As adorable as it is memorable, Pandora looks like it just fell out of a comic book – maybe *Tintin and the Mystery of Surprisingly Cheap Accommodation in Chaweng*? Rooms are outfitted with cheerful pastels, wooden mouldings and the occasional stone feature. It's about a five-minute walk to the beach.

Tango Beach Resort RESORT $$
(Map p534; ☎0 7742 2470; www.tangobeachsamui. com; r 1700-7400B; ❄@☎☲) Tango features a string of bungalows arranged along a teak boardwalk that meanders away from an excellent but busy stretch of beach. The dark tinted windows make the place look a little tacky from the outside (and the 1980s-era pool doesn't help) but bright paint and wood floors make the rooms feel fresh.

Hat Chaweng

Activities, Courses & Tours

Sleeping

Eating

Drinking & Nightlife

Entertainment

Ark Bar
RESORT $$

(Map p534; ☑0 7742 2047; www.ark-bar.com; r 1630-4200B; ✳🛜❄) You'll find two of every party animal at Ark Bar – frat boys, chilled-out hippies, teenagers, 40-somethings and so on. Contemporary, brightly painted rooms are staggering distance from the bar that pumps out techno all day and well into the night. Beds are hard but chances are you'll be too drunk to care.

★Library
RESORT $$$

(Map p534; ☑0 7742 2767; www.thelibrary.name; r from 9140B; ✳@🛜❄) This library is too cool for school. The entire resort is a sparkling white mirage accented with black trimming and slatted curtains. Besides the futuristic iMac computer in each page (rooms are 'pages' here), our favourite feature is the large monochromatic wall art – it glows brightly in the evening and you can adjust the colour to your mood.

Life-size statues are engaged in the act of reading, and if you too feel inclined to pick up a book, the on-site library houses an impressive assortment of colourful art and design books. The large rectangular pool is not to be missed – it's tiled in piercing shades of red, making the term 'bloodbath' suddenly seem appealing. It has an on-site restaurant (p542).

Buri Rasa Village
RESORT $$$

(Map p534; ☑0 7723 0222; samui.burirasa.com; r 4900-6900B; ✳🛜❄) Thai-style wooden doors lead to private villa patios and simple yet elegant rooms. This Zen-feeling place is beautifully landscaped with palms and frangipani, central, well-priced and on a good stretch of busy beach, but the real reason to stay here is the bend-over-backwards friendly and helpful service.

Baan Haad Ngam
RESORT $$$

(Map p534; ☑0 7723 1500; www.baanhaadngam. com; bungalows 6250-14,000B; ✳@🛜❄) Classy yet simple lime green rooms and villas are tucked into a veritable botanical garden cut with mini waterfalls and streams that lead to a small infinity pool that gazes over aqua sea. Its best asset, however, is its location, close to the action yet quiet and private.

Kirikayan Boutique Resort
RESORT $$$

(Map p534; ☑0 7733 2299; www.kirikayan.com; r from 6840B; ✳@🛜❄) Simple whites, lacquered teak and blazing red accents set the colour scheme at this small, hip address along Hat Chaweng's southern sands. Wander past thick palm trunks and sky-scraping foliage to find the relaxing pool deck at the back.

Centara Grand
RESORT $$$

(Map p534; ☑0 7723 0500; www.centralhotels resorts.com; r 8900-21,500B; ✳@🛜❄) Centara is a massive, manicured compound in the heart of Hat Chaweng, but the palm-filled property is so large you can safely escape the street-side bustle. Rooms are found in a hotel-like building that is conspicuously Western in theme and decor. Babysitting and family-friendly services abound. Check online for big discounts out of high season.

Baan Chaweng Beach Resort   RESORT $$$
(Map p534; ☑0 7742 2403; www.baanchaweng beachresort.com; bungalows 4500-13,600B; ❄@☎☀) A bit of luxury without the hefty bill, Baan Chaweng draws in families and retiree bargain-seekers who roast themselves on loungers along the lovely beach. The immaculate rooms are painted in various shades of peach and pear, with teak furnishings that feel both modern and traditional.

Hat Lamai

The central, powdery white area of Hat Lamai is packed with an amazing quantity of sunburned souls lounging on beach chairs, but head to the grainier northern or southern extremities and things get much quieter. Ban Lamai runs back from the main beach area. Unlike Hat Chaweng, the main party in Lamai takes place off the beach so the sand here is generally free of a dance-beat soundtrack. However, the party scene that is here, mostly along the town's main drag and its smaller arteries, is of the seedier bar-girl-oriented variety.

Beer's House   BUNGALOW $
(☑0 7723 0467; 161/4 Moo 4, Lamai North; bungalows 600-700B, r 1000B) One of the last of a dying breed on Ko Samui, this old-school-backpacker, low-key village of coconut bark huts sits right on a beautiful, sandy beach. Some huts have a communal toilet, but all have plenty of room to sling a hammock and laze the day away.

If the huts are too basic for you, check out the plain air-con rooms at Beer & Wine's Hut, across the road and away from the beach.

Amarina Residence   HOTEL $
(www.amarinaresidence.com; r 900-1200B; ❄☎) A two-minute walk to the beach, this excellent-value small hotel has two storeys of big, tastefully furnished, tiled rooms encircling the lobby and an incongruous dipping pool.

New Hut   BUNGALOW $
(☑0 7723 0437; newhutlamai@yahoo.co.th; Lamai North; huts 300-500B; ☎) A-frame huts right on the beach all share a big, clean block of bathrooms. There's a lively restaurant,

friendly staff and one of the most simple and happy backpacker vibes on the island.

Spa Resort   BUNGALOW $$
(☑0 7723 0855; www.spasamui.com; Lamai North; bungalows 1000-3500B; ❄☎) Programs at this practical, not glamorous spa include colonics, massage, aqua detox, hypnotherapy and yoga, just to name a few. The bathrooms leave a bit to be desired, but (colonics aside) who needs a toilet when you're doing a week-long fast? Accommodation books up quickly. Nonguests are welcome to partake in the programs and dine at the excellent (and healthy) restaurant.

★**Rocky Resort**   RESORT $$$
(☑0 7741 8367; www.rockyresort.com; Hua Thanon; r 6800-11,800B; ❄☎☀) Our favourite spot in Lamai (well, actually just south of Lamai), Rocky finds the right balance between an upmarket ambience and unpretentious, sociable atmosphere. During the quieter months the prices are a steal, since ocean views abound, and each room is furnished with beautiful Thai-inspired furniture that seamlessly incorporates a modern twist.

The pool has been carved in between a collection of boulders mimicking the rocky beach nearby (hence the name).

Banyan Tree Koh Samui   RESORT $$$
(☑0 7791 5333; www.banyantree.com/en/samui/overview; villas from 23,300B; ❄@☎☀) Occupying an entire bay, this sprawling over-the-top luxury delight encompasses dozens of pool villas hoisted above the foliage by spiderlike stilts. Golf carts zip around the grounds carrying jet-setters between the myriad dining venues and the gargantuan spa (which sports a relaxing rainforest simulator).

Samui Jasmine Resort   RESORT $$$
(☑0 7723 2446; 131/8 Moo 3, Lamai; r & bungalows 4600-12,000B; ❄☎☀) Smack dab in the middle of Hat Lamai, varnished-teak yet frilly Samui Jasmine is a great deal. Go for the lower-priced rooms – most have excellent views of the ocean and the crystal-coloured lap pool.

Choeng Mon

Choeng Mon is actually an area that holds several beaches that span the northeastern nub of the island. Samrong and Ton Son to the north are home to small communities and some of the most luxurious resorts in the world. Those with mortal budgets tend to stay on the beach at Choeng Mon proper whose perfect (although busy) half-moon of sand is considered by many to be the most beautiful beach on the island.

Ô Soleil
BUNGALOW $

(⚡0 7742 5232; osoleilbungalow@yahoo.fr; Choeng Mon; r fan/air-con from 500/700B; ❄🛜) Located in a sea of luxury resorts, Thai-Belgian family-run stalwart Ô Soleil offers a welcome scatter of budget concrete bungalows and semidetached rooms extending inland from a gorgeous stretch of sand. As long as your expectations keep in line with what you're paying, this simple place will charm you.

Honey Resort
RESORT $$

(⚡0 7742 7094; www.samuihoney.com; Choeng Mon; r 3500-6500B; ❄🛜⛵) At the quieter southern part of the beach, this small resort (with an equally small pool) isn't anything that special but it's nicer than some of the other mediocre offerings in this price range on this beach. Expect classic Zen-style rooms with black and white decor.

★ Six Senses Samui
RESORT $$$

(⚡0 7724 5678; www.sixsenses.com/hideaway-samui/index.php; Samrong; bungalows from 13,000B; ❄@🛜⛵) This hidden bamboo paradise is worth the once-in-a-lifetime splurge. Set along a rugged promontory, Six Senses strikes the perfect balance between opulence and rustic charm, and defines the term 'barefoot elegance'. Most of the villas have stunning concrete plunge pools and offer magnificent views of the silent bay below.

The regal, semi-outdoor bathrooms give the phrase 'royal flush' a whole new meaning. Beige golf buggies move guests between their hidden cottages and the stunning amenities strewn around the property – including a world-class spa and two excellent restaurants.

Tongsai Bay
RESORT $$$

(⚡0 7724 5480, 0 7724 5500; www.tongsaibay.co.th; Tong Son; ste 9800-34,000B; ❄🛜⛵) For serious pampering, head to this secluded luxury gem. Expansive and impeccably maintained, the hilly grounds make the cluster of bungalows look more like a small village. All the extra-swanky split-level suites have day-bed rest areas, gorgeous romantic decor, stunning views, large terraces and creatively placed bathtubs (you'll see).

Facilities include salt- and freshwater pools, a tennis court, the requisite spa, a dessert shop and also several restaurants.

Sala Samui
RESORT $$$

(⚡0 7724 5888; www.salasamui.com; Choeng Mon; r 6200B, villas 8400-20,100B; ❄@🛜⛵) Is the hefty price tag worth it? Definitely. The dreamy, modern design scheme is exquisite – clean whites and lacquered teaks are lavish throughout, while subtle turquoise accents draw on the colour of each villa's private plunge pool. It feels like a surreal white dream of a futeristic regal Asia.

🏖 Big Buddha Beach (Hat Bang Rak)

This area gets its moniker from the huge golden Buddha that acts as overlord from the small nearby quasi-island of Ko Fan. The western half of the beach is by far the best with its relatively empty stretch of white sand and although the main road runs just parallel so parts of the beach is buzzed by traffic. The closer you get to the busy pier areas, the coarser and browner the sand becomes and the murkier the water. Big Buddha Beach's proximity to the airport means some noise overhead but quick and cheap taxi rides if you're flying in or out.

Secret Garden Bungalows
BUNGALOW $$

(⚡tel, info 0 7724 5255; www.secretgarden.co.th; bungalows 750-1600B; ❄🛜) The deals here are no secret, so book in advance. This UK-run establishment has an excellent beach restaurant and bar and well-equipped, good-value yet simple bungalows in the eponymous garden. There's live music on Sundays when locals, expats and tourists come to chill out and imbibe, but it's fairly subdued the rest of the time.

★ Scent
RESORT $$$

(⚡0 7796 0123; www.thescenthotel.com; ste 8500-10,500B) Find a taste (and scent if you light your complimentary incense) of *Indochine* at this resort that recreates the elegance of 1940s and '50s colonial Asia. The tall grey concrete structure is cut by elongated teak framed windows and surrounds a courtyard swimming pool and ornamental trees and plants.

Guests choose between European, Chinese or Thai-Chinese style rooms but all are spacious and decorated with tasteful opulence. Catch a classic film in the 'tea foyer' to really get into the old time groove.

Prana

RESORT $$$

(✆ 0 7724 6362; www.pranaresorts.com; r 6650-13,100B; ❄🛜🏊) Sharp lines, polished cement and a skinny, rectangular infinity pool overlooking white sand make this place feel like the love child of an urban-chic upstairs lounge and a cushion-clad beach pad. Sophisticated bright rooms, a luxurious beachside spa and excellent service seal the deal.

🏛 Bo Phut

And now for something completely different. Bo Phut's Fisherman's Village is a collection of narrow Chinese shophouses that have been transformed into some of the island's best trendy (and often midrange) boutique hotels and eateries. The beach along most of this stretch, particularly the eastern part, is slim and coarse but it becomes whiter and lusher further west. The combination of pretty beach and gussied-up old village is beguiling.

Khuntai

GUESTHOUSE $

(Map p539; ✆ 0 7724 5118; r fan/air-con 600/750B; ❄🛜) A block away from the beach, right in the Fisherman's Village, Khuntai's massive 2nd-floor fan rooms are drenched in afternoon sunshine and sea breezes. All rooms have hot-water bathrooms, fridges and TVs. It's a local family run place with plenty of heart.

★Samui-Ley

GUESTHOUSE $$

(Map p539; ✆ 0 7724 5647; samuileyhouse@gmail.com; r 2300-2500B; ❄🛜) This tiny boutique guesthouse is shabby chic at its finest. Stylishly kistch wallpaper is paired with white walls, rag-woven rugs, paint-chipped furniture and retro Asian advert posters as well as modern art, checked and striped paint and more. Although it sounds headache-inducing, in fact the effect is soothing, especially with all the light pouring in from the sea-view terraces.

It's very laid-back and not a top choice for luxury hounds, but we love it.

Hacienda

GUESTHOUSE $$

(Map p539; ✆ 0 7724 5943; www.samui-hacienda.com; r 1000-3400B, f 3300-3900B; ❄🛜🏊) Polished terracotta and rounded archways give the entrance a Spanish mission motif. Similar decor permeates the adorable rooms, which sport touches such as pebbled bathroom walls and translucent bamboo lamps. Hacienda Suites, the overflow property a few doors down, holds the cheaper 'eco' rooms which are minuscule and mostly window-less, but still clean and comfortable. The tiny rooftop pool has gorgeous ocean views.

The Lodge

HOTEL $$

(Map p539; ✆ 0 7742 5337; www.lodgesamui.com; r 2300-3000B; ❄🛜) The Lodge feels like a colonial hunting chalet with pale walls and dark wooden beams jutting across the ceiling, except it all looks out over blue-green sea. Each of the eight rooms has scores of wall hangings and a private balcony overlooking the beach; the 'pent-huts' on the top floor are particularly spacious.

You're really in the heart of the Fisherman's Village making this a lively spot but somehow still intimate. It's extremely popular so reservations are a must.

Eden

BUNGALOW $$

(Map p539; ✆ 0 7742 7645; www.edenbungalows.com; bungalows 1500-1900B; ❄🛜🏊) Eden is an exceptional find. The 10 bungalows and five rooms are all tucked away in a gorgeous tangle of garden with a small pool at its centre. Cheaper options are fairly plain but an upgrade gets you a stylish suite with yellow walls and naturalistic wood furniture. It's about a two-minute walk to the beach.

Cocooning

HOTEL $$

(Map p539; ✆ 08 5781 4107; cocooning.samui@hotmail.com; r/ste 1000/1800B; ❄🛜🏊) New owners have spiffed up this small hotel with teak windows aplenty, which let in lovely muted light. Decor is a tasteful mix of Thai and a touch of Ikea thanks to the Swedish half of the British/Swede ownership. Service is exceptionally friendly and you'll find yourself making friends around the little green plunge pool. The beach is but a skip away.

★Anantara

RESORT $$$

(Map p539; ✆ 0 7742 8300; samui.anantara.com; r 5300-18,600B; ❄@🛜🏊) Anantara's stunning palanquin entrance satisfies fantasies of a far-flung oriental kingdom. Clay and copper statues of grimacing jungle creatures abound on the property's wild acreage, while guests savour wild teas in an open-air pagoda, swim in the lagoonlike infinity-edged swimming pool or indulge in a relaxing spa treatment.

The new wing of adjacent whitewashed villas brings the resort up to another level of opulence and the whole place was upgraded in 2013.

Bo Phut

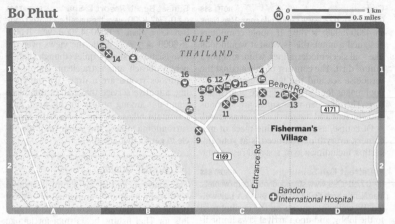

Bo Phut

Sleeping
1 Anantara	B1
2 Cocooning	C1
3 Eden	C1
4 Hacienda	C1
5 Khuntai	C1
6 Samui-Ley	C1
7 The Lodge	C1
8 Zazen	B1

Eating
9 69	C2
10 Karma Sutra	C1
11 Shack Bar & Grill	C1
12 Starfish & Coffee	C1
13 The Hut	D1
14 Zazen	B1

Drinking & Nightlife
15 Billabong Surf Club	C1
16 Coco Tam's	B1

Zazen RESORT $$$

(Map p539; ☑ 0 7742 5085; www.samuizazen.com; r 6160-17,200B; ✿ @ 🛜 🐾) Welcome to one of the boutique-iest boutique resorts on Samui – every inch of this charming getaway has been thoughtfully and creatively designed. It's 'Asian minimalism meets modern roco-co' with a scarlet accent wall, terracotta goddesses, a dash of feng shui and a generous smattering of good taste.

Guests relax poolside or on loungers gently shaded by canvas parasols on the very best stretch of this beach. Even better, the service is as luxe as the setting.

🛏 Mae Nam & Bang Po

Mae Nam's slim stretch of white that slopes down to a calm, swimmable aqua sea is one of the island's prettiest. It's popular with families and older couples, that give it a quiet yet still vibrant ambience perfect for reading under the shade of a palm tree, sleeping and indulging in beach massages.

Bang Po, just around the tiny peninsula, is even quieter.

Shangri-la BUNGALOW $

(☑ 0 7742 5189; Mae Nam; bungalows fan/air-con from 500/1300B; ✿) A backpacker's Shangri La indeed – these are some of the cheapest huts around and they're on a sublime part of the beach. Grounds are sparsely landscaped but the basic concrete bungalows, all with attached bathrooms (only air-con rooms have hot water), are well-kept and the staff is pleasant.

Coco Palm Resort BUNGALOW $$

(☑ 0 7742 5095; www.cocopalmbeachresort.com; Mae Nam; bungalows 2500-9000B; ✿ 🛜 🐾) The huge array of bungalows at Coco Palm have been crafted with hard wood, bamboo and rattan touches. A rectangular pool is the centrepiece along the beach, and the price is right for a resortlike atmosphere. The cheapest choices are the furthest from the beach but even these are comfy and pleasant.

Code
HOTEL $$$

(☎0 7760 2122; www.samuicode.com; Mae Nam; ste 4300-7500B; ✳☎🛜❄) If Apple computers designed a hotel, this is what it would look like – all sleek modern lines, white and not a hint of dust. The contrast of this against the turquoise sea and the hotel's large infinity pool makes for a stunning piece of architecture. The all-ocean-view suites are spacious and efficient and the service is just as grand.

Of course, as with any fine piece of machinery, everything you need is at your fingertips, including a gym, spa and restaurant.

W Retreat Koh Samui
RESORT $$$

(☎0 7791 5999; www.starwoodhotels.com/whotels; Mae Nam; r from 13,000B; ✳@☎🛜❄) A bejewelled 'W' welcomes guests on the curling road to the lobby, and upon arrival jaws immediate drop while staring out over the glittering infinity pools and endless horizon. The trademark 'W glam' is palpable throughout the resort, which does its darnedest to fuse an urban vibe with tropical serenity. Do note that this hotel is on a hill and not on a beach.

Napasai By Orient Express
RESORT $$$

(☎0 7742 9200; www.napasai.com; Bang Po; r from 9100B; ✳@☎🛜❄) Gorgeously manicured grounds welcome weary travellers as they glide past grazing water buffalo and groundsmen donning cream-coloured pith helmets. A generous smattering of villas dot the expansive landscape – all sport traditional Thai-style decorations, from the intricately carved wooden ornamentation to streamers of luscious local silks.

West Coast

Largely the domain of Thai tourists, Samui's west coast has skinny beaches of grainy sand but the sunsets, sandy-bottom blue seas and views out to the Five Islands and the shadowy greens of the mainland more than make up for this. It's a welcome escape from the east-side bustle.

Am Samui
BUNGALOW $$

(☎0 7723 5165; www.amsamuiresort.com; Taling Ngam; bungalows 1600-6000B; ✳🛜❄) Cast modesty aside, spread your curtains wide, and welcome sunshine and sea views in through your floor-to-ceiling windows. Getting out of the main tourist areas to this private beach with fantastic sunset views means your baht goes miles further in terms of room quality. Expect quiet nights and a less manicured beach.

Sunset Beach Resort & Spa
RESORT $$$

(☎0 7742 8200; www.thesunsetbeachresort.com; Ban Taling Nam; r 6000-14,300B, villa 11,000-35,800B; ✳☎🛜❄) While the views over the Five Islands at sunset, quiet (though slightly pebbly) beach and extra-clean, simple yet luxurious rooms are a draw, it's the smiling, attentive service that makes this place stand out among resorts in this area. Free mountain bikes get you around the sleepy surrounding village, but you'll want a vehicle to get further afield.

South Coast

The southern end of Ko Samui is spotted with rocky headlands and smaller coves of pebble sand that are used more as parking lots for Thai fishing boats than for lounge chairs. It's a great area to take a leisurely cycle through coconut palm groves and small Thai villages that aren't ruled by tourism.

Easy Time
BUNGALOW $$

(☎0 7792 0110; www.easytimesamui.com; Phang Ka; villas 2100-3850B; ✳@☎🛜❄) Safely tucked away from the throngs of tourists, this little haven – nestled a few minutes' walk to the beach around a serene swimming pool – doesn't have well-oiled service so be prepared to be master of your own off-the-beaten-path getaway. Duplex villa units and a chic dining space create an elegant mood that is refreshingly unpretentious.

Elements
RESORT $$$

(☎0 7791 4678; www.elements-koh-samui.com; Phang Ka; r 8000-21,500B; ✳@☎🛜❄) Peaceful Elements occupies a lonely strand of palm-studded sand with views of the stunning Five Islands, and is the perfect place for a meditative retreat or quiet couples romantic getaway. Chic rooms are arranged in condo-like blocks while hidden villas dot the path down to the oceanside lounge area. Free kayaks and bikes plus excellent service add to the calm.

We were quoted walk-in rates over 50% below the rack rates we list above, so call ahead and try your luck.

✗ Eating

If you thought it was hard to pick a place to sleep, the island has even more options when it comes to dining. From roasted crickets to beluga caviar, Samui's got it and is not afraid to flaunt it.

SALT AND SPICE IN SOUTHERN THAI CUISINE

Don't say we didn't warn you: southern Thai cooking is undoubtedly the spiciest regional cooking style in a land of spicy regional cuisines. The food of Thailand's southern provinces also tends to be very salty, and seafood, not surprisingly, plays an important role, ranging from fresh fish that is grilled or added to soups, to pickled or fermented fish served as sauces or condiments.

Two of the principal crops in the south are coconuts and cashews, both of which find their way into a variety of dishes. In addition to these, southern Thais love their greens, and nearly every meal is accompanied by a platter of fresh herbs and veggies and a spicy 'dip' of shrimp paste, chillies, garlic and lime.

Dishes you are likely to come across in southern Thailand include the following:

➡ *Gaang đai blah* – An intensely spicy and salty curry that includes đai blah (salted fish stomach); much tastier than it sounds.

➡ *Gaang sôm* – Known as *gaang lěu·ang* (yellow curry) in central Thailand, this sour/spicy soup gets its hue from the liberal use of turmeric, a root commonly used in southern Thai cooking.

➡ *Gài tôrt hàht yài* – The famous deep-fried chicken from the town of Hat Yai gets its rich flavour from a marinade containing dried spices.

➡ *Kà·nŏm jeen nám yah* – This dish of thin rice noodles served with a fiery currylike sauce is always accompanied by a tray of fresh vegetables and herbs.

➡ *Kôo·a glîng* – Minced meat fried with a fiery curry paste is a southern staple.

➡ *Kôw yam* – A popular breakfast, this dish includes rice topped with sliced herbs, bean sprouts, dried prawns, toasted coconut and powdered red chilli, served with a sour/sweet fish-based sauce.

➡ *Pàt sà·đor* – This popular stir-fry of 'stink beans' with shrimp, garlic, chillies and shrimp paste is both pungent and spicy.

Influenced by the mainland, Samui is peppered with *kôw gaang* (rice and curry) shops, usually just a wooden shack displaying large metal pots of southern Thai-style curries. Folks pull up on their motorcycles, lift up the lids to survey the vibrantly coloured contents, and pick one for lunch. *Kôw gaang* shops are easily found along the Ring Rd (Rte 4169) and sell out of the good stuff by 1pm. Any build-up of local motorcycles is usually a sign of a good meal in progress.

The upmarket choices are even more numerous and although Samui's swank dining scene is laden with Italian options, visitors will have no problem finding flavours from around the globe. Lured by high salaries and spectacular weather, world-class chefs regularly make an appearance on the island.

✕ Hat Chaweng

Dozens of the restaurants on the 'strip' serve a mixed bag of local bites, international cuisine and greasy fast food. For the best ambience head to the beach, where many bungalow operators set up tables on the sand and have glittery fairy lights at night.

Laem Din Market　　　　　　MARKET $
(Map p534; dishes from 35B; ⊘ 4am-6pm, night market 6pm-2am) A busy day market, Laem Din is packed with stalls that sell fresh fruits, vegetables and meats and stock local Thai kitchens. Pick up a kilo of sweet green oranges or wander the stalls trying to spot the ingredients in last night's curry. For dinner, come to the adjacent night market and sample the tasty southern-style fried chicken and curries.

Ninja Crepes　　　　　　　　　THAI $
(Map p534; dishes from 75B; ⊘ 11am-midnight) Even though this basic food hall gets packed nightly and the multiple woks at the centre work double-time to keep the pace, the owners welcome and chat with nearly every one of their customers; it's a miracle of friendly service. The food, from Thai seafood and classics to sweet and savoury pancakes, is a delectable bargain.

Khaosan Restaurant & Bakery
INTERNATIONAL $

(Map p534; dishes from 70B; ☺ breakfast, lunch & dinner) From *filet mignon* to flapjacks and everything in between, this chow house is popular with those looking for cheap nosh. Hang around after your meal and catch a newly released movie on the big TV. It's everything you'd expect from a place called 'Khaosan'.

Wave Samui
INTERNATIONAL $

(Map p534; dishes from 60B; ☺ breakfast, lunch & dinner; 🛜) This jack-of-all-trades (guest-house-bar-restaurant) serves honest food at honest prices and fosters a travellers' ambience with an in-house library and a popular happy hour (3pm to 7pm). Basic, cheap rooms upstairs are 350B.

Page
ASIAN FUSION $$$

(Map p534; dishes 280-1650B; ☺ breakfast, lunch & dinner) If you can't afford to stay at the ultra-swanky Library (p535), have a meal at its beachside restaurant. The food is expensive (of course) but you'll receive glances from the beach bums on the beach as they try to figure out if you're a jet-setter or movie star. Lunch is a bit more casual and affordable, but you'll miss the designer lighting effects in the evening.

Dr Frogs
STEAKHOUSE $$$

(mains 220-1350B; ☺ lunch & dinner) Perched atop a rocky overlook, Dr Frogs combines incredible ocean vistas with delicious international flavours (namely Italian and Thai favourites). Delectable steaks and crab cakes, and friendly owners, put this spot near the top of our dining list.

Prego
ITALIAN $$$

(Map p534; www.prego-samui.com; mains 200-700B; ☺ dinner) This smart ministry of culinary style serves up fine Italian cuisine in a barely there dining room of cool marble and modern geometry. Reservations are accepted for seatings at 7pm and 9pm.

✗ Hat Lamai

As Samui's second-most populated beach, Hat Lamai has a surprisingly limited assortment of decent eateries when compared to Hat Chaweng next door. Most nights a few noodle and pancake stalls open up around the 'Lady Boxing' bars in the centre of town, and sell dishes from 50B that you can eat at outdoor plastic tables.

Hua Thanon Market
MARKET $

(dishes from 30B; ☺ 6am-6pm) Slip into the rhythm of this village market that's slightly south of Lamai; it's a window into the food ways of southern Thailand. Vendors shoo away the flies from the freshly butchered meat and housewives load bundles of vegetables into their baby-filled motorcycle baskets.

Follow the market road to the row of food shops delivering edible Muslim culture: chicken *biryani*, fiery curries or toasted rice with coconut, bean sprouts, lemon grass and dried shrimp.

Lamai Day Market
MARKET $

(dishes from 30B; ☺ 6am-8pm) Lamai's market is a hive of activity, selling food necessities and takeaway food. Visit the covered area to pick up fresh fruit or to see vendors shredding coconuts to make coconut milk. Or hunt down the ice-cream seller for homemade coconut ice cream. It's next door to a petrol station.

Radiance
INTERNATIONAL $$

(meals 100-400B; ☺ breakfast, lunch & dinner; 🛜🍽) Even if you're not staying at the Spa, or not even a vegetarian for that matter, healthy food never tasted this good. You'll find everything from an amazing raw *thom kha* (coconut green curry soup) to chocolate smoothies that can jive with anyone's dietary restrictions. Plus the semi-outdoor Zenlike setting is relaxing without a hint of pretension.

French Bakery
BAKERY $$

(set breakfasts from 120B; ☺ breakfast & lunch) The expat's breakfast choice is away from the main zone, near Wat Lamai on Rte 4169, but it's worth the 10-minute walk. Choose from fresh bread and pastries or unusually good set breakfasts that include fresh fruit and well-cooked eggs. Wash down your meal with espressos or a selection of teas.

Rocky's
INTERNATIONAL $$$

(dishes 300-950B; ☺ lunch & dinner) Easily the top dining spot on Lamai. Try the signature beef tenderloin with blue cheese – it's like sending your taste buds on a Parisian vacation. On Tuesdays diners enjoy a special Thai-themed evening with a prepared menu of local delicacies. Rocky's is at the like-named resort just south of Lamai.

✕ Choeng Mon & Big Buddha Beach (Hat Bang Rak)

Choeng Mon's lively main drag that runs parallel to this main northern beach has lots of eating options, although price tags are high even without the beach view. There are fewer eating options around Big Buddha Beach, west of Choeng Mon, where the setting is less glamorous, but prices are more reasonable.

BBC
INTERNATIONAL $$

(Big Buddha Beach; dishes 70-300B; ☺ breakfast, lunch & dinner) No, this place has nothing to do with *Dr Who* – BBC stands for Big Buddha Café. It's popular with the local expats, the international menu is large and there are exquisite ocean views from the patio.

Antica Locanda
ITALIAN $$

(www.anticasamui.com; Hat Bang Rak; dishes 170-280B; ☺ dinner) This friendly trattoria has pressed white tablecloths and caskets of Italian wine. Try the *vongole alla marinara* (clams in white wine) and don't forget to check out the succulent specials of the day.

Catcantoo
WESTERN $$

(http://catcantoo.net; Hat Bang Rak; mains 90-350B; ☺ breakfast, lunch & dinner) Enjoy a bargain-basement breakfast (99B) in the morning, succulent ribs at noon, or shoot some pool later in the day.

★ Dining On The Rocks
ASIAN FUSION $$$

(☏ 0 7724 5678; reservations-samui@sixsenses.com; Choeng Mon; menus from 2200B; ☺ dinner) Samui's ultimate dining experience takes place on nine cantilevered verandahs of weathered teak and bamboo that yawn over the gulf. After sunset (and wine), guests feel like they're dining on a barge set adrift on a starlit sea. Each dish on the six-course prix-fixe menu is the brainchild of the cooks who regularly experiment with taste, texture and temperature.

If you're celebrating a special occasion, you'll have to book well in advance if you want to sit at 'table 99' (the honeymooners' table) positioned on a private terrace. Dining On The Rocks is at the isolated Six Senses Samui.

✕ Bo Phut

The Fisherman's Village is the nicest setting for a meal but you'll find heaps of cheaper options on the road leading inland towards the main road.

The Hut
THAI $

(Map p539; mains 80-300B; ☺ dinner) You'll find basic Thai specialities at reasonable prices (for the area) as well as more expensive fresh seafood treats. If you're a fisherman this is the place to get your own catch cooked up. There are only about a dozen tables and they fill fast so get here early or late if you don't want to wait.

★ 69
THAI FUSION $$

(Map p539; mains 179-550B; ☺ 11am-11pm Mon-Thu, 6-11pm Fri; 🖘) Imagine the best Thai green curry you ever had stuffed inside an Indian roti and topped with fresh mango – and this is just the beginning. Vivian is a food genius who is constantly coming up with creative twists on Thai favourites and she'll even encourage you to come up with your own ideas as you order.

The roadside setting isn't the best but the decor is as *vavoom* as the food: a cabaret of sequined tablecloths, bouquets of feathers and hanging tassels.

Karma Sutra
INTERNATIONAL $$

(Map p539; mains 180-700B; ☺ breakfast, lunch & dinner; 🖘) A haze of purples and pillows, this charming chow spot straddles the heart of Bo Phut's Fisherman's Village and serves up very good international and Thai eats. Try the Mediterranean starter plate (300B), a beautifully arranged tray of olive tapenades, marinated peppers, eggplant caviar and more.

Starfish & Coffee
THAI $$

(Map p539; mains 150-280B; ☺ breakfast, lunch & dinner) This streamer-clad eatery was probably named after the Prince song, since we couldn't find any starfish on the menu (there's loads of coffee though). Evenings feature standard Thai fare and sunset views of rugged Ko Pha-Ngan.

Shack Bar & Grill
STEAKHOUSE $$$

(Map p539; www.theshackgrillsamui.com; mains 450-800B; ☺ dinner) With hands-down the best steaks on the island, the Shack imports the finest cuts of meat from Australia and slathers them in a rainbow of tasty sauces from red wine to blue cheese. Booth seating and jazz over the speakers give the joint a distinctly Western vibe, though you'll find all types of diners coming here to splurge.

'WALKING STREET' NIGHT MARKETS

The most fun dining experiences on Ko Samui are on 'Walking Streets', where once (or more) per week each beach village sets up a food-filled marketplace where you can sample local delicacies at hawker stalls, shop for crafts and trinkets and mingle with tourists and locals. All the markets are on or near the host village's main drag so they're hard to miss, and they all start setting up around 4pm to 5pm and run till 11pm or midnight. If you want to avoid the crowds count on arriving before 6pm or after about 10pm.

This was the schedule at the time of research but the popularity of these markets means that some are considering opening more frequently:

➡ **Ban Chaweng** Every night except Friday and Sunday. This is the biggest market with tonnes of food and seating (which is still hard to nab during peak hours)

➡ **Ban Lamai** Sunday

➡ **Ban Meanam** Thursday

➡ **Bo Phut** Friday

➡ **Ban Choeng Mon** Friday

Zazen ASIAN FUSION **$$$**
(Map p539; dishes 540-900B; set menu from 1300B; ☺lunch & dinner) The chef describes the food as 'organic and orgasmic', and the ambient 'yums' from elated diners confirm the latter. This romantic dining experience comes complete with ocean views, dim candle lighting and soft music. Thai dancers animate things on Thursday and Sunday nights. Reservations recommended.

✗ Mae Nam & Bang Po

Mae Nam has tonnes of eating options from beach-side, palm-thatch and driftwood affairs serving a mix of Thai, Western and seafood dishes to classier places tucked along the inland, lily-pad pond-dotted tangle of roads. It's a lovely place to wander and find your own surprises.

Bang Po Seafood SEAFOOD **$$**
(Bang Po; dishes from 100B; ☺dinner) A meal at Bang Po Seafood is a test for the taste buds. It's one of the only restaurants that serves traditional Ko Samui fare: recipes call for ingredients such as raw sea urchin roe, baby octopus, sea water, coconut and local turmeric.

Farmer INTERNATIONAL **$$$**
(☑0 7744 7222; Mae Nam; mains 350-1000B; ☺lunch & dinner) Magically set in a rice field, the Farmer is a refreshing change of setting and a romantic one at that, especially when the candlelight flickers on a clear starry night. The mostly European-inspired food is tasty and well-presented and there's a free

pick-up for nearby beaches since this place is far from the main tourist areas.

✗ West & South Coasts

The quiet west coast features some of the best seafood on Samui. Na Thon has a giant **day market** on Th Thawi Ratchaphakdi – it's worth stopping by to grab some snacks before your ferry ride.

★Ging Pagarang SEAFOOD **$**
(Thong Tanote; meals from 50B; ☺11.30am-8pm) Locals know this is one of the island's best beachside places to sample authentic Samui-style seafood. It's simple and family-run, but the food and views are extraordinary. Try the sea algae salad with crab, fried dried octopus with coconut or the spectacular fried fish or prawns with lemon grass. The English translations on the menu will keep you giggling.

About Art & Craft Café VEGETARIAN **$$**
(Na Thon; dishes 80-180B; ☺breakfast & lunch;) An artistic oasis in the midst of hurried Na Thon, this cafe serves an eclectic assortment of healthy and wholesome food, gourmet coffee and, as the name states, art and craft, made by the owner and her friends. Relaxed and friendly, this is also a gathering place for Samui's dwindling population of bohemians and artists.

Five Islands SEAFOOD **$$$**
(www.thefiveislands.com; Taling Ngam; dishes 250-630B; tours not incl/incl meal 3500/6900B; ☺lunch & dinner) Five Islands offers Samui's most unique (yet pricey) eating experience.

First, a long-tail boat will take you out into the turquoise sea to visit the haunting Five Sister Islands, where you'll learn about the ancient art of harvesting bird nests to make bird's-nest soup, a Chinese delicacy. When you return a deluxe meal is waiting for you on the beach.

Lunch tours departs around 10am, and the dinner programs leave around 3pm. Customers are also welcome to dine without going on the tour and vice versa.

🍷 Drinking & Nightlife

Samui's biggest party spot is, without a doubt, noisy Hat Chaweng. Lamai and Bo Phut come in second and third respectively, while the rest of the island is generally quiet, as the drinking is usually focused around self-contained resort bars.

🍸 Hat Chaweng & Lamai

Making merry in Chaweng is a piece of cake. Most places are open until 2am and there are a few places that go strong all night long. Soi Green Mango has loads of girly bars. Soi Colibri and Soi Reggae Pub are raucous as well.

Every Saturday night around dinner hours it's lady boxing time at Lamai's thus named 'Lady Boxing' bars, when two bar girls duke it out in the ring after weeks of training. The rest of the week the girls writhe and dance at these central open-air bars, which is particularly depressing when there are no clients.

Beach Republic   BAR
(www.beachrepublic.com; 176/34 Moo 4, Hat Lamai) Recognised by its yawning thatch-patched awnings, Beach Republic could be the poster-child of a made-for-TV, beachside, booze swilling holiday. There's a wading pool, comfy lounge chairs, an endless cocktail list and even a hotel if you never, ever want to leave the party. The Sunday brunches here are legendary.

Ark Bar   BAR
(Map p534; www.ark-bar.com; Hat Chaweng) Drinks are dispensed from the multicoloured bar draped in paper lanterns, guests recline on loungers on the beach, and the party is on day and night. If you ever dreamed of being part of an MTV spring break special, well remember this *is* Thailand, but it's getting awfully similar.

Bar Solo   BAR
(Map p534; Hat Chaweng) A future-fitted outdoor beer hall in an urban setting with sleek cubist decor and a cocktail list that doesn't scream holiday hayseed. The evening drink specials lure in the front-loaders preparing for a late, late night at the dance clubs on Soi Solo and Soi Green Mango.

Tropical Murphy's Irish   BAR
(Map p534; Hat Chaweng) A popular *fa·ràng* (Westerner) joint, Tropical Murphy's dishes out steak-and-kidney pie, fish and chips, lamb chops and Irish stew (mains 60B to 300B). Come night-time, the live music kicks on and this place turns into the most popular Irish bar on Ko Samui (yes, there are a few).

Green Mango   BAR
(Map p534; Hat Chaweng) This place is so popular it has an entire soi named after it. Samui's favourite power drinking house is very big, very loud and very *fa·ràng*. Green Mango has blazing lights, expensive drinks and masses of sweaty bodies swaying to dance music.

Reggae Pub   BAR
(Map p534; Hat Chaweng) This fortress of fun sports an open-air dance floor with music spun by foreign DJs. It's a towering two-storey affair with long bars, pool tables and a live-music stage. The whole place doubles as a shrine to Bob Marley.

🍷 Northern & West Coast Beaches

Woo Bar   BAR
(Mae Nam) The W Retreat's signature lobby bar gives the word 'swish' a whole new meaning with cushion-clad pods of seating plunked in the middle of an expansive infinity pool that stretches out over the infinite horizon. This is, without a doubt, the best place on Samui for a sunset cocktail. On Monday nights get two-for-the-price-of-one mojitos.

Nikki Beach   BAR
(www.nikkibeach.com/kohsamui; Lipa Noi) The acclaimed luxury brand has brought its international *savoir faire* to the secluded west coast of Ko Samui. Expect everything you would from a chic address in St Barts or St Tropez: haute cuisine, chic decor and gaggles of jet-setters. Themed brunch and dinner specials keep the masses coming

POP'S CULTURE: LIFE AS A LADYBOY

Pop, age 45, is what Thais call a *gà·teu·i*, usually referred to as a 'ladyboy' in English. Thailand's transgender population is the subject of many debates and conversations, especially among tourists. Although tolerance is widespread in Buddhist Thailand, concealed homophobia prevails – for *gà·teu·i*, this can be a challenging life, with the entertainment and sex industries the only lucrative career avenues. We spent the day with Pop and got the skinny on what life was really like as a member of Thailand's oft-talked-about 'third sex'.

Let's start with a question that many tourists in Thailand would like to ask: why does there seem to be so many ga·teu·i in Thailand?

Well, that's like asking me why I am a ladyboy! I have no idea. I didn't ask to have these feelings. I think the more important thing to notice is why there are so many ladyboys in the cabaret or sex industry. First, however, let me start by staying that the word *gà·teu·i* is the informal way of saying 'person with two sexes'; the term *pôo yĭng kâhm pêt* is generally more polite. Also, *gà·teu·i* is strictly reserved for people who still have male body parts but dress as female, so I am not technically *gà·teu·i* anymore.

Most tourists think that there are tonnes of ladyboys in Thailand because they are in places that many tourists visit. Yes, some ladyboys want to be cabaret dancers, just like some women want to be cabaret dancers, but most of them don't. These types of jobs are the only ones available to ladyboys, and the pay is lousy. Life is not as 'Hollywood' for a ladyboy as it may seem on stage. Most ladyboys don't have the chance to have a job that is respected by the community. We are not allowed to become doctors or psychologists and most corporations do not allow ladyboy employees because they don't want *gà·teu·i* to be associated with their company's image. Since many of us cannot have proper jobs, many ladyboys drop out of school at a young age, and lately this educational gap in the culture has become huge. Ladyboys work in the sex industry because they aren't given the opportunity to make a lot of money doing something else. I feel like a second-class citizen; we are not allowed to use male *or* female bathrooms! I used to have to climb 14 flights of stairs to use the special ladyboys' bathroom at my old job! Also, Thai law states that my ID cards and passport must always have an 'M' for male because the definition of a female in Thailand is someone who can bear children. It's hard for me to leave the country because my passport says 'male' but I look like a female. They will never let me through security because it looks like a fraudulent passport.

How does one tell the difference between a ladyboy and a woman?

Sometimes it's really hard to tell...a ladyboy can be more beautiful than a woman! There is no set way to figure it out, unless you ask them for their ID card. These days, doctors are really starting to perfect the operations, and the operations are expensive – mine was 150,000B! I had the 'snip', then I had breast implants, my Adam's apple was shaved off, and I also had a nose job (I didn't like my old nose anyway). Other operations available include silicone implants in the hips, jaw narrowing, cheekbone shaving and chin sculpting – to make it rounder. But before anyone can have an operation, you have to have a psych evaluation. The operation was extremely painful. I spent seven days in the hospital and it took me about two months to fully recover. Younger patients tend to heal faster – I was about 40 years old when I had the operation.

What do you feel is the biggest misconception about gà·teu·i?

This is an easy question. The biggest misconception is that we are all promiscuous whores and liars. Like any human being, we are just looking for love. It is true that many ladyboys do try to trick the people around them, but this is because they are afraid of being rejected for who they really are. Also, many of them lie because they desperately want to be real women, but they will never be real women. I know that – that's why I always show the real me – I am comfortable with who I am. I wish everyone else would be too.

As told to Brandon Presser

throughout the week, and sleek bungalow accommodation is also on offer.

Coco Tam's
BAR

(Map p539; Bo Phut; shisha pipes 500B) Plop yourself on a beanbag on the sand, order a giant cocktail served in a jar and take a toke on a shisha (water pipe). It's a bit pricey, but this boho, beach bum-chic spot oozes relaxation. There are fire dancers most nights.

Billabong Surf Club
BAR

(Map p539; Bo Phut) Billabong's all about Aussie Rules football – it's playing on the TV and the walls are smothered with memorabilia from Down Undah. There are great views of Ko Pha-Ngan and hearty portions of ribs and chops to go with your draught beer.

☆ Entertainment

Moulin Rouge
CABARET

(Map p534; Hat Chaweng) This flashy joint offers free *gà·teu·i* (ladyboys; also spelled *kàthoey*) cabaret every night at 11pm and attracts a mixed clientele of both sexes. Other ladyboys loiter out front and try to drag customers in, so to speak.

ℹ Information

DANGERS & ANNOYANCES

The rate of road accident fatalities on Ko Samui is quite high. This is mainly due to the large number of tourists who rent motorcycles only to find out that the winding roads, sudden tropical rains and frenzied traffic can be lethal. If you decide to rent a motorcycle, protect yourself by wearing a helmet, and ask for one that has a plastic visor.

Beach vendors are registered with the government and should all be wearing a numbered jacket. No peddler should cause an incessant disturbance – seek assistance if this occurs.

EMERGENCY

Tourist Police (☑ 0 7742 1281, emergency 1155) Based at the south of Na Thon.

IMMIGRATION

Located about 2km south of Na Thon is Ko Samui's **Immigration Office** (☑ 0 7742 1069; ☺ 8.30am-noon & 1-4.30pm Mon-Fri). Officials here tend to issue the minimum rather than maximum visa extensions. During our visits here we've watched dozens of tourists wait through exhausting lines only to be curtly denied an extension for no particular reason. On a particularly bad day expect extensions to take the entire afternoon.

INTERNET ACCESS

There are countless places all over the island for internet access, even at the less popular beaches. Prices range from 1B to 2B per minute. Keep an eye out for restaurants that offer complimentary wi-fi service. Most accommodation offers a wi-fi connection; ironically you'll pay extra for it at high-end hotels.

MEDIA

The **Siam Map Company** (www.siammap.com) puts out quarterly booklets including a *Spa Guide, Dining Guide,* and an annual directory, which lists thousands of companies and hotels on the island. Its *Siam Map Company Samui Guide Map* is fantastic, free and easily found throughout the island. Also worth a look is the **Samui Navigator** (www.samuinavigaot.com) pamphlet. **Essential** (www.essential-samui) is a pocket-sized pamphlet focused on promoting Samui's diverse activities. **Samui Guide** (www.samuiguide.com) looks more like a magazine and features mostly restaurants and attractions.

MEDICAL SERVICES

Ko Samui has four private hospitals, all near Chaweng's Tesco-Lotus supermarket on the east coast (where most of the tourists tend to gather). The government hospital (Samui Hospital) in Na Thon has seen significant improvements in the past couple of years but the service is still a bit grim because funding is based on the number of Samui's legal residents (which doesn't take into account the many illegal Myanmar workers).

Bandon International Hospital (Map p539; ☑ 0 7742 5840, emergency 0 7742 5748)

Bangkok Samui Hospital (Map p534; ☑ 0 7742 9500, emergency 0 7742 9555) Your best bet for just about any medical problem.

Hyperbaric Chamber (☑ 0 7742 7427; Big Buddha Beach) The island's dive medicine specialists.

Samui International Hospital (Map p534; ☑ 0 7742 2272; www.sih.co.th; Hat Chaweng) Emergency ambulance service is available 24 hours and credit cards are accepted. It's near the Amari Resort in Hat Chaweng.

MONEY

Changing money isn't a problem on the east and north coasts, and in Na Thon. Multiple banks and foreign-exchange booths offer daily services and there's an ATM. You should not have to pay credit card fees as you do on neighbouring Ko Tao.

POST

In several parts of the island there are privately run post-office branches charging a small commission. You can almost always leave your stamped mail with your accommodation.

ℹ️ RENTAL SCAMS

Even if you escape unscathed from a motorbike riding experience (or hire a car), some shops will claim that you damaged your rental and will try to extort some serious cash. The best way to avoid this is to take copious photos of your vehicle at the time of rental, making sure the person renting you the vehicle sees you do it (they will be less likely to make false claims against you if they know you have photos). If they still make a claim against you, keep your cool. Losing your temper won't help you win the argument and could significantly escalate the problem. The situation is just as bad on Ko Pha-Ngan, a bit less so on Ko Tao.

If things get really bad call the tourist police (p547), not the regular police.

Main Post Office Near the TAT office; not always reliable.

TOURIST INFORMATION

Tourism Authority of Thailand (TAT; ☑ 0 7742 0504; Na Thon; ⊙ 8.30am-4.30pm) At the northern end of Na Thon; this office is friendly, helpful and has handy brochures and maps, although travel agents throughout the island can provide similar information.

ℹ️ Getting There & Away

AIR

Ko Samui's airport is in the northeast of the island near Big Buddha Beach. **Bangkok Airways** (www.bangkokair.com) operates flights roughly every 30 minutes between Samui and Bangkok's Suvarnabhumi International Airport (50 minutes). Bangkok Airways also flies direct from Samui to Phuket, Pattaya, Chiang Mai, Singapore and Hong Kong. **Firefly** (www.fireflyz.com.my) operates direct flights from Ko Samui to Kuala Lumpur's Subang airport.

There is a **Bangkok Airways Office** (Map p534; ☑ 0 7742 0519, 0 7742 0512) in Hat Chaweng and another at the **airport** (Map p534; ☑ 0 7742 5011). The first (at 6am) and last (10pm) flights of the day are always the cheapest.

During the high season, make your flight reservations far in advance as seats often sell out. If the Samui flights are full, try flying into Surat Thani from Bangkok and taking a short ferry ride to Samui instead. Flights to Surat Thani are generally cheaper than a direct flight to the island, although they are much more of a hassle.

BOAT

To reach Samui, the four main piers on the mainland are Ao Ban Don, Tha Thong, Don Sak and Khanom – Tha Thong (in central Surat) and Don Sak being the most common. On Samui, the three oft-used ports are Na Thon, Mae Nam and Big Buddha Beach. Expect complimentary taxi transfers with high-speed ferry services.

To/From the Mainland

There are frequent boat departures between Samui and the mainland. Two options are the high-speed **Lomprayah** (☑ 077 4277 656; www.lomprayah.com; 450B), which departs from Na Thon, and the slower, stinkier **Raja** (☑ 02 2768 2112; www.rajaferryport.com) car ferry (150B), which departs from Thong Yang. Ferries take one to five hours, depending on the boat. A couple of these departures can connect with the train station in Phun Phin (for a nominal extra fee). The slow night boat to Samui (200B) leaves from central Surat Thani each night at 11pm, reaching Na Thon around 5am. It returns from Na Thon at 9pm, arriving at around 3am. Watch your bags on this boat.

To/From Ko Pha-Ngan & Ko Tao

There are almost a dozen daily departures between Ko Samui and Thong Sala on the west coast of Ko Pha-Ngan and many of these continue on to Ko Tao. These leave from the Na Thon, Mae Nam or Big Buddha Beach pier, take from 20 minutes to one hour and cost 200 to 300B to Ko Pha-Ngan, depending on the boat.

To go directly to Hat Rin, the *Haad Rin Queen* goes back and forth between Hat Rin and Big Buddha Beach four times a day. The voyage takes 50 minutes and costs 200B.

Also for Hat Rin and the more remote east coast beaches of Ko Pha-Ngan, the small and rickety *Thong Nai Pan Express* runs once a day at noon from Mae Hat on Ko Samui to Hat Rin and then up the east coast, stopping at all the beaches as far as Thong Nai Pan Noi. Prices range from 200B to 400B, depending on the destination. The boat won't run in bad weather.

BUS & TRAIN

A bus-ferry combo is more convenient than a train-ferry package for getting to Ko Samui because you don't have to switch transportation in Phun Phin. However, the trains are much more comfortable and spacious – especially at night. If you prefer the train, you can get off at Chumphon and catch the Lomprayah catamaran service the rest of the way.

Several services offer these bus-boat combo tickets, the fastest and most comfortable being the Lomprayah which has two daily departures from Bangkok at 6am and 9pm and two from Samui to Bangkok at 8am and 12.30pm. The total voyage takes about 13½ hours and costs 1450B.

Getting Around

You can rent motorcycles (and bicycles) from almost every resort on the island. The going rate is 200B per day, but for longer periods try to negotiate a better rate.

Drivers of *sŏrng·tăa·ou* (pick-up trucks) love to try to overcharge you, so it's always best to ask a third party for current rates, as they can change with the season. These vehicles run regularly during daylight hours. It's about 50B to travel between beaches, and no more than 100B to travel halfway across the island. Figure about 20B for a five-minute ride on a motorcycle taxi.

Taxi service is quite chaotic due to the plethora of cabs. In the past taxi fares were unwieldy; these days prices are more standardised across the islands (though fares are still ridiculously inflated compared to Bangkok). Taxis typically charge around 500B for an airport transfer. Some Hat Chaweng travel agencies can arrange minibus taxis for less.

Ko Pha-Ngan   เกาะพะงัน

POP 12,500

Slacker, hippie-at-heart Ko Pha-Ngan has become so synonymous with the wild and massive Full Moon Party on Hat Rin that the rest of the island – and even Hat Rin outside of full moon week – gets forgotten. It's a strange juxtaposition where for one week the island has some 30,000 people crammed on one beach partying their minds out and then off they all go on the next boat, leaving the beaches and accommodations half empty. It's at this time that budgeting serenity seekers can retreat into a fog (perhaps with a slight herbal scent) of the backpacker days of old and nab a fan-cooled beach shack from 400B (on the northern beaches at least). This will probably change quickly with the imminent opening of the island's airport in late 2014, but for now this exceptionally gorgeous

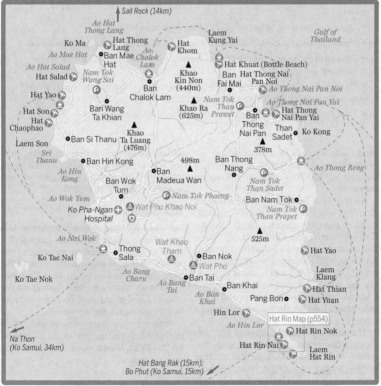

Ko Pha-Ngan

THE TEN COMMANDMENTS OF FULL MOON FUN

No one knows exactly when or how these crazy parties started – many believe they began in 1987 or 1988 as someone's 'going away party', but none of that is relevant now. Today, thousands of bodies converge monthly on the kerosene-soaked sands of Sunrise Beach for an epic trance-a-thon. Crowds can reach an outrageous 40,000 partiers during high season, while the low season still sees a respectable 5000 pilgrims.

If you can't make your trip coincide with a full moon but still want to cover yourself in fluorescent paint, fear not – enterprising locals have organised a slew of other reasons to get sloshed. There are Black Moon Parties (at Ban Khai), Half Moon Parties (at Ban Tai) and Moon-set Parties (at Hat Chaophao) just to name a few.

Some critics claim the party is starting to lose its carefree flavour, especially after increasing violence and the fact that the island's government now charges a 100B entrance fee to partygoers (the money goes towards needed beach cleaning and security). Despite changes, the night of the full moon is still the ultimate partying experience, as long as one follows the unofficial Ten Commandments of Full Moon fun:

➡ Thou shalt arrive in Hat Rin at least three days early to nail down accommodation during the pre-full moon rush of backpackers.

➡ Thou shalt double-check the party dates as sometimes they coincide with Buddhist holidays and are rescheduled.

➡ Thou shalt secure all valuables, especially when staying in budget bungalows.

➡ Thou shalt savour some delicious fried fare in Chicken Corner before the revelry begins.

➡ Thou shalt wear protective shoes during the sandy celebration, unless thou wants a tetanus shot.

➡ Thou shalt cover thyself with swirling patterns of neon body paint.

➡ Thou shalt visit Mellow Mountain or the Rock for killer views of the heathens below.

➡ Thou shalt not sample the drug buffet, nor shalt thou swim in the ocean under the influence of alcohol.

➡ Thou shalt stay in a group of two or more people, especially if thou art a woman, and especially when returning home at the end of the evening.

➡ Thou shalt party until the sun comes up and have a great time.

island is in a sleepy sweet spot where you can even find a solid bungalow on Hat Rin for around 1000B outside of full moon mania.

Ko Pha-Ngan has plenty to offer the more clean-cut, comfort-seeking traveller as well; its peace and quiet make it a great choice for families. Remote Hat Thong Nai Pan Noi in particular feels like a miniature version of Ko Samui with its elegant resorts fronted by rows of cushion-clad beach loungers, while the easier-to-access west coast has attracted a handful of new upscale resorts and a few older places have been revamped to attract a more ritzy market.

The phrase 'private infinity pool' and 'personal butler' may soon be heard more frequently than 'magic milkshake' and 'another whisky bucket please'. But whatever happens, chances are that the vast inland jungle

will continue to feel undiscovered, and there will still be plenty of stunning, secluded bays where you can string up a hammock and watch the tide roll in. Enjoy.

◉ Sights

For those who tire of beach-bumming, this large jungle island has many natural features to explore including mountains, waterfalls and, most importantly, some of the most spectacular beaches in all of Thailand.

There are many waterfalls throughout the island's interior, although most are reduced to a trickle during the dry season.

Remember to change out of your beach clothes when visiting one of the 20 wát on Ko Pha-Ngan. Most temples are open during daylight hours.

Nam Tok Than Sadet WATERFALL

These falls feature boulders carved with the royal insignia of Rama V, Rama VII and Rama IX. King Rama V enjoyed this hidden spot so much that he returned over a dozen times between 1888 and 1909. The river waters of Khlong Than Sadet are now considered sacred and used in royal ceremonies. Also near the eastern coast, Than Prawet is a series of chutes that snake inland for approximately 2km.

Nam Tok Phaeng WATERFALL

In the centre of the island, Nam Tok Phaeng is protected by a national park; this waterfall is a pleasant reward after a short, but rough, hike. Continue the adventure and head up to Khao Ra, the highest mountain on the island at 625m. Those with eagle-eyes will spot wild crocodiles, monkeys, snakes, deer and boar along the way, and the viewpoint from the top is spectacular – on a clear day you can see Ko Tao. Although the trek isn't arduous, it is very easy to lose one's way, and we *highly* recommend hiring an escort in Ban Madeua Wan (near the falls). The local guides have crude signs posted in front of their homes, and, if they're around, they'll take you up to the top for 500B. Most of them only speak Thai.

Hat Khuat BEACH

Also called Bottle Beach, Hat Khuat is a classic fave. Visitors flock to this shore for a relaxing day of swimming and snorkelling, and some opt to stay the night in one of the several bungalow operations along the beach. For additional seclusion, try the isolated beaches on the east coast, which include Than Sadet, Hat Yuan, Hat Thian and the teeny Ao Thong Reng. For additional enchanting beaches, consider doing a day trip to the stunning Ang Thong Marine National Park (p580).

Wat Phu Khao Noi BUDDHIST TEMPLE

(Map p549) The oldest temple on the island is Wat Phu Khao Noi, near the hospital in Thong Sala. While the site is open to visitors throughout the day, the monks are only around in the morning.

Wat Pho BUDDHIST TEMPLE

(Map p549; herbal sauna admission 50B; ☺ herbal sauna 3-6pm) Wat Pho, near Ban Tai, has a herbal sauna accented with natural lemon grass. The Chinese Temple is believed to give visitors good luck. It was constructed about 20 years ago after a visiting woman had a vision of the Chinese Buddha, who instructed her to build a fire-light for the island.

Wat Khao Tham BUDDHIST TEMPLE

(Map p549) Wat Khao Tham, near Ban Tai, sits high on a hill and has resident female monks. At the temple there is a bulletin board detailing a meditation retreat taught by an American-Australian couple. For additional information, write in advance to Wat Khao Tham, PO Box 8, Ko Pha-Ngan, Surat Thani 84280.

🏃 Activities

With Ko Tao, the high-energy diving behemoth, just a few kilometres away, Ko Pha-Ngan enjoys a much quieter, more laid-back diving scene focused on fun diving rather than certifications. A recent drop in Open Water certification prices has made local prices competitive with Ko Tao. Group sizes tend to be smaller on Ko Pha-Ngan since the island has fewer divers in general.

Like the other islands in the Samui Archipelago, Pha-Ngan has several small reefs dispersed around the island. The clear favourite snorkelling spot is Ko Ma, a small island in the northwest connected to Ko Pha-Ngan by a charming sandbar. There are also some rock reefs of interest on the eastern side of the island.

A major perk of diving from Ko Pha-Ngan is the proximity to Sail Rock (Hin Bai), the best dive site in the Gulf of Thailand and a veritable beacon for whale sharks. This large pinnacle lies about 14km north of the island. An abundance of corals and large tropical fish can be seen at depths of 10m to 30m, and there's a rocky vertical swim-through called 'The Chimney'.

Dive shops on Ko Tao sometimes visit Sail Rock, however the focus tends to be more on swallow reefs (for newbie divers) and the shark-infested waters at Chumphon Pinnacle. The most popular trips departing from Ko Pha-Ngan are three-site day trips which stop at Chumphon Pinnacle, Sail Rock and one of the other premier sites in the area. These three-stop trips cost from around 3650B to 4000B and include a full lunch. Two-dive trips to Sail Rock will set you back around 2500B to 2800B.

Reefers, Lotus Diving and Haad Yao Divers are the main operators on the island with a solid reputation.

Hiking and snorkelling day trips to Ang Thong Marine National Park generally

KO SAMUI & THE LOWER GULF KO PHA-NGAN

depart from Ko Samui, but recently tour operators are starting to shuttle tourists from Ko Pha-Ngan as well. Ask at your accommodation for details about boat trips as companies often come and go due to unstable petrol prices.

Many of the larger accommodation options can hook you up with a variety of aquatic equipment such as jet skis and kayaks, and the friendly staff at Backpackers Information Centre can attend to any of your other water-sports needs.

Chaloklum Diving
DIVING

(☑ 0 7737 4025; www.chaloklum-diving.com) One of the more established dive shops on the island, these guys (based on the main drag in Ban Chalok Lam) have quality equipment and high standards in all that they do.

Reefers
DIVING

(☑ 08 6471 4045; www.reefersdiving.com) Vic, the owner, and his gaggle of instructors are chilled and professional. Recommended.

Lotus Diving
DIVING

(☑ 0 7737 4142; www.lotusdiving.net) This dive centre owns not one, but two beautiful boats (that's two more vessels than most of the other operations on Ko Pha-Ngan). Trips can be booked at their office in Ban Chalok Lam, or at the Backpackers Information Centre.

Haad Yao Divers
DIVING

(☑ 08 6279 3085; www.haadyaodivers.com; Hat Yao) Established in 1997, this dive operator has garnered a strong reputation by maintaining European standards of safety and customer service.

Wake Up
WAKEBOARDING

(☑ 08 7283 6755; www.wakeupwakeboarding.com; ☉ Jan-Oct) Jamie passes along his infinite wakeboarding wisdom to eager wannabes at his small water sports school in Chalok Lam. Fifteen minutes of 'air time' will set you back 1200B, which is excellent value considering you get one-on-one instruction. Kiteboarding, wake-skating and waterskiing sessions are also available.

Jungle Gym
GYM

(Map p554; Hat Rin) One of several Thai boxing places on Ko Pha Ngan, this very conveniently located gym was one of the island's first and also offers yoga and well-maintained fitness equipment.

☞ Tours

Eco Nature Tour
ECO TOUR

(☑ 08 4850 6273) This exceedingly popular oufit offers a 'best of' island trip, which includes elephant trekking, snorkelling and a visit to the Chinese temple, a stunning viewpoint and Nam Tok Phaeng. The day trip, which costs 1500B, departs at 9am and returns around 3pm. Bookings can be made at its office in Thong Sala or at the Backpackers Information Centre. **Pha-Ngan Safari** (☑ 08 1895 3783, 0 7737 4159) offers a similar trip for 1900B.

🛏 Sleeping

Ko Pha-Ngan's legendary history of laid-back revelry has solidified its reputation as *the* stomping ground for the gritty backpacker lifestyle. Even so, many local mainstays have recently collapsed their bamboo huts and constructed newer, sleeker accommodation aimed at the ever-growing legion of 'flashpackers'.

On other parts of the island, new tracts of land are being cleared for Samui-esque five-star resorts. But backpackers fear not; it will still be a while before the castaway lifestyle goes the way of the dodo. For now, Ko Pha-Ngan can revel in having excellent choices to suit every budget. Pha-Ngan also caters to a subculture of seclusion-seekers who crave a deserted slice of sand. The northern and eastern coasts offer just that – a place to escape.

Sleeping options start in Hat Rin, move along the southern coast, head up the west side, across the northern beaches and down the quiet eastern shore. The accommodation along the southern coast is the best bang for your baht on Ko Pha-Ngan, while the west coast is seeing a lot of development. The atmosphere here is a pleasant mix of quiet seclusion and a sociable vibe, although some of the beaches, particularly towards the south, aren't as picturesque as other parts of the island. Price tags are also higher than north or south of here.

Stretching from Chalok Lam to Thong Nai Pan, the dramatic northern coast is a wild jungle with several stunning and secluded beaches – it's the most scenic coast on the island.

The east coast is the ultimate hermit hang-out. For the most part you'll have to hire a boat to get to these beaches from Thong Sala, Chalok Lam and Hat Rin and 4WD taxis from Thong Sala are an option for the few that have dirt roads. The *Thong Nai Pan Express* boat runs daily at noon from Hat Mae Nam on Ko Samui stopping at Hat Rin and the east coast beaches as far as Thong Nai Pan Noi. The boat is a casual, rickety fishing-style vessel and won't run in rough weather.

Hat Rin

The thin peninsula of Hat Rin features three separate beaches. Beautiful blond Hat Rin Nok (Sunrise Beach) is the epicentre of full moon tomfoolery, Hat Rin Nai (Sunset Beach) is the much less impressive stretch of sand on the far side of the tiny promontory, and Hat Seekantang (also known as Hat Leela), just south of Hat Rin Nai, is a smaller, lovely white and more private beach. The three beaches are linked by Ban Hat Rin (Hat Rin Town) – a small inland collection of restaurants and bars. It takes only a few minutes to walk from one beach to another.

Hat Rin sees Thailand's greatest accommodation crunch during the full moon festivities. At this time, bungalow operations expect you to stay for a minimum number of days (usually five). If you plan to arrive the day of the party (or even the day before), we strongly suggest booking a room in advance, or else you'll probably have to sleep on the beach (which you might end up doing anyway). There's a new breed of cattle car–style dorms where a seemingly impossible number of beds are stacked and crammed into dark small rooms and shared toilets are few. These start at around 200B outside of the full moon chaos then escalate to 650B and up for party times. Even though these grim options have added a significant number of beds to the town, everything still manages to fill up. Check hostel booking websites for dorm bed availability.

Full-mooners can also stay on Ko Samui or other beaches on Ko Pha-Ngan and take speedboat shuttles to access the festivities – prices will depend on how far away you're staying but the money you'll save on staying anywhere besides Hat Rin itself will probably make it worth it. Driving on Ko Pha-Ngan during the festivities is an absolutely terrible idea and there are gory and often fatal accidents monthly.

Needless to say, the prices listed here are meaningless during periods of maximum lunar orbicularity. Expect rates to increase by 20% to 300% during full moon.

★ **Lighthouse Bungalows** BUNGALOW $
(✆0 7737 5075; www.lighthousebungalows.com; Hat Seekantang; bungalows 500-1200B; ❋ ⎙) This hidden, low-key collection of hip huts gathers along a sloping, bouldered terrain punctuated by towering palms. The fan options are rustic but the newest, spacious air-con bungalows are terrific value. Every option has a terrace and sweeping view of the sea plus there's a cushion-clad restaurant/common area. To get there, follow the wooden boardwalk southeast from Hat Leela.

Blue Marine BUNGALOW $
(Map p554; ✆0 7737 5079; www.blue marinephangan.com; Hat Rin Nai; bungalows 600-1200B; ❋ ⎙) This cluster of identical concrete bungalows with blue-tiled roofs surrounds a manicured green lawn; the best have dreamy views over the whitest and cleanest part of quiet Sunset Beach. Every unit is spacious, clean and has air-con, fridge, hot water and TV. Staff is exceptionally helpful and friendly which helps create a neighborhood vibe among guests.

Seaview Sunrise BUNGALOW $
(Map p554; www.seaviewsunrise.com; Hat Rin Nok; r 500-1400B; ❋ ⎙) Budget full moon revellers who want to sleep inches from the tide, apply here. Some of the options back in the jungle are dark and musty but the solid, beachfront models have bright, polished wooden interiors often splashed with the occasional burst of neon paint from the ghosts of parties past.

Paradise Bungalows BUNGALOW $
(Map p554; ✆0 7737 5244; Hat Rin Nok; bungalows 650-2500B; ❋) The world-famous Full Moon Party was hatched at this scruffy batch of bungalows, and the place has been living on its fame ever since. The backpackers keep on coming to wax nostalgic, although the grounds are starting to look more like a junkyard now that the family has divvied up the land into several small 'resorts'. Paradise lost.

Same Same GUESTHOUSE $
(Map p554; ✆0 7737 5200; www.same-same.com; Ban Hat Rin; dm 500B, r 550-850B; ❋ ⎙) A supersociable spot for Scandinavians during the full moon madness, Same Same offers simple but bright rooms and plenty of party preparation fun.

Hat Rin

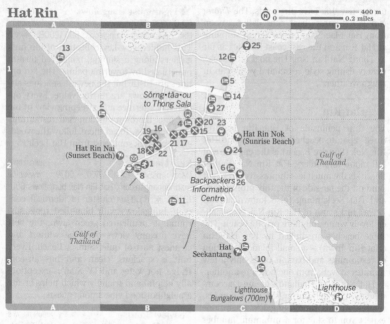

Hat Rin

Activities, Courses & Tours
1 Jungle Gym	B2

Sleeping
2 Blue Marine	B1
3 Cocohut Village	C3
4 Delight	B2
5 Palita Lodge	C1
6 Paradise Bungalows	C2
7 Pha-Ngan Bayshore Resort	C1
8 Rin Beach Resort	B2
9 Same Same	C2
10 Sarikantang	C3
11 Sea Breeze Bungalow	B2
12 Seaview Sunrise	C1
13 The Coast	A1
14 Tommy Resort	C1

Eating
15 Kawee	B2
16 Lazy House	B2
17 Little Home	B2
18 Lucky Crab	B2
Mama Schnitzel	(see 20)
19 Monna Lisa	B2
20 Mr K Thai Food	C2
21 Nic's	B2
22 Om Ganesh	B2

Drinking & Nightlife
23 Cactus Bar	C2
24 Drop-In Bar	C2
25 Mellow Mountain	C1
26 Rock	C2
27 Sunrise	C1
Tommy	(see 14)

Cocohut Village　　　　　　RESORT **$$**
(Map p554; ☑ 0 7737 5368; www.cocohut.com; Hat Seekantang; bungalows 1300-12,000B; ❋@❞❋) This super-social place on a stunning stretch of sand is popular with Israelis. Plans to expand further down the beach were under way when we passed. The priciest options, including the cliff villas and beachfront bungalows, are some of the best bets in Hat Rin, while the budget choices are dark and dismal. Fantastic buffet breakfasts are included in the price.

Pha-Ngan Bayshore Resort　　RESORT **$$**
(Map p554; ☑ 0 7737 5227; www.phanganbayshore. com; Hat Rin Nok; r 2500-8400B; ❋@❞❋) After a much-needed overhaul in 2009, this hotel-style operation has primed itself for the ever-increasing influx of flashpackers in Hat Rin. Sweeping beach views and a giant swimming pool make Pha-Ngan Bayshore one of the top

addresses on Sunrise Beach, especially if you can nab a special promotion.

Delight
GUESTHOUSE $$

(Map p554; ☑ 0 7737 5527; www.delightresort.com; Ban Hat Rin; r 1400-5400B; ✳ ☎ ☲) Secretly tucked behind the bright yellow Kodak sign in the centre of Hat Rin, Delight offers some of the best lodging around. Spic-and-span rooms in a Thai-style building come with subtle designer details (such as peacock murals) and are sandwiched between an inviting swimming pool and a lazy lagoon peppered with lily pads.

Tommy Resort
RESORT $$

(Map p554; ☑ 0 7737 5215; www.phangantommyresort.com; Hat Rin Nok; r 2100-7000B; ✳ ☎ ☲) Tommy is a trendy address in the heart of Hat Rin, striking a balance between chic boutique and carefree flashpacker hang-out. The rectangular swimming pool changes things up, since every other man-made body of water on the island looks like it was manufactured at the kidney-shaped pool factory.

Palita Lodge
BUNGALOW $$

(Map p554; ☑ 0 7737 5172; www.palitalodge.com; Hat Rin Nok; bungalows 1800-5900B; ✳ ☎ ☲) Smack in the heart of the action, Palita is a tribute to the never-ending party that is Hat Rin's Sunrise Beach. Spacious concrete bungalows look a bit ramshackle from the outside but the wooden accents and modern design elements make the interiors very comfy. It's on a beachy wedge of sand and the restaurant serves good Thai food.

Sea Breeze Bungalow
BUNGALOW $$

(Map p554; ☑ 0 7737 5162; Ban Hat Rin; bungalows 1500-8000B; ✳ ☎ ☲) Sea Breeze gets a good report card from our readers, and we agree; the labyrinth of secluded hillside cottages is a pleasant hammocked retreat for any type of traveller. Several bungalows, poised high on stilts, deliver stunning views of Hat Rin and the sea. There's a big range of options here.

Rin Beach Resort
RESORT $$

(Map p554; ☑ 0 7737 5112; www.rinbeachresort.com; Hat Rin Nai; bungalows 1100-8000B; ✳ ☎ ☲) Giant amphorae, spewing forth gushes of water, welcome weary travellers as they tumble off the wooden ferry. Even if you don't stay here, please take a minute to appreciate the kistch catastrophe of the candy-coloured, two-storey Spanish galleon replica bungalows along the beachfront.

Sarikantang
RESORT $$$

(Map p554; ☑ 0 7737 5055; www.sarikantang.com; Hat Seekantang; bungalows 2500-6200B; ✳ ☎ ☲) Cream-coloured cabins, framed with teak posts and lintels, are sprinkled among swaying palms and crumbling winged statuettes on one of Hat Rin's best stretches of beach. Inside, the rooms are an Ikea chic that's not ageing well but still offers a comfy stay.

The Coast
RESORT $$$

(Map p554; ☑ 07795 1567; www.thecoastphangan.com; Hat Rin Nai; 3500-10,000B; ✳ ☎ ☲) Yes, Hat Rin is going upscale. This dark grey, sharp-angled resort is on a slim but OK stretch of beach away from the party hub. Swanky room interiors are polished cement and beds are topped with white duvets. An infinity pool overlooks the sea and service is grand. Materials are a bit flimsy, however, and it was already showing signs of wear mere months after opening.

🛏 Ban Khai to Ban Tai

The waters at Ban Tai tend to be shallow and opaque, especially during low season, but lodging options are well-priced compared to other parts of the island, and you're not too far from Hat Rin. Like Ban Tai, Ban Khai's beaches aren't the most stunning, but the accommodation is cheap and there are beautiful views of Ang Thong Marine National Park in the distance.

These beaches are where many of the moon-but-not-full-moon parties happen so even if your resort seems quiet, there's probably some boozed-up action nearby.

Boom's Cafe Bungalows
BUNGALOW $

(☑ 0 7723 8318; www.boomscafe.com; Ban Khai; bungalows 600-1200B; ✳) Staying at Boom's is like visiting the Thai family you never knew you had. The friendly owners lovingly tend their sandy acreage and dote on the contented clientele. No one seems to mind that there's no swimming pool, since the curling tide rolls right up to your doorstep. Boom's is at the far eastern corner of Ban Khai, near Hat Rin.

⭐ Divine Comedie
RESORT $$

(☑ 08 0885 8789; info@divine-resort.com; Ban Tai; ste 3000-4000B; ✳ ☎ ☲) A mix of 1920s sino and perhaps Mexican hacienda architecture with a colour palette that shifts from mint to ochre – it not only works, it's beguiling. Junior suites have rooftop terraces, the elongated pool runs to the slim beach and there's an on-site restaurant serving Myanmar specialities. It's expertly run by a hip French and Corsican couple.

There's no website; contact them directly or reserve via a booking site.

Bay Lounge & Resort
RESORT $$

(☑0 7737 7892; www.baylounge.com; Ban Khai; bungalows 1600-3800B; ❄️🛜🏊) On a private white nugget of beach sandwiched by jungle-topped boulders, this is an intimate, chic choice. Bungalows mingle with the natural surroundings yet inside look quite urban with distressed concrete and bright modern art. It's midway between Hat Rin's Full Moon Party and the Half Moon Party in Ban Khai – the resort offers transport to each.

Mac Bay
BUNGALOW $$

(☑0 7723 8443; bungalows 1200-8500B; ❄️🛜🏊) Home to the Black Moon Party (another lunar excuse for Ko Pha-Ngan to go wild), Mac Bay is a sandy slice of Ban Khai where even the cheaper bungalows are spic and span. At beer o'clock, grab a shaded spot on the sand and watch the sun dance amorphous shadows over the distant islands of Ang Thong Marine National Park.

Milky Bay Resort
RESORT $$$

(☑0 7723 8566; http://milkybaythailand.com; Ban Tai; bungalows 1800-13,200B; ❄️@🛜🏊) Several differnt types of minimalist chic bungalows with dark-tinted glass hide in the shade of tall stands of bamboo. Wood chip paths link everything and lead to a skinny beach and somehow the ensemble is very stylish. It's a busy, well-run place.

Thong Sala

Thong Sala's beach is really just an extension of Ban Tai but the beaches are a bit wider up this way and have the advantage of being walking distance to Ko Pha-Ngan's main town, its restaurants and services.

★ Coco Garden
BUNGALOW $

(☑08 6073 1147, 0 7737 7721; www.cocogardens. com; Thong Sala; bungalows 450-1250B; ❄️🛜) The best budget hang-out along the southern coast, Coco Garden one-ups the nearby resorts with well-manicured grounds and sparkling bungalows. As such, it's really popular with the backpacker set and is a fun scene.

Blue Parrot
BUNGALOW $

(☑0 7723 8777; www.theblueparrotphangan.com; Thong Sala; r fan/air-con 450/750B; ❄️🛜) Two cute lines of good-sized, clean bungalows – some tiled with burnt yellow exteriors and others of grey polished cement – lead to the beach. There's a little on-site cafe that travellers say serves great Western and Thai food.

Lime n Soda
RESORT $$

(www.limesodathailand.com; bungalows 700-4400B; ❄️🛜🏊) Clean and simple tiled bungalows hide in the shade of bamboo and coconut palms along a breakwater above the beach. They call themselves an 'eco resort', but it's unclear why.

Ao Nai Wok to Ao Sri Thanu

Close to Thong Sala, the resorts peppered along this breezy west-coast strip mingle with small beaches between patches of gnarled mangroves. Despite the lack of sand, the prices are cheap and the sunsets are memorable.

Chills Resort
RESORT $$

(☑08 9875 2100; Ao Sri Thanu; r 1000-2500B; ❄️🛜🏊) Set along a stunning and secluded stretch of stony outcrops, Chills' cluster of delightfully simple-but-modern rooms all have peaceful ocean views letting in plenty of sunlight and sea breezes. It went under new management in 2013 that will hopefully improve the suffering service standards. Book through www.Agoda.com.

Shambhala Bungalow Village
BUNGALOW $$

(☑08 9875 2100; www.shambhala-phangan.com; Ao Nai Wok; bungalows 850-2300B; ❄️🛜) The owners of Shambhala have lovingly restored a batch of huts and added loads of personal touches that make this a memorable place to stay. Expect fresh linen, carved wood, artistic lighting and neatly designed bathrooms, but also isolation and a very small beach.

Loyfa Natural Resort
BUNGALOW $$

(☑0 7737 7319; loyfabungalow@yahoo.com; Ao Sri Thanu; r 750B, bungalows 1300-3100B, f villas from 3825B; ❄️🛜) Loyfa scores high marks for its friendly, French-speaking Thai staff, charming gardens and sturdy huts guarding sweeping ocean views. Modern bungalows tumble down the promontory onto an uberprivate sliver of ash-coloured sand. Cheapest rooms are in a hotel block.

Kupu Kupu Phangan Beach Villa RESORT $$$
(☑0 7737 7384; www.kupuphangan.com; Ao Nai Wok; villas from 6000B; ❀ ☎ ✹) Opened in December 2012, this Balinese-style resort is possibly the island's most swoon-worthy, with lily ponds, tall palms, a swimming pool right off the pages of a luxury magazine and rocky boulders that meet the sea. The gorgeous wooden villas all have dipping pools and spacious, elegant interiors. They're not very private, however, and management is still finding its feet.

Hat Chaophao

Like Hat Yao up the coast, this rounded beach on the west coast is lined with a variety of bungalow operations.

Sunset Cove BUNGALOW $$
(☑0 7734 9211; www.thaisunsetcove.com; bungalows 1200-3850B; ❀ @ ☎ ✹) There's a feeling of Zen symmetry among the forested assortment of boutique, but ageing bungalows; the towering bamboo shoots are evenly spaced along the cobbled paths weaving through brush and boulders. The beachside abodes are particularly elegant, sporting slatted rectangular windows and barrel-basined bathtubs.

Pha-Ngan Paragon BUNGALOW $$$
(☑08 4728 6064; www.phanganparagon.com; bungalows 2500-15,000B; ❀ @ ☎ ✹) A tiny hideaway with seven rooms, the Paragon has decor that incorporates stylistic elements from ancient Khmer, India and Thailand, without forfeiting any modern amenities. The 'royal bedroom' deserves a special mention – apparently the canopied bed was imported from Kashmir.

Hat Yao & Hat Son

One of the busier beaches along the west coast, Hat Yao sports a swimmable beach, numerous resorts and a few extra services such as ATMs and convenience stores. Hat Son is a quiet, much smaller beach that feels like a big secret.

Tantawan Bungalows BUNGALOW $
(☑0 7734 9108; www.tantawanbungalow.com; Hat Son; bungalows 600-1200B; ✹) This charming teak nest, tucked among jungle fronds, is dripping with clinking chandeliers made from peach coral and khaki-coloured seashells. It had changed management and big changes were planned when we passed.

High Life BUNGALOW $
(☑0 7734 9114; www.highlifebungalow.com; Hat Yao; fan bungalows 500B, air-con bungalows 800-2200B; ❀ ☎ ✹) We can't decide what's more conspicuous: the dramatic ocean views from the infinity-edged swimming pool, or the blatant double entendre in the resort's name. True to its moniker, the 25 bungalows, of various shapes and sizes, sit on a palmed outcropping of granite soaring high above the cerulean sea.

Shiralea BUNGALOW $
(☑08 0719 9256; www.shiralea.com; Hat Yao; bungalows 600-1000B; ❀ ☎ ✹) The fresh-faced poolside bungalows here are simple but the ambience, with an onsite bar with draught beer, is convivial. It's about 100m away from the beach and it fills up every few weeks with Contiki student tour groups.

Haad Son Resort & Restaurant RESORT $$
(☑0 7734 9104; www.haadson.info; Hat Son; bungalows 1000-8000B; ❀ @ ☎ ✹) There's a mixed bag of rooms here from big, older wooden bungalows with terraces on the hillside to brand-new polished cement suites and rooms along the beachfront. The secluded beach setting is spectacular and is highlighted by one of the most beachy-chic restaurants on the island on a jungle- and boulder-clad peninsula overlooking the sea.

Haad Yao Bay View Resort RESORT $$$
(☑0 7734 9193; www.haadyao-bayviewresort.com; Hat Yao; r & bungalows 1500-7000B; ❀ @ ☎ ✹) This conglomeration of bungalows and hotel-style accommodation looks like a tropical mirage on Hat Yao's northern headland. There's a huge array of options but our pick are the tiny but good-value rooms (from 1500B in low season) that hover right over the sea. For more luxe head up to the hillside sea-view bungalows. It's a busy, businesslike place.

Haad Yao See Through Boutique Resort HOTEL $$
(☑0 7734 9315; www.haadyao.net; Hat Yao; r 1200-3800B; ❀ ☎) A towering polished cement double-storey complex with elongated Chinese-style wooden doors. Though the uninviting pool is hard to access and the building itself looks bizarrely placed, room interiors are comfortable and the resort has a central beachfront location.

Hat Salad

This slim, pretty beach on the northwest coast is fronted by shallow blue water – a clutch of photogenic long-tail boats tend to park at the southern end. It's slightly rustic, with local Thai fishermen coming out to throw their nets out at sunset, yet with plenty of amenities and comfortable accommodation.

Cookies Salad   RESORT $$
(☑08 3181 7125, 0 7734 9125; www.cookies phangan.com; bungalows 1600-5000B; ❖❄) The resort with a tasty name has delicious, private Balinese-styled bungalows on a steep hill, orbiting a two-tiered lap pool tiled in various shades of blue. Shaggy thatching and dense tropical foliage give the realm a certain rustic quality, although you won't want for creature comforts. It's super friendly and books up fast.

Salad Hut   BUNGALOW $$
(☑0 7734 9246; www.saladhut.com; bungalows 2200-5000B; ❄@❖❄) Wholly unpretentious yet sharing a beach with some distinctly upscale options, this small clutch of Thai-style bungalows sits but a stone's throw from the rolling tide. Watch the sun gently set below the waves from your lacquered teak porch.

Salad Beach Resort   BUNGALOW $$
(☑0 7734 9149; www.phangan-saladbeachresort. com; bungalows 2000-4900B; ❄@❖❄) A full-service retreat along the sands of Salad. Room decor employs an unusual palette of colours, but the grounds are tasteful and understated – especially around the pool.

Green Papaya   BUNGALOW $$$
(☑0 7737 4182; www.greenpapayaresort.com; bungalows 4300-8500B; ❄@❖❄) The polished wooden bungalows at Green Papaya are a clear standout along the lovely beach at Hat Salad; however, they come at quite a hefty price and you'll need a posh attitude to fit in.

Ao Mae Hat

The relatively undeveloped northwest tip of the island has excellent ocean vistas, plenty of white sand and little Ko Ma is connected to Pha-Ngan by a stunning sandbar.

Island View Cabana   BUNGALOW $
(☑0 7737 4173; islandviewcabana@gmail.com; Ao Mae Hat; bungalows 400-1500B; ❖) It's a bit overpriced but the bungalows here are really big, relatively new and on a truly wonderful slice of beach right at the isthmus to Ko Ma. The copious staff seem to have been trained to be exuberant although not necessarily helpful.

Mae Hat Beach View Resort   BUNGALOW $
(☑08 9823 9756; bungalows 400-600B) Hidden behind the dune of the beach's southern end, this lost-in-time cluster of bungalows was empty when we passed save a few friendly Myanmar staff. The bamboo, fan-cooled bungalows with solid tiled floors are the perfect place to disappear into tropical mode with a good book for a few days.

Ban Chalok Lam (Chaloklum) & Hat Khom

In the north of the island, the cramped fishing village at Ban Chalok Lam is like no other place on Ko Pha-Ngan. The conglomeration of teak shanties and huts has just started to be infiltrated with the occasional (and so far welcome) European-style coffeehouse or authentic Italian restaurant. For the most part though, locals still far outnumber tourists and that's refreshing. There's not much of a beach however.

Sŏrng·tăa·ou ply the route from here to Thong Sala for around 150B per person. There's a dirt road leading from Chalok Lam to Hat Khom, and water taxis are available to a number of beaches.

Fantasea   BUNGALOW $
(☑08 9443 0785; www.fantasea.asia; Chalok Lam; bungalows fan/air-con 400/700B; ❖) One of the better of a string of family-run bungalow operations along the quiet, eastern part of Chalok Lam. There's a thin beach out front with OK swimming, an elevated Thai-style restaurant area to chill out in, and you may even get a dog who sleeps on your terrace and barks at passersby.

Mandalai   HOTEL $$$
(☑0 7737 4316; www.mymandalai.com; Chalok Lam; r 1800-5600B; ❄@❄) Like an ash-white Riyadh from a distant Arabian land, this small boutique hotel quietly towers over the surrounding shantytown of fishermen's huts. Floor-to-ceiling windows command views of tangerine-coloured fishing boats in the bay, and there's an intimate wading pool hidden in the inner cloister. It's all very out of place in this rickety town.

Hat Khuat (Bottle Beach)

This isolated dune in the north of the island has garnered a reputation as a low-key getaway, and has thus become quite popular. During high season, places can fill up fast so it's best to try to arrive early. Grab a long-tail taxi boat from Chalok Lam for 100B to 150B (depending on the boat's occupancy).

Smile Bungalows   BUNGALOW $
(☏08 1956 3133; smilebeach@hotmail.com; Bottle Beach/Hat Khuat; bungalows 400-700B) At the far western corner of the beach, Smile features an assortment of wooden huts that climb up a forested hill. The two-storey bungalows (700B) are our favourite. Listen for the Bottle Beach song by Bottle Beach lover and musician John Nicholas, playing on the stereo in the loungable beach cafe.

Bottle Beach II   BUNGALOW $
(☏0 7744 5156; Bottle Beach/Hat Khuat; bungalows 300-500B; ☎) At the far eastern corner of the beach, this double string of very basic, turquoise bungalows is the ideal place to chill out – for as long as you can – if you don't need many creature comforts.

Thong Nai Pan

The pair of rounded bays at Thong Nai Pan, in the northeast of the island, are some of the most remote yet busy beaches on the island; Ao Thong Nai Pan Yai (*yai* means 'big') is the southern half that has some excellent budget and midrange options, and Ao Thong Nai Pan Noi (*noi* means 'little') is Pha-Ngan's most upscale beach that curves just above. Both bays are equally beautiful and great for swimming and hiking.

The road from Thong Sala to Thong Nai Pan was in the process of being widened so it could be paved when we passed. The completion will most likely increase development on these beaches.

Longtail Beach Resort   BUNGALOW $
(☏0 7744 5018; www.longtailbeachresort.com; Thong Nai Pan; bungalows fan/air-con from 490/890B; ☎☎) Tucked at the lovely southern end of the beach and effortlessly adorable, Longtail offers backpackers charming thatch-and-bamboo abodes that wind up a lush garden path. The lounge area is strewn with cushions and very busy.

Dolphin   BUNGALOW $
(Thong Nai Pan; bungalows 500-1800B; ☎☎) This hidden retreat gives you a chance to rough it in style. Quiet afternoons are spent lounging on the comfy cushions in one of the small pagodas hidden throughout the jungle and bungalows are quite private. Lodging is only available on a first-come, first-served basis.

Anantara Rasananda   RESORT $$$
(☏0 7723 9555; www.rasananda.com; villas from 7500B; ☎@☎☎) Blink and you'll think you've been transported to Ko Samui. This five-star luxury resort is a sweeping sandside property with a smattering of semi-detached villas – many bedecked with private plunge pools. A savvy mix of modern and traditional *săh·lah* styling prevails, and great Anantara management means that this high-end stalwart is here to stay.

Than Sadet

From Thong Sala a 4WD taxi leaves for Than Sadet on the east coast daily at 1pm for 200B per person. If you miss the taxi, resorts can arrange a private 4WD pick-up for 800B for the whole car. Otherwise catch the *Thong Nai Pan Express* boat from Ko Samui.

Mai Pen Rai   BUNGALOW $
(☏0 7744 5090; www.thansadet.com; Than Sadet; bungalows 500-1200B; ☎) This quiet, beachy bay elicits nothing but sedate smiles. Trek up to Nam Tok Than Sadet falls, hike an hour to Thong Nai Pan or explore by sea with a rented kayak. Bungalows mingle with Plaa's next door on the hilly headland, and sport panels of straw weaving with gabled roofs. Family bungalows are available for 900B and there's a friendly on-site restaurant.

Hat Thian & Hat Yuan

Both Hat Thian and Hat Yuan, near the southeastern tip of the island, have a few bungalow operations, and are quite secluded. You can walk between the two in under 10 minutes via the rocky outcrop that seperates them. Hat Yuan is the more developed beach and has the whiter, wider stretches of sand, while Hat Thain is relatively empty and is back-to-nature pretty.

To get here hire a long-tail from Hat Rin (300B to 400B for the whole boat) or organise a boat pick-up from your resort. A dirt road to Hat Yuan has been cleared for 4WDs, but is only passable in the dry season; even then the voyage by sea is much easier.

Bamboo Hut
BUNGALOW $

(☑ 08 7888 8592; Hat Yuan; bungalows 350-1000B; 🛜) Beautifully lodged up on the bouldery outcrops that overlook Hat Yuan and back into the jungle, groovy, hippie village, Bamboo Hut is a favourite for yoga retreats and meditative relaxation. Dark wood bungalows are small and have terraces and the patrons all float around the property high on fasting.

Barcelona
BUNGALOW $

(☑ 0 7737 5113; Hat Yuan; bungalows 400-700B) Old, rickety wood bungalows climb up the hill on stilts behind a palm garden and have good vistas. Price depends on the view, but there's not that much variation so grab a cheap one.

★ Sanctuary
BUNGALOW $$

(☑ 08 1271 3614; www.thesanctuarythailand.com; Hat Thian; dm 220B, bungalows 770-6000B) A friendly forested enclave of relaxed smiles, the Sanctuary is a haven of splendid lodgings, yoga classes and detox sessions. Accommodation, in various manifestations of twigs, is scattered along a tangle of hillside jungle paths while Hat Thian is wonderfully quiet and is great for swimming. You'll want to Nama-stay forever.

Pariya Resort & Villas
RESORT $$$

(☑ 08 7623 6678; www.pariyahaadyuan.com; Hat Yuan; villas 8000-17,000B; 🌬🛜🌊) The swankiest option on these beaches is found right in front of the softest sands of Hat Yuan in magestic burnt-yellow painted concrete. Octagonal, pagoda-topped bungalows are spacious yet sparsely furnished. If you can find a promotion this may be worth it but, otherwise, the resort is overpriced.

✖ Eating

Ko Pha-Ngan is no culinary capital, especially since most visitors quickly absorb the lazy lifestyle and wind up eating at their accommodation. Those with an adventurous appetite should check out the island's centre of local commerce, Thong Sala, although there are a few surprises elsewhere as well.

✖ Hat Rin

This bustling 'burb has the largest conglomeration of restaurants and bars on the island, yet most of them are pretty lousy. The infamous Chicken Corner is a popular intersection stocked with several faves such as **Mr K Thai Food** (Map p554; Ban Hat Rin; dishes 30-80B) and **Mama Schnitzel** (Map p554; Ban Hat Rin; dishes 40-100B), which promise to cure any case of the munchies, be it noon or midnight.

For the cheapest eats head to 'Thai Street', running roughly between Nic's and Kawee, a row of basic eateries serving noodles and curries for around 40B.

Little Home
THAI $

(Map p554; Ban Hat Rin; mains from 40B; ⊙ breakfast, lunch & dinner) Little Home woos the masses with cheap, flavourful Thai grub that's gobbled up with alacrity among wooden tables and flimsy plastic chairs.

★ Kawee
THAI, FRENCH $$

(Map p554; dishes 100-350B) Calling itself an 'art-mosphere', this French-run place raises the bar for Hat Rin both with its jungle-y, dimly lit, bookstore-attached decor and its fantastic French- and Thai-inspired dishes. The *ho mok* (a savoury steamed pudding of coconut milk, curries and meat) and Kawee skewers (crispy white fish on lemon grass blades) are not to be missed.

Nic's
INTERNATIONAL $$

(Map p554; Ban Hat Rin; mains 80-280B; ⊙ dinner) A dizzying realm of polished concrete and coloured pillows, Nic's – at the back of Hat Rin's lake – slings tasty pizzas and tapas every evening. Slurp a Singha during the 6pm-to-8pm happy hour. New management hopes to make it shine even more.

Lazy House
INTERNATIONAL $$

(Map p554; Hat Rin Nai; dishes 90-270B; ⊙ lunch & dinner) Back in the day, this joint was the owner's apartment – everyone liked his cooking so much that he decided to turn the place into a restaurant and hang-out spot. Today, Lazy House is easily one of Hat Rin's best places to veg out in front of a movie with a scrumptious shepherd's pie.

Lucky Crab
SEAFOOD $$

(Map p554; Hat Rin Nai; dishes 100-450B; ⊙ lunch & dinner) Rows of freshly caught creatures are presented nightly atop miniature long-tail boats loaded with ice. Once you've picked your prey, grab a table inside amid dangling plants and charming stone furnishings.

Om Ganesh
INDIAN $$

(Map p554; Hat Rin Nai; dishes 70-200B; ⊙ breakfast, lunch & dinner) Customers meditate over curries, *biryani* rice, roti and lassis (though the local expats joke that every dish tastes the same). Platters start at 350B.

Monna Lisa
ITALIAN $$

(Map p554; Hat Rin Nai; pizza & pasta from 200B; ☺breakfast, lunch & dinner) Travellers rave about the pizza here, but we found it mediocre, so you be the judge (but definitely skip the lasagne). It's run by a team of friendly Italians and has a basic, open-air atmosphere.

✖ Southern Beaches

On Saturday evenings from 4pm to 10pm, a side street in the eastern part of Thong Sala becomes **Walking Street** – a bustling pedestrian zone mostly filled with locals hawking their wares to other islanders. There's plenty on offer, from clothing to food. Be sure to try the delicious red pork with gravy (40B) at Lang Tang – you'll find it in glass cases next to a large English sign saying 'Numpanich'.

Night Market
MARKET $

(Thong Sala; dishes 25-180B; ☺dinner) A heady mix of steam and snacking locals, Thong Sala's night market is a must for those looking for a dose of culture while nibbling on a low-priced snack. The best place to grab some cheap grub is the stall in the far right corner with a large white banner. Hit up the vendor next door for tasty seafood platters, such as red snapper served over a bed of thick noodles. Banana pancakes and fruit smoothies abound for dessert.

Ando Loco
MEXICAN $

(Ban Tai; mains from 59B; ☺dinner) This outdoor Mexican hang-out looks like an animation cell from a vintage Hanna-Barbera cartoon, with assorted kitschy accoutrements such as papier-mâché cacti. Jibing with the look, one of its catchphrases is 'cheese on tap'. Down a super-sized margarita and show your skills on the beach volleyball court.

★Fisherman's Restaurant
SEAFOOD $$

(✆08 4454 7240; Thong Sala; dishes 50-600B; ☺1-10pm) Wooden tables on a sand floor look out over the sunset and a rocky pier. Lit up at night, it's one of the island's nicest settings and the food, from the addictive yellow curry crab to the massive seafood platter to share (with all assortment of critters; 800B to 900B), is as wonderful as the ambience.

★Fabio's
ITALIAN $$

(✆08 3389 5732; Ban Khai; dishes 150-400B; ☺1-10pm Mon-Sat) An intimate, authentic and truly delicious Italian place with golden walls, cream linens and bamboo furniture. There are only seven tables so reserve in advance. House-made delicacies like seafood risotto, pizzas and iced limoncello are as artfully presented as they are fresh and amazing. One of the island's best restaurants.

Mason's Arms
BRITISH $$

(Thong Sala; mains 160-350B; ☺lunch & dinner) Suddenly, a clunky structure emerges from the swaying palms; it's a Tudor-style manse, plucked directly from Stratford-upon-Avon and plunked down in the steamy jungle. This lodge-like lair is one blood pudding away from being an official British colony. The fish 'n' chips is a local favourite.

✖ Other Beaches

★Sanctuary
HEALTH FOOD $$

(Hat Thian; mains from 130B) Forget what you know about health food: the Sanctuary's restaurant proves that wholesome eats can also be delicious. Enjoy a tasty parade of plates – from Indian pakoras to crunchy Vietnamese spring rolls – as an endless playlist of music (undoubtedly the island's best) wafts overhead. Don't forget to wash it all down with a shot of neon-green wheatgrass. Yum!

★Cucina Italiana
ITALIAN $$

(Jenny's; Chalok Lam; pizzas 180-200B; ☺dinner) If it weren't for the sand between your toes and the long-tail boats whizzing by, you might think you had been transported to the Italian countryside. The friendly Italian chef is passionate about his food, and creates everything from his pasta to his tiramisu daily, from scratch. The rustic, thin-crust pizzas are out-of-this-world good.

Peppercorn
STEAKHOUSE $$

(www.peppercornphangan.com; Hat Salad; mains 160-400B; ☺4-10pm Mon-Sat; ✐) Escargot and succulent steaks in a rickety jungle cottage? You bet. Peppercorn may be tucked in the brush away from the sea, but that shouldn't detract foodies from seeking out one of Phangan's best attempts at highbrow international cuisine. There's also a fine selection of very good vegetarian dishes. No artificial ingredients.

Bamboo Hut
WESTERN, THAI $$

(Hat Yuan; dishes 100-300B; ☺breakfast, lunch & dinner; ☎✐) Lounge on a Thai-style cushion or sit at a teak table that catches sea breezes and looks over infinite blue. There are plenty of options from vegetarian specialities and fresh juices for those coming off a fast or cleanse, to classic, very well-prepared Thai dishes with all assortment of beef, chicken and prawns.

Dolphin Bar & Cafe WESTERN, THAI $$
(Hat Thong Nai Pan Noi; dishes 80-350B; ⊙ breakfast, lunch & dinner) Fresh baked bread, mostly locally sourced produce and a healthy flair make up delicious international food enjoyed in a waterfront, old teak wood structure. There's also great coffee and cocktails.

Two Brothers SEAFOOD $$
(Chalok Lam; barbecue sets from 250B; ⊙ breakfast, lunch & dinner)   One of the best of a string of Chalok Lam's seafood restaurants where fisher families serve you their bounty straight off the boats. Bamboo furniture sits on the sand and you can watch the boat action in the busy bay.

🍷 Drinking & Nightlife

Every month, on the night of the full moon, pilgrims pay tribute to the party gods with trancelike dancing, wild screaming and glow-in-the-dark body paint. The throngs of bucket-sippers and fire twirlers gather on the infamous Sunrise Beach (Hat Rin Nok) and party until the sun replaces the moon in the sky.

A few other noteworthy spots can be found around the island for those seeking something a bit mellower.

📍 Hat Rin

Hat Rin is the beating heart of the legendary full moon fun. When the moon isn't lighting up the night sky, partygoers flock to other spots on the island's south side. Most party venues flank Hat Rin's Sunrise Beach from south to north.

Rock BAR, NIGHTCLUB
(Map p554) Great views of the party from the elevated terrace on the far south side of the beach. Also, the best cocktails in town.

Drop-In Bar BAR, NIGHTCLUB
(Map p554) This dance shack blasts the chart toppers that we all secretly love. This is one of the liveliest places and even non-full-moon nights can get boisterous.

Cactus Bar BAR, NIGHTCLUB
(Map p554) Smack in the centre of Hat Rin Nok, Cactus pumps out a healthy mix of old

-school tunes, hip-hop and R&B. It's also very popular and always happening.

Sunrise BAR, NIGHTCLUB
(Map p554) A spot on the sand where trance beats shake the graffiti-ed walls.

Tommy BAR, NIGHTCLUB
(Map p554) One of Hat Rin's largest venues lures the masses with black lights and trance music blaring on the sound system. Drinks are dispensed from a large arklike bar.

Mellow Mountain BAR, NIGHTCLUB
(Map p554) Also called 'Mushy Mountain' (you'll know why when you get there), this trippy hang-out sits at the northern edge of Hat Rin Nok, delivering stellar views of the shenanigans below. One of those places you need to at least see if you're on Hat Rin.

📍 Other Beaches

Eagle Pub BAR
(Hat Yao) At the southern end of Hat Yao, this drink-dealing shack, built right into the rock face, is tattooed with the neon graffiti of virtually every person who's passed out on the lime green patio furniture after too many caipirinhas.

Jam BAR
(www.thejamphangan.com; Hin Wong) It's DIY live music at this friendly nightspot on the west coast. Saturday nights are open mic, and the rest of the week you'll usually catch a few locals jamming on their guitars.

Pirates Bar BAR
(Hat Chaophao) This wacky drinkery is a replica of a pirate ship built into the cliffs. When you're sitting on the deck and the tide is high (and you've had a couple of drinks), you can almost believe you're out at sea. These guys host the well-attended Moon Set parties, three days before Hat Rin gets pumpin' for the full moon fun.

Flip Flop Pharmacy BAR
(Thong Nai Pan) This open-air bar on the sands of Thong Nai Pan is the area's preferred hang-out spot.

Amsterdam BAR
(Ao Plaay Laem) Near Hat Chaophao on the west coast, Amsterdam attracts tourists and locals from all over the island, who are looking for a chill spot to watch the sunset.

ℹ Information

DANGERS & ANNOYANCES

Some of your fondest vacation memories may be forged on Ko Pha-Ngan; just be mindful of the following situations that can seriously tarnish your experience.

Drugs You're relaxing on the beach when suddenly a local walks up and offers you some local herb at a ridiculously low price. 'No thanks,' you say, knowing that the penalties for drug use in Thailand are fierce. But the vendor drops his price even more and practically offers you the weed for free. Too good to be true? Obviously. As soon as you take a toke, the seller rats you out to the cops and you're whisked away to the local prison where you must pay a wallet-busting fine. This type of scenario happens all the time on Ko Pha-Ngan so it's best to avoid the call of the ganja.

Here's another important thing to remember: your travel insurance does not cover any drug-related injury or treatment. Drug-related freak-outs *do* happen – we've heard firsthand accounts of partiers slipping into extended periods of delirium. Suan Saranrom (Garden of Joys) Psychiatric Hospital in Surat Thani has to take on extra staff during full-moon and other party periods to handle the number of *fa·ràng* who freak out on magic mushrooms, acid or other abundantly available hallucinogens.

Women travellers Female travellers should be extra careful when partying on the island. We've received many reports about drug- and alcohol-related situations (and these situations are not limited to Full Moon Parties). Another disturbing problem is the unscrupulous behaviour of some of the local motorcycle taxi drivers. Several complaints have been filed about drivers groping female passengers; there are even reports of severe sexual assaults.

Motorcycles Ko Pha-Ngan has more motorcycle accidents than injuries incurred from full moon tomfoolery. Nowadays there's a system of paved roads, but much of it is a labyrinth of rutty dirt-and-mud paths. The island is also very hilly, and even if the road is paved, it can be too difficult for most to take on. The *very* steep road to Hat Rin is a perfect case in point. The island now has a special ambulance that trawls the island helping injured bikers.

EMERGENCY

Main Police Station (☑191, 0 7737 7114) Located about 2km north of Thong Sala. The police station in Hat Rin (near Hat Rin school) will not let you file a report; to do so you must go to Thong Sala. Local police have been known to charge 200B to file a report. Do not pay this – it should be free. Note that if you are arrested you do have the right to an embassy phone call; you do not have to agree to accept the 'interpreter' you are offered.

INTERNET ACCESS

Hat Rin and Thong Sala are the main centres of internet activity, but every beach with development now offers access. Rates are generally 2B per minute, with a 10B to 20B minimum and discounts if you stay on for more than an hour. Places offering a rate of 1B per minute usually have turtle-speed connections.

LAUNDRY

If you got fluorescent body paint on your clothes during your full-moon romp, don't bother sending them to the cleaners – the paint will never come out. Trust us, we've tried. For your other washing needs, there are heaps of places that will gladly wash your clothes. Prices hover around 40B per kilo, and express cleanings shouldn't be more than 60B per kilo.

MEDICAL SERVICES

Medical services can be a little crooked in Ko Pha-Ngan – expect unstable prices and under-qualified doctors. Many clinics charge a 3000B entrance fee before treatment. Serious medical issues should be dealt with on nearby Ko Samui.

Ko Pha-Ngan Hospital (Map p549; ☑0 7737 7034; Thong Sala; ⊙24hr) About 2.5km north of Thong Sala; offers 24-hour emergency services.

MONEY

Thong Sala, Ko Pha-Ngan's financial 'capital', has plenty of banks, currency converters and several Western Union offices. Hat Rin has numerous ATMs and a couple of banks at the pier. There are also ATMs in Hat Yao, Chalok Lum and Thong Nai Pan.

POST

Main Post Office (⊙8.30am-4.30pm Mon-Fri, 9am-noon Sat) In Thong Sala; there's a smaller office right near the pier in Hat Rin.

TOURIST INFORMATION

There are no government-run Tourist Authority of Thailand (TAT) offices on Ko Pha-Ngan; instead tourists get their information from local travel agencies and brochures. Most agencies are clumped around Hat Rin and Thong Sala. Agents take a small commission on each sale, but collusion keeps prices relatively stable and standardised. Choose an agent you trust if you are spending a lot of money – faulty bookings do happen on Ko Pha-Ngan, especially since the island does not have a unit of tourist police.

Several mini-magazines also offer comprehensive information about the island's accommodation, restaurants, activities and Full Moon Parties. Our favourite option is the pocket-sized **Phangan Info** (www.phangan.info).

Backpackers Information Centre (Map p554; ☏ 0 7737 5535; www.backpackersthailand.com; Hat Rin) A must for travellers looking to book high-quality tours (diving, live-aboards, jungle safaris etc) and transport. Not just for backpackers, it's an expat-run travel agency that offers peace of mind with every purchase – travellers are provided with the mobile phone number of the owners should any problems arise. It also runs the Crystal Dive shop next door.

Backpackers Thailand (www.backpackersthailand.com) Everything you need to know about Ko Pha-Ngan, from booking accommodation to finding out the Full Moon Party schedule. Doubles as a vast resource for the whole country as well.

ⓘ Getting There & Away

As always, the cost and departure times are subject to change. Rough waves are known to cancel ferries between October and December.

AIR

Ko Pha-Ngan's new airport is scheduled to open in September 2014 with two daily flights to/from Bangkok on **Kan Air** (www.kanairlines.com). The flight will take 80 minutes. It's expected that services will increase over the next few years to include more Bangkok flights and other destinations as well.

BOAT

To/From Bangkok, Hua Hin & Chumphon

The **Lomprayah** (☏ 077 4277 656; www.lomprayah.com) and **Seatran Discovery** (☏ 0 2240 2582; www.seatrandiscovery.com) services have bus-boat combination packages (from around 1500B) that depart from the Th Khao San area in Bangkok and pass through Hua Hin and Chumphon. The whole voyage takes about 17 hours.

It is also quite hassle-free (unless your train breaks down, which happens a lot) to take the train from Bangkok or Hua Hin to Chumphon and switch to a ferry service. In this case expect to pay 300B for a train from Bangkok to Chumphon (about 8½ hours); the boat from Chumphon to Ko Pha-Ngan takes around 2½ hours and costs 800B to 1000B depending on the boat.

To/From Ko Samui

There are around a dozen daily departures between Thong Sala on Ko Pha-Ngan and Ko Samui. These boats leave throughout the day from 7am to 6pm, take from 20 minutes to an hour and cost 200B to 300B depending on the boat.

The **Haad Rin Queen** (☏ 0 7748 4668) goes back and forth between Hat Rin and Big Buddha Beach on Ko Samui four times a day. The voyage takes 50 minutes and costs 200B.

The *Thong Nai Pan Express* is a wobbly old fishing boat (not for the faint-hearted) that runs once a day from Mae Hat on Ko Samui to Hat Rin on Ko Pha-Ngan and then up the east coast, stopping at all the beaches as far as Thong Nai Pan Noi. Prices range from 200B to 400B depending on the destination. The boat won't run in bad weather.

To/From Ko Tao

Ko Tao-bound **Lomprayah** ferries (500B) depart from Thong Sala on Ko Pha-Ngan at 8.30am and 1pm and arrive at 9.45am and 2.15pm. The **Seatran** service (430B) departs from Thong Sala at 8.30am and 2pm daily. Taxis depart Hat Rin for Thong Sala one hour before the boat departure. The cheaper-but-slower **Songserm** (350B) leaves Ko Pha-Ngan at 12.30pm and alights at 2.30pm.

To/From Surat Thani & the Andaman Coast

There are about eight daily departures between Ko Pha-Ngan and Surat Thani on the **Songserm** (☏ 0 7737 7704; www.songserm-expressboat.com; 350B, 4½ hours) or **Lomprayah** (550B, 2¾ hours) services, both travelling via Ko Samui. These boats leave from Thong Sala throughout the day from 7am to 8pm. Every night, depending on the weather, a boat runs from Surat (350B, seven hours), departing at 11pm. Boats in the opposite direction leave Ko Pha-Ngan at 10pm.

Combination boat-bus tickets are available at any travel agency. Simply tell them your desired destination and they will sell you the necessary links in the transport chain. Most travellers will pass through Surat Thani as they swap coasts.

ⓘ Getting Around

You can rent motorcycles all over the island for 150B to 250B per day. Always wear a helmet – it's the law on Ko Pha-Ngan, and local policemen are starting to enforce it. If you plan on riding over dirt tracks it is imperative that you rent a bike comparable to a Honda MTX125 – gearless scooters cannot make the journey. Bicycle rentals are discouraged unless you're fit enough to take on Lance Armstrong.

Pick-up trucks and *sŏrng·tǎa·ou* chug along the island's major roads and the riding rates double after sunset. Ask your accommodation about free or discount transfers when you leave the island. The trip from Thong Sala to Hat Rin is 100B; further beaches will set you back around 150B to 200B.

Long-tail boats depart from Thong Sala, Chalok Lam and Hat Rin, heading to a variety of far-flung destinations such as Hat Khuat (Bottle Beach) and Ao Thong Nai Pan. Expect to pay anywhere from 50B for a short trip, and up to 300B for a lengthier journey. You can charter a private boat ride from beach to beach for about 150B per 15 minutes of travel.

Ko Tao เกาะเต่า

POP 1500

Once the baby of the Samui, Pha-Ngan, Tao trio, Ko Tao may still be the smallest in size but in many other ways it's grown up. The island is consistently gaining popularity and going more upscale, but for now this jungle-topped cutie has the busy vibe of Samui mixed with the laid-back nature of Pha-Ngan. But Tao also has its wildcard, something the others don't: easy-to-get-to, diverse diving right off its shores. Cavort with sharks and rays in a playground of tangled neon coral, toast the day with sunset cocktails on a white

beach then get up and do it all over again the next day. But even while the island may be synonymous with diving, there is much more to the place. Hikers and hermits can re-enact an episode from *Lost* in the dripping coastal jungles. And when you're Robinson Crusoe-ed out, hit the pumpin' bar scene that rages on until dawn.

🏃 Activities

Diving

If you've never been diving before, Ko Tao is *the* place to lose your scuba virginity. The shallow bays scalloping the island are perfect for newbie divers to take their first stab

Ko Tao

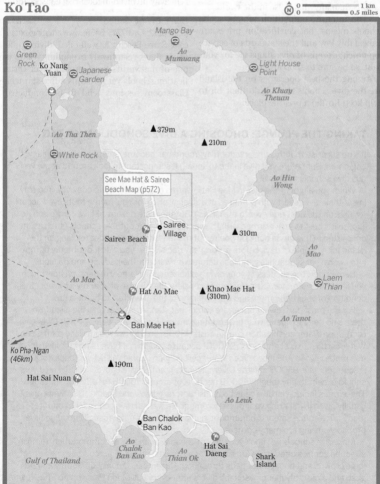

at scuba; the waters are crystal clear, there are loads of neon reefs and the temperatures feel like bathwater. The best dive sites are found at offshore pinnacles within a 20km radius of the island, but seasoned scubaholics almost always prefer the top-notch sites along the Andaman coast. The local marine wildlife includes groupers, moray eels, batfish, bannerfish, barracudas, titan triggerfish, angelfish, clownfish (Nemos), stingrays, reef sharks and frequent visits by mighty whale sharks.

Onshore, over 40 dive centres are ready to saddle you up with gear and teach you the ropes in a 3½-day Open Water certification course. The island issues more scuba certifications than anywhere else in the world.

The intense competition among scuba schools means that certification prices are unbeatably low and the standards of service top-notch; dozens of dive shops vie for your baht, so be sure to shop around.

Among the best operators on the island are the dive schools that all do their bit to help keep Ko Tao a pristine place:

ACE Marine Expeditions
DIVING

(Map p572; www.divephotothai.com) The luxe choice. Go out on this James Bond-worthy speedboat and get to sites in a fraction of the time. The ingenious 'Whaleshark Watch' program keeps up-to-the-moment tabs on where sightings are taking place – they'll whisk you out to where the creatures are so you're chances of seeing them are greatly increased.

Roctopus
DIVING

(Map p572; ☑ 0 7745 6611; www.roctopusdive.com; Sairee Beach) One of the newer places on the scene, Roctopus already has a near legendary reputation for its great staff and high standards. Groups are small and the centre is heavily involved in local reef conservation.

Ban's Diving School
DIVING

(Map p572; ☑ 0 7745 6466; www.amazingkohtao. com; Sairee Beach) A well-oiled diving machine that's relentlessly expanding, Ban's is one of the world's most prolific diver certification schools yet it retains a five-star feel. Classroom sessions tend to be conducted

---

TAKING THE PLUNGE: CHOOSING A DIVE SCHOOL ON KO TAO

It's no surprise that this underwater playground has become exceptionally popular with beginners. But before you dive in (so to speak) it's important to look around at the various dive schools available.

When you alight at the pier in Mae Hat, swarms of touts will try to coax you into staying at their dive resort with promises of a 'special price for you' (some touts even accost tourists on the boat ride over to the island). But there are dozens of dive centres on Ko Tao, so it's best to arrive armed with the names of a few reputable schools (such as the ones listed in this guide book). If you're not rushed for time, consider relaxing on the island for a couple of days before making any decisions – you will undoubtedly bump into swarms of scubaphiles and instructors who will offer their advice and opinions.

Remember: the success of your diving experience will largely depend on how much you like your instructor. Other factors to consider are the size of your diving group, the condition of your equipment and the condition of the dive sites, to name a few.

For the most part, diving prices are somewhat standardised across the island, so there's no need to spend your time hunting around for the best deal. A **PADI** (www.padi. com) Open Water certification course costs 9800B; an **SSI** (www.ssithailand.com) Open Water certificate is slightly less (9000B) because you do not have to pay for instruction materials. An Advanced Open Water certification course will set you back 8500B, a rescue course is 9500B and the Divemaster program costs a cool 25,000B. Fun divers should expect to pay roughly 1000B per dive, or around 7000B for a 10-dive package. These rates include all dive gear, boat, instructors/guides and snacks. Discounts are usually given if you bring your own equipment. Be wary of dive centres that offer too many price cuts – safety is paramount, and a shop giving out unusually good deals is probably cutting too many corners.

Most dive schools will hook you up with cheap or even free accommodation. Almost all scuba centres offer gratis fan rooms for anyone doing beginner coursework. Expect large crowds and booked-out beds throughout December, January, June, July and August, and a monthly glut of wannabe divers after every Full Moon Party on Ko Pha-Ngan.

in large groups, but there's a reasonable amount of individual attention in the water. A breadth of international instructors means that students can learn to dive in their native tongue.

Big Blue Diving
DIVING

(Map p572; ☑ 0 7745 6772, 0 7745 6415; www.bigbluediving.com; Sairee Beach) If Goldilocks were picking a dive school, she'd probably pick Big Blue – this midsize operation (not too big, not too small) gets props for fostering a sociable vibe while maintaining a high standard of service. Divers of every ilk can score dirt-cheap accommodation at their resort.

Buddha View
DIVING

(☑ 0 7745 6074; www.buddhaview-diving.com; Chalok Ban Kao) Another big dive operation on Ko Tao, Buddha View offers the standard fare of certification and special programs for technical diving (venturing beyond the usual parameters of recreational underwater exploration). Discounted accommodation is available at its friendly resort.

Crystal Dive
DIVING

(Map p572; ☑ 0 7745 6107; www.crystaldive.com; Mae Hat) Crystal is the Meryl Streep of diving operators, winning all the awards for best performance year after year. It's one of the largest schools on the island (and around the world), although high-quality instructors and intimate classes keep the school feeling quite personal. Multilingual staff members, air-conditioned classes and two on-site swimming pools sweeten the deal. Highly recommended.

New Heaven
DIVING

(☑ 0 7745 6587; www.newheavendiveschool.com; Chalok Ban Kao) The owners of this small diving operation dedicate a lot of their time to preserving the natural beauty of Ko Tao's underwater sites by conducting regular reef checks and contributing to reef restoration efforts. A special CPAD research diver certification program is available in addition to the regular order of programs and fun dives.

Scuba Junction
DIVING

(Scuba J; Map p572; ☑ 0 7745 6164; www.scubajunction.com; Sairee Beach) A groovy new storefront and a team of outgoing instructors lure travellers looking for a more intimate dive experience. Scuba Junction guarantees a maximum of four people per diving group.

ZERO TO HERO

It's the oldest story in the book: 'I came to Ko Tao on vacation and six months later I'm still here!' Seems like the island's magical magnetic energy catches hold of everyone, so don't be surprised if you too find yourself altering flight plans.

For those of you who anticipate embracing the castaway lifestyle, consider going from 'Zero to Hero' as they call it on Ko Tao. Over the last few years, several of the savvier diving operators started package deals where you can go from scuba newbie to pro over the course of a couple of months. You'll graduate through four levels of diving certifications, 'intern' as a divemaster at your dive school, then take a stab at the instructor program. Prices hover around 80,000B and include all the bells and whistles necessary to turn you into a fish. Accommodation is not included.

Snorkelling

Snorkelling is a popular alternative to diving, and orchestrating your own snorkelling adventure here is simple, since the bays on the east coast have small bungalow operations offering equipment rental for between 100B and 200B per day.

Most snorkel enthusiasts opt for the do-it-yourself approach on Ko Tao, which involves swimming out into the offshore bays or hiring a long-tail boat to putter around further out. Guided tours are also available and can be booked at any local travel agency. Tours range from 500B to 800B (usually including gear, lunch and a guide/boat captain) and stop at various snorkelling hotspots around the island. **Laem Thian** is popular for its small sharks, **Shark Island** has loads of fish (and ironically no sharks), **Ao Hin Wong** is known for its crystalline waters, and **Light House Point**, in the north, offers a dazzling array of colourful sea anemones. Dive schools will usually allow snorkellers on their vessels for a comparable price – but it's only worth snorkelling at the shallower sites such as Japanese Gardens. Note that dive boats visit the shallower sites in the afternoons.

Freediving

Over the last couple of years freediving (exploring the sea using breath-holding techniques rather than scuba gear) has grown rapidly in popularity. Several small schools have opened up across the island. We recommend the capable staff at **Apnea Total** (Map p572; ☏08 7183 2321; www.apnea-total.com; Sairee Beach) who have earned several awards in the freediving world and possess a special knack for easing newbies into this heart-pounding sport. The student-teacher ratio of three to one also ensures plenty of attention to safety. Also worth a special mention is **Blue Immersion** (Map p572; ☏08 7682 1886; www.blue-immersion.com; Sairee Beach) run by friendly Akim, a martial arts expert and a freediving pro – he was one of the first people in the world to freedive below 100m. Freediving prices are standardised across the island as well – a 2½-day SSI beginner course will set you back 5500B.

Technical Diving & Cave Diving

Well-seasoned divers and hardcore Jacques Cousteaus should contact **Tech Thailand** (www.techthailand.com) or one of a handful of other tech diving schools if they want to take their underwater exploration to the next level and try a technical dive. According to PADI, tec diving, as it's often known, is 'diving other than conventional commercial or recreational diving that takes divers beyond recreational diving limits'. Technical diving exceeds depths of 40m and requires stage decompressions, and a variety of gas mixtures are often used in a single dive.

Several years ago, Tech Thailand's old boat, MS *Trident,* made a name for itself in the diving community after successfully locating dozens of previously undiscovered wrecks in the Gulf of Thailand. Its most famous discovery was the USS *Lagarto,* an American naval vessel that sank during WWII. The gulf has long been an important trading route and new wrecks are being dis-

---

DIVE SITES AT A GLANCE

In general, divers don't have a choice as to which sites they explore. Each dive school chooses a smattering of sites for the day depending on weather and ocean conditions. Deeper dive sites such as Chumphon Pinnacle are usually visited in the morning. Afternoon boats tour the shallower sites such as Japanese Gardens. Recently, two large vessels have been sunk off the coast, providing scubaphiles with two new wreck dives. Divers hoping to spend some quality time searching for whale sharks at Sail Rock should join one of the dive trips departing daily from Ko Pha-Ngan.

➜ **Chumphon Pinnacle** (36m maximum depth), 13km west of Ko Tao, has a colourful assortment of sea anemones along the four interconnected pinnacles. The site plays host to schools of giant trevally, tuna and large grey reef sharks. Whale sharks are known to pop up once in a while.

➜ **Green Rock** (25m maximum depth) is an underwater jungle gym featuring caverns, caves and small swim-throughs. Rays, grouper and triggerfish are known to hang around. It's a great place for a night dive.

➜ **Japanese Gardens** (12m maximum depth), between Ko Tao and Ko Nang Yuan, is a low-stress dive site perfect for beginners. There's plenty of colourful coral, and turtles, stingray and pufferfish often pass by.

➜ **Mango Bay** (16m maximum depth) might be your first dive site if you are putting on a tank for the first time. Lazy reef fish swim around as newbies practise their skills on the sandy bottom.

➜ **Sail Rock** (34m maximum depth), best accessed from Ko Pha-Ngan, features a massive rock chimney with a vertical swim-through, and large pelagics like barracuda and kingfish. This is one of the top spots in Southeast Asia to see whale sharks.

➜ **Southwest Pinnacle** (33m maximum depth) offers divers a small collection of pinnacles that are home to giant groupers and barracudas. Whale sharks and leopard sharks are sometimes spotted (pun partially intended).

➜ **White Rock** (29m maximum depth) is home to colourful corals, angelfish, clown fish and territorial triggerfish. Another popular spot for night divers.

covered all the time, from old Chinese pottery wrecks to Japanese *marus* (merchant ships). In 2011 the *Trident* was purposefully sunk off the coast of Ko Tao to create an artificial reef. A miscalculation with the explosives has left the wreck a bit too deep for beginners.

Recently, cave diving has taken Ko Tao by storm, and the most intrepid scuba buffs are lining up to make the half-day trek over to Khao Sok National Park. Beneath the park's main lake lurks an astonishing submarine world filled with hidden grottos, limestone crags and skulking catfish. In certain areas divers can swim near submerged villages that were flooded in order to create a reservoir and dam. Most cave-diving trips depart from Ko Tao on the afternoon boat service and return to the island on the afternoon boat service of the following day. Overnight stays are arranged in or near the park.

Underwater Photography & Videography

If your wallet is already full of PADI certification cards, consider renting an underwater camera or enrolling in a marine videography course. Many scuba schools hire professional videographers to film Open Water certifications, and if this piques your interest, you could potentially earn some money after completing a video internship. Your dive operator can put you in touch with any of the half-dozen videography crews on the island. We recommend ACE Marine Images (Map p572; ✆0 7745 7054; www.acemarineimages.com; Sairee Beach), one of Thailand's leading underwater videography studios. An introductory course including camera, diving and instruction is 4500B and can also be used towards an Advanced PADI certification. Deep Down Productions (✆08 7133 4102; www.deepdown-productions.com) and Oceans Below (✆08 6060 1863; www.oceansbelow.net) offer videography courses and internships and each have their own special options.

Other Activities

★Flying Trapeze Adventures ACROBATICS (FTA; Map p572; ✆08 0696 9269; www.flyingtrapezeadventures.com; Sairee Beach; ⊘4-8pm, lessons 4pm, 5pm & 6pm) Find out if you're a great catch during a one-hour group trapeze lesson (950B). Courses are taught by superfriendly Gemma and her posse of limber sidekicks, who take you from circus neophyte to soaring savant in four jumps or less. Book over the phone or show up at one

of the nightly demos, which start at 7.30pm. Participants must be at least six years old.

Goodtime Adventures
HIKING, ADVENTURE SPORTS
(Map p572; ✆08 7275 3604; www.gtadventures.com; Sairee Beach; ⊘noon-late) Hike through the island's jungly interior, swing from rock to rock during a climbing and abseiling session (from 2000B), or unleash your inner daredevil during an afternoon of cliff jumping (at your own risk). The Goodtime office, along the Sairee sands, doubles as a friendly cafe serving an assortment of international nibbles (including dip coffee!).

Shambhala
YOGA
(Map p572; ✆08 4440 6755; Sairee Beach) Ko Tao's full-time yoga centre is housed in beautiful wooden *săh·lah* on the forested grounds of Blue Wind in Sairee Beach. The two-hour classes, led by Kester, the energetic yogi, cost 300B.

Ko Tao Bowling & Mini Golf
BOWLING, MINIGOLF
(✆0 7745 6316; ⊘noon-midnight) Located on the main road between Mae Hat and Chalok Ban Kao, Ko Tao Bowling & Mini Golf has several homemade bowling lanes where the employees reset the pins after every frame (300B per hour). The 18-hole minigolf course has a landmark theme – putt your ball through Stonehenge or across the Golden Gate Bridge.

🛌 Sleeping

If you are planning to dive while visiting Ko Tao, your scuba operator will probably offer you free or discounted accommodation to sweeten the deal. Some schools have on-site lodging, while others have deals with nearby bungalows. It's important to note that you only receive your scuba-related discount on the days you dive. So, for example, if you buy a 10-dive package, and decide to take a day off in the middle, your room rate will not be discounted on that evening. Also, a restful sleep is important before diving, so scope out these 'great room deals' before saying yes – some of them are one cockroach away from being condemned.

There are also many sleeping options that have absolutely nothing to do with the island's diving culture. Ko Tao's secluded eastern coves are dotted with stunning retreats that still offer a true getaway experience, but these can be difficult to reach due to the island's dismal network of roads. You can often call ahead of time and arrange to be picked up from the pier in Mae Hat.

Note that many budget rooms are only available on a first come, first served basis and often aren't even advertised on hotel websites. Many midrange resorts offer budget rooms so take a look at all our listings to see each resort's (usually very big) price range. These rooms book fast so it can be prudent to call ahead and find out what may be available before you arrive.

Sairee Beach

Giant Sairee is the longest and most developed strip on the island, with a string of dive operations, bungalows, travel agencies, minimarkets and internet cafes. The northern end is the prettiest and quietest while there's more of a party scene and noise from the bars to the south. For most people, this is the choice beach to stay at since it has a great blend of scenery and action.

Blue Wind   BUNGALOW $
(Map p572; ☑ 0 7745 6116; bluewind_wa@yahoo.com; bungalows 350-1400B; ❄ ⓢ) Blue Wind offers a breath of fresh air from the high-intensity dive resorts strung along Sairee Beach. Sturdy bamboo huts are peppered along a dirt trail behind the beachside bakery. Large, tiled air-conditioned cabins are also available, boasting hot showers and TVs. It's rustic but relaxing.

Spicytao Backpackers   HOSTEL $
(Map p572; ☑ 08 1036 6683; www.spicyhostels.com; dm 200-250B; ❄ ⓢ) Like your own supersocial country hang-out, Spicytao is hidden off the main drag in a rustic garden setting. Backpackers rave about the ambience and staff who are always organising activities. Book in advance!

Ban's Diving Resort   RESORT $$
(Map p572; ☑ 0 7745 6466; www.amazingkohtao.com; r 600-29,700B; ❄ @ ⓢ ⌘) This dive-centric party palace offers a wide range of quality accommodation from basic backpacker digs to sleek hillside villas, and it's getting bigger all the time. Post-scuba chill sessions happen on Ban's prime slice of beach or at one of the two swimming pools tucked within the strip of jungle between the two-storey, pillared and terraced white hotel blocks.

Sairee Cottage   BUNGALOW $$
(Map p572; ☑ 0 7745 6126; www.saireecottagediving.com; bungalows 350-2800B; ❄ ⓢ) Bungalows are connected by a sand path through a sun-splotched garden of palms and hibiscus. Even the smallest, most budget options here are of higher standard than most and very good value. The beach out front is slim and under the shade of a giant ironwood tree.

Big Blue Resort   BUNGALOW $$
(Map p572; ☑ 0 7745 6050; www.bigbluediving.com; dm 400B, r 2000-7000B; ❄ @) This scuba-centric resort has a summer camp vibe – diving classes dominate the daytime, while evenings are spent en masse, grabbing dinner or watching fire twirling. Both the basic fan bungalows and motel-style air-con rooms offer little when it comes to views, but who has the time to relax when there's an ocean out there to explore?

Palm Leaf & Bow Thong   BUNGALOW $$
(Map p572; ☑ 0 7745 6266; www.bowthongresort.com; bungalows 700-4900B; ❄ ⓢ ⌘) Palm Leaf is the swankier part of these conjoined resorts; Bow Thong has more popular lower-priced digs. Reception is a little awkward, the rooms are good though nothing spectacular, but the location, at the quieter northern section of silky Sairee Beach simply can't be beat. The lowest-priced bungalows are on a first come, first served basis.

In Touch Resort   BUNGALOW $$
(Map p572; ☑ 0 7745 6514; www.intouchresort.com; bungalows 800-2500B; ❄ ⓢ) Older bungalows

are a mishmash of bamboo and dark wood, while several rounded air-con rooms have a cave theme – it's all very *Flintstones*. This is as far south as you can get on Sairee, at the end of a skinny motorbike path, with a groovy bar and lush beach right out front and not too much of a racket.

Seashell Resort
BUNGALOW $$

(Map p572; ☑0 7745 6271; www.seashell-kohtao. com; bungalows 1000-4800B; ❄☎) Another place with a huge mix of lodging from simple wood bungalows to hotel-style rooms in a block. This is a busy resort with nicely tended grounds but we found the prices out of whack with what you can find elsewhere. It's a good backup that welcomes divers and non-divers.

★Place
RESORT $$$

(www.theplacekohtao.com; villas 8000B; ❄☎) Honeymooners will delight in this unique option – several private luxury villas nestled in the leaf-clad hills with sweeping ocean views down below. A private plunge pool is standard – naturally – and private chef services are available for those who choose to remain in their love nest instead of sliding down to Sairee for restaurant eats. It's about a 15-minute walk or five-minute taxi ride from this hilltop location to Sairee Beach.

Ko Tao Cabana
BUNGALOW $$$

(Map p572; ☑0 7745 6250; www.kohtaocabana. com; bungalows 5300-14,000B; ❄@☎≋) This prime piece of quiet beachside property offers timber-framed villas and crinkled white adobe huts with woven roofs dotted along the boulder-strewn beach and up the hill. Paths wind through the fern-laden, manicured jungle. The private villas are one of the more upscale options on the island although service isn't quite yet on par with what you'd hope for in this price bracket.

Koh Tao Coral Grand Resort
BUNGALOW $$$

(Map p572; ☑0 7745 6431; www.kohtaocoral.com; bungalows 2600-9300B; ❄☎≋) The plethora of pink facades at this family-friendly option feels a bit like Barbie's dream Thai beach house. Cottage interiors are coated in cheery primary colours framed by white truncated beams while pricier digs have a more distinctive Thai flavour, boasting dark lacquered mouldings and gold-foiled art. The setting is lovely, though the service is not all it could be.

🛏 Mae Hat

All ferry arrivals pull into the pier at the busy village of Mae Hat and nearly all the resorts on this beach will have a view and be in earshot of the constant ebb and flow of boat arrivals and departures. As such this isn't the best beach for a tranquil getaway although it's a good hub if your main goal is diving. Accommodation is spread throughout, but the more charming options extend in both directions along the sandy beach, both north and south of the pier.

Sai Thong Resort
BUNGALOW $

(☑0 7745 6868; Hat Sai Nuan; bungalows 500-2000B; ❄) As the rush of Mae Hat dwindles away along the island's southwest shore, Sai Thong emerges along quiet, sandy Hat Sai Nuan. Bungalows, in various, rustic incarnations of weaving and wood, have colourful porch hammocks and palm-filled vistas. Guests frequent the restaurant's relaxing sun deck – a favourite spot for locals too. The resort is accessed by a quick ride from the Mae Hat pier in a boat taxi.

Tao Thong Villa
BUNGALOW $

(☑0 7745 6078; Ao Sai Nuan; bungalows 400-1800B; ❄@☎) Very popular with long-termers seeking peace and quiet, these funky, no-frills bungalows have killer views. Tao Thong actually straddles two tiny beaches on a craggy cape about halfway between Mae Hat and Chalok Ban Kao. To reach it, grab a boat taxi for a short ride from the Mae Hat pier.

Crystal Dive Resort
BUNGALOW $$

(Map p572; ☑0 7745 6107; www.crystaldive.com; bungalows 800-1500B; ❄☎≋) The bungalow and motel-style accommodation at Crystal is reserved for its divers, and prices drop significantly for those taking courses. Guests can take a dip in the refreshing pool when it isn't overflowing with bubble-blowing newbie divers.

Ananda Villa
HOTEL $$

(Map p572; ☑0 7745 6478; www.anandavilla.com; r 500-2000B; ❄☎) This two-storey cream and white hotel has a colonial feel and is lined with decorative palms and plumeria. The cheapest rooms are fan only and are in another older block a bit further from the beach. Friendly reception.

Mae Hat & Sairee Beach

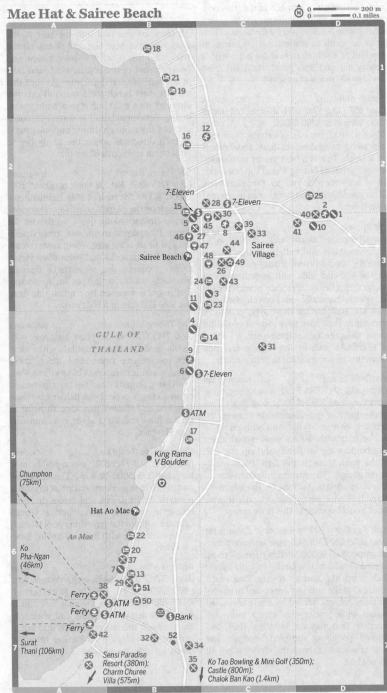

Mae Hat & Sairee Beach

Regal Resort RESORT $$
(Map p572; 0 7745 6007; www.kohtaoregal.com; r 1900-3500B; ✳@🛜🏊) This resort is just north of the pier so you get all the commotion along with your pretty stretch of white sand – the main pool is filled with divers most of the day. Rooms are large and some have beautiful sea views but it's all *Fawlty Towers*-esque with amenities breaking down etc. Decent value for the price though.

Montra Resort & Spa RESORT $$$
(Map p572; 0 7745 7057; www.kohtaomontra.com; r 4200-12,800B; ✳@🛜🏊) The big, imposing Montra encircles an equally huge pool with a swim-up bar. This is a good location for Mae Hat, on the beach and steps away from all the action, although note that this is very close to the port.

Charm Churee Villa RESORT $$$
(0 7745 6393; www.charmchureevilla.com; bungalows 4300-18,700B; ✳🛜🏊) Tucked under sky-scraping palms away from the bustle of the pier, the luxuriant villas of Charm Churee are dedicated to the flamboyant spoils of the Far East. Staircases, chiselled into the rock face, dribble down a palmed slope revealing teak huts strewn across smoky boulders. The villas' unobstructed views of the swishing waters are beguiling.

Sensi Paradise Resort RESORT $$$
(0 7745 6244; www.sensiparadise.com; bungalows 2100-7000B; ✳🛜🏊) 'Natural chic' on the prettiest stretch of Mae Hat proper, right up against some boulder outcrops. You won't escape the noise of the pier, however. Rooms on the hillside are worn and not worth the price while newer models closer to the beach are quite lovely. Friendly caretakers and several airy teak *săh·lah* add an extra element of charm.

Chalok Ban Kao

Ao Chalok Ban Ko, about 1.7km south of Mae Hat by road, has the third-largest concentration of accommodation on Ko Tao. This is a slim stretch of sand in a scenic half-circle bay framed by boulders at either end. The milky blue water here is quite shallow and at low tide a sandbar is exposed that's fun to wade out to for prime sun bathing. This is the quietest of the main beaches but there's still a good selection of restaurants, diving and a more mellow but fun nightlife scene.

Tropicana GUESTHOUSE $
(☑0 7745 6167; www.koh-tao-tropicana-resort.com; r 500-1500B) Low-rise, basic hotel units peppered across a sandy, shady garden campus that provide fleeting glimpses of the ocean between fanned fronds and spiky palms.

JP Resort GUESTHOUSE $
(☑0 7745 6099; r from 600-1300B; ❄@☎) A colourful (some may say old-fashioned) menagerie of prim motel-style rooms stacked on a small scrap of jungle across the street from the sea.

★ **Viewpoint Resort** RESORT $$
(☑0 7745 6666; www.kohtaoviewpoint.com; bungalows 1200-14,000B; ❄☎✉) Lush grounds of ferns and palms meander across a boulder-studded hillside offering stunning views over the sea and the bay. All options, from the exquisite private suites that feel like Tarzan and Jane's love nest gone luxury to the huge, view-filled bungalows, use boulders, wood and concrete to create comfortable, naturalistic abodes. It's under new management and fantastic value.

Freedom Beach BUNGALOW $$
(☑0 7745 6596; bungalows 700-3500B; ❄☎) On its own secluded beach shaded by tall, pretty bushes and connected to Ao Chalok Ban Kao by a boardwalk, Freedom feels like a classic backpacker haunt. Steep, concrete paths link the seaside bar to the accommodation (from wooden shacks to sturdier huts with air-con) that runs from the beach to high on the cliff. Reception is at Taahtoh Resort.

New Heaven Resort BUNGALOW $$
(☑0 7745 6422; www.newheavenkohtao.com; r & bungalows 700-3800B; ❄☎) Just beyond the clutter of Chalok Ban Kao, New Heaven delivers colourful huts perched on a hill over impossibly clear waters. A steep path of chiselled stone tumbles down the shrubby rock face revealing views ripped straight from the pages of *National Geographic*.

Buddha View Dive Resort BUNGALOW $$
(☑0 7745 6074; www.buddhaview-diving.com; r 800-1500B; ❄@☎✉) Like the other large diving operations on the island, Buddha View offers its divers discounted on-site digs in a super-social atmosphere.

Ko Tao Resort RESORT $$$
(☑0 7745 6133; www.kotaoresort.com; r & bungalows 1850-9500B; ❄@☎✉) The entrance is a throwback to the days when taste and architecture weren't particularly synonymous, but inside the facilities fit the true definition of a resort. Rooms are split between 'pool side' and 'paradise zone' – all are well stocked, water sports equipment is on offer, and there are several bars primed to serve an assortment of fruity cocktails.

Chintakiri Resort RESORT $$$
(☑0 7745 6133; www.chintakiri.com; r & bungalows 2900-7000B; ❄@☎✉) Perched high over the gulf waters overlooking Chalok Ban Kao, Chintakiri is one of Ko Tao's more luxurious properties, helping the island furtively creep upmarket. Rooms are spread around the inland jungle, and sport crisp white walls with lacquered finishing.

🛏 Hin Wong

A sandy beach has been swapped for a boulder-strewn coast on the serene east side of the island, but the water is crystal clear. The road to Hin Wong is paved in parts, but sudden sand pits and steep hills can toss you off your motorbike.

Hin Wong Bungalows BUNGALOW $
(☑0 7745 6006; Hin Wong; bungalows 350-700B; ☎) Pleasant wooden huts are scattered across vast expanses of untamed tropical terrain – it all feels a bit like *Gilligan's Island*. A rickety dock, jutting out just beyond the breezy restaurant, is the perfect place to dangle your legs and watch schools of black sardines slide through the cerulean water.

View Rock BUNGALOW $
(☑0 7745 6549, 0 7745 6548; viewrock@hotmail.com; Hin Wong; bungalows 500-2000B; ❄☎) When coming down the dirt road into Hin Wong, follow the signs as they lead you north of Hin Wong Bungalows. View Rock is precisely that: views and rocks; the hodgepodge of wooden huts, which looks like a secluded fishing village, is built into the steep crags offering stunning views of the bay.

🛏 Ao Tanot (Tanote Bay)

Tanote Bay is more populated than some of the other eastern coves, but it's still rather quiet and picturesque. It is the only bay on the east coast that is accessible by a decent road. Discounted taxis (around 100B) bounce back and forth between Tanote Bay and Mae Hat; ask at your resort for a timetable.

Poseidon   BUNGALOW $
(☑0 7745 6735; poseidonkohtao@hotmail.com; Ao Tanot; bungalows 400-1200B; ☎) Poseidon keeps the tradition of the budget bamboo bungalow alive with a dozen basic-but-sleepable huts scattered near the sand.

Family Tanote   BUNGALOW $$
(☑0 7745 6757; Ao Tanot; bungalows 800-3500B; ✳@☎) As the name suggests, this scatter of hillside bungalows is run by a local family who take pride in providing comfy digs to solitude seekers. Strap on a snorkel mask and swim up with the fish at your doorstep, or climb up to the restaurant for a tasty meal and pleasant views of the bay.

Ao Leuk & Ao Thian Ok

Jamahkiri Resort & Spa   RESORT $$$
(☑0 7745 6400; www.jamahkiri.com; bungalows 6900-30,000B; ✳@☎) Wooden gargoyle masks and stone fertility goddesses abound amid swirling mosaics and multi-armed statues at this whitewashed estate. Feral hoots of distant monkeys confirm the jungle theme, as do the thatched roofs and tiki-torched soirees. The resort's seemingly infinite number of stone stairways can be a pain, so it's a good thing Ko Tao's most luxurious spa is on the premises.

Ko Nang Yuan

Photogenic Ko Nang Yuan, just off the northwest coast of Ko Tao, is easily accessible by the Lomprayah catamaran, and by water taxis that depart from Mae Hat and Sairee (100B each way). There's a 100B tax for all visitors to the island.

Ko Nangyuan Dive Resort   BUNGALOW $$$
(☑0 7745 6088; www.nangyuan.com; bungalows 1500-9000B; ✳☎) The rugged collection of wood and aluminium bungalows winds its way across three coolie-hatlike conical islands connected by an idyllic beige sandbar. Yes, this is a private island paradise but note it gets busy with day-trippers. The resort also boasts the best restaurant on the island, but then again, it's the only place to eat...

✕🍴 Eating

With super-sized Ko Samui lurking on the horizon, it's hard to believe that quaint little Ko Tao holds its own in the gastronomy category. Most resorts and dive operators offer on-site dining, and stand-alone establishments are multiplying at lightning speed in Sairee Beach and Mae Hat. The diverse population of divers has spawned a broad range of international cuisine dining options, including Mexican, French, Italian, Indian and Japanese. On our quest to find the tastiest Thai fare on the island, we discovered, not surprisingly, that our favourite local meals were being dished out at small, unnamed restaurants on the side of the road.

✕ Sairee Beach

Su Chili   THAI $
(Map p572; dishes 70-150B; ☉lunch & dinner; ☎) Fresh and tasty Thai food served by friendly waitstaff who always ask how spicy you want your food and somehow get it right. Try the delicious northern Thai specialities or Penang curries.

ZanziBar   CAFE $
(Map p572; sandwiches 90-150B; ☉breakfast, lunch & dinner) The island's outpost of sandwich yuppie-dom slathers an array of yummy ingredients between two slices of wholegrain bread.

Blue Wind Bakery   INTERNATIONAL $
(Map p572; mains 50-180B; ☉breakfast, lunch & dinner) This beachside shanty dishes out Thai favourites, Western confections and freshly blended fruit juices. Enjoy your thick fruit smoothie and flaky pastry while reclining on tattered triangular pillows and watching the waves roll in and out.

★Barracuda
Restaurant & Bar   ASIAN FUSION $$
(Map p572; ☑08 0146 3267; mains 180-400B; ☉dinner) Chef Ed Jones caters for the Thai princess when she's in town but you can sample his exquisite cuisine for mere pennies in comparison to her budget. Locally sourced ingredients are used to make creative, fresh, fusion masterpieces. Try the seafood platter, basil stuffed fish or sashimi bruchetta – then wash it down with a lemon grass, ginger mojito.

The Gallery
THAI FUSION **$$**

(Map p572; [☎] 0 7745 6547; mains 100-350B) One of the nicer settings in town, next to owner Chris Clark's gallery of beautiful island photography, the food here is equally special. The signature dish is *mok maprao* (chicken, shrimp and fish curry served in a young coconut) but the green curry red snapper is also phenomenal.

Taste of Home
INTERNATIONAL **$$**

(Map p572; mains 180-250B; ⊙ lunch & dinner; 🛜) German-run and serving a bit of everything (Swedish meatballs, Turkish kofta, Greek salads and Weiner schnitzel to name a few), but everything is delicious and prepared with heart. It's a small, simple setting popular with expats. Don't forget to finish your meal with the owner's homemade Bailey's!

Darawan
INTERNATIONAL **$$**

(Map p572; mains 120-450B; ⊙ lunch & dinner) Like a top-end dining venue plucked from the posh shores of Ko Samui, regal Darawan is the island's best place to take a date. Perched atop the trees at the back of Ban's sprawling resort, the outdoor balcony offers beautiful views of the setting sun (come around 6pm). Designer lighting, efficient waiters and two-for-one sunset gin and tonics seal the deal.

Chopper's Bar & Grill
INTERNATIONAL **$$**

(Map p572; dishes 60-200B; ⊙ breakfast, lunch & dinner) So popular that it has become a local landmark, Chopper's is a two-storey hangout where divers and travellers can widen their beer belly. There's live music, sports on the TVs, billiards and a cinema room. On Friday nights the drinks are 'two for one', and dishes are half-priced as well. Cheers for scored goals are interspersed with chatter about the day's dive.

Café Corner
CAFE **$$**

(Map p572; snacks & mains 30-180B; ⊙ breakfast & lunch) Prime real estate, mod furnishings and tasty iced coffees have made Café Corner a Sairee staple over the last few years. Swing by at 5pm to stock up for tomorrow morning's breakfast; the scrumptious baked breads are buy-one-get-one-free before being tossed at sunset.

Big Blue East
THAI, INTERNATIONAL **$$**

(Map p572; dishes 70-250B; ⊙ breakfast, lunch & dinner) Big Blue Resort's busy chow house, located about 2m from the crashing tide, dispatches an assortment of Thai and international eats, including tasty individual pizzas. The joint fills up around sunset with divers chuckling at the daily dive bloopers shown on the big-screen TV.

El Gringo
MEXICAN **$$**

(Map p572; dishes 80-200B; ⊙ breakfast, lunch & dinner) As if there aren't already enough nicknames in Thailand for *fa·ràng*. The self-proclaimed 'funky Mexican joint' slings burritos of questionable authenticity in both Sairee Beach and Mae Hat. Delivery is available.

✕ Mae Hat

Bizzaro Tapas
TAPAS **$**

(dishes 60-140B; ⊙ 4pm-1am, closed Tue) It's a bit out of the way, on the road between Mae Hat and Chalok Ban, but the setting in bamboo huts with cross-legged seating is great and the fun food – from ceviche and stuffed eggplant to barbecued pork ribs – is worth the drive.

Pim's Guesthouse
THAI **$**

(Map p572; curry 70B; ⊙ lunch) Everyday Pim makes a curry (the massaman is everyone's favourite) at this humble spot, and everyday she sells out before the lunch hour is over. People from all over the island flock here. It's that good.

★ Whitening
INTERNATIONAL **$$**

(Map p572; dishes 150-400B; ⊙ dinner; 🛜) This starched, white, beachy spot falls somewhere between being a restaurant and a chic seaside bar – foodies will appreciate the tasty twists on indigenous and international dishes. Dine amid dangling white Christmas lights while keeping your bare feet tucked into the sand. And the best part? It's comparatively easy on the wallet.

Café del Sol
INTERNATIONAL **$$**

(Map p572; dishes 70-320B; ⊙ breakfast, lunch & dinner; 🛜) Just steps away from the pier is our favourite breakfast spot on the island – go for the 'Del Sol breakfast' (delicious fruit salad, yoghurt and coffee) with a scrumptious spinach omelette on the side. Lunch and dinner dishes range from hearty pepper hamburgers to homemade pasta, though prices tend to be quite inflated.

Zest Coffee Lounge
CAFE **$**

(Map p572; dishes 70-190B; ⊙ breakfast & lunch; 🛜) Indulge in the street-cafe lifestyle at Zest – home to the best cup of joe on the island. Idlers can nibble on ciabatta sandwiches or sticky confections while nursing their creamy caffe latte. There's a second branch in Sairee, although we prefer this location.

Dolce Vita
ITALIAN $$
(Map p572; pizzas 170-270B; ⊘noon-10pm) For the best Italian on Ko Tao, come and taste Dolce Vita's homemade pastas and fine pizzas.

Safety Stop Pub
INTERNATIONAL $
(Map p572; mains 60-250B; ⊘breakfast, lunch & dinner; ☎) A haven for homesick Brits, this pier-side restaurant and bar feels like a tropical beer garden. Stop by on Sundays to stuff your face with an endless supply of barbecued goodness; and the Thai dishes also aren't half bad.

Pranee's Kitchen
THAI $
(Map p572; dishes 50-150B; ⊘breakfast, lunch & dinner; ☎) An old Mae Hat fave, Pranee's serves scrumptious curries and other Thai treats in an open-air pavilion sprinkled with lounging pillows, wooden tables and TVs. English movies (with hilariously incorrect subtitles) are shown nightly at 6pm.

Food Centre
THAI $
(Map p572; mains from 30B; ⊘breakfast, lunch & dinner) An unceremonious gathering of hot-tin food stalls, Food Centre – as it's come to be known – lures lunching locals with veritable smoke signals rising up from the concrete parking lot abutting Mae Hat's petrol station. You'll find some of the island's best papaya salad here.

Greasy Spoon
BREAKFAST $
(Map p572; English breakfast 140B; ⊘breakfast & lunch) Although completely devoid of character, Greasy Spoon stays true to its name by offering a variety of heart-clogging breakfast treats: eggs, sausage, stewed vegies and chips (their speciality) that'll bring a tear to any Brit's eye.

✕ Chalok Ban Kao

I ♥ Salad
CAFE $$
(salads 160-200B; ⊘breakfast & lunch; ☎) A healthy array of salads and wraps use fresh ingredients and are big and filling. There are also real fruit juices and healthy egg white-only breakfasts.

Viewpoint Restaurant
INTERNATIONAL $$$
(☏0 7745 6444; 250-1250B; ⊘breakfast, lunch & dinner) On a beautiful, wooden deck overlooking Ao Chalok Ban Kao, this is one of the most romantic settings on the island. The food is also the most upscale and holds its own against Samui's best – try the slow-roasted pork or the red snapper in green curry. Apart from the beef dishes, the prices are reasonable for the high standards.

Long Pae
STEAKHOUSE $$$
(mains 100-430B; ⊘dinner) Situated off the radar from most of the island's tourist traffic, 'Uncle Pae' sits on a scruffy patch of hilly jungle with distant views of the sea down below. The speciality here is steak, which goes oh-so-well with a generous smattering of pan-Asian appetisers.

🍷 Drinking & Nightlife

After diving, Ko Tao's favourite pastime is drinking, and there's definitely no shortage of places to get tanked. In fact, the island's three biggest dive centres each have bumpin' bars – **Fish Bowl**, **Crystal Bar** and **Buddha On The Beach** in Chalok Bak Kao – that attract swarms of travellers and expats alike. It's well worth stopping by even if you aren't a diver.

Flyers detailing upcoming parties are posted on various trees and walls along the island's west coast (check the two 7-Elevens in Sairee). Also keep an eye out for posters touting 'jungle parties' held on nondescript patches of scrubby jungle in the centre of the island. There's also a **Koh Tao Pub Crawl** (www.kohtaopubcrawl.com) that starts at Chopper's Bar & Grill (p576) on Hat Sairee every Monday, Wednesday and Friday at 7pm and bounces around to the most happening spots. The 380B cover includes a bucket, two shots and a T-shirt, so it's not a bad deal.

Several places, such as Chopper's and Safety Stop Pub, double as great hang-out joints for a well-deserved post-dive beer.

Just remember: don't drink and dive.

Clumped at the southern end of Sairee Beach, **AC Party Pub**, **In Touch** and **Maya Bar** take turns reeling in the partiers throughout the week.

Castle
NIGHTCLUB
(www.thecastlekohtao.com; Mae Hat) Located along the main road between Mae Hat and Chalok Ban Kao, the Castle has quickly positioned itself as the most-loved party venue on the island, luring an array of local and

international DJs to its triad of parties each month.

Fizz
BAR

(Map p572; Sairee Beach) Recline on mattress-sized pillows and enjoy designer cocktails while listening to Moby or Enya, mixed with hypnotic gushes of the rolling tide.

Lotus Bar
BAR

(Map p572; Sairee Beach) Lotus is the de facto late-night hang-out spot along the northern end of Sairee. Muscular fire twirlers toss around flaming batons, and the drinks are so large there should be a lifeguard on duty.

Office Bar
BAR

(Map p572; Sairee Beach) With graffiti proudly boasting 'No Gaga, and no Black Eyed F*^£*£ Peas', this hexagonal hut lures regulars with grunge beats and rickety wooden seats.

Diza
BAR

(Map p572; Sairee Beach) Once a tatty shack that blasted music as it sold pirated DVDs, Diza has evolved into a casual hang-out at the crossroads of Sairee Village. Locals lounge on plastic chairs as they slurp their beer and people-watch.

☆ Entertainment

★ Queen's Cabaret
CABARET

(Map p572; ⊙10.15pm nightly) **FREE** Wow! Every night is different at this intimate bar where acts range from your standard sparkling Abba and leg kicks extravaganza to steamy topless croons. If you're male, note you may get 'dragged' into the performance if you're sitting near the front. Drinks are pricey but worth it for the show.

Raw Art Moovment
LIVE MUSIC

(⊙10am-late) **FREE** A place for art, music, socialising, drinking and, most importantly, the Sunday Art Jam when the island's talented musicians perform and the vibe is like a big, fun party at someone's house (in fact the venue is part of owner's Denny and Lisa's house). The first chords are strummed at 7.30pm, but come by any time.

🛍 Shopping

Although most items are cheap when compared to prices back home, diving equipment is a big exception to the rule. On Ko Tao you'll be paying Western prices plus shipping plus commission on each item (even with 'discounts') so it's better to do your scuba shopping at home or on your computer.

Avalon
HAIR CARE

(Map p572; Mae Hat; ⊙10am-7pm Mon-Sat) If you're having trouble scrubbing the sea salt out of your hair, then stop by Avalon for some locally made (and eco-friendly) body and hair-care products.

❶ Information

The ubiquitous *Koh Tao Info* booklet lists loads of businesses on the island and goes into some detail about the island's history, culture and social issues.

DANGERS & ANNOYANCES

There's nothing more annoying than enrolling in a diving course with your friends and then having to drop out because you scraped your knee in a motorcycle accident. The roads on Ko Tao are slowly being paved but are still horrendous. While hiring a moped is extremely convenient, this is not the place to learn how to drive. The island is rife with abrupt hills and sudden sand pits along gravel trails. Even if you escape unscathed from a riding experience, scamming bike shops may claim that you damaged your rental and will try to extort some serious cash from you.

Travellers should also be aware that mosquito-borne dengue fever (and a similar but less-severe cousin) is a real and serious threat. The virus can spread quickly due to tightly packed tourist areas and the small size of the island.

EMERGENCY

Police Station (Map p572; ☏ 0 7745 6631) Between Mae Hat and Sairee Beach along the rutted portion of the beachside road.

INTERNET ACCESS

Rates are generally 2B per minute, with a 20B minimum and discounts if you log on for one hour or longer. You may find, however, that certain useful tourism websites have been firewalled at internet cafes affiliated with travel agencies. The larger dive schools on the island usually have a wireless connection available for laptop-toting travellers.

MEDICAL SERVICES

All divers are required to sign a medical waiver before exploring the sea. If you have any medical condition that might hinder your ability to dive (including mild asthma), you will be asked to get medical clearance from a doctor on Ko Tao. If you're unsure about whether or not you are fit to dive, consider seeing a doctor before your trip as there are no official hospitals on the island, and the number of qualified medical professionals is limited. Also, make sure your traveller's insurance covers scuba diving. On-island medical 'consultations' (and we use that term very lightly) cost 300B. There are several walk-in clinics and mini-hospitals scattered around Mae Hat and Sairee. All serious medical needs should be dealt with on Ko Samui. If you are diving, ask your outfitter to point you in the proper direction of medical advice.

Diver Safety Support (Map p572; ☏08 1083 0533; kohtao@sssnetwork.com; Mae Hat; ☉on call 24hr) Has a temporary hyperbaric chamber and offers emergency evacuation services.

MONEY

There are 24-hour ATMs at the island's 7-Elevens. There's also a cluster of ATMs orbiting the ferry docks at Mae Hat. There is a money exchange window at Mae Hat's pier and a second location near Chopper's in Sairee Beach. There are several banks near the post office in Mae Hat, at the far end of town along the island's main inland road. They are usually open 9am to 4pm on weekdays. Almost all dive schools accept credit cards, however there is usually a 3% or 4% handling fee.

POST

Post Office (Map p572; ☏0 7745 6170; ☉9am-5pm Mon-Fri, 9am-noon Sat) A 10- to 15-minute walk from the pier; at the corner of Ko Tao's main inner-island road and Mae Hat's 'down road'.

TOURIST INFORMATION

There's no government-run TAT office on Ko Tao. Transportation and accommodation bookings can be made at most dive shops or at any of the numerous travel agencies, all of which take a small commission on services rendered.

Koh Tao Online (www.kohtaoonline.com) An online version of the handy *Koh Tao Info* booklet.

❶ Getting There & Away

As always, costs and departure times are subject to change. Rough waves are known to cancel ferries between the months of October and December. When the waters are choppy we recommend taking the **Seatran** (☏0 2240 2582; www.seatrandiscovery.com) rather than the **Lomprayah** (☏077 4277 656; www.lomprayah. com) catamaran if you are prone to seasickness. The catamarans ride the swell, whereas the Seatran cuts through the currents as it crosses the sea. Note that we highly advise purchasing your boat tickets *several* days in advance if you are accessing Ko Tao from Ko Pha-Ngan after the Full Moon Party.

AIR

Nok Air (p590) jets passengers from Bangkok's Don Muang airport to Chumphon once daily in each direction from Monday to Saturday while **Happy Air** (www.happyair.co.th) has one to two flights per day from Bangkok's Suvarnabhumi International Airport and a flight five days a week to Ranong. Flights to/from Bangkok are usually around 3300B. Upon arriving in Chumphon, travellers can make a seamless transfer to the catamaran service bound for Ko Tao.

BOAT
To/From Ko Pha-Ngan

The **Lomprayah** catamaran offers a twice-daily service (500B), leaving Ko Tao at 9.30am and 3pm and arriving on Ko Pha-Ngan around 10.50am and 4.10pm. The **Seatran Discovery Ferry** (430B) offers an identical service. The **Songserm** express boat (350B) departs daily at 10am and arrives on Ko Pan-Ngan at 11.30am. Hotel pick-ups are included in the price.

To/From Ko Samui

The **Lomprayah** catamaran offers a twice-daily service (600B), leaving Ko Tao at 9.30am and 3pm and arriving on Ko Samui via Ko Pha-Ngan, around 11.30am and 4.40pm. The **Seatran Discovery Ferry** (600B) offers an identical service. The **Songserm** express boat (450B) departs daily at 10am and arrives on Samui (again via Ko Pha-Ngan) at 12.45pm. Hotel pick-ups are included in the price.

To/From Surat Thani & the Andaman Coast

The easiest option is to stop over on either Ko Pha-Ngan or Ko Samui to shorten the trip and lessen the number of connections. Otherwise, a combination bus-boat ticket from travel agents around the island shouldn't cost more than going it alone. But if you don't feel like being herded like a sheep onto a tourist bus, there are two routes you can take. The first, and more common, approach is to board a Surat-bound boat (you may have to transfer boats on Ko Pha-Ngan or Ko Samui), then transfer to a bus upon arrival.

The second option is to take a ferry to Chumphon on the mainland and then switch to a bus or train bound for the provinces further south.

BUS

Bus-boat package tickets to/from Bangkok are available from travel agencies all over Bangkok and the south; tickets cost about 1000B and the whole journey takes about 12 hours. Buses switch to boats in Chumphon and Bangkok-bound passengers can choose to disembark in Hua Hin (for the same price as the Ko Tao–Bangkok ticket).

TRAIN

Travellers can plan their own journey by taking a boat to Chumphon, then making their way to Chumphon's town centre to catch a train up to Bangkok (or any town along the upper southern gulf); likewise in the opposite direction. A

2nd-class ticket to Bangkok will cost around 300B and the trip takes around 8½ hours.

From Ko Tao, the high-speed catamaran departs for Chumphon at 10.15am and 2.45pm (600B, 1½ hours), and a Songserm express boat makes the same journey at 2.30pm (500B, three hours). There may be fewer departures if the swells are high.

ⓘ Getting Around

MOTORCYCLE

Renting a motorcycle is a dangerous endeavour if you're not sticking to the main, well-paved roads. Daily rental rates begin at 150B for a scooter. Larger bikes start at 350B. Discounts are available for weekly and monthly rentals. Try **Lederhosenbikes** (Map p572; ☑ 08 1752 8994; www.lederhosenbikes.com; Mae Hat; ⊙ 8.30am-6pm Mon-Sat). Do not rent all-terrrain-vehicles (ATVs) or jet skis – they are unsafe.

SŎRNG·TĂA·OU

In Mae Hat *sŏrng·tăa·ou*, pick-up trucks and motorbikes crowd around the pier as passengers alight. If you're a solo traveller, you will pay 200B to get to Sairee Beach or Chalok Ban Kao. Groups of two or more will pay 100B each. Rides from Sairee to Chalok Ban Kao cost 150B per person, or 300B for solo tourists. These prices are rarely negotiable, and passengers will be expected to wait until their taxi is full unless they want to pay an additional 200B to 300B. Prices double for trips to the east coast, and the drivers will raise the prices when rain makes the roads harder to negotiate. If you know where you intend to stay, we highly recommend calling ahead to arrange a pick up. Many dive schools offer free pick-ups and transfers as well.

WATER TAXI

Boat taxis depart from Mae Hat, Chalok Ban Kao and the northern part of Sairee Beach (near Vibe Bar). Boat rides to Ko Nang Yuan will set you back at least 100B. Long-tail boats can be chartered for around 1500B per day, depending on the number of passengers carried.

Ang Thong Marine National Park

อุทยานแห่งชาติหมู่เกาะอ่างทอง

The 40-some jagged jungle islands of Ang Thong Marine National Park stretch across the cerulean sea like a shattered emerald necklace – each piece a virgin realm featuring sheer limestone cliffs, hidden lagoons and perfect peach-coloured sands. These dream-inducing islets inspired Alex Garland's cult classic *The Beach,* about dope-dabbling backpackers.

February, March and April are the best months to visit this ethereal preserve of greens and blues; crashing monsoon waves mean that the park is almost always closed during November and December.

◉ Sights

Every tour stops at the park's head office on **Ko Wua Talap**, the largest island in the archipelago.

The naturally occurring stone arches on **Ko Samsao** and **Ko Tai Plao** are visible during seasonal tides and weather conditions. Because the sea is quite shallow around the island chain, reaching a maximum depth of 10m, extensive coral reefs have not developed, except in a few protected pockets on the southwest and northeast sides. There's a shallow coral reef near Ko Tai Plao and Ko Samsao that has decent but not excellent snorkelling. There are also several novice dives for exploring shallow caves and colourful coral gardens and spotting banded sea snakes and turtles. Soft powder beaches line **Ko Tai Plao, Ko Wuakantang** and **Ko Hintap**.

Viewpoint   VIEWPOINT
The island's viewpoint might just be the most stunning vista in all of Thailand. From the top, visitors will have sweeping views of the jagged islands nearby as they burst through the placid turquoise water in easily anthropomorphised formations. The trek to the lookout is an arduous 450m trail that takes roughly an hour to complete. Hikers should wear sturdy shoes and walk slowly on the sharp outcrops of limestone. A second trail leads to **Tham Bua Bok**, a cavern with lotus-shaped stalagmites and stalactites.

Emerald Sea   LAKE
The Emerald Sea (also called the Inner Sea) on **Ko Mae Ko** is another popular destination. This large lake in the middle of the island spans an impressive 250m by 350m and has an ethereal minty tint. You can look but you can't touch; the lagoon is strictly off limits to the unclean human body. A dramatic **viewpoint** can be found at the top of a series of staircases nearby.

☞ Tours

The best way to experience Ang Thong is by taking one of the many guided tours departing Ko Samui and Ko Pha-Ngan. The tours usually include lunch, snorkelling equipment, hotel transfers and (with fingers crossed) a knowledgeable guide. If you're staying in luxury accommodation, there's a good chance that your resort has a private boat for providing group tours. Some mid-range and budget places also have their own boats, and if not, they can easily set you up with a general tour operator. Dive centres on Ko Samui and Ko Pha-Ngan offer **scuba trips** to the park, although Ang Thong doesn't offer the world-class diving that can be found around Ko Tao and Ko Pha-Ngan.

Due to tumultuous petrol prices, tour companies tend to come and go like the wind. Ask at your accommodation for a list of current operators.

Sleeping

Ang Thong does not have any resorts; however, on Ko Wua Talap the national park has set up five bungalows, each housing between two and eight guests. Campers are also allowed to pitch a tent in certain designated zones. Online bookings are possible, although customers must forward a bank deposit within two days of making the reservation. For advance reservations contact the **National Parks Services** (☑0 7728 6025; www.dnp.go.th; bungalows 500-1400B).

Getting There & Around

The best way to reach the park is to take a private day tour from Ko Samui or Ko Pha-Ngan (28km and 32km away, respectively). The islands sit between Samui and the main pier at Don Sak; however, there are no ferries that stop off along the way.

The park officially has an admission fee (adult/child 400/200B), although it should be included in the price of every tour (ask your operator if you are unsure). Private boat charters are also another possibility, although high petrol prices will make the trip quite expensive.

SURAT THANI PROVINCE

Surat Thani   อำเภอเมืองสุราษฎร์ธานี

POP 128,990

Known in Thai as 'City of Good People', Surat Thani was once the seat of the ancient Srivijaya empire. Today, this unglamorous, busy junction has become a transport hub that indiscriminately moves cargo and people around the country. Travellers rarely linger here as they make their way to the popular islands of Ko Samui, Ko Pha-Ngan and Ko Tao, but it's a great stop if you enjoy real Thai working cities and good southern-style street food.

Sleeping

Staying in central Surat puts you in a bustling Thai city that can be refreshing after days in the primped-for-tourists gulf islands. Between the late-running markets, karaoke bars and frequent festivals, nights up to around midnight can be noisy and it's hard to escape the sounds of revelry even in high-rise hotels. Prices, however, are very low and you get a lot for relatively few baht.

For a quieter night and more modern amenities, escape the city centre and hop on a sŏrng·tăa·ou heading towards the Phang-Nga district. When you climb aboard, tell the driver 'Tesco-Lotus', and you'll be taken about 2km to 3km out of town to a large, boxlike shopping centre. A handful of hotel options orbit the mall.

If you're on a very tight budget, consider zipping straight through town and taking the night ferry to reach your island destination.

My Place @ Surat Hotel   HOTEL $

(☑0 7727 2288; www.myplacesurat.com; 247/5 Na Meuang Rd; fan r with/without bathroom 260/199B, air-con r with bathroom 490B; ❄ ☎) This spiffed-up Chinese hotel has surprising touches like bright paint, colourful throw cushions and modern art on the walls. It's clean, very central and the best bargain in town.

100 Islands Resort & Spa   RESORT $

(☑0 7720 1150; www.roikoh.com; 19/6 Moo 3, By-pass Rd; r 900-1800B; ❄@☎☀) Across the street from the suburban Tesco-Lotus, 100 Islands is as good as it gets around here for a reasonable price. This teak palace looks out of place along the highway, but inside the immaculate rooms surround an overgrown garden and lagoonlike swimming pool.

Eating

Surat Thani is packed with delicious street food at lunch and then even more at dinner. Aside from the central night market listed below, stalls near the departure docks open for the daily night boats to the islands, and there's an afternoon **Sunday market** (☉4-9pm) near the TAT office. During the day many food stalls near the downtown bus terminal sell kôw gài òp (marinated baked chicken on rice).

Surat Thani

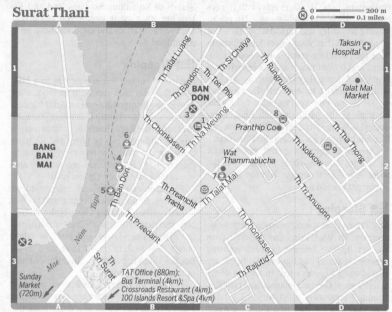

Surat Thani

Sleeping
1 My Place @ Surat Hotel B2

Eating
2 Crossroads Restaurant.......................... A3
3 Night Market.. B1

Transport
4 Ko Tao Night Ferry Pier........................ B2
  Lomprayah ....(see 6)
5 Night Boat to Ko Pha-Ngan B2
6 Seatran Discovery B2
7 Seatran Office C2
  Songserm ....(see 6)
8 Talat Kaset 1 Bus Terminal................... C2
9 Talat Kaset 2 Bus Terminal D2

★ **Night Market**   MARKET **$**

(Sarn Chao Ma; Th Ton Pho; dishes from 35B; ⊘ 6-11pm) A truly fantastic smorgasborg of food including lots of melt-in-your-mouth marinated meats on sticks, fresh fruit juices, noodle dishes and desserts. It's not that big so it's easy to browse the stalls before choosing what to eat.

Crossroads Restaurant   INTERNATIONAL **$$**

(Bypass Rd; dishes 50-200B; ⊘ lunch & dinner) Located southwest of Surat across from the Tesco-Lotus mall, Crossroads has a quaint bluesy vibe enhanced by dim lighting and live music. Try the oysters – Surat Thani is famous for its giant molluscs, and the prices are unbeatable.

ℹ Information

Th Na Meuang has a bank on virtually every corner in the heart of downtown. If you're staying near the 'suburbs', the Tesco-Lotus has ATMs as well.

Post Office (☑ 0 7728 1966, 0 7727 2013; ⊘ 8.30am-4.30pm Mon-Fri, 8.30am-12.30pm Sat) Across from Wat Thammabucha. The local One Tambon One People (OTOP) craft house is inside.

Taksin Hospital (☑ 0 7727 3239; Th Talat Mai) The most professional of Surat's three hospitals. Just beyond the Talat Mai Market in the northeast part of downtown.

Tourism Authority of Thailand (TAT; ☑ 0 7728 8817; tatsurat@samart.co.th; 5 Th Talat Mai; ⊘ 8.30am-4.30pm) Friendly office southwest of town. Distributes plenty of useful brochures and maps, and staff speak English very well.

ℹ Getting There & Away

In general, if you are departing Bangkok or Hua Hin for Ko Pha-Ngan or Ko Tao, consider taking the train or a bus-boat package that goes through Chumphon rather than Surat. You'll save time, and the journey will be more comfortable. Travellers heading to/from Ko Samui will most likely pass through. If you require any travel services, try **Pranthip Co** (Th Talat Mai) – both are reliable and English is spoken.

AIR

Although flights from Bangkok to Surat Thani are cheaper than the flights to Samui, it takes quite a bit of time to reach the gulf islands from the airport. Air Asia offers a convenient bus and boat shuttle with their flights that can alleviate some of the stress. There are daily shuttles to Bangkok on **Thai Airways International** (THAI; ☑ 0 7727 2610; 3/27-28 Th Karunarat), Air Asia (p590) and Nok Air (p590).

BOAT

Various ferry companies offer services to the islands. Try **Lomprayah** (☑ 077 4277 656; www. lomprayah.com), **Seatran Discovery** (☑ 0 2240 2582; www.seatrandiscovery.com) or **Songserm** (☑ 0 7737 7704; www.songsermexpressboat.com).

Bus-boat Combination Tickets

In the high season travellers can usually find bus-boat services to Ko Samui and Ko Pha-Ngan directly from the Phun Phin train station (which is 14km west of Surat). These services don't cost any more than those booked in Surat Thani and can save you some serious waiting time.

There are also several ferry and speedboat operators that connect Surat Thani to Ko Tao, Ko Pha-Ngan and Ko Samui. Most boats – such as the Raja and Seatran services – leave from Don Sak (about one hour from Surat; bus transfers are included in the ferry ticket) although the Songserm leaves from the heart of Surat town. Be warned that the Raja service can be a very frustrating experience, especially for travellers who are tight on time. The boat trip usually takes around 1½ hours to Ko Samui and 2½ hours to Ko Pha-Ngan, although often the captain will cut the engines to half propulsion, which means the journey can take up to five hours.

Night Ferry

From the centre of Surat there are nightly ferries to Ko Tao (eight hours, departs at 10pm), Ko Pha-Ngan (seven hours, departs at 10pm) and Ko Samui (six hours, departs at 11pm). These are cargo ships, not luxury boats, so bring food and water and watch your bags.

BUS & MINIVAN

The most convenient way to travel around the south, frequent buses and minivans depart from two main locations in town known as Talat Kaset 1 and Talat Kaset 2. Talat Kaset 1, on the north side of Th Talat Mai (the city's main drag) offers speedy service to Nakhon (120B, 1½ hours). This is also the location of Pranthip Co, one of the more trustworthy agencies in town. Buses to Phun Phin also leave from Talat Kaset 1.

At Talat Kaset 2, on the south side of Th Talat Mai, you'll find frequent transportation.

The 'new' bus terminal (which is actually a few years old now, but still referred to as new by the locals) is 7km out of town on the way to Phun Phin. This hub services traffic to and from Bangkok (380B to 800B, 11 to 14 hours).

TRAIN

BUSES & MINIVANS FROM SURAT THANI

DESTINATION	FARE	DURATION
Bangkok	421-856B	10hr
Hat Yai	160-240B	5hr
Khanom	100B	1hr
Krabi	150B	2½hr
Phuket	200B	6hr
Trang	190B	2hr 10min

When arriving by train you'll actually pull into Phun Phin, a nondescript town 14km west of Surat. From Phun Phin, there are buses to Phuket, Phang-Nga and Krabi – some via Takua Pa, a junction for Khao Sok National Park. Transport from Surat moves with greater frequency, but it's worth checking the schedule in Phun Phin first – you might be lucky and save yourself a slow ride between towns.

If you plan on travelling during the day, go for the express railcars. Night travellers should opt for the air-con couchettes. Trains passing through Surat stop in Chumphon and Hua Hin on their way up to the capital, and in the other direction you'll call at Trang, Hat Yai and Sungai Kolok before hopping across the border. The train station at Phun Phin has a 24-hour left-luggage room that charges around 20B a day. The advance ticket office is open from 6am to 6pm daily (with a nebulous one-hour lunch break somewhere between 11am and 1.30pm). The trip to Bangkok takes over 8½ hours and costs 107B to 1379B depending on class.

ⓘ Getting Around

Air-conditioned vans to/from Surat Thani airport cost around 100B per person and they'll drop you off at your hotel.

To travel around town, *sŏrng·tăa·ou* cost 10B to 30B (it's 15B to reach Tesco-Lotus from the city centre).

Fan-cooled Orange buses run from Phun Phin train station to Surat Thani every 10 minutes (15B, 25 minutes). For this ride, taxis charge a cool 200B for a maximum of four people, while share taxis charge 100B per person. Other taxi rates are posted just north of the train station (at the metal pedestrian bridge).

WÁT SUAN MOKKHAPHALARAM

Surrounded by lush forest, **Wát Suan Mokkhaphalaram** (www.suanmokkh.org; Wat Suanmokkh), whose name means 'Garden of Liberation', charges 2000B for a 10-day program that includes food, lodging and instruction (although technically the 'teaching' is free). English retreats, run by the International Dhamma Hermitage, begin on the first day of every month and registration takes place the afternoon before. Founded by Ajan Buddhadasa Bhikkhu, arguably Thailand's most famous monk, the temple's philosophical teachings are ecumenical in nature, comprising Zen, Taoist and Christian elements, as well as the traditional Theravada schemata.

For details on reaching the temple, located 7km outside of Chaiya, check out www.suanmokkh-idh.org/idh-travel.html.

NAKHON SI THAMMARAT PROVINCE

Ao Khanom   อ่าวขนอม

Lovely Ao Khanom, halfway between Surat Thani and Nakhon Si Thammarat, quietly sits along the blue gulf waters. Overlooked by tourists who flock to the jungle islands nearby, this pristine region, simply called Khanom, is a worthy choice for those seeking a serene beach setting unmarred by enterprising corporations.

The beach area is actually quite long and is comprised of two beaches: the main, long Hat Nadan and the smaller and more out of the way Hat Naiplau.

◉ Sights

This area is home to a variety of pristine geological features including **waterfalls** and **caves** but the highlight for many are the pink dolphins.

Caves   CAVE

There are two beautiful caves along the main road (Hwy 4014) between Khanom and Don Sak. **Khao Wang Thong** has a string of lights guiding visitors through the network of caverns and narrow passages. A metal gate covers the entrance; stop at the house at the base of the hill to retrieve the key (and leave a small donation). Turn right off the main highway at Rd 4142 to find **Khao Krot**, which has two large caverns, but you'll have to bring a torch (flashlight).

Samet Chun Waterfall   WATERFALL

This is the largest waterfall in the area with tepid pools for cooling off, and great views of the coast. To reach the falls, head south from Ban Khanom and turn left at the blue Samet Chun sign. Follow the road for about 2km and, after crossing a small stream, take the next right and hike up into the mountain following the dirt road. After about a 15-minute walk, listen for the waterfall and look for a small trail on the right.

Hin Lat Falls   WATERFALL

The scenic Hin Lat Falls is the smallest cascade, but it's also the easiest to reach. There are pools for swimming and several huts providing shade. It's south of Nai Phlao.

Dat Fa Mountain   MOUNTAIN

For a postcard-worthy vista of the undulating coastline, head to Dat Fa Mountain, about 5km west of the coast along Hwy 4014. The hillside is usually deserted, making it easy to stop along the way to snap some photos.

☞ Tours

Pink Dolphin Viewing Tours   WILDLIFE

(day tours 1700B) The most special inhabitants of Khanom are the pink dolphins – a rare albino breed with a stunning pink hue. They are regularly seen from the old ferry pier and the electric plant pier around dawn and dusk but resorts are now offering full-day tours that include viewing the dolphins by boat and a car tour to the area's caves and waterfalls.

If you just want to see the dolphins you can hire a boat for a few hours (for up to six people) for 1000B. Enquire at your hotel.

🛏 Sleeping & Eating

In the last few years, there has been talk of further developing Khanom's beaches into a more laid-back alternative to the islands nearby. A recent surge in gulf oil rigging means developers are eyeing Khanom as a potential holiday destination for nearby workers, but for now it's still a very low-key retreat.

Many of the resorts see very few customers and the constant disuse (not regularly flushing the toilets etc) means that some rooms are dank as the relentless jungle reclaims them. It's best to stay away from the large hotels and stick to beachside bungalow operations. Note that all options are spaced very far apart so unless you have your own wheels don't expect to just show up and wander around looking for a place to stay.

For some cheap eats, head to **Hat Kho Khao** at the end of Rd 4232. You'll find a steamy jumble of barbecue stands offering some tasty favourites such as *mŏo nám dòk* (spicy pork salad) and *sôm·đam*. On Wednesday and Sunday there are markets further inland near the police station.

Suchada Villa   BUNGALOW **$**
(📞0 7552 8459; www.suchadavilla.com; Hat Naiplau; bungalows 800B; ❄️) Right off the main road and a short walk to the beach, Suchada is recognisable by its cache of brightly coloured bungalows. Rooms are cute and clean with quirky designer details such as strings of shells dangling in front of the bathroom doors. Friendly, English-speaking staff.

Khanom Hill Resort   BUNGALOW **$$**
(📞0 7552 9403; www.khanom.info; Hat Naiplau; bungalows 2800-3800B; ❄️🛜🏊) Travellers rave about this spot on a very small hill, that leads to a half-circle of dreamy white beach. Choose from modern, concrete villas with thatched roofs, cheaper models with Thai-style architecture or big family-sized apartments; all are clean and comfy.

Talkoo Beach Resort   BUNGALOW **$$**
(📞0 7552 8397; yok_hana@yahoo.com; Hat Nadan; bungalows 1000-1500B; ❄️🛜🏊) Probably the most efficiently run place on Hat Nadan. Talkoo has a range of bungalows in a garden on the beach and cheaper ones across the main road in a more dry, sparse area. All are in great shape, spacious, comfortable and have charming touches like naturalistic bathrooms. The owner is a character who engages with all her guests.

CC Beach Bar & Bungalows   BUNGALOW **$$**
(www.ccbeachbarthai.wordpress.com; bungalows from 1500B; ❄️🛜🏊) A social spot that's sprung from a friendly, fun beach bar on a stunning stretch of Hat Nadan. The clean and modern concrete bungalows are priced higher for what you can find elsewhere, with a foreigner-specific, chummy ambience.

Racha Kiri   RESORT **$$$**
(📞0 7530 0245; www.rachakiri.com; bungalows 3550-18,500B; ❄️🛜🏊) Khanom's upscale retreat is a beautiful campus of rambling villas. The big price tag means no crowds, which can be nice, although the resort feels like a white elephant when the property isn't being used as a corporate retreat.

ℹ️ Information

The police station and hospital are just south of Ban Khanom at the junction leading to Hat Kho Khao. There's a 7-Eleven (with an ATM) in the heart of Khanom town.

ℹ️ Getting There & Away

Minivans from both Surat Thani and Nakhon leave every hour on the hour from 5am to 5pm daily and drop passengers off in Khanom town, which is several kilometres from the beach. From Khanom town you can hire motorcycle taxis out to the beaches for about 20B to 80B depending on the distance you're going. If you've booked in advance your hosts may offer to pick you up in Khanom town for free.

A taxi to/from Don Sak pier for the gulf islands is 1000B and a motorcyle taxi is 300B.

Once at your lodging you'll be stranded unless you hire your own transport or take a tour with your hotel.

Nakhon Si Thammarat
อำเภอเมืองนครศรีธรรมราช

POP 120,836

The bustling city of Nakhon Si Thammarat (usually shortened to 'Nakhon') won't win any beauty pageants. However, travellers who stop in this historic town will enjoy a decidedly cultural experience amid some of the most important *wát* in the kingdom.

Hundreds of years ago, an overland route between the western port of Trang and the eastern port of Nakhon Si Thammarat functioned as a major trade link between Thailand and the rest of the world. This ancient influx of cosmopolitan conceits is still evident today in the local cuisine, and housed in the city's temples and museums.

⊙ Sights

Most of Nakhon's commercial activity (hotels, banks and restaurants) takes place in the northern part of the downtown. South of the clock tower, visitors will find the city's historic quarter with the oft-visited Wat Mahatat. Th Ratchadamnoen is the main thoroughfare and teems with cheap *sŏrng·tǎa·ou* heading both north and south.

★ **Wat Phra Mahathat Woramahawihaan** TEMPLE
(Th Si Thamasok; ☺ 8.30am-4.30pm) The most important wát in southern Thailand, stunning Wat Phra Mahathat Woramahawihaan (simply known as Mahathat) boasts 77 *chedi* (stupa) and an imposing 77m *chedi* crowned by a gold spire. According to legend, Queen Hem Chala and Prince Thanakuman brought relics to Nakhon over 1000 years ago, and built a small pagoda to house the precious icons.

The temple has since grown into a rambling site, and today crowds gather daily to purchase the popular Jatukham amulets. Don't miss the museum inside featuring antique statues from all eras and corners of Thailand.

Shadow Puppets MUSEUM
(Th Si Thamasok Soi 3; ☺ 8.30am-4pm) There are two styles of local shadow puppets: *nǎng dà·lung* and *nǎng yài*. At just under 1m tall, the former feature movable appendages and parts; the latter are nearly life-sized, and lack moving parts. Both are intricately carved from cow hide. Suchart Subsin's puppet house has a small museum where staff

can demonstrate the cutting process and performances for visitors (50B).

National Museum MUSEUM
(Th Ratchadamnoen; admission 30B; ☺ 9am-4pm Wed-Sun) When the Tampaling (also known as Tambralinga) kingdom traded with merchants from Indian, Arabic, Dvaravati and Champa states, the region around Nakhon became a melting pot of crafts and art. Today, many of these relics are on display behind the run-down facade of the national museum.

🛏 **Sleeping & Eating**

Nakhon is a great place to sample cuisine with a distinctive southern twist. In the evening, Muslim food stands sell delicious *kôw mòk gài* (chicken *biryani*), *má·dà·bà* (*murdabag*; Indian pancake stuffed with chicken or vegetables) and roti. A good hunting ground is along Th Neramit, which turns into Th Pak Nakhon – the street bustles with food stalls every night.

Thai Hotel HOTEL $
(☎ 0 7534 1509; fax 0 7534 4858; 1375 Th Ratchadamnoen; fan/air-con r 350/500B; ❄ ☎) Thai Hotel is the most central sleeping spot in town. The lobby is musty, the walls are thin, but the rooms are clean, freshly painted and a good deal for the price. Each room has a TV

JATUKHAM RAMMATHEP

If you've spent more than 24 hours in Thailand, you've probably seen a Jatukham Rammathep dangling around someone's neck – these round amulets are everywhere.

The bearers of the Jatukham Rammathep are supposed to have good fortune and protection from any harm. The origin of the amulet's name remains a mystery, although a popular theory suggests that Jatukham and Rammathep were the aliases of two Srivijayan princes who buried relics under Nakhon's Wat Phra Mahathat some 1000 years ago.

A notorious Thai police detective first wore the precious icon, and firmly believed the guardian spirits helped him solve a particularly difficult murder case. He tried to popularise the amulet, but it wasn't a market success until his death in 2006. Thousands of people attended his funeral, including the crown prince, and the Jatukham Rammathep took off.

The talismans are commissioned at Wat Phra Mahathat, and in the last several years southern Thailand has seen a spike in economic activity. The first amulet was sold in 1987 for 39B, and today over 100 million baht are spent on the town's amulets every *week*. The desire for these round icons has become so frenzied that a woman was crushed to death on the temple grounds during a widely publicised discount sale (she was not wearing her talisman).

Every day, trucks drive along Nakhon's main roads blaring loud music to promote new shipments. These thumping beats have started to shake the ground beneath the temple, and the repeated hammering has, in an ironic metaphor, bent the main spire of Wat Phra Mahathat.

and the higher floors have good views of the urban bustle.

Nakorn Garden Inn
HOTEL $

(☑0 7532 3777; 1/4 Th Pak Nakhon; r 450B; ❀ ☎) With all the foliage, this place feels more like a shady jungle than its location in the centre of town. All rooms have air-con, TV, hot water, fridge, tiled floors and bamboo-plaited walls, although most are quite dark and a little musty. It's a nice change from a cement block, though, a good deal and friendly.

Twin Lotus Hotel
HOTEL $$

(☑0 7532 3777; www.twinlotushotel.net; 97/8 Th Phattanakan Khukhwang; r 1200-8200B; ❀ ☎ ☎) Its age is showing, but Twin Lotus is still the place to go a little more upscale when in Nakhon. This 16-storey behemoth sits 2km southeast of the city centre.

Khrua Nakhon
THAI $$

(Bovorn Bazaar; dishes 60-200B; ⊙ breakfast & lunch) This joint has a great selection of traditional Nakhon cuisine. Order a sharing platter, which comes with five types of curry (including an unpalatable spicy fish sauce), or try the *kôw yam* (southern-style rice salad). There's one at a second location in Robinson Ocean shopping mall.

Rock 99
INTERNATIONAL $

(1180/807 Bovorn Bazaar; dishes 60-150B; ⊙ 4pm-midnight) The choice *fa·ràng* hang-out in Nakhon, Rock 99 has a good selection of international fare, from taco salads to pizzas (avoid the Thai fare though). There's live music on Wednesday, Friday and Saturday nights, but expect to bump into friendly expats almost all the time.

ⓘ Information

Several banks and ATMs hug Th Ratchadamnoen in the northern end of downtown. There is an English-language bookstore on the 3rd floor of Robinson Ocean shopping mall.

Most hotels have free, useful city maps to give to guests.

Bovorn Bazaar (Th Ratchadamnoen) A mall housing a few internet cafes.

Police Station (☑1155; Th Ratchadamnoen) Opposite the post office.

Post Office (Th Ratchadamnoen; ⊙8.30am-4.30pm)

Tourism Authority of Thailand (TAT; ☑0 7534 6515; ⊙8.30am-4.30pm) Housed in a 1926-vintage building in the northern end of the Sanam Na Meuang (City Park). Has some useful brochures in English.

ⓘ Getting There & Away

AIR

Several carriers such as Nok Air, Air Asia and Orient Thai Airlines (plus Thai Airways) fly from Bangkok to Nakhon daily. There are about six daily one-hour flights. One-way fares are around 1500B.

BUS

Ordinary buses to Bangkok leave from the bus terminal (mostly in the afternoon or evening), but a couple of private buses leave from booking offices on Th Jamroenwithi, where you can also buy tickets. The journey takes 12 hours and costs 454B to 1142B depending on the class of bus.

When looking for minivan stops to leave Nakhon, keep an eye out for small desks along the side of the downtown roads (minivans and waiting passengers may or may not be present nearby). It's best to ask around as each destination has a different departure point. Krabi and Don Sak minivans are grouped together – just make sure you don't get on the wrong one. Stops are scattered around Th Jamroenwithi, Th Wakhit and Th Yommarat.

TRAIN

There are two daily train departures to/from Bangkok to Nakhon (133B to 652B; stopping at Hua Hin, Chumphon and Surat Thani along the way). All are 12-hour night trains. These trains continue on to Hat Yai and Sungai Kolok.

ⓘ Getting Around

Sŏrng·tǎa·ou run north–south along Th Ratchadamnoen and Th Si Thammasok for 10B (a bit more at night). Motorcycle-taxi rides start at 30B and cost up to 50B for longer distances.

SONGKHLA PROVINCE

Songkhla's postal code is 90210, but this ain't no Beverly Hills! The province's two main commercial centres, Hat Yai and Songkhla, are less affected by the political turmoil plaguing the cities further south. Intrepid travellers will be able to count the number of other tourists on one hand as they wander through local markets, savour Muslim-Thai fusion cuisine and relax on breezy beaches.

Songkhla & Around
สงขลา

POP 90,780

'The great city on two seas' lends itself perfectly to the click of a visitor's camera; however, slow-paced Songkhla doesn't see much

DON'T MISS

KHAO LUANG NATIONAL PARK

Known for its beautiful mountain and forest walks, cool streams, waterfalls and orchards, **Khao Luang National Park** (อุทยานแห่งชาติเขาหลวง; ☑ 0 7530 0494; www.dnp. go.th; adult/child 400/200B) surrounds the 1835m peak of Khao Luang. This soaring mountain range is covered in virgin forest. An ideal source for streams and rivers, the mountains show off impressive waterfalls and provide a habitat for a plethora of bird species – this place is a good spot for any budding ornithologist. Fans of flora will also get their kicks here; there are over 300 species of orchid in the park, some of which are found nowhere else on earth.

It's possible to rent **park bungalows** (per night 600-2000B), sleeping six to 12 people. There's a **restaurant** at park headquarters. **Camping** is permitted along the trail to the summit. To reach the park, take a *sŏrng·tǎa·ou* (around 35B) from Nakhon Si Thammarat to Lan Saka; drivers will usually take you the extra way to park headquarters. The entrance to the park and the offices of the Royal Forest Department are 33km from the centre of Nakhon on Rte 4015, an asphalt road that climbs almost 400m in 2.5km to the office and a further 450m to the car park. Plenty of up-to-date details are available on the park's website.

in the way of foreign tourist traffic. Although the town hasn't experienced any of the Muslim separatist violence plaguing the provinces further south, it's still catching the same bad press. This is a shame, since it's the last safe city where travellers can experience the unique flavour of Thailand's predominately Muslim Deep South.

The population is a mix of Thais, Chinese and Malays, and the local architecture and cuisine reflect this fusion at every turn.

⊙ Sights

There's a **zoo** (สวนสัตว์สงขลา; www.songkhla zoo.com; Khao Rup Chang; admission adult/child 100/50B; ⊙ 9am-6pm) and **aquarium** (สงขลา อะควาเรียม; www.songkhlaaquarium.com; admission adult/child 300/200B; ⊙ 9.30am-4pm Tue-Fri, 9.30am-5pm Sat & Sun), both good outings if you have kids in tow.

★ **National Museum**   MUSEUM
(พิพิธภัณฑสถานแห่งชาติสงขลา; Th Wichianchom; admission 150B; ⊙ 9am-4pm Wed-Sun, closed public holidays) This 1878 building was originally built in a Chinese architectural style as the residence of a luminary. The museum is easily the most picturesque national museum in Thailand and contains exhibits from all Thai art-style periods, particularly the Srivijaya. Walk barefoot on the wood floors to view elaborate wood carvings, historical photos and pottery salvaged from a shipwreck.

Hat Samila   BEACH
(หาดสมิหลา) Stroll this beautiful strip of white sand with the giggling local couples

and enjoy the kite flying (a local obsession). A bronze **Mermaid sculpture**, in tribute to Mae Thorani (the Hindu-Buddhist earth goddess), sits atop some rocks at the northern end of the beach. Locals treat the figure like a shrine, tying the waist with coloured cloth and rubbing the breasts for good luck.

Don't expect to sunbathe here – the local dress code is too modest – but it's a wholesome spot to meet locals and enjoy a distinctly Thai beach scene.

Ko Yo   ISLAND
(เกาะยอ) A popular day trip from Songkhla, this island in the middle of Thale Sap is actually connected to the mainland by bridges and is famous for its cotton-weaving industry. There's a roadside market selling cloth and ready-made clothes at excellent prices.

If you visit Ko Yo, don't miss **Wat Phrahorn Laemphor**, with its giant reclining Buddha, and check out the **Thaksin Folklore Museum** (☑ 0 7459 1618; admission 100B; ⊙ 8.30am-4.30pm), which actively aims to promote and preserve the culture of the region, and is a must-see. The pavilions here are reproductions of southern Thai–style houses and contain folk art, handicrafts and traditional household implements.

⊊ Tours

Singora Tram Tour   TRAM TOUR
(⊙ 6 tours daily btwn 9am & 3pm) **FREE** These 40-minute tours in an open-air tram leave from next to the National Museum. You'll be lucky if you get any English narration but you will get a drive through the old part

of town past the Songkhla mosque, a Thai temple, Chinese shrine and then out to Hat Samila.

Sleeping & Eating

Songkhla's hotels tend to be lower priced than other areas in the gulf, which makes going up a budget level a relatively cheap splurge.

For quality seafood, head to the street in front of the BP Samila Beach Hotel – the best spot is the restaurant directly in the roundabout. If market munching is your game, you'll find a place to sample street food every day of the week. On Sundays try the bustling market that encircles the Pavilion Hotel. Monday, Tuesday and Wednesday feature a night market (which closes around 9pm) near the local fish plant and bus station, and the Friday morning market sits diagonally opposite the City Hall.

Queen Hotel GUESTHOUSE $
(☑0 7431 1138; 20 Th Traiburi; s/d/ste 330/380/550B; ☀) Central with basic, ageing but clean rooms with air-con, private hot-water bathrooms and friendly staff who speak minimal English. You can't beat the price.

BP Samila Beach Hotel HOTEL $$
(☑0 7444 0222; www.bphotelsgroup.com; 8 Th Ratchadamnoen; r 1600-2500B; ☀@☀) A landmark in quaint Songkhla, the city's poshest address is actually a great deal – you'd pay nearly double for the same amenities on the islands. The beachfront establishment offers large rooms with fridges, satellite TVs and a choice of sea or mountain views (both are pretty darn good).

Khao Noy THAI $
(☑0 7431 1805; 14/22 Th Wichianchom; dishes 30-50B; ⊙ breakfast & lunch Thu-Tue) Songkhla's most lauded *ráhn kôw gaang* (curry shop) serves up an amazing variety of authentic southern-style curries, soups, stir-fries and salads. Look for the glass case holding several stainless-steel trays of food just south of the sky-blue Chokdee Inn.

Information

Banks can be found all over town.
Indonesian Consulate (☑0 7431 1544; Th Sadao)
Malaysian Consulate (☑0 7431 1062; 4 Th Sukhum)

Police Station (☑0 7432 1868; Th Laeng Phra Ram) North of the town centre.
Post Office (Th Wichianchom) Opposite the market; international calls can be made upstairs.

Getting There & Around

BUS
The bus and minibus station is a few hundred metres south of the Viva Hotel. Three 2nd-class buses go daily to Bangkok (1126B), stopping in Nakhon Si Thammarat and Surat Thani, among other places. For Hat Yai, buses (19B to 21B) and minivans (30B) take around 40 minutes, and leave from Th Ramwithi. *Sŏrng·tăa·ou* also leave from here for Ko Yo.

TRAIN
From Songkhla you'll have to go to Hat Yai to reach most long-distance destinations in the south (trains no longer pass through town).

Hat Yai หาดใหญ่
POP 191,696

Welcome to the urban hub of southern Thailand where Western-style shopping malls mingle with wafts of curry from the incredible range of busy street food stalls. Teenagers text each other between shopping and coffee shops and old Chinese men sit and watch the world go by on rickety chairs outside their junk shops – it's a lively mix of busy city and laid-back tropics. The town has long been a favourite stop for Malaysian men on their weekend hooker tours and you'll notice that the town's tourism scene is still predominantly Malaysian mixed with a few Western expats. An evening bar scene includes cosy pubs and bouncing discos.

The town is often said to be safe from the violent hullabaloo of the far south, however it hasn't been ignored. On March 31, 2012 the Lee Gardens Plaza Hotel was bombed, killing three people and injuring 400. In the past banks, malls and the airport have been targeted in more minor incidents. It's up to you if you want to stop here, but changing transport shouldn't be too risky. Those who get out and explore will be rewarded with some of the best food in the region and the dynamic flavour of the big smoke of southern Thailand.

Sleeping & Eating

Hat Yai has dozens of business-style hotels in the town centre, within walking distance of the train station. The city is the unofficial capital of southern Thailand's cuisine, offering Muslim roti and curries, Chinese noodles, duck rice and dim sum, and fresh Thai-style seafood from both the gulf and Andaman coasts. You'll find hawker stalls everywhere but a particularly good hunting ground is along Th Supasarnrangsan. Meals here cost between 25B to 80B.

Tune Hotel   HOTEL $

(☑0 2613 5888; www.tunehotels.com; 152-156 Th Niphat Utit 2; r from 800B; ✱ ☎) In a great, central location, Air Asia's cookie cutter hotel chain works well in Hat Yai, with its affordable, extremely clean and slick rooms. Hopefully you like red and white. Prices change a lot depending on how far in advance you book and/or promotions and you save if you book a room with an Air Asia flight.

Night Market   MARKET $

(Th Montri 1) The night market boasts heaps of local eats including several stalls selling the famous Hat Yai-style deep-fried chicken and *kà·nŏm jeen* (fresh rice noodles served with curry), as well as a couple of stalls peddling grilled seafood.

ⓘ Information

Immigration Office (Th Phetkasem) Near the railway bridge, it handles visa extensions.

Tourism Authority of Thailand (TAT; tatsgkhla@tat.or.th; 1/1 Soi 2, Th Niphat Uthit 3; ☺8.30am-4.30pm) The very helpful staff here speak excellent English and have loads of info on the entire region.

Tourist Police (Th Niphat Uthit 3; ☺24hr) Near the TAT office.

ⓘ Getting There & Away

AIR

Air Asia (www.airasia.com) Daily flights from Hat Yai to Bangkok and Kuala Lumpur.

Nok Air (www.nokair.com) Daily flights between Hat Yai and Bangkok's Don Muang Airport.

Thai Airways International (THAI; 182 Th Niphat Uthit 1) Operates several flights daily between Hat Yai and Bangkok.

Nearly all of the low-cost airlines now operate flights to and from Bangkok:

BUS

Most interprovincial buses and southbound minivans leave from the bus terminal 2km southeast of the town centre, while most northbound minivans now leave from a minivan terminal 5km west of town at Talat Kaset, a 60B túk-túk ride

from the centre of town. Buses link Hat Yai to almost any location in southern Thailand.

Prasert Tour (Th Niphat Uthit 1) runs quicker minibuses to Surat Thani (4½ hours, 8am to 5pm), and **Cathay Tour** (93/1 Th Niphat Uthit 2) can also arrange minivans to many destinations in the south.

TRAIN

There are four overnight trains to/from Bangkok each day (146B to 825B), and the trip takes at least 16 hours. There are also seven trains daily that run along the east coast to Sungai Kolok and two daily trains running west to Butterworth and Padang Besar, both in Malaysia.

There is an advance booking office and left-luggage office at the train station; both are open 7am to 5pm daily.

ⓘ Getting Around

An **Airport Taxi Service** (☑0 7423 8452; 182 Th Niphat Uthit 1) makes the run to the airport four times daily (80B per person, 6.45am, 9.30am, 1.45pm and 6pm). A private taxi for this run costs 320B.

Sŏrng·tăa·ou run along Th Phetkasem (10B per person). Túk-túk and motorcycle taxis around town cost 20B to 40B per person.

DEEP SOUTH

Yala   ยะลา

POP 76,853

Landlocked Yala wiggles its way south to the Malaysian border, making it Thailand's southernmost province. Its eponymous capital appears very different from other Thai metropolises. The city's big boulevards and well-organised street grid are set around a huge circular park and feel distinctly Western. Around three-quarters of the population are Muslim and it is a university town; the educational centre of the Deep South.

BUSES FROM HAT YAI

DESTINATION	PRICE	DURATION
Bangkok	688-1126B	15hr
Krabi	82-535B	5hr
Phuket	344-535B	8hr
Songkhla	19-21B	1½hr
Sungai Kolok	200B	4hr
Surat Thani	160-240B	6hr

◎ Sights

Yala's biggest attraction is **Wat Kuha Pi Muk** (also called Wat Na Tham or Cave-front Temple), one of the most important pilgrimage points in southern Thailand. Located 8km west of town on the road connecting Yala to Hat Yai (Rte 409), the Srivijaya-period cave temple features a reclining Buddha that dates back to AD 757. A statue of a giant guards the temple's entrance, and inside small natural openings in the cave's roof let in the sun's rays to illuminate a variety of ancient Buddhist cave drawings.

Further south, Betong is home to the largest **mail box** in Thailand, first built in 1924. Betong also functions as a legal, but inconvenient, border crossing to Malaysia; contact Yala's **immigration office** (☎ 0 7323 1292).

⊨ Sleeping & Eating

Many of Yala's cheapest lodgings double as unofficial brothels. There are excellent restaurants scattered around the park's perimeter.

Yala Rama HOTEL **$**
(☎ 0 7321 2815; 21 Th Sri Bumrung; r 500-600B; ❄ ☎) Like most hotels in the region, this central and reputable place would be more expensive if it wasn't in the tourist-free Deep South. Clean, comfortable rooms and an OK attached restaurant.

ⓘ Getting There & Around

There are five daily buses to and from Bangkok's southern bus terminal (689B to 1218B, 14 hours). The 2.30pm bus from Bangkok carries onto Betong.

Yala's bus station is south of the city centre. Four trains a day run between Bangkok and Yala (22 hours). Six trains travel daily from Yala to Sungai Kolok (three to four hours). The train station is just north of the city centre.

Buses to Hat Yai (160B, 2½ hours) stop several time a day on Th Sirirot, outside the Prudential TS Life office.

Minivans to Betong and Sungai Kolok (120B, two hours) depart hourly from opposite the train station.

Four trains a day run between Bangkok and Yala (22 hours). Six trains travel daily from Yala to Sungai Kolok (three to four hours).

Pattani ปัตตานี
POP 43.631

Once the heart of a large Muslim principality that included the neighbouring provinces of Yala and Narathiwat, Pattani Province has never adjusted to Thai rule. Although today's political situation has stunted the area's development, Pattani Town has a 500-year history of trading with the world's most notorious imperial powerhouses. The Portuguese established a trading post here in 1516, the Japanese passed through in 1605, the Dutch in 1609 and the British flexed their colonial muscle in 1612.

Yet despite the city's fascinating past, there's little of interest in Pattani except its access to some decent nearby beaches. The ongoing insurgency has made all but a handful of these sandy destinations unsafe for the independent traveller.

◎ Sights

The Mae Nam Pattani (Pattani River) divides the older town to the east and the newer town to the west. Along Th Ruedi you can see what is left of old Pattani **architecture** – the Sino-Portuguese style that was once so prevalent in this part of southern Thailand. On Th Arnoaru there are several ancient but still quite intact Chinese-style homes.

Pattani could be one of the better beach destinations in the region. The coastline between Pattani Town and Narathiwat Province is stunning: untouched and deserted apart from fishing villages. But exploring much of this area independently is not a safe option at this time (see the boxed text on p594), nor is there any tourist infrastructure once you get to the beaches.

Locals frequent **Laem Tachi**, a sandy cape that juts out over the northern end of Ao Pattani. It can be reached by boat taxi from Pattani pier. **Hat Talo Kapo**, 14km east of Pattani near Yaring Amphoe, is another hotspot. Although it's technically in Songkhla Province, **Thepha district**, 35km northwest of Pattani, is the most developed beach destination in the area. There you'll find a few slightly aged resorts that cater mostly to middle-class Thais. At **Hat Soi Sawan**, near the Songkhla–Pattani border, several families have set up informal beachfront restaurants that are popular with weekend visitors. To reach Thepha, hop on any Songkhla-bound bus from Pattani (or vice versa); mention the name of your resort and you'll be deposited at the side of the road for the brief walk to the beach.

Matsayit Klang
MOSQUE

(Th Naklua Yarang) Thailand's second-largest mosque is the Matsayit Klang, a traditional structure with a green hue that is probably still the south's most important mosque. It was built in the 1960s.

🛏️ Sleeping & Eating

Palace Hotel
HOTEL $

(☑ 0 7334 9171; 10-12 Pipit Soi Talattewiwat 2; r 200-350B; ❄) There's nothing palatial about this place. But it is the only budget option in town for foreigners and close to the night market. Go for the air-con rooms with hot water.

CS Pattani Hotel
HOTEL $$

(☑ 0 7333 5093; www.cspattanihotel.com; 299 Moo 4, Th Nong Jik; r from 1100B; ❄ @ 🛜 ☀) The safest hotel, with soldiers outside and a metal detector in the lobby, this is where Thai politicians stay on their rare visits to the Deep South. The paucity of tourists means you get great rooms and facilities for a bargain price. It's about 2km west of the centre of town. The area around the hotel has a number of restaurants and bars.

Sakom Cabana
RESORT $$

(☑ 0 7431 8065; 136 Moo 4, Tambon Sakom; r 600-1000B; ❄) Located about 40km from Pattani town in the Thepha district, this basic resort features a clean compound with several attractive wooden duplex bungalows a short walk from the beach.

ℹ️ MOBILE PHONES

When you arrive in the Deep South, you'll notice that your mobile (cell) phone won't work, whether or not you have a Thai SIM card. Mobile phone signals are routinely jammed to prevent insurgents using them to set off bombs. If you have a Thai SIM, you can reactivate it by visiting a local phone shop and handing over your passport and 50B. They'll make a note of your details, so that the authorities know whose phone it is should it be used for anything illegal, and an hour later your phone will work again.

Night Market
SOUTHERN THAI $

(Soi Talattewiwat; ⊙ 4-9pm) Pattani shuts down far earlier than most Thai towns, but the night market offers solid seafood, as well as southern Thai-style curries and the usual noodle and fried rice options.

ℹ️ Information

There are several banks along the southeastern end of Th Pipit, near the Th Naklua Yarang intersection.

Pattani Hospital (☑ 0 7332 3414, 0 7332 3411; Th Nong Jik)

Police Station (☑ 0 7334 9018; Th Pattani Phirom) In a central location.

ℹ️ Getting There & Around

Minivans are the region's most popular mode of transport and there are frequent daytime departures to Hat Yai (100B, 1½ hours), Narathiwat (100B, two hours) and Sungai Kolok (130B, 2½ hours). Ask at your hotel for the departure points.

There is one daily bus to and from Bangkok's southern bus terminal (763B, 15 hours).

Motorbike taxis charge 10B to 30B for hops around town, but they become very scarce after dark.

Narathiwat
นราธิวาส

POP 40,521

Sitting on the banks of the Bang Nara River, Narathiwat is probably the most Muslim city in Thailand, with many mosques scattered around town. There are still a few old Sino-Portuguese buildings lining the riverfront (although blink and you'll miss them), and there are some excellent beaches just outside town. But few tourists pass through, due to the security situation.

👁️ Sights

Matsayit Klang
MOSQUE

Towards the southern end of Th Pichitbumrung stands Matsayit Klang, a wooden mosque built in the Sumatran style and known locally as the 'central mosque'. It was reputedly built by a prince of the former kingdom of Pattani over a hundred years ago.

Ao Manao
BEACH

Five kilometres south of town, Ao Manao is a superb strip of palm tree-fringed sand. You'll likely have it all to yourself.

TRAVEL IN THE DEEP SOUTH: SHOULD YOU GO?

Despite the conflict, almost everyone in the Deep South – whether ethnic Malay Muslim or a Thai soldier – is happy to see a *fa·ràng*. So few foreigners make it here that you're guaranteed a lot of attention from the locals. Nor have tourists, or any Westerners, ever been targeted by the insurgents; this is a very insular war.

Yet by nature insurgencies are unpredictable, and bombs kill indiscriminately. Explosive devices planted on parked motorbikes outside shops are a common tactic of the separatists and have been used in the city centres of Yala, Pattani and Narathiwat on a number of occasions.

It's best not to linger on the streets for too long; you could be in the wrong place at the wrong time. Nor is travel in the countryside in the early morning or after dark advisable. This isn't an area to be riding a motorbike in if you can't be identified as a foreigner.

But perhaps the biggest drawback to travel in the region is that the insurgency has stifled tourism to such an extent that there is very little infrastructure for visitors. Apart from travelling between the major centres, you'll need private transport to get around. There are few hotels and restaurants and precious little nightlife, and hardly anyone speaks English. And those beautiful beaches have absolutely no facilities.

If you do want to travel here, research the current situation carefully and take advice from your embassy.

Hat Narathat
BEACH

Just north of town is Hat Narathat, a 5km-long sandy beach fronted by towering pines, which serves as a public park for locals. The beach is only 2km from the town centre – you can easily walk there or take a *săhm·lór*.

Wat Khao Kong
BUDDHIST TEMPLE

(⊗9am-5pm) **FREE** The tallest seated-Buddha image in southern Thailand is at Wat Khao Kong, 6km southwest on the way to the train station in Tanyongmat. Located in a park, the image is 17m long and 24m high, and made of reinforced concrete covered with tiny gold-coloured mosaic tiles that glint magically in the sun.

🛏 Sleeping & Eating

Most of the town's accommodation is located on and around Th Puphapugdee along the Bang Nara river. There are a few riverfront Thai restaurants which serve alcohol; the Muslim ones in town are booze-free.

Ocean Blue Mansion
HOTEL $

(☑ 0 7351 1109; 297 Th Puphapugdee; r 400-500B; ❄ 🛜) Sound budget choice with a riverfront location. Rooms are decent-sized and come with fridges and cable TV.

Imperial
HOTEL $$

(☑ 0 7351 5041; narathiwat@imperialhotels.com; 260 Th Pichitbumrung; r 1000B; ❄ @ 🛜) Not the most exclusive hotel in town, but still a snip at the price and centrally located and secure. Rooms are large and comfortable. There are a few Thai restaurants/bars close by.

Jay Sani
MUSLIM-THAI $

(50/1 Th Sophaphisai; dishes 40-80B; ⊗10am-9pm) This is where locals go for excellent Thai-Muslim food. Point to whatever curry or stir-fry looks good, but be sure not to miss the sublime beef soup.

Ang Mo
CHINESE-THAI $

(cnr Th Puphapugdee & Th Chamroonnara; dishes 50-150B; ⊗10am-10pm) This exceedingly popular Chinese restaurant is both cheap and tasty, and has even fed members of the Thai royal family.

ⓘ Information

The **Tourism Authority of Thailand** (TAT; ☑ Narathiwat 0 7352 2411, nationwide call centre 1672) is inconveniently located a few kilometres south of town, just across the bridge on the road to Tak Bai.

ⓘ Getting There & Around

Air Asia (☑ nationwide call centre 0 2515 9999; www.airasia.com; Narathiwat Airport) flies daily to and from Bangkok (from 2390B, 1½ hours).

Two buses daily travel to and from Bangkok's southern bus terminal (685B to 1369B, 15 to 17 hours). Narathiwat's **bus terminal** (☑ 0 7351 1552) is 2km south of town on Th Rangae Munka.

THAILAND'S FORGOTTEN WAR

It may seem fantastic as you laze on the beach, or meditate at a peaceful hilltop temple, but the Deep South of Thailand is home to one of Southeast Asia's longest-running and bloodiest conflicts.

Just 300km or so south of the party islands of Ko Samui and Ko Pha-Ngan, a guerrilla war between ethnic Malay Muslims and the overwhelmingly Buddhist Thai state has claimed almost 5500 lives since 2004 and left close on 10,000 people injured.

The Deep South, which borders Malaysia, is a different world to the rest of the country. Foreign visitors are nonexistent and the pristine beaches deserted. Military convoys rumble through the villages and towns, checkpoints dominate the roads and mobile phone signals are jammed to prevent the insurgents from using them to set off bombs.

Around 80% of the 1.8 million people who live in Thailand's three southernmost provinces of Pattani, Narathiwat and Yala are ethnic Malay Muslims. They speak a Malay dialect and many want their own independent state, as the region once was hundreds of years ago.

For the estimated 12,500 to 15,000 separatist fighters here, the Deep South is 'Patani'; this is the name given to the Qatar-sized sultanate during its glory days in the 14th and 15th centuries. The separatists view the Thai government as a colonial power and Thai Buddhists as interlopers in their land.

Ranged against the insurgents are around 150,000 soldiers, police and militias. Targeted in ambushes along the coconut tree-lined roads of the region, or by increasingly sophisticated IEDs (improvised explosive devices), barely a day goes by without a member of the Thai security forces being killed or wounded.

At the same time, the insurgency has set neighbours against each other. Gruesome tit-for-tat killings occur, with both Buddhist and Muslim civilians being gunned down as they ride home on their motorbikes, or beheaded in the rubber plantations that are the mainstay of the local economy. Bombs are planted outside shops and in the markets of the towns, claiming random victims. The few remaining Buddhist monks in the region have to be escorted by the army when they collect alms every morning for fear they will be assassinated, while mosques are riddled with bullet holes.

Yet despite the appalling violence – one 2012 Australian study revealed that 5% of all global terrorist attacks between 2002 and 2009 occurred in the Deep South – the insurgency remains little-known both at home and overseas. With 24 million visitors a year, Thailand is fiercely proud and protective of its reputation as the 'Land of Smiles'. The media downplays the security situation, while Thai politicians act as if they are in denial about the sheer scale of the conflict.

The insurgents, too, have resisted attacking targets outside the Deep South, a tactic that would do huge damage to the Thai psyche and would garner them far more attention

Minivans heading to Hat Yai (160B, three hours), Pattani (100B, two hours), Songkhla (150B, two hours), Sungai Kolok (80B, one hour) and Yala (100B, 1½ hours) leave on an hourly basis from 5am to 5pm from the bus terminal.

Narathiwat is small enough to navigate by foot, although motorcycle taxis only charge 20B to 30B to get around.

Sungai Kolok   สุไหงโกลก
POP 42,776

It's not the most prepossessing place to enter or exit the 'Land of Smiles', but Sungai Kolok is the main gateway between Thailand and Malaysia. As such, it's a scuzzy border town best known for smuggling and prostitution. Far less of a target than the other major towns in the region, the unstable situation in the Deep South has nevertheless severely diminished its 'sin city' reputation in recent years, with the Malaysian men who once came here for wild weekends now favouring safer Hat Yai. But there's still a small strip of booming bars on Th Charoenkhet, Soi 3 and behind the Marina Hotel. Fewer travellers, too, leave Thailand here now; more come in the opposite direction and immediately hop a train north.

around the world. Nor do they appear to be connected to the more radical Islamic militants of Indonesia and the Philippines.

Instead, they stay in the shadows, rarely issuing statements or talking to the press. Operating in independent cells, they belong to three different organisations all likely linked to each other. But there seems to be no common leader of the groups. That renders the sporadic peace talks that take place between the separatists and the Thai government meaningless, as no one is really sure if the representatives of the insurgents have any true control over them.

While the insurgency kicked into life in earnest in 2004, after 32 suspected Muslim rebels were cornered in an ancient mosque in Pattani Town and brutally killed by the Thai army, its roots go back hundreds of years. From the 16th century on, the sultanate of Patani was unwillingly under Thai rule for brief periods. But it wasn't until the Anglo-Siamese Treaty of 1909 that the Deep South was absorbed into Thailand proper. Britain recognised Thai sovereignty over the region, in return for Bangkok abandoning its claims to other parts of what were then the British-ruled Malay States.

Since then, Thailand, the most populous Buddhist country in the world, has set about attempting to remake the Deep South in its own image. Muslim schools have been shut down and all children made to study in Thai, even though most of them speak it only as a second language. They are also forced to learn about Buddhism, a part of the Thai national curriculum, despite following Islam. Officials from other parts of the country are imported to run the region.

By turns heavy-handed and paternalistic, the Thai government's policies began to fuel a separatist movement. Even now, there are no media outlets in the Malay dialect spoken by the majority of people in the Deep South. Having their children subject to the Thai school system remains a huge source of resentment for many Muslims. Regarded as symbols of the hated Thai state by the insurgents, over 300 schools have been burned down in recent years, while more than 150 Buddhist teachers have been assassinated.

But with the insurgency entirely confined to just three provinces, and a small part of neighbouring Songkhla Province, few Thais are even aware of why the fighting is taking place. Nor are they willing to contemplate giving into the separatists' demands. Imbued with the nationalism taught in their schools, the idea that the Deep South should want to secede from Thailand is unthinkable, both to ordinary Thais and the authorities.

Yet some form of autonomy for the region is likely the only way to end the violence. Until that happens, Thailand's forgotten war will carry on and the grim list of casualties will continue to grow.

🛏 Sleeping & Eating

Most hotels here are uniform in quality and price. Many of the real cheapies won't accept foreigners.

Stand-out restaurants are in short supply, although there is some tasty Malaysian and Chinese food around.

Tara Regent HOTEL **$**
(☑ 0 7361 1401; 45 Th Charoenkhet; r 600B; ❄ 🛜) Functional but clean and reasonably sized rooms are at this Malay-Chinese-owned place 400m walk from the train station. Little English spoken.

Genting Hotel HOTEL **$$**
(☑ 0 7361 3231; 250 Th Asia 18; r 700-800B; ❄ @ 🛜 ☎) More respectable than most hotels in town and, if you're the nervous type, the security is efficient. But the mid-range rooms are rather scuffed for the price. It's a few hundred metres west of the train station on the other side of the road.

Kakyah Restaurant MALAYSIAN **$**
(43/11 Th Charoenkhet; dishes from 30B; ⏰ 10am-10pm) Decent Malaysian food is on offer at this reliable, alcohol-free, Muslim-run place.

GETTING TO MALAYSIA: SUNGAI KOLOK TO RANTAU PANJANG

Getting to the Border The Thai border (open 5am to 9pm) is about 1.5km from the centre of Sungai Kolok or the train station. Motorbike taxis charge 30B.

At the Border This is a hassle-free, straightforward border crossing. After completing formalities, walk across the Harmony Bridge to the Malaysian border post.

Moving On Shared taxis and buses to Kota Bharu, the capital of Malaysia's Kelantan State, can be caught 200m beyond the Malaysian border post. Shared taxis cost RM$8 per person (80B) or RM$40 (400B) to charter the whole car yourself. The ride takes around 40 minutes. Buses make the hour-long journey for RM$5.10 (50B).

It's possible to continue south by the so-called 'jungle train', but the closest station is at Pasir Mas, located along taxi/bus routes to Kota Bharu.

Tak Bai, also in Narathiwat Province, and Betong, further south in Yala, are also legal crossing points for foreigners, but Sungai Kolok is by far the most convenient place to cross the border.

Night Market MARKET $

It's a small night market, but exceptionally good and cheap eats can be found at the stall in the centre that only has Chinese characters.

ⓘ Information

In addition to the one at the border, there is an **immigration office** (☑ 0 7361 4114; Th Charoenkhet; ☉ 8am-5pm Mon-Fri) opposite the night market with helpful, English-speaking staff. A tourist police office sits at the border. There are plenty of ATMs in town as well as foreign-exchange booths, which are open during border-crossing hours.

ⓘ Getting There & Away

The long-distance **bus station** (☑ 0 7361 2045) is an office on the corner of Th Wongwiwat and Th Worakamin in the east of town.

There are four buses daily to and from Bangkok's southern bus terminal (741B to 1481B, 17 to 20 hours).

Minivans heading north to Narathiwat (80B, one hour), Pattani (130B, 2½ hours), Yala (120B, two hours) and Hat Yai (200B, four hours) depart frequently during the day across the road from the Genting Hotel.

Two daily trains connect Sungai Kolok with Bangkok (607B to 1753B, 24 hours, departures at 11.20am and 2.20pm). Very slow local trains run to other points north. Trains in the Deep South are often delayed and subject to army and police searches.

ⓘ Getting Around

Motorcycle taxis zoom around town for a flat rate of 30B.

Phuket & the Andaman Coast

Includes ➡

Best Places to Eat

➡ Kruthara (p649)

➡ Nee Papaya (p683)

➡ Siam Indigo (p624)

➡ Suay (p624)

➡ Pad Thai Shop (p632)

Best Places to Stay

➡ Six Senses Hideaway (p616)

➡ Sabai Corner (p630)

➡ Pak-up Hostel (p644)

➡ Railei Beach Club (p652)

Why Go?

The Andaman is Thailand's turquoise coast, that place on a 'Travel to Paradise' postcard that makes you want to leave your job and live in flip-flops...forever. And for once, the beauty exceeds the hype. White beaches, cathedral-like limestone cliffs and hundreds of jungle-covered isles extend down the Andaman Sea from the border of Myanmar to Malaysia. Photographs haven't yet fully captured the array of blues and greens, let alone the soft fingers of humidity on the skin or the feel of the world's softest sands between your toes. For this, you'll need to visit.

The catch? The destination is no secret and the beaches are becoming more crowded with backpackers, package tourists and everyone in between. Flashy resorts are pushing out the bamboo shacks and authenticity now hides in the backwaters. But your postcard dream is still here – if you're willing to look.

When to Go

➡ May to October is the rainy season. At this time, swells kick up surf, many resorts close and others slash their prices. The Vegetarian Festival is held in late September or October and involves parades of pierced-faced worshippers, endless firecrackers and great meatless food.

➡ December to January is the peak season for tourism. Prices soar, and accommodation and transport need to be booked well in advance.

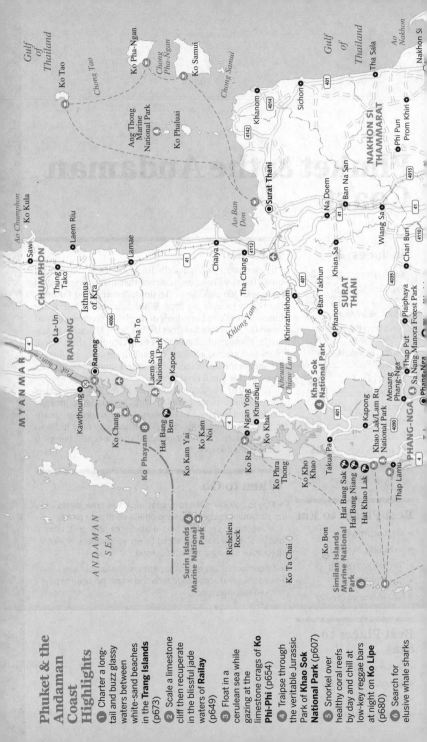

Phuket & the Andaman Coast Highlights

1 Charter a long-tail and buzz glassy waters between white-sand beaches in the Trang Islands (p673)

2 Scale a limestone cliff then recuperate in the blissful jade waters of Railay (p649)

3 Float in a cerulean sea while gazing at the limestone crags of Ko Phi-Phi (p654)

4 Traipse through the veritable Jurassic Park of Khao Sok National Park (p607)

5 Snorkel over healthy coral reefs by day and chill at low-key reggae bars at night on Ko Lipe (p680)

6 Search for elusive whale sharks

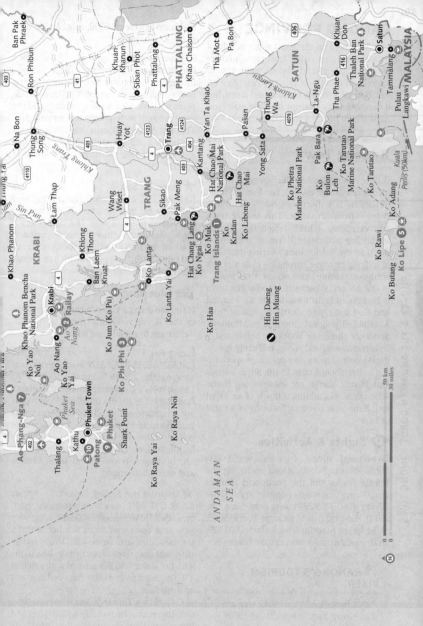

and swim with fish at the **Surin** (p611) and **Similan Islands** (p612)

7 Kayak into the spectacular *hóngs* in the jaw-dropping **Ao Phang-Nga** (p613)

8 Fall into the snoozy, beach-bar vibe and lounge on the white sand of **Ko Phayam** (p604)

9 Tempt your taste buds with a heady mix of gourmet treats and street food at **Phuket** (p621)

10 Find gluttonous hedonism in the hair-raising clubs and packed beaches of **Hat Patong** (p632)

RANONG PROVINCE

The first piece in the Andaman's puzzle of coastal provinces is the least-populated region in Thailand and also its wettest, with up to eight months of rain per year. As a result, Ranong's forests are lush and green, but it means that it's swampy near the mainland coast where beaches are scarce.

Ranong Town
ระนอง

POP 24,500

On the eastern bank of the Sompaen River's turbid, tea-brown estuary, the frontier town of Ranong is a short boat ride – or a filthy swim – from Myanmar. This border town *par excellence* (shabby, frenetic, slightly seedy) has a thriving Burmese population (keep an eye out for men wearing traditional *longyi*; Burmese sarong), a clutch of hot springs and some tremendous street food.

Once a gritty backwater, today the town is basking in transit tourism to Ko Phayam and Ko Chang, and clearly benefiting from a stabilised political situation in Myanmar. Suddenly there are boutique hotels and a style-conscious local scene, relatively speaking. More and more dive operators specialising in live-aboard trips to the Surin Islands and Burma Banks are establishing themselves here too, adding a pinch of an expat feel. Ranong is absolutely worthy of a night or two.

⊙ Sights & Activities

Live-aboard diving trips to world-class bubble-blowing destinations, including the Burma Banks and the Surin and Similan Islands, are deservedly popular. Try **A-One-Diving** (✆0 7783 2984; www.a-one-diving.com; 256 Th Ruangrat; 3-night packages from 16,900B; ☺Oct-Apr) or **Aladdin Dive Safari** (✆08 7288 6908; www.aladdindivesafari.com; Ko Phayam Pier;

ⓘ RANONG'S TOURISM FIXER

Pon's Place (✆08 1597 4549; www.pon-place-ranong.com; Th Ruangrat; ☺7.30am-midnight) is the go-to spot in Ranong for everything from Western breakfasts (from 40B) to Ranong Air bookings and information about bus schedules. Pon himself is a high-energy, friendly guy. If you need help with anything, consider Pon your fixer.

---

live-aboard trips from 14,900B; ☺Oct-Apr) located at the Ko Phayam pier.

Rakswarin Hot Springs   HOT SPRINGS
(Th Petchkasem; ☺8am-5pm) **FREE** Ranong healing waters bubble from a sacred spring hot enough to boil eggs (65°C). The riverside pools have received a recent update and are now blessed with chequered mosaic tile. That hot concrete floor is essentially one giant heating pad – stretch out your bad back and let the heat penetrate your gnarliest knots.

★**Siam Hot Spa**   SPA
(✆0 7781 3551; www.siamhotsparanong.com; 73/3 Th Petchkasem; treatments from 300B) Opposite the public springs, Siam Hot Spa offers a more sterilised mineral-bath experience. You can dip into a Jacuzzi (600B) or standard tubs (300B), and pair it with a salt scrub (550B) or a massage (200B).

🛏 Sleeping

If you are doing a visa run through an agency, they'll ship you in and out of town without having to spend the night.

Luang Poj   GUESTHOUSE $
(✆08 7266 6333, 0 7783 3377; www.facebook.com/luangpojhostel; 225 Th Ruangrat; r 500B; ❋🛈) Luang Poj is a gorgeous remodel of Ranong's first hotel: a 1920s-era building. Most rooms are windowless and all share warm-water bathrooms and are decorated in a signature colour (we like the purple room). It's further highlighted with modern flair: think Indian art, birdcages, one-of-a-kind light fixtures and retro photography.

★**Thansila Hot Spring Resort**   HOTEL $$
(✆08 1797 4674; www.thansila-hotspring-resort.com; 129/2 Th Petchkasem; r 700-900B) A groovy new spot downriver from the hot springs, the best digs are stone-wall lodge rooms with fantastic river views, grotto-like baths with hot water, and flat screens with satellite TV. The hotel rooms offer high ceilings and an artsy flair.

Owned by a Thai architect who renovated over two years, she recently added a hip and homey cafe here, serving Western breakfasts and simple Thai meals.

The B   HOTEL $$
(✆0 7782 3111; www.thebranong.com; 295/1-2 Th Ruangrat; superior/deluxe 1100/1300B) This chunk of polished concrete modernism is proof of a new era in Ranong. Rooms have floating beds,

Ranong

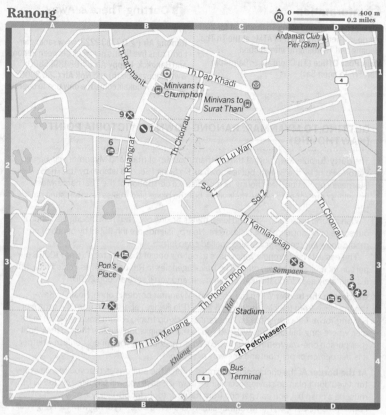

flat-screen TV, rain showers, high ceilings and excellent service. They also have a billiards and snooker bar, an open-air restaurant and a rooftop infinity pool overlooking town and the surrounding green hills.

🍴 Eating & Drinking

Ranong has a lively, young and very local drinking scene involving lots of karaoke.

Night Market NIGHT MARKET
On Th Kamlangsap, there is a night market not far from Hwy 4 that sells great Thai dishes at low prices.

Day Market DAY MARKET
The day market on Th Ruangrat offers inexpensive Thai and Burmese meals.

Sophon's Hideaway THAI, INTERNATIONAL **$$**
(📞 0 7783 2730; www.sophonshideaway.asia; 323/7 Th Ruangrat; mains 45-350B; ⏰ 10am-11pm; 🛜)

This expat favourite has everything, including internet access, a free pool table, a pizza oven, full bar, water features and rattan furnishings aplenty.

ℹ Information

Internet can be found along Th Ruangrat for 20B per hour. There's a cluster of ATMs at the Th Tha Meuang and Th Ruangrat intersection.

Main Post Office (Th Chonrau; ⊙9am-4pm Mon-Fri, to noon Sat)

ℹ Getting There & Away

AIR

Ranong Air (📞0 7783 2222; www.ranongair. com) runs five flights per week between Ranong and Bangkok. **Happy Air** (📞08 1891 5800; www.happyair.co.th) and **Nok Air** (📞0 2900 9955; www.nokair.com), the only one to operate

---

GETTING TO MYANMAR: RANONG TOWN TO VICTORIA POINT (KAWTHOUNG)

The dusty, tumbledown port at the southernmost tip of mainland Myanmar was named Victoria Point by the British, but is known as Ko Song (Second Island) by the Thais. The Burmese appellation, Kawthoung, is most likely a corruption of the Thai name. Most travellers come here to renew their visas, but the place also makes an interesting day trip.

Fishing and trade with Thailand keep things ticking over, but Kawthoung also churns out some of Myanmar's best kickboxers. Nearby islands are inhabited by bands of nomadic *chow lair* (sea gypsies; also spelled *chao leh*).

The easiest way to renew your visa is to opt for one of the 'visa trips' (from 1000B per person including visa fees) offered by travel agencies in Ranong such as Pon's Place, but it's relatively easy to do the legwork yourself, and you'll save around 200B.

Getting to the border When the Thailand–Myanmar border is open, boats to Kawthoung leave from the pier at **Saphan Plaa** (Pla Bridge) about 5km from the centre of Ranong Town. Take *sŏrng·tǎa·ou* (passenger pick-up truck) 3 from Ranong (20B) to the pier, where long-tail captains will lead you to the immigration window then to their boat (per person one-way/return 150/300B). When negotiating your price, confirm whether it is per person or per ride, and one-way or return.

At the border At the checkpoint, you must inform the authorities that you're a day visitor if you don't plan on staying overnight – in which case you will pay a fee of US$10 (it must be a crisp bill, you can get one from harbour touts for 500B). The only big hassles come from 'helpers' on the Myanmar side who offer to do everything from carrying your day pack to collecting forms, then ask for tips, but they're generally more friendly than aggravating.

If you're just coming to renew your Thai visa, the whole process will take a minimum of two hours. Bear in mind when you are returning to Thailand that Myanmar's time is 30 minutes behind Thailand's. This has caused problems in the past for returning visitors who got through Burmese immigration before its closing time only to find the **Thai Immigration office** (⊙8.30am-4.30pm) closed. It's a good idea to double-check Thai immigration closing hours when leaving the country – if you don't get stamped in you'll have to return to Myanmar again the next day.

A quicker, easier (especially for self-drivers) and much more polished alternative – albeit sterilised and less interesting – is to find the **Andaman Club** (www.andamanclub. com; Hwy 4; 850B; ⊙8.30am-3.30pm) pier, just north of town, off Hwy 4. At the terminal, you'll get your passport stamped in minutes, and a Myanmar bound ferry (25 min each way) leaves hourly from 8.30am to 3.30pm, docking at a flash casino resort. The whole trip costs 850B, and for an additional 490B you can take a half-day tour along the Myanmar coast from the casino.

Moving on It's possible to stay overnight in one of Victoria Point's dingy, overpriced hotels, but you'd probably rather not. If you have a valid Myanmar visa in your passport, which you'll have to apply for at the Myanmar Embassy in Bangkok (or a third country), you'll be permitted to stay for up to 28 days and exit anywhere you like, taking your passport with you. If not, you'll have to leave your passport at the border and grab it on your way back to Ranong.

out of Don Muang Airport, also make the run. Book flights at Pon's Place. The airport is 22km south of town.

BUS

The **bus terminal** is on Th Petchkasem 1km from town, though some Bangkok-bound buses stop at the main market. *Sŏrng·tăa·ou 2* (blue) passes the terminal.

DESTINATION	FARE (B)	DURATION (HR)
Bangkok	360-725	10
Chumphon	130	3
Hat Yai	420	5
Khao Lak	180	3½
Krabi	210	6
Phang-Nga	190	5
Phuket	260	5-6
Surat Thani	190	4-5

Minivans head to Surat Thani (190B, 3½ hours, four times daily) and Chumphon (120B, three hours, hourly from 6am to 5pm).

Getting Around

Motorcycle taxis will take you almost anywhere in town for 50B, and to the pier for boats to Ko Chang, Ko Phayam and Myanmar for 70B. Pon's Place can assist with motorcycle and car rentals and offers shuttle vans from its office to the ferry docks for 70B. Minivan shuttles (per person 350B) meet flights and run from the airport to the Ko Phayam pier.

Ko Chang   เกาะช้าง

This little-visited rustic isle is a long way – in every respect – from its much more popular Trat Province namesake. Its speciality is no-frills living, and yes, electricity is a frill here, but it's absence gives as much as it denies. The whole island is saturated in an all-pervading quiet, where the blip and buzz of modern life are replaced with the slosh of the sea, the intoxicating murmur of the cicadas and the far off rumbling of a long-tail.

Pass the time exploring the island's tiny village capital (where the boats dock during the wet season) or wend your way around the island on one of the dirt trails. Sea eagles, Andaman kites and hornbills all nest here and, if you're lucky, you'll catch sight of them floating above the mangroves and the jungled east coast. The wide, west-coast beach of **Ao Yai** has gorgeous marbled white and black sand in the south, which obscures

the otherwise clear water. A short trail leads over the bluff to **Ao Tadeng**, another marbled beach strewn with boulders and the island's best sunset spot. White-sand snobs will be happiest on Ao Yai's north end. In the dry season you'll be dropped off directly in front of your bungalow.

There are no banks or cars on Ko Chang, but internet has arrived at **Cashew Resort** (Ao Yai; per min 2B) and Crocodile Rock (1B per minute). Yoga and tai chi classes are held at **Om Tao** (☑ 08 5470 9312; www.omtao.net; Ao Yai), next door.

Trails lead south from the village in the island's interior to the national park station on the east coast. That's where you'll find the island's best stretch of intact jungle. Elsewhere it's all been tamed into cashew orchards and rubber plantations.

Sleeping & Eating

Basic bamboo huts reign supreme on Ko Chang and, for the most part, they're only open from November to mid-April. Electricity is limited, though a few places have solar and wind power.

Ao Yai is where you'll find most lodging options; a few more places are tucked away on Ao Tadaeng, to the south, which is linked to Ao Yai via a short walking track. More isolated options can be found on the beaches to the north and far south of the island.

★**Crocodile Rock**   GUESTHOUSE $
(☑ 08 0533 4138; tonn1970@yahoo.com; Ao Yai; bungalows 400-500B; @) Outstanding bamboo bungalows hover on Ao Yai's serene southern headland with superb bay views through gentle foliage. Its classy kitchen turns out homemade yoghurt, bread, cookies, good espresso and a variety of veggie and seafood dishes.

Sawasdee   GUESTHOUSE $
(☑ 08 1803 0946, 08 6906 0900; www.sawadeekohchang.com; Ao Yai; bungalows 350-600B) The A-frame wooden bungalows have vented walls to keep things cool. Every option has sunken bathrooms painted bright colours and hammocks on the terraces.

Sunset Bungalows   GUESTHOUSE $
(☑ 08 0693 8577, 08 4339 5224; Ao Yai; bungalows 250-500B) Sweet wooden bungalows with bamboo decks and attached Thai-style bathrooms sit back in the trees along Ao Yai's best stretch of beach.

Mama's GUESTHOUSE **$**

(☑08 0530 7066, 0 7782 0180; mamasbunga-lows@yahoo.com; Ao Tadaeng; huts 250-500B) One of three good choices on Ao Tadaeng, Mama's is tucked into a pretty corner on a rocky, hibiscus-laden hillside.

❶ Getting There & Away

From Ranong take a *sŏrng·tăa·ou* (25B) from the day market on Th Ruangrat to Tha Ko Phayam near Saphan Plaa. Alternatively, most Ranong guesthouses will arrange for a taxi to shuttle you to the pier for 50 to 100B.

Two speedboats to Ao Yai (per person 350B, 45 minutes, 9.30am and 2pm) leave daily from late October to April. They return to Ranong at 9am and 1pm. It's cheaper and just as conven-ient to travel on one of two daily long-tail taxi boats (per person 150B, two hours, 8.30am and 2pm). In the dry season, they stop at all the west-coast beaches. Taxi boats return at 7.30am and 1.30pm. During the monsoon months only morning boats make the crossing three days a week, docking at the main pier on the northeast coast.

You can also charter a long-tail boat to Ko Phayam through Koh Chang Resort (1500B). In high season inquire about a once daily taxi boat to the island.

Ko Phayam เกาะพยาม

Technically part of Laem Son National Park, little Ko Phayam is fringed with beautiful beaches and – for now – is managing to go mainstream while still holding onto its soul. The spectacular northwest and southwest coasts are dotted with beach bungalows, breezy restaurants and bars, and its wood-ed interior is laced with narrow concrete streets, so you can certainly understand the appeal. Fauna in the area includes wild pigs, monkeys and snakes, and there is tremen-dous bird life. Look for sea eagles, toucans and hornbills. The one 'village' on the island, where you will also find the main pier and a majestic golden Buddha at **Wat Phayam**, caters mostly to tourists, but hit it during a festival (such as the Cashew Festival in April) and you'll see that islanders still have a firm grip on their homeland. Motorcycle pathways run down the middle of the island, feeding smaller concrete roadways and dirt trails, some of which can be rutted to the point of hazardous – drive slowly.

The main drawback of Ko Phayam is that the snorkelling isn't great, as high sea tem-peratures have killed off all the coral. But the Surin Islands are closer to here than any-where else and you can hop on live-aboard dive expeditions or speedboat transfers. For dive trips and PADI courses, contact **Phay-am Divers** (☑08 6995 2598; www.phayamlodge. com; Ao Yai).

🛏 Sleeping & Eating

Room capacity has doubled in the past four years, and most resorts are now open year-round with attached eateries serving mid-dling Thai fare. Most places have wi-fi or internet for 2B per minute. The cheapest and some of the best Thai eats are found in town near the pier. Electricity is often only available from sunset to 10pm or 11pm.

Aow Yai Bungalows GUESTHOUSE **$**

(☑08 9819 8782, 0 7787 0216; Ao Yai; bungalows 200-400B) This is the thatched bamboo-bungalow pioneer that started it all here in the late 1980s. Choose between small wooden and bamboo bungalows in the palm grove and a larger beachfront model on the southern end of Ao Yai.

★ **June Horizon** BUNGALOWS **$**

(☑08 0145 9771; Ao Khao Kwai; bungalows 450-600B; ☺Nov-May) A joyful addition tucked into a mangrove inlet at the south end of the beach. Bunk in one of their creative circular concrete bungalows brushed with fanciful murals, or grab a beach hut nailed together with reclaimed and distressed wood panels and crowned with a grass ceiling. All have outdoor baths. The wonderful 'gypsy bar' is worth a tipple.

PP Land HOTEL **$**

(☑08 1678 4310; www.payamppplandbeach.com; Ao Hin-Khow; bungalows from 650B) This is a stunning ecolodge, north of the pier on the little-visited windward side of the island. The stylish concrete bungalows are powered by the wind and sun and have terraces that overlook the sea. The owners have set up an organic garden, make their own all-natural laundry detergent and treat the sewage with a cutting-edge grey-water system.

Heaven Beach GUESTHOUSE **$$**

(☑08 2806 0413; www.ppland-heavenbeach.com; Ao Khao Kwai; r 2000B; ☺) A two-year-old re-sort with an idyllic slice of real estate on lus-cious Ao Khao Kwai. Their tiled bungalows are spacious with outdoor baths, hot show-ers, all day electricity and wide decks with rattan lounges. Enjoy a coconut shake at the cute beachfront restaurant with turquoise

KO PHAYAM'S BEACHES

Ko Phayam has many small beaches but these two long stretches of sandy bliss are where most folks end up.

➡ **Ao Khao Kwai (Buffalo Bay)** is a golden white cove with jungled bluffs and a rock reef offshore – it's the most stunning location on the island. Lovers of peace and quiet head here along with some hippies and the occasional German package tourist. It's a terrific swimming beach, too, except at low tide, when the sea recedes leaving mud flats on the southern end.

➡ **Ao Yai** is long, wide and chilled out yet social, attracting everyone from gap-year backpackers and glampacking couples to young families and retirees. The surf kicks up in the fringe and low seasons and you can rent boogie boards and surfboards at guesthouses along the beach. At other times the swimming is great here and the island's best snorkelling (don't expect much) is found off **Leam Rung**, Ao Yai's northernmost point.

benches, hand-painted menu boards and tables sunk in the sand.

Buffalo Bay Vacation Club HOTEL $$
(☏08 5107 9473; www.buffalobayclub.com; Ao Khao Kwai; bungalows 1300-2500B; ✳@☎) Buffalo's spotless, airtight concrete bungalows with sliding glass doors, hot water and TVs are posh by Phayam standards and a decent value. Their restaurant serves everything from fajitas to authentic Thai curries.

ⓘ Getting There & Around

There is a daily ferry from Phayam Pier in Ranong to Ko Phayam's main pier (150B, 1½ to two hours) at 9.30am and speedboats (350B, 45 minutes) at 10am, noon, 2.30pm & 4pm. From Ko Phayam back to Ranong the boats run at 9am, noon and 3.30pm. Long-tail boat charters to Ko Chang are 1500B.

Motorcycle taxis provide transport around Ko Phayam; there are no cars. A motorcycle taxi from the pier to the main beaches costs 50B to 80B per person each way, depending on the beach. Walking is possible but distances are long – it's about 45 minutes from the pier to Ao Khao Kwai, the nearest bay. Motorbike rentals (200B) are available in the village and from most of the larger resorts, and you'll need one to properly explore the island. It's best to rent yours immediately after getting off the boat in the village. Bicycles are widely available as well.

Laem Son National Park

อุทยานแห่งชาติแหลมสน

This **national park** (☏0 7786 1431; www.dnp.go.th; adult/child 200/100B) covers 315 sq km. It includes about 100km of Andaman Sea coastline – the longest protected shore in the country – and more than 20 islands. Much of the coast here is edged with mangroves and laced with tidal channels, which are home to various species of birds, fish, deer and monkeys. Sea turtles nest on Hat Praphat.

The most accessible beach is the gorgeous 3km white sweep of **Hat Bang Ben**, where the park headquarters are located. Look south and peninsulas jut out into the ocean like so many fingers, hiding isolated coves accessible only by long-tail boat. All of the beaches are said to be safe for swimming year-round. From here you can also see several islands, including the nearby Ko Kam Yai, Ko Kam Noi, Mu Ko Yipun, Ko Khang Khao and, to the north, Ko Phayam. Park staff arrange boat trips to any of these islands for 1500B to 1800B depending upon the destination. If there is a prettier sunset picnic spot on the north Andaman coast, we missed it.

🛏 Sleeping & Eating

Most accommodation options are at Hat Bang Ben. At research time, the national park bungalows were closed and camping was no longer available on the beach

Wasana Resort GUESTHOUSE $
(☏0 7786 1434; bungalows 400-600B; ✳☎) The Wasana is a family-run ring of cosy bungalows wrapping around the colourful on-site restaurant. The owners, a Dutch–Thai couple, have plenty of great ideas for exploring Laem Son (ask about the stunning 10km trek around the headland) and can take you out on a day trip to the islands.

ℹ️ Getting There & Away

The turn-off for Laem Son National Park is about 58km from Ranong down Hwy 4 (Petchkasem Hwy), between the Km 657 and Km 658 markers. Buses heading south from Ranong can drop you off here (ask for Hat Bang Ben). Once you're off the highway, however, you'll have to flag down a pickup truck going towards the park. If you can't get a ride all the way, it's a 10km walk from Hwy 4 to the park entrance. The road is paved, so if you're driving it's a breeze.

PHANG-NGA PROVINCE

POP 9700

Phang-Nga's lush jungle-draped mountains rise like a beautiful jigsaw. It's carved by thick muddy rivers, studded with limestone karst scenery that will make you weak in the knees and blessed with a cerulean bay dotted with dozens of spectacular *horng* islands drilled with caves that lead to pristine ecosystems, which you can glimpse on popular kayak tours.

Phang-Nga's worst days, the Boxing Day Tsunami in 2004, are now a decade in the past, and though tales are still being told about that day, there's a palpable sense of progress as Khao Lak's economy and growth – for better and worse – has surpassed its pre-tragedy potential.

Most of the province remains seasonal. From November to April the water is very clear, the sun shines and soda-white beaches and offshore islands and reefs beckon. In the rainy season, however, many places shut down and the area can feel a bit haunted.

COMMUNITY-BASED TOURISM IN KO PHRA TONG

Andaman Discoveries (☑ 08 7917 7165; www.andamandiscoveries.com; Khuraburi) runs highly recommended three-day, four-night community-based tours that visit homestays in remote villages on Ko Phra Tong. Trips include learning local fishing techniques, mangrove tours and fresh seafood dinners served by your Moken hosts.

Andaman Discoveries also manages three community-service projects: a learning centre for children of Burmese migrant workers, an orphanage outside of Khao Lak and a school for children with learning disabilities in Ranong.

Ko Phra Thong & Ko Ra เกาะพระทอง/เกาะระ

Legend has it that many centuries ago, pirates docked and buried a golden Buddha beneath the sands at Ko Phra Thong, translated as 'Golden Buddha Island'. The legendary statue has never been found, but Ko Phra Thong has modern-day treasures aplenty: endless sandy beaches, mangroves, vast birdlife and rare orchids.

Nearby and even quieter is Ko Ra, encircled by golden beaches and mangroves. This small isle is a mountainous jungle with an impressive array of wildlife (including leopard cats, flying lemurs, scaly anteaters and slow loris) and has a welcoming local population of fisherfolk.

Locals of Tung Dap village on the southern tip of Ko Phra Thong have requested that tourists not visit their area, so please be respectful and avoid this corner.

🛏️ Sleeping

Ko Ra Eco-Resort　　　　　BUNGALOWS $$
(☑ 08 9867 5288; www.kohraecolodge.com; bungalows 1400-2800B) 🌿 Nestled in the trees on a small private beach, this older place offers everything from meditation retreats to spectacular wildlife hikes. Diving and snorkelling tours – including to the relatively nearby Surin Islands – are available.

★ **Golden Buddha Beach Resort**　　　　　BUNGALOWS $$$
(☑ 08 1892 2208; www.goldenbuddharesort.com; bungalows 3200-14,000B) The area's poshest resort attracts a stream of yoga aficionados keen for a spiritual getaway. Accommodation is in naturalistic-chic privately owned wooden houses rented out short- or long-term. There's also a dive centre.

ℹ️ Getting There & Away

There are no regular boats to Ko Phra Thong or Ko Ra, but you could theoretically charter a longtail from the Kuraburi pier for around 1500B each way – though boatmen are hard to find. It's far better and cheaper to contact your resort in advance to arrange transport.

Khao Sok National Park
อุทยานแห่งชาติเขาสก

If your leg muscles have atrophied after one too many days of beach-bumming, consider venturing inland to the wondrous **Khao Sok National Park** (☑0 7739 5025; www.khaosok. com; park admission adult/child 200/100B). Many believe this lowland jungle – the wettest spot in Thailand – to be over 160 million years old, making it one of the oldest rainforests on the globe. It features dramatic limestone formations and waterfalls that cascade through juicy thickets drenched with rain. A network of dirt trails snakes through the quiet park, allowing visitors to spy on the exciting array of indigenous creatures.

The best time of year to visit is the dry season (Dec–Apr). During the wet season (Jun–Oct), trails can be extremely slippery, flash flooding is common and leeches come out in force. On the other hand, animals leave their hidden reservoirs throughout the wet months, so you're more likely to stumble across big fauna.

Sights & Activities

Khao Sok's vast terrain makes it one of the last viable habitats for **large mammals**. During the wetter months you may happen upon bears, boars, gaurs, tapirs, gibbons, deer, wild elephants and perhaps even a tiger. There are more than 300 bird species, 38 bat varieties and one of the world's largest flowers, the rare *Rafflesia kerrii,* which, in Thailand, is found only in Khao Sok. These **giant flowers** can reach 80cm in diameter.

Chiaw Lan, created in 1982 by an enormous shale-clay dam called Ratchaprapha (Kheuan Ratchaprapha or Chiaw Lan), sits about an hour's drive (65km) east of the visitors centre. The limestone outcrops protruding from the lake reach a height of 960m, over three times higher than the formations in the Phang-Nga area.

Tham Nam Thalu cave contains striking limestone formations and subterranean streams, while **Tham Si Ru** features four converging passageways used as a hideout by communist insurgents between 1975 and 1982. The caves can be reached on foot from the southwestern shore of the lake. You can rent boats from local fishermen to explore the coves, canals, caves and cul-de-sacs along the lakeshore.

Elephant trekking, kayaking and rafting are popular park activities. The hiking is also excellent, and you can arrange park tours from any guesthouse in or around the park. Various trails, which you can hike independently from the visitors centre, lead to the waterfalls of **Sip-Et Chan** (4km), **Than**

KHAO SOK TOURS

Tours in and around Khao Sok can be up to 50% cheaper when booked at guesthouses or travel agents near the park itself. Tours booked from further-afield destinations such as Phuket or Khao Lak will include higher-priced transport and tour-agent commissions.

Sawan (9km) and **Than Kloy** (9km), among other destinations. The park office hands out free trail maps.

Sleeping & Eating

The road leading into the park is lined with simple, charming guesthouses, all of which offer a variety of park tours and guide services. We recommend going on a two-day, one-night trip (2500B per person) to Chiaw Lan where you sleep in floating huts on the lake and go on a variety of canoe and hiking excursions.

Most guesthouses have their own eateries (also open to non-guests) and there are a few restaurants on the road as well.

Art's Riverview Jungle Lodge GUESTHOUSE $$
(☑09 0167 6818; http://krabidir.com/artsriverviewlodge; 54/3 Moo 6; bungalows 650-1500B) In a monkey-filled jungle bordering a river with a natural limestone cliff–framed swimming hole, this is the prettiest location in Khao Sok. Wood bungalows are simple but big; all have river views.

Tree House GUESTHOUSE $$
(☑0 7739 5169; ww.khaosok-treehouse.com; 233 Moo 6; r with fan/air-con 1000/2000B; ✦🛜❄) Don't be dissuaded by the Disney-esque facade, here is a complex of rather excellent and spacious bungalows connected by raised paths and bridges. The best nests have flat screens, air-con and two terraces. Fan rooms are simpler and smaller but very clean.

⭐**Elephant Hills** RESORT $$$
(☑0 7638 1703; www.elephant-hills.com; 170 Moo 7 Tambon Klong Sok; d all-inclusive from 12,500B; 🅿🛜) 🍃 Whether you are a family of five, honeymooning backpackers or a soloist, this is one of those resorts that makes everyone smile. Set above the Sok River, at the base of stunning limestone mountains draped in misty jungle, the area's only tented camp offers the kind of rootsy luxury you'd most

associate with the Serengeti. Airy tents have wood floors, stone baths, skylights, wood furnishings and hammocks on the porch.

It's all inclusive and the price includes average meals, guided hikes through the jungle and a canoe trip downriver to their elephant camp where 15 lovely ladies – rescues from other camps where they were forced to carry tourists around – are treated kindly. You can't ride them. But you do get to feed, bathe and spend some quality time with them. The kids love it. The inner-kid loves it. It really is a special experience. And after a few days in the hills, consider adding a night at their **Rainforest Camp** (www.rainforestcamp.com; Chiaw Lan Lake), a floating tented camp on Chiaw Lan Lake. Reservations only.

❶ Information

The park headquarters and visitors centre are 1.8km off Rte 401, close to the Km 109 marker.

There's an ATM outside the Morning Mist Mini-Mart and internet is available near the park entrance for 2B per minute.

❶ Getting There & Around

Minivans to Surat Thani (250B, one hour), Krabi (300B, two hours) and a handful of other destinations leave daily from the park. Otherwise, from Surat catch a bus going towards Takua Pa; from the Andaman coast, take a Surat Thani–bound bus. Buses drop you off along the highway (Rte 401), 1.8km from the visitors centre. If guesthouse touts don't meet you, you'll have to walk to your chosen nest (from 50m to 2km).

To explore Chiaw Lan lake on your own, charter a long-tail (2000B per day) at the dam's entrance.

Khao Lak & Around   เขาหลัก

Hat Khao Lak is a beach for folks who shun the glitz of Phuket's bigger resort towns, but still crave comfort, shopping and plenty of facilities. With warm waves to frolic in, long stretches of golden sand backed by forested hills, and easy day trips to the Similan and Surin Islands, Khao Sok and Khao Lak/Lam Ru National Parks, and even Phuket, the area is a central base for exploring the North Andaman – above and below the water.

About 2.5km north of Hat Khao Lak, **Hat Bang Niang** is an even quieter version of sandy bliss with skinnier beaches but fewer people. Khao Lak proper (also called Khao Lak Town locally) – a hodgepodge of restaurants, tourist markets and low-rise hotels along a grey highway – isn't exactly pretty, but it is convenient.

⊙ Sights

Khao Lak/Lam Ru
National Park   NATIONAL PARK

(☎0 7642 0243; www.dnp.go.th; adult/child 200/100B; ⊙8am-4.30pm) The area immediately south of Hat Khao Lak has been incorporated into the vast 125-sq-km **Khao Lak/Lam Ru National Park**, a collage of sea cliffs, 1000m-high hills, beaches, estuaries, forested valleys and mangroves. Wildlife includes hornbills, drongos, tapirs, gibbons, monkeys and Asiatic black bears.

The visitors centre, just off Hwy 4 between the Km 56 and Km 57 markers, has a very nice open-air restaurant on a shady slope overlooking the sea. From the restaurant you can take a fairly easy 3km round-trip nature trail that heads along the cape and ends at often-deserted Hat Lek beach.

Boat 813   MONUMENT

FREE In an open field nearly 1km from shore, this boat is a testament to the force of the 2004 Boxing Day Tsunami. Nearly 10 years later, it remains the region's most prominent reminder of the disaster. There's an information booth nearby with a tsunami timeline in both Thai and English. It's a 50B *sŏrng·tăa·ou* ride between here and Khao Lak.

🏃 Activities

Diving or snorkelling day excursions to the Similan and Surin Islands are immensely popular but, if you can, opt for a live-aboard. Since the islands are around 60km from the mainland (about three hours by boat), you'll have a more relaxing trip and experience the islands sans day trippers. All dive shops offer live-aboard trips from around 17,000/29,000B for three-/five-day packages and day trips for 4900B to 6500B.

On these two-, three-, four- or five-day trips, you'll wake up with the dawn and slink below the ocean's surface up to four times per day in what's commonly considered to be one of the top 10 diving realms in the world. While both the Similan and Surin Islands have experienced vast coral bleaching recently, **Richelieu Rock** is still the crème de la crème of the region's sites. **Ko Bon** and **Ko Ta Chai** are two other good sites due to the traffic of giant manta rays.

Although geared towards divers, all dive shops welcome snorkellers who can hop on selected dive excursions or live-aboars for a discount of around 40%; otherwise, tour agencies all around town offer even cheaper snorkelling trips to the Similan Islands for around 3200B. PADI Open Water certification courses cost anywhere from 10,000B to 18,000B depending on where you dive. You can go on a 'discover scuba' day trip to the Similans for around 6000B to 6500B.

★**Wicked Diving** DIVING
(☑ 0 7648 5868; www.wickeddiving.com) An exceptionally well-run and environmentally conscious outfit that runs diving and snorkelling overnight trips offering a range of live-aboard options including Whale Sharks & Mantas, Turtle & Reefs and Sharks & Rays conservation trips, run in conjunction with **Ecocean** (www.whaleshark.org). It does all the PADI courses, too.

Sea Dragon Diver Centre DIVING
(☑ 0 7648 5420; www.seadragondivecenter.com; Th Phetkasem) One of the older operations in Khao Lak, Sea Dragon has maintained high standards throughout the years.

Similan Seven Sea Club DIVING
(☑ 0 7648 5237; www.similansevenseaclub.com; Th Phetkasem) A new, highly recommended dive outfitter for day trips and live-aboards to the Similans.

IQ Dive DIVING
(☑ 0 7648 5614; www.iq-dive.com; Th Phetkasem; diving day trips from 5100B) A quality operation that focuses on diving and snorkelling day trips. The website has good information about the gamut of live-aboards operating in the region.

★**Fantastic** SNORKELLING
(☑ 0 7648 5998; www.fantasticsimilan.com; adult/child 3200/2200B) Fantastic is a campy frolic of a Similans snorkelling tour featuring players from the local cross-dressing cabaret as guides. It's a trip duplicated nowhere else on earth: lunch is served on a pristine white-sand beach and they get you to the prime snorkel sites, too. No booking office; meet at the pier or Fantastic can arrange pick-ups from your hotel.

🛏 Sleeping

For the cheapest sleeps in town, head to Sea Dragon Diver Centre and ask about the dorm beds at Tiffy's Café, which go for 180B per night.

Walker's Inn GUESTHOUSE $
(☑ 08 6281 7668, 08 4840 2689; www.walkersinn.com; Th Phetkasem; dm/r 200/600B; ❄ 🖥) A long-running backpacker fave and classic

Khao Lak

old-school guesthouse that offers bright and spacious air-con rooms, decent dorms and a fine downstairs pub serving full English breakfasts. They offer laundry service and motorbike rental, too.

Khaolak Banana Bungalows BUNGALOWS $
(☑ 0 7648 5889; www.khaolakbanana.com; 4/147 Moo7; r 500-1200B; ❄ 🏊) These adorable little bungalows have swirls painted on the

cement floors and sun-filled indoor-outdoor bathrooms. A cute pool with deckchairs sweetens the deal.

Fasai House
GUESTHOUSE $

(☑ 0 7648 5867; r 500-700B; ❄ @) The best budget choice in Khao Lak, Fasai has immaculate motel-style rooms and smiling staff members.

Greenbeach
HOTEL $$

(☑ 0 7648 5845; www.khaolakgreenbeachresort.com; bungalows 1400-2300B; ❄) On an excellent stretch of Khao Lak beach and extending back into a garden, this place has a warm family-style soul. The wooden bungalows have glass doors, air-con and fan, shady terraces and views of a towering, ancient banyan tree. Even the cheapest rooms have sea views.

Nangthong Bay Resort
HOTEL $$

(☑ 0 7648 5088; www.nangthong.com; r 1800B, bungalows 2500-3000B; ❄ @ ☎ ⛱) Rooms are designed with a sparse black-and-white chic decor. The cheapest rooms are set back from the beach, but are fantastic value. Grounds are lush and service is excellent.

Monochrome
BOUTIQUE HOTEL $$$

(☑ 0 7642 7700; www.monochromeresort.com; 67/238 Moo 5, Ban Niang; r/ste from 3900/7900B; P ❄ @ ☎ ⛱) Just four months old at research time, the newest splashy address in Khao Lak is set on the road to Bang Niang, about 200m from the beach. It's modern, with a vertical louvred facade, a beer garden off the entryway and pool in the courtyard, with lots of charcoal grey and natural cherrywood to soothe the eye.

Pricier suites include a full living room and soaker tub in the bedroom. Yes the bedroom. It's unique, yet strangely alluring.

Sarojin
HOTEL $$$

(☑ 0 7642 7901, 0 7642 7900; www.sarojin.com; Hat Pakarang; r 12,500-22,250B; ❄ @ ☎ ⛱) A quiet retreat 15km north of Khao Lak with a Japanese-meets-modern-Thai style, the service here is stellar and the setting is elegant and intimate. The very private spa (treatments from 2300B), which takes in views of coconut groves and is nestled at the edge of the mangroves, is one of the best on the Andaman coast.

We especially love the pool with its stylish lounging huts that hover above the crystal-blue water, and a cooking class takes place on the banks of the Takuapa River, where you can watch water buffalo amble by. No kids allowed.

✕ Eating & Drinking

This is no culinary capital, but there are a few local haunts where tourists congregate to rehash the day's diving yarns. Early-morning divers will be hard-pressed to find a place to grab a bite before 8.30am.

Go Pong
THAI $

(Th Phetkasem; dishes 30-100B; ⊙ noon-10pm) Get off the tourist taste-bud tour at this terrific little streetside diner where they stir-fry noodles and spicy rice dishes, and simmer an aromatic noodle soup that attracts a local lunch following. If you dig the pig, try the stewed pork leg with rice or the Chinese broccoli with crispy pork. Both are worthy.

Jumbo Steak & Pasta
ITALIAN $$

(☑ 08 7269 3928; Th Phetkasem, Ban Khukkhuk; mains 70-220B; ⊙ 10.30am-10pm Thu-Tue) A hole-in-the-wall joint in Ban Khukkhuk, just past the police boat, launched by a former line chef at Le Meridian who does beautiful pasta dishes of all varieties: penne arrabiata, spaghetti alla carbonara, a host of pizzas and some terrific steaks. Dishes are an incredible value (hence the local expat scene), though portions aren't huge.

Phu Khao Lak
INTERNATIONAL, THAI $$

(☑ 0 7648 5141; Th Phetkasem; dishes 80-300B; ⊙ 8am-10pm) With its cloth tables spilling to the edges of a lawn at the southern end of the Khao Lak strip, this place is hard to miss. And you shouldn't pass it by – there's a huge menu of Western and Thai dishes here with ample descriptions, all cooked to perfection.

★ Takieng
THAI $$

(☑ 08 6952 7693; 26/43 Moo 5, Bang Niang; dishes 80-350B; ⊙ 11am-10pm) Set on the east side of highway just before the Bang Niang turn are two open-air Thai restaurants beneath stilted tin roofs. This is the more visually appealing of the two, and the dishes are also stylish. They steam fresh fish in green curry, do a scintillating chicken and pork larb, and fry squid in chilli paste. Service is impeccable.

Happy Snapper
BAR

(☑ 0 7648 5500; www.happysnapperbar.com; Th Phetkasem) Here's a bar stocked with good liquor, a map of the world on the ceiling, the tree of life on the wall and a rockin' house band on stage six nights a week in the high season, led by the owner, a Bangkok-born bass legend.

ℹ Information

For diving-related emergencies, call the **SSS Ambulance** (☏ 08 1081 9444), which rushes injured persons down to Phuket for treatment. The ambulance can also be used for car or motorcycle accidents. There is also one nurse in Bang Niang who treats diving-related injuries.

There are numerous travel agencies scattered about – the best is **Khao Lak Land Discoveries** (☏ 0 7648 5411; www.khaolaklanddicovery. com; Th Petchkasem) – that rent motorbikes for around 250B per day.

ℹ Getting There & Away

Any bus running along Hwy 4 between Takua Pa (60B, 45 minutes) and Phuket (100B, two hours) will stop at Hat Khao Lak if you ask the driver.

Khao Lak Land Discoveries runs hourly minibuses to Phuket International Airport (600B, one hour 15 minutes). Alternatively, you can take **Cheaper Than Hotel** (☏ 08 6276 6479, 08 5786 1378), which admittedly is an odd name for a taxi and transport service. They make the run to the Phuket airport (1000B) and points south. Or tell a Phuket-bound bus driver to drop you at the 'airport' – you'll be let off at an intersection from which motorcycle taxis will take you to the airport (10 minutes, 100B). It sounds sketchy, but works every time.

Surin Islands Marine National Park

อุทยานแห่งชาติหมู่เกาะสุรินทร์

The five gorgeous islands that make up the **Surin Islands Marine National Park** (www.dnp.go.th; admission adult/child 500/300B; ⊙mid-Nov–mid-May) sit 60km offshore, just 5km from the Thailand–Myanmar marine border. Healthy rainforest, pockets of white-sand beach in sheltered bays and rocky headlands that jut into the ocean characterise these granite-outcrop islands. The clearest of water makes for great marine life, with underwater visibility often up to 35m. The islands' sheltered waters also attract *chow lair* – sea gypsies – who live in a village onshore during the monsoon season from May to November. Around here they are known as Moken, from the local word *oken* meaning 'salt water'.

Ko Surin Neua (north) and Ko Surin Tai (south) are the two largest islands. Park headquarters and all visitor facilities are at Ao Chong Khad and Ao Mai Ngam on Ko Surin Neua, near the jetty. The shapes and colours are what you'll remember most. The flaxen sand and sparkling blue-green bays, the purpling depths, and sheer granite peninsulas that tumble down in a permanent geological avalanche forming arrow-like points and natural breakwaters are spectacular.

Khuraburi is the jumping-off point for the park. The pier is about 9km north of town, as is the mainland **national park office** (☏ 0 7649 1378; ⊙8am-5pm), with good information, maps and helpful staff.

◉ Sights & Activities

Several tour operators run day tours from Khao Lak and Khuraburi (2900B including food and park lodging) to the park.

Greenview   TOUR
(☏ 0 7640 1400; Khuraburi Pier) The best in safety, service and value is Greenview. Agencies dealing with diving in Hat Khao Lak, Phuket and Ranong are the most convenient options for booking live-aboard dive trips. Transfers from the place of purchase are always included.

Diving & Snorkelling

Dive sites in the park include **Ko Surin Tai** and **HQ Channel** between the two main islands. **Richelieu Rock** (a seamount 14km southeast) is also technically in the park and happens to be one of the best dive sites, if not the best, on the Andaman coast. Whale sharks are sometimes spotted here during March and April. There's no dive facility in the park itself, so dive trips (four-day live-aboards around 20,000B) must be booked from the mainland.

Bleaching has damaged the hard corals but you'll see plenty of fish and soft corals. Two-hour snorkelling trips (per person 100B, gear per day 40B) leave the park headquarters at 9am and 2pm daily. Expect to be in the company of mostly Thais who swim fully clothed. If you'd like a more serene snorkelling experience, charter your own long-tail from the national park (half day 1500B), or better yet, directly from the Moken themselves in **Ban Moken** (Moken Village). The most beautiful, vibrant soft corals we saw were at **Ao Mae Yai**, an enormous North Island bay around the corner from Chong Khod. The best section of reef is between the white buoys along the northern peninsula. There are more fish off tiny **Ko Pajumba**, but the coral isn't in great shape. **Ao Suthep**, off the South Island, has vast schools of iridescent fish and shallow blue holes with milky bottoms.

Wildlife & Hiking

Around park headquarters you can explore the forest fringes, looking out for crab-eating macaques and some of the 57 resident bird species, which include the fabulous Nicobar pigeon, endemic to the Andaman islands. Along the coast you're likely to see the Brahminy kite in the air and reef herons on the rocks. Twelve species of bat live here, most noticeably the tree-dwelling fruit bats (also known as flying foxes).

A rough-and-ready **walking trail** winds 2km along the coast, through forest and back down to the beach at **Ao Mai Ngam**, where there's camping facilities and its own canteen. At low tide it's easy to walk along the coast between the two campsites.

Village Tour

Ban Moken at Ao Bon on the South Island welcomes visitors. Post-tsunami, Moken have settled in this one sheltered bay where a major ancestral worship ceremony (Loi Reua) takes place in April. The national park offers a **Moken Village Tour** (per person 300B). You'll stroll through the village where you should ask locals for permission to hike the 800m **Chok Madah trail** over the jungled hills to an empty beach. Tours depart at 9.15am and must be reserved the day before. You can also organise a ride over from the park's HQ (per person 100B). If you do visit the village, bring cash to buy handicrafts to help support its economy. There's also a clothing donation box at park headquarters for the Moken, so this is a good, responsible place to lighten your load.

🛏 Sleeping & Eating

Park accommodation is decent, but because of the island's short, narrow beaches it can feel seriously crowded when full (around 300 people). Book online at www.dnp.go.th or with the mainland national park office (p611) in Khuraburi. The clientele is mostly Thai, giving the place a lively holiday-camp feel. You can camp on both Ao Chong Klod and Ao Mae Ngam. The former has the more spectacular beach, the latter fills up last, is more secluded, and with its narrow white-sand shallow bay, it feels a bit wilder. There are no bungalows on Ao Mae Ngam.

Bungalows (weekday/weekend 1400/2000B) have wood floors and private terraces, as well as private terracotta bathrooms and fans that run all night. **Tents** (2-/4-person 300/450B, bedding per person 60B) are available for rent or you can pitch your own **tent** (per night 80B). There's generator power until 10pm.

A park **restaurant** (dishes from 80B, set menus 170-200B) serves decent Thai food.

ℹ Getting There & Away

Tour operators use speedboats (return 1700-1900B; 60-75 minutes one-way) exclusively. They leave around 9am and honour open tickets. Return whenever you please, but ask the park office to confirm your ticket the night before.

Similan Islands Marine National Park

อุทยานแห่งชาติหมู่เกาะสิมิลัน

Known to divers the world over, beautiful **Similan Islands Marine National Park** (www.dnp.go.th; admission adult/child 400/200B; ⊙ Nov-May) is 70km offshore. Its smooth granite islands are as impressive above water as below, topped with rainforest, edged with white-sand beaches and fringed with coral reefs. Unfortunately, recent coral bleaching has killed off many of the hard corals but soft corals are still intact, the fauna is there and it's still a lovely place to dive.

Two of the nine islands, Island 4 (Ko Miang) and Island 8 (Ko Similan), have ranger stations and accommodation; park headquarters and most visitor activity centres are on Island 4. 'Similan' comes from the Malay word *sembilan,* meaning 'nine', and while each island is named, they're more commonly known by their numbers. Relatively recently, the park was expanded to included Ko Bon and Ko Tachai, and both have remained unscathed by coral bleaching making them some of the better diving and snorkelling areas.

Hat Khao Lak is the jumping-off point for the park. The pier is at Thap Lamu, about 10km south of town.

◉ Sights & Activities

Diving & Snorkelling

The Similans offer diving for all levels of experience, at depths from 2m to 30m. There are rock reefs at **Ko Payu** (Island 7) and divethroughs at **Hin Pousar** (Elephant Head), with marine life ranging from tiny plume worms and soft corals to schooling fish and whale sharks. There are dive sites at each of the six islands north of Ko Miang (Island 4); the southern part of the park (Islands 1, 2 and 3) is a turtle nesting ground and off-limits to divers. No facilities for divers exist in the national park itself, so you'll need to take a dive tour. Agencies in Hat Khao Lak and Phuket book dive trips (three-day live-aboards from around 15,000B, but you'll pay more to rent gear).

You can hire snorkelling gear (per day 150B) from the park headquarters. Day-tour operators usually visit three or four different snorkelling sites. Plenty of tour agencies in Hat Khao Lak offer snorkelling-only day/overnight trips (from around 3000/5000B), and the beach can become positively packed. It's clear that nobody is really monitoring the numbers of day trip visitors, to the park's detriment. Some snorkelling outfits go so far as to feed the fish, which is a big ecological no-no. That would never happen if this place were a national park! Oh, wait...

Wildlife & Hiking

The forest around the park headquarters on Ko Miang (Island 4) has a couple of walking trails and some great wildlife. The fabulous Nicobar pigeon, with its wild mane of grey-green feathers, is common here. Endemic to the islands of the Andaman Sea, it's one of some 39 bird species in the park. Hairy-legged land crabs and fruit bats (flying foxes) are relatively easily seen in the forest, as are flying squirrels.

A small **beach track**, with information panels, leads 400m to a tiny, pretty snorkelling bay. Detouring from the track, the **Viewpoint Trail** – 500m or so of steep scrambling – has panoramic vistas from the top. A 500m walk to **Sunset Point** takes you through forest to a smooth granite platform facing west.

On Ko Similan (Island 8) there's a 2.5km forest hike to a **viewpoint**, and a shorter, steep scramble off the main beach to the top of **Sail Rock** (aka Balance Rock).

🛏 Sleeping & Eating

Accommodation in the park is available for all budgets. Book online at www.dnp.go.th or with the mainland **national park office** (☑ 0 7645 3272) at Hat Khao Lak. Tour agents in Hat Khao Lak also arrange overnight to

multiday trips that include transport, food and lodging at the park – these cost little more than it would to go solo.

On Ko Miang there are sea-view **bunga-lows** (2000B; ❇ 🤶) with balconies, two dark five-room wood-and-bamboo **longhouses** (r 1000B; ❇) with fans, and **tents** (2-/4-person 300/450B). There's electricity from 6pm to 6am.

Tents are also available on Ko Similan. You can pitch your own **tent** (per night 80B) on either island.

A **restaurant** (dishes 100-150B) near the park headquarters serves simple Thai food.

ℹ Getting There & Away

There's no public transport to the park, but theoretically independent travellers can book a speedboat transfer (return 1700B, 1½ hours one way) with a Hat Khao Lak snorkelling operator, though they much prefer that you join the snorkelling tour and generally discourage independent travel to the Similans.

Agencies in Khao Lak and Phuket book day/overnight tours (from around 3000/5000B) and dive trips (three-day live-aboards from around 15,000B) – this is about how much you would pay if you tried to get to the islands on your own steam. You can try to link up with a dive trip and pay for the excursion sans diving equipment, but operators will only cooperate if their boats are relatively empty.

Phang-Nga Town & Ao Phang-Nga พังงา/อ่าวพังงา

With turquoise bays peppered with craggy limestone rock towers, brilliant-white beaches and tumbledown fishing villages, Ao Phang-Nga is one of the region's most spectacular landscapes. Little wonder then that it was here, among the towering cliffs and swifts' nests, that James Bond's nemesis, Scaramanga (*The Man with the Golden Gun*), chose to build his lair. Wanted assassins with goals of world domination would not be recommended to hide out here nowadays, since the area is swarming with tourists in motorboats and sea kayaks nearly year-round. Much of the bay, and some of the coastline, has now been incorporated into the Ao Phang-Nga Marine National Park.

◎ Sights & Activities

Phang-Nga is a scruffy town with little going for it, backed up against sublime limestone

Ao Phang Nga

PHANG-NGA
Wat Tham Suwankhuha
Phang-Nga
Thap Put
Sa Nang Manora Forest Park
Takua Thung
Tha Dan
Ao Phang-Nga Marine National Park
Ao Leuk
Krabi (17km)
Ko Panyi
Ko Phing Kan
Ao Phang-Nga
Ao Luk
KRABI
Thai Muang (23km)
Ko Yao Noi
Tha Manok
Tha Khao
Bang Rong
Tha Klong Hia
Tha Len
Ko Yao Yai
PHUKET
Phuket Town
ANDAMAN SEA
Ao Por Pier
Ko Phi-Phi National Park (40km)

cliffs. There isn't a whole lot to see or do unless you happen to be here during the annual **Vegetarian Festival** in late September or October.

Boat Tours

About 8.5km south of the town centre is Tha Dan. From here, you can charter boats to see half-submerged **caves**, oddly shaped islands and **Ko Panyi**, a Muslim village on stilts. There are tours to the well-trodden **Ko Phing Kan** (James Bond Island) and **Ao Phang-Nga National Marine Park** (500B per person for a two- to three-hour tour). Takua Thung, another pier area about 10km further west of Tha Dan, also has private boats for hire at similar prices to tours. The park office, inside Ao Phang-Nga National Marine Park, also offers boat tours.

Although it can be a pain to haggle with boatmen, it's nice to create your own itinerary. Of course, it's easier (and cheaper) to go with an organised tour through an agency in town. Several are clustered around the bus station. **Sayan Tours** (08 1397 4717, 08 3692 0537; www.sayantour.com) has been doing tours of Ao Phang-Nga for many years, and continues to receive good reviews from travellers. **Mr. Kean Tour** (08 9871 6092, 0 7643 0619), owned by the man himself, is an-

other great choice. He's been running tours in the area for over 20 years. Half-/full-day tours cost from 700B to 1600B per person and include **Tham Lawt** (a large water cave), Ko Phing Kan and Ko Panyi, among other destinations. You can even add a bit of kayaking.

Sleeping & Eating

Phang-Nga doesn't have much in the way of quality sleeping and most folks just choose to swing by on a day trip. Several food stalls on the main street of Phang-Nga sell delicious *kà·nŏm jeen* (thin wheat noodles) with chicken curry, *nám yah* (spicy ground-fish curry) or *nám prík* (spicy sauce). There's a morning market open from 5am to 10am daily and a small night market on Tuesday, Wednesday and Thursday evenings, located just south of Soi Lohakit.

Baan Phang Nga GUESTHOUSE $$
(0 7641 3276; 100/2 Th Petchkasem; r 650-850B;) It's a mom and pop kind of place with spacious, spotless rooms in an old relic. Ceilings are high, the concrete floors are painted and they even have rain showers and hot water in the bathrooms. Good coffee and Western breakfasts are served in the downstairs bakery.

Phang-Nga Inn HOTEL $$
(0 7641 1963; 2/2 Soi Lohakit; r 700-1500B;) This converted residential villa features heavy wood staircases, louvred cabinets and peaceful gardens. It's well furnished, there's a little eatery and the staff are gracious.

Getting There & Away

Phang-Nga's bus terminal is located just off the main street on Soi Bamrung Rat. Bangkok buses to/from Phang-Nga include VIP class (960B, 12 hours, one daily), 1st class (600B, 12 to 13 hours, two daily) and 2nd class (480B, 12 hours, three to four daily).

There are several other bus services available:

DESTINATION	PRICE	FREQUENCY	DURATION
Hat Yai	237-306B	2 daily	6hr
Krabi	80B	frequent	1½hr
Phuket	90B	frequent	1½hr
Ranong	170B	4 daily	5hr
Surat Thani	150B	frequent	3hr
Trang	200B	frequent	3½hr

Around Phang-Nga

Ao Phang-Nga Marine National Park อุทยานแห่งชาติอ่าวพังงา

Established in 1981 and covering an area of 400 sq km, **Ao Phang-Nga Marine National Park** (☎0 7641 1136; www.dnp.go.th; adult/child 200/100B; ⊙8am-4pm) is noted for its classic karst scenery. There are over 40 islands with huge vertical cliffs, some with caves that are accessible at low tide and lead into hidden *hôrngs* (lagoons surrounded by solid rock walls). The bay itself is composed of large and small tidal channels including Khlong Ko Phanyi, Khlong Phang-Nga, Khlong Bang Toi and Khlong Bo Saen. These channels run through vast mangroves in a north–south direction and today are used by fisherfolk and island inhabitants as aquatic highways. These are the largest remaining primary mangrove forests in Thailand.

In the peak season, the bay can become a package-tourist superhighway. But if you explore in the early morning (best done from Ko Yao Noi or Ko Yao Yai) or stay out a bit late, you'll find a slice of beach, sea and a limestone karst to call your own. The best way to experience the park is by kayak.

◉ Sights & Activities

Ko Nok & Ko Klui ISLANDS
Set halfway between Phuket and Krabi, these two islands are far enough from tour epicentres that you'll usually have them to yourself. **Ko Klui**, the big island north of Ko Yao Noi, has tidal access to a huge *hôrng*, which some call the **Blue Room**, and a pristine white-sand beach with plenty of hornbills and monkeys.

Ko Phing Kan (James Bond Island) ISLAND
The biggest tourist drawcard in the park is the so-called James Bond Island, known to Thais as **Ko Phing Kan** (literally 'Leaning on Itself Island'). Once used as a location setting for *The Man with the Golden Gun,* the island is now full of vendors hawking coral and shells that should have stayed in the sea.

★ **John Gray's Seacanoe** BOATING
(☎0 7622 6077; www.johngray-seacanoe.com) John Gray was the first kayak outfitter in the bay and remains the most ecologically minded. He's constantly clamouring for more protection for his beloved *hôrngs* among local national-park rangers and their supervisors in Bangkok. His **Hong By Starlight trip** (per person 3950B) dodges the crowds, involves plenty of sunset paddling and will introduce you to Ao Phang-Nga's famed bio-luminescence once night falls.

❶ Getting There & Around

If you have your own vehicle, drive about 6km south on Hwy 4 from the centre of Phang-Nga, turn left onto Rte 4144 (the road to Tha Dan) and travel 2.6km to the park headquarters. Without your own transport you'll need to take a *sŏrng·tăa·ou* to Tha Dan (30B).

From the park office, you can hire a boat (1500-2000B, maximum four passengers) for a three-hour tour of the surrounding islands.

Ko Yao เกาะยาว

With mountainous backbones, unspoilt shorelines, a large variety of birdlife and a population of friendly Muslim fisherfolk, **Ko Yao Yai** and **Ko Yao Noi** are laid-back vantage points for soaking up Ao Phang-Nga's beautiful scenery. The islands are part of the

---

WILDLIFE IN AO PANG-NGA NATIONAL PARK

The marine limestone environment here favours a long list of reptiles, including Bengal monitor lizards, flying lizards, banded sea snakes, dogface water snakes, shore pit vipers and Malayan pit vipers. Keep an eye out for a two-banded monitor (*Varanus salvator*), which looks like a crocodile when seen swimming in the mangrove swamp and can measure up to 2.2m in length.

Amphibians in the Ao Phang-Nga region include marsh frogs, common bush frogs and crab-eating frogs. Avian residents of note are helmeted hornbills (the largest of Thailand's 12 hornbill species, with a body length of up to 127cm), the edible-nest swiftlets (*Aerodramus fuciphagus*), white-bellied sea eagles, ospreys and Pacific reef egrets.

In the mangrove forests and on some of the larger islands reside over 200 species of mammals, including white-handed gibbons, serows, dusky langurs and crab-eating macaques.

Ao Phang-Nga National Park but are most easily accessed from Phuket.

Despite being the relative pipsqueak of the Ko Yao Islands, Ko Yao Noi is the main population centre, with fishing, coconut farming and tourism sustaining its small, year-round population. Bays on the east coast recede to mud flats at low tide but the beaches are still splendid. Ko Yao Yai is far less developed than Ko Yao Noi; it offers an even more remote and wild getaway.

Please remember to respect the beliefs of the local Muslim population and wear modest clothing when away from the beaches.

◉ Sights & Activities

Cycling

Bring along or rent (200B per day from most guesthouses) a mountain bike if you want to explore each of the islands' numerous dirt trails, or join up with Phuket's **Amazing Bike Tours** (☑ 08 7263 2031; www.amazingbiketoursthailand.com; day trip 2900B).

Diving & Snorkelling

Half-day three-island snorkelling tours (1700B, maximum six passengers) through Ao Phang-Nga are easily organised from any guesthouse or with long-tail captains on the beaches. **Koh Yao Diver** (☑ 076 597 406, 08 7895 7515; http://kohyaodiver.com) leads dive trips from both islands.

Rock Climbing

Mountain Shop Adventures (☑ 08 3969 2023; www.themountainshop.org; Tha Khao) offers half-day and full-day rock-climbing trips for 2500B and 4000B respectively. There are over 150 climbs on Ko Yao Noi and owner Mark has routed most of them himself – many trips involve boat travel to get to remote limestone cliff faces. Most climbs are equipped with titanium bolts and beginner to advanced trips are available.

🛏 Sleeping & Eating

🛏 Ko Yao Noi

Ulmur's Nature Lodge   BUNGALOWS $$
(☑ 0 7658 2728, 08 9290 0233; ulmar_nature_lodge@hotmail.com; Hat Tha Khao; bungalows with fan/air-con 1000/1600B; ❄☎) Set in a mangrove-shrouded toe of the bay are a collection of nice octagonal bungalows made of wood with sliding glass doors that peel back onto marvellous views. All are super

clean, with hot water and hardwood floors. There's an onsite yoga studio (classes 7.30am & 4.30pm) here, too.

Ko Yao Beach Bungalows   GUESTHOUSE $$
(☑ 0 7645 4213, 08 1693 8935; www.kohyaobeach.com; Hat Tha Khao; bungalows 1500B; ❄☎) They offer attractive, spacious tiled bungalows with hot water and air-con, as well as smaller, older thatched wooden huts. The whole compound is set across the road from a fantastic swimming beach, and either choice is a great value.

Lom Lea   BUNGALOWS $$$
(☑ 0 7659 7486; www.lomlae.com; Ko Yao Noi; bungalows 2500-6000B) Stylish, natural wooden bungalows are fronted by a stunning and secluded beach with views of Phang-Nga's signature karst islands. There's a dive centre, a good restaurant and plenty of activities on offer.

★ **Six Senses Hideaway**   HOTEL $$$
(☑ 0 7641 8500; www.sixsenses.com/hideaway-yaonoi; Ko Yao Noi; villas from 20,377B; ❄@☎) 🌿 This swanky five-star property – where 56 hillside pool villas (and their tremendous spa) have been built to resemble an old *chow lair* village – doesn't disappoint. Views of distant limestone formations are jaw dropping, the Thai kitchen is tantalising and its commitment to sustainability is unparalleled among global five-star chains.

Rice Paddy   THAI, INTERNATIONAL $$
(☑ 08 2331 6581, 0 7645 4255; Hat Pasai; mains 150-250B; ⊘6-10pm Tue-Sun; ☑) Just around the corner from Pasai Beach, this cute, all-wood Thai and international kitchen is German owned, and all the dishes are special. They fry barracuda fillets and smother them in curry, flash fry *sôm·đam*, and the felafel and hummus get high marks too. In fact, they do a number of veggie dishes featuring chicken, lamb and seafood substitutes.

🛏 Ko Yao Yai

Thiwson Beach Resort   GUESTHOUSE $$$
(☑ 08 1737 4420; www.thiwsonbeach.com; Ko Yao Yai; bungalows 3200B; ❄) Easily the cleanest and sweetest of Ko Yao Yai's bungalow properties. Here are proper wooden bungalows with polished floors, outdoor baths and wide patios facing the best beach on the island. Beachfront bungalows are the largest, but fan rooms are tremendous value.

Elixir HOTEL $$$

(☑08 7808 3838; www.elixirresort.com; Ko Yao Yai;
bungalows 3331-9000B; ❄@☒) The first of
Yao Yai's two four-star resorts offers taste-
ful beachfront and hillside peaked-roof vil-
las steeped in classic Thai style. There are
dark-wood floors and high ceilings, indoor
and outdoor showers and ceramic-bowl
sinks. It's set on a private beach, where you'll
also find a common pool, dive centre, mas-
sage pagodas and spectacular sunsets over
Phuket.

❶ Information

In **Ta Khai**, the largest settlement on Ko Yao Noi,
there's a 7-Eleven with an attached ATM, one of
five on the island. You won't be cash poor here.

On Ko Yao Yai, there were three ATMs operat-
ing at research time, but it would still be wise
to carry plenty of cash in the low season, when
re-supply can be an issue.

❶ Getting There & Away

TO/FROM PHUKET

To get to Ko Yao Noi from Phuket, take a taxi
(600B to 800B) to Tha Bang Rong. From here,
there are hourly long-tails (120B, 20 minutes)
or three daily speedboats (200B, 20 minutes)
between 7.15am and 5.40pm. They dock at Tha
Klong Hia on Ko Yao Yai upon request before
crossing to Ko Yao Noi. Boats begin returning
to Phuket at 6.30am. Returning to Phuket from
Ko Yao Noi, taxis run from Tha Bang Rong to the
resort areas for 600B to 800B, or there's one
sŏrng·tăa·ou (80B) to Phuket Town at 2.30pm
daily.

The best way to reach Ko Yao Yai from Phuket
is to catch a speedboat or ferry from Tha Rasada
near Phuket Town. Ferries depart at 8.30am,
10.30am and 2pm (one hour, 100B). Speedboats
(30 minutes, 150B) make the run at 4pm and
5pm. On Fridays, the schedule shifts to accom-
modate prayer times.

TO/FROM KRABI

There are four 'express' boats (470B, 1½ hours)
and two speedboats (600B, 45 minutes) per day
from Krabi's Tha Len pier to Ko Yao Noi piers at
Tha Manok and Tha Khao.

TO/FROM PHANG-NGA

From Tha Sapan Yao in Phang-Nga there's a
9am ferry to Ko Yao Noi continuing to Ko Yao Yai
(200B, 1½ hours) that makes an excellent budg-
et cruise of Ao Phang-Nga. It leaves Ko Yao Noi
for the return trip at 7:30am the next morning.

❶ Getting Around

To get from Ko Yao Noi to Ko Yao Yai, catch a
shuttle boat from Tha Manok (100B to 150B, 15
minutes) to Tha Klong Hia. On the islands, you
can travel by túk-túk for about 150B per ride or
rent a motorbike from most guesthouses for
around 200-300B per day. It's 100B for túk-túk
transport to the resorts.

PHUKET ISLAND ภูเก็ต

POP 83,800

The island of Phuket has long been misun-
derstood. Firstly, the 'h' is silent. Ahem. And
secondly, Phuket doesn't feel like an island
at all. It's so huge (the biggest in Thailand)
that you rarely get the sense that you're sur-
rounded by water, which is probably the
reason why the Ko (meaning 'island') was
dropped from its name. Dubbed the 'pearl
of the Andaman' by marketing execs, this
is Thailand's original flavour of tailor-made
fun in the sun.

The island's sin city of Patong is the big-
gest town and busiest beach. It's the ulti-
mate gong show where beachaholics sizzle
off their hangovers and go-go girls play ping-
pong...without paddles. But ultimately the
island's affinity for luxury far outshines its
other stereotypes. Jet-setters come through
in droves, getting pummelled during swanky
spa sessions and swigging sundowners at
one of the many fashion-forward nightspots
or on their rented yacht. But you don't have
to be an heiress to tap into Phuket's trendy
to-do list. With deep-sea diving, high-end
dining and white beaches all within reach,
it really is hard to say farewell.

🏃 Activities

Diving & Snorkelling

Phuket enjoys an enviable central location
relative to the Andaman's top diving desti-
nations. The much-talked-about Similan Is-
lands sit to the north, while dozens of dive
sites orbit Ko Phi-Phi and Ko Lanta to the
south. Of course, this means that trips from
Phuket to these awesome destinations cost
slightly more than from places closer to
the sites, since you'll be forking over extra
dough for your boat's petrol. Most Phuket
operators take divers to the nine decent sites
orbiting the island, like Ko Raya Noi and Ko
Raya Yai (also called Ko Racha Noi and Ko
Racha Yai), but these spots rank lower on
the wow-o-meter. The reef off the southern

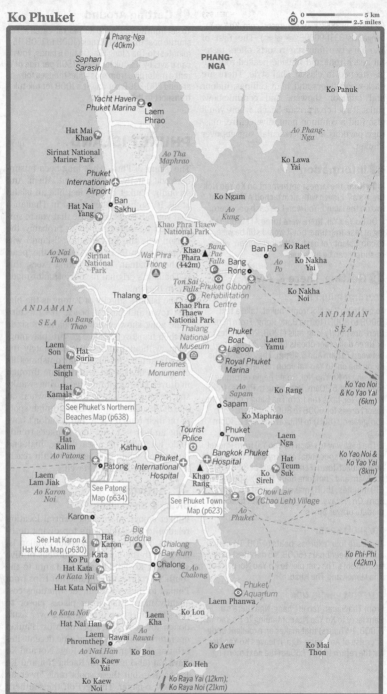

0 ____ 5 km
0 ____ 2.5 miles

Phang-Nga
(40km)

Saphan
Sarasin

**PHANG-
NGA**

Ko Panuk

Yacht Haven
Phuket Marina
Laem
Phrao

Hat Mai
Khao

Sirinat National
Marine Park

Ao Phang-
Nga

Phuket
International
Airport

Ao Tha
Maphrao

Ko Lawa
Yai

Ban
Sakhu

Hat Nai
Yang

Ko Ngam

Ao
Kung

Ao Nai
Thon

Sirinat
National
Park

Khao Phra Thaew
National Park

Wat Phra
Thong

Khao
Phara
(442m)

Bang
Pae
Falls

Ban Po

Ko Raet

Bang
Rong

Ao
Po

Ko Nakha
Yai

**ANDAMAN

SEA**

Thalang

Ton Sai
Falls

Phuket Gibbon
Rehabilitation
Centre

Ko Nakha
Noi

**ANDAMAN

SEA**

Ao Bang
Thao

Khao Phra
Thaew
National Park

Thalang
National
Museum

Phuket
Boat
Lagoon

Laem
Yamu

Laem
Son

Hat
Surin

Heroines
Monument

Royal Phuket
Marina

Ko Yao Noi
& Ko Yao Yai
(6km)

Laem
Singh

Ao
Sapam

Ko Rang

Hat
Kamala

Sapam

Ko Maphrao

See Phuket's Northern
Beaches Map (p638)

Tourist
Police

Phuket
Town

Laem
Nga

Hat
Kalim

Kathu

Phuket
International
Hospital

Bangkok Phuket
Hospital

Hat
Teum
Suk

Ko Yao Noi &
Ko Yao Yai
(8km)

Ao Patong

Patong

Khao
Rang

Ko
Sireh

Laem
Lam Jiak

See Patong
Map (p634)

See Phuket Town
Map (p623)

Chow Lair
(Chao Leh) Village

Ao Karon
Noi

Karon

Big
Buddha

Ao
Phuket

See Hat Karon &
Hat Kata Map (p630)

Hat
Karon

Chalong
Bay Rum

Ko Pu

Kata

Chalong

Ko Phi-Phi
(42km)

Hat Kata
Ao Kata Yai

Ao
Chalong

Hat Kata Noi

Phuket
Aquarium

Ao Kata Noi

Laem Phanwa

Hat Nai Han

Laem
Kha

Ko Lon

Laem
Phromthep

Rawai

Ao
Rawai

Ko Aew

Ko Mai
Thon

Ao Nai Han

Ko Bon

Ko Kaew
Yai

Ko Heh

Ko Kaew
Noi

Ko Raya Yai (12km);
Ko Raya Noi (21km)

tip of Raya Noi is the best spot, particularly good for experienced divers, with soft corals and pelagic fish species aplenty. Manta and marble rays are also frequently glimpsed here and, if you're very lucky, you might even see a whale shark.

Typical one-day dive trips to nearby sites cost about 3500B to 4000B, including two dives and equipment. Nondivers (and snorkellers) are permitted to join these trips for a significant discount. PADI Open Water certification courses cost around 15,000B to 17,000B for three days of instruction and equipment hire.

Snorkelling isn't wonderful off Phuket proper, though mask, snorkel and fins can be rented for around 250B a day in most resort areas. As with scuba diving, you'll find better snorkelling, with greater visibility and variety of marine life, along the shores of small outlying islands such as Ko Raya Yai and Ko Raya Noi.

As is the case elsewhere in the Andaman Sea, the best diving months are December to May when the weather is good and the sea is smooth and clear.

Sea Kayaking

Several companies based on Phuket offer canoe tours of scenic Ao Phang-Nga. Kayaks can enter semisubmerged caves inaccessible to long-tail boats. A day paddle costs from 3950B per person and includes meals, equipment and transfer. Many outfits also run all-inclusive, three-day (from 13,700B) or six-day (from 23,400B) kayak and camping trips.

Surfing

Phuket is an undercover surf destination. Once the monsoons bring their midyear swell, glassy seas fold into barrels. The best waves arrive between June and September, when annual competitions are held in Kata and Kalim. **Phuket Surf** (Map p630; ☑ 08 1611 0791, 08 7889 7308; www.phuketsurf.com; Th Kok-tanod, Kata; lessons 1500B, board rental per hr/day 150/500B; ☺ Apr–late-Oct) is based in Kata, at the south end of the bay near the best break, which typically tops out at 2m. Hat Nai Han can get bigger waves (up to 3m) near the yacht club. Be warned: both Kata and Nai Han have vicious undertows that can claim lives.

Hat Kalim, just north of Patong, is sheltered and has a consistent break that also gets up to 3m. This is a hollow wave and considered the best break on the island.

Kamala's northernmost beach has a nice 3m beach break, and Laem Singh, just up the coast in front of the Amanpuri, gets very big and fast, plus it's sheltered from wind by the massive headland.

Hat Nai Yang has a consistent if soft wave that breaks more than 200m offshore. Hat Nai Thong gets better shape. Swells get up to 3m high a few times per year.

Kiteboarding

One of the world's fastest-growing sports is also one of Phuket's latest fads. The three best spots are Hat Nai Yang, Karon (in the low season) and Rawai (ideal conditions for beginners in the high season). Phuket's three kiteboarding outfitters are all affiliated with the International Kiteboarding Organization (think: PADI for kites).

Yachting

Phuket is one of Southeast Asia's main yachting destinations, and you'll find all manner of craft anchored along its shores – from 80-year-old wooden sloops to the latest in high-tech motor cruisers.

Marina-style facilities with year-round anchorage are presently available at a few locations.

Port clearance is rather complicated; the marinas will take care of the paperwork (for a fee, of course) if notified of your arrival in advance. Expect to pay from 17,000B per day for a high-season, bareboat charter.

Royal Phuket Marina BOATING
(☑ 0 7636 0811; www.royalphuketmarina.com) The US$25 million Royal Phuket Marina is located just south of Phuket Boat Lagoon. It's more luxurious with shiny new townhouses, upscale restaurants and a convention centre overlooking 190 berths.

Yacht Haven Phuket Marina BOATING
(☑ 0 7620 6704; www.yacht-haven-phuket.com) This marina is at Laem Phrao on the northeastern tip of Phuket. The Yacht Haven boasts 130 berths with deep-water access and a scenic restaurant. It also does yacht maintenance.

Asia Marine BOATING
(www.asia-marine.net; Yacht Haven Phuket Marina) One of the first yacht charters in Phuket and with the most diverse fleet cruising the Andaman Sea, Asia Marine has a boat for everyone – from sleek fibreglass catamarans to wooden junks. Reservations and enquiries are available online only.

◈ Courses

Popular Thai cooking classes are held in Kata, Phuket Town, Ko Sireh and Patong.

☞ Tours

It's not hard to find elephant rides and 4WD tours of the island's interior, though none of those will win their way into the hearts of animal rights activists or environmentalists, so why not take a bike ride?

Amazing Bike Tours   CYCLING
(☑ 0 7628 3436; www.amazingbiketoursthailand. asia; 32/4 Moo 9, Th Chaofa, Chalong; day trips adult/child from 1600/1400B) Amazing Bike Tours, Phuket's best new adventure outfitter, leads small groups on half-day bicycle tours through the Khao Phra Thaew Royal Wildlife & Forest Reserve, and it offers terrific day trips around Ko Yao Noi and the gorgeous beaches and waterfalls of Thai Muang in nearby Phang-Nga province.

❶ Information

DANGERS & ANNOYANCES

During the May to October monsoon, large waves and fierce undertows sometimes make it too dangerous to swim. Dozens of drownings occur every year on Phuket's beaches, especially on Laem Singh, Kamala and Karon. Red flags are posted to warn bathers of serious rip tides.

Keep an eye out for jet skis when you are in the water. Although the Phuket governor declared jet skis illegal in 1997, enforcement of the ban is another issue. Long-tails can be hazardous too. Do not expect the boat to see you!

Renting a motorcycle or motorbike can be a high-risk proposition. Thousands of people are injured or killed every year on Phuket's high-

ways. If you must rent one, make sure you at least know the basics and wear a helmet.

There have been late-night motorbike muggings and stabbings on the road leading from Patong to Hat Karon, and on the road between Kata and the Rawai–Hat Nai Han area. Random sexual assaults on women can happen as well. Women should think twice before sunbathing topless (a big no-no in Thailand anyway) or alone, especially on an isolated beach. It can also be dangerous to run alone at night or early in the morning.

MEDICAL SERVICES

Local hospitals are equipped with modern facilities, emergency rooms and outpatient-care clinics. Both of the following, which are near Phuket Town, have hyperbaric chambers:

Bangkok Phuket Hospital (☑ 0 7625 4425; www.phukethospital.com; Th Yongyok Uthit) Reputedly the favourite with locals.

Phuket International Hospital (☑ 0 7624 9400; www.phuketinternationalhospital.com; Th Chalermprakiat) International doctors rate this hospital as the best on the island.

TOURIST INFORMATION

The weekly English-language *Phuket Gazette* (www.phuketgazette.net) publishes information on activities, events, dining and entertainment around the island, as well as the latest scandals. *Phuket Wan* (www.phuketwan.com) is frequently juicier – and more newsworthy.

WEBSITES

Jamie's Phuket (www.jamie-monk.com) A fun insider's blog written by a long-time Phuket expat resident with excellent photos and travel tips.

One Stop Phuket (www.1stopphuket.com) A user-friendly travel guide and internet-booking referral service.

FLIGHTS TO/FROM PHUKET

DESTINATION	AIRLINE	FREQUENCY	PRICE
Bangkok	Air Asia	several daily	around 1480B
	Bangkok Airways	daily	1725B
	Nok Air	3-4 daily	1488B
	THAI	seven daily	3000B
Ko Samui	Bangkok Airways	daily	2380B
Hong Kong	Air Asia	daily	5000-10740B
Chiang Mai	Air Asia	twice daily	1600B
Singapore	Air Asia	daily	1400B
Jakarta	Air Asia	Sun, Wed & Fri	from 2730B
Seoul	Korean Air	daily	roundtrip US$660
Kuala Lumpur	Air Asia	four daily	1712B

Phuket Dot Com (www.phuket.com) Offers a sophisticated compendium of many kinds of information, including accommodation on the island.

ⓘ Getting There & Away

AIR

Phuket International Airport (📞 0 7632 7230; www.phuketairportonline.com) is 30km northwest of Phuket Town and it takes around 45 minutes to an hour to reach the southern beaches from here.

Bangkok Airways (Map p623; 📞 0 7622 5033; www.bangkokair.com; 58/2-3 Th Yaowarat, Phuket Town) and **THAI** (Map p623; 📞 0 7621 1195; www.thaiairways.com; 78/1 Th Ranong, Phuket Town) have offices on Phuket.

BUS

All buses depart from the **bus terminal** (Map p623; 📞 0 7621 1977; Th Thepkrasattri), to the east of Phuket Town's centre.

DESTINATION	BUS TYPE	FARE (B)	DURATION (HR)
Bangkok	2nd class	543	15
	air-con	680	13-14
	VIP	1058	13
Hat Yai	air-con	556	6-7
Ko Samui	air-con	430	8 (bus/boat)
Krabi	air-con	150	3½
Phang-Nga	ordinary	90	2½
Ranong	ordinary	209	6
	air-con	270	5
Surat Thani	ordinary	195	6
	air-con	220	5
Trang	air-con	240	5

FERRY & SPEEDBOAT

Phuket's Tha Rasada, southeast of Phuket Town, is the main pier for boats to Ko Phi-Phi, connecting onward to Krabi, Ko Lanta, the Trang Islands, Ko Lipe and even as far as Langkawi Island in Malaysia (where there are further ferry connections to Penang). For additional services to Krabi and Ao Nang via the Ko Yao Islands, boats leave from Tha Bang Rong north of Tha Rasada.

MINIVAN

Phuket travel agencies all around the island sell tickets (including ferry fare) for air-con minivans down to Ko Samui and Ko Pha-Ngan. Air-con minivan services to Krabi, Ranong, Trang, Surat Thani and several other locations are also available. Prices are slightly more than the buses, which all stop in Phuket Town.

ⓘ METERED TAXIS

To escape Phuket's 'taxi mafia' (an organisation of overpriced chartered cars that are often the only means of transport in the beach areas) get the phone number of a metered taxi and use the same driver throughout your stay in Phuket. The easiest way to do this is to take a metered taxi from the airport (one of the only places where you'll find them) when you arrive, then take down your driver's phone number. Metered taxis are found about 50m to the right as you exit the arrivals hall.

ⓘ Getting Around

Local Phuket transport is terrible. The systems in place make tourists either stay on their chosen beach, rent a car or motorbike (which can be hazardous) or take overpriced private car 'taxis' or túk-túk (pronounced *đúk đúk*). There are *sŏrng·tăa·ou* (passenger pick-up trucks) which run to the beaches from Phuket Town but often you'll have to go via Phuket Town to get from one beach to another (say Hat Surin to Hat Patong), which can take hours.

That said, when it comes to transport to and from the airport, the stranglehold local drivers have enjoyed may be coming to an end. At research time, Phuket authorities had evicted the legions of drivers who used to gather at the doors to baggage claim and haggle and tug for passengers. Now, just seven drivers, of metered taxis only, will be allowed in at any one time, making for a far more soothing first step on the island.

Phuket Town เมืองภูเก็ต

POP 94,325

Long before tourist T-shirts or flip-flops, Phuket was an island of rubber trees, tin mines and cash-hungry merchants. Attracting entrepreneurs from as far away as the Arabian Peninsula, China, India and Portugal, Phuket Town was a colourful blend of cultural influences, cobbled together by tentative compromise and cooperation. Today the city is proof of the island's historical soul. Wander down streets clogged with Sino-Portuguese architecture housing arty coffee shops, galleries, wonderful inexpensive restaurants and hip little guesthouses; peek down alleyways to find Chinese Taoist shrines shrouded in incense smoke.

WORTH A TRIP

BIG BUDDHA

Set on a hilltop just northwest of Chalong circle and visible from almost half of the island, the **Big Buddha** (พระใหญ่; mingmongkolphuket.com; off Hwy 402) **FREE** has the best view on Phuket. Once you're up here, pay your respects at the golden shrine, then step up to Big Buddha's glorious plateau where you can peer into Kata's bay, glimpse the shimmering Karon strand and, on the other side, survey the serene Chalong harbour where the channel islands look like pebbles. Over the last 20 years construction on Phuket hasn't stopped, so it means something when locals refer to the Big Buddha project as Phuket's most important development in the last 100 years.

But it's not just some lost-in-time cultural archive. Bubbling up throughout the emerging Old Town is an infusion of current art, music and food that attracts a very hip crowd, most of it Thai. Investors have finally caught on that culture, not just slinky beaches and girly bars, is a commodity. Old shophouses and homes, once left to rot, are being bought up and restored, resulting in flash-forward gentrification.

Despite inflated real estate prices, if you're on a budget, Phuket Town has the best lodging bargains on the island. From here you can hop on regular *sŏrng·tăa·ou* to any of Phuket's beaches (which will take between 30 minutes and 1½ hours).

◉ Sights

Sino-Portuguese Architecture ARCHITECTURE
Stroll along Ths Thalang, Dibuk, Yaowarat, Ranong, Phang-Nga, Rasada and Krabi for a glimpse of some of the best architecture on offer. Soi Romanee off of Th Thalang is the most ambient area of town. The most magnificent examples of buildings are the **Standard Chartered Bank** (Map p623; Th Phang-Nga), Thailand's oldest foreign bank; the **THAI office**; and the **old post office building**, which now houses the **Phuket Philatelic Museum** (Map p623; Th Montri; ⊙9.30am-5.30pm) **FREE**.

The best-restored residential properties are found along Th Dibuk and Th Thalang. The fabulous **Phra Phitak Chyn Pracha Mansion** (Map p623; www.blueelephant.com; 9 Th Krabi) has been restored and turned into a branch of the upscale Blue Elephant restaurant chain and culinary school.

Khao Rang VIEWPOINT
(เขารัง; Phuket Hill) For a bird's-eye view of the city, climb up pretty Khao Rang, northwest of the town centre. It's at its best during the week, when the summit is relatively peaceful, but keep an eye out for the mobs of snarling dogs.

Phuket Thaihua Museum MUSEUM
(พิพิธภัณฑ์ภูเก็ตไทยหัว; Map p623; 28 Th Krabi; admission 200B; ⊙9am-5pm) This flashy new museum, set in an old Sino-Portuguese home, is filled with photos and exhibits on Phuket's history. The last room is covered in photos of local dishes – and if this makes you hungry, info on where to find the food stalls is listed.

🏃 Activities & Courses

★ John Gray's Seacanoe BOATING
(☑0 7625 4505; www.johngray-seacanoe.com; 124 Soi 1, Th Yaowarat; adult/child from 3950/1975B) The original, still the most reputable and by far the most ecologically sensitive sea-kayaking company on the island. Like any good brand in Thailand, his 'Seacanoe' name and itineraries have been frequently copied. He's north of Phuket Town.

★ Suay Cooking School COOKING
(Map p623; ☑08 1797 4135; www.suayrestaurant. com; 50/2 Th Takuapa; per person 1800B) Learn from one of the best chefs on the island. Noy Tammasak will lead you through the local market, and teach you how to make three dishes before opening a bottle of wine for you to enjoy with your culinary creations. Highly recommended.

🎉 Festivals & Events

The **Vegetarian Festival** is Phuket's most important event and usually takes place during late September or October.

🛏 Sleeping

Phuket Town is the cheapest place on the island to get some zzz's and is a treasure trove of budget lodging. Head out to the beaches for more midrange and top-end options.

Phuket Town

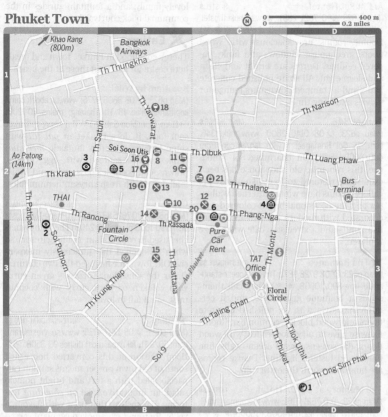

Phuket Town

👁 Sights

1	Bang Niew Shrine	D4
2	Jui Tui Tao Bo Keng Shrine	A3
3	Phra Phitak Chyn Pracha Mansion	A2
4	Phuket Philatelic Museum	C2
5	Phuket Thaihua Museum	B2
6	Standard Chartered Bank	C2

⚙ Activities, Courses & Tours

| | Suay Cooking School | (see 15) |

🛏 Sleeping

7	99 Old Town Boutique Guesthouse	C2
8	Ai Phuket Hostel	B2
9	Phuket 346	B2
10	The Memory at On On Hotel	B2
11	The Romanee	B2

✕ Eating

12	Cook	C2
13	Kopitiam by Wilai	B2
14	Siam Indigo	B2
15	Suay	B3

🍸 Drinking & Nightlife

16	Juice Raw	B2
17	Sanaeha	B2
18	Timber Hut	B1

🛍 Shopping

19	Ban Boran Textiles	B2
20	Drawing Room	C2
21	Ranida	C2

Ai Phuket Hostel
HOSTEL $

(Map p623; ☑ 0 7621 2881; www.aiphukethostel. com; 88 Th Yaowarat; dm 299B, d 699B; ❄️@🛜) Double rooms are spacious with wood floors, greenhouse windows and funky papered ceilings. Dorms are bright and clean and sleep eight. All share polished concrete baths and a cramped downstairs lounge for movies and hang time.

Phuket 346
GUESTHOUSE $

(Map p623; ☑ 08 0146 2800; www.phuket346. com; 15 Soi Romanee; r with fan/air-con from 400/800B; ❄️🛜) On charming Soi Romanee, this romantic old shophouse has been exquisitely restored to look like a cosy art gallery. Rooms have white-patterned wallpaper and the occasional bright-coloured wall decorated with modern art. Downstairs are fish ponds and a streetside cafe where jazz is played.

★ The Romanee
GUESTHOUSE $$

(Map p623; ☑ 08 9728 9871; Th Romanee; r standard/deluxe 890/1090B; ❄️🛜) They call themselves a boutique guesthouse, and it certainly has style with its polished concrete floors and wood block reception bar. Rooms likewise have an airy modern feel with wood floors, flat screens, pastel accent walls, fine linens and tasteful lighting. Deluxe rooms are huge and worth the extra coin.

The Memory at On On Hotel
HOTEL $$

(Map p623; ☑ 0 7621 6161; www.thememoryhotel. com; 19 Th Phang-Nga; dm 400B, r 1600B; 🅿️❄️🛜) This longtime bare-bones classic snapped up a cameo in *The Beach* (2000), playing a shitty backpacker dive. And that's what it was until a recent refurbish put the antiquated shine on Phuket's first hotel. Private rooms have concrete floors, rain showers, flat screens and gorgeous shutters. Though some smell musty.

Dorms are even better, with wood floors, old-school office desks, draped bunks and a fantastic lounge area, kitchen and laundry facilities.

99 Old Town Boutique Guesthouse
GUESTHOUSE $$

(Map p623; ☑ 08 1693 2423, 0 7622 3800; 99old town@hotmail.co.th; 99 Th Thalang; s/d from 650/790B; ❄️@🛜) Another shophouse-turned-B&B that's unpretentious at first glance but has surprisingly sumptuous rooms with four-poster beds and large polished-cement bathrooms. It's run by a lovely family, and a fountain gurgles in the communal back courtyard.

✕ Eating

There's good food in Phuket Town and meals here cost a lot less than those at the beach.

Kopitiam by Wilai
THAI $

(Map p623; ☑ 08 3606 9776; www.facebook.com/ kopitiambywilai; 18 Th Thalang; mains 70-120B; ⏲ 11am-10pm Mon-Sat; 🛜) Wilai serves Phuket soul food. It does Phuketian *pàt tai* with some kick to it, and a fantastic *mèe sua*: think noodles sautéed with egg, greens, prawns, chunks of sea bass and squid. Wash it all down with fresh chrysanthemum juice.

Cook
INTERNATIONAL-THAI $

(Map p623; ☑ 0 7625 8375; 101 Th Phang-Nga; pasta dishes 90-160B, pizzas 160-240B) The Thai owner-chef used to cook Italian at a megaresort, so when he opened this ludicrously inexpensive Old Town cafe he fused the two cultures. Order the sensational pizzas – green curry with chicken or pork curry with coconut milk – and fall in love.

★ Suay
INTERNATIONAL-THAI $$

(Map p623; ☑ 08 1797 4135; www.suayrestaurant. com; 50/2 Th Takuapa; most dishes 90-350B; ⏲ 5-11pm) Fusion at this converted house just south of old town proper means salmon carpaccio piled with a tart and bright pomelo salad, an innovative take on *sôm·dam* featuring mangosteen that pops with flavour, a yellowfin tuna *larb*, smoked eggplant served with roast chilli paste and crab meat, and a massaman curry with lamb chops.

But do not skip on the mango with sticky rice. The rice is wrapped in a spring roll, fried and stuffed with mango. Plated with more mango, it's paired with black sesame ice cream that may have you hugging the chef with gratitude. We sure did. Tables are sprinkled inside the house and on the wrap around porch. The wine list is proper, and the chef/owner also offers cooking classes.

★ Siam Indigo
INTERNATIONAL-THAI $$

(Map p623; ☑ 0 7625 6697; www.siamindigo.com; 8 Th Phang-Nga; dishes 120-280B; ⏲ 2-11pm) One of Phuket's most stylish gems is set in an 80-year-old Sino-Portuguese relic and specialises in Thai cuisine – including classic recipes rarely seen these days, with a French-International twist. Meals are plated on gorgeous china, the room is glorious and the food is exceptional.

🍷 Drinking & Nightlife

This is where you can party like a local. Bars buzz until late, patronised almost exclusively by Thais and local expats.

⭐ **Sanaeha**   BAR
(Map p623; ☑ 08 1519 8937; 83, 85 Th Yaowarat, Phuket Town; ⊙ 6pm-late) Sanaeha is an up-

scale bohemian joint lit by seashell chandeliers, with plenty of dark corners where you can sip, snuggle, snack and dig that soulful crooner on stage.

Timber Hut   CLUB
(Map p623; ☑ 0 7621 1839; 118/1 Th Yaowarat, Phuket Town; ⊙ 6pm-2am) Thai and expat locals have been filling this old clubhouse every

---

VEGETARIAN FESTIVAL

Loud popping sounds similar to machine-gun fire fill the streets, the air is nearly opaque with grey-brown smoke and men and women traipse along blocked-off city roads, their cheeks pierced with skewers and knives or, more surprisingly, lamps and tree branches. Some of the flock have blood streaming down their fronts or open lashes across their backs. No this isn't a war zone, this is the **Vegetarian Festival**, one of Phuket's most important festivals, centred in Phuket Town.

The festival, which takes place during the first nine days of the ninth lunar month of the Chinese calendar – usually late September or October – celebrates the beginning of 'Taoist Lent', when devout Chinese abstain from eating meat. But more obvious to the outsider are the daily processions winding their way through town with floats of ornately dressed children and ladyboys (gà·teu·i, also spelt kàthoey), near armies of flag-bearing colour-coordinated young people and, most noticeably, men and women engaged in outrageous acts of self-mortification. Shopowners along Phuket's central streets set up altars in front of their shopfronts offering nine tiny cups of tea, incense, fruit, firecrackers, candles and flowers to the nine emperor gods invoked by the festival.

Those participating as mediums bring the nine deities to earth by entering into a trance state, piercing their cheeks with an impressive variety of objects, sawing their tongues or flagellating themselves with spiky metal balls. Whatever form the self-flagellation takes, the mediums (primarily men) walk in procession, stopping at shopfront altars, where they pick up the offered fruit. They also drink one of the nine cups of tea, grab some flowers to stick in their waistbands or set strings of firecrackers alight. The shop owners and their families stand by with their palms together in a wâi gesture, out of respect for these mediums who are temporarily possessed by deities. Surreal and overwhelming hardly describes it.

In Phuket Town, the festival activities are centred around five Chinese temples, with the **Jui Tui temple** (Map p623; Soi Puthon; ⊙ 6am-6pm) FREE on Th Ranong the most important, followed by **Bang Niew** (Map p623; Th Ong Sim Phai; ⊙ 6am-6pm) FREE and **Sui Boon Tong** temples. There are also events at temples in the nearby towns of **Kathu** (where the festival originated) and **Ban Tha Reua**. If you stop by the procession's starting point early enough in the morning, you may see a surprisingly professional, latex-glove-clad crew piercing the devotee's cheeks – not for the faint-hearted. Other ceremonies occur throughout the festival at the temples and can include firewalking and knife-ladder climbing. Beyond the headlining gore, fabulous vegetarian food stalls line the side streets offering a perfect opportunity to sample cheap local treats and strike up interesting conversations with the locals.

The TAT office (p626) in Phuket prints a helpful schedule of events for the Vegetarian Festival each year. The festival also takes place in Trang, Krabi and other southern Thai towns.

Oddly enough, there is no record of these sorts of acts of devotion associated with Taoist Lent in China. The local Chinese claim the festival was started by a theatre troupe from China that stopped off in Kathu around 150 years ago. The story goes that the troupe was struck seriously ill because the members had failed to propitiate the nine emperor gods of Taoism. The nine-day penance they performed included self-piercing, meditation and a strict vegetarian diet.

For more info, visit www.phuketvegetarian.com.

night for nearly 20 years. They gather at long wooden tables on two floors, converge around thick timber columns, swill whiskey and sway to live bands that swing from hard rock to funk to hip-hop.

Juice Raw JUICE

(Map p623; 91 Th Yaowarat; ☺ 10am-9pm) A new and ambitious cafe serving fresh pressed hangover tonics, pomelo-, tomato- or cucumber-based detox drinks and some outrageous smoothies. The J Passion is a blend of passionfruit, dates, orange, ginger and banana. Carrot Lava blends carrot, pineapple, ginger and almond milk. You can also customise your juice. As if you could do better.

🔒 Shopping

There are some fabulous bohemian-chic boutiques scattered throughout the Old Town selling jewellery, women's fashions, fabrics and souvenirs. Some whimsical art galleries tucked behind charming Chinese shopfronts are mostly found on Th Yaowarat.

★ Drawing Room GALLERY

(Map p623; ☑ 08 6899 4888; isara380@gmail. com; 56 Th Phang Nga; ☺ 9am-11pm) With a vibe reminiscent of pre-boom Brooklyn or East London, this wide-open, almost reclaimed, co-operative is by far the most interesting gallery in a town full of them. Canvasses can be colourful abstract squiggles or dreamy pen-and-ink meanderings. A street art aesthetic pervades; house music thumps at low levels. Find it.

Ban Boran Textiles TEXTILES

(Map p623; ☑ 0 7621 1563; 51 Th Yaowarat; ☺ 10.30am-6.30pm Mon-Fri) Simply put, this dusty hole-in-the-wall is the best shop on the island for silk, raw silk, cotton textiles and sarongs.

Ranida GALLERY

(Map p623; 119 Th Thalang; ☺ 10am-6pm) An exquisite antique gallery featuring antiquated Buddha statues and sculpture, organic textiles and interesting fashions inspired by vintage Thai garments and fabrics. The clothing is striking and ambitious, but on the right woman it can be a tasteful high fashion statement.

ℹ️ Information

There are numerous internet cafes and ATMs around Th Phuket, Th Ranong, Th Montri and Th Phang-Nga.

Main Post Office (Map p623; Th Montri; ☺ 8.30am-4pm Mon-Fri, 9am-noon Sat)

Police (Map p623; ☑ 0 7622 3555, 191; cnr Th Phang-Nga & Th Phuket)

TAT Office (Map p623; ☑ 0 7621 2213; www. tat.or.th; 73-75 Th Phuket, Phuket Town; ☺ 8.30am-4.30pm) Has maps, information brochures, a list of standard *sŏrng·tăa·ou* fares out to the various beaches and the recommended charter costs for a vehicle.

ℹ️ Getting There & Around

TO/FROM THE AIRPORT

Despite what airport taxi touts would like you to believe, a bright-orange **government airport bus** (☑ 0 7623 2371; www.airportbusphuket. com; tickets 90B) runs between the airport and Phuket Town via the Heroines Monument about every hour between 6am and 7pm. There's also a minibus service at the airport that will take you into Phuket Town for 150B per person. Services to Patong, Kata and Karon beaches cost 180B if there are enough passengers. Chartered cars between the airport and Phuket Town cost 500B; between the airport and beaches is 700B to 1000B. Metered taxis should cost no more than 550B (including airport tax) to anywhere around the island.

BUS

You'll find the bus terminal (p621) just to the east of the town centre, within walking distance of the many hotels. See the Getting There & Away section on p621 for more information on bus services from Phuket.

CAR

There are cheap car-rental agencies on Th Rasada near **Pure Car Rent** (Map p623; ☑ 0 7621 1002; www.purecarrent.com; 75 Th Rasada), which is a good choice. Suzuki jeeps go for about 1200B per day (including insurance), though in the low season the rates can go down to 750B. And if you rent for a week or more, you should get a discount.

The rates are always better at local places than at the better-known international firms, though you may be able to get deals with the familiar companies if you reserve in advance.

MOTORCYCLE

You can rent motorcycles on Th Rasada near Pure Car Rent, or from various places at the beaches. Costs are anywhere from 200B to 300B per day, and can vary depending on the season. Bigger bikes (over 125cc) can be rented at shops in Patong, Kata, Rawai and Karon.

SŎRNG·TĂA·OU & TÚK-TÚK

Large bus-sized *sŏrng·tăa·ou* run regularly from Th Ranong near the market to the various Phuket beaches (25B to 40B per person). These run from around 7am to 5pm; outside these times you have to charter a túk-túk to the beaches, which will set you back 500B to Patong, Kata and Rawai, and 600B to Karon and Kamala. You'll have to bargain. Beware of tales about the tourist office being 5km away, or that the only way to reach the beaches is by taxi, or even that you'll need a taxi to get from the bus terminal to the town centre (it is more or less in the town centre). For a ride around town, túk-túk drivers should charge 100B to 200B.

Motorcycle taxis around town cost 30B.

Ko Sireh   เกาะสิเหร่

This tiny island, 4km east of the district capital and connected to the main island by a bridge, is known for its *chow lair* (also spelt *chao leh*) village and a hilltop reclining Buddha at **Wat Sireh**.

The largest settlement of *chow lair* in Thailand is little more than a poverty-stricken cluster of tin shacks on stilts, plus one seafood restaurant. The Urak Lawoi, the most sedentary of the three *chow lair* groups, are found only between the Mergui Archipelago and the Tarutao-Langkawi Archipelago, and speak a pidgin mix of Malay and Mon-Khmer.

A single road loops the island, passing a few residences, prawn farms, lots of rubber plantations and a bit of untouched forest. On the east coast there's a public beach called **Hat Teum Suk**, as well as a terrific cooking school, the **Phuket Thai Cookery School** (☑ 0 7625 2354; www.phuketthaicookery school.com; Ko Sireh; courses per day from 2900B; ☺ 8.30am-5pm). Here you can get intimate with aromatic Thai spices at this popular cooking school set on a quiet seafront plot on Ko Sireh's east coast. Courses can last up to six hours. The school provides hotel pick-ups, market tours and a cookbook.

Laem Phanwa   แหลมพันวา

Laem Phanwa is a wooded, elongated cape, jutting into the sea south of Phuket. Some say this is the last vestige of Phuket as it once was. It's an all-natural throwback and just 15 minutes from wonderful Phuket Town. The biggest bloom of development can be found near the harbour at the cape's tip. That's where you'll find **Phuket Aquarium**

(☑ 0 7639 1126; www.phuketaquarium.org; adult/child 100/50B; ☺ 8.30am-4.30pm), which displays a varied collection of tropical fish and other marine life. The **seafood restaurants** along the Laem Phanwa waterfront are a great place to hang and watch the pleasure skiffs and painted fishing boats passing by.

On either side of the harbour, the beaches and coves remain rustic and protected by rocky headlands and mangroves. The sinuous coastal road is magic. If you just can't leave, check into the family-friendly **Panwha Beach Hotel** (☑ 0 7639 3300; www. marcopolohotels.com; 5/3 Moo 8, Ao Yon; r from 4000B; 🅿 ❄ 🛜 ☎), on the east cape, for four-star setting and service at a three-star price tag. Or go with the adults only **Cloud 19** (☑ 0 7620 0920; www.cloud19phuket.com; 30/10 Moo 8, Th Bor Rae-Ao Yon; r from 4150B; ❄ 🛜 ☎), a boutique hotel. For a splash of serious luxury above the main strip, find **Sri Panwha** (☑ 0 7637 1000; www.sripanwa.com; 88 Moo 8, Th Sakdidej; d from 14,280B; ❄ 🛜 ☎). This is as decadent as the cape gets.

To get to the cape, take Rte 4021 south and then turn down Rte 4023 just outside Phuket Town.

Rawai   ราไวย์

Now this is a place to live, which is exactly why Phuket's rapidly developing south coast is teeming with retirees, Thai and expat entrepreneurs, and a service sector that, for the most part, moved here from somewhere else.

The region is defined not only by its beaches but also by the lush coastal hills that rise steeply and tumble into the Andaman Sea forming **Laem Promthep**, Phuket's southernmost point. These hills are home to pocket neighbourhoods and cul de sacs that are knitted together by just a few roads. So even with the growth you can feel nature, especially when you hit the beach.

⊙ Sights & Activities

Hat Nai Han, with its crescent of white sand backed by causarinas, bobbing yachts, seafront temple Wat Nai Han and a monsoon-season surf break, is the best beach in the area, but there are smaller, hidden beaches that are just as beautiful. **Hat Rawai** lacks Nai Han's good looks. It's a rocky harbour for long-tails and speedboats, which makes it the perfect place to open up a seafood grill – and,

PHUKET FOR CHILDREN

There's plenty for kids to do on Phuket. And while the seedier face of the sex industry is on full show in Patong (we wouldn't bring our kids there, although many people do), the rest of the island is fairly G-rated.

Elephant treks are always a big hit with kids, with the best options available on the Kata-Hat Nai Han road. Phuket Aquarium (p627) and a visit to the tiny Phuket Gibbon Rehabilitation Centre (p643) are also terrific animal-themed activities that are sure to please.

The main family-flogged feature of Phuket is Phuket Fantasea (p637), which is a pricey extravaganza of animals, costumes, song, special effects, pyrotechnics, and a lousy dinner.

The newest attractions for kids of all ages, but especially for tweeners and above is the **Phuket Wake Park** (☑ 0 7620 2527; www.phuketwakepark.com; 86/3 Moo 6, Th Wichitsongkram, Kathu; two hours 500-650B, day pass 1200B; ☺ 7.30am-11pm), where you can learn to wake board by buzzing a lake nestled in the mountains of Kathu.

indeed, there is a string of them here. All are locally owned and equally delicious.

Long-tail and speedboat charters are available from Hat Rawai. Destinations include the quiet snorkelling islands of Ko Bon (long-tail/speedboat 1000/2000B), Coral Island (1500/4000B) and Ko Kai (4000/9000B). Maximum six passengers.

Rawai is a fine place to learn how to kiteboard and is also abundant with *moo•ay tai* (also spelt *muay Thai*) boxing gyms.

Chalong Bay Rum
DISTILLERY

(☑ 09 3575 1119; www.chalongbayrum.com; 14/2 Moo 2, Soi Palai 2; ☺ tours 4-6pm Mon-Sat) FREE Nearby Chalong is home to Phuket's only working distillery, open for tours six days weekly. You have to reserve ahead, mostly because you'll need directions as it can be hard to find. But upon arrival you'll be awarded a mojito, made with their delicious product, and escorted on a delightful 30-minute tour. Then you'll get a refill.

Sleeping

All the lodging in lovely Hat Nai Han is reached via a skinny, rutted paved road that begins from the Phuket Yacht Club parking lot (yes, you can drive past the guard). Alternatively, charter a long-tail from Rawai for 500B.

Ao Sane Bungalows
HOTEL $

(☑ 0 7628 8306; 11/2 Moo 1, Th Viset, Hat Nai Han; bungalows 600-1200B) The rickety cold-water, fan-cooled wooden bungalows are on a secluded beach, with million-dollar views of Ao Sane and Ao Nai Han. There's a beachside restaurant, dive centre and an old-hippie vibe.

Vijitt
HOTEL $$$

(☑ 0 7636 3600; www.vijittresort.com; 16 Moo 2, Th Viset; villas from 6700B; ❀) Arguably the area's most elegant property, Vijitt is sprinkled with deluxe villas that boast limestone floors, large bathtubs, outdoor showers and gorgeous sea views from private terraces. The stunning black-bottom infinity pool overlooks Friendship Beach.

Eating & Drinking

Besides the restaurants listed here, there are a dozen tasty **seafood grills** roasting fresh catch along the roadside at the northern end of Hat Rawai.

Roti House
SOUTHERN THAI $

(81/6 Soi Sameka; mains 20-40B; ☺ 7-11am) If you like French toast or croissants in the morning, you'll love roti, Thailand's Muslim morning delicacy. You'll receive a plate of savoury crepes and a bowl of sweet breakfast curry. Dunk, munch, repeat. They also do martabak, tea and sugary, milky coffee too.

Som Tum Lanna
THAI $

(☑ 08 6593 2711; 2/16 Th Sai Yuan; mains 50-150B; ☺ 8am-5pm Tue-Sun) When it comes to *sôm·đam*, don't be a hero. Order it mild. It will still bring some serious heat. And while the fish at this Isan soul food shack is very good, its equal exists elsewhere. The chicken on the other hand...well, heed the words of another blissed-out, greasy-mouthed customer: 'This is some fucking killer fucking chicken!'

★ Rum Jungle
INTERNATIONAL $$$

(☑ 0 7638 8153; 69/8 Th Sai Yuan; meals 300-500B; ☺ 11.30am-10.30pm) The best restaurant in the area and one of the best in all of

Phuket is family run and spearheaded by a terrific Aussie chef. The New Zealand lamb shank is divine, as are the steamed clams, and the pasta sauces are all made from scratch. Everything – including the Pampero rocks – is served under a thatched roof to an exceptional world-beat soundtrack.

Orange PUB

(41/7-8 Th Viset; ⊘ 5pm-2am; 🛜) Billed as an Irish pub, though it doesn't look the part, this polished concrete block of a building offers a happening night scene thanks its incredible house band imported from the Philippines. Fronted by a soulful diva as beautiful as she is talented, this is a serious group playing anything and everything from Deep Purple to Beyoncé.

❶ Getting There & Away

Rawai is about 18km from Phuket Town. *Sŏrng·tǎa·ou* (30B) run from Phuket's fountain circle at Th Ranong – some continue to Hat Nai Han, but not all of them, so ask first. The túk-túk trip from Rawai to Nai Han is a hefty 200B.

You can hire taxis (or sometimes actually just chartered cars) from Rawai and Hat Nai Han to the airport (800B), Patong (700B) and Phuket Town (500B).

Hat Kata หาดกะตะ

Travellers of all ages, styles and tastes descend on this tourist enclave with its bustling restaurants, wet season surfing and luscious beach, which is without the seedy hustle endemic to Patong. While you might not find a secluded strip of sand, you will find lots to do and plenty of easy-going folks to clink beers with. There's even a top-notch yoga studio.

The beach is divided in two by a rocky headland, and the road between them is home to Phuket's original millionaire's row. Hat Kata Yai is on the north end, while the more secluded Hat Kata Noi unfurls to the south. Both offer soft golden sand and attract a bohemian crowd.

The main commercial street of Th Thai Na is perpendicular to the shore and has most of its restaurants and shops, along with some cheaper places to stay.

◉ Sights & Activities

The small island of **Ko Pu** is just off shore, but be careful of rip tides, heed the red flags and don't go past the breakers in the wet season unless you are a strong ocean swimmer with experience. Both Hat Kata Yai and Hat Kata Noi offer decent surfing from April to November. Board rental costs 100B to 150B for one hour or 300B to 600B for the whole day. **Surf House** (Map p630; ☑ 08 1979 7737; www.surfhousephuket.com; 4 Moo 2, Th Kata; ⊘ 10am-midnight), a bar across the street from Hat Kata, has a man-made surf park (per hour 800B) that kids love.

If it's heat and sweat you crave, drop into **Kata Hot Yoga** (Map p630; ☑ 0 7660 5950; www.katahotyoga.com; 217 Th Khoktanod; per class 500B; ⊘ classes 9am, 5.15pm & 7.15pm).

🛏 Sleeping

High season is from May to October. Like Patong, it's getting harder and harder to find anything under 1000B during the high season, but prices drop radically when tourism is down.

Just before the turn toward Karon, hang a right into the Beach Center, a complex of new townhouses packed with way too many guesthouses to list. If you're stuck without shelter, you should find a room here.

Rumblefish Adventure HOSTEL $

(Map p630; ☑ 0 7633 0315; http://scubatuna.com; 98/79 Th Kata, Hat Kata; dm 250B, s/d 600/700B; 🄿 ❋ 🛜) A water-sports flophouse offering reasonably clean doubles with private baths, hot water and air con. Dorms sleep six and are airy with turquoise accent walls. There's a mini living area upstairs, too. Why not get certified by day and crash here by night? It's in the Beach Center complex.

Fantasy Hill Bungalow HOTEL $

(Map p630; ☑ 0 7633 0106; fantasyhill@hotmail.com; 8/1 Th Patak West, Hat Kata; r with fan 600B, air-con 1000-1200B; 🄿 ❋ 🛜) Sitting in a lush garden on a hill, the older but well-maintained bungalows here are great value. The place is peaceful but central and the staff super sweet. Angle for a corner room with air-con and a view.

Chanisara Guesthouse GUESTHOUSE $

(Map p630; ☑ 08 5789 5701; 48/5 Soi Casa del Sol, Hat Kata; r from 1000B; ❋ 🛜) One of several townhouse-style guesthouses on the Casa Del Sol cul de sac. Rooms are super bright, tiled affairs with air-con flat screen TVs, recessed lighting and a little balcony. Beds are dressed in Thai linens and bottled water is delivered daily. Low season rates drop to 600B per night.

Hat Karon & Hat Kata

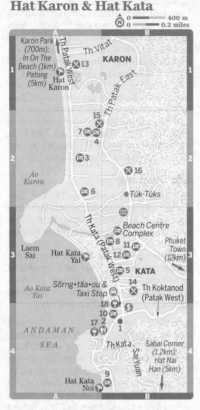

and full of character. Their in-house country restaurant offers a cheap and authentic steam table pick-and-mix option at lunch.

Sawasdee Village
HOTEL $$$

(Map p630; ☑ 0 7633 0979; www.phuketsawasdee.com; 38 Th Ked Kwan; bungalows from 5940B; ✳@ 🛜 ⚊) This lush, opulent boutique resort is built in the classic Thai style but with a compact footprint. Ornate, peaked-roof bungalows have wood floors, beamed ceilings and doors that open onto a thick tropical landscape laced with *koi* (carp) canals and gushing waterfalls. Not to mention those Buddhist art installations. Throw in its quality spa and this place is unique and inviting in every way.

Mom Tri's Boathouse
BOUTIQUE HOTEL $$$

(Map p630; ☑ 0 7633 0015; www.boathousephuket.com; 2/2 Th Kata (Patak West); r from 6000B; ✳🛜⚊) For Thai politicos, pop stars, artists and celebrity authors, the intimate boutique Boathouse is still the only place to stay on Phuket. Rooms are spacious and gorgeous, some sporting large breezy verandahs. Critics complain that the Boathouse is a bit stiff-lipped and old-fashioned for this century, but no-one can deny that the main reason to stay here is for the food.

The on-site restaurant, Boathouse Wine & Grill, is among the best on the island.

Katathani Resort & Spa
HOTEL $$$

(Map p630; ☑ 0 7633 0124; www.katathani.com; 14 Th Kata Noi; r from 7800B; ✳🛜⚊) Taking over a huge portion of lush, relatively quiet Hat Kata Noi, this glitzy spa resort offers all the usual trimmings in stylish surrounds. It features a spa, a handful of pools and heaps of space. Excellent low-season deals are often available here.

✖ Eating

There's some surprisingly classy food in Kata, though you'll be paying for it. For cheaper eats, head to Th Thai Na and the cluster of affordable, casual seafood restaurants on Th Kata (Patak West) near the shore.

★ Sabai Corner
INTERNATIONAL-THAI $$

(☑ 0 9875 5525; www.sabaicorner.com; Th Karon Lookout; mains 200-499B; ☉10am-10pm; 🅿🛜) There is no better view on the island than the one you'll glimpse from the deck at this superlative pub. From here you can see all the way to Patong in one direction, and an endless horizon of wide rippling blue ocean

★ Sabai Corner
BUNGALOWS $$

(☑ 0 9875 5525; www.sabaicorner.com; Th Karon Lookout; r 1950B) No room on this sweet island offers the view available from the two chalets set on the hillside above Sabai Corner. Each is an independent studio with granite tile in the baths, canopied bed, wall-mounted flat screen with satellite TV, sofa, wardrobe and security boxes. They also have wide outdoor patios that function as an outdoor living room.

And about that 270-degree ocean view. Yeah, you may want to look into that. There's a great restaurant on-site, too.

Kata Country House
HOTEL $$

(Map p630; ☑ 0 7633 3210; www.katacountryhouse.com; 82 Th Kata; r 1600-2600B; ✳⚊) Whether or not the retro '60s kitsch is intentional or just a lovely accident, the leafy setting, wagon-wheel railings, water-lily ponds and tiki-style (Polynesian) lounge are inviting

Hat Karon & Hat Kata

as it unfurls west and wraps around Phuket in the other. Sunsets just don't get any better.

Yet it's rare that a location like this gets the restaurant it deserves. That's why this Thai-Swiss-American owned indoor-outdoor patio restaurant is such a stellar find. Here is a soaring thatched roof, an island bar and wide deck to take in the sun and stars. There's also a pool table, a flat screen for ball games and the best service staff in town. The menu isn't innovative – wandering from grilled and fried fish to searing Thai curries to salads, pastas and some damn good pizza – but it satisfies. It's no wonder they lure such a consistent local expat scene. You'll find it downhill and around a bend from the Karon Lookout, a little over halfway between Rawai and Kata.

Capannina　　　　　　　　　ITALIAN **$$**
(Map p630; ☎ 0 7628 4318; www.capannina-phuket.com; 30/9 Moo 2, Th Kata (Patak West); mains 200-700B) Everything here – from the pastas to the sauces – is made fresh and you can taste it. The ravioli and gnocchi are memorable, the risotto comes highly recommended, and it has great pizzas, calzones and veal Milanese, too. It gets crowded during the high season, so you may want to reserve ahead.

★**Boathouse Wine & Grill**　INTERNATIONAL **$$$**
(Map p630; ☎ 0 7633 0015; www.boathousephuket.com; 2/2 Th Kata (Patak West); mains 450-950B; ☉11am-11pm) The perfect place to wow a fussy date, the Boathouse is the pick of the bunch for most local foodies. The atmosphere can be a little stuffy – this is the closest Phuket gets to old-school dining – but the Mediterranean fusion food is fabulous, the wine list expansive and the sea views sublime.

🍷 Drinking & Nightlife

Kata's nightlife tends to be pretty mellow.

★**Ska Bar**　　　　　　　　　　　　　BAR
(Map p630; 186/12 Th Koktanod, Kata; ☉ noon-late) At Kata's southernmost cove, tucked into the rocks and seemingly intertwined with the trunk of a grand old banyan tree, this is our choice for oceanside sundowners. The Thai bartenders add to Ska's funky Rasta vibe, and the canopy dangles with buoys, paper lanterns and the flags of 10 countries.

ℹ Information

There are plenty of ATMs along Kata's main drag.
Post Office (Map p630; ☉ 9am-4.30pm Mon-Fri, to noon Sat) On Rte 4028, at the end of Th Thai Na.

ℹ Getting There & Around

Sŏrng·tăa·ou to both Kata and Karon (per person 25B) leave frequently from the day market on Th Ranong in Phuket from 7am to 5pm. The main *sŏrng·tăa·ou* stop in Kata is in front of Kata Beach Resort.

Taxis from Kata go to Phuket Town (600B), Patong (600B) and Karon (200B).

Motorbike rentals (per day 300B) are widely available.

Hat Karon　　　　　　　　　หาดกะรน

Hat Karon is like Hat Patong and Hat Kata's love child: it's chilled-out, a touch glamorous and a tad sleazy. There are two mega-resorts and package tourists aplenty, but there's still more sand space per capita than at either Patong or Kata. The further north you go the more beautiful the beach gets, culminating at the northernmost edge, accessible from a rutted road that extends past the vendors and food stalls, where the water is like turquoise glass. Within the inland network of streets and plazas you'll find a blend of good local food, more Russian signage than seems reasonable, low-key girly bars, T-shirt vendors and lovely Karon Park, with its artificial lake and mountain backdrop. Fronting the whole mess is a fine stretch of sand.

Sleeping

★ Bazoom Haus   GUESTHOUSE $
(Map p630; ☑ 08 9533 0241; www.bazoomhostel.com; 269/5 Karon Plaza, Hat Karon; dm 300B, r 2700B; ❄@ ⚘) The fabulous private rooms offer wood floors and furnishings, recessed lighting, flat screens and mosaic showers. There's a Jacuzzi and barbecue on the rooftop deck, DJ decks in the in-house Korean restaurant (the owners are from Korea) and a dive shop, too. Dorms have six beds to a room. Discounts of up to 65% off in low season.

Kangaroo Guesthouse   GUESTHOUSE $$
(Map p630; ☑ 0 7639 6517; www.kangarooguesthouse.com; 269/6-9 Karon Plaza, Hat Karon; r 1200B; ❄⚘) Basic, but very clean and sun-filled tiled rooms with hot water, air-con, a cute breakfast nook and balconies overlooking a narrow, slightly seedy soi.

In On The Beach   HOTEL $$$
(☑0 7639 8220; www.karon-inonthebeach.com; 695-697 Moo 1, Th Patak; r from 3500B; ❄@ ⚘ ☒) This is a sweet, tasteful inn on Karon Park. The location is sublime, and the rooms feature marble floors and sea views. Other perks include wi-fi, air-con, ceiling fans and a horseshoe-shaped pool. With substantial low-season discounts, this is the perfect surf lair.

Andaman Seaview Hotel   HOTEL $$$
(Map p630; ☑0 7639 8111; www.andamanphuket.com; 1 Soi Karon, Th Kata (Patak West); r from 4600B; ❄@ ⚘ ☒) The design here is sort of Cape Cod with a sky-blue-and-white exterior and chequerboard marble floors in the lobby. The rooms have a turn-of-the-20th-century Americana theme with marble tables, antiquated ceiling fans, art deco–style bathroom tiles and white-shutter cabinet doors. There's a bubbling kids pool, an adult pool and an overall family vibe.

✖ Eating & Drinking

There are a few cheap Thai and seafood places off the roundabout at the north end of Hat Kata (including a number of beach-side seafood houses under one louvred roof a further 100m north) and a similar group on the main road near the southern end of Hat Karon.

★ Pad Thai Shop   THAI $
(Map p630; Th Patak East; dishes 50-60B; ⊙9am-8pm) On the busy main road behind Karon, just north of the tacky Ping Pong Bar, is this glorified food stand where you can find rich and savoury chicken stew (worthy of rave reviews in its own right) and the best *pàt tai* on planet earth: spicy and sweet, packed with prawns, tofu, egg and peanuts, and wrapped in a fresh banana leaf.

You will be grateful. It closes around 7pm.

Mama Noi's   THAI, ITALIAN $
(Map p630; Karon Plaza; mains 60-185B; ⊙8am-10pm; ⚘) A simple tiled cafe with a handful of plants out front that has been feeding the expat masses for nearly a generation. They do all the Thai dishes and some popular pasta dishes too. It's all cheap and tasty, and arrives in ample portions

Bai Toey   THAI $$
(Map p630; ☑08 1691 6202; www.baitoeyrestaurant.com; 192/36 Th Patak West; meals 200-300B; ⊙11am-10pm; ⚘) This is a charming Thai bistro with shaded outdoor patio and indoor seating. It has the traditional curry, stir-fry and noodle dishes, but you'd do well to sample the Thai-style grilled beef. It's a sliced filet brushed in oyster sauce and served with sticky rice.

Hat Patong   หาดป่าตอง

Sun-seared Russians in bad knock-off T-shirts, beach-buzzing wave runners, a complete disregard for managed development and a knack for turning the midlife crisis into a full-scale industry (sorry, Cialis, Patong was here first) make Patong rampant with unintentional comedy. But for all the concrete, silicon and moral and gender bending, there's something honest about this place.

Patong is a free-for-all. Anything, from a Starbucks venti latte to an, ahem, companion for the evening is available for the right price. And while that's true of dozens of other, phonier destinations, Patong doesn't try to hide it. Patong is what it is. And that's refreshing.

Of course, that doesn't mean you're going to like it. But when you arrive you'll take one look at the wide, white-sand beach and its magnificent crescent bay, and you'll understand how the whole thing started.

Diving and spa options abound, as well as upscale dining, street-side fish grills, campy cabaret, Thai boxing, dusty antique shops and one of Thailand's coolest shopping malls.

🏃 Activities & Courses

Sea Fun Divers   DIVING
(Map p630; ☑ 0 7634 0480; www.seafundivers.com; 29 Soi Karon Nui, Patong; 2/3 dives per day 4100/4500B, open-water course 18,400B) This is an outstanding and very professional diving operation. Its standards are extremely high and the service is impeccable. There's an office at Le Meridien resort in Patong and a second location at the Katathani Resort (p630).

Pum Thai Cooking School   COOKING
(Map p634; ☑ 0 7634 6269; www.pumthaifoodchain.com; 204/32 Th Rat Uthit, Patong; classes from 500-7500B) This restaurant chain (three locations in Thailand and two in France) holds several daily one- to six-hour classes. Longer classes begin with a market tour and end with a meal.

Swasana Spa   SPA
(Map p634; ☑ 0 7634 0138; www.impiana.com; 41 Th Thawiwong) treatments from 850B; ⊙10am-9pm) This four-star spa at Impiana Phuket Cabana (p633) is right on the beach at the quiet north end of Patong. The best deal is the traditional Thai massage (850B). You'll be nestled in a cool glass cube on a cushy floor mat with ocean views.

🛏 Sleeping

It's getting pretty difficult to find anything in Patong costing less than 1000B from about November to April, but outside this time period rates drop by 40% to 60%.

Patong Backpacker Hostel   HOSTEL $
(Map p634; ☑ 0 7625 6680; www.phuketbackpacker.com; 140 Th Thawiwong; dm 250-450B; ❀🛜) This is a great location near the beach and the owner offers info on all the best and cheapest places to eat in town. Dorm prices vary depending on the number of beds in the room (three to 10). The top floor is

the brightest but dorm rooms on the lower floors each have their own attached bathroom. Skip the overpriced room.

Merrison Inn   HOTEL $$
(Map p634; ☑ 0 7634 0383; www.merrisoninn.com; 5/35 Th Hat Patong; r 1300B; ❀🛜) Polished concrete floors, terrazzo bathrooms, wall-mounted flat-screen TVs, queen-sized beds and more than a little Asian kitsch make this place a real bargain.

Tune Hotel   HOTEL $$
(Map p634; ☑ 0 7634 1936; www.tunehotels.com; 56 Th Rat Uthit; 1500B; 🅿❀) Brand-new at research time, the Tune is a budding Southeast Asian brand. They offer small but comfy rooms with wood floors, satellite TV and plush linens. It's no-frills, tidy three-star living. And it works.

Baipho, Baithong & Sala Dee   GUESTHOUSE $$
(Map p634; ☑ 0 7629 2738, 0 7629 2074; www.baipho.com; 205/12-13 & 205/14-15 Th Rat Uthit 200 Pee; r 1800-3300B; ❀🛜) These three arty guesthouses are all on the same little soi under the same friendly, organised management. Rooms and common areas are filled with Buddha imagery and Zen-like trimmings mingling with modern art and urban touches. The dimly lit, nestlike rooms are all unique so ask to see a few if possible.

The Lounge, downstairs at Baithong, serves cocktails and very good Italian and Thai food as well as gourmet snacks. Guests can use the pool at the unsightly Montana Grand Phuket next door.

The Kee   RESORT $$$
(Map p634; ☑ 0 7633 5888; www.thekeeresort.com; 152/1 Th Thawiwong; d from 3600B; 🅿❀🛜🏊) A splashy, sprawling chic spread for the masses. It's not uber exclusive or swanky, though it does feel that way compared to most Patong nests. There's a rooftop lounge and restaurant, and four-star rooms horseshoe a shallow blue pool. Promotional rates are terrific, but they'll probably climb soon.

Impiana Phuket Cabana   HOTEL $$$
(Map p634; ☑ 0 7634 0138; www.impiana.com; 41 Th Thawiwong; r from 4500-7000B; ❀🛜🏊) Cabana-style and plumb on the best part of the beach, the rooms here are laden with chic comforts and close to all the action.

BYD Lofts   HOTEL $$$
(Map p634; ☑ 0 7634 3024; www.bydlofts.com; 5/28 Th Rat Uthit; apt 4900-19,500B; ❀@🛜🏊) If style and comfort are more important to

Patong

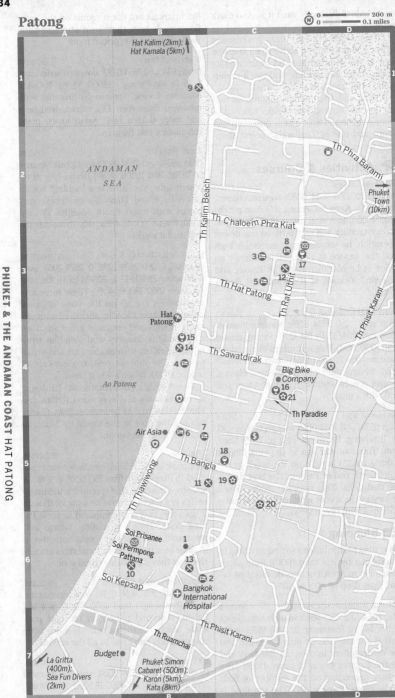

Hat Kalim (2km);
Hat Kamala (5km)

ANDAMAN
SEA

Th Phra Barami

Phuket
Town
(10km)

Th Kalim Beach

Th Chaloem Phra Kiat

8

3

17

5   12

Th Hat Patong

Th Rat Uthit

Th Phisit Karani

Hat
Patong

15

14

4

Th Sawatdirak

Ao Patong

Big Bike
Company

16

21

Th Paradise

Air Asia   6   7

Th Bangla

18

Th Thawiwong

11   19

20

Soi Prisanee

1

Soi Permpong
Pattana

13

10

2

Soi Kepsap

Bangkok
International
Hospital

Th Phisit Karani

Th Ruamchai

La Gritta
(400m);
Sea Fun Divers
(2km)

Budget

Phuket Simon
Cabaret (500m);
Karon (5km);
Kata (8km)

0   200 m
0   0.1 miles

Patong

you than the beachfront (although it's only a minute's walk to the beach), look no further. Urban-style apartments with lots of white (floors, walls, blinds) and sharp lines feel angelic compared with the seedy world of Patong on the streets below. There's a day spa, a rooftop pool and an excellent restaurant on the premises.

 Eating

Patong has stacks of restaurants: the trick is to steer around the abundant watered-down Thai and poorly executed Western kitchens. The most glamorous restaurants are in a little huddle above the cliffs on the northern edge of town.

Bargain seafood and noodle stalls pop up across town at night – try the lanes on and around Th Bangla, or venture over to the **Patong Food Park** (Map p634; Th Rat Uthit; meals 100-200B; ⊘4pm-midnight) once the sun drops.

Chicken Rice Briley　　　　　THAI $
(Map p634; ☎0 7634 4079; Patong Food Park, Th Rat Uthit; meals 35-45B; ⊘9am-3pm) The only diner in the Patong Food Park to offer sustenance when the sun shines. Steamed chicken breast is served on a bed of rice with a bowl of chicken broth and crumbled bits of meat, bone and roast pork. Dip in the fantastic chilli sauce. There's a reason it's forever packed with locals.

Mengrai Seafood　　　　　SEAFOOD $$
(Map p634; ☎08 7263 7070; Soi Tun; meals 120-300B) Located down a sweaty, dark soi off Th Bangla is a wonderful food court serving fresh, local food. The stalls towards the end of the soi serve daily curries that local ex-

pats swear by. This restaurant specialises in (very) fresh fish, prawns and mussels.

Ella　　　　　INTERNATIONAL $$
(Map p634; ☎08 1540 1267; www.theellagroup. org; 100/19-20 Th Permpong Pattana, (Soi Post Office); mains 150-250B; ⊛) A funky moulded concrete bar and bistro with creative all-day breakfasts featuring Rajisthani scrambled eggs, omelettes stuffed with chicken and peas, and baguette french toast. At lunch and dinner they fire up the grill to barbecue everything from pork ribs to blackened slabs of tuna. They have guest rooms of a similar style and decor upstairs.

Shalimar　　　　　INDIAN $$
(Map p634; 207/7, 8 Soi Patong Lodge, 200 Pee; dishes 120-600B; buffet 300B; ⊘11am-11:30pm) This Indian kitchen offers a daily veggie lunch buffet and a half-dozen dishes off the menu, ranging from samosas and butter chicken to tandoori mixed grill and biryani. In a town with a hefty share of Indian joints, these wood tables and leather seats are consistently packed with Indians.

The Beach　　　　　THAI $$
(Map p634; ☎0 7634 5944; 49 Th Thawiwong; mains 180-350B; ⊘8am-midnight) If you want decent Thai food and an array of seafood choices on the beach, come to this long-running shack. There are a string of choices here that are all slightly overpriced, but the setting is terrific.

Baan Rim Pa　　　　　THAI $$$
(Map p634; ☎0 7634 4079; Th Kalim Beach; dishes 215-475B) Stunning Thai food is served with a side order of spectacular views at this institution. Standards are high, with prices

GAY PRIDE IN PHUKET

Although there are big gay pride celebrations in Bangkok and Pattaya, the **Phuket Gay Pride Festival** is considered by many to be the best in Thailand, maybe even Southeast Asia. The date has changed several times, but it usually lands between February and April. Whenever it blooms, the whole island – but the town of Patong specifically – is packed with (mostly male) revellers from all over the world.

The main events of the four-day weekend party are a huge beach volleyball tournament and, of course, the Grand Parade, featuring floats, cheering crowds and beautiful costumes in the streets of Patong. In recent years, the festival has also included social-responsibility campaigns to increase awareness of child prostitution, substance abuse and HIV.

Any other time of year, the network of streets that link the Royal Paradise Hotel with Th Rat Uthit in Patong is where you'll find Phuket's gay pulse. The **Boat Bar** (Map p634; ☑ 0 7634 2206; www.boatbar.com; 125/20 Th Rat Uthit; ⊙ 9pm-late), Phuket's original gay nightspot and still its only disco, is usually jumping with a lively, mostly gay crowd. Make sure to arrive before the midnight cabaret! There's another good cabaret, some might say the original, at nearby **My Way** (Map p634; 125/15-17 Th Rat Uthit; ⊙ 9pm-late). For updates on future festivals or for more information about the scene in general, go to **Gay Patong** (www.gaypatong.comn).

to match, but romance is in the air, with candlelight and piano music aplenty. Book ahead and tuck in your shirt.

🍷 Drinking & Nightlife

Some visitors may find that Patong's bar scene is enough to put them off their *pàt tai*, but if you're in the mood for plenty of beer, winking neon and short skirts, it is certainly worth sampling.

Th Bangla is Patong's beer and bar-girl mecca and features a number of spectacular go-go extravaganzas, where you can expect the usual mix of gyrating Thai girls and often red-faced Western men. The music is loud (expect techno), the clothes are all but nonexistent and the decor is typically slapstick with plenty of phallic imagery. That said, the atmosphere is more carnival than carnage and you'll find plenty of peers pushing their way through the throng to the bar.

★ Seduction   NIGHTCLUB
(Map p634; www.facebook.com/seductiondisco; 39/1 Th Bangla; ⊙ 10pm-4am) International DJs, professional grade sound system and the best dance party on Phuket, without question. Winner and still champion.

La Gritta   BAR
(☑ 0 7634 0106; www.amari.com; 2 Th Meun-ngern; ⊙ 10.30am-11.30pm) A spectacular modern restaurant in the town's southwest that doesn't fit in with the ageing bones of this once-great property, but who cares? With

tiered booths, massive yet muted light boxes and a deck that is just centimetres above the boulder-strewn shore, there is no better place for a sunset cocktail.

Barefoot Beach Shack   BAR
(Map p634; ☑ 08 9697 2337; www.facebook.com/BarefootBeachShack; Th Thawiwong; ⊙ 10am-10pm; ☎) A whimsically decorated retro bar with a Caribbean feel, crafted from reused corrugated tin and reclaimed wood. It's right on the beach, pulses with palatable pop tunes and is irrigated with middling cocktails and Chang draught. There are worse ways to spend an afternoon.

Nicky's Handlebar   BAR
(Map p634; ☑ 08 9866 9302, 0 7634 3211-3; www.nickyhandlebars.com; 41 Th Rat Uthit) Catch a blast of *Easy Rider* nostalgia at this biker bar. Ashtrays made from bike parts rest on the pressed metal bar and careful lifting those menus, they weigh a ton (they're made from hubcaps and heavy disc brakes). You can get your own wheels by asking about the Harleys for hire.

☆ Entertainment

Cabaret and Thai boxing are something of a speciality here.

Phuket Simon Cabaret   CABARET
(☑ 0 7634 2011; www.phuket-simoncabaret.com; Th Sirirach; admission 700-800B; ⊙ performances 6pm, 7.45pm & 9.30pm nightly) About 300m south of town, this cabaret offers entertain-

ing transvestite shows. The 600-seat theatre is grand, the costumes are gorgeous and the ladyboys (gà·teu·i) are convincing. The house is often full – book ahead.

Bangla Boxing Stadium THAI BOXING
(Map p634; ☑ 0 7282 2348; 198/4 Th Rat Uthit; admission 1000-1500B; ◷ 9-11.30pm Tue, Wed, Fri & Sun) Old name, new stadium, same game: a packed line-up of competitive moo·ay tai (Thai boxing) bouts.

Jung Ceylon CINEMA
(Map p634; Th Rat Uthit) You can catch new Hollywood releases in pristine, amphitheatre-style cinemas at the shopping mall.

❶ Information

There are internet cafes and banks with ATM and currency-exchange facilities across town.

Post Office (Map p634; Th Thawiwong; ◷ 9am-4.30pm Mon-Fri, to noon Sat)

Tourist Police (Map p634; ☑ 1699; cnr Th Thawiwong & Th Bangla, Patong)

❶ Getting There & Around

Air Asia (Map p634; ☑ 0 7634 1792; www.air asia.com; 39 Th Thawiwong; ◷ 9am-9pm) has an office in town.

Túk-túks circulate around Patong for 50B to 100B per ride. There are numerous places to rent 125cc motorbikes and jeeps. **Big Bike Company** (Map p634; ☑ 0 7634 5100; 106 Th Rat Uthit) rents proper motorcycles (500B to 1000B per day) and Nicky's Handlebar rents Harleys. Keep in mind that the mandatory helmet law is strictly enforced in Patong, where roadblocks and checkpoints can spring up at a moment's notice. **Budget** (Map p634; ☑ 0 7629 2389; 44 Th Thawiwong; ◷ 9am-4pm) has an office in the Patong Merlin Hotel.

Sŏrng·tăa·ou from Phuket Town to Patong leave from Th Ranong, near the day market and fountain circle; the fare is 25B. The after-hours charter fare is 500B. Sŏrng·tăa·ou then drop off and pick up passengers at the southern end of Patong beach. From here you can hop on a motorbike taxi (20B to 40B per ride), flag down a túk-túk (prices vary widely) or walk till your feet hurt.

Hat Kamala หาดกมลา

A chilled-out hybrid of Hat Karon and Hat Surin, calm but fun Kamala tends to lure a mixture of longer-term, lower-key partying guests, families and young couples. The bay is magnificent, turquoise and serene with shore breakers that lull you to sleep. Palms and pines mingle on the leafy and rocky northern end where the water is a rich emerald green and the snorkelling around the rock reef is halfway decent, while new resorts are ploughed into the southern bluffs above the gathering long-tails. The entire beach is backed with lush rolling hills, which one can only hope are left alone... forever. And it's the only beach with a walking path lined with this many restaurants, resorts and shops. Ditch the motorbike and step into Kamala bliss.

◉ Sights & Activities

Local beach boffins will tell you that **Laem Singh**, just north of Kamala, is one of the best capes on the island. Walled in by cliffs, there is no road access so you have to park your car (40B) or motorbike (20B) on the headland and clamber down a narrow path, or you could charter a long-tail (1000B) from Hat Kamala. It gets crowded.

Phuket Fantasea THEATRE
(Map p638; ☑ 0 7638 5000; www.phuket-fantasea. com; admission with/without dinner 1900/1500B; ◷ shows 7pm & 9pm Wed & Fri, 9pm only Sat-Tue) This is a US$60 million 'cultural theme park' located just east of Hat Kamala. Despite the billing, there aren't any rides, but there is a show that takes the colour and pageantry of Thai dance and combines this with state-of-the-art light-and-sound techniques that rival anything found in Las Vegas (think 30 elephants). All of this takes place on a stage dominated by a full-scale replica of a Khmer temple.

Kids especially will be captivated by the spectacle, but it is over-the-top cheesy. Cameras are forbidden.

🛏 Sleeping & Eating

Clear House HOTEL $$
(Map p638; ☑ 0 7638 5401; www.clearhousephuket. com; 121/2, 121/10 Th Rimhaad, Hat Kamala; r 1300B; ❋ ☯ ⊕) Shabby chic with a mod twist, the whitewashed rooms have pink feature walls, plush duvets, flat-screen TVs, wi-fi and huge pebbled baths. This place just feels good.

Layalina Hotel HOTEL $$$
(Map p638; ☑ 0 7638 5942; www.layalinahotel.com; r incl breakfast 5500-7700B; ❋ @ ⊕ ☷) Nab one of the split-level suites with private rooftop terraces at this small boutique hotel for romantic sunset views over white sand and blue sea. The decor is simple, Thai and chic,

Phuket's Northern Beaches

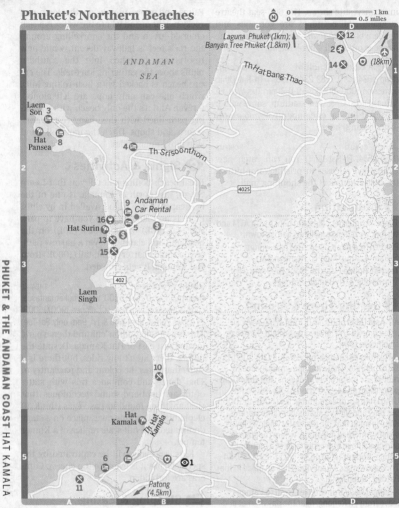

Phuket's Northern Beaches

with fluffy white duvets and honey-toned wood furniture. Room rates include a one-hour couple's massage at the on-site spa. The pool is ridiculously small, but that turquoise ocean *is* only steps away.

Beach Restaurants THAI, INTERNATIONAL **$**
(Map p638; Hat Kamala; dishes 50-250B; ⊙11am-9pm) One of Kamala's highlights is its long stretch of eateries where you can dine in a swimsuit with your feet in the sand. There's everything from Thai to pizza, and plenty of cold beer. **Ma Ma Fati Ma**, at the far northern part of the beach, is our favourite.

Rockfish FUSION **$$**
(Map p638; ☑0 7627 9732; www.rockfishrestaurant.com; 33/6 Th Kamala Beach; dishes 170-1000B; ⊙noon-late; 🛜🍴) Perched above the river mouth and the bobbing long-tails is Kamala's best dining room, with beach, bay and mountain views. It rolls out gems such as braised duck breast with kale and prosciutto-wrapped scallops.

ⓘ Getting There & Away

To catch a regular *sŏrng·tăa·ou* from Kamala to Patong costs 50B per person, while a *sŏrng·tăa·ou* charter (starting in the evenings) costs 250B.

Hat Surin หาดสุรินทร์

Like that hot boy or girl in school who also happens to have style, soul, a fun personality and wealthy parents, Surin beach is the kind of place that can inspire (travel) lust in anyone who meets him or her. With a wide, blonde beach, water that blends from pale turquoise in the shallows to a deep blue on the horizon, and two lush, boulder-strewn headlands, Surin could easily attract tourists on looks alone. Ah, but there are stunning galleries, five-star spa resorts and wonderful beachfront dining options, too. So by the time you're done swimming, sunbathing, snacking at local fish grills and sipping cocktails at barefoot-chic beach clubs, don't be surprised if you've fallen in love.

🛏 Sleeping

Hat Surin is home to some of Phuket's classiest resorts, but there's little available for those on a budget.

Benyada Lodge HOTEL **$$**
(Map p638; ☑0 7627 1261; www.benyadalodgephuket.com; 106/52 Moo 3, Th Chengtalay; r from

2800B; 🌑🛜❄) Chic, modern rooms – with black louvred closets, terracotta-tiled bathrooms and silk, pastel-coloured throw pillows scattered in the lounging corner – are a great bargain for this area. The service is stellar. Take in the sunset and have a dip in the pool at the rooftop bar. It's only a few minutes' walk to the beach.

★Surin Phuket HOTEL **$$$**
(Map p638; ☑0 7662 1579; www.thesurinphuket. com; 118 Moo 3, Hat Pansea; r 17,000-58,000B; 🌑🛜❄) Almost any place located on a private beach this quiet and stunning would have be a top pick. But the bungalows at the Surin (previously known as the Chedi), with naturalistic wooden exteriors that hide beneath hillside foliage, and earthy, luxurious interiors, make the site that much better.

You'll have to be in decent shape for walking around the resort, since it can be quite a hoof up hills and over wooden walkways to get to many of the bungalows.

★Twin Palms RESORT **$$$**
(Map p638; ☑0 7631 6500; www.twinpalmsphuket.com; 106/46 Moo 3, Th Surin Beach; r 8100-25,850B; 🌑@🛜❄) This is the Audrey Hepburn of Phuket's hotels: it's classic yet completely contemporary. There's a pervasive feeling of space with minimalist, artsy swimming pools everywhere that are fringed by delicate white frangipani. Even the simplest rooms are extra spacious and have oversized bathrooms, sublimely comfortable beds and a supreme sense of calm.

It's a few minutes' walk to the beach. Expats from all over Phuket can be found here on Sunday at the island's most popular brunch (open noon to 2pm; buffet 1300B).

Amanpuri Resort RESORT **$$$**
(Map p638; ☑0 7632 4333; www.amanresorts.com; Hat Pansea; villas from US$1050; 🌑@🛜❄) To experience one of Phuket's most exclusive hotels (and celebrity magnets) stay at the over-the-top luxurious Amanpuri Resort.

🍴 Eating & Drinking

There are plenty of excellent restaurants in and around Surin. For cheap seafood, your first stop should be the numerous, fun and delicious seafront dining rooms.

Twin Brothers THAI **$$**
(Map p638; Hat Surin; mains 150-350B; ⊙10.30am-10.30pm) By day, one brother mans the wok, cooking up decent Thai food at local prices. At night, the other fires up a fresh seafood

grill for beachside diners. It's a bit more down to earth than other Surin choices.

★ Taste
INTERNATIONAL-THAI $$

(Map p638; ☑08 7886 6401; tapas 160-225B) The best of a new breed of urban-meets-surf eateries along the beach. Dine indoors or alfresco on meal-sized salads, perfectly cooked filet mignon or a variety of Thai-Mediterranean starters and mains. Service is outstanding and there's an enticing attached gallery selling Tibetan, Nepali and local jewellery and art.

The Catch
BEACH CLUB

(Map p638; ☑0 7631 6567; www.catchbeachclub. com; Hat Surin; beach club access per day 1500B; ◷10.30am-10.30pm; ☏⚗) Slip on your breeziest linen to dine at this draped, cabana-style eatery right on the beach. It's part of Twin Palms, even though it's not attached, and has all the same classy attributes as the hotel in both ambience and cuisine.

ⓘ Information

There is an ATM at Surin Plaza, just east of the beach on Rte 4025. Internet access is available at most hotels for 1B per minute.

ⓘ Getting There & Away

A regular *sǒrng·tǎa·ou* from Phuket Town's Th Ranong to Hat Surin costs 40B per person, and túk-túk or *sǒrng·tǎa·ou* charters cost 600B.

Rent cars from **Andaman Car Rental** (Map p638; ☑0 7662 1600; www.andamancarrent. com; ◷9am-9pm), opposite the entrance to Twin Palms. Vehicles can be rented from 1400B per day.

Ao Bang Thao
อ่าวบางเทา

Almost as large and even more beautiful than Ao Patong, the stunning, 8km-long white-sand sweep of Ao Bang Thao is the glue that binds the region's disparate elements. The southern half is home to a sprinkling of three-star bungalow resorts. Further inland you'll find an old fishing village laced with canals along with a number of upstart villa subdivisions. Don't be alarmed if you see a herd of water buffalo grazing just 100m from a gigantic construction site. That's how fast Bang Thao has changed.

Smack in the centre of it all is the somewhat absurd Laguna Phuket complex – a network of five four- and five-star resort properties and an ageing shopping mall knitted together by an artificial lake (patrolled by tourist shuttle boats) and a paved nature trail. But in the north, Mother Nature asserts herself once more, and a lonely stretch of powder-white sand and tropical blue sea extends past all the bustle and change, delivering the kind of peace you imagined when you booked your trip.

The **Hideaway Day Spa** (Map p638; ☑08 1750 0026; www.phuket-hideaway.com; 382/33 Th Srisoontorn, Chergtalay; treatments from 1500B) has an excellent reputation. It offers traditional Thai massage, sauna and mud body wraps in a tranquil wooded setting at the edge of a lagoon. The Hideaway also has its own line of spa products.

🛌 Sleeping

Laguna Phuket is home to five luxury resorts, an 18-hole golf course and 30 restaurants. Guests at any one of the resorts can use the dining and recreation facilities at all of them. Frequent shuttle buses make the rounds of all the hotels, as do pontoon boats (via the linked lagoons).

Andaman Bangtao Bay Resort
HOTEL $$$

(Map p638; ☑0 7627 0246; www.andamanbang taobayresort.com; bungalows 2900-5900B; ⚗⚗) Every bungalow has a sea view and there's a summer-camp vibe at this pleasant little resort. The design is very Thai, with wood-carvings on the walls and coconuts hanging from the eaves of the roofs, but for this price we expect a little more luxury.

Banyan Tree Phuket
RESORT $$$

(☑0 7632 4374; www.banyantree.com; villas from 16,200B; ⚗@☏⚗) One of Phuket's finest hotels, and the first to introduce bungalows with their own private pool, the Banyan Tree Phuket (in Laguna Phuket) is an oasis of sedate, understated luxury. Accommodation is in villas – and, as long as you're here, the on-site spa should not be missed.

🍴 Eating

Many of Phuket's finest eateries are found just outside Laguna's main gate. There are even more at the seafood-oriented beach cafes south of the Banyan Tree.

Cafe de Bangtao
INTERNATIONAL $$

(69/19 Moo 3, Hat Bang Tao; mains 130-450B; ◷8am-1am; ☏) A cute terracotta tiled cafe with wood tables and a tiki bar, this is the most appealing eatery on this end of Bang Tao. Dishes range from Western breakfasts to tasty, reasonably priced Thai dishes and pork tenderloin to tamarind-glazed spare ribs.

Tawai
THAI $$$

(☑ 0 7632 5381; Moo 1, Laguna Resort Entrance; mains 180-300B) Set in a lovely old house decorated with traditional art is this gem of a Thai kitchen, serving classics like roast duck curry and pork *lâhp*. A free shuttle service is available to and from the Laguna hotels.

Tatonka
INTERNATIONAL $$$

(Map p638; ☑ 0 7632 4349; Th Srisoonthorn; dishes 180-790B; ⊙ 6pm-late Thu-Tue) This is the home of 'globetrotter cuisine', which owner-chef Harold Schwarz developed by taking fresh local products and combining them with cooking techniques learned in Europe, Colorado and Hawaii. The eclectic, tapas-style selection includes creative vegetarian and seafood dishes and such delights as Peking duck pizza (220B).

There's also a tasting menu (750B per person, minimum two people), which lets you try a little of everything. Call ahead during the high season.

Siam Supper Club
INTERNATIONAL $$$

(Map p638; ☑ 0 7627 0936; Hat Bang Thao; dishes 290-1290B; ⊙ 6pm-1am) One of the hippest spots on Phuket, this is where the 'infamous' come to sip cocktails, listen to jazz and eat an excellent meal. The menu is predominantly Western with gourmet pizzas, seafood *cioppino* (stew) and hearty mains such as veal tenderloin with wild mushrooms on truffle mash. Don't miss the insane cheesecake.

❶ Getting There & Away

A *sŏrng·tăa·ou* between Ao Bang Thao and Phuket Town's Th Ranong costs 40B per person. Túk-túk charters are 700B.

Sirinat National Park อุทยาน
แห่งชาติสิรินาถ

Comprising the exceptional beaches of Nai Thon, Nai Yang and Mai Khao, as well as the former Nai Yang National Park and Mai Khao wildlife reserve, **Sirinat National Park** (☑ 0 7632 8226; www.dnp.go.th; adult/child 200/100B; ⊙ 8am-5pm) encompasses 22 sq km of coastal land, plus 68 sq km of sea.

The whole area is 15 minutes or less from Phuket International Airport, which makes it particularly convenient for a first stop after a long trip. This is one of the sweetest slices of the island.

◉ Sights & Activities

If you're after a lovely arc of fine golden sand, away from the buzz of Phuket busyness, **Hat Nai Thon** is it. One of the best beaches on the island, swimming is exceptional here except at the height of the monsoon, and there is some coral near the headlands at either end of the bay. The closest ATM is in Nai Yang, so stock up on baht before you come. There are a handful of beach restaurants strung along the sand.

Hat Nai Yang's bay is sheltered by a reef that slopes 20m below the surface – which makes for both good snorkelling in the dry season and fantastic surfing in the monsoon season. Along the dirt road at the very southern end is a seemingly endless strip of seafood restaurants, beach bars and, oddly enough, tailor shops. It's all refreshingly rough around the edges.

Hat Nai Yang is also a great place to go kiteboarding. Three fine operators with offices here are **Bob's Kite School Phuket** (www.kiteschoolphuket.com; Nai Yang; 1hr discovery lesson 1000B, 3hr course 3300B), **Kiteboarding Asia** (☑ 08 1591 4594; www.kiteboardingasia.com; lessons from 4000B) and **Kite Zone** (☑ 08 3395 2005; www.kitesurfingphuket.com; 1hr beginner lessons from 1100B; half-day lesson 4400B; ⊙ May-late-Oct).

About 5km north of Hat Nai Yang is **Hat Mai Khao**, Phuket's longest beach. Sea turtles lay their eggs here between November and February. Take care when swimming, as there's a strong year-round undertow. Except on weekends and holidays, you'll have this place almost to yourself.

⛺ Sleeping & Eating

⛺ Hat Nai Thon หาดในทอน

Phuket Naithon Resort
HOTEL $$

(☑ 0 7620 5233; www.phuketnaithonresort.com; 24 Moo 4; r 2500B; ✳ 🗢) A great midrange choice set across from the beach and smack in the middle of the strip. Rooms are spacious tiled affairs with floating queen beds, built-in day beds, mini fridge, desk, tub and shower. Check-in at the **Wiwan Restaurant**.

★ Pullman
RESORT $$$

(☑ 0 7630 3299; www.pullmanphuketarcadia.com; 22/2 Moo 4, Hat Nai Thon; r from 3100B; 🅿 ✳ @ 🗢 ☄) The area's newest resort is a stunner. Set high on the cliff above Hat Nai Thon, the lobby alone will make you weak in the knees, with its soothing grey and lavender colour scheme, hardwood floors and exposed rough cut limestone walls. A dreamy network of reflection pools extend out above the sea, 180 degrees to the horizon.

Rooms, set in two- and three-storey wood chalets, are spacious with wide terraces that function as outdoor living areas. It's big (277 rooms), but it sure is pretty and service is divine.

🛏 Hat Nai Yang & Hat Mai Khao หาดในยาง/หาดไม้ขาว

Sirinat National Park　　CAMPING, BUNGALOWS $
(📞 0 7632 7152; www.dnp.go.th/parkreserve; campsites 30B, bungalows 700-1000B) There are campsites (bring your own tent) and large concrete bungalows at the park headquarters on a gorgeous and shady white-sand bluff. Check in at the visitors centre or book online.

Discovery Beach Resort　　GUESTHOUSE $
(65/17 Moo 5, Hat Nai Yang; r with fan/air-con 800/1500B; ❄🖵) With wooden Thai accents on the facade and lacquered timber handrails and furnishings, this spotless, budget three-star spot has enough motel kitsch to make it interesting, and its location – right on the beach – makes it a terrific value.

★ Dewa　　RESORT $$$
(📞 0 7637 2300; www.dewaphuketresort.com; 65 Tambon Sakoo; condos & villas from 7000B; 🅿❄🖵🏊) An independently owned boutique resort with one- and two-bedroom condos and luscious pool villas, steps from the virgin national park beach. You'll have more space (and a full kitchen) in the condos, but the villas are secluded pods with reclaimed wood accents, vintage wrought-iron motifs and a wall-mounted flat screen.

Huge outdoor baths with a soaker tub and rain shower spill into a garden with a sizable plunge pool. The restaurant is sensational and borders the sexy common pool area, blessed with magnificent sunset views. Service could not be better.

Indigo Pearl　　HOTEL $$$
(📞 0 7632 7006; www.indigo-pearl.com; r 8250-16,500B; ❄@🖵🏊) One of the most unique of Phuket's high-end resorts takes its design cues from the island's tin-mining history. Although it sounds weird, the industrial theme melded with tropical luxe creates a spectacularly soothing place to stay. Hardware, such as vices, scales and other mining tools, is

used in the decor down to the tiniest detail – even the toilet-paper rolls are big bolts.

The gardens are modern and lush and surround an oasis-like pool with a big waterfall.

★ Ban Ra Tree　　THAI $$
(Hat Nai Yang; mains 90-350B; ⏱11am-10.30pm) The best choice on the Hat Nai Yang strip, the plastic tables are elegantly dressed in turquoise and white linen and sunk in the sand beneath parasols. The seafood is dynamite: think green curry fried rice topped with coconut milk. Ask for yours with crab, and it will be topped with a whole, meaty cracked crab for just 220B!

They also do fresh fish in myriad ways – try it fried in yellow or red curry. They steam and sauce Phuket lobster, slather prawns in tamarind sauce and make wonderful smoothies. Service is superb.

ℹ Getting There & Away

If you're coming from the airport, a taxi costs about 200B. There is no regular sŏrng·tăa·ou, but a túk-túk charter from Phuket Town costs about 800B.

Khao Phra Taew Royal Wildlife & Forest Reserve
อุทยานสัตว์ป่าเขาพระแทว

Phuket's not all sand and sea. In the north of the island, this park protects 23 sq km of virgin island rainforest (evergreen monsoon forest). There are some pleasant hikes over the hills and a couple of photogenic waterfalls, including **Nam Tok Ton Sai** and **Nam Tok Bang Pae**. The falls are at their most impressive during the rainy season between June and November. The highest point in the park is **Khao Phara** (442m). Because of its royal status, the reserve is better protected than the average national park in Thailand.

A German botanist discovered a rare and unique species of palm in Khao Phra Taew in the mid-1900s. Called the white-backed palm or langkow palm, the fan-shaped plant stands 3m to 5m tall and is found only here and in Khao Sok National Park.

Nowadays resident mammals are limited to humans, pigs, monkeys, slow loris, langurs, civets, flying foxes, squirrels, mousedeer and other smaller animals. Watch out for cobras and wild pigs.

Park rangers may act as guides for hikes in the park on request; payment for services is negotiable.

To get to Khao Phra Taew from Phuket Town by vehicle, take Th Thepkasatri north about 20km to Thalang District and turn right at the intersection for Nam Tok Ton Sai, which is 3km down the road. Some travel agencies run day tours to the park.

Phuket Gibbon Rehabilitation Centre
ANIMAL SHELTER

(☑0 7626 0492; www.gibbonproject.org; admission 10B; ☺9am-4pm) This tiny sanctuary in the park, near Nam Tok Bang Pae, is open to the public. Financed by donations (1500B will care for a gibbon for a year), the centre adopts gibbons that have been kept in captivity in the hopes they can be reintroduced to the wild. The centre also has volunteer opportunities that include providing educational information to visitors, cleaning cages and feeding the animals as well as tracking the released animals.

Thalang District
อำเภอถลาง

A few hundred metres northeast of the famous **Heroines Monument** in Thalang District on Rte 4027, and about 11km northwest of Phuket Town, is **Thalang National Museum** (☑0 7631 1426; admission 30B; ☺9am-4pm). The museum contains five exhibition halls chronicling southern themes such as the history of Thalang-Phuket and the colonisation of the Andaman Coast, and describing the various ethnicities found in southern Thailand. The legend of the 'two heroines' (memorialised on the nearby monument), who supposedly drove off an 18th-century Burmese invasion force by convincing the island's women to dress as men, is also recounted in detail. The focal point of one hall is the impressive 2.3m-tall statue of Vishnu, which dates to the 9th century and was found in Takua Pa early in the 20th century.

Also in Thalang District, about 5km north of the crossroads near Thalang town, is **Wat Phra Thong** (admission by donation; ☺dawn-dusk), Phuket's 'Temple of the Gold Buddha'. The image is half buried so that only the head and shoulders are visible. According to local legend, those who have tried to excavate the image have become very ill or encountered serious accidents. The temple is particularly revered by Thai-Chinese, many of whom believe the image hails from China.

During the Chinese New Year pilgrims descend from Phang-Nga, Takua Pa and Krabi.

KRABI PROVINCE

When travellers talk about the amazing Andaman, they are probably talking about Krabi, with its trademark karst formations curving along the coast like a giant limestone fortress. Rock-climbers will find their nirvana in Railay, while castaway wannabes should head to Ko Lanta, Ko Phi-Phi or any of the other 150 islands swimming off the bleach-blonde shores.

Krabi Town
กระบี่

POP 27,500

Krabi Town is majestically situated among impossibly angular limestone karsts jutting from the mangroves, but mid-city you're more likely to be awe struck by the sheer volume of guesthouses and travel agencies packed into this compact, quirky little town. Western restaurants are ubiquitous, as are gift shops that all sell the same old trinkets. Yet if you hang out a while, you'll also see that there's a very real provincial scene going on between the cracks. Lately, it is the increasingly moneyed side of Krabi Town that seems to be blooming and growing.

◉ Sights & Activities

Wat Tham Seua
TEMPLE

(วัดถ้ำเสือ) Wat Tham Seua (Tiger Cave Temple) is a sprawling hill and cave temple complex 8km northwest of Krabi and is an easy day trip from Krabi Town. The best part of the grounds can be found by following a loop trail through a little forest valley behind the ridge where the *bòht* (central sanctuary) is located. You'll find several limestone caves hiding Buddha images, statues and altars, as well as troops of monkeys cackling from the trees.

Back near the park entrance you'll come to a gruellingly steep 1237-stair case leading to a 600m karst peak. The fit and fearless are rewarded with a Buddha statue, a gilded stupa and spectacular views. Motorcycle taxis or túk-túk to the wát from Krabi cost 100B each way; a *sŏrng·tăa·ou* from Th Utarakit is 50B. Please, please dress appropriately when visiting the wát by covering shoulders to knees.

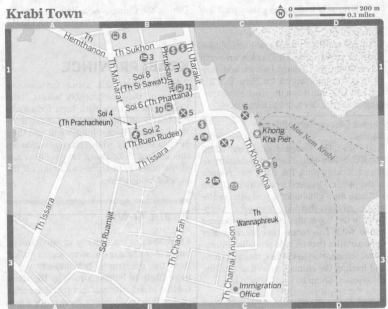

Krabi Town

Krabi Town

Activities, Courses & Tours	
1 Sea Kayak Krabi	B2
Sleeping	
2 Chan Cha Lay	C2
3 Hometel	B1
4 Pak-up Hostel	C2
Eating	
5 Cucina Italiana Viva	B1
6 Night Market	C1
7 Relax Coffee	C2
Drinking & Nightlife	
Playground	(see 4)
Transport	
8 Minivans to Ao Luk	B1
9 PP Family Co	C2
10 Sŏrng·tăa·ou to Ao Nang	B1
11 Sŏrng·tăa·ou to Ao Nang & Hat Nopphrat Thara	B1

Sea Kayak Krabi

BOATING

(☑ 0 7563 0270; www.seakayak-krabi.com; 40 Th Ruen Rudee) They offer a wide variety of sea-kayaking tours, including to Ao Thalane (half/full day 900/1500B), which has looming sea cliffs; Ko Hong (full day 1800B), famed for its emerald lagoon; and Ban Bho Tho (full day 1700B), which has sea caves

with 2000- to 3000-year-old cave paintings. All rates include guides, lunch, fruit and drinking water.

Tours

Various companies offer day trips to Khlong Thom, about 45km southeast of Krabi on Hwy 4, taking in some nearby hot springs and freshwater pools. Expect to pay around 1000B to 1200B, including transport, lunch and beverages; bring a swimsuit and good walking shoes. Various other 'jungle tour' itineraries are available.

Sleeping

Krabi has an exceptional guesthouse scene that continues to improve, but go to nearby Ao Nang if you crave luxury. In the low season, guesthouse room prices can plummet to as low as 150B.

★ Pak-up Hostel

HOSTEL $

(☑ 0 7561 1955; www.pakuphostel.com; 87 Th Utarakit; dm 220-270B; d 500-600B; ❀@☎) This snazzy hostel features several uberhip 10-bed dorms with big wooden bunks built into the wall, each equipped with a personal locker. Massive, modern shared bathrooms have cold-water stalls as well as a few hot-water rain showers. There are two on-site bars (one with nightly live music) and a young, hip, clublike vibe.

Chan Cha Lay
GUESTHOUSE $

(☑ 0 7562 0952; www.chanchalay.com; 55 Th Utarakit; r with shared/private baths 200/400B; ❄ ☎) The rooms here are Krabi's most stylish and comfortable, with gorgeous Mediterranean blues and polished-concrete semi-outdoor bathrooms. The shared-bathroom, fan-only rooms are plain, but spotless with firm beds.

Hometel
HOTEL $

(☑ 0 7562 2301; 7 Soi 2, Th Maharat ; r 750B; ❄ ☎) A modern and funky boutique sleep with 10 rooms on three floors crafted entirely from polished concrete. Abstract art brings colour, there are rain showers, some rooms have two terraces and all have high ceilings. There's a tour desk which can arrange any and all transport wishes as well as a sunny cafe serving Western breakfasts.

✗ Eating & Drinking

★ Night Market
THAI $

(Th Khong Kha; meals 20-50B) The most popular and pleasant place for an evening meal is near the Khong Kha pier. Menus are in English but the food is authentic: try papaya salad, fried noodles, *đôm yam gûng* (prawn and lemongrass soup) and sweet milky Thai desserts.

Relax Coffee
CAFE $

(Th Chao Fah; mains 45-220B; ⊙7:30am-6pm; ☎) Krabi's best coffee shop offers both Thai and Western breakfasts and ample salads, sandwiches and curries at lunch, and they do pizza too. All of it served in a charming, restored wooden storefront near the river.

Cucina Italiana Viva
ITALIAN $$

(☑ 0 7563 0517; 29 Th Phruksauthit; mains 120-560B) This is the place to sample tasty, thin-crust pizza, with a variety of cheeses and toppings to choose from. It has calzones, Italian wine, ice cream and coffee, and it delivers.

Playground
BAR

(87 Th Utarakit; ☎) Pak-up's rollicking downstairs courtyard bar is where the fun and games gather and bloom. From beer pong and open-mic nights to live music and game nights, there is always something on and new friends to enjoy.

ℹ Information

Many of Krabi's guesthouses and restaurants offer free wi-fi. There are numerous banks and ATMs.

Immigration Office (☑ 0 7561 1350; Th Chamai Anuson; ⊙8.30am-4pm Mon-Fri) Handles visa extensions.

Krabi Hospital (☑ 0 7561 1210; Th Utarakit) About 1km north of town.

Post Office (Th Utarakit) Just south of the turn-off to Khong Kha pier.

ℹ Getting There & Away

AIR

Most domestic carriers offer flights between Bangkok and Krabi International Airport (one-way around 4400B, 1¼ hours). **Bangkok Air** (www.bangkokair.com) has a daily service to Ko Samui for around 3800B.

BOAT

Boats to Ko Phi-Phi and Ko Lanta leave from the passenger pier at Khlong Chilat, about 4km southwest of Krabi. Travel agencies will arrange free transfers when you buy a boat ticket with them.

The largest boat operator is **PP Family Co** (☑ 0 7561 2463; www.phiphifamily.com; Th Khong Kha), which has a ticket office right beside the pier in town. In the high season there are boats to Ko Phi-Phi (300B, 1½ hours) at 9am, 10.30am, 1.30pm and 3pm, while in low season the schedule is reduced to two boats per day.

From November to May, there is only one daily boat to Ko Lanta (400-450B, two hours) leaving Krabi at 11.30am. These can also stop at Ko Jum (one hour), where long-tails shuttle you to shore (though you'll pay the full fare). During the wet season, you can only get to Ko Lanta by frequent air-con vans (300B, 2½ hours), which also run throughout the high season.

If you want to get to Railay, long-tail boats leave from Krabi's Khong Kha pier to Hat Railay East (150B, 45 minutes) from 7.45am to 6pm. The boatmen will wait until they can fill a boat with 10 people before they leave; if you're antsy to go before then, you can charter the whole boat for 1500B. Boats to Hat Railay West leave from Ao Nang.

To get to Phuket or the Ko Yao Islands, the quickest route is with direct boats from the pier at Ao Nang. *Sŏrng·tăa·ou* run between the two piers for 50B, or a taxi costs 400B to 500B.

BUS

The **Krabi bus terminal** (☑ 0 7561 1804; cnr Th Utarakit & Hwy 4) is in nearby Talat Kao, about 4km north of Krabi. Air-conditioned government buses leave for Bangkok (720B, 12 hours) at 7am, 4pm and 5.30pm. There's a very plush

24-seat VIP bus to Bangkok (1100B) departing at 5.30pm daily. From Bangkok's southern bus terminal, buses leave at 7.30am and between 7pm and 8pm. Regular air-conditioned government buses from Talat Kao also service Hat Yai (170B, three hours), Phuket (145B, 3½ hours), Surat Thani (140B, 2½ hours) and Trang (90B, two hours).

MINIVAN

Dozens of travel agencies in Krabi run air-con minivans and VIP buses to popular tourist centres throughout southern Thailand, but you may end up crammed cheek to jowl with other backpackers. Most travel agencies also offer combined minivan and boat tickets direct to Ko Samui (550B, 5½ hours) and Ko Pha-Ngan (700B, 7½ hours). Destinations include the following:

DESTINATION	FARE (B)	DURATION (HR)
Ao Luk	80	1
Hat Yai	350	3
Ko Lanta	300	1½
Phuket	300-350	2-3
Satun	600-650	5
Trang	350	2

SŎRNG·TĂA·OU

Sŏrng·tăa·ou run from the bus station to central Krabi and on to Hat Noppharat Thara (50B), Ao Nang (50B) and the Shell Cemetery at Ao Nam Mao (50B). There are services from 6am to 6.30pm. In the high season there are more frequent services until 10pm for a 10B surcharge. For Ao Luk (80B, one hour) there are frequent *sŏrng·tăa·ou* from the corner of Th Phattana and Th Phruksauthit; the last service leaves at around 3pm.

❶ Getting Around

Central Krabi is easy to explore on foot, but the bus terminal and airport are both a long way from the town centre. A taxi from the airport to town will cost 400B. In the reverse direction, taxis cost 350B, while motorcycle taxis cost 300B. Agencies in town can arrange seats on the airport bus for 100B. *Sŏrng·tăa·ou* between the bus terminal and central Krabi cost 50B.

CAR & MOTORCYCLE

Hiring a vehicle is an excellent way to explore the countryside around Krabi. Most of the travel agencies and guesthouses in town can rent you a Yamaha motorbike for 150B to 200B per day. Pak-up Hostel (p644) has a gleaming fleet and provides helmets. They also rent push bikes for 120B per day. A few of the travel agencies along Th Utarakit rent out small 4WDs for 1200B to 1800B per day.

Ao Nang อ่าวนาง

POP 12,400

First, the hard truths. Thanks to its unchecked and rather unsightly development huddled in the shadows of stunning karst scenery, Ao Nang is ugly pretty, and there's a touch of Twilight Zone living in the air here, too, with its countless Indian-owned 'Italian' restaurants and naughty bar-girl sois. So yes, it's a little trashy, but if you forgive all that and focus on the beaches, framed by limestone headlands tied together by narrow strips of golden sand, there's an awful lot to like here. In the dry season the sea glows a turquoise hue; in the wet season, riptides stir up the mocha shallows. If you're hankering for a swim in crystalline climes at any time of year, you can easily book a trip to the local islands that dot the horizon.

Ao Nang is compact and easy to navigate, and with the onrush of attractive midrange development, accommodation standards are high, with substantial discounts possible. It's not nearly as cheap (or authentic) as Krabi town, but it's cleaner and sunnier. There's plenty to do (mangrove tours, snorkelling trips) and it's only 40 minutes away from Krabi airport and a smooth 20-minute longtail boat ride from stunning Railay.

◉ Sights

Shell Cemetery NATURE RESERVE

(สุสานหอย; admission 50B, visitors centre admission 50B; ⏰8.30am-4.30pm, visitors centre 8.30am-4.30pm) About 9km east of Ao Nang at the western end of Ao Nam Mao is the **Shell Cemetery**, also known as Gastropod Fossil or Su-San Hoi. Here you can see giant slabs formed from millions of tiny 75-million-year-old fossil shells. There's a small **visitors centre**, with geological displays and various stalls selling snacks. *Sŏrng·tăa·ou* from Ao Nang cost 30B.

🏃 Activities

Loads of activities are possible at Ao Nang, and children under 12 typically get a 50% discount.

Kayaking

Several companies offer kayaking tours to mangroves and islands around Ao Nang. Popular destinations include the scenic sea lagoon at Ko Hong (1500B to 1800B) to view collection points for sea-swallow nests (spurred by demand for bird's nest soup).

There are also trips to the lofty sea cliffs and wildlife-filled mangroves at Ao Thalane (half/full day 500/800B) and to the sea caves and 2000- to 3000-year-old paintings at Ban Bho Tho (half/full day 700/900B). Rates will vary slightly, but always include lunch, fruit, drinking water, sea kayaks and guides.

Diving & Snorkelling

Ao Nang has numerous dive schools offering trips to 15 local islands, including Ko Si, Ko Ha, Yava Bon and Yava Son. It costs about 2500B to 3300B for two local dives. Ko Mae Urai is one of the more unique local dives, with two submarine tunnels lined with soft and hard corals. Other trips run further afield to King Cruiser (three dives from 4200B) and Ko Phi-Phi (two dives 3400-3900B). A PADI Open Water course will set you back 14,900B to 16,000B. Reliable dive schools include **Kon-Tiki Diving & Snorkelling** (✓0 7563 7826; www.kontiki-thailand. com; 161/1 Moo 2 Tambon Ao Nang; dive trips from 3900B; ◷9am-1pm & 4-9pm), **The Dive** (✓08 2282 2537; www.thediveaonang.com; 249/2 Moo 2; Dive trips 2500-4200B) and **Aqua Vision** (✓0 7563 7415; www.aqua-vision.net; Ao Nang; around 3000B for two dives). Most dive companies can also arrange snorkelling trips in the area.

Cycling

Krabi Eco Cycle   CYCLING
(✓0 7563 7250; www.krabiecocycle.com; 41/2 Moo 5; half-/full-day tour 800/1700B) Take a Tour de Krabi by hooking up with Krabi Eco Cycle. The recommended full-day 15.5km pedal takes you through rubber plantations, small villages, hot springs and, finally, a cooler dip at the aptly named Emerald Pool. Lunch is included on all tours except the half-day bike-only tour.

☞ Tours

Any travel agency worth its salt can book you on one of the popular four- or five-island tours for around 2500B. The **Ao Nang Long-Tail Boat Service** (✓0 7569 5313) offers private charters for up to six people to Hong Island (2500B) and Bamboo Island (3800B), and the standard five-island tour, of course. You can also book half-day trips to Poda and Chicken Islands (2000B, four hours) for up to four people.

Several tour agencies offer tours to **Khlong Thom**, including visits to freshwater pools, hot springs and the **Wat Khlong Thom Museum**; the price per adult/child is 1500/1000B. So-called mystery tours visit local snake farms, rural villages, crystal pools and rubber, pineapple, banana and papaya plantations; they cost around 900/450B per adult/child. Tour agencies also offer trips to attractions around Ao Phang-Nga and to a number of dubious animal shows.

You can also arrange day tours to Ko Phi-Phi on the **Ao Nang Princess** (adult/child 1400/1000B). The boat leaves at 9am from the Hat Noppharat Thara National Park headquarters and visits Bamboo Island, Phi-Phi Don and Phi-Phi Leh. Free transfers from Ao Nang to Hat Noppharat Thara are included in the price.

🛏 Sleeping

Prices at all these places drop by 50% during the low season.

★ Glur   HOSTEL $
(✓08 9001 3343, 0 7569 5297; www.krabiglur hostel.com; 22/2 Moo 2, Soi Ao Nang; dm 600B, d 1300-1500B; P❄@🛜🏊) Another sneaky, great Krabi-area hostel. Designed, built, owned and operated by a talented Thai architect and his wife, the gleaming white complex incorporates shipping containers, glass and moulded and polished concrete to create sumptuous dorms, with curtained off turquoise beds and airy private rooms. The pool was under construction at research time. Glur also runs a seasonal sandwich shop that makes some of the best sandwiches and burgers in all of Krabi.

The Nine @ Ao Nang   HOTEL $$
(✓0 7569 5668; www.thenineaonang.com; 348 Moo 2, Soi Ao Nang; d 1700-2200B; ❄🛜) Dig the dancing Ganesh statues framed in the lobby and the floating beds and slightly sunken baths in the stylish guest rooms. The latter also have private terraces (some with cliff views), mini-fridges, wall-mounted flat screens and their own little Ganesh standing sentry on the desk. It all adds up to one of Ao Nang's most stylish 3-star sleeps.

Somkiet Buri Resort   HOTEL $$
(✓0 7563 7320; www.somkietburi.com; 236 Moo 2, Ao-Nang; r from 1800-3000B; ❄🛜🏊) This place just might inspire you to slip into a yoga pose. The lush jungle grounds are filled with ferns and orchids, while lagoons, streams and meandering wooden walkways guide you to the 26 large and creatively designed rooms. A great swimming pool is set amid it all – balconies either face this pool or a peaceful pond. The service is first-rate.

Apasari
HOTEL **$$**

(0 7563 7188; www.apasari.com; 178 Th Ao Nang; r 1800-5200B; ✳@🛜🌊) One of a handful of stylish midrangers on Ao Nang's newest boulevard. Rooms have high-end tiled floors, flat-screen TVs and built-in desks and wardrobes. All rooms have balconies overlooking the lap pool. It's exceptional value in the low season.

Ban Sainai
RESORT **$$$**

(0 7581 9333; 11/1 Soi Ao Nang; bungalows from 3000B; P✳🛜🌊) One of the newest properties in town sports cushy, thatched faux-adobe bungalows sprinkled amid the palms and set so close to the cliffs you can almost kiss them. Expect high-end tiled floors, polished concrete baths, timber wash basins and pebbled showers. Low season deals (1750B) are fabulous.

Golden Beach Resort
HOTEL **$$$**

(0 7563 7871, 0 7563 7870; www.goldenbeach-resort.com; 254 Moo2, Th Ao-Nang; r 3500-6100B; bungalows 5100-8500B; ✳🌊) This sprawling, unpretentious resort dominates the southernmost 400m of Ao Nang's beachfront – the best part of the beach. It's made up of large hotel blocks and stylish wood-trimmed bungalows arranged in garden foliage around a big pool. It's not quite hip but it definitely feels good to be here. Check the website for specials.

Phra Nang Inn
HOTEL **$$$**

(0 7563 7130; www.phranonghotels.com; Th Ao Nang; r incl breakfast from 3600B; ✳@🌊) It's an artistic explosion of rustic coconut wood, bright orange and purple paint, and plenty of elaborate Thai tiles. There are two pools, and a similarly designed branch is across the road from the original.

✗ Eating

Ao Nang is full of mediocre roadside restaurants serving Italian, Scandinavian, Indian, Thai and fast food. Prices are a bit inflated but you won't go hungry. For budget meals, a few stalls pop up at night on the road to Krabi (near McDonald's). You'll find *roti* (pancakes), *gài tôrt* (fried chicken), hamburgers and the like, and around lunch time street stalls also set up just north of Krabi Resort. Of course, the best meal in the Ao Nang area (and beyond) can be found at Kruthara in nearby Nopparat Thara. It's well worth the trip.

Soi Sunset
SEAFOOD **$$**

(0 7569 5260; Soi Sunset; dishes 60-400B; ⊙noon-10pm) At the western end of the beach is this narrow pedestrian-only alley housing several romantic seafood restaurants with gorgeous views of an island-dotted ocean. They all have model ice boats at the entrance showing off the day's catch while smiling staff beckon you to take a seat. One of the best (and most popular) is Krua Ao Nang at the end of the strip.

Jeanette's Restaurant
SWEDISH, THAI **$$**

(08 9474 6178; www.jeanettekrabi.com; dishes 120-350B; ⊙8am-10pm) The most popular place in town thanks to its signature bench seating, ink-blot art on the walls and traditional Thai menu augmented with Swedish hits (that apple pie does sound good).

🍺 Drinking & Nightlife

There's no shortage of bars in Ao Nang.

Last Café
CAFE, BAR

(⊙11am-7pm) At the far southern end of Hat Ao Nang is this barefoot beach cafe, with cold beer and cool breezes. Come here for a welcome blast of Ao Nang natural.

ℹ Information

All the information offices on the strip, including the **Ao Nang Visitor Center** (0 7562 8221), are private tour agencies. Most offer international calls and internet access for around 1B per minute.

Several banks have ATMs and foreign-exchange windows (open from 10am to 8pm) on the main drag.

ℹ Getting There & Around

BUS, CAR & MINIVAN

Sŏrng·tǎa·ou run to and from Krabi (50B, 20 minutes). The route goes from the Krabi bus terminal (add 10B to the fare) via Th Maharat, the Khong Kha pier in Krabi and on to Hat Noppharat Thara, Ao Nang and finally the Shell Cemetery. From Ao Nang to Hat Noppharat Thara or the Shell Cemetery it's 40B.

Airport buses to and from Ao Nang cost 80B to 100B and leave throughout the day. Private taxis from the airport cost about 800B. Minibuses go to destinations all over the south including Phuket (350B to 400B, three to four hours), Pak Bara (300B, 3½ hours) and Ko Lanta (400B, two hours).

Dozens of places along the strip rent out small motorcycles for 150B to 200B. Budget Car Hire charges around 1600B.

BOAT

Boats to Railay's Hat Railay West are run by the **Ao Nang Long-Tail Boat Service** (☑ 0 7569 5313; www.aonangboatco-op.com); rates are 100B per person from 7.30am to 6pm or 150B per person from 6pm to 6am. It's a 15-minute journey. Boats leave when there are a minimum six people, or you can charter the whole boat by paying for the equivalent of eight people. During rough seas, boats leave from a sheltered cove about 200m west of Ao Nang – you can get here from Ao Nang by motorcycle taxi (30B), *sŏrng·tăa·ou* (10B) or on foot.

Ferries and speedboats leave from the nearby pier at Hat Nopphrat Thara to Ko Phi-Phi, Ko Lanta, Phuket and the Ko Yao Islands.

Around Ao Nang

Hat Nopphrat Thara หาดนพรัตน์ธารา

North of Ao Nang, the golden beach gets a bit more *au naturel* as it curves around a headland for 4km, where the sea eventually spills into a natural lagoon at the Hat Nopphrat Thara National Park headquarters. Here, scores of long-tails mingle with fishing boats and speedboats against a stunning limestone backdrop. The small **visitors centre** has displays on coral reefs and mangrove ecology, labelled in Thai and English.

Several resorts falsely advertise a 'central Ao Nang' location – if you don't read the fine print, you may end up sleeping out here (though you might prefer it anyway).

Around the national park headquarters are several **restaurants** serving snacks such as fried chicken and papaya salad.

🛌 Sleeping

Government Bungalows   BUNGALOWS $$
(☑ 0 7563 7200; bungalows 1000B) These wooden, fan-cooled bungalows across the street from the beach are rustic yet well maintained and a terrific budget choice. Prices don't go up in the high season, but you'd better book ahead. Check in at national park headquarters near the harbour.

Sabai Resort   HOTEL $$
(☑ 0 7563 7791; www.sabairesort.com; bungalows 1300-1600B; ❄ @ ☎) This is the most professionally run of the area's bungalow properties. The tiled-roof bungalows are fan cooled with pebbled concrete patios overlooking a palm-shaded swimming pool and a flower garden.

⭐ Kruthara   SEAFOOD $$
(☑ 0 7563 7361; Hat Nopparat Thara; meals from 300B; ⏰ 11am-10pm; P) This cavernous, tin-roof delight is the best restaurant in the South Andaman, and one of the best seafood kitchens in Thailand, which places it high in the running for best worldwide. There is no pretension here, just the freshest fish, crab, clams, oysters, lobster and prawns done dozens of ways, some of which are very special.

The crab fried in yellow curry is spectacular – with meaty legs half cracked and waiting, and the guts and roe scrambled in eggs which are drenched in curry and piled on top of the crab itself. The fried rice is fluffy and light, and the snapper fried in red curry is scintillating and moist and one of the best fish dishes we've ever eaten in Thailand (and we've had hundreds). Simply put, this is a meal that can turn enemies into friends, friends into lovers and lovers into life partners.

ℹ Getting There & Away

Sŏrng·tăa·ou between Krabi and Ao Nang stop in Hat Nopphrat Thara; the fare is 50B from Krabi or 20B from Ao Nang.

From November to May the *Ao Nang Princess* runs between Ko Phi-Phi Marine National Park headquarters and Ko Phi-Phi (400B, two hours). The boat leaves from the national park jetty at 9am, returning from Ko Phi-Phi at 1.30pm. It also stops at Hat Railay West. This boat can also be used for day trips to Ko Phi-Phi. During the same high-season months, there's also a 3pm boat to Phuket (700B, four hours) leaving from the same pier and a 10.30am boat to Ko Lanta (470B, 1½ hours).

A faster alternative to Phuket is to take the *Green Planet* speedboat (950B, 75 minutes), which goes from Hat Nopphrat Thara to Bang Rong Pier, north of Phuket Town via Ko Yao Noi and Ko Yao Yai (both 470B, 45 minutes). The boat leaves Hat Nopphrat Thara at 10.30am and 4pm and transport to your Phuket accommodation is included in the fare.

Railay   ไร่เล

Krabi's fairy-tale limestone crags come to a dramatic climax at Railay (also spelt Rai Leh), the ultimate jungle gym for rock-climbing fanatics. This quiet slice of paradise fills in the sandy gaps between each craggy flourish, and although it's just around the bend from chaotic tourist hustle in Ao Nang, the atmosphere here is nothing short of laid-back, Rasta-Thai heaven.

⊙ Sights

Tham Phra Nang   CAVE

(Princess Cave) At the eastern end of Hat Phra Nang is Tham Phra Nang, an important shrine for local fishermen. Legend has it that a royal barge carrying an Indian princess foundered in a storm here during the 3rd century BC. The spirit of the drowned princess came to inhabit the cave, granting favours to all who came to pay respect.

Local fishermen – Muslim and Buddhist – place carved wooden phalluses in the cave as offerings in the hope that the spirit will provide plenty of fish.

Sa Phra Nang   LAGOON

(Holy Princess Pool) About halfway along the path from Hat Railay East to Hat Phra Nang, a crude path leads up the jungle-cloaked cliff wall to a hidden lagoon known as Sa Phra Nang. There's a dramatic viewpoint over the peninsula from the nearby clifftop, but be warned that this is a strenuous hike with some serious vertigo-inducing sections.

Tham Phra Nang Nai   CAVE

(Inner Princess Cave; adult/child 40/20B; ⊙ 5am-8pm) Above Hat Railay East is another large cave called Tham Phra Nang Nai, also known as Diamond Cave. A wooden boardwalk leads through a series of caverns full of beautiful limestone formations but, with shifting rain patterns, the water is now gone and with it the illuminated effects that won the diamond moniker. But even in monochrome conditions, it's still worth a stroll.

🏃 Activities

Rock Climbing

With nearly 500 bolted routes, ranging from beginner to advanced, and all with unparalleled clifftop vistas, it's no surprise that Railay is among the top climbing spots in the world. You could spend months here climbing and exploring – and many people do. Deep-water soloing offers the biggest thrill. That's where free-climbers scramble up ledges over deep water sans rope – if you fall you will most likely just get wet, so even daring beginners can give this a try.

Most climbers start off at **Muay Thai Wall** and **One, Two, Three Wall**, at the southern end of Hat Railay East, which have at least 40 routes graded from 4b to 8b on the French system. The mighty **Thaiwand Wall** sits at the southern end of Hat Railay West and offers a sheer limestone cliff with some of the most challenging climbing routes.

Other top climbs include **Hidden World** (some classic routes for intermediate climbers), **Wee's Present Wall** (an overlooked 7c+ gem), **Diamond Cave** (another beginner-to-intermediate favourite) and **Ao Nang Tower** (a three-pitch climbing wall reached only by long-tail).

The going rate for climbing courses is 800B to 1000B for a half-day and 1500B to 2000B for a full day. Private instruction runs 3000B for a half-day and 5000B for a full-day. Three-day courses (6000B) involve lead climbing, where you clip into bolts on the rock face as you ascend. Experienced climbers can rent gear sets for two people from any of the climbing schools for 800/1300B for a half/full day – the standard set consists of a 60m rope, two climbing harnesses and climbing shoes. If you're planning to climb independently, you're best off bringing your own gear from home; be sure to bring plenty of slings and quickdraws, chalk (sweaty palms are inevitable in the tropics) and a small selection of nuts and cams as backup for thinly protected routes. If you forget anything, some climbing schools sell a small range of imported climbing gear but they might not have exactly what you need or the right size. A woven rattan mat (available locally for 100-150B) will help keep the sand out of your gear.

Several locally published books detail climbs in the area, but *Rock Climbing in Thailand*, by Elke Schmitz and Wee Changrua, is one of the more complete guides. There's a similar book by a non-resident author available through traditional booksellers.

★ Base Camp Ton Sai   ROCK CLIMBING

(☑ 08 1149 9745; www.tonsaibasecamp.com; Hat Ton Sai; ⊙ 8am-9:30pm) Arguably the most professional outfit in the area.

Highland Rock Climbing   ROCK CLIMBING

(☑ 08 0693 0374; highlandrockclimbingthailand. weebly.com; Hat Railay East) If you're bunking on the mountain, the owner of this outfit is the man to climb with.

Hot Rock   ROCK CLIMBING

(☑ 0 7562 1771; www.railayadventure.com; Hat Railay West) Has a very good reputation and is owned by one of the granddaddies of Railay climbing.

King Climbers   ROCK CLIMBING

(☑ 0 7563 7125; www.railay.com; Hat Railay East) One of the biggest, oldest and most reputable schools.

Railay

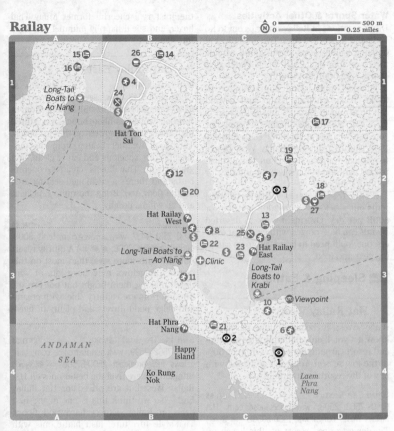

N 0 _____ 500 m
0 _____ 0.25 miles

Long-Tail Boats to Ao Nang
Hat Ton Sai
Hat Railay West
Long-Tail Boats to Ao Nang
Clinic
Hat Railay East
Long-Tail Boats to Krabi
Viewpoint
Hat Phra Nang
ANDAMAN SEA
Happy Island
Ko Rung Nok
Laem Phra Nang

Railay

Water Sports & Other Activities

Dive operations in Railay run trips out to Ko Poda and other dive sites. Two local dives at outlying islands costs about 2000B while a three- or four-day PADI Open Water dive course is 12,000B to 15,000B.

Full-day, multi-island **snorkelling** trips to Ko Poda, Chicken Island and beyond can be arranged through any of the resorts for about 2000B (maximum six people) or you can charter a long-tail (half-/full-day 1800/2500B) from Hat Railay West beach. If you just want to snorkel off Railay, most resorts can rent you a mask set and fins for 100B to 150B each.

Flame Tree Restaurant (Hat Rai Leh West) rents out **sea kayaks** for 200B per hour or 800B per day. Overnight trips to deserted islands can be arranged with local boat owners, but you'll need to bring your own camping gear and food.

🛏 Sleeping & Eating

🛏 Hat Railay West

Railay West is beautiful and developers know it – you'll only find midrange and top-end resorts around here. Rates drop by 30% in the low season. You can't go wrong with any of the resorts' restaurants.

Sand Sea Resort   HOTEL $$
(☑ 0 7562 2608; www.krabisandsea.com; Hat Railay West; bungalows 1950-5950B; ✳@✲) The lowest-priced resort on this beach offers everything from ageing fan-only bungalows to newly remodelled cottages with every amenity. There's a peaceful karst-view, foliage-enclosed pool – if you're able to tear yourself away from that sublime beach out front, that is.

★ Railei Beach Club   VILLA RENTAL $$$
(☑ 08 6685 9359; www.raileibeachclub.com; houses from 3000B; 🛜) At the northern end of the beach is this collection of Thai-style homes, each unique in size and design, rented out on behalf of absentee owners. They come with patios, kitchens and amenities, and some have pools to make extended stays very comfortable. They're hidden in forested grounds that stretch all the way back to luscious limestone cliffs.

Houses sleep between two and eight people comfortably. It's a superb deal and a romantic location, so book well in advance for the high season. Their in-house massage

therapist is a cheerful former Muay Thai boxer, and she'll happily pummel you deep into wellness.

🛏 Hat Railay East

Railay Garden View   BUNGALOWS $$
(☑ 08 5888 5143; www.railaygardenview.com; Hat Railay East; bungalows 1300B) A collection of tin-roof, woven-bamboo bungalows, stilted high above the mangroves on the east beach. They look weather beaten from the outside, but are spacious and super clean, and graced with Thai linens, creative concrete baths and there's a cushioned seating area on the floor, too. Bring mosquito repellent, and all will be peachy.

Anyavee   HOTEL $$
(☑ 0 7581 9437; www.anyavee.com; tents 300B, bungalows from 1700B; ✳@✲) A quirky resort but one with more style than most on this beach. Bungalows here have lots of windows, making them bright but not private. The interiors are country chic, with cream-and-beige plaid duvets and plenty of hardwoods.

Sunrise Tropical Resort   HOTEL $$
(☑ 0 7562 2599; www.sunrisetropical.com; bungalows incl breakfast 2500-6750B; ✳@🛜✲) Bungalows here rival the better ones on Hat Railay West but are priced for Hat Railay East – so we think this is one of the best deals in Railay. Expect hardwood floors, Thai-style furniture, lush bathrooms with bright aqua tiles, and private balconies or patios.

Mangrove Restaurant   THAI $
(dishes 70-120B; ⊗8am-10pm) This humble, local-style place, set beneath a stilted thatched roof on the recently detoured trail between the east and west beaches turns out all your spicy Thai faves cheaply, from beef salad and noodles to curries and *sôm dam*. Praise goes to the kitchen's matriarch. She means business, and her husband can turn a spoon just fine, too.

🛏 Railay Highlands

Railay Cabana   GUESTHOUSE $
(☑ 08 45341928, 0 7562 1733; Railay Highlands; bungalows 350-600B) Superbly located high in the hills in a bowl of karst cliffs, this is your hippie tropical mountain hideaway. Simple, clean thatched bungalows are surrounded by mango, mangosteen, banana and guava

WHERE TO STAY IN RAILAY

There are four beaches around Railay, or you can choose to stay up on the headland. It's only about a five-minute walk between Hat Railay East, Hat Railay West, Hat Phra Nang and the headlands. Hat Ton Sai is more isolated and to get to the other beaches you'll need to take a long-tail (50B) or hike – it takes about 20 minutes to scramble over the rocks from Hat Railay West.

➡ **Hat Railay East** is the most developed beach. The shallow, muddy bay lined with mangroves is not appealing for swimming, but the beach is lined with hotels and guesthouses, and those headlands and limestone cliffs are miraculous.

➡ **Hat Railay West** is a near-flawless white wonder and the best place to swim, join an afternoon pick-up football game or just watch the sun go down. Tastefully designed midrange resorts are sprinkled throughout, and long-tail boats pick up and drop off here to/from nearby Ao Nang.

➡ **Hat Phra Nang** is quite possibly one of the world's most beautiful beaches, with a crescent of pale, golden sand, framed by karst cliffs carved with caves. Those distant limestone islets peeking out of the cerulean sea are Chicken (Ko Hua Khwan) and Poda Islands. Rayavadee, the peninsula's most exclusive resort, is the only one on this beach, but anyone can drop a beach towel.

➡ **Hat Ton Sai** is the grittier climbers' retreat. The beach here isn't spectacular, but with so many good climbs all around, most people don't mind. Bars and bungalows are nestled in the jungle behind the beach and it's a lively, fun scene.

➡ **The Railay Headlands** catch sea breezes. Since it's the most recent place to be developed, it feels like a frontier with plantations, jungle and some very friendly locals. To get here you'll have to walk about 500m from either Hat Railay West or East. From Hat Railay West follow 'Walking Street,' veer left onto a dirt path then follow the signs to Ya-Ya Bar. From Hat Railay East turn right on the cement road accessible via the beachside Diamond Cave Restaurant.

groves. The only sounds are birds chirping and children laughing.

Railay Phutawan Resort   HOTEL **$$**
(☑ 0 7581 9479, 08 4060 0550; www.railayphutawan. com; r from 1850B, bungalows from 2150B; ❉ @) The best options here are the super-spacious polished-cement bungalows highlighted with creamy yellow walls, big rain-shower bathrooms and all the trimmings of a high-end resort. Tiled rooms in an apartment-style block are a step down in luxury but very comfortable; fan-cooled bungalows with bamboo ceilings are musty but good value.

🛏 Hat Phra Nang หาดถ้ำพระนาง

⭐ **Rayavadee**   HOTEL **$$$**
(☑ 0 7562 0741, 0 7562 0740; www.rayavadee. com; pavilions from 14,500B, villas from 75,000B; ❉ 🛜 ≋) This exclusive resort has sprawling banyan tree- and flower-filled grounds navigated by golf buggies. The two-storey mushroom-domed pavilions are filled with antique furniture and every mod con – as well as the occasional private Jacuzzi, swim-

ming pool or butler service. Two restaurants grace Hat Phra Nang (one is half inside an illuminated cave) and non-guests can stop in for pricey but divine Thai or Mediterranean meals.

🛏 Hat Ton Sai หาดต้นไทร

Paasook   HOTEL **$**
(☑ 08 9648 7459; Hat Ton Sai; bungalows 200–900B) Definitely the most stylish budget establishment on Ton Sai: wooden bungalows have elongated floor-to-ceiling windows and concrete floors. The gardens are lush, management is friendly and there's a rustic-chic outdoor restaurant, perfect for steamy evenings.

Forest Resort   HOTEL **$$**
(☑ 08 0143 8261; Hat Ton Sai; bungalows 400–1000B) The concrete floor cells are mouldy and uninhabitable, though the bamboo bungalows are slightly less scruffy. The best bet are the wood-and-brick tiled bungalows with tiled floors and tin roofs. All are fan cooled when electricity is running (5pm–6am daily).

Mountain View Resort
HOTEL $$

(☑08 9783 4008, 0 7581 9819; www.citykrabi.com; bungalows 1300-1900B; ❋) This place is bright, cheery and immaculate with mint-green walls, tiled floors and crisp sheets in lodge-like environs. Some rooms are slightly musty, so sniff around.

Mama's Chicken
THAI $

(Hat Ton Sai; 50-90B; ⊙7:30am-10pm) One of the more popular of the Ton Sai beach stalls offers Western breakfasts, fruit smoothies and a range of cheap Thai dishes, including a massaman tofu, which is a rarity. Grab a table and watch management engage in their daily battle with a thieving mob of macaques, who do love their mangoes.

🍷 Drinking

There's a bunch of places on the beaches where you can unwind and get nicely inebriated.

★ Lucky Last Bar
BAR

(⊙11am-late) A multi-level tiki bar that rambles to the edge of the mangroves on Hat Railay East, they have cushioned seating on one deck, candlelit tables on another and a bandstand closer to the walking street. It's no wonder the crowds gather here.

Backyard Bar & Cafe
CAFE

(Hat Ton Sai; ⊙8am-9pm) Good coffee, organic teas, a tasty chai, and a range of cakes and cookies, including 'Happy Cookies.' Which are, well, quite happy. Or so we hear. Brunch is served between 8am and 2pm.

Highland Rock Climbing
CAFE

(☑08 0693 0374; Railay Highlands) Part climbing school, part cafe, this place has been cobbled together from driftwood and dangles with orchids. The owner, Chaow, sources his beans from sustainable farms in Chiang Rai and serves the best coffee on the peninsula.

ℹ️ Information

The website www.railay.com has lots of information about Railay. There are two ATMs along Hat Railay East. On Hat Ton Sai there is one ATM near the Ton Sai Bay Resort. Several of the bigger resorts can change cash and travellers cheques. For minor climbing injuries there's a small clinic at Railay Bay Resort & Spa.

Wi-fi is widely available in hotels and cafes.

ℹ️ Getting There & Around

Long-tail boats to Railay run from Khong Kha pier in Krabi and from the seafronts of Ao Nang and Ao Nam Mao. Boats between Krabi and Hat Railay East leave every 1½ hours from 7.45am to 6pm when they have six to 10 passengers (150B, 45 minutes). Chartering the whole boat costs 1500B.

Boats to Hat Railay West or Hat Ton Sai from Ao Nang cost 100B (15 minutes) from 7.30am to 6pm or 150B at other times; boats don't leave until eight people show up. Private charters cost 800B. During exceptionally high seas the boats from Ao Nang and Krabi stop running, but you may still be able to get from Hat Railay East to Ao Nam Mao (100B, 15 minutes), where you can pick up a *sŏrng·tăa·ou* to Krabi or Ao Nang.

From October to May the *Ao Nang Princess* runs from Hat Noppharat Thara National Park headquarters to Ko Phi-Phi with a stop at Hat Railay West. Long-tails run out to meet the boat at around 9.15am from in front of the Sand Sea Resort in Hat Railay West. The fare to Ko Phi-Phi from Railay is 350B.

Ko Phi-Phi Don
เกาะพีพีดอน

Oh, how beauty can be a burden. Like Marilyn Monroe, Phi-Phi Don's stunning looks have become its own demise. Everyone wants a piece of her. Though not exactly Hollywood, this is Thailand's Shangri-La: a hedonistic paradise where tourists cavort in azure seas and snap pictures of long-tails puttering between craggy cliffs. With its flashy, curvy blonde beaches and bodacious jungles it's no wonder that Phi-Phi has become the darling of the Andaman coast. And, like any good starlet, this island can party hard all night and still look like a million bucks the next morning. Unfortunately, nothing can withstand this glamorous pace and unless limits are set, Phi-Phi is in for an ecological crash.

Ko Phi-Phi Don is practically two islands joined together by a narrow isthmus flanked by the stunning **Ao Ton Sai** and **Ao Lo Dalam** on either side. Boats dock at the large concrete pier at Ao Ton Sai and a narrow path, crammed full of tour operators, bungalows, restaurants, bars and souvenir shops, stretches east along the beach towards **Hat Hin Khom**. The maze of small streets in the middle of this sandbar is equally packed and is known as **Tonsai Village** (or the Tourist Village). The swimmer-friendly **Hat Yao** (Long Beach) faces south and has some of Phi-Phi Don's best coral. The beautifully languid and long eastern bays of **Hat Laem Thong** and **Ao Lo Bakao** are reserved for several top-end resorts, while the smaller bays of **Hat Phak Nam** and **Hat Rantee** play host to a few simple, low-key bungalow affairs.

◉ Sights & Activities

The strenuous and sweaty climb to Phi-Phi's **viewpoint** (Map p656) is a rewarding short and steep hike. Most people will need to stop for a short break (don't forget to bring some water), but once you reach the top you'll be treated to postcard-worthy views of the twin bays, soaring karst formations and quiet Ko Phi-Phi Leh off in the distance.

Diving

Crystal-clear Andaman water and abundant marine life make the perfect recipe for top-notch scuba. Popular sights include the **King Cruiser Wreck**, sitting a mere 12m below the surface; **Anemone Reef**, teeming with hard corals and clownfish; **Hin Bida**, a submerged pinnacle attracting turtles and large pelagic fish; and **Ko Bida Nok**, with its signature karst massif luring leopard sharks. Hin Daeng and Hin Muang, about 70km south, are expensive ventures from Ko Phi-Phi – it's cheaper to link up with a dive crew in Ko Lanta.

An Open Water certification course costs around 12,900B to 13,800B, while the standard two-dive trips cost from 2500B to 3200B. Trips out to Hin Daeng/Hin Muang will set you back 5500B.

Adventure Club　　　　　　DIVING
(Map p658; ☑08 1970 0314; www.phi-phi-adventures.com) Our favourite diving operation on the island runs an excellent assortment of educational, eco-focused diving, hiking and snorkelling tours. You won't mind getting up at 6am for the much-loved shark-watching snorkel trips on which you're guaranteed to cavort with at least one reef shark.

Sea Frog Diving　　　　　　DIVING
(Map p658; ☑0 756 01073; www.ppseafrog.com) A long-running dive shop, with a solid reputation.

Snorkelling

A popular snorkelling destination is **Ko Mai Phai** (Bamboo Island), 5km north of Phi-Phi Don. There's a shallow area here where you may see small sharks. Snorkelling trips cost between 600B to 2400B, depending on whether you travel by long-tail or motor-boat. There is also good snorkelling along the eastern coast of **Ko Nok**, near Ao Ton Sai, and along the eastern coast of **Ko Nai**. If you're going on your own, most bungalows and resorts rent out a snorkel, mask and fins for 150B to 200B per day.

Rock Climbing

Yes, there are good limestone cliffs to climb on Ko Phi-Phi, and the views are spectacular. The main climbing areas are **Ton Sai Tower** (Map p656), at the western edge of Ao Ton Sai, and **Hin Taak** (Map p656), a short long-tail boat ride around the bay. Climbing shops on the island charge around 1200B for a half-day of climbing or 2000B for a full day, including instruction and gear. **Spider Monkey** (Map p658; ☑0 7581 9384; www.spidermonkeyphiphi.com) is run by Soley, one of the most impressive climbers on Phi-Phi. **Ibex Climbing & Tours** (Map p658; ☑08 4309 0445, 0 7560 1423; www.ibexclimbingandtours.com) is one of the newest and best outfitters in the Village.

◈ Courses

Pum Restaurant & Cooking School　　　　　COOKING
(Map p658; ☑08 1521 8904; www.pumthaifoodchain.com; classes 399-1200B; ⊙classes 1pm & 4pm) Thai-food fans can take cooking courses at the recommended Pum Restaurant & Cooking School in the tourist village. You'll learn to make some of the excellent dishes that are served in its restaurant and home with a great cookbook.

☞ Tours

Ever since Leo smoked a spliff in Alex Garland's *The Beach,* Phi-Phi Leh has become somewhat of a pilgrimage site. Aside from long-tail boat tours to Phi-Phi Leh and Ko Mai Phai (Bamboo Island), tour agencies can arrange sunset tours to Monkey Bay and the beach at Wang Long, both on Phi-Phi Leh, for 600B. Adventure Club is a good choice. **U-Rip** (☑0 7560 1075; per person 600B) offers the same trip and is also highly recommended.

You can no longer camp on Maya Beach, but you can join the **Plankton Sunset Cruise** (www.mayabaytours.com; per person 1200B) and sleep aboard the boat just offshore. They only take online bookings.

Captain Bob's Booze Cruise (☑08 4848 6970; www.phiphiboozecruise.com; men/women 3000/2500B; ⊙departs at 1pm, returns at 7pm) is the latest buzz-worthy excursion and is

Ko Phi-Phi Don

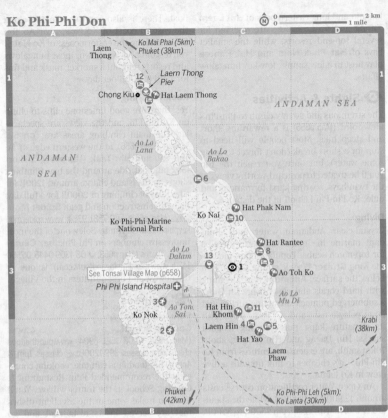

Ko Phi-Phi Don

exactly what it sounds like. You're cruising the waters around Phi Phi Don and Phi Phi Leh, on a sailboat, adult beverage in hand.

Another unique choice is the **Watersports Experience** (www.facebook.com/watersportsexperience; per person with/without sports 2500/1500B), where guests can stand-up paddle (SUP), wake board, water ski and snorkel the waters around Phi Phi Don and Phi Phi Leh. You'll lunch on Ao Rantee. You'll be zip-ping around in the Ali Baba speedboat, and guests who only wish to cruise are welcome at a discount. Best booked at any of the tour offices in the village.

🛏 Sleeping

Finding accommodation on this ever-popular island has never been easy and you can expect serious room shortages at peak holiday times. Masses of touts meet incoming boats and, while often annoying, can make your life easier.

Be sure you lock the door while you sleep and close all the windows when you go out. Break-ins can be a problem.

Tonsai Village บ้านต้นไทร

The flat, hourglass-shaped land between Ao Ton Sai and Ao Lo Dalam is crowded with loads of lodging options.

Blanco HOSTEL $
(Map p658; ☑ 0 7562 8900; Tonsai Village; dm 300B; ☎) This bare bones (better bring your own top sheet) yet stylish hostel offers 8-bed dorms in bamboo chalets with concrete floors. Digs are cramped and mattresses are gym-mat hard, but this is where the cool kids stay, thanks to fun-loving Thai ownership and a super groovy beach bar.

The bar itself is arced concrete, there are cushioned lounges and a handful of candle-lit white tables sunk in the sand with Dalam views. The food is good, too. Of course, with this location you'll be keeping vampire hours. But how sexy is that?

Rock Backpacker HOSTEL $
(Map p658; ☑ 08 1607 3897; Tonsai Village; dm 300B; r from 400-600B) A proper hostel on the village hill, with clean dorms lined with bunk beds, tiny private rooms, an inviting restaurant-bar and a rugged, graffiti-scrawled exterior.

Oasis Guesthouse GUESTHOUSE $
(Map p658; ☑ 0 7560 1207; Tonsai Village; r 800-900B; ☒) It's worth the walk up the side road east of the village centre to find this cute guesthouse with wooden shutters surrounded by trees. The innkeeper can be surly, but freshly painted rooms have sparkling bathrooms. It's first come, first serve only.

Tee Guesthouse GUESTHOUSE $
(Map p658; ☑ 08 4851 5721; Tonsai Village; r with fan/air-con 800/1200B; ☒) A fun and funky choice tucked down a side road. Rooms are simple with graceful touches like exposed brick and lavender walls, queen beds, mosaic-tiled baths, and a welcome blast of graffiti on the exterior. They have a darling little cafe (p661) here too.

★ JJ Residence GUESTHOUSE $$
(Map p658; ☑ 0 7560 1098; d 1900-2500B; ☒☎☒) Expect spacious tiled rooms with funky wood panelling, beamed ceilings, duvee, mini fridge, flat screen, built-in desk and wardrobe and private terrace. Those on the first floor spill right onto the pool. One of the nicer choices in Ton Sai.

Orange Tree GUESTHOUSE $$
(Map p658; ☑ 08 1439 3924; www.orangetree-phiphi.com; r 1300-1500B; ☒☎) A chic four-room guesthouse tucked down a narrow soi, with windowless dark pods for rooms that still feel really good thanks to high-end tiled floors, exposed concrete and brick walls, flat screens and tastefully tiled baths. From a design point of view, it's by far the best option in the village. But it's not for light sleepers.

Hat Hin Khom หาดหินคม

This area has a few small white-sand beaches in rocky coves that are relatively quiet. It's about a 15-minute jungle walk from both Hat Yao and the Ao Ton Sai bustle.

Viking Natures Resort HOTEL $$
(Map p656; ☑ 0 7581 9399; www.vikingnaturesresort.com; bungalows 1500-12,000B; ☎) OK, it's funky (in all senses of the word), but the wood, thatch and bamboo bungalows here are dreamily creative and stylish with lots of driftwood, shell mobiles and hammock-decked lounging spaces with outrageous views of Ko Phi-Phi Leh. All bungalows have mosquito nets and balconies, but the cheaper rooms don't have their own bathrooms.

Hat Yao หาดยาว

You can either walk here in about 30 minutes from Ton Sai via Hat Hin Khom or take a long-tail (100B to 150B) from Ton Sai pier. This long stretch of pure-white beach is perfect for swimming and well worth the walk but don't expect to have it to yourself – it's popular with families and sporty types playing volleyball.

Paradise Pearl Resort RESORT $$
(Map p656; ☑ 0 7560 1246; www.phiphiparadise pearl.com; d from 2000-3000B; ☒☎) A collection of dark wood Thai chalets tucked into the rocky headland on the southern curl of Hat Yao, the Paradise is decked out with tasteful art and updated electronics. There are chic lounges on the beach and a restaurant that rambles on timber tables to the edge of the sand; it's typically packed with young couples. Free wi-fi is available in the lobby only.

Tonsai Village

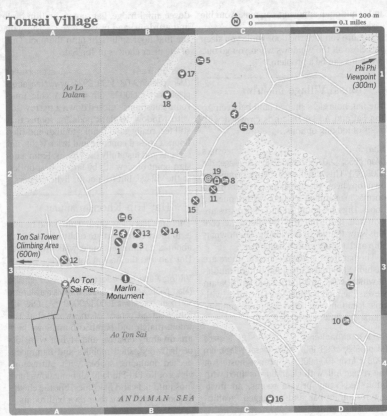

★ **Paradise Resort Phi Phi** HOTEL $$$
(Map p656; ☎ 08 1968 3982; www.paradiseresort.
co.th; bungalows from 3000B; ❋❄☎) Rooms in
the uber-white lodge have South Beach ech-
oes and are plush with granite-tiled floors,
wood panelled walls, floating beds, flat
screens and desks. They also have stand-
alone beach cottages with similar furnish-
ings in older bones. Low season deals are
superb.

ℹ️ SLEEPING (OR TRYING TO) ON KO PHI-PHI

Noise pollution on Phi-Phi is bad and centred around central Ao Ton Sai and Ao Lo Dalam – although don't expect an early night on Hat Hin Khom either. At the time of writing, bars had a 2am curfew in Ao Lo Dalam and 1.30am in Ton Sai, but that doesn't stop inebriated revellers from making plenty of other noises (door slamming seems to be a late-night island pastime).

The most peaceful accommodation can be found on:

➡ Phi-Phi's east coast

➡ The back road that connects the southeast end of Ao Ton Sai with Ao Lo Dalam (and passes Chunut House)

➡ The hill near the road up to the viewpoint

➡ The far western section of Ao Ton Sai

➡ Hat Yao

Of course, the best option may simply be to grab a bucket and join the scrum.

🛏 Hat Rantee & Ao Toh Ko

Still fairly low-key, this series of small, remote grey-gold beaches has good snorkelling. You can either get here by long-tail from Ao Ton Sai pier (300B – although most resorts provide free pick-up if you reserve; the return trip is 150B) or by making the strenuous 45-minute hike over the viewpoint.

PP Rantee BUNGALOWS **$$**
(Map p656; ☑ 08 1597 7708; Hat Rantee; bungalow with fan 1200-1600B, air-con 2000B; ⊘ restaurant 7am-10pm; ✳🛜) Here are basic but acceptable woven-bamboo bungalows and newer tiled bungalows with wide porches overlooking a trim garden path that leads to the sand. They also have the best restaurant on the beach and a big wooden swing on the tree out front.

Rantee Cliff Beach Resort BUNGALOWS **$$**
(Map p656; ☑ 08 9725 4411; www.ranteecliffbeach.com; bungalows 2000-5800B; ✳🛜) The newest offering on Phi Phi was nearing completion at research time. Expect stylish bamboo bungalows with soaring thatched roofs, french doors opening onto private patios, gauzy mosquito netting and sunken baths. It's tucked into the headland at the southern end of Hat Rantee.

🛏 Hat Phak Nam & Ao Lo Bakao

Hat Phak Nam is a gorgeous white-sand beach sharing the same bay as a small fishing hamlet. To get here, either charter a long-tail from Ao Ton Sai for around 500B (150B by shared taxi boat upon your return) or make the very sweaty one-hour hike over the viewpoint.

Ao Lo Bakao's fine stretch of palm-backed sand, ringed by dramatic hills, is one of Phi-Phi's most lovely beaches, with offshore views over aqua bliss to Bamboo and Mosquito Islands. Phi-Phi Island Village arranges transfers for guests; on your own a charter from Ao Ton Sai will cost 800B.

★ Relax Beach Resort HOTEL **$$**
(Map p656; ☑ 08 9475 6536, 08 1083 0194; www.phiphirelaxresort.com; bungalows 1800-4900B; @✉) There are 47 unpretentious but pretty Thai-style bungalows with wood floors, two-tiered terraces with lounging cushions, and mosaic bathrooms in the newest nests. All are rimmed by lush jungle – there's a good restaurant and breezy bar, and it's run by incredibly charming staff who greet and treat you like family.

Phi-Phi Island Village HOTEL **$$$**
(Map p656; ☑ 0 7636 3700; www.ppisland.com; bungalows 7200-21,500B; ✳🛜✉) This place really is a village unto itself: its whopping 100 bungalows take up much of the beachfront with palms swaying between them. Facilities vary from casual family-friendly activities to romantic dining experiences and pampering spa treatments. It adds up to good living with a whiff of old-school luxury if you have the means.

Hat Laem Thong หาดแหลมทอง

The beach here is long, white and sandy with a small *chow lair* (sea gypsy) rubbish-strewn settlement at the north end. Despite the upmarket offerings here, the beach is really busy and all the hotels are packed together. A long-tail charter from Ao Ton Sai costs 800B. Operators can also arrange transfers.

PP Erawan   HOTEL $$$
(Map p656; ✆08 1968 5690; www.pperawanpalms.com; r 3000-4000B; ❈@❅❆) Step onto the grounds here and let the stress fall away, as you follow a meandering path through the garden to bright modern rooms decorated with Thai art and handicrafts. There's an inviting pool bar and excellent service, too. Breakfast is included.

Zeavola   HOTEL $$$
(Map p656; ✆0 7562 7000; www.zeavola.com; bungalows 9900-26,900B; ❈@❅❆) Hibiscus-lined pathways lead to shady teak bungalows with sleek, distinctly Asian indoor-outdoor floorplans. Each comes with glass walls on three sides (with remote-controlled bamboo shutters for privacy), beautiful 1940s fixtures and antique furniture, a patio and impeccable service.

✗ Eating

Most of the resorts, hotels and bungalows around the island have their own restaurants. Ao Ton Sai is home to some reasonably priced restaurants, but don't expect haute cuisine.

Local Food Market   THAI $
(Map p658; Ao Ton Sai; meals 30-60B; ⊘8am-8pm) The cheapest and most authentic eats are at the market. A handful of local stalls huddle on the narrowest sliver of the isthmus and serve up scrumptious *pàt tai,* fried rice, *sôm·đam* (spicy green papaya salad) and smoked catfish.

La Mamita   ITALIAN, MEXICAN $
(Map p658; mains 80-250B; ⊘11am-11pm) The latest offering from the Cosmic family, this atmospheric room, tucked down a narrow soi, feels like a grotto, and is known for pasta, pizza, fajitas and burritos. They reportedly do a nice moussaka here, too.

Papaya Restaurant   THAI $
(Map p658; ✆08 7280 1719; dishes 80-300B; ⊘11am-11pm) Here's some real-deal Thai food

served in heaping portions that's cheap, tasty and spicy. It has your basil and chilli, all the curries and *đôm yam,* too. They're so popular they decided to open **Papaya 2** (Map p658; ✆08 7280 1719; Ton Sai Village; dishes 80-300B), a block away.

Le Grand Bleu   INTERNATIONAL-THAI $$
(Map p658; ✆08 1979 9739; mains 140-265B; ⊘11am-2pm, 6:30-10pm) This place serves Thai-European fusion dishes and is set in a charming wooden house just off the main pier. It features French and Aussie wines, and you can get your duck wok-fried with basil or oven-roasted and caramelised with mango.

Unni's   INTERNATIONAL $$
(Map p658; mains 200-320B; ⊘8am-10pm) Come here for lunch to dine on homemade bagels topped with everything from smoked salmon to meatballs. There are also massive salads, Mexican food, tapas, cocktails and more.

🍷 Drinking & Nightlife

A rowdy nightlife saturates Phi-Phi. Sticky-sweet cocktails and buckets of cheap whiskey and Red Bull make this the domain for spring-break wannabes and really bad hangovers. The truth is that if you're nesting within earshot of the partying, you may as well enjoy the chaos.

★ Sunflower Bar   BAR
(Map p656; Ao Lo Dalam) Poetically ramshackle, this driftwood gem is still the chillest bar in Phi-Phi. Destroyed in the tsunami, the owner rebuilt it with reclaimed wood. The long-tail booths are named for the four loved ones he lost in the flood.

Slinky Bar   NIGHTCLUB
(Map p658; Ao Lo Dalam) This was the beach dance floor of the moment when we visited. Expect the standard fire show, buckets of candy juice and throngs of people mingling, flirting and flailing to throbbing bass on the sand.

Ibiza   NIGHTCLUB
(Map p658; Ao Lo Dalam) Another of Dalam's beach dens of inebriation and inequity (but, you know, in a good way). Relax on beachside cushions, toke a shisha pipe and marvel at expert fire twirlers and drunken daredevils as they jump through fiery hoops, limbo beneath a fiery cane and jump a fiery rope to bone-rattling bass.

Chukit Bar & Karaoke
BAR

(Map p658; ⊘ 11am-2am) Part of the otherwise forgettable Chukit Resort complex, this fine bar extends over a long-tail harbour on the lip of Ao Ton Sai. In addition to bar stools with a supreme view, they have a pool table, live bands and a happy hour crowd. Don't worry, it's not that kind of karaoke joint.

Tee Cafe
CAFE

(Map p658; ⊘ 8am-4pm) They do crepes and salads, but we love this intimate Moroccan-themed cafe for its selection of coffee, tea and fresh-pressed juices.

ℹ Information

ATMs are spread thickly throughout the Tourist Village but aren't available on the more remote eastern beaches. Wi-fi is widely available, so Insta your hearts out. **D's Bookshop** (Map p658; ⊘ 7am-10pm), in the heart of the Tourist Village, sells new and used fiction and pours a decent espresso. **Phi Phi Island Hospital** (Map p656) offers some emergency care, but for anything truly serious, you'll be on the first boat back to Krabi. It's set beyond the beach bars from town on Ao Ton Sai.

ℹ Getting There & Away

Ko Phi-Phi can be reached from Krabi, Phuket, Ao Nang, Railay and Ko Lanta. Most boats moor at Ao Ton Sai, though a few from Phuket use the isolated northern pier at Laem Thong. The Phuket and Krabi boats operate year-round, while the Ko Lanta and Ao Nang boats only run in the October-to-April high season.

Krabi Boats depart from Krabi for Ko Phi-Phi (300B, 1½ hours) at 9am, 10.30am, 1.30pm and 3.30pm, and return at 7.30am, 10.30am, 1.30pm, 3.30pm.

Ao Nang Boats leave Ao Nang for Ko Phi-Phi (350B, 1½ hours) at 3.30pm and leave Ko Phi-Phi for Ao Nang at the same time.

Phuket From Phuket (250-350B, 1¾ to two hours), boats leave at 9am, 2pm, and 2.30pm, and return from Ko Phi-Phi at 10am, 3.30pm and 4pm.

Ko Lanta From Ko Lanta (350B, 1½ hours), boats leave at 1pm, 3.30pm and 4.30pm, and return from Ko Phi-Phi at 11.30am, 2pm and 3pm.

Railay For Railay (350B, 1¼ hours), take the Ao Nang–bound ferry.

ℹ Getting Around

There are no roads on Phi-Phi Don so transport on the island is mostly by foot, although long-tails can be chartered at Ao Ton Sai for short hops around Ko Phi-Phi Don and Ko Phi-Phi Leh.

Long-tails leave from the Ao Ton Sai pier to Hat Yao (100-150B), Laem Thong (800B), Hat Rantee (500B) and Viking Cave (on Ko Phi-Phi Leh; 500B). Chartering speedboats for six hours costs around 6500B, while chartering a long-tail boat costs 1500B for three hours or 3000B for the whole day.

Ko Phi-Phi Leh
เกาะพีพีเล

Rugged Phi-Phi Leh is the smaller of the two islands and is protected on all sides by soaring cliffs. Coral reefs crawling with marine life lie beneath the crystal-clear waters and are hugely popular with day-tripping snorkellers. Two gorgeous lagoons await in the island's interior – **Pilah** on the eastern coast and **Ao Maya** on the western coast. In 1999 Ao Maya was controversially used as the setting for the filming of *The Beach,* based on the popular novel by Alex Garland. Visitor numbers soared in its wake.

At the northeastern tip of the island, **Viking Cave** (Tham Phaya Naak) is a big collection point for swifts' nests. Nimble collectors scamper up bamboo scaffolding to gather the nests. Before ascending, they pray and make offerings of tobacco, incense and liquor to the cavern spirits. This cave gets its misleading moniker from 400-year-old graffiti left by Chinese fishermen.

There are no places to stay on Phi-Phi Leh and most people come here on one of the ludicrously popular day trips out of Phi-Phi Don. Tours last about half a day and include snorkelling stops at various points around the island, with detours to Viking Cave and Ao Maya. Long-tail trips cost 800B; by speedboat you'll pay around 2400B. Expect to pay a national park day-use fee (adult/ child 400/200B) upon landing.

It is no longer possible to camp on Phi-Phi Leh, but you can still visit Maya Beach at dusk and sleep on board a boat bobbing just offshore with Plankton Sunset Cruise (p655).

Ko Jum & Ko Si Boya
เกาะจำ/ เกาะศรีบอยา

Just north of Ko Lanta, Ko Jum and its neighbour Ko Si Boya have surprisingly little development; what's there is tucked away in the trees.

Ko Jum was once the exclusive domain of Lanta's *chow lair* people, but ethnic Chinese began arriving after Chairman Mao assumed power in the 1950s. At the time there were no Thai people living here at all, but eventually the three cultures merged into one, which is best sampled in the warm early morning, amid the ramshackle poetry of Ban Ko Jum, the island's fishing village.

Although technically one island, the locals consider only the flatter southern part of Ko Jum to be Ko Jum; the northern hilly bit is called Ko Pu.

🛏 Sleeping & Eating

Most accommodation options have on-site restaurants.

Bodaeng BUNGALOWS $
(☑ 08 1494 8760; Hat Yao; bungalow with shared/private bath 150/200B) A good old-fashioned hippie vortex with dirt-cheap lean-to wood and bamboo bungalows sprinkled in the trees. It ain't fancy – expect squat toilets in the corrugated bathrooms. It is open year-round and there's a restaurant too.

Siboya Resort HOTEL $
(☑ 08 1979 3344, 0 7561 8026; www.siboyabungalows.com; bungalows 350B, houses 600-1200B; @ 🕾) OK, Ko Si Boya's beach isn't spectacular. But the mangrove setting is wild and full of life, and the wood bungalows are large and tasteful. No wonder ever-smiling, secretive 50-somethings flock here like it's a retirees' version of Alex Garland's *The Beach*.

★ Woodland Lodge GUESTHOUSE $$
(☑ 08 1893 5330; www.woodland-koh-jum.com; Hat Yao; standard/family bungalows 1000/1500B) This place has tasteful, clean huts with polished wood floors and verandahs. The exceptionally friendly British–Thai owners can organise boat trips and fishing and have an excellent, sociable restaurant.

Koh Jum Lodge HOTEL $$$
(☑ 0 7561 8275; www.kohjumlodge.com; Hat Yao; bungalows 4500-5500B; 🕾🕾) 🍃 An ecolodge with style: imagine lots of hardwoods and bamboo, gauzy mosquito netting, potted orchids, Thai carvings, manicured grounds and a hammock-strewn curve of white sand out the front. It strikes that hard-to-get-perfect balance of authenticity and comfort.

🛈 Getting There & Away

From December to April, boats between Krabi and Ko Lanta can drop you at Ko Jum, but you'll pay full fare (400B, one hour). In the fringe months of November and May only the early boat will drop you. In the high season there's a

long-tail ferry to Ko Phi Phi (600B, 1½ hours) that leaves between 8am and 9am and picks guests up from the Hat Yao resorts.

There are also small boats to Ko Jum from Ban Laem Kruat, a village about 30km southeast of Krabi, at the end of Rte 4036, off Hwy 4. The boat (100B) leaves at 9am, 10am, 11.30am, 1pm, 2pm, 4pm, 5.30pm and 6.15pm, and returns the following day at 6.30am, 7.15am, 7.35am, 7.55am, 8.15am, 1.30pm, 2.30pm and 4pm. Private charters cost 1200B to 1500B.

If you plan to arrive in Ko Jum via Laem Kruat, make sure to call your guesthouse in advance so they can arrange your transfer from the pier. Otherwise, you may be relying on the kindness of drunk strangers with a motorbike (helmet not included). A handful of places on the main road in Ban Ko Jum rent out bicycles (100B), mountain bikes (130B to 150B) and motorbikes (250B) at standard rates.

Boats to Ko Si Boya (50B) make the 10-minute hop from Laem Hin, just north of Ban Laem Kruat hourly between 8am and 5pm. Call Siboya Resort to arrange transfer from the pier.

Ko Lanta เกาะลันตา
POP 20,000

Once the domain of backpackers and sea gypsies, Lanta hasn't just gentrified, it's morphed almost completely from a luscious southern Thai backwater into a midrange getaway for French, German and Swedish package tourists who come for the divine beaches (though the northern coast is eroding rapidly) and the nearby dive spots of Hin Daeng, Hin Muang and Ko Ha. Within eyeshot of Phi Phi, Lanta remains far more calm and real, however, and caters to all budget types. It's also flat compared to the karst formations of its neighbours and laced with good roads. A quick loop by motorbike reveals a colourful crucible of cultures – fried-chicken stalls sit below slender minarets, stilted *chow lair* villages cling to the island's east side, and small Thai *wát* hide within green-brown tangles of curling mangroves.

Ko Lanta is technically called Ko Lanta Yai, the largest of 52 islands in an archipelago protected by the Mu Ko Lanta Marine National Park. Almost all boats pull into Ban Sala Dan, a dusty two-street town at the northern tip of the island.

🔍 Sights

Ban Ko Lanta TOWN
Halfway down the eastern coast, Ban Ko Lanta (Lanta Old Town) was the original

port and commercial centre for the island, and provided a safe harbour for Arabic and Chinese trading vessels sailing between Phuket, Penang and Singapore. Some of the gracious and well-kept wooden stilt houses and shopfronts here are over 100 years old.

Pier restaurants offer a fresh catch and have views over the sea. There's a small afternoon market on Sundays, and if you're looking for hip, handmade goods, stop by **Malee Malee** (☑ 08 4443 8581; 55/3 Moo 2, Ban Ko Lanta; ⊙ 9am-9pm), a bohemian wonderland trading in silk scarves, journals, toys, baby clothes, paintings, handbags and silk-screened and hand-painted T-shirts. Prices are low and it's a fun browse. For quality hammocks don't miss **Hammock House** (www.jumbohammock.com; ⊙ 10am-5pm).

Ko Lanta Marine National Park NATIONAL PARK
(อุทยานแห่งชาติเกาะลันตา; www.dnp.go.th; adult/child 200/100B) Established in 1990, this marine national park protects 15 islands in the Ko Lanta group, including the southern tip of Ko Lanta Yai. The park is increasingly threatened by the runaway development on the western coast of Ko Lanta Yai. The other islands in the group have fared slightly better – **Ko Rok Nai** is still very beautiful, with a crescent-shaped bay backed by cliffs, fine coral reefs and a sparkling white-sand beach.

Camping is permitted on **Ko Rok Nok** and nearby **Ko Haa**, with permission from the national-park headquarters. On the eastern side of Ko Lanta Yai, **Ko Talabeng** has some dramatic limestone caves that you can visit on sea-kayaking tours. The national park fee applies if you visit any of these islands.

The **national park headquarters** is at Laem Tanod, on the southern tip of Ko Lanta Yai, reached by a steep and corrugated 7km dirt track from Hat Nui; túk-túk can take you there. There are some basic hiking trails and a scenic lighthouse, and you can hire long-tails here for island tours during the low season.

Tham Khao Maikaeo CAVE
(ถ้ำเขาไม้แก้ว) Monsoon rains pounding away at limestone cracks and crevices for millions of years have created this complex of forest caverns and tunnels. There are chambers as large as cathedrals that are dripping with stalactites, and tiny passages you have to squeeze through on hands and knees.

There's even a subterranean pool you can take a chilly swim in. Sensible shoes are essential and getting totally covered in mud is almost guaranteed.

Tham Khao Maikaeo is reached via a guided trek through the jungle. A local family runs treks to the caves (with torches) for around 200B. The best way to get here is by rented motorcycle, or most resorts can arrange transport.

Close by, but reached by a separate track from the dirt road leading to the marine national park headquarters, **Tham Seua** (Tiger Cave) also has interesting tunnels to explore; elephant treks run up here from Hat Nui.

🏃 Activities
Diving & Snorkelling
Some of Thailand's top diving spots are within arm's reach of Ko Lanta. The best diving can be found at the undersea pinnacles called **Hin Muang** and **Hin Daeng**, about 45 minutes away by speedboat. These world-class dive sites have lone coral outcrops in the middle of the sea and act as important feeding stations for large pelagic fish such as sharks, tuna and occasionally whale sharks and manta rays. Hin Daeng is considered by many to be Thailand's second-best dive site after Richelieu Rock, near the Burmese border. The sites around **Ko Haa** have consistently good visibility, with depths of 18m to 34m, plenty of marine life and a cave known as the Cathedral. There are also trips to the King Cruiser Wreck, Anemone Reef and Ko Phi-Phi.

Trips out to Hin Daeng and Hin Muang cost around 4500B to 5500B, while trips to Ko Haa tend to be around 3300B to 4000B. PADI Open Water courses will set you back around 14,000B to 17,000B.

Numerous tour agencies in the main tourist areas can organise snorkelling trips out to Ko Rok Nok, Ko Phi-Phi and other nearby islands.

Scubafish DIVING
(☑ 0 7566 5095; www.scuba-fish.com; Ban Sala Dan) One of the best dive operations on the island is located at Baan Laanta Resort (p667) on Ao Kantiang; there's also a small second office at the Narima resort. Unlike some of the large and impersonal operators based in Ban Sala Dan, Scubafish runs personable programs tailored to one's needs, including the Liquid Lense underwater photography program.

Ko Lanta

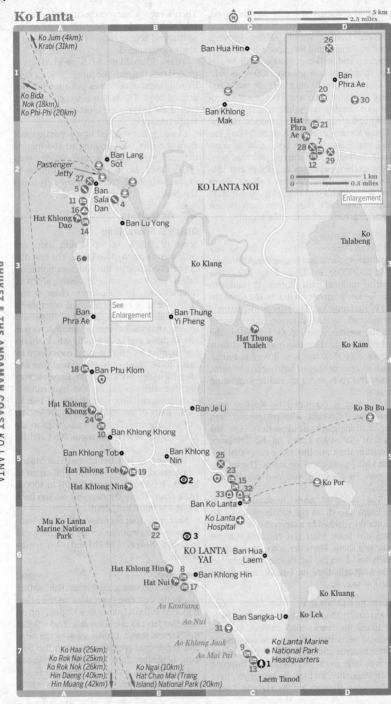

Ko Jum (4km);
Krabi (31km)

Ko Bida
Nok (18km);
Ko Phi-Phi (20km)

Ban Hua Hin

Ban Khlong
Mak

Ban Lang
Sot

Passenger
Jetty

27

5

Ban
Sala
Dan

4

11

16

Hat Khlong
Dao

14

6

Ban Lu Yong

KO LANTA NOI

Ko
Talabeng

Ko Klang

Ban
Phra Ae

See
Enlargement

Ban Thung
Yi Pheng

Hat Thung
Thaleh

Ko Kam

18

Ban Phu Klom

Hat Khlong
Khong

24

10

Ban Je Li

Ko Bu Bu

Ban Khlong Khong

Ban Khlong Tob

Ban Khlong
Nin

25

Hat Khlong Tob

19

23

15

32

Hat Khlong Nin

2

33

Ko Por

Ban Ko Lanta

Mu Ko Lanta
Marine National
Park

22

3

Ko Lanta
Hospital

KO LANTA
YAI

Ban Hua
Laem

Hat Khlong Hin

8

Ban Khlong Hin

Hat Nui

17

Ko Kluang

Ao Kantiang

Ban Sangka-U

Ko Lek

Ko Haa (25km);
Ko Rok Nai (25km);
Ko Rok Nok (26km);
Hin Daeng (40km);
Hin Muang (42km)

Ao Nui

31

Ao Khlong Jaak

Ko Ngai (10km);
Hat Chao Mai (Trang
Island) National Park (20km)

Ao Mai Pai

9

13

1

Laem Tanod

Ko Lanta Marine
National Park
Headquarters

Enlargement

26

Ban
Phra Ae

20

30

Hat
Phra Ae

21

7

28

29

12

Ko Lanta

The three-day dive packages (9975B) are quite popular.

Blue Planet Divers DIVING
(✆0 7566 2724; www.blueplanetdivers.net; Ban Sala Dan) The only school that specialises in free diving instruction.

Go Dive DIVING
(✆0 7566 8321; www.godive-lanta.com; Ban Sala Dan) One of the island's newest outfitters.

🎓 Courses

Time for Lime COOKING
(✆0 7568 4590; www.timeforlime.net; per class 1800B) On Hat Khlong Dao, this place has a huge professional kitchen with plenty of room to run amok. It offers cooking courses with a slightly more exciting selection of dishes than most cookery schools in Thailand; five-hour courses cost 1800B with substantial discounts if you take more than one class. Profits from the school help finance Lanta Animal Welfare.

⊟ Sleeping

Ko Lanta is home to many long stretches of beach packed with accommodation. Some resorts close down for the May-to-October low season, others drop their rates by 50% or more. Resorts usually have their own restaurants and tour-booking facilities that can

arrange island snorkelling, massages, tours and motorcycle rental.

The building boom means that in addition to the waterfront resorts suggested here, there are now dozens of good value roadside spots available, though views will probably leave you wanting. Reservations are a must in high season.

🛏 Hat Khlong Dao หาดคลองดาว

Once an outstanding 2km stretch of white sand with no rocks and perfect for swimming, erosion has gotten so bad that at high tide there is no beach here at all, just a sea wall. That's a big issue throughout northern Lanta.

Lanta Bee Garden GUESTHOUSE **$$**
(✆08 1606 6344; www.lantabeegarden.com; Hat Khlong Dao; bungalows with fan/air-con 800/1500B; ❄️❄️) A mix of concrete fan-cooled rooms with tinted windows, just off the main road, and newer air-con rooms in the two-storey annex, with burgundy accent walls, hot water and air-con. There is no beach here.

⭐ **Costa Lanta** HOTEL **$$$**
(✆0 7566 8168; www.costalanta.com; Hat Khlong Dao; r from 6800B; ❄️@🔊❄️) These Zen-like abodes are nestled in a coconut-palm garden laced with tidal canals at the north end of Hat Khlong Dao. Everything from the floors and walls to the washbasins is polished concrete;

the barn doors of each cabana open on two sides to maximise air flow.

The restaurant is stunning, as is the black spill-over pool at the edge of the sand. Discounts are available if booked online: the low-season rates are a steal.

Hat Phra Ae หาดพระแอ

The beach at Hat Phra Ae (Long Beach) is only mediocre, but the ambience is lively. A large travellers' village has set up camp here and there are loads of *fa·ràng*-oriented restaurants, beach bars, internet cafes and tour offices.

Hutyee Boat
GUESTHOUSE $

(✆08 9645 1083, 08 3633 9723; Hat Phra Ae; bungalows 350-400B) A hidden hippie paradise of big solid bungalows with tiled bathrooms and mini-fridges in a forest of palms and bamboo. It's behind Nautilus Bungalows.

Sanctuary
GUESTHOUSE $

(✆08 1891 3055; sanctuary_93@yahoo.com; Hat Phra Ae; bungalows 600-1200B) The original Phra Ae resort is still a delightful place to stay. There are artistically designed wood-and-thatch bungalows with lots of grass and a hippie-ish atmosphere that's low-key and friendly. The restaurant offers Indian and vegetarian eats and the Thai usuals. It also holds yoga classes.

Andaman Sunflower
BUNGALOWS $

(✆0 7568 4668; Hat Phra Ae; bungalows 850B; ☉Oct-Apr; ☎) A terrific collection of wood and bamboo bungalows with built-in platform beds, high palm-leaf ceilings, polished wood floors and glass bowl sinks in the bath. Set back from the beach, these are some of the best budget bungalows around.

Somewhere Else
GUESTHOUSE $

(✆08 1536 0858; Hat Phra Ae; bungalows 600-1200B; ☎) Big octagonal bamboo huts grace a shady lawn right on a very social and lounge-worthy stretch of beach.

Relax Bay
HOTEL $$

(✆0 7568 4194; www.relaxbay.com; bungalows with fan 1550-2100B, air-con 2450-4050B, luxury tents 2750B; ❄☎❀) This gorgeous French-run place is spread out over a tree-covered headland near a small beach. Its wooden bungalows sit on stilts with large decks; for a more unique experience sleep in a seaview luxury tent perched over the rocks on a wooden platform.

Hat Khlong Khong หาดคลองโขง

This is thatched-roof, Rasta-bar bliss with plenty of beach volleyball games, moon parties and the occasional well-advertised mushroom shake (imbibe at your own risk). Still, it's all pretty low-key and all ages are present. The beach goes on forever in either direction.

★ Bee Bee Bungalows
BUNGALOWS $

(✆08 1537 9932; www.beebeebungalows; Hat Khlong Khong; bungalows 900B; @☎) One of the best budget spots on the island, Bee Bee's super friendly staff care for a dozen creative bamboo cabins – every one is unique and a few are up on stilts in the trees. The on-site restaurant has a library of tattered paperbacks to keep you busy while you wait for your delicious Thai staples.

Where Else?
BUNGALOWS $

(✆0 756 67173, 08 1536 4870; www.lanta-where-else.com; Hat Khlong Khong; bungalows 300-800B) One of Ko Lanta's little slices of bohemia. The bungalows may be a bit shaky but there is great mojo here and the place buzzes with backpackers. The restaurant is a growing piece of art in itself. The pricier bungalows are all unique multilevel abodes sleeping up to four people.

Hat Khlong Nin หาดคลองนิน

After Hat Khlong Tob, the main road heading south forks: head left for the inland road which runs to the east coast, go right and the country road hugs the coastline for 14km to the tip of Ko Lanta. The first beach here is lovely, white Hat Khlong Nin. There are lots of small inexpensive guesthouses at the north end of the beach that are usually attached to restaurants – it's easy to get dropped off here then shop around for a budget place to stay.

Round House
GUESTHOUSE $

(✆08 1606 0550; www.lantaroundhouse.com; Hat Khlong Nin; r/bungalow/house 800/1000/2400B; ❄☎) A cute little find on the north end of this beach with three options. The wooden and bamboo bungalows are closest to the beach, just behind the breezy restaurant. They also have a cool adobe round house (hence the name) off the road and a nearby beach house perfect for families.

Sri Lanta

HOTEL $$

(☑ 0 7566 2688; www.srilanta.com; Hat Khlong Nin; cottages from 1800-6200B; ❄ @ 🛜 ⅏) 🏖 At the southern end of the beach, this decadent resort consists of minimalist wooden villas in wild gardens stretching from the beach to a landscaped jungle hillside. There's a very stylish beachside area with a restaurant, infinity pool and private drapery-swathed massage pavilions. The resort strives for low environmental impact by using biodegradable products and minimising energy use and waste.

🛏 Ao Kantiang อ่าวกันเตียง

This superb sweep of sand backed by mountains is also its own self-contained little village complete with minimarts, internet cafes, motorbike rental and restaurants. Much of the beach here is undeveloped, although there are lots of sailboats and motorboats anchored in the bay. It's far from everything; if you land here don't expect to move much.

Baan Laanta Resort & Spa

HOTEL $$

(☑ 0 7566 5091; www.baanlaanta.com; Ao Kantiang; bungalow pool/seaview from 2000/3000B; ❄ @ 🛜 ⅏) Landscaped grounds wind around stylish wooden bungalows and a pool that drops off to a stretch of white sand beach. The room's centrepiece is a futon-style bed on a raised wooden platform under a gauzy veil of mosquito netting.

★ Phra Nang Lanta

RESORT $$$

(☑ 0 7566 5025; Ao Kantiang; studios 2500-8500B; ❄ @ 🛜 ⅏) The gorgeous Mexican-style adobe concrete studios are huge and straight off the pages of an architectural mag. Interiors are decorated with clean lines, hardwoods and whites accented with bright colours. Outside, flowers and foliage climb over bamboo lattice sunshades, and the pool and lush restaurant-bar look over the beautiful beach.

🛏 Ao Khlong Jaak & Laem Tanod อ่าวคลองจาก/แหลมโตนด

The splendid beach at Ao Khlong Jaak is named after the inland waterfall.

Mu Ko Lanta Marine National Park Headquarters

CAMPING GROUND $

(☑ in Bangkok 0 2561 4292; www.dnp.go.th; with own tent per person 30B, with tent hire 225B, 2-/4-

room bungalows 1500/3000B) The secluded jungle grounds of the national park headquarters are a wonderfully serene and wild place to camp. There are toilets and running water, but you should bring your own food. You can also get permission for camping on Ko Rok or Ko Haa here. National-park entry fees apply.

The road to the marine national park headquarters fords the *klong* (canal), which can get quite deep in the wet season.

Baan Phu Lae

BUNGALOWS $

(☑ 08 5474 0265, 0 7566 5100; www.baanphulae. com; Ao Mai Pai; bungalows 800-1000B) Set on the rocks at the end of this tiny beach, the last before the cape, are a collection of romantic, canary-yellow concrete bungalows with thatched roofs, bamboo beds and private porches. The restaurant's rickety deck juts over the sea; they also arrange trips with Go Dive (p665), offer cooking classes and massage, and book transport.

★ La Laanta

BOUTIQUE HOTEL $$$

(☑ 0 7566 5066; www.lalaanta.com; Ao Mai Pai; bungalows 2800-6200B; ❄ @ 🛜 ⅏) Owned and operated by a young English-speaking Thai–Vietnamese couple, this is the grooviest spot on the entire island. Thatched bungalows have polished-concrete floors, platform beds, floral-design motifs and decks overlooking a pitch of sand, which blends into a rocky fishermen's beach. Set down a rutted dirt road, it's also the closest resort to the marine national park.

🛏 Ban Ko Lanta บ้านเกาะลันตา

There are a handful of guesthouses open for business on Lanta's oft-ignored, wonderfully dated and incredibly rich Old Town.

Sriraya

GUESTHOUSE $

(☑ 0 7569 7045; Ban Ko Lanta; r with shared bathrooms 500B) Sleep in a simple but beautifully restored, thick-beamed Chinese shophouse. Walls are black and the sheets are white. Angle for the street-front balcony room that overlooks the old town's ambient centre.

★ Mango House

GUESTHOUSE $$

(☑ 0 7569 7181; www.mangohouses.com; Ban Ko Lanta; suites 1500-3000B; ⊙ Oct-April) These 100-year-old Chinese teak pole houses and a former opium den are stilted over the harbour. The original time-worn wooden floors are still intact, ceilings soar and the house-sized rooms are decked out with satellite TVs, DVD players and ceiling fans. The restaurant is just as sea-shanty chic and serves Thai and Western dishes with panache.

✗ Eating

Ban Sala Dan has plenty of restaurants and minimarts. Don't miss the seafood restaurants along the northern edge of the village. With tables on verandahs over the water, they offer fresh seafood sold by weight (which includes cooking costs).

Beautiful Restaurant SEAFOOD $$
(✆0 7569 7062; www.beautifulrestaurantkolanta. com; Ban Ko Lanta; mains 100-200B; ✐) This is the best of the Old Town's seafood houses. Tables are scattered on four piers that extend into the sea. The fish is fresh and exquisitely prepared.

★ Lanta Seafood SEAFOOD $$
(✆0 7566 8411; Ban Sala Dan; mains 80-300B) The best option of the seafood-by-weight options. Order the *blah tôrt kà mîn* – it's white snapper rubbed with fresh, hand-ground turmeric and garlic, then deep fried.

Lym's Rice Bowl THAI $$
(Hat Phra Ae; mains 80-180, seafood dinners 450B; ⊙8am-10pm Oct-Apr; ✐) Authentic curries, noodles, soups and stir-fries are served under the casuarinas, right on the beach. At dinner time they also do fresh fish, steamed, grilled and fried. If you eat and drink here you are welcome to their beach lounges all day long.

Country Lao THAI $$
(✆08 5796 3024; Ban Phra Ae; mains 80-400B) A huddle of bamboo umbrellas and thatched pagodas on the main road notable for its house speciality: crispy papaya salad (150B). Green papaya shreds are battered and crispy fried. They're served in a heap alongside a bowl of lime dressing swimming with peanuts, green beans and juicy cherry tomatoes, and three tiger prawns. Your job: combine, devour.

Red Snapper INTERNATIONAL $$$
(✆0 7885 6965; www.redsnapper.lanta.com; Hat Phra Ae; tapas 35-295B; mains 295-525B; ⊙5-11pm Thu-Tue) A Dutch-run tapas restaurant on the roadside in Hat Phra Ae with a romantic garden setting. The duck breast with shiitake mushrooms comes highly recommended.

♥ Drinking & Nightlife

If you're looking for roaring discotheques, pick another island. If you want a more low-key bar scene with music wafting well into the night, then head to Hat Phra Ae, where you'll find a cluster of fun spots.

Same Same But Different BAR
(✆08 1787 8670; Ao Kantiang; ⊙8am-11pm) In a sweet seaside setting, you can sample middling Thai cuisine and sip cocktails beneath massive trees, thatched pagodas or in a bamboo chair sunk into the sand. The location is the thing.

Opium Bar NIGHTCLUB
(www.opiumbarkohlanta.com; Hat Phra Ae; ⊙from 6pm) This chic club has live music some nights, guest DJs and a big dance floor. It's still the top party spot on Lanta.

ℹ Information

Ban Sala Dan village has a number of internet cafes (1B per minute), travel agencies, dive shops and motorcycle rental joints. There are five 7-Elevens spread along the island's west coast – each one has an ATM.

Ko Lanta Hospital (✆0 7569 7085) Located 1km south of Ban Ko Lanta (Old Town).
Police Station (✆0 7569 7017) North of Ban Ko Lanta.

ℹ Getting There & Away

Most people come to Ko Lanta by boat or air-conditioned minivan. If you're coming under your own steam, you'll need to use the frequent **vehicle ferries** (motorcycle 10B, pedestrian 23B, car 170B; ⊙7am-8pm) between Ban Hua Hin and Ban Khlong Mak (Ko Lanta Noi) and on to Ko Lanta Yai.

BOAT

There are two piers at Ban Sala Dan. The passenger jetty is about 300m from the main strip of shops; vehicle ferries leave from a second jetty that's several kilometres further east.

There is one passenger ferry connecting Krabi's Khlong Chilat pier with Ko Lanta departing from Ko Lanta at 8am (400B, two hours) and returning from Krabi at 11am. It also stops at Ko Jum (for the full 400B fare).

Boats between Ko Lanta and Ko Phi-Phi technically run year-round, although service can peter out in the low season if there are not enough passengers. Ferries usually leave Ko Lanta at 8am and 1pm (300B, 1½ hours); in the opposite direction boats leave Ko Phi-Phi at 11.30am and 2pm. From here you can transfer to ferries to Phuket.

From around 21 October to May, you can join a four-island snorkelling tour to the Trang Islands and hop off with your bags at any destination you choose (350B). Boats stop on Ko Ngai (two hours), Ko Muk (three hours) and Ko Kradan (four hours).

There are also several speedboats that go from Ko Lanta to the Trang islands, the fastest being the **Satun-Pak Bara Speedboat Club** (☑ 08 2433 0114, 0 7475 0389; www.tarutao ipeisland.com) that stops in Ko Ngai (650B, 30 minutes), Ko Muk (900B, one hour) and Ko Bulon Leh (1600B, two hours) then continues on to Ko Lipe (1900B, three hours).

Tigerline (☑ 08 1092 8800; www.tigerline travel.com), a high-speed ferry, runs between Ban Sala Dan on Ko Lanta and Ko Lipe (1500B, four hours), stopping at Ko Ngai (500B, 30 minutes), Ko Kradan (750B, 1½ hours) and Ko Muk (750B, two hours). The service leaves at 1pm. The next day the same boat makes the return trip from Ko Lipe departing at 9am and arriving in Ban Sala Dan after noon.

MINIVAN

Minivans run year-round and are your best option from the mainland. Daily minivans to Krabi airport (300B, 1½ hours) and Krabi Town (250B, 1½ hours) leave hourly between 7am and 3.30pm. From Krabi, minivans depart hourly from 8am till 4pm.

Minivans to Phuket (500B, four hours) leave Ko Lanta every two hours or so, but are more frequent in the high season. There are also several daily air-conditioned minivans to Trang (300B, 2½ hours) and less frequent services to Khao Lak (500B, six hours), Ko Samui (800B including boat ticket) and other popular destinations.

❶ Getting Around

Most resorts send vehicles to meet the ferries – a free ride *to* your resort. In the opposite direction expect to pay 80B to 350B. Alternatively, you can take a motorcycle taxi from opposite the 7-Eleven in Ban Sala Dan; fares vary from 50B to 350B depending on distance.

Motorcycles (250B per day) can be rented all over the island. Unfortunately, very few places provide helmets and none provide insurance, so take extra care on the bumpy roads.

Several places rent out small 4WDs for around 1600B per day, including insurance.

TRANG PROVINCE

With its own set of jagged jungly karst formations and lonely islets in the crystalline sea, Trang is experiencing a tourist boom like neighbouring Krabi did several years back. Its shining stars are the constellation of fabled offshore isles known simply as the Trang Islands.

Trang Town ตรัง

POP 64,700

Most visitors to Trang are in transit to nearby islands, but if you're an aficionado of culture, Thai food or markets, plan to stay a day or more. It's an easy-to-manage town where you can get lost in wet markets by day and hawker markets and late-night Chinese coffee shops by night; at nearly any time of the year, there's likely to be some minor festival that oozes local colour.

Most of the tourist facilities lie along the main drag, Th Praram VI, between the clock tower and the train station.

◉ Sights

Trang is more of a business centre than a tourist town. **Wat Tantayaphirom** (Th Tha Klang) has a huge white *chedi* (stupa) enshrining a footprint of the Buddha that's mildly interesting. The Chinese **Meunram Temple**, between Th Wisek-kul and Th Ratsada, sometimes sponsors performances of southern Thai shadow theatre. It's also worth strolling around the large **wet and dry markets** on **Th Ratchadamnoen** and **Th Sathani**.

✦ Activities & Tours

Tour agencies around the train station and along Th Praram VI offer various tours around Trang. **Boat trips** to Hat Chao Mai National Park and the Trang Islands start at 750B plus national park fees. **Snorkelling** trips on private long-tails to Ko Rok (per person 1300B) and trips to local **caves and waterfalls** (1800B, maximum three people) by private car can also be arranged by most agencies.

🛏 Sleeping & Eating

Trang is famous for its *mǒo yâhng* (crispy barbecued pork) and *ráhn go·Ƀii* (coffee shops) that serve real filtered coffee. You can find *mǒo yâhng* in the mornings at some coffee shops or by weight at the wet market on Th Ratchadamnoen. To really get into the local scene, stay out late at the coffee shops along Th Ratsada.

Sri Trang Hotel
HOTEL $$

(☑ 0 7521 8122; www.sritrang.com; 22-26 Th Praram VI; r 640-840B; ❈ 🤶) There is a range of fan-cooled and air-conditioned rooms in this renovated 60-year-old building with high ceilings, a winding wooden staircase, groovy paint jobs, and wi-fi throughout. There's also a cafe-bar downstairs that's ideal for hanging out.

Rua Rasada Hotel
HOTEL $$$

(☑ 0 7521 4230; www.ruarasadahotel.com; 188 Th Trang-Phattalung; r incl breakfast from 2600B; ❈ 🤶 ⛱) Trang's slickest choice is a 10-minute (25B) túk-túk ride from the train station. The chic rooms have large tiles, comfortable beds and a dark mauve-and-grey colour scheme. It's a five-minute walk to Robinson's Shopping Mall and Cinema City.

★ Night Market
MARKET $

(btwn Th Praram VI & Th Ratchadamnoen; meals around 30B) The best night market on the Andaman coast will have you salivating over bubbling curries, fried chicken and fish, *pàt tai* and an array of Thai desserts. Go with an empty stomach and a sense of adventure. On Friday and Saturday nights there's a second night market right in front of the train station.

Asia Ocha
THAI $

(Th Kantang; meals from 35-40B; ⏱ 7am-10pm) In business since the mid-1940s, this place serves filtered coffee to an all-Thai clientele who sit at vintage marble tables in this antiquated building. Don't miss the food either – the roast duck is delectable.

ⓘ Information

You'll find several internet cafes and various banks with ATMs and foreign-exchange booths on Th Praram VI.

Post Office (cnr Th Praram VI & Th Kantang) Also sells CAT cards for international phone calls.

ⓘ Getting There & Away

AIR

Nok Air (www.nokair.com) operates daily flights from Bangkok (Don Muang) to Trang, but note that flights may be cancelled due to heavy rain. The airport is 4km south of Trang; minivans meet flights and charge 80B to town. In the reverse direction a taxi or túk-túk will cost 100B to 120B.

BUS

Buses leave from the Trang **bus terminal** (Th Huay Yot). Air-con buses from Trang to Bangkok cost 600B to 680B (12 hours, morning and afternoon). More comfortable are the VIP 24-seater buses at 5pm and 5.30pm (1050B). From Bangkok, VIP/air-con buses leave between 6.30pm and 7pm.

Other services include the following:

DESTINATION	FARE (B)	DURATION (HR)	FREQUENCY
Hat Yai	110	3	frequent
Krabi	90-115	2	frequent
Phang-Nga	200	3½	hourly
Phuket	240	5	hourly
Satun	110	3	frequent

MINIVAN & SHARE TAXI

Hourly vans heading to Surat Thani (180B, 2½ hours), with connections to Ko Samui and Ko Pha-Ngan, leave from a **depot** just before Th Tha Klang crosses the railway tracks. Several daily air-conditioned minivans between Trang and Ko Lanta (250B, 2½ hours) leave from the travel agents across from the train station. There are shared taxis to Krabi (150B, two hours) and air-conditioned minivans to Hat Yai (150B, two hours) from offices just south of the Trang bus terminal.

Local transport is mainly by air-conditioned minivan rather than *sŏrng·tăa·ou*. Minivans leave regularly from the depot on Th Tha Klang for Pak Meng (100B, 45 minutes), Hat Chao Mai (150B, one hour) and the Kuantungku pier (150B, one hour) for onward boat travel.

TRAIN

Only two trains go all the way from Bangkok to Trang: the express 83 and the rapid 167, which both leave from Bangkok's Hualamphong station in the afternoon and arrive in Trang the next morning.

From Trang, trains leave in the early and late afternoon. Fares are around 1480B/831B for a 1st-/2nd-class air-conditioned sleeper and 285B for 3rd class.

ⓘ Getting Around

Túk-túk and their drivers mill around near the train station and should charge about 30B for local trips or 250B per hour. Motorbike taxis charge the same price.

Motorcycles can be rented at travel agencies for about 200B per day. Most agencies can also help you arrange car rental for around 1500B per day.

Trang

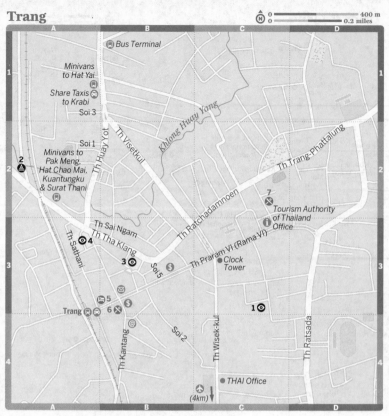

Trang Beaches

Think of limestone karsts rising from steamy palm-studded valleys and swirling seas. Trang's beaches are mostly just jumping-off points to the islands, but if you have the time, stop and enjoy the scenery.

Hat Pak Meng & Hat Chang Lang
หาดปากเมง/หาดฉางลาง

Thirty-nine kilometres west of Trang in Sikao District, Hat Pak Meng is the main jumping-off point for Ko Ngai. There's a wild-looking stretch of coastline here, and though the beach is scruffy, the backdrop – jutting limestone karsts on all sides that rival the best of Railay and Phi-Phi – is spectacular. The main pier is at the northern end of the beach and there are several seafood restaurants with deck chairs under casuarinas where Rte 4162 meets the coast.

Trang

Sights
1. Meunram Temple C3
2. Wat Tantayaphirom A2
3. Wet & Dry Market (Th Ratchadamnoen) B3
4. Wet & Dry Market (Th Sathani) A3

Sleeping
5. Sri Trang Hotel B3

Eating
6. Asia Ocha B3
7. Night Market C2

Tour agencies at the jetty organise one-day boat tours to Ko Muk, Ko Cheuk, Ko Ma and Ko Kradan for 750B per person (minimum three people), including lunch and beverages. There are also snorkelling day tours to Ko Ngai (750B) and Ko Rok (1200-1400B, plus national-park fees). Mask and

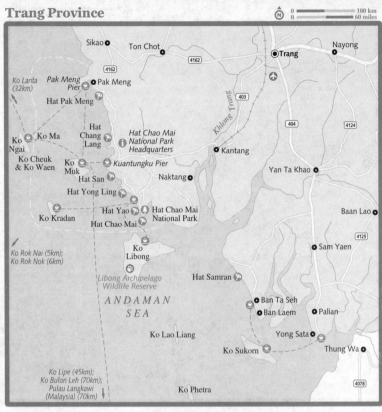

snorkel sets and fins can be rented by the pier for 50B each.

Hat Chang Lang is the next beach south from Hat Pak Meng and it continues the casuarina-backed beach motif. At the southern end of Hat Chang Lang, where the beachfront road turns inland, is the headquarters of **Hat Chao Mai National Park** (⤷0 7521 3260; adult/child 200/100B; ⊘6am-6pm).

The 231-sq-km park covers the shoreline from Hat Pak Meng to Laem Chao Mai and encompasses the islands of Ko Muk, Ko Kradan and Ko Cheuk plus a host of small islets. In various parts of the park you may see endangered dugong and rare black-necked storks, as well as more common species such as sea otters, macaques, langurs, wild pigs, pangolins, little herons, Pacific reef egrets, white-bellied sea eagles and monitor lizards.

🛌 Sleeping

National Park
Headquarters
CAMPING, CABINS **$**

(⤷0 7521 3260; www.dnp.go.th; camping with own tent 30B, with tent hire 200B, cabins 800B) Simple cabins sleep up to six people and have fans. You can also camp under the casuarinas. There's a restaurant and a small shop here, too.

Anantara Sikao
HOTEL **$$$**

(⤷0 7520 5888; www.sikao.anantara.com; Hat Cheng Leng; r from 5100B; ⓟ❄☎☲) Set on the northern edge of Hat Chang Leng, Anantara's glamorous yet hip vibe has refreshed these old bones (it was once an Amari Resort). Deluxe oceanfront rooms have wood floors, floating desks, flat-screen TVs and amazing views of Pak Meng's signature karsts.

There are impressive timber columns and Balinese wood furnishings in the lobby, and the view from the Acqua restaurant is jaw dropping. Take the free shuttle to its guests-only beach club on seductive Ko Kradan.

❶ Getting There & Away

Regular air-conditioned minivans from Th Kha Klang in Trang run to Hat Pak Meng (60B, 45 minutes) and Chao Mai (80B, one hour). Or you can charter a taxi from Trang for around 800B.

The Chao Mai National Park headquarters is about 1km off Rte 403, down a clearly sign-posted track.

There are several daily boats from Pak Meng to Ko Ngai (450B) at noon; they depart Ko Ngai at 8.30am. A long-tail charter is 1500B.

Trang Islands

The mythical Trang Islands feel like the lost fragments of the Andaman's iconic limestone that have tumbled into the sea. Most have pure white-sand beaches home to roving sea gypsies.

Ko Ngai   เกาะไหง (ไห)

The long, blonde, wind-swept beach along the developed east coast of Ko Ngai (often called Ko Hai) extends into blue water with a sandy bottom (perfect for children) that ends at a reef drop-off with excellent snorkelling. Coral and clear waters actually encircle the entire densely forested island – it's a stunning place. With no indigenous population living here, several spiffy resorts have the whole island to themselves. There is one dive centre (dives from 1500B), mask and snorkel sets and fins can be rented from resorts for 100B each, sea kayaks rent for around 150B to 180B per hour, or you can take half-day snorkelling tours of nearby islands (850B per person). Internet at the big resorts is slow and costs 100B to 150B per hour. Wi-fi is iffy.

Even though it's technically a part of Krabi Province, the island's mainland link is with Pak Meng.

🛏 Sleeping

Most places are decidedly midrange and come with restaurants and 24-hour electricity. The boat pier is at Koh Ngai Resort, but if you book ahead resorts on the other beaches will arrange transfers.

Ko Hai Camping   CAMPING GROUND **$**
(☑ 08 1970 9804; seamoth2004@yahoo.com; tent 500-600B) Big, clean fan-cooled tentalos on the beach have shared bathrooms and are

run by friendly Tu, who also manages the adjacent Sea Moth Dive Center.

★**Coco Cottages**   HOTEL **$$$**
(☑ 08 9724 9225; www.coco-cottage.com; bunga-lows 3600-4800B; ❀ 🖥) As the name suggests, these cottages are coconut extravaganzas with thatched roofs, coconut-wood walls and coconut-shell lanterns. Grab a sea-view fan bungalow if you can.

❶ Getting There & Away

Ko Ngai Villa runs the daily boats from Ko Ngai to Hat Pak Meng at 8.30am, returning to Ko Ngai at noon. Transfers cost 450B (1½ hours). You can also privately charter a long-tail to and from Pak Meng for 1500B, as well as Ko Muk (1500B) and Ko Kradan (1800B). Ko Ngai Seafood and Ko Ngai Villa are the best sources for long-tail charters.

In the high season, the **Tigerline** (☑ 08 1092 8800; www.tigerlinetravel.com) high-speed ferry runs between Ban Sala Dan (750B, 30 minutes) on Ko Lanta and Ko Lipe (1600B, four hours), stopping at the pier on Ko Muk, where you can connect to Ko Ngai. **Satun Pakbara Speedboat Club** (☑ 08 2433 0114, 0 7475 0389; www.tarutaolipeisland.com) is the more direct and comfortable choice from Ko Lanta (650B, 30 minutes). You can charter a long-tail to Lanta for 2000B to 2500B.

Ko Muk   เกาะมุก

Motoring into Ko Muk is unforgettable whether you land on the sugary white sandbar of **Hat Sivalai** or spectacular **Hat Faràng** (aka Hat Sai Yao, aka Charlie's Beach) where jade water kisses a perfect beach. Unfortunately, the lodging options aren't tremendous, and you won't be alone. Still, the west coast sunsets are glorious, it's easy to hop from here to any and every island in the province, and you may feel Ko Muk's topography stir something deep and wild within your primordial soul.

◉ Sights & Activities

Tham Morakot (Emerald Cave) is a beautiful limestone tunnel that leads 80m into a *hôrng*. No wonder long-gone pirates buried treasure here. You have to swim or paddle through the tunnel, part of the way in pitch blackness, to a small white-sand beach surrounded by lofty limestone walls; a piercing shaft of light illuminates the beach around midday. The cave features prominently on most tour itineraries, so it can get ridiculously crowded in the high season. Better to arrange a long-tail boat (600-800B) or rent a kayak (hour/day 150/500B) to zip over to the cave at daybreak or late afternoon when you'll have it to yourself – but note you can't get inside the cave at high tide.

Between Ko Muk and Ko Ngai are the small karst islets of **Ko Cheuk** and **Ko Waen**, both of which have good snorkelling and small sandy beaches.

Ko Mook Garden Resort rents out **bikes** (per day 100B) with maps for self-guided island tours, and you can also spend hours walking through rubber plantations and the island's devout Muslim sea shanty villages (please cover up).

🛏 Sleeping

Ko Mook Garden Resort   GUESTHOUSE $
(☏09 0703 3570; Hat Lodung; r 400-800B) Wooden rooms are large while bamboo bungalows are small and basic. Staying here means you'll be with a local family who take guests snorkelling, rent bikes (100B) and give out detailed maps of all the island's secret spots.

Pawapi Resort   BUNGALOWS $$
(☏08 6444 7543; www.pawapi.com; Hat Sivalai; bungalows incl breakfast from 1600B; ✳) The upscale bamboo bungalows here hover on stilts about 1.5m off the ground so that breezes ventilate the room from all sides and the insanely gorgeous view sits 180 degrees in front of you.

Sivalai   HOTEL $$$
(☏08 9723 3355; www.komooksivalai.com; Hat Sivalai; bungalows incl breakfast 4000-8000B; ✳🛜🏊) Straddling an arrow-shaped peninsula of white sand and surrounded by views of karst islands and the mainland, this location is mind-bogglingly sublime. Elegant thatched-roof cottages are almost encircled with glass doors so you can let in as much of the view as you want.

ℹ Getting There & Away

Boats to Ko Muk leave from the pier at Kuantungku. There are daily departures at 8am, 9am and 2pm (200-300B, 30 minutes), which make the return trip to the mainland an hour later; the early morning ferry is the cheapest. Minibuses to/from Trang (350-450B, one hour) meet the 9am and 3pm boats. Minivans to the Trang airport (550B) meet the 2pm boat only. You can charter a long-tail from Kuantungku to Ko Muk (800B, 30 minutes) and to either Pak Meng or Hat Yao (around 1200B, 45 minutes to one hour).

Long-tail charters to Ko Kradan (600B, 30 minutes) and Ko Ngai (1000B, one hour) are easily arranged on the pier or at the Rubber Tree Bungalow or Ko Yao Restaurant on Hat Farang.

From November to May, Ko Muk is one of the stops on the speedboats connecting Ko Lanta and Ko Lipe.

Lanta Garden Hill's (www.lantaisland tours.com; long-tail/big boat/speedboat 850/900/1500B) speedboat makes the Lanta–Ngai–Muk connection leaving Ko Muk daily at 10.30am.

Ko Kradan   เกาะกระดาน

Kradan is dotted with slender, silky white-sand beaches, bathtub-warm shallows and limestone karst views. There's a small but lush tangle of remnant jungle inland, where a short track leads past Paradise Lost over the ridge to **Sunset Beach**, a mostly wet and rocky beach with open seas in the offing, and a fun place to get a little beachside privacy.

Sadly, although the water is clean, clear, warm and inviting on Kradan, the coral structure has been decimated and the snorkelling is a major disappointment. Nevertheless, it is nice to splash, wade and swim here.

For internet and boat tickets go to Kradan Beach Resort, the biggest spread of mediocre bungalows on the main beach.

🛏 Sleeping

Paradise Lost   GUESTHOUSE $$
(☏08 9587 2409; www.kokradan.wordpress.com; bungalows with/without bath 1200/600B) One of the first places built on Kradan and still one of the best, this groovy, inland US-owned bungalow property has easy access to the island's more remote beaches. Small bamboo nests have solid wood floors and shared bathrooms. Larger bungalows are all wood and have private facilities, and dorms are on an open verandah.

The guesthouse's kitchen (dishes 120B to 1800B) is the best on the island.

Coral Garden   COTTAGES $$$
(www.coralgardenresort.com; cottages from 3000B) A rather stunning collection of spacious, multi-hued natural wood cottages decked out with floating queen beds, rattan wardrobes, recessed lighting and private pa-

tios, set at the wooded northwestern end of the island. Online reservations only.

ℹ️ Getting There & Away

Daily boats to Kuantungku leave at 9am and noon; tickets include the connecting minibus to Trang (450B). A chartered long-tail from Kuantungku will cost around 800B to 1000B one-way (45 minutes to one hour); you can also charter boats from Kradan to other islands within the archipelago.

Tigerline (☎ 08 1092 8800; www.tigerline travel.com) connects Kradan with Ko Lanta (850B, 1½ hours) and Hat Yao (1050B, one hour).

Ko Libong   เกาะลิบง

Trang's largest island is just 20 minutes by long-tail from Hat Yao. Less visited than neighbouring isles, it's a gorgeous, lush mountainous pearl wrapped in rubber trees, thick with mangroves and known for its captivating flora and fauna (especially the resident dugong). The island is home to a small Muslim fishing community and has a few resorts on the west coast. Libong's scruffy sweetness and backwater charm has a way of making you feel humble, grateful and open, if you let it.

🛏️ Sleeping

Le Dugong Resort   HOTEL **$**
(☎ 08 7475 8310, 08 7475 8310; www.libongresort. com; Ko Libong; bungalows 900B) The best digs are rustic yet stylish wood-and-bamboo bungalows with terracotta sinks, woven walls and shuttered doors that open the whole room to the sea and setting sun.

Libong Beach Resort   BUNGALOWS **$$**
(☎ 08 4849 0899, 08 9647 7030; www.libong beachresort.com; Ko Libong; bungalows with fan 800-1000B, air-con 2000B; ❄️@) There are several options here, from bland slap-up shacks behind a murky stream to beach-front and very comfortable varnished wood-and-thatch chalets. It offers a slew of trips, motorbike rental (300B) and internet access (per hour 100B); the **Jolly Roger Dive Center** is based here too. The kitchen rocks. Order the *tom yom ka min* (turmeric fish soup).

ℹ️ Getting There & Away

Long-tail boats to Ban Ma Phrao on the east coast of Ko Libong leave regularly from Hat Yao (20 minutes) during daylight hours for 50B per person; the long-tail jetty at Hat Yao is just west of the newer Yao pier. On Ko Libong, motorcycle taxis run across to the resorts on the west coast for 100B. A chartered long-tail directly to the resorts will cost 800B each way.

Ko Sukorn   เกาะสุกร

Sukorn is a cultural paradise of tawny beaches, light-green sea, black-rock headlands and stilted-shack neighbourhoods that are home to about 2800 Muslim inhabitants – their rice fields, watermelon plots and rubber plantations unfurl on narrow concrete roads. Cycle past fields occupied only by water buffalo, through pastel villages where folk are genuinely happy to see you and sleep soundly through deep black nights. Sukorn's simple stillness is breathtaking, its authenticity a tonic to the jaded, road-weary soul.

With few hills, stunning panoramas, lots of shade and plenty of opportunities to meet locals, renting a bike (150B) is the best way to see the island. Covering up is an absolute must when you leave the beach – be respectful of the locals.

NICE DAY FOR A WET WEDDING

Every Valentine's Day, Ko Kradan is the setting for a rather unusual wedding ceremony. Around 35 brides and grooms don scuba gear and descend to an underwater altar amid the coral reefs, exchanging their vows in front of the Trang District Officer. How the couples manage to say, 'I do,' underwater has never been fully explained, but the ceremony has made it into the *Guinness Book of Records* for the world's largest underwater wedding. Before and after the scuba ceremony, the couples are paraded along the coast in a flotilla of motorboats. If you think this might be right for your special day, visit the website www.trangonline.com/underwaterwedding.

🛏 Sleeping

Sukorn Cabana BUNGALOWS $$
(☑08 9724 2326; www.sukorncabana.com; Ko
Sukorn; bungalows 800-1500B; ❄@) Sloping
landscaped grounds dotted with papaya,
frangipani and bougainvillea hold large
and clean bungalows with thatched roofs,
varnished-wood interiors and plush veran-
dahs. The gorgeous beach has stunning
views over Ko Phetra.

★ Sukorn Beach Bungalows HOTEL $$
(☑08 1647 5550, 0 7520 7707; www.sukorn-island-
trang.com; Ko Sukorn; bungalows 1000-2200B;
❄🛜) Easily the most professionally run
place on this island, the concrete-and-wood
bungalows all have comfy verandahs and
a long swimming beach out the front from
which you can watch the sun set over outlying islands. The friendly Dutch and Thai
owners are chock-full of information, arrange excellent island-hopping tours and
offer guided tours of Sukorn (per person
350B).

Oh, and the food (mains 180 to 300B) is
the best in the Trang Islands.

ⓘ Getting There & Away

The easiest way to get to Sukorn is by private
transfers from Trang, available with the resorts
for 1850B per person. The cheapest way is to
take a *sŏrng·tǎa·ou* from Trang to Yan Ta Khao
(40 minutes, 80B), then transfer to Ban Ta Seh
(45 minutes, 50B), where long-tails (50B) leave
from the pier when full.

Otherwise, book a private taxi or *sŏrng·tǎa·ou*
from Trang to Ban Ta Seh (800B), where you
can charter a long-tail to Ban Saimai (300B),
the main village on Ko Sukorn. The resorts are
a 20-minute walk or 50B motorcycle-taxi ride
from Ban Saimai. You can also charter long-tails
directly to the beach resorts (750B).

From Ko Sukorn you can charter long-tails
to meet the high-speed **Tigerline** (☑08 1092
8800; www.tigerlinetravel.com) ferry that connects Lanta with Lipe.

SATUN PROVINCE

Until recently, Satun was mostly overlooked,
but that's all changed thanks to the dynamic
white sands of Ko Lipe – a one-time backpacker secret turned mainstream beach
getaway. Beyond Ko Lipe, the rest of the
province often passes by in the blink of an
eye as visitors rush north to Ko Lanta or
south to Pulau Langkawi in Malaysia. This
means, of course, that most people miss the
untrammelled beaches and sea caves on Ko
Tarutao, the rugged trails and ribbon waterfalls of Ko Adang and the rustic beauty of
Ko Bulon Leh.

Pak Bara ปากบารา

The small fishing community of Pak Bara is
the main jumping-off point for the islands
in the Mu Ko Phetra and Ko Tarutao Marine
National Park. Tourist facilities are slowly
improving as Pak Bara becomes increasingly
busy with tourists discovering these dazzling isles. The peaceful town has forgettable
sleeping options and, aside from the great
seafood, there's no pressing reason to stick
around.

The main road from La-Ngu terminates
at the pier where there are several travel
agencies, internet cafes, cheap restaurants
and shops selling beach gear. There's a
brand-new **visitors centre** (☑0 7478 3485)
for Ko Tarutao Marine National Park just
back from the pier, which is really more of
a massive passenger waiting terminal for
Lipe and Tarutao bound speedboats. You can
book Tarutao accommodation and obtain
permission for camping here as well. Local
travel agencies can also arrange tours to the
islands in the national park.

ⓘ Getting There & Away

There are hourly buses between 7am and 4pm
from Hat Yai to the pier at Pak Bara (100B, 2½
hours). Coming from Satun, you can take an
ordinary bus towards Trang and get off at La-Ngu
(70B, 30 minutes), continuing by *sŏrng·tǎa·ou* to
Pak Bara (20B, 15 minutes).

Air-conditioned minivans leave hourly for Hat
Yai (150B, two hours) from travel agencies near
Pak Bara pier. There are also minivans to Trang
(200B, 1½ hours), which connect to numerous
destinations such as Krabi (450B, four hours)
and Phuket (650B, six hours).

From 21 October to the end of May there are
several speedboats to Ao Pante Malacca on
Ko Tarutao and on to Ko Lipe. Boats depart
from Pak Bara at 11.30am, 2.30pm, 3pm and
sometimes 5pm (return 1300B, one hour); in
the reverse direction boats leave fro Ko Lipe
at 9.30am and 1.30pm only. From 16 November these boats also stop at Ko Adang for the
same price. For Ko Bulon Leh, boats depart at
12.30pm, arriving in Ko Bulon Leh one hour later
(return 800B), before buzzing on to Ko Lipe. If
you miss the Bulon boat, you can easily charter
a long-tail from local fishermen (2000B, 1½

hours). During the wet season, services to Ko Lipe are weather and demand dependent, but generally operate daily. All boats depart from the new national park office.

Ko Bulon Leh   เกาะบุโหลนเล

This pretty island, 23km west of Pak Bara, is surrounded by the Andaman's signature clear waters and has its share of faultless beaches with swaying casuarinas. Gracious Ko Bulon Leh is in that perfect phase of being developed enough to offer comfortable facilities, yet not so popular that you have to book beach-time days in advance.

The exceptional white-sand beach extends along the east coast from Bulone resort, on the northeast cape, to Pansand. At times the beach narrows a bit, especially where buffered by gnarled mangroves and strewn with thick sun-bleached logs. But those nooks and crannies make it easy to find a secret shady spot with dreamy views.

Bulon's lush interior is interlaced with a few tracks and trails that are fun to explore – though the dense, jungled rock that makes up the western half remains inaccessible on foot. Bulon's wild beauty is accessible on the southern coast at Ao Panka Yai, which is blue and laden with coral gravel. There's good snorkelling around the western headland, and if you follow the trails through remnant jungle and rubber plantations – with eyes wide lest you miss glimpsing one of Bulon's enormous monitor lizards – you'll wind your way to Ao Muang (Mango Bay), where you'll find an authentic *chow lair* squid-fishing camp.

Resorts can arrange snorkelling trips (2000B, four hours) to other islands in the Ko Bulon group for a maximum of six people, and fishing trips for 400B per hour. Bulone Resort also offers internet (per minute 3B), and battery-charging services for laptops (50B) and digital cameras (10B).

🛏 Sleeping & Eating

Most places here shut down in the rainy season (May to October). There are a few local restaurants and a small shop in the Muslim village next to Bulon Viewpoint.

Bulon Hill Resort   BUNGALOWS **$$**
(📞 08 6960 3890, 08 0709 8453; www.bulonhill.com; bungalows 1000-1500B) A collection of decent and spacious wooden and smaller bamboo bungalows stilted on the hill just inland from Bulone Resort. They are only open in high season.

Pansand Resort   RESORT **$$**
(📞 0 7521 1010; www.pansand-resort.com; cottages from 1800B; @) Pansand sits on the south end of the island's gorgeous white-sand beach. Brick-and-bamboo bungalows are fan cooled and come with sea views. The actual lodging isn't any better than elsewhere on the island – you're paying for a sublime location and a larger, organised resort setting. Cheaper wooden bungalows are set back in the trees.

Bulone Resort   HOTEL **$$**
(📞 08 6960 0468; www.bulone-resort.com; bungalows 2500-3500B) Perched on the northeast cape with access to two exquisite stretches of white sand, these cute wooden bungalows have the best beachside location on Bulon. Queen-sized beds come with iron frames and ocean breezes.

❶ Getting There & Away

The boat to Ko Bulon Leh (450B) leaves from Pak Bara at 12.30pm daily if there are enough takers. Ship-to-shore transfers to the beach by long-tail cost 50B – save yourself some sweat and ask to be dropped off on the beach closest to your resort. In the reverse direction, the boat moors in the bay in front of Pansand Resort at 9.30am. You can charter a long-tail from Pak Bara for 1500B to 2000B.

From November to May there is a daily speedboat (600B, one hour) from Ko Bulon Leh to Ko Lipe in Ko Tarutao Marine National Park. Boats, which originate in Ko Lanta and make stops in the Trang Islands, depart from in front of the Pansand resort at 3pm. It returns from Lipe at 9am.

Ko Tarutao Marine National Park
อุทยานแห่งชาติหมู่เกาะตะรุเตา

One of the most exquisite and unspoilt regions in all of Thailand, **Ko Tarutao Marine National Park** (📞 0 7478 1285; adult/child 400/200B; ☉ Nov–mid-May) encompasses 51 islands covered with well-preserved virgin rainforest teeming with fauna, and surrounded by healthy coral reefs and radiant beaches. Pressure from big developers to build resorts on the islands has so far (mostly) been ignored, though concessions were made for the filming of the American reality-TV series *Survivor* in 2001. And there is the minor issue of a private fishing resort on Ko Adang, which is supposed to be off-limits to developers. It was originally slated to open in 2010, but local environmentalists have

Ko Tarutao National Park & Around

PHUKET & THE ANDAMAN COAST KO TARUTAO MARINE NATIONAL PARK

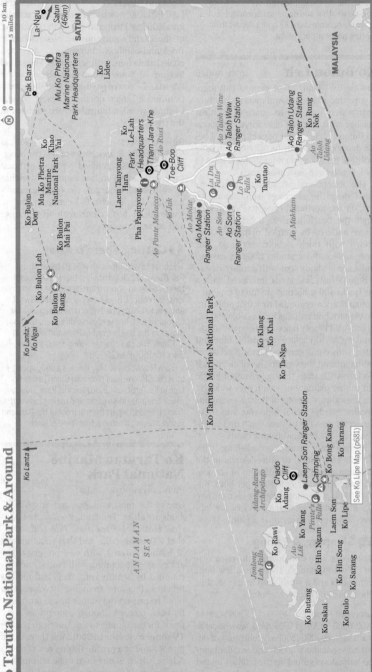

See Ko Lipe Map (p681)

appealed to the Thai courts to keep it shuttered.

Ko Tarutao is the biggest and second-most-visited island in the group. It's home to the park headquarters and government accommodation. Note that there are no foreign-exchange facilities at Ko Tarutao – you can change cash and travellers cheques at travel agencies in Pak Bara and there's an ATM at La-Ngu.

Many travellers choose to stay on Ko Lipe which, despite being part of the park, is fast becoming a popular and increasingly paved resort island with tourist facilities and bungalows aplenty. Curiously, the island has managed to evade the park's protection because it is home to communities of *chow lair* people, making it exempt from zero development laws.

Ko Tarutao เกาะตะรุเตา

Most of Ko Tarutao's whopping 152 sq km is covered in old-growth jungle, which rises sharply up to the park's 713m peak. Mangrove swamps and typically impressive limestone cliffs circle much of the island, and the western coast is pocked with caves and lined with quiet white-sand beaches. This is one of Thailand's wildest islands. The park entrance fee, payable on arrival, is 400B (200B for children).

Tarutao's sordid history partly explains its preservation. Between 1938 and 1948, more than 3000 Thai criminals and political prisoners were incarcerated here, including interesting inmates such as So Setabutra, who compiled the first Thai–English dictionary while imprisoned on Tarutao, and Sittiporn Gridagon, son of Rama VII. During WWII, food and medical supplies from the mainland were severely depleted and hundreds of prisoners died from malaria. The prisoners and guards mutinied, taking to piracy in the nearby Strait of Malacca until they were suppressed by British troops in 1944.

◎ Sights & Activities

The overgrown ruins of the camp for political prisoners can be seen at **Ao Taloh Udang**, in the southeast of the island, reached via a long overgrown track. The prison camp for civilian prisoners was over on the eastern coast at **Ao Taloh Waw**, where the big boats from Satun's Tammalang pier now dock.

Next to the **park headquarters** (Map p678) at Ao Pante Malacca, a steep trail leads through the jungle to **Toe-Boo Cliff** (Map p678), a dramatic rocky outcrop with fabulous views towards Ko Adang and the surrounding islands.

Ao Pante Malacca has a lovely alabaster beach shaded by pandanus and casuarinas. If you follow the large stream flowing inland through here, you'll reach **Tham Jara-Khe** (Map p678) (Crocodile Cave), once home to deadly saltwater crocodiles. The cave is navigable for about 1km at low tide and can be visited on long-tail tours from the jetty at Ao Pante Malacca.

Immediately south of Ao Pante Malacca is **Ao Jak**, which has another fine sandy beach, and **Ao Molae**, which also has fine white sand and a **ranger station** (Map p678) with bungalows and a camping ground. A 30-minute boat ride or 8km walk south of Ao Pante is **Ao Son**, an isolated sandy bay where turtles nest between September and April. You can camp here but there are no facilities. Ao Son has decent snorkelling, as does **Ao Makham**, further south. From the small **ranger station** (Map p678) at Ao Son you can walk inland to **Lu Du Falls** (about 1½ hours) and **Lo Po Falls** (about 2½ hours).

🛏 Sleeping & Eating

There's accommodation both at Ao Pante Malacca and Ao Molae, open mid-November to mid-May. Water is rationed, rubbish is (sporadically) transported back to the mainland, lighting is provided by power-saving lightbulbs and electricity is available between 6pm and 7am only.

The biggest spread of options is at Ao Pante Malacca, conveniently near all the facilities, where there are bungalows, simple longhouse rooms sleeping up to four people with shared bathrooms and **camp sites** (with/without tent rental 375/150B).

Ao Molae is quieter, much more isolated and arguably prettier. But that's splitting hairs. Basic and reasonably clean (but not spotless) one- and two-room **duplexes** (r 600-1000B) are right on the beach. Accommodation can be booked at the park office in Pak Bara. National park entry fees can be paid at Ao Pante Malacca or Ao Taloh Waw.

Camping is also permitted under casuarinas at Ao Molae and Ao Taloh Waw, where there are toilet and shower blocks, and on the wild beaches of Ao Son, Ao Makham and Ao Taloh Udang, where you will need to be self-sufficient. The cost is 30B per person with your own tent, or you can hire tents for 225B. Camping is also permitted on Ko Adang and other islands in the park. Note that local monkeys have a habit of going into tents and destroying or eating everything they find inside – shut everything tight.

The park authorities run **canteens** (dishes 40-120B; ☉7am-2pm & 5-9pm) at Ao Pante Malacca and Ao Molae. The food is satisfying, but you can find beer only at Ao Molae.

ⓘ Getting There & Around

Boats connecting Pak Bara and Ko Lipe stop at Ko Tarutao (450B each way, at least four times daily). Oddly, though, only the 9.30am boat directly from Lipe drops passengers at Tarutao. The island officially closes from the end of May to 15 September. Regular boats run from 21 October to the end of May. During the high season, you can also come here on speedboat day tours from Pak Bara for 2000B, including national park fees, lunch, drinks and snorkelling.

With a navigable river and plenty of long paved roads, the island lends itself to self-propulsion: hire a kayak (per hour/day 100B/300B) or mountain bike (50/200B) – or if it's just too darned hot, you can charter a vehicle (per day 600B). Long-tails can be hired for trips to Ao Taloh Udang (2000B), Ao Taloh Waw (1500B), and Tham Jara-Khe or Ao Son for around 800B each.

If you're staying at Ao Molae, take a park car (per person 60B) from the jetty at Ao Pante Malacca.

Ko Lipe เกาะหลีเป๊ะ

Ko Lipe is this decade's poster child for untamed development in the Thai Islands. Blessed with two wide white-sand beaches separated by jungled hills, and within spitting distance of protected coral reefs, five or six years ago the island was only spoken about in secretive whispers. But then the whispers became small talk, which quickly turned into a roar – you know, the kind generally associated with bulldozers. The biggest losers have been the 700-strong community of *chow lair* villagers, whose ancestors had been gifted Lipe as a home base by King Rama V in 1909. They eventually sold to a Thai developer with suspected mafia ties in the 1970s. Back in 2009, the big fear was that Lipe would become another Phi Phi. Those fears were stoked when a bass-heavy nightclub arrived on Hat Pattaya, but the club was shut down and those fears have mellowed somewhat.

Which is a relief, because there's still plenty to love, and love deeply, about Lipe.

The gorgeous white-sand crescent of **Hat Pattaya** on the southern coast has some terrific beach bars, seafood and a party vibe during the high season. Windswept **Sunrise Beach**, another sublime long stretch of sand, juts to the north where you'll have spectacular Adang views. A drawback of both of the busy beaches is the preponderance of long-tails that crowd out swimmers. **Sunset Beach**, with its golden sand, gentle jungled hills and serene bay that spills into the Adang Strait, has an altogether different feel and retains Lipe's wild soul. In between there's an ever-expanding concrete maze of cafes, travel agencies, shops and salons. More resorts are opting to stay open year-round.

There are no banks or ATMs on the island, though several of the bigger resorts can change travellers cheques and cash or give advances on credit cards – all for a hefty fee. Internet is available along the cross-island path for 3B per minute and a few places behind Sunrise Beach charge 2B per minute, though most hotels and several restaurants offer free wi-fi.

🏃 Activities

There's good coral all along the southern coast and around **Ko Kra**, the little island opposite Sunrise Beach. But be careful while swimming, especially in low season. A swimmer was killed when a long-tail ran him down in 2013. Keep your eyes open and don't expect boats to avoid you!

There are few experiences as relaxing as put-putting between jungled gems on board a long-tail. Most resorts rent out mask and snorkel sets and fins for 50B each, and can arrange four-point snorkel trips to Ko Adang, Ko Rawi and other coral-fringed islands for around 1500B (up to five people). The best way to see the archipelago, however, is to hire a local *chow lair* captain from the **Taxi Boat** (Map p681) stand on Sunrise Beach.

While it would be a stretch to call the diving here world class most of the year, it is outstanding when the visibility clarifies, somewhat counterintuitively, in the early part of the wet season (mid-April–mid-June). There are some fun drift dives and two rock-star dive sites. **Eight Mile Rock** is a deep pinnacle that attracts devil rays and the (very) rare whale shark. It's the only site in the area to see pelagics. **Stonehenge** is popular because of its beautiful

Ko Lipe

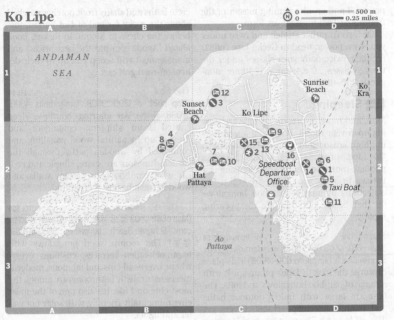

```
N          0 _____ 500 m
           0 _____ 0.25 miles
```

ANDAMAN
SEA

Sunset
Beach

Sunrise
Beach

Ko
Kra

Ko Lipe

Hat
Pattaya

Speedboat
Departure
Office

Taxi Boat

Ao
Pattaya

Ko Lipe

🟢 Activities, Courses & Tours

1 Castaway Divers	D2
2 Chao Shop Thai Massage	C2
Forra Dive	(see 6)
3 Sabye Divers	C1

🛏 Sleeping

4 Bila Beach	B2
5 Castaway Resort	D2
6 Forra Dive	D2
7 Forra Dive 2	C2
8 Forra Dive 3	B2

9 Gecko Lipe	C2
10 Mali Resort	C2
11 Serendipity	D2
12 Sunset Beach	C1
13 The Box	C2

⊗ Eating

14 Nee Papaya	D2
15 Papaya Mom	C2

🟢 Drinking & Nightlife

16 Pooh's Bar	D2

---

soft corals, resident seahorses and rare leopard sharks, and also because it resembles that (possibly) alien-erected monstrosity that inspired Spinal Tap's greatest work. **Ko Sorong** is another stunner with amazing soft corals, a ripping current and solar flares of fish.

On Sunrise and Pattaya beaches, French-run **Forra Dive** (Map p681; ☎ 08 4407 5691; www.forradiving.com; 2/3 dives 2500/3200B) is Lipe's least expensive choice. They offer snorkelling trips and have Lipe's only liveaboard dive operation. They visit Hin Daeng and Hin Muang, one of the best dives in Thailand on the way north to Ko Phi Phi. **Castaway Divers** (Map p681; ☎ 08 7478 1516;

www.kohlipedivers.com), based on Sunrise Beach, offers PADI and SDI training, and more intimate dive trips (two dives 2800B) off long-tail boats. **Sabye Divers** (Map p681; ☎ 08 9464 5884; www.sabye-sports.com) is the small Greenfins-certified shop on Sunset Beach owned by a long-time expat.

While it may look inviting, do not try to swim the narrow strait between Lipe and Adang at any time of year. Currents are swift and can be deadly.

After all that activity you may need a little recovery time. That's when you should find Kun Rund at **Chao Shop Thai Massage** (Map p681; 300B). She may be small but she's powerful and an unassuming master of the traditional Thai massage art form.

Or if you'd rather stretch and twist under your own power, head to Gecko Lipe (p682) for their twice daily yoga classes under the trees (classes at 6.45am & 7.30pm; non-guests 300-400B)

🛏 Sleeping

More and more resorts on Ko Lipe are staying open year-round. Book well ahead during high season and around Thai holidays. On Lipe, progress means big charmless package-tour type resorts are colonising Hat Pattaya in a big way. There are still a few collections of humble bamboo bungalows on that beach, but they are disappearing rapidly.

Forra Dive   BUNGALOWS $$
(Map p681; ☑ 08 0545 5012; www.forradiving.com; Sunrise Beach; bungalows 600-1400B) This place captures the look of Lipe's pirate spirit with a range of bamboo bungalows and lofts. The best are large with indoor-outdoor baths and hammock-strung terraces. Divers get 25% off lodging. There's a second location (Map p681) with similar bungalows on Hat Pattaya, and a new third location (Map p681) on Hat Sunset.

Gecko Lipe   BUNGALOWS $$
(Map p681; ☑ 09 0716 6883; www.geckolipe.com; small/large 1300/1950B; 🛜) Here is a wonderful hilltop collection of bamboo bungalows in two sizes nestled in the trees. The smaller white-washed varietal offers blonde floors and cold water baths. The shaggy haired, golden bamboo edition is larger and offers stylish hot-water baths and thicker mattresses. Expect deep discounts in the low season. They offer yoga classes here too.

Bila Beach   BUNGALOWS $$
(Map p681; ☑ 08 7570 3684; www.bilabeach.com; Sunset Beach; bungalow 1500B) A killer bamboo reggae bar and beachfront restaurant lurk below stylish cliffside, shaggy haired bungalows set above a private white-sand cove, which is strewn with boulders and adjacent to Sunset Beach. It's the perfect setting for your hippy honeymoon and a short jog over the hill from Pattaya.

Sunset Beach   BUNGALOWS $$
(Map p681; ☑ 08 7479 5326; www.lipesunsetbeach. com; bungalows 1800B; 🛜) Here's a refreshing collection of damn fine braided-bamboo bungalows with king beds, moulded concrete baths and shady front porches perched above the rocky far end of Hat Sunset, just before the curve to Mountain Resort. Book ahead (Agoda.com has the best prices) and management will scoop you up in their deluxe off-road golf cart.

The Box   HOTEL $$
(Map p681; d 1200-2900B, family units 4600-5200B; ❄🛜) An alluring boutique sleep crafted from shipping containers and dressed up in natural wood panelling and connected by wooden paths through the garden. Interiors are spare, simple and stylish with bamboo beds, accent walls and wooden wash basins. A great find.

Castaway Resort   HOTEL $$$
(Map p681; ☑ 08 3138 7472; www.castaway-resorts. com; Sunrise Beach; bungalows 3500-5000B; @🛜) The roomy wood bungalows with hammock-laden terraces, cushions everywhere, overhead fans and fabulous, modern-meets-naturalistic bathrooms are among the most chic on Lipe. It's also one of the most environmentally friendly, with solar hot water and lights.

Mali Resort   RESORT $$$
(Map p681; www.maliresortkohlipe.com; bungalows from 3800B) Chic and laid back, the gorgeous new bungalows at this rebranded, American-owned resort on Pattaya offer dark wood floors, thatched beamed ceilings, built-in day beds and huge outdoor baths with dual shower heads. They also have older and more affordable garden cottages with plush linens and flat screens.

All offer access to the stunning beach bar – the best on the island bar none – and an ideal slab of Pattaya beachfront.

Serendipity   BUNGALOWS $$$
(Map p681; ☑ 074 783 322, 088 395 5158; www.serendipityresort-kohlipe.com; bungalows from 4500B; ❄🛜🏊) An amazing new spot, isolated and set above the boulder-strewn southwest point of Hat Sunrise. They feature spacious dark wood, thatched bungalows with private patios, seating areas inside and out, brass bowl sinks, and some of the units have air-con. The Big Lebowski unit is their take on a penthouse suite and includes a private pool with a commanding view.

🍴 Eating & Drinking

Hat Pattaya's resorts put on nightly fresh seafood barbecues; Daya's is arguably the best. Cheap eats are best found at the roti stands and small Thai cafes along Walking Street.

For drinking, driftwood-clad Rasta bars are found on all beaches. At least some things never change.

Papaya Mom
THAI $

(Map p681; mains 80-160B; ⊙10am-10pm) Another cute Isan food stall between two beaches, notable for authentic eats popular with locals, like grilled spicy pork neck and *larb*. Meat dishes are so varied and succulent they may make an omnivore out of even the least-conflicted vegan. Okay, maybe not. Vegans can raid the luscious fruit stand.

★ Nee Papaya
THAI $

(Map p681; ☑08 7714 5519; mains 80-200B; ⊙8am-10pm; 🛜) Delightful Nee offers an affordable fish grill nightly, all the standard curries (including a dynamite *pá·naang* vegetable), noodles, stir-fries with beef, chicken, seafood or veggie, as well as a tremendous array of fiery Isan dishes. Ask for a *larb pla*, one of her new off-menu specialities.

She will tone down the spice upon request, but her food is best when spiced for the local palate, which is why she attracts droves of Thai tourists, who know what good is.

Pooh's Bar
BAR

(Map p681; ☑0 7472 8019; www.poohlipe.com; ⊙7am-10pm; 🛜) This massive complex was built by a Lipe pioneer and includes bungalows, a dive shop and several restaurants. It's a very popular local expat hang-out, especially in the low season. Each night it projects films onto its big screen.

ℹ Getting There & Away

From 21 October through to the end of May, several speedboats run from Pak Bara to Ko Lipe via Ko Tarutao or Ko Bulon Leh at 9.30am, 11am, 12.30pm and 2pm (550B to 650B, 1½ hours); in the reverse direction boats leave at 9.30am, 10am and 1.30pm. Low-season transport depends on the weather, but there are usually three direct boats per week. A boat charter to Ko Lipe from Pak Bara is a hefty 4000B each way.

Tigerline (☑08 1092 8800; www.tigerlinetravel.com) offers the cheapest high-speed ferry service to Ko Lanta (1700B, five hours), stopping at Ko Muk (1600B, 3½ hours), Ko Kradan (1800B, 3½ hours) and Ko Ngai (1600B, four hours). It departs from Ko Lipe at 9.30am.

You'll net up to 20% discounts when booked online.

The daily and more comfortable **Satun-Pak Bara Speedboat Club** (☑08 2433 0114, 0 7475 0389; www.tarutaolipeisland.com) speedboat departs from Ko Lipe for Ko Lanta (1900B, three hours) at 9am, stopping at Ko Bulon Leh (600B, one hour), Ko Muk (1400B, two hours) and Ko Ngai (1600B, 2½ hours). The same boat makes the return trip from Ko Lanta at 1pm.

No matter which boat you end up deciding to use, you will have to take a long-tail shuttle (per person 50B) to and from the floating pier at the edge of the bay. Yes, it's a minor inconvenience, but It's also part of a local agreement to share the flow. Though it's really more of a trickle.

Ko Adang & Ko Rawi
เกาะอาดัง/เกาะราวี

The island immediately north of Ko Lipe, **Ko Adang** has brooding, densely forested hills, white-sand beaches and healthy coral reefs. Lots of snorkelling tours make a stop here. Inland are a few short jungle trails and tumbling waterfalls, including the ramble up to **Pirate's Falls**, which is rumoured to have been a freshwater source for pirates. There are great views from **Chado Cliff** (Map p678), above the main beach, where green turtles lay their eggs between September and December.

Ko Rawi, a long rocky, jungled ellipse 11km west of Ko Adang, has first-rate beaches and large coral reefs offshore. Camping at Ao Lik is allowed, with permission from the national-park authorities. Excellent snorkelling spots include the northern side of **Ko Yang** and tiny **Ko Hin Ngam**, which has underwater fields of giant clams, vibrant anemones and striped pebble beaches. A legend has it that the stones are cursed and anyone who takes one away will experience bad luck until the stone is returned to its source. Even a short stop on the island will cost you the park's entrance fee (adult/child 200/100B).

Park accommodation on Ko Adang is located near the **ranger station** (Map p678) at Laem Son. There are new and attractive **bungalows** (3-9 people 600-1800B), scruffier **longhouses** (3-bed dm 300B) with attached bathrooms, and facilities for **camping** (Map p678; sites per person 30B, with tent hire 250B). A small canteen provides good Thai meals.

Long-tails from Ko Lipe will take you to Ko Adang and Ko Rawi for 50B per person, although you might have to do a little bargaining.

Satun

สตูล

POP 33,400

Lying in a steamy jungle valley surrounded by limestone cliffs and framed by a murky river, isolated Satun is a surprisingly bustling little city – the focal point of a province that's home to a quarter million people. Malaysia-based yachties, passing through for cheap repairs in Satun's acclaimed boat yard, are the only travellers who seem to hang around, but if you wander a bit before you leave, you'll see some interesting religious architecture, lots of friendly smiles and plenty of gritty charm.

⊙ Sights

Monkey Mountain   WALK

This jungled mound of limestone, teeming with primates, winds around **Spirit Rock**, a kitschy but locally beloved Buddhist shrine. You can also walk over a bridge to stroll through a stilted fishing village just a kilometre west of town.

Mangrove Walk   WALK

A self-guided walk along a boardwalk with a river viewpoint behind the football stadium. It's especially popular at sunset.

🛏 Sleeping & Eating

Chinese and Muslim bites can be scouted on Th Burivanich and Th Samanta Prasit.

On's Guesthouse   GUESTHOUSE $$

(☑ 0 7472 4133; 36 Th Burivanich; r with/without bath 750/650B) Satun's dynamic tourism matriarch, On, has redone an old downtown shophouse and turned it into a sparkling and affordable guesthouse with spacious rooms featuring wood furnishings, cute end tables and desks, and other homey touches. The second-floor room has a private bath down the hall, and good wi-fi connectivity. Cheaper rooms on the third floor share a bath.

Sinkiat Buri Hotel   HOTEL $$

(☑ 0 7472 1055; www.sinkiathotel.com; 20 Th Aphinurartumuluk; r with/without breakfast 1400/1200B; ❄🞬🛜🞬) Just five months old at research time, rooms are fresh and bright with granite desktops and wood floors, aircon and wardrobes, rain shower heads and flat screens. It's new, modern and a welcome addition.

Night Market   NIGHT MARKET $

(off Th Satun Thanee) Satun's popular night market comes to life around 5pm and serves great Thai curries.

The Kitchen   THAI, INTERNATIONAL $$

(☑ 0 7472 4133; 36 Th Burivanich; mains 100-300B; ⊗8am-10pm; 🛜) The ground-floor cafe in On's Guesthouse produces tasty pizzas and standard Thai mains, as well as popular steak dinners and a Thursday night poker

Satun

```
                              ⬡ 0        200 m
                              Ⓝ 0        0.1 miles
```

Monkey Mt Forest Park · Th Yatrasawat · Soi 5 · Th Satun Thanee · Soi 8 · Soi 6 · Khlong Bambang · Th Hatthakam Seuksa · Aphinurartumuluk · Th Burivanich · Th Phuminat · Th Siriwithi · Th Tirasathit · Soi 4 · Soi 1 · Th Samanta Prasit · Soi 6 · Soi 3 · Soi 8 · Soi 10 · 8 · (1.8km)

GETTING TO MALAYSIA

Keep in mind that Malaysia is one hour ahead of Thai time.

Ko Lipe to Pulau Langkawi

Getting to the border Tigerline (☎ 08 1092 8800; www.tigerlinetravel.com) and **Satun-Pak Bara Speedboat Club** (☎ 08 2433 0114, 0 7475 0389; www.tarutaolipeisland.com) offer daily trips to Pulau Langkawi (1400B, one hour) in Malaysia; departure is at 7.30am, 10.30am and 4pm. Head to the immigration office at the Bundhaya Resort in Ko Lipe ahead of time to get stamped out. In reverse, boats leave from Pulau Langkawi for Ko Lipe at 7.30am, 9.30am and 2.30pm Malay time.

At the border Visas are available on arrival for citizens of the US, EU and several other countries once you get to Langkawi and are good for up to 90 days. If you have questions about your eligibility, check with the Malaysian Embassy and apply for a visa in advance. There are no visa fees.

Satun to Kuala Perlis or Pulau Langkawi

Getting to the border Head to the **immigration office** (☎ 0 7471 1080; Th Burivanich; ⊗ 8.30am-4.30pm Mon-Fri) ahead of time to get stamped out. Boats to Malaysia leave from Tammalang pier, 7km south of Satun. Large long-tail boats run at 9.30am and 4:30pm daily to Kuala Perlis in Malaysia (300B, one hour). From Malaysia the fare is M$30.

For Pulau Langkawi in Malaysia, boats leave from Tammalang pier at 9.30am, 1.30pm and 4pm daily (300B, 1½ hours). In the reverse direction, boats leave from Pulau Langkawi at 8.30am, 12.30pm and 3pm and cost M$27.

At the border Visas are available on arrival for citizens of the US, EU and several other countries once you get to Langkawi and are good for up to 90 days. If you have questions about your eligibility, check with the Malaysian Embassy and apply for a visa in advance. There are no visa fees.

game, frequented by visiting yachties and young expat English teachers. Don't tell them we told you.

ⓘ Getting There & Away

BUS
Buses leave from the **bus terminal** (Th Samanta Prasit), 2km east of the town centre. Air-con services to Bangkok (800-1200B, 14 hours) leave at 7am, 7.30am, 3pm and 4pm. Air-conditioned buses to Trang (120B, 1½ hours) leave hourly. There are also a few daily buses to Krabi (250B, four hours) and Phuket (360B, seven hours). **Buses** to Hat Yai (70B, two hours) and local buses without air-con to Trang (85B, two hours) will stop and pick up passengers on Th Satun Thanee.

MINIVAN & SHARE TAXI
There are regular **minivans** to the train station in Hat Yai (80B, one hour) from a depot south of Wat Chanathipchaloem on Th Sulakanukoon. Occasional minivans run to Trang, but buses are much more frequent. If you're arriving by boat at Tammalang pier, there are direct air-con minivans to Hat Yai and Hat Yai airport (90B).

ⓘ Getting Around

Small orange **sŏrng·tǎa·ou** to Tammalang pier (for boats to Malaysia) cost 40B and leave from the 7-Eleven on Th Sulakanukoon 40 minutes before ferry departure. A motorcycle taxi from the same area costs 60B.

Understand
Thailand

Thailand Today

Thailand continues to ride a wave of prosperity. The standard and cost of living has increased, the coming ASEAN Economic Community (AEC) promises expanded business opportunities and tourism has discovered a new supply of visitors from China. Relations with its neighbours, especially once cloistered Myanmar, have never been better, enabling more open borders and trade. And the cities continue to modernise, replacing soot-stained shophouses with fashionable shopping centres filled with cafes and boutiques.

Best Non-Fiction Books

Very Thai (Philip Cornwell-Smith) Colourful photos and essays on Thailand's quirks.

Chronicle of Thailand (William Warren) History of the last 50 years.

King Bhumibol Adulyadej: A Life's Work (Nicholas Grossman et al.) The official biography of the king.

Best Thai Literature

Pisat, Evil Spirits (Seni Saowaphong) Deals with conflicts between the old and new generations.

Lai Chiwit (Many Lives; by Kukrit Pramoj) A collection of short stories.

Monsoon Country (Pira Sudham) Brilliantly captures the northeast's struggles against nature and nurture.

The Judgement (Chart Korbjitti) A drama about a young village man wrongly accused of a crime.

Jasmine Nights (SP Somtow) An upbeat coming-of-age novel that fuses traditional ideas with modern Thai pop culture.

Married to the Demon King (Sri Doruang) Adapts the *Ramayana* into modern Bangkok.

The Post Coup Years

Though Thaksin Shinawatra was removed from the prime minister's position by a military coup in 2006 and later self-exiled from the country, he still exerts a sunlike gravitational pull on Thailand's political process. His politically allied party, Puea Thai, won a clear majority of parliamentary seats in 2011, and his sister Yingluck Shinawatra was elected prime minister. She is Thailand's first female prime minister and this is the fifth straight electoral win for a Thaksin-backed political party. She is often viewed as a proxy for her brother and Thais refer to the brother and sister as one and the same, rarely distinguishing between the two. Despite the unusual balance of power, Yingluck's administration has brought about a degree of political unity with the military and could finish its term without the interference of a coup, a meaningful milestone in Thai politics.

Meanwhile, the legislature has spent two years debating the details of the so-called amnesty bill that would allow Thaksin to return to the country by absolving him of criminal charges, which he is now evading through self-imposed exile. The bill, which would also pardon government officials who ordered the 2010 military crackdown on civilian (Red Shirt) demonstrators, passed the lower house. The Senate ultimately rejected the bill but it is unclear if amnesty is dead or just resting. There was also a related political manoeuvre to ensure a more supportive legislature for Thaksin and his allies by changing the make-up of the Senate to a fully elected body, but the charter amendment was rejected by the constitutional court. Pro- and anti-government groups (sporting bells and whistles, respectively) have once again flooded the streets of Bangkok.

As a concession to the anti-government protestors, prime minister Yingluck called for new elections in February 2014 but this gesture did little to solve the political stalemate as Thaksin-allied politicians handily win the popular vote. Instead anti-government groups see reforms of democracy as the only solution for their persistent Thaksin problem. By staging large-scale political demonstrations, anti-government groups hope to provoke the military to stage a coup in an attempt to restore peace and order. In January 2014, protestors organised as the People's Democratic Reform Committee (PDRC) staged nearly a dozen rallies at key intersections and important government buildings designed to shutdown Bangkok. As this book was going to press, the outcome of the so-called Bangkok Shutdown was uncertain, but many European nations issued travel warnings to their citizens to avoid travel in Bangkok during the shutdown. It is imperative to monitor to the situation and to avoid any political demonstrations as violence does occur.

Other major hurdles for Yingluck's administration were the record-setting 2011 floods that spread from the north through the manufacturing centres surrounding Bangkok and beyond. International factories producing cars and computer drives suspended operations during the floods and suffered damage to their factories. The most iconic image of the natural disaster was submerged planes on the tarmac of Bangkok's second airport, Don Muang, designated a flood-relief centre. By 2012, though, manufacturing had recovered and international investors remain committed to Thailand for its skilled workforce and technology, according to a *Wall Street Journal* article. Flood mitigation projects totalling US$11.7 billion were allocated by the government.

Thailand has also lost ground as one of the world's leading rice exporters thanks to an ill-fated government scheme to boost rice revenues by buying the domestic product at 50% above market value, hoping that market prices would follow. Instead India and Vietnam supplied the missing inventory at lower prices, leaving Thailand with stockpiles of an overvalued product and billions of dollars in subsidies. The scheme was designed to boost incomes for rural rice farmers, a strong political base for the Puea Thai party.

Hello, Neighbour

At the end of 2015, the ASEAN Economic Community (AEC) will unite the association's 10 Southeast Asian countries into a liberalised marketplace where goods, services, capital and labour are shared across borders with little or no country-specific impediments. In theory the AEC will make it easier to buy and sell goods, hire non-nationals and invest within ASEAN. Each member country is required to meet certain standards in order to comply with AEC agreements. Thailand is completing work on two new Mekong River bridges to facilitate trade with Laos and has worked with Myanmar for open borders. It is anticipated that the Thailand–Cambodia border of Aranya Prathet–Poipet will see a business boom for trade between the two countries.

POPULATION: **67.4 MILLION**

AREA: **513,120 SQ KM**

GDP: **US$662.6 BILLION**

GDP PER CAPITA: **US$10,300**

UNEMPLOYMENT: **0.7%**

LIVING IN POVERTY: **13.2%**

if Thailand were 100 people

75 would be Thai
14 would be Chinese
11 would be Other

belief systems
(% of population)

95 Buddhist
5 Muslim
1 Christian

population per sq km

THAILAND   USA   UK

≈ 33 people

But there are still impediments ranging from restrictive labour codes (Thai law excludes non-nationals from 39 occupations), undeveloped infrastructure (in countries like Laos, Cambodia and Myanmar) and language barriers. Thailand is expected to benefit from its proximity and ties to Myanmar for future business investments, but critics are concerned that the kingdom lags behind its neighbours in English and Chinese language skills, making it less competitive in the common pool. Many analysts cite the EU as a model, but it is unclear how effective a single market will be in a region with greater disparity.

Riding the Wealth Wave

Smartphones everywhere, cars instead of motorcycles and the need for immigrant labour – there is no doubt about it, Thailand is getting richer. In 2011, the World Bank upgraded the country's category from a lower-middle economy to an upper-middle income economy, a designation based on gross national income (GNI) per capita. Thailand's GNI is US$4210, almost double what it was a decade ago.

Certainly there have been huge gains at the top of the economic heap. Ten Thais (up from five) now rank on *Forbes*' 2013 list of global billionaires. The richest residents of Thailand are 16% richer than they were a year ago (combined wealth increased from US$95 billion to US$110 billion), representing Southeast Asia's biggest wealth gain. The combined wealth of Thailand's top families equals 12% of GDP.

Though not an equitable jump, the rise in prosperity has not been limited to the elites. Thailand's poverty rate in 2011 was 13.2%, continuing a downward trend from 42.6% in 2000. Disparity of wealth persists in rural areas, especially in the north and northeast, where about 88% of the country's poor live. Another metric is the Gini coefficient, which measures income equality (based on a scale of 0, perfect equality, to 100, perfect inequality). Inequality is shrinking in Thailand sitting at a score of 39.4 in 2010. This score gains it few global bragging rights, but it does represent a steady improvement from 2000 when it was 43.

Making good on one of her campaign promises, Yingluck passed a minimum wage hike to 300B per day. Though the increase hurt small and mid-sized labour-intensive factories, the unemployment rate remains extremely low at 0.7% in 2012 and economic growth remains strong at 5% for 2013. Thai workers might earn more, but costs have also risen: cooking gas, fuel, utilities and food items have all increased in price. A bowl of noodles in Bangkok now costs 60B instead of 40B two years ago. Household debt has also increased thanks to easier access to credit cards and tax rebates on first-time car purchases, introduced to spur domestic spending after the 2011 floods. Due to a combination of factors, Thais have a higher standard of living than a decade ago.

History & Politics

Thai history begins as a story of migrants heading into a frontier land claimed by distant empires for trade, forced labour and patronage. Eventually the nascent country develops its own powerful entities that unite feuding localities and begins to fuse a national identity around language, religion and monarchy. The kings resist colonisation from the expansionist Western powers on its border only to cede their absolute grip on the country when challenged from forces within. Since the transition to a constitutional monarchy in 1932, the military predominantly rules the country with a few democratic hiccups in between.

History

Ancient History

Little evidence remains of the cultures that existed in Thailand before the middle of the 1st millennium AD. *Homo erectus* fossils in Thailand's northern province of Lampang date back at least 500,000 years, and the country's most important archaeological site is Ban Chiang, outside Udon Thani, which provides evidence of one of the world's oldest agrarian societies. It is believed that the Mekong River Valley and Khorat Plateau were inhabited as far back as 10,000 years ago by farmers and bronze-workers. Cave paintings in Pha Taem National Park near Ubon Ratchathani date back some 3000 years.

Early Empires

Starting around the 10th century, the 'Tai' people, considered to be the ancestors of the contemporary Thais, began migrating from southern China into present-day Southeast Asia. These immigrants spoke Tai-Kadai, said to be the most significant ethno-linguistic group in Southeast Asia. Some settled in the river valleys of modern-day Thailand while others chose parts of modern-day Laos and the Shan state of Burma (present-day Myanmar).

They settled in villages as farmers, hunters and traders and organised themselves into administrative units known as *meu·ang,* under the rule of a lord, that became the building blocks of the Tai state. Over time, the

> Relief carvings at Angkor Wat depict Tai mercenaries serving in Khmer armies. The Khmer called them 'Syam'. The name was transliterated to 'Siam' by the English trader James Lancaster in 1592.

TIMELINE	4000–2500 BC	6th–11th centuries	9th–13th centuries
	Prehistoric people develop pottery, rice cultivation and bronze metallurgy in northeastern Thailand.	Dvaravati establish city-states in central Thailand, develop trade routes and Mon culture and practise Theravada Buddhism.	Angkor extends control across parts of Thailand, building Hindu-Buddhist sanctuaries.

Tai expanded from the northern mountain valleys into the central plains and northeastern plateau, where there existed several important trading centres ruled by various indigenous and 'foreign' empires, including the Mon-Dvaravati, Khmer (Cambodia) and Srivijaya (Malay).

Dvaravati

The Mon dominated parts of Burma, western Thailand and into the central plains. In the 6th to 9th centuries, the Dvaravati culture emerged as a distinct Buddhist culture associated with the Mon people. Little is known about this period but it is believed that Nakhon Pathom might have been the centre, and that overland trade routes extended to Burma, Cambodia, Chiang Mai and Laos as evidenced by findings of distinctive Dvaravati Buddha images, temples and stone inscriptions in the Mon language.

The Dvaravati was one of many Indian-influenced cultures that established themselves in Southeast Asia, but scholars single out the Dvaravati because of its artistic legacy and the trade routes that might have provided an early framework for what would become the core of the modern-day Thai state.

Khmer

The Khmers were Southeast Asia's equivalent of the Roman Empire. This kingdom became famous for its extravagant sculpture and architecture and had a profound effect on the art and religion of the region. Established in the 9th century, the Khmer kingdom built its capital in Angkor (modern-day Cambodia) and expanded westward across present-day central and northeastern Thailand. Administrative centres anchored by Angkor-style temples were built in Lopburi (then known as Lavo), Sukhothai and Phimai (near Nakhon Ratchasima) and linked by road to the capital.

The Khmer's large-scale construction projects were a symbol of imperial power in its frontier lands and examples of the day's most advanced technologies. Khmer elements – Hinduism, Brahmanism, Theravada Buddhism and Mahayana Buddhism – mark this period in Thailand.

Srivijaya

While mainland Thailand was influenced by forces from the north and west, the Malay Peninsula was economically and culturally fused to cultures further south. Between the 8th and 13th centuries, the Malay Peninsula was under the sway of the confederation of the Srivijaya, which controlled maritime trade between the South China Sea and Indian Ocean. The Srivijaya capital is believed to have been in Palembang on Sumatra.

King Naresuan is portrayed as a national hero and became a cult figure, especially worshipped by the Thai army. His story inspired a high-budget, blockbuster film trilogy, *King Naresuan*, funded in part by the Thai government.

In 1868 King Mongkut (Rama IV) abolished a husband's right to sell his wife or her children without her permission. The older provision, it was said, treated the woman 'as if she were a water buffalo'.

10th century	1240–1438
Arrival of Tai peoples in Thailand.	Approximate dates of Sukhothai kingdom.

➜ Ruins at Sukhothai Historical Park (p354)

Of the series of Srivijaya city-states along the Malay Peninsula, Tambralinga established its capital near present-day Nakhon Si Thammarat and adopted Buddhism in the 13th century, while the states further south adopted Islam, creating a religious boundary which persists to this day. Remains of Srivijaya culture can be seen around Chaiya and Nakhon Si Thammarat. Many art forms of the Srivijaya kingdom – such as *năng dà·lung* (shadow theatre) and *lá·kon* (classical dance-drama) – persist today.

Emerging Tai Kingdoms

In the 13th century, the regional empires started to decline and prosperous Tai city-states emerged with localised power and military might. The competing city-states were ultimately united into various kingdoms that began to establish a Thai identity. Scholars recognise Lanna, Sukhothai and Ayuthaya as the unifying kingdoms of the period.

> Phibul Song-khram officially changed the name of the country in 1939 from Siam to Prathet Thai (or 'Thailand' in English); it was considered an overt nationalistic gesture intended to unite all the Tai-speaking people.

Lanna

The Lanna kingdom, based in northern Thailand, dates its formation to the upper Mekong River town of Chiang Saen in the middle of the 12th century by King Mengrai. He migrated south to Chiang Mai (meaning 'New City') in 1292 to establish his capital. The king was a skilled diplomat and forged important alliances with potential rivals, such as King Ngam Muang of Phayao and King Ramkhamhaeng of Sukhothai; a bronze statue commemorating this confederation stands in Chiang Mai today. King Mengrai is also credited for successfully repulsing the Mongol invasions in the early 14th century.

The Lanna kingdom is recognised for its royal patronage of the Sinhalese tradition of Theravada Buddhism that is now widely practised in Thailand and of the distinctive northern Thai culture of the region. The Lanna kingdom didn't experience an extensive expansion period as it was plagued by dynastic intrigues and wars with rival powers.

RAMKHAMHAENG'S STONE INSCRIPTION

In an inscription of 1292, King Ramkhamhaeng gives a picture of his kingdom as idyllic and free of constraints, and of himself as a benevolent patriarch:

In the time of King Ramkhamhaeng this land of Sukhothai is thriving. There are fish in the water and rice in the fields...whoever wants to trade in elephants, does so; whoever wants to trade in horses, does so;...if any commoner in the land has a grievance...it is easy; he goes and strikes the bell which the king has hung there; King Ramkhamhaeng... hears the call; he goes and questions the man, examines the case, and decides it justly for him.

Translation by AB Griswold and Prasert Na Nagara, Journal of the Siam Society (July 1971)

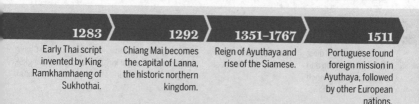

1283	1292	1351–1767	1511
Early Thai script invented by King Ramkhamhaeng of Sukhothai.	Chiang Mai becomes the capital of Lanna, the historic northern kingdom.	Reign of Ayuthaya and rise of the Siamese.	Portuguese found foreign mission in Ayuthaya, followed by other European nations.

Sukhothai

During the 13th century, several principalities in the central plains united and wrested control from the dying Khmer empire, making their new capital at Sukhothai (meaning 'Rising of Happiness'). Thais consider Sukhothai the first true Thai kingdom and the period is recognised as an artistic and cultural awakening.

The most revered of the Sukhothai kings was Ramkhamhaeng, who is credited for developing the modern Thai writing system, which is based on Indian, Mon and Khmer scripts. He also established Theravada Buddhism as the official religion.

In its prime, the Sukhothai kingdom extended as far as Nakhon Si Thammarat in the south, to the upper Mekong River Valley in Laos and to Bago (Pegu) in southern Burma. For a short time (1448–86), the Sukhothai capital was moved to Phitsanulok, but by that time another star was rising in Thailand, the kingdom of Ayuthaya.

Ayuthaya

In the mid-14th century, the Ayuthaya kingdom began to dominate the Chao Phraya River basin during the twilight of the Khmer period. It survived for 416 years, defining itself as Siam's most important kingdom with an expansive sphere of influence (including much of the former

FREE NOT TO SPEAK

Press intimidation in Thailand is made easier because of the country's lèse-majesté laws – causing offence against the dignity of the monarchy – which carries a jail term of between three and 15 years. Often the media exercises self-censorship with regard to the monarchy, mainly out of respect for the crown, but also out of fear of political retribution.

Filing of lèse-majesté charges has increased since 2006 against media, academics and political figures. Even average citizens are vulnerable: charges have been filed against a Thai Facebook user who posted a negative comment about the king and an overseas Thai with US citizenship who posted translations of a banned book about the king on his blog. The most recent high-profile conviction has been Sondhi Limthongkul, a former media tycoon who led the charge against the then prime minister Thaksin Shinawatra via the now defunct People's Alliance for Democracy (aka Yellow Shirts). The court found that Sondhi told his supporters at a rally about remarks made by the opposition Red Shirt leader; repeating these monarchy-defaming comments earned him a two-year prison sentence. The original Red Shirt commentator received a 15-year sentence though she plans to petition for a royal pardon after five years.

1688	1767	1768	1782
King Narai dies; Palace Revolution and expulsion of the French follows.	Ayuthaya is sacked by the Burmese.	King Taksin establishes a new capital in Thonburi.	Founding of the Chakri dynasty and Bangkok as the new capital.

Khmer empire) and a fundamental role in organising the modern Thai state and social structure.

With a strategic island location formed by encircling rivers, Ayuthaya grew wealthy through international trade during the 17th century's age of commerce and fortified itself with superior Portuguese-supplied firearms and mercenaries. The river system connected to the Gulf of Thailand and to the hinterlands as well.

This is the period when Western traders 'discovered' Southeast Asia, and Ayuthaya hosted many foreign settlements. Accounts by foreign visitors mention Ayuthaya's cosmopolitan markets and court. In 1690 Londoner Engelbert Campfer proclaimed, 'Among the Asian nations, the kingdom of Siam is the greatest'.

Ayuthaya adopted Khmer court customs, honorific language and ideas of kingship. The monarch styled himself as a Khmer *devaraja* (divine king) rather than Sukhothai's *dhammaraja* (righteous king); Ayuthaya continued to pay tribute to the Chinese emperor, who rewarded this ritualistic submission with generous gifts and commercial privileges.

The kingdom functioned according to a strict and complex hierarchy, much of which was defined by King Trailok (r 1448–88). Elaborate lists of official posts with specific titles and ranks were established. Individual social status was measured in numerical units of how much land one possessed. Fines and punishments were proportional to the person's rank. Ayuthaya society consisted of royalty, nobility and commoners. Commoners were further divided into freemen and slaves. Freemen were assigned to a royal or noble overseer. For six months of each year they owed labour to the ruling elite, doing personal errands, public works or military service. Despite the clear social hierarchy, social mobility was possible, depending on personal skills, connections (including marriage) and royal favour. These societal divisions highlight the feudal elements that persist in Thai society today.

The glories of Ayuthaya were interrupted by the expansionist Burmese. In 1569 the city had fallen to the great Burmese king, Bayinnaung, but regained independence under the leadership of King Naresuan. Then, in 1765, Burma's ambitious and newly established Kongbaung dynasty pushed eastward to eliminate Ayuthaya as a political and commercial rival. Burmese troops laid siege to the capital for a year before destroying it in 1767. The city was devastated, its buildings and people wiped out. The surrounding areas were deserted. So chilling was this historic sacking and razing of Ayuthaya that the perception of the Burmese as ruthless aggressors still persists in the minds of many Thais to this day.

1851–68	1855	1868–1910	1874
Reign of King Mongkut (Rama IV) and a period of Western influence.	Bowring Treaty concluded between Siam and Britain stimulating the Thai economy and granting extraterritorial rights to British subjects in Siam.	Reign of King Chulalongkorn (Rama V) and increased European imperialism in neighbouring countries.	Slavery is abolished.

FRIENDS OF THE KING

In the 1680s many foreign emissaries were invited to Ayuthaya by King Narai, who was keen to acquire and consume foreign material, culture and ideas. His court placed orders for spyglasses, hourglasses, paper, walnut trees, cheese, wine and marble fountains. He joined the French Jesuits to observe the eclipse at his palace in Lopburi and received a gift of a globe from France's King Louis XIV.

In the 1680s, Narai recruited the services of the Greek adventurer Constantine Phaulkon, who was later accused of conspiring to overthrow the ailing king. Instead, the accusers led a coup and executed Constantine.

The Bangkok Era

With Ayuthaya in ruins, the line of succession of the kings was broken and chaos ensued. A former general, Taksin, claimed his right to rule, defeated potential rivals and established his new capital in Thonburi, a settlement downriver from Ayuthaya with better access to trade. King Taksin, the son of a Chinese father and Thai mother, strongly promoted trade with China. After 15 years, the king was deposed in 1782 by the military.

One of the coup organisers, Chao Phraya Chakri, assumed the throne as King Yot Fa (Rama I) and established the Chakri dynasty, which still rules today. The new monarch moved the capital across the Chao Phraya River to modern-day Bangkok. The first century of Bangkok rule focused on rebuilding the cultural, political and military might of Ayuthaya. The new rulers extended their influence in every direction. Destroying the capital cities of both Laos and Cambodia, Siam contained Burmese aggression and made a vassal of Chiang Mai. Defeated populations were resettled and played an important role in increasing the rice production of Siam, much of which was exported to China.

Unlike the Ayuthaya rulers who identified with the Hindu god Vishnu, the Chakri kings positioned themselves as defenders of Buddhism. They undertook compilations and Thai translations of essential Buddhist texts and constructed many royal temples.

In the meantime, a new social order and market economy was taking shape in the mid-19th century. Siam turned to the West for modern scientific and technological ideas and reforms in education, infrastructure and legal systems. One of the great modernisers, King Mongkut (Rama IV; r 1851–68) never expected to be king. Before his ascension he had spent 27 years in the monastery, founding the Thammayut sect based on the strict disciplines of the Mon monks.

1890
Siam's first railway connects Bangkok with Nakhon Ratchasima.

1893
French blockade Chao Phraya River over disputed Indochina territory, intensify threat of colonisation.

➡ Wat Arun (p68) on the Chao Phraya River

During Mongkut's reign, Siam concluded treaties with Western powers that integrated the kingdom into the world market system, ceded royal monopolies and granted extraterritorial rights to British subjects.

Mongkut's son, King Chulalongkorn (Rama V) was to take much greater steps in replacing the old political order with the model of the nation-state. He abolished slavery and the corvée system (state labour), which had lingered on ineffectively since the Ayuthaya period. Chulalongkorn's reign oversaw the creation of a salaried bureaucracy, a police force and a standing army. His reforms brought uniformity to the legal code, law courts and revenue offices. Siam's agricultural output was improved by advances in irrigation techniques and increasing peasant populations. Schools were established along European lines. Universal conscription and poll taxes made all men the king's men.

In 'civilising' his country, Chulalongkorn relied greatly on foreign advisers, mostly British. Within the royal court, much of the centuries-old protocol was abandoned and replaced by Western forms. The architecture and visual art of state, like the new throne halls, were designed by Italian artists.

Like his father, Chulalongkorn was regarded as a skilful diplomat and is credited for successfully playing European powers off one another to avoid colonisation. In exchange for independence, Thailand ceded territory to French Indochina (Laos in 1893, Cambodia in 1907) and British Burma (three Malayan states in 1909). In 1902, the former Patani kingdom was ceded to the British, who were then in control of Malaysia, but control reverted back to Thailand five years later. (The Deep South region continues to consider itself occupied by the Thai central government.)

Defying old traditions, Chulalongkorn allowed himself to be seen in public and photographed in peasant garb; he also allowed his image to be reproduced on coins, stamps and postcards. (Though his father, King Mongkut, was the first Siamese monarch to allow himself to be photographed and seen by commoners in public.) He was also well travelled and visited Europe, Singapore, Java, Malaya, Burma and India. He collected art and inspiration from these travels and built fanciful palaces as architectural scrapbooks.

Siam was becoming a geographically defined country in a modern sense. By 1902, the country no longer called itself Siam but Prathet Thai (the country of the Thai) or Ratcha-anachak Thai (the kingdom of the Thai). By 1913, all those living within its borders were defined as 'Thai'.

Democracy vs Military

In 1932 a group of young military officers and bureaucrats calling themselves Khana Ratsadon (People's Party) mounted a successful, bloodless coup which marked the end of absolute monarchy and introduced

Landmarks of the Bangkok Era

Wat Arun

Wat Phra Kaew & Grand Palace

Dusit Palace Park

1902	1909	1913	1916
Siam annexes Yala, Pattani and Narathiwat from the former sultanate of Patani.	Anglo-Siamese Treaty outlines Siam's boundaries.	King Vajiravudh requires all citizens to adopt surnames.	The first Thai university, Chulalongkorn University, is established.

a constitutional monarchy. The leaders of the group were inspired by the democratic ideology they had encountered during their studies in Europe.

In the years after the coup, rival factions (royalists, military, civilians) struggled for the upper hand in the new power regime. Even the People's Party was not unified in its vision of a democratic Thailand, and before general elections were held the military wing of the party seized control of the government. The leader of the civilian wing of the People's Party, Pridi Phanomyong, a French-educated lawyer, was forced into exile in 1933 after introducing a socialist-leaning economic plan that angered the military generals. Thailand's first popular election was held in 1937 for half of the seats in the People's Assembly, the newly instated legislative body. General Phibul Songkhram, one of the military leaders, became prime minister, a position he held from 1938 to 1944 and again from 1948 to 1957.

Phibul's regime coincided with WWII and was characterised by strong nationalistic tendencies of 'nation' and 'Thai-ness'. He collaborated with

THE THAI MONARCHY

After the 1932 revolution, King Prajathipok (Rama VII) abdicated the throne in 1935, but was replaced shortly thereafter by Ananda Mahidol, the nephew of the abdicated king. He was crowned Rama VIII, though he was only 10 years old and had spent much of his childhood studying abroad. After returning to Thailand, he was shot dead under mysterious circumstances in his bedroom in 1946.

That same year, his brother, Bhumibol Adulyadej (pronounced *phuumíphon adunyádèt*), assumed the throne – he has gone on to become the longest-reigning king in Thai history, as well as the world's longest-reigning living monarch. Though he had no direct role in politics, His Majesty Bhumibol Adulyadej (Rama IX) often served as a stabilising force in times of political crisis. The king enjoys great respect, even worship, among his subjects and served as a role model for the modern Thai man (educated, family oriented, philanthropic and even stylish). His Royal Project Foundation started in 1969 is often credited for the eradication of opium cultivation among the northern hill tribes.

Now in his mid-80s, the king has receded from public view. He was hospitalised for nearly four years and was recently released to his seaside palace. His last public appearances was in 2012. Queen Sirikit is also struggling with old age having suffered a stroke.

The heir apparent, his son the Crown Prince Vajiralongkorn, has assumed many of the royal duties. The Crown Prince's daughter Princess Bajraktiyabha (also known as 'Princess Patty') has also taken on a public role. She is well educated with a doctorate degree in law from Cornell University and is currently serving as Thailand's ambassador to Austria. Her philanthropic work includes various campaigns for women's rights.

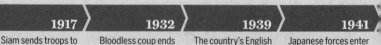

1917	1932	1939	1941
Siam sends troops to join the Allies in WWI.	Bloodless coup ends absolute monarchy.	The country's English name is officially changed from Siam to Thailand.	Japanese forces enter Thailand during WWII.

the Japanese and allowed them to use Thailand as a staging ground for its invasion of other Southeast Asian nations. The Phibul government was hoping the allegiance would restore historical territory lost during France's expansion of Indochina. Thailand intended to declare war on the US and Britain during WWII. But Seni Pramoj, the Thai ambassador in Washington and a member of Seri Thai (the Thai liberation movement), refused to deliver the formal declaration of war, thus saving Thailand from bearing the consequences of defeated-nation status. Phibul was forced to resign in 1944 and was tried for war crimes.

For a brief period after the war, democracy flourished: full elections for the people's assembly were held and the 1946 constitution sought to reduce the role of the military and provide more democratic rights. And it all lasted until the death of King Ananda, the pretext the military used to return to power with Phibul at the helm.

Military Dictatorships

In 1957 Phibul's successor General Sarit Thanarat subjected the country to a true military dictatorship: abolishing the constitution, dissolving the parliament and banning all political parties. In the 1950s, the US partnered with Sarit and subsequent military dictators, Thanom Kittikachorn and Praphat Charusathien (who controlled the country from 1964 to 1973), to allow the US military to develop bases in Thailand during the war in Vietnam in exchange for economic incentives.

By 1973, an opposition group of left-wing activists, mainly intellectuals and students, organised political rallies demanding a constitution from the military government. On 14 October that year the military brutally suppressed a large demonstration in Bangkok, killing 77 people and wounding more than 800. The event is commemorated by a monument on Th Ratchadamnoen Klang in Bangkok, near the Democracy Monument. King Bhumibol stepped in and refused to support further bloodshed, forcing Thanom and Praphat to leave Thailand.

In the following years, the left-oriented student movement grew more radical, creating fears among working-class and middle-class Thais of home-grown communism. In 1976 Thanom returned to Thailand (ostensibly to become a monk) and was received warmly by the royal family. In response, protesters organised demonstrations at Thammasat University against the perceived perpetrator of the 14 October massacre. Right-wing, anti-communist civilian groups clashed with the students, resulting in bloody violence. In the aftermath, many students and intellectuals were forced underground, and joined armed communist insurgents – known as the People's Liberation Army of Thailand (PLAT) – based in the jungles of northern and southern Thailand.

MILITARY COUPS

Thailand has had 17 constitutions, all rewritten as a result of 18 (this number is debatable) coups. Each reincarnation seeks to allocate power within the branches of government with a bias for the ruling interest (military, royalist or civilian) and against their political foes.

1945	1946	1957	1959
WWII ends; Thailand cedes seized territory from Laos, Cambodia and Malaysia.	King Bhumibol Adulyadej (Rama IX) ascends the throne; Thailand joins the UN.	Sarit Thanarat leads a coup that introduces military rule that lasts until 1973.	The first tourist authority is created.

LIBERAL COUNTERWEIGHT

Pridi Phanomyong (1900–83) was a French-educated lawyer and a civilian leader in the 1932 revolution and People's Party. His work on democratic reforms in Thailand was based on constitutional measures and attempts to restrict by law military involvement in Thai politics. He supported nationalisation of land and labour, state-led industrialisation and labour protection. In 1934, he founded Thammasat University. He also served as the figurehead of Seri Thai (the resistance movement against WWII Japanese occupation of Thailand) and was Thai prime minister in 1946.

Though acknowledged as a senior statesman, Pridi Phanomyong was a controversial figure and a major foe of Phibul Songkhram and the military regimes. He was accused of being a communist by his critics and forced out of the country under suspicion of regicide. Since the thawing of the Cold War, his legacy has been re-examined and recognised for its democratic efforts and the counterbalancing effects it had on military interests. He was named one of Unesco's great personalities of the 20th-century world in 2000.

Military control of the country continued through the 1980s. The government of the 'political soldier', General Prem Tinsulanonda, enjoyed a period of political and economic stability. Prem dismantled the communist insurgency through military action and amnesty programs. But the country's new economic success presented a challenging rival: prominent business leaders who criticised the military's role in government and their now-dated Cold War mentality. Communists, they maintained, should be business partners, not enemies.

It's Just Business

In 1988, Prem was replaced in fair elections by Chatichai Choonhavan, leader of the Chat Thai Party, who created a government dominated by well-connected provincial business people. His government shifted power away from the bureaucrats and set about transforming Thailand into an 'Asian Tiger' economy. But the business of politics was often bought and sold like a commodity and Chatichai was overthrown by the military on grounds of extreme corruption. This coup demarcated an emerging trend in Thai politics: the Bangkok business community and educated classes siding with the military against provincial business-politicians and their money politics.

In 1992, after reinstating elections, an unelected military leader inserted himself as prime minister. This was met with popular resistance and the ensuing civilian-military clash was dubbed 'Black May'. Led by former Bangkok mayor Chamlong Srimuang, around 200,000 protesters (called the 'mobile phone mob', representing their rising urban affluence)

Thaksin Shinawatra was the first prime minister in Thai history to complete a four-year term of office.

1965	1968	1973	1976
Thailand hosts US military bases during the Vietnam War.	Thailand is a founding member of the Association of Southeast Asian Nations (ASEAN).	Thai students, workers and farmers demonstrate for the reinstallation of a democratic government.	Violent suppression of the student movement by the military.

launched a mass demonstration in Bangkok that resulted in three nights of violence with armed soldiers. On the night of 20 May, King Bhumibol called an end to the violence.

After Black May, a new wave of democracy activists advocated for constitutional reforms. For most of the 1990s, the parliament was dominated by the Democrat Party, which represented the urban middle class and business interests. Its major base of support came from the southern Thai population centres, formerly port towns now dominated by tourism and exports (rubber, tin and fishing). On the other side of the spectrum were the former pro-military politicians based in the central plains and the people of the agrarian northeast in new provincial towns who focused on state-budget distributions. These political lines still exist today.

In 1997, the boom years went bust and the Asian economic crisis unfolded. The country's economy was plagued by foreign-debt burdens, an overextension in the real-estate sector and a devalued currency. Within months of the crisis, the Thai currency plunged from 25B to 56B per US$1. The International Monetary Fund (IMF) stepped in to impose financial and legal reforms and economic liberalisation programs in exchange for more than US$17 billion to stabilise the Thai currency.

In the aftermath of the crisis, the Democrats returned to power uncontested, but were viewed as ineffective as the economy worsened.

Thaksinocracy & the 2006 Coup

In 2000, the economic slump began to ease. The telecommunications billionaire and former police officer Thaksin Shinawatra, through his Thai Rak Thai (TRT or 'Thai Loving Thai') party, won a majority in the elections of 2001. Self-styled as a CEO-politician, Thaksin swiftly delivered on his campaign promises for rural development, including agrarian debt relief, village capital funds and cheap health care.

Thanks to the 1997 constitutional reforms designed to strengthen the prime minister's position, his was one of Thai history's most stable elected governments. The surging economy and his bold, if strong-arm, leadership won an outright majority in 2005, introducing one-party rule. His popularity among the working class and rural voters was immense.

In 2006 Thaksin was accused of abusing his powers and of conflicts of interest, most notably in his family's sale of their Shin Corporation to the Singaporean government for 73 billion baht (US$1.88 billion), a tax-free gain thanks to legislation he helped craft. Demonstrations in Bangkok called for his ousting and on 19 September 2006, the military staged a bloodless coup that forced Thaksin into exile. General elections were held shortly thereafter with Thaksin's political allies forming a government led by Samak Sundaravej.

The Thai national anthem is played on TV and radio stations at 8am and 6pm. The video that accompanies the TV broadcast shows a multi-ethnic, multi-religious Thailand living in harmony under the national flag.

Student protest attack in 1976

1979	1980
After three years of military rule, elections and parliament restored.	Prem Tinsulanonda's government works to undermine the communist insurgency movement and eventually ends it with a political solution.

AFP / GETTY IMAGES ©

This was an unsatisfactory outcome to the military and the anti-Thaksin group known as People's Alliance for Democracy (PAD), consisting of mainly urban elites nicknamed 'Yellow Shirts' because they wore yellow (the king's birthday colour). It was popularly believed that Thaksin was consolidating power during his tenure so that he could interrupt royal succession.

In September 2008, Samak Sundaravej was unseated by the Constitutional Court on a technicality: while in office, he hosted a TV cooking show deemed to be a conflict of interest. Concerned that another election would yield another Thaksin win, the Yellow Shirts seized control of Thailand's main airports, Suvarnabhumi and Don Muang, for a week in November 2008 until the military manoeuvred a silent coup and another favourable court ruling that further weakened Thaksin's political proxies. Through last-minute coalition building, Democrat Abhisit Vejjajiva was elected in a parliamentary vote, becoming Thailand's 27th prime minister.

Thaksin supporters organised their own counter-movement as the United Front for Democracy Against Dictatorship (UDD), better known as the 'Red Shirts'. Supporters hailed mostly from the north and northeast, and include anti-coup, pro-democracy activists; anti-royalists; and die-hard Thaksin fans. There is a degree of class struggle, with many working-class Red Shirts expressing bombastic animosity towards the aristocrats.

The Red Shirts' most provocative demonstration came in 2010 after Thailand's Supreme Court ordered the seizure of US$46 billion of Thaksin's assets after finding him guilty of abusing his powers as prime minister. The Red Shirts occupied Bangkok's central shopping district for two months and demanded the dissolution of the government and re-instatement of elections. In May 2010 the military used force to evict the protesters, resulting in bloody clashes where 91 people were killed and shopping centres were set ablaze (US$1.5 billion of crackdown-related arson damage was estimated).

In 2011, general elections were held and Thaksin's politically allied Puea Thai party won a parliamentary majority with Thaksin's sister Yingluck Shinawatra elected as prime minister.

Troubles in the Border Regions

Since 2001, Thailand has been fighting a low-scale war with Muslim separatist insurgents in the southernmost provinces of Pattani, Narathiwat and Yala, collectively known as the Deep South. These provinces once made up the historic sultanate of Patani until it was conquered by the Chakri kings. During WWII, a policy of nation-building set out to transform the multi-ethnic, multi-religious society into a unified and homoge-

1988	1991–2	1997	2001
Chatichai Choonhavan becomes first elected prime minister since 1976.	General Suchinda attempts to seize power; King Bhumibol intervenes to halt civil turmoil surrounding 'Black May' protests.	Asian economic crisis; passage of historic 'people's constitution'.	Telecommunications tycoon Thaksin Shinawatra is elected prime minister.

neous Thai Buddhist nation. This policy was resisted in the Deep South and gave birth to an ongoing separatist movement. In the 1980s and '90s, the assimilation policy was abandoned and then prime minister Prem brokered peace through support for Muslim cultural rights and religious freedoms, amnesty to the armed insurgents and economic development for the historically impoverished region.

The Thaksin regime took another approach to the region. Greater central control from Bangkok was exerted and was viewed as a thinly disguised policy to break up the traditional stronghold of the Democrat Party. The sensitive and tenacious Muslim culture of the Deep South did not respond favourably. In 2002, the government dissolved the long-standing inspectorate and the army-run joint civilian-police-military border security office – a unit often lauded for maintaining peace and stability and providing a communication link between the Thai government and the southern Muslims. In its place the Thai provincial police assumed control of security, though they lacked perceived moral authority and the support of the local population. In 2004, the government responded harshly to demonstrations that resulted in the Krue Se Mosque and Tak Bai incidents, which together cost the lives of at least 180 Muslims, many of them unarmed civilians. In 2005, martial law was declared in the area.

After more than a decade of violence, Thailand's national government announced peace talks with Barisan Revolusion Nasional (BNR), a Malaysian-based insurgent group claiming a leading role in the southern war. But meetings have been suspended due to spikes in violence and concerns that BNR doesn't exert significant organisational control.

Another troublesome spot is an ongoing border dispute with Cambodia. In 2008 Cambodia successfully petitioned Unesco to list the ancient Khmer temple of Khao Phra Wihan ('Preah Vihear' in Cambodian) as an official World Heritage Site. Remote and seemingly insignificant, the temple has long been a contentious issue between Cambodia and Thailand. A 1969 International Court of Justice case awarded Cambodia ownership of the temple, but both countries lay claim to a 4.6-sq-km area surrounding it. Four years since the Unesco petition, troops have been deployed to the border and periodically exchange fire, including clashes in 2011. In 2013, the International Court of Justice ruled in favour of Cambodia's claim on the disputed territory and ordered the two countries to make a bilateral agreement on amended boundary lines.

Voting in Thailand is compulsory for all eligible citizens, which excludes monks and other religious figures.

Politics & Government

Much of the political drama that has unfolded since the 2006 coup involves a long-standing debate about how to structure Thailand's legislative body and, ultimately, who gets greater control. The National Assembly

2004	2006	2008	2010
Indian Ocean tsunami kills over 5000 people in Thailand and damages tourism and fishing industries; Muslim insurgency reignites in the Deep South.	King Bhumibol celebrates 60th year on the throne; Thaksin government overthrown in a coup and prime minister forced into exile.	Cambodia successfully petitions Unesco to list Khao Phra Wihan as a World Heritage Site, reigniting border tensions; pro-royalist Yellow Shirt activists, seize Bangkok's international airports, causing a week-long shut-down.	Pro-Thaksin Red Shirt activists occupy central Bangkok for two months; military crackdown results in 91 deaths.

MASKED MASSES

Thailand's obsession with mass political rallies has been dominated by colour-coded activists (Yellow versus Red Shirts). But there is a new arrival to the protest movement: a group calling itself 'V for Thailand' has donned Guy Fawkes masks and convened demonstrations in Bangkok's shopping malls, a near-permanent encampment in Lumphini Park and Phuket. The group charges Yingluck's administration with corrupt policies designed to reward base supporters.

(or parliament of Thailand) currently has 630 members divided into two chambers (House of Representatives and the Senate) with a mix of seats being popularly elected and elected by party vote. The ratio of seats being popularly elected changes with each replacement constitution. The 1997 constitution, dubbed the People's Constitution, called for both chambers to be fully elected by popular vote. This power to the people paved the way for Thaksin and his well-loved Thai Rak Thai party to gain nearly complete control. The military and the elites have since questioned the benefits of full democracy in Thailand.

When Thai voters go to the polls they cast a ballot for the constituency member of parliament (MP) and for their preferred party, the results of which are used to determine individual winners and proportional representation outcomes for the positions assigned by party vote. The prime minister is the head of the government and is elected via legislative vote by the majority party.

Voting in Thailand is compulsory for all eligible citizens (over the age of 18) but members of the clergy are not allowed to vote. Voter turnout for national elections was 75% in 2011, down from 78% in 2007. Charges of vote-buying typically accompany every election. Anecdotally, local party leaders make their rounds through the villages handing out money for the promise of a vote. In some cases, villagers will accept money from competing parties and report that they have no loyalty at the ballot box.

The ballots include a 'no' vote if the voter wishes to choose 'none of the above' intended as an option for compulsory voters who dislike all of their options. It is also common to 'spoil' the ballot, or disqualify it, by writing on it or defacing it. During the 2005 general election a large number of ineligible ballots contained anti-Thaksin messages. In the 2011 election, Yellow Shirts mounted a 'vote no' campaign as a political demonstration against the current political system that they charged was corrupt. The campaign was unsuccessful in nullifying the election, and is often credited for contributing to the losses of the previously allied Democrats.

The Democrat Party (Phak Prachathipat) founded in 1946 is now the longest-surviving political party in Thailand.

2011	2013	2015
Yingluck Shinawatra becomes Thailand's first female prime minister; devastating floods inundate industrial region.	Peace talks start then stall with southern militants.	Scheduled start of the ASEAN Economic Community (AEC).

AFP / GETTY IMAGES ©

➜ Yingluck Shinawatra

Above Young girls from the Hmong hill tribe

People & Culture

Thailand's cohesive national identity provides a unifying patina for ethnic and regional differences that evolved through historical migrations and geographic kinships with ethnically diverse neighbours.

Ethnic Make-up

Some 75% of the citizens of Thailand are ethnic Thais, providing a superficial view of sameness. But subtle regional differences exist. In the central plains (Chao Phraya delta), Siamese Thais united the country through its historic kingdoms and promulgated its culture and language. Today the central Thai dialect is the national standard and Bangkok exports unify culture through popular media and standardised education.

The northeast (Isan) has always stood apart from the rest of the country, sharing closer ethnic and cultural ties with Laos and the Thai

Traditional Lisu clothing

Lao people. In the northeastern provinces that border Cambodia, there is a distinct Khmer influence as many families migrated across the border during historical tumult. A minority tribe, known as Suay, lives near Surin and Khorat (Nakhon Ratchasima) and are traditional elephant mahouts.

Thai Pak Tai people define the characteristics of the south. The dialect is a little faster than standard Thai and there is more mixing of Muslim folk beliefs into the regional culture thanks to the geographic proximity to Malaysia and the historic Muslim population.

If you were to redraw Thailand's borders according to ethnicity, northern Thailand would be united with parts of southern China and northern Myanmar. The traditional homeland of the Tai people was believed to be the Yunnan region of China. There are also many sub-groups, including the Shan (an ethnic cousin to the Thais who settled in the highlands of Burma) and the Tai Lü (who settled in Nan and Chiang Rai Provinces as well as the Vietnamese highlands).

People of Chinese ancestry – second- or third-generation Hakka, Teochew, Hainanese or Cantonese – make up 14% of the population. Bangkok and the nearby coastal areas have a large population of immigrants from China who came for economic opportunities in the early to mid-20th century. In northern Thailand there is also a substantial number of Chinese Muslims who emigrated from Yunnan in the late 19th century. Historically wealthy Chinese introduced their daughters to the royal court as consorts, developing royal connections and adding a Chinese bloodline that extends to the current king.

The second-largest ethnic minority are the Malays (4.6%), most of whom reside in the provinces of the Deep South. The remaining minority

ECONOMIC MIGRANTS

Thailand unofficially hosts up to 3 million migrant workers, mainly from Myanmar and to a lesser extent Laos and Cambodia. The majority are low-skilled workers with little to no formal education from economically depressed or politically unstable areas. They are usually in the country illegally, which means that they have no labour protections and employers can pay them less than Thai workers (if they pay them at all). Fisheries, garment factories and construction sites depend heavily on migrant labour.

Although the Thai government maintains a national verification process that has registered about half of the estimated guest workers, the rules require them to return home for up to four years before being allowed to return for a renewed work permit. Such punitive measures and expensive brokerage fees deters many migrants from becoming legitimate workers.

groups include smaller percentages of non-Thai-speaking people such as the Vietnamese, Khmer, Mon, Semang (Sakai), Moken (*chow lair,* also spelt *chao leh;* people of the sea, or 'sea gypsies'), Htin, Mabri, Khamu and a variety of hill tribes. A small number of Europeans and other non-Asians reside in Bangkok and the provinces.

Hill Tribes

Ethnic minorities in the mountainous regions of northern Thailand are often called 'hill tribes', or in Thai vernacular, *chow kŏw* (mountain people). Each hill tribe has its own language, customs, mode of dress and beliefs Most are of seminomadic origin, having come from Tibet, Myanmar, China and Laos during the past 200 years or so. They are 'fourth-world' people in that they belong neither to the main aligned powers nor to the developing nations. Language and culture constitute the borders of their world. Some groups are caught between the 6th and 21st centuries, while others have assimilated into modern life. The Tribal Research Institute in Chiang Mai recognises 10 different hill tribes but there may be up to 20. Hill tribes are increasingly integrating into the Thai mainstream and many of the old ways are disappearing.

> Thais are fastidious in their personal appearance, often bathing twice a day, and are confused that seemingly wealthy foreigners are so unkempt.

Akha (I-kaw)

Population: 70,000
Origin: Tibet
Present locations: Thailand, Laos, Myanmar, Yunnan (China)
Belief system: Animism with an emphasis on ancestor worship; some groups are Christian
Cultural characteristics: The Akha are among the poorest of Thailand's ethnic minorities and reside mainly in Chiang Mai and Chiang Rai Provinces, along mountain ridges or steep slopes 1000m to 1400m in altitude. They're regarded as skilled farmers but are often displaced from arable land by government intervention. The well-known Akha Swing Ceremony takes place from mid-August to mid-September, between rice planting and harvest time. Akha houses are constructed of wood and bamboo, usually atop short wooden stilts and roofed with thick grass. At the entrance of every traditional Akha village stands a simple wooden gateway. Akha shamans affix various charms made from bamboo strips to the gateway to prevent malevolent spirits from en-

Traditional Akha clothing

tering. Standing next to each village gateway are the crude wooden figures of a man and a woman, each bearing exaggerated sexual organs, in the belief that human sexuality is abhorrent to the spirit world.

Akha are focused on family ties and will recite their personal genealogies upon first meetings to determine a shared ancestor. Their traditional clothing consists of a headdress of beads, feathers and dangling silver ornaments.

LAHU CULTURE

The Lahu people are known for their strict adherence to gender equality.

Hmong (Mong or Maew)

Population: 151,000
Origin: South China
Present locations: South China, Thailand, Laos, Vietnam
Belief system: Animism
Cultural characteristics: The Hmong are Thailand's second-largest hill-tribe group and are especially numerous in Chiang Mai Province with smaller enclaves in the other northern Thai provinces. They usually live on mountain peaks or plateaus above 1000m. Kinship is patrilineal and polygamy is permitted.

Hmong tribespeople wear simple black jackets and indigo or black baggy trousers with striped borders (White Hmong) or indigo skirts (Blue Hmong) and silver jewellery. Sashes may be worn around the waist, and embroidered aprons draped front and back. Most women wear their hair in a bun.

Karen (Yang or Kariang)

Population: 420,000
Origin: Myanmar
Present locations: Thailand, Myanmar
Belief system: animism, Buddhism, Christianity, depending on the group
Cultural characteristics: The Karen are the largest hill-tribe group in Thailand and number about half of the total tribal population. They tend to live in lowland valleys and practise crop rotation rather than swidden agriculture. Their numbers and proximity to mainstream society have made them the most integrated and financially successful of the hill-tribe groups. Karen homes are built on low stilts or posts, with the roofs swooping quite low. There are four distinct Karen groups: the Skaw (White) Karen, Pwo Karen, Pa-O (Black) Karen and Kayah (Red) Karen.

Thickly woven V-neck tunics of various colours are typically worn (though unmarried women wear white). Kinship is matrilineal and marriage is monogamous.

Traditional Karen clothing

Lahu (Musoe)

Population: 103,000
Origin: Tibet
Present locations: Southwest China, Thailand, Myanmar
Belief system: Theistic animism; some groups are Christian
Cultural characteristics: The Thai term for this tribe, *moo·seu*, is derived from a Burmese word meaning 'hunter', a reference to their skill in the forest. The Lahu tend to live at about 1000m altitude and can be found in remote areas of Chiang Mai, Chiang Rai and Tak Provinces. They typically live in mixed ethnic villages and are an ethnically diverse group with five main subsets: Red Lahu (the most

numerous Lahu group in Thailand), Black Lahu, White Lahu, Yellow Lahu and Lahu Sheleh.

Houses are built of wood, bamboo and grass, and usually stand on short wooden posts. Lahu food is probably the spiciest of all the hill-tribe cuisines.

Traditional dress consists of black-and-red jackets with narrow skirts worn by women and bright green or blue-green baggy trousers worn by men.

Lisu (Lisaw)

Population: 55,000
Origin: Tibet
Present locations: Thailand, Yunnan (China)
Belief system: animism with ancestor worship and spirit possession
Cultural characteristics: Lisu villages are usually in the mountains at an elevation of about 1000m and occur in eight Thai provinces: Chiang Mai, Chiang Rai, Mae Hong Son, Phayao, Tak, Kamphaeng Phet, Sukhothai and Lampang. Patrilineal clans have pan-tribal jurisdiction, which makes the Lisu unique among hill-tribe groups (most of which have power centred with either a shaman or a village headman).

Traditional Lahu clothing

Homes are built on the ground and consist mostly of bamboo and thatched grass.

The women wear long multicoloured tunics over trousers and sometimes black turbans with tassels. Men wear baggy green or blue pants pegged in at the ankles.

Mien (Yao)

Population: 35,500
Origin: Central China
Present locations: Thailand, south China, Laos, Myanmar, Vietnam
Belief system: Animism with ancestor worship, Taoism, Buddhism and Christianity
Cultural characteristics: The Mien are highly skilled at crafts such as embroidery and silversmithing. They settle near mountain springs at between 1000m and 1200m with a concentration in Nan, Phayao and Chiang Rai Provinces and a few communities elsewhere. Migration into Thailand increased during the Vietnam War era when the Mien collaborated with the CIA against Pathet Lao; 50,000 Mien refugees were resettled in the US. The Mien are influenced by Chinese traditions and use Chinese characters to write their language. Kinship is patrilineal and marriage is polygamous.

Houses are built at ground level, out of wood or bamboo thatch.

Women wear trousers and black jackets with intricately embroidered patches and red furlike collars, along with large dark-blue or black turbans. Men wear black tunics and black pants.

A MODERN PERSPECTIVE ON THE HILL TRIBES

Hill tribes tend to have among the lowest standards of living in Thailand. Although it could be tempting to correlate this with traditional lifestyles, their situation is compounded, in most cases, by not having Thai citizenship. Without the latter, they are technically illegal residents in the country of their birth. Without legal status they don't have the right to own land, educate their children, earn a minimum wage or access health care. In the last decades some hill-tribe groups have been issued Thai identification cards, which enable them to access national programs (in theory, though, extra 'fees' might prevent families from being able to afford public schooling and health care). Other hill-tribe families have received residency certificates that restrict travel outside of an assigned district, in turn limiting access to job opportunities associated with a mobile modern society.

Furthermore, the Thai government has pursued a 30-year policy of hill-tribe relocation, often moving villages from fertile agricultural land to infertile land, in turn removing the tribes from a viable subsistence system in which tribal customs were intact to a market system in which they can't adequately compete and in which tribal ways have been fractured.

In the past decade, the expansion of tourism into the mountainous regions of the north presents a complicating factor to the independence of hill-tribe villages. City speculators will buy land from hill-tribe farmers for fairly nominal sums only to be resold, usually to resorts, for much higher costs if the documentation of ownership can be procured. (In many cases the hill-tribe farmer doesn't own the land rights and has very little bargaining power when approached by outsiders.) The displaced farmer and his family might then migrate to the city, losing their connection to their rural and tribal lifestyle with few resources to succeed in the lowland society.

The Thai Character

Much of Thailand's cultural value system is hinged upon respect for the family, religion and monarchy. Within that system each person knows his or her place and Thai children are strictly instructed in the importance of group conformity and suppressing confrontational views. In most social situations, establishing harmony often takes a leading role and Thais take personal pride in making others feel at ease.

Sà·nùk

In general, Thais place high value on *sà·nùk*, which means 'fun'. It is often regarded as a necessary underpinning of anything worth doing. Even work and studying should have an element of *sà·nùk*, otherwise it automatically becomes drudgery. This doesn't mean Thais don't want to work, but they labour best as a group, so as to avoid loneliness and ensure an element of playfulness. Nothing condemns an activity more than *mâi sà·nùk* (no fun). Thais often mix their job tasks with a healthy dose of socialising, from the back-breaking work of rice farming to the tedium of long-distance bus driving.

Saving Face

Thais believe strongly in the concept of saving face: avoiding confrontation and endeavouring not to embarrass themselves or other people (except when it's *sà·nùk* to do so). The ideal face-saver doesn't bring up negative topics in conversation, doesn't express firm convictions or opinions and doesn't claim to have an expertise. Agreement and harmony are considered to be the most important social graces.

While Westerners might think of heated discussion as social sport, Thais regard any instance where voices are raised as rude and potentially volatile. Losing your temper causes a loss of face for everyone and Thais

Above Colourful Hmong-tribe clothing
Right Karen woman smoking a pipe

Family riding a motorbike in Chiang Rai

who have been crossed may react in extreme ways. Minor embarrassments, such as tripping or falling, might elicit giggles from a crowd of Thais. In this case they aren't taking delight in your mishap, but helping you save face by laughing it off.

The TV show *Hormones* is a new-generation hit about high-school students dealing with sex, drugs and parents.

Status & Obligation

All relationships in traditional Thai society – and those in the modern Thai milieu as well – are governed by social rank defined by age, wealth, status and personal or political position. The elder position is called *pôo yài* (literally the 'big person') and is used to describe parents, bosses, village heads, public officials etc. The junior position is called *pôo nóy* ('little person') and describes anyone who is subservient to the *pôo yài*. Although this tendency towards social ranking is to some degree shared by many societies around the world, the Thai twist lies in the set of mutual obligations linking the elder to the junior.

Pôo nóy are supposed to show obedience and respect (together these concepts are covered by the single Thai term *greng jai*) towards the elder. Those with junior status are not supposed to question or criticise those with elder status. In the workplace, this means younger staff members are not encouraged to speak during meetings and are expected to do their bosses' bidding.

In return *pôo yài* are obligated to care for or 'sponsor' the *pôo nóy*. It is a paternalistic relationship in which *pôo nóy* can ask for favours involving money or job access. *Pôo yài* reaffirm their rank by granting requests when possible; to refuse would risk a loss of face and status.

The protocol defined by the social hierarchy governs almost every aspect of Thai behaviour. Elected or appointed officials occupy one of the highest rungs on the social ladder and often regard themselves as caretakers of the people, a stark contrast to the democratic ideal of being the voice of the people. The complicated personal hierarchy in Thailand often prevents collaboration, especially between those with competing status. This is why Bangkok has several modern-art museums with somewhat anaemic collections rather than one consolidated powerhouse.

Most foreign visitors will interact with a simplified version of this elder-junior relationship in the form of *pêe* (elder sibling) and *nórng* (younger sibling). All Thais refer to each other using familial names. Even people unrelated by blood quickly establish who's *pêe* and who's *nórng*. This is why one of the first questions Thais ask new acquaintances is 'How old are you?'

Lifestyle

Individual lifestyles vary according to family background, income and geography. In many ways Bangkok is its own phenomenon where upper- and middle-class Thais wake up to an affluent and modern lifestyle: smartphones, fast food, K-pop music and fashion addictions. The amount of disposable income in Bangkok is unparalleled elsewhere in the country, though affluence is on the rise.

There continues to be a migration from the countryside or small towns to the urban job centres. It was once standard for Thais to send a portion of their pay home to support their parents or dependent children left behind to be raised in the village. This still happens today in some socio-economic strata, but increasingly affluent parents don't need financial help from their adult children. In fact an important social shift has occurred: parents continue to support their adult children with big-ticket purchases of cars and real estate that entry-level salaries can't afford. As a result, the older generation often criticises today's youth as having an inflated sense of entitlement.

> The Thai equivalent of giving someone the middle finger is to show them the bottom of the foot.

In the provincial capitals, life is more traditional, relatively speaking. The civil servants – teachers and government employees – make up the backbone of the Thai middle class and live in nuclear families in terrace housing estates outside the city centre. Some might live in the older in-town neighbourhoods filled with front-yard gardens growing papayas, mangoes and other fruit trees. The business class lives in the city centre, usually in apartments above shopfronts, making for an easy commute but a fairly urban life. In the cool hours of the day, the wage earners and students head to the nearest park to jog, play badminton or join in the civic-run aerobics classes.

One of the best places to view the Thai 'lifestyle' is at the markets. Day markets sell kitchen staples as well as local produce and regional desserts. Night markets are good for dinner and people-watching as few Thais bother to cook for themselves.

THE NICKNAME GAME

At birth Thai babies are given auspicious first names, often bestowed by the family patriarch or matriarch. These poetic names are then relegated to bureaucratic forms and name cards, while the child is introduced to everyone else by a one-syllable nickname. Thai nicknames are usually playful and can be inspired by the child's appearance (Moo, meaning 'pig', if he/she is chubby) or a favourite pastime (Toon, short for 'cartoon' for avid TV-watchers). Girls will typically be named Lek or Noi (both of which mean 'small'). Some parents even go so far as imprinting their interests on their children's names: Golf (as in the sport) and Benz (as in the car).

Thailand at a Glance

Population:
67 million

Fertility rate: 1.6

Percentage of people over 65: 9.5%

Urbanisation rate: 34%

Life expectancy: 73 years

Though fewer people toil in the rice paddies than in the past, the villages still survive on the outskirts of the urban grid. Here life is set to the seasons, the fashions are purchased from the market and if the water buffaloes could talk they'd know all the village gossip.

From a demographic perspective, Thailand, like most of Asia, is greying. Women pursue careers instead of husbands; unmarried women now make up 30% of the population (plus they start to outnumber men in their 30s). Successful government-sponsored family-planning efforts and professional opportunities have reduced the fertility rate so successfully – from six children in the 1960s to 1.6 children today – that analysts are now warning of future labour shortages and overextended pension systems.

Religion

Religion is alive and well in Thailand and colourful examples of daily worship can be found on nearly every corner. Walk the streets early in the morning and you'll see the solemn procession of Buddhist monks, with shaved heads and orange-coloured robes, engaged in *bin·dá·bàht*, the daily house-to-house alms food gathering.

Although the country is predominantly Buddhist, the minority religions often practise alongside one another.

Buddhism

Approximately 95% of Thai people are Theravada Buddhists, a branch of Buddhism that came from Sri Lanka during the Sukhothai period.

The ultimate end of Theravada Buddhism is *nibbana* ('nirvana' in Sanskrit), which literally means the 'blowing out' or extinction of all grasping and thus of all suffering (*dukkha*). Effectively, *nibbana* is also an end to the cycle of rebirths (both moment-to-moment and life-to-life) that is

Getting soaked during Songkran (p29)

Young boy with an incense sticks

existence. In reality, most Thai Buddhists aim for rebirth in a 'better' existence rather than the supramundane goal of *nibbana*. The concept of rebirth is almost universally accepted in Thailand, even by non-Buddhists.

The idea of reincarnation also provides Thais with a sense of humility and interconnectedness. They might observe a creepy-crawly in the bushes and feel that perhaps they too were once like that creature or that a deceased relative now occupies a non-human body. Reflecting Thailand's social stratification, reincarnation is basically a reward or punishment. This is essentially the Buddhist theory of karma, expressed in the Thai proverb *tam dee, dâi dee; tam chôo·a, dâi chôo·a* (good actions bring good results; bad actions bring bad results). A good person can improve their lot in life today and in future lives by making merit *(tam bun)*.

The Buddhist hierarchy in Thailand is made up of the Tiratana (Triple Gems) – the Buddha, the *dhamma* (the teachings) and the *sangha* (the Buddhist community). Historically, the Thai king has occupied a revered position in Thai Buddhism, often viewed as semi-divine. Thai royal ceremonies remain almost exclusively the domain of Brahman priests, bestowed with the duty of preserving the three pillars of Thai nationhood, namely sovereignty, religion and the monarchy.

Thai Buddhism has no particular Sabbath day but there are holy days *(wan prá)*, which occur every seventh or eighth day depending on phases of the moon. There are also religious holidays, typically marking important events in the Buddha's life.

Merit-Making

Thais visit temples for spiritual enlightenment as well as cultural entertainment. Pilgrimages to famous temples are an important feature of domestic tourism. During these visits, merit-making is an individual

BUDDHIST ERA

The official year in Thailand is reckoned from 543 BC, the beginning of the Buddhist Era, so that AD 2013 is BE 2556, AD 2014 is BE 2557 etc.

ritual rather than a congregational affair. Worshippers buy offerings such as lotus buds, incense and candles and present these symbolic gifts to the temple's primary Buddha image. Other merit-making activities include offering food to the temple *sangha*, meditating (individually or in groups), listening to monks chanting *suttas* (Buddhist discourse), and attending a *têht* or *dhamma* talk by the abbot or another respected teacher. Though Thailand is increasingly secular, merit-making remains an important cultural activity often linked to wish fulfilment (finding love or academic success) rather than religious devotion.

Monks & Nuns

Socially, every Thai male is expected to become a monk (*bhikkhu* in Pali; *prá* or *prá pík·sù* in Thai) for a short period in his life, optimally between the time he finishes school and the time he starts a career or marries. A family earns great merit when one of its sons 'takes robe and bowl'. Traditionally, the length of time spent in the wát is three months, during the *pan·săh* (Buddhist Lent), which begins in July and coincides with the rainy season. However, nowadays men may spend as little as a week to accrue merit as monks. Most temporary ordinations occur under the age of 20 years old, when a man may enter the *sangha* as a 10-vow novice (*nairn*).

Monks are required to shave their heads, eyebrows and any facial hair during their residence in the monastery as a sign of renouncing worldly concerns. They are also required to live an ascetic life free of luxury and eat one meal per day (sometimes two, depending on the temple traditions). Monks who live in the city usually emphasise study of the Buddhist scriptures, while those who opt for the forest temples tend to emphasise meditation. Fully ordained monks perform funeral and marriage rites, conduct sermons and instruct monastic teachings.

The monastery sometimes still serves its traditional role as a social welfare institution. Male children can enter the monastery and receive a free education, a tradition that has been largely replaced by public schooling.

In Thai Buddhism, women who seek a monastic life are given a minor role in the temple that is not equal to full monkhood. A Buddhist nun is known as *mâa chee* (mother priest) and lives as an *atthasila* (eight-precept) nun, a position traditionally occupied by women who had no other place in society. Thai nuns shave their heads, wear white robes and take care of temple chores. Generally speaking, *mâa chee* aren't considered as prestigious as monks and don't have a function in the merit-making rituals of lay people.

HOUSES OF THE HOLY

Many homes or inhabited dwellings in Thailand have an associated 'spirit house', built to provide a residence for the plot of land's *prá poom* (guardian spirits). Based on animistic beliefs that predate Buddhism, guardian spirits are believed to reside in rivers, trees and other natural features and need to be honoured (and placated). The guardian spirit of a particular plot of land is the supernatural equivalent of a mother-in-law, an honoured but sometimes troublesome family member. To keep the spirits happily distracted, Thais erect elaborate dollhouse-like structures where the spirits can 'live' comfortably separated from humans. To further cultivate good relations and good fortune, daily offerings of rice, fruit, flowers and water are made to the spirit house. If the human house is enlarged the spirit house must also be enlarged, so that the spirits do not feel slighted. Spirit houses must be consecrated by a Brahman priest.

Above Lotus bud rests in the hand of a golden Buddha statue
Right Buddhist monks

Islam

At around 4% of the population, Muslims make up Thailand's largest religious minority, living side by side with the Buddhist majority. There are some 3000 mosques in Thailand – over 200 in Bangkok alone. Of these mosques, 99% are associated with the Sunni branch of Islam (in which Islamic leadership is vested in the consensus of the Ummah, or Muslim community), and 1% with the Shi'ite branch (in which religious and political authority is given to descendants of the Prophet Mohammed).

Islam was introduced to Thailand's southern region between AD 1200 and 1500 through the influence of Indian and Arab traders and scholars. To this day, most of Thailand's Muslims reside in the south. Most of Thailand's southern Muslims are ethnically Malay and speak Malay or Yawi (a dialect of Malay written in the Arabic script) in addition to Thai.

Good Reads

Being Dharma: The Essence of the Buddha's Teachings (2001; Ajahn Chah)

Thai Folk Wisdom: Contemporary Takes on Traditional Proverbs (2010; Tulaya Pornpiriyakulchai and Jane Vejjajiva)

Sacred Tattoos of Thailand (2011; Joe Cummings)

The Sex Industry in Thailand

Prostitution has been widespread in Thailand since long before the country gained a reputation among international sex tourists. Throughout Thai history the practice was accepted and common, though it has not always been respected by society as a whole. Today prostitution is technically illegal but anti-prostitution laws are ambiguous and often unenforced.

History & Cultural Attitudes

Prostitution was declared illegal in 1960 under pressure from the UN. But a separate law passed in 1966 allows for entertainment places (go-go bars, beer bars, massage parlours, karaoke bars and bathhouses) that can legally provide nonsexual services (such as dancing, massage, a drinking buddy); sexual services are brokered through these venues but they are not technically the businesses' primary purpose.

With the arrival of the US military forces in Southeast Asia during the Vietnam War era, enterprising forces adapted the existing framework to a new clientele. The industry targeted to foreigners is very visible with multiple red-light districts in Bangkok alone, but there is also a more clandestine domestic sex industry and myriad informal channels of sex-for-hire.

In 1998 the International Labour Organization, a UN agency, advised Southeast Asian countries, including Thailand, to recognise prostitution as an economic sector and income generator. It is estimated that one-third of the entertainment establishments are registered with the government and the majority pay an informal tax in the form of police bribes. In 2003, measures to legalise prostitution cited the Thai sex industry as being worth US$4.3 billion (about 3% of GDP), employing roughly 200,000 sex workers. A study conducted in 2003 by Thailand's Chulalongkorn University estimated 2.8 million sex workers, of which 1.98 million were adult women, 20,000 were adult men and 800,000 were children, defined as any person under the age of 18.

> Entertainment places fine a worker if she doesn't smile enough, arrives late or doesn't meet the drink quota. These deductions often exceed the worker's monthly base salary.

PROS & CONS

Women's rights groups take oppositional approaches to the question of prostitution. Abolitionists see prostitution as exploitation and an infraction of basic human rights. Meanwhile, mitigators recognise that there is demand and supply and try to reduce the risks associated with the activity, through HIV/AIDS prevention and education programs (especially for economic migrants). Sex-worker organisations argue that prostitution is a legitimate job and the best way to help women is to treat the issue from a workers' rights perspective, demanding fair pay and compensation, legal redress and mandatory sick and vacation time. According to pro-sex worker unions, the country's quasi-legal commercial sex establishments provide service industry jobs (dishwashers, cooks, cleaners) to non sex workers, who would otherwise qualify for employment protection if the employer were a restaurant or hotel.

HIV/AIDS

Thailand was lauded for its rapid and effective response to the AIDS epidemic through an aggressive condom-use campaign in the 1990s. But infection rates throughout the population have spiked as public education has declined. A 2007 study found that HIV prevalence among sex workers is highest in the freelance community (at a rate of 19%) compared to sex workers in commercial establishments (4.3%). Of the country's 490,000 people living with HIV/AIDS, intravenous drug users (22%) and gay men (between 20% to 31%) made up the largest portion of HIV prevalence.

Economic Motivations

NGOs

Ecpat (www.ecpat. net): anti-child prostitution and trafficking group.

Coalition Against Trafficking in Women (CATW; www.catwinter national.org): anti-trafficking NGO.

Empower Foundation (www.empowerfoundation.org): sex workers union.

Regardless of their background, most women in the sex industry are there for financial reasons: many find that sex work is one of the highest-paying jobs for their level of education, and they have financial obligations (be it dependents or debts). The most comprehensive data on the economics of sex workers comes from a 1993 survey by Kritaya Archavanitkul. The report found that sex workers made a mean income of 17,000B per month (US$18 per day), the equivalent of a mid-level civil servant job, a position acquired through advanced education and family connections. At the time of the study, most sex workers did not have a high-school degree.

These economic factors provide a strong incentive for rural, unskilled women (and to a lesser extent, men) to engage in sex work.

As with many in Thai society, a large percentage of sex workers' wages are remitted back to their home villages to support their families (parents, siblings and children). Kritaya's 1993 report found that between 1800B and 6100B per month was sent back to rural communities. The remittance-receiving households typically bought durable goods (TVs and washing machines), bigger houses and motorcycles or automobiles. Their wealth displayed their daughters' success in the industry and acted as free advertisement for the next generation of sex workers.

Child Prostitution & Human Trafficking

According to Ecpat (End Child Prostitution & Trafficking), there are currently 30,000 to 40,000 children involved in prostitution in Thailand, though estimates are unreliable. According to Chulalongkorn University, the number of children is as high as 800,000, though this number includes anyone under the age of 18.

In 1996, Thailand passed a reform law to address the issue of child prostitution defined into two tiers: 15 to 18 years old and under 15. Fines and jail time are assigned to customers, establishment owners and even parents involved in child prostitution. Under the old law only prostitutes were culpable. Many countries also have extraterritorial legislation that allows nationals to be prosecuted in their own country for such crimes committed in Thailand.

Suspicious behaviour involving child-sex tourism can be reported on a dedicated hotline (☏1300).

Urban job centres such as Bangkok have large populations of displaced and marginalised people (migrant workers, ethnic hill-tribe members and impoverished rural Thais). Children of these fractured families often turn to street begging, which is an entryway into prostitution usually through low-level criminal gangs.

Thailand is also a conduit and destination for people trafficking from Myanmar, Laos, Cambodia and China. In 2007, the US State Department labelled Thailand as not meeting the minimum standards of prevention of human trafficking. Reliable data about trafficked people, including minors, does not exist.

Food & Drink

There's an entire universe of amazing dishes once you get beyond pát tai ('pad Thai') and green curry, and for many visitors food is one of the main reasons for choosing Thailand as a destination. Even more remarkable, however, is locals' own love for Thai food. This unabashed enthusiasm for eating, not to mention an abundance of fascinating ingredients and influences, has resulted in one of the most fun and diverse food scenes anywhere in the world.

Staples & Specialities

Rice & Noodles

Rice is so central to Thai food culture that the most common term for 'eat' is *gin kôw* (literally, 'consume rice') and one of the most common greetings is *Gin kôw rĕu yang?* (Have you consumed rice yet?). To eat is to eat rice, and for most of the country, a meal is not acceptable without this staple.

There are many varieties of rice in Thailand and the country has been among the world leaders in rice exports since the 1960s. The highest grade is *kôw hŏrm má·lí* (jasmine rice), a fragrant long grain that is so coveted by neighbouring countries that there is allegedly a steady underground business in smuggling out fresh supplies. Residents of Thailand's north and northeast eat *kôw nĕe·o* (sticky rice), a glutinous short-grained rice that is cooked by steaming, not boiling. In Chinese-style eateries, *kôw dôm* (boiled rice), a watery porridge sometimes employing brown or purple rice, is a common carb.

Rice is customarily served alongside main dishes like curries, stir-fries or soups, which are lumped together as *gàp kôw* (with rice). When you order plain rice in a restaurant you use the term *kôw plòw* (plain rice) or *kôw sŏo·ay* (beautiful rice).

> Thailand is the world's third-largest exporter of rice and in 2012 exported 6.9 million tonnes of the grain.

You'll find four basic kinds of noodle in Thailand. Hardly surprising, given the Thai fixation on rice, is the overwhelming popularity of *sên gŏo·ay dĕe·o*, noodles made from rice flour mixed with water to form a paste, which is then steamed to form wide, flat sheets. The sheets are folded and sliced into various widths.

Also made from rice is *kà·nŏm jeen*, which is produced by pushing rice-flour paste through a sieve into boiling water, much the way Italian-style pasta is made. *Kà·nŏm jeen* is a popular morning market meal that is eaten doused with various spicy curries and topped with a self-selection of fresh and pickled vegetables and herbs.

The third kind of noodle, *bà·mèe*, is made from wheat flour and egg. It's yellowish in colour and sold only in fresh bundles.

Finally there's *wún·sên*, an almost clear noodle made from mung-bean starch and water. Often sold in dried bunches, *wún·sên* (literally 'jelly thread') is prepared by soaking in hot water for a few minutes. The most common use of the noodle is in *yam wún sên*, a hot and tangy salad made with lime juice, fresh sliced *prík kêe nŏo* (tiny chillies), shrimp, ground pork and various seasonings.

STREET FOOD

Curries & Soups

Thai Food by David Thompson is widely considered the most authoritative English-language book on Thai cooking. Thompson's latest book, *Thai Street Food*, focuses on less formal street cuisine.

In Thai, *gaang* (it sounds somewhat similar to the English 'gang') is often translated as 'curry', but it actually describes any dish with a lot of liquid and can thus refer to soups (such as *gaang jèut*) as well as the classic chilli paste-based curries for which Thai cuisine is famous. The preparation of the latter begins with a *krêu·ang gaang,* created by mashing, pounding and grinding an array of fresh ingredients with a stone mortar and pestle to form an aromatic, extremely pungent-tasting and rather thick paste. Typical ingredients in a *krêu·ang gaang* include dried chilli, galangal, lemongrass, kaffir lime zest, shallots, garlic, shrimp paste and salt.

Another food celebrity that falls into the soupy category is *dôm yam,* the famous Thai spicy and sour soup. Fuelling the fire beneath *dôm yam's* often velvety surface are fresh *prík kêe nöo* (tiny chillies) or, alternatively, half a teaspoonful of *nám prík pöw* (a roasted chilli paste). Lemongrass, kaffir lime leaf and lime juice give *dôm yam* its characteristic tang.

Stir-Fries & Deep-Fries

The simplest dishes in the Thai culinary repertoire are the various stir-fries *(pàt)* introduced to Thailand by the Chinese, who are world famous for being able to stir-fry a whole banquet in a single wok.

The list of *pàt* dishes seems endless. Many cling to their Chinese roots, such as the ubiquitous *pàt pàk bûng fai daang* (morning glory flash-fried with garlic and chilli), while some are Thai-Chinese hybrids, such as *pàt pèt* (literally 'hot stir-fry'), in which the main ingredients, typically meat or fish, are quickly stir-fried with red curry paste.

Tôrt (deep-frying in oil) is mainly reserved for snacks such as *glôo·ay tôrt* (deep-fried bananas) or *pò·pée·a* (egg rolls). An exception is *plah tôrt* (deep-fried fish), which is a common way to prepare fish.

Hot & Tangy Salads

Standing right alongside curries in terms of Thai-ness is the ubiquitous *yam,* a hot and tangy 'salad' typically based around seafood, meat or vegetables.

Lime juice provides the tang, while the abundant use of fresh chilli generates the heat. Most *yam* are served at room temperature or just slightly warmed by any cooked ingredients. The dish functions equally well as part of a meal or on its own as snack food *(gàp glâam)* to accompany a night of boozing.

Nám Prík

Pok Pok, by Andy Ricker and JJ Goode (and photographed by the author of this chapter), features recipes of the rustic regional Thai dishes served at Ricker's eponymous Portland, Oregon, and New York City restaurants.

Although they're more home than restaurant food, *nám prík,* spicy chilli-based 'dips', are, for the locals at least, among the most emblematic of all Thai dishes. Typically eaten with rice and steamed or fresh vegetables and herbs, they're also among the most regional of Thai dishes, and you could probably pinpoint the province you're in by simply looking at the *nám prík* on offer.

Fruits

Being a tropical country, Thailand excels in the fruit department. *Má·môo·ang* (mangoes) alone come in a dozen varieties that are eaten at different stages of ripeness. Other common fruit include *sàp·bà·rót* (pineapple), *má·lá·gor* (papaya) and *daang moh* (watermelon), all of which are sold from ubiquitous vendor carts and accompanied by a dipping mix of salt, sugar and ground chilli. Yet a highlight of visiting Thailand is sampling the huge variety of obscure and indigenous fruits; for a rundown on these, see the boxed text.

Sweets

English-language Thai menus often have a section called 'Desserts', but the concept takes two slightly different forms in Thailand. *Kŏrng wăhn*, which translates as 'sweet things', are small, rich sweets that often boast a slightly salty flavour. Prime ingredients for *kŏrng wăhn* include grated coconut, coconut milk, rice flour (from white rice or sticky rice), cooked sticky rice, tapioca, mung-bean starch, boiled taro and various fruits. Egg yolks are a popular ingredient for many *kŏrng wăhn* – including the ubiquitous *fŏy torng* (literally 'golden threads') – probably influenced by Portuguese desserts and pastries introduced during the early Ayuthaya era.

Thai sweets similar to the European concept of pastries are called *kà·nŏm*. Probably the most popular type of *kà·nŏm* in Thailand are the bite-sized items wrapped in banana leaves, especially *kôw đôm gà·tí* and *kôw đôm mát*. Both consist of sticky rice grains steamed with *gà·tí* (coconut milk) inside a banana-leaf wrapper to form a solid, almost taffylike, mass.

Maintained by a Thai woman living in the US, She Simmers (www.shesimmers.com) is a good resource for those making Thai food outside of Thailand.

FRUIT FOR THOUGHT

Thailand is home to an entire repertoire of fruit you probably never knew existed. Many are available year-round nowadays, but April and May is peak season for several of the most beloved varieties, including durian, mangoes and mangosteen.

Custard apple Known in Thai as *nóy nàh*; the knobbly green skin of this fruit conceals hard black seeds and sweet, gloopy flesh with a granular texture.

Durian Known in Thai as *tú·ree·an*, the king of fruit is also Thailand's most infamous, due to its intense flavour and odour, which can suggest everything from custard to onions.

Guava A native of South America, *fa·ràng* is a green, applelike ball containing a pink or white flesh that's sweet and crispy.

Jackfruit The gigantic green pod of *kà·nŭn* – it's generally considered the world's largest fruit – conceals dozens of waxy yellow sections that taste like a blend of pineapple and bananas (it reminds us of Juicy Fruit chewing gum).

Langsat Strip away the yellowish peel of this fruit, known in Thai as *long·gong*, to find a segmented, perfumed pearlescent flesh with a lychee-like flavour.

Longan *Lam yai* takes the form of a tiny hard ball; it's like a mini lychee with sweet, perfumed flesh. Peel it, eat the flesh and spit out the hard seeds.

Lychee The pink skin of *lín·jèe* conceals an addictive translucent flesh similar in flavour to a grape; it's generally only available between April and June.

Mangosteen The hard purple shell of *mang·kút*, the queen of Thai fruit, conceals delightfully fragrant white segments, some containing a hard seed.

Pomelo Like a grapefruit on steroids, *sôm oh* takes the form of a thick pithy green skin hiding sweet, tangy segments; cut into the skin, peel off the pith and then break open the segments and munch on the flesh inside.

Rambutan People have different theories about what *ngó* look like, not all repeatable in polite company. Regardless, the hairy shell contains sweet translucent flesh that you scrape off the seed with your teeth.

Rose apple Known in Thai as *chom·pôo*, rose apple is an elongated pink or red fruit with a smooth, shiny skin and pale, watery flesh; a good thirst quencher on a hot day.

Salak Also known as snake fruit because of its scaly skin; the exterior of *sàlà* looks like a mutant strawberry and the soft flesh tastes like unripe bananas.

Starfruit The star-shaped cross-section of *má·feu·ang* is the giveaway; the yellow flesh is sweet and tangy and believed by many to lower blood pressure.

Regional Variations

One little-known (at least outside of Thailand) characteristic aspect of Thai food is its regional diversity. Despite having evolved in a relatively small area, Thai cuisine is anything but a single entity, and takes a slightly different form every time it crosses a provincial border. For more on the regional specialities of Thailand, see p38.

Drinks

Coffee, Tea & Fruit Drinks

Bangkok's Top 50 Street Food Stalls, by Chawadee Nualkhair, also functions well as a general introduction and guide to Thai-style informal dining.

Thais are big coffee drinkers, and good-quality arabica and robusta are cultivated in the hilly areas of northern and southern Thailand. The traditional filtering system is nothing more than a narrow cloth bag attached to a steel handle. This type of coffee is served in a glass, mixed with sugar and sweetened with condensed milk – if you don't want either, be sure to specify *gah·faa dam* (black coffee) followed with *mâi sài nám·đahn* (without sugar).

Black tea, both local and imported, is available at the same places that serve real coffee. *Chah tai* derives its characteristic orange-red colour from ground tamarind seed added after curing.

Fruit drinks appear all over Thailand and are an excellent way to re-hydrate after water becomes unpalatable. Most *nám pŏn·lá·mái* (fruit juices) are served with a touch of sugar and salt and a whole lot of ice. Many foreigners object to the salt, but it serves a metabolic role in helping the body to cope with tropical temperatures.

Beer & Spirits

There are several brands of beer in Thailand, ranging from domestic brands (Singha, Chang, Leo) to foreign-licensed labels (Heineken, Asahi, San Miguel). They are all largely indistinguishable in terms of taste and quality.

Domestic rice whisky and rum are favourites of the working class, struggling students and family gatherings as they're more affordable than beer. Once spending money becomes a priority, Thais often upgrade to imported whiskies. These are usually drunk with lots of ice, soda water and a splash of coke. On a night out, buying a whole bottle is the norm in most of Thailand. If you don't finish it, it will simply be kept at the bar until your next visit.

Where to Eat & Drink

Appon's Thai Food (www. khiewchanta. com) features nearly 1000 authentic and well-organised Thai recipes – many with helpful audio recordings of their Thai names – written by a native Thai.

Prepared food is available just about everywhere in Thailand, and it shouldn't come as a surprise that the locals do much of their eating outside the home. In this regard, as a visitor, you'll fit right in.

Open-air markets and food stalls are among the most popular places where Thais eat. In the morning, stalls selling coffee and Chinese-style doughnuts spring up along busy commuter corridors. At lunchtime, midday eaters might grab a plastic chair at yet another stall for a simple stir-fry, or pick up a foam box of noodles to scarf down at the office. In most small towns, night markets often set up in the middle of town with a cluster of vendors, metal tables and chairs, and some shopping as an after-dinner mint.

There are, of course, restaurants *(ráhn ah·hăhn)* in Thailand that range from simple food stops to formal affairs. Lunchtime is the right time to point and eat at the *ráhn kôw gaang* (rice-and-curry shop), which sells a selection of premade dishes. The more generic *ráhn ah·hăhn đahm sàng* (food-to-order shop) can often be recognised by a display of raw ingredients – Chinese kale, tomatoes, chopped pork, fresh or dried fish, noodles, eggplant, spring onions – and serve a standard repertoire of Thai and Chinese dishes. As the name implies, the cooks attempt to prepare any dish you can name, a slightly more difficult operation if you can't speak Thai.

Vegetarians & Vegans

Vegetarianism isn't a widespread trend in Thailand, but many of the tourist-oriented restaurants cater to vegetarians. That doesn't mean that all Thais are monogamous carnivores; there are several non-profit *ráhn ah·hǎhn mang·sà·wí·rát* (vegetarian restaurants) in Bangkok and several provincial capitals where the food is served buffet-style and is very inexpensive. Dishes are almost always 100% vegan (ie no meat, poultry, fish or fish sauce, dairy or egg products).

The phrase 'I'm vegetarian' in Thai is *pǒm gin jair* (for men) or *dì·chǎn gin jair* (for women). Loosely translated this means 'I eat only vegetarian food', which includes no eggs and no dairy products – in other words, total vegan.

Habits & Customs

Like most of Thai culture, eating conventions appear relaxed and informal but are orchestrated by many implied rules.

Whether at home or in a restaurant, Thai meals are always served 'family-style' (from common serving platters) and the plates appear in whatever order the kitchen can prepare them. When serving yourself from a common platter, put no more than one spoonful onto your plate at a time. Heaping your plate with all 'your' portions at once will look greedy to Thais unfamiliar with Western conventions.

Originally Thai food was eaten with the fingers, and it still is in certain regions of the kingdom. In the early 1900s, Thais began setting their tables with fork and spoon to affect a 'royal' setting, and it wasn't long before fork-and-spoon dining became the norm in Bangkok and later spread throughout the kingdom. To use these tools the Thai way, use a serving spoon, or alternatively your own, to take a single mouthful of food from a central dish, and ladle it over a portion of your rice. The fork is then used to push the now food-soaked portion of rice back onto the spoon before entering the mouth.

If you're not offered chopsticks, don't ask for them. Thai food is eaten with fork and spoon, not chopsticks. When *fa·ràng* (Westerners) ask for chopsticks to eat Thai food, it only puzzles restaurant proprietors. Chopsticks are reserved for eating Chinese-style food from bowls, or for eating in all-Chinese restaurants. In either case you will be supplied with chopsticks without having to ask. Unlike their counterparts in many Western countries, restaurateurs in Thailand won't assume you don't know how to use them.

Thai Hawker Food, by Kenny Yee and Catherine Gordon, is an illustrated guide to recognising and ordering street food in Thailand.

Thai Food Master (www.thaifoodmaster.com), maintained by a longtime foreign resident of Thailand, contains helpful step-by-step photos that illustrate the making of a variety of Thai dishes.

Food Spotter's Guide

Spanning four distinct regions, influences from China to the Middle East, a multitude of ingredients and a reputation for spice, Thai food can be more than a bit overwhelming. So to point you in the direction of the good stuff, we've put together a shortlist of the country's must-eat dishes.

1. Đôm yam
The 'sour Thai soup' moniker featured on many English-language menus is a feeble description of this mouth-puckeringly tart and intensely spicy herbal broth.

2. Pàt tai
Thin rice noodles fried with egg, tofu and shrimp, and seasoned with fish sauce, tamarind and dried chilli, have emerged as the poster boy for Thai food – and justifiably so.

3. Gaang kĕe·o wăhn
Known outside of Thailand as green curry, this intersection of a piquant, herbal spice paste and rich coconut milk is single-handedly emblematic of Thai cuisine's unique flavours and ingredients.

4. Yam
This family of Thai 'salads' combines meat or seafood with a tart and spicy dressing and fresh herbs.

5. Lâhp
Minced meat seasoned with roasted rice powder, lime, fish sauce and fresh herbs is a one-dish crash course in the strong, rustic flavours of Thailand's northeast.

AUSTIN BUSH ©

6. Bà·mèe

Although Chinese in origin, these wheat-and-egg noodles, typically served with roast pork and/or crab, have become a Thai hawker-stall staple.

7. Kôw mòk

The Thai version of *biryani* couples golden rice and tender chicken with a sweet and sour dip and a savoury broth.

8. Sôm·đam

'Papaya salad' hardly does justice to this tear-inducingly spicy dish of strips of crunchy unripe papaya pounded in a mortar and pestle with tomato, long beans, chilli, lime and fish sauce.

9. Kôw soy

Even outside of its home in Thailand's north, there's a cult following for this soup that combines flat egg-and-wheat noodles in a rich, spice-laden, coconut-milk-based broth.

10. Pàt pàk bûng fai daang

'Morning glory', a crunchy green vegetable, flash-fried with heaps of chilli and garlic, is, despite the spice, Thai comfort food.

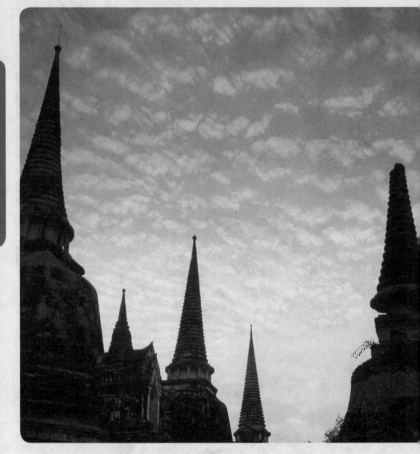

Arts & Architecture

Thailand has an intensely visual culture and an appreciation of beauty that infuses audacious temple buildings, humble old-fashioned houses and the high arts developed for the royal court. Temple architecture and Buddhist sculpture define the bulk of Thailand's ancient arts but the modern era has branched into many forms of expression from social commentary in contemporary paintings to sky-piercing towers in Bangkok. Musical traditions range from classical orchestras to teenage anthems with a great dance beat.

Architecture

Above Wat Phra Si Sanphet, Ayuthaya (p154)

Most striking of Thailand's architectural heritage are the Buddhist temples, which dazzle in the tropical sun. A classic component of temple architecture is the *chedi* (stupa), a mountain-shaped monument that pays tribute to the enduring stability of Buddhism. Many contain relics of important kings or the historical Buddha.

Thai temples rely heavily on Hindu-Buddhist iconography. *Naga,* a mythical serpentlike creature, guarded Buddha during meditation and is often depicted in entrance railings and outlining roof gables. On the tip of the roof is the *chôr fáh:* a golden bird-shaped silhouette suggesting flight.

The lotus bud is another sacred motif that is often used to decorate the tops of the temple gates, verandah columns and the spires of Sukhothai-era *chedi*. Images of the Buddha often depict him meditating in a lotus pedestal. It carries with it a reminder of the tenets of Buddhism. The lotus can bloom even in a rancid pond, illustrating the capacity for religious perfection in unlikely situations.

Thais began mixing traditional architecture with European forms in the late 19th and early 20th centuries. The port cities, including Bangkok and Phuket, acquired fine examples of Sino-Portuguese architecture – buildings of stuccoed brick decorated with an ornate facade – a style that followed the sea traders during the colonial era. It is locally known as 'old Bangkok' or 'Ratanakosin'.

Bangkok Today

Bangkok's skyscrapers are textbook examples of postmodern dos and don'ts. In the 1960s and '70s Thai architecture was inspired by the European Bauhaus movement with stark functionalism – the average building looked like a giant egg carton turned on its side. When Thai architects began experimenting with form over function during the building boom of the mid-1980s, the result was high-tech designs such as

THAILAND'S ARTISTIC & ARCHITECTURAL PERIODS

PERIOD	TEMPLE & CHEDI STYLES	BUDDHA STYLES	EXAMPLES
Dvaravati Period (7th–11th centuries)	Rectangular-based *chedi* with stepped tiers	Indian influenced; thick torso, large hair curls, arched eyebrows (like flying birds), protruding eyes, thick lips and flat nose	Phra Pathom Chedi, Nakhon Pathom; Lopburi Museum, Lopburi; Wat Chama Thewi, Lamphun
Srivijaya Period (7th–13th centuries)	Mahayana Buddhist–style temples; Javanese-style *chedi* with elaborate arches	Indian influenced; heavily ornamented, humanlike features and slightly twisted at the waist	Wat Phra Mahathat Woramahawihaan and National Museum, Nakhon Si Thammarat
Khmer Period (9th–11th centuries)	Hindu-Buddhist temples; corn-cob-shaped *prang* (Khmer-styled *chedi*)	Buddha meditating under a canopy of the seven-headed *naga* and atop a lotus pedestal	Phimai Historical Park, Phimai; Phanom Rung Historical Park, Surin
Chiang Saen–Lanna Period (11th–13th centuries)	Teak temples; square-based *chedi* topped by gilded umbrella; also octagonal-based *chedi*	Burmese influences with plump figure, round, smiling face and footpads facing upwards in meditation pose	Wat Phra Singh, Chiang Mai; Chiang Saen National Museum, Chiang Saen
Sukhothai Period (13th–15th centuries)	Khmer-inspired temples; slim-spired *chedi* topped by a lotus bud	Graceful poses, often depicted 'walking', no anatomical human detail	Sukhothai Historical Park, Sukhothai
Ayuthaya Period (14th–18th centuries)	Classical Thai temple with three-tiered roof and gable flourishes; bell-shaped *chedi* with tapering spire	Ayuthaya-era king, wearing a gem-studded crown and royal regalia	Ayuthaya Historical Park, Ayuthaya
Bangkok-Ratanakosin Period (19th century)	Colourful and gilded temple with Western-Thai styles; mosaic-covered *chedi*	Reviving Ayuthaya style	Wat Phra Kaew, Wat Pho and Wat Arun, Bangkok

Above Bangkok Art & Culture Centre (p81)
Left Ananta Samakhom Throne Hall (p86)

Above Bangkok skyline

ML Sumet Jumsai's famous 'Robot Building' on Th Sathon Tai in Bangkok. Rangsan Torsuwan, a graduate of the Massachusetts Institute of Technology (MIT), introduced the neoclassic (or neo-Thai) style. Today, Bangkok is more sophisticated in its architectural aesthetic. Shopping malls, skyscrapers and hotels all demonstrate the latest architectural trends: rounded glass towers, patterned facades, hyper geometry and stark minimalism. Adapting modern architecture to the extremes of a tropical climate has restored some of the functionalism that was lost during the country's rush towards modernisation in decades past. Reclaiming and restoring old buildings is another architectural trend for the vintage-oriented youth who view traditional architecture as novel and sentimental instead of outdated.

Arts

Much of Thailand's best ancient art is on display inside the country's many famous temples, while Bangkok's many national and commercial museums curate contemporary collections.

Traditional Painting & Sculpture

Thailand's artistic repository resides in the temples where Buddha sculptures and murals communicate a visual language of the religion. These Buddha images trace Thailand's historical and artistic evolution from a conquered backwater to a sovereign nation. The period when the country first defined its own artistic style was during the Sukhothai era, famous for its graceful and serene Buddha figures.

Temple murals are the main form of ancient Thai art. Always instructional in intent, murals often depict the *jataka* (stories of the Buddha's past lives) and the Thai version of the Hindu epic *Ramayana*. Lacking the durability of other art forms, pre-20th-century religious painting

Bangkok Art Museums & Galleries

National Museum

Bangkok Art & Culture Centre

100 Tonson Gallery

H Gallery

Kathmandu Photo Gallery

Museum of Contemporary Art

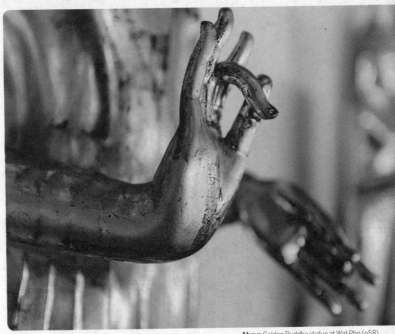

Above Golden Buddha statue at Wat Pho (p58)

is limited to very few surviving examples. The earliest examples are found at Ayuthaya's Wat Ratburana, but Bangkok has some of the best surviving examples.

The development of Thai religious art and architecture is broken into different periods defined by the patronage of the ruling capital. The best examples of a period's characteristics are seen in the variations of the *chedi* shape and in the features of the Buddha sculptures, including facial features, the top flourish on the head, the dress and the position of the feet in meditation.

Contemporary Art

Adapting traditional themes to the secular canvas began around the turn of the 20th century as Western influence surged in the region. In general, Thai painting favours abstraction over realism and continues to preserve the one-dimensional perspective of traditional mural paintings. There are two major trends in Thai art: the updating of religious themes and tongue-in-cheek social commentary. Some artists overlap the two.

Italian Corrado Feroci is often credited as the father of modern Thai art. He was invited to Thailand by Rama VI in 1923 and built Bangkok's Democracy Monument and other monuments in the city.

In the 1970s Thai artists tackled the modernisation of Buddhist themes through abstract expressionism. Leading works include the colourful surrealism of Pichai Nirand and the mystical pen-and-ink drawings of Thawan Duchanee. Internationally known Montien Boonma uses the ingredients of Buddhist merit-making, such as gold leaf, bells and candle wax, to create installation pieces.

Politically motivated artwork defined a parallel movement in Thai contemporary art. In Thailand's rapidly industrialising society, many artists watched as the rice fields became factories, the forests became as

Above Buddha statues at dusk
Right Ceramic sculptures

FRANK CARTER / GETTY IMAGES ©

Above Thai xylophone
Left Live music in Phuket

> ## HANDMADE ART
>
> Thailand has a long tradition of handicrafts, often regionally and even village specific. Ceramics include the greenish celadon products, the red-earth clay pots of Dan Kwian, and central Thailand's *ben·jà·rong* or 'five-colour' style. *Ben·jà·rong* is based on Chinese patterns while celadon is of Thai origin.
>
> Northern Thailand has long produced regionally distinctive lacquerware thanks to the influence of Burmese artisans.
>
> Each region in Thailand has its own silk-weaving style. In ancient times woven textiles might have functioned much like business cards do today – demarcating tribal identity and sometimes even marriage status. Today, village weaving traditions continue but have become less geographically specific.

đà·pohn
(tohn)

rá·nâht èhk

phalt and the spoils went to the politically connected. Manit Sriwanichpoom is best known for his Pink Man on Tour series, in which he depicted artist Sompong Thawee in a pink suit with a pink shopping cart amid Thailand's most iconic attractions. Vasan Sitthiket is more blatantly controversial and uses mixed-media installations to condemn the corruption. His works have been banned in Thailand and criticised as anti-Thai.

In the 1990s there was a push to move art out of museums and into public spaces. Navin Rawanchaikul started his 'in-the-streets' collaborations in his hometown of Chiang Mai and then moved to Bangkok where he filled the city's taxi cabs with art installations, a show that literally went on the road. His other works have a way with words, such as the 2002 mixed-media piece *We Are the Children of Rice (Wine)* and his rage against the commercialisation of museums in his epic painting entitled *Super (M)art Bangkok Survivors* (2004). Up-and-coming artists use a variety of media and take on more introspective topics, like Maitree Siriboon who uses collage and photography to explore personal identity and sexuality. Thai-Japanese artist Yuree Kensaku creates cartoon-like paintings with pop-culture references.

pèe

Thai sculpture is often considered to be the strongest of the contemporary arts. Khien Yimsiri creates elegant human and mythical forms out of bronze. Manop Suwanpinta moulds the human anatomy into fantastic shapes that often intersect with technology, such as hinged faces that open to reveal inanimate content. Kamin Lertchaiprasert explores the subject of spirituality and daily life in his sculptures. His *Ngern Nang* (Sitting Money) installation included a series of figures made from discarded paper bills from the national bank embellished with poetic instructions on life and love.

sor

Music

Throughout Thailand you'll find a diversity of musical genres and styles, from the serene court music that accompanies classical dance-drama to the bass-heavy house music played at dance clubs.

klòo·i

Classical Music

The classical orchestra is called the *pèe pâht* and was originally developed to accompany classical dance-drama and shadow theatre, but these days can be heard in straightforward performances at temple fairs and tourist attractions. The ensemble can include from five to more than 20 players. Prior to a performance the players offer incense and flowers to the *đà·pohn*.

kórng wong
yài

The standard Thai scale divides the eight-note octave into seven full-tone intervals, with no semitones. Thai scales were first transcribed by the Thai-German composer Peter Feit (also known by his Thai name, Phra Chen Duriyang), who composed Thailand's national anthem in 1932.

Thailand Playlist

That Song (Modern Dog)

The Sound of Siam: Leftfield Luk Thung, Jazz & Molam in Thailand 1964–1975 (Soundway Records compilation)

Made in Thailand (Carabao)

Best (Pumpuang Duangjan)

Romantic Comedy (Apartment Khunpa)

Lôok Tûng & Mŏr Lam

The bestselling modern musical genre in Thailand is *lôok tûng* (literally 'children of the fields'), which dates to the 1940s. Analogous to country-and-western music in the USA, it appeals to working-class Thais. Traditional subject matter are tales of lost love, tragic early death, and the dire circumstances of struggling farmers. The plaintive singing style ranges from sentimental to anguish and singers are often backed by Las Vegas–style showgirl dancers.

Mŏr lam is Thailand's blues; it's a folk tradition firmly rooted in northeast Thailand and Laos and is based on the songs played on the *kaan* (a wind instrument devised of a double row of bamboo-like reeds fitted into a hardwood soundbox). The oldest style is most likely to be heard at a village gathering with a simple but insistent bass beat and is often sung in Isan dialect. *Mŏr lam* has jumped the generational fence and now has an electrified pop version and a seriously silly side.

As economic migrants from across the country have moved to Bangkok, the two genres have merged with each other as well as with other forms. Contemporary singers might sing about city woes, factory work or being too fat backed up by a dance club beat.

Thailand's most famous *lôok tûng* singer was Pumpuang Duangjan, who received a royally sponsored cremation when she died in 1992 and a major shrine at Suphanburi's Wat Thapkradan. Gravelly voiced Siriporn Ampaipong helped carry the tradition afterwards and is still beloved. The new *lôok tûng* princesses are Yingli Sijumpon, a sweetheart from Buriram, and Baitoi R Siam, who has crossed over into sexy pop. Pai Pongsaton and Tai Orathai are other stalwarts. Auu Jeerawat has an acoustic take on the genre.

Thai Rock & Pop

The 1970s ushered in the politically conscious folk rock of the USA and Europe, which the Thais dubbed *pleng pêu·a chee·wít* ('songs for life'). Chiefly identified with the Thai band Caravan, this style defined a major contemporary shift in Thai music. Songs of this nature have political and environmental topics rather than the usual love themes. During the authoritarian dictatorships of the '70s many of Caravan's songs were officially banned. Another longstanding example of this style, Carabao, mixed in rock and heavy metal and spawned a whole generation of imitators.

TRADITIONAL INSTRUMENTS

➡ **þèe** High-pitched woodwind, often heard at Thai-boxing matches

➡ **rá·nâht èhk** Bamboo-keyed percussion that resembles a xylophone

➡ **kórng wong yài** Tuned gongs arranged in a semicircle

➡ **đà·pohn (tohn)** A double-headed hand-drum

➡ **pĭn** Four-stringed instrument plucked like a guitar

➡ **sor** Slender bowed instrument with a coconut-shell soundbox

➡ **klòo·i** Wooden flute

HIPSTER CRAZE: SIAMESE SOUL

Pop music from the 1960s and '70s has gained an international cult following thanks to overseas collectors Sublime Frequencies. Compilations from the era include *Siamese Soul: Thai Pop Spectacular*, which includes groovy tunes crowded with horns and funky beats. The track 'E-Saew Tam Benha Huajai' inspired the music for My Morning Jacket's song 'Holding on to Black Metal'.

Thailand also has a thriving teen-pop industry – sometimes referred to as T-pop – centred on artists chosen for their good looks, which often means they are half-Thai, half-*fa·ràng* and sport English names. Thailand's king of pop is Thongchai 'Bird' McIntyre (also known as Pi Bird). His first album came out in 1986 and he has followed up with an album almost every year since. With Madonna's staying power coupled with a nice-guy persona, he is very popular with Thais in their 30s and 40s.

The current crop of pop stars are imitating the signature dance moves of Korean pop stars (Japan pop, or J-pop, is out). The most curious of them all is Apple Girl Band (as in Apple products): they use Apple apps to make music. Endorphine is a feel-good band led by sweet-faced Da with almost a decade's worth of hits.

The 1990s gave birth to an alternative pop scene – known as 'indie' – pioneered by the independent record label Bakery Music. During indie's heyday, Modern Dog, composed of four Chulalongkorn University graduates, orchestrated the generation's musical coming of age. Another indie fixture was Loso (from 'low society' as opposed to 'hi-so' or socialites), which updated Carabao's affinity for Thai folk melodies and rhythms. But the past decade has moved these bands into classic rock status and Bakery Music was bought by a conglomerate.

The alt scene lives in a variety of forms – lounge pop, garage rock and electronica. Tattoo Colour hailing from Khon Kaen managed to score several hits from a small indie label. The female trio Yellow Fang has a following for its once-a-year single releases. The revived disco sound of Groove Riders has brought down the tempo but upped the funky factor. Their hit 'Disco' was a wedding-song staple.

Music Sources

E Thai Music (www.ethaicd.com) is an online Thai music store.

Popular Thai radio stations include Fat FM 104.5 (alt-rock), Seed FM 97.5 (T-pop), and Luk Thung FM95.0 (lôok tûng and mŏr lam).

Dance & Theatre

Thailand's high arts have been in decline since the palace transitioned from a cloistered community. Some of the endangered art forms have been salvaged and revived for the tourist community. Folk traditions have a broader appeal, though the era of village stage shows is long gone.

Thailand's most famous dance-drama is *kŏhn*, which depicts the *Ramakian*, the Thai version of India's *Ramayana*. Dancers wear elaborate costumes and some characters are masked. The central story revolves around Prince Rama's search for his beloved Princess Sita, who has been abducted by the evil 10-headed demon Ravana and taken to the island of Lanka.

Every region has its own traditional dance style performed at temple fairs and provincial parades. School-aged children often take traditional Thai dance lessons. Occasionally temples will also provide shrine dancers, who are commissioned by merit-makers to perform.

Most often performed at Buddhist festivals, *lí·gair* is a gaudy, raucous theatrical art form thought to have descended from drama rituals brought to southern Thailand by Arab and Malay traders. It contains a colourful mix of folk and classical music, outrageous costumes, melodrama, slapstick comedy, sexual innuendo and up-to-date commentary.

Puppet theatre also enjoyed royal and common patronage. *Lá·kon lék* (little theatre) used marionettes of varying sizes for court performances similar to *kŏhn*. Two to three puppet masters are required to manipulate the metre-high puppets by means of wires attached to long poles. Stories are drawn from Thai folk tales, particularly *Phra Aphaimani*, and occasionally from the *Ramakian*.

Shadow-puppet theatre – in which two-dimensional figures are manipulated between a cloth screen and a light source at night-time performances – has been a Southeast Asian tradition for perhaps five centuries originally brought to the Malay Peninsula by Middle Eastern traders. In Thailand it is mostly found in the south. As in Malaysia and Indonesia, shadow puppets in Thailand are carved from dried buffalo or cow hides (*năng*).

Cinema

When it comes to Thai cinema, there are usually two concurrent streams: the movies that are financially successful and the movies that are considered cinematically meritorious. Only occasionally do these overlap.

Popular Thai cinema ballooned in the 1960s and '70s, especially when the government levied a tax on Hollywood imports which spawned a home-grown industry. The majority of films were cheap action flicks that were often dubbed *nám nôw* (stinking water), but the fantastic (even nonsensical) plots and rich colours left a lasting impression on modern-day Thai filmmakers.

Thai cinema graduated into international film circles in the late 1990s and early 2000s, thanks in part to director Pen-ek Ratanaruang and his gritty and engrossing films. Apichatpong Weerasethakul is Thailand's leading *cinéma-vérité* director and has received two Cannes accolades. Today the international film festivals host a new crop of experimental directors. Nawapol Thamrongrattanrit gained acclaim for his modern-girl-in-the-city screenplay *Bangkok Traffic Love Story* (2009) and followed up with his directorial debut *36* (2012), which uses 36 static camera shots to explore lost love and lost memories. *Mary is Happy, Mary is Happy* (Nawapol Thamrongrattanarit; 2013) is a film festival hit that adapted the Twitter feed of a Thai teen into a movie.

Film fest fare has been bolstered by independent film clubs and self-promotion through social media. This is how low-budget filmmakers bypass the big studios, the cinema censors (who are ever vigilant) and the skittish, controversy-averse movie theatres. In 2007 the film board introduced a rating system (five levels indicated by appropriate age of viewer) to provide more predictability. Being censored often equals immediate indie success. Two political documentaries of 2013 challenged the board's sensitivities. Pen-ek's historical *Paradoxocracy* had to mute objectionable dialogue while Nontawat Numbenchapol's *Boundary* was initially banned, though that was lifted after an appeal.

The big studios like ghost stories, horror flicks, historic epics, sappy love stories and camp comedies. Elaborate historical movies serve a dual purpose: making money and promoting national identity. Criticised as a propaganda tool, the *Legend of King Naresuan* epic, which comprises five instalments, focuses on the Ayuthaya-era king who repelled an attempted Burmese invasion. Each chapter (four have been released so far) has been a box-office winner.

Literature

The written word has a long history in Thailand, dating back to the 11th or 12th century when the first Thai script was fashioned from an older Mon alphabet. The 30,000-line *Phra Aphaimani*, composed by poet Sunthorn Phu in the late 18th century, is Thailand's most famous classical literary work. Like many of its epic predecessors around the world, it tells the story of an exiled prince who must complete an odyssey of love and war before returning to his kingdom in victory.

Of all classical Thai literature, however, *Ramakian* is the most pervasive and influential in Thai culture. The Indian source, *Ramayana,* came to Thailand with the Khmers 900 years ago, first appearing as stone reliefs on Prasat Hin Phimai and other Angkor temples in the northeast. Eventually the Thais developed their own version of the epic, which was first written down during the reign of Rama I (r 1782–1809). This version contained 60,000 stanzas and was a quarter longer than the Sanskrit original.

Although the main themes remained the same, the Thais embroidered the *Ramayana* with more biographical detail on arch-villain Ravana (called Thotsakan, or '10-necked' in the *Ramakian*) and his wife Montho. Hanuman, the monkey god, differs substantially in the Thai version in his flirtatious nature (in the Hindu version he follows a strict vow of chastity). One of the classic *Ramakian* reliefs at Bangkok's Wat Pho depicts Hanuman clasping a maiden's bared breast as if it were an apple.

Environment & Wildlife

Thailand spans a distance of 1650km from its northern tip to its southern tail, a distance that encompasses 16 latitudinal degrees and a variety of ecological zones, making it one of the most environmentally diverse countries in Southeast Asia.

The Land

Thailand's odd shape is often likened to the head of an elephant, with the shaft of the trunk being the Malay Peninsula and the head being the northern mountains. Starting at the crown of the country, northern Thailand is dominated by the Dawna-Tenasserim mountain range, a southeast-trending extension of the Himalayan mountains. Dropping into the central region, the topography mellows into rice-producing plains fed by rivers that are as revered as the national monarchy. Thailand's most exalted river is the Chao Phraya, which is formed by the northern tributaries of Ping, Wang, Yom and Nan – a lineage as notable as any aristocrat's. The country's early kingdoms emerged around the Chao Phraya basin, still the seat of the monarchy today. The river delta is in cultivation for most of the year.

Tracing the contours of Thailand's northern and northeastern border is another celebrated river: the Mekong. As the artery of Southeast Asia, the Mekong both physically separates and culturally fuses Thailand with its neighbours. It is a workhorse river that has been dammed for hydroelectric power, and swells and contracts based on the seasonal rains. In the dry season, farmers plant vegetables in the muddy floodplain, harvesting their crops before the river reclaims its territory.

The landscape of Thailand's northeastern border is occupied by the arid Khorat Plateau rising some 300m above the central plain. This is a hardscrabble land where the rains are meagre, the soil is anaemic and the red dust stains as stubbornly as the betel nut chewed by the ageing grandmothers.

The kingdom's eastern rivers dump their waters into the Gulf of Thailand, a shallow basin off the neighbouring South China Sea. The warm, gentle gulf is an ideal cultivation ground for coral reefs. Sliding further south is the Malay Peninsula, a long trunklike landmass. On the western side is the Andaman Sea, a splendid tropical setting of stunning blue waters and dramatic limestone islands. Onshore, the peninsula is dominated by some final remaining stands of rainforest and ever-expanding rubber and palm-oil plantations.

Statistics

Thailand encompasses 513,120 sq km, equal to the size of France.

Bangkok sits at a latitude of 14° north, level with Chennai, Manila, Guatemala City and Khartoum.

Flora & Fauna

In the northern half of Thailand, most indigenous species are classified zoologically as Indo-Chinese, referring to fauna originating from mainland Asia, while those of the south are generally Sundaic, typical of peninsular Malaysia, Sumatra, Borneo and Java. There is also an interesting overlap that provides habitat for plants and animals from both zones

WHERE THE WILD ELEPHANTS ROAM

Many of the national parks host wild elephant herds that congregate in the evenings at salt ponds and watering holes. Here are a few parks known for their elephant herds:

➡ **Kuiburi National Park** (p516), near Prachuap Khiri Khan.

➡ **Khao Yai National Park** (p419), northeast of Bangkok in Nakhon Ratchasima Province.

➡ **Kaeng Krachan National Park** (p499), south of Bangkok in Phetchaburi.

starting in Uthai Thani and extending south to the gulf region around Prachuap Khiri Khan.

Thailand is particularly rich in bird life, with over a thousand recorded resident and migrating species, approximately 10% of the world's bird species. The cool mountains of northern Thailand are populated by montane species and migrants with clear Himalayan affinities such as flycatchers and thrushes. The arid forests of Khao Yai National Park in northeastern Thailand are favourites for hornbills. Marshland birds prefer the wetlands of the central region, while Sundaic species such as Gurney's pitta flock to the wetter climate of southern Thailand.

In addition to abundant bird life, visitors to the country's national parks are most likely to spot monkeys. Thailand is home to five species of macaque, four species of the smaller leaf-monkey and three species of gibbon. Although they face the same habitat loss as other native species, monkeys sometimes survive in varying states of domestication with humans. The long-armed gibbons were once raised alongside children in rural villages, and macaques can be found living in small wooded patches or unused temples in population centres.

Other species found in the kingdom's parks and sanctuaries include gaur (Indian bison), banteng (wild cattle), serow (an Asiatic goat-antelope), sambar deer, muntjac (barking deer), mouse deer and tapir – to name a few.

Thailand has six venomous snakes: the common cobra, king cobra, banded krait, green viper, Malayan viper and Russell's pit viper. Although the relatively rare king cobra can reach up to 6m in length, the nation's largest snake is the reticulated python, which can reach a whopping 10m.

The country's many lizard species include two common varieties – *dúk·gaa,* a reclusive and somewhat homely gecko heard in the early evening coughing its name; and *jîng·jòk,* a spirited house lizard that is usually spotted on ceilings and walls chasing after bugs. The black jungle monitor, which looks like a miniature dinosaur, lives in some of the southern forests.

The oceans are home to hundreds of species of coral, and the reefs created by these tiny creatures provide the perfect living conditions for fish, crustaceans and tiny invertebrates. You can find the world's smallest fish (the 10mm-long goby) and the largest (the 18m-long whale shark), plus reef denizens such as clownfish, parrotfish, wrasse, angelfish, triggerfish and lionfish. Deeper waters are home to grouper, barracuda, sharks, manta rays, marlin and tuna. You might also encounter turtles, whales and dolphins.

Thailand's most famous animals are also its most endangered. The Asian elephant, a smaller cousin to the African elephant, once roamed the forests of Indochina in great herds. But the wild elephant faces extinction due to habitat loss and poaching. The population of wild elephants in Thailand is estimated at about one thousand.

Reclusive wild tigers stalk the hinterlands between Thailand and Myanmar, but in ever-decreasing numbers. It is difficult to obtain

BIODIVERSITY

The Mekong River rivals the Amazon River in terms of biodiversity, and shelters endangered and newly discovered species, such as the Khorat big-mouthed frog, which uses fangs to catch prey.

an accurate count, but experts estimate that around 200 to 300 wild tigers remain in Thailand. Although tiger hunting and trapping is illegal, poachers continue to kill the cats for the overseas wildlife trade.

The rare dugong (also called manatee or sea cow), once thought extinct in Thailand, survives in a few small pockets around Trang, but is increasingly threatened by habitat loss and the lethal propellers of tourist boats.

The remaining jungles of Thailand can be divided into two forest types: monsoon (with a distinct dry season of three months or more) and rainforest (where rain falls more than nine months per year). The most heavily forested provinces are Chiang Mai and Kanchanaburi.

Monsoon forests in the northern parts of the country are composed of deciduous trees, which are green and lush during the rainy season but dusty and leafless during the dry season. Teak is one of the most highly valued monsoon forest trees, but it now exists only in limited quantities.

In southern Thailand, where rainfall is plentiful and distributed evenly throughout the year, forests are classified as rainforests with a few areas of monsoon forest. One remarkable plant found in some southern forests is *Rafflesia kerrii*, a squat plant with a huge flower that reaches 80cm across; you can see it at Khao Sok National Park near Surat Thani.

Thailand is home to nearly 75 coastal mangrove species, small salt-tolerant trees that provide an incubator for many coastal fish and animal species. Reforestation programs of mangrove areas have gained popularity thanks to their protective role during the 2004 Asian tsunami.

Orchids are Thailand's most exquisite native flora. There are over 1100 native species and they live in a variety of habitats: some are ground dwellers, while others anchor high up in trees, and still others cling to rocky outcrops.

Queen Sirikit Botanic Gardens (p280), outside of Chiang Mai, includes a beautiful collection of orchids and lotus.

Environmental Issues

Deforestation

Thailand has put enormous pressure on its ecosystems through cultivation of land into cities and farms. Natural forest cover now makes up about 28% of land area, compared to 70% some 50 years ago. The rapid depletion of the country's forests coincided with the shift towards industrialisation, urbanisation and commercial logging. Although these statistics are alarming, forest loss has slowed since the turn of the millennium to about 0.4% per year.

In response to environmental degradation, the Thai government created a large number of protected areas, starting in the 1970s, and set a goal of 40% forest cover by the middle of this century. In 1989 all logging was banned in Thailand following disastrous mudslides in Surat Thani Province that buried villages and killed more than a hundred people. It is now illegal to sell timber felled in the country, but this law is frequently flouted by local populations living near forest complexes and by those with well-connected interests.

A corollary problem to deforestation is habitat loss. Wildlife experts agree that the greatest danger faced by Thai fauna and flora is neither hunting nor the illegal wildlife trade, but habitat loss. Species that are notably extinct in Thailand include the kouprey (a type of wild cattle), Schomburgk's deer and the Javan rhino, but innumerable smaller species have also disappeared with little fanfare.

Coastal & Marine Degradation

Thailand's coastal region has experienced higher population and economic growth than the national average, and the majority of the country's manufacturing industry is located along the eastern seaboard and the upper Gulf of Thailand. With increased population comes increased environmental pressure.

Soil erosion is a major coastal problem. According to the World Bank, Thailand is losing 2 sq km from its coastline every year. This is due in part to coastal development (construction of jetties, breakwaters, ocean-front hotels and roads), land subsiding (due to groundwater depletion) and rising sea levels. Accurate data is lacking on coastal water quality, but analysts admit that wastewater treatment facilities are outpaced by the area's population and that industrial wastewater is often insufficiently treated.

Coastal degradation puts serious pressure on Thailand's diverse coral reef system and marine environment. It is estimated that about half of Thailand's coral reefs are classified as highly threatened, indicating a disproportionate number of dead coral to living coral, according to a World Bank 2006 environmental report. The 2010 global bleaching phenomenon, in which El Niño weather conditions contributed to warmer sea temperatures, exacerbated the health problems of Thailand's reefs. Eighteen areas in seven marine parks that had experienced widespread bleaching were closed to tourism by the Thai government. Many of the reefs, especially in shallow water, will never recover.

The overall health of the ocean is further impacted by large-scale fishing, an important part of the Thai economy. Fisheries continue to experience declining catches, and an industry once dominated by small family fisherfolk has now shifted to big commercial enterprises that can go into deeper waters and devote more resources to a profitable catch.

Energy Consumption

Thailand's increasingly affluent society is expected to consume 75% more energy in the forthcoming decades, according to the Oxford Business Group. As Southeast Asia's second-largest energy consumer (Indonesia ranks first in the region), Thailand is looking to increase its energy supply and production by expanding oil and gas resources or developing alternative fuel sources. Most of the existing fields are in the Gulf of Thailand in an area known as the Pattani Trough and the government is working with Cambodia on the development of reserves in the upper Gulf of Thailand near the border of the two countries. Thailand is the leading producer of biofuels, including ethanols from molasses and cassava, and biodiesel from palm oil. Power generation, agriculture and industrial activity account for the largest proportion of the country's greenhouse gas emissions. While the energy sector searches for additional fuel supplies to feed the economy, the country's greenhouse gas management division is pushing for a voluntary carbon market in an attempt to meet international standards set for 2020.

Flooding

Seasonal flooding is a common natural occurrence in some parts of Thailand due to the nature of the monsoon rains. But high-level floods are an almost annual occurrence. The record-busting 2011 floods were unlike anything the country has ever experienced before. Prior to the start of the rainy season, a two-week period of heavy rainfall presaged trouble ahead, causing flooding in southern Thailand, and temporarily stranding tourists on resort islands. By midyear, tropical storms brought an inundation of rain that triggered a domino flood effect spanning nearly three months and drowning almost every region of the country. Of Thailand's 77 provinces, 65 were declared flood disaster zones; there were 815 deaths and an estimated US$45.7 billion worth of damages, one of the world's costliest natural disasters. Flood waters collapsed the barriers protecting the country's industrial estates north of Bangkok,

ENVIRONMENT & WILDLIFE ENVIRONMENTAL ISSUES

In 2013 a pipeline unloading an oil tanker off the coast of Rayong spilled 50,000L of crude into the sea, coating the western side of Ko Samet.

Bangkok has been sinking at a rate of 10cm per year, and some scientists estimate that the city may face submersion within 20 years due to rising sea levels.

ILLEGAL WILDLIFE TRADE

Thailand is a signatory to the UN Convention on International Trade in Endangered Species (Cites), but the country remains an important transport link and marketplace for the global wildlife trade, which is the third-largest black-market activity after drugs and arms dealing. Endangered animals and animal parts are poached from local forests or smuggled from neighbouring countries through Thailand en route to the lucrative markets of China or the US. Despite police efforts, Bangkok's Chatuchak Market contains a clandestine exotic species section.

In 2013, Thailand hosted the UN Cites meeting, where Prime Minister Yingluck Shinawatra promised tighter controls on the local ivory trade, which is presently allowed from domesticated stock, and eventually a national ban though she gave no timeline. Leading up to the meeting, more enforcement efforts were made to curtail wildlife smuggling, and so many animals were seized that government wildlife centres are now overwhelmed by their new charges, according to a New York Times article.

Though the country's efforts to stop the trade are more impressive than those of its neighbours, corruption and weak laws hinder law enforcement. Another complicating factor is that Thai law allows the trade of wild species bred in captivity, designed ostensibly to take the pressure off wild populations. This is especially problematic with elephants; criminal gangs steal baby elephants from wild herds or smuggle them across Myanmar's borders and then forge registration papers so that the elephant appears to have been born to a captive mother and can be 'legally' sold to elephant camps.

Most agree that the enforcement alone is not the answer and that the real solution is decline in demand. Without buyers, there will be no trade. On a small scale, several NGOs work on the attendant problems. **WARF** (Wild Animal Rescue Foundation of Thailand; www.warthai.org) was started by a Bangkok housewife who converted her backyard into a makeshift sanctuary for unwanted wild pets some 30 years ago. Today the NGO works with the forestry department on sting operations, job-skills training and educational workshops in Thai public schools. Some of the students who attend WARF workshops have parents who are poachers, and WARF hopes that the message of conservation (and maybe even a little environmental peer pressure) will be brought home to those students. With better education and job training, WARF hopes to dissuade future poachers and to turn current poachers into conservationists.

causing water inundation of international factories and a disruption in the global supply chain, including hard disc drives and automobile components. In the aftermath of the 2011 floods, residents of severely affected communities charged the national government of protecting Bangkok by redirecting water into their backyards.

The 2011 flood trumped the previous year's record-setting event in which the late-arriving rains transformed reservoirs in Nakhon Ratchasima Province from parched pits into overflowing disaster zones. There were 177 deaths in the 2010 floods, and a massive disaster relief response that lasted for several months after waters subsided. Another record flood occurred in 2006 with 46 affected provinces, mainly in the north, and again in 2008 along the Mekong.

There are myriad suspected reasons for these extreme weather patterns. Many environmental experts attribute human alteration of natural flood barriers and watercourses and deforestation as potential causes. Increased incidents of flooding along the Mekong is often linked to upstream infrastructure projects, such as dams and removal of rapids for easier navigation, and increasing human populations along the river that infringe on forested floodplains and wetlands. Another emerging component is the role of climate change in the increase of seasonal rains.

Survival Guide

Responsible Travel

Cultural Etiquette

The monarchy and the religion (which are interconnected) are treated with extreme deference in Thailand. Thais avoid criticising or disparaging the royal family for fear of offending someone or, worse, being charged with lèse majesté, which carries a jail sentence.

Buddha images are sacred objects. Thais consider it bad form to pose in front of one for a photo or to clamber upon them (in the case of temple ruins), instead they would show respect by performing a *wâi* (a prayer-like gesture) to the figure no matter how humble it is. As part of their ascetic vows, monks are not supposed to touch or be touched by women. If a woman wants to hand something to a monk, the object is placed within reach of the monk or on the monk's 'receiving cloth'.

From a spiritual viewpoint, Thais regard the head as the highest and most sacred part of the body and the feet as the dirtiest and lowest. Many of the taboos associated with the feet have a practical derivation as well. Traditionally Thais ate, slept and entertained on the floor of their homes with little in the way of furniture. To keep their homes and eating surfaces clean, the feet (and shoes) contracted a variety of rules.

Shoes aren't worn inside private homes and temple buildings, as a sign of respect and for sanitary reasons. Thais can kick off their shoes in one fluid step and many lace-up shoes are modified by the wearer to become slip-ons. Thais also step over – not on – the threshold, which is where the spirit of the house is believed to reside. On some buses and 3rd-class trains, you'll see Thais prop up their feet on the adjacent bench; while this isn't the height of propriety, do notice that they always remove their shoes before doing so. Thais also take off their shoes if they need to climb up onto a chair or seat.

Thais don't touch each other's head or ruffle their hair as a sign of affection. Occasionally you'll see young people touching each other's head, which is a teasing gesture, maybe even a slight insult, between friends.

Social Conventions & Gestures

The traditional Thai greeting is made with a prayerlike palms-together gesture known as *wâi*. The depth of the bow and the placement of the fingers in relation to the face is dependent on the status of the person receiving the *wâi*. Adults don't *wâi* children and in most cases service people (when they are doing their jobs) aren't *wâi-ed*, though this is a matter of personal discretion.

In the more traditional parts of the country, it is not proper for members of the opposite sex to touch one another, either as lovers or as friends. Hand-holding is not acceptable behaviour outside of the major cities such as Bangkok. But same-sex touching is quite common and

ESSENTIAL ETIQUETTE

Do

Stand respectfully for the national anthem It is played on TV and radio stations as well as public and government places at 8am and 6pm. If you're inside a building you don't have to stand.

Rise for the royal anthem It is played in movie theatres before every screening.

Smile a lot It puts Thais at ease.

Bring a gift if you're invited to a Thai home Fruit, drinks or snacks would be acceptable; flowers are usually for merit-making purposes not home decor.

Take off your shoes When you enter a home, temple building or wherever there are sandals piled up at the door.

Lower your head slightly When passing between two people having a conversation or when passing near a monk; it is a sign of respect.

Dress modestly for temple visits Cover to the elbows and ankles and always remove your shoes when entering any building containing a Buddha image.

Give and receive politely Extend the right hand out while the left hand gently grips the right elbow when handing an object to another person or receiving something – truly polite behaviour.

Respect all Buddha images and pictures of the monarchy Signs of disrespect can have serious consequences.

Sit in the 'mermaid' position inside temples Tuck your feet beside and behind you so that your feet aren't pointing at the Buddha image.

Don'ts

Don't get a tattoo of the Buddha It is considered sacrilegious.

Don't criticise the monarchy The monarchy is revered and protected by defamation laws.

Don't prop your feet on tables or chairs Feet are considered dirty and people don't want to sit or eat where feet have been.

Don't step on a dropped bill/note to prevent it from blowing away Thai money bears a picture of the king. Feet + monarchy = grave offence.

Never step over someone or their personal belongings Aaah, attack of the feet.

Avoid tying your shoes to the outside of your backpack They might accidentally brush against someone, gross.

Don't touch a Thai person on the head It is considered rude, not chummy.

Women cannot touch monks or their belongings Step out of the way when passing one on the footpath and do not sit next to them on public transport.

is typically a sign of friendship, not sexual attraction. Older Thai men might grab a younger man's thigh in the same way that buddies slap each other on the back. Thai women are especially affectionate with female friends, often sitting close to one another or linking arms.

Thais hold modesty in personal dress in high regard, though this is changing among the younger generation. The importance of modesty extends to the beach as well. Except for urbanites, most provincial Thais swim fully clothed. For this reason, sunbathing nude or topless is not acceptable and in some cases is even illegal. Remember that swimsuits are not proper attire off the beach; wear a cover-up in between the sand and your hotel.

Tourism

Most forms of tourism, despite the prevailing prejudices, have a positive economic effect on the local economy in Thailand: they provide jobs for young workers and business opportunities for entrepreneurs. But in an effort to be more than just a consumer, many travellers look for opportunities to spend where their money might be needed, either on charitable causes or activities that preserve traditional ways of life. Thailand has done a surprisingly good job at adapting to this emerging trend by promoting village craft programs and homestays (see p752). Unfortunately, much of this is aimed at the domestic market rather than international visitors. But more and more, foreign tourists can engage in these small-scale tourism models that offer an insight into traditional ways.

Diving

The popularity of Thailand's diving industry places immense pressure on fragile coral sites. To help preserve the ecology, adhere to these simple rules.

➡ Avoid touching living marine organisms, standing on coral or dragging equipment (such as fins) across the reef. Coral polyps can be damaged by even the gentlest contact.

➡ When treading water in shallow reef areas, be careful not to kick up clouds of sand, which can easily smother the delicate reef organisms.

➡ Take great care in underwater caves where your air bubbles can be caught within the roof and leave previously submerged organisms high and dry.

➡ Join a coral clean-up campaign sponsored by local dive shops.

➡ Don't feed the fish or allow your dive operator to dispose of excess food in the water. The fish become dependent on this food source and don't tend eat the coral, causing harm to the reef.

Elephant Encounters

Throughout Thai history, elephants have been revered for their strength, endurance and intelligence, working alongside their mahouts to harvest teak, transport goods through mountains or fight ancient wars.

But many of the elephant's traditional roles have either been outsourced to machines or outlawed (logging was banned in 1989), leaving the domesticated animals and their mahouts without work. Some mahouts turned to begging on the streets in Bangkok and other tourist centres, a dangerous practice that the government is working to curb through fines and incentive programs. But most elephants, like many human migrants, found work in Thailand's tourism industry, which varies from circus-like shows to elephant camps giving rides to tourists. Other elephant encounters include mahout-training schools, while sanctuaries and rescue centres provide modest retirement homes to animals that can no longer work and are no longer profitable for their owners.

Working elephants have a career of about 50 years and are trained at a young age by two mahouts, usually a father-and-son team, who can see the animal through its lifetime. Thai law requires that elephants be retired and released into the wild at age 61. They often live for 80 years or more. It costs about 30,000B (US$1000) per month to provide a comfortable living standard for an elephant; this is equivalent to the salary of Thailand's upper middle class. It is an expensive proposition to provide a comfortable life for an elephant, and the welfare standards within the tourism industry are not standardised or subject to government regulations. It is up to the conscientious consumer to encourage the industry to make safe working conditions for elephants the norm, not the exception. For more on this issue, see The Elephant Debate boxed text in the Chiang Mai chapter.

Here are some questions to ask the elephant camps to make sure you've chosen a well-run operation.

➡ **Does the camp employ a veterinarian?** Good camps keep their elephants under regular medical supervision.

➡ **What is its policy on procuring new elephants?** Some camps buy illegally caught wild elephants with forged registration so they appear to be born in captivity.

➡ **How many hours per day do the elephants work?** A brisk-paced walk for about four hours per day (with breaks for eating and drinking) is considered adequate exercise.

➡ **How many adults do the elephants carry?** An elephant can carry a maximum of 150kg (330lb) on its back, plus a mahout on its neck. Tally up you and your partner's combined weight and request a separate elephant if you tip the scales.

➡ **Are the elephants kept in a shady spot near fresh water and a food source?** What do they eat? A balanced diet includes a mixture of fruit, grasses, bamboo and pineapple shoots.

➡ **Do the elephants have noticeable wounds?** This is often a sign of mistreatment.

➡ **What kind of a seat is used for elephant riding?** Wooden seats, custom-made to fit the elephant's back, cause less irritation and stress on the animal.

➡ **What is the camp's birth rate?** Happy elephants have babies.

Hill-Tribe Trekking

Though marginalised within mainstream society, the hill-tribe minorities remain a strong tourism draw, with large and small businesses organising trekking tours to villages for cultural displays and interactions. Economically, it is unclear whether hill-tribe trekking helps alleviate the poverty of the hill-tribe groups, thus helping maintain their ethnic identity. Most agree that a small percentage of the profits from trekking filters down to individual families within hill-tribe villages, giving them a small source of income that might prevent urban migration. One guide we spoke to estimated that 50% of the tour budget was spent on purchasing food, lodging and supplies from hill-tribe merchants at the host village.

In general the trekking business has become more socially conscious compared to previous decades. Most companies now tend to limit the number of visits to a particular area to lessen the impact of outsiders on the daily lives of ordinary villagers, but the industry still has a long way to go. It should be noted that trekking companies are Thai owned and employ Thai guides, another bureaucratic impediment regarding citizenship for ethnic minorities. Without an identification card, guides from the hill tribes do not qualify for a Tourist Authority of Thailand (TAT) tour guide licence and so are less than desirable job candidates.

Trekkers should also realise that the minority tribes maintain their own distinct cultural identity and many continue their animistic traditions, which define social taboos and conventions. If you're planning on visiting hill-tribe villages on an organised trek, ask your guide about acceptable behaviour.

TOP PLACES FOR HILL-TRIBE TREKKING

➡ Chiang Mai

➡ Chiang Rai

➡ Mae Hong Son

➡ Mae Sariang

➡ Tha Thon

Here is a general guide to get you started.

➡ Always ask for permission before taking any photos of tribes people, especially at private moments inside their dwellings. Many traditional belief systems regard photography with suspicion.

➡ Show respect for religious symbols and rituals. Don't touch totems at village entrances or sacred items hanging from trees. Don't participate in ceremonies unless invited to.

➡ Avoid encouraging the practice of begging, especially among children. Talk to your guide about donating to a local school instead.

➡ Avoid public nudity and be careful not to undress near an open window where village children might be able to peep in.

➡ Don't flirt with members of the opposite sex unless you plan on marrying them.

➡ Don't drink or do drugs with the villagers; altered states sometimes lead to culture clashes.

➡ Smile at villagers even if they stare at you. Ask your guide how to say 'hello' in the local language.

➡ Avoid public displays of affection, which in some traditional systems are viewed as offensive to the spirit world.

➡ Don't interact with the villagers' livestock, even the free-roaming pigs; these creatures are valuable possessions, not entertainment. Also avoid interacting with jungle animals, which in some belief systems are viewed as visiting spirits.

➡ Adhere to the same feet taboos that apply to Thai culture. Don't step on the threshold of a house, prop your feet up against the fire or wear your shoes inside.

Homestays

You can travel independently without isolating yourself from the culture by staying at Thailand's local homestays. More popular with domestic tourists, homestays differ from guesthouses in that visitors are welcomed into a family's home, typically in a small village that isn't on the tourist trail. Accommodation is basic: usually a mat or foldable mattress on the floor, or occasionally a family will have a private room. Rates include lodging, meals with the family, and cultural activities that highlight the region's traditional way of life, from rice farming to silk weaving. English fluency varies, so homestays are also an excellent way to exercise your spoken Thai.

Volunteering

When you travel to another country it is easier to see the areas of suffering and injustice more clearly than you can in your own country. And Thailand is still technically a developing country, lacking a tight-knit welfare system, an executed environmental protection program and equal labour protections. There are a myriad organisations in Thailand to address both the needs of the locals and visitors' desire to help. Be aware, though, that so-called 'voluntourism' has become a big business and that not every organisation fulfills its promise of meaningful experiences. Before making a commitment, do your homework on the tour organiser and the volunteer facility.

TOP HOMESTAYS

➡ **Ban Prasat** (p417), Nakhon Ratchasima

➡ **Ban Kham Pia** (p475), Bueng Kan

➡ **Ban Ta Klang** (p429), Surin

➡ **Ban Mae Kampong** (p288), Chiang Mai

Environmental & Animal Welfare Work

A number of NGOs undertake local conservation efforts, and run rescue and sanctuary centres for wild animals that have been adopted as pets, or veterinarian clinics that tend to the domesticated population of dogs and cats. At centres and sanctuaries that rely on volunteer labour, your hard work is often rewarded with meaningful interactions with the animals.

Highland Farm Gibbon Sanctuary (www.gibbonathighlandfarm.org; Mae Sot) Gives a permanent home to orphaned, abandoned and mistreated gibbons; volunteers are asked for a one-month commitment and to help with farm chores.

Starfish Ventures (www.starfishvolunteers.com) Places volunteers in conservation, teaching and animal welfare programs throughout Thailand.

Wild Animal Rescue Foundation (WARF; www.warthai.org) Operates the Phuket Gibbon Rehabilitation Centre and a conservation education centre in Ranong Province on the Andaman Coast. Job placements include assisting with the daily care of gibbons that are being rehabilitated for life in the wild or counting and monitoring sea-turtle nests.

Wildlife Friends of Thailand Rescue Centre (www.wfft.org; Phetchaburi) Volunteers care for sun bears, macaques and gibbons at an animal rescue centre.

There are also smaller organisations listed in the On the Road chapters.

Humanitarian & Educational Work

Northern Thailand, especially Chiang Mai and Chiang Rai, has a number of volunteer opportunities to work with disadvantaged hill-tribe groups. Chiang Mai, Mae Sot and Sangkhlaburi have communities of Burmese refugees and migrants. There are also many volunteer teaching positions in northeastern Thailand. Organisations require varying time commitments but in order to be an effective volunteer, you should dedicate at least a month to the program. You should also have some experience in education or humanitarian work, so that you aren't a burden to the host community. Voluntourism is very popular these days and there are many pay-to-play opportunities of varying legitimacy. Investigate the organisation's reputation, costs and services provided (training, lodging, support). The following grassroots organisations are worth investigating.

Andaman Discoveries (08 7917 7165; www.andamandiscoveries.com; Phang-Nga) Manages a learning centre for children of Burmese migrants, an orphanage and a school for disabled children in southern Thailand.

Ban Thor Phan (www.banthorphan.com; Sangkhlaburi) One of the few children's home in the area run by a local.

Cultural Canvas Thailand (www.culturalcanvas.com; Chiang Mai) Places volunteers in migrant learning centres, art programs and other social-justice projects in northern Thailand.

Dragonfly Volunteer Projects (08 7963 0056; http://thai-dragonfly.com; Nakhon Ratchasima) Trains and places volunteers in building, teaching and animal-welfare projects throughout the country.

Isara (Map p458; 0 4246 0827; www.isara.org) Places teachers in underprivileged schools around Thailand; one of the few volunteer programs that is free and placements include housing and some meals.

LemonGrass (08 1977 5300; www.lemongrass-volunteering.com) A well-run Surin-based outfit places native English speakers in local primary schools where they work alongside the regular teachers.

Open Mind Projects (08 7233 5734; www.openmindprojects.org) Offers volunteer positions in IT, health care, education and community ecotourism.

Travel to Teach (www.travel-to-teach.org; Chiang Mai) Offers flexible volunteering positions in schools, English camps or temples with placements in Mae Hong Son and Chiang Mai.

Volunthai (www.volunthai.com) A family-run operation that places volunteers in teaching positions at rural schools with homestay accommodation.

Directory A-Z

Accommodation

Thailand offers a wide variety of accommodation from cheap and basic to pricey and luxurious. Accommodation rates listed here are high-season prices.

In places where spoken English might be limited, it is handy to know the following: *hôrng pát lom* (room with fan) and *hôrng aa* (room with air-con).

Guesthouses

Guesthouses are generally the cheapest accommodation in Thailand and can be found all along the backpacker trail. In areas like the northeast and parts of the southeast, guesthouses (as well as tourists) are not widespread.

BOOK YOUR STAY ONLINE

For more accommodation reviews by Lonely Planet authors, check out http://lonelyplanet.com/hotels/. You'll find independent reviews, as well as recommendations on the best places to stay. Best of all, you can book online.

Rates vary according to facilities and location. In small towns between 150B to 200B are about the cheapest rates around and usually have shared bathroom and a rickety fan. Private facilities, air-con and sometimes a TV can be had for 600B to 800B. But prices are much higher in the beach resorts, where a basic fan room starts at 700B to 800B. Many guesthouses make their bread and butter from

their on-site restaurants that serve the classic backpacker fare (banana pancakes and fruit shakes). Although these restaurants are convenient and a good way to meet other travellers, don't measure Thai food based on these dishes.

Most guesthouses cultivate a travellers' ambience with friendly knowledgeable staff and book exchanges. But there are also plenty of guesthouses with grumpy, disgruntled clerks who let customers know that they dislike their jobs. In these cases, the boss, not the customer, is the culprit for the the staff's bad attitude.

Increasingly, guesthouses can handle advance reservations, but due to inconsistent cleanliness and quality it is advisable to always look at a room in person before committing. In tourist centres, if your preferred place is full, there are usually alternatives nearby. Guesthouses typically only accept cash payments.

Hotels

In provincial capitals and small towns, the only options

SLEEPING PRICE RANGES

A two-tiered pricing system has been used to determine the accommodation price ranges (budget, midrange, top end) in this book.

Big Cities & Beach Resorts

$ less than 1000B

$$ 1000–3000B

$$$ more than 3000B

Small Towns

$ less than 600B

$$ 600–1500B

$$$ more than 1500B

are often older Thai-Chinese hotels, once the standard in all of Thailand. Most cater to Thai guests and English is usually limited.

These hotels are multistorey buildings and might offer a range of rooms from midrange options with private bathrooms, air-con and TV to cheaper ones with shared bath facilities and a fan. In some of the older hotels, the toilets are squats and the 'shower' is a *klong* jar (a large terracotta basin from which you scoop out water for bathing). Although the Thai-Chinese hotels have got tonnes of accidental retro charm, unless the establishment has been recently refurbished, we've found that they are too old and worn to represent good value compared to the guesthouses.

The new hotel norm is the 'flashpacker' hotel, which has dressed up the utilitarian options of the past with stylish decor and more creature comforts. Expect an upper budget or lower midrange price tag.

International chain hotels can be found in Bangkok, Chiang Mai, Phuket and other high-end beach resorts. Many of these upscale resorts incorporate traditional Thai architecture with modern minimalism.

Most top-end hotels and some midrange hotels add a 7% government tax (VAT) and an additional 10% service charge. The additional charges are often referred to as 'plus plus'. A buffet breakfast will often be included in the room rate. If the hotel offers a Western breakfast, it is usually referred to as 'ABF', meaning 'American breakfast'.

Midrange and chain hotels, especially in major tourist destinations, can be booked in advance and some offer internet discounts through their websites or online agents. They also accept most credit cards, but only a few deluxe places accept American Express.

COMMISSION HASSLES

In the popular tourist spots you'll be approached, sometimes surrounded, by touts or transport drivers who get a commission from the guesthouse for bringing in potential guests. While it is annoying for the traveller, this is an acceptable form of advertising among small-scale businesses in Thailand. As long as you know the drill, everything should work out in your favour. Touts get paid for delivering you to a guesthouse or hotel (whether you check in or not). Some places refuse to pay commissions so in return the touts will steer customers away from those places (saying it is closed or burned down). In less scrupulous instances, they'll tell you that the commission-paying hotel is the one you requested. If you meet with resistance, call the guesthouse for pick-up as they are often aware of aggressive business tactics.

Climate

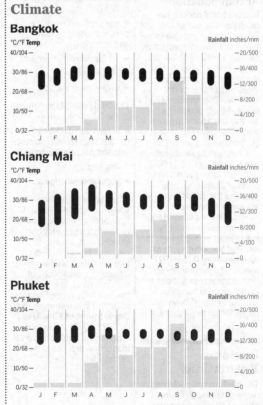

Bangkok

Chiang Mai

Phuket

National Parks Accommodation

Most national parks have bungalows or campsites. Bungalows typically sleep as many as 10 people and rates range from 800B to 2000B, depending on the park and the size of the bungalow. These are popular with extended Thai families who bring enough provisions to survive the Apocalypse. A few parks also have *reu·an tăa·ou* (longhouses).

Camping is available at many parks for 60B to 90B per night. Some parks rent tents and other sleeping gear, but the condition of the equipment can be poor.

Reservations for all park accommodation must be made in advance through the **central booking system** (☎reservations 0 2561 0777; www.dnp.go.th/parkreserve). Do note that reservations for campsites and bungalows are handled on different pages within the website.

Customs Regulations

The **customs department** (www.customs.go.th) maintains a helpful website with specific information about customs regulations for travellers. Thailand allows the following items to enter duty free:

➡ reasonable amount of personal effects (clothing and toiletries)

➡ professional instruments

➡ 200 cigarettes

➡ 1L of wine or spirits

Thailand prohibits the import of the following items:

➡ firearms and ammunition (unless registered in advance with the police department)

➡ illegal drugs

➡ pornographic media

When leaving Thailand, you must obtain an export licence for any antique reproductions or newly cast Buddha images (except personal amulets). Submit two front-view photos of the object(s), a photocopy of your passport, along with the purchase receipt and the object(s) in question, to the **Department of Fine Arts** (0 2628 5032). Allow four days for the application and inspection process to be completed.

Electricity

Thailand uses 220V AC electricity; power outlets most commonly feature two-prong round or flat sockets.

220V/50Hz

220V/50Hz

Embassies & Consulates

Foreign embassies are located in Bangkok; some nations

also have consulates in Chiang Mai, Phuket or Pattaya.

Australia (Map p83; ☑0 2344 6300; www.thailand. embassy.gov.au; 37 Th Sathon Tai; MLumphini exit 2)

Cambodia (☑0 2957 5851; 518/4 Th Pracha Uthit/Soi Ramkhamhaeng 39; MPhra Ram 9 exit 3 & taxi) Consulate in Sa Kaew.

Canada Bangkok (Map p83; ☑0 2646 4300; www.canadainternational.gc.ca; 15th fl, Abdulrahim Pl, 990 Th Phra Ram IV; MSi Lom exit 2, ⊠Sala Daeng exit 4); Chiang Mai (☑0 5385 0147; 151 Superhighway, Tambon Tahsala)

China Bangkok (☑0 2245 7044; www.fmprc.gov.cn; 57 Th Ratchadaphisek; Chiang Mai (Map p240;☑0 5327 6125; chiangmai.chinsesconsulate. org; 111 Th Chang Lor, Tambon Haiya)

Denmark (Map p83; ☑0 2343 1100; thailand.um.dk; 10 Soi 1, Th Sathon Tai) Consulates in Phuket and Pattaya.

France (Map p76; ☑0 2657 5100; www.ambafrance-th.org; Th Charoen Krung, 35 Soi 36); Bangkok Visa & Culture Services (☑0 2627 2150; ambafrance-th.org; 29 Th Sathon Tai); Chiang Mai (Map p234; ☑0 5328 1466; 138 Th Charoen Prathet) Consulates also in Phuket, Pattaya & Surat Thani.

Germany (Map p83; ☑0 2287 9000; www.bangkok.diplo.de; 9 Th Sathon Tai; MLumphini exit 2)

India (Map p90; ☑0 2258 0300-6; indianembassy.in.th; 46 Soi Prasanmit/Soi 23, Th Sukhumvit; Bangkok Visa Centre (Map p90; ☑0 2664 1200; www.indiavisathai.com; Th Sukhumvit, 253 Soi 21/ Asoke; ⊙IVS Global Services, 22nd fl); Chiang Mai (Map p234; ☑0 5324 3066; 33/1 Th Thung Hotel, Wat Gate)

Indonesia (Map p84; ☑0 2252 3135; www.kemlu.go.id/ bangkok; 600-602 Th Phetchaburi)

Ireland (Map p78; ☑0 2632 6720; www.irelandinthailand. com; 62 Th Silom, 4th fl, Thaniya Bldg) Consulate only: the nearest Irish embassy is in Kuala Lumpur.

Israel (Map p90; ☑0 2204 9200; bangkok.mfa.gov.il; 25 Soi 19, Th Sukhumvit, Ocean Tower 2, 25th fl)

Japan Bangkok (Map p83; ☑0 2207 8500; www.th.emb-japan. go.jp; 177 Th Witthayu/Wireless Rd); Chiang Mai (Map p234; ☑0 5320 3367; 104-107 Th Mahidon, Airport Business Park)

Laos (☑0 2539 6678; www. laoembassybkk.com; Th Ramkamhaeng, 502/1-3 Soi Sahakarnpramoon, Pracha Uthit/Soi 39)

Malaysia (Map p83; ☑0 2629 6800; www.kln.gov.my; 35 Th Sathon Tai, Bangkok; Mmetro Lumphini exit 2) Consulate in Songkhla.

Myanmar (Map p78; ☑0 2233 2237; www.myanmarembassybkk.com; 132 Th Sathon Neua; ⊠Surasak exit 3)

Nepal (☑0 2391 7240; nepalembassybangkok.com; 189 Soi 71, Th Sukhumvit)

Netherlands (Map p84; ☑0 2309 5200; www.netherlandsembassy.in.th; 15 Soi Tonson; ⊠Chit Lom exit 4)

New Zealand (Map p84; ☑0 2254 2530; www.nzembassy. com/thailand; 87 Th Witthayu (Wireless Rd), 14th fl, M Thai Tower, All Seasons Pl; ⊠Phloen Chit exit 5)

Philippines (Map p90; ☑0 2259 0139; www.bangkokpe. com; 760 Th Sukhumvit)

Russia (Map p78; ☑0 2234 9824; www.thailand.mid.ru; 78

Soi Sap, Th Surawong) Consulates in Pattaya and Phuket.

Singapore (Map p78; ☑0 2286 2111; www.mfa.gov.sg/ bangkok; 129 Th Sathon Tai)

South Africa (Map p84; ☑0 2659 2900; www.dirco.gov. za; 87 Th Witthayu (Wireless Rd), 12th A fl, M Thai Tower, All Seasons Pl)

Spain (Map p90; ☑0 2661 8284; es.embassyinformation. com; 193 Th Ratchadaphisek, 23 fl, Lake Ratchada Office Complex)

Switzerland (Map p84; ☑0 2674 6900; www.eda.admin. ch/bangkok; 35 Th Witthayu/ Wireless Rd)

UK Bangkok (Map p84;☑0 2305 8333; www.gov.uk; 14 Th Witthayu/Wireless Rd; ⊠Phloen Chit exit 5); Chiang Mai (Map p234;☑0 5326 3015; www.british-consulate.net; 198 Th Bamrungrat) Consulate also in Pattaya.

USA Bangkok (Map p84;☑0 2205 4049; http://bangkok. usembassy.gov; 95 Th Witthayu/Wireless Rd); Chiang Mai (Map p240;☑0 5310 7700; chiangmai.usconsulate.gov; 387 Th Wichayanon)

Vietnam (Map p84; ☑0 2251 5838, 0 2251 5836; www. vietnamembassy-thailand.org; 83/1 Th Witthayu (Wireless Rd))

Food

For in-depth information on Thailand's glorious cuisine, see Food & Drink (p721).

EATING PRICE RANGES

The following price ranges indicate how much you should expect to pay for a meal in Thailand.

$ less than 150B

$$ 150–350B

$$$ more than 350B

Gay & Lesbian Travellers

Thai culture is relatively tolerant of both male and female homosexuality. There is a fairly prominent gay and lesbian scene in Bangkok, Pattaya and Phuket. With regard to dress or mannerism, lesbians and gays are generally accepted without comment. However, public displays of affection – whether heterosexual or homosexual – are frowned upon. **Utopia** (www. utopia-asia.com) posts lots of Thailand information for gay and lesbian visitors and publishes a guidebook to the kingdom for homosexuals.

Insurance

A travel insurance policy to cover theft, loss and medical problems is a good idea. Policies offer differing medical-expense options. There is a wide variety of policies available, so check the small print. Be sure that the policy covers ambulances or an emergency flight home. Some policies specifically exclude 'dangerous activities', which can include scuba diving, motorcycling or even trekking. A locally acquired motorcycle licence is not valid under some policies. You may prefer a policy that pays doctors or hospitals directly rather than you having to pay on the spot and claim later. If you have to claim later make sure you keep all documentation.

Worldwide travel insurance is available at www.lonely planet.com/travel-insurance. You can buy, extend and claim online any time – even if you're already on the road.

Internet Access

As more and more people travel with mobile devices, internet cafes have begun to disappear. Some guesthouses still have computer terminals, however, charging between 60B to 150B an hour, depending on how much competition there is. Wi-fi is becoming commonplace in guesthouses, restaurants and cafes. Signal strength deteriorates in the upper floors of a multi-storey building; so request a room near a router.

Legal Matters

In general, Thai police don't hassle foreigners, especially tourists. They usually go out of their way to avoid having to speak English with a foreigner, especially regarding minor traffic issues.

One major exception is drugs, which most Thai police view as either a social scourge against which it's their duty to enforce the letter of the law, or an opportunity to make untaxed income via bribes.

If you are arrested the police will allow you to make a phone call, either to your embassy or consulate in Thailand if you have one, or to a friend or relative if not. There's a whole set of legal codes governing the length of time and manner in which you can be detained before being charged or put on trial, but a lot of discretion is left to the police. In the case of foreigners the police are more likely to bend these codes in your favour. However, as with police worldwide, show respect or it will make matters worse.

Thai law does not presume an indicted detainee to be either 'guilty' or 'innocent' but rather a 'suspect', whose guilt or innocence will be decided in court. Trials are usually speedy.

The **tourist police** (☏1155) can be very helpful in cases of arrest. Although they typically have no jurisdiction over the kinds of cases handled by regular cops, they may be able to help with translations or with contacting your embassy. You can call the hotline number 24 hours a day to lodge complaints or to request assistance with regards to personal safety.

Maps

ThinkNet (www.thinknet. co.th) produces high-quality, bilingual city and country maps, including interactive-map CDs.

Money

The basic unit of Thai currency is the baht. There are 100 satang in one baht; coins include 25-satang and 50-satang pieces and baht in 1B, 2B, 5B and 10B coins. Older coins have Thai numerals only, while newer coins have Thai and Arabic numerals. The 2B coin is similar in size to the 1B coin but it is gold in colour. The two satang coins are typically only issued at supermarkets where prices aren't rounded up to the nearest baht.

Paper currency is issued in the following denominations: 20B (green), 50B (blue), 100B (red), 500B (purple) and 1000B (beige).

ATMs & Credit/Debit Cards

Debit and ATM cards issued by a bank in your own country can be used at ATMs around Thailand to withdraw cash (in Thai baht only) directly from your account back home. ATMs are widespread throughout the country and can be relied on for the bulk of your spending cash.

Thai ATMs now charge a 150B foreign-transaction fee on top of whatever currency conversion and out-of-network fees your home bank charges. That means that ATMs are now a lot more expensive to use than in the past. Before leaving home, shop around for a bank account that has free international ATM usage and reimburses fees incurred at other institution's ATMs.

Aeon is the only bank that we know of in Thailand that doesn't charge the 150B usage fee on foreign accounts, but their distribution of national ATMs is limited and often located in Big C stores.

Credit cards as well as debit cards can be used for purchases at some shops, hotels and restaurants. The most commonly accepted cards are Visa and Master-Card. American Express is typically only accepted at high-end hotels and restaurants.

Contact your bank and your credit card company before you leave home and notify them of your upcoming trip so that your accounts aren't suspended due to suspicious overseas activity.

To report a lost or stolen credit/debit card, call the following hotlines in Bangkok:

American Express (☏0 2273 5544)

MasterCard (☏001 800 11887 0663)

Visa (☏001 800 11 535 0660)

Changing Money

Banks or private money-changers offer the best foreign-exchange rates. When buying baht, US dollars are the most accepted currency, followed by British pounds and euros. Most banks charge a commission and duty for each travellers cheque cashed. Current exchange rates are posted at exchange counters.

Foreign Currency Regulations

There is no limit on the amount of foreign currency that can be brought into Thailand, but people arriving or departing with amounts over US$20,000 need to declare this to the customs officer. Foreigners need to demonstrate adequate funds for their visit. Usually this is only required when applying in advance for a Tourist or other type of visa.

It's legal to open a foreign-currency account at any commercial bank in Thailand. If the funds originate from out of the country there aren't any

restrictions on maintenance or withdrawal.

Tipping

Tipping is not generally expected in Thailand, though it is appreciated. The exception is loose change from a large restaurant bill; if a meal costs 488B and you pay with a 500B note, some Thais will leave the 12B change. It's not so much a tip as a way of saying 'I'm not so money grubbing as to grab every last baht'. At many hotel restaurants or other upmarket eateries, a 10% service charge will be added to your bill.

Opening Hours

The following are standard hours for businesses in Thailand. All government offices and banks are closed on public holidays.

Banks 9.30am to 3.30pm Monday to Friday; ATMs accessible 24 hours.

Bars 6pm to midnight (officially); closing times vary due to local enforcement of curfew laws; bars close during elections and certain religious public holidays.

Clubs (discos) 8pm to 2am; closing times vary due to local enforcement of curfew laws; clubs close during elections and certain religious public holidays.

Government offices 8.30am to 4.30pm Monday to Friday; some close for lunch (noon to 1pm) while others are open Saturday (9am to 3pm).

Live-music venues 6pm to 1am; closing times vary due to local enforcement of curfew laws; clubs close during elections and certain religious public holidays.

Restaurants 8am to 10pm; some local restaurants or those that specialise in morning meals close by 3 pm or 4pm.

Stores local stores 10am or 11am to 6pm; department stores 10am to 8pm. In some small towns, local stores close on Sunday.

Photography

Memory cards for digital cameras are widely available in the electronic sections of most shopping malls.

Be considerate when taking photographs of the locals. Learn how to ask politely in Thai and wait for an embarrassed nod. In some of the regularly visited hill-tribe areas be prepared for the photographed subject to ask for money in exchange for a picture. Other hill tribes will not allow you to point a camera at them.

Post

Thailand has a very efficient postal service and local postage is inexpensive. Typical provincial post offices keep the following hours: 8.30am to 4.30pm weekdays and 9am to noon on Saturdays. Larger main post offices in provincial capitals may also be open for a half-day on Sundays.

PRACTICALITIES

➡ *Bangkok Post* and the *Nation* publish English-language news daily.

➡ There are more than 400 AM and FM radio stations; short-wave radios can pick up BBC, VOA, Radio Australia, Deutsche Welle and Radio France International.

➡ Six VHF TV networks carry Thai programming, plus TrueVision cable with international programming.

➡ Thailand follows the international metric system. Gold and silver are weighed in *bàat* (15g).

Most provincial post offices will sell do-it-yourself packing boxes. Don't send cash or other valuables through the mail.

Thailand's poste restante service is generally very reliable, though these days few tourists use it. When you receive mail, you must show your passport and fill out some paperwork.

Public Holidays

Government offices and banks close on public holidays.

1 January New Year's Day

February (date varies) Makha Bucha Day, Buddhist holy day

6 April Chakri Day, commemorating the founder of the Chakri dynasty, Rama I

13–14 April Songkran Festival, traditional Thai New Year and water festival

5 May Coronation Day, commemorating the 1946 coronation of HM the King and HM the Queen

1 May Labour Day

May/June (date varies) Visakha Bucha, Buddhist holy day

July (date varies) Asahna Bucha, Buddhist holy day

12 August Queen's Birthday

23 October Chulalongkorn Day

October/November (date varies) Ork Phansaa, the end of Buddhist 'lent'

5 December King's Birthday

10 December Constitution Day

31 December New Year's Eve

Safe Travel

Although Thailand is not a dangerous country to visit, it is smart to exercise caution, especially when it comes to dealing with strangers (both Thai and foreigners) and travelling alone. In reality, you are more likely to be ripped off or have a personal possession surreptitiously stolen than you are to be physically harmed.

Motorcycle accidents are another common injury.

Assault

Assault of travellers is rare in Thailand, but it does happen. Causing a Thai to 'lose face' (feel public embarrassment or humiliation) can sometimes elicit an inexplicably strong and violent reaction. Oftentimes alcohol is the number one contributor to bad choices and worse outcomes.

Women, especially solo travellers, need to be smart and somewhat sober when interacting with the opposite sex, be they Thai or *fa·ràng* (foreigners). Opportunists pounce when too many whisky buckets are involved. Also be aware that an innocent flirtation might convey firmer intentions to a recipient who does not share your culture's sexual norms.

Border Issues & Hot Spots

Thailand enjoys much better relations with its neighbours and most land borders are fully functional passages for goods and people. However, the ongoing violence in the Deep South has made the crossing at Sungai Kolok into Malaysia completely off limits and the entire Muslim-majority provinces (Yala, Pattani and Narathiwat) should be avoided by casual visitors.

Cross-border relations between Thailand and Myanmar have normalised with unprecedented open land access. The long-contested area at Khao Phra Wihan (known as 'Preah Vihear' in Cambodia), along the Thai-Cambodian border, is still a source of military clashes and should be avoided until a lasting peace is found.

Check with your government's foreign ministry for current travel warnings.

Drug Possession

Belying Thailand's anything-goes atmosphere are severely strict punishments for possession and trafficking that are not relaxed for foreigners.

It is illegal to buy, sell or possess opium, heroin, amphetamines, hallucinogenic mushrooms and marijuana in Thailand. Possession of drugs can result in at least one year or more of prison time. Drug smuggling – defined as attempting to cross a border with drugs in your possession – carries considerably higher penalties, including execution.

Scams

Thais can be so friendly and laid-back that some visitors are lulled into a false sense of security, making them vulnerable to scams of all kinds. Bangkok is especially good at long-involved frauds that dupe travellers into thinking that they've made a friend and are getting a bargain when in fact they are getting ripped off.

Follow Tourism Authority of Thailand's (TAT) number-one suggestion to tourists: *Disregard all offers of free shopping or sightseeing help from strangers*. These invariably take a commission from your purchases.

Theft & Fraud

Exercise diligence when it comes to your personal belongings. Ensure that your room is securely locked and carry your most important effects (passport, money, credit cards) on your person. Take care when leaving valuables in hotel safes.

Follow the same practice when you're travelling. A locked bag will not prevent theft on a long-haul bus.

When using a credit card, don't let vendors take your card out of your sight to run it through the machine. Unscrupulous merchants have been known to rub off three or four or more receipts with one purchase. Sometimes they wait several weeks – even months – between submitting each charge receipt to the bank, so that you can't remember whether you'd been billed by the same vendor more than once.

To avoid losing all of your travel money in an instant,

use a credit card that is not directly linked to your bank account so that the operator doesn't have access to immediate funds.

Contact the **tourist police** (☑1155) if you have any problems with consumer fraud.

Touts & Commissions

Touting is a longtime tradition in Asia, and while Thailand doesn't have as many touts as, say, India, it has its share. In Bangkok, túk-túk drivers and other 'new' friends often take new arrivals on city tours; these almost always end up in high-pressure sales situations at silk, jewellery or handicraft shops.

Touts also steer customers to certain guesthouses that pay a commission. Travel agencies are notorious for talking newly arrived tourists into staying at badly located, overpriced hotels.

Some travel agencies often masquerade as TAT, the government-funded tourist information office. They might put up agents wearing fake TAT badges or have signs that read TAT in big letters to entice travellers into their offices where they can sell them bus and train tickets for a commission. Be aware that the official TAT offices do not make hotel or transport bookings. If such a place offers to do this for you then they are a travel agent, not a tourist information office.

When making transport arrangements, talk to several travel agencies to look for the best price, as the commission percentage varies. Also resist any high-sales tactics from an agent trying to sign you up for everything: plane tickets, hotel, tours etc. The most honest Thais are often subpar salespeople.

Shopping

Many bargains await you in Thailand but don't go shopping in the company of touts, tour guides or friendly strangers as they will inevitably take a commission on anything you buy, thus driving prices up beyond an acceptable value and creating a nuisance for future visitors.

Antiques

Real Thai antiques are increasingly rare. Today, most dealers sell antique reproductions or items from Myanmar. Bangkok and Chiang Mai are the two centres for the antique and reproduction trade.

Real antiques cannot be taken out of Thailand without a permit. No Buddha image, new or old, may be exported without the permission of the Department of Fine Arts.

Ceramics

Many kinds of hand-thrown pottery, old and new, are available throughout the kingdom. Bangkok is full of modern ceramic designs while Chiang Mai sticks to traditional styles. Ko Kret and Dan Kwian are two traditional pottery villages.

Clothing

Clothes tend to be inexpensive in Thailand but ready-made items are not usually cut to fit Westerners' body types. Increasingly, larger-sized clothes are available in metropolitan malls or tourist centres. Markets sell cheap everyday items and are handy for picking up something when everything else is dirty. For chic clothes, Bangkok and Ko Samui lead the country with design-minded fashions. Finding shoes that fit larger feet is also a problem. The custom of returns is not widely accepted in Thailand, so be sure everything fits before you leave the store.

Thailand has a long sartorial tradition, practised mainly by Thai-Indian Sikh families. But this industry is filled with cut-rate operators and commission-paying scams. Be wary of the quickie 24-hour tailor shops; they often use inferior fabric and have poor workmanship. It's best to ask longtime foreign residents for a recommendation and then go for two or three fittings.

Fake Goods

In Bangkok, Chiang Mai and other tourist centres there's a thriving black-market street trade in fake designer goods. No one pretends they're the real thing, at least not the vendors. Technically it is illegal for these items to be produced and sold and Thailand has often been pressured by intellectual-property enforcement agencies to close down the trade. Rarely does a crackdown by the police last, however, and often the vendors develop more surreptitious means of distribution. In the Patpong market, for example, a vendor might show you a picture

---

BARGAINING

If there isn't a sign stating the price for an item then the price is negotiable. Bargaining is common in street markets and some small shops. Prices in department stores, minimarts, 7-Elevens and so forth are fixed.

Thais respect a good haggler. Always let the vendor make the first offer, then ask 'Can you lower the price?'. This usually results in a discount. Now it's your turn to make a counteroffer; always start low but don't bargain at all unless you're serious about buying.

It helps immeasurably to keep the negotiations relaxed and friendly, and always remember to smile. Don't lose your temper or raise your voice as drama is not a good leverage tool.

of a knock-off watch, you pay for it and they go around the corner to fetch it. They usually come back, but you'll wait long enough to wonder.

Furniture

Rattan and hardwood furniture items are often good purchases and can be made to order. Chiang Mai is the country's primary furniture producer with many retail outlets in Bangkok. Due to the ban on teak harvesting and the subsequent exhaustion of recycled teak, 70% of export furniture produced in Thailand is made from parawood, a processed wood from rubber trees that can no longer be used for latex production.

Gems & Jewellery

Thailand is a leading exporter of gems and ornaments, rivalled only by India and Sri Lanka. Although rough-stone sources in Thailand have decreased dramatically, stones are now imported from Myanmar, Sri Lanka and other countries to be cut, polished and traded.

Although there are a lot of gem and jewellery stores in Thailand, it has become so difficult to dodge the scammers that the country no longer represents a safe and enjoyable place to buy these goods. It is better just to window shop.

Lacquerware

Chiang Mai is known for gold-on-black lacquerware. Lacquerware furniture and decorative items were traditionally made from bamboo and teak, but these days mango wood might be used as the base. If the item is top quality, only the frame is bamboo and horse or donkey hairs will be wound round it. With lower-quality lacquerware, the whole object is made from bamboo. The lacquer is then coated over the framework and allowed to dry. After several days it is sanded down with ash from rice husks, and another coating of lacquer is applied. A high-quality

item may have seven layers of lacquer. The piece is then engraved, painted and polished to remove the paint from everywhere except in the engravings. Multicoloured lacquerware is produced by repeated applications.

From start to finish it can take five or six months to produce a high-quality piece of lacquerware, which may have as many as five colours. Flexibility is one characteristic of good lacquerware: a well-made bowl can have its rim squeezed together until the sides meet without suffering damage. The quality and precision of the engraving is another thing to look for.

Textiles

The northeast is famous for *mát·mèe* cloth – a thick cotton or silk fabric woven from tie-dyed threads, similar to Indonesia's *ikat* fabrics. Surin Province is renowned for its *mát·mèe* silk often showcasing colours and geometric patterns inherited from Khmer traditions.

In the north, silks reflect the influence of the Lanna weaving traditions, brought to Chiang Mai and the surrounding mountains by the various Tai tribes.

Fairly nice *bah·dé* (batik) is available in the south in patterns that are more similar to the batik found in Malaysia than in Indonesia.

Each hill tribe has a tradition of embroidery that has been translated into the modern marketplace as bags and jewellery. Much of what you'll find in the marketplaces has been machine made, but there are many NGO cooperatives that help villagers get their handmade goods to the consumers. Chiang Mai and Chiang Rai are filled with handicraft outlets.

Telephone

The telephone country code for Thailand is ☎66 and is used when calling the country from abroad. All Thai

telephone numbers are preceded by a '0' if you're dialling domestically (the '0' is omitted when calling from overseas). After the initial '0', the next three numbers represent the provincial area code, which is now integral to the telephone number. If the initial '0' is followed by an '8' or a '9', then you're dialling a mobile phone.

International Calls

If you want to call an international number from a telephone in Thailand, you must first dial an international access code plus the country code followed by the subscriber number.

In Thailand, there are various international access codes charging different rates per minute. The standard direct-dial prefix is ☎001; it is operated by CAT and is considered to have the best sound quality; it connects to the largest number of countries but is also the most expensive. The next best is ☎007, a prefix operated by TOT with reliable quality and slightly cheaper rates. Economy rates are available through different carriers; do an internet search to determine promotion codes.

The following are some common international country codes: ☎61 Australia, ☎44 UK and ☎1 US.

Dial ☎100 for operator-assisted international calls or reverse-charges (collect) call. Alternatively, contact your long-distance carrier for their overseas operator number, a toll-free call, or try ☎001 9991 2001 from a CAT phone and ☎1 800 000 120 from a TOT phone.

Mobile Phones

The easiest phone option in Thailand is to acquire a mobile (cell) phone equipped with a local SIM card.

Thailand is on the GSM network and mobile phone providers include AIS (1 2 Call), DTAC and True Move.

You have two hand-phone options: you can buy a mobile phone in Thailand at one of the urban shopping malls or phone stores near the markets in provincial towns. Or you can use an imported phone that isn't SIM-locked (and one that supports the GSM network). To get started, buy a SIM card of a particular carrier, which includes an assigned telephone number. Once your phone is SIM-enabled you can buy minutes with prepaid phonecards. SIM cards and refill cards (usually sold in 300B to 500B denominations) can be bought from 7-Elevens throughout the country.

Thailand finally has a 3G network and True Move is offering 4G LTE coverage in Bangkok. Coverage and quality of the different carriers varies from year to year based on network upgrades and capacity. As of 2013 True was regarded with the highest data connectivity, though this could change. Carriers usually sell talk-data packages based on usage amounts.

Calling overseas through phones in most hotel rooms usually incurs additional surcharges (sometimes as much as 50% over and above the CAT rate). Some guesthouses will have a mobile phone or landline that customers can use for a per-minute fee for overseas calls.

Time

Thailand's time zone is seven hours ahead of GMT/UTC (London). Times are expressed according to the 24-hour clock, eg 11pm is written '23.00' in most cases.

Toilets

Increasingly, the Asian-style squat toilet is less of the norm in Thailand. There are still specimens in rural places, provincial bus stations, older homes and modest restaurants, but the Western-style toilet is becoming more prevalent and appears wherever foreign tourists can be found.

If you encounter a squat, here's what you should know. You should straddle the two footpads and face the door. To flush use the plastic bowl to scoop water out of the adjacent basin and pour into the toilet bowl. Some places supply a small pack of toilet paper at the entrance (5B), otherwise bring your own stash or wipe the old-fashioned way with water.

Even in places where sit-down toilets are installed, the septic system may not be designed to take toilet paper. In such cases there will be a waste basket where you're supposed to place used toilet paper and feminine hygiene products. Some toilets also come with a small spray hose – Thailand's version of the bidet.

Tourist Information

The government-operated tourist information and promotion service, **Tourism Authority of Thailand** (TAT; www.tourismthailand.org), was founded in 1960 and produces excellent pamphlets on sightseeing. TAT's head office is in Bangkok and there are 35 regional offices throughout the country.

TAT has more than 35 overseas information offices; check TAT's website for contact information.

Travellers with Disabilities

Thailand presents one large, ongoing obstacle course for the mobility impaired. With its high curbs, uneven footpaths and nonstop traffic, Thai cities can be particularly difficult. In Bangkok many streets must be crossed via pedestrian bridges flanked with steep stairways, while buses and boats don't stop long enough even for the fully abled. Rarely are there any ramps or other access points for wheelchairs.

A number of more expensive top-end hotels make consistent design efforts to provide disabled access to their properties. Other deluxe hotels with high employee-to-guest ratios are usually good about accommodating the mobility impaired by providing staff help where building design fails. For the rest, you're pretty much left to your own resources.

Counter to the prevailing trends, **Worldwide Dive & Sail** (www.sirenfleet.com) offers live-aboard diving programs for the deaf and hard of hearing.

Some organisations and publications that offer tips on international travel include the following:

Accessible Journeys (www.disabilitytravel.com)

Mobility International USA (www.miusa.org)

Society for Accessible Travel & Hospitality (SATH; www.sath.org)

Visas

The **Ministry of Foreign Affairs** (www.mfa.go.th) oversees immigration and visa issues. Check the website or the nearest Thai embassy or consulate for application procedures and costs.

Tourist Visas & Exemptions

The Thai government allows entry to 55 different nationalities, including those from Australia, New Zealand, the USA and most of Europe without prior visa arrangements for a set period of time. Some Eastern Europeans, Indians and Chinese qualify for a visa on arrival valid for 15 days, though talks are under way to allow Chinese visa exemptions. ASEAN countries are moving towards visa-waiving programs.

For most Western nationalities arriving in the kingdom by air, a 30-day visa is issued without a fee. For those arriving via a land border, the arrival visa is 15 days. Some countries (including Brazil, South Korea, Argentina, Chile and Peru) receive a 90-day free visa at all borders.

Without proof of an onward ticket and sufficient funds for one's projected stay any visitor can be denied entry, but in practice this is a formality that is rarely checked.

If you plan to stay in Thailand longer than 30 days (or 15 days for land arrivals), you should apply for the 60-day Tourist Visa from a Thai consulate or embassy before your trip. Contact the nearest Thai embassy or consulate to obtain application procedures and determine fees for tourist visas.

Non-Immigrant Visas

The Non-Immigrant Visa is good for 90 days and is intended for foreigners entering the country for business, study, retirement and extended family visits. There are multiple-entry visas available in this visa class. If you plan to apply for a Thai work permit, you'll need to possess a Non-Immigrant Visa first.

Visa Extensions & Renewals

If you decide you want to stay longer than the allotted time, you can extend your visa by applying at any immigration office in Thailand. The usual fee for a visa extension is 1900B. Those issued with a standard stay of 15 or 30 days can extend their stay for seven to 10 days (depending on the immigration office) if the extension is handled before the visa expires. The 60-day tourist visa can be extended by up to 30 days at the discretion of Thai immigration authorities.

Another visa-renewal option is to cross a land border. A new 15-day visa will be issued upon your return and some short-term visitors make a day trip out of the 'visa run'.

If you overstay your visa, the usual penalty is a fine of 500B per day, with a 20,000B limit. Fines can be paid at the airport or in advance at an immigration office. If you've overstayed only one day, you don't have to pay. Children under 14 travelling with a parent do not have to pay the penalty.

Foreign residents in Thailand should arrange visa extensions at the immigration office closest to their in-country address.

Volunteering

There are many wonderful volunteering organisations in Thailand that provide meaningful work and cultural engagement. **Volunteer Work Thailand** (www.volunteerworkthailand.org) maintains a database of opportunities with grassroots organisations.

Women Travellers

Women face relatively few problems in Thailand. With the great amount of respect afforded to women, an equal measure should be returned.

Thai women, especially the younger generation, are showing more skin these days. That means almost everyone is now dressing like a bar girl and you can wear spaghetti strap tops and navel-bearing shirts without offending Thais' modesty streak. But to be on the safe side, cover up if you're going deep into rural communities. And certainly cover up if visiting temples.

Attacks and rapes are not common in Thailand, but incidents do occur, especially when an attacker observes a vulnerable target: a drunk or solo woman. If you return home from a bar alone, be sure to have your wits about you. Avoid accepting rides from strangers late at night or travelling around in isolated areas by yourself – common sense stuff that might escape your notice in a new environment filled with hospitable people.

While Bangkok might be a men's paradise to some, foreign women are finding their own Romeos on the Thai beaches. As more couples emerge, more Thai men will make themselves available. Women who aren't interested in such romantic encounters should not presume that Thai men have merely platonic motives. Frivolous flirting could unintentionally cause a Thai man to feel a loss of face if attention is then diverted to another person and, in some cases where alcohol is involved, the spurned man may become unpleasant or even violent.

76

Transport

GETTING THERE & AWAY

Flights and tours can be booked online at www.lonely planet.com/bookings.

Entering the Country

Entry procedures for Thailand, by air or by land, are straightforward: you'll have to show your passport and you'll need to present completed arrival and departure cards.

You do not have to fill in a customs form on arrival unless you have imported goods to declare. In that case, you can get the proper form from Thai customs officials at your point of entry.

Air

Airports

Bangkok is Thailand's primary international and domestic gateway. There are also smaller airports throughout the country serving domestic and sometimes regional routes.

Suvarnabhumi International Airport (BKK; ☑0 2132 1888; www.bangkokair portonline.com) Receives nearly all international flights and most domestic flights. It is located in Samut Prakan – 30km east of Bangkok and 110km from Pattaya. The airport name is pronounced sù·wan·ná·poom.

Don Muang Airport (DMK; ☑0 2535 1111; www.donmuan gairportonline.com) Bangkok's second airport is used by Air Asia, Nok Air and Orient Thai (formerly One-Two-Go).

Phuket International Airport (☑0 7632 7230; www.phuketairportonline. com) International destinations include Seoul, Hong Kong, Kuala Lumpur, Singapore, Abu Dhabi, Chengdu, Shanghai and other Chinese cities. Direct charter flights from Europe are also available.

Chiang Mai International Airport (Map p234; www. chiangmaiairportonline.com) International destinations include Kunming, Seoul, Hong Kong, Macau, Kuala Lumpur and Singapore.

Airlines

The following airlines fly to and from Bangkok and international destinations.

Air Asia (☑0 2515 9999; www.airasia.com)

Air Berlin (☑001 800 12 0666 375; www.airberlin.com)

Air Canada (Map p78;☑0 2718 1839; www.aircanada.com)

Air China (Map p78;☑0 2108 1888; www.airchina.com)

Air France (☑001 800 441 0771; www.airfrance.fr)

Bangkok Airways (Map p112;☑1771; www.bangkokair. com)

British Airways (Map p78; ☑001 800 441 5906; www. britishairways.com)

CLIMATE CHANGE & TRAVEL

Every form of transport that relies on carbon-based fuel generates CO_2, the main cause of human-induced climate change. Modern travel is dependent on aeroplanes, which might use less fuel per kilometre per person than most cars but travel much greater distances. The altitude at which aircraft emit gases (including CO_2) and particles also contributes to their climate change impact. Many websites offer 'carbon calculators' that allow people to estimate the carbon emissions generated by their journey and, for those who wish to do so, to offset the impact of the greenhouse gases emitted with contributions to portfolios of climate-friendly initiatives throughout the world. Lonely Planet offsets the carbon footprint of all staff and author travel.

Cathay Pacific Airways (Map p84; ☎0 2263 0606; www.cathaypacific.com)

China Airlines (Map p84; ☎0 2250 9898; www.china-airlines.com)

Delta Airlines (☎001 800 658 228; www.delta.com)

Emirates (Map p90; ☎0 2664 1040; www.emirates.com)

Eva Air (☎0 2269 62300; www.evaair.com)

Garuda Indonesia (Map p83; ☎0 2285 6470; www.garuda-indonesia.com)

Japan Airlines (Map p84; ☎001 800 811 0600; www.jal.co.jp)

Jetstar Airways (☎0 2267 5125; www.jetstar.com)

KLM Royal Dutch Airlines (Map p83; ☎001 800 441 5560; www.klm.com)

Korean Air (☎0 2620 6900; www.koreanair.com)

Lao Airlines (☎0 2236 9822; www.laoairlines.com)

Lufthansa Airlines (Map p90; ☎0 2264 6800; www.lufthansa.com)

Malaysia Airlines (Map p84; ☎0 2263 0565; www.mas.com.my)

Myanmar Airways International (Map p90; ☎0 2261 5060; www.maiair.com)

Nepal Airlines (☎0 2266 7146; www.nepalairlines.com.np)

Philippine Airlines (☎0 2633 5713; www.philippineairlines.com)

Qantas Airways (Map p78; ☎0 2632 6611; www.qantas.com.au)

Royal Brunei Airlines (Map p83; ☎0 2638 3050; www.bruneiair.com)

Scandinavian Airlines (Map p90; ☎0 2693 7888; www.flysas.com)

Singapore Airlines (Map p78; ☎0 2353 6000; www.singaporeair.com)

South African Airways (Map p78; ☎0 2635 1414; www.flysaa.com)

Thai Airways International (THAI; Map p78; ☎0 2288 7000; www.thaiair.com; 485 Th Silom; ☉8am-5pm Mon-Sat; Ⓢ Chong Nonsi exit 3)

United Airlines (Map p84; ☎0 2353 3939; www.united.com)

Vietnam Airlines (Map p84; ☎0 2655 4137; www.vietnam-air.com)

Tickets

In some cases – when travelling to neighbouring countries or to domestic destinations – it is still convenient to use a travel agent in Thailand. The amount of commission an agent will charge varies so shop around to gauge the discrepancy in prices. Paying by credit card generally offers purchasing protection, because most card issuers provide refunds if you can prove you didn't get what you paid for. Agents who accept only cash should hand over the tickets straightaway and not tell you to 'come back tomorrow'. After you've made a booking or paid your deposit, call the airline and confirm that the booking was made.

Air fares during the high season (December to March) can be expensive.

Land

Thailand shares land borders with Laos, Malaysia, Cambodia and Myanmar. Travel between all of these countries can be done by land via sanctioned border crossings. With improved highways, it is also becoming easier to travel from Thailand to China via Laos.

Border Crossings

CAMBODIA

Cambodian tourist visas are available at the border for US$20, though some borders charge 1500B. Bring a passport photo and try to avoid some of the runner boys who want to issue a health certificate or other paperwork for additional fees.

Aranya Prathet to Poipet The most direct land route between Bangkok and Angkor Wat (Siem Reap), now connected by direct government bus.

Hat Lek to Krong Koh Kong The coastal crossing for travellers heading to/from Ko Chang/Sihanoukville.

Ban Pakard/Pong Nam Ron to Psar Pruhm A backdoor route from Ko Chang (via Chanthaburi) to Battambang and Angkor Wat.

Remote crossings include O Smach to Chong Chom (periodically closed due to fighting at Khao Phra Wihan) and Chong Sa to Ngam Choam, but they aren't as convenient as you'll have to hire private transport on the Cambodian side of the border.

CHINA

The interior of southern China is now linked with Laos and northern Thailand, making it possible to travel somewhat directly between the two countries. You'll need to arrange your Chinese visa prior to departure, ideally in Bangkok or Chiang Mai.

Chiang Khong to Mengla The China–Thailand highway (Rte 3) was a former opium smuggling trail that has been modernised into a major transnational shipping route. The 1800km of paved road between Kunming, in China's Yunnan Province, to Bangkok is still missing one vital link: the fourth Thai-Lao Friendship Bridge (at Chiang Khong–Huay Xai) across the Mekong River, which is projected to be completed at the end of 2014.

Chiang Saen to Jinghong It was once possible to take a slow boat along the Mekong River from northern Thailand to China's Yunnan Province, but service has been suspended.

LAOS

It is fairly hassle free to cross into Laos from northern and northeastern Thailand. Lao visas (US$35 to US$50) can be obtained on arrival and applications require a passport photo. Try to have crisp, clean bills. There are increasing amounts of direct buses that link major towns on both sides of the border, making the border towns just a formality stop.

Nong Khai to Vientiane The first Thai–Lao Friendship Bridge to span the Mekong River is one of the main gateways between the two countries. Nong Khai is easily reached by train or bus from Bangkok.

Chiang Khong to Huay Xai The fourth Thai–Lao Friendship Bridge increases the popularity of this crossing that links northern Thailand with Luang Prabang via boat. Direct buses from Chiang Mai to Laos use this crossing.

Mukdahan to Savannakhet The second Thai–Lao Friendship Bridge provides a trilateral link between Thailand, Laos and Vietnam.

Nakhon Phanom to Tha Khaek The third Thai–Lao Friendship Bridge connects northeastern Thailand to southern Laos.

Chong Mek to Vangtao The border is best accessed via Ubon Ratchathani (Thailand) and is a good option for transiting to Pakse (Laos). Direct buses from Ubon are now available.

In northeastern Thailand, remote crossings include Bueng Kan to Paksan (Lao visas must be arranged in advance) and Tha Li to Kaen Thao (requires chartered transport). In northern Thailand, a remote crossing includes Ban Huay Kon to Muang Ngeun.

MALAYSIA

Malaysia, especially the west coast, is easy to reach via bus, train and even boat.

Hat Yai to Butterworth The western spur of the train line originating in Bangkok terminates at Butterworth, the mainland transfer point to Penang.

Hat Yai to Padang Besar Buses originate out of the southern transit town of Hat Yai en route to a variety of Malaysian destinations. Border formalities are handled at Padang Besar.

Sungai Kolok to Kota Bahru While this border crossing is a possibility, the continued violence in Thailand's Deep South means that we do not recommend it.

Ko Lipe to Langkawi Boats provide a convenient high-season link between these two Andaman islands.

There is also boat service from the mainland port of Satun (Thailand) to the Malaysian island of Langkawi and the mainland town of Kuala Perlis, but most travellers transit to Malaysia via Ko Lipe (Thailand).

MYANMAR

As part of the AEC (ASEAN Economic Community) integration goals, Myanmar has lifted travel restrictions at four of its borders with Thailand, meaning that foreign visitors can now enter the country with a pre-arranged Myanmarese visa and exit via a different border (previously all visitors had to enter and exit via the same controlled point). Of the four borders, Ban Phu Nam Ron to Htee-Khee is a new crossing requiring major infrastructure investment; the Thai government intends to develop this route as a link between Bangkok and Myanmar's Dawei port in the Andaman Sea.

Mae Sai to Tachileik This is a popular border-run crossing. It also hosts a popular border market that can be visited on a day trip from Thailand without a pre-arranged visa. For further travel, a pre-arranged visa is required.

Ranong to Kawthoung This is a popular visa-renewal point in the southern part of Thailand and can be used to enter/exit southern Myanmar.

Mae Sot to Myawaddy One of the most accessible land borders for points within Myanmar.

Bus, Car & Motorcycle

Road connections exist between all of Thailand's neighbours, and these routes can be travelled by bus, shared taxi and private car. In some cases, you'll take a bus to the border point, pass through immigration and then pick up another bus or shared taxi on the other side. In other cases, especially when crossing the Malaysian border, the bus will stop for immigration formalities and then continue to its destination across the border.

Train

Thailand's and Malaysia's state railways meet at Butterworth (93km south of the Thai–Malaysian border), which is a transfer point to Penang (by boat) or to Kuala Lumpur and Singapore (by Malaysian train).

There are several border crossings for which you can take a train to the border and then switch to automobile transport on the other side. The Thai–Cambodian border crossing of Aranya Prathet to Poipet and the Thai–Lao crossing of Nong Khai to Vientiane are two examples.

Another rail line travels to the Malaysian east coast border town of Sungai Kolok, but because of ongoing violence in Thailand's Deep South we don't recommend this route for travellers.

GETTING AROUND

Air

Hopping around the country by air continues to be affordable. Most routes originate from Bangkok, but Chiang Mai, Ko Samui and Phuket all have a few routes to other Thai towns. See the Thai Airfares map for routes and estimated costs.

THAI, Bangkok Air, Orient Thai and Nok Air all operate many domestic routes from Bangkok to provincial capitals.

Boat

The true Thai river transport is the *reu·a hăhng yow* (long-tail boat), so-called because the propeller is mounted at the end of a long drive shaft extending from the engine. The long-tail boats are a staple of transport on rivers and canals in Bangkok and neighbouring provinces.

Between the mainland and small, less touristed islands, the standard craft is a wooden boat, 8m to 10m long, with an inboard engine, a wheelhouse and a simple roof to shelter passengers and cargo. But faster, more expensive hovercraft (jet-foils) and speedboats are the norm these days.

Bus & Minivan

The bus network in Thailand is prolific and reliable. The Thai government subsidises the Transport Company (*bò·rí·sàt kŏn sòng*), usually abbreviated to Baw Khaw Saw (BKS). Every city and town in Thailand linked by bus has a BKS station, even if it's just a patch of dirt by the side of the road.

By far the most reliable bus companies in Thailand are the ones that operate out of the government-run BKS stations. In some cases the companies are entirely state owned, in others they are private concessions.

We do not recommend using bus companies that operate directly out of tourist centres, like Bangkok's Th Khao San, because of repeated instances of theft and commission-seeking stops. Be sure to be aware of bus scams and other common problems.

Minivans are increasingly becoming the middle-class option. Minivans are run by private companies and because their vehicles are smaller, they can depart from the market (instead of the out-of-town bus stations) and will deliver guests directly to their hotel. Just don't sit in the front – that way you can avoid having to watch the driver's daredevil techniques.

Bus Classes

The cheapest and slowest buses are the *rót tam·má·dah* (ordinary fan buses) that stop in every little town and for every waving hand along the highway. Only a few of these ordinary buses, in rural locations or for local destinations, still exist since most have been replaced by air-con buses.

Rót aa (air-con buses) come in a variety of classes, depending on the destination's distance. Short distances are usually covered by the basic 2nd class bus, which does not have an on-board toilet on board. For longer routes, the buses increase in comfort and amenities, ranging from 1st class to 'VIP' and 'Super VIP'. The latter two have fewer seats so that each seat reclines further; sometimes these are called *rót norn* (sleeper buses).

Bring along a jacket for long-distance bus trips as air-con keeps the cabin at arctic temperatures. The service on these buses is usually quite good and on certain routes sometimes includes a beverage and video, courtesy of an 'air hostess'.

On overnight journeys the buses usually stop somewhere en route for 'midnight kôw dôm', when passengers are awakened to get off the bus for a free meal of rice and soup.

Reservations

You can book air-con BKS buses at any BKS terminal. Ordinary (fan) buses cannot be booked in advance. Privately run buses can be booked through most hotels or any travel agency, but it's best to book directly through a bus office to be sure that you get what you pay for.

Car & Motorcycle

Driving Licence

In theory short-term visitors who wish to drive vehicles (including motorcycles) in Thailand need an International Driving Permit, however this isn't always enforced.

BICYCLE TRAVEL IN THAILAND

For travelling just about anywhere outside Bangkok, bicycles are an ideal form of local transport – cheap, non-polluting and slow moving enough to allow travellers to see everything. Bicycles can be hired from guesthouses for as little as 50B per day, though they aren't always high-quality. A security deposit isn't usually required.

Bicycle touring is also a popular way to see the country, and most roads are sealed and have roomy shoulders. Because duties are high on imported bikes, you'll do better to bring your own bike to Thailand rather than purchasing locally. No special permits are needed for bringing a bicycle into the country, although it may be registered by customs – which means if you don't leave the country with your bicycle, you'll have to pay a customs duty. It's advisable to bring a well-stocked repair kit.

Air-Fares & Train Routes Map

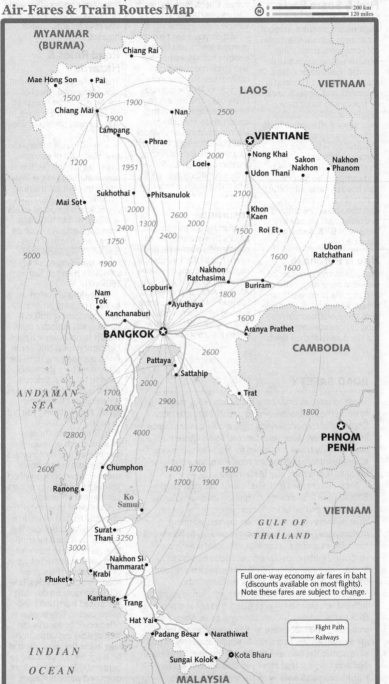

MYANMAR (BURMA)

LAOS

VIETNAM

Chiang Rai

Mae Hong Son • Pai

1500 *1900*

Chiang Mai •
1900
Lampang
1200
• Nan
1900
2500

• Phrae

⊙ **VIENTIANE**

2000
Loei •
• Nong Khai
Sakon Nakhon
Nakhon Phanom

• Udon Thani

1951

Sukhothai •
• Phitsanulok

Mai Sot •

2000
2100

Khon Kaen

2600
2400 *1300*
2000
1500
Roi Et •

1750

2400

1600
Ubon Ratchathani

1900
1600

5000

Nakhon Ratchasima
Buriram

Nam Tok
Lopburi •
• Ayuthaya
1800

Kanchanaburi
BANGKOK ⊙
1600
Aranya Prathet

CAMBODIA

Pattaya •
2600
• Sattahip

ANDAMAN SEA
1700
2000
• Trat

2000
2900
1800

2800
4000

PHNOM PENH ✹

2600
• Chumphon
1400 *1700* *1500*
1700 *1900*

Ranong •

Ko Samui

VIETNAM

GULF OF THAILAND

Surat Thani *3250*

3000

Nakhon Si Thammarat •

Phuket •
• Krabi

Kantang •
• Trang

Full one-way economy air fares in baht (discounts available on most flights). Note these fares are subject to change.

Hat Yai •

• Padang Besar   • Narathiwat

INDIAN OCEAN

Sungai Kolok ⊙ Kota Bharu

MALAYSIA

Flight Path
Railways

Fuel & Spare Parts

Modern petrol (gasoline) stations are plentiful. In more rural areas *ben·sin/nám·man rót yon* (petrol containing benzine) is usually available at small roadside or village stands. All fuel in Thailand is unleaded, and diesel is used by trucks and some passenger cars. Thailand also uses several alternative fuels, including gasohol (a blend of petrol and ethanol that comes in different octane levels, either 91% or 95%) and compressed natural gas, used by taxis with bifuel capabilities. For news and updates about fuel options and other car talk, see the website of **BKK Auto** (www.bkkautos.com).

Hire & Purchase

Cars, jeeps and vans can be rented in most major cities and airports from local companies as well as international chains. Local companies tend to have cheaper rates, but the quality of their fleet varies. Check the tyre treads and general upkeep of the vehicle before committing.

Motorcycles can be rented in major towns and tourist centres from guesthouses and small mum-and-dad businesses. Renting a motorcycle in Thailand is relatively easy and a great way to independently tour the countryside. For daily rentals, most businesses will ask that you leave your passport as a deposit. Before renting a motorcycle, check the vehicle's condition and ask for a helmet (which is required by law).

Insurance

Thailand requires a minimum of liability insurance for all registered vehicles on the road. The better hire companies include comprehensive coverage for their vehicles. Always verify that a vehicle is insured for liability before signing a rental contract; you should also ask to see the dated insurance documents.

If you have an accident while driving an uninsured vehicle, you're in for some major hassles.

Road Rules & Hazards

Thais drive on the left-hand side of the road (most of the time!). Other than that, just about anything goes, in spite of road signs and speed limits.

The main rule to be aware of is that right of way goes to the bigger vehicle; this is not what it says in the Thai traffic law, but it's the reality. Maximum speed limits are 50km/h on urban roads and 80km/h to 100km/h on most highways – but on any given stretch of highway you'll see various vehicles travelling as slowly as 30km/h and as fast as 150km/h.

Indicators are often used to warn passing drivers about oncoming traffic. A flashing left indicator means it's OK to pass, while a right indicator means that someone's approaching from the other direction. Horns are used to tell other vehicles that the driver plans to pass. When drivers flash their lights, they're telling you not to pass.

In Bangkok traffic is chaotic, roads are poorly signposted and motorcycles and random contra flows mean you can suddenly find yourself facing a wall of cars coming the other way.

Outside of the capital, the principal hazard when driving in Thailand, besides the general disregard for traffic laws, is having to contend with so many different types of vehicles on the same road – trucks, bicycles, túk-túk ('pronounced *đúk dúk;* motorised transport) and motorcycles. This danger is often compounded by the lack of working lights. In village areas the vehicular traffic is lighter but you have to contend with stray chickens, dogs and water buffaloes.

ROAD SAFETY

Thailand rates as one of the most dangerous places to be on the road, according to a recent World Health Organization report. Several high-profile bus accidents involving foreign tourists prompted some Western nations to issue travel advisories for highway safety due to disregard for speed limits, reckless driving and long-distance bus drivers' use of stimulants.

Fatal bus crashes make headlines, but more than 80% of vehicle accidents in Thailand involve motorcycles. Less than half of the motorcyclists in the country wear helmets and many tourists are injured riding motorcycles because they don't know how to handle the vehicles and are unfamiliar with local driving conventions. British consular offices cited Thailand as a primary destination for UK citizens experiencing road traffic accidents, often involving motorcyclists.

If you are a novice motorcyclists, familiarise yourself with the vehicle in an uncongested area of town and stick to the smaller 100cc automatic bikes. Drive slowly, especially when roads are slick or when there is loose gravel. Remember to distribute weight as evenly as possible across the frame of the bike to improve handling. And don't expect that other vehicles will look out for you. Motorcycles are low on the traffic totem pole.

Hitching

Hitching is never entirely safe in any country and we don't recommend it. Travellers who decide to hitch should understand that they are taking a small but potentially serious risk. Hitching is rarely seen these days in Thailand, so most passing motorists might not realise the intentions of the foreigner standing on the side of the road with a thumb out. Thais don't 'thumb it'; instead, when they want a ride they wave their hand with the palm facing the ground. This is the same gesture used to flag a taxi or bus, which is why some drivers might stop and point to a bus stop if one is nearby.

In some of the national parks where there isn't public transport, Thais are often willing to pick up a passenger standing by the side of the road.

Local Transport

City Bus & Sŏrng·tăa·ou

Bangkok has the largest city-bus system in the country, while Udon Thani and a few other provincial capitals have some city-bus services. The etiquette for riding public buses is to wait at a bus stop and hail the vehicle by waving your hand palm-side downward. You typically pay the fare once you've taken a seat or, in some cases, when you disembark.

Elsewhere, public transport is provided by sŏrng·tăa·ou (a small pick-up truck outfitted with two facing rows of benches for passengers). They sometimes operate on fixed routes, just like buses, but they may also run a share-taxi service where they pick up passengers going in the same general direction. In tourist centres, sŏrng·tăa·ou can be chartered just like a regular taxi, but you'll need to negotiate the fare before-

hand. You can usually hail a sŏrng·tăa·ou anywhere along its route and pay the fare when you disembark.

Depending on the region, sŏrng·tăa·ou might also run a fixed route from the centre of town to outlying areas or even points within the provinces. Sometimes these vehicles are larger six-wheeled vehicles (sometimes called 'rót hòk lór').

Mass Transit

Bangkok is the only city in Thailand to have an above-ground (BTS) and underground light-rail (MRT) public transport system.

Motorcycle Taxi

Many cities in Thailand have mor·deu·sai ráp jâhng (100cc to 125cc motorcycles) that can be hired, with a driver, for short distances. If you're empty-handed or travelling with a small bag, they can't be beaten for transport in a pinch.

In most cities, you'll find motorcycle taxis clustered near street intersections. Usually they wear numbered jerseys. Fares tend to run from 10B to 50B, depending on distance and you'll need to establish the price beforehand.

Taxi

Bangkok has the most formal system of metered taxis. In other cities, a taxi can be a private vehicle with negotiable rates and there are a variety of shared taxis in which the fare is split among a group of passengers.

Tours

Many operators around the world can arrange guided tours of Thailand. Most of them simply serve as brokers for tour companies based in Thailand. The better tour companies build their own Thailand itineraries from scratch and choose their local suppliers based on which best serve these itineraries. Many are now offering 'voluntourism' programs, which means that you might buy lunch for an orphanage, visit a hospital or teach an English class in addition to sightseeing.

Asian Trails (www.asiantrails.info) Tour operator that runs programs for overseas brokers; trips include a mix of on- and off-the-beaten-path destinations.

Hands Up Holidays (www.handsupholidays.com) Volunteer tourism and village sightseeing programs.

SĂHM·LÓR & TÚK-TÚK

Săhm·lór are three-wheeled pedicabs that are typically found in small towns where traffic is light and old-fashioned ways persist.

The modern era's version of the human-powered săhm·lór is the motorised túk-túk. They're small utility vehicles, powered by screaming engines (usually LPG-powered) with a lot of flash and sparkle.

With either form of transport the fare must be established by bargaining before departure. In tourist centres, túk-túk drivers often grossly overcharge foreigners, so have a sense of how much the fare should be before soliciting a ride. Hotel staff are helpful in providing reasonable fare suggestions.

Readers interested in pedicab lore and design may want to have a look at Lonely Planet's hardcover pictorial book, Chasing Rickshaws, by Lonely Planet founder Tony Wheeler.

I-to-I (www.i-to-i.com) Volunteer tourism and gap-year programs.

Intrepid Travel (www.intrepidtravel.com) Specialises in small-group travel geared towards young people.

Isan Explorer (www.isanexplorer.com) Custom tours to the northeast.

Mekong Cruises (www.cruisemekong.com) Float down the mighty river aboard an elegant vessel.

Orient Express (www.orient-express.com) High-end luxury tours of common and uncommon places in Thailand.

Spice Roads (www.spiceroads.com) Variety of regional cycling programs.

Tour de Thailand (www.tourdethailand.com) Charity bike ride organiser covering touring routes throughout the country.

Tours with Kasma Loha-Unchit (www.thaifoodandtravel.com) Thai cookbook author offers personalised 'cultural immersion' tours of Thailand.

Train

Thailand's train system connects the four corners of the country and is most convenient as an alternative to buses for the long journey north to Chiang Mai or south to Surat Thani. The train is also ideal for short trips to Ayuthaya and Lopburi from Bangkok where traffic is a consideration.

The 4500km rail network is operated by the **State Railway of Thailand** (SRT; ☑1690; www.railway.co.th) and covers four main lines: the northern, southern, northeastern and eastern lines. All long-distance trains originate from Bangkok's Hualamphong station.

Classes

The SRT operates passenger trains in three classes – 1st, 2nd and 3rd – but each class varies considerably depending on whether you're on an ordinary, rapid or express train.

First Class – Private cabins define the 1st-class carriages, which are available only on rapid, express and special-express trains.

Second Class – The seating arrangements in a 2nd-class, non-sleeper carriage are similar to those on a bus, with pairs of padded seats, usually recliners, all facing towards the front of the train. On 2nd-class sleeper cars, pairs of seats face one another and convert into two fold-down berths. The lower berth has more headroom than the upper berth and this is reflected in a higher fare. Children are always assigned a lower berth. Second-class carriages are found only on rapid and express trains. There are air-con and fan 2nd-class carriages.

Third Class – A typical 3rd-class carriage consists of two rows of bench seats divided into facing pairs. Each bench seat is designed to seat two or three passengers, but on a crowded rural line nobody seems to care. Express trains do not carry 3rd-class carriages at all. Commuter trains in the Bangkok area are all 3rd class.

Costs

Fares are determined on a base price with surcharges added for distance, class and train type (special express, express, rapid, ordinary). Extra charges are added if the carriage has air-con and for sleeping berths (either upper or lower).

Reservations

Advance bookings can be made from one to 60 days before your intended date of departure. You can make bookings in person from any train station. Train tickets can also be purchased at travel agencies, which usually add a service charge to the ticket price. If you are planning long-distance train travel from outside the country, you should email SRT (passenger-ser@railway.co.th) at least two weeks before your journey. You will receive an email confirming the booking. Pick up and pay for tickets an hour before leaving at the scheduled departure train station.

It is advisable to make advanced bookings for long-distance sleeper trains between Bangkok and Chiang Mai or from Bangkok to Surat Thani as seats fill up quickly.

For short-distance trips you should purchase your ticket at least a day in advance for seats (rather than sleepers).

Partial refunds on tickets are available depending on the number of days prior to your departure you arrange for a cancellation. These arrangements can be handled at the train station booking office.

Station Services

You'll find that all train stations in Thailand have baggage-storage services (or 'cloak rooms'). Most stations have a ticket window that will open between 15 and 30 minutes before train arrivals. There are also newsagents and small snack vendors, but no full-service restaurants.

Most train stations have printed timetables in English; although this isn't always the case for smaller stations.

Health

Health risks and the quality of medical facilities vary depending on where and how you travel in Thailand. The majority of cities and popular tourist areas have adequate and even excellent medical care. However, travel to remote rural areas can expose you to some health risks and less adequate medical care.

Travellers tend to worry about contracting exotic infectious diseases when visiting the tropics, but these are far less common than problems with pre-existing medical conditions such as heart disease, and accidental injury (especially as a result of traffic accidents).

Other common illnesses are respiratory infections, diarrhoea and dengue fever. Fortunately most common illnesses can be prevented or are easily treated.

The advice given here is a general guide and does not replace the advice of a doctor trained in travel medicine.

BEFORE YOU GO

Pack medications in clearly labelled original containers and obtain a signed and dated letter from your physician describing your medical conditions, medications and syringes or needles. If you have a heart condition, bring a copy of your electrocardiography (ECG) taken just prior to travelling.

If you take any regular medication bring double your needs in case of loss or theft. In Thailand you can buy many medications over the counter without a doctor's prescription, but it can be difficult to find the exact medication you are taking.

Contact your home country's Department of Foreign Affairs or the equivalent and register your trip; this is a helpful precaution in the event of a natural disaster.

Insurance

Even if you're fit and healthy, don't travel without health insurance – accidents *do* happen. You may require extra cover for adventure activities such as rock climbing or diving, as well as scooter/motorcycle riding. If your health insurance doesn't cover you for medical expenses abroad, ensure you get specific travel insurance. Most hospitals require an upfront guarantee of payment (from yourself or your insurer) prior to admission. Inquire before your trip about payment of medical charges and retain all documentation (medical reports, invoices etc) for claim purposes.

Recommended Vaccinations

You should arrange your vaccines six to eight weeks prior to departure though a specialised travel-medicine clinic.

FURTHER READING

➡ **International Travel & Health** (www.who.int/ith) Published by the World Health Organization (WHO).

➡ **Centers for Disease Control & Prevention** (CDC; www.cdc.gov) Country-specific advice.

➡ *Healthy Travel – Asia & India* (by Lonely Planet) Pretrip planning, emergency first aid, immunisation and disease information.

➡ *Traveller's Health: How to Stay Healthy Abroad* (by Dr Richard Dawood) Considered the 'health bible' for international holidays.

➡ *Travelling Well* (by Dr Deborah Mills) Health guidebook and website (www.travellingwell.com.au).

➡ *Healthy Living in Thailand* (published by the Thai Red Cross) Recommended for long-term travellers.

The **Centers for Disease Control and Prevention** (CDC; www.cdc.gov) has a traveller's health section that contains recommendations for vaccinations. The only vaccine required by international regulations is yellow fever. Proof of vaccination will only be required if you have visited a country in the yellow-fever zone within the six days prior to entering Thailand. If you are travelling to Thailand *from* Africa or South America you should check to see if you require proof of vaccination.

Medical Checklist

Recommended items for a personal medical kit include the following; most of these medicines are available in Thailand:

➡ antifungal cream, eg Clotrimazole

➡ antibacterial cream, eg Muciprocin

➡ antibiotic for skin infections, eg Amoxicillin/ Clavulanate or Cephalexin

➡ antibiotics for diarrhoea include Norfloxacin, Ciprofloxacin or Azithromycin for bacterial diarrhoea; for giardiasis or amoebic dysentery take Tinidazole

➡ antihistamine – there are many options, eg Cetirizine for daytime and Promethazine for night-time

➡ antiseptic, eg Betadine

➡ antispasmodic for stomach cramps, eg Buscopan

➡ contraceptives

➡ decongestant

➡ DEET-based insect repellent

➡ oral rehydration solution for diarrhoea (eg Gastrolyte), diarrhoea 'stopper' (eg Loperamide) and antinausea medication

➡ first-aid items such as scissors, Elastoplasts, bandages, gauze, thermometer (but not one with mercury), sterile needles and syringes (with a doctor's letter), safety pins and tweezers

➡ hand gel (alcohol based) or alcohol-based hand wipes

➡ ibuprofen or another anti-inflammatory

➡ indigestion medication, eg Quick Eze or Mylanta

➡ laxative, eg Coloxyl

➡ migraine medicine – for migraine sufferers

➡ paracetamol

➡ Permethrin to impregnate clothing and mosquito nets if at high risk

➡ steroid cream for allergic/ itchy rashes, eg 1% to 2% hydrocortisone

➡ sunscreen, sunglasses and hat

➡ throat lozenges

➡ thrush (vaginal yeast infection) treatment, eg Clotrimazole pessaries or Diflucan tablet

➡ Ural or equivalent if prone to urine infections

IN TRANSIT

Deep Vein Thrombosis

Deep vein thrombosis (DVT) occurs when blood clots form in the legs during long trips such as flights, chiefly because of prolonged immobility. The longer the journey, the greater the risk. Though most blood clots are reabsorbed uneventfully, some may break off and travel through the blood vessels to the lungs, where they can cause life-threatening complications.

The chief symptom of DVT is swelling or pain of the foot, ankle or calf, usually but not always on one side. When a blood clot travels to the lungs, it may cause chest pain and difficulty in breathing. Travellers with any of these symptoms should immediately seek medical attention.

To prevent the development of DVT on long flights you should walk about the cabin, perform isometric compressions of the leg muscles (ie contract the leg muscles while sitting) and drink plenty of fluids (nonalcoholic). Those at higher risk should speak with a doctor.

Jet Lag & Motion Sickness

Jet lag is common when crossing more than five time zones; it results in insomnia, fatigue, malaise or nausea. To avoid jet lag drink plenty of fluids (nonalcoholic) and eat light meals. Upon arrival, seek exposure to natural sunlight and readjust your schedule. Some people find melatonin helpful.

Sedating antihistamines such as dimenhydrinate (Dramamine) or Prochlorperazine (Phenergan) are usually the first choice for treating motion sickness. Their main side effect is drowsiness. A herbal alternative is ginger. Scopolamine patches are considered the most effective prevention.

IN THAILAND

Availability & Cost of Health Care

Bangkok is considered a centre of medical excellence in Southeast Asia. Private hospitals are more expensive than other medical facilities but offer a superior standard of care and English-speaking staff. The cost of health care is relatively cheap in Thailand compared to most Western countries.

RARE BUT BE AWARE

➡ Avian Influenza – Most of those infected have had close contact with sick or dead birds.

➡ Filariasis – A mosquito-borne disease that is common in the local population; practise mosquito-avoidance measures.

➡ Hepatitis E – Transmitted through contaminated food and water and has similar symptoms to hepatitis A; can be a severe problem in pregnant women. Follow safe eating and drinking guidelines.

➡ Japanese B Encephalitis – Viral disease transmitted by mosquitoes, typically occurring in rural areas; vaccination is recommended for travellers spending more than one month outside cities or for long-term expats.

➡ Meliodosis – Contracted by skin contact with soil. Affects up to 30% of the local population in northeastern Thailand. The symptoms are very similar to those experienced by tuberculosis (TB) sufferers. There is no vaccine but it can be treated with medications.

➡ Strongyloides – A parasite transmitted by skin contact with soil; common in the local population. It is characterised by an unusual skin rash – a linear rash on the trunk which comes and goes. An overwhelming infection can follow. It can be treated with medications.

➡ Tuberculosis – Medical and aid workers and long-term travellers who have significant contact with the local population should take precautions. Vaccination is recommended for children spending more than three months in Thailand. The main symptoms are fever, cough, weight loss, night sweats and tiredness. Treatment is available with long-term multidrug regimens.

➡ Typhus – Murine typhus is spread by the bite of a flea; scrub typhus is spread via a mite. Symptoms include fever, muscle pains and a rash. Following general insect-avoidance measures and Doxycycline will also prevent it.

Infectious Diseases

Cutaneous Larva Migrans

This disease, caused by dog or cat hookworm, is particularly common on the beaches of Thailand. The rash starts as a small lump, and then slowly spreads like a winding line. It is intensely itchy, especially at night. It is easily treated with medications and should not be cut out or frozen.

Dengue Fever

This mosquito-borne disease is increasingly problematic in Thailand, especially in the cities. As there is no vaccine it can only be prevented by avoiding mosquito bites. The mosquito that carries dengue is a daytime biter, so use insect-avoidance measures at all times. Symptoms include high fever, severe headache (especially behind the eyes), nausea and body aches (dengue was previously known as 'breakbone fever'). Some people develop a rash (which can be very itchy) and experience diarrhoea. Chiang Mai and the southern islands are particularly high-risk areas. There is no specific treatment, just rest and paracetamol – do not take aspirin or ibuprofen as they increase the risk of haemorrhaging. See a doctor to be diagnosed and monitored.

Dengue can progress to the more severe and life-threatening dengue haemorrhagic fever; however this is very uncommon in tourists. The risk of this increases substantially if you have previously been infected with dengue and are then infected with a different serotype.

Hepatitis A

The risk in Bangkok is decreasing but there is still significant risk in most of the country. This food- and waterborne virus infects the liver, causing jaundice (yellow skin and eyes), nausea and lethargy. There is no specific treatment for hepatitis A. In rare instances, it can be fatal for those over the age of 40. All travellers to Thailand should be vaccinated against hepatitis A.

Hepatitis B

The only sexually transmitted disease (STD) that can be prevented by vaccination, hepatitis B is spread by body fluids. In some parts of Thailand up to 20% of the population are carriers of hepatitis B, and are usually unaware of this. The long-term consequences can include liver cancer, cirrhosis and death.

HIV

HIV is now one of the most common causes of death in people under the age of 50 in Thailand. Always practise safe sex; avoid getting tattoos or using unclean syringes.

Influenza

Present year-round in the tropics, influenza (flu) symptoms include high fever, muscle aches, runny nose, cough and sore throat. Flu is the most common vaccine-preventable disease contracted by travellers and everyone should consider vaccination. There is no specific treatment, just rest and paracetamol. Complications such as bronchitis or middle-ear infection may require antibiotic treatment.

Leptospirosis

Leptospirosis is contracted from exposure to infected surface water – most commonly after river rafting or canyoning. Early symptoms are very similar to flu and include headache and fever. It can vary from a very mild ailment to a fatal disease. Diagnosis is made through blood tests and it is easily treated with Doxycycline.

Malaria

There is an enormous amount of misinformation concerning malaria. Malaria is caused by a parasite transmitted by the bite of an infected mosquito. The most important symptom of malaria is fever, but general symptoms such as headache, diarrhoea, cough or chills may also occur – the same symptoms as many other infections. A diagnosis can only be made by taking a blood sample.

Most parts of Thailand visited by tourists, particularly city and resort areas, have minimal to no risk of malaria, and the risk of side effects

from taking antimalarial tablets is likely to outweigh the risk of getting the disease itself. If you are travelling to high-risk rural areas (unlikely for most visitors), seek medical advice on the right medication and dosage for you.

Measles

This highly contagious viral infection is spread through coughing and sneezing. Most people born before 1966 are immune as they had the disease in childhood. Measles starts with a high fever and rash and can be complicated by pneumonia and brain disease. There is no specific treatment. Ensure you are fully vaccinated.

Rabies

This disease, fatel if untreated, is spread by the bite or lick of an infected animal – most commonly a dog or monkey. You should seek medical advice immediately after any animal bite and commence postexposure treatment. Having a pretravel vaccination means the postbite treatment is greatly simplified.

If an animal bites you, gently wash the wound with soap and water, and apply iodine-based antiseptic. If you are not prevaccinated you will need to receive rabies immunoglobulin as soon as possible, followed by five shots of vaccine over 28 days. If prevaccinated you need just two shots of vaccine given three days apart.

STDs

Sexually transmitted diseases most common in Thailand include herpes, warts, syphilis, gonorrhoea and chlamydia. People carrying these diseases often have no signs of infection. Condoms will prevent gonorrhoea and chlamydia but not warts or herpes. If after a sexual encounter you develop any rash, lumps, discharge or pain when passing urine seek immediate medical attention. If you have been sexually active during your travels have

an STD check on your return home.

Typhoid

This serious bacterial infection is spread through food and water. It gives a high and slowly progressive fever, severe headache, and may be accompanied by a dry cough and stomach pain. It is diagnosed by blood tests and treated with antibiotics. Vaccination is recommended for all travellers spending more than a week in Thailand, or travelling outside of the major cities. Be aware that vaccination is not 100% effective so you must still be careful with what you eat and drink.

Traveller's Diarrhoea

Traveller's diarrhoea is by far the most common problem affecting travellers. In over 80% of cases, traveller's diarrhoea is caused by a bacteria (there are numerous potential culprits), and responds promptly to treatment with antibiotics.

Here we define traveller's diarrhoea as the passage of more than three watery bowel movements within 24 hours, plus at least one other symptom such as vomiting, fever, cramps, nausea or feeling generally unwell.

Treatment consists of staying well hydrated; rehydration solutions such as Gastrolyte are the best for this. Antibiotics such as Norfloxacin, Ciprofloxacin or Azithromycin will kill the bacteria quickly. Seek medical attention if you do not respond to an appropriate antibiotic.

Loperamide is just a 'stopper' that only treats the symptoms. It can be helpful, for example if you have to go on a long bus ride. Don't take Loperamide if you have a fever, or blood in your stools.

Giardia lamblia is a parasite that is relatively common. Symptoms include nausea, bloating, excess gas, fatigue and intermittent diarrhoea. 'Eggy' burps are often attributed solely to giardiasis. The treatment of choice is Tinidazole, with Metronidazole being a second-line option.

Amoebic dysentery is very rare in travellers but poor-quality labs tests may not recognise it when it's actually present. Symptoms are similar to bacterial diarrhoea. You should always seek reliable medical care if you have blood in your diarrhoea. Treatment involves two drugs; Tinidazole or Metronidazole to kill the parasite in your gut and then a second drug to kill the cysts. If left untreated complications, such as liver abscesses, can occur.

MOSQUITO AVOIDANCE TIPS

Travellers are advised to prevent mosquito bites by taking these steps:

➡ use a DEET-containing insect repellent on exposed skin

➡ sleep under a mosquito net, ideally impregnated with Permethrin

➡ choose accommodation with screens and fans

➡ impregnate clothing with Permethrin in high-risk areas

➡ wear long sleeves and trousers in light colours

➡ use mosquito coils

➡ spray your room with insect repellent before going out

Environmental Hazards

Food

Eating in restaurants is the biggest risk factor for contracting traveller's diarrhoea. Ways to avoid it include eating only freshly cooked food, and avoiding food that has been sitting around in buffets. Peel all fruit and cook vegetables. Eat in busy restaurants with a high turnover of customers.

Heat

For most people it takes at least two weeks to adapt to the hot climate. Prevent swelling of the feet and ankles as well as muscle cramps caused by excessive sweating by avoiding dehydration and excessive activity in the heat of the day.

Heat stroke requires immediate medical treatment. Symptoms come on suddenly and include weakness, nausea, a hot dry body with a body temperature of over 41°C, dizziness, confusion, loss of coordination, fits and eventually collapse and loss of consciousness.

Insect Bites & Stings

Bedbugs live in the cracks of furniture and walls and then migrate to the bed at night to feed on humans. You can treat the itch with an antihistamine.

Ticks are contracted when walking in rural areas. They are commonly found behind the ears, on the belly and in armpits. If you've been bitten by a tick and a rash develops at the site of the bite or elsewhere, along with fever or muscle aches, see a doctor. Doxycycline prevents tickborne diseases.

Leeches are found in humid rainforests. They do not transmit disease but their bites are often itchy for days or weeks afterwards and can easily become infected. Apply an iodine-based antiseptic to the bite to help prevent infection.

Bee and wasp stings mainly cause problems for people who are allergic to them. Anyone with a serious allergy should carry an injection of adrenaline (eg an Epipen) for emergencies. For others, pain is the main problem – apply ice to the sting and take painkillers.

Parasites

Numerous parasites are common in local populations in Thailand, but most of these are rare in travellers. To avoid parasitic infections, wear shoes and avoid eating raw food, especially fish, pork and vegetables.

Skin Problems

Prickly heat is a common skin rash in the tropics, caused by sweat being trapped under the skin. Treat by taking cool showers and using powders.

Two fungal rashes commonly affect travellers. The first occurs in the groin, armpits and between the toes. It starts as a red patch that slowly spreads and is usually itchy. Treatment involves keeping the skin dry, avoiding chafing and using an antifungal cream such as Clotrimazole or Lamisil. The fungus *Tinea versicolor* causes small and light-coloured patches, most commonly on the back, chest and shoulders. Consult a doctor.

Cuts and scratches become easily infected in humid climates. Immediately wash all wounds in clean water and apply antiseptic. If you develop signs of infection, see a doctor. Coral cuts can easily become infected.

Snakes

Though snake bites are rare for travellers, there are over 85 species of venomous snakes in Thailand. Always wear boots and long pants if walking in an area that may have snakes.

The Thai Red Cross produces antivenom for many of the poisonous snakes in Thailand.

JELLYFISH STINGS

Box jellyfish stings range from minor to deadly. It is best to presume a box jelly is dangerous until proven otherwise. There are two main types of box jellyfish – multitentacled and single-tentacled.

Multitentacled box jellyfish are present in Thai waters – these are the most dangerous and a severe envenomation can kill an adult within two minutes. They are generally found on sandy beaches near river mouths and mangroves during the warmer months.

There are many types of single-tentacled box jellyfish, some of which can cause severe symptoms known as the Irukandji syndrome. The initial sting can seem minor; however severe symptoms such as back pain, nausea, vomiting, sweating, difficulty breathing and a feeling of impending doom can develop between five and 40 minutes later.

There are many other jellyfish in Thailand that cause irritating stings but no serious effects. The only way to prevent these stings is to wear protective clothing.

First Aid for Severe Stings

For severe life-threatening envenomations the first priority is keeping the person alive. Send someone to call for medical help, and start immediate CPR if they are unconscious. If the victim is conscious douse the stung area liberally with vinegar for 30 seconds.

Vinegar can also reduce irritation from minor stings as well. It is best to seek medical care quickly in case any other symptoms develop over the next 40 minutes.

Australia and Thailand are now working in close collaboration to identify the species of jellyfish in Thai waters, as well as their ecology – hopefully enabling better prediction and detection of the jellyfish.

Thanks to Dr Peter Fenner for the information on jellyfish stings.

Sunburn

Even on a cloudy day sunburn can occur rapidly. Use a strong sunscreen (at least factor 30), making sure to reapply after a swim, and always wear a wide-brimmed hat and sunglasses outdoors. If you become sunburnt stay out of the sun until you have recovered, apply cool compresses and take painkillers for the discomfort. One per cent hydrocortisone cream applied twice daily is also helpful.

Travelling With Children

Thailand is relatively safe for children. Consult a doctor who specialises in travel medicine prior to travel to ensure your child is appropriately prepared. A medical kit designed specifically for children includes liquid medicines for children who can not swallow tables. Azithromycin is an ideal paediatric formula used to treat bacterial diarrhoea, as well as ear, chest and throat infections.

Good resources are the Lonely Planet publication *Travel with Children*, and for those spending longer away Jane Wilson-Howarth's book *Your Child's Health Abroad* is excellent.

Women's Health

Pregnant women should receive specialised advice before travelling. The ideal time to travel is in the second trimester, when pregnancy-related risks are low. Avoid rural areas with poor transport and medical facilities. Ensure travel insurance covers all pregnancy-related possibilities, including premature labour.

Malaria is a high-risk disease in pregnancy. Pregnant women should *not* travel to areas with Chloroquine-resistant malaria. None of the more effective antimalarial drugs is completely safe in pregnancy.

Traveller's diarrhoea can quickly lead to dehydration and result in inadequate blood flow to the placenta. Azithromycin is considered one of the safest anti-diarrhoea drugs in pregnancy.

In Thailand's urban areas, supplies of sanitary products are readily available; stock up before travelling to rural areas. Bring adequate supplies of your personal birth-control option. Heat, humidity and antibiotics can all contribute to thrush, which can be treated with antifungal creams and Clotrimazole. A practical alternative is one tablet of fluconazole (Diflucan). Urinary-tract infections can be precipitated by dehydration or long bus journeys without toilet stops; bring suitable antibiotics for treatment.

Language

Thailand's official language is effectively the dialect spoken and written in central Thailand, which has successfully become the lingua franca of all Thai and non-Thai ethnic groups in the kingdom.

In Thai the meaning of a single syllable may be altered by means of different tones. In standard Thai there are five: low tone, mid tone, falling tone, high tone and rising tone. The range of all five tones is relative to each speaker's vocal range, so there is no fixed 'pitch' intrinsic to the language.

➡ **low tone** – 'Flat' like the mid tone, but pronounced at the relative bottom of one's vocal range. It is low, level and has no inflection, eg bàht (baht – the Thai currency).

➡ **mid tone** – Pronounced 'flat', at the relative middle of the speaker's vocal range, eg dee (good). No tone mark is used.

➡ **falling tone** – Starting high and falling sharply, this tone is similar to the change in pitch in English when you are emphasising a word, or calling someone's name from afar, eg mâi (no/not).

➡ **high tone** – Usually the most difficult for non-Thai speakers. It's pronounced near the relative top of the vocal range, as level as possible, eg máh (horse).

➡ **rising tone** – Starting low and gradually rising, sounds like the inflection used by English speakers to imply a question – 'Yes?', eg sǎhm (three).

WANT MORE?

For in-depth language information and handy phrases, check out Lonely Planet's *Thai Phrasebook*. You'll find it at **shop.lonelyplanet.com**, or you can buy Lonely Planet's iPhone phrase-books at the Apple App Store.

The Thai government has instituted the Royal Thai General Transcription System (RTGS) as a standard method of writing Thai using the Roman alphabet. It's used in official documents, road signs and on maps. However, local variations crop up on signs, menus etc. Generally, names in this book follow the most common practice.

In our coloured pronunciation guides, the hyphens indicate syllable breaks within words, and some syllables are further divided with a dot to help you pronounce compound vowels, eg mêu·a·rai (when).

The vowel a is pronounced as in 'about', aa as the 'a' in 'bad', ah as the 'a' in 'father', ai as in 'aisle', air as in 'flair' (without the 'r'), eu as in 'new' (with rounded lips), oh as the 'o' in 'toe', or as in 'torn' (without the 'r') and ow as in 'now'.

Most consonants correspond to their English counterparts. The exceptions are b (a hard 'p' sound, almost like a 'b', eg in 'hip-bag'); d (a hard 't' sound, like a sharp 'd', eg in 'mid-tone'); ng (as in 'singing'; in Thai it can occur at the start of a word) and r (as in 'run' but flapped; in everyday speech it's often pronounced like 'l').

BASICS

The social structure of Thai society demands different registers of speech depending on who you're talking to. To make things simple we've chosen the correct form of speech appropriate to the context of each phrase.

When being polite, the speaker ends his or her sentence with kráp (for men) or kâ (for women). It is the gender of the speaker that is being expressed here; it is also the common way to answer 'yes' to a question or show agreement.

The masculine and feminine forms of phrases in this chapter are indicated where relevant with 'm/f'.

Hello.	สวัสดี	sà-wàt-dee
Goodbye.	ลาก่อน	lah gòrn
Yes./No.	ใช่/ไม่	châi/mâi
Please.	ขอ	kŏr
Thank you.	ขอบคุณ	kòrp kun
You're welcome.	ยินดี	yin dee
Excuse me.	ขออภัย	kŏr à-pai
Sorry.	ขอโทษ	kŏr tôht

How are you?
สบายดีไหม — sà-bai dee măi

Fine. And you?
สบายดีครับ/ค่ะ / — sà-bai dee kráp/
แล้วคุณล่ะ — kâ láa-ou kun lâ (m/f)

What's your name?
คุณชื่ออะไร — kun chêu à-rai

My name is ...
ผม/ดิฉันชื่อ... — pŏm/dì-chăn chêu ... (m/f)

Do you speak English?
คุณพูดภาษา — kun pôot pah-săh
อังกฤษได้ไหม — ang-grìt dâi măi

I don't understand.
ผม/ดิฉันไม่ — pŏm/dì-chăn mâi
เข้าใจ — kôw jai (m/f)

ACCOMMODATION

Where's a ...? — ... อยู่ที่ไหน — ... yòo têe năi

campsite	ค่ายพักแรม	kâi pák raam
guesthouse	บ้านพัก	bâhn pák
hotel	โรงแรม	rohng raam
youth hostel	บ้าน	bâhn
	เยาวชน	yow-wá-chon

Do you have — มีห้อง ... — mee hôrng ...
a ... room? — ไหม — măi

single	เดี่ยว	dèe·o
double	เตียงคู่	đee·ang kôo
twin	สองเตียง	sŏrng đee·ang

air-con	แอร์	aa
bathroom	ห้องน้ำ	hôrng nám
laundry	ห้องซักผ้า	hôrng sák pâh
mosquito net	มุ้ง	múng
window	หน้าต่าง	nâh đàhng

Question Words

What?	อะไร	à-rai
When?	เมื่อไร	mêu·a-rai
Where?	ที่ไหน	têe năi
Who?	ใคร	krai
Why?	ทำไม	tam-mai

DIRECTIONS

Where's ...?
... อยู่ที่ไหน — ... yòo têe năi

What's the address?
ที่อยู่คืออะไร — têe yòo keu à-rai

Could you please write it down?
เขียนลงให้ได้ไหม — kĕe·an long hâi dâi măi

Can you show me (on the map)?
ให้ดู (ในแผนที่) — hâi doo (nai păan têe)
ได้ไหม — dâi măi

Turn left/right.
เลี้ยวซ้าย/ขวา — lée·o sái/kwăh

It's ...	อยู่ ...	yòo ...
behind	ที่หลัง	têe lăng
in front of	ตรงหน้า	đrong nâh
next to	ข้างๆ	kâhng kâhng
straight ahead	ตรงไป	đrong bai

EATING & DRINKING

I'd like (the menu), please.
ขอ (รายการ — kŏr (rai gahn
อาหาร) หน่อย — ah-hăhn) nòy

What would you recommend?
คุณแนะนำอะไรบ้าง — kun náa-nam à-rai bâhng

That was delicious!
อร่อยมาก — à-ròy mâhk

Cheers!
ไชโย — chai-yoh

Please bring the bill.
ขอบิลหน่อย — kŏr bin nòy

I don't eat ...	ผม/ดิฉัน	pŏm/dì-chăn
	ไม่กิน ...	mâi gin ... (m/f)
eggs	ไข่	kài
fish	ปลา	blah
red meat	เนื้อแดง	néu·a daang
nuts	ถั่ว	tòo·a

Key Words

bar	บาร์	bah
bottle	ขวด	kòo·at
bowl	ชาม	chahm
breakfast	อาหารเช้า	ah-hăhn chów
cafe	ร้านกาแฟ	ráhn gah-faa
chopsticks	ไม้ตะเกียบ	mái đà-gèe·ap
cold	เย็น	yen
cup	ถ้วย	tôo·ay
dessert	ของหวาน	kŏrng wăhn
dinner	อาหารเย็น	ah-hăhn yen
drink list	รายการ เครื่องดื่ม	rai gahn krêu·ang dèum
fork	ส้อม	sôrm
glass	แก้ว	gâa·ou
hot	ร้อน	rórn
knife	มีด	mêet
lunch	อาหาร กลางวัน	ah-hăhn glahng wan
market	ตลาด	đà-làht
menu	รานการ อาหาร	rai gahn ah-hăhn
plate	จาน	jahn
restaurant	ร้านอาหาร	ráhn ah-hăhn
spicy	เผ็ด	pèt
spoon	ช้อน	chórn
vegetarian (person)	คนกินเจ	kon gin jair

with	มี	mee
without	ไม่มี	mâi mee

Meat & Fish

beef	เนื้อ	néu·a
chicken	ไก่	gài
crab	ปู	boo
duck	เป็ด	bèt
fish	ปลา	blah
meat	เนื้อ	néu·a
pork	หมู	mŏo
seafood	อาหารทะเล	ah-hăhn tá-lair
squid	ปลาหมึก	blah mèuk

Fruit & Vegetables

banana	กล้วย	glôo·ay
beans	ถั่ว	tòo·a
coconut	มะพร้าว	má-prów
eggplant	มะเขือ	má-kĕu·a
fruit	ผลไม้	pŏn-lá-mái
guava	ฝรั่ง	fa-ràng
lime	มะนาว	má-now
mango	มะม่วง	má-môo·ang
mangosteen	มังคุด	mang-kút
mushrooms	เห็ด	hèt
nuts	ถั่ว	tòo·a
papaya	มะละกอ	má-lá-gor
potatoes	มันฝรั่ง	man fa-ràng
rambutan	เงาะ	ngó
tamarind	มะขาม	má-kăhm
tomatoes	มะเขือเทศ	má-kĕu·a têt
vegetables	ผัก	pàk
watermelon	แตงโม	đaang moh

Other

chilli	พริก	prík
egg	ไข่	kài
fish sauce	น้ำปลา	nám blah
ice	น้ำแข็ง	nám kăang

noodles	เส้น	sên
oil	น้ำมัน	nám man
pepper	พริกไทย	prík tai
rice	ข้าว	kôw
salad	ผักสด	pàk sòt
salt	เกลือ	gleu·a
soup	น้ำซุป	nám súp
soy sauce	น้ำซีอิ๊ว	nám see-éw
sugar	น้ำตาล	nám đahn
tofu	เต้าหู้	đôw hôo

Drinks

beer	เบียร์	bee·a
coffee	กาแฟ	gah-faa
milk	นมจืด	nom jèut
orange juice	น้ำส้ม	nám sôm
soy milk	น้ำเต้าหู้	nám đôw hôo
sugarcane juice	น้ำอ้อย	nám ôy
tea	ชา	chah
water	น้ำดื่ม	nám dèum

EMERGENCIES

Help!	ช่วยด้วย	chôo·ay dôo·ay
Go away!	ไปให้พ้น	ɓai hâi pón

Call a doctor!
เรียกหมอหน่อย — rêe·ak mŏr nòy

Call the police!
เรียกตำรวจหน่อย — rêe·ak đam·ròo·at nòy

I'm ill.
ผม/ดิฉันป่วย — pŏm/dì-chăn ɓòo·ay (m/f)

I'm lost.
ผม/ดิฉัน
หลงทาง — pŏm/dì-chăn lŏng tahng (m/f)

Where are the toilets?
ห้องน้ำอยู่ที่ไหน — hôrng nám yòo têe năi

SHOPPING & SERVICES

I'd like to buy ...
อยากจะซื้อ ... — yàhk jà séu ...

I'm just looking.
ดูเฉย ๆ — doo chĕu·i chĕu·i

Can I look at it?
ขอดูได้ไหม — kŏr doo dâi măi

How much is it?
เท่าไร — tôw-rai

That's too expensive.
แพงไป — paang ɓai

Can you lower the price?
ลดราคาได้ไหม — lót rah-kah dâi măi

There's a mistake in the bill.
บิลใบนี้ผิด — bin bai née pit ná
นะครับ/ค่ะ — kráp/kâ (m/f)

TIME & DATES

What time is it?
กี่โมงแล้ว — gèe mohng láa·ou

morning	เช้า	chów
afternoon	บ่าย	bài
evening	เย็น	yen
yesterday	เมื่อวาน	mêu·a wahn
today	วันนี้	wan née
tomorrow	พรุ่งนี้	prûng née

Monday	วันจันทร์	wan jan
Tuesday	วันอังคาร	wan ang-kahn
Wednesday	วันพุธ	wan pút
Thursday	วันพฤหัสฯ	wan pá-réu-hàt
Friday	วันศุกร	wan sùk
Saturday	วันเสาร์	wan sŏw
Sunday	วันอาทิตย์	wan ah-tít

TRANSPORT

Public Transport

bicycle rickshaw	สามล้อ	săhm lór
boat	เรือ	reu·a
bus	รถเมล์	rót mair
car	รถเก๋ง	rót gĕng
motorcycle	มอร์เตอร์ไซค์	mor-đeu-sai
taxi	รับจ้าง	ráp jâhng
plane	เครื่องบิน	krêu·ang bin
train	รถไฟ	rót fai
túk-túk	ตุ๊ก ๆ	đúk đúk

Numbers

1	หนึ่ง	nèung
2	สอง	sŏrng
3	สาม	săhm
4	สี่	sèe
5	ห้า	hâh
6	หก	hòk
7	เจ็ด	jèt
8	แปด	bàat
9	เก้า	gôw
10	สิบ	sìp
11	สิบเอ็ด	sìp-èt
20	ยี่สิบ	yêe-sìp
21	ยี่สิบเอ็ด	yêe-sìp-èt
30	สามสิบ	săhm-sìp
40	สี่สิบ	sèe-sìp
50	ห้าสิบ	hâh-sìp
60	หกสิบ	hòk-sìp
70	เจ็ดสิบ	jèt-sìp
80	แปดสิบ	bàat-sìp
90	เก้าสิบ	gôw-sìp
100	หนึ่งร้อย	nèung róy
1000	หนึ่งพัน	nèung pan
10,000	หนึ่งหมื่น	nèung mèun
100,000	หนึ่งแสน	nèung săan
1,000,000	หนึ่งล้าน	nèung láhn

When's the ... bus?	รถเมล์คัน ... มาเมื่อไร	rót mair kan ... mah mêu·a rai
first	แรก	râak
last	สุดท้าย	sùt tái
next	ต่อไป	dòr bai

A ... ticket, please.	ขอตั๋ว ...	kŏr dŏo·a ...
one-way	เที่ยวเดียว	têe·o dee·o
return	ไปกลับ	bai glàp

I'd like a/an ... seat.	ต้องการ ที่นั่ง ...	dôrng gahn têe nâng ...
aisle	ติดทางเดิน	dìt tahng deun
window	ติดหน้าต่าง	dìt nâh dàhng
platform	ชานชาลา	chan-chah-lah

ticket window	ช่องขายตั๋ว	chôrng kăi dŏo·a
timetable	ตารางเวลา	đah-rahng wair-lah

What time does it get to (Chiang Mai)?

ถึง (เชียงใหม่) กี่โมง	tĕung (chee·ang mài) gèe mohng

Does it stop at (Saraburi)?

รถจอดที่ (สระบุรี) ไหม	rót jòrt têe (sà-rà-bù-ree) măi

Please tell me when we get to (Chiang Mai).

เมื่อถึง (เชียงใหม่) กรุณาบอกด้วย	mêu·a tĕung (chee·ang mài) gà-rú-nah bòrk dôo·ay

I'd like to get off at (Saraburi).

ขอลงที่ (สระบุรี)	kŏr long têe (sà-rà-bù-ree)

Driving & Cycling

I'd like to hire a ...	อยากจะ เช่า ...	yàhk jà chôw ...
car	รถเก๋ง	rót gĕng
motorbike	รถ มอร์เตอร์ไซค์	rót mor-đeu-sai

I'd like ...	ต้องการ ...	đôrng gahn ...
my bicycle repaired	ซ่อมรถ จักรยาน	sôrm rót jàk-gà-yahn
to hire a bicycle	เช่ารถ จักรยาน	chôw rót jàk-gà-yahn

Is this the road to (Ban Bung Wai)?

ทางนี้ไป (บ้านบุ่งหวาย) ไหม	tahng née bai (bâhn bùng wăi) măi

Where's a petrol station?

ปั๊มน้ำมันอยู่ที่ไหน	bâm nám man yòo têe năi

Can I park here?

จอดที่นี้ได้ไหม	jòrt têe née dâi măi

How long can I park here?

จอดที่นี้ได้นานเท่าไร	jòrt têe née dâi nahn tôw-rai

I need a mechanic.

ต้องการช่างรถ	đôrng gahn châhng rót

I have a flat tyre.

ยางแบน	yahng baan

I've run out of petrol.

หมดน้ำมัน	mòt nám man

Do I need a helmet?

ต้องใช้หมวก กันน็อกไหม	đôrng chái mòo·ak gan nórk măi

GLOSSARY

This glossary includes Thai, Pali (P) and Sanskrit (S) words and terms frequently used in this guidebook. For definitions of food and drink terms, see p780.

ajahn – *(aajaan)* respectful title for 'teacher'; from the Sanskrit term *acarya*

amphoe – *(amphur)* district, the next subdivision down from province

AUA – American University Alumni

bâhn – *(ban)* house or village

baht – *(bàat)* the Thai unit of currency

bàht – a unit of weight equal to 15g; rounded bowl used by monks for receiving alms food

BKS – Baw Khaw Saw (Thai acronym for the Transport Company)

bodhisattva (S) – in Theravada Buddhism, the term used to refer to the previous lives of the Buddha prior to his enlightenment

bòht – central sanctuary in a Thai temple used for the monastic order's official business, such as ordinations; from the Pali term *uposatha* (*ubohsòt*); see also *wí·hǎhn*

bòr nám rórn – hot springs

Brahman – pertaining to Brahmanism, an ancient religious tradition in India and the predecessor of Hinduism; not to be confused with 'Brahmin', the priestly class in India's caste system

BTS – Bangkok Transit System (Skytrain); Thai: *rót fai fáh*

bah·dé – batik

CAT – CAT Telecom Public Company Limited

chedi – see *stupa*

chow – folk; people

chow lair – *(chow nám)* sea gypsies

CPT – Communist Party of Thailand

doy – mountain in the Northern Thai dialect; spelt 'Doi' in proper names

dròrk – *(trok)* alley, smaller than a soi

fa·ràng – a Westerner (person of European origin); also guava

gà·teu·i – *(kàthoey)* Thailand's 'third gender', usually cross-dressing or transsexual males; also called ladyboys

gopura (S) – entrance pavilion in traditional Hindu temple architecture, often seen in Angkor-period temple complexes

hàht – beach; spelt 'Hat' in proper names

hǒr drai – a Tripitaka (Buddhist scripture) hall

hôrng – *(hong)* room; in southern Thailand this refers to semi-submerged island caves

Isan – *(ee·sǎhn)* general term used for northeastern Thailand

jataka (P) – *(chah·dòk)* stories of the Buddha's previous lives

jeen – Chinese

jeen hor – literally 'galloping Chinese', referring to horse-riding Yunnanese traders

kàthoey – see *gà·teu·i*

klorng – canal; spelt 'Khlong' in proper nouns

kǒhn – masked dance–drama based on stories from the Ramakian

kǒw – hill or mountain; spelt 'Khao' in proper names

KMT – Kuomintang

KNU – Karen National Union

ku – small *stupa* that is partially hollow and open

kùti – monk's dwelling

lǎam – cape; spelt 'Laem' in proper names

làk meu·ang – city pillar

lék – little, small (in size); see also *noi*

longyi – Burmese sarong

lôok tûng – Thai country music

lôw kŏw – white whisky, often homemade rice brew

mâa chee – Thai Buddhist nun

mâa nám – river; spelt Mae Nam in proper names

mahathat – *(má·hǎh tâht)* common name for temples containing Buddha relics; from the Sanskrit–Pali term *mahadhatu*

masjid – *(mát·sà·yít)* mosque

mát·mèe – technique of tie-dyeing silk or cotton threads and then weaving them into complex patterns, similar to Indonesian *ikat*; the term also refers to the patterns themselves

meu·ang – city or principality

mon·dòp – small square, spired building in a wát; from Sanskrit *mandapa*

moo·ay tai – *(muay thai)* Thai boxing

mŏr lam – an Isan musical tradition akin to *lôok tûng*

naga (P/S) – *(nâhk)* a mythical serpent-like being with magical powers

ná·kon – city; from the Sanskrit-Pali *nagara*; spelt 'Nakhon' in proper nouns

nám – water

nám đòk – waterfall; spelt 'Nam Tok' in proper nouns

neun – hill; spelt 'Noen' in proper names

nibbana (P/S) – nirvana; in Buddhist teachings, the state of enlightenment; escape from the realm of rebirth; Thai: *níp·pahn*

noi – *(nóy)* little, small (amount); see also *lék*

nôrk – outside, outer; spelt 'Nok' in proper names

ow – bay or gulf; spelt 'Ao' in proper nouns

pâh mát·mèe – *mát·mèe* fabric

pěe – ghost, spirit

pík·sù – a Buddhist monk; from the Sanskrit *bhikshu*, Pali *bhikkhu*

PLAT – People's Liberation Army of Thailand

prá – an honorific term used for monks, nobility and Buddha images; spelt 'Phra' in proper names

prá krêu·ang – amulets of monks, Buddhas or deities worn around the neck for spiritual protection; also called *prá pim*

prá poom – earth spirits or guardians

prang – (*bràhng*) Khmer-style tower on temples

prasat – (*bràh·sàht*) small ornate building, used for religious purposes, with a cruciform ground plan and needlelike spire, located on temple grounds; any of a number of different kinds of halls or residences with religious or royal significance

rót aa – blue-and-white air-con bus

rót norn – sleeper bus

săh·lah – open-sided, covered meeting hall or resting place; from Portuguese term *sala*, literally 'room'

săhm·lór – three-wheeled pedicab

samsara (P) – in Buddhist teachings, the realm of rebirth and delusion

sangha – (P) the Buddhist community

satang – (*sà·dahng*) a Thai unit of currency; 100 satang equals 1 baht

serow – Asian mountain goat

sêua môr hôrm – blue cotton farmer's shirt

soi – lane or small street

Songkran – Thai New Year, held in mid-April

sŏrng·tăa·ou – (literally 'two rows') common name for small pick-up trucks with two benches in the back, used as buses/taxis; also spelt 'săwngthăew'

SRT – State Railway of Thailand

stupa – conical-shaped Buddhist monument used to inter sacred Buddhist objects

tâh – pier, boat landing; spelt 'Tha' in proper nouns

tâht – four-sided, curvilinear Buddha reliquary, common in Northeastern Thailand; spelt 'That' in proper nouns

tâm – cave; spelt 'Tham' in proper nouns

tam bun – to make merit

tambon – see *đam·bon*

TAT – Tourism Authority of Thailand

Thammayut – one of the two sects of Theravada Buddhism in Thailand; founded by King Rama IV while he was still a monk

thanŏn – (*tà·nŏn*) street; spelt 'Thanon' in proper noun and shortened to 'Th'

T-pop – popular teen-music

tràwk – see *đròrk*

trimurti (S) – collocation of the three principal Hindu deities, Brahma, Shiva and Vishnu

Tripitaka (S) – Theravada Buddhist scriptures; (Pali: *Tipitaka*)

túk–túk – (*dúk–dúk*) motorised săhm·lór

vipassana (P) – (*wí·bàt·sà·nah*) Buddhist insight meditation

wâi – palms–together Thai greeting

wan prá – Buddhist holy days, falling on the days of the main phases of the moon (full, new and half) each month

wang – palace

wát – temple–monastery; from the Pali term *avasa* meaning 'monk's dwelling'; spelt 'Wat' in proper nouns

wí·hăhn – (*wihan, viharn*) any large hall in a Thai temple, usually open to laity; from Sanskrit term *vihara*, meaning 'dwelling'

Yawi – traditional language of Malay parts of Java, Sumatra and the Malay Peninsula, widely spoken in the most southern provinces of Thailand; the written form uses the classic Arabic script plus five additional letters

yài – big

Behind the Scenes

SEND US YOUR FEEDBACK

We love to hear from travellers – your comments keep us on our toes and help make our books better. Our well-travelled team reads every word on what you loved or loathed about this book. Although we cannot reply individually to postal submissions, we always guarantee that your feedback goes straight to the appropriate authors, in time for the next edition. Each person who sends us information is thanked in the next edition – the most useful submissions are rewarded with a selection of digital PDF chapters.

Visit **lonelyplanet.com/contact** to submit your updates and suggestions or to ask for help. Our award-winning website also features inspirational travel stories, news and discussions.

Note: We may edit, reproduce and incorporate your comments in Lonely Planet products such as guidebooks, websites and digital products, so let us know if you don't want your comments reproduced or your name acknowledged. For a copy of our privacy policy visit lonelyplanet.com/privacy.

OUR READERS

Many thanks to the travellers who used the last edition and wrote to us with helpful hints, useful advice and interesting anecdotes:

A Adeline, Aileen, Alex Moore, Alice Hedger, Anais, Andre Schmidt, Andrea Fisher, Andrew Bustamante, Andrew Dean, Andrew Jennings, Angelika Scheack, Anglade, Anna Fulton, Annalisa Cavallini, Annelies Heeman, Anneloes Maas Geesteranus, Arie van Oosterwijk, Armando, Arnold Huber **B** Ben Greenslade, Bert Theunissen, Bertrand Thierry, Bjoern Olsson, Bret Sauels, Brian Knight, Burghard Thiele **C** Carl Danzig, Carol Doyle, Carter Castor, Casper, Cecilie Normand, Chris Pitt, Christian Holtzmann, Christopher Byrd, Christopher Hemsley, Clare Hall **D** Daniel, Daniel Davis, Dario, David Hogan, Dawn Bragg, Dawn Marie Cooper, Detig, Dinesh, Dominique Lavallée, Dorle Schreiber **E** Elisabeth Nielsen, Emma Dale **F** Mr Fhu, Francis Rigal, Francoise Pigeaud, Fred Fickera, Fred Robert Munger, Fred Tiedemann Croese, Freddy Bradley **G** Geoff Mead, Georgina Madison, Gims Resort, Goon, Gordon Hague (Blacktip), Greg Taylor **H** Hanne Knoebel, Heather Johnson, Helen Shih, Hubris18 **I** Irene van Baarsen **J** James Adams, Jan Mulder, Jasdeep Jolly, Jean-Daniel Champod, Jihi Bustamante, Jim White, Joana Correia, Jonathan Preboy, Jonathan Russell, Jouni

Remes, Judy Smart, Julien Gamba, Justin Thornberry **K** Kat, Katia Moretti, KB, Kevin Carty, Kevin Smith, Kimberley Lorimer, Koen Bart, Kristin Malenfant, Kristine Smiltniece, Kurt Gruen **L** Les Dunning, Lisa Tsang, Luigi Huikeshoven **M** Maaike Bosschart, Marc Mochel, Marco Ooms, Marcus Sutor, Marie Eaton, Mark Britowich, Marloes Fortuijn, Mathias, Matthea Stoter, Mehmet, Menard, Michael Falvella, Michael Novack, Mike Seaberg, Murat Mirata **N** Nicole Humphreys, Nidhi Akkaravivat, Nikki Buran **O** Oihane, Oli Brown, Ms Oy **P** Padungsak, Paolo Borraccetti, Parawat Poungpiam, Pascal Ancher, Pat Cox, Patrick Heathcott, Patty, Paul de Havilland, Paul Reardon, Peter Buckland, Peter Ogier, Peter R. Sibbald **Q** Queenie Szeto **R** Rachel Loo, Rebecca Ayres, Rebecca Brickson, Renate Lang, Rich, Rick Borgia, Rob de Ruiter, Rob Peterside, Robert Mavric, Roo du Jardin, Rowan Gibbons, Ryan **S** Sam Crisp, Shane M Spencer, Shireen Hussein, Shoaban Nair, Siegfried Bolek, Simon Bevan-Davies, Spencer Harrison, Stefan Gerke, Stefano Tirelli, Steve Hollins, Stony, Suwatchai Praesomboon **T** Theodore Gemmer, Thippakomut, Thomas Stegemann, Tung **U** Uschi Gaida, Uwe Düffert **V** Valerie Koller, Valy Nicolas, Vincent Schoonhoven **W** Wera, Werner Bruyninx, Wido Teriet, Wim Dohmen **Y** Yan Giroud

AUTHOR THANKS

China Williams

Many thanks to my good buddy Nong, the gals at TJR, Candyhome nursery school, Pong at Libernard Café, Andrew Bond, Pim of CityLife, Aidan from Chiang Mai Mountain Bikes and Pat of Patara Elephant Farm. In Bangkok, many thanks to Ruengsang, Mai, Jane, Kanchana and Austin. Thanks to Matt and Felix for taking care of each other and to Mandy for taking care of them. Applause to the co-authors, Ilaria, Bruce and the now-dismissed LP production staff. I heart old-fashioned publishing.

Mark Beales

Enormous thanks to Ilaria for asking me to return to Central Thailand for a third time and to China and Bruce for their excellent support. In Kanchanaburi, K.Chalee, Apple and Noi were as hospitable as ever, while in Sangkhlaburi, Charlie and Sai were charming hosts. Thanks also to the TAT staff for their insight, especially Kook in Lopburi. Lastly, thanks to Ann.

Tim Bewer

A hearty *kòrp jai lǎi lǎi dêu* to the perpetually friendly people of Isan who rarely failed to live up to their reputation for friendliness and hospitality when faced with my incessant questions. In particular Chommanaad Booanree, Julian Wright, June Niampan, Prapaporn Sompakdee, Supakorn Kongsuwan and Traimat Wongwai all provided great help and/or good company. Special thanks to Suttawan Intarapanich-Bewer for everything.

Celeste Brash

Thanks to Samui Steve, Johnny, Kirk Stucker, Rachel and Stephen and Nick Ray for help on Samui. On Ko Pha-Ngan a huge thanks to my friend Marissa Bright and to the folks at Chaloklam Diving who, despite going out of their way to help, never found out who I was. On Tao thanks to Heather and Andy Keeler, Chris and Pu, Gemma and Ed. Huge thanks to Brandon Presser for great base text and tips

and as always to my family for holding the fort at home without me.

Austin Bush

A massive shout out to LPers for Life, Ilaria Walker and Bruce Evans, a huge thanks to dedicated Coordinating Author China Williams and the kind folks on the ground in Thailand, with a special debt to Joe Cummings and Kitty Chirapongse for their helpful contributions.

David Eimer

Much gratitude to Khun Morn for her Trat tips and islands advice. Thanks to China Williams and to Ilaria Walker, Bruce Evans, Diana Von Holdt and Lorna Goodyer at Lonely Planet. As ever, thanks to the many people who passed on information along the way, whether knowingly or unwittingly.

Adam Skolnick

As is always the case for me in Thailand, I received far too many friendly smiles and welcome insights to thank everyone appropriately. So allow me to give one giant hug to this fun, strange, spicy and soothing country that is so easy to adore. I'd also like to thank Sienna Lee, Aleesha Wilson and Annie Lim for your assistance; Pak and James in Krabi; Chawalit 'Lek' Ratanachinakorn at Saneha; Wilai and family in Phuket Town; Nico, Diane, Scott and Chaini at my new Phuket home; Tony and Jo at Rum Jungle; Wan Phakawan, James Hembrow, Ja and Thanasin; and the wonderful Celine Masson, Claude Sauter and your sweet children for our continued, valued and deepening friendship.

ACKNOWLEDGMENTS

Climate map data adapted from Peel MC, Finlayson BL & McMahon TA (2007) 'Updated World Map of the Köppen-Geiger Climate Classification', *Hydrology and Earth System Sciences*, 11, 1633–44.

Illustrations pp60-1 and pp70-1 by Michael Weldon.

Cover photograph: Wat Pho, Bangkok, Shaun Egan/AWL.

THIS BOOK

This 15th edition of Lonely Planet's *Thailand* guidebook was researched and written by China Williams, Mark Beales, Tim Bewer, Celeste Brash, Austin Bush, David Eimer and Adam Skolnick. This guidebook was commissioned in Lonely Planet's Melbourne office, and produced by the following:

Commissioning Editor
Ilaria Walker

Coordinating Editors
Lorna Goodyer, Anne Mason

Senior Cartographer
Diana Von Holdt

Book Designer Wendy Wright

Assisting Editors Penny Cordner, Paul Harding, Helen Koehne, Jodie Matire, Anne Mulvaney, Maryanne Netto, Chris Pitts, Alison Ridgway, Luna Soo, Gabbi Stefanos, Tracy Whitmey

Assisting Cartographers
Jeff Cameron, Julie Dodkins, Mick Garrett, Jennifer Johnston, James Leversha, Gabe Lindquist

Cover Research Naomi Parker

Language Content Branislava Vladisavljevic

Thanks to Anita Banh, Elin Berglund, Bruce Evans, Ryan Evans, Larissa Frost, Errol Hunt, Genesys India, Jouve India, Wayne Murphy, Mazzy Prinsep

Index

Map Legend

Sights

- Beach
- Bird Sanctuary
- Buddhist
- Castle/Palace
- Christian
- Confucian
- Hindu
- Islamic
- Jain
- Jewish
- Monument
- Museum/Gallery/Historic Building
- Ruin
- Sento Hot Baths/Onsen
- Shinto
- Sikh
- Taoist
- Winery/Vineyard
- Zoo/Wildlife Sanctuary
- Other Sight

Activities, Courses & Tours

- Bodysurfing
- Diving
- Canoeing/Kayaking
- Course/Tour
- Skiing
- Snorkelling
- Surfing
- Swimming/Pool
- Walking
- Windsurfing
- Other Activity

Sleeping

- Sleeping
- Camping

Eating

- Eating

Drinking & Nightlife

- Drinking & Nightlife
- Cafe

Entertainment

- Entertainment

Shopping

- Shopping

Information

- Bank
- Embassy/Consulate
- Hospital/Medical
- Internet
- Police
- Post Office
- Telephone
- Toilet
- Tourist Information
- Other Information

Geographic

- Beach
- Hut/Shelter
- Lighthouse
- Lookout
- Mountain/Volcano
- Oasis
- Park
- Pass
- Picnic Area
- Waterfall

Population

- Capital (National)
- Capital (State/Province)
- City/Large Town
- Town/Village

Transport

- Airport
- Border crossing
- Bus
- Cable car/Funicular
- Cycling
- Ferry
- Metro/MRT station
- Monorail
- Parking
- Petrol station
- Skytrain/Subway station
- Taxi
- Train station/Railway
- Tram
- Underground station
- Other Transport

Note: Not all symbols displayed above appear on the maps in this book

Routes

- Tollway
- Freeway
- Primary
- Secondary
- Tertiary
- Lane
- Unsealed road
- Road under construction
- Plaza/Mall
- Steps
- Tunnel
- Pedestrian overpass
- Walking Tour
- Walking Tour detour
- Path/Walking Trail

Boundaries

- International
- State/Province
- Disputed
- Regional/Suburb
- Marine Park
- Cliff
- Wall

Hydrography

- River, Creek
- Intermittent River
- Canal
- Water
- Dry/Salt/Intermittent Lake
- Reef

Areas

- Airport/Runway
- Beach/Desert
- Cemetery (Christian)
- Cemetery (Other)
- Glacier
- Mudflat
- Park/Forest
- Sight (Building)
- Sportsground
- Swamp/Mangrove

Austin Bush

Bangkok, Northern Thailand Austin Bush came to Thailand in 1999 as part of a language study programme hosted by Chiang Mai University. The lure of city life, employment and spicy food eventually led Austin to Bangkok. City life, employment and spicy food have managed to keep him there since. Austin is a native of Oregon and a writer and photographer who often focuses on food. Samples of his work can be seen at www.austinbushphotography.com. Austin also wrote the Eat Like a Local, Food & Drink and Food Spotter's Guide chapters.

David Eimer

Ko Chang & Eastern Seaboard, Hua Hin & the Upper Gulf, and Ko Samui & the Lower Gulf A decade of visiting Thailand in search of beaches and fine food prompted David to relocate to Bangkok in 2012. Since then, his work as a journalist for a variety of newspapers and magazines has taken him from the far south of Thailand, to its northernmost extremities, with many stops in between. Originally from London, David spent seven years living in Beijing, and another five in LA, prior to moving to Bangkok. He has contributed to 11 Lonely Planet books.

Adam Skolnick

Phuket & the Andaman Coast Adam Skolnick writes about travel, culture, health, sports, human rights and the environment for Lonely Planet, Outside, Travel & Leisure, Salon.com, BBC.com and ESPN.com. He has authored and co-authored two dozen Lonely Planet guidebooks. On this research trip he drove over 3000 km and hopped more than 50 long-tails. His debut novel, *Middle of Somewhere*, is set to publish in 2014. Read more of his work at www.adamskolnick.com, and find him on Twitter and Instagram (@adamskolnick).

OUR STORY

A beat-up old car, a few dollars in the pocket and a sense of adventure. In 1972 that's all Tony and Maureen Wheeler needed for the trip of a lifetime – across Europe and Asia overland to Australia. It took several months, and at the end – broke but inspired – they sat at their kitchen table writing and stapling together their first travel guide, *Across Asia on the Cheap*. Within a week they'd sold 1500 copies. Lonely Planet was born.

Today, Lonely Planet has offices in Melbourne, London and Oakland, with more than 600 staff and writers. We share Tony's belief that 'a great guidebook should do three things: inform, educate and amuse'.

OUR WRITERS

China Williams

Coordinating Author, Chiang Mai Every two years, China Williams leaves her quiet suburban life for a guidebook deployment to Thailand. This time she brought along her one-year old daughter as her research assistant and to boost her cuteness factor. It worked; the Thais were smitten. She first came to Thailand in 1997 to teach English in Surin. Since then she has shuttled across the Pacific for more than a decade working on various Thailand and Southeast Asia titles. Thailand gets richer and happier with every visit. China lives in Catonsville, Maryland (USA) with her husband, Matt, son, Felix, and daughter, Phoebe.

Mark Beales

Central Thailand After working as a journalist for 13 years, Mark swapped the chilly shores of England for the sunnier coasts of Thailand. Since 2004 he has lived in Thailand, where he has written several books for Lonely Planet, tried his hand at being a TV presenter and is currently Head of English at an international school in Rayong. Highlights on this trip included triumphing in a chilli-eating competition with voluntary workers in Sangkhlaburi. For more on Mark's work, visit www.markbeales.com.

Tim Bewer

Northeastern Thailand While growing up, Tim didn't travel much except for the obligatory pilgrimage to Disney World and an annual summer week at the lake. He's spent most of his adult life making up for this, and has since visited over 80 countries, including most in Southeast Asia. After university he worked briefly as a legislative assistant before quitting capitol life to backpack around West Africa. It was during this trip that the idea of becoming a freelance travel writer and photographer was hatched, and he's been at it ever since. He has lived in Khon Kaen, Thailand since 2007.

Celeste Brash

Ko Samui & the Lower Gulf Celeste first arrived in Thailand as a student of Thai language, history and culture at Chiang Mai University. She's come back countless times since and has done the gamut from wild nights on Ko Pha-Ngan to weeks of silence at a Buddhist Wat. Her writing has appeared in publications ranging from *Islands Magazine* to newspapers and anthologies. She's contributed to around 50 Lonely Planet guides but her heart is irrevocably stuck on Southeast Asia. When not in exotic places, she and her family live in Portland, Oregon. Find her on the web at www.celestebrash.com.

OVER MORE
PAGE WRITERS

Published by Lonely Planet Publications Pty Ltd
ABN 36 005 607 983
15th edition – July 2014
ISBN 978 1 74220 580 9
© Lonely Planet 2014 Photographs © as indicated 2014
10 9 8 7 6 5 4 3 2 1
Printed in China